# LONGMAN
# Elementary
# Dictionary
## and Thesaurus

**With color photographs and illustrations**

PEARSON
Longman

Pearson Education Limited
Edinburgh Gate
Harlow
Essex CM20 2JE, England, UK
and associated Companies throughout the world

Visit our website: http://www.pearsonlongman.com/dictionaries

First edition published 2010

ISBN    978-1-4082-2521-9

Words that the editors have reason to believe constitute trademarks have been described as such. However, neither the presence nor the absence of such a description should be regarded as affecting the legal status of any trademark.

1 2 3 4 5 6 CRK 15 14 13 12 11 10

Set in Frutiger by Letterpart, UK
Printed by Courier, U.S.

## Acknowledgements

**Editorial Director**
Michael Mayor

**Publishing Manager**
Laurence Delacroix

**Managing Editor**
Chris Fox

**Senior Editor**
Karen Cleveland-Marwick

**Editors**
Evadne Adrian-Vallance
Elizabeth Beizai
Rosalind Combley
Stephen Handorf
Lucy Hollingworth
Elizabeth Manning
Michael Murphy
Dr Martin Stark
Laura Wedgeworth

**Project Management**
Alan Savill

**Appendix**
Stephen Handorf

**Production**
Keeley Everitt

**Editorial Manager**
Paola Rocchetti

**Production Editor**
Anna Bardong
Debora Ferrari Haines

**Pronunciation Editor**
Dinah Jackson

**Proofreaders**
Pat Dunn
Karin Fischer-Buder
Isabel Griffiths

**Design**
Matthew Dickin

**Computational Linguist**
Allan Ørsnes

**Project and Databases Administrator**
Denise McKeough

**Picture Research**
Sandra Hilsdon

**Illustrations**
Maurizio De Angelis
(Beehive Illustration)
Wes Lowe (Beehive Illustration)
Claire Mumford (Beehive Illustration)
Chris Pavely
Mark Turner (Beehive Illustration)
Laszlo Veres (Beehive Illustration)
Tony Wilkins
John Carrozza

**The publishers would like to thank**

- their special consultant Dr Kate Kinsella, Teacher Educator and National Academic Language and Literacy Consultant, for her support and highly informed guidance on this project.

- all the dedicated elementary teachers who have participated in focus groups and given their informed feedback on the text throughout the development of this project:
  Melissa Waters, Elizabeth Morris, Mike Della Penna, Joal Arvanigian, Alison Merz, Jennifer Almer, Carol Kinzel, Darleen Osorio, Sharon Moya, Gissela Dillow, Mary Murphy, Trina Meyer, Martha Gray, Penny Church, Chris Copeland, Tafar Topalian, Kirsten Jackson, Debbie Winstein, Jessica Kern, Elyse Thompson, Marcia McGee, Kathy Segal, Angela D'Mello, Shari Anderson, Lisa Almgren, Nicole Rios, Pamela, Williamson, Monja Torres, Kristin Puls, Sharon Lyle, Pearl Santiago, Arnold Eclarinal, Judy Williams, Gay Thompkins, Anne Farwell, Edwardo Munoz, Nabila Massourni, Claire Trepanier, Carla Llewelyn-Vasquez, Yun Ji Chai, Jacqueline Omaria, Susan Graubard Archuletta, Mary Burmester, Renee Harris, Virginia Muller, Sean Nakamura, Tiffany Durand, Julie Alexander, Noah Mock, Ann Snelling, Pat Kelly, Amber Keeney, Jami Arsnt, Stephanie Beall, Maria Espinosa, Iris Halliburton, Cheryl Strause, Yuri Zaragoza, Maria Del Rocio Vargas, Judith Levy, Elisa Reyes, Cherylholly Baron, Norman Dittmeier, Jasmin Guzman, Tanya Henry, Aleiva Kopenec, David Lujan, Janie Pribanic, Dalia Sandoval, Marion Smith, Karen Stika, Carol Leonard, Eric Ramos, Paul Haupt

- Averil Coxhead for permission to reproduce the Academic Word list (AWL, compiled in 2000), in the back of this dictionary.

# Table of Contents

# How To Use Your Dictionary

**Guide Words** tell you the first and last word on the page.

**Definitions** are written in clear, simple language.

**Index Tabs** help you find the letter you are looking for FAST!

**Pictures** help you understand the meaning of a word.

The **part of speech** is clearly labeled to help you learn the differences between nouns, verbs, adjectives, and adverbs.

The **different meanings** of a word are clearly numbered. The most common meaning is shown first

When you see the word **Thesaurus**, go to the red **Thesaurus** section at the back of the book to help you build your vocabulary and make your language more interesting.

**Word Origin** boxes have interesting and fun facts explaining where a word comes from and when it started to be used.

## dolphin ▶ domino

**dol·phin** /**dahl**-fin/ *noun* a large gray animal that lives in the ocean. Dolphins look like large fish, but they are a kind of mammal. They breathe through a hole on their head. They are very smart: *The dolphins came right up to the side of the boat and swam around it.*

a
b
c
**d**
e
f
g
h

**dolphin**

**camp** /kamp/
● *noun*
**1** a place where people stay in tents, or in temporary buildings: *We put up our tents at the camp.* | *an army camp*
**2** a place where children stay and do activities during their vacation: *At summer camp, I did a lot of swimming.*
● *verb*
to live in a tent for a short time, usually on vacation: *We camped by the river so we could go fishing.*

**en·e·my** /**en**-uhm-ee/ *noun* (plural **enemies**)
**1** someone who hates you and wants to harm you or prevent you from being successful: *Everyone likes her. She doesn't have any enemies.* (ANTONYM: **friend**) ▶ see **Thesaurus**
**2** the people that you are fighting in a war: *The soldiers started shooting at the enemy.*
(ANTONYM: **ally**)

### Word Origin: enemy

**Enemy** came into English from Old French. It comes from a Latin word that means "not friend."

**for·tu·nate** /**forch**-uhn-it/ *adjective* in a good situation because of luck: *You're fortunate that you have such wonderful parents.*
(SYNONYM: **lucky**) (ANTONYM: **unfortunate**)

Synonyms and Antonyms show words that are the same or opposite and are listed at the end of the definition.

**crit·i·cize** /**krit**-uh-sīz/ *verb* to say that someone or something is bad: *My brother is always criticizing me and saying that I'm stupid.*
(ANTONYM: **praise**)
—**criticism** /**krit**-uh-siz-uhm/ *noun* remarks that say that someone or something is bad: *His criticism of my work really upset me.*

Simple respell system helps with **pronunciation**.

Simple **example** sentences show you how to use the word and help explain the meaning.

**Word Family:** criticize

**criticize** *verb* | **criticism** *noun* | **critical** *adjective* | **critic** *noun*

**Word Family** boxes show related words with the same roots and different parts of speech.

**-less** /liss/

**Word Building**

**-less** is a suffix. It is used in adjectives.
breath**less** | care**less** | motion**less** | pain**less** | spot**less**
**-less** means "without." If you are *breathless*, you can't breathe normally because you have been running. You are without breath. If an operation is *painless*, the patient does not feel any pain. If a house is *spotless*, it is very clean. The house is without any spots of dirt.

**Word Building** boxes explain how words are created using prefixes and suffixes.

**fun** /fuhn/
● *noun* something you enjoy doing: *Everyone was out having fun in the snow.* | *This game is a lot of fun.*

IDIOM with **fun**
**make fun of** to make unkind jokes about someone: *The other kids made fun of the way I talked.*
● *adjective* enjoyable: *There are lots of fun things to do at the beach.*

**Idioms** and idiomatic phrases are groups of words with a special meaning that is different than the meaning of the separate words. **Idioms** help make your language sound more natural.

**Word Choice:** fun, funny

You use **fun** to talk about situations or activities that you enjoy: *I have a lot of fun when I play with Brandon.* | *The art project was fun to do.*
You use **funny** to say that someone or something makes you laugh: *The movie was so funny we couldn't stop laughing.* | *Brandon is really funny. He's always telling jokes.*

**Word Choice** boxes explain the difference between words with similar meanings and help you choose the correct word.

# Preface

by
Dr. Kate Kinsella
Teacher Educator and National Academic Language
and Literacy Consultant

Elementary school students can surely benefit from a child-friendly dictionary that helps them tackle the vocabulary demands of their academic literacy tasks. However, children in grades 3–5 tend to be caught between two target dictionary markets. Students in the intermediate grades require a lexical resource that is considerably more robust than a primary grades picture dictionary targeting everyday vocabulary but far less daunting than an abridged desktop dictionary intended for adolescents. As a parent of two school-age youths, one an English learner and one a native English speaker, I am elated to have a dictionary that they can actually explore independently, understand and enjoy! Because my son still has critical gaps in his English word knowledge, he can become easily discouraged by unintelligible definitions including yet more unfamiliar words. I am confident that the *Longman Elementary Dictionary and Thesaurus*' carefully crafted explanations and examples anchored in familiar contexts will help children like my own more readily access new word meaning. I also understand the importance of a considerate page layout for younger word learners that doesn't require an over-the-shoulder mature reader to navigate. The visually appealing *Longman Elementary Dictionary and Thesaurus* pages were designed to help young vocabulary scholars readily locate a word and easily comprehend the most essential information.

As a teacher educator, I am eager to get the *Longman Elementary Dictionary and Thesaurus* into the hands of the many elementary school teachers I support. It is time-consuming and arduous to prepare to teach lesson terms to a mixed-ability class including students with diverse language backgrounds and literacy skills. The *Longman Elementary Dictionary and Thesaurus* will help make vocabulary instruction more efficient and engaging because so much thought has already been devoted to conjuring up accessible word meanings, familiar contextualized examples, and related word knowledge. The additional Writer's Thesaurus will be appreciated by teachers and students alike. This practical resource was included to help aspiring young writers like my daughter replace overused everyday words with more precise and dynamic word choices. As we developed the LEDT, I asked my children to review the sample pages and offer feedback from a young reader's perspective. My nine year-old daughter delved into the Writer's Thesaurus entries and exclaimed that she was planning to use several of the new "sparkle words" she found for the word nice in her assigned paragraph about a close friend.

Vocabulary knowledge is the single most reliable predictor of school achievement in grades 4–12. It would therefore seem to be an educational imperative for every classroom to be equipped with a rich and reliable vocabulary resource like the *Longman Elementary Dictionary and Thesaurus*, to expand children's linguistic horizons and support their teachers in effectively delivering robust instruction.

# Elementary Dictionary

# Aa

**a** /uh, ay/ (also **an**) *indefinite article*
**1** used when you are saying what someone or something is: *My dad's a doctor.* | *She was wearing a red skirt.*
**2** one: *She won a thousand dollars (=$1,000).* | *Can I have two hamburgers, a hot dog and three coffees?*
**3** each: *The candy costs 75 cents a bag.* | *We go swimming once a week.*

## Grammar: a, an

Use **a** if the word that is after it starts with a consonant sound: *a toy* | *a white egg* | *a horse*
Use **an** if the word that is after it starts with a vowel sound (the sounds shown by the letters a, e, i, o, or u): *an apple* | *an orange sweater* | *an honor*

**A** /ay/ *noun* the best grade that you can get on a test or in a class: *I got an A in English.*

**aard·vark** /**ard**-vark/ *noun* an African animal with a long thin tongue for eating insects

**ab·a·cus** /**ab**-uhk-uhss/ *noun* a wooden frame with small balls on wires, used for counting

**a·ban·don** /uh-**band**-uhn/ *verb*
**1** to leave something or someone and not go back: *The thieves abandoned the car beside the road.*
**2** to stop doing or thinking about something because of problems: *We abandoned the idea of a picnic because of the rain.*

**ab·bre·vi·a·tion** /uh-breev-ee-**aysh**-uhn/ *noun* a short way of writing a word: *"Mr." is the abbreviation of "Mister."*

**ABC's** /ay bee **seez**/ *noun* the letters of the English alphabet: *My little brother already knows his ABC's.*

**ab·do·men** /**abd**-uhm-uhn/ *noun*
**1** the front part of your body between your chest and your legs: *These exercises are good for the muscles in your abdomen.*
**2** the back part of an insect's body: *An insect's abdomen is just behind its thorax.*
—**abdominal** /ab-**dahm**-uhn-uhl/ *adjective* relating to the abdomen: *abdominal pain*

**ab·duct** /uhb-**duhkt**/ *verb* to kidnap someone: *A group of men abducted him and took him away in their car.*
—**abduction** /uhb-**duhk**-shuhn/ *noun* the act of kidnapping someone: *The police arrested him for the abduction of a young girl.*

**a·bil·i·ty** /uh-**bil**-uht-ee/ *noun* (plural **abilities**)
**1** if you have the ability to do something, you can do it: *Young children have the ability to learn fast.*
**2** skill at doing something: *Laura has great musical ability.*

**a·ble** /**ayb**-uhl/ *adjective*
**1** if you are able to do something, you can do it: *She's able to speak Spanish and Italian.*
**2** good at doing something: *In math, the less able children get extra help.*

## Word Family: able

**able** *adjective* | **unable** *adjective* | **ability** *noun* | **enable** *verb*

**-able** /uhb-uhl/

## Word Building

**-able** is a suffix. It changes the root word into an adjective.
**1** wash**able** | port**able** | ador**able**
**-able** means that something can be done. A *washable jacket* can be washed. A *portable television* can be moved. An *adorable baby* makes you want to adore it.
**2** valu**able** | knowledge**able** | comfort**able**
**-able** means that something has a particular quality. A *valuable ring* has value because it is worth a lot of money. Someone who is *knowledgeable* knows a lot about something. A *comfortable chair* has the quality of comfort, so it makes your body feel relaxed.

**ab·nor·mal** /ab-**norm**-uhl/ *adjective* not normal compared to what is usual: *A body temperature over 99°F is abnormal.* (ANTONYM: **normal**)
—**abnormally** /ab-**norm**-uhl-ee/ *adverb* in an abnormal way: *His blood pressure was abnormally high so the doctor gave him medicine.*
—**abnormality** /ab-nor-**mal**-uht-ee/ *noun* something that is not normal: *The disease is caused by an abnormality in the skin cells.*

**a·board** /uh-**bord**/ *adverb, preposition* on a ship, airplane, or train: *There were 150 passengers aboard the ship.*

**a·bol·ish** /uh-**bahl**-ish/ *verb* to end a law or system: *The U.S. abolished slavery in 1865.*
—**abolition** /ab-uh-**lish**-uhn/ *noun* the ending of a law or system: *The group campaigns for the abolition of the death penalty.*

**ab·o·li·tion·ist** /ab-uh-**lish**-uhn-ist/ *noun* someone who worked to abolish slavery in the U.S. during the 1800s

**a·bout** /uh-**bowt**/ *adverb, preposition*
**1** used to say what the subject of something is: *I'm reading a book about space travel.*
**2** around a number or amount: *Dad's about six feet tall.* (SYNONYM: **approximately**)
**3** **about to** almost ready to do something: *We were about to go out, when the phone rang.*
**4** **what about/how about** used to suggest doing something: *How about going for a walk?*
**5** **what about/how about** used to ask a question about something or someone: *What about David? Is he coming too?*

**a·bove** /uh-**buhv**/ *adverb, preposition*
**1** higher than something: *Raise your arm above your head.* | *The plane flew above the house.* (ANTONYM: **below**)
**2** more than something: *The temperature went above 100 degrees today.* | *The game is for kids age eight and above.* (ANTONYM: **below**)

**above**

The mirror is above the fireplace.

**a·bridged** /uh-**brijd**/ *adjective* an abridged book or play has been made shorter than the original one: *The abridged version of the book is shorter and easier for children to understand.*

**a·broad** /uh-**brod**/ *adverb* in or to a foreign country: *Have you ever traveled abroad?*

**a·brupt** /uh-**bruhpt**/ *adjective*
**1** sudden and unexpected: *The road came to an abrupt end.*
**2** speaking with few words in a way that seems rude or unfriendly: *He seemed annoyed and was very abrupt with me.*
—**abruptly** /uh-**bruhpt**-lee/ *adverb* in an abrupt way: *The meeting was canceled abruptly, just minutes before it was due to start.*

**ab·sence** /**ab**-suhnss/ *noun* a time when you are not at school or work: *What was the reason for his absence from school?*

**ab·sent** /**ab**-suhnt/ *adjective* not at school, work, or a meeting when you should be there: *She was absent from school for three weeks because she was sick.* (ANTONYM: **present**)
—**absentee** /ab-suhn-**tee**/ *noun* someone who is absent

**ab·so·lute** /**ab**-suh-loot/ *adjective* complete or total: *There was absolute silence.*

**ab·so·lute·ly** /ab-suh-**loot**-lee/ *adverb*
**1** completely or totally: *Are you absolutely sure?*
**2** used to say that you strongly agree: *"He's nice, isn't he?" "Absolutely."*

**ab·so·lute val·ue** /ab-suh-loot **val**-yoo/ *noun* the value of a number in relation to zero. The value is the same for positive and negative numbers. For example, the absolute value of +3 and −3 is 3.

**ab·sorb** /uhb-**sorb**/ *verb*
**1** to take in liquid or other substances: *The sponge will absorb the water.*
**2** if you are absorbed in something, you are very interested in it and not paying attention to anything else: *Emma was so absorbed in her book that she forgot about the time.*
—**absorbent** /uhb-**sorb**-uhnt/ *adjective* able to absorb liquids: *The paper towels are very absorbent and will soak up a lot of liquid.*
—**absorption** /uhb-**sorp**-shuhn/ *noun* the act of absorbing liquids or other substances: *Vitamin C increases the body's iron absorption.*

**ab·stain** /uhb-**stayn**/ *verb* to not do something that you normally enjoy: *Muslims abstain from food all day during a religious festival.*

**ab·stract** /uhb-**strakt**/ *adjective*
**1** based on ideas rather than real things: *"Thoughts" are abstract – you cannot see or touch them.*
**2** abstract art is made of shapes and patterns that do not look like real things or people: *He does abstract paintings using colored dots.*

**abstract**
an abstract painting

**ab·surd** /uhb-**surd**/ *adjective* very silly: *That is an absurd idea!*
—**absurdly** /uhb-**surd**-lee/ *adverb* in an absurd way: *The price was absurdly high.*

**a·bun·dance** /uh-**buhnd**-uhnss/ *noun* a lot of something: *There is an abundance of fresh fruit and vegetables at the farmers' market.*

**a·bun·dant** /uh-**buhnd**-uhnt/ *adjective* more than enough: *They had an abundant supply of food.* ( SYNONYM: **plentiful** )

**a·buse**
● *noun* /uh-**byooss**/
**1** cruel or violent treatment of someone: *His father was accused of child abuse.*
**2** the use of something in a wrong or harmful way: *Alcohol abuse has damaged his life.*
● *verb* /uh-**byooz**/
**1** to do cruel or violent things to someone: *The boy had been abused and neglected.*
**2** to use something in a wrong or harmful way: *He abused his power to get what he wanted.*
—**abusive** /uh-**byooss**-iv/ *adjective* cruel or violent: *abusive behavior*

**ac·a·dem·ic** /ak-uh-**dem**-ik/ *adjective* relating to work in schools, colleges, and universities: *The academic year starts in September.*

**a·cad·e·my** /uh-**kad**-uhm-ee/ *noun* (plural **academies**)
**1** a school, especially a school you pay for, or one that teaches a special subject: *He learned about being a soldier at a military academy.*

**2** an organization for artists, professors, or scientists: *The Academy of Motion Picture Arts and Sciences gives Oscars for the best movies.*

**ac·cel·er·ate** /uhk-**sel**-uh-rayt/ *verb* to start to go faster in a vehicle: *He accelerated and tried to pass the car in front.*
—**acceleration** /uhk-sel-uh-**raysh**-uhn/ *noun* the action of going faster

**ac·cent** /**ak**-sent/ *noun*
**1** the way you pronounce words, which shows where you come from: *He spoke English with a strong French accent.*
**2** a mark above a letter that shows how to pronounce it: *There is an accent over the "e" in the name José.*

**ac·cept** /uhk-**sept**/ *verb*
**1** to take something that someone offers you: *Please accept this small gift.* ( ANTONYM: **refuse** )
**2** to agree to an invitation or suggestion: *I accepted Daniel's invitation to his party.*
**3** to admit that something is true: *He refused to accept that he was wrong.*
**4** to let someone join a university or other organization: *My sister has been accepted into Harvard University.* ( ANTONYM: **reject** )

**ac·cept·a·ble** /uhk-**sept**-uhb-uhl/ *adjective* good enough: *This behavior is not acceptable in class.*

**ac·cept·ance** /uhk-**sept**-uhnss/ *noun*
**1** agreement to an offer or suggestion: *Olivia's family moved after her father's acceptance of a new job.*
**2** agreement that something is true or cannot be changed: *There is acceptance among scientists that the Earth is becoming warmer.*

**ac·cess** /**ak**-sess/
● *noun*
**1** a way that you can use or have something: *Do you have Internet access at home?*
**2** a way of getting to or into a place: *The school has access for people in wheelchairs.*
● *verb*
to find and use information on a computer: *You can access the information on our website.*

**ac·ces·si·ble** /uhk-**sess**-uhb-uhl/ *adjective* if something is accessible, you can get to it or find it: *The beach is only accessible by boat.*

3

**a**
b
c
d
e
f
g
h
i
j
k
l
m
n
o
p
q
r
s
t
u
v
w
x
y
z

**ac·ces·so·ry** /uhk-**sess**-uhr-ee/ *noun* (plural **accessories**) something that you wear or carry because it is attractive: *The store sells accessories such as jewelry and handbags.*

**ac·ci·dent** /**akss**-uhd-uhnt/ *noun* something bad that happens by chance and hurts someone or damages something: *His friend was hurt in a car accident.* | *I'm sorry I broke the cup – it was an accident.*

> **IDIOM with accident**
> **by accident** if something happens by accident, it was not planned and was a mistake: *I dropped a plate by accident.*
> ( SYNONYM: **accidentally** ) ( ANTONYM: **on purpose** )

**ac·ci·den·tal** /akss-uh-**dent**'l/ *adjective* not intended or planned: *We hadn't arranged to meet – it was completely accidental.*
( ANTONYM: **deliberate** )

**ac·ci·den·tal·ly** /akss-uh-**dent**'l-ee/ *adverb* by mistake: *I accidentally dialed Mom's number when I meant to call Chris.*
( ANTONYM: **deliberately** )

**ac·com·mo·date** /uh-**kahm**-uh-dayt/ *verb*
**1** to have enough space for a number of people or things: *The theater can accommodate 800 people.*
**2** to do what someone wants or needs: *It isn't easy to accommodate everyone's wishes.*

**ac·com·mo·da·tions** /uh-kahm-uh-**daysh**-uhnz/ *plural noun* a place to live or stay: *The price of the trip includes accommodations and meals.*

**ac·com·pa·ny** /uh-**kuhmp**-uhn-ee/ *verb* (**accompanies, accompanied**)
**1** to go somewhere with someone: *Five parents accompanied the Boy Scouts on the hike.*
**2** to play music while someone is playing or singing the main tune: *My sister sang, and I accompanied her on the piano.*

**ac·com·plish** /uh-**kahmp**-lish/ *verb* to succeed in doing or learning something: *He has accomplished a lot and his English has really improved.*
—**accomplishment** /uh-**kahmp**-lish-muhnt/ *noun* something that you have succeeded in doing: *Winning the game was a great accomplishment.*

**ac·cord·ing to** /uh-**kord**-ing too/ *preposition*
**1** from what someone says or what something

shows: *According to our teacher, the test's not very difficult.* | *According to the map, we're almost there.*
**2** in a way that obeys a rule or follows a plan: *Everything went according to plan.*

**ac·cor·di·on** /uh-**kord**-ee-uhn/ *noun* a musical instrument that you play by squeezing the sides together and pressing keys

**accordion**

**ac·count** /uh-**kownt**/
● *noun*
**1** an arrangement with a bank to keep your money for you: *I opened a savings account, so I can put a little money in the bank every month.*
**2** a description of something that has happened: *In his book he gives an account of his trip through South America.*
**3 accounts** a record of the money that a business has received and spent: *Companies must keep accurate accounts.*

> **IDIOMS with account**
> **on account of** because of something: *School was closed on account of the snow.*
> **take into account** to consider something when you make a decision: *You have to take her age into account – she's only six.*
● *verb*
**1 account for** to explain the reason for something: *Can you account for your absence from school?*
**2 account for** to be a part of an amount: *Girls account for 60% of the class.*

**ac·count·ant** /uh-**kownt**-uhnt/ *noun* someone whose job is to keep records of the money a business receives and spends

**ac·cu·mu·late** /uh-**kyoom**-yuh-layt/ *verb* if something accumulates, there is gradually more and more of it: *If you save money, it accumulates in the bank.*
—**accumulation** /uh-kyoom-yuh-**laysh**-uhn/ *noun* a situation in which there is more and more of something: *An accumulation of snow was making driving very difficult.*

**ac·cu·rate** /**ak**-yuhr-it/ *adjective*
**1** exactly correct: *I'm sure that all my measurements are accurate.*
( ANTONYM: **inaccurate** )
**2** an accurate throw or shot hits the thing you are trying to hit: *He made an accurate throw to first base.*
—**accurately** /**ak**-yuhr-it-lee/ *adverb* in an accurate way: *She accurately described what had happened.*
—**accuracy** /**ak**-yuhr-uhss-ee/ *noun* the quality of being accurate: *Check the accuracy of your answer.*

**Word Family:** accurate

accurate *adjective* | **inaccurate** *adjective* | **accurately** *adverb* | **accuracy** *noun*

**ac·cu·sa·tion** /ak-yuh-**zaysh**-uhn/ *noun* a statement saying that someone has done something wrong: *There were accusations that he stole money from people.*

**ac·cuse** /uh-**kyooz**/ *verb* to say that someone has done something wrong: *She was upset when Michael accused her of lying.*

**Word Family:** accuse

accuse *verb* | **accusation** *noun*

**ace** /ayss/ *noun* a playing card with one symbol on it. An ace can have the highest or lowest value in a game: *I had the ace of hearts so I won the game.*

**ache** /ayk/
● *verb* if part of your body aches, it hurts for a long time: *My legs were aching after walking so far.*
● *noun* a continuous pain: *She felt an ache in her chest where she had been hit.*

**a·chieve** /uh-**cheev**/ *verb* to succeed in doing or getting something you want: *She achieved her goal of becoming a lawyer.*
—**achievable** /uh-**cheev**-uhb-uhl/ *adjective* able to be achieved: *an achievable goal*

**Word Family:** achieve

achieve *verb* | **achievable** *adjective* | **achievement** *noun*

**a·chieve·ment** /uh-**cheev**-muhnt/ *noun* something important or difficult that you do successfully: *One of his greatest achievements was to win a gold medal at the Olympics.*

**ac·id** /**ass**-id/ *noun* a liquid chemical substance that can burn things: *The acid has burned a hole in the metal.*
—**acidic** /uh-**sid**-ik/ *adjective* containing acid: *The plant will not grow in acidic soil.*
—**acidity** /uh-**sid**-uht-ee/ *noun* the amount of acid in something: *The high acidity of the water means that few fish live in it.*

**ac·id rain** /**ass**-id **rayn**/ *noun* rain that contains pollution. Acid rain damages plants, trees, and rivers.

**ac·knowl·edge** /uhk-**nahl**-ij/ *verb*
**1** to accept or admit that something is true or correct: *Angie acknowledged that she had made a mistake and apologized.*
**2** to show someone that you have seen or heard him or her: *She didn't even acknowledge me when I said "hi."*
**3** to let someone know that you have received something from him or her: *She never acknowledged my letter, so I don't know if she got it.*
—**acknowledgment** /uhk-**nahl**-ij-muhnt/ *noun* the act of acknowledging someone or something

**ac·ne** /**ak**-nee/ *noun* a skin problem that makes a lot of red spots appear on your face, and is common among teenagers: *She had terrible acne when she was a teenager and she tried to cover her face with her hair.*

**a·corn** /**ay**-korn/ *noun* the nut of an oak tree
▶ see picture at **tree**

**ac·quaint·ance** /uh-**kwaynt**-uhnss/ *noun* someone you have met, but do not know well: *He's not really a friend. He's an acquaintance who I see sometimes at church.*

**ac·quire** /uh-**kwī**-ur/ *verb* to get or buy something: *The museum acquired the painting for $5.6 million.*
—**acquisition** /ak-wuh-**zish**-uhn/ *noun* something that you have acquired: *The painting is a new acquisition.*

**a·cre** /**ayk**-ur/ *noun* a unit for measuring an area of land, equal to 4,840 square yards, or 4,047 square meters: *The park has around 300 acres of forest.*

a
b
c
d
e
f
g
h
i
j
k
l
m
n
o
p
q
r
s
t
u
v
w
x
y
z

a
b
c
d
e
f
g
h
i
j
k
l
m
n
o
p
q
r
s
t
u
v
w
x
y
z

**ac·ro·bat** /**ak**-ruh-bat/ *noun* someone who entertains people in a circus. Acrobats can walk on a high rope, jump through the air, or do other special things: *The acrobat was walking on his hands.*

acrobat

**ac·ro·nym** /**ak**-ruhn-im/ *noun* a word made from the first letters of the name of something: *NASA is an acronym for the National Aeronautics and Space Administration.*

**a·cross** /uh-**kross**/ *adverb, preposition*
**1** from one side to the other: *A boy suddenly ran across the road.* | *The river is two miles across.*
**2** on the opposite side of something: *Ben lives across the street from us.*

**act** /akt/
● *verb*
**1** to do something: *If there's a fire, you need to act fast.*
**2** to behave in a particular way: *Terry was shouting and acting like an idiot.*
**3** to perform in a play or movie: *She has acted in a couple of Hollywood movies.*
**4** to have an effect: *The medicine acted quickly and Sara was soon asleep.*
● *noun*
**1** something that you do: *His act of courage saved the child.*
**2** a law that the government makes. First Congress passes it and then the president signs it: *The Education Act was passed by Congress in 1994.*
**3** one of the main parts of a play: *The king dies in Act 5.*
**4** a short performance that is part of a television or theater show: *Ross did a very funny comedy act.*

**Word Family:** act

act *noun* | act *verb* | action *noun* | activity *noun* | active *adjective*

**act·ing** /**akt**-ing/ *noun* the activity of performing in plays or movies: *Hannah loves acting and she's in the school play.*

**ac·tion** /**ak**-shuhn/ *noun*
**1** something that you do: *She explained the reason for her actions.*
**2** the effect that something has: *The action of the yeast makes the bread rise and become bigger.*

IDIOMS with action
**course of action** a way of dealing with a situation: *If you are upset, the best course of action is to talk to someone.*
**take action** to do something in order to deal with something: *We need to take action to protect the environment.*

**ac·tive** /**akt**-iv/ *adjective*
**1** moving around a lot, or doing a lot: *The little girl is very active and she's always running around doing things.* ( ANTONYM: **inactive** )
**2** if a verb or sentence is active, the subject of the verb does the action: *In the sentence "The boy kicked the ball," the verb is active. In the sentence "The ball was kicked by the boy," the verb is passive.* ( ANTONYM: **passive** )

**ac·tiv·i·ty** /ak-**tiv**-uht-ee/ *noun* (plural **activities**)
**1** something that you do for enjoyment: *The boys love outdoor activities like biking and swimming.*
**2** a situation in which a lot of things are happening: *There's always a lot of activity at the end of the school year.*

**ac·tor** /**akt**-ur/ *noun* someone who performs in plays, movies, or television shows: *Johnny Depp is a very good actor.*

**ac·tress** /**ak**-triss/ *noun* a woman who performs in plays, movies, or television shows

**ac·tu·al** /**ak**-choo-uhl/ *adjective* real or exact: *There were a lot of people there – I'm not sure what the actual number was.*

**ac·tu·al·ly** /**ak**-choo-uhl-ee/ *adverb*
**1** used when saying that something is true,

especially something surprising: *I know she doesn't look very old, but she is actually 18.*
**2** used when giving more information, or when giving your opinion: *Actually, we have two cats as well as a dog.* | *I like the green T-shirt, actually.*

**a·cute** /uh-**kyoot**/ *adjective*
**1** very serious or severe: *He has acute stomach pains and it is difficult for him to eat anything.*
**2** an acute sense makes you notice something very easily: *Dogs have an acute sense of smell and they can follow people over a long distance.*
**3** an acute angle is an angle of less than 90°

**ad** /ad/ *noun* a short word for advertisement: *I saw an ad for a really cheap computer.*

**A.D.** /ay **dee**/ used to show that a year was after the birth of Jesus Christ. A.D. is short for the Latin "Anno Domini" and means "in the year of our Lord": *He became emperor of Rome in 161 A.D.*

**a·dapt** /uh-**dapt**/ *verb*
**1** to change because you are in a new situation: *My family quickly adapted to living in this country.*
**2** to change something so that you can use it in a different way: *Some of her books have been adapted into movies.*

### Word Family: adapt

**adapt** *verb* | **adaptable** *adjective*

**a·dapt·a·ble** /uh-**dapt**-uhb-uhl/ *adjective* able to change and deal with new situations: *When animals' environment changes, they need to be adaptable to survive.*

**ad·ap·ta·tion** /ad-uhp-**taysh**-uhn/ *noun*
**1** a movie, play, or television program that is made from a book: *The movie is based on an adaptation of a book by Alice Walker.*
**2** the process of changing to suit a new situation: *The animal's survival depends on adaptation to the environment.*

**add** /ad/ *verb*
**1** to put numbers together to get the total: *If you add 5 and 3, you get 8.* | *Add up your scores and see who has won.* (ANTONYM: **subtract**)
**2** to put something with another thing: *Mix the butter and sugar and then add the eggs.*

**3** to say one more thing: *"Remember to lock the door," she added.*
**4** **add up** to seem true or reasonable: *Her explanation of what happened doesn't add up.*

### Word Family: add

**add** *verb* | **addition** *noun* | **additional** *adjective*

**ad·dend** /**ad**-end/ *noun* a number that you add to another number: *The missing addend in 5 + = 7 is 2.*

**ad·dict** /**ad**-ikt/ *noun*
**1** someone who cannot stop taking harmful drugs: *She became a drug addict and lost her home and her friends.*
**2** someone who likes using or doing something a lot: *My brother is always playing computer games. He's a real addict.*
—**addicted** /uh-**dikt**-id/ *adjective* unable to stop taking drugs, or unable to stop doing something: *He is addicted to drugs.*
—**addiction** /uh-**dik**-shuhn/ *noun* the problem when someone cannot stop taking drugs, or does something too much: *Drug addiction is a very serious problem.*

**ad·dic·tive** /uh-**dikt**-iv/ *adjective* very hard to stop doing or using: *Smoking is very addictive.*

**ad·di·tion** /uh-**dish**-uhn/ *noun*
**1** in math, the process of adding numbers together to get a total: *Here is an addition question: What do you get when you add 12 and 19?* (ANTONYM: **subtraction**)
**2** a person or thing that is added to something: *Matthew is a great addition to the team.*

**IDIOM with addition**
**in addition** as well as something else: *In addition to football, the children can play baseball or basketball.*

**ad·di·tion·al** /uh-**dish**-uhn-uhl/ *adjective* more than you already have: *For additional information, visit our website.* (SYNONYM: **extra**)

**ad·di·tive** /**ad**-uht-iv/ *noun* a chemical substance that is added to food. Additives can be used to preserve food or to make the color nicer: *I prefer fresh food, without any additives.*

**a**
**b**
**c**
**d**
**e**
**f**
**g**
**h**
**i**
**j**
**k**
**l**
**m**
**n**
**o**
**p**
**q**
**r**
**s**
**t**
**u**
**v**
**w**
**x**
**y**
**z**

**ad·dress** /uh-**dress**/
● *noun*
**1** the number of the building, and the name of the street and town of someone's home or business: *My address is 271 Dexter Avenue, Seattle.*
**2** the letters or numbers you use to send an email to someone: *What is your email address?*
**3** the letters or numbers you use to get to a website: *Do you have the school's web address?*
**4** a formal speech: *The president made an address to the nation.*
● *verb*
**1** to write a name and address on an envelope or package: *The letter was addressed to my brother.*
**2** to speak to a group of people: *The principal addressed the whole school.*
**3** to start trying to solve a problem: *We need to address this problem.*

**ad·e·quate** /**ad**-uh-kwit/ *adjective* enough or good enough: *It is important to eat an adequate amount of fresh fruit and vegetables every day if you want to be healthy.* (ANTONYM: **inadequate**)
—**adequately** /**ad**-uh-kwit-lee/ *adverb* in an adequate way

**Word Family:** adequate

**adequate** *adjective* | **inadequate** *adjective* |
**adequately** *adverb* | **inadequately** *adverb*

**ADHD** /ay dee aych **dee**/ *noun* a medical condition that makes children unable to pay attention or sit quietly for long. ADHD is short for Attention Deficit Hyperactivity Disorder: *Her youngest son has ADHD.*

**ad·ja·cent** /uh-**jayss**-uhnt/ *adjective* next to something: *The baseball field is adjacent to the main school building.*

**ad·jec·tive** /**aj**-ikt-iv/ *noun* a word that describes a person or thing. In the sentence "We want a new car," "new" is an adjective.

**ad·just** /uh-**juhst**/ *verb*
**1** to change something a little to make it better: *You can adjust the color on your computer screen.*
**2** to gradually become accustomed to a new or difficult situation: *It took me a long time to adjust to living in the city.*
—**adjustable** /uh-**juhst**-uhb-uhl/ *adjective* able to

be adjusted: *The straps are adjustable and you can make them tighter or looser.*

**ad·just·ment** /uh-**juhst**-muhnt/ *noun* a small change you make to something: *There have been a few adjustments to the plan.*

**ad·min·is·tra·tion** /uhd-min-uh-**straysh**-uhn/ *noun*
**1** the U.S. president and the people who work for him or her: *The administration wants everyone to have good health care.*
**2** the job of organizing the work of a business or organization: *My dad has a college degree in business administration.*

**Word Family:** administration

**administration** *noun* | **administrator** *noun*

**ad·min·is·tra·tor** /uhd-**min**-uhss-trayt-ur/ *noun* someone whose job is organizing the work in a business or organization: *The school administrator is responsible for organizing everything that happens at the school.*

**ad·mi·ra·ble** /**ad**-muhr-uhb-uhl/ *adjective* very good in a way that people admire: *The new principal has done an admirable job and we are very pleased with her.*

**ad·mi·ral** /**ad**-muhr-uhl/ *noun* an important officer in the navy or coast guard. An admiral is above a vice admiral.

**ad·mi·ra·tion** /ad-muh-**raysh**-uhn/ *noun* the feeling you have when you think someone or something is very good, beautiful, or intelligent: *The girls thought he was very good-looking and they looked at him with admiration.*

**ad·mire** /uhd-**mī**-ur/ *verb*
**1** to think someone or something is very good, beautiful, or intelligent: *Ethan was great at sports – everyone admired him.*
▶ see **Thesaurus**
**2** to look at something that you think is beautiful or impressive: *At the top of the hill, we stopped to admire the view.*

**Word Family:** admire

**admire** *verb* | **admiration** *noun* | **admirable** *adjective*

**ad·mis·sion** /uhd-**mish**-uhn/ *noun*
**1** the price you pay to go to something, for example a movie or sports event: *Admission to the museum is $8.*
**2** the right to become a student at a college or school: *Tom has applied for admission to City College.*
**3** something that you say or do, that shows you have done something bad: *I was shocked by his admission that he had lied.*

**ad·mit** /uhd-**mit**/ *verb* (**admitting, admitted**)
**1** to say that you have done something wrong, or that something bad is true: *Two of the boys admitted taking the money.*
**2** to allow someone to enter a place: *You will not be admitted without a ticket.*

**a·do·be** /uh-**dohb**-ee/ *noun* mud and straw that are made into bricks for building: *The old church was made of adobe.*

### Word Origin: adobe

**Adobe** buildings are common in Mexico and the southwestern U.S. The word adobe comes from ancient Egypt, from about 2,000 B.C. The Egyptian word meant "mud brick." Arabic people began using the Egyptian word, and then the word passed into Spanish. When the Spanish explorers saw the buildings in the New World, they used the word adobe to say what the buildings were made of. And now we use adobe in English.

**ad·o·les·cent** /ad'l-**ess**-uhnt/ *noun* a young person between 12 and 17 who is becoming an adult: *At 15, Bill was a shy adolescent.*
—**adolescence** /ad'l-**ess**-uhnss/ *noun* the time of your life when you are an adolescent

**a·dopt** /uh-**dahpt**/ *verb*
**1** to become the legal parents of a child that is not your own child: *Our neighbors have adopted a new baby.*
**2** to begin to use a new way of doing something: *Some schools have adopted a new approach to homework.*
—**adoption** /uh-**dahp**-shuhn/ *noun* the act of adopting a child: *They considered adoption because they were unable to have a child of their own.*

**a·dor·a·ble** /uh-**dor**-uhb-uhl/ *adjective* very pretty or easy to love: *Look at that adorable puppy!*

**a·dore** /uh-**dor**/ *verb* to love someone or something very much: *Billy adores sports.*

**a·dult** /uh-**duhlt**/ *noun* someone who has finished growing and is not a child. You become an adult when you are 18 years old: *The tickets are $8 for adults and $5 for children.*
( SYNONYM: **grown-up** )

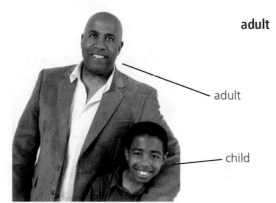

adult

adult

child

**ad·ult·hood** /uh-**duhlt**-hud/ *noun* the time in your life when you are an adult: *School prepares young people for adulthood.*

**ad·vance** /uhd-**vanss**/
● *noun*
**1** a change that brings progress: *There have been huge advances in computers and modern computers are much faster and more powerful.*
**2** a movement forward to a new position, especially by soldiers: *They were trying to prevent the army's advance.*

IDIOM with **advance**
**in advance** before something happens, or before you go somewhere: *You must reserve your tickets in advance.*
● *verb*
**1** to improve – used especially about science and medicine: *Our medical knowledge has advanced greatly in the past 100 years.*
**2** to move forward to a new position: *The soldiers advanced south.* ( ANTONYM: **retreat** )

**ad·vanced** /uhd-**vanst**/ *adjective*
**1** very modern, or developed to a high level: *Schools today use a lot of advanced technology. | The U.S. is one of the most advanced nations in the world.*
**2** studying a subject at a difficult level: *The class is for advanced students.*

**ad·van·tage** /uhd-**vant**-ij/ *noun*
**1** something that helps you to be successful: *It's a big advantage if you can speak a second language.* ( ANTONYM: **disadvantage** )
**2** something that is good or useful: *Our new house has a lot of advantages. It's near my school and it's also much bigger than our old house.* ( ANTONYM: **disadvantage** )
▶ see **Thesaurus**
**3** in tennis, the point that a player wins after the score is 40–40

IDIOM with **advantage**
**take advantage**
**1** to use an opportunity: *We decided to take advantage of the good weather and go to the beach.*
**2** to use a person in a way that is not fair: *Don't let other people take advantage of you.*

**ad·ven·ture** /uhd-**vench**-ur/ *noun* an exciting thing that you do: *Our trip to Canada was a real adventure.*
—**adventurous** /uhd-**vench**-uhr-uhss/ *adjective* wanting to do exciting or dangerous things: *The boys are very adventurous and they like going into the forest near our house.*

**ad·verb** /**ad**-vurb/ *noun* a word that describes a verb, an adjective, or another adverb. In the sentence "He walks slowly," "slowly" is an adverb.

**ad·ver·sar·y** /**ad**-vur-sair-ee/ *noun* someone you are fighting or competing against: *He looked across the boxing ring at his adversary.*

**ad·ver·tise** /**ad**-vur-tīz/ *verb*
**1** to try to make people buy a product by telling them good things about it: *The company advertises its pizzas on television.*
**2** to try to find someone to do a job by putting a public announcement somewhere: *The restaurant is advertising for a new waiter.*
—**advertising** /**ad**-vur-tīz-ing/ *noun* the business of advertising products and services: *My dad works in advertising.*

**Word Family: advertise**
**advertise** *verb* | **advertisement** *noun* | **advertising** *noun*

**ad·ver·tise·ment** /ad-vur-**tīz**-muhnt/ *noun* a picture or short movie that tries to make people buy something: *There are a lot of advertisements for cars on the TV.* ( SYNONYM: **ad** )

**ad·vice** /uhd-**vīss**/ *noun* ideas that help you to decide what you should do: *My grandma gave me some good advice about taking care of cats.*
▶ see **Thesaurus**

**Word Family: advice**
**advice** *noun* | **advise** *verb* | **adviser** *noun*

**ad·vise** /uhd-**vīz**/ *verb* to tell someone what you think he or she should do: *Dan advised us to take the earlier train.*
—**adviser**, **advisor** /uhd-**vīz**-ur/ *noun* someone whose job is to advise people

**aer·o·sol** /**air**-uh-sol/ *noun* a container with liquid such as paint or hairspray inside. When you press a button on the top, the liquid comes out in a spray.

**aerosol**

**aer·o·space** /**air**-oh-spayss/ *noun* the industry that designs and builds aircraft and space vehicles: *the U.S. aerospace industry*

**af·fair** /uh-**fair**/ *noun*
**1** a special event such as a party or wedding: *Thanksgiving is always a big family affair.*
**2** **affairs** things that relate to a particular subject: *Dad never really talked to us about his business affairs.*

**af·fect** /uh-**fekt**/ *verb* to have an effect on someone or something, especially in a bad way: *His illness affects his eyes.*

**Word Family: affect**
**affect** *verb* | **effect** *noun*

**af·fec·tion** /uh-**fek**-shuhn/ *noun* a feeling of liking or loving someone: *He treated his grandchildren with great affection and he was always buying them gifts.*
—**affectionate** /uh-**fek**-shuhn-it/ *adjective* showing that you like or love someone: *Michelle gave me an affectionate hug.*
—**affectionately** /uh-**fek**-shuhn-it-lee/ *adverb* in an affectionate way: *She smiled at him affectionately.*

**af·ford** /uh-**ford**/ *verb*
**1** to have enough money to buy something: *The cars are very expensive and most people can't afford them.*
**2** to have the time or ability to do something: *During the test, you can't afford to spend too much time on one question.*

**af·ford·a·ble** /uh-**ford**-uhb-uhl/ *adjective* not too expensive: *The store sells T-shirts at very affordable prices.*

**a·fraid** /uh-**frayd**/ *adjective*
**1** frightened of something that may hurt you or be dangerous: *Are you afraid of spiders?*
SYNONYMS: **scared, frightened**
**2** worried about something that may happen: *I was afraid she'd be mad at me.*
**3** I'm afraid sorry: *I'm afraid we can't go on the school trip after all.*

**Word Origin:** afraid

**Afraid** comes from an English word *afray*, which means "to frighten." People used the word "afray" until the 1800s, but we do not use it any more. Before people started saying "afraid," they used the older English word "afeared."

**Af·ri·can** /**af**-rik-uhn/
● *adjective* relating to Africa: *Kenya is an African country.*
● *noun* someone from Africa

**Af·ri·can-A·mer·i·can** /af-rik-uhn uh-**merr**-ik-uhn/ *noun* an American with dark skin, whose family first came to the U.S. from Africa
—**African-American** *adjective* relating to African-Americans: *She's an African-American woman.*

**af·ter** /**aft**-ur/ *preposition, conjunction, adverb*
**1** later than something: *Do you want to come to my house after school?*
**2** following someone or something to stop or catch them: *I ran after him and asked him to wait.*
**3** used to say how many minutes past the hour it is: *"What time is it?" "It's twenty after two (=2:20)."* SYNONYM: **past**

**af·ter·noon** /aft-ur-**noon**/ *noun* the time between 12 noon and the evening: *We went swimming in the afternoon.*

**af·ter·shock** /**aft**-ur-shahk/ *noun* a small earthquake that comes after a stronger earthquake: *Several aftershocks were felt after the earthquake.*

**af·ter·ward** /**aft**-ur-wurd/ (also **afterwards**) *adverb* after an event or time: *We'll go see a movie and have some pizza afterward.*

**a·gain** /uh-**gen**/ *adverb* one more time: *Could you say that again? I didn't hear.*

**a·gainst** /uh-**genst**/ *preposition*
**1** next to a surface, or touching it: *We pushed the table up against the wall.*
**2** competing with a team in a game: *Did you watch the Cowboys against the Eagles last night?*
**3** not allowed by the law or the rules: *Running in school is against the rules.*
**4** not agreeing with or supporting something: *Most of the class were against the idea.*
ANTONYM: **for**
**5** fighting with a country in a war: *They fought against Germany.*

**age** /ayj/ *noun*
**1** the number of years that someone has lived: *Most kids start school at the age of five.*
**2** a time in someone's life: *People often need more help in their old age.*
**3** a period of time in history: *The Ice Age ended 10,000 years ago.*
**4** ages a long time: *We had to wait ages for a bus.*

**a·gen·cy** /**ayj**-uhnss-ee/ *noun* (plural **agencies**)
**1** a business that provides a service to people: *We arranged our vacation through a travel agency.*
**2** a part of a government that does a special job: *NASA is the name of the U.S. space agency.*

**a·gen·da** /uh-**jend**-uh/ *noun*
**1** a list of the subjects that people will discuss at a meeting: *There are six items on the agenda.*
**2** a list of things that an organization is planning to do: *The principal said that buying new computers is high on the agenda.*

**a·gent** /**ayj**-uhnt/ *noun*
**1** a person or company that arranges things for other people: *A travel agent found the hotel for us.*
**2** someone whose job is to get secret information: *The government used secret agents to collect information on its enemies.*

**ag·gres·sive** /uh-**gress**-iv/ *adjective* behaving in an angry or violent way: *The driver of the truck became rude and aggressive.*
—**aggression** /uh-**gresh**-uhn/ *noun* angry or violent behavior: *The apes show aggression to male apes who do not belong to the group.*

**a·go** /uh-**goh**/ *adverb* used to say when something happened in the past: *Anna called ten minutes ago.*

**Word Choice:** ago, for, since

**Ago**, **for**, and **since** are all used to talk about time.

**Ago** is used to say how far back in the past something happened. You say the amount of time, and then the word **ago**: *I moved here two years ago.* | *The movie started 15 minutes ago.*

**For** is used to say how long something has lasted. You say the word **for** and then the amount of time: *I have lived here for three years.* | *She waited for ten minutes.*

**Since** is used to say when something started. You say the word **since** and then say the day, date, or time after it: *It's been raining since Monday.* | *I've been going to school here since 2010.*

**ag·o·ny** /**ag**-uhn-ee/ *noun* very bad pain or worry: *He was screaming in agony.*
—**agonizing** /**ag**-uh-nīz-ing/ *adjective* very painful or worrying: *After an agonizing wait, we finally got the news.*

**a·gree** /uh-**gree**/ *verb*
**1** to think the same as someone else, or to think that something is right: *Dad liked the blue car best and I agreed.* | *I don't agree with their decision.* ( ANTONYM: **disagree** )
**2** to say that you will do something: *I agreed to stay and help after school.* ( ANTONYM: **refuse** )
**3** to decide something together: *They still haven't agreed on a name for the baby.*

**a·gree·a·ble** /uh-**gree**-uhb-uhl/ *adjective*
**1** pleasant: *Minnie was always cheerful and agreeable.*
**2** willing to agree to an idea: *The teacher was agreeable to our plan.*

**a·gree·ment** /uh-**gree**-muhnt/ *noun*
**1** an arrangement or promise: *The two countries reached an agreement to stop fighting.*
**2** the situation when people think the same about an idea: *We were all in agreement about who should be team captain.*
( ANTONYM: **disagreement** )

**ag·ri·cul·ture** /**ag**-ri-kuhlch-ur/ *noun* the activity of growing crops or keeping animals for food on a farm: *The trees were cut down so that farmers could use the land for agriculture.*
( SYNONYM: **farming** )
—**agricultural** /ag-ri-**kuhlch**-uhr-uhl/ *adjective* relating to agriculture: *agricultural land*

agriculture

**a·head** /uh-**hed**/ *adverb*
**1** in front of someone or something: *Rob was ahead of me in the race.* | *You can see the school straight ahead.*
**2** in the future: *Try to plan ahead.*

aim

**IDIOMS with ahead**
**ahead of schedule/time** earlier than people had planned: *The plane arrived ahead of schedule.*
**get ahead** to be successful in your work or life: *You need to work hard if you want to get ahead.*
**go ahead** used when telling someone that he or she can do something: *"Can I use your phone?" "Sure, go ahead."*

ahead

Rob is ahead of Chris.

**aid** /ayd/
● *noun* money, food, medicine, or equipment that is sent to people in a difficult situation: *The U.S. sends a lot of aid to help people in poor countries.*
● *verb* to help someone: *The website aids the students with their research.*

**AIDS** /aydz/ *noun* a very serious disease that makes the body unable to fight other diseases. It is caused by the HIV virus. AIDS is short for Acquired Immune Deficiency Syndrome.

**aim** /aym/
● *noun*
**1** something that you want to achieve: *Our aim is to win the competition.* (SYNONYM: **goal**)
**2** the action of pointing a gun or throwing a ball in the direction of someone or something: *He lifted the gun, took aim, and fired.*
● *verb*
**1** to point a gun, ball, arrow, etc. at someone or something. You then try to hit that person or thing: *I aimed the ball at the basket.* | *Police officers were aiming their guns at the robbers.*
**2** to plan or intend to do something: *I aim to finish my homework by six o'clock, so I should be free after that time.*

**air** /air/ *noun*
**1** the gases around you, which you breathe: *Go outside and get some fresh air.*
**2** if something goes up in the air, it goes up into the sky: *The balloon went up into the air.*

**IDIOMS with air**
**by air** using an airplane: *It's quicker to go by air.*
**on the air** being broadcast on television or on the radio: *"Sesame Street" has been on the air for more than 40 years.*

**air con·di·tion·er** /air kuhn-dish-uhn-ur/ *noun* a machine that makes the air in a building or car become cool

**air con·di·tion·ing** /air kuhn-dish-uhn-ing/ *noun* a system of machines that makes the air in a building or car become cool: *It was getting hotter, so he turned the air conditioning on.*
—**air-conditioned** /air kuhn-dish-uhnd/ *adjective* having air conditioning: *an air-conditioned office*

**air·craft** /air-kraft/ *noun* (plural **aircraft**) an airplane or other vehicle that can fly: *How many people were on the aircraft?*

**air·fare** /air-fair/ *noun* the price of an airplane ticket: *He got a cheap airfare to New York.*

**air force** /air forss/ *noun* the group of people who fight for their country using airplanes

**air·line** /air-līn/ *noun* a company that takes people and things to different places by airplane: *Which airlines have flights to Hawaii?* | *an airline pilot*

**air·mail** /air-mayl/ *noun* the system of sending letters and packages to another country by airplane: *She sent the book airmail.* | *an airmail envelope*

**air·plane** /**air**-playn/ *noun* a vehicle with wings that flies through the air: *I watched the airplane go up into the sky.* (SYNONYM: **plane**)

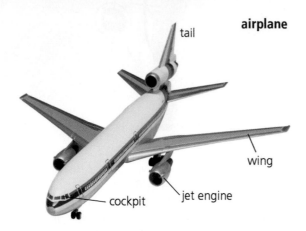

airplane

tail

wing

jet engine

cockpit

**air·port** /**air**-port/ *noun* a place where airplanes take off and land. An airport has buildings for people to wait in before they fly: *The plane landed at Los Angeles airport.*

**air·tight** /**air**-tīt/ *adjective* something that is airtight does not allow air to get in: *Store the crackers in an airtight container so they don't go soft.*

**aisle** /īl/ *noun* a long space that you can walk along between rows of seats or shelves: *The bride and her father walked down the aisle of the church.* | *The ice cream is down this aisle.*

aisle

aisle

**a·jar** /uh-**jar**/ *adjective* a door that is ajar is open a little bit: *He left the door ajar so that the cat could come in.*

ajar

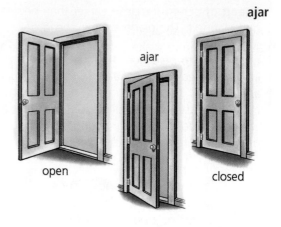

ajar

open

closed

**-al** /-uhl/

## Word Building

**-al** is a suffix. It changes the root word into an adjective.

**logical | magical | structural**

**-al** means that something is related to something. A *logical explanation* is an explanation that makes sense and is based on good thinking, so it is related to logic. Someone who has *magical powers* is able to do things relating to magic. A *structural problem* in a building is a problem that relates to the building's structure.

**a·larm** /uh-**larm**/
● *noun*
**1** a piece of equipment that makes a noise to warn people of danger: *Smoke set the fire alarm off.*
**2** a feeling of fear that something bad might happen: *We watched with alarm as the water started to come into the kitchen.*
● *verb*
to make someone feel very worried or frightened: *He spoke quietly so he wouldn't alarm the little boy.*
—**alarmed** /uh-**larmd**/ *adjective* worried or frightened: *His mother was alarmed when she saw the bruises on his leg.*
—**alarming** /uh-**larm**-ing/ *adjective* worrying or frightening: *The fire is spreading at an alarming rate through the forest.*

**a·larm clock** /uh-**larm** klahk/ *noun* a clock that will make a noise at a particular time to wake you up: *I set the alarm clock for 7:00.*

alarm clock

**al·bum** /**alb**-uhm/ *noun*
**1** the group of songs or pieces of music on a CD: *She wrote all the songs on her new album.*
**2** a book that you put things in, such as photographs or stamps: *We put the photographs of our vacation in a photo album.*

**al·co·hol** /**alk**-uh-hol/ *noun* drinks such as beer or wine that can make you drunk: *You're not allowed to buy alcohol unless you're over 21.*

**al·co·hol·ic** /alk-uh-**hol**-ik/
● *adjective* an alcoholic drink has alcohol in it
● *noun* someone who drinks a lot of alcohol and finds it hard to stop drinking it: *He was an alcoholic, but now he doesn't drink at all.*
—**alcoholism** /**alk**-uh-hol-iz-uhm/ *noun* the problem of being an alcoholic

**a·lert** /uh-**lurt**/ *adjective* always watching and ready to move or do something: *I'm always alert in case a car comes toward me.*

**al·gae** /**al**-jee/ *noun* a plant that does not have roots, stems, or leaves. Algae grows on the surface of water and rocks: *Many small fish eat algae.*

algae

algae

**al·ge·bra** /**alj**-uh-bruh/ *noun* a type of mathematics that uses letters and symbols to represent numbers, for example $x^2 + y^2 = 25$

**a·li·en** /**ayl**-ee-uhn/ *noun*
**1** a creature from another planet: *The movie was about aliens who land on earth.*
**2** someone who is from a different country than the one he or she is living in or visiting: *Some of the workers were illegal aliens and they had entered the U.S. illegally.*

**a·like** /uh-**līk**/ *adjective, adverb* almost the same: *Steve and his brother look very alike.*

**a·live** /uh-**līv**/ *adjective* living and not dead: *He's been badly injured but he's still alive.*

**all** /ol/
● *adjective, pronoun*
**1** every thing or person in a group, or every part of something: *There's enough room for all of us.* | *Have you spent all the money already?* | *We all liked him.*
**2** the only thing or things: *All I want to do is sleep.*
**3 all kinds/sorts of** a lot of different types of things or people: *We talked about all kinds of things: sports, movies, music.*
**4 at all** used to emphasize "not," "no," and "no one": *The test is not easy at all.* | *I got no presents at all.*
● *adverb*
**1** completely or entirely: *The chocolate cake is all gone.*
**2** used when saying that two teams or people have an equal number of points in a game: *The score was 9 all at halftime.*

**Word Choice:** all, each, every

**All**, **each**, and **every** are all used to talk about every person or thing in a group.

When you are thinking about the whole group together, use **all**: *All the children had math books.*

When you are thinking about the people or things in the group separately, use **every** or **each**: *Every child had a math book.* | *Each child had a math book.*

**Al·lah** /**al**-uh/ the Muslim name for God

**al·le·giance** /uh-**leej**-uhnss/ *noun* loyalty to a leader or country: *We pledge allegiance to the flag of the United States of America* (=we promise to be loyal to our country).

**al·ler·gy** /**al**-urj-ee/ *noun* (plural **allergies**) if you have an allergy, you get sick when you eat, touch, or breathe something: *A lot of people have nut allergies and can't eat peanut butter.* —**allergic** /uh-**lurj**-ik/ *adjective* having an allergy: *She started sneezing because she was allergic to cats.*

**al·ley** /**al**-ee/ (also **al·ley·way** /**al**-ee-way/) *noun* a narrow passage between buildings: *The garbage trucks picked up the trash cans in the alley.*

alley

**al·li·ga·tor** /**al**-uh-gayt-ur/ *noun* a large animal with a long body and a big mouth with sharp teeth. Alligators live in hot wet places in the U.S., South America, and China: *We saw a 13-foot alligator in the zoo.*

## Word Origin: alligator

When Spanish explorers first saw an **alligator**, they called it **el lagarto**. This means "the big lizard." English people heard "el lagarto" and started calling the animal "alligarter." Later, people changed the word to "alligator."

alligator

**al·low** /uh-**low**/ *verb* to say that someone can do something: *We aren't allowed to wear jewelry at school.* (ANTONYM: **forbid**)
▶ see Thesaurus

**al·low·ance** /uh-**low**-uhnss/ *noun* money that your parents give you regularly: *Jacob gets an allowance of two dollars a week from his parents.*

**al·loy** /**al**-oy/ *noun* a metal that is a mixture of two or more different metals: *Brass is an alloy of copper and zinc.*

**all right** /ol **rīt**/ *adjective, adverb*
**1** used to say "yes," when someone asks or suggests something: *"Can I ask you something?" "All right."* (SYNONYM: **okay**)
**2** fairly good or fairly well, but not great: *"How was the movie?" "It was all right, I guess."* | *Don't worry – everything will be all right.* (SYNONYM: **okay**)
**3** not sick, hurt, or upset: *You look terrible – are you all right?* (SYNONYM: **okay**)
**4** acceptable to you: *Is it all right if I close the window?* | *"Sorry I'm late!" "That's all right."* (SYNONYM: **okay**)

**al·ly** /uh-**lī**/ *noun* (plural **allies**) a country that helps and supports another country: *England and the U.S. were allies during the Iraq war.*

**al·ma·nac** /**ol**-muh-nak/ *noun* a book with lists of the latest information about different subjects. It is published every year: *I looked up the capital of South Africa in the almanac.*

**al·mond** /**ahm**-uhnd/ *noun* a white nut with brown skin and a slightly sweet taste. Almonds have an oval shape: *Do you like chocolate with almonds in it?*

almond

**al·most** /**ol**-mohst/ *adverb* nearly, or close to something: *We see each other almost every day.* | *Are we almost home?*

**a·lone** /uh-**lohn**/ *adjective, adverb* without any other people: *He lives alone and has no one to talk to.* ▶ see Thesaurus

**a·long** /uh-**long**/ *adverb, preposition*
**1** moving forward toward one end of something: *We took a walk along the river.* (SYNONYM: **down**)

**2** next to something: *They put up a fence along the sidewalk.* ( SYNONYM: **beside** )

**3** with someone: *You're welcome to come along to the party.*

**a·long·side** /uh-long-**sīd**/ *adverb, preposition*
**1** next to something: *I ran alongside Grandpa's car, shouting goodbye.*
**2** together with someone: *Scientists from many countries worked alongside each other.*

**a·loud** /uh-**lowd**/ *adverb* using your voice: *Each child reads part of the story aloud.*

**al·pha·bet** /**alf**-uh-bet/
*noun* the letters of a language: *The English alphabet has 26 letters.*
—**alphabetical**
/alf-uh-**bet**-ik-uhl/
*adjective* in the order of the letters of the alphabet: *The words in this dictionary are arranged in alphabetical order.*

**alphabet**

**al·pine** /**al**-pīn/
*adjective* living in high mountains, or relating to high mountains: *Alpine flowers like to have a lot of sunlight.*

**al·read·y** /ol-**red**-ee/ *adverb*
**1** before now: *I've seen that movie twice already.* | *When I got there, Ricky had already left.*
**2** used when something happens sooner than you expected: *It was only 4:00, but the store was already closed.*

**Word Choice: already, all ready**

**Already** is used when you talk about something that has happened: *I've already read the book that the teacher is reading to our class.*

**All ready** is used when you say that someone is ready to do something, or that something is ready to be used: *Are you all ready for school?* | *Dinner is all ready.*

**al·so** /**ol**-soh/ *adverb* used when you mention

another thing: *Jenny sings and she also plays the guitar.* ( SYNONYM: **too** )

**Grammar: also**

Use **also** before a verb, unless the verb is "be": *Diana's sister also plays soccer.*
Use **also** after the word "be": *Two other girls were also late.* | *He's good-looking and he is also very intelligent.*

**al·tar** /**olt**-ur/ *noun* a table used by the priest in religious services: *There were two candles on the altar at the church.*

**al·ter** /**olt**-ur/ *verb* to change something: *We had to alter our plans because of the rain.*
—**alteration** /olt-uh-**raysh**-uhn/ *noun* a change: *He made several alterations to his work.*

**al·ter·nate**
● *verb* /**olt**-ur-nayt/
to do one thing, then a different thing, and then do the first thing again: *She alternated between feeling happy and feeling sad.*
● *adjective* /**olt**-urn-it/
**1** an alternate plan, idea, etc. can be used instead of another one: *If things go wrong, do you have an alternate plan?*
( SYNONYM: **alternative** )
**2** if you do something on alternate days, you do it on one day, but not the next day, and then do it again on the following day: *I see my dad on alternate weekends.*

**al·ter·na·tive** /ol-**turn**-uht-iv/
● *noun*
something you can choose to do or use instead of something else: *As a snack, carrots are a healthy alternative to potato chips.*
● *adjective*
**1** an alternative way or plan can be used instead of another one: *Can you think of an alternative way of measuring the liquid?*
**2** different from the usual type, but doing the same thing: *Corn is used to make an alternative fuel for cars, instead of gasoline.*
—**alternatively** /ol-**turn**-uht-iv-lee/ *adverb* used for suggesting something different: *We could go to the movies. Alternatively, we could go to the park.*

a
b
c
d
e
f
g
h
i
j
k
l
m
n
o
p
q
r
s
t
u
v
w
x
y
z

**a**

**al·though** /ol-**thoh**/ *conjunction*
**1** used when you say a fact that makes the other part of your sentence seem surprising: *Although it was snowing, I didn't feel cold.*
**2** but: *He's good at running, although not as good as I am.*

**al·ti·tude** /**alt**-uh-tood/ *noun* the height of something above sea level: *The plane was flying at an altitude of 30,000 feet.*

**al·to·geth·er** /ol-tuh-**geth**-ur/ *adverb*
**1** including everyone or everything: *There are 20 people altogether.*
**2** completely: *I stopped talking to him altogether.*

**a·lu·mi·num** /uh-**loom**-uhn-uhm/ *noun* a metal that is a silver-gray color. Aluminum is used to make cans and foil. The symbol for aluminum is Al.

**al·ways** /**ol**-wayz/ *adverb*
**1** every time, or at all times: *I always brush my teeth before I go to bed.* | *It's always very cold in the Arctic.*
**2** for a very long time: *I've always wanted to go to New York.*
**3** used when making a suggestion: *You could always come over next weekend instead.*

**Word Choice: always, still, yet**

**Always** means "all the time" or "every time": *She is always so nice to me.* | *I always go swimming on Thursdays.*

You use **still** to say that a situation that began in the past has not changed and is continuing: *He is still sick.*

You use **yet** in sentences with "not" in them. You also use **yet** in questions to talk about something that you think will happen, but which has not happened at the time you are talking: *I haven't seen that movie yet.* | *Is mom home from work yet?*

**Alz·heim·er's dis·ease** /**ahlts**-hīm-urz di-zeez/ *noun* a serious disease that damages people's brains and makes them unable to remember things. Alzheimer's disease usually affects old people.

**am** /m, am/ *verb* the present form of the verb "be" that is used with "I": *I am ten years old.*

**a.m.** /ay **em**/ used to show that a time is in the morning. The letters stand for "ante meridiem." In Latin, that means "before midday": *I catch the school bus at 8 a.m.*

**am·a·teur** /**am**-uhch-ur/
● *adjective* doing a sport or activity because you enjoy it, not as a job for money: *The race is for amateur athletes, not professionals.*
ANTONYM: **professional**
● *noun* someone who does something for enjoyment, not as a job for money: *The photograph was taken by an amateur.*

**a·maze** /uh-**mayz**/ *verb* to make someone very surprised: *She amazed all her friends by winning the race.*
—**amazed** /uh-**mayzd**/ *adjective* very surprised: *I was amazed at how good his English was.*
—**amazing** /uh-**mayz**-ing/ *adjective* very good in a surprising way: *Your hair looks amazing!*

**a·maze·ment** /uh-**mayz**-muhnt/ *noun* the feeling when you are very surprised: *To my amazement, I won the competition.*

**am·bas·sa·dor** /am-**bass**-uhd-ur/ *noun* an important person whose job is to represent his or her country in another country: *She is the U.S. ambassador to France and she lives in Paris.*

**am·big·u·ous** /am-**big**-yoo-uhss/ *adjective* if something is ambiguous, it can have more than one meaning, and you can easily misunderstand what someone is saying: *The phrase "soon" is ambiguous. It can mean "in a few minutes," "in a few days," or "in a few weeks."*

**am·bi·tion** /am-**bish**-uhn/ *noun*
**1** something that you want to achieve in the future: *My ambition is to become a doctor.*
**2** a strong feeling that you want to be successful: *You need to have a lot of ambition if you want to be a famous singer.*
—**ambitious** /am-**bish**-uhss/ *adjective* wanting very much to be successful: *She's very ambitious and she wants to study at Harvard University.*

**am·bu·lance**
/**am**-byuh-luhnss/ *noun* a vehicle for taking sick or injured people to the hospital: *The ambulance came quickly and took him to the emergency room.*

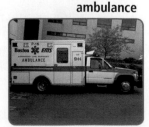
ambulance

18

## am·bush /**amb**-ush/
● *verb* to suddenly attack someone after waiting in a hidden place: *The police officers were hiding behind a fence so they could ambush the robbers.*
● *noun* a sudden attack by someone who has been waiting in a hidden place: *The soldiers walked into an ambush by the enemy.*

## a·mend·ment /uh-**mend**-muhnt/ *noun* a
change to a law or to an important document: *The First Amendment to the Constitution protects freedom of speech.*
—**amend** /uh-**mend**/ *verb* to make a change to a law or to an important document: *Congress is going to amend the law.*

## a·men·i·ties /uh-**men**-uh-teez/ *plural noun*
things in a place that make it nice to live in or stay in: *The town has amenities such as a park and a swimming pool.*

## A·mer·i·can /uh-**merr**-ik-uhn/
● *adjective* from or in the United States: *I feel proud to be American.* | *American food*
● *noun* someone from the United States

## am·mu·ni·tion /a-myuh-**nish**-uhn/ *noun* bullets:
*The soldiers don't have enough ammunition for a long battle.*

## am·nes·ty /**am**-nuhst-ee/ *noun* (plural
**amnesties**) an order from a government that lets prisoners leave prison, or that says people will not be punished for a crime: *Some people who came to the U.S. illegally were given an amnesty.*

## a·moe·ba /uh-**meeb**-uh/ *noun* (plural **amoebas**
or **amoebae** /uh-**meeb**-ee/) a very small creature that has only one cell. You can only see an amoeba through a microscope.

**amoeba**

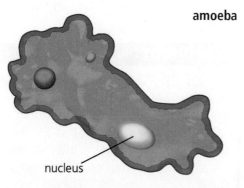

nucleus

## a·mong /uh-**muhng**/ (also a·mongst /uh-**muhngst**/) *preposition*
**1** in the middle of a lot of people or things: *He was standing among a group of trees.*
**2** included in a larger group of people or things: *Karen was among the ten students who received the award.*

### Word Choice: among, between

**Among** and **between** are both used to talk about where someone or something is.

You use **among** when there are two or more people or things on each side or all sides of someone or something: *The teacher stood among all the children.* | *There were some red flowers among the yellow ones.*

Use **between** when there is one other person or thing on each side of someone or something: *I sit between Luis and Emily in class.* | *The blue book was between two red books.*

## a·mor·al /ay-**mor**-uhl/ *adjective* not caring if
your behavior is right or wrong: *His attitude is amoral and he is only interested in making himself rich.*

## a·mount /uh-**mownt**/
● *noun*
an amount of something is how much there is: *$80,000 is a very large amount of money.*
● *verb*
**1 amount to** to make a total: *My birthday money amounted to $55.*
**2** amount to be the same as something: *If you borrow someone's pen that doesn't amount to stealing.*

### Word Choice: amount, number

Use **amount** with nouns that are things you cannot count: *a large amount of food* | *Mom limits the amount of time I can watch TV.*

Use **number** with nouns that are things you can count: *a small number of cookies* | *I talked to a number of people about the idea.*

## amp /amp/ (also am·pere /**amp**-eer/) *noun* a unit
for measuring an electric current

**am·phib·i·an** /am-**fib**-ee-uhn/ *noun* an animal, such as a frog, that starts its life living in water. When it is young, an amphibian breathes through gills like fish do. Amphibians later grow legs, breathe air, and live on land: *The smallest amphibian in the world is a tiny frog that lives in Cuba.*

**amphibian**

frog

newt

toad

**am·phi·the·a·ter** /**amf**-uh-thee-uht-ur/ *noun* a large theater that has no roof. The seats go around the stage in a circle or half a circle.

**amphitheater**

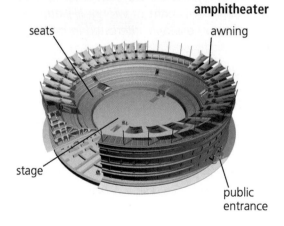

seats

awning

stage

public entrance

**am·ple** /**am**-puhl/ *adjective* more than enough: *We had ample time to answer all the test questions.*

**am·pu·tate** /**amp**-yuh-tayt/ *verb* to cut off a part of someone's body: *His leg was so badly injured it had to be amputated.*
—**amputation** /amp-yuh-**taysh**-uhn/ *noun* the act of amputating something

**a·muse** /uh-**myooz**/ *verb*
**1** to make someone laugh or smile: *Uncle Bill makes funny faces to amuse the kids.*

**2** to do things so that you do not get bored: *We amused ourselves by playing computer games on longer car trips.*
—**amused** /uh-**myoozd**/ *adjective* if you are amused, you think that something is funny: *Everyone was very amused when they saw his new yellow pants.*

**a·muse·ment** /uh-**myooz**-muhnt/ *noun* the feeling you have when you think something is funny: *There was a smile of amusement on her face.*

**a·muse·ment park** /uh-**myooz**-muhnt park/ *noun* a place where people go to enjoy themselves by riding on large machines that go fast or turn around, for example a merry-go-round or a roller coaster: *My favorite ride at the amusement park is the roller coaster.*

**amusement park**

roller coaster

ferris wheel

**a·mus·ing** /uh-**myooz**-ing/ *adjective* funny: *I didn't think his jokes were amusing | an amusing story*

**an** /uhn, an/ *indefinite article* used instead of "a" before a word beginning with a vowel sound: *an animal | an X-ray | an hour | an excellent meal*

**Grammar: a, an**

Use **an** if the word that is after it starts with a vowel sound (the sounds shown by the letters a, e, i, o, or u): *an apple | an orange sweater | an honor*

Use **a** if the word that is after it starts with a consonant sound: *a toy | a white egg | a horse*

**-an** /-uhn/, **-ian**

## Word Building

**-an** or **-ian** is a suffix.

**1** American | San Franciscan | vegetarian | electrician

**-an** or **-ian** means "a person." It is used in nouns. An *American* is a person who comes from America. A *San Franciscan* is a person who lives in the city of San Francisco. A *vegetarian* is someone who only eats vegetables and other food from plants, not meat. An *electrician* is someone whose job is to put in and fix electrical equipment, such as lights.

**2** American | Victorian | Christian

**-an** or **-ian** means "relating to" or "belonging to." It is used in adjectives. An *American flag* relates to the country of America. A *Victorian novel* is a book that was written when Victoria was queen of Great Britain, in the 1800s. A *Christian church* is a church that people go to if they believe in Jesus Christ.

**a·nal·y·sis** /uh-**nal**-uhss-iss/ *noun* if you do an analysis of something, you examine it carefully: *The scientist did an analysis of the blood found at the crime scene.*

**an·a·lyst** /**an**'l-ist/ *noun*
**1** someone whose job is to study a subject carefully, in order to give other people information about it: *Business analysts are saying that the economic situation will get better.*
**2** a doctor who helps people with problems by listening to them talk about their lives

**an·al·yze** /**an**'l-īz/ *verb* to examine something carefully: *Scientists analyzed the water and found that it had harmful chemicals in it.*

## Word Family: analyze

analyze *verb* | analysis *noun* | analyst *noun*

**a·nat·o·my** /uh-**nat**-uhm-ee/ *noun*
**1** the structure of the body of a person or animal: *The anatomy of men and women is slightly different.*
**2** the study of the structure of the body: *Student nurses have to take classes in anatomy.*

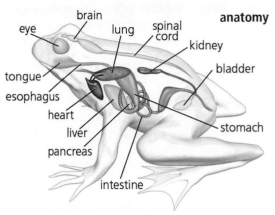

**anatomy**

brain
eye
lung
spinal cord
kidney
tongue
esophagus
bladder
heart
liver
stomach
pancreas
intestine

anatomy of a frog

**an·ces·tor** /**anss**-est-ur/ *noun* a member of your family who lived a long time before you were born: *His ancestors came to the U.S. from Germany over 100 years ago.*
—**ancestry** /**anss**-ess-tree/ *noun* your ancestors: *She is of Korean ancestry.*

**an·chor** /**angk**-ur/ *noun*
**1** someone who reads the news on television or radio: *She is the anchor on the ten o'clock news program.*
**2** a heavy metal object that you put in the water to stop a boat from moving: *"Lower the anchor!" shouted the ship's captain.*

**anchor**

anchor

**an·cient** /**aynsh**-uhnt/ *adjective* thousands of years old: *The explorers found an ancient city in the middle of the jungle.*

**and** /uhn, uhnd, and/ *conjunction*
**1** used to join two words or two parts of a sentence: *I like pizza and pasta.* | *He fell off his bicycle and hurt his knee.*
**2** used when one number is added to another: *7 and 8 is 15.* (SYNONYM: **plus**)

**an·es·thet·ic** /an-uhss-**thet**-ik/ *noun* a drug that stops you from feeling pain during a medical operation: *The doctors gave me a general anesthetic and I didn't feel anything.*
—**anesthesia** /an-uhss-**theezh**-uh/ *noun* the use of drugs to stop someone from feeling pain during a medical operation

21

a
b
c
d
e
f
g
h
i
j
k
l
m
n
o
p
q
r
s
t
u
v
w
x
y
z

**an·gel** /**aynj**-uhl/ *noun* in the Christian religion, a spirit that lives with God in heaven. Angels in pictures usually look like people with wings.

### Word Origin: angel

**Angel** comes from an ancient Greek word that means "messenger." People believed that angels bring messages from God to people on Earth.

**an·ger** /**ang**-gur/
● *noun* angry feelings: *Her face turned red with anger.* ▶ see **Thesaurus**
● *verb* to make someone angry: *He was angered by their rudeness.*

**an·gle** /**ang**-guhl/ *noun*
**1** the shape that is formed when two straight lines meet each other. You measure the shape in degrees: *The top part of the triangle has an angle of 45 degrees.*
**2** a way of thinking about a situation: *I want to look at the problem from a different angle.*

IDIOM with **angle**
**at an angle** sloping, not straight: *The ladder is at an angle against the wall.*

angle

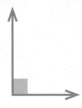  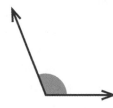

**right angle**
makes a
square corner

**acute angle**
opens less than
a right angle

**obtuse angle**
opens more than
a right angle

**an·gry** /**ang**-gree/ *adjective* feeling like you want to shout or hurt someone: *I was angry at my dad for leaving us.* (SYNONYM: **mad**)
▶ see **Thesaurus**
—**angrily** /**ang**-gruh-lee/ *adverb* in an angry way: *"You lied to me!" he said angrily.*

**an·guish** /**ang**-gwish/ *noun* a very strong feeling of unhappiness: *He caused a lot of anguish to his family because they did not know where he was.*

**an·i·mal** /**an**-uhm-uhl/ *noun* a creature that

breathes and moves: *My favorite animals are horses.* ▶ see **Thesaurus**

**an·i·ma·tion** /an-uh-**maysh**-uhn/ *noun* animation is making movies with a lot of drawings. When the drawings are shown quickly one after another, they seem to move: *"The Incredibles" was made using computer animation.*
—**animated** /**an**-uh-mayt-id/ *adjective* using animation: *Pixar makes animated movies like "Up."*

**an·kle** /**angk**-uhl/ *noun* the part of your body between your foot and your leg: *I fell and hurt my ankle.* ▶ see picture at **foot**

**an·ni·ver·sa·ry** /an-uh-**vurss**-uhr-ee/ *noun* (plural **anniversaries**) a day when you remember something important that happened on the same date in the past, for example the day when someone got married: *My mom and dad are celebrating their 15th wedding anniversary.*

**an·nounce** /uh-**nownss**/ *verb* to tell people some important news: *The coach announced that he was leaving the team.*
—**announcement** /uh-**nownss**-muhnt/ *noun* something important that someone tells people: *The principal will make an important announcement.*

**an·noy** /uh-**noy**/ *verb* to make someone feel a little bit angry: *My little brother was annoying me by making stupid noises.* (SYNONYM: **irritate**)
—**annoyed** /uh-**noyd**/ *adjective* a little angry: *The teacher got annoyed when Luis wouldn't stop talking.*
—**annoying** /uh-**noy**-ing/ *adjective* making someone feel a little angry: *I wish you wouldn't eat and talk at the same time. It's really annoying.*

**an·noy·ance** /uh-**noy**-uhnss/ *noun* the feeling of being a little bit angry: *She stamped her foot in annoyance.* (SYNONYM: **irritation**)

**an·nu·al** /**an**-yoo-uhl/ *adjective* happening once a year: *We're having our annual Halloween party next week.*
—**annually** /**an**-yoo-uhl-ee/ *adverb* once a year: *The report is published annually.*

**a·no·rex·i·a** /an-uh-**rekss**-ee-uh/ *noun* a medical condition in which someone stops wanting to eat. People with anorexia become very thin but

are sometimes worried about being fat. Anorexia usually affects teenagers and young people.
—**anorexic** /an-uh-**rekss**-ik/ *adjective* having anorexia: *She lost a lot of weight when she was anorexic.*

**an·oth·er** /uh-**nuth**-ur/ *adjective, pronoun*
**1** one more person or thing of the same kind: *Can I have another cookie?*
**2** a different person or thing: *He moved to another city last year.*

**an·swer** /**anss**-ur/
● *noun*
**1** something that you say or write when someone asks you a question or gives you a test: *His answer was "yes." | I don't know the answer to question three on the test.*
**2** something that solves a problem: *Money is not the answer to every problem.* (SYNONYM: **solution**)
● *verb*
**1** to say or write something after you have been asked a question or given a test: *I couldn't answer all the questions on the test.*
▶ see **Thesaurus**
**2** to pick up the telephone when it rings: *Juan's mother answered the phone.*
**3** to go to the door when someone knocks or rings a bell: *I rang the doorbell but no one answered.*

**an·swer·ing ma·chine** /**anss**-ur-ing muh-**sheen**/ *noun* a machine that records phone messages when someone is not at home: *I left a message on her answering machine.*

**ant** /ant/ *noun* a very small black or red insect that lives in groups under the ground: *There were ants crawling all over our picnic blanket.*

ant

**an·tac·id** /ant-**ass**-id/ *noun* a medicine that you take when your stomach hurts because you have eaten too much

**Ant·arc·tic** /ant-**arkt**-ik/ (also **Antarctica**) *noun* the area around the South Pole: *Penguins live in the Antarctic.* ▶ see picture at **globe**

**ant·eat·er** /**ant**-eet-ur/ *noun* an animal that has a very long tongue, which uses to eat ants and other insects. An anteater also has a very long nose. Anteaters live in South America.
▶ see picture on page **A2**

**an·te·lope** /**ant**'l-ohp/ *noun* an animal that has long horns and can run very fast. An antelope looks like a large deer and lives in Africa and parts of Asia.

antelope

horn

**an·ten·na** /an-**ten**-uh/ *noun*
**1** a metal object for receiving radio or television signals: *The television antenna is on the roof of the house.*
**2** (plural **antennae** /an-**ten**-ee/) one of two long thin things on an insect's head that it uses to feel things: *Do you see the beetle moving its antennae?*
▶ see picture at **hornet**

antenna

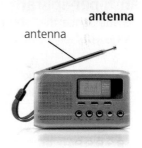
antenna

**an·them** /**anth**-uhm/ *noun* a song that people sing on special occasions. The national anthem is a country's national song: *The band played the national anthem before the game.*

**an·thro·pol·o·gy** /an-thruh-**pahl**-uhj-ee/ *noun* the study of people in different places around the world and how they live
—**anthropologist** /an-thruh-**pahl**-uhj-ist/ *noun* someone who studies people

**anti-** /ant-i/

## Word Building

**anti-** is a prefix.
**antibody** | **antifreeze** | **anti**-war
**anti-** means "against". An *antibody* is a cell in your body that fights against diseases. *Antifreeze* stops an engine from freezing. An *anti-war protester* is someone who is against a war.

**an·ti·bi·ot·ic** /ant-i-bī-**aht**-ik/ *noun* a medicine that kills the bacteria causing an illness or infection: *Penicillin is an antibiotic.*

**an·tic·i·pate** /an-**tiss**-uh-payt/ *verb* to expect something to happen: *The coach doesn't anticipate any problems during tomorrow's game.*
—**anticipation** /an-tiss-uh-**paysh**-uhn/ *noun* the feeling you have when you expect something exciting to happen: *We waited with anticipation for the movie to start.*

**an·ti·freeze** /**ant**-i-freez/ *noun* a liquid that stops water from freezing. You put antifreeze into the water in a car's radiator.

**an·ti·per·spi·rant** /ant-i-**pursp**-uhr-uhnt/ *noun* a substance that you put under your arms to stop yourself from sweating

**an·tique** /an-**teek**/
● *noun* an old and valuable object such as a piece of furniture or jewelry
● *adjective* antique objects are old and valuable: *My grandmother gave me an antique necklace which is over 100 years old.*

**antique**

an antique desk

a modern desk

**an·ti·sep·tic** /ant-i-**sept**-ik/ *noun* a chemical that you put on a cut or wound to stop it from becoming infected. An antiseptic kills germs: *I scraped my knee, and Mom put antiseptic on it.*
▶ see picture at **kit**

**an·ti·so·cial** /ant-i-**sohsh**-uhl/ *adjective* behaving in a way that annoys or causes problems for other people: *It's antisocial to drop litter in the playground.*

**ant·ler** /**ant**-lur/ *noun* the hard pointed parts on the heads of animals such as deer or moose: *The deer's antlers looked like tree branches.*
▶ see picture at **deer**

**antler**

**an·to·nym** /**ant**-uh-nim/ *noun* a word that means the opposite of another word: *"Long" is an antonym of "short."* ( ANTONYM: **synonym** )

**anx·i·e·ty** /ang-**zī**-uht-ee/ *noun* a strong feeling of worry about something: *My parents were full of anxiety because they did not know where I was.* ( SYNONYM: **worry** )

**anx·ious** /**angksh**-uhss/ *adjective*
**1** very worried about something: *I was anxious about being late.* ( SYNONYM: **worried** )
**2** feeling strongly that you want to do something or want something to happen: *She was anxious to make new friends.* ( SYNONYM: **eager** )
—**anxiously** /**angksh**-uhss-lee/ *adverb* in an anxious way: *They waited anxiously for news.*

**an·y** /**en**-ee/
● *adjective, pronoun*
**1** some: *Is there any more ice cream?*
**2** none: *I haven't seen any of his movies.*
**3** used when it does not matter which thing or person: *You can write about any subject you want.*
● *adverb*
even a small amount: *She couldn't walk any farther.*

**Grammar:** any, a

In questions and sentences with "not" in them, we use **any** with nouns that you cannot count. We also use **any** with nouns that show that there is more than one thing: *I don't have any homework.* | *Are there any movies you want to see?*

We use **a** in the same type of sentences when there is only one thing: *Do you have a bike?*

**an·y·bod·y** /**en**-ee-bahd-ee/ *pronoun* anyone: *Is anybody home?*

**an·y·how** /**en**-ee-how/ *adverb* anyway

**an·y·more**, any more /en-ee-**mor**/ *adverb* if something does not happen anymore, it has stopped happening: *I used to be scared of spiders, but I'm not scared of them anymore.*

**an·y·one** /**en**-ee-wuhn/ *pronoun* any person: *I haven't told anyone else.* | *The game is so easy that anyone can play it.*

---

**Grammar:** anyone, someone

In questions and sentences with "not" in them, we usually use **anyone**: *Did you ask anyone to help you?* | *I didn't see anyone there.*

In other sentences, we use **someone**: *There's someone knocking on the door.*

---

**an·y·place** /**en**-ee-playss/ *adverb* anywhere: *I can't find my book anyplace.*

**an·y·thing** /**en**-ee-thing/ *pronoun* a thing of any kind: *Did he say anything else?* | *I listened, but I couldn't hear anything.* | *My dog will eat anything, even things like rocks.*

---

**Word Choice:** anything, something

In questions and sentences with "not" in them, we usually use **anything**: *Mrs. Hogan did not say anything.* | *Do you know anything about dinosaurs?*

In other sentences, we use **something**: *There's something on the table for you.*

---

**an·y·time**, any time /**en**-ee-tīm/ *adverb* at a time, day, hour, etc. that you want, when it does not matter which one: *You can call me anytime.*

( SYNONYM: **whenever** )

**an·y·way** /**en**-ee-way/ *adverb*
**1** even though something else is true: *I didn't like the stew, but I ate it anyway.*
**2** used when you are starting to talk about something different: *Anyway, where's mom?*

**an·y·where** /**en**-ee-wair/ *adverb*
**1** in or to any place: *I'm not allowed to go anywhere by myself.* | *Have you looked anywhere else for your book?*
**2** between two numbers or amounts: *My trip to school takes anywhere from 15 to 25 minutes.*

---

**Grammar:** anywhere, somewhere

In questions and sentences with "not" in them, we usually use **anywhere**: *I couldn't find my hairbrush anywhere.* | *Have you seen my keys anywhere?*

In other sentences, we use **somewhere**: *You all need to find somewhere to sit.*

---

**a·part** /uh-**part**/ *adverb*
**1** not close together: *Stand with your legs apart.*
**2** into many pieces or parts: *He took the old clock apart to see how it worked.*
**3** except for something: *I liked the book apart from the ending.*

**a·part·ment** /uh-**part**-muhnt/ *noun* a set of rooms in a large building where someone lives: *I live in a two-bedroom apartment on the second floor.*

apartment

**a·pat·o·saur·us** /uh-pat-uh-**sor**-uhss/ *noun* a very large dinosaur with a long neck and tail and a small head. ▶ see picture at **dinosaur**

**ape** /ayp/ *noun* a large animal like a monkey but with no tail: *Apes, such as gorillas and chimpanzees, have long arms so that they can climb trees in the jungle.*

ape

gorilla

chimpanzee

orangutan

**a·piece** /uh-**peess**/ *adverb* each: *The apples are 25 cents apiece.*

**a·pol·o·gize** /uh-**pahl**-uh-jīz/ *verb* to say that you are sorry about something that you have done: *He apologized to his mom for shouting at her.*
—**apologetic** /uh-pahl-uh-**jet**-ik/ *adjective* saying or showing that you are sorry about something: *She was very apologetic for being late.*

**a·pol·o·gy** /uh-**pahl**-uhj-ee/ *noun* (plural **apologies**) something that you say or write when you are sorry about what you have done: *Please accept my apologies for the mistake.*

**a·pos·tro·phe** /uh-**pahss**-truhf-ee/ *noun*
**1** the mark ('), which shows that letters have been left out of a word, or numbers have been left out of a date: *don't* (=do not) | *He was born in '96 (=1896 or 1996).*
**2** the mark ('), which is used before an "s" to show that something belongs to someone: *Sarah's coat* (=the coat that belongs to Sarah)

**ap·par·ent** /uh-**parr**-uhnt/ *adjective*
**1** easy to see: *It was apparent to everyone that he was sick.* ( SYNONYMS: **clear, obvious** )
**2** seeming to be true or real: *Despite his apparent calmness, he felt very nervous.*

**ap·par·ent·ly** /uh-**parr**-uhnt-lee/ *adverb* used when you are mentioning something that other people say is true: *He was late for school today. Apparently, he didn't hear his alarm clock.*

**ap·peal** /uh-**peel**/
● *verb*
**1** to ask people for something urgently: *The boy appealed for food for his family.*
**2** to ask a court to change a decision by a different court: *His lawyers appealed the court's decision.*
**3** **appeal to** if something appeals to you, you like it or it seems interesting: *Playing soccer just doesn't appeal to me.*
● *noun*
**1** if someone makes an appeal, he or she asks for money or help from other people: *The charity made an appeal for food and warm clothes.*
**2** the act of asking a court to change a decision by a different court: *His appeal against the court's decision was unsuccessful.*
**3** the quality that makes someone like or want

something: *The show is very popular and it has great appeal for children.*

**ap·peal·ing** /uh-**peel**-ing/ *adjective* making you like or want something, or think it is interesting: *The idea of a day at the beach was very appealing.*

**ap·pear** /uh-**peer**/ *verb*
**1** to seem: *His eyes are closed and he appears to be asleep.*
**2** to begin to be seen: *A message suddenly appeared on my computer screen.*
**3** to take part in a movie or show: *He appeared in over 30 movies.*

**Word Family:** appear

**appear** *verb* | **disappear** *verb* | **appearance** *noun* | **disappearance** *noun*

**ap·pear·ance** /uh-**peer**-uhnss/ *noun*
**1** the way someone or something looks: *The new haircut really changed her appearance.*
**2** a time when someone or something can be seen somewhere: *His first TV appearance was in 1990.*

**ap·pen·di·ci·tis** /uh-pend-uh-**sīt**-iss/ *noun* if you have appendicitis, your appendix gets bigger and becomes painful. It usually has to be taken out in an operation.

**ap·pen·dix** /uh-**pend**-ikss/ *noun*
**1** a small closed tube that is part of your intestine: *The doctors removed his appendix because he had very bad stomach pains.*
**2** (plural **appendices** /uh-**pend**-uh-seez/) a part at the end of a book that has extra information: *A list of useful books is given in the appendix.*

**ap·pe·tite** /**ap**-uh-tīt/ *noun* the feeling that you want to eat something: *When I was sick, I lost my appetite and hardly ate anything.*

**ap·pe·tiz·er** /**ap**-uh-tīz-ur/ *noun* a small amount of food that you eat before the main part of a meal: *I want to have garlic bread as an appetizer.*

**ap·plaud** /uh-**plod**/ *verb* to hit your hands together many times to show that you think something is good: *Everyone applauded him and said that it was a very good speech.*
( SYNONYM: **clap** )

**ap·plause** /uh-**ploz**/ *noun* the sound of people

hitting their hands together many times to show that they think something is good: *There was loud applause at the end of the concert.*

**ap·ple** /**ap**-uhl/ *noun* a hard round red or green fruit that is white inside: *apple juice*

apple

**ap·ple·sauce** /**ap**-uhl-soss/ *noun* cooked apples that have been crushed until they are smooth

seed

**ap·pli·ance** /uh-**pli**-uhnss/ *noun* a machine that is used in someone's home, for example a refrigerator or a dishwasher

core

**ap·pli·ca·tion** /ap-li-**kaysh**-uhn/ *noun*
**1** a form that you write on when you are asking for a job, asking to join something, etc.: *If you want to attend the sports camp, here's the application.*
**2** a computer program that you can use for doing something: *This application is used for making web pages.*

**ap·ply** /uh-**pli**/ *verb* (**applies**, **applying**, **applied**)
**1** to ask for something by writing a letter or filling out a form: *My brother applied to study at four colleges.*
**2** to affect a particular person or situation: *The rule applies to everyone.*
**3** to spread something on a surface, for example paint: *She applied her lipstick.*
—**applicant** /**ap**-lik-uhnt/ *noun* someone who is applying for something: *job applicants*

**Word Family:** apply

**apply** *verb* | **application** *noun* | **applicant** *noun*

**ap·point** /uh-**poynt**/ *verb* to choose someone for a job: *A new principal has just been appointed at the school.*

**ap·point·ment** /uh-**poynt**-muhnt/ *noun*
**1** a meeting that you have planned to happen at a particular time and place: *I have a doctor's appointment at 5:00.*

**2** the act of choosing someone for a job: *The appointment of a new coach took several months.*

**ap·pre·ci·ate** /uh-**preesh**-ee-ayt/ *verb* to feel thankful for something: *Thanks for your help. I appreciate it.*

**Word Family:** appreciate

**appreciate** *verb* | **appreciation** *noun*

**ap·pre·ci·a·tion** /uh-prish-ee-**aysh**-uhn/ *noun* the feeling of being thankful for something: *How can I show my appreciation for all your hard work?* ( SYNONYM: **gratitude** )

**ap·pren·tice** /uh-**prent**-iss/ *noun* someone who is learning how to do a job by working with someone who can do it: *He is an apprentice to a carpenter.*

**ap·proach** /uh-**prohch**/
● *verb*
**1** to move closer to someone or something: *Don't cross the street when a car is approaching.*
**2** to be going to happen soon: *Winter was approaching and it was getting colder.*
● *noun*
a way of doing something or dealing with a problem: *The treatment didn't work, so the doctor tried a different approach.*

**ap·pro·pri·ate** /uh-**proh**-pree-it/ *adjective* correct or good for a person or situation: *Scary movies are not appropriate for young children.*
( ANTONYM: **inappropriate** )
—**appropriately** /uh-**proh**-pree-it-lee/ *adverb* in an appropriate way: *He was very short and was appropriately called Mr. Small.*

**ap·prov·al** /uh-**proov**-uhl/ *noun*
**1** actions that show you think someone or something is good: *Children always want their parents' approval.*
**2** if you have approval for something, you are allowed to do it: *You must get approval from the school if you want to go on vacation early.*

**ap·prove** /uh-**proov**/ *verb*
**1** to think that someone or something is good: *My mother doesn't approve of boys having long hair.* ( ANTONYM: **disapprove** )
**2** to allow someone to do something, or allow something to happen: *Has your teacher approved your science project?*

**ap·prox·i·mate·ly** /uh-**prakss**-uhm-it-lee/ *adverb* used when a number or amount is not exactly right: *The test will take approximately 15 minutes.* (SYNONYM: **around**)
—**approximate** /uh-**prahkss**-uhm-it/ *adjective* not exact: *The approximate cost of the air ticket will be $150.*

**ap·ri·cot** /**ay**-pri-kaht/ *noun* a small soft fruit with a yellow-orange skin and one large seed ▶ see picture on page **A7**

**A·pril** /**ayp**-ruhl/ *noun* (ABBREVIATION: **Apr.**) the fourth month of the year. April is between March and May: *In April, the flowers start to appear.* | *Mom's birthday is on April 15.*

---

**Word Origin:** April

**April** comes from the Latin name for this month, **Aprilis**. The name of the month may come from another Latin word meaning "to open." Flowers and leaves grow and start to open in April. Or, the name April may come from the Greek goddess called Aphrodite. Many of the months in the Roman calendar were named after gods or goddesses.

---

**A·pril Fools' Day** /ayp-ruhl-**foolz** day/ *noun* April 1, when people play tricks on each other: *On April Fools' Day, my brother put a plastic snake in my bed.*

**a·pron** /**ayp**-ruhn/ *noun* a piece of clothing that covers your other clothes when you are cooking or painting: *I usually wear an apron when I'm in the kitchen.*

**ap·ti·tude** /**apt**-uh-tood/ *noun* a natural ability that makes it easy for you to do something well: *She has a real aptitude for math and she gets good grades on all her tests.*

**a·quar·i·um** /uh-**kwair**-ee-uhm/ *noun*
**1** a glass container for keeping fish in: *Change the water in the aquarium once a week.*
**2** a building where people go to look at fish or other sea animals: *I saw a shark at the aquarium.*

**aq·ue·duct** /**ak**-wuh-duhkt/ *noun* a long bridge or channel that carries water from one place to another: *The aqueduct carries water from the mountains to Los Angeles.*

**Ar·ab** /**arr**-uhb/
● *adjective* from or in the Middle East or North Africa: *Some Arab countries have become very rich because of oil.*
● *noun* someone from the Middle East or North Africa: *The Arabs made many important discoveries in mathematics and science.*

**Ar·a·bic** /**arr**-uhb-ik/ *noun* the language spoken in the Middle East and North Africa: *In Arabic, people write from right to left.*

**ar·a·ble** /**arr**-uhb-uhl/ *adjective* arable land is used for growing crops

**ar·bi·trar·y** /**arb**-uh-trair-ee/ *adjective* done without any good reason: *The rules seem arbitrary and it's difficult to know why some things are allowed and other things aren't.*

**arc** /ark/ *noun* a curved line, especially one that is part of a circle: *The rainbow forms a big arc in the sky.*

**ar·cade** /ar-**kayd**/ *noun* a place where people pay to play video games

**arch** /arch/ *noun* (plural **arches**) a curved shape at the top of a door or window, or supporting a bridge: *The weight of the bridge is supported by huge stone arches.*

arch

arch

**ar·che·ol·o·gy**, **archaeology** /ark-ee-**ahl**-uhj-ee/ *noun* the study of people who lived a long time ago. You do this by digging to find old buildings and tools that people used.
—**archeologist** /ark-ee-**ahl**-uhj-ist/ *noun* someone who studies archeology: *Archeologists have found a Mayan city in the jungle.*

**ar·chi·tect** /**ark**-uh-tekt/ *noun* someone whose job is to design buildings: *These are the architect's drawings of the new school.*

**ar·chi·tec·ture** /**ark**-uh-tek-chur/ *noun* the style and design of a building: *The city is famous for its beautiful architecture.*

**Arc·tic** /**arkt**-ik/ *noun* the area around the North Pole: *Polar bears live in the Arctic.* ▶ see picture at **globe**

**are** /ur, ar/ *verb* the present form of the verb "be" that is used with plurals and "you": *Robert and Ray are in the kitchen.* | *Are you hungry?*

**ar·e·a** /**air**-ee-uh/ *noun*
**1** a part of a place: *Our house is in a quiet area of town.* | *the children's play area*
▶ see **Thesaurus**
**2** the size of a flat surface or shape: *The area of a rectangle is the length multiplied by the height.*

**ar·e·a code** /**air**-ee-uh kohd/ *noun* the three numbers that come before a telephone number. You use the area code when you call someone who lives in a different area than you: *My area code is 818.*

**a·re·na** /uh-**reen**-uh/ *noun* a large building where people go to watch sports or concerts: *The arena was full of fans.*

**aren't** /**ar**-uhnt/ *contraction*
**1** short for "are not": *My aunt and uncle aren't here yet.*
**2** the short form of "am not," used in questions: *I'm right, aren't I?*

**ar·gue** /**arg**-yoo/ *verb*
**1** if people argue, they shout or say angry things because they do not agree with each other: *My brothers are always arguing with each other.*
▶ see **Thesaurus**
**2** to explain why you think something is true: *He argued that it wouldn't be right to keep the money.*

**ar·gu·ment** /**arg**-yuh-muhnt/ *noun*
**1** if people have an argument, they shout or say angry things because they do not agree with each other: *Mom and Dad had a big argument about money.* ▶ see **Thesaurus**
**2** a reason that you give to show that something is right or wrong: *His argument was that the plan was too expensive.*

**a·rise** /uh-**rīz**/ *verb* (**arose** /uh-**rohz**/, **arisen** /uh-**riz**-uhn/) to happen: *Problems sometimes arise in any school.*

**a·rith·me·tic** /uh-**rith**-muht-ik/ *noun* the activity of adding, subtracting, multiplying, or dividing numbers: *The students practice doing simple arithmetic, like adding three plus four.*

**arm** /arm/ *noun*
**1** the part of your body between your shoulder and your hand: *She held the baby in her arms.*
▶ see picture on page **A13**
**2** the part of a chair or sofa that you rest your arm on
**3** **arms** weapons such as guns and bombs: *He ordered the soldiers to put down their arms.*

**ar·ma·dil·lo** /arm-uh-**dil**-oh/ *noun* an animal with a pointed nose and a hard shell. Armadillos live in hot dry parts of North and South America.

**Word Origin:** armadillo

Spanish explorers in the 1500s had never seen an **armadillo** before, so they did not have a name for it. They thought that an armadillo looked like it was wearing armor, like a knight. In Spanish, armadillo means "the little armored one."

**armadillo**

**arm·chair** /**arm**-chair/ *noun* a chair with sides that you can rest your arms on: *He was sitting in an armchair by the fireplace.*

**armed** /armd/ *adjective* carrying a weapon such as a gun or knife: *A gang of armed robbers took all his money.*

**armed forc·es** /armd **forss**-iz/ *plural noun* a country's army, navy, air force, etc.: *All his brothers were in the armed forces.*

**ar·mor** /**arm**-ur/ *noun*
**1** metal clothing that protects your body if you are attacked: *Knights used to wear metal armor.*
**2** a strong metal layer that protects a vehicle if it is attacked
—**armored** /**arm**-urd/ *adjective* having armor: *an armored truck*

**armor**

helmet
visor
shield
sword

**arm·pit** /**arm**-pit/ *noun* the place under your arm where it joins your body

**ar·my** /**arm**-ee/ *noun* (plural **armies**) the large group of people who fight for their country on land: *My grandfather was in the army and he fought in the Vietnam War.*

**a·ro·ma** /uh-**rohm**-uh/ *noun* a strong good smell: *The aroma of freshly baked cookies filled the house.*

**a·rose** /uh-**rohz**/ *verb* the past tense of **arise**

**a·round** /uh-**rownd**/ *adverb, preposition*
**1** surrounding a place or person: *There was a high wall around the house.* | *Mom put her arms around Joey.*
**2** in many parts of a place: *Everyone was running around on the playground.*
**3** somewhere in an area: *She lives around here.*
**4** used when saying that a number is not exact: *It's around five o'clock.* ( SYNONYM: **about** )
**5** in the opposite direction: *The car turned around and drove away.*
**6** moving in a circle: *What makes the wheels go around?*

**a·rouse** /uh-**rowz**/ *verb* to make someone have a feeling: *A strange sound outside his window aroused his curiosity.*

**ar·range** /uh-**raynj**/ *verb*
**1** to put a group of things in an order or place: *The desks are arranged in rows.*
**2** to make plans for something to happen: *The doctor arranged for my grandmother to have some tests.*

**ar·range·ment** /uh-**raynj**-muhnt/ *noun*
**1** if you make arrangements for something, you do things so that it will happen: *Mom made all the arrangements for my birthday party.*
**2** the way that things are put into an order or position: *The arrangement of the desks made it easy for the children to work together.*

**ar·ray** /uh-**ray**/ *noun*
**1** a group of people or things, especially one that is good or has many parts: *The museum has an impressive array of dinosaur bones.*
**2** a set of numbers that are in a pattern, especially in columns or rows

**ar·rest** /uh-**rest**/
● *verb* if the police arrest someone, they take the person away because they think that he or she has done something illegal: *He was arrested for stealing.*
● *noun* a situation when the police arrest someone: *After his arrest, the officers took him to the police station.*

**ar·riv·al** /uh-**rīv**-uhl/ *noun*
**1** the act of arriving somewhere: *He met Beth soon after his arrival in Boston.*
( ANTONYM: **departure** )

30

**2** a person or thing that has come to a place only a short time ago: *The principal welcomed the new arrivals to the school.*

**ar·rive** /uh-**rīv**/ *verb* to get to a place: *What time does the plane arrive in Chicago?*
▶ see **Thesaurus**

**ar·ro·gant** /**arr**-uhg-uhnt/ *adjective* rude and not friendly because you think you are better than other people: *He's so arrogant! He'll never admit he's wrong.*
—**arrogantly** /**arr**-uhg-uhnt-lee/ *adverb* in an arrogant way: *"Do it this way," she said arrogantly.*
—**arrogance** /**arr**-uhg-uhnss/ *noun* arrogant behavior: *His arrogance made him unpopular.*

**ar·row** /**arr**-oh/ *noun*
**1** a long thin piece of wood or metal with a point at one end. You shoot it from a bow: *Native Americans used bows and arrows to hunt deer and other animals for food.*
**2** a sign in the shape of an arrow which tells you where to go: *An arrow on the map shows where the hidden treasure is.*

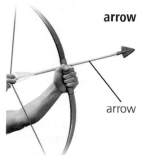
**arrow**
arrow

**ar·row·head** /**arr**-oh-hed/ *noun* the pointed part of an arrow: *The Indians made arrowheads from stone.*

**ar·son** /**arss**-uhn/ *noun* the crime of making a building start burning: *The church was damaged by arson last year.*
—**arsonist** /**arss**-uhn-ist/ *noun* someone who commits arson: *Arsonists started a fire at the school.*

**art** /art/ *noun*
**1** things such as paintings, drawings, and sculptures: *You can see works of art at the museum.* ▶ see **Thesaurus**
**2** the activity of making paintings, drawings, and sculptures: *I love doing art at school.*
**3 the arts** the group of subjects that includes painting, music, and literature: *He's interested in the arts and he likes going to concerts and exhibitions.*

**Word Family:** art

art *noun* | artist *noun* | artistic *adjective*

**ar·ter·y** /**art**-uhr-ee/ *noun* one of the tubes that carries blood from your heart around your body
▶ see picture at **heart**

**ar·thri·tis** /ar-**thrit**-iss/ *noun* a disease that makes people's joints painful and swollen. Arthritis mainly affects older people: *Grandma has arthritis in her knees.*

**ar·thro·pod** /**arth**-ruh-pahd/ *noun* a type of animal that has a hard skeleton on the outside of its body, pairs of legs, and no backbone. Spiders, beetles, and crabs are arthropods.

**ar·ti·choke** /**art**-i-chohk/ *noun* a round green vegetable with pointed leaves. You can cook and eat the leaves and the soft bottom.

**ar·ti·cle** /**art**-ik-uhl/ *noun*
**1** a piece of writing about a subject in a newspaper or magazine: *There was an article about our school in the newspaper.*
**2** a thing: *an article of clothing*
**3** the word "the," "a," or "an" that goes before a noun. "The" is the definite article and "a" and "an" are the indefinite articles.

**ar·ti·fact** /**art**-i-fakt/ *noun* an object that was made and used a long time ago: *There are many interesting artifacts in the museum.*

**ar·ti·fi·cial in·tel·li·gence** /**art**-uh-fish-uhl in-tel-uhj-uhnss/ *noun* the use of computer technology to make computers think and make decisions like humans

**ar·ti·fi·cial** /art-uh-**fish**-uhl/ *adjective* not real or natural, but made by people: *Real flowers are nicer than artificial ones.* | *an artificial leg*
▶ see **Thesaurus**
—**artificially** /art-uh-**fish**-uhl-ee/ *adverb* in an artificial way: *The water was artificially blue.*

**art·ist** /**art**-ist/ *noun*
**1** someone who paints pictures, does drawings, makes sculptures, etc.: *Picasso was a famous artist.*
**2** someone who writes music or books, sings, etc.: *This artist writes all her own songs.*

**ar·tis·tic** /ar-**tist**-ik/ *adjective*
**1** good at art: *I'm not very artistic – my picture of a dog looked like a horse!*
**2** relating to art: *His latest artistic creation is a car made out of soda cans.*

**a** b c d e f g h i j k l m n o p q r s t u v w x y z

**as** /uhz, az/ *adverb, preposition, conjunction*
**1** used for saying what someone's job is: *My father works as a doctor.*
**2** used for saying what something is used for: *We used our coats as blankets.*
**3** while something is happening: *As I walked home, I thought about Mary.*
**4** because: *I decided to go to bed, as I was very tired.* ( SYNONYM: **since** )
**5 as . . . as** used for comparing people or things: *The house was almost as big as a castle.* | *I'm not as pretty as you.*
**6 as if/as though** used when you are saying how someone looks or how something seems: *She looked as if she had been crying.* | *It felt as though something exciting was going to happen.*

**ASAP** /ay ess ay **pee**/ *adverb* ASAP is short for "as soon as possible": *Please reply ASAP.*

**as·cend** /uh-**send**/ *verb* to go up higher: *The president ascended the steps.* ( SYNONYM: **rise** )
( ANTONYM: **descend** )
—**ascent** /uh-**sent**/ *noun* the act of ascending: *The hikers began their ascent of the mountain.*

**ash** /ash/ *noun* the gray powder that is left after something has burned: *She swept up the ashes from the fire.* ▶ see picture at **volcano**

**a·shamed** /uh-**shaymd**/ *adjective* feeling sad and embarrassed about something wrong you did: *I was ashamed about lying to my mother.*

**A·sia** /**ayzh**-uh/ *noun* the area of land that has China, Japan, Korea, Vietnam, India, and other countries in it. Asia is one of the seven continents: *Pakistan is in Asia.* ▶ see picture at **continent**

**A·sian** /**ayzh**-uhn/
● *adjective* from Asia: *An Asian family has moved here from Thailand.*
● *noun* someone from Asia: *There are a lot of Asians in my school.*

**a·side** /uh-**sīd**/ *adverb* to one side: *Please move aside so I can pass.*

**ask** /ask/ *verb*
**1** to say something that is a question: *My little sister is always asking questions.* | *You can ask the teacher to help you.* | *"Can I have a drink?" he asked.* ▶ see **Thesaurus**
**2** to invite someone to go somewhere: *I'm going to ask all my friends to my party.*

**a·sleep** /uh-**sleep**/ *adjective* sleeping: *The baby is asleep in the back of the car.* | *Is Dad asleep?*
( ANTONYM: **awake** )

asleep

asleep

awake

**as·par·a·gus** /uh-**sparr**-uhg-uhss/ *noun* a long thin green vegetable with a pointed top

asparagus

**as·pect** /**asp**-ekt/ *noun* one part of something: *Religion is an important aspect of his life.*

**as·pen** /**asp**-uhn/ *noun* a type of tree that grows in western North America

**as·phalt** /**ass**-folt/ *noun* a hard black substance used for covering roads: *an asphalt playground*

**as·pirin** /**asp**-rin/ *noun* a medicine that makes you feel less pain: *Mom took two aspirins for her headache.*

**as·sas·sin** /uh-**sass**-uhn/ *noun* someone who kills an important person: *The king was killed by an assassin.*

**as·sas·si·nate** /uh-**sass**-uh-nayt/ *verb* to kill an important person: *President Kennedy was assassinated in 1963.*
—**assassination** /uh-sass-uh-**naysh**-uhn/ *noun* the killing of an important person: *The assassination of Martin Luther King in 1968 shocked America.*

**as·sault** /uh-**solt**/
● *verb* to attack and hurt someone: *They were arrested for assaulting him.* ( SYNONYM: **attack** )
● *noun* an act of attacking someone and hurting them: *She was injured in an assault downtown.*

## as·sem·ble

/uh-**sem**-buhl/ *verb*
**1** to put the different parts of something together: *Dad helped me to assemble the model airplane.*

SYNONYM: **put together**

**2** if people assemble, they come together in a group: *All the students assembled in front of the school.*

**assemble**

## as·sem·bly /uh-**sem**-blee/ *noun*

**1** a meeting of a large group of people: *I had to give a talk during a school assembly.*
**2** the process of putting the parts of something together: *The assembly of the tent takes about 30 minutes.*

## as·sess /uh-**sess**/ *verb* to judge how good or bad something is: *The teacher assesses your work then gives you a grade.*

—**assessment** /uh-**sess**-muhnt/ *noun* the act of assessing something: *After an assessment of the evidence, the judge decided she was guilty.*

## as·set /**ass**-et/ *noun* someone or something that helps you to be successful: *Kevin is a really good player and he is the team's greatest asset.*

## as·sign /uh-**sīn**/ *verb* to give someone work to do: *The teacher assigned a lot of homework.*

## as·sign·ment /uh-**sīn**-muhnt/ *noun* a piece of work that your teacher has told you to do: *You can use a computer for your homework assignments.*

## as·sim·i·late /uh-**sim**-uh-layt/ *verb* to become part of a country or group and be accepted in it: *His family assimilated easily into American life.*

## as·sist /uh-**sist**/ *verb* to help someone do something: *You can use a calculator to assist you.* SYNONYM: **help**

## as·sist·ance /uh-**sist**-uhnss/ *noun* help for someone: *Press the buzzer if you need assistance.* SYNONYM: **help**

## as·sist·ant /uh-**sist**-uhnt/ *noun* someone who helps a more important person with their work: *For this experiment, I need an assistant.*

## as·so·ci·ate

● *verb* /uh-**sohsh**-ee-ayt/ to think of two things as connected with each other: *Lung cancer is associated with smoking cigarettes.*

SYNONYM: **connect**

● *noun* /uh-**sohsh**-ee-it/ someone that you work with or do business with: *He is one of my father's business associates.*

## as·so·ci·a·tion /uh-sohss-ee-**aysh**-uhn/ *noun* an organization of people who do the same type of work or activity: *the United States Tennis Association*

## as·sort·ed /uh-**sort**-id/ *adjective* of different types: *I got a bag of assorted candy.*

**assorted**

## as·sume /uh-**soom**/ *verb* to think that something is probably true: *I assumed that they were sisters because they look so alike.*

assorted candy

—**assumption** /uh-**suhmp**-shuhn/ *noun* something that you think is probably true: *He made the assumption that the two boys knew each other.*

## as·sure /uh-**shoor**/ *verb* to tell or promise someone something to stop them from worrying: *The doctor assured me that I was fine.*

—**assurance** /uh-**shoor**-uhnss/ *noun* something you say that assures someone: *Can you give me an assurance that this will not happen again?*

## as·ter·isk /**ast**-uh-risk/ *noun* a mark like a star (*), used to show there is more information somewhere else: *There were asterisks next to some of the names on the list.*

## as·te·roid /**ast**-uh-royd/ *noun* an object like a small planet that goes around the Sun: *Asteroids are made of rock and metal.*

## asth·ma /**az**-muh/ *noun* a medical problem that makes it difficult for someone to breathe sometimes. The tubes in the lungs become narrow and swollen, and the person breathes very noisily: *Dust makes my asthma worse.*

—**asthmatic** /az-**mat**-ik/ *adjective* having asthma: *Pedro is asthmatic so he carries an inhaler.*

a
b
c
d
e
f
g
h
i
j
k
l
m
n
o
p
q
r
s
t
u
v
w
x
y
z

**as·ton·ish** /uh-**stahn**-ish/ *verb* to surprise someone very much: *He astonished them with his knowledge of baseball.* ( SYNONYM: **amaze** )
—**astonished** /uh-**stahn**-isht/ *adjective* very surprised: *She's very intelligent and I will be astonished if she doesn't know the right answer.* ( SYNONYM: **amazed** )
—**astonishing** /uh-**stahn**-ish-ing/ *adjective* very surprising: *The store has an astonishing range of toys – you can get almost anything.* ( SYNONYM: **amazing** )
—**astonishment** /uh-**stahn**-ish-muhnt/ *noun* the feeling you have when you are very surprised: *"Have you really met the President?" he asked in astonishment.* ( SYNONYM: **amazement** )

**as·trol·o·gy** /uh-**strahl**-uhj-ee/ *noun* the study of how the position of the stars and planets may affect people's lives: *In astrology, people born between July 23 and August 22 are Leos.*

**as·tro·naut** /**ass**-truh-not/ *noun* someone who travels in space: *Neil Armstrong was the first astronaut to walk on the moon.*

**astronaut**

**as·tron·o·my** /uh-**strahn**-uhm-ee/ *noun* the study of space, stars, and planets: *I was interested in astronomy, so my dad bought me a telescope.*
—**astronomer** /uh-**strahn**-uhm-ur/ *noun* a scientist who studies astronomy

**at** /uht, at/ *preposition*
**1** in a particular place: *I'm having a party at my house.*
**2** used when saying the time when something happens: *The movie starts at 8:00.*
**3** toward: *That boy keeps looking at me.*

**4** used when saying the price of something: *The jeans are selling at $25 a pair.*
**5** doing something: *He's good at soccer.* | *The two countries are at war.*

**ate** /ayt/ *verb* the past tense of **eat**

**a·the·ism** /**ayth**-ee-iz-uhm/ *noun* the belief that there is no god
—**atheist** /**ayth**-ee-ist/ *noun* someone who believes that there is no god

**ath·lete** /**ath**-leet/ *noun* someone who is good at sports and often plays sports: *Athletes from all over the world take part in the Olympic Games.*

**ath·let·ic** /ath-**let**-ik/ *adjective*
**1** an athletic person has a strong body and is good at playing sports: *He is tall and athletic and he likes playing basketball.*
**2** relating to sports: *athletic shoes*

**ath·let·ics** /ath-**let**-ikss/ *noun* sports and other activities you do to keep your body healthy: *My sister is good at athletics and she wins all her races.*

**At·lan·tic** /uht-**lant**-ik/ *noun* the ocean that is between America and Europe: *He crossed the Atlantic in a sailing ship.* ▶ see picture at **continent**

**at·las** /**at**-luhss/ *noun* a book of maps: *Find Canada in the atlas.*

**Word Origin:** atlas

The word **atlas** was first used in the title of a book of maps in 1595. Many other map makers also started using atlas in the title of their map books, until atlas began to mean "a book of maps." The word **atlas** may come from two different stories. The first story is a legend about King Atlas, who made the first globe. The second story is a Greek myth. In the story, Atlas was an old Greek god called a Titan. The Titans fought against the newer Greek gods called the Olympians. Atlas was punished for fighting the Olympians. He had to hold up the sky to keep it separate from the Earth.

**ATM** /ay tee **em**/ *noun* a machine that you put your bank card in to get money from your bank account. ATM stands for "automatic teller machine."

**at·mos·phere** /**at**-muhss-feer/ *noun*
**1** the air around the Earth or around another planet: *Most of the Earth's atmosphere is made of oxygen and nitrogen.*
**2** the feeling that a place or situation gives you: *The school has a very friendly atmosphere.*

**at·om** /**at**-uhm/ *noun*
the smallest possible amount of an element (=a chemical substance that is not made of other substances). Atoms join together to make different substances: *Each hydrogen atom is only about a ten millionth of a millimeter in size.*

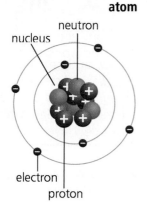
**atom**
neutron
nucleus
electron
proton

**a·tom·ic** /uh-**tahm**-ik/
*adjective* relating to atoms: *the atomic weight of carbon*

**a·tom·ic en·er·gy** /uh-tahm-ik **en**-urj-ee/ *noun*
the energy that comes when scientists split atoms: *Electricity can be produced by atomic energy.* (SYNONYM: **nuclear energy**)

**at·tach** /uh-**tach**/ *verb*
**1** to fasten one thing to another: *They attached a rope to the front of the car.*
**2** to put a computer file with an email in order to send them together: *Attach your report to an email.*
**3** be attached to to like something or someone: *I'm very attached to this house.*

**Word Family:** attach
attach *verb* | attachment *noun*

**at·tach·ment** /uh-**tach**-muhnt/ *noun*
**1** a computer file that you put with an email in order to send them together: *I sent the pictures as an attachment.*
**2** a strong feeling that you like someone or something very much: *People feel a strong attachment to their pets.*

**at·tack** /uh-**tak**/
● *verb*
**1** to try to hurt someone: *The man attacked Ray with a stick.*
**2** to fight people in a place and damage the buildings there: *Enemy soldiers attacked the town.*
**3** to say bad things about someone: *It's wrong to attack people for being different.*
(SYNONYM: **criticize**)
● *noun*
**1** an attempt to hurt another person: *The men who started the attack have been punished.*
**2** a fight with an enemy in a war: *The planes started their attack at dawn.*
**3** a time when you suddenly get sick: *I can't breathe when I have an asthma attack.*

**at·tack·er** /uh-**tak**-ur/ *noun* someone who tries to hurt another person: *Her attackers ran off with her purse.*

**at·tain** /uh-**tayn**/ *verb* to get something you want, especially after a lot of work: *I hope my students will attain good grades this year.*
(SYNONYM: **achieve**)
—**attainment** /uh-**tayn**-muhnt/ *noun* the act of attaining something: *For Juan, the attainment of a high school diploma was an important goal.*
(SYNONYM: **achievement**)

**at·tempt** /uh-**tempt**/
● *verb* to try to do something: *Do not attempt to light a fire without an adult.* (SYNONYM: **try**)
● *noun* the act of trying to do something: *His first attempt at the test was unsuccessful.*

**at·tend** /uh-**tend**/ *verb*
**1** to go to an event or a place: *Why didn't you attend school yesterday?*
**2** to deal with something: *The doctor will attend to you in a few minutes.*

**at·tend·ance** /uh-**tend**-uhnss/ *noun* the act of going regularly to an event or place: *Her attendance at school is good.*

**at·tend·ant** /uh-**tend**-uhnt/ *noun* someone whose job is to take care of a place and the people who use it: *A flight attendant serves drinks and takes care of passengers on a plane.*

**at·ten·tion** /uh-**tensh**-uhn/ *noun*
**1** listening or looking carefully: *I waved at Joe because I wanted to get his attention and make him look at me.* | *You must pay attention to what the teacher is saying and listen carefully.*
**2** care or treatment: *The cut on your arm needs attention.*

**at·ten·tive** /uh-**tent**-iv/ *adjective* listening and looking carefully: *The class was very attentive and they listened to every word of the story.*
—**attentively** /uh-**tent**-iv-lee/ *adverb* in an attentive way: *The children were listening very attentively.*

**at·tic** /**at**-ik/ *noun* a space or room under the roof of a house: *There are a lot of old toys up in the attic.*

**at·ti·tude** /**at**-uh-tood/ *noun* the way you think or feel about something: *Her attitude toward her schoolwork is very good.*

**at·tor·ney** /uh-**turn**-ee/ *noun* someone whose job is to give people advice about the law: *He hired an attorney to defend him in court.*
( SYNONYM: **lawyer** )

**at·tract** /uh-**trakt**/ *verb*
**1** to make someone feel interested in something, or want to visit something: *The library wants to attract more young people.*
**2** if you are attracted to someone, you like that person: *I was very attracted to her.*
**3** if something attracts an object, it pulls the object toward itself: *The needle is attracted by the magnet and moves toward it.*

**Word Family:** attract

**attract** *verb* | **attraction** *noun* | **attractive** *adjective* | **unattractive** *adjective*

**at·trac·tion** /uh-**trak**-shuhn/ *noun*
**1** the feeling when you like someone or something very much: *Kids feel a strong attraction to superheroes like Spider-Man.*
**2** something that people want to see or do: *The zoo is a good tourist attraction.*

**at·trac·tive** /uh-**trakt**-iv/ *adjective*
**1** pretty or nice to look at: *She is a very attractive woman.* ( ANTONYM: **unattractive** )
**2** interesting or exciting: *A picnic in the rain was not a very attractive idea.* ( ANTONYM: **unattractive** )

**auc·tion** /**ok**-shuhn/
● *noun* an event at which things are sold. The person who offers the most money for something can buy it: *My mother bought the painting at an auction.*
● *verb* to sell something at an auction: *They auctioned my grandfather's war medals.*

**audi-** /**od**-ee/

**Word Building**

**audi**ence | **audi**torium | **audi**ble | **audi**tion
These words all have the Latin word root **audi** in them. **Audi** means "to hear." An *audience* listens to a concert or play. An *auditorium* is a place where you listen to a concert or play. If a sound is *audible*, you can hear it.

**au·di·ble** /**od**-uhb-uhl/ *adjective* loud enough to be heard: *Your voice must be clearly audible when you read out your story.*

**au·di·ence** /**od**-ee-uhnss/ *noun* the people watching a performance such as a play or a speech: *The audience stood up and clapped.*

**au·di·o** /**od**-ee-oh/ *adjective* relating to sound, especially sound that is played on electronic equipment: *The audio quality of the radio is good.*

**au·di·o·vis·u·al** /od-ee-oh-**vizh**-oo-uhl/ *adjective* playing recorded pictures and sound: *Audiovisual equipment such as TVs and computers are sometimes used in class.*

**au·di·tion** /o-**dish**-uhn/
● *noun* a short performance that you do to try to be in a play or singing group: *Auditions for the school play are on Tuesday.*
● *verb* to do a short performance to try to be in a play or singing group: *I auditioned for the school choir.*

**au·di·to·ri·um** /od-i-**tor**-ee-uhm/ *noun* a large room used for concerts or public meetings: *The audience was seated in the auditorium.*

**Au·gust** /**og**-uhst/ *noun* ( ABBREVIATION: **Aug.** ) the eighth month of the year. August is between July and September: *New York is very hot in August. | My birthday is on August 18.*

> ### Word Origin: August
>
> The month of **August** is named after Augustus Caesar. He was the first emperor of the Roman empire.

**aunt** /ant/ *noun* the sister of your mother or of your father. Your aunt can also be the wife of your uncle: *Aunt Grace is my mom's younger sister.*

> ### Word Origin: aunt
>
> **Aunt** comes from an Old French word, **ante**. The French word came from Latin. The Latin word for aunt may have come from a word used by children that meant "mother."

**au·thor** /**oth**-ur/ *noun* someone who writes books: *The author writes books for children.*

**au·thor·i·ty** /uh-**thor**-uht-ee/ *noun*
**1** if someone has authority, he or she has the right to make important decisions and control people: *You need to speak to someone in authority.*
**2** an organization or government department that controls something: *We reported the accident to the authorities.*

> ### Word Family: authority
>
> **authority** *noun* | **authorize** *verb* | **authorization** *noun*

**au·thor·ize** /**oth**-uh-rīz/ *verb* to give someone permission to do something: *You are not authorized to leave the school at lunchtime.*
—**authorization** /oth-ur-uh-**zaysh**-uhn/ *noun* permission: *You need special authorization to park here.*

**au·tis·m** /**ot**-iz-uhm/ *noun* a medical condition in the brain that makes it difficult for someone to communicate and have relationships with other people
—**autistic** /o-**tist**-ik/ *adjective* having autism: *My*

younger brother goes to a special school for autistic children.

**au·to** /**ot**-oh/ *adjective* relating to cars: *General Motors is an auto company.*

> ### Word Building
>
> **auto**mobile | **auto**biography | **auto**graph | **auto**matic
> These words all have the Greek word root **auto** in them. **Auto** means "self." An *automobile* uses its own engine to make itself move. You write an *autobiography* about yourself and your life. An *autograph* is a famous person's name, written by that person himself or herself. If a machine is *automatic*, it works by itself after you start it.

**au·to·bi·og·ra·phy** /ot-uh-bī-**ahg**-ruhf-ee/ *noun* a book that someone writes about his or her own life: *The president has written his autobiography.*
—**autobiographical** /ot-uh-bī-uh-**graf**-ik-uhl/ *adjective* an autobiographical book is about the writer's own life: *an autobiographical novel*

**au·to·graph** /**ot**-uh-graf/ *noun* a famous person's name, written by him or her: *Fans were asking for the singer's autograph.*

**au·to·mat·ic** /ot-uh-**mat**-ik/ *adjective*
**1** an automatic machine works on its own, without people operating it: *Most homes have automatic washing machines.*
**2** done without thinking: *I screamed – it was an automatic reaction.*

**au·to·mat·i·cally** /ot-uh-**mat**-ik-lee/ *adverb*
**1** without thinking: *I automatically put my glasses on as soon as I wake up.*
**2** without being operated by someone: *The lights turn on automatically when you enter the room.*

**au·to·mation** /ot-uh-**maysh**-uhn/ *noun* the use of machines to do a job: *Automation makes factories able to produce things more quickly.*

**au·to·mo·bile** /ot-uh-muh-**beel**/ *noun* a car: *Steel is used for making automobiles.*

**au·top·sy** /**ot**-ahpss-ee/ *noun* an examination of a dead body, in order to find out how that person died: *An autopsy showed that she died from a heart attack.*

**au·tumn** /**ot**-uhm/ *noun* the season before winter, when the leaves fall off the trees: *New England is beautiful in the autumn.*
SYNONYM: **fall**

**a·vail·a·ble** /uh-**vayl**-uhb-uhl/ *adjective* if something is available, you can have it, buy it, or use it: *The book will be available in stores soon.*
—**availability** /uh-vayl-uh-**bil**-uht-ee/ *noun* the state of being available: *You can check the availability of our products on our website.*

**av·a·lanche**
/**av**-uh-lanch/ *noun* a large amount of snow or rocks that falls down a mountain: *Avalanches are dangerous because they can move very fast.*

avalanche

**av·e·nue** /**av**-uh-noo/ *noun* a wide street in a town or city: *He lives on Melrose Avenue.*

**av·erage** /**av**-rij/
● *noun*
the amount that you get by adding a group of numbers together, then dividing the total by the number of things in the group: *The average of 2, 9, and 10 is 7* (=because 2 + 9 + 10 = 21, divided by 3 = 7).

IDIOMS with average
**above average** higher than the usual number or level: *Her test scores were well above average.*
**below average** lower than the usual number or level: *Temperatures have been below average this summer.*
**on average** usually: *On average, I play sports four times a week.*
● *adjective*
**1** calculated by adding a group of numbers together, then dividing the total by the number of things in the group: *The average age of the students is 12.*
**2** typical or ordinary: *We live in an average house on an average street.*

**a·vi·a·tion** /ayv-ee-**aysh**-uhn/ *noun* the activity of flying aircraft or making aircraft: *We're studying the history of aviation.*

**av·o·ca·do**
/av-uh-**kah**-doh/ *noun* (plural **avocados**) a fruit with a green or dark purple skin and a large seed in the middle: *The salad had avocados and tomatoes in it.*

avocado
seed

**a·void** /uh-**voyd**/ *verb*
**1** to stay away from someone or something: *We had a fight and now she's avoiding me.*
**2** to try not to do something because it might cause problems: *I want to avoid talking about things that will upset him.*
—**avoidable** /uh-**voyd**-uhb-uhl/ *adjective* possible to avoid: *Most of these mistakes were avoidable.*
—**avoidance** /uh-**voyd**-uhnss/ *noun* the act of avoiding something: *the avoidance of accidents*

**a·wait** /uh-**wayt**/ *verb* to wait for something: *We are awaiting the arrival of a special visitor.*

**a·wake** /uh-**wayk**/
● *adjective* not asleep: *The children are often awake till midnight.*
● *verb* (**awoke** /uh-**wohk**/, **awoken** /uh-**wohk**-uhn/) to wake up: *I was awoken by the sound of the phone.*

**a·ward** /uh-**word**/
● *noun* a prize given to someone for doing something good: *She has won many awards for her dancing.* SYNONYM: **prize**
● *verb* to give someone an award: *The student who writes the best story will be awarded a prize.*

**a·ware** /uh-**wair**/ *adjective* knowing that something exists or that something is happening: *He was aware that someone was in the room.*
ANTONYM: **unaware**
—**awareness** /uh-**wair**-niss/ *noun* knowledge that something exists or that something is happening: *Very young children have no awareness of danger.*

**a·way** /uh-**way**/ *adverb*
**1** further from a person, place, or thing: *Go away!* | *I pushed him away from the fire.*
**2** used when saying how far something is from somewhere: *The nearest town is ten miles away.*
**3** not at home, at work, or in school: *I didn't see Brad at school today. He was away.*

**4** used when saying how much time will pass before something happens: *My birthday is only five days away.*

**5** into the place where something is kept: *You can put your books away now.*

**awe** /o/ *noun* a feeling of great admiration or respect: *The sight of the Grand Canyon filled us with awe.*

**awe·some** /**o**-suhm/ *adjective*

**1** very good: *This pie's awesome! Can I have some more?*

**2** very big or difficult: *Building a sports stadium is an awesome task.*

**aw·ful** /**of**-uhl/ *adjective*

**1** very bad: *There's an awful smell in here! Can we open the window?*

**2 an awful lot** very much or a great amount: *Our cat eats an awful lot of food and he's very fat.*

**3 feel awful** to feel very sick: *My throat hurts and I feel awful. I think I'm getting a cold.*

**aw·fully** /**of**-lee/ *adverb* very: *He works awfully hard.*

**a·while** /uh-**wil**/ *adverb* for a short time: *I decided to rest awhile.*

**awk·ward** /**ok**-wurd/ *adjective*

**1** not able to relax and talk to people easily: *I always feel a little awkward when I meet someone for the first time.*

**2** embarrassing or difficult: *My mom asked me some awkward questions about what had happened to her best plates.*

**3** difficult to use or hold: *The backpack was big and awkward to carry.*

—**awkwardly** /**ok**-wurd-lee/ *adverb* in an awkward way: *"It's my first time here," he said rather awkwardly.*

—**awkwardness** /**ok**-wurd-niss/ *noun* an awkward quality: *After some awkwardness at first, they began to chat.*

**awn·ing** /**on**-ing/ *noun* a sheet of material that sticks out like a small roof over a door or window. An awning keeps the sun or the rain off.

awning

**a·woke** /uh-**wohk**/ *verb* the past tense of **awake**

**ax**, **axe** /akss/ *noun* a tool used for cutting wood. An ax has a metal blade on a long handle: *He was chopping up logs with an ax.*

**ax·is** /**akss**-iss/ *noun* (plural **axes** /**akss**-eez/)

**1** a line at the side or bottom of a graph, where you put numbers: *The x-axis goes from left to right on the graph, and the y-axis goes from top to bottom.*

**2** an imaginary line through the middle of something that is turning, for example the Earth: *The Earth turns on its axis.* ► see picture at **globe**

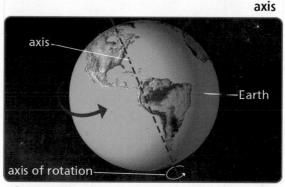
axis
axis
Earth
axis of rotation

**ax·le** /**akss**-uhl/ *noun* a long thin part that connects two wheels on a vehicle. The axle goes through the center of the two wheels and they turn around it at the same speed: *There was a problem with the car's front axle.*

*a*
**b**
*c*
*d*
*e*
*f*
*g*
*h*
*i*
*j*
*k*
*l*
*m*
*n*
*o*
*p*
*q*
*r*
*s*
*t*
*u*
*v*
*w*
*x*
*y*
*z*

# Bb

**B** /bee/ *noun* a grade that you get on a test or in a class. If you get a B, your work is good, but not excellent: *If you get a B, try to get an A next time.*

**ba·boon** /ba-**boon**/ *noun* a large monkey that lives in Africa and south Asia

**baboon**

**ba·by** /**bayb**-ee/ *noun* a very young child: *He is a beautiful little baby boy. | Mom told us she was going to have a baby.* ▶ see **Thesaurus**

**ba·by car·riage** /**bayb**-ee karr-ij/ (also **ba·by bug·gy** /**bayb**-ee buhg-ee/) *noun* a thing used for pushing a baby from one place to another. It has a part for the baby to lie on and four wheels at the bottom.

**ba·by·sit** /**bayb**-ee-sit/ *verb* (**babysitting**, **babysat** /**bayb**-ee-sat/) to take care of a child while his or her parents are not at home: *My grandma comes to babysit when my mom is at the gym.*
—**babysitter** /**bayb**-ee-sit-ur/ *noun* someone who babysits: *We have a babysitter when Mom and Dad go out.*
—**babysitting** /**bayb**-ee-sit-ing/ *noun* the job of babysitting a child: *Babysitting is one way teenagers can earn money.*

**ba·by tooth** /**bayb**-ee tooth/ *noun* one of a child's first set of teeth. Baby teeth fall out and are replaced by new adult teeth.

**back** /bak/
● *noun*
**1** the rear part of your body between your neck and your waist. Your back is on the other side from your chest and stomach: *He was lying on his back, looking up at the sky.* (ANTONYM: **front**)
▶ see picture at **horse**
**2** the part of something that is farthest from the front: *The answers to the quiz are in the back of the book.* (ANTONYM: **front**)
● *adverb*
**1** in the place where someone or something was before: *Put those books back on the shelf. | She went out but she should be back soon.*
**2** into the condition that someone or something was in before: *I woke up at 5 a.m. and couldn't get back to sleep.*
**3** in the direction that is behind you: *She fell back onto the floor and hit her head.*
**4** doing the same thing to someone as he or she has done to you: *He hit me, so I hit him back.*
**5 back and forth** in one direction and then in the opposite direction several times: *He went back and forth on the swing.*
● *verb*
**1** to move backward: *The car is backing into the driveway. | He backed away when he saw the snake.*
**2** to support someone or something: *The president backed the plan and said that he wanted it to succeed.*
**3 back down** to stop arguing and insisting that you are right: *Everyone disagreed with her, but she refused to back down.*
**4 back out** to decide not to do something you promised to do: *I feel nervous about singing on stage, but it is too late to back out now.*
**5 back up** to show that what someone is saying is true: *Give examples to back up your ideas.*
● *adjective*
**1** in or on the back of something: *the back door | the back page of the magazine*
(SYNONYM: **rear**) (ANTONYM: **front**)
**2 a back street/road** a street or road that is not a main one: *We drove through the back streets, looking for her house.*

**back·board** /**bak**-bord/ *noun* the piece of wood or plastic behind a basketball net: *The ball bounced off the backboard.* ▶ see picture on page **A10**

**back·bone** /**bak**-bohn/ *noun* the line of bones down the middle of your back. Each bone is connected to the one next to it: *He was so thin you could see his backbone sticking out.*
( SYNONYM: **spine** )

**back·fire** /**bak**-fī-ur/ *verb* to not happen in the way that you wanted it to: *I pretended to be sick, but my plan backfired when Mom said I had to go to the doctor.*

**back·ground** /**bak**-grownd/ *noun*
**1** the part of a picture that is behind the main part: *This is a photo of me with the White House in the background.*
**2** someone's family, education, and past experience: *She comes from a very religious background and her parents go to church every Sunday.*

**background**

There is a house in the background.

**back·pack** /**bak**-pak/ *noun* a bag that you carry on your back: *I carry my books in my backpack.*

**backpack**

**back·stroke** /**bak**-strohk/ *noun* a way of swimming on your back. You move one arm up and over your head and then the other: *He swam the backstroke across the pool.*
▶ see picture at **swim**

**back·up** /**bak**-uhp/ *noun* a copy of something, that you can use if there is a problem: *Make a backup of your work in case the computer crashes.*

**back·ward** /**bak**-wurd/ (also **backwards**)
● *adverb*
**1** in the direction that is behind you: *I walked two steps backward.* ( ANTONYM: **forward** )
**2** toward the beginning: *Can you say the alphabet backward?* ( ANTONYM: **forward** )
**3** with the back part in front: *He always wears his baseball cap backward.*
● *adjective*
toward the direction that is behind you: *She turned and took a backward look at the other runners behind her.* ( ANTONYM: **forward** )

**back·yard** /**bak**-**yard**/ *noun* the area of land behind a house: *The kids were playing in the backyard.*

**ba·con** /**bayk**-uhn/ *noun* meat from the back or sides of a pig which has been preserved using salt or smoke: *We had bacon and eggs for breakfast.*

**bac·te·ri·a** /**bak**-**teer**-ee-uh/ *plural noun* (singular **bacterium** /**bak**-**teer**-ee-uhm/) living things that are too small to see but that are all around you. Some kinds of bacteria cause disease: *Wash your hands to remove harmful bacteria.*

**bad** /**bad**/ *adjective* (**worse** /wurss/, **worst** /wurst/)
**1** not nice or enjoyable: *I have some bad news – we lost the game.* | *The weather is very bad and it has been raining all day.* ( ANTONYM: **good** )
▶ see **Thesaurus**
**2** not able to do something well: *He's a bad driver and he often has accidents.* | *I'm very bad at math.* ( ANTONYM: **good** )
**3** of low quality: *Her singing was so bad I walked out of the concert.* ( ANTONYM: **good** )
**4** not healthy: *Sugar is bad for your teeth.* ( ANTONYM: **good** )
**5** serious or severe: *There was a bad accident on the freeway.*
**6** morally wrong or evil: *A bad man locked the princess in a tower.* ( ANTONYM: **good** )
**7 feel bad** to feel sorry or ashamed about something: *I feel bad about forgetting your birthday.*
**8 too bad** used to say that you are sorry about a sad situation: *It's too bad your grandma is sick.*
**9 not bad** fairly good, but not very good: *"How was the food?" "Not bad."*

**badge** /baj/ *noun* a small piece of metal or plastic with a picture or sign on it. You wear it or carry it to show who you are or who you work for: *The police officer was wearing a badge on his uniform.*

**badg·er** /**baj**-ur/ *noun* a medium-sized animal with black and white fur. Badgers live underground and look for food at night.

**bad·ly** /**bad**-lee/ *adverb* (**worse** /wurss/, **worst** /wurst/)

**1** in a way that is not good: *The children are behaving very badly and they keep shouting all the time.* (ANTONYM: **well**)

**2** very severely: *He was badly injured in a car accident and he broke his leg.*
(SYNONYM: **seriously**)

**bad·min·ton** /**bad**-mint-uhn/ *noun* a game like tennis, with two or four players. You use a racket to hit a small object with feathers on it over a net: *Let's play a game of badminton.*

**bag** /bag/ *noun* a soft container made of paper, plastic, cloth, or leather. You carry things in a bag: *Here's a bag of jelly beans. | I carried some shopping bags for Mom.* ▶ see **Thesaurus**

**ba·gel** /**bayg**-uhl/ *noun* a type of bread that is round with a hole in the center: *I sometimes have a bagel with cream cheese for breakfast.*

### Word Origin: bagel

**Bagels** are shaped like rings. The word bagel comes from an Old German word that meant "ring." The Old German word moved into Yiddish, which was spoken by Jewish people in Europe. These Jewish people came to the U.S. and brought bagels with them.

**bag·gage** /**bag**-ij/ *noun* the bags or suitcases that you take with you when you travel on an airplane, train, or bus: *The men are putting our baggage onto the airplane.*

**bag·gy** /**bag**-ee/ *adjective* big and loose: *He is wearing a pair of baggy jeans.* (ANTONYM: **tight**)

**bail** /bayl/
● *noun* money that someone pays to leave prison until his or her trial. If he or she does not come to the trial, the court keeps the money: *The police released the man on $10,000 bail.*

● *verb* **bail out** to help someone get out of trouble: *Joe owed the bank a lot of money, and his parents had to bail him out.*

**bait** /bayt/ *noun* a small amount of food that you use to catch fish or animals: *I use worms as bait when I'm fishing.*

**bake** /bayk/ *verb* to cook something such as bread or cakes in an oven: *Let's bake a cake for Sam's birthday.*

**bak·er** /**bayk**-ur/ *noun* someone whose job is making things such as bread or cakes

**bak·er·y** /**bayk**-uhr-ee/ *noun* a place where bread and cakes are made or sold: *The bakery sells freshly made bread every day.*

**bal·ance** /**bal**-uhnss/
● *noun*
**1** the ability to stand or walk steadily, without falling: *When you stand on one leg it's hard to keep your balance.*
**2** a situation in which different things are in the right amounts: *You need to get the right balance between study and play.*
● *verb*
**1** to stay in a steady position, without falling: *Can you balance on one foot?*
**2** to keep something in a steady position so that it does not fall: *She was balancing a plate of food on her knees.*

**bal·anced** /**bal**-uhnst/ *adjective* including different things in the right amounts: *A balanced diet includes food from all the different food groups.*

**bal·co·ny** /**balk**-uhn-ee/ *noun* (plural **balconies**)
**1** a small floor that sticks out from the outside of a building. You can sit or stand on a balcony: *Our apartment has a balcony with chairs and a table on it.*
**2** the seats upstairs in a theater: *I had a good view of the show from the balcony.*
▶ see picture at **theater**

**bald** /bold/ *adjective* having little or no hair on your head: *Underneath his hat he was completely bald.*

### bald ea·gle /**bold**
eeg-uhl/ *noun* a large North American bird with a white head and neck. The bald eagle is a symbol of the United States.

bald eagle
beak
talon

### ball /bol/ *noun*
**1** a round object that you throw, hit, or kick in some games: *Try to throw the ball through the hoop.* | *a tennis ball* ▶ see picture at **racket**
**2** something made into a round shape: *Shape the cookie mixture into balls.* | *a ball of string*
**3** in baseball, a time when a ball is thrown and the hitter does not try to hit it because it is not in the correct area: *The first pitch was a ball.*
**4** a large formal party at which people dance: *At the ball, Cinderella danced with the prince all night.* ( SYNONYM: **dance** )

> **IDIOMS with ball**
> **have a ball** to have a lot of fun: *We were having a ball playing in the snow.*
> **be on the ball** to be able to think or act quickly: *The kids were really on the ball and caught on to the idea quickly.*

### bal·le·ri·na /bal-uh-**reen**-uh/ *noun* a woman
who dances in ballets. A ballerina plays the most important part in the ballet: *The ballerina danced on her toes.*

### bal·let /ba-**lay**/ *noun*
**1** a type of dancing: *She goes to ballet classes because she loves dancing.* | *a ballet dancer*
**2** a performance in which the dancers do this type of dancing to tell a story: *We saw a ballet at the theater.*

ballet
a ballet dancer

### bal·loon /buh-**loon**/
*noun* a colored rubber bag that you fill with air. Balloons are often used at parties as a decoration: *We blew up balloons and played games with them.*

balloon

**Word Origin: balloon**

**Balloon** first meant a game that was played with a large ball filled with air. The word balloon probably came from an Italian word that meant "a large ball." In the 1700s, people started using the word balloon about hot-air balloons. Rubber balloons were invented in England in the 1800s, and that was when the name balloon was given to them.

### bal·lot /**bal**-uht/ *noun*
**1** a piece of paper used for voting. You mark on the ballot who you want to vote for then put it in a box: *They are counting the ballots to see who has won the election.*
**2** a system in which people vote: *We have a ballot to choose the leader.*

**Word Origin: ballot**

**Ballot** comes from an Italian word that means "little ball." A long time ago, people dropped a little ball into a pot to vote for someone.

### ball·park /**bol**-park/ *noun* a place for playing
baseball: *He hit the ball out of the ballpark.*

### ball·point pen /bol-poynt **pen**/ *noun* a pen
with a small ball at the end. The ball rolls ink onto the paper.

### ball·room /**bol**-room/ *noun* a large room for
formal dances: *The party will be in the hotel ballroom.*

### bam·boo /bam-**boo**/ *noun* a tall plant with hard
hollow stems that grows in hot countries. Bamboo is often used for making furniture: *Pandas like to eat bamboo.*

a
**b**
c
d
e
f
g
h
i
j
k
l
m
n
o
p
q
r
s
t
u
v
w
x
y
z

### ban /ban/
● *noun* an official order saying that something is not allowed: *There is a ban on cell phones at our school because they make too much noise in class.*
● *verb*, (**banning**, **banned**) to say that something is not allowed: *Mom banned me from watching TV for a week because she thinks I watch too much TV.*

### ba·nan·a /buh-**nan**-uh/ *noun* a long curved fruit with a yellow skin: *She picked up a bunch of bananas.* ▶ see picture on page **A7**

### band /band/ *noun*
**1** a group of musicians that plays popular music: *The band has a singer, two guitar players, and a drummer.*
**2** a small group of people who do something together: *The team has a loyal band of fans.*
( SYNONYM: **group** )
**3** a narrow piece of something which goes around something else to hold it or decorate it: *He wore a leather band around his wrist.*

### ban·dage /**band**-ij/
● *noun* a long piece of cloth that you put around a wound: *He had a bandage around his head.* ▶ see picture at **kit**
● *verb* to put a bandage around a wound: *The nurse bandaged his arm.*

### Band-Aid /**band** ayd/ *noun trademark* a small piece of material that you stick over a small cut on your skin: *Do you need a Band-Aid for your finger?*

### ban·dan·na /ban-**dan**-uh/ *noun* a square piece of colored cloth that you wear around your head or neck: *He covered his face with his bandanna.*

### bang /bang/
● *verb*
**1** to make a loud noise by hitting something: *We banged on the door, but no one answered.*
**2** to hit a part of your body on something by accident: *I banged my head on the shelf.*
● *noun*
a sudden loud noise: *The door closed with a bang because of the wind.*

### bangs /bangz/ *plural noun* hair that is cut so that it covers your forehead

bangs

bangs

### ban·is·ter /**ban**-uhst-ur/ *noun* a bar that you hold onto when you go up or down stairs ▶ see picture at **staircase**

### ban·jo /**ban**-joh/ *noun* (plural **banjos**) a musical instrument with strings and a round body: *My uncle plays the banjo in a country and western band.*

**Word Origin:** banjo

The word **banjo** probably comes from an African language. Banjos are similar to instruments that are used in Africa. African people who became slaves in the U.S. made their own instruments like the ones they had used in Africa.

banjo

### bank /bangk/
● *noun*
**1** a place where you can keep your money or borrow money: *Dad went to the bank to get some money.*
**2** land along the side of a river: *We went for a walk along the river bank.*
**3** a place where a large quantity of something is stored for people to use: *The blood is kept in a blood bank at the hospital.*
● *verb*
to use a particular bank: *Mom banks with First National.*

**bank·er** /**bangk**-ur/ *noun* someone who has an important job in a bank

**bank·ing** /**bangk**-ing/ *noun* the business of banks, for example lending money

**bank·rupt** /**bangk**-ruhpt/
● *adjective* not able to pay the money you owe other people or companies: *The company lost a lot of money and it went bankrupt.*
● *verb* to make a person or business unable to pay the money owed to other people or companies: *The medical bills bankrupted them.*
—**bankruptcy** /**bangk**-ruhptss-ee/ *noun* a situation in which a person or company cannot pay the money owed to other people or companies: *Sales have been poor and the company is facing bankruptcy.*

**ban·ner** /**ban**-ur/ *noun* a long piece of cloth with writing on it: *The banner said "Welcome Home!"*

**ban·quet** /**bangk**-wit/ *noun* a big formal meal for a lot of people: *The mayor invited city leaders to the banquet.*

**bap·tize** /**bap**-tīz/ *verb* to put water on someone in a religious ceremony, so that he or she becomes a member of the Christian church: *He was baptized when he was six months old.*
—**baptism** /**bap**-tiz-uhm/ *noun* a religious ceremony in which water is put on someone. Baptism makes someone a member of the Christian religion.

**bar** /bar/
● *noun*
**1** a small block of something: *He was eating a candy bar. | a bar of soap*

bar
a bar of chocolate

a bar of soap

**2** a place where people can buy and drink alcohol: *The men were drinking beer in a bar.*
**3** a long thin stick of metal: *The fence was made with iron bars.*
**4** a group of notes in music: *We sang a few bars of the song.*

IDIOM with **bar**
**behind bars** in prison: *The bank robber is now behind bars.*

● *verb*, (**barring**, **barred**)
**1** to officially stop someone from doing something: *The judge barred the man from driving for six months.*
**2** to put a piece of wood or metal across a door or window to stop people from going in or out: *The windows were all barred.*

**bar·be·cue**
/**barb**-i-kyoo/ *noun*
**1** a meal or party where you cook food outside: *My parents are having a barbecue tonight.*
**2** a piece of equipment you use to cook food outside: *There were hamburgers and hotdogs cooking on the barbecue.*

barbecue

**Word Origin:** barbecue

The word **barbecue** comes from the language of a tribe who lived in the Caribbean islands. The people in that tribe put meat on a set of sticks and then cooked the meat over a fire.

**barbed wire** /**barbd**-wī-ur/ *noun* wire with short sharp points on it: *There was a barbed wire fence around the prison.*

**bar·ber** /**barb**-ur/ *noun* a man whose job is to cut men's hair
—**barber shop** /**barb**-ur shahp/ *noun* a store where men's hair is cut

**bar code** /**bar** kohd/ *noun* a row of black lines on something that is sold in a store. The bar code gives a computer information about the thing being sold, for example how much it costs.

**bare** /bair/ *adjective*
**1** not covered by clothes: *I like walking on the sand in bare feet.*
**2** if a place is bare, it has nothing in it or on it: *The walls of the classroom were bare and there were no pictures.* (SYNONYM: **empty**)

a b c d e f g h i j k l m n o p q r s t u v w x y z

**a b c d e f g h i j k l m n o p q r s t u v w x y z**

**bare·foot** /**bair**-fut/
*adjective*, *adverb* not wearing any shoes or socks: *We took off our shoes and walked barefoot on the beach.*

barefoot

**bare·ly** /**bair**-lee/
*adverb* almost not: *I could barely sleep the night before my birthday.*
SYNONYM: **hardly**

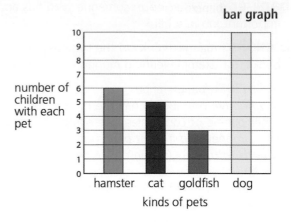
bar graph

number of children with each pet

kinds of pets

**bar·gain** /**barg**-uhn/
● *noun* something you buy for a price that is cheaper than normal: *The bike was a bargain – it was only $60.*
● *verb* to try to get someone to sell you something for a lower price: *Sometimes you can bargain with the salesman to get a good price.*

**barge** /barj/
● *noun* a large boat with a flat bottom. A barge carries goods on a river: *The barge was carrying coal.*
● *verb* to walk quickly and carelessly, so that you push someone or something: *He barged into me and almost knocked me over.*

barge

**bar graph** /**bar** graf/ *noun* a graph that uses pictures of boxes that are different heights to show different amounts. For example, a tall box means a larger amount than a short box: *The bar graph shows what kind of pets the children have. Dogs are the most popular pets.*

**bark** /bark/
● *verb*
if a dog barks, it makes a short loud sound: *Our dog always barks at the mailman.*
● *noun*
**1** the sound a dog makes: *The dog gave a loud bark.*
**2** the part that covers the outside of a tree: *The bark of a birch tree is smooth.* ▶ see picture at **tree**

**bar·ley** /**barl**-ee/ *noun* a grain used in making some foods: *barley soup*

**bar mitz·vah** /bar **mitss**-vuh/ *noun* a religious ceremony that takes place when a Jewish boy is 13 years old. After this ceremony, he can take part in his religion as an adult.

**barn** /barn/ *noun* a large building on a farm for storing crops or keeping animals in: *The straw is kept in a big barn.*

barn

**ba·rom·e·ter** /buh-**rahm**-uht-ur/ *noun* an instrument that measures the pressure of the air around us. When the air pressure is low, the weather will be rainy.

**bar·racks** /**barr**-uhkss/ *noun* a group of buildings where soldiers live

**bar·ra·cu·da** /barr-uh-**kood**-uh/ *noun* a large ocean fish that eats other fish. Barracudas have sharp teeth and live in warm areas of the ocean.

**bar·rel** /**barr**-uhl/ *noun*
**1** a large container for liquids, for example oil or beer. A barrel is like a very large tube with a flat top and bottom: *The wine is kept in big barrels for two years.*
**2** the part of a gun that the bullets are shot through

**bar·rette** /buh-**ret**/ *noun* a small metal or plastic clip that a girl uses to keep her hair in place: *A red barrette keeps her hair out of her eyes.*

**bar·ri·er** /**barr**-ee-ur/ *noun*
**1** a fence or wall that stops people from going into a place: *There was a barrier between the crowd and the stage.*
**2** a problem that stops people from doing something: *If you don't speak good English, this can be a barrier to getting a good job.*

**bar·ri·o** /**barr**-ee-oh/ *noun* (plural **barrios**) an area in a city where many Spanish-speaking people live

**bar·tend·er** /**bar**-tend-ur/ *noun* someone whose job is to make and serve drinks in a bar

**bar·ter** /**bart**-ur/
● *verb* to pay for something by giving other things or doing work, rather than by using money: *The Indians bartered animal skins for cloth and guns.*
● *noun* the system of paying for something by giving other things or doing work, instead of using money: *In the past, people used barter to get the things they needed.*

**base** /bayss/
● *noun*
**1** the lowest part of something: *His name is written on the base of the statue.*
**2** one of the four places that a baseball player must run to in order to score a point: *I ran to second base.*
**3** the main place used by a company or person: *The company has its base in Oregon.*
**4** a place where soldiers live and work: *an army base*
**5** a substance that will form a salt if it is combined with an acid: *Bases have a pH higher than 7, so they will turn litmus paper blue.*
**6** the number that a mathematical system is built on: *The decimal system uses a base of 10.*
● *verb*
**1** to have your main office or home in a place: *Dad's company is based in Houston.*
**2** to use an idea or fact as a start for making something new: *The movie is based on a true story.*

**base·ball** /**bayss**-bol/ *noun*
**1** a game played by two teams of nine players. The players try to get points by hitting a ball with a bat and running around four bases: *Do you want to play baseball?* | *the baseball team*
▶ see picture on page **A10**
**2** the ball used in this game

**base·ment** /**bayss**-muhnt/ *noun* the part of a building that is below the level of the ground: *The storeroom is in the basement.*

**bash** /bash/
● *verb* to hit something hard: *I bashed my head when I fell down.*
● *noun* a party: *Are you coming to my birthday bash?*

**bash·ful** /**bash**-fuhl/ *adjective* shy and embarrassed: *She was very nervous and she gave him a bashful smile.* (SYNONYM: **shy**)
—**bashfully** /**bash**-fuhl-ee/ *adverb* in a bashful way

**ba·sic** /**bayss**-ik/ *adjective* simple but important and necessary: *Today we are going to learn some basic facts about using computers.*

**Word Family: basic**

**basic** *adjective* | **base** *verb* | **base** *noun* | **basis** *noun* | **basically** *adverb*

**ba·si·cally** /**bayss**-ik-lee/ *adverb*
**1** used when you are giving the most important reason or fact about something: *Basically, I don't have enough money to buy a new bike.*
**2** in the most important ways: *The teacher said that my answer was basically right.*

**ba·sics** /**bayss**-ikss/ *plural noun* the most important facts or things that you need to know: *Everyone needs to learn the basics – reading, writing, and math.*

**ba·sil** /**bayz**-uhl/ *noun* a plant with leaves that are used in cooking. The leaves are green and smell sweet: *Put some basil in the spaghetti sauce.*

**ba·sin** /**bayss**-uhn/ *noun*
**1** a large area of land around a river. The water from the land in the basin goes into the river: *The Amazon basin covers parts of Brazil, Peru, and other countries.*
**2** a large bowl, especially one for water: *I washed my hands in a basin of water.*

**ba·sis** /**bayss**-iss/ *noun* (plural **bases** /**bayss**-eez/)
**1** the idea or reason that something comes from: *These ideas were the basis for the U.S. Constitution.*
**2** the most important part of something: *Grass forms the basis of a rabbit's diet.*

> **IDIOM with basis**
> **on a daily/weekly/monthly, etc. basis** every day, week, month, etc.: *The swim club meets on a weekly basis.*

**bas·ket** /**bask**-it/ *noun*
**1** a container that you can carry or hold things in. A basket is made of thin pieces of wood, plastic, or wire: *Her shopping basket was full.*
**2** a round metal ring with a net hanging from it. You throw the ball through the basket when you play basketball. ▶ see picture on page **A10**
**3** a point scored in basketball when the ball passes through the net

**bas·ket·ball** /**bask**-it-bol/ *noun*
**1** a game played by two teams of five players. The players try to get points by throwing a ball into a high net at each end of the court: *Do you want to play basketball? | the school basketball team* ▶ see picture on page **A10**
**2** the ball used in this game

**bass** *noun*
**1** /bayss/ (also **bass guitar** /bayss gi-**tar**/) a type of guitar that plays low notes: *My older brother plays bass in a band.*
**2** /bayss/ a very large musical instrument that looks like a violin. You stand up to play a bass.
**3** /bass/ a type of fish that you can eat. Bass live in rivers and in the ocean.
▶ see picture on page **A3**

**bas·soon** /buh-**soon**/ *noun* a long wooden musical instrument shaped like a tube. It makes a very low sound. You play it by blowing into it and pressing keys.

bassoon

**bat** /bat/
● *noun*
**1** a long wooden stick that you use to hit the ball in baseball: *a baseball bat*
**2** a small animal that flies at night. It looks like a mouse with wings: *Bats use sound to help them find food and avoid flying into objects.*
● *verb* (**batting**, **batted**)
to take your turn to try to hit the ball with a bat in baseball: *You're the next person to bat, so you had better get ready.*

bat

**batch** /bach/ *noun*
**1** a group of things that are made at the same time: *Mom made another batch of pancakes.*
**2** a group of things or people that arrive or are dealt with at the same time: *Another batch of kids arrived at the camp.*

**bath** /bath/ *noun* (plural **baths** /bathz/)
**1** if you take a bath, you wash your body while sitting in a bathtub: *I take a bath every day.*
**2** the water that you sit in to wash yourself: *I love to soak in a hot bath.*

**bathe** /bayth/ *verb* to wash yourself or someone else in a bath: *She bathed the baby in warm water.*

**bath·ing suit** /**bayth**-ing soot/ *noun* a piece of

clothing that you wear for swimming: *I'm going to wear my new bathing suit.*

( SYNONYM: **swimsuit** )

**bath·robe** /**bath**-rohb/ *noun* a long piece of clothing that you wear after you take a bath. A bathrobe fits loosely and has a belt you tie around your waist.

**bath·room** /**bath**-room/ *noun* a room where there is a toilet and sink, and usually a bathtub or a shower: *The girls' bathroom is over there.*

⎰ IDIOM with **bathroom**
⎱ **go to the bathroom** to use a toilet: *I need to go to the bathroom.*

**bath·tub** /**bath**-tuhb/ *noun* a long container that you fill with water, sit in, and wash yourself in ( SYNONYM: **tub** )

**bat mitz·vah** /baht **mitss**-vuh/ *noun* a religious ceremony that takes place when a Jewish girl is 12 or 13 years old. After this ceremony, she can take part in her religion as an adult.

**bat·ter** /**bat**-ur/
● *noun*
**1** a mixture of flour, eggs, milk, etc. You make batter when you make cakes or similar foods: *pancake batter* | *Pour the batter into the cake pan.*
**2** the person who is trying to hit the ball in baseball: *The batter missed the ball.*
▶ see picture on page **A10**
● *verb*
to hit something many times: *The waves battered against the rocks.*

**bat·tered** /**bat**-urd/ *adjective* old and damaged from being used many times: *This suitcase is very old and battered. We need to get a new one.*

**bat·ter·y** /**bat**-uhr-ee/ *noun* (plural **batteries**) an object that provides electricity for a radio, camera, toy, etc.: *The radio has stopped working – it needs new batteries.*

**bat·tle** /**bat**'l/
● *noun*
**1** a fight between two armies: *The British army won the Battle of Bunker Hill in 1775.*

**2** a situation in which people are trying hard to do something, or to stop something from happening: *Scientists are trying to win the battle against the disease.*
● *verb*
to try very hard to do or get something: *The team is battling to stay in the tournament.*

**bat·tle·ship** /**bat**'l-ship/ *noun* a very large ship used in wars

**bawl** /bol/ *verb*
**1** to cry loudly: *The baby started bawling.*
**2** **bawl out** to shout at someone because he or she has done something bad: *Mom bawled me out for not cleaning my room.*
( SYNONYM: **scold** )

**bay** /bay/ *noun* a part of an ocean that is partly surrounded by land: *The boat was sailing in the bay.* | *the Hudson Bay*

**bay**

bay

**bay·ou** /**bī**-oo/ *noun* a large area of water in the southeast U.S. It moves very slowly and has many water plants.

**ba·zaar** /buh-**zahr**/ *noun*
**1** an event at which people sell things to collect money for an organization: *They are selling cakes and cookies at the church bazaar.*
**2** a market in Asian and Middle Eastern countries

**B.C.** /bee **see**/ *adverb* used after a date to show that something happened before Jesus Christ was born. B.C. is short for "before Christ": *The temple was built around 530 B.C.*

**be** /bee/ *verb* (**am**, **is**, **are**, **being**, **was**, **were**, **been**)

**1** used when describing or giving information: *I'm really tired.* | *The movie was really good.* | *Is it Tuesday today?* | *It's two o'clock.*

**2** used when saying that someone or something is in a place: *Is Luisa here?* | *There were a lot of people at the party.* | *"Where's the milk?" "It's in the fridge."*

**3** used with the "-ing" form of other verbs to show that something is in progress or was in progress: *It's snowing.* | *We were eating dinner when he arrived.*

**4** used with the "-ed" form of other verbs to show that something happens or happened to a person or thing: *The room is painted yellow.* | *What was that movie called?*

**5** used when saying how someone should behave, or how someone is behaving: *Be careful!* | *Stop being so silly.*

**beach** /beech/ *noun* an area of sand next to the ocean: *We walked along the beach and looked at the ocean.*

**bead** /beed/ *noun* a small ball of plastic, wood, or glass with a hole in the middle. Beads are used for making jewelry: *She wore a string of beads around her neck.*

**beak** /beek/ *noun* the hard pointed mouth of a bird: *The parrot is holding a seed in its beak.*
▶ see picture at **eagle**

**beak·er** /**beek**-ur/ *noun*
a glass or plastic cup with straight sides. You use it in chemistry to measure liquids: *I poured the liquid into a big glass beaker.*

**beaker**

**beam** /beem/
● *noun*
**1** a line of light shining from something: *A beam of light is shining through the curtains.*
**2** a long piece of wood or metal that is used when building houses, bridges, etc.: *The roof is supported by wooden beams.*
● *verb*
**1** to smile in a happy way: *He was beaming proudly because he won the race.*
**2** to send out a line of light or heat: *The sun was beaming down on us and it felt very hot.*

**3** to send a radio or television signal through the air: *Television pictures are beamed across the country by satellite.*

**bean** /been/ *noun*
**1** a seed from a bean plant that you can cook and eat, or the seed and the part that covers the seed that you cook and eat together: *We had green beans at dinnertime.* ▶ see picture on page **A7**
**2** a seed from some other kinds of plants, used to make other foods or drinks: *coffee beans*

**bear** /bair/
● *noun*
a large strong animal with thick fur: *Black bears eat plants, meat, and insects.* ▶ see picture on page **A2**
● *verb* (**bore** /bor/, **borne** /born/)
**1** to accept something that is painful or difficult: *The little girl couldn't bear to leave her mom.*
**2** to support the weight of something: *The old bridge couldn't bear the weight of the truck.*
**3** to produce fruit or flowers: *The orange trees bear fruit in the winter.*

**Word Origin: bear**

**Bear** comes from a very old word that means "the brown one." A very long time ago, hunters thought that it was unlucky to say the name of the animal they were hunting. So instead they called the animal "the brown one." The language that "bear" comes from is so old that it came before English, German, Dutch, and Swedish started, and no one speaks it now.

**beard** /beerd/ *noun* the hair that grows on a man's chin: *Santa Claus has a long white beard.*

**beast** /beest/ *noun* a wild animal: *The forest was full of wild beasts.*

**beat** /beet/
● *verb* (**beat**, **beaten** /beet'n/)
**1** to get more points, votes, etc. than someone else in a game or competition: *I beat my brother at pool.*
**2** to hit someone or something many times: *The men beat him and stole his money.* | *The waves were beating against the rocks.*
**3** to mix food together quickly using a fork or a

kitchen tool: *Beat the eggs and pour them into a pan.*
**4** to make a regular sound or movement: *Your heart beats fast when you have been running.*
● *noun*
**1** the regular pattern of sounds in a piece of music: *This kind of dance music has a fast beat.*
**2** one of many regular movements or sounds: *His heart rate is 120 beats a minute.*

**beau·ti·ful** /**byoot**-uh-fuhl/ *adjective*
**1** very nice to look at: *Once upon a time, a beautiful princess lived in a castle.* | *The mountains are beautiful.* ▶ see **Thesaurus**
**2** a beautiful song, book, or poem gives you a lot of pleasure: *He played a beautiful song on his guitar.*
—**beautifully** /**byoot**-uh-flee/ *adverb* in a beautiful way: *She plays the piano beautifully.*

**beau·ty** /**byoot**-ee/ *noun* (plural **beauties**) the quality of being beautiful: *The movie star was famous for her beauty.*

**bea·ver** /**beev**-ur/ *noun* a North American animal that has thick fur and a wide flat tail. Beavers use their sharp teeth to cut down trees to build their lodges (=homes): *Beavers build dams to stop water from flowing and make ponds that they can build their lodges in.*

beaver

**be·came** /bi-**kaym**/ *verb* the past tense of **become**

**be·cause** /bi-**koz**/ *conjunction* used when you are giving the reason for something: *I did well on the test because I studied hard.* | *The game was canceled because of the rain.*

**be·come** /bi-**kuhm**/ *verb* (**became** /bi-**kaym**/, **become**)
**1** to start to be: *The man became angry and started shouting at me.* ▶ see **Thesaurus**

**2** to start to have a job: *I want to become a doctor when I'm older.*

**bed** /bed/ *noun*
**1** a piece of furniture for sleeping on: *It's time to go to bed.* | *She got into bed and turned off the light.*
**2** the ground at the bottom of the ocean, a river, or a lake: *The boat had sunk and was now lying on the river bed.*
**3** an area of ground where you have planted flowers: *We planted some seeds in the flower beds.*

**bed·room** /**bed**-room/ *noun* a room that you sleep in: *My brother and I share a bedroom.*

**bed·spread** /**bed**-spred/ *noun* a large cover that goes on top of a bed: *She put the bedspread over her head and went to sleep.*

**bed·time** /**bed**-tīm/ *noun* the time when you usually go to bed: *Mom used to read me stories at bedtime.*

**bee** /bee/ *noun* a yellow and black insect that flies and makes honey: *Bees make a buzzing sound.*

bee

**beech** /beech/ (also **beech tree** /**beech**-tree/) *noun* a tree with smooth gray bark: *Beech nuts have a sweet taste.*

beech

**beef** /beef/ *noun* meat from a cow: *a roast beef sandwich*

**bee·hive** /**bee**-hīv/ *noun* a place where bees live
SYNONYM: **hive**

**been** /bin/ *verb* the past participle of be

> ## Grammar: been and gone
>
> **Been** and **gone** are used as past participles of **go**. A past participle is a form of a verb that shows an action happening in the past.
>
> **Has been** is the way you say that someone has visited a place in the past: *Jordan has been to Florida* (=Jordan has visited Florida before, but he is not there now).
>
> **Has gone** is the usual way to say that someone has traveled to a place in the past: *Jordan has gone to Florida* (=Jordan has traveled to Florida and is there now).

**beep** /beep/
- *verb* to make a short high noise. Car horns and machines beep: *The taxi driver beeped his horn outside our house.*
- *noun* the sound that an electronic machine or a car horn makes: *The computer makes a beep if you hit the wrong key.*

**beer** /beer/ *noun* a yellow or brown alcoholic drink: *a bottle of beer*

**beet** /beet/ *noun* a round dark red vegetable that grows under the ground ▶ see picture on page **A7**

**bee·tle** /**beet**'l/ *noun*
an insect with a hard round back that covers its wings: *I found a small brown beetle on a lettuce leaf.*

**beetle**

**be·fore** /bi-**for**/
- *preposition, conjunction*
**1** earlier than: *I usually get up before seven o'clock.* | *We lived in Chicago before we moved to Los Angeles.* ( ANTONYM: **after** )
**2** in front of someone or something: *The teacher stood before the class.* | *A comes before B in the alphabet.* | *Turn left just before the traffic lights.*
( ANTONYM: **after** )
- *adverb*
at an earlier time: *I've never eaten this kind of cake before.*

**be·fore·hand** /bi-**for**-hand/ *adverb* before something happens: *He told me beforehand that he was going to be late.*

**beg** /beg/ *verb* (**begging**, **begged**)
**1** to ask someone for food or money because you are very poor: *In poor countries you see children begging for food in the street because they do not have enough to eat.*
**2** to ask for something in a way that shows you want it very much: *I begged my parents to let me go to the party.*

> **IDIOM with beg**
> **I beg your pardon**
> **1** used when asking someone politely to say something again: *"It's raining outside." "I beg your pardon?" "I said it's raining outside."*
> ( SYNONYM: **excuse me** )
> **2** used when saying you are sorry: *Oh, I beg your pardon! Did I step on your foot?*
> ( SYNONYM: **sorry** )

**be·gan** /bi-**gan**/ *verb* the past tense of **begin**

**beg·gar** /**beg**-ur/ *noun* someone who asks people for food and money in order to live: *I feel sorry for the beggars in the street who ask tourists for money.*

**be·gin** /bi-**gin**/ *verb* (**beginning**, **began** /bi-**gan**/, **begun** /bi-**guhn**/) to start: *The baby began to cry.* | *The word "boat" begins with a "b."*
( ANTONYMS: **end, stop, finish** )

**be·gin·ner** /bi-**gin**-ur/ *noun* someone who is starting to do something or learn something: *I go to the beginners' class in judo.*

**be·gin·ning** /bi-**gin**-ing/ *noun* the start or first part of something: *We moved to San Diego at the beginning of the year.* | *At the beginning of the Harry Potter story, Harry doesn't know he's a wizard.* ( SYNONYM: **start** ) ( ANTONYM: **end** )
▶ see Thesaurus

**be·gun** /bi-**guhn**/ *verb* the past participle of begin

**be·have** /bi-**hayv**/ *verb*
**1** to be polite and not cause trouble: *The children were very noisy and their mom told them to behave.* ( ANTONYM: **misbehave** )
**2** to do or say things in a particular way: *Some boys behaved badly at the party.*

**be·hav·ior** /bi-**hayv**-yur/ *noun* the things that a

person or animal does: *Her behavior in class is much better, and she doesn't argue with the other students anymore.*

**be·hind** /bi-**hīnd**/ *preposition, adverb*
**1** at the back of: *I sat behind Dylan. | She found some money behind the couch.*
**2** less successful than someone else: *The Rams were 21 points behind the Falcons.*
**3** supporting someone, or supporting an idea: *The whole team is behind the captain.*
**4** late in doing something: *I'm behind on my homework.*

> **IDIOM with behind**
> **behind someone's back** if you do something bad or not nice behind someone's back, you do it without him or her knowing: *I don't like talking about him behind his back.*

**beige** /bayzh/ *noun, adjective* a pale brown color: *The dead grass was a beige color.*

**be·ing** /**bee**-ing/
● *verb* the present participle of be
● *noun* a living thing: *Do you think there are intelligent beings on other planets?*

**be·lief** /buh-**leef**/ *noun* a strong feeling that something is true or right: *We must respect other people's religious beliefs. | It is our belief that every child is important.*

**be·lieve** /buh-**leev**/ *verb*
**1** to feel sure that something is true: *You cannot believe everything Alyssa tells you.*
**2** to feel sure that something or someone is real: *Do you believe in ghosts?*
**3** to feel sure that someone or something is good or right: *My parents believe in the importance of a good education.*

**be·liev·er** /buh-**leev**-ur/ *noun* someone who believes in God or a religion: *Believers go to the mosque to pray.*

**bell** /bel/ *noun*
**1** a metal object that makes a musical sound when you hit it or shake it: *The church bells were ringing.* ▶ see picture at **bicycle**
**2** a piece of electrical

bell

equipment that makes a ringing sound: *I heard the doorbell ring.*

**bel·ly** /**bel**-ee/ *noun* (plural **bellies**) your stomach: *My belly hurts.*

**bel·ly but·ton** /**bel**-ee buht'n/ *noun* the small hollow place in the middle of your stomach
( SYNONYM: **navel** )

**be·long** /bi-**long**/ *verb*
**1** if something belongs somewhere, that is its correct place: *The toys belong in the box.*
**2** if something belongs to you, you own it: *Does this pen belong to you?*
**3** to be a member of a group: *I belong to the Cub Scouts.*

**be·long·ings** /bi-**long**-ingz/ *noun* the things that you own, or the things that you have taken with you: *Make sure you take all your belongings home.*

**be·lov·ed** /bi-**luhv**-id/ *adjective* loved very much: *His beloved wife died.*

**be·low** /bi-**loh**/ *adverb, preposition*
**1** lower than something, or under it: *I looked out of the plane window and saw the mountains below us. | Read the story and then answer the questions below.* ( SYNONYM: **under** )
( ANTONYM: **above** )
**2** less than an amount: *The temperature was below zero.* ( ANTONYM: **above** )

**belt** /belt/ *noun*
**1** a long piece of leather or cloth that you wear around your waist. A belt holds up your pants or skirt: *He was wearing a leather belt with his jeans.* ▶ see picture at **pirate**
**2** a circular piece of rubber or some other material that goes around and moves parts of a machine: *This belt connects the fan to the engine.*

**be·mused** /bi-**myoozd**/ *adjective* slightly confused

**bench** /bench/ *noun* a long seat for two or more people, especially outdoors: *The rest of the team sat on the bench.*

**bend** /bend/ (**bent** /bent/)

● *verb*

**1** to move the top of your body and your head down: *He bent over to pick up the ball.*

**2** to move a part of your body so that it is not straight: *Bend your knees.*

**3** to push or press something so that it is no longer flat or straight: *He was strong enough to bend a piece of metal with his hands.*

**4** to change direction: *After the bridge, the road bends to the right.*

● *noun*

a curve in something such as a road or river: *A car came around the bend on the other side of the road.*

**be·neath** /bi-**neeth**/ *adverb, preposition* under or below something: *He is sitting beneath the tree.* | *A mole is an animal that lives beneath the ground.* ( SYNONYM: **under** )

**ben·e·fi·cial** /ben-uh-**fish**-uhl/ *adjective* helpful or useful: *Regular exercise is beneficial to your health.*

**ben·e·fit** /**ben**-uh-fit/

● *noun*

**1** something good or useful that you get from something: *One of the benefits of education is the chance to get good jobs.*

**2** money or insurance that you get from the government or the company you work for: *Dad gets medical benefits through his work.*

● *verb*

if you benefit from something, it helps you: *People benefit from eating healthy food.*

**Word Family:** benefit

**benefit** *noun* | **benefit** *verb* | **beneficial** *adjective*

**bent** /bent/

● *verb* the past tense and past participle of **bend**

● *adjective* not straight – use this about things that are usually straight: *The front wheel on my bike is bent because I ran into a tree.*

**ber·ry** /**berr**-ee/ *noun* (plural **berries**) a small soft fruit with very small seeds. There are many kinds of berries: *My favorite berries are strawberries and blueberries.*

**be·side** /bi-**sīd**/ *preposition* next to someone or something: *I sat beside Steve.* | *There is a picnic area beside the river.*

IDIOM with **beside**

**be beside the point** to not be important compared to something else: *He's only eight, but that's beside the point. He still knows he shouldn't lie.*

**be·sides** /bi-**sīdz**/ *preposition, adverb*

**1** as well as someone or something: *Besides playing the guitar, she also plays the piano.* | *Who's going to the party besides Tim and me?*

SYNONYMS: **as well as, in addition to**

**2** used when giving another reason: *I don't feel like playing outside. Besides, it's too cold.*

**best** /best/

● *adjective*

**1** better than anyone or anything else: *She is the best student in her class.* ( ANTONYM: **worst** )

**2** your best friend is the friend you know and like the most: *Sofia is my best friend.*

● *noun*

someone or something that is better than all the others: *Which song is the best?* ( ANTONYM: **worst** )

● *adverb*

**1** in a way that is better than any other: *Logan did best on the math test.* ( ANTONYM: **worst** )

**2** most: *Which part of the movie did you like best?*

IDIOMS with **best**

**at best** the most you can expect: *I'll probably get a C, or at best, a B.*

**do your best** to try very hard to do something: *I did my best in the race, but I only came third.*

**best man** /best **man**/ *noun* a man who stands next to the groom (=man who is getting married) at a wedding. The best man is a friend or relative of the groom.

**bet** /bet/

● *verb* (**betting, bet**) to try to win money by guessing who will win a game or competition:

*He bet $20 that the Steelers would win.*
SYNONYM: **gamble**

IDIOMS with **bet**
**I bet ...** used when saying that you think something will happen: *I bet Dad won't let us stay up late.*
**you bet!** used when saying that you agree: *"Would you help me?" "You bet."*
● *noun* if you make a bet, you try to win money by guessing who will win a game or competition: *He made a bet on the winner of the Super Bowl.*

**be·tray** /bi-**tray**/ *verb* to not be loyal to your country or to another person, when they trust you: *The spy betrayed his country by selling secrets to the enemy.*
—**betrayal** /bi-**tray**-uhl/ act of betraying a person: *The spy helped the enemy, which was a betrayal of his country.*

**bet·ter** /**bet**-ur/
● *adjective*
**1** more useful, skillful, or of a higher quality than something else: *Your computer is much better than mine.* ( ANTONYM: **worse** )
**2** less sick than before: *I had a cold, but I'm better now.* ( ANTONYM: **worse** )
● *adverb*
**1** more: *Which shirt do you like better?*
**2** in a more skillful way: *I play the guitar better than my brother.*

IDIOMS with **better**
**be better off** to have more money now than you did in the past: *My family is better off than it used to be.*
**had better** used when saying that someone should do something: *You'd better hurry or you'll be late for school.*

**be·tween** /bi-**tween**/ *preposition, adverb*
**1** with one thing or person on each side: *I sat between Bethany and Ava.*
**2** after one time and before another: *The library is open between nine and five o'clock.*
**3** in the space in the middle of two places: *Phoenix is between Las Vegas and Tucson.*
**4** used to show a range of amounts, from the smallest amount to the largest amount: *My walk to school takes between 15 and 20 minutes.*

**5** used when you have two choices and must choose one of them: *You can choose between chocolate and vanilla ice cream.*

**between**

The cat is sitting between the dog and the rabbit.

**bev·erage** /**bev**-rij/ *noun* a drink: *The restaurant has cola, juice, and other beverages.*

**be·ware** /bi-**wair**/ *verb* used when you are warning someone to be careful: *Beware of the dog. He is very fierce and he sometimes bites people.*

**be·wil·dered** /bi-**wild**-uhrd/ *adjective* very confused and not sure what to do or think: *She had a bewildered expression on her face.*

**be·yond** /bi-**yahnd**/ *preposition, adverb*
**1** on the other side of something: *Beyond the baseball field there's a small pond.*
**2** later than a time or date: *In the 1800s, many children did not live beyond age five.*
**3** if something is beyond you, it is too difficult for you to understand: *Advanced math is beyond some of the students in my class.*

**bi-** /bi-, bī/

## Word Building

**bi-** is a prefix.
**bicycle** | **binoculars** | **biweekly**
**bi-** means "two." A *bicycle* has two wheels. *Binoculars* have two parts that let you see things that are far away. If something happens *biweekly*, it happens every two weeks.

**bi·as** /bī-uhss/ *noun* an unfair opinion about someone that makes you treat that person differently: *There is still a bias in favor of men and they usually get the best jobs.*
—**biased** /bī-uhst/ *adjective* thinking that one person or thing is better than another, and treating them differently or unfairly: *The referee was biased against our team and he refused to allow the goal.*

### Word Family: bias

**bias** *noun* | **biased** *adjective* | **unbiased** *adjective*

**bib** /bib/ *noun* a piece of cloth or plastic that stops food from getting on a baby's clothes when you feed it. You put the bib around the baby's neck.

**Bi·ble** /bīb-uhl/ *noun* the holy book of the Christian religion: *He's very religious and he reads the Bible every day.*

**bib·li·og·ra·phy** /bib-lee-**ahg**-ruhf-ee/ *noun* (plural **bibliographies**) a list of books on a subject: *The bibliography at the back of the book lists more books about dinosaurs.*

**bi·cy·cle** /bīss-ik-uhl/ *noun* a vehicle with two wheels that you ride by pushing the pedals with your feet: *The kids were riding their bicycles up and down the street.* ( SYNONYM: **bike** )

gear shift  handlebars  saddle  **bicycle**
brake
light
fender
pump
tire
pedal
spoke
wheel  valve  chain

**bid** /bid/
● *noun* an offer to pay a particular price for something that several people want to buy: *The house will be sold to the person who makes the highest bid.*
● *verb* (**bidding**, **bid**) to offer to pay a particular price for something that several people want to buy: *He bid $200 for the painting at an*

auction.
—**bidder** /bid-ur/ *noun* someone who bids for something: *The painting was sold to the highest bidder.*

**big** /big/ *adjective* (**bigger**, **biggest**)
**1** large: *Our dog is really big. He weighs over 150 pounds.* | *I ate a big piece of chocolate cake.* ( ANTONYM: **small** ) ▶ see Thesaurus
**2** important or serious: *I made a big mistake – I put salt in his coffee instead of sugar.* | *We had a big problem when the car broke down.* ( ANTONYM: **small** )
**3** successful or popular: *The movie was a big hit.*

**big·ot** /big-uht/ *noun* someone who does not like people who belong to a different race, religion, or country: *His family members were all bigots and they hated people of different races.*
—**bigoted** /big-uht-id/ *adjective* someone who is bigoted dislikes people who belong to a different race, religion, or country: *He is a bigoted man who does not like foreigners.*
—**bigotry** /big-uhtr-ee/ *noun* the actions or beliefs of a bigot: *Bigotry against people because of their religion is wrong.*

**bike** /bīk/ *noun*
**1** a bicycle: *I rode my bike to the park.*
**2** a motorcycle
—**biker** /bīk-ur/ *noun* someone who rides a motorcycle or a bicycle

**bi·ki·ni** /bi-**keen**-ee/ *noun* a swimming suit in two pieces, that women or girls wear

### Word Origin: bikini

The **bikini** was invented in France in the 1940s. The man who made the first bikini named it after an island in the Pacific Ocean. A nuclear bomb was tested on Bikini Island in 1946.

**bi·lin·gual** /bī-**ling**-gwuhl/ *adjective*
**1** able to speak two languages: *Maria is bilingual. She can speak English and German.*
**2** written or spoken in two languages: *a Spanish–English bilingual dictionary*

**bill** /bil/
● *noun*
**1** a piece of paper money: *I found a ten-dollar bill.*

**2** a list that shows how much you have to pay for something: *The bill for the repairs was over $700.*
**3** a plan for a new law: *Congress is discussing a bill to increase spending on health care.*
**4** a bird's hard mouth: *The duck was holding a big fish in its bill.* (SYNONYM: **beak**)
● *verb*
to send a bill to someone to tell them how much money they must pay: *We will bill you for the cost of the repairs to the car.*

**bill·board** /**bil**-bord/ *noun* a big sign next to a road, used for advertising something: *I passed a big billboard with an advertisement for Levi jeans.*

**bil·lion** /**bil**-yuhn/ *number* (plural **billion** or **billions**) 1,000,000,000: *There are 6.5 billion people living on the Earth.*
—**billionth** /**bil**-yuhnth/ *number* 1,000,000,000th or 1/1,000,000,000

**bin** /bin/ *noun* a large container for keeping things in: *Put the bottles in the recycling bin.*

**bind** /bīnd/ *verb* (**bound** /bownd/) to tie someone or something with rope or string: *The newspapers were bound with string.*

**bind·er** /**bīnd**-ur/ *noun* a cover that you can keep papers in: *He bought a three-ring binder for school.*

**binge** /binj/
● *noun* if someone goes on a binge, he or she does too much of something in a short time, especially eating or drinking: *She went on a shopping binge and bought lots of expensive clothes.*
● *verb* to do too much of something in a short time, especially eating or drinking: *Some people binge on chocolate and then feel sick because they have eaten so much.*

**bin·go** /**bing**-goh/ *noun* a game in which someone says numbers, and players mark the numbers on a card. If you have the right numbers in a line on your card, you are the winner.

**bin·oc·u·lars** /bi-**nahk**-yuhl-urz/ *plural noun* an object that you look through with both eyes to see things that are far away: *If you look at the birds through binoculars, you can see the beautiful feathers on their wings.*

**binoculars**
binoculars

**bio-** /bī-oh/

## Word Building

**bio**logy | **bio**graphy | **bio**me
These words all have the Greek word root **bio-** in them. **Bio-** means "life." *Biology* is the study of living things, such as plants and animals. A *biography* is a book about someone's life. A *biome*, such as a desert or forest, is a place where animals and plants live.

**bi·o·de·grad·a·ble** /bī-oh-di-**grayd**-uhb-uhl/ *adjective* something that is biodegradable will disappear into the ground naturally, and will not harm the environment: *Paper is biodegradable and is much better for the environment than plastic.*

**bi·og·ra·phy** /bī-**ahg**-ruhf-ee/ *noun* (plural **biographies**) a book about a person's life: *I'm reading a biography of Martin Luther King.*

**bi·ol·o·gy** /bī-**ahl**-uhj-ee/ *noun* the scientific study of living things: *In our biology class, we're studying how plants get energy from sunlight.*
—**biologist** /bī-**ahl**-uhj-ist/ *noun* someone whose job involves studying biology: *Marine biologists study life in the oceans.*
—**biological** /bī-uh-**lahj**-ik-uhl/ *adjective* relating to biology: *Your body's growth and ageing is a biological process.*

**bi·ome** /bī-ohm/ *noun* all the plants and animals that live in an area that has its own type of weather and environment. A forest or an ocean can be a biome: *Each biome is home to many different animals and plants.*

**birch** /burch/ *noun*
**1** a tree with smooth bark that feels like paper
**2** the wood from this tree: *a birch table*

**bird** /burd/ *noun* an animal with wings and feathers. Most birds can fly. Female birds lay eggs: *The birds are singing in the trees outside our house.*

bird

**birth** /burth/ *noun*
**1** the time when a baby is born: *At birth, the baby weighed seven pounds.*
**2** the beginning of something new: *The birth of the Internet has changed the way we communicate with each other.*

> IDIOM with **birth**
> **give birth** if a woman gives birth, a baby comes out of her body: *She gave birth to a baby boy.*

**birth·day** /**burth**-day/ *noun* the date when you were born, or a celebration of that day: *My birthday is August 8. | I blew out the candles on my birthday cake. | Happy Birthday, Suzy!*

**bis·cuit** /**bisk**-it/ *noun* a type of bread that is baked in small round pieces: *We had soup and biscuits for dinner.*

**bish·op** /**bish**-uhp/ *noun* an important Christian priest. A bishop is in charge of all the churches and priests in a large area.

**bi·son** /**bīss**-uhn/ *noun* an animal that looks like a large cow with a big head. It has thick brown hair on its neck and shoulders: *The American bison is the largest land animal in North America.*
( SYNONYM: **buffalo** )

bison

**bit** /bit/
● *noun*
**1** a small piece of something: *The floor was covered with bits of broken glass.*

**2** the smallest unit of information that a computer uses: *Each picture contains over ten million bits of data.*
**3** a metal bar that you put inside a horse's mouth. The bit is attached to the reins, so that you can make the horse go straight forward or turn.
**4 a little bit** slightly: *We were all a little bit nervous before the game.*
**5 quite a bit** rather a lot: *Dale's gained quite a bit of weight.*
● *verb*
the past tense of **bite**

**bite** /bīt/
● *verb* (**bit** /bit/, **bitten** /bit′n/)
**1** to cut something with your teeth: *Kirsty bit off a piece of banana. | A dog bit his leg badly.*
**2** if an insect bites you, it hurts you by making a small hole in your skin: *The mosquito bit me and there was a big red mark on my arm.*
● *noun*
**1** if you take a bite of something, you bite a small piece from it: *I took a small bite of apple pie.*
**2** a wound made when an animal or insect bites you: *We arrived home covered in mosquito bites.*

bite

**bit·ten** /**bit**′n/ *verb* the past participle of bite

**bit·ter** /**bit**-ur/ *adjective*
**1** angry and unhappy for a long time: *He felt bitter because he thought they had treated him unfairly.*
**2** having a strong sharp taste, like the taste of very dark chocolate: *If the coffee tastes bitter, you can add a little sugar before you drink it.*
( ANTONYM: **sweet** )
**3** bitter weather is extremely cold: *The bear's thick fur protects it from the bitter cold.*
—**bitterly** /**bit**-ur-lee/ *adverb* in a way that shows

sadness or anger: *I was bitterly disappointed when the trip was canceled.*
—**bitterness** /**bit**-ur-niss/ *noun* a bitter quality: *Anger and bitterness are common after a divorce.* | *the bitterness of the coffee*

**bi·zarre** /bi-**zar**/ *adjective* very unusual and strange: *There's a bizarre picture of a frog dressed like a cowboy.*

**black** /blak/
● *adjective*
**1** having the darkest color, like the sky at night: *He has black hair and brown eyes.*
**2** having dark brown skin – used about people whose families originally came from Africa: *Barack Obama is our first black president.*
● *noun*
**1** the darkest color, like the color of the sky at night: *She likes to wear black.*
**2** someone with dark brown skin, whose family originally came from Africa

**black·ber·ry** /**blak**-berr-ee/ *noun* a small sweet dark purple fruit that grows on a bush

**black·bird** /**blak**-burd/ *noun* a common American and European bird with black feathers

**black·board** /**blak**-bord/ *noun* a dark smooth board that you write on with chalk: *Miss Wright wrote the answer on the blackboard.*

**black eye** /blak ī/ *noun* a dark bruise around someone's eye where he or she has been hit: *He came home with a black eye after a fight with one of the other boys.*

**black·mail** /**blak**-mayl/
● *noun* the crime of saying you will tell someone's secret unless that person does what you want: *"I'll tell the police about you, if you don't give me some money." "But that's blackmail!"*
● *verb* to use blackmail
—**blackmailer** /**blak**-mayl-ur/ *noun* someone who uses blackmail

**black·out** /**blak**-owt/ *noun*
**1** if a place has a blackout, all the lights go out because electricity stops reaching the area: *There was a blackout last night and the air conditioning stopped working.*
**2** if you have a blackout, you become

unconscious: *Since he hurt his head in a car accident, Sam has suffered from blackouts.*

**black·smith** /**blak**-smith/ *noun* someone who makes horseshoes and other things made of iron: *The local blacksmith has been making and fitting horseshoes all his life.*

**black·top** /**blak**-tahp/ *noun* a black substance used for making the surface of roads, pavements, and parking lots

**blad·der** /**blad**-ur/ *noun* the part inside your body that holds urine. Urine is liquid waste that comes out of your body when you use the toilet.
▶ see picture at **anatomy**

**blade** /blayd/ *noun*
**1** the flat cutting part of a knife: *The blade of the knife is very sharp.*
**2** one piece of grass: *She picked a blade of grass.*

**blame** /blaym/
● *verb* to say that someone is responsible for something bad that has happened: *The man blamed me for breaking his window. He said I threw a rock at it.*
● *noun* if you get the blame for something bad that has happened, other people say you are responsible for it: *I always get the blame, even when it's not my fault.*

**bland** /bland/ *adjective* bland food has very little taste: *The soup is very bland and you can't taste the vegetables in it.*

**blank** /blangk/
● *adjective*
**1** a blank sheet of paper, disk, space, etc. has nothing on it: *She started writing on a blank page.*
**2** if your mind goes blank, you suddenly cannot remember something: *When the teacher asked me the question, my mind went blank and I couldn't remember the answer.*
● *noun*
an empty space on a piece of paper where you write something: *Fill in the blanks with your name and address.*

**blan·ket** /**blangk**-it/ *noun*
**1** a thick warm cover for a bed: *I can put another blanket on the bed if you're cold.*
**2** a thick covering of snow, fog, etc.: *The hills were covered in a blanket of fresh snow.*

**a**
**b**
**c**
**d**
**e**
**f**
**g**
**h**
**i**
**j**
**k**
**l**
**m**
**n**
**o**
**p**
**q**
**r**
**s**
**t**
**u**
**v**
**w**
**x**
**y**
**z**

**blare** /blair/ *verb* to make a very loud unpleasant noise: *The fire truck came up the hill with its sirens blaring.*

**blast** /blast/
● *noun*
**1** an explosion: *The force of the blast broke the windows.*
**2** a sudden strong movement of the air: *When I opened the door, a blast of cold air hit my face.*
● *verb*
**1** to break something into pieces by making it explode: *The railroad workers blasted through the mountains to make tunnels.*
**2** to make a very loud noise: *Music was blasting out from two huge speakers.*
**3** **blast off** if a spacecraft blasts off, it leaves the ground: *The space shuttle is due to blast off in 24 hours.*

**blast-off** /**blast**-of/ *noun* the moment when a spacecraft leaves the ground: *The countdown begins when it is ten seconds to blast-off.*

**blaze** /blayz/
● *verb* to burn or shine very brightly and strongly: *The light from the sun blazed down on them and it was very hot.*
● *noun* a big fire: *The blaze spread very quickly.*

**blaz·ing** /**blayz**-ing/ *adjective* very hot: *It was a blazing hot day in the middle of the summer.*

**bleach** /bleech/
● *noun*
a strong chemical used to make clothes white or to kill germs: *We use bleach to clean the toilet.*
● *verb*
**1** to make something lighter in color: *She bleaches her hair to make it look blonde.*
**2** to use bleach when you are cleaning or washing clothes: *Mom bleached the sink to kill all the germs.*

**bleach·ers** /**bleech**-urz/ *plural noun* rows of seats where people sit to watch sports: *We sat in the bleachers watching the basketball game.*

**bleak** /bleek/ *adjective*
**1** seeming bad and not likely to get better: *With no job and no money, the future looked bleak for Carrie.* ( ANTONYM: **bright** )
**2** cold and with no sun: *It was a bleak day in the middle of winter.* ( ANTONYM: **bright** )

**bleed** /bleed/ *verb* (**bled** /bled/) if part of your body is bleeding, blood is coming out of it: *I cut my finger and it started bleeding.*

**Word Family:** bleed
**bleed** *verb* | **blood** *noun* | **bloody** *adjective*

**blem·ish** /**blem**-ish/ *noun* a small mark on something that spoils the way it looks: *She covered the blemish on her face with makeup.*

**blend** /blend/
● *verb* to mix foods or other things together: *You blend the eggs and the sugar together when you are making the cake.*
● *noun* a mixture of things: *Their songs are a blend of rock music and country music.*

**blend·er** /**blend**-ur/ *noun* a small electric machine that you use to mix foods together: *You can mix bananas and orange juice in a blender to make a smoothie.*

**bless** /bless/ *verb*
**1** to ask God to protect and help someone or something: *May God bless you and keep you safe.*
**2** to make something holy: *At Mass, the priest blesses the bread and the wine.*
**3** **Bless you!** you say "bless you" when someone sneezes

**bless·ing** /**bless**-ing/ *noun*
**1** something good that you are thankful for: *It's a blessing that he wasn't hurt.*
**2** someone's approval: *She got married with her parents' blessing.*
**3** if a priest or minister gives a blessing, he asks God to protect and help someone or something: *The priest gave a blessing and asked God to help their son.*

**blew** /bloo/ *verb* the past tense of **blow**

**blimp** /blimp/ *noun* an aircraft like a very large balloon, with a room for people to sit in below it

**blind** /blīnd/
● *adjective* not able to see: *Josh is blind and he needs someone to tell him what is written on the board.*
—**blindness** /**blīnd**-niss/ *noun* the state when someone is not able to see: *The disease can cause blindness.*

● *verb* to make someone not able to see: *He was blinded by the bright light for a moment.*

● *noun* a piece of material that you pull down to cover a window: *We always close the blinds at night.*

## blind·fold /**blīn**-fohld/

● *noun* a piece of cloth that is used to cover someone's eyes: *Someone puts a blindfold over your eyes and you have to guess what the picture is.*

● *verb* to cover someone's eyes with a blindfold: *We blindfolded her at the beginning of the game.*

## blink /blingk/ *verb*

**1** to open and close your eyes very quickly: *The sudden bright light made me blink for a few seconds.*

**2** if a light blinks, it goes on and off quickly: *The light blinks on the machine when there is a message for you.*

## blink·er /**blingk**-ur/ *noun* a light on a car that the driver turns on to show that the car is going to turn

## bliss /bliss/ *noun* complete happiness: *My idea of bliss is a big tub of ice cream and a box of chocolate chip cookies.*

## blis·ter /**blist**-ur/ *noun* a sore area on your skin, caused by something burning or rubbing against your skin. Blisters are filled with liquid: *New shoes always give me blisters.*

## bliz·zard /**bliz**-urd/ *noun* a very bad storm with a lot of snow and wind

## blob /blahb/ *noun* a small drop of a thick liquid: *There's a blob of ice cream on the table.*

## block /blahk/

● *noun*

**1** a square area of a city with streets on all four sides: *Dad took the dog for a walk around the block.*

**2** the distance from one street to another in a city: *I live three blocks from the subway.*

**3** a piece of something hard: *The wall was made of blocks of concrete.*

**4** a small piece of wood that children use to build things: *My little sister made a tower out of her blocks.*

● *verb*

**1** to stop something from moving through somewhere: *Someone's car was blocking our driveway.*

**2** to stop something from happening or someone from doing something: *Parents can block websites they don't want their children to see.* | *A guy with a big hat was blocking my view of the game.*

## block·ade /blah-**kayd**/

● *noun* the action of surrounding a place, in order to stop people or things from going into it or coming out of it: *The president ordered a blockade of the port to stop the enemy's ships from leaving.*

● *verb* to put a blockade around a place: *Warships blockaded the harbor.*

## blog /blahg/ *noun* a web page in which you write about your opinions and what you have been doing: *She writes a blog about life with her family in China.*

—**blogger** /**blahg**-ur/ *noun* someone who writes a blog

## blonde /blahnd/

● *adjective* (also **blond** /blahnd/) blonde hair is light yellow: *She has long blonde hair.*

● *noun* a woman who has pale yellow hair: *He always dates blondes.*

## blood /bluhd/ *noun* the red liquid in your body: *There was blood all over his hand from the cut.*

## blood pres·sure /**bluhd** presh-ur/ *noun* the force with which blood moves around your body. High blood pressure can make someone have a heart attack. Low blood pressure can make someone faint.

## blood·shed /**bluhd**-shed/ *noun* the killing of people in a war or fight: *The war ended after years of bloodshed.*

## blood·stream /**bluhd**-streem/ *noun* blood that is flowing around the body: *Bacteria can enter the bloodstream through a tiny cut.*

## blood ves·sel /**bluhd** vess'l/ *noun* one of the tubes that blood flows through in your body

## blood·y /**bluhd**-ee/ *adjective*

**1** covered in blood: *Scott got a bloody nose in the fight.*

**2** violent, and killing a lot of people: *The battle was long and bloody.*

a
**b**
c
d
e
f
g
h
i
j
k
l
m
n
o
p
q
r
s
t
u
v
w
x
y
z

**bloom** /bloom/
- *verb* if a plant blooms, its flowers open: *The daffodils are blooming in the park.*
- *noun* **be in bloom** if a plant is in bloom, its flowers are open: *It is spring, and the lilacs are in bloom.*

**blos·som** /**blahss**-uhm/
- *noun* a flower on a tree or bush: *In April, the cherry trees are covered in blossoms.*
- *verb* if a tree or a bush blossoms, it produces flowers: *The apple trees are starting to blossom.*

**blouse** /blowss/ *noun* a shirt for a woman or girl: *Maria put on a clean white blouse.*

**blow** /bloh/
- *verb* (**blew** /bloo/, **blown** /blohn/)
**1** if the wind blows, it makes the air move: *A cold wind was blowing from the east.*
**2** to send out air through your mouth: *I blew the dust off the book.*
**3** to make a whistle, car horn, etc. make a sound: *The referee blew the whistle to start the game.*
**4** **blow it** to make a mistake and not succeed in doing something: *I blew it and failed the test.*
**5** **blow your nose** to clear your nose by blowing air through it into a piece of cloth or tissue: *She blew her nose loudly on a tissue and then threw it away.*
**6** **blow out** to blow air on a flame and make it stop burning: *She blew out all the candles on her birthday cake.*
**7** **blow up** to fill something with air or gas, especially a balloon: *We blew up the balloons for the party.*
**8** **blow up** to destroy something by making it burst into small pieces: *The plane dropped a bomb that blew up the ship.* (SYNONYM: **explode**)
- *noun*
**1** a hard hit: *The boxer received a blow to the head.*
**2** something very sad and upsetting that happens to you: *His dog's death was a terrible blow.*

**blow**

She is blowing out the candles.

**blow dry·er** /**bloh** drī-ur/ *noun* a piece of equipment that dries your hair by blowing hot air
—**blow dry** /**bloh** drī/ *verb* to dry your hair using a blow dryer

**blown** /blohn/ *verb* the past participle of blow

**blue** /bloo/
- *adjective*
**1** having the same color as the sky on a sunny day: *The walls are painted blue.*
**2** sad: *She is feeling blue because her friends have all gone on vacation.* (SYNONYM: **depressed**)
- *noun*
**1** the color of the sky on a sunny day: *Blue is my favorite color and I like to wear a lot of blue clothes.*
**2** **blues** a slow sad type of music that comes from African-American culture

**blue·ber·ry** /**bloo**-berr-ee/ *noun* a dark blue berry that grows on a bush. Blueberries are small, round, and sweet: *We had blueberry pancakes.* ▶ see picture on page **A7**

**blue·bird** /**bloo**-burd/ *noun* a small bird that has blue feathers on its back and wings

**blue·jay** /**bloo**-jay/ (also **jay**) *noun* (plural **bluejays**) a common North American bird with blue and white feathers that form a point on the top of its head ▶ see picture on page **A4**

**blue jeans** /**bloo** jeenz/ *plural noun* pants made of dark blue denim: *On weekends he mostly wears blue jeans and sneakers.* (SYNONYM: **jeans**)

**bluff** /bluhf/
- *verb* to pretend that you will do something, or that something is true: *She is bluffing when she says that she will tell the teacher.*
- *noun* if something is a bluff, it is not true and it is intended to trick someone: *He said he didn't have much money, but it was just a bluff to make them reduce the price.*

**blunt** /bluhnt/ *adjective*
**1** a blunt object is not sharp: *The knife is too blunt to cut the rope.* ▶ see picture at **sharp**
**2** saying something in a very honest way, even when this upsets people: *The coach is very blunt and he says exactly what he thinks is wrong with your game.*
—**bluntly** /**bluhnt**-lee/ *adverb* in an honest way

that may upset someone: *She told him bluntly that he had failed the test.*

**blur** /blur/
- *verb* (**blurring, blurred**) to make something hard to see because the edges are not clear: *The mist blurred our view of the buildings.* | *She tried to blur the truth, by saying that she wasn't sure what happened.*
- *noun* something that you cannot see or remember clearly: *The horses were just a blur because they were running so fast.*
—**blurred** /blurd/ (also **blurry** /blur-ee/) *adjective* not clear: *The photographs were blurred because his hand was shaking when he took the picture.*

**blurt** /blurt/ *verb* to say something suddenly and without thinking about it first: *She blurted out the truth and said that she hated him.*

**blush** /bluhsh/ *verb* if you blush, your face becomes red because you are embarrassed: *When I said she was pretty, she blushed and shook her head.*

**Blvd.** the written abbreviation of **boulevard**

**boa con·stric·tor** /**boh**-uh kuhn-strikt-ur/ *noun* a very large snake that kills animals by crushing them

**boar** /bor/ *noun*
**1** a wild pig
**2** a male pig ( ANTONYM: **SOW** )

**board** /bord/
- *noun*
**1** a flat piece of wood or plastic that you use for writing or doing things on: *The teacher wrote a math problem on the board.* | *a chess board*
▶ see picture at **chess**
**2** a long flat piece of wood that you use for making floors, houses, etc.: *The floor boards in the gym are made of thick strong wood.*
**3** a group of people who control an organization: *The school board decided to build a new school in the area.*

IDIOM with **board**
**on board** on an airplane, ship, train, or bus: *There were more than 200 passengers on board the plane.*
- *verb*
**1** to get on an airplane, ship, or train: *What time do we board our flight?* ( SYNONYM: **get on** )
**2 board up** to cover a window or door with

wooden boards: *A lot of the store windows were boarded up.*

**boast** /bohst/ *verb* to tell other people how smart or good you are, or about how much money you have: *He's always boasting about how good he is at soccer.* ( SYNONYM: **brag** )

**boat** /boht/ *noun* a small vehicle that you use to travel over water: *We went up the river by boat.* | *a fishing boat* ▶ see **Thesaurus**
▶ see picture on page **A10**

**bob** /bahb/ *verb* (**bobbing, bobbed**) to move up and down on water: *Boats were bobbing up and down on the waves.*

**bob·by pin** /**bahb**-ee pin/ *noun* a U-shaped piece of metal that a woman uses to hold her hair in place

**bob·cat** /**bahb**-kat/ *noun* a wild cat that has a short tail and lives in North America. A bobcat is a type of lynx: *A bobcat is twice the size of a house cat.*

**bod·y** /**bahd**-ee/ *noun*
**1** all of the parts of a person or animal, including the head, chest, legs, arms, etc.: *He has a big strong body.* | *I had spots all over my body.*
▶ see picture on page **A13**
**2** a dead person: *The soldier's body was flown home to be buried.* ( SYNONYM: **corpse** )
**3** the main part of something: *The body of the airplane was not damaged in the crash.*

**bod·y·guard** /**bahd**-ee-gard/ *noun* someone whose job is to protect an important person from being attacked: *The president's bodyguards go with him wherever he goes.*

**bo·gus** /**bohg**-uhss/ *adjective* not real or true: *He was arrested for using a bogus passport.*
( SYNONYMS: **fake, false** )

**boil** /boyl/
- *verb*
**1** if a liquid boils, it starts to bubble and make steam: *When the water boils, add the rice.*
**2** to cook food in boiling water: *Boil the spaghetti for 8 minutes.* ▶ see picture at **cook**
- *noun*
a big sore lump on your skin, where there is an infection

**boil·er** /**boyl**-ur/ *noun* a big container that heats the water for a building

**boil·ing point** /**boyl**-ing poynt/ *noun* the temperature of a liquid when it begins to boil. Water boils at 100° Celsius, or 212° Fahrenheit.

**bois·ter·ous** /**boyst**-uhr-uhss/ *adjective* noisy and full of energy: *The kids were running around the store and behaving in a very boisterous way.*

**bold** /bohld/ *adjective*
**1** confident and not afraid: *Columbus was bold enough to cross the Atlantic Ocean in a small ship.*
**2** bold colors or letters are very bright and easy to see: *Her name was shown in big bold letters outside the movie theater.*
—**boldly** /**bohld**-lee/ *adverb* in a bold way: *He walked boldly to the door and opened it.*

**bo·lo·gna**, **baloney** /buh-**lohn**-ee/ *noun* a type of sausage meat used for making sandwiches

**bolt** /bohlt/

**bolt**

● *noun*
**1** a piece of metal that you slide across to lock a door: *I shut the stable door and pushed the bolt across.*
**2** a piece of metal like a screw that goes inside a nut. You use it to hold pieces of metal or wood together: *One of the bolts on the engine has become loose.*

**3** a sudden flash of lightning in the sky during a storm: *A bolt of lightning struck the house and it burned down.*
● *verb*
**1** to lock a door with a bolt: *She closed the door and bolted it so no one could get in.*
**2** to suddenly run somewhere very quickly: *A dog bolted into the road and the driver had to brake suddenly.*

**bomb** /bahm/
● *noun* a weapon that explodes: *The bomb went off in a crowded street and a lot of people were hurt.*
● *verb* to attack a place with bombs: *Planes bombed the city.*

**bomb·er** /**bahm**-ur/ *noun*
**1** an airplane that drops bombs on a place
**2** someone who puts a bomb somewhere

**bond** /bahnd/ *noun* a strong feeling of love and trust that people have for each other: *There was a bond of friendship between the two brothers, and they always helped each other in times of trouble.*

**bone** /bohn/ *noun* one of the hard white parts inside the body that form a skeleton: *I broke a bone in my arm when I was skateboarding.*

**bon·gos** /**bahng**-gohz/ (also **bongo drums** /**bahng**-goh druhmz/) *noun* a pair of small drums that you play with your hands

**bon·net** /**bahn**-it/ *noun* a hat for a baby that ties under the chin. Bonnets were also worn by women in the past.

**bo·nus** /**bohn**-uhss/ *noun* something good that you get as an extra reward: *You will get a bonus point if you can answer this question correctly.*

**bon·y** /**bohn**-ee/ *adjective* very thin: *She had long bony arms.*

**boo** /boo/
● *noun*
**1** a word you shout to surprise someone who does not know you are there: *Tammy was hiding behind the door, and she suddenly shouted "Boo!"*
**2** a word people shout to show that they do not like someone or something: *The movie was terrible and there were boos from the audience.*
● *verb*
to shout "boo" to show that you do not like someone or something: *The other team was booed by the home fans.* (ANTONYM: **cheer**)

**book** /buk/
● *noun* a set of pages inside a cover, that you read or write in: *Mark Twain wrote a lot of other books as well as "The Adventures of Huckleberry Finn."* | *an address book*
● *verb* to arrange to do something in the future: *My parents have booked a vacation in Colorado.*

**book·case** /**buk**-kayss/ *noun* a piece of furniture with shelves for books

**book·keep·er** /**buk**-keep-ur/ *noun* someone whose job is keeping a record of the money that a business receives and spends
—**bookkeeping** /**buk**-keep-ing/ *noun* the work a bookkeeper does

**book·let** /**buk**-lit/ *noun* a short book that has information about something: *The instruction booklet tells you how to use the camera.*

**book·mark** /**buk**-mark/
● *noun* a piece of paper, leather, etc. that you put in a book to show you the last page you have read: *My bookmark fell out and now I can't find the page I was on.*
● *verb* to put a website in your list of favorite websites: *Do you know how to bookmark a website?*

**book·mo·bile** /**buk**-moh-beel/ *noun* a vehicle that is used as a traveling library: *Folks who live in the country rely on the bookmobile for their books.*

**book·shelf** /**buk**-shelf/ *noun* (plural **bookshelves** /**buk**-shelvz/) a shelf that you keep books on

**book·store** /**buk**-stor/ *noun* a store that sells books

**book·worm** /**buk**-wurm/ *noun* someone who enjoys reading and reads a lot of books: *My sister is a real bookworm, but I prefer playing outside.*

**boom** /boom/
● *noun*
**1** a deep loud sound, for example an explosion: *Suddenly there was a big boom and the chemistry lab was filled with smoke.*
**2** a sudden increase in something: *A lot of babies were born during the baby boom after World War II.*
● *verb*
**1** to make a deep loud sound: *His voice boomed around the hall.*
**2** to increase suddenly: *The population of California boomed when gold was discovered there.*

**boo·mer·ang** /**boom**-uh-rang/ *noun* a curved stick that flies in a circle and comes back to you when you throw it: *Boomerangs were originally used for hunting birds and animals in Australia.*

**boost** /boost/
● *verb*
**1** to help someone reach a higher place by lifting them: *Dad boosted me up so I could reach the branch.*

**2** to increase or improve something: *You can boost your chances of winning the game by practicing every day.*
● *noun*
**1** if you give someone a boost, you lift them up: *I put my foot in his hands and he gave me a boost.*
**2** an increase or improvement in something: *He got a good grade, and that gave his confidence a real boost.*

**booster** /**boost**-ur/ (also **booster shot** /**boost**-ur shaht/) *noun* a substance that a doctor puts into your body with a needle. The substance stops you from getting a disease. Boosters make the substance that you were given before continue to work: *You should have a tetanus booster every ten years.*

**boot** /boot/
● *noun* a shoe that covers your ankle and sometimes part of your leg: *He wore black jeans and cowboy boots.* ▶ see picture at **pirate**
● *verb* to make a computer start working: *I waited while the computer was booting up.*

**booth** /booth/ *noun*
**1** a small area that is surrounded by thin walls, where you go to do something: *Mom went into the voting booth.*
**2** a small place where you can buy something. The booth is open at the front and has a roof and walls: *You can buy a ticket from the booth at the bus station.*
**3** an area you sit in at a restaurant, that is separated from the next area by the high back of the seat: *We sat together in the booth and ordered a shake.*

**bor·der** /**bord**-ur/ *noun*
**1** the line between two states or countries: *We crossed the border between the U.S. and Canada.*
**2** a thin area around the edge of something: *The paper has a blue border around it.*

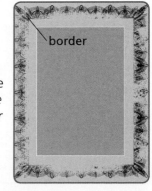

border

**b**

**bore** /bor/
● *verb*
**1** the past tense of **bear**
**2** if something bores you, you are not interested in it: *The conversation bored me and I kept looking at my watch.*
● *noun*
someone or something that is not interesting: *Washing dishes is such a bore!*

**Word Family: bore**

**bore** *noun* | **bore** *verb* | **bored** *adjective* | **boring** *adjective* | **boredom** *noun*

**bored** /bord/ *adjective* if you are bored, you feel that something is not interesting: *She was bored with the party and wanted to go home.*

**bore·dom** /**bord**-uhm/ *noun* the feeling you have when you are bored: *I started falling asleep with boredom.*

**bor·ing** /**bor**-ing/ *adjective* not interesting: *It was a boring game and nothing exciting happened.* ▶ see **Thesaurus**

**born** /born/ *adjective*
**1** if a baby is born, it comes out of its mother's body: *I was born in California in 2002. | Where were you born?*
**2** naturally good at doing something: *He's a born athlete and he has big shoulders and strong legs.*

**borne** /born/ *verb* the past participle of bear

**bor·row** /**bar**-oh/ *verb* to use something that belongs to someone and give it back later: *Can I borrow your pen? | Ellen borrowed $8,000 from the bank to buy a car.*

**Word Choice: borrow, lend**

If you **borrow** something from someone, you take something that someone gives you for a short time, and then you give it back: *Can I borrow your bike?*

You cannot say "Can I lend your bike?"

If you **lend** something to someone, you give it to him or her so that he or she can use it for a short time: *I lent my book to Elena. | Mom, could you lend me some money?*

You cannot say "Could you borrow me some money?"

**bor·row·er** /**bar**-oh-ur/ *noun* someone who borrows money from a bank

**boss** /boss/
● *noun* the person who is in charge of a group of people, and tells them what to do: *Laura asked her boss if she could go home early.*
● *verb* **boss around** to keep telling someone what to do in an annoying way: *My brother thinks he can boss me around, just because he's older than me.*

**boss·y** /**boss**-ee/ *adjective* a bossy person keeps telling other people what to do in an annoying way: *She is a very bossy little girl and she is always telling people where to put everything.*

**bot·a·ny** /**baht**'n-ee/ *noun* the study of plants
—**botanist** /**baht**'n-ist/ *noun* a scientist who studies plants

**both** /bohth/ *adjective, pronoun* used for talking about two people or things: *We both go to the same school. | Hold the cup in both hands. | Both of my parents are teachers.*

**Grammar: both, both of**

Do not say "The both boys were at school." Say *Both of the boys were at school*, *Both boys were at school*, or *Both the boys were at school.*
Do not say "his both sisters." Say *both of his sisters* or *both his sisters.*

**both·er** /**bahth**-ur/ *verb*
**1** to annoy someone by talking when he or she is busy: *Don't bother your dad while he's working.*
**2** if something bothers you, it makes you worried or upset: *It really bothered me that she didn't listen to me.*
**3** to make an effort to do something: *I didn't bother to do my homework.*

**bot·tle** /**baht**'l/ *noun* a glass or plastic container that holds liquid: *a bottle of water*
—**bottled** /**baht**'ld/ *adjective* bottled drinks are sold in bottles

**bot·tom** /**baht**-uhm/
● *noun*
**1** the lowest part of something: *Some strange fish live at the bottom of the ocean.*
**ANTONYM: top**

66

**2** the part of your body that you sit on
● *adjective*
the bottom shelf, drawer, step, etc. is the lowest one: *Your T-shirts are in the bottom drawer.*
( ANTONYM: **top** )

**bought** /bot/ *verb* the past tense and past participle of **buy**

**boul·der** /**bohld**-ur/ *noun* a large rock

**bou·le·vard** /**bul**-uh-vard/ *noun* a wide road in a city: *We drove down Sunset Boulevard.*

**bounce** /bownss/
● *verb*
**1** if a ball bounces, it hits the ground or wall and moves away again: *In tennis, the ball must bounce only once. | He bounced the ball against the wall and caught it again.*
**2** to jump up and down on something soft: *Don't bounce on the sofa!*
● *noun*
an action in which a ball hits a surface and moves away again: *The ball took a bad bounce and went under my mitt.*

**bound** /bownd/
● *adjective*
**1** if something is bound to happen, it is certain to happen: *Mom is bound to find out that I lied.*
**2** traveling toward a particular place: *The train was bound for New York.*
● *verb*
**1** to move forward by running and jumping: *The dog bounded across the lawn.*
**2** the past tense and past participle of **bind**
● *noun*
a big jump into or over something: *The horse was over the gate in one bound.*

⌐ IDIOM with **bound**
  **out of bounds**
  **1** if a place is out of bounds, you are not allowed to go there: *The classrooms are out of bounds to students during lunch.*
  **2** if a ball is out of bounds, it is outside the playing area, and you cannot play the ball: *He missed the pass and the ball went out of bounds.*

**bound·a·ry** /**bownd**-uhr-ee/ *noun* (plural **boundaries**) the line that separates two areas of land: *The Rio Grande forms the boundary between Texas and Mexico.*

**bou·quet** /boh-**kay**/
*noun* some flowers that are tied together: *The bride carried a bouquet of roses.*

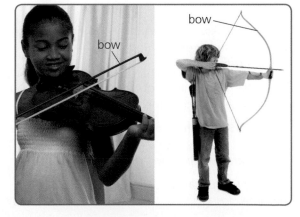
bouquet

**bout** /bowt/ *noun*
**1** a short period of time when you are sick: *I had a bout of the flu.*
**2** a fight in boxing or wrestling

**bou·tique** /boo-**teek**/ *noun* a small store that sells fashionable clothes

**bow**
● *verb* /boh/
to bend your head and the top part of your body down. You bow after you have performed in front of people, or to show respect for someone: *The dancers bowed and left the stage. | We bowed our heads in prayer.*
● *noun* /bow/
**1** the action of bending your head and the top part of your body down: *The actors stepped forward and took a bow at the end of the performance.*
**2** the front part of a ship or boat: *A dolphin jumped in the water near the bow of the ship.*
● *noun* /boh/
**1** a knot with two loops (=circles) and two free ends: *Tie your shoelaces in a bow.*
**2** a weapon that you use to shoot arrows: *Native Americans hunted with bows and arrows.*
**3** a thing that you use for playing instruments with strings, such as the violin. It is a long thin piece of wood with hair stretched from one end to the other.

bow

bow

bow

**bow·el** /**bow**-uhl/ *noun* the long tube inside your body that food goes through after it leaves your stomach. Food is digested in your bowel before waste material goes out of your body.
( SYNONYM: **intestine** )

**bowl** /bohl/ *noun* a round dish. You put food or liquid in a bowl: *a bowl of soup*

**bowl**

a bowl of cereal

**bowl·ing** /**bohl**-ing/ *noun* an indoor game in which you roll a heavy ball at ten objects called pins, in order to knock them down: *Do you want to go bowling with us?*

**bow tie** /**boh** tī/ *noun* a man's necktie that is tied in the shape of a bow

**box** /bahkss/
● *noun* a container with four sides: *I put the books in a cardboard box. | a box of cookies*
● *verb* to fight someone while wearing big leather gloves, as a sport

**box**

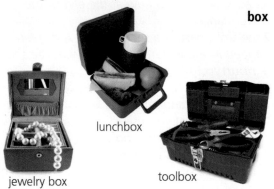

jewelry box

lunchbox

toolbox

**box·car** /**bahkss**-kar/ *noun* a type of railroad car with a large sliding door. Boxcars are used for carrying goods.

**box·er** /**bahkss**-ur/ *noun* someone who boxes as a sport: *The boxers went into the ring and prepared to fight.*

**box·ing** /**bahkss**-ing/ *noun* the sport of fighting while wearing big leather gloves

**box of·fice** /**bahkss** of-iss/ *noun* a place where you can buy tickets to a movie, concert, etc.: *Tickets are on sale now at the box office.*

**boy** /boy/ *noun* a male child: *The two boys became close friends. | How old is your little boy*

(=your young son)?
—**boyish** /**boy**-ish/ *adjective* looking or behaving like a boy: *The police officer had a boyish face and looked very young.*

**Word Origin:** boy

The word **boy** started being used in English in the 1100s. The word boy may come from a word that meant "servant." Or, boy may come from another word that meant "a young gentleman."

**boy·cott** /**boy**-kaht/
● *verb* to refuse to buy something or do something as a protest: *During the 1960s, African-Americans boycotted the city's buses because black people were not allowed to ride in any seat they wanted.*
● *noun* a protest in which you refuse to buy or do something

**boy·friend** /**boy**-frend/ *noun* a boy or man that someone is having a romantic relationship with: *My sister has a boyfriend and they want to get married one day.*

**bra** /brah/ *noun* a piece of underwear that a woman wears to support her breasts

**brace·let** /**brayss**-lit/ *noun* a piece of jewelry that you wear around your wrist

**bra·ce·ro** /brah-say-ro/ *noun* someone who came to the U.S. from Mexico for a limited period to work on a farm

**brac·es** /**brayss**-iz/ *plural noun* wires that a dentist puts on your teeth to make them straight

**brack·et** /**brak**-it/ *noun*
**1** one of the pair of marks [ ] that are put around extra information
**2** a group: *The toy is for children in the 8–10 age bracket.*

**brag** /brag/ *verb* (**bragging**, **bragged**) to tell other people how smart or good you are, or about how much money you have: *He was bragging about how good he was at baseball.*
( SYNONYM: **boast** )

## braid /brayd/

● *verb* to twist together three pieces of hair, rope, or cloth so that they form one piece: *Her mother was braiding her hair.*
● *noun* three pieces of hair that you twist together: *My sister wears her hair in braids.*

**braid**

## Braille /brayl/ *noun* an alphabet that is written as round bumps on paper. Blind people read by feeling the bumps: *The elevator buttons have the floor numbers in Braille, so that blind people can feel which floor they are on.*

**Braille**

## brain /brayn/ *noun*

**1** the part inside your head that controls how you think, feel, and move: *If your brain is damaged, this can affect your ability to communicate.* ► see picture at **anatomy**
**2** **brains** the ability to think and learn well: *The boy has brains and he will do well in college.*
SYNONYM: **intelligence**

**brain**

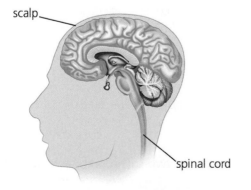

scalp

spinal cord

## brain·wash /brayn-wahsh/ *verb* to make someone believe something that is not true, by telling him or her many times that it is true: *People are brainwashed into believing that money will make them happy.*

## brake /brayk/

● *noun* a piece of equipment that makes a vehicle go more slowly or stop: *My dad put his foot on the brake pedal, to make the car slow down.* ► see picture at **bicycle**
● *verb* to make a vehicle go more slowly or stop by using its brakes: *She braked when a dog ran into the road.*

## bran /bran/ *noun* the outer skin of wheat or another grain. In white flour, the bran is taken out: *Bran is good for you because it helps your stomach to digest food.*

## branch /branch/ *noun*

**1** a part of a tree that grows out from the main trunk: *The branches of the tree are covered in leaves.* ► see picture at **tree**
**2** if a company has branches, it has stores or offices in many different places: *The store has branches in most cities.*

## brand /brand/

● *noun*
**1** a type of product made by a company: *It's the most popular brand of cola in America.*
**2** a mark on a cow or horse that shows who it belongs to
● *verb*
to burn a mark onto the skin of a cow or horse to show who it belongs to: *The cowboys branded all the calves.*

## brand-new /brand **noo**/ *adjective* new and never used before: *The toys are brand-new and still in their boxes.*

## brass /brass/ *noun*

**1** a very hard yellow metal that is a mixture of copper and zinc: *a brass doorknob*
**2** the people in an orchestra who play musical instruments such as the trumpet and the trombone. These instruments are called brass instruments.

## brat /brat/ *noun* a child who behaves badly: *A noisy little brat was screaming in the supermarket.*

a
b
c
d
e
f
g
h
i
j
k
l
m
n
o
p
q
r
s
t
u
v
w
x
y
z

a
**b**
c
d
e
f
g
h
i
j
k
l
m
n
o
p
q
r
s
t
u
v
w
x
y
z

**brave** /brayv/

● *adjective* if you are brave, you do something difficult or dangerous even when you are afraid: *The brave firefighters went into the burning building to rescue the people inside.*
( SYNONYM: **courageous** ) ▶ see **Thesaurus**
—**bravely** /brayv-lee/ *adverb* in a way that shows you are brave: *He bravely helped the other soldiers to escape, even though he was badly injured.*
● *noun* a Native American man who fought for his tribe in the past

**brav·er·y** /brayv-uhr-ee/ *noun* actions that show that you are brave: *He showed great bravery in the battle and saved many lives.*
( SYNONYM: **courage** ) ( ANTONYM: **cowardice** )

**bread** /bred/ *noun* a food made by baking a mixture of flour and water: *I had a ham sandwich made with white bread. | a loaf of bread*

**breadth** /bredth/ *noun*
**1** the distance from one side of something to the other: *The breadth of the pool is 20 meters.*
( SYNONYM: **width** )
**2** the breadth of someone's knowledge or experience is how many different things they know about or have done: *He has an enormous breadth of knowledge about baseball and he knows all the different players.*

**break** /brayk/
● *verb* (**broke** /brohk/, **broken** /brohk-uhn/)
**1** if something breaks, it separates into pieces after being hit or dropped: *If the cup falls on the floor, it will break. | Who broke the bathroom window? | I broke my arm when I was skateboarding.* ▶ see **Thesaurus**
**2** to damage a machine or piece of equipment, so that it stops working: *I lent Jimmy my video game console and he broke it. | I dropped the camera and now it's broken.*
**3 break a law/rule** to not obey a law or rule: *Students who break the rules will be punished.*
**4 break your promise/word** to not do what you promised to do: *He said he would take me to the baseball game, but he broke his promise.*
**5 break a record** to do something faster or better than it has ever been done before: *Jones broke the world record in the 400 meters.*
**6 break down** if a car or a machine breaks

down, it stops working: *Dad's truck broke down on the way to work.*
**7 break in** to enter a building using force: *Burglars broke into the house while we were on vacation.*
**8 break out** if something bad such as a fire, war, or disease breaks out, it begins to happen: *The fire broke out on the second floor.*
**9 break up** to stop having a romantic relationship with someone: *My brother and his girlfriend broke up last week.*
● *noun*
a short rest from studying or working: *I'm tired. Let's take a break. | What time does your lunch break start?*

**break·danc·ing** /brayk-danss-ing/ *noun* a kind of dancing. The dancers often stand on their hands or their heads and turn around: *Breakdancing is done to hip hop music.*

**break·down** /brayk-down/ *noun*
**1** if a vehicle or piece of machinery has a breakdown, it stops working: *Our car had a breakdown and we had to call someone to come and fix the engine.*
**2** if someone has a breakdown, he or she becomes mentally ill because problems in life seem too difficult to deal with: *She's working too hard. I'm worried she'll have a breakdown.*

**break·fast** /brek-fuhst/ *noun* the meal you eat in the morning: *I had cereal for breakfast.*

**break-in** /brayk in/ *noun* a crime in which someone breaks a door or window of a building in order to go in and steal things: *There was a break-in at the school and some computers were stolen.*

**break·through** /brayk-throo/ *noun* an important discovery: *Scientists made a breakthrough in the search for a cure for the disease.*

**break·up** /brayk-uhp/ *noun* the ending of a romantic relationship or a marriage: *He was really unhappy over the breakup of his parents' marriage.*

**breast** /brest/ *noun*
**1** one of the two soft round parts on a woman's chest
**2** the part of a bird's body between the neck and

the stomach: *Cut up the chicken breast and put it in the pan.*
**3** a person's body between the neck and the stomach

**breast·stroke** /**brest**-strohk/ *noun* a way of swimming. You push both your arms forward, and then move them around to your sides: *She swam the breaststroke in the race.*
▶ see picture at **swim**

**breath** /breth/ *noun* the air that you take in and let out when you breathe: *I took a deep breath, and dived into the ocean.* | *He has very bad breath – it smells terrible.*

> IDIOMS with **breath**
> **catch your breath** to breathe normally again, after you have been running or exercising: *I had to sit down to catch my breath.*
> **hold your breath** to breathe in a lot of air, and then not breathe it out again for a short time: *How long can you hold your breath under water?*
> **be out of breath** to have difficulty breathing because you have been running or exercising: *My grandmother was out of breath from climbing so many stairs.*

**breathe** /breeth/ *verb* to take air into your body and let it out again: *Shut your eyes and breathe slowly and deeply.* | *I breathed in the cold night air.*
—**breathing** /**breeth**-ing/ *noun* the act of taking air into your body and letting it out again: *His breathing became deeper as he fell asleep.*

**breath·less** /**breth**-liss/ *adjective* not able to breathe easily: *I was breathless from running.*

**breath·tak·ing** /**breth**-tayk-ing/ *adjective* very beautiful or exciting: *From the top of the hill, there is a breathtaking view of the ocean.*

**breed** /breed/
● *noun*
one type of a particular animal: *Labradors are a good breed of dog for a family pet.*
● *verb* (**bred** /bred/)
**1** if animals breed, they have babies: *Birds breed in the spring.*
**2** to keep animals so that they will have baby animals that you can sell: *He breeds horses for racing.*

**breeze** /breez/ *noun* a gentle wind: *There was a nice cool breeze blowing through the window.*
—**breezy** /**breez**-ee/ *adjective* with a lot of gentle wind: *Breezy days are good for drying clothes.*

**brew** /broo/ *verb*
**1** to make a drink of tea or coffee: *She brewed a pot of coffee.*
**2** to make beer: *They brew the beer in big containers.*
**3** if something bad is brewing, it will happen soon: *The sky became dark and I knew there was a storm brewing.* | *The problems at the bank had been brewing for a long time before it failed.*

**brew·er·y** /**broo**-uhr-ee/ *noun* a place where beer is made

**bribe** /brīb/
● *verb* to give money or a gift to someone so that they will do something you want, especially something illegal: *The men bribed a prison officer to help them to escape from the prison.* | *He bribed his sister not to tell his parents about what he had done.*
—**bribery** /**brīb**-uhr-ee/ *noun* the action of bribing someone: *Officials were accused of bribery and corruption.*
● *noun* money or a gift that is used to bribe someone: *It is illegal to offer a bribe to a police officer.*

**brick** /brik/ *noun* a hard block of baked clay. Bricks are used to build houses and walls.

**bride** /brīd/ *noun* the woman at a wedding who is getting married: *The bride and groom were just leaving the church.*
—**bridal** /**brīd**'l/ *adjective* relating to a bride or a wedding: *She was wearing a long white bridal gown.*

**bride·groom** /**brīd**-groom/ *noun* the man at a wedding who is getting married
SYNONYM: **groom**

**brides·maid** /**brīdz**-mayd/ *noun* a woman who helps a bride at her wedding: *The bridesmaids carried pink flowers.*

a
**b**
c
d
e
f
g
h
i
j
k
l
m
n
o
p
q
r
s
t
u
v
w
x
y
z

**bridge** /brij/ *noun* a structure built over a river or road. You use the bridge to cross over the river or road: *The Golden Gate Bridge crosses from one side of the bay to the other.*

**bridge**

**brief** /breef/ *adjective*
**1** continuing for a short time: *We'll have a brief rest before the next game.* ( ANTONYM: **long** )
**2** using only a few words: *His instructions were very brief and I wasn't sure what to do.*
—**briefly** /breef-lee/ *adverb* in a brief way: *The teacher briefly explained how to use the computers.*

**brief·case** /breef-kayss/ *noun* a bag that people carry papers in for work. A briefcase is flat and has a handle, and often has hard sides: *He put the documents back in his briefcase and shut the lid.*

**bright** /brīt/ *adjective*
**1** having a lot of light, or shining so there is a lot of light: *She could see the bright lights of the city.* | *The afternoon was brighter and sunnier.*
▶ see **Thesaurus**
**2** bright colors are strong and easy to see: *a bright red sweater* ( ANTONYM: **pale** )
**3** quick at learning things: *Emma is a bright student and she gets good grades on all her tests.* ( SYNONYMS: **smart, intelligent** )
—**brightly** /brīt-lee/ *adverb* in a bright way: *The sun shone brightly.* | *The children wore brightly colored T-shirts.*
—**brightness** /brīt-niss/ *noun* a bright quality: *Sunglasses protect your eyes from the sun's brightness.*

**bright·en** /brīt'n/ *verb*
**1** to make something brighter or lighter: *The moon brightened the dark sky.*

**2** to make something look more colorful and pretty: *The yellow paint really brightened up the room.*
**3** to become or look happier: *His face brightened when he heard the good news that he had passed his test.*

**bril·liant** /bril-yuhnt/ *adjective*
**1** very smart or very good at your work: *He was a brilliant scientist who made some amazing discoveries.*
**2** showing that you are smart or good at something: *That's a brilliant idea!*
**3** a brilliant light or color is very bright: *The plant has brilliant red berries.*
—**brilliantly** /bril-yuhnt-lee/ *adverb* in a brilliant way: *The book is brilliantly written.* | *The jewels were brilliantly colored.*
—**brilliance** /bril-yuhnss/ *noun* greatness or brightness: *Picasso was famous for the brilliance of his paintings.*

**brim** /brim/ *noun*
**1** the part of a hat that sticks out around your head: *A cowboy hat has a big brim.*
**2** the top of a container, such as a glass: *My cup was filled to the brim.*

**brim**

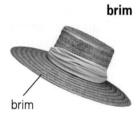

brim

**bring** /bring/ *verb* (**brought** /brot/)
**1** to take someone or something with you: *Bring your reading books to school.* | *My father brought this doll back from Japan.* | *She brought out a picture to show me.*
**2** to make something happen or come: *Winter brings snow to the mountains.* | *Bring the water to a boil.*
**3** to make someone have a feeling, or to cause something to happen: *His music has brought joy to many people.* | *The hurricane brought disaster to the city.*
**4** **bring up a child** to take care of a child until he or she is an adult: *She brought up three children by herself.* ( SYNONYM: **raise** )
**5** **bring up a subject** to mention something you want to talk about: *I hope Mom doesn't bring up the subject of homework again.*
( SYNONYM: **raise** )

## Word Choice: bring, get, take

You use **bring** when you take something or someone to the place where you are now, or a place where you are going with other people: *Did you bring your homework to school?* | *Elise brought her friend with her to the party.*

You use **get** when you go to another place and come back with something or someone: *I'll get my soccer ball.*

You use **take** when you move something from the place you are to a different place, or help someone go from one place to a different place: *Mrs. Muñoz will take you home after school.* | *Don't forget to take your coat with you.*

**brink** /bringk/ *noun* if you are on the brink of something, it may happen soon: *The country is on the brink of war.*

**bris·tle** /**briss**-uhl/ *noun* a short stiff hair or wire: *The brush had short bristles.*

**Brit·ish** /**brit**-ish/
● *adjective* from Great Britain: *British people*
● *noun* people from Great Britain

**brit·tle** /**brit**'l/ *adjective* hard or stiff, but easily broken: *The paper was old and brittle.*

**broad** /brod/ *adjective*
**1** wide: *She had a broad smile on her face.*
( ANTONYM: **narrow** )
**2** including many different kinds of things or people: *There's a broad range of things you can do at summer camp.* ( SYNONYM: **wide** )
( ANTONYM: **narrow** )

IDIOM with **broad**
**in broad daylight** during the day, when other people can easily see what you are doing: *The robbery took place in broad daylight.*

**broad·cast** /**brod**-kast/
● *verb* (**broadcast**) to show a program on the television, or to put a program on the radio: *The game will be broadcast on CBS.*
—**broadcaster** /**brod**-kast-ur/ *noun* someone who talks on the radio or on television programs, or someone who is in the radio or television business
—**broadcasting** /**brod**-kast-ing/ *noun* the business

of showing programs on the television or playing them on the radio
● *noun* a program on the radio or television: *a news broadcast*

**broc·co·li** /**brahk**-uhl-ee/ *noun* a green vegetable with thick round bunches of small green flowers on stalks. ▶ see picture on page **A7**

**bro·chure** /broh-**shoor**/ *noun* a thin paper book with pictures. A brochure gives information or advertises something: *Look in the brochure for the days and times of the dance classes.*

**broil** /broyl/ *verb* to cook something by putting the food directly over or under flames or heat: *He broiled steak for his dinner.*

**broil·er** /**broyl**-ur/ *noun* the part of an oven where you cook food under heat: *Put the chicken breasts under the broiler.*

**broke** /brohk/
● *verb* the past tense of **break**
● *adjective* having no money: *I spent all my money, so now I'm broke.*

**bro·ken** /**brohk**-uhn/
● *verb* the past participle of break
● *adjective* damaged or in pieces: *One of the boys had a broken leg.* | *a broken toy*

**bro·ker** /**brohk**-ur/ *noun* someone whose job is to buy and sell houses, insurance, stocks, etc.: *My father's a real estate broker.*

**bron·to·sau·rus** /brahnt-uh-**sor**-uhss/ *noun* a very large dinosaur with a long neck and tail and a small head. Brontosauruses probably ate plants. Scientists now usually call this dinosaur an apatosaurus.

**bronze** /brahnz/ *noun* a metal made by mixing copper and tin. Bronze is a brown-red color: *About 4,000 years ago, men began making tools out of bronze.*

bronze

a bronze pot

**brooch** /brohch/ *noun* a piece of jewelry with a pin on the back. Women fasten brooches to their clothes: *Mary was wearing a silver brooch on her dress.*

**brook** /bruk/ *noun* a small stream: *The water in the brook was clear and running fast.*

**broom** /broom/ *noun* a brush with a long handle, used for sweeping floors

broom

broom

**Word Origin: broom**

**Broom** comes from the Old English name for a plant with long twigs and yellow flowers. The twigs of the plant were tied together and used to sweep floors.

**broth·er** /**bruth**-ur/ *noun* a boy or man who has the same parents as you: *My older brother is 12.* | *This is my little brother, Charlie.*
—**brotherly** /**bruth**-ur-lee/ *adjective* kind, helpful, and loyal in the way a brother behaves: *Joe was filled with brotherly pride about what Dan had done.*

**Word Origin: brother**

**Brother** comes from Old English. The word for brother in many other languages sounds a little like the English word for brother. This is because the words for brother come from a language that people used many thousands of years ago. English, Greek, Latin, Hindi, and many other languages developed from this very old language.

**broth·er-in-law** /**bruth**-ur in lo/ *noun*
**1** the brother of someone's husband or wife
**2** the husband of someone's sister

**brought** /brot/ *verb* the past tense and past participle of **bring**

**brow** /brow/ *noun* the part of your face above your eyes and below your hair: *She wiped the sweat off her brow.* (SYNONYM: **forehead**)

**brown** /brown/ *adjective, noun* the color of dirt, wood, or coffee: *Ellana has brown hair and brown eyes.*

**browse** /browz/ *verb*
**1** to look at things in a store, or to look at a magazine, when you do not plan to buy anything or read anything carefully: *A boy was browsing through the comic books on the rack.*
**2** to look for information on the Internet: *You can get facts for your project by browsing the Internet.*

**brows·er** /**browz**-ur/ *noun* a computer program that lets you find and use information on the Internet

**bruise** /brooz/
● *noun* a dark mark on your skin where it has been hit: *She had cuts and bruises from when she fell off her bike.*
● *verb* to get a bruise: *I bruised my knee when I hit it on the table.*
—**bruised** /broozd/ *adjective* having one or more bruises: *His legs were bruised after the soccer game.*

**bru·nette** /broo-**net**/ *noun* a woman with brown hair

**brush** /bruhsh/
● *noun*
**1** an object that you use for cleaning, painting, or making your hair smooth. A brush is made of pieces of hair or plastic that are fastened to a handle: *He picked up his brush and started painting a picture of a lake.* | *I use this brush to clean the kitchen floor.*
▶ see picture at **dustpan**
**2** small plants and trees that cover an area of land: *The fire started in some brush near the campsite.*
● *verb*
**1** to use a brush, for example to clean your teeth or to make something look neat: *Brush your teeth twice a day.*
**2** to use your hand or a brush to move something off a surface: *Kim brushed the crumbs off the table.*
**3** to touch something gently with your fingers: *His fingers brushed her cheek.*

brush

toothbrush

paintbrushes

hairbrush

**bru·tal** /**broot**'l/ *adjective* very cruel or violent: *The long and brutal war has finally ended.*
—**brutally** /**broot**'l-ee/ *adverb* in a brutal way: *The man was brutally attacked by a gang of robbers.*
—**brutality** /broo-**tal**-uht-ee/ *noun* brutal behavior

**bub·ble** /**buhb**-uhl/
● *noun* a ball of air in a liquid, or a ball of air in something soft such as gum: *If you see bubbles in a river or lake, there's often a fish under the water. | The soda has bubbles in it.*
● *verb* to make bubbles: *When the milk gets hot, it starts to bubble.*

**buck** /buhk/ *noun*
**1** a dollar: *The DVD cost 20 bucks.*
**2** a male deer or rabbit

**buck·et** /**buhk**-it/ *noun* a deep round container with a handle on the top. You use a bucket for carrying water and other liquids: *We always wash the car with a bucket instead of a hose to save water.* ( SYNONYM: **pail** )

**buck·le** /**buhk**-uhl/
*noun* a metal object used to fasten a belt, shoe, or bag: *Taylor undid his belt buckle and took his pants off.*
▶ see picture at **watch**

buckle

buckle

**bud** /buhd/ *noun* a young flower or leaf that has just started growing and is a small round shape: *In spring, the buds on the trees start to open.* ▶ see picture at **flower**

bud

bud

**Bud·dha** /**bood**-uh/ *noun*
**1** the person who started the religion of Buddhism. His name was Siddhartha Gautama and he lived in India 2,500 years ago.
**2** a picture or statue of Buddha

**Bud·dhis·m** /**bood**-iz-uhm/ *noun* a religion based on the teachings of Buddha. Buddhists believe that if people stop wanting things, they will no longer have pain or problems. They also believe that you live many different lives.
—**Buddhist** /**bood**-ist/ *noun* someone whose religion is Buddhism

**bud·dy** /**buhd**-ee/ *noun* (plural **buddies**) a friend: *Todd is my best buddy and we've known each other for a long time.*

**budge** /buhj/ *verb* if someone or something does not budge, they do not move when you want them to: *She pushed the door but it wouldn't budge.*

**budg·et** /**buhj**-it/
● *noun* an amount of money that a person or company can spend: *My parents try to keep to their budget, so we don't go out to eat much.*
● *verb* to plan how much money you can spend: *The school has budgeted $5,000 for new sports equipment.*

**buff** /buhf/ *noun* someone who is very interested in something and knows a lot about it: *My brother is a movie buff and he has a huge collection of movies.*

**buf·fa·lo** /**buhf**-uh-loh/ *noun* a wild animal that looks like a large cow with a big head. Buffaloes have thick brown hair on their neck and shoulders: *The Native American tribes on the plains hunted the buffalo for food.*
( SYNONYM: **bison** )

## Word Origin: buffalo

The word **buffalo** probably comes from the Portuguese word for "water buffalo." It may also come from a French word that means "ox" or "male cow". An American buffalo is not the same as a water buffalo, and it is not a kind of cow. An American buffalo is really a kind of bison.

**buf·fet** /buh-**fay**/ *noun* a meal where all the dishes are on a table and you go and take what you want: *There's a buffet where you can choose any salad you want and put it on your plate.*

**bug** /buhg/
● *noun*
**1** an insect: *Bugs were crawling on the plant's leaves.*
**2** an illness that passes from one person to another easily: *I had a stomach bug and stayed home from school.*
**3** a small problem in a computer program that stops it from working well: *There was a bug in the software and I kept having problems with my computer.*
● *verb* (**bugging**, **bugged**)
to annoy someone: *Stop bugging me!*

## Word Origin: bug

Once, an insect was found inside a computer that wasn't working correctly. Some people think that the word **bug** started being used about computer problems then. But the word was used a long time before that. Thomas Edison, the man who invented the light bulb and many other things in the 1870s, was maybe the first person to use **bug** to mean "a small problem that stops something from working."

**build** /bild/ *verb* (**built** /bilt/)
**1** to make a building, a bridge, or another structure: *They're going to build some new houses next to our house.* | *The girl built a tower out of blocks.*
▶ see **Thesaurus**
**2** to make something get bigger or stronger: *Exercise will help to build up your muscles.*

build

The girl built a tower out of blocks.

**build·ing** /**bild**-ing/ *noun*
**1** a house, school, or anything with a roof and walls: *The Sears Tower in Chicago is one of the tallest buildings in the world.* | *an apartment building*
**2** the process of making a house, school, road, etc.: *The building of the railroad took many years.* ( SYNONYM: **construction** )

**built** /bilt/ *verb* the past tense and past participle of **build**

**bulb** /buhlb/ *noun*
**1** the glass part of an electric light, where the light shines from: *This new kind of bulb saves electricity.*
( SYNONYM: **light bulb** )
**2** the round root of some kinds of plants. Tulips and onions grow from bulbs: *If you plant the bulbs in the fall, you will have beautiful yellow flowers in the spring.*
▶ see picture at **flower**

bulb

bulb

**bulge** /buhlj/
● *verb* to curve out in a round shape: *The shopping bag was very full and it was bulging with cakes and cookies.*
● *noun* the curved shape something makes when it bulges: *The wallet made a big bulge in his pocket.*

**bulk** /buhlk/ *noun*
**1** most of something: *He spends the bulk of his time playing computer games.*
**2** the large size of something or someone: *Dinosaurs moved slowly because of their bulk.*

**bulk·y** /**buhlk**-ee/ *adjective* big and heavy: *She wore a bulky winter jacket.*

**bull** /bul/ *noun*
**1** a male cow
**2** the male of some other large animals, for example an elephant or whale

**bull·doz·er** /**bul**-dohz-ur/ *noun* a big strong vehicle used for moving dirt and rocks

**bulldozer**

**bul·let** /**bul**-it/ *noun* the small hard metal thing that comes out of a gun when you fire it: *The police officer fired two bullets at the robbers.*

**bul·le·tin** /**bul**-uht-in/ *noun*
**1** a short news program on television or radio: *There was a news bulletin about the storm on the TV.*
**2** a short letter that gives information: *The meeting was listed in the church bulletin.*

**bul·le·tin board** /**bul**-uht-in bord/ *noun* a board on a wall where people put information. Bulletin boards are covered with a soft material called cork that you can pin papers to: *There is a poster about the karate class on the bulletin board.*

**bull·frog** /**bul**-frog/ *noun* a large frog that makes a loud noise

**bull's-eye** /**bulz**-ī/ *noun* the center of a target. You try to hit the bull's-eye when you shoot a gun or arrow, or play the game of darts: *Her first shot hit the bull's-eye.*

**bul·ly** /**bul**-ee/ (plural **bullies**)
● *noun* someone who frightens or hurts people who are smaller or not as strong: *The bullies made the little boy give them all his lunch money every day.*
● *verb* (**bullies**, **bullying**, **bullied**) to frighten or hurt people who are smaller or not as strong:

*She's unhappy because she's being bullied by one of the older girls.*
—**bullying** /**bul**-ee-ing/ *noun* the activity of frightening or hurting people who are smaller or not as strong: *What does the school do about bullying on the playground?*

**bum·ble·bee** /**buhm**-buhl-bee/ *noun* a large bee

**bump** /buhmp/
● *verb*
**1** to hit something by accident: *Joey fell and bumped his head on the table.* | *I bumped into the door and hurt my nose.*
**2 bump into someone** to meet someone you know when you are not planning to: *We bumped into my teacher at the airport.*
● *noun*
**1** a raised area on your skin. A bump comes up when you hit part of your body on something: *I had a big bump on my head from falling off the bed.*
**2** a hard raised area on the ground: *There were a lot of bumps in the road, so we drove slowly.*

**bump·er** /**buhmp**-ur/ *noun* the part of a car that protects it if it hits anything. The bumper is a bar of metal or rubber that goes across the front or back of the car: *He damaged the front bumper when he drove into a wall.*

**bump·y** /**buhmp**-ee/ *adjective* not smooth and having a lot of bumps: *The road was very bumpy and the car kept going up and down.*

**bun** /buhn/ *noun*
**1** a small round piece of bread: *I want my hamburger in a bun.* (SYNONYM: **roll**)
**2** if a woman's hair is in a bun, it is tied in a round shape at the back of her head: *Kelly put her hair up in a bun.*

**bunch** /buhnch/ *noun*
**1** a group of things that are held together, such as bananas or flowers: *I always buy a big bunch of roses for my mom on Mother's Day.* | *a bunch of grapes*
**2** a lot of something: *A bunch of people were waiting at the bus stop.* | *There's a whole bunch of pens in the box.*

**bunch**

a bunch of grapes

**bun·dle** /**buhnd**'l/ *noun* a group of papers, clothes, sticks, etc. that are tied together: *The truck was filled with bundles of newspapers.*

**bunk** /buhngk/ *noun*
**1** a bed that is above or below another bed: *At camp, I slept on the top bunk.*
**2** a bed that is joined to the wall on a train or ship

**bunk beds** /**buhngk** bedz/ *noun* two beds with one above the other: *My brother and I sleep on bunk beds.*

**bun·ny** /**buhn**-ee/ (also **bun·ny rab·bit** /**buhn**-ee rab-it/) *noun* (plural **bunnies**) a rabbit

**buoy** /**boo**-ee/ *noun* an object that floats on water. Buoys show where it is safe or dangerous for boats or swimming, or show where something is: *Swimmers must not swim beyond the buoys.*

**bur·den** /**burd**'n/ *noun* something difficult or worrying that you have to deal with: *Some children have the burden of caring for a sick parent.*

**bu·reau** /**byoor**-oh/ *noun*
**1** a piece of furniture that you keep clothes in. A bureau has drawers that slide in and out: *Put your T-shirts in the bureau.*
(SYNONYMS: **chest of drawers, dresser**)
**2** an organization that does something or gives information: *You can pick up a free map at the tourist bureau.* | *the Federal Bureau of Investigation*

**bu·reauc·ra·cy** /byu-**rahk**-ruhss-ee/ *noun* an official system for doing something. These systems have a lot of rules so it can take a long time to do things: *It took three months to get a visa because of all the bureaucracy.*

**burg·er** /**burg**-ur/ *noun* a round flat piece of beef between pieces of round bread: *Could I get a burger and fries, please?* (SYNONYM: **hamburger**)

**bur·glar** /**burg**-lur/ *noun* someone who goes into a building to steal things: *Burglars broke into the house and stole the TV.*
—**burglary** /**burg**-luhr-ee/ *noun* an occasion when someone steals things from a building: *Several paintings were stolen in the burglary.*

—**burglarize** /**burg**-luh-rīz/ *verb* to go into a building to steal things: *Our neighbor's house was burglarized while he was on vacation.*

**bur·i·al** /**berr**-ee-uhl/ *noun* the act of putting a dead person in a box into the ground: *The coffin was taken to the cemetery for burial.*

**burn** /burn/
● *verb* (**burned** or **burnt** /burnt/)
**1** to destroy or damage something with fire or heat: *She burned the old letters.* | *The house burned down in a fire.* | *I burned the toast.*
▶ see **Thesaurus**
**2** to hurt your body with fire or something hot: *She burned her hand on the iron.*
**3** if a fire, candle, or wood burns, it produces flames and heat: *There's a wood fire burning in the living room.*
● *noun*
an injury caused by fire, heat, or the sun: *He picked up a hot plate and he got a burn on his hand.*

**burp** /burp/
● *verb* to make a noise when you let air come out from your stomach through your mouth: *It is not polite to burp when you've finished eating.*
● *noun* the noise you make when you burp

**bur·row** /**bur**-oh/
● *noun* a hole in the ground that a rabbit or other small animal lives in: *Prairie dogs live in large burrows.*
● *verb* if an animal burrows, it digs a hole in the ground: *The rabbit was burrowing in the ground.*

**burst** /burst/
● *verb* (**burst**)
**1** to break open suddenly: *The balloon burst with a loud bang.*
**2** **burst into tears** to start crying suddenly: *She fell down and burst into tears.*
**3** **burst out laughing** to start laughing suddenly: *He burst out laughing when he heard the joke.*
● *noun*
a sudden short period of noise or activity: *He won the race with a sudden burst of speed.*

**bur·y** /**berr**-ee/ *verb* (**buries, burying, buried**)
**1** to put a dead person into the ground: *My grandparents are buried next to each other.*
**2** to hide something by putting it in the ground or covering it with something: *The dog buried a bone in the backyard.*

**bus** /buhss/ *noun* (plural **buses**) a large vehicle that many people can travel on. You usually pay to ride on a bus: *The school bus comes at eight o'clock.* | *Five people got on the bus.*

**bush** /bush/ *noun* a large plant with a lot of branches: *There are a lot of flowers growing on the bush.*

**bush·y** /**bush**-ee/ *adjective* bushy hair or fur grows very thickly: *Our cat has a big bushy tail.*

**bus·i·ly** /**biz**-uhl-ee/ *adverb* in a busy way: *The children were busily writing down notes.*

**busi·ness** /**biz**-niss/ *noun*
**1** a company that makes or sells things: *My mom has her own business and she sells jewelry on the Internet.*
**2** the work of buying and selling goods or services: *The bank does business all over the world.* | *A lot of companies have gone out of business and closed down, because they do not have enough customers.*

> **IDIOM with business**
> **mind your own business/it's none of your business** used when something is private and you do not want to talk about it: *"Where are you going this evening?" "Mind your own business!"*

**busi·ness·man** /**biz**-niss-man/ *noun* (plural **businessmen** /**biz**-niss-men/) someone who works in business or who owns a business

**busi·ness·wom·an** /**biz**-niss-wum-uhn/ *noun* (plural **businesswomen** /**biz**-niss-wim-in/) a woman who works in business or who owns a business

**bus stop** /**buhss** stahp/ *noun* a place where buses stop so people can get on and off: *About ten people were waiting at the bus stop.*
SYNONYM: **stop**

**bust** /buhst/
● *noun* a model of someone's head and shoulders: *A marble bust of Saint John was in the church.*
● *adjective* a business that goes bust stops working because it does not have enough money: *People stopped using the store and the business went bust.*

bust

**bus·tle** /**buhss**-uhl/ *verb*
**1** to be full of people who are moving around: *The airport was bustling with travelers.*
**2** to move around in a busy way: *The teacher was bustling around, handing out papers.*

**bus·y** /**biz**-ee/ *adjective* (**busier, busiest**)
**1** someone who is busy is working or has a lot to do: *Dad is very busy at work and he won't be home till late.*
**2** if a telephone line is busy, someone is talking on it when you try to call him or her: *Her phone is busy; I'll try again later.*
**3** a busy place or time is full of people or full of things happening: *The freeway is really busy at six o'clock and there are a lot of cars.* | *Christmas is a busy time of year.* ANTONYM: **quiet**

**but** /buht/
● *conjunction*
**1** used before you say something that is different or surprising: *I was tired, but I still had fun.* | *He's not good at baseball, but he's really good at basketball.*
**2** used before you give the reason why you cannot do something: *I want to go, but Mom says I can't.*
● *preposition*
except for someone or something: *There's nobody here but me.*

**butch·er** /**buch**-ur/ *noun* a person who cuts and sells meat

**butt** /buht/ *noun* the part of your body that you sit on: *I slipped on the ice and fell on my butt.*
SYNONYM: **buttocks**

**but·ter** /**buht**-ur/ *noun* a yellow food that you spread on bread or use in cooking. Butter is made from milk: *He ate a piece of toast with butter and jam.*

**but·ter·fly** /**buht**-ur-flī/ *noun* (plural **butterflies**) an insect with wings
▶ see **Thesaurus**

**butterfly**

**but·ter·milk** /**buht**-ur-milk/ *noun* the liquid that is left after butter has been made. You can drink it or use it in cooking.

**but·ter·scotch** /**buht**-ur-skahch/ *noun* a type of candy made from butter and sugar cooked together

**but·tocks** /**buht**-uhkss/ *plural noun* the part of your body that you sit on ( SYNONYM: **butt** )

**but·ton** /**buht**'n/
● *noun*
**1** a small round object that you use to fasten your shirt, coat, etc. You put the button through a hole to hold the two sides of the shirt together: *One of the buttons has come off my shirt.*
**2** a small part of a machine that you press to make it work: *Press the blue button to turn on the DVD player.*
**3** a small metal or plastic pin with words or a picture on it: *She has a happy-face button on her backpack.*
● *verb*
to fasten clothes using buttons: *Button up your coat – it's cold outside.*

**buy** /bī/ *verb* (**buying**, **bought** /bot/) to get something by paying money for it: *My parents bought me a new bike!* ▶ see **Thesaurus**
—**buyer** /**bī**-ur/ *noun* someone who wants to buy something from another person: *They can't find a buyer for the house.*

**buzz** /buhz/
● *verb* to make a noise like the sound of a bee: *A fly was buzzing around the room.*
● *noun* a noise like the sound of a bee: *There was a constant buzz of traffic outside the school.*
▶ see picture on page **A16**

**buz·zard** /**buhz**-urd/ *noun* a large wild bird that eats dead animals

**buzz·er** /**buhz**-ur/ *noun* a button that makes a buzzing sound when you press it: *I pressed the buzzer next to the door and waited for someone to come.*

**by** /bī/ *preposition, adverb*
**1** near or beside: *Who's standing by Lisa?*
**2** past: *We drive by your house on the way to school.* | *Lee ran by really fast.*
**3** used when saying who or what does something: *Her car was hit by a truck.* | *The Harry Potter books were written by J.K. Rowling.*
**4** using something: *I go to school by bus.*
**5** not later than a time: *Dad's usually home from work by 7:00.*
**6** used when giving the two parts of a measurement: *The rectangle is two inches by four inches.*
**7 by yourself** alone or without help: *I was scared to go there by myself.*

**bye** /bī/ (also **bye-bye** /bī bī/) goodbye: *I'd better go. Bye, Tania.*

**by·pass** /**bī**-pass/ *noun* an operation on someone's heart, when a tube carrying blood is getting blocked. Doctors put in another tube so that blood can flow through it instead: *My grandfather had a heart bypass operation.*

**by·stand·er** /**bī**-stand-ur/ *noun* someone who is in a place when something happens: *A bystander was hurt during the robbery.*

**byte** /bīt/ *noun* a unit for measuring the amount of information a computer can use. A byte is equal to eight bits: *There are one million bytes in a megabyte.*

# Cc

**C** /see/ *noun*
**1** a grade that you get on a test or in a class. If you get a C, your work is neither very good nor very bad: *I only got a C for my math homework.*
**2** the written abbreviation of **Celsius** or **Centigrade**: *The temperature is 30°C.*

**cab** /kab/ *noun*
**1** a car with a driver that you pay to take you somewhere: *We can take a cab to the airport.*
( SYNONYM: **taxi** )
**2** the part of a truck or train where the driver sits

**cab·bage** /**kab**-ij/ *noun* a large round vegetable with thick green or purple leaves

> ## Word Origin: cabbage
>
> **Cabbage** comes from an old French word that means "head." A cabbage is round like a person's head.

**cab·in** /**kab**-in/ *noun*
**1** a small house made of wood, usually in a forest or the mountains: *They have a log cabin in Montana.*
**2** a small room that you sleep in on a ship: *Our cabin is on the top deck of the ship.*

cabin
a log cabin

**3** the area inside an airplane where the passengers sit: *The passenger cabin was almost full when we got on the plane.*

**cab·i·net** /**kab**-uhn-it/ *noun*
**1** a piece of furniture with shelves or drawers and a door: *We keep the bandages in the medicine cabinet in the bathroom.*
**2** an important group of politicians who help the leader of a government: *The president met with his cabinet to discuss the situation.*

**ca·ble** /**kayb**-uhl/ *noun*
**1** a tube containing wires that carry electricity, telephone signals, or television signals: *This cable connects your games console to your TV.*
**2** a system of broadcasting television using cables: *We watched the movie on cable.*
**3** a thick strong metal rope: *The skiers sit in a seat that is pulled up the mountain on steel cables.*

**cac·tus** /**kakt**-uhss/ *noun* (plural **cacti** /**kak**-tī/ or **cactuses**) a plant that has thick stems covered with sharp points. Cactuses grow in hot dry places such as deserts.

cactus

**ca·fe**, **café** /ka-**fay**/ *noun* a small restaurant where you can buy drinks and simple meals: *We had a drink at a cafe.*

**caf·e·te·ri·a** /kaf-uh-**teer**-ee-uh/ *noun* a restaurant in a school, office, etc., where people take the food and drink they want from a counter and then sit down: *All the children eat in the school cafeteria.*

> ## Word Origin: cafeteria
>
> **Cafeteria** comes from a Spanish word that means "coffee store." The word cafeteria started to be used in English in the 1800s.

**caf·feine** /ka-**feen**/ *noun* a substance in coffee, and cola that makes people feel more awake

**cage** /kayj/ *noun* a container made of wires or bars, used for keeping birds or animals in: *I think it's wrong to keep wild animals in cages.*

**cake** /kayk/ *noun*
**1** a sweet food made by baking a mixture of flour, fat, sugar, and eggs: *We made a chocolate cake for his birthday. | Would you like a piece of cake?*
▶ see Thesaurus ▶ see picture at **dessert**
**2** a flat round piece of food made from fish, rice, or potato: *It's fish cakes for lunch.*

**IDIOM with cake**
**be a piece of cake** to be very easy: *The test will be a piece of cake.*

a b c d e f g h i j k l m n o p q r s t u v w x y z

**cal·ci·um** /**kalss**-ee-uhm/ *noun* a white-gray substance that is necessary for strong teeth and bones. Calcium is a chemical element. The symbol for calcium is Ca: *You get calcium from food such as milk and cheese.*

**cal·cu·late** /**kalk**-yuh-layt/ *verb* to find out a number or amount using mathematics: *Calculate how many apples you can buy with $4 if they cost 50 cents each.* ▶ see **Thesaurus**

**cal·cu·la·tion** /kalk-yuh-**laysh**-uhn/ *noun* if you do a calculation, you use mathematics to find a number or amount: *The teacher did a few calculations on the blackboard.*

**cal·cu·la·tor**

/**kalk**-yuh-layt-ur/ *noun* a small machine that can add numbers and multiply them: *You can use a calculator to work out your math problems.*

**calculator**

**cal·en·dar** /**kal**-uhnd-ur/

*noun* a set of pages that show all the days in a year: *I looked at the calendar to find out what date it was.*

**calf** /kaf/ *noun* (plural **calves** /kavz/)

**1** a young cow
**2** the back of your leg between your knee and your foot

**calf**

cow

calf

**call** /kol/

● *verb*

**1** to telephone someone: *I'll call you tomorrow.*
**2** to give someone or something a name or description: *Rob calls his little sister Squeaky.* | *New York is sometimes called The Big Apple.*
**3** to shout or say something loudly: *Mrs. Smithson called out my name.*

**4** to tell someone to come to you: *The principal called her into his office.*
**5 call off** to decide that an event will not happen: *The game was called off because of the rain.*
**6 call on** if a teacher calls on a student, he or she asks that student to answer a question: *I didn't want the teacher to call on me because I didn't know the answer.*

● *noun*

**1** if you make a call, you talk to someone by telephone: *Give me a call this evening.* | *Mom was making a few phone calls.*
**2** the high sound that a bird or animal makes: *I could hear the call of seagulls outside my window.*
**3** an announcement: *This is the last call for flight 506 to Chicago.*

**call·er** /**kol**-ur/ *noun* someone who makes a telephone call: *The caller didn't give his name.*

**calm** /kahm/

● *adjective*

**1** feeling peaceful or relaxed: *Mom is always calm and never gets angry with anyone.*
▶ see **Thesaurus**
**2** with no big waves: *It was sunny and the ocean was calm.*
**3** peaceful, or without any fighting: *The fighting has stopped and the situation is calm.*
**4** not windy: *It was a calm day.*
—**calmly** /**kahm**-lee/ *adverb* in a calm way: *She calmly continued talking.*
—**calmness** /**kahm**-niss/ *noun* a calm quality: *I really admire his calmness under pressure.*
● *verb*
**calm down** to stop being angry or upset: *Calm down – we can easily fix this.*

**cal·o·rie** /**kal**-uhr-ee/ *noun* a unit for measuring the amount of energy food will produce: *A potato has about 90 calories.*

**calves** /kavz/ *noun* the plural of **calf**

**came** /kaym/ *verb* the past tense of **come**

**cam·el** /**kam**-uhl/ *noun* a large animal with one or two humps on its back. Camels live in hot dry places in North Africa and Western Asia. Camels are used to carry goods or people: *Camels can survive without water for many days.*

humps     **camel**

### cam·era /**kam**-ruh/

*noun* a piece of equipment used for taking photographs or making movies: *I brought the camera to take pictures at her birthday party.*

**camera**

digital camera

### cam·ou·flage /**kam**-uh-flahzh/

● *noun* clothes or colors that hide you by making you look like the things around you: *Soldiers often wear camouflage so that the enemy cannot see them.* ▶ see picture at **soldier**
● *verb* to hide something by using camouflage: *A chameleon is a kind of lizard that camouflages itself by changing color.*

### camp /kamp/

● *noun*
**1** a place where people stay in tents, or in temporary buildings: *We put up our tents at the camp. | an army camp*
**2** a place where children stay and do activities during their vacation: *At summer camp, I did a lot of swimming.*
● *verb*
to live in a tent for a short time, usually on vacation: *We camped by the river so we could go fishing.*

### cam·paign /kam-**payn**/

● *noun* a series of things that you do, to try to persuade people to do something: *The school is having a campaign to get money for a new gymnasium.*
● *verb* to try to persuade the public or politicians to do something: *Parents campaigned for the school to stay open.*

### camp·er /**kamp**-ur/ *noun*

**1** a vehicle you can live in while you are on vacation: *We usually take our vacations in our camper.*
**2** someone who is staying in a tent on vacation: *The forest is visited by nearly four million campers each year.*

### camp·ground /**kamp**-grownd/ *noun* a place where there are many places for people to camp

### camp·ing /**kamp**-ing/ *noun* the activity of living in a tent for a short time: *In the summer, we often go camping.*

### camp·site /**kamp**-sīt/ *noun* a place where people can camp: *The park has about 300 campsites.*

### cam·pus /**kamp**-uhss/ *noun* the land or buildings belonging to a college: *Most students here live on campus.*

### can /kuhn, kan/

● *verb*
**1** to be able to do something: *Sam can run really fast. | Can you speak Spanish?*
**2** to be allowed to do something: *You can go home now.*
**3** used when asking someone to do something: *Can you help me with my homework?*
● *noun* /kan/
a metal container that holds food: *Mom opened up a can of soup.*

**can**

a can of soup

> **IDIOM with can**
> **a can of worms** a complicated situation that causes a lot of problems when you try to deal with it: *When I asked why she was unhappy, I didn't realize that I was opening up a can of worms.*

### Ca·na·di·an /kuh-**nayd**-ee-uhn/

● *adjective* from Canada: *He's a Canadian singer.*
● *noun* someone from Canada: *Many Canadians speak French.*

a b **c** d e f g h i j k l m n o p q r s t u v w x y z

**ca·nal** /kuh-**nal**/ *noun* a man-made river. Canals are dug through land so that boats can go from one lake or ocean to another one: *The Panama Canal connects the Atlantic and Pacific Oceans.*

canal

canal

**ca·nar·y** /kuh-**nair**-ee/ *noun* (plural **canaries**) a small yellow bird that sings and is often kept as a pet

canary

**can·cel** /**kanss**-uhl/ *verb* to stop something you had planned from happening: *The game was canceled because of bad weather.* —**cancellation** /kanss-uh-**laysh**-uhn/ *noun* the act of canceling something: *Storms caused the cancellation of many flights.*

**can·cer** /**kanss**-ur/ *noun* a serious illness that makes the cells in the body grow in a way that is not normal: *He is sick with lung cancer.*

**can·di·date** /**kand**-uh-dayt/ *noun*
**1** someone who is trying to win an election: *He's the Democratic candidate for governor.*
**2** someone who is trying to get a job: *There were four candidates for the waitress job.*

**Word Origin:** candidate

**Candidate** comes from a Latin word that means "dressed in white." In ancient Rome, someone who wanted to be elected wore white clothes called a toga.

**can·dle** /**kand**'l/ *noun* a thing that you burn to produce light. A candle is a stick of wax with string through the middle: *There were nine candles on my birthday cake.*

**can·dy** /**kand**-ee/ *noun* (plural **candies**) a sweet food made of sugar or chocolate: *Would you like a piece of candy?*

**Word Origin:** candy

**Candy** comes from an Arabic word, *qandi*. The Arabic word came from a word used in India that meant "piece of sugar." The word candy first started being used in English about 800 years ago. Then, candy meant sugar that had been cooked with water or milk until it formed pieces. Today, we use the word candy to talk about many different kinds of sweet foods, like chocolate bars or caramels.

**can·dy bar** /**kand**-ee bar/ *noun* a long thin piece of candy, usually covered with chocolate

**cane** /kayn/ *noun*
**1** a thin stick that you use to help you walk: *She has a bad leg so she walks with a cane.*
**2** a plant that farmers grow to produce sugar
( SYNONYM: **sugar cane** )

**ca·nine** /**kay**-nīn/ *adjective* relating to dogs: *Our dog has lots of other canine friends.*

**canned** /kand/ *adjective* canned food is sold in a can: *We use canned tomatoes for making pasta sauce.*

**can·nery** /**kan**-uh-ree/ *noun* a factory where food is put into cans

**can·ni·bal** /**kan**-uhb-uhl/ *noun* a person who eats human flesh: *There used to be cannibals on the island.*

**can·non** /**kan**-uhn/ *noun* a large gun that fires heavy metal balls, used in past times: *The soldiers attacked the fort with cannons.*

**can·not** /**kan**-aht/ *verb* can not, the negative of can: *If you cannot come on the trip, please let your teacher know.* ( SYNONYM: **can't** )

**ca·noe** /kuh-**noo**/ *noun*
a light narrow boat
which you move
through the water using
a paddle: *They paddled
up the river in their
canoe.*

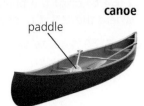
canoe
paddle

—**canoeing** /kuh-**noo**-ing/
*noun* the activity of
moving through water in a canoe: *We
sometimes go canoeing on the lake.*

**can o·pen·er** /**kan**ohp-uhn-uhr/ *noun* a tool
used for opening cans of food

**can·o·py** /**kan**-uh-pee/ *noun* a cover above
something, especially one that provides shelter:
*I stood under the canopy outside the hotel and
waited for the rain to stop.*

**can't** /kant/ *contraction* short for "cannot":
*I can't remember her name.*

**can·ta·loupe** /**kant**'l-ohp/ *noun* a sweet
melon that is orange inside ▶ see picture on
page **A7**

**can·vas** /**kan**-vuhss/
*noun*
**1** a type of strong cloth
that is used to make
bags, shoes, sails, and
tents: *She carries her
books in a big canvas
bag.*
**2** a piece of canvas cloth
on a wooden frame.
Artists paint pictures on canvas: *The artist began
painting on the blank canvas.*

canvas
canvas
easel

**can·yon** /**kan**-yuhn/ *noun* a deep valley with very
steep sides. Canyons are usually made by a river
over a long time: *The Colorado River flows
through the Grand Canyon.*

**Word Origin:** canyon

Canyon comes from a Spanish word,
**cañon**. The Spanish word means a deep
valley, and because English did not have a
special word for this, we borrowed the
Spanish word.

canyon

cap

**cap** /kap/ *noun*
**1** a cloth hat with a
curved part that sticks
out at the front: *a
baseball cap | a wool ski
cap*
**2** a cover that goes on a
bottle or pen: *The cap
on the medicine bottle can't be opened by small
children.*

**ca·pa·ble** /**kayp**-uhb-uhl/ *adjective*
**1** able to do something: *The team is capable of
winning the game, but they will need to play
really well.* ( ANTONYM: **incapable** )
**2** able to do something well: *Brett is a very
capable student and I'm sure he will get good
grades on his test.*
—**capability** /kayp-uh-**bil**-uht-ee/ *noun* the ability
to do something: *Children have the capability to
learn very fast.*

**Word Family:** capable

**capable** *adjective* | **incapable** *adjective* |
**capability** *noun*

**ca·pac·i·ty** /kuh-**pass**-uht-ee/ *noun* (plural
**capacities**)
**1** the amount that something can hold: *The tank
has a capacity of 20 gallons* (=it can hold 20
gallons of liquid).
**2** the ability to do or produce something: *I think
that he has the capacity to be a great leader one
day.*

a
b
c
d
e
f
g
h
i
j
k
l
m
n
o
p
q
r
s
t
u
v
w
x
y
z

### cape /kayp/ *noun*
**1** a long loose piece of clothing without sleeves. It fastens around your neck and is worn over your clothes: *The hero wears a big black cape.*
**2** a large area of land that has ocean on three sides of it: *Cape Cod goes out into the Atlantic Ocean.*

cape

cape

cape

### cap·i·tal /**kap**-uht'l/ *noun*
**1** the city where a country's or state's main government is: *Tokyo is the capital of Japan.*
**2** the large form of a letter, for example B rather than b: *He wrote the title in capitals.* | *Start your name with a capital letter.*
**3** money that you can use to start a business or make more money: *She needed capital to start up her company.*

### cap·i·tal·ism /**kap**-uht'l-iz-uhm/ *noun* a system where most businesses in a country belong to private owners, not to the government
—**capitalist** /**kap**-uht'l-ist/ *adjective* supporting or based on capitalism: *In capitalist countries, land, factories, and transport systems are not owned by the government.*

### cap·i·tal·ize /**kap**-uht'l-īz/ *verb* to put a capital letter at the beginning of a word or sentence: *The names of countries must be capitalized.*

### cap·i·tol /**kap**-uht'l/ *noun*
**1** the building in each U.S. state where the people who make laws meet: *the Virginia state capitol*

**2** **the Capitol** the building in Washington D.C. where the U.S. Congress meets

### cap·size /**kap**-sīz/ *verb* if a boat capsizes, it turns over in the water: *The big waves caused the boat to capsize.*

**capsize**

### cap·sule /**kapss**-uhl/ *noun*
**1** a small round container with medicine in it, that you swallow: *I had to take two capsules every day.*
**2** the part of a spacecraft that people travel in: *The astronauts are in the space capsule.*

### cap·tain /**kapt**-uhn/ *noun*
**1** someone who is in charge of a ship or airplane: *The captain welcomed passengers on board the ship.*
**2** the leader of a sports team: *Daniel is the captain of the basketball team.*
**3** an officer in the army, air force, or navy: *He became a captain in the army.*

### cap·tion /**kap**-shuhn/ *noun* words printed above or below a picture or photograph. The words give a short description: *The caption under the picture says: "Sunrise over Central Park."*

### cap·tive /**kapt**-iv/ *noun* someone who is kept as a prisoner: *The captives were never released.*

### cap·tiv·i·ty /kap-**tiv**-uht-ee/ *noun* if a person or animal is in captivity, they are kept somewhere and are not free: *The lion cubs were raised in captivity, then returned to the wild.*

### cap·ture /**kap**-chur/
● *verb*
**1** to catch a person or animal that you intend to keep somewhere: *Two police officers captured the thieves.* (SYNONYM: **catch**)
**2** to get control of a place during a war: *The town was captured by the enemy.*

**3** to get someone's attention: *Their music soon captured the attention of the world.*
● *noun*
the act of capturing a person or place: *The soldiers managed to avoid capture.*

**car** /kar/ *noun*
**1** a vehicle with four wheels and an engine. You use a car to travel from one place to another: *He was driving a blue car.*
**2** a part of a train that carries passengers or things: *The train had 14 cars.*

**Word Origin: car**

**Car** comes from a Latin word that means "vehicle with wheels." Car may be a short way of saying "carriage," which is a vehicle with wheels that was pulled by horses. When cars were first invented, some people called them "horseless carriages."

**car·a·mel** /**karr**-uhm-uhl/ *noun*
**1** a candy made of cooked sugar, butter, and milk
**2** a flavor used in cakes and sweet food, made from burned sugar: *ice cream with caramel sauce*

**car·bo·hy·drate** /kar-boh-**hī**-drayt/ *noun* a substance in foods such as sugar, rice, bread, or potatoes that gives your body energy. Carbohydrates are made of carbon, hydrogen, and oxygen: *Your body needs protein and fat as well as carbohydrates.*

**car·bon** /**karb**-uhn/ *noun* a chemical element that is found in all living things, and in coal and diamonds. The symbol for carbon is C.

**car·bon di·ox·ide** /karb-uhn-dī-**ahkss**-īd/ *noun* a gas that is a mixture of carbon and oxygen. It has no color and no smell. People breathe this gas out and plants take it in through their leaves: *Plants take in carbon dioxide from the air and produce oxygen as a result of photosynthesis.*

**car·bon mo·nox·ide** /karb-uhn muh-**nahkss**-īd/ *noun* a poisonous gas that is produced when engines burn gasoline: *Cars produce over 70% of the carbon monoxide in the air.*

**card** /kard/ *noun*
**1** a folded piece of stiff paper with a picture on the front. You send cards to people at special times such as birthdays: *I have to buy a birthday card for my sister.*
**2** a small flat piece of plastic that someone uses to pay for something: *I don't have any cash, so I'll pay by card.*
**3** a small piece of stiff paper that is used for playing games: *When you land on this space, take a card.* | *Do you want to play cards?*

card
card
envelope
card

**card·board** /**kard**-bord/ *noun* very thick stiff paper: *All the books were in cardboard boxes.*

cardboard

a cardboard box

**car·di·nal** /**kard**'n-uhl/ *noun*
**1** a wild bird that sings and has feathers that stick up on its head. The male bird is bright red.
**2** a priest of very high rank in the Roman Catholic Church

cardinal

**car·di·o·vas·cu·lar** /kard-ee-oh-**vask**-yuhl-ur/ *adjective* relating to the heart and the tubes that take blood to and from the heart: *Exercise can help prevent you from getting cardiovascular disease.*

a b **c** d e f g h i j k l m n o p q r s t u v w x y z

**care** /kair/

● *verb*

**1** to feel that someone or something is important to you: *I care about my family a lot. | I don't care about the money. I just want you to be happy.*

**2 care for** to do things to help someone who is old, sick, or very young: *She has two little kids to care for.*

● *noun*

**1** things you do to help someone who is old, sick, or very young: *He needed constant care when he came out of the hospital.*

**2** careful attention so that you do not make a mistake or damage something: *On the box it said "Handle with care."*

**3** something that you are worried about: *A vacation in the sun is a good way to forget about your cares.*

> IDIOMS with **care**
>
> **take care** used when saying goodbye to someone you know well: *"I'll talk to you soon." "Yeah, take care."*
>
> **take care of** to watch someone or something and make sure they are safe, or have the things they need: *Who can take care of the cat while we are away?*

**ca·reer** /kuh-**reer**/ *noun* a job or type of work that you do for a long time: *I'm interested in a career as a teacher.*

**care·ful** /**kair**-fuhl/ *adjective* thinking about what you are doing, so you do not make mistakes or damage things: *Be careful with those scissors! | He was careful to spell everything correctly.* (ANTONYM: **careless**) ▶ see Thesaurus

—**carefully** /**kair**-fuhl-ee/ *adverb* in a careful way: *Listen carefully.*

**care·less** /**kair**-liss/ *adjective* not thinking about what you are doing, so that you make mistakes or damage things: *She is a very careless driver and she often has accidents.* (ANTONYM: **careful**) ▶ see Thesaurus

—**carelessly** /**kair**-liss-lee/ *adverb* in a careless way: *He carelessly left the gate open, and the dog got out.*

—**carelessness** /**kair**-liss-niss/ *noun* careless behavior: *Carelessness can cause accidents.*

**car·go** /**karg**-oh/ *noun* (plural **cargoes**) the goods that a ship or airplane carries: *The ship was carrying a cargo of oil.*

**Car·ib·be·an** /karr-uh-**bee**-uhn/

● *noun* the part of the Atlantic Ocean between Central America and South America. There are many small islands in the Caribbean: *They had a vacation in the Caribbean.*

● *adjective* relating to the Caribbean: *Jamaica is a Caribbean island.*

**car·i·bou** /**karr**-uhb-oo/ *noun* (plural **caribou**) a large deer with antlers that look like the branches on a tree. Caribou live in the cold parts of North America. (SYNONYM: **reindeer**)

**car·ni·val** /**karn**-uhv-uhl/ *noun* an outdoor event where people can ride on special machines and play games: *There were lots of rides and a live band at the carnival.* (SYNONYM: **fair**)

**car·ni·vore** /**karn**-uh-vor/ *noun* an animal that eats meat: *Dogs are carnivores and they need to eat meat every day.*

—**carnivorous** /kar-**niv**-uhr-uhss/ *adjective* carnivorous animals eat meat: *Wolves are carnivorous animals.*

**car·ol** /**karr**-uhl/ *noun* a song that people sing at Christmas: *In church we all sang Christmas carols.*

**car·pen·ter** /**karp**-uhnt-ur/ *noun* someone whose job is making things from wood: *Our desks were made by a local carpenter.*

—**carpentry** /**karp**-uhn-tree/ *noun* the activity of making things out of wood: *Jude is learning carpentry.*

**car·pet** /**karp**-it/ *noun*

**1** a thick material used for covering the floor of a room: *We had to buy a new carpet for the living room floor.*

**2** a thick layer of something on the ground: *There was a carpet of leaves in the forest.*

**car·pool** /**kar**-pool/

● *noun* a group of people who ride together to work or school in one car: *We're in a carpool with three other families.*

● *verb* to ride with other people in a car to work or school: *We carpool to school.*

**car·riage** /**karr**-ij/ *noun* a vehicle with wheels that is pulled by horses, for people to ride in

carriage

**car·rot** /**karr**-uht/ *noun* a long orange vegetable that grows under the ground ► see picture on page **A7**

**car·ry** /**karr**-ee/ *verb* (**carries**, **carrying**, **carried**)
**1** to hold something in your hands or in your clothes as you go somewhere: *Will you carry my bag for me?* | *Dad carries his wallet in his back pocket.*
**2** if a vehicle, pipe, or wire carries something, it takes it from one place to another: *The bus was carrying 25 passengers.* | *The electric lines carry electricity to the houses.*
**3** if a store carries something, it has it for sale: *They don't carry children's toys.*
**4** if you carry a disease, you can give it to other people: *Many diseases are carried by insects.*
**5 carry on** to continue doing something: *It was too noisy to carry on a conversation.*
**6 carry out** to do something in a planned and organized way: *The children carried out experiments with the magnets.*

carry

She is carrying her books.

**cart** /kart/ *noun*
**1** a metal basket or table on wheels: *Our shopping cart was full.*
**2** a vehicle with two wheels that is pulled by a horse. It is used for carrying heavy things: *A pony was pulling a wooden cart.*

cart

cart

**car·ton** /**kart**'n/ *noun* a small cardboard box that contains something such as juice, milk, or soup: *Each child had a small carton of milk.*

**car·toon** /kar-**toon**/ *noun*
**1** a movie or television program with characters that are drawn and not real: *The kids were watching a Disney cartoon.*
**2** a funny drawing in a newspaper: *I like the cartoons at the back of the magazine.*
—**cartoonist** /kar-**toon**-ist/ *noun* someone who draws cartoons

**cart·wheel** /**kart**-weel/ *noun* a movement you make by putting your hands on the floor and your feet in the air. You then turn your body sideways until your feet are on the floor again: *Ellie's really good at doing cartwheels.*

**carve** /karv/ *verb*
**1** to cut a piece of wood or stone into a shape: *A sculptor carves statues out of stone.*
**2** to cut a large piece of cooked meat into smaller pieces: *Mom carved the turkey.*
—**carving** /**karv**-ing/ *noun* something made by cutting a piece of wood or stone: *There was a wood carving of an elephant on the wall.*

**cas·cade** /ka-**skayd**/ *noun*
**1** a waterfall
**2** something that hangs down in large quantities: *A cascade of pink flowers was growing over the wall.*

**case** /kayss/ *noun*
**1** a container that you keep something in: *Put your pens away in your pencil case.*
**2** an example of an event, situation, or thing: *In this particular case, the artist has used oil paints, not watercolors.*
**3** a crime that the police are trying to find out the truth about: *The police are trying to solve a robbery case.*
**4** a trial or question that a court of law deals with: *Did he win the court case?*

case

glasses case

pencil case

**IDIOM with case**

**in case** in order to be ready for something that might happen: *I'll take an umbrella just in case it rains.*

**cash** /kash/
- *noun* coins and paper money that you use for buying things: *I only have $10 in cash.*
- *verb* if you cash a check, you exchange it for money: *You can cash a check at the bank.*

**cash crop** /**kash**crahp/ *noun* a crop that farmers grow to sell

**cash·ier** /ka-**sheer**/ *noun* someone whose job is taking the money that customers pay: *Dad gave the cashier a $100 bill.*

**cash reg·is·ter** /**kash** rej-ist-ur/ *noun* a machine in a store that shows how much you must pay, and is used to keep the money in

**cas·ket** /**kask**-it/ *noun* a box that a dead body is put in to be buried ( SYNONYM: **coffin** )

**cas·se·role** /**kass**-uh-rohl/ *noun* food that is cooked slowly in liquid in an oven, especially meat or fish with vegetables: *For dinner we had chicken casserole with rice.*

**cast** /kast/ *verb*
- *verb* (**cast**)
**1** to choose an actor for a part in a movie or play: *Daniel Radcliffe was cast as Harry Potter.*
**2** if you cast your ballot or vote, you vote in an election: *Most of the students cast their ballots for Doug for class president.*
**3** to throw your fishing line or net into the water, in order to catch fish: *Fishermen were casting their nets into the ocean.*
**4** to make something by pouring hot metal or plaster into a container: *The sculpture was cast in bronze.*
- *noun*
**1** a hard cover that doctors put around a broken bone until it gets better: *His leg was in a cast.*
**2** all the actors in a play, movie, or television show: *I'm in the cast for the school play.*

cast

cast

**cas·tle** /**kass**-uhl/ *noun* a large stone building with high walls around it. A castle can also have water in a moat around it. Castles were built in the Middle Ages to protect the people inside during wars ► see **Thesaurus**

**cas·u·al** /**kazh**-oo-uhl/ *adjective*
**1** casual clothes are the kind you usually wear, but that you do not wear to special occassions such as weddings: *I like wearing casual clothes, like jeans and a T-shirt.*
**2** relaxed and not worried about things: *Rick was in trouble, but he was trying to act casual.*

**cas·u·al·ty** /**kazh**-uhlt-ee/ *noun* (plural **casualties**) someone who is hurt or killed in an accident or war: *Luckily there were no casualties in the accident.*

**cat** /kat/ *noun*
**1** a small animal with soft fur and pointed ears. People often keep cats as a pet.
**2** any large wild animal that is related to cats: *In Africa you can see big cats such as lions and leopards.*

cat

kitten

cat

**cat·a·log**, catalogue /**kat**'l-og/ *noun*
**1** a book with a list of things you can buy from a company: *Mom bought me a sweater from a mail-order catalog.*
**2** a list of all the books in a library, or all the things in an exhibition: *You can check the library catalog online.*

**ca·tas·tro·phe** /kuh-**tass**-truhf-ee/ *noun* a terrible event that causes a lot of damage or suffering: *The fire was a catastrophe, and many people lost everything.* ( SYNONYM: **disaster** )

**catch** /kach/
- *verb* (**caught** /kot/)
**1** to use your hands to stop and hold something that is moving through the air: *Craig jumped into*

the air and caught the ball. (ANTONYM: **drop**)
▶ see picture on page **A15**

**2** to stop a person or animal that wants to escape from you: *A police officer ran after the thief and caught him.* ▶ see **Thesaurus**

**3** to get a fish or animal by using a net, hook, or trap: *I caught three big fish today.*

**4** to get an illness from someone else: *I don't want to catch chickenpox from you!*

**5** to get on a bus, train, or plane to go somewhere: *Alex catches the bus to school at seven o'clock.*

**6** to see something on television or at the movie theater: *I want to catch the movie on TV tonight.*

**7** to see someone doing something bad or wrong: *I caught him reading my diary!*

**8** **catch on** to become a popular idea or thing to do: *The new game soon caught on at school.*

**9** **catch up** to reach a person who was in front of you: *Nick was ahead of me, but then I caught up.*

**10** **catch up** to reach the same standard as other people: *I missed a month of school, and it was hard to catch up.*

● **noun**

**1** the act of catching a ball: *That was a great catch! Did you see how high he jumped?*

**2** a hidden problem in a situation that seems to be very good: *The tickets are very cheap. The catch is that you can only travel after midnight.*

**3** a game in which two people throw a ball to each other: *The kids were in the yard playing catch.*

**catch·er** /**kach**-ur/ *noun* the baseball player who stays behind the batter, to catch the balls that the batter misses ▶ see picture on page **A10**

**cat·e·go·ry** /**kat**-uh-gor-ee/ *noun* (plural **categories**) a group of people or things that are similar to each other: *This book belongs in the category of reference books.*

—**categorize** /**kat**-uhg-uh-rīz/ *verb* to put people or things into categories: *We categorize the boxes according to size.*

**cat·er·pil·lar** /**kat**-ur-pil-ur/ *noun* the young form of a butterfly or moth. It has a long soft body and many legs but no wings. When the caterpillar is big enough, it makes a hard shell for itself called a chrysalis. Later, a butterfly or moth comes out of the chrysalis.

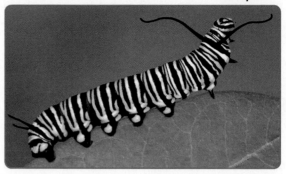

caterpillar

**cat·fish** /**kat**-fish/ *noun* a fish with long things like hairs around its mouth. It lives mainly in rivers and lakes.

catfish

**ca·the·dral** /kuh-**theed**-ruhl/ *noun* a big important church: *There was a special service for the soldiers at the National Cathedral in Washington.*

cathedral

**Cath·o·lic** /**kath**-lik/

● *adjective* belonging to the part of the Christian religion that has the Pope as its leader: *A Catholic priest said mass.*

(SYNONYM: **Roman Catholic**)

—**Catholicism** /kuh-**thahl**-uh-siz-uhm/ *noun* the Catholic religion

● *noun* someone who believes in the Catholic religion

**cat·sup** /**kech**-uhp/ *noun* another spelling of ketchup

**cat·tle** /**kat**'l/ *plural noun* cows and bulls that are kept on a farm

**Cau·ca·sian** /ko-**kayzh**-uhn/
- *noun* a person who belongs to a race of people with pale skin. Caucasians are originally from Europe. (SYNONYM: **white**)
- *adjective* having pale skin: *49% of the city's population is Caucasian.*

**cau·cus** /**kok**-uhss/ *noun* a meeting of the members of a political party, to choose a representative or decide on their plans

**caught** /kot/ *verb* the past tense and past participle of **catch**

**caul·dron** /**kol**-druhn/ *noun* a big round cooking pot, used over a fire: *The witch stirred the liquid in her cauldron.*

**cau·li·flow·er** /**kol**-i-flow-ur/ *noun* a white vegetable with green leaves around the outside
▶ see picture on page **A7**

**cause** /koz/
- *noun*
**1** the thing that makes something happen: *What was the cause of the accident?*
**2** a reason for doing or feeling something: *There is no cause for alarm.*
**3** a goal or idea that people support, or fight for: *The money will be used for a good cause – it will pay for a new sports hall at the school.*
- *verb*
to make something happen: *One of the other boys caused the fight.*

**cau·tion** /**kosh**-uhn/ *noun* carefulness to avoid danger or risks: *Always approach big animals with caution.*
—**cautionary** /**kosh**-uhn-uhr-ee/ *adjective* giving a warning about the need to be careful: *The story is a cautionary tale about accepting help from strangers.*

**cau·tious** /**kosh**-uhss/ *adjective* careful to avoid danger or problems: *You must be more cautious when you cross the road.*
—**cautiously** /**kosh**-uhss-lee/ *adverb* in a cautious way: *Lizzy cautiously put one foot in the water.*

**cav·al·ry** /**kav**-uhl-ree/ *noun* soldiers who fought on horses in wars in the past: *The cavalry charged towards the enemy guns.*

cavalry

a cavalry soldier

**cave** /kayv/ *noun* a big hole in the side of a cliff or under the ground: *The cave goes 500 feet into the side of the mountain.*
▶ see **Thesaurus**

cave

cave

**cav·ern** /**kav**-urn/ *noun* a big cave, often under the ground: *The underground cavern reaches deep into the earth.*

**cav·i·ty** /**kav**-uht-ee/ *noun* (plural **cavities**) a hole inside something: *The dentist said there was a cavity in one of my teeth.*

**cc** /see **see**/
**1** the abbreviation for **cubic centimeter**: *The car has a 2,000cc engine.*
**2** used on emails or in business letters to show that you are sending a copy to someone. The letters cc are written before the person's name.

**CD** /see **dee**/ *noun* a small round piece of plastic that records and plays music or computer information. CD is short for "compact disc": *Do you want to listen to my new CD?*

**CD-ROM** /see dee **rahm**/ *noun* a CD that you can use on a computer. It can store a large amount of information: *You can buy the encyclopedia as a CD-ROM.*

**cease** /seess/ *verb* to stop: *The old house has ceased to exist.*

**cease·fire** /seess-**fī**-ur/ *noun* a time during a war when the enemies agree to stop fighting: *Both governments agreed to a ceasefire.*

**ce·dar** /**seed**-ur/ *noun* a tall tree with thin leaves like needles. The wood from this tree is used in furniture: *She keeps extra blankets in a cedar chest.*

**cedar**

**ceil·ing** /**seel**-ing/ *noun* the top surface of a room, above your head: *He is so tall that he can touch the ceiling.*

**cel·e·brate** /**sel**-uh-brayt/ *verb* to do something enjoyable because it is a special occasion: *All our family gets together to celebrate Thanksgiving every year.*

**cel·e·bra·tion** /sel-uh-**braysh**-uhn/ *noun* something enjoyable, especially a party, that you do on a special occasion: *We're having a birthday celebration for David.*

**ce·leb·ri·ty** /suh-**leb**-ruht-ee/ *noun* (plural **celebrities**) a famous person: *There were lots of celebrities at the first night of the show.*

**cel·er·y** /**sel**-uhr-ee/ *noun* a vegetable with long green stems that you can eat uncooked
▶ see picture on page **A7**

**cell** /sel/ *noun*
**1** the smallest part that forms an animal or plant that can function by itself: *All living things are made of cells.*
**2** a small room where a prisoner is kept: *The prisoners were locked up in their cells 24 hours a day.*

**cell**

nucleus

an animal cell

nucleus          vacuole

a plant cell

**cel·lar** /**sel**-ur/ *noun* a room under a house, where you can store things: *The empty boxes are in the cellar.*

**cel·lo** /**chel**-oh/ *noun* a big musical instrument that you hold between your knees. You play it by moving a bow over its strings.
—**cellist** /**chel**-ist/ *noun* someone who plays the cello: *She is a cellist in the New York Symphony Orchestra.*

**cello**

**cell phone** /**sel**-fohn/ (also **cell·u·lar phone** /sel-yuhl-ur **fohn**/) *noun* a small telephone that you carry with you: *Mom was talking on her cell phone while she was walking down the street.*

**cell phone**

a b c d e f g h i j k l m n o p q r s t u v w x y z

**cel·lu·lar** /**sel**-yuhl-ur/ *adjective*
**1** relating to the cells of plants or animals: *Cellular biology is the study of cells.*
**2** a cellular phone is a cell phone: *Please do not use cellular phones inside the building.*

**cel·lu·lar res·pi·ra·tion** /**sel**-yuhl-ur resp-uh-raysh-uhn/ *noun* the process in which a cell changes sugar and other substances into energy

**Cel·si·us** /**selss**-ee-uhss/ *noun* a scale used to measure temperature. On this scale, water freezes at 0° Celsius (=32° Fahrenheit) and boils at 100° (=212° Fahrenheit). The short form of Celsius is C. In the U.S., most temperatures are given in Fahrenheit, but scientists often use Celsius measurements: *In summer, the temperature reaches 40 degrees Celsius (40°C).*
( SYNONYM: **Centigrade** )

**ce·ment** /si-**ment**/ *noun* a material used for building. It is made of a powder mixed with water and sand. Cement becomes hard when it is dry: *The bricks are stuck together with cement.*

**cem·e·ter·y** /**sem**-uh-terr-ee/ *noun* (plural **cemeteries**) a place where dead people are buried: *We put flowers on my grandfather's grave at the cemetery.*

**cen·sus** /**senss**-uhss/ *noun* (plural **censuses**) an official count of how many people live in a country and what they have or do: *According to the census, 97% of all homes have telephones.*

**cent** /sent/ *noun* a unit of money. One hundred cents are equal to one dollar or one euro. Cents are used in the United States, Canada, Australia, New Zealand, the European Union, and other countries: *I bought a chocolate bar for 75 cents.*

## Word Building

**cent** | **cent**ury | **cent**imeter | **cent**ipede
These words all have the Latin word root ***cent*** in them. ***Cent*** means 100. There are 100 *cents* in one dollar. A *century* is a period of time that is 100 years long.

**cen·taur** /**sent**-or/ *noun* a creature in old Greek stories. It has the head, chest, and arms of a man, and the body and legs of a horse.

**cen·ter** /**sent**-ur/ *noun*
**1** the middle of something: *There's a park in the center of town.*
**2** a big building where people go to do a particular activity: *The city has a sports center.*
**3** a town or area that is important for a particular activity: *Phoenix is an important business center.*
**4** the player in basketball who plays near the basket: *I'm tall so I usually play center.*

**cen·ter field** /**sent**-ur feeld/ *noun* the area in baseball in the center of the outfield

**Cen·ti·grade** /**sent**-uh-grayd/ *noun* another word for Celsius

**cen·ti·me·ter** /**sent**-uh-meet-ur/ *noun* a unit in the metric system for measuring length. There are 100 centimeters in one meter: *My sister is 122 centimeters tall.*

**cen·ti·pede**
/**sent**-uh-peed/ *noun* a small creature that has a long soft body and many tiny legs

centipede

**cen·tral** /**sen**-truhl/ *adjective*
**1** in the center of an area: *They live in the central part of the city.*
**2** most important: *Love is the central subject of the book.*

**cen·tu·ry** /**sench**-uhr-ee/ *noun* (plural **centuries**) a period of 100 years: *The church was built in the 18th century (=between 1700 and 1799). | I was born at the start of the 21st century.*

**ce·re·al** /**seer**-ee-uhl/ *noun*
**1** food made from grain that people eat for breakfast with milk: *I usually have a bowl of cereal for breakfast.*
**2** a plant grown to produce grain for food, for example wheat, corn, or oats: *The farmers here grow cereals and vegetables.*

**cer·e·mo·ny** /**serr**-uh-mohn-ee/ *noun* (plural **ceremonies**) a formal event, for example when people get married, or students graduate from high school: *The wedding ceremony will be in the local church.*
—**ceremonial** /serr-uh-**mohn**-ee-uhl/ *adjective* relating to a ceremony: *The soldiers were wearing ceremonial uniforms.*

**cer·tain** /surt'n/ *adjective*
**1** completely sure: *Are you certain you mailed that letter?* ( SYNONYM: **sure** )
**2** definitely going to happen: *It's almost certain to rain.*
—**certainty** /surt'n-tee/ *noun* the feeling you have when you are sure about something: *He spoke with certainty and everyone believed him.*

> **IDIOM with certain**
> **make certain** to do what is necessary to be sure about something: *I made certain that all the doors were locked.*

## Word Family: certain

**certain** *adjective* | **uncertain** *adjective* |
**certainly** *adverb* | **uncertainly** *adverb* |
**certainty** *noun* | **uncertainty** *noun*

**cer·tain·ly** /surt'n-lee/ *adverb*
**1** definitely: *The book was certainly interesting.*
**2** of course: *"Could you help me lift this box?" "Certainly."*

**cer·tif·i·cate** /sur-**tif**-uhk-it/ *noun* an official document showing that something has happened or is true: *You will need your birth certificate in order to get a passport.*

**cer·ti·fy** /**surt**-uh-fī/ *verb* (**certifies**, **certified**) to officially say that something is true: *You have to sign here to certify that you have read the document.*

**ce·sar·e·an** /si-**zair**-ee-uhn/ (also **ce·sa·re·an sec·tion** /si-zair-ee-uhn **sek**-shuhn/) *noun* an operation to help a baby to be born. A cut is made in the front of the mother's body and the baby is taken out: *When my brother was born, my mom had a cesarean.*

**chain** /chayn/
● *noun*
**1** a line of metal rings joined together: *A chain with a lock held the bike to the rack.*
▶ see picture at **bicycle**
**2** a number of events that make something happen: *A chain of events led to the war.*
**3** a group of stores, restaurants, or hotels that are owned by the same company: *The restaurant is part of a large chain and you can find one in almost every big city.*
**4** a line of mountains or islands: *Hawaii is part of a chain of islands.*

● *verb*
to tie people or things together, using a chain: *The prisoners were chained together.*

**chain·saw** /**chayn**-so/ *noun* a tool for cutting wood, that works using a motor: *They cut down the trees with chainsaws.*

**chair** /chair/ *noun*
**1** a piece of furniture that you sit on: *There were six chairs around the kitchen table.*
**2** another word for chairman or chairwoman

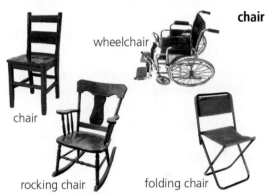

chair

wheelchair

chair

rocking chair

folding chair

**chair·man** /**chair**-muhn/ *noun* (plural **chairmen** /**chair**-muhn/) someone who is in charge of a meeting, organization, or university department: *Mr. Carper is chairman of the school board.*
—**chairmanship** /**chair**-muhn-ship/ *noun* the position of a chairman: *He took over the chairmanship in May.*

**chair·per·son** /**chair**-purss-uhn/ *noun* (plural **chairpersons**) a chairman or chairwoman

**chair·wom·an** /**chair**-wum-uhn/ *noun* (plural **chairwomen** /**chair**-wim-in/) a woman who controls a meeting, organization, or university department: *The chairwoman asked Mrs. Robbins to speak.*

**chalk** /chok/ *noun*
**1** a stick of soft rock that you use for writing or drawing on a special board: *I wrote on the blackboard with a piece of chalk.*
**2** soft white rock that is used to make chalk for writing: *The cliffs here are made of chalk.*

chalk

chalk

**chalk·board** /**chok**-bord/ *noun* a hard smooth dark surface that you write on with chalk: *Mrs. Gibbs wrote our homework on the chalkboard.*
SYNONYM: **blackboard**

**chal·lenge** /**chal**-uhnj/
● *noun*
something difficult that needs skill or effort to do: *It will be a real challenge to get to the top of the mountain.*
● *verb*
**1** to ask someone to compete or fight against you: *He challenged me to beat him at a computer game.*
**2** to question whether something is right: *You shouldn't challenge what your mother says.*

**Word Family: challenge**

**challenge** *noun* | **challenge** *verb* | **challenging** *adjective*

**chal·leng·er** /**chal**-uhnj-ur/ *noun* someone who is competing against other people to win a game, title, or election: *John is one of the strongest challengers for the championship.*

**chal·leng·ing** /**chal**-uhnj-ing/ *adjective* difficult in an interesting way: *A teacher's job is challenging but very satisfying.*

**champ** /champ/ *noun* another word for a champion: *She was the diving champ.*

**cham·pi·on** /**champ**-ee-uhn/ *noun* a person or team that has won an important sports competition or game: *She is the women's world swimming champion.*

**cham·pi·on·ship** /**champ**-ee-uhn-ship/ *noun* a competition to find the best player or team in a sport: *Their team won the Indiana state basketball championship.*

**chance** /chanss/ *noun*
**1** an opportunity to do something: *I'd love to have the chance to go to Disney World.*
SYNONYM: **opportunity**
**2** a possibility that something will happen: *There's a chance it will snow later.*

IDIOMS with **chance**
**by chance** in a way that was not planned: *By chance, she saw him at the bus stop.*
**take a chance** to do something that is a risk: *Don't take any chances – wear your helmet when you are out on your bike.*

**chan·de·lier** /shand-uh-**leer**/ *noun* a type of light that hangs from the ceiling. It holds many small lights and is decorated with pieces of glass: *The hall had a huge chandelier in the middle.*

**change** /chaynj/
● *verb*
**1** to become different, or to make something different: *The school has changed a lot recently.* | *Leaves change color in the fall.* | *I wish I could change the situation, but I can't.*
▶ see **Thesaurus**
**2** to exchange something you have for a new or different one: *We've changed classrooms.*
**3** to put on different clothes: *Go and change your clothes – they're all muddy.*
**4** to exchange money for different notes or coins: *Can you change a $10 bill?*

IDIOM with **change**
**change your mind** to change your ideas about something: *Donna changed her mind and decided to stay home.*
● *noun*
**1** something that is different: *There's been a change in our plans.*
**2** the money you get back when you pay more than something costs: *The salesperson gave me my change.*
**3** coins, not bills: *Do you have any change for the candy machine?*

**chan·nel** /**chan**'l/ *noun*
**1** a television station: *"Scooby Doo" is on Channel 2.*
**2** a long area of water between two areas of land: *The English Channel is between England and France.*

**chant** /chant/
● *verb* to say the same word or phrase many times: *The crowd was chanting "USA, USA!"*
● *noun* something people say or sing many times: *Everyone joined in the chant.*

**Cha·nu·kkah** /**hahn**-uhk-uh/ *noun* another spelling of Hanukkah

**cha·os** /**kay**-ahss/ *noun* a very confused situation: *The storms caused chaos. Many roads were blocked and the electricity stopped working for three days.*

**cha·os the·o·ry** /kay-ahss thee-uhr-ee/ *noun* the study of systems in which small changes can have a big effect, in a way that you cannot guess before the changes happen. For example, chaos theory says scientists cannot always be sure that it will rain. So rain can happen if there is a small change in temperature or in the amount of water in the air.

**chap·el** /**chap**-uhl/ *noun*
**1** a small church
**2** a small separate part of a large church

**chap·ter** /**chapt**-ur/ *noun* one of the parts of a book: *For homework, read chapter 3.*

**char·ac·ter** /**karr**-ikt-ur/ *noun*
**1** the type of person that you are: *My brother and I have very different characters. I'm very quiet, but he likes to talk a lot.*
( SYNONYM: **personality** )
**2** a person in a book, play, television program, or movie: *SpongeBob SquarePants is my favorite cartoon character.*
**3** the qualities that a particular place or thing has: *The new buildings will change the character of the school and make it seem much more modern.*
**4** a letter or other mark used to mean something in writing: *Chinese characters are very different from the English alphabet.*

**Word Family:** character

character *noun* | characteristic *noun* | characteristic *adjective*

**char·ac·ter·is·tic** /karr-ikt-uh-**rist**-ik/
● *noun* something that is typical about someone or something: *One of his worst characteristics is that he is very lazy.*
● *adjective* typical of someone or something: *Her kindness is very characteristic of Lisa.*

**char·coal** /**char**-kohl/ *noun* a black substance used as fuel, or for drawing. It is made from burned wood: *Charcoal is the best fuel for barbecues.*

**charge** /charj/
● *verb*
**1** to ask people to pay a particular amount of money for something: *The theater charges $4 for a child's ticket.*

**2** to buy something with a credit card: *"How would you like to pay?" "I'll charge it."*
**3** if the police charge someone, they say that he or she has done something wrong: *A local man has been charged with stealing the car.*
**4** to move forward fast in an angry way: *The bull charged toward us.*
**5** to fill a battery with electricity: *I need to charge my cell phone.*
● *noun*
**1** the amount of money you pay to do something: *There's a $3 charge to rent a DVD.*
**2** a statement that someone has done something wrong. The police make a charge against someone: *The man faced two charges of theft.*
**3** the amount of electricity stored in something: *There's no charge left in my MP3 player.*

**IDIOM with charge**
**be in charge** to be the person who controls or organizes something: *Mrs. Jackson is in charge of the library.*

**char·i·ty** /**charr**-uht-ee/ *noun* (plural **charities**) an organization that gives money or help to people who need it: *The charity provides food and shelter to people with no homes.*

**charm** /charm/
● *noun*
**1** a personal quality that makes people like you: *Her natural charm made her very popular with the other students.*
**2** an object that you believe brings you good luck: *Ruby wore the silver bracelet as a charm.*
● *verb*
to make people like you a lot: *José was good-looking and charmed all the girls.*

**charm·ing** /**charm**-ing/ *adjective* very pleasing or attractive: *He is a charming young man and very popular.*

**chart** /chart/ *noun*
**1** a drawing that shows information: *We made a chart of our heights and put it on the classroom wall.*
**2** a map, especially of oceans or stars: *This chart shows the position of the sun and the planets.*

**char·ter school** /**chart**-ur skool/ *noun* a school that is controlled by parents or companies rather than the public school system. The state gives it permission to operate and some money.

**chase** /chayss/
- *verb* to quickly follow someone or something because you want to catch him, her, or it: *I chased my brother but he was too fast.* | *The dog chased the cat out of the yard.*
- *noun* a situation in which someone tries to catch another person, car, or animal: *There was a really exciting car chase in the movie.*

**chat** /chat/
- *verb* (**chatting**, **chatted**)
**1** to talk with friends or in a friendly way: *Mom was chatting to one of the neighbors about the weather.*
**2** to quickly send messages back and forth with someone on the Internet: *Kids love to chat on the Internet.*
- *noun*
a friendly talk: *Marsha and I had a long chat on the phone.*

**chat room** /**chat** room/ *noun* a place on the Internet where you can chat by sending and receiving messages: *My sister spends lots of time in chat rooms.*

**chauf·feur** /**shohf**-ur/ *noun* someone whose job is to drive a car for someone else: *Her chauffeur opened the door of the limousine.*

**cheap** /cheep/ *adjective*
**1** costing very little money: *I bought two pairs of jeans because they were really cheap.*
( SYNONYM: **inexpensive** ) ( ANTONYM: **expensive** )
▶ see Thesaurus
**2** someone who is cheap does not like to spend money: *He was too cheap to get her a birthday gift.* ( ANTONYM: **generous** )

**cheap·ly** /**cheep**-lee/ (also **cheap**) *adverb* for a low price: *You can buy vegetables more cheaply at the farmers' market.*

**cheat** /cheet/ *verb*
- *verb*
**1** to do something dishonest to help you succeed or win: *She cheated on the test and copied another student's work.*
**2** to get something from someone by doing something dishonest: *He lied to people and cheated them out of thousands of dollars.*
**3 feel cheated** to feel that you have been treated badly or unfairly and have not been given something you deserve: *The team's poor performance left many fans feeling cheated.*

- *noun* (also **cheat·er** /cheater/) someone who does dishonest things to help them win or succeed: *I'm not going to play with you – you're a cheat!*

**check** /chek/
- *verb*
**1** to make sure that something is correct or as it should be: *Check your spelling before you hand your work in.* | *I'll check that the door is locked.*
**2 check in** to go to the desk at a hotel or airport to say that you have arrived: *You should check in an hour before the flight.*
**3 check off** to put a mark (✔) next to something on a list: *The teacher checked the kids' names off as they came in.*
**4 check out** to look at something or try to find out about it: *You can check out the band's website for more information.*
**5 check out of a hotel** to pay the bill and leave a hotel: *You must check out before 12 o'clock.*
**6 check out a book** to borrow a book from a library: *You can check out four books at one time.*
- *noun*
**1** a piece of printed paper that you use to pay for things. The check has your name and bank account number on it. You write an amount of money on the check and sign it: *Mom paid by check.*
**2** a mark (✔) next to an answer that is correct, or next to something on a list: *The teacher put a check by each right answer.*
**3** a piece of paper you get in a restaurant or hotel. The check shows how much you must pay: *Can I have the check, please?* ( SYNONYM: **bill** )
**4** a pattern of squares on something: *Tom was wearing a shirt with blue and white checks.*

**check·book** /**chek**-buk/ *noun* a book of checks that you use to pay for things

**check·ers** /**chek**-urz/ *noun* a game for two people, played on a board with a pattern of squares. Each player has 12 round pieces.

**check-in** /**chek**-in/ *noun*
**1** (also **check-in counter/desk**) a place at an airport or a hotel where you go to say that you have arrived: *There was a long line of people at the check-in counter at the airport.*

**2** the process of telling someone at a hotel or airport that you have arrived: *Please allow at least an hour for check-in before your flight.*

**check·out** /**chek**-owt/ *noun*
**1** (also **checkout counter**) a place in a store where you pay for things you have bought: *I waited for a long time at the checkout.*
**2** the time by which you must leave a hotel room: *Checkout is at noon.*

**check·up** /**chek**-uhp/ *noun* an examination by a doctor or dentist to see if you are healthy: *You should have regular checkups.*

**ched·dar** /**ched**-ur/ (also **ched·dar cheese** /**ched**-ur cheez/) *noun* a hard yellow cheese

**cheek** /cheek/ *noun* the part of your face under each eye: *Tears ran down her cheeks.*
▶ see picture on page **A13**

**cheek·bone** /**cheek**-bohn/ *noun* the bone in your cheek, or the top part of your cheek: *She has a beautiful face with high cheekbones.*

**cheep** /cheep/ *verb* if a young bird cheeps, it makes high sounds

**cheer** /cheer/
● *verb*
**1** to shout to show that you like something: *The fans cheered when Brown scored a touchdown.*
**2 cheer up** to make someone feel happier: *I bought you some candy to cheer you up.*
● *noun*
a shout showing that you like something: *When the band came on stage, there was a loud cheer from the crowd.*

**cheer·ful** /**cheer**-fuhl/ *adjective* happy: *The sunshine made me feel cheerful.*
—**cheerfully** /**cheer**-fuhl-lee/ *adverb* in a cheerful way: *"I'm fine," she said cheerfully.*
—**cheerfulness** /**cheer**-fuhl-niss/ *noun* a cheerful attitude: *His cheerfulness created a nice atmosphere.*

**cheer·lead·er**
/**cheer**-leed-ur/ *noun* someone who helps a crowd to cheer at sports games

cheerleader

**cheese** /cheez/ *noun* a solid food made from milk: *He asked for extra cheese on his pizza.*

**cheese·cake** /**cheez**-kayk/ *noun* a sweet food made with soft white cheese

**chee·tah** /**cheet**-uh/ *noun* a large wild cat with black spots that lives in Africa and southwest Asia. Cheetahs can run faster than any other animal.

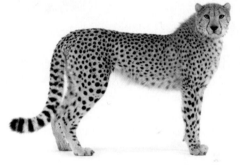
cheetah

**chef** /shef/ *noun* someone whose job is cooking in a restaurant

**chem·i·cal** /**kem**-ik-uhl/
● *noun* a substance that is used in chemistry or for doing something such as cleaning: *Dangerous chemicals are locked up in the lab where students can't reach them.*
● *adjective* relating to substances or to the ways that they mix with each other: *We watched a chemical reaction.*

**Word Family:** chemical

**chemical** *noun* | **chemical** *adjective* | **chemistry** *noun*

**chem·ist** /**kem**-ist/ *noun* a scientist who does work related to chemistry

**chem·is·try** /**kem**-uhss-tree/ *noun* the science in which you study substances and the ways that they mix with each other: *In our chemistry class, we left different metals in water to see if they would rust.*

**cher·ry** /**cherr**-ee/ *noun* (plural **cherries**) a small round fruit with dark red skin and a long stem. A cherry has a hard round seed inside: *a cherry tree* ▶ see picture on page **A7**

**chess** /chess/ *noun* a game for two people who have 16 pieces each. You play chess by moving the pieces on a board that has black and white squares. The aim of the game is to trap the other player's king: *Do you want to play chess?*

chess

chess pieces

chessboard

**chest** /chest/ *noun*
**1** the front part of your body, between your neck and stomach: *Boys wear shorts to swim, so nothing covers their chest.* ▶ see picture on page **A13**
**2** a large strong box that you keep things in: *I found some old photos in a chest in the attic.*

**chest·nut** /**chess**-nuht/ *noun*
**1** a type of tree that grows nuts
**2** the nut that grows on a chestnut tree. A chestnut is red-brown on the outside, and you can cook and eat it.

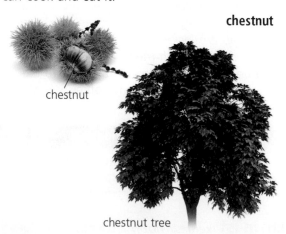
chestnut

chestnut

chestnut tree

**chest of drawers**
/chest uhv **drorz**/ *noun* (plural **chests of drawers**) a piece of furniture with drawers that clothes can be kept in ( SYNONYM: **dresser** )

chest of drawers

**chew** /choo/ *verb* to crush food between your back teeth several times: *Daniel chewed his sandwich slowly.*

**chew·ing gum** /**choo**-ing guhm/ *noun* a type of candy that you chew for a long time but do not swallow: *Do you want a piece of chewing gum?*

**chew·y** /**choo**-ee/ *adjective* food that is chewy has to be chewed a lot before it is soft: *The meat was very tough and chewy.*

**Chi·ca·no** /chi-**kahn**-oh/ *noun* someone living in the U.S. who was born in Mexico or whose family came from Mexico
—**Chicana** /chi-**kahn**-uh/ *noun* a woman living in the U.S. who was born in Mexico or whose family came from Mexico

**chick** /chik/ *noun* a baby bird: *The hen had six chicks.*

chick

chick          chicken

**chick·en** /**chik**-uhn/
● *noun* a farm bird that is kept for its eggs and meat: *His favorite food is fried chicken.*
▶ see picture at **chick**
● *adjective* afraid to do something: *She was too chicken to dive in the lake.*
● *verb* **chicken out** to decide not to do something because you are too afraid: *He was going to ask her out on a date, but he chickened out.*

**chick·en·pox** /**chik**-uhn-pahkss/ *noun* a disease that gives you itchy red spots on your skin. Children often get chickenpox from each other.

**chief** /cheef/
● *noun*
**1** the leader of a group or organization: *Brown became chief of police in Houston.*
**2** the leader of a tribe: *an American Indian chief*
● *adjective*
most important: *Their chief aim is to protect the forest.* ( SYNONYM: **main** )

**chief·ly** /**cheef**-lee/ *adverb* mainly: *This bird feeds chiefly on insects.*

**chig·ger** /**chig**-ur/ *noun* a very small creature that bites people and makes their skin itch

**child** /chīld/ *noun* (plural **children** /**childr**-uhn/)
**1** a young person who is not yet fully grown: *Children love playing with toys.* | *She is the youngest child in her class.* ( SYNONYM: **kid** )
▶ see picture at **adult**
**2** a son or daughter: *The couple have two children.* ( SYNONYM: **kid** )

**child·birth** /**chīld**-burth/ *noun* the act of having a baby: *A doctor helps a woman during childbirth.*

**child·care** /**chīld**-kair/ *noun* an arrangement in which someone takes care of children while their parents are at work: *Childcare can be very expensive.*

**child·hood** /**chīld**-hud/ *noun* the time when you are a child: *I had a very happy childhood.*

**child·ish** /**chīld**-ish/ *adjective* behaving in a silly way like a young child: *He was being very childish and wouldn't sit with the girls.*

**chil·dren** /**childr**-uhn/ *noun* the plural of **child**

**chil·i** /**chil**-ee/ *noun* (plural **chilies**)
**1** (also **chili pepper**) a small red or green vegetable with a very hot taste
**2** a dish made with beans, chilis, and usually meat: *He was making a big pot of chili.*

### Word Origin: chili

**Chili** comes from an Aztec word for a hot pepper. Until the explorers came to Central America, no one in the rest of the world had ever eaten a chili. Now chilies are used all over the world.

**chill** /chil/
● *verb*
**1** to make something cold: *She chilled the lemonade in the refrigerator.*
**2** to relax: *After school I like to chill out with my friends.*
● *noun*
**1** a feeling of being frightened: *Whenever I pass the dark old house, a chill goes down my spine and I feel very frightened.*
**2 chills** a cold feeling that makes you shake, when you are sick: *Sam is in bed with the chills.*
**3** if there is a chill somewhere, it is cold: *It was October and there was a chill in the air.*

**chill·y** /**chil**-ee/ *adjective* cold: *It's a little chilly in here. I'll turn the heater on.*

**chime** /chīm/ *verb* if a clock or a bell chimes, it makes a ringing sound: *The clock chimed six.*

**chim·ney** /**chim**-nee/ *noun* a structure that smoke from a fire in a fireplace passes through to get out of a building and into the air

**chim·pan·zee**
/chim-pan-**zee**/ *noun* an African animal that is like a monkey without a tail. Chimpanzees are very intelligent animals.

**chimpanzee**

**chin** /chin/ *noun* the front part of your face below your mouth: *You have some food on your chin.* ▶ see picture on page **A13**

**chi·na** /**chīn**-uh/ *noun* plates, cups, or other things made from white clay: *a delicate china cup*

**Chi·nese** /chī-**neez**/
● *adjective*
from or in China: *We eat Chinese food with chopsticks.* | *Her mom is Chinese.*
● *noun*
**1** any of the languages that are spoken in China, such as Mandarin or Cantonese: *Chinese is a difficult language to learn because it has a very complicated writing system.*
**2 the Chinese** people from China

a b c d e f g h i j k l m n o p q r s t u v w x y z

**chip** /chip/
● *noun*
**1** a thin piece of potato or tortilla that has been cooked in oil until it is hard: *We shared a bag of potato chips.*
**2** a small object containing electronic connections or information. Chips are made of a mineral called silicon and are used especially in computers: *The new chips allow computers to process information much more quickly.*
( SYNONYM: **microchip** )
**3** a small piece of something such as chocolate, wood, or stone: *Add the chocolate chips to the cookie dough.*
● *verb* (**chipping**, **chipped**)
to break a small piece off something:
*I accidentally chipped a plate when I was washing the dishes.*
—**chipped** /chipt/ *adjective* having a small piece that has broken off: *I fell on the sidewalk and got a chipped tooth.*

**chip·munk** /chip-muhngk/ *noun* a small brown animal with stripes on its back, that looks like a small squirrel. Chipmunks live in North America and northeast Asia: *Chipmunks live in holes in the ground called burrows.*

**Word Origin:** chipmunk

**Chipmunk** comes from a Native American word that means "red squirrel." It also means something like "the one who goes down trees head first." The first time it was written in English it was spelled "chipmonk."

**chi·ro·prac·tor** /kī-ruh-prakt-ur/ *noun* someone who treats back pain by moving and pressing a person's back

**chirp** /churp/ *verb* if a bird or insect chirps, it makes short high sounds: *I was woken up by the sound of birds chirping.*

**chlo·rine** /klor-een/ *noun* a gas with a strong smell. Chlorine is added to the water in swimming pools to keep it clean.

**chlo·ro·phyll** /klor-uh-fil/ *noun* the green substance in plants. Chlorophyll helps plants get energy from sunlight, in order to make the food they need.

**choco·late** /chahk-lit/ *noun*
**1** a sweet brown food that is eaten as candy and used in cooking: *The piece of chocolate had melted in her hand.* | *a chocolate cake*
**2** a small candy that is covered with chocolate: *He gave me a box of chocolates.*

**Word Origin:** chocolate

**Chocolate** comes from the language spoken by the Aztecs. The words it came from meant "bitter water." When it is not mixed with sugar, chocolate is very bitter. Chocolate was brought to Spain by explorers in 1520. The word chocolate first started being used in English in the 1600s.

**choice** /choyss/ *noun*
**1** the chance to choose between things or people: *I'm going to give you a choice. You can either have pasta or rice.*
**2** the person or thing that someone chooses: *I think you made a good choice.*
**3** a number of things that someone can choose from: *There's a wide choice of things to eat at the restaurant.*

**choir** /kwī-ur/ *noun* a group of people who sing together: *She sings in the church choir.*

**choke** /chohk/ *verb*
**1** to have difficulty breathing because your throat is blocked: *She choked on a fish bone.*
**2** to press someone's throat so that he or she cannot breathe: *This scarf feels like it's choking me!* ( SYNONYM: **strangle** )

**chol·er·a** /kahl-uhr-uh/ *noun* a very serious disease that people usually get from drinking dirty water. It causes diarrhea and vomiting.

**cho·les·ter·ol** /kuh-lest-uh-rol/ *noun* a substance in your blood and in foods such as meat, eggs, and cheese. Too much cholesterol may cause heart disease: *Bacon has a lot of cholesterol.*

**choose** /chooz/ *verb* (**chose** /chohz/, **chosen** /chohz-uhn/) to decide to have or do something: *Why did you choose that book?* | *Michael chose to stay home rather than go to the game.*
▶ see **Thesaurus**

**chop** /chahp/
● *verb* (**chopping**, **chopped**) to cut something into smaller pieces using a knife or an ax: *Chop the carrots into small pieces and fry them in a little oil.* | *They are chopping down the trees next to our house.*
● *noun* a small flat piece of meat with the bone attached to it: *a pork chop*

**chop·sticks**
/chahp-stikss/ *plural noun* a pair of thin sticks for eating food, used mainly by people in Asia

**chopstick**

chopsticks

**chord** /kord/ *noun*
**1** three or more musical notes played at the same time: *I can play a few chords on the guitar.*
**2** a straight line that joins two points on a curve

**chore** /chor/ *noun* a job that you have to do regularly in your home, such as washing dishes: *I want you to do some chores. Can you wash the dishes and clean the kitchen floor?*

**cho·rus** /kor-uhss/ *noun*
**1** the part of a song that is repeated after each verse: *I want everyone to sing the chorus together.*
**2** a large group of people who sing together: *He sings in the school chorus.* ( SYNONYM: **choir** )

**chose** /chohz/ *verb* the past tense of **choose**

**chos·en** /chohz-uhn/ *verb* the past participle of choose

**chow·der** /chowd-ur/ *noun* a thick soup made with milk, potatoes, and often fish: *clam chowder*

**Christ** /krīst/ Jesus, who Christians believe is the son of God

**Chris·tian** /kriss-chuhn/
● *adjective* relating to the religion that is based on the life and ideas of Jesus Christ: *She has strong Christian beliefs.*
● *noun* someone who believes in the Christian religion: *Some Christians read the Bible every day.*

**Chris·ti·an·i·ty** /kriss-chee-**an**-uht-ee/ *noun* the religion that is based on the life and ideas of Jesus Christ

**Christ·mas** /**kriss**-muhss/ *noun*
**1** December 25, when Christians celebrate the birth of Jesus Christ: *My parents gave me a guitar for Christmas.*
**2** the time around December 25: *We get a week off school at Christmas.* | *a Christmas party*

**Christ·mas Eve** /kriss-muhss **eev**/ *noun* December 24, the day before Christmas: *On Christmas Eve, I was too excited to sleep.*

**chro·mo·some** /**krohm**-uh-sohm/ *noun* a part of each cell in a living thing which contains genes. Genes control the size, shape, color, etc. of a living thing.

**chron·ic** /**krahn**-ik/ *adjective* a chronic illness or problem is one that continues for a long time and cannot be cured: *She has chronic back pain and is never comfortable.*

**chron·o·log·i·cal** /krahn'l-**ahj**-ik-uhl/ *adjective* with things arranged according to the order in which they happened: *Make a list of presidents in chronological order, starting with George Washington.*

**chrys·a·lis** /**kriss**-uhl-iss/ *noun* a butterfly or moth at the time when it has a hard covering and is changing from a caterpillar into an adult

**chry·san·the·mum** /kri-**santh**-uhm-uhm/ *noun* a garden plant which has large brightly colored flowers with many petals ▶ see picture on page **A6**

**chub·by** /**chuhb**-ee/ *adjective* slightly fat: *The baby has chubby little fingers.*

**chuck·le** /**chuhk**-uhl/
● *verb* to laugh quietly: *She chuckled to herself when she read the letter.*
● *noun* a quiet laugh: *The man gave a little chuckle.*

**chunk** /chuhngk/ *noun* a thick piece of something, which does not have an even shape: *The stew had big chunks of meat in it.*

**chunk·y** /**chuhngk**-ee/ *adjective*
**1** thick: *She wore a chunky silver bracelet.*
**2** chunky food has big pieces in it: *chunky peanut butter*

**church** /church/ *noun*
**1** a building where Christians go to worship God and pray: *On Sunday, we usually go to church.*
**2** a group in the Christian religion that has its own beliefs: *the Catholic Church*

church

**ci·der** /**sīd**-ur/ (also **apple cider**) *noun* a drink made from apples

**ci·gar** /si-**gar**/ *noun* a thick object that some people smoke, made of tobacco leaves: *He is smoking a big cigar.*

**cig·a·rette** /sig-uh-**ret**/ *noun* a thin paper tube containing tobacco that some people smoke: *Smoking cigarettes is bad for your health.*

**cin·e·ma** /**sin**-uhm-uh/ *noun* movies: *In the early years of cinema, movies did not have sound.*

**cin·na·mon** /**sin**-uhm-uhn/ *noun* a sweet brown spice used in baking: *The buns have cinnamon on top.*

**circ-** /surk/, **cir·cum** /surk-uhm/

## Word Building

**circ**uit | **circ**ulate | **circum**ference

These words all have the Latin word root ***circ-*** in them. ***Circ-*** means "go around." A *circuit* is the path that an electric current goes around. Your blood *circulates* in your body by going out of your heart, around your body, and back to your heart. The *circumference* of a circle is the distance around the outside of it.

**cir·cle** /**surk**-uhl/
● *noun*
**1** a round shape like the letter O: *Draw a circle around a cup.*
**2** a group of people who are friends, or who know each other: *She has a big circle of friends at school.*
● *verb*
**1** to draw a circle around something: *Circle the correct answer.*
**2** to move in a circle: *A big bird is circling in the sky above us.*

## Word Family: circle

**circle** *noun* | **circle** *verb* | **circular** *adjective* | **semicircle** *noun*

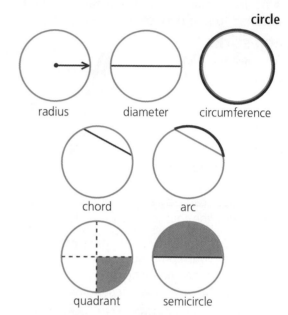

circle

radius        diameter        circumference

chord                    arc

quadrant              semicircle

**cir·cle graph** /**surk**-uhl graf/ *noun* a circle divided into different parts by lines coming from the center. Circle graphs are used to show the sizes of different amounts compared with each other. SYNONYM: **pie chart**

**cir·cuit** /**surk**-it/ *noun* the path that an electric current travels around: *When you complete the circuit, the bulb lights up.*

**cir·cu·lar** /**surk**-yuhl-ur/ *adjective* shaped like a circle: *They sat around a circular table.*
SYNONYM: **round**

**cir·cu·late** /**surk**-yuh-layt/ *verb* to go around inside something: *Blood circulates around the body.*

**cir·cu·la·tion** /surk-yuh-**laysh**-uhn/ *noun*
**1** the movement of blood around your body: *Exercise can improve your circulation.*
**2** the number of copies of a newspaper or magazine that are sold each time it is printed: *The newspaper has a circulation of 400,000.*

**cir·cu·la·tor·y sys·tem** /**surk**-yuhl-uh-tor-ee sist-uhm/ *noun* your heart and the tubes through which blood moves around your body

**cir·cum·ference** /sur-**kuhm**-fruhnss/ *noun* the distance around the outside of a circle or a round object: *What is the circumference of the lake?*

**cir·cum·stan·ces** /**surk**-uhm-stanss-iz/ *plural noun* the conditions that affect a situation or event: *Under normal circumstances, Tony would have won the game easily.*

**cir·cus** /**surk**-uhss/ *noun* a show given by a group of performers and sometimes animals that travel from one town to another: *We saw clowns, acrobats, and elephants at the circus.*

**ci·ta·tion** /sī-**taysh**-uhn/ *noun* words from a book or speech by someone else, which you mention: *Don't forget to say which page the citation comes from.*

**cite** /sīt/ *verb* to mention something as an example or as proof of something: *The principal cites three reasons for the school's success.*

**cit·i·zen** /**sit**-uhz-uhn/ *noun* someone who lives in a town, state, or country and has legal rights there: *He has the right to live here because he is an American citizen.*
—**citizenship** /**sit**-uhz-uhn-ship/ *noun* if you have citizenship of a country, you are a citizen of that country: *She has applied for U.S. citizenship.*

**cit·rus fruit** /**sitr**-uhss froot/ *noun* a fruit such as an orange or a lemon: *Citrus fruits contain a lot of vitamin C.*

**cit·y** /**sit**-ee/ *noun* (plural **cities**) a very large town: *New York is the biggest city in the United States.*

**cit·y hall** /**sit**-ee **hol**/ *noun*
**1** the building that has the offices of the mayor and other people who run a city: *The mayor held a news conference at city hall.*
**2** the local government of a city: *What is City Hall going to do about the crime problem?*

**civ·ic** /**siv**-ik/ *adjective* relating to a city or the people who live in it: *The mayor and other civic leaders were at the ceremony.*

**civ·ics** /**siv**-ikss/ *plural noun* the study of the rights and duties of citizens and the way government works: *We learned about elections in civics class.*

**civ·il** /**siv**-uhl/ *adjective*
**1** polite but not very friendly: *I was always civil to her, even though I didn't like her.*
**2** relating to the government or people of a country, not a religious or military organization: *Civil servants work for government departments such as the Department of Education.* | *We were married in a civil ceremony, not in church.*
**3** relating to laws about business and property, rather than laws about crimes: *Some customers wanted to bring a civil lawsuit against the company.*

**ci·vil·ian** /suh-**vil**-yuhn/ *noun* anyone who is not in the army, navy, or air force: *He left the army and became a civilian again.*

**civ·i·li·za·tion** /siv-uhl-uh-**zaysh**-uhn/ *noun* a society that is well organized and developed: *We learned about the ancient civilizations of Greece and Rome.*

**civ·i·lized** /**siv**-uh-līzd/ *adjective*
**1** a civilized society is well organized, and has good laws and ways of living: *All civilized societies have laws against people stealing things.*
**2** behaving in a polite and reasonable way: *They got divorced, but they were very civilized about it.*

**civ·il lib·er·ties** /siv-uhl **lib**-uhr-teez/ *plural noun* the right of citizens to do whatever they want if it does not harm the rights of other people: *Our civil liberties include the right to a fair trial.*

**civ·il rights** /siv-uhl **rītss**/ *plural noun* the legal rights that every citizen of a country has, for example the right to be treated fairly: *Martin Luther King was involved in the struggle for African-American civil rights.*

**Civil Rights Move·ment** /siv-uhl **rītss** moov-muhnt/ *noun* the organized political effort to get equal rights for African-Americans and for people of all races in the U.S.: *Martin Luther King was one of the leaders of the Civil Rights Movement in the 1960s.*

a b **c** d e f g h i j k l m n o p q r s t u v w x y z

### civ·il war /siv-uhl **wor**/ noun

**1** a war between groups of people who live in the same country: *The hatred between the two groups may cause a civil war.*
**2 the Civil War** the war between the southern and northern states of the United States. The war was from 1861 to 1865. The southern states were called the Confederacy and the northern states were called the Union.

**Civil War**

a Union soldier    a Confederate soldier

### clad /klad/ adjective
wearing or covered in something: *The man was clad in black.*

### claim /klaym/

● *verb*

**1** to say that something is true, even though it might not be: *He claims that he is the tallest man in the world. | Some people claim that they have seen flying saucers.*
**2** to ask for something that belongs to you or that you have a right to have: *Josh went up on stage to claim his prize.*
**3** to cause people to die: *The accident claimed 30 lives.*

● *noun*

**1** a statement that something is true, even though it might not be: *Nobody believed her claim that it was an accident.*
**2** an official request for something that you think you have a right to have: *If your bike is damaged, you can make a claim to the insurance company to get some money to pay for the repairs.*

### clam /klam/ noun
a small shellfish with two round shells that are joined in one place and tightly closed. You can eat the meat inside the shell. ▶ see picture at **shellfish**

**clam**

clam

### clam·my /**klam**-ee/
*adjective* clammy skin feels cold and wet because you have been sweating: *I was very nervous and my hands were all clammy.*

### clamp /klamp/

● *verb*

**1** to put or hold something firmly in a particular position: *He clamped the wood to the bench before cutting it. | I clamped my mouth shut.*
**2 clamp down** to become very strict in order to stop people from doing something: *The school is clamping down on bullying.*

● *noun*

a tool used for holding things together tightly

### clan·des·tine /klan-**dest**-in/ adjective
a clandestine organization or meeting is one that is secret: *The spies had clandestine meetings at a hotel in Washington.*

### clap /klap/ verb
(**clapping, clapped**) to hit your hands together to show that you like something, or to get someone's attention: *The show ended and everyone clapped loudly.*

**clap**

### clar·i·fy /**klarr**-uh-fī/
*verb* (**clarifies, clarified**) to make something easier to understand: *Can you clarify that last sentence for me?*
—**clarification** /klarr-uhf-uh-**kaysh**-uhn/ *noun* an explanation that makes something clearer: *Ask for clarification if there is anything you don't understand.*

### clar·i·net /klarr-uh-**net**/ noun
a musical instrument like a long black tube. You play a clarinet by blowing into it and pressing keys and

covering holes with your fingers. It is a woodwind instrument.

**clarinet**

**clar·i·ty** /**klarr**-uht-ee/ *noun* clearness that makes something easy to understand: *He explained the instructions with great clarity.*

**clash** /klash/
● *verb*
**1** if colors or patterns clash, they look bad together: *That orange T-shirt clashes with your red skirt.*
**2** to fight or argue with someone: *They often clashed with each other about money.*
● *noun*
a fight or argument: *Sometimes my parents and I have angry clashes about my homework.*

**class** /klass/ *noun*
**1** a group of students who are taught together: *He's the tallest kid in his class.*
**2** a period of time when students are taught: *She loved science classes in high school.* | *Bob wasn't in class today.*
**3** a group of people in a society that earn about the same amount of money or have the same types of jobs: *Teachers and office workers are members of the middle class.*
**4** a group of things that are like each other in some way: *This new class of drugs is more effective against cancer.*

**clas·sic** /**klass**-ik/
● *adjective*
**1** something that is classic is very good and well known, and usually old: *"E.T." is a classic kids' movie.*
**2** very typical: *This is a classic example of a beginner's mistake.*
● *noun*
a book, movie, or song that is very good and

well known: *"The Adventures of Tom Sawyer" is a classic.*

**clas·si·cal** /**klass**-ik-uhl/ *adjective*
**1** classical music is serious, and is often played by orchestras: *Mozart and Beethoven were famous for writing classical music.*
**2** relating to ancient Greece and Rome: *Many movies are based on stories from classical mythology.*

**clas·si·fied** /**klass**-uh-fīd/ *adjective* classified information is information that the government wants to be kept secret: *He works for the Pentagon and he has access to classified information about U.S. military plans.*

**clas·si·fy** /**klass**-uh-fī/ *verb* (**classifies**, **classified**) to decide which group something belongs to: *The books are classified into fiction and nonfiction.*
—**classification** /klass-uhf-uh-**kaysh**-uhn/ *noun* a group that something or someone is put into: *Federal forms ask for your racial classification.*

**class·mate** /**klass**-mayt/ *noun* someone who is in the same class as you at school: *I'm younger than most of my classmates.*

**class·room** /**klass**-room/ *noun* a room in a school, where you have classes: *The teacher puts the children's artwork on the walls of the classroom.*

**clause** /kloz/ *noun*
**1** a group of words that contains a subject and a verb. A clause can be a sentence or part of a sentence: *The sentence "You can play if you want" contains two clauses: "You can play" and "if you want."*
**2** a part of a legal document: *Read every clause in the agreement before you sign.*

**claw** /klo/ *noun* a sharp curved nail on an animal's or bird's foot: *The cat scratched the door with its claws.* ▶ see picture at **lobster**

**clay** /klay/ *noun* a type of sticky earth. Clay is used for making objects such as pots, dishes, or bricks: *In our art class, we were making things from clay.* | *a clay pot*

**clay**

a clay pot

a
b
**c**
d
e
f
g
h
i
j
k
l
m
n
o
p
q
r
s
t
u
v
w
x
y
z

**clean** /kleen/
● *adjective*
**1** not dirty: *Make sure your hands are clean before you start cooking.*
(ANTONYM: **dirty**) ► see picture at **dirty**
**2** not involving anything bad or illegal: *He lived a good clean life.*
—**cleanliness** /klen-lee-niss/ *noun* being clean: *Cleanliness is very important in a hospital.*
● *verb*
to remove dirt from something: *You need to clean your shoes.* ► see **Thesaurus**
—**cleaning** /kleen-ing/ *noun* the work of cleaning a house: *I help mom and dad with the cleaning.*

**clean·er** /kleen-ur/ *noun*
**1** a machine or substance that is used to clean things: *She sprayed some glass cleaner on the window.*
**2** someone whose job is to clean houses or other buildings: *She works as a house cleaner.*
**3** a business that cleans clothes with chemicals: *Dad went to pick up his suit from the cleaners.*
(SYNONYM: **dry cleaners**)

**cleanse** /klenz/ *verb* to make something completely clean: *This cream will cleanse your skin.* (SYNONYM: **clean**)

**cleans·er** /klenz-ur/ *noun*
**1** a substance used for cleaning your skin
**2** a substance used for cleaning surfaces in houses

**clear** /kleer/
● *adjective*
**1** easy to understand, hear, or see: *The instructions are very clear and they show you exactly how to play the game.*
**2** easy to see through: *Windows are usually made of clear glass.* (SYNONYM: **transparent**)
**3** without any clouds: *The sky is clear and the sun is shining.* (ANTONYM: **cloudy**)
**4** not blocked by anything: *The road is clear and the cars are all moving again.*
● *verb*
**1** to move things from a place so that it is neat

**clean**

or empty: *Can you clear the table and take away the dishes?*
**2** to say officially that someone has not done something wrong: *He was cleared of all charges against him.*

**clear·ance** /kleer-uhnss/ *noun* official permission to do something: *The pilot is waiting for clearance to take off from the airport.*

**clear·ing** /kleer-ing/ *noun* a small area in a forest where there are no trees: *The deer stopped at the edge of the clearing.*

**clear·ly** /kleer-lee/ *adverb*
**1** in a way that is easy to understand, hear, or see: *Our teacher is good at explaining things clearly.*
**2** without any doubt: *Clearly, the computer doesn't work properly.* (SYNONYM: **obviously**)

**clench** /klench/ *verb* to close your hand or mouth tightly: *The boxer clenched his fists.*

**cler·gy** /klurj-ee/ *plural noun* official religious leaders, such as priests: *Members of the clergy can perform wedding ceremonies.*

**clerk** /klurk/ *noun*
**1** someone whose job is to keep records or deal with documents in an office or bank
**2** someone who deals with people arriving at a hotel: *Please return your keys to the clerk at the front desk.*

**clev·er** /klev-ur/ *adjective*
**1** a clever person is intelligent and good at thinking of ideas or ways of doing things: *The men tried to trick him, but he was too clever for them.* (SYNONYM: **smart**)
**2** a clever idea, plan, or method shows a lot of intelligence and careful thought: *He thought of a clever way of making money.* (SYNONYM: **smart**)
—**cleverly** /klev-ur-lee/ *adverb* in a clever way: *The toy is cleverly designed.*

**cli·ché** /klee-shay/ *noun* a phrase that has been used many times before, and so is now boring: *His writing is full of clichés.*

**click** /klik/
● *verb*
**1** to make a very short sound: *Her heels clicked on the floor.*
**2** to press a button on a computer mouse in

order to choose something on a computer screen: *Click on the link to visit our website.*
● *noun*
a clicking sound: *I heard the click of a light switch.* ▶ see picture on page **A16**

**cli·ent** /**klī**-uhnt/ *noun* someone who pays to have work done by a professional person or a business: *He was a good lawyer, and his clients trusted him.*

**cliff** /klif/ *noun* a high area with a very steep rocky side, especially by the ocean: *Don't go too near the edge of the cliff!*

**cli·mate** /**klīm**-it/ *noun* the type of weather that a place usually has: *The climate in Texas is hot.*

**cli·max** /**klīm**-akss/ *noun* the most important or exciting thing that happens: *The climax of the movie is a big battle between two armies.*

**climb** /klīm/
● *verb*
**1** to go up toward the top of a high place: *Jake's really good at climbing trees.*
**2** to use your hands and feet to move somewhere: *I climbed through a hole in the fence.*
● *noun*
the act of going up toward the top of a hill or mountain: *We were exhausted after the long climb.*

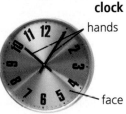
climb

**climb·er** /**klīm**-ur/ *noun* someone who climbs mountains: *a rock climber*

**climb·ing** /**klīm**-ing/ *noun* the sport of climbing mountains: *She doesn't want him to go climbing because she thinks it's too dangerous.*

**cling** /kling/ *verb* (**clung** /kluhng/) to hold onto someone or something tightly: *The little boy is clinging onto his mother's arm because he's very frightened.*

**clin·ic** /**klin**-ik/ *noun* a place where people can get medical treatment or advice: *She went to the clinic for a blood test.*

**clin·i·cal** /**klin**-ik-uhl/ *adjective* relating to treating people who are sick: *Doctors are doing clinical tests to find out if the drug is effective.*

**clip** /klip/
● *noun*
**1** a small object used for holding things together: *Fasten the pictures together with a paper clip.*
**2** a short section taken from a movie or television program: *Tonight on the show we're going to show you some clips from Tom's new movie.*
● *verb* (**clipping**, **clipped**)
**1** to hold things together with a clip: *She clipped a note to the front of his book.*
**2** to cut small pieces off something to make it look neater: *Dad was clipping the hedge.*

**clip·board** /**klip**-bord/ *noun* a flat board with a clip at the top that holds paper onto it. People have clipboards when they need to write things while walking around.

**clip·pers** /**klip**-urz/ *plural noun* a tool for cutting small pieces off something: *I use nail clippers to make my nails look neat.*

**cloak** /klohk/ *noun* a piece of clothing like a big coat with no sleeves: *She was wearing a big black cloak.*

**clock** /klahk/ *noun* an instrument on a wall or table that shows the time: *I looked at the clock by my bed. It was only 6:15.*

clock
hands
face

┌ **IDIOM with clock**
│ **around the clock** all
│ day and night: *Some*
└ *stores are open around the clock.*

**clock·wise** /**klahk**-wīz/ *adverb* moving in the same direction as the hands of a clock: *Turn the faucet clockwise.* (ANTONYM: **counterclockwise**)
▶ see picture at **counterclockwise**

**clog** /klahg/
● *noun* a shoe that covers your toes but is open at the back
● *verb* (**clogging**, **clogged**) to block something such as a pipe or road, so that things cannot move through it: *The drain was clogged with toilet paper.*

clog

## close

● *verb* /klohz/

**1** to shut something: *Stop writing and close your books.* ( SYNONYM: **shut** ) ( ANTONYM: **open** )
▶ see Thesaurus

**2** when a place such as a store or museum closes, people cannot visit it any more that day: *We'd better hurry – the store closes at 5:00.*
( ANTONYM: **open** )

**3** if a store or factory closes, it stops doing business forever: *The factory may have to close down.* ( ANTONYM: **open** )

● *adjective* /klohss/

**1** not far from someone or something: *My school is very close to my house and it only takes me five minutes to walk there.* ( SYNONYM: **near** )

**2** almost: *It's 11:45. It's getting close to lunchtime.*

**3** people who are close like each other a lot and talk to each other a lot: *Debbie is my closest friend and we tell each other all our secrets.*

**4** a close game, race, or competition is one which the winner does not win easily: *It was a close game, but we lost 2–1.*

## closed /klohzd/ *adjective*

**1** not open: *Her eyes are closed and she seems to be asleep.* ( SYNONYM: **shut** )

**2** not doing business: *The store is closed on Sundays.*

## close·ly /klohss-lee/ *adverb* if you look at someone or something closely, you look very carefully: *If you look closely at this leaf, you can see tiny hairs.*

## clos·et /klahz-it/ *noun* a space like a small room where you keep your clothes: *She put the dress back in the closet.*

## close-up /klohss uhp/ *noun* a photograph or a picture in a movie that is taken very near to someone or something: *The program ends with a close-up of the woman's face.*

## clos·ing /klohz-ing/ *noun* the last words written in a letter: *"Lots of love" is not a suitable closing for a formal letter.*

## clot /klaht/

● *noun* some blood that has become solid: *He had a blood clot in his leg.*

● *verb* (**clotting**, **clotted**) if blood clots, it becomes solid: *The blood will clot and the cut will stop bleeding.*

## cloth /kloth/ *noun*

**1** material used for making clothes and other things: *She sewed pieces of cloth together to make a bag.*

**2** a piece of material that you use for doing something: *I wiped my face with a cloth.*

## clothe /klohth/ *verb*

**1** to provide clothes for someone to wear: *We didn't have enough money to feed and clothe our family.*

**2** **fully clothed** wearing all of your clothes: *He jumped into the water fully clothed!*

## clothes /klohz/ *plural noun* things that you wear, for example pants, dresses, underwear, and coats: *Put on your clothes. It's time to get dressed.* ▶ see Thesaurus

### Grammar: clothes, clothing

**Clothes** means all the things people can wear: *Her clothes are really pretty.*
Don't say "Her clothing is really pretty."
You use clothing when you are talking about clothes in a general way, not about someone's clothes: *The children need food and clothing.*

## clothes·line /klohz-līn/ *noun* a rope that you hang wet clothes on so they will dry: *Mom hung the towels on the clothesline.*

## clothes·pin /klohz-pin/ *noun* something you use to fasten wet clothes to a line so they will dry

## cloth·ing /klohth-ing/ *noun* clothes: *If you're going skiing, you'll need warm clothing.*

## cloud /klowd/

● *noun*

**1** a white or gray thing in the sky, that rain sometimes falls from. Clouds are made of many tiny drops of water or tiny pieces of ice: *Luke saw the dark clouds and knew it was going to rain.*

**2** a lot of smoke or dust in a shape like a cloud: *I hit the old sofa and a cloud of dust rose into the air.*

● *verb*

**cloud up/over** to become cloudy: *The sky was clear in the morning but it started to cloud up in the afternoon.*

**cloud·y** /**klowd**-ee/ *adjective*
**1** if it is cloudy, there are a lot of clouds in the sky: *Tomorrow will be cloudy with some rain.*
**2** cloudy liquids are not clear: *His drink was cloudy with bits of orange floating in it.*

**clove** /klohv/ *noun*
**1** a piece of garlic
**2** a strong sweet spice: *The cake has cinnamon and cloves in it.*

**clo·ver** /**klohv**-ur/ *noun*
a small green plant with three round leaves and white or pink flowers: *People say it's lucky if you find a clover with four leaves.*

**clover**

**clown** /klown/ *noun* a person who makes people laugh by wearing funny clothes and a big red nose, and by doing silly things. You see clowns at the circus: *The clown fell over and all the children laughed.*

**club** /kluhb/ *noun*
**1** a group of people who meet so that they can do an activity: *I'm in the school cooking club.*
**2** a card used in card games. The cards have pictures on them that look like this: (♣): *My last card was the king of clubs.*
**3** a metal stick you use to hit a golf ball: *He carried his own clubs in a bag.*
**4** a place where people go to dance or listen to music: *Mom and dad sometimes go to a jazz club.*

**club sand·wich** /kluhb **sand**-wich/ *noun* a large sandwich. It has three pieces of bread with meat and cheese between them.

**cluck** /kluhk/ *verb* if a chicken clucks, it makes short low sounds

**clue** /kloo/ *noun* some information that helps you find the truth or the right answer: *The police are looking for clues to who started the fire.*

> **IDIOM with clue**
> **I don't have a clue** I do not know something at all: *"Where does Jay live?" "I don't have a clue."*

**Word Origin: clue**

**Clue** comes from an Old English word that means "a ball of yarn." Clue started to mean "information that helps you solve a puzzle or a mystery" because of a Greek myth. In the myth, Theseus, a hero, ties the end of a ball of yarn to the door before he goes into a kind of maze called a labyrinth. He goes into the labyrinth and kills a monster. Then Theseus uses the ball of yarn to find his way back out of the labyrinth. So, the ball of yarn helped Theseus solve the puzzle of the labyrinth, and now a clue helps us solve other kinds of puzzles.

**clump** /kluhmp/ *noun* a group of things growing close together: *The bear went behind a clump of trees.*

**clum·sy** /**kluhmz**-ee/ *adjective* someone who is clumsy drops things or falls down a lot: *My clumsy little brother dropped his plate on the floor.*
—**clumsily** /**kluhmz**-uhl-ee/ *adverb* in a clumsy way: *She clumsily knocked the glass over with her elbow.*
—**clumsiness** /**kluhmz**-ee-niss/ *noun* clumsy behavior

**clung** /kluhng/ *verb* the past tense and past participle of **cling**

**clus·ter** /**kluhst**-ur/ *noun* a group of things that are close together: *This cluster of stars is called "the Big Dipper."*

**clutch** /kluhch/ *verb* to hold something tightly: *The little boy clutched his mother's hand.*

**clut·ter** /**kluht**-ur/ *noun* a lot of things that fill a place and make it messy: *We cleared the clutter out of my closet.*
—**cluttered** /**kluht**-urd/ *adjective* if a place is cluttered, it is messy because it is full of things: *My bedroom is always cluttered with toys and clothes.*

**cm** the written abbreviation of **centimeter**: *The cut on his leg was 4 cm long.*

a b **c** d e f g h i j k l m n o p q r s t u v w x y z

**co-** /koh/

**Word Building**

**co-** is a prefix.

**cooperate** | **co-**star | **correspond**

**co-** means "together." If you *cooperate* with someone, you work together with that person. If two actors *co-star*, they work together in the same TV program or movie. If one thing *corresponds* with another thing, the two things match or go together.

**co.** the written abbreviation of **company**

**coach** /kohch/
● *noun*
**1** someone who helps people to get better at a sport or at a subject: *The coach says I need to hit the ball harder.*
**2** the type of seats on an airplane that cost the least money: *We always fly coach in order to save money.* ( SYNONYM: **economy** )
● *verb*
to help people to get better at a sport or at a subject: *Mr. Davis coaches our soccer team.*

**coal** /kohl/ *noun* a hard black substance from below the ground that people burn to produce heat: *He works underground at the coal mine.*

**coarse** /korss/ *adjective* rough and thick: *The sacks were made of coarse brown cloth.*
( ANTONYM: **smooth** )

**coast** /kohst/ *noun* the land next to the ocean: *We usually go to the coast on vacation.*
▶ see picture on page **A11**

**coast guard** /**kohst** gard/ *noun* the people whose job is to watch ships in the ocean and protect a country's coast. The coast guard is part of the armed forces: *The coast guard stopped a ship that did not have permission to sail in American waters.*

**coast·line** /**kohst**-līn/ *noun* the land at the edge of the ocean: *There are some beautiful beaches along this coastline.*

**coat** /koht/ *noun*
**1** something that you wear over other clothes to keep you warm outdoors: *It's cold outside. Put on your coat.* ▶ see picture at **pirate**

**2** an animal's hair or fur: *The dog was black with a smooth coat.*
**3** a thin layer on the surface of something: *He gave the boat a new coat of paint.*

**coax** /kohkss/ *verb* to try to make someone do something by talking to them gently and kindly: *We tried to coax the cat to come into the house.*

**cob** /kahb/ *noun* the long hard part of a corn plant on which the yellow grains grow: *We had hot dogs and corn on the cob for dinner.*

**cob·ble·stone** /**kahb**-uhl-stohn/ *noun* a small round stone that was used for making roads in the past: *In the old part of the city you can still see cobblestone streets.*

**co·bra** /**kohb**-ruh/ *noun* a big poisonous snake that lives in Africa and Asia. When a cobra is angry or afraid, it raises its head high and spreads its neck wide.

cobra

**cob·web** /**kahb**-web/ *noun* a net of fine threads made by a spider. This word is used when the cobweb makes a place look dirty: *The old barn was full of cobwebs.*

**Word Origin:** cobweb

The "cob" in **cobweb** is from an Old English word for a spider. The Old English word was **atorcoppe**, and it meant "poison-head."

**cock·pit** /**kahk**-pit/ *noun* the part of an airplane where the pilot sits: *There are usually two pilots in the cockpit.* ▶ see picture at **airplane**

**cock·roach** /**kahk**-rohch/ *noun* a dark brown insect that lives in dark or dirty places: *A big cockroach ran across the kitchen floor.*
▶ see picture on page **A15**

**co·coa** /**kohk**-oh/ *noun*
**1** a hot chocolate drink: *I often have a cup of cocoa at bedtime.*
**2** a brown powder that tastes like chocolate and is used in cooking. Cocoa is made from the beans of the cacao tree: *Add three tablespoons of cocoa to the cake mix.*

## co·co·nut

/**kohk**-uh-nuht/ *noun* a large brown nut with a hairy shell. It has liquid inside that you can drink and white flesh that you can eat: *Coconuts grow on palm trees.*

coconut

## co·coon

/kuh-**koon**/ *noun* a bag of threads that a caterpillar makes to protect itself. The caterpillar stays inside the cocoon when it is changing from a caterpillar into a moth.

## cod

/kahd/ *noun* (plural **cod**) a fish that has white meat and is found mainly in the northern Atlantic Ocean

## code

/kohd/ *noun*
**1** a way of using words, numbers, or symbols to send secret messages: *The message was written in code, and they couldn't understand it.*
**2** a set of rules that tells people how they must behave: *The school has a dress code that says what you are allowed to wear to school.*

## co·erce

/koh-**urss**/ *verb* to force someone to do something, by saying you will hurt or punish him or her if he or she does not do it: *No one was coerced into taking part in the research; they were all volunteers.* ( SYNONYM: **force** )

## cof·fee

/**kof**-ee/ *noun*
**1** a hot brown drink that is made from roasted brown beans: *She likes cream in her coffee.*
**2** the brown beans of a plant. Coffee beans are cooked and crushed and used to make the hot drink called coffee: *Put one spoonful of instant coffee into each cup.*

### Word Origin: coffee

The English word **coffee** comes from the Italian word **caffè**. The Italian word was borrowed from Arabic. The Arabic word for coffee may come from "Kaffa," which is the place in Ethiopia where coffee plants were first found. Or, coffee may come from an Arabic word that means "wine of the bean," because coffee is made from crushed coffee beans.

## cof·fin

/**kof**-in/ *noun* a long box in which a dead person is buried: *They carried the coffin into the church.* ( SYNONYM: **casket** )

## cog

/kahg/ *noun* a wheel on a machine. The cog has a special edge that fits into another wheel and makes it turn.

## co·her·ent

/koh-**heer**-uhnt/ *adjective* clear and easy to understand: *Try to write your story in a coherent way.*
—**coherently** /koh-**heer**-uhnt-lee/ *adverb* in a coherent way: *When you give a talk, you need to speak coherently so that everyone can understand you.*

## coil

/koyl/
● *noun* a long piece of rope or wire that is wound around in a circle: *There was a big coil of rope in the bottom of the boat.*
● *verb* to wind something long and thin into a circle shape: *Paul coiled up the hose and put it in the shed.*

coil

## coin

/koyn/ *noun* a piece of money made of metal: *Suzie put some coins in the soda machine.*

## co·in·cide

/koh-in-**sīd**/ *verb* to happen at the same time as something: *Grandpa's visit coincided with my birthday and he brought me a gift.*

## co·in·ci·dence

/koh-**inss**-uhd-uhnss/ *noun* a surprising situation in which the same thing happens twice, without anyone planning this: *Today we are both wearing yellow dresses. What a coincidence!*

## co·la

/**kohl**-uh/ *noun* a sweet brown drink full of bubbles: *a can of cola*

## col·an·der

/**kahl**-uhnd-ur/ *noun* a metal or plastic bowl with a lot of small holes in it. You use a colander to separate liquid from food: *I put the spaghetti in a colander to drain the water.*

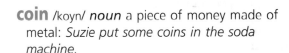

**cold** /kohld/
● *adjective*
**1** if something is cold, it has a low temperature: *The weather is very cold in January.* | *I want a nice cold drink.* ( ANTONYMS: **hot, warm** )
▶ see Thesaurus
**2** if you feel cold, you feel uncomfortable because you are not warm enough: *If you are cold, put on a sweater.* ( ANTONYM: **hot** )
**3** not friendly: *He gave her a cold look.*
● *noun*
**1** a common illness that gives you a blocked nose and a sore throat, and makes you sneeze: *She kept blowing her nose because she had a cold.*
**2** cold weather: *Don't stay outside in the cold – come in!*

**cold-blood-ed** /kohld **bluhd**-uhd/ *adjective*
**1** a cold-blooded animal has a body temperature that changes. If the air or ground around the animal gets warmer, the animal also gets warmer. If the air or ground gets colder, the animal also gets colder: *Snakes are cold-blooded.*
( ANTONYM: **warm-blooded** )
**2** done in a way that shows you do not care if someone is hurt: *The boss made the cold-blooded decision to fire all the workers.*

**cold-ly** /**kohld**-lee/ *adverb* in a way that is not at all friendly: *"I'm busy. Go away," Jon said coldly.*

**cold-ness** /**kohld**-niss/ *noun*
**1** low temperature: *The coldness of the wind hurt my face.*
**2** behavior that is not at all friendly: *I felt hurt by her coldness.*

**cole-slaw** /**kohl**-slo/ *noun* a salad made of uncooked cabbage that has been cut into thin strips and put in a white sauce

**col-lage** /kuh-**lahzh**/ *noun* a picture made by sticking many pieces of cloth, paper, photographs, or other things onto a piece of paper: *We made a collage of a face, using pieces of colored paper.*

**col-lapse** /kuh-**lapss**/ *verb*
**1** if a building or bridge collapses, it suddenly falls down and is destroyed: *The earthquake shook the bridge and made it collapse.*
**2** to suddenly fall down or become unconscious because you are sick or very weak: *He collapsed in the street and was taken to the emergency*
room.
**3** if a business or system collapses, it fails and cannot continue: *The bank collapsed because people took out all their money.*

**col-lar** /**kahl**-ur/ *noun*
**1** the part of a shirt or coat that fits around your neck and that usually folds down: *My shirt collar is too tight around my neck.*
**2** a thing that a cat or dog wears around its neck. A collar is made of a thin piece of leather, cloth, or plastic: *I held the dog by its collar to keep it from jumping up.*

**col-lar-bone** /**kahl**-ur-bohn/ *noun* a bone that goes from the bottom of your neck to your shoulder. You have two collarbones, one on each side of your body.

**col-league** /**kahl**-eeg/ *noun* someone who works with you: *Mr. Smith is one of dad's work colleagues.*

**col-lect** /kuh-**lekt**/ *verb*
**1** to get things and bring them together: *They collected wood for the fire.*
**2** to get and keep objects of the same type because you like them: *She collects toy animals.*
**3** to come together and form a large amount: *Dirt collects in the corners of the windows.*
( SYNONYM: **gather** )

**col-lec-tion** /kuh-**lek**-shuhn/ *noun* a group of similar things that you keep together after getting them over a period of time: *He has a toy train collection.*

**col-lege** /**kahl**-ij/ *noun* a school where you can study after you have finished high school: *I want to go to college when I'm older.*
( SYNONYM: **university** )

**col-lide** /kuh-**lïd**/ *verb* to crash into something with a lot of force: *His car collided with a tree and was badly damaged.* ( SYNONYM: **crash** )

**col-li-sion** /kuh-**lizh**-uhn/ *noun* a crash between two cars, planes, or trains: *A collision on the freeway caused a huge traffic jam.*
( SYNONYM: **crash** )

**co-lon** /**kohl**-uhn/ *noun*
**1** the mark (:). You use a colon in writing before a list or before giving some examples.
**2** a part inside your body where food turns into

waste that will leave your body. The colon is the bottom part of a long tube called the intestine.

**colo·nel** /**kurn**'l/ *noun* an important officer in the army, air force, or Marine Corps: *Colonel Parker told his men to stop shooting.*

**co·lo·ni·al** /kuh-**lohn**-ee-uhl/ *adjective* relating to the control of a place by a more powerful country: *We learned about life in colonial America, when the country was ruled by Britain.*

**col·o·nist** /**kahl**-uhn-ist/ *noun* someone who comes to live in a new colony: *The first colonists came to America in the 1600s.*

**col·o·nize** /**kahl**-uh-nīz/ *verb* to start to control another country or area, and to send people to live there: *Argentina was colonized by Spain.*

**col·o·ny** /**kahl**-uhn-ee/ *noun* (plural **colonies**) a country or area that is ruled by a more powerful country. The powerful country is usually far away from the colony: *Maryland used to be a British colony.*

**col·or** /**kuhl**-ur/
● *noun* red, blue, yellow, green, orange, etc.: *"What's your favorite color?" "Yellow."*
● *verb* to add colors to a picture on a piece of paper using colored pencils or paint: *When you've finished your picture, color it in.*

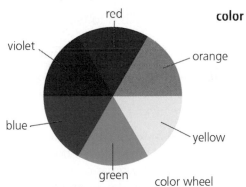

color

red
orange
yellow
green
blue
violet

color wheel

**col·or·blind** /**kuhl**-ur-blind/ *adjective* not able to see the difference between some colors: *If you are colorblind, red and green look the same.*

**col·or·ful** /**kuhl**-ur-fuhl/ *adjective* having a lot of bright colors: *The ocean is full of colorful fish.*

**col·or·ing** /**kuhl**-uhr-ing/ *noun*
**1** the color of something, especially someone's hair, skin, or eyes: *Anna and her sister have similar coloring – very dark hair and brown eyes.*
**2** something that makes something else have a

color: *Use food coloring to make the cupcakes pink.*

**col·or·less** /**kuhl**-ur-liss/ *adjective* not having any color: *Water is colorless.*

**colt** /kohlt/ *noun* a young male horse

**col·umn** /**kahl**-uhm/ *noun*
**1** a tall stone post that supports a building or statue: *26 columns support the roof of the temple.*
**2** a long narrow area of writing that goes down a page or computer screen: *The first column listed the names of all the kids in the class.*
**3** an article by someone who writes regularly in a newspaper or magazine: *He writes a sports column for the newspaper.*

column

column

**co·ma** /**kohm**-uh/ *noun* if someone is in a coma, he or she is not conscious for a long time: *After the accident, he was in a coma for two weeks.*

**comb** /kohm/
● *noun* an object you use to make your hair neat. A comb is a flat piece of plastic with a row of very thin sticks on one side: *Your hair is a mess. Here, use my comb.*
● *verb* to make your hair neat with a comb: *I washed my face and combed my hair.*

**com·bat** /**kahm**-bat/ *noun* fighting during a war: *The soldiers were wounded in combat.*

**com·bi·na·tion** /kahm-buh-**naysh**-uhn/ *noun* two or more different things that are used together: *A football team needs the right combination of players.*

**com·bine** /kuhm-**bīn**/
● *verb* to join or mix two things together: *The show combines music and entertainment.*
● *noun* a large machine used on a farm to cut the grain and take the seeds off at the same time

a
b
**c**
d
e
f
g
h
i
j
k
l
m
n
o
p
q
r
s
t
u
v
w
x
y
z

**come** /kuhm/ *verb* (**came** /kaym/, **come**)

**1** to move toward a place: *Come here. I need to talk to you.* | *Do you want to come over to my house?* | *Is Dan coming with you?*

**2** to arrive somewhere: *I'm waiting for the pizza man to come.* | *She came home late.*

**3** to be in a place or position: *The runner who comes first gets a gold medal.* | *The water came up to my knees.* | *"B" comes after "A" in the alphabet.*

**4** to happen: *Spring came early this year.*

**5 come down with** to get an illness: *I think I'm coming down with the flu.*

**6 come from** if you come from a place, you were born there: *"Where do you come from?" "Ohio."*

**7 come on!** used when telling someone to be quick: *Come on! We're late!*

**8 come to** used when saying what the total of something is: *Four candy bars comes to $2.45.*

**9 come up with** to think of an idea: *Have you come up with a title for your story?*

**co·me·di·an** /kuh-**meed**-ee-uhn/ *noun* someone whose job is to tell funny stories and make people laugh: *The comedian told some really funny jokes.* ( SYNONYM: **comic** )

**com·e·dy** /**kahm**-uhd-ee/ *noun* (plural **comedies**) a funny movie, play, or television program that makes people laugh: *"Hannah Montana" is a comedy about a school girl who becomes a pop singer at night.*

**com·et** /**kahm**-it/ *noun* an object in the sky that looks like a very bright ball with a long tail. A comet moves slowly around the Sun: *The comet can be seen from Earth every 75 or 76 years.*

**com·fort** /**kuhmf**-urt/

● *noun*

**1** a feeling of being relaxed: *The car has big leather seats and you can travel in comfort.* ( ANTONYM: **discomfort** )

**2** something or someone that makes you feel less upset or worried: *It was a comfort to have my parents with me at the hospital.*

● *verb*

to make someone feel less worried or unhappy: *Sasha was crying and her mother was trying to comfort her.*

**Word Family: comfort**

**comfort** *noun* | **comfort** *verb* | **comfortable** *adjective* | **uncomfortable** *adjective* | **discomfort** *noun*

**com·fort·a·ble** /**kuhmft**-uhb-uhl/ *adjective*

**1** if a chair, bed, or room is comfortable, it makes you feel relaxed: *The chair was really soft and comfortable.* ( ANTONYM: **uncomfortable** )

▶ see Thesaurus

**2** if you are comfortable, you feel relaxed and have no pain: *I felt warm and comfortable when I was lying on the sofa.*

( ANTONYM: **uncomfortable** )

—**comfortably** /**kuhmft**-uhb-lee/ *adverb* in a comfortable way: *He was sitting comfortably in a soft chair.*

**com·ic** /**kahm**-ik/

● *adjective*

funny: *There are some comic moments in the movie.*

● *noun*

**1 comics** the different comic strips that are printed in the newspaper: *I read some of the comics every day.*

**2** a comic book: *He was reading an X-Men comic.*

**3** someone whose job is to tell funny stories and make people laugh: *She is a very funny comic and I like her jokes.* ( SYNONYM: **comedian** )

**com·ic book** /**kahm**-ik buk/ *noun* a magazine that tells a story using drawings: *He was sitting on his bed reading a Superman comic book.*

**com·ic strip** /kahm-ik **strip**/ *noun* a set of pictures that are drawn inside boxes and tell a story: *"Peanuts" is a great comic strip. It's the one that has Charlie Brown and Snoopy.*

**com·ma** /**kahm**-uh/ *noun* the mark (,). Commas are used in writing to separate parts of a sentence or to separate words in a list.

**com·mand** /kuh-**mand**/

● *noun*

**1** an order from an important person to do something: *Soldiers must obey their leaders' commands.* ( SYNONYM: **order** )

**2** if you are in command of something, you control something such as an army or group of

police officers: *The general was in command of more than a thousand soldiers.*
● *verb*
**1** to tell someone that he or she must do something, when you are more important than him or her: *The police officer commanded him to stop.* ( SYNONYM: **order** )
**2** to be the leader of a group of soldiers: *Who commands the army?*

**com·mand·er** /kuh-**mand**-ur/ *noun* an important officer who is in charge of a group of soldiers: *The commander ordered his men to attack.*

**com·mence** /kuh-**menss**/ *verb* to begin: *The play will commence at 7:30.* ( SYNONYM: **start** )

**com·mence·ment** /kuh-**menss**-muhnt/ *noun*
**1** the beginning of something: *Please buy a ticket before the commencement of the show.*
( SYNONYM: **start** )
**2** an event at which students get their diplomas to show they have finished high school or college: *Two students gave speeches at commencement.* ( SYNONYM: **graduation** )

**com·ment** /**kahm**-ent/
● *noun* something that you say about something: *He made a rude comment about my dress.*
● *verb* to say something about something: *Grown-ups often comment on how tall I am.*

**com·men·tar·y** /**kahm**-uhn-lair-ee/ *noun* (plural **commentaries**) if someone gives a commentary, he or she tells about what is happening during an event such as a game: *We were listening to the commentary of the game on the car radio.*

**com·men·ta·tor** /**kahm**-uhn-tayt-ur/ *noun* someone on television or radio who talks about an event: *The commentator got very excited when Atlanta scored.*

**com·merce** /**kahm**-urss/ *noun* the activity of buying and selling things: *There has been an increase in the amount of commerce between the U.S. and China.* ( SYNONYM: **trade** )

**com·mer·cial** /kuh-**mursh**-uhl/
● *noun* an advertisement on television or radio: *Kids want toys that they see in commercials.*
( SYNONYMS: **ad, advertisement** )
● *adjective* relating to business and making money: *The movie was a commercial success.*

**com·mit** /kuh-**mit**/ *verb* (**committing, committed** )
**1** to do something that is against the law: *The police do not know who committed the crime.*
**2** to say that you will definitely do something: *If you want to play the guitar, you have to commit yourself to practicing every day.*

**Word Family: commit**

**commit** *verb* | **commitment** *noun*

**com·mit·ment** /kuh-**mit**-muhnt/ *noun*
**1** a promise to do something: *The couple made a commitment to love each other for the rest of their lives.*
**2** hard work and effort that shows you feel enthusiastic about doing something: *If you get up early every day to swim, that shows commitment.*

**com·mit·tee** /kuh-**mit**-ee/ *noun* a group of people who have been chosen to do something or decide something: *Mom is on the committee that raises money for the school.*

**com·mon** /**kahm**-uhn/ *adjective* often seen or often happening: *Black bears are common in Yosemite National Park. | a common illness*
( ANTONYM: **rare** )
—**commonly** /**kahm**-uhn-lee/ *adverb* often: *Pepper is the most commonly used spice.*

**com·mon de·nom·i·na·tor** /**kahm**-uhn di-**nahm**-uh-nayt-ur/ *noun* a number that more than one fraction in a set has as its denominator. In the fractions 1/3 and 2/3, 3 is the common denominator.

**com·mon fac·tor** /**kahm**-uhn **fakt**-ur/ *noun* a number that divides exactly into all the numbers in a set. For example, 3 is the common factor of 9, 12, and 18.

**com·mon mul·ti·ple** /**kahm**-uhn **muhlt**-uhp-uhl/ *noun* a number that can be divided by every number in a set. For example, 12 is a common multiple of 3, 6, and 12.

**com·mon sense** /**kahm**-uhn **senss**/ *noun* the ability to think and behave in a sensible way. If you have common sense, you do not do stupid things: *Everyone knows that you shouldn't walk in the middle of the road – it's common sense.*

**commun-** /kuh-myoon, kahm-yoon/

## Word Building

**commun**icate | **commun**ity | **commun**ism
These words all have the Latin word root **commun-** in them. **Commun-** means "to share." If you *communicate* with someone, you talk to that person and share information. A *community* is all the people who live in the same area, who share schools, parks, etc. *Communism* is a political system where the government owns everything, and shares it with the people who live in the country.

**com·mu·ni·cate** /kuh-**myoon**-uh-kayt/ *verb* to tell someone something, for example by talking or writing, or in another way: *We communicate with each other by email.*

## Word Family: communicate

**communicate** verb | **communication** noun

**com·mu·ni·ca·tion** /kuh-myoon-uh-**kaysh**-uhn/ *noun*
**1** if there is communication, people talk or write to each other and understand each other: *Communication is hard when people speak different languages.*
**2 communications** ways of sending information between places, using computers, telephones, radios, etc.: *The police department is trying out a new communications system.*

**com·mu·nism** /**kahm**-yuh-niz-uhm/ *noun* a political system in which the government of a country owns all the land and businesses: *Communism ended in Hungary in 1989.*
—**communist** /**kahm**-yuhn-ist/ *noun* someone who believes communism is a good political system
—**communist** /**kahm**-yuhn-ist/ *adjective* supporting or based on communism: *Cuba is a communist country.*

**com·mu·ni·ty** /kuh-**myoon**-uht-ee/ *noun* (plural **communities**)
**1** all of the people who live in the same town or area: *All the children in our community go to the same school.*
**2** a group of people in an area who belong to the same religion, come from the same country,

or do the same activity: *Dallas has a large Jewish community.*

**com·mu·ni·ty col·lege** /kuh-**myoon**-uht-ee kahl-ij/ *noun* a school where people can learn a skill or prepare to go to university. People usually go to a community college for two years: *He is studying chemistry at Bronx Community College.*

**com·mute** /kuh-**myoot**/ *verb* to go in a car, bus, or train every day to get to work: *He commutes to work by car.*
—**commuter** /kuh-**myoot**-ur/ *noun* someone who travels to work each day: *The subway was full of commuters.*

**com·pact** /**kahm**-pakt/
● *adjective* small and designed to use only a little space: *The camera is very compact and fits in your pocket.*
● *noun* an agreement between two or more people or countries: *The governors signed a compact to protect the Great Lakes.*

**com·pact disc** /kahm-pakt **disk**/ *noun* a small round piece of plastic that records and plays music or computer information: *You can copy files from your computer onto a compact disc.*
( SYNONYM: **CD** )

**com·pan·ion** /kuhm-**pan**-yuhn/ *noun* someone you spend a lot of time with: *The dog was the old man's only companion.*

**com·pa·ny** /**kuhmp**-uhn-ee/ *noun* (plural **companies**)
**1** a business organization: *Dad works for a computer company.*
**2** if you have company, there are friends with you at your home: *We're having company for dinner.*
**3** a group of 100 to 200 soldiers: *Two companies returned home from the war.*

IDIOM with **company**
**keep someone company** to stay with you, so you are not alone: *Pedro will be there to keep you company.*

**com·par·a·tive** /kuhm-**parr**-uht-iv/ *noun* the form of an adjective or adverb that you use when saying that someone or something is bigger, better, older, etc. than another thing or person: *The comparative of "good" is "better."*

**com·pare** /kuhm-**pair**/ *verb* to think about how two or more things are different or the same: *If* you compare the two boys, you'll see that Jordan is much taller.

## Word Family: compare

**compare** verb | **comparison** noun |
**comparative** noun

**com·par·i·son** /kuhm-**parr**-uhss-uhn/ *noun* if you make a comparison between two things, you say how you think they are the same or different: *It's hard to make a comparison between the two students because Anna is ten and John is only six.* | *Their house is really big – ours is tiny in comparison.*

**com·part·ment** /kuhm-**part**-muhnt/ *noun* a separate area inside a large container: *There's a compartment in your backpack for your pens.*

**com·pass** /**kuhmp**-uhss/ *noun*

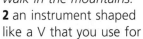
compass

**1** an instrument with a magnetic needle that always points north. You use a compass to see which direction you should go: *Always take a map and compass with you when you walk in the mountains.*
**2** an instrument shaped like a V that you use for drawing circles. It has one sharp point and another part that you attach a pen or pencil to: *Draw a two-inch circle using your compass.*

**com·pas·sion** /kuhm-**pash**-uhn/ *noun* the feeling that you are sorry for someone who is hurt or upset, and you want to help them: *I felt compassion for the people who had lost their homes in the earthquake.*

**com·pas·sion·ate** /kuhm-**pash**-uhn-it/ *adjective* feeling sorry for people who are hurt or upset, and wanting to help them: *My teacher was very compassionate and she offered to help me with my problems.*

**com·pen·sate** /**kahmp**-uhn-sayt/ *verb* to do something so that something bad has a smaller effect, for example to pay someone money: *You will be compensated if your flight is canceled.*

**com·pen·sa·tion** /kahmp-uhn-**saysh**-uhn/ *noun* money that is paid to someone because

something bad has happened to them: *He got compensation after a wall fell down on him.*

**com·pete** /kuhm-**peet**/ *verb* to take part in a race or competition and try to win: *How many runners will be competing in the race?*

## Word Family: compete

**compete** verb | **competition** noun |
**competitor** noun | **competitive** adjective

**com·pe·tent** /**kahmp**-uht-uhnt/ *adjective* having enough skill or knowledge to do something: *If you want to become a competent player, it can take many years of hard work.*
—**competently** /**kahmp**-uht-uhnt-lee/ *adverb* in a way that shows you have skill or knowledge: *The work was done competently.*
—**competence** /**kahmp**-uht-uhnss/ *noun* skill or knowledge: *This test is to find out your competence in English.*

**com·pe·ti·tion** /kahmp-uh-**tish**-uhn/ *noun*
**1** an event in which people or teams try to be the best at doing something: *I entered the spelling competition.* ▶ see **Thesaurus**
**2** if there is competition for something, a lot of people are all trying to get the same thing, but not everyone can get it: *There is a lot of competition for places on the football team.*

**com·pet·i·tive** /kuhm-**pet**-uht-iv/ *adjective*
**1** a competitive person wants to win: *Steve is very competitive. He hates to lose.*
**2** a competitive sport or business is done by people or companies who are all trying hard to be best: *Ice hockey is a very competitive sport and it is difficult to get to the top.*

**com·pet·i·tor** /kuhm-**pet**-uht-ur/ *noun* a person, team, or company that is trying to win against another person, team, or company: *The competitors lined up for the race.* | *Their main competitor is a Japanese company.*

**com·plain** /kuhm-**playn**/ *verb* to say that you are not happy about something: *They complained about the food.* ▶ see **Thesaurus**

**com·plaint** /kuhm-**playnt**/ *noun* something that you say or write when you are not happy about something: *There have been a lot of complaints about the noise.*

**com·plete** /kuhm-**pleet**/
- *adjective*

**1** including everything or everyone: *This is a complete list of all the people in the class.*
( ANTONYM: **incomplete** )
**2** in every way: *The day was a complete disaster – everything went wrong.* ( SYNONYM: **total** )
**3** finished: *When your work is complete, give it to the teacher.* ( ANTONYM: **incomplete** )
- *verb*

to finish doing something: *Have you completed your homework?*

**com·plete·ly** /kuhm-**pleet**-lee/ *adverb* in every way: *I trust you completely.*

**com·plete sen·tence** /kuhm-pleet **sent**-uhnss/ *noun* a sentence that has a subject and a verb and that can be understood without any extra information: *Please answer the questions in complete sentences.*

**com·plex**
- *adjective* /kuhm-**plekss**/ having a lot of different parts and difficult to understand: *The rules of the game are very complex.*
( SYNONYM: **complicated** ) ( ANTONYM: **simple** )
—**complexity** /kuhm-**plekss**-uht-ee/ *noun* the quality of being complex: *The complexity of the problem makes it difficult to deal with.*
- *noun* /kahm-plekss/ a group of buildings or one large building that is used for a purpose: *They're building a new sports complex.*

**com·plex·ion** /kuhm-**plek**-shuhn/ *noun* the color of the skin on your face and the way that it looks: *She has a very dark complexion.*

**com·pli·cate** /**kahmp**-luh-kayt/ *verb* to make something more difficult: *Do not complicate things – keep it simple.*

**com·pli·cat·ed** /**kahmp**-luh-kayt-id/ *adjective* having a lot of different parts, and difficult to understand: *This game is very complicated and there are a lot of rules.* ( SYNONYM: **complex** )
( ANTONYM: **simple** )

**com·pli·ca·tion** /kahmp-luh-**kaysh**-uhn/ *noun* something that makes a situation more difficult: *The illness should go away on its own, with no complications.*

**com·pli·ment**
- *noun* /**kahmp**-luh-muhnt/ something nice that you say to someone about how they look or

what they have done: *Anna is very pretty and gets a lot of compliments.*
- *verb* /**kahmp**-luh-ment/ to say something nice to someone about the way they look or what they have done: *He complimented me on how well I played the guitar.*

**com·pose** /kuhm-**pohz**/ *verb*
**1 be composed of** to be made of two or more things: *Water is composed of hydrogen and oxygen.*
**2** to write a piece of music: *We all had to compose our own song.*
—**composer** /kuhm-**pohz**-ur/ *noun* someone who writes music: *Mozart is a famous composer.*

**com·pos·ite num·ber** /kuhm-pahz-uht **nuhm**-buhr/ *noun* a number that can be divided by another number that is not itself or 1: *9 is a composite number – it can be divided by 3.*

**com·po·si·tion** /kahmp-uh-**zish**-uhn/ *noun*
**1** a piece of music, a poem, or an essay that someone has written: *The song was one of his first compositions.*
**2** the things something is made of: *What is the composition of water?*

**com·post** /**kahm**-pohst/ *noun* a mixture of leaves and plants that are rotting. You put the compost on the soil to make it better for growing new plants.

**com·pound** /**kahm**-pownd/ *noun*
**1** a substance that is made of two or more different substances: *Carbon dioxide is a chemical compound. It is made of carbon and oxygen.*
**2** (also **compound noun** /kahm-pownd **nown**/) two or more words that are used together as a noun that means one thing: *The noun "ice cream" is a compound.*

**com·pound sen·tence** /kahm-pownd **sent**-uhnss/ *noun* a sentence that has two or more shorter sentences in it. The shorter sentences are joined together by a word such as "and" or "but": *"The dog ran away and the boy ran after him" is a compound sentence.*

**com·pound word** /kahm-pownd **wurd**/ *noun* a word made from two or more words that are joined together: *"Fireman" is a compound word.*

**com·pre·hend** /kahmp-ri-**hend**/ *verb* to understand something: *It is difficult to*

comprehend why anyone would want to do such a terrible thing. (SYNONYM: **understand**)
—**comprehension** /kahmp-ri-**hensh**-uhn/ *noun* someone's ability to understand something: *The teacher asked some questions in order to test our reading comprehension.*

**com·pre·hen·sive** /kahmp-ri-**henss**-iv/ *adjective* including everything that is needed: *This is not a comprehensive list – it does not have the names of all the students.*

**com·prise** /kuhm-**prīz**/ *verb* to consist of something: *Each team comprises six players.*

**com·pro·mise** /**kahmp**-ruh-mīz/
● *noun* if two people reach a compromise, they both accept something different from what they wanted at the beginning: *We worked out a compromise – I'll wash the dishes every night, and mom will give me a bigger allowance.*
● *verb* to agree to something that is different from what you wanted at the beginning: *You will both need to compromise if you want to reach an agreement with each other.*

**com·pul·so·ry** /kuhm-**puhlss**-uhr-ee/ *adjective* if something is compulsory, it must be done because of a rule or law: *School is compulsory until you finish 12th grade.*
(SYNONYM: **mandatory**) (ANTONYM: **voluntary**)

**com·put·er** /kuhm-**pyoot**-ur/ *noun* an electronic machine that stores information. You use a computer for writing, finding information, or playing games: *We can play math games on the computer in class.*

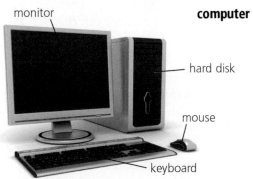

monitor

**computer**

hard disk

mouse

keyboard

**con** /kahn/ *noun* one of the bad things about something that is good in some ways and bad in other ways: *Football has its pros and cons – it's fun to play but it can be dangerous.*
(ANTONYM: **pro**)

**con·ceal** /kuhn-**seel**/ *verb* to hide something: *Was she trying to conceal the truth?*

**con·ceit·ed** /kuhn-**seet**-id/ *adjective* too proud of what you can do or how you look: *He's very conceited and he is always talking about how good he is at sports.*

**con·ceive** /kuhn-**seev**/ *verb*
**1** to become pregnant
**2** to have an idea or think of a plan: *A hundred years ago, people could not conceive of space travel.*

**con·cen·trate** /**kahnss**-uhn-trayt/ *verb* to think very carefully about what you are doing: *You can't concentrate on your homework when the TV is on.*

**con·cen·tra·tion** /kahnss-uhn-**traysh**-uhn/ *noun* the ability to think carefully about what you are doing: *The accident happened after the driver lost his concentration and went on to the other side of the road.*

**con·cept** /**kahn**-sept/ *noun* a general idea about how something is or should be: *The children understand the concept of addition. They know that if you have three beads and add two more beads, you have five beads altogether.*

**con·cern** /kuhn-**surn**/
● *noun*
**1** a feeling of worry about something important: *Her teacher expressed concern about her schoolwork.*
**2** something that you feel worried about: *My main concern is that I pass the test.*
● *verb*
**1** to be about something or someone: *The story concerns a group of friends.*
**2** to involve someone: *Go away – this doesn't concern you.*
**3** to make someone feel worried: *It concerns me that he is always so tired.*

**con·cerned** /kuhn-**surnd**/ *adjective*
**1** worried: *Her parents were concerned about her because she seemed unhappy.*
**2** thinking that something is important: *He's more concerned about sports than about his schoolwork.*
**3** involved in something: *The principal listened to the opinions of everyone concerned.*

a
b
c
d
e
f
g
h
i
j
k
l
m
n
o
p
q
r
s
t
u
v
w
x
y
z

a
b
**c**
d
e
f
g
h
i
j
k
l
m
n
o
p
q
r
s
t
u
v
w
x
y
z

> **IDIOM with concerned**
> **as far as I'm concerned** in my opinion: *As far as I'm concerned, the whole idea is crazy.*

**con·cern·ing** /kuhn-**surn**-ing/ *preposition*
about: *Does anyone have any questions concerning the trip?*

**con·cert** /**kahnss**-urt/ *noun* a performance given by musicians or singers: *We went to a concert last night. | a rock concert*

**con·cise** /kuhn-**sīss**/ *adjective* not containing too many words: *The instructions should be clear and concise.*

**con·clude** /kuhn-**klood**/ *verb*
**1** to decide that something must be true: *When she didn't answer the door, he concluded that she was out of the house.*
**2** to finish something: *I'm afraid we have to conclude our discussion now.*
( SYNONYMS: **finish, end** ) ( ANTONYMS: **begin, start** )
**3** to end: *The book concludes with a chapter on global warming.* ( SYNONYM: **end** )
( ANTONYMS: **begin, start** )

**Word Family:** conclude

**conclude** *verb* | **conclusion** *noun*

**con·clu·sion** /kuhn-**kloozh**-uhn/ *noun*
**1** a decision that something must be true: *I came to the conclusion that she was telling lies.*
**2** the last part of something: *The conclusion of the book starts on page 212.*

**con·crete** /**kahng**-kreet/
● *noun* a substance that is used for making buildings. Concrete is a mixture of a gray powder with sand and water, which becomes hard when it dries: *The bridge is made of concrete and steel.*
● *adjective* real and able to be touched or seen: *A sticker is a concrete reward for behaving well. Praise is a reward too, but the child can show his parents the sticker.* ( ANTONYM: **abstract** )

**con·cus·sion** /kuhn-**kuhsh**-uhn/ *noun* a small injury to the brain, caused by hitting your head: *One player had a concussion after being knocked over.*

**con·demn** /kuhn-**dem**/ *verb*
**1** to say very strongly that you do not approve of someone or something: *We condemn all kinds of violence.*
**2** to give someone a severe punishment: *The criminal was condemned to life in prison.*

**con·den·sa·tion** /kahnd-uhn-**saysh**-uhn/ *noun* small drops of water that appear on a cold surface when warm air touches it: *There was a lot of condensation on the window, which made it difficult to see out.*

**con·dense** /kuhn-**denss**/ *verb*
**1** to make a speech or piece of writing shorter: *Can you condense the paragraph into one sentence?*
**2** if gas or wet air condenses, it becomes a liquid as it becomes cooler: *The steam condenses on the glass.*
**3** to make a liquid thicker by removing some water: *condensed soup*

**con·de·scend·ing** /kahn-di-**send**-ing/ *adjective* showing that you think you are better than someone else: *His big sister told him in a condescending tone that he was wrong.*

**con·di·tion** /kuhn-**dish**-uhn/ *noun*
**1** the state of something: *The car is in very good condition.*
**2** **conditions** the situation in which someone lives, or in which something happens: *The living conditions are better in the U.S. than in many other countries.*
**3** a medical problem that you have for a long time: *My father has a heart condition and he has to take a lot of pills every day.*
**4** something that you must agree to or that must happen before you can do something: *You can have a dog on one condition: that you take it for a walk every day.*

**con·di·tion·er** /kuhn-**dish**-uhn-ur/ *noun* a thick liquid that you can put on your hair when you wash it. Conditioner makes your hair softer and easier to comb: *Do you use conditioner as well as shampoo?*

**con·do·min·i·um** /kahnd-uh-**min**-ee-uhm/ (also **con·do** /**kahnd**-oh/) *noun*
**1** a building with a number of apartments owned by different people
**2** an apartment in a building like this

**con·duct**
● *verb* /kuhn-**duhkt**/
**1** to do something in an organized way: *The*

police are conducting an investigation into the accident.
**2** if something conducts electricity or heat, it allows electricity or heat to go through it: *Gold conducts electricity better than most other metals.*
**3** to stand in front of an orchestra and show the musicians when and how they should play: *He conducts the orchestra by waving a small stick.*
● *noun* /**kahnd**-uhkt/
the way someone behaves: *Her conduct has been very bad.* ( SYNONYM: **behavior** )

**con·duc·tiv·i·ty** /kahnd-uhk-**tiv**-uht-ee/ *noun*
how easily electricity or heat goes through a particular substance: *We did experiments to test the conductivity of different materials.*

**con·duc·tor** /kuhn-**duhkt**-ur/ *noun*
**1** a person who sells and checks tickets on a train
**2** someone who conducts the musicians in an orchestra
**3** a substance that allows electricity or heat to go through it: *Metal is a good conductor of heat.*

**cone** /kohn/ *noun*
**1** an object that is round at one end and pointed at the other: *an ice cream cone* ▶ see picture at **ice cream cone**
**2** the hard brown fruit of a pine or fir tree, which has the seed in it

cone

**Con·fed·er·a·cy** /kuhn-**fed**-uhr-uhss-ee/ *noun* the southern states of the U.S. that fought against northern states in the Civil War: *Four more states joined the Confederacy after the war started.*

**Con·fed·er·ate** /kuhn-**fed**-uhr-it/
● *adjective* belonging or relating to the Confederacy: *the Confederate army*
● *noun* a Confederate soldier ▶ see picture at **soldier**

**con·ference** /**kahn**-fruhnss/ *noun*
**1** an event where people can listen to talks and discuss ideas: *She is giving a talk at a conference on cancer research.*
**2** a meeting at which a small group of people discuss something: *a parent–teacher conference*

**con·fess** /kuhn-**fess**/ *verb* to tell someone that you have done something wrong: *I confessed that I had broken the bowl.* | *He has confessed to the robbery.*

**con·fes·sion** /kuhn-**fesh**-uhn/ *noun* a statement that you have done something wrong: *He made a full confession at the police station.*

**con·fi·dence** /**kahn**-fuhd-uhnss/ *noun*
**1** the feeling that you are able to do something well: *If you practice your speech at home, it will give you more confidence.*
**2** the feeling that you can trust someone or something to be good: *I have confidence in the team and I'm sure that they can win.*

IDIOM with **confidence**
**in confidence** if you tell someone something in confidence, you do not want him or her to tell anyone else

**Word Family: confidence**
**confidence** *noun* | **confidential** *adjective* | **confidentially** *adverb*

**con·fi·dent** /**kahn**-fuhd-uhnt/ *adjective*
**1** believing that you can do something well: *You will feel more confident about riding when you have been on a horse a few times.*
**2** sure that something will happen: *I am confident that we can succeed.*
—**confidently** /**kahn**-fuhd-uhnt-lee/ *adverb* in a confident way: *She walked confidently up onto the stage.*

**con·fi·den·tial** /kahn-fuh-**densh**-uhl/ *adjective* if information is confidential, you must not show it or talk about it to other people: *The letter from the doctor was marked "Confidential."*
—**confidentially** /kahn-fuh-**densh**-uhl-ee/ *adverb* in a way that you must not talk about to other people: *I'm telling you this confidentially.*

**con·firm** /kuhn-**furm**/ *verb* to say or show that something is definitely true: *Sarah has confirmed that she will come to the wedding.*

**Word Family: confirm**
**confirm** *verb* | **confirmation** *noun*

**con·fir·ma·tion** /kahn-fur-**maysh**-uhn/ *noun* something that says or shows that something is definitely true: *We are waiting for confirmation of this news.*

**con·fis·cate** /**kahn**-fuh-skayt/ *verb* to take away something that belongs to you because you should not have it: *The teacher confiscated my cell phone because I was using it in class.*

**con·flict**

● *noun* /**kahn**-flikt/

**1** a serious disagreement about something: *He's a very gentle person and he always tries to avoid conflict.*

**2** a war or a period of fighting: *Many people died in the conflict.*

● *verb* /kuhn-**flikt**/

if two ideas or statements conflict, they are completely different: *The two boys' stories conflicted with each other, and we didn't know which one to believe.*

**con·form** /kuhn-**form**/ *verb* to behave in the way that most people behave: *There's a lot of pressure on kids to conform.*

**con·front** /kuhn-**fruhnt**/ *verb*

**1** to speak to someone strongly about something serious and bad: *His father confronted him about his stealing.*

**2** to think about and try to deal with a difficult feeling or situation: *It is best to confront your fears rather than pretending you're not scared.*

**con·fron·ta·tion** /kahn-fruhn-**taysh**-uhn/ *noun* an angry argument or fight: *He tried to avoid confrontations with his parents.*

**con·fuse** /kuhn-**fyooz**/ *verb*

**1** to make you feel that you do not know what to do: *Don't give him too many things to do – you will only confuse him.*

**2** to think incorrectly that a person or thing is someone or something else: *I always confuse him with his brother because they look so similar.*

—**confusing** /kuhn-**fyooz**-ing/ *adjective* making you feel confused: *The map was confusing because it wasn't clear which direction was north.*

**Word Family: confuse**

**confuse** *verb* | **confusion** *noun* | **confusing** *adjective* | **confused** *adjective*

**con·fused** /kuhn-**fyoozd**/ *adjective* if you are confused, you do not know what to do: *I got confused when I read the directions and turned left instead of right.*

▶ see **Thesaurus**

**con·fu·sion** /kuhn-**fyoozh**-uhn/ *noun* the feeling that you do not know what to do: *The changes at school have caused a lot of confusion.*

**con·grat·u·late** /kuhn-**grach**-uh-layt/ *verb* to tell someone that you are pleased about something good that he or she has done: *The principal congratulated the softball team on their win.*

**con·grat·u·la·tions** /kuhn-grach-uh-**laysh**-uhnz/ *interjection* used when congratulating someone: *Congratulations! I hear you passed your test.*

**con·gre·ga·tion** /kahng-gruh-**gaysh**-uhn/ *noun* the people who are in a church for a religious ceremony: *The congregation started praying.*

**Con·gress** /**kahng**-griss/ *noun* the group of people that make laws in the U.S. The Congress consists of the Senate and the House of Representatives.

**con·gress·man** /**kahng**-griss-muhn/ *noun* (plural **congressmen** /**kahng**-griss-muhn/) a man who is a member of the House of Representatives

**con·gress·wom·an** /**kahng**-griss-wum-uhn/ *noun* (plural **congresswomen** /**kahng**-griss-wim-in/) a woman who is a member of the House of Representatives

**con·gru·ent** /kuhng-**groo**-uhnt/ *adjective* congruent triangles are the same size and shape

**co·nif·e·rous** /kuh-**nif**-uhr-uhss/ *adjective* coniferous trees have leaves that look like needles. They do not lose their leaves in winter, and produce cones containing their seeds.

ANTONYM: **deciduous**

**con·junc·tion** /kuhn-**juhngk**-shuhn/ *noun* a word such as "but," "and," or "while" that connects parts of sentences

IDIOM with **conjunction**

**in conjunction with** together with someone or something else: *The school is working in conjunction with sports clubs to provide more opportunities for students to play sports.*

**con·nect** /kuh-**nekt**/ *verb*
**1** to join one thing to another: *You can connect a speaker to your MP3 player.* | *I'm having trouble connecting to the Internet.*
( ANTONYM: **disconnect** )
**2** to think that things are related: *I didn't connect the two events.*

**con·nect·ed** /kuh-**nekt**-id/ *adjective*
**1** if two things or events are connected, there is some kind of relationship between them: *The students all became sick at the same time and the doctors think that these cases are connected with each other.* ( SYNONYM: **related** )
**2** joined: *Make sure the printer is connected to your computer.*

**con·nec·tion** /kuh-**nek**-shuhn/ *noun*
**1** a relationship between things: *There is a connection between smoking and heart disease.*
**2** the state of being joined to something electrical: *How much do you pay for your Internet connection?*
**3** another airplane, bus, or train that people can change to in order to continue their trip quickly: *The plane was late and we missed our connection at the airport.*

**con·quer** /**kahng**-kur/ *verb* to defeat a group of people in a war and take their land: *The Romans conquered most of Europe and established the Roman Empire.*
—**conqueror** /**kahng**-kuhr-ur/ *noun* a leader or nation that conquers a place

**con·quest** /**kahng**-kwest/ *noun* the defeat and control of a country or group of people: *The Roman conquest of Britain began in 43 A.D.*

**con·quis·ta·dor** /kahn-**keest**-uh-dor/ *noun* one of the Spanish people who conquered Mexico and Peru in the 1500s

**con·science** /**kahnsh**-uhnss/ *noun* the feeling inside you that tells you whether it is right or wrong to do something: *I had a clear conscience because I knew I had done the right thing.*

**con·sci·en·tious** /kahnsh-ee-**ensh**-uhss/ *adjective* careful to do everything that you have been asked to do in the correct way: *She is a very conscientious student and she always hands in her assignments on time.*
—**conscientiously** /kahnsh-ee-**ensh**-uhss-lee/ *adverb* in a conscientious way

**con·scious** /**kahnsh**-uhss/ *adjective*
**1** awake and able to understand what is happening: *Two hours after her surgery she was conscious and feeling fine.*
( ANTONYM: **unconscious** )
**2** if you are conscious about something, you know about it and this affects what you decide to do: *Teenagers are very conscious about fashion and they like to wear all the latest clothes.* ( SYNONYM: **aware** )

**Word Family: conscious**

**conscious** *adjective* | **unconscious** *adjective* | **consciously** *adverb* | **unconsciously** *adverb* | **consciousness** *noun* | **unconsciousness** *noun*

**con·scious·ly** /**kahnsh**-uhss-lee/ *adverb* deliberately: *I consciously tried not to look at him.*

**con·scious·ness** /**kahnsh**-uhss-niss/ *noun* the state of being awake and able to understand what is happening: *I lost consciousness for a few seconds when I hit my head.*

**con·sent** /kuhn-**sent**/
● *noun* permission to do something: *You need to have your parents' consent to get medical treatment.*
● *verb* to say that you will allow something to be done: *He hadn't consented to being filmed.*

**con·se·quence** /**kahnss**-uh-kwenss/ *noun* something that happens as a result of an action: *She never thinks about the consequences of her actions.*

**Word Family: consequence**

**consequence** *noun* | **consequently** *adverb*

**con·se·quent·ly** /**kahnss**-uh-kwent-lee/ *adverb* as a result of something: *He didn't study and consequently failed the test.*

**con·ser·va·tion** /kahnss-ur-**vaysh**-uhn/ *noun*
**1** the activity of protecting wild plants and animals: *Conservation groups campaigned to save the trees.*
**2** the activity of using energy, water, or fuel carefully without wasting any: *This area does not get a lot of rain and water conservation is very important.*

a b c d e f g h i j k l m n o p q r s t u v w x y z

**con·serv·a·tive** /kuhn-**surv**-uht-iv/ *adjective*
**1** believing that the government should not make too many laws and that society should not change too much: *He is conservative, and always votes Republican.* ( SYNONYM: **right-wing** )
**2** not wanting to change what you do because you prefer traditional things: *Old people are often very conservative and they don't like to try eating new foods.*

**con·serve** /kuhn-**surv**/ *verb*
**1** to protect wild plants and animals and stop them from being destroyed: *We must do everything we can to conserve wildlife.*
**2** to use energy, water, or fuel carefully and not waste it: *You can turn your refrigerator down to conserve energy.*

**con·sid·er** /kuhn-**sid**-ur/ *verb*
**1** to think about something carefully: *She is considering buying a new car.*
**2** to have an opinion about something or someone: *I consider myself to be a pretty good singer.*

**con·sid·er·a·ble** /kuhn-**sid**-uhr-uhb-uhl/ *adjective* a considerable amount is a lot: *We could save a considerable amount of money by doing it this way.*

**con·sid·er·a·bly** /kuhn-**sid**-uhr-uhb-lee/ *adverb* a lot: *He is considerably older than his wife.*

**con·sid·er·ate** /kuhn-**sid**-uhr-it/ *adjective* a considerate person thinks about what other people feel or need: *It was considerate of them to keep quiet while I was trying to sleep.*
( ANTONYM: **inconsiderate** )
—**considerately** /kuhn-**sid**-uhr-it-lee/ *adverb* in a way that shows someone is thinking about what other people feel or need: *"Would you like me to carry your bag?" he asked considerately.*

**con·sid·e·ra·tion** /kuhn-sid-uh-**raysh**-uhn/ *noun*
**1** careful thought about something: *His suggestion deserves serious consideration.*
**2** one of the things you think about when trying to make a decision: *The cost is an important consideration.*

**con·sid·er·ing** /kuhn-**sid**-uhr-ing/ *preposition, conjunction* used when mentioning something that has an important effect on what you have just said: *You've done really well, considering that you had nobody to help you.*

**con·sist** /kuhn-**sist**/ *verb* **consist of** to be formed of something: *The school consists of two buildings.*

**con·sis·ten·cy** /kuhn-**sist**-uhnss-ee/ *noun*
**1** the ability to always do something in the same way, or to always do something well: *There were doubts about the team's consistency last year and they lost a lot of games.*
**2** how thick, smooth, or sticky a substance is: *The sauce should have a smooth consistency.*

**con·sist·ent** /kuhn-**sist**-uhnt/ *adjective*
**1** always doing something in the same way or always doing something well: *He is very consistent and he has scored a home run in every game this season.* ( ANTONYM: **inconsistent** )
**2** the same as something else: *The result of this experiment is consistent with our previous results.*
—**consistently** /kuhn-**sist**-uhnt-lee/ *adverb* in a consistent way: *You consistently spell this word wrong.*

**con·sole** /kuhn-**sohl**/ *verb* to help someone to feel less sad: *When he lost his dog, his mother tried to console him by saying that they would get another one.*

**con·so·nant** /**kahnss**-uhn-uhnt/ *noun* a letter such as b, c, or d, that is not a vowel: *The word "bird" begins and ends with a consonant.*

**con·spic·u·ous** /kuhn-**spik**-yoo-uhss/ *adjective* very easy to notice: *I felt very conspicuous in my yellow coat.*

**con·spir·a·cy** /kuhn-**spirr**-uhss-ee/ *noun* (plural **conspiracies**) a secret plan between a group of people to do something bad: *Four people were involved in the conspiracy to steal the money.*

**con·stant** /**kahnst**-uhnt/ *adjective*
**1** happening all the time: *After the accident, he was in constant pain.*
**2** staying at the same level: *The fish need the water to be kept at a constant temperature.*
—**constantly** /**kahnst**-uhnt-lee/ *adverb* all the time: *He and his brother argue constantly.*

**con·stel·la·tion** /kahnst-uh-**laysh**-uhn/ *noun* a group of stars that form a pattern in the sky and have a name: *The Big Dipper is a constellation that consists of seven stars in the shape of a big ladle.*

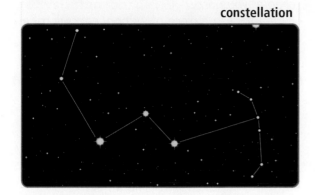

**constellation**

**con·sti·pa·tion** /kahnst-uh-**paysh**-uhn/ *noun* if you have constipation, it is difficult for you to make solid waste leave your body: *Eating fruit helps to prevent constipation.*
—**constipated** /**kahnst**-uh-payt-id/ *adjective* having constipation: *If you're constipated, you should eat more fiber.*

**con·sti·tute** /**kahnst**-uh-toot/ *verb* to form part of something: *Women constitute 51% of the population.*

**con·sti·tu·tion** /kahnst-uh-**toosh**-uhn/ *noun* a document that describes the set of basic laws and ideas in a country. The constitution says which rights the people should have and which powers the government should have: *The U.S. Constitution says that everyone should have the right to free speech.*
—**constitutional** /kahnst-uh-**toosh**-uhn-uhl/ *adjective* relating to a constitution: *the constitutional rights of the people*

**con·struct** /kuhn-**struhkt**/ *verb* to build something: *We constructed a table out of pieces of old wood.*

**Word Family:** construct

**construct** *verb* | **construction** *noun*

**con·struc·tion** /kuhn-**struhk**-shuhn/ *noun* the process of building something: *A new library is now under construction.*

**con·sult** /kuhn-**suhlt**/ *verb* to ask someone for advice or information: *You should consult your doctor before you start a diet.*
—**consultation** /kahnss-uhl-**taysh**-uhn/ *noun* a discussion that you have to get advice or information: *The rules were changed after consultation with teachers and students.*

**Word Family:** consult

**consult** *verb* | **consultation** *noun* | **consultant** *noun*

**con·sult·ant** /kuhn-**suhlt**-uhnt/ *noun* someone whose job is to give advice about something: *A financial consultant gives people advice about what to do with their money.*

**con·sume** /kuhn-**soom**/ *verb*
**1** to use something such as energy, fuel, or electricity: *The U.S. consumes more energy than any other country in the world.*
**2** to eat or drink something: *Penguins consume a lot of fish.*

**con·sum·er** /kuhn-**soom**-ur/ *noun* anyone who buys things or uses services: *Consumers always want prices to be as low as possible.*

**con·sump·tion** /kuhn-**suhmp**-shuhn/ *noun*
**1** the amount of fuel or electricity that something uses: *Turn the air conditioning down to reduce your energy consumption.*
**2** the amount of something that someone eats or drinks: *If he wants to lose weight, he needs to reduce his consumption of fatty foods.*

**con·tact** /**kahn**-takt/
● *verb*
to telephone or write to someone: *You can contact me at this number.*
● *noun*
**1** if you have contact with someone, you sometimes see them, speak to them, or write to them: *He doesn't have much contact with his grandparents.*
**2** if things are in contact, they are touching each other: *If the two wires come into contact, they could cause a fire.*

**con·tact lens** /**kahn**-takt lenz/ *noun* a thin round piece of plastic you put on your eye to help you see clearly: *I used to wear glasses but now I wear contact lenses.*

**con·ta·gious** /kuhn-**tayj**-uhss/ *adjective* if a disease is contagious, you can easily catch it from another person: *Measles is highly contagious so, if you get it, you should stay home.*

a b **c** d e f g h i j k l m n o p q r s t u v w x y z

**con·tain** /kuhn-**tayn**/ *verb*
**1** to have something inside: *The purse contained a lot of money.*
**2** to include something: *The movie contains some scary scenes.*

**con·tain·er** /kuhn-**tayn**-ur/ *noun* something that you keep things in: *The toys are in a plastic container.*

**con·tam·i·nated** /kuhn-**tam**-uh-nayt-id/ *adjective* if something is contaminated, it contains dirty or dangerous substances and you should not use it: *The water is contaminated, so you must not drink it.*
—**contaminate** /kuhn-**tam**-uh-nayt/ *verb* to make something dirty or harmful: *Flies carry disease and can contaminate food.*
—**contamination** /kuhn-tam-uh-**naysh**-uhn/ *noun* the act of contaminating something: *Pollution can lead to the contamination of land.*

**con·tem·po·ra·ry** /kuhn-**temp**-uh-rair-ee/
● *adjective* modern: *The museum has a show of contemporary art.*
● *noun* (plural **contemporaries**) someone who lives at the same time as another person: *He had very different ideas from his contemporaries.*

**con·tempt** /kuhn-**tempt**/ *noun* a complete lack of respect for someone or something: *He treated his wife with contempt and ignored everything that she said.*
—**contemptuous** /kuhn-**temp**-choo-uhss/ *adjective* showing contempt: *The clerk gave me a contemptuous look.*

**con·tend** /kuhn-**tend**/ *verb* to compete to get something: *Eight teams are contending for the championship.*
—**contender** /kuhn-**tend**-ur/ *noun* someone who is competing to get something: *She's a strong contender to win the race and she could easily win.*

**con·tent**
● *adjective* /kuhn-**tent**/
happy with a situation: *He was content to let his brother have the best room.*
● *noun* /**kahn**-tent/
**1** **contents** the things inside a container: *She emptied the contents of the bag onto the table.*
**2** **contents** a list at the front of a book that says what is in it: *Look in the contents to find the*
chapter you need.
**3** the things in a piece of writing, a movie, or a television program: *The content of the program is not suitable for young children.*

**con·tent·ed** /kuhn-**tent**-id/ *adjective* happy and not wanting anything else: *He fell asleep immediately, like a contented baby.*
—**contentedly** /kuhn-**tent**-id-lee/ *adverb* in a contented way: *The cat was purring contentedly.*
—**contentment** /kuhn-**tent**-muhnt/ *noun* happiness and satisfaction: *His children brought him contentment.*

**con·test** /**kahn**-test/ *noun* a competition: *He entered a poetry contest and won first prize.*

**con·test·ant** /kuhn-**test**-uhnt/ *noun* someone who takes part in a contest: *Contestants on the game show can win a lot of money.*

**con·text** /**kahn**-tekst/ *noun*
**1** the words before and after a word or sentence: *You need to study the context, if you want to understand the meaning of a word.*
**2** the situation in which something happens: *The book explains the context behind the Pilgrims' decision to leave England: they wanted to worship God in their own way.*

**con·ti·nent** /**kahnt**-uhn-uhnt/ *noun* one of the seven large areas of land on the Earth. They are North America, South America, Europe, Africa, Asia, Australia, and Antarctica.
—**continental** /kahnt-uh-**nent**'l/ *adjective* relating to a continent, but not its islands: *A map of the continental United States does not include Hawaii.*

**con·tin·u·al** /kuhn-**tin**-yoo-uhl/ *adjective* happening a lot or all the time: *After two days of continual rain, the streets were flooded.*
—**continually** /kuhn-**tin**-yoo-uhl-ee/ *adverb* a lot or all the time: *She shouts at me continually.*

**con·tin·ue** /kuhn-**tin**-yoo/ *verb*
**1** to not stop: *Although we were tired, we continued working.* ▶ see **Thesaurus**
**2** to start again after stopping for a little time: *He picked up the book and continued reading.*
—**continuation** /kuhn-tin-yoo-**aysh**-uhn/ *noun* an act of continuing something: *We do not want a continuation of the war.*

**Word Family: continue**

continue *verb* | **continuation** *noun* | **continuity** *noun* | **continual** *adjective* | **continuous** *adjective* | **continuously** *adverb*

**con·tin·u·i·ty** /kahnt-uh-**noo**-uht-ee/ *noun* a situation in which something continues without stopping or changing: *Our traditions give us a sense of continuity.*

**con·tin·u·ous** /kuhn-**tin**-yoo-uhss/ *adjective* happening without stopping: *Learning is a continuous process.*
—**continuously** /kuhn-**tin**-yoo-uhss-lee/ *adverb* without stopping: *It rained continuously for two days.*

**con·tour** /**kahn**-toor/ *noun*
**1** the curved lines that form the shape of something: *The clothes are designed to fit the contours of your body.*
**2** a line on a map that shows places of the same height: *If you look at the contours on the map, you can see where the highest points are.*

**contra-** /kahn-truh/, **contro-** /kahn-troh/

**Word Building**

**contradict** | **controversy** | **contrary**
These words all have the Latin word root **contra-** in them. **Contra-** means "against" or "opposite." If you *contradict* someone, you say the opposite of what someone else says about the same thing. A *controversy* is a subject that people often have opposite opinions about. *Contrary* is used when the opposite of something is true.

**con·tract**
● *noun* /**kahn**-trakt/
a legal agreement: *The band signed a contract with a record company.*
● *verb* /kuhn-**trakt**/
**1** to get a serious disease: *She contracted the disease when she was bitten by a dog.*
**2** to become smaller: *The hot metal contracts when it becomes cooler.* (ANTONYM: **expand**)

**con·trac·tion** /kuhn-**trak**-shuhn/ *noun* a short form of a word or words: *"Don't" is a contraction of "do not."*

**continent**

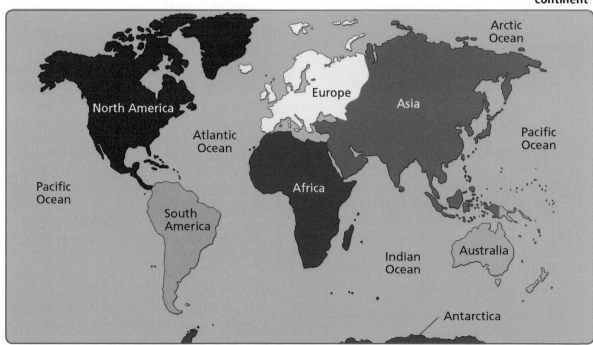

### con·tra·dict /kahn-truh-**dikt**/ *verb*
**1** to say that what someone has just said is wrong: *My sister always contradicts everything I say.*
**2** to be very different from what someone else has said: *Andy's description of the fight contradicted Matt's.*
—**contradiction** /kahn-truh-**dik**-shuhn/ *noun* a difference between two statements that means they cannot both be true: *There were contradictions between the two boys' descriptions. One said the man had brown hair and the other said he had blond hair.*
—**contradictory** /kahn-truh-**dikt**-uhr-ee/ *adjective* contradictory statements are different and cannot both be true: *There is contradictory information about the safety of nuclear power.*

### con·tra·ry /**kahn**-trair-ee/ *noun, adjective*

**IDIOMS with contrary**
**on the contrary** used when saying that the opposite of something is true: *"Was he disappointed?" "On the contrary, he was really pleased."*
**contrary to** the opposite of something such as an idea or statement: *Contrary to what most people think, a little fat is good for you.*

### con·trast
● *noun* /**kahn**-trast/
a big difference between people or things: *There was a big contrast between city life and life on the farm.*
● *verb* /kuhn-**trast**/
**1** if two things contrast, they are very different: *Her yellow top contrasts with her green skirt.*
**2** to show how two things are different: *In science, we compared and contrasted two leaves.*

### con·trib·ute /kuhn-**trib**-yoot/ *verb*
**1** to give money or help for something: *Parents contribute money to buy computers for the school.*
**2** to take part in a class or discussion by saying something: *She contributes a lot in class and she is always the first one to answer the teacher's questions.*
—**contributor** /kuhn-**trib**-yuht-ur/ *noun* someone who gives money or help for something

**Word Family: contribute**
**contribute** *verb* | **contribution** *noun* | **contributor** *noun*

### con·tri·bu·tion /kahn-truh-**byoosh**-uhn/ *noun*
**1** money that you give to help pay for something: *Would you like to make a contribution to buy the coach a present?*
**2** something you do that helps something be successful: *He makes a big contribution to the team.*

### con·trol /kuhn-**trohl**/
● *verb* (**controlling**, **controlled**)
to make someone or something do what you want: *You need to be able to control your dog and you shouldn't let him run in the street.*
● *noun*
**1** the ability to make someone or something do what you want: *My teacher has good control over the class and the students are always well behaved.*
**2** the ability to stay calm when you are angry or upset: *I just lost control and started yelling.*
**3** controls the things that you move to make an airplane, car, or machine work: *He showed me how to operate the controls of the plane.*

**IDIOMS with control**
**out of control** if something is out of control, you cannot make it do what you want: *The car went out of control and hit a tree.*
**under control** happening in the way that you want: *Don't worry – everything is under control.*

### con·tro·ver·sy /**kahn**-truh-vurss-ee/ *noun* (plural **controversies**) a lot of disagreement among people: *The decision to close the school caused a lot of controversy and many people said they wanted it to stay open.*
—**controversial** /kahn-truh-**vursh**-uhl/ *adjective* causing disagreement among people: *Politics is a controversial subject.*

### con·vec·tion /kuhn-**vek**-shuhn/ *noun* movement of a gas or liquid that happens because different parts of it are at different temperatures: *Warm air rises by convection.*

**con·ven·ience** /kuhn-**veen**-yuhnss/ *noun*
**1** the quality of being easy or quick to use: *People like the convenience of shopping online.*
( ANTONYM: **inconvenience** )
**2** something that is useful and makes your life easier: *We wouldn't want to give up modern conveniences such as washing machines and refrigerators.*

**con·ven·ience store** /kuhn-**veen**-yuhnss stor/ *noun* a small store where you buy food, newspapers, and other everyday things: *Many convenience stores are open 24 hours each day.*

**con·ven·ient** /kuhn-**veen**-yuhnt/ *adjective*
**1** easy to use or get to: *The park is near both our homes, so it is a convenient place to meet.* ( ANTONYM: **inconvenient** )
**2** a convenient time is good for you to do something because you are not busy then: *"Is tomorrow morning convenient?" "Yes, that's fine."* ( ANTONYM: **inconvenient** )

**con·ven·tion** /kuhn-**vensh**-uhn/ *noun* a large meeting of people who are members of the same group: *She gave a speech to the Republican National Convention.*

**con·ver·sa·tion** /kahn-vur-**saysh**-uhn/ *noun* a talk between two or more people: *We had a long conversation about our favorite movies.*

**con·verse** /kuhn-**vurss**/ *verb* to have a conversation with someone: *She usually conversed with her mother by phone.*
( SYNONYM: **talk** )

**con·verse·ly** /kuhn-**vurss**-lee/ *adverb* used when mentioning the opposite of something: *Which is your best subject at your school, and conversely which is your worst?*

**con·vert** /kuhn-**vurt**/ *verb*
**1** to change something into something else: *Dad wants to convert the spare bedroom into an office.*
**2** to change your religion: *She was a Christian before she converted to Islam.*
—**conversion** /kuhn-**vurzh**-uhn/ *noun* the act of converting: *His conversion to Judaism took place after he married a Jewish woman.*

**con·ver·ti·ble** /kuhn-**vurt**-uhb-uhl/ *noun* a car with a roof that you can fold back or take off

**convertible**

**con·vey** /kuhn-**vay**/ *verb* to give information or show what you mean: *You can convey ideas with a picture as well as with words.*

**con·vict**
● *verb* /kuhn-**vikt**/ to decide that someone is guilty of a crime in a court of law: *He was convicted of stealing from a store.*
● *noun* /**kahn**-vikt/ a criminal who has been sent to prison: *The police are looking for a convict who has escaped from prison.*

**con·vic·tion** /kuhn-**vik**-shuhn/ *noun*
**1** a strong belief: *He recycles paper and cans because of his convictions about taking care of the Earth.*
**2** a decision made in a court of law that someone is guilty of a crime: *The man has several convictions for burglary.*

**con·vince** /kuhn-**vinss**/ *verb*
**1** to make someone believe something: *She convinced me that she was telling the truth.*
**2** to persuade someone to do something: *We convinced dad to exercise more.*
—**convincing** /kuhn-**vinss**-ing/ *adjective* making you believe that something is true: *I tried to think of a convincing excuse for being late.*

**con·vinced** /kuhn-**vinst**/ *adjective* certain that something is true: *I am convinced that we will win the game.* ( SYNONYM: **sure** )

**con·voy** /**kahn**-voy/ *noun* a group of trucks, cars, or ships that are traveling together: *A convoy of military trucks drove into town.*

**cook** /kuk/
- *verb* to make food ready to eat by cutting, mixing, and heating it: *I'm cooking dinner for my family this evening.* ▶ see **Thesaurus**
- *noun* someone who makes food ready to eat: *My mom is a good cook.*

cook

boil

roast

fry

steam

**cook·book** /**kuk**-buk/ *noun* a book that tells you how to make different foods: *I got this pasta recipe from an Italian cookbook.*

**cook·ie** /**kuk**-ee/ *noun* a flat sweet food that is baked in an oven: *She's making chocolate chip cookies.*

**cook·ing** /**kuk**-ing/ *noun* the activity of making food ready to eat: *The kids are doing the cooking tonight.*

**cool** /kool/
- *adjective*
**1** used to show that you like or admire someone or something: *I like Sam – he's cool.*
**2** acceptable to you: *"Is it OK if I sit here?" "Yeah, that's cool."* ( SYNONYMS: **OK, fine** )
**3** a little cold: *There was a nice cool breeze.*
**4** calm: *I stayed cool and I didn't get angry with her.*
- *verb*
to become colder: *Take the cake out of the oven and let it cool. | We ran into the ocean to cool off.*
- *noun*

IDIOMS with **cool**
**keep your cool** to stay calm in a difficult situation: *She kept her cool and in the end she won.*
**lose your cool** to become angry or upset in a difficult situation: *He lost his cool and started yelling.*

**cool·er** /**kool**-ur/ *noun* a box in which you can keep food or drinks cool

**co·op·er·ate** /koh-**ahp**-uh-rayt/ *verb* to work with someone else or do as they ask: *If we all cooperate, we can get this done faster.*

**Word Family:** cooperate

**cooperate** *verb* | **cooperation** *noun* | **cooperative** *adjective*

**co·op·er·a·tion** /koh-ahp-uh-**raysh**-uhn/ *noun* if you give someone your cooperation, you work with them or do as they ask: *Teachers depend on the cooperation of students in class.*

**co·op·er·a·tive** /koh-**ahpr**-uht-iv/ *adjective* if you are cooperative, you do as you are asked: *She was very cooperative and answered all my questions.*

**co·or·di·nate**
- *verb* /koh-**ord**'n-ayt/ to organize something that involves a lot of people: *Mrs. Walker will be coordinating all the events.*
- *noun* /koh-**ord**'n-it/ one of a set of numbers that tell you exactly where something is on a map or graph: *We have the coordinates of the place where the money is buried.*

**Word Family:** coordinate

**coordinate** *verb, noun* | **coordination** *noun* | **coordinated** *adjective*

**co·or·di·na·tion** /koh-ord'n-**aysh**-uhn/ *noun*
**1** the ability to use the different parts of your body together well: *I'm no good at sports because my coordination is terrible.*
**2** the organizing of something complicated: *She is involved in the coordination of the school music festival.*
—**coordinated** /koh-**ord**'n-ayt-id/ *adjective* able to use the different parts of your body together well: *Very young children aren't coordinated enough to catch a ball.*

**cop** /kahp/ *noun* a police officer: *If you come here again, I'll call the cops!*

**cope** /kohp/ *verb* to deal successfully with a difficult situation: *I don't know how she copes with all the housework.*

**cop·i·er** /**kahp**-ee-ur/ *noun* a machine for copying pieces of writing or pictures
( SYNONYM: **photocopier** )

**cop·per** /**kahp**-ur/ *noun* an orange-brown metal that allows heat and electricity to pass through it easily: *Electrical wires are often made of copper.*

**cop·y** /**kahp**-ee/
● *verb* (**copies, copying, copied**)
**1** to make something that is the same as something else: *Copy this picture of a dinosaur.* | *The computer copies the file into a new folder.*
**2** to deliberately do what someone else has done: *He copies everything his brother does.*
● *noun* (plural **copies**)
**1** something that is made to look exactly the same as something else: *This is a copy of a famous painting.* ▶ see **Thesaurus**
**2** one of many books, magazines, or newspapers that are exactly the same: *We both have a copy of the book.*

**cor·al** /**kor**-uhl/ *noun*
**1** a small sea creature that lives in groups in warm ocean water. When the coral dies, it forms a hard substance that is sometimes used for making jewelry: *She was wearing a coral necklace.*
**2** **coral reef** a line of coral and other material that has become like a rock: *There were lots of beautiful fish swimming around the coral reef.*

coral

**cord** /kord/ *noun*
**1** a piece of wire covered with plastic, used for connecting electrical equipment: *Make sure that the phone cord is connected to the wall.*
**2** thin rope: *They tied the wood together with cord.*

**cor·du·roy** /**kord**-uh-roy/ *noun* cloth with big soft lines along it: *brown corduroy pants*

**core** /kor/
● *noun*
**1** the most important part of something: *We need to get to the core of the problem.*
**2** the hard part in the center of an apple or pear: *Stella threw the apple core away.* ▶ see picture at **apple**
**3** the central part of the Earth: *The Earth's core is very hot.* ▶ see picture at **earth**
● *adjective*
most important and basic: *You have to take four core classes.*

**cork** /kork/ *noun*
**1** the soft bark of a type of tree, used for making things: *The bulletin board is covered in cork.*
**2** a piece of this material that goes in the top of a wine bottle to close it: *The cork came out of the bottle with a loud pop.*

cork
cork

**corn** /korn/ *noun* a tall plant with yellow seeds that people eat as a vegetable: *In Iowa, farmers grow a lot of corn.*

corn

**corn·bread** /**korn**-bred/ *noun* bread made from cornmeal (=flour made from dried corn)

**cor·ner** /**korn**-ur/ *noun* the point where two roads or two sides of something meet: *I waited on the corner of Main Street and Canal Street.* | *There is a computer in the corner of the classroom.*

**corn·flakes** /**korn**-flaykss/ *plural noun* a breakfast food consisting of small flat pieces of crushed corn. You eat cornflakes with milk.

**corn·meal** /**korn**-meel/ *noun* a type of flour made from dried corn

**cor·po·ral** /**korp**-uhr-uhl/ *noun*
( ABBREVIATION: **Cpl.** ) an officer with a low rank in the army or Marines

**cor·po·ra·tion** /korp-uh-**raysh**-uhn/ *noun* a large business: *The corporation has 200,000 employees.*

**corpse** /korpss/ *noun* a dead human body
( SYNONYM: **body** )

**cor·ral** /kuh-**ral**/ *noun* an area with a fence around it where cattle or horses are kept

**cor·rect** /kuh-**rekt**/
● *adjective* without any mistakes: *Can anyone tell me the correct answer?* ( SYNONYM: **right** )
( ANTONYMS: **incorrect, wrong** )
—**correctly** /kuh-**rekt**-lee/ *adverb* in the correct way: *Did I say your name correctly?*
● *verb* to change something so that there are no mistakes in it: *The teacher corrected my spelling mistakes.*

**cor·rec·tion** /kuh-**rek**-shuhn/ *noun* a change that makes something right: *The teacher made some corrections to my work.*

**cor·re·spond** /kor-uh-**spahnd**/ *verb*
**1** if two people correspond, they write letters to each other: *My mom corresponds with a friend in Texas.* ( SYNONYM: **write** )
**2** to match something else: *The seat number corresponded to the number on his ticket.*

**cor·re·spond·ence** /kor-uh-**spahnd**-uhnss/ *noun*
**1** letters that people send and receive: *There was a pile of correspondence on the desk.*
**2** a connection between two things: *There is a correspondence between the letters of the alphabet and the sounds they represent.*

**cor·re·spond·ent** /kor-uh-**spahnd**-uhnt/ *noun* someone whose job is to report news: *She was the war correspondent for the "New York Times."*

**cor·ri·dor** /**kor**-uhd-ur/ *noun* a long hall between two rows of rooms in a large building: *Amy walked down the corridor to the principal's office.* ( SYNONYM: **hall** )

**cor·rupt** /kuh-**ruhpt**/
● *adjective* a corrupt official uses his or her power in a way that is wrong, in order to get money or more power: *Corrupt police officers were protecting the gang.*
● *verb* to make someone dishonest: *Power often corrupts people.*
—**corruption** /kuh-**ruhp**-shuhn/ *noun* corrupt behavior: *The country's government is full of corruption.*

**cos·met·ics** /kahz-**met**-ikss/ *plural noun* things such as lipstick or eyeshadow that people put on their faces to make them look pretty
( SYNONYM: **makeup** )

**cost** /kost/
● *verb* (**cost**)
**1** to have a price: *The book costs $15.*
**2** to make someone lose something important: *One little mistake cost him the game.*
● *noun*
**1** the amount of money you must pay for something: *The cost of a new computer has gone down.* ▶ see **Thesaurus**
**2** something that is damaged when you are doing something else: *There are costs to the environment when new roads are built.*

**co-star** /**koh** star/
● *noun* one of the actors who have important parts in the same movie, play, or television program: *The two girls are co-stars in a new TV series.*
● *verb* (**co-starring, co-starred**) to be one of the important actors in the same movie, play, or television program: *Efron co-starred with Vanessa Hudgens in "High School Musical."*

**cost·ly** /**kost**-lee/ *adjective* costing a lot of money: *The fuel is costly to produce.*
( SYNONYM: **expensive** )

**cost of liv·ing** /kost uhv **liv**-ing/ *noun* the amount of money that people have to spend in order to buy food, clothes, and a place to live: *The cost of living is higher in California than in Iowa.*

**cos·tume** /**kahst**-oom/ *noun*
**1** the special clothes you wear to look like a different type of person: *I went to the Halloween party in a pirate costume.*
**2** the special clothes that actors wear: *We made our own costumes for the play.*

**cot** /kaht/ *noun* a small bed that you can fold and put away

**cot·tage** /**kaht**-ij/ *noun* a small house in the country: *We went to my grandparents' cottage by Lake Huron.*

**cot·tage cheese** /**kaht**-ij cheez/ *noun* a soft white cheese that looks like little round balls

**cot·ton** /**kaht**′n/ *noun*
**1** soft cloth made from the white threads around the seeds of a plant: *a cotton shirt* ▶ see picture at **kit**
**2** the plant used for making this cloth: *Cotton is still an important crop in the southern U.S.*

**cot·ton can·dy** /**kaht**′n kand-ee/ *noun* sticky candy that you buy as a big soft ball on a stick. Cotton candy is often pink: *Dad bought us some cotton candy at the fair.*

**cot·ton gin** /**kaht**′n jin/ *noun* a machine for separating cotton threads from the seeds of the cotton plant

**couch** /kowch/ *noun* a long comfortable seat for two or more people: *She was lying on the couch and watching TV.* ( SYNONYM: **sofa** )

**cou·gar** /**koog**-ur/ *noun* a large brown wild cat. Cougars live in the mountains in North and South America. ( SYNONYM: **mountain lion** )

**cougar**

**cough** /kof/
● *verb*
if you cough, air suddenly comes out of your throat with a short sound: *The smoke made him cough.*
● *noun*
**1** the sound made when you cough: *I heard a cough behind me.*
**2** an illness that makes you cough a lot: *Jenna was home from school with a cold and a cough.*

**could** /kuhd, kud/ *verb*
**1** used when saying what someone was able to do: *I could hear my sister singing.*
**2** used when saying that something might happen: *The new drug could save lives.*
**3** used when asking someone something politely: *Could you tell me where the library is?*
**4** used when suggesting something: *We could*

have a barbecue.
**5** **could have** used when saying that something was possible, but did not happen: *He could have been hurt!*

**could·n't** /**kud**′nt/ *contraction* short for "could not": *It was dark and I couldn't see anything.*

**could've** /**kud**-uhv/ *contraction* short for "could have": *I could've done better on the math test.*

**coun·cil** /**kownss**-uhl/ *noun* a group of people who have been chosen to make decisions for a town or organization: *The city council has approved plans for the new football stadium.*

**coun·sel** /**kownss**-uhl/ *verb* to listen to someone who has a problem and to give him or her advice: *He counsels students with personal problems.*
—**counseling** /**kownss**-uhl-ing/ *noun* the job or activity of listening to someone who has a problem and giving him or her advice: *Counseling can help children whose parents are getting divorced.*

**coun·sel·or** /**kownss**-uhl-ur/ *noun*
**1** someone whose job is to listen to people who have problems and to give them advice: *Dan talked to the school counselor about being bullied.*
**2** someone who takes care of a group of children at a camp: *Camp counselors will help you if you're homesick.*

**count** /kownt/
● *verb*
**1** to find out how many things there are: *I counted the money in my piggy bank.*
**2** to say numbers in the right order: *Can you count to 100?*
**3** to be important: *You're safe, and that's the only thing that really counts.*
**4** **count on** to depend on someone or something: *I know I can count on you to help me when I'm in trouble.*
● *noun*
**1** the action of finding out how many of something there are: *They did a count of the city's population.*
**2** **lose count** to forget how many things you have counted: *I lost count of how many emails I received.*

**count·down** /**kownt**-down/ *noun* a countdown is when someone counts from a number down to zero, so that people know when something will happen: *The countdown for the launch of the space shuttle has begun.*

**coun·ter** /**kownt**-ur/ *noun*
**1** a flat surface in a kitchen where you make food: *There was a chocolate cake on the kitchen counter.*
**2** the place like a long table in a store or restaurant, where you pay for something or eat: *I sat down at the counter and ordered a milkshake.*

**counter-** /kownt-ur/

> ## Word Building
>
> **counter-** is a prefix.
> **counter**attack | **counter**terrorism
> **counter-** means "against." If an army *counterattacks*, it fights back against another army. *Counterterrorism* is all the things the government does to stop terrorism.

**coun·ter·clock·wise** /kownt-ur-**klahk**-wīz/ *adjective*, *adverb* in the opposite direction to the hands of a clock: *Turn the handle counterclockwise.* ( ANTONYM: **clockwise** )

**counterclockwise**

counterclockwise

clockwise

**coun·ter·feit** /**kownt**-ur-fit/ *adjective* made to look exactly like something else in order to trick people: *The tickets were counterfeit and we could not use them to get into the game.*

**count·less** /**kownt**-liss/ *adjective* very many: *I've told you countless times to clean your room!*

**coun·try** /**kuhn**-tree/ *noun* (plural **countries**)
**1** a large area of land with its own government: *China is a very big country.* ▶ see **Thesaurus**
**2** areas that are not near towns and cities: *Her cousins live in the country on a farm.*
**3** a type of music that is popular especially in the southern and western U.S. Country music has people playing guitars and sometimes violins and banjos: *Dolly Parton is a country singer.*

**coun·try·side** /**kuhn**-tree-sīd/ *noun* land that is not near towns and cities: *We drove through the hills of the Virginia countryside.*

**coun·ty** /**kownt**-ee/ *noun* (plural **counties**) a part of a state with its own government: *Orange County is one of the 58 counties in the state of California.*

**cou·ple** /**kuhp**-uhl/ *noun*
**1** two, or a small number: *A couple of kids in my class have rabbits.*
**2** two people who are in a romantic relationship: *The couple were laughing and kissing.*

**cou·pon** /**koop**-ahn/ *noun* a piece of paper that you use at a store so you pay less money for something: *The coupon gives you $1 off a pizza.*

**cour·age** /**kur**-ij/ *noun* if you have courage, you are not afraid to do something difficult or dangerous: *I don't have the courage to tell him that he is wrong.* | *The soldiers continued to fight with great courage.*
—**courageous** /kuh-**rayj**-uhss/ *adjective* brave: *Dr. King was a courageous man who fought for the things that he believed in.*
—**courageously** /kuh-**rayj**-uhss-lee/ *adverb* in a brave way: *He fought very courageously against cancer.*

**course** /korss/ *noun*
**1** a class in a particular subject: *My parents are taking an English course in night school.*
**2** an area of land where people play golf or where races take place: *The homes are near a golf course.*
**3** one of the parts of a meal: *We had fish for the main course.*
**4** the direction that a boat or airplane takes to reach a place: *The airplane changed course to fly around a big storm.*

IDIOMS with **course**
**of course**
**1** used when saying "yes" to show that you agree: *"Can I come with you?" "Of course."*
**2** used when saying that something is not surprising: *Of course dad was mad when I lost his keys.*
**of course not** used when saying "no" in a very firm way: *"Are you angry with me?" "Of course not."*

**court** /kort/ *noun*
**1** an area where you play a game such as tennis or basketball: *The players were practicing on the tennis court.* ▶ see picture on page **A10**
**2** a place where people decide whether someone is guilty of a crime: *She said in court that she was at home on the night of the murder.*

**cour·te·ous** /**kurt**-ee-uhss/ *adjective* polite: *He is very courteous and he always says "good morning" to me.*
—**courteously** /**kurt**-ee-uhss-lee/ *adverb* in a polite way: *Raj courteously thanked her for the gift.*

**cour·te·sy** /**kurt**-uhss-ee/ *noun* behavior that is polite: *You should treat your teachers with courtesy and respect.*

**court·house** /**kort**-howss/ *noun* the building where law courts are

**court-mar·tial** /**kort**-marsh-uhl/
● *noun* a trial in which a military court decides whether a soldier has done something wrong: *The soldier is facing a court-martial for disobeying orders.*
● *verb* if a soldier is court-martialed, he or she has a trial in a military court

**court·room** /**kort**-room/ *noun* a room where a law case is decided: *The judge came into the courtroom.*

**court·yard** /**kort**-yard/ *noun* an area of ground with walls or buildings around it: *There is a courtyard in the middle of the college, where you can sit outside.*

**cous·in** /**kuhz**-uhn/ *noun* a child of your aunt or uncle: *My aunt had a baby, so I have a new cousin to play with.*

**cov·er** /**kuhv**-ur/
● *verb*
**1** to put something over something or someone: *She covered the baby with a blanket.*

**2** **be covered in/with** to have a lot of something on the surface: *Your hands are covered with paint!*
**3** to include or deal with something: *The book covers the period in history from 1945 to 1968.*
**4** to travel a particular distance: *We covered around 15 miles on our bikes.*
**5** **cover up** to stop people from discovering something bad: *She stole some money, and then she tried to cover it up.*
● *noun*
**1** the outside of a book or magazine: *The principal's photo was on the cover of the school magazine.*
**2** protection from attack or bad weather: *The soldiers ran for cover when the shooting started.*
**3** something that is used to cover something else: *a cushion cover*
**4** **covers** the sheets and blankets on a bed: *I pulled the covers up to my chin.*

**cover**

His hands are covered with paint.

**cov·er·age** /**kuhv**-uhr-ij/ *noun*
**1** if an event gets coverage in newspapers or on television, there are news reports about it: *The trial got a lot of media coverage.*
**2** if you have coverage from insurance, you get money from the insurance company if you are sick, or if something is stolen or damaged: *Some families have no health coverage and they cannot afford to go the doctor.*

**cov·ered wag·on** /**kuhv**-urd **wag**-uhn/ *noun* a wooden vehicle with a cloth cover, which was pulled by horses or oxen. Covered wagons were used by the people who traveled across the U.S. to the West to start farms and towns in the 1800s.

**cov·er·ing** /**kuhv**-uhr-ing/ *noun* something that covers something else: *Curtains are one kind of window covering.*

**cov·er-up** /**kuhv**-ur uhp/ *noun* if there is a cover-up, someone tries to stop other people from finding out about something: *The mayor refused to answer questions about the situation and some people think there was a cover-up.*

**cow** /kow/ *noun* a large farm animal that we get milk and meat from. A female cow is called a cow, a male cow is called a bull, and a group of cows are called cattle: *There were cows eating grass in the field.* ▶ see picture at **calf**

**cow·ard** /**kow**-urd/ *noun* someone who is not brave: *The boys called him a coward because he wouldn't fight.*
—**cowardly** /**kow**-urd-lee/ *adjective* not brave: *He was too cowardly to admit that he was wrong.*
—**cowardice** /**kow**-urd-iss/ *noun* behavior that is not brave

**Word Origin:** coward

**Coward** comes from an Old French word that means "tail." So a coward is someone who runs away, so that you only see his or her tail.

**cow·boy** /**kow**-boy/ *noun* a man whose job is to take care of cattle: *The cowboys were riding horses.*

**cow·girl** /**kow**-gurl/ *noun* a woman whose job is to take care of cattle

**coy·o·te** /kī-**oht**-ee/ *noun* a wild animal that looks like a small wolf. Coyotes live in western North America, Canada, and Mexico: *We heard the howl of a coyote.*

**Word Origin:** coyote

People who spoke English did not have a name for this animal when they first saw it. So they used the Spanish word **coyote**. The Spanish word comes from the Aztec language called Nahuatl.

**co·zy** /**kohz**-ee/ *adjective* warm and comfortable, and making you feel relaxed: *There was a big armchair next to the fire and the room felt very cozy.*

**crab** /krab/ *noun* a sea animal with ten legs and a round flat shell around its body. Most crabs are fairly small. You can eat the meat from a crab: *Crabs have large front claws called pincers.*

**crack** /krak/
● *verb*
**1** to break something and make a line on its surface: *I dropped something on the plate and cracked it.* | *The ice cracked when John stepped on it.*
**2 crack down** to start dealing with a crime or problem more severely: *The teachers are cracking down on bullying in the playground.*
**3 crack up** to start laughing: *He told a really funny joke and we all cracked up.*
● *noun*
**1** a thin line where something is broken: *That cup has a crack in it.*
**2** a very narrow space between two parts of something: *A light shone through the crack between the curtains.* (SYNONYM: **gap**)
**3** a sudden short loud noise: *The branch broke with a loud crack.*
—**cracked** /krakt/ *adjective* something that is cracked has a thin line in it where it has broken: *The window was cracked.*

crack

crack

**crack·er** /**krak**-ur/ *noun* a small thin hard type of bread: *We're having soup and crackers for lunch.*

**cra·dle** /**krayd**'l/ *noun* a bed for a baby. A cradle can move from side to side: *She rocked the cradle until the baby went to sleep.*

**craft** /kraft/ *noun* an activity in which you make something using your hands: *The Navajo Indians still do traditional crafts such as rug-making and pottery.*

**crafts·man** /**kraftss**-muhn/ *noun* (plural **craftsmen** /**kraftss**-muhn/) someone who is good at making things with his or her hands: *The jewelry is made by a local craftsman.*

—**craftsmanship** /**kraftss**-muhn-ship/ *noun* the skill that someone has when making something with his or her hands: *You can see the craftsmanship in his work.*

**cram** /kram/ *verb* (**cramming**, **crammed**) to put a lot of things or people into a small space, so that the space is full: *Alyson crammed all the books into her school backpack.*

**cramp** /kramp/ *noun* a bad pain that you get when a muscle suddenly becomes too tight: *One runner got leg cramps and had to leave the race.*

**cramped** /krampt/ *adjective* a cramped room is small and does not have enough space for everything: *He shares a cramped bedroom with his brother.*

**cran·ber·ry**
/**kran**-berr-ee/ *noun*
(plural **cranberries**) a
small sour red fruit that
grows on a bush: *We
always have cranberry
sauce with the turkey
on Thanksgiving.*

cranberry

**crane** /krayn/ *noun*
**1** a tall machine for lifting heavy things. Cranes have a long metal arm: *Cranes were used to lift the roof beams.*
**2** a bird with long legs that lives near water
▶ see picture on page **A4**

**crash** /krash/
● *verb*
**1** if a vehicle crashes, it hits something in an accident: *The plane crashed in a field and the wings were badly damaged.* | *He crashed his car into a wall.*
**2** to hit something hard and make a loud noise: *Waves crashed onto the beach.*
**3** if a computer crashes, it suddenly stops working: *My computer crashed and I lost all of my homework.*
● *noun*
**1** an accident in which a vehicle hits something: *The car was wrecked in the crash.*
**2** a sudden loud noise when something falls or breaks: *The tree fell over with a loud crash.*

**crate** /krayt/ *noun* a large box for carrying fruit, bottles, etc.: *The men are unloading crates of bananas from the ship.* | *He was carrying a big crate of beer.*

**cra·ter** /**krayt**-ur/ *noun*
**1** the round hole at the top of a volcano: *Clouds of black smoke are coming out of the crater of the volcano.* ▶ see picture at **volcano**
**2** a large hole in the ground made by a meteorite from space, or by a bomb: *It's possible to see the craters on the moon from Earth.* | *The explosion made a big crater in the road.*

crater

**crawl** /krol/
● *verb*
**1** to move along on your hands and knees: *Babies usually start to crawl at around six to nine months.*
**2** if an insect or spider crawls somewhere, it moves there: *A spider was crawling up my leg.*
**3** to move somewhere very slowly: *The cars were crawling along at ten miles per hour.*
● *noun*
a way of swimming. You move one arm up next to your head and then the other arm: *Can you do the crawl?* ▶ see picture at **swim**

crawl

**cray·on** /**kray**-ahn/ *noun* a stick of colored wax or a colored pencil that children use to draw pictures: *She took a pink crayon and colored the nose of the rabbit.* ▶ see picture on page **A9**

**craze** /krayz/ *noun* something that is very popular for a short time: *The toys are the latest craze and every kid wants to have one.*

**cra·zy** /**krayz**-ee/ *adjective*
**1** not thinking or behaving in a reasonable way: *It was crazy to jump in the water when you can't swim.*
**2** liking someone or something very much: *He's crazy about basketball.*
**3** mentally ill: *She went crazy and started hearing voices that weren't really there.*

IDIOM with **crazy**
**like crazy** very much or very quickly: *He's growing like crazy – four inches this year.*

**creak** /kreek/
● *verb* if a door, floor, etc. creaks, it makes a long high noise when it moves: *The stairs creak when you step on them.*
● *noun* a long high noise that something makes when it moves: *There was a creak as the door slowly opened.* ▶ see picture on page **A16**

**cream** /kreem/
● *noun*
**1** the thick part of milk, which is usually separated from the milk we drink: *I like to eat strawberries with cream and sugar.*
**2** a yellowish-white color: *The walls were painted cream.*
**3** a thick smooth substance that you put on your skin: *Dad put shaving cream on his face.*
SYNONYM: **lotion**
● *adjective*
having a yellowish-white color: *He is wearing a cream shirt.*

**cream cheese** /**kreem** cheez/ *noun* a soft white cheese that you spread: *Can I have some cream cheese on my bagel?*

**crease** /kreess/ *noun* a deep line in clothes, paper, or someone's skin: *His pants had a sharp crease down the front.*
—**creased** /kreest/ *adjective* creased clothes, paper, or skin have deep lines in them: *The paper was creased and dirty.*

**cre·ate** /kree-**ayt**/ *verb* to make something new: *She helped create the costumes for the play.* | *The new rules created a lot of problems.*

**Word Family:** create
**create** verb | **creator** noun | **creative** adjective | **creation** noun | **creativity** noun | **creatively** adverb

**cre·a·tion** /kree-**aysh**-uhn/ *noun*
**1** the act of making something new: *Different religions have different stories about the creation of the world.*
**2** something new or different that someone has made: *His latest creation is a movie about a group of penguins.*

**cre·a·tive** /kree-**ayt**-iv/ *adjective* thinking of new ideas or making new things: *My sister is very creative and she makes all her own jewelry.*
—**creatively** /kree-**ayt**-iv-lee/ *adverb* in a creative way: *She had creatively made a bag from some material she had bought.*
—**creativity** /kree-ay-**tiv**-uht-ee/ *noun* the skill of being creative: *In the art class, students are encouraged to develop their creativity.*

**cre·a·tor** /kree-**ayt**-ur/ *noun* the person who has made something: *Mark Twain was the creator of the character "Huckleberry Finn."*

**crea·ture** /**kreech**-ur/ *noun* an animal, fish, or insect: *The pond is full of creatures such as water snails and dragonflies.*

**cred·it** /**kred**-it/
● *noun*
**1** praise for doing something: *I think we should give him credit for all his hard work.*
**2** a way of buying things in which you pay for them later: *My parents bought the car on credit and they have to pay $150 every month for the next three years.*
**3** an amount of money that is put into someone's bank account: *A credit of $65 has been added to your account.* ANTONYM: **debit**
● *verb*
to add money to a bank account: *The money will be credited to your account.* ANTONYM: **debit**

**cred·it card** /**kred**-it kard/ *noun* a small plastic card that people use to buy things and pay for them later: *Dad paid for the clothes with a credit card.*

**creed** /kreed/ *noun* a set of beliefs: *There are students of all races and creeds at the school – Muslims, Hindus, and Christians.*

**creek** /kreek/ *noun* a small river: *The boys went fishing in the creek.*

**creep** /kreep/ *verb* (**crept** /krept/) to move slowly and quietly: *Ben crept down the hall without his parents noticing.*

**creep·y** /**kreep**-ee/ *adjective* making you feel a little frightened: *There is something strange and rather creepy about him.*

**cremate** /**kree**-mayt/ *verb* to burn the body of a dead person: *When my grandmother died, she was cremated.*
—**cremation** /kri-**maysh**-uhn/ *noun* the act or ceremony of burning the body of a dead person

**cre·ma·to·ri·um** /kreem-uh-**tor**-ee-uhm/ *noun* a building where the bodies of dead people are burned

**crept** /krept/ *verb* the past tense and past participle of **creep**

**cres·cent** /**kress**-uhnt/ *noun* a curved shape that is pointed on the ends, like a thin moon: *The beach was a crescent of white sand.*

crescent

crescent

**crest** /krest/ *noun* the top of a hill or a wave: *We finally reached the crest of the hill.*

**crew** /kroo/ *noun*
**1** the people who work on a ship or airplane: *The ship has a crew of 18 officers and 260 sailors.*
**2** a group of people who are making a movie or television program: *A TV news crew filmed the fight.*

**crib** /krib/ *noun* a small bed for a baby. A crib has high sides made of bars: *The baby was asleep in his crib.*

crib

**crick·et** /**krik**-it/ *noun*
**1** a small brown insect that jumps. Crickets make a short high noise by rubbing their wings together.
**2** a game played by two teams of 11 players. You hit a ball with a flat bat and run between two wickets (=sets of sticks): *Cricket is a popular game in England.*

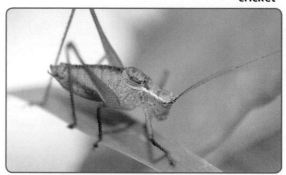
cricket

**cried** /krīd/ *verb* the past tense and past participle of **cry**

**cries** /krīz/ *noun*
● *noun* the plural of **cry**
● *verb* the third person singular of the present tense of cry

**crime** /krīm/ *noun* an action that the law does not allow: *Stealing is a crime.* | *Crime is a big problem in this part of the city.*
▶ see **Thesaurus**

**crim·i·nal** /**krim**-uhn-uhl/
● *noun* someone who often breaks the law: *Violent criminals should go to prison for a long time.* ▶ see **Thesaurus**
● *adjective* relating to crime: *Stealing a car is a criminal offense.*

**crim·son** /**krimz**-uhn/ *noun, adjective* a dark red color: *The plant has crimson flowers.*

**crip·ple** /**krip**-uhl/ *verb* to injure someone so that he or she cannot walk anymore: *He was crippled in a car accident and he has to use a wheelchair.*

**cri·sis** /**krīss**-iss/ *noun* (plural **crises** /**krīss**-eez/) a very bad and very upsetting situation: *Many people lost their jobs during the economic crisis.*

**crisp** /krisp/ *adjective*
**1** crisp food is hard and makes a noise when you bite it: *The carrots were nice and crisp.*
**2** crisp air or weather is cold and dry: *It was a crisp winter morning and I was wearing my warm coat.*

a b **c** d e f g h i j k l m n o p q r s t u v w x y z

**crisp·y** /**krisp**-ee/ *adjective* crispy food is hard and makes a noise when you bite it: *The bacon was nice and crispy.*

**cri·te·ri·a** /krī-**teer**-ee-uh/ *plural noun* (singular **criterion** /krī-**teer**-ee-uhn/) rules that you use when making a decision or judgment: *The criteria for being able to vote are that you must be 18 and a U.S. citizen.*

**crit·ic** /**krit**-ik/ *noun*
**1** someone whose job is writing about books, movies, plays, etc., and saying whether they are good or bad: *Critics loved the movie and said that it was the best movie of the year.*
**2** someone who says that someone or something is bad: *He is a strong critic of the war.*

**crit·i·cal** /**krit**-ik-uhl/ *adjective*
**1** saying that you think something is bad: *My sister is always very critical of my clothes and she doesn't like my T-shirt.*
**2** very important or serious: *Teachers and parents have a critical role in a child's life.*
—**critically** /**krit**-ik-lee/ *adverb* in a critical way: *"I don't like your painting," he said critically.* | *He was critically injured.*

**crit·i·cize** /**krit**-uh-sīz/ *verb* to say that someone or something is bad: *My brother is always criticizing me and saying that I'm stupid.*
( ANTONYM: **praise** )
—**criticism** /**krit**-uh-siz-uhm/ *noun* remarks that say that someone or something is bad: *His criticism of my work really upset me.*

**Word Family: criticize**

**criticize** verb | **criticism** noun | **critical** adjective | **critic** noun

**croak** /krohk/ *verb*
**1** if a frog croaks, it makes a low sound
**2** to speak in a low rough voice: *"I have a terrible cold," he croaked.*

**croc·o·dile** /**krahk**-uh-dīl/ *noun* an animal with a big mouth and many sharp teeth, that lives in or near water. It has a long body, short legs, and a hard skin. Crocodiles are reptiles. ▶ see picture at **reptile**

crocodile

**cro·cus** /**krohk**-uhss/ *noun* a small plant with a purple, yellow, or white flower. Crocuses have flowers in the early part of spring. ▶ see picture on page **A6**

**crook** /kruk/ *noun* a dishonest person or a criminal: *The police are there to catch the crooks.*

**crook·ed** /**kruk**-id/ *adjective*
**1** not straight: *The old woman had crooked teeth.* ▶ see picture at **straight**
**2** not honest: *Crooked police officers took money from criminals.*

**crop** /krahp/ *noun*
**1** a plant such as corn, wheat, etc. that farmers grow: *Farmers planted their crops in the spring.*
**2** the amount of food that is grown in one year: *There was a good wheat crop that year.*

**cross** /kross/
● *verb*
**1** to move from one side of something to the other: *Look carefully before you cross the street.*
**2** if roads or lines cross, they go across each other: *Springfield Road crosses the highway.*
**3** to draw a line through something: *Remember to cross your t's.* | *If you make a mistake, cross it out.*

IDIOMS with **cross**
**cross my heart** used when you promise to do something, or when you promise that something is true: *I'll bring you the book tomorrow. I cross my heart.*
**cross your legs/arms** to put one leg or arm over the other one: *Dad sat down and crossed his legs.*
**cross your mind** if something crosses your mind, you think of it: *A strange idea suddenly crossed my mind.*

● *noun*

**1** the shape x or +: *Put a cross next to the person you want to vote for.*

**2** an object that is the symbol of the Christian religion. It has the shape **✝**: *There was a wooden cross in the church.*

**3** something that is a mixture of one thing and another: *A mule is a cross between a horse and a donkey.*

**cross**

They are crossing the street.

**cross·ex·am·ine** /**kross**ig-zam-in/ *verb* to ask someone a lot of questions, especially in a court: *The lawyer cross-examined the witness.*

**cross·leg·ged** /**kross** leg-id/ *adjective, adverb* if you sit cross-legged, you sit on the ground with your knees apart and with one foot crossing over your other foot: *We sat cross-legged on the floor.*

**cross-legged**

**cross·walk** /**kross**-wok/ *noun* a place where people can cross the street. A crosswalk is marked with lines: *Watch out for cars when you are on the crosswalk.*

**cross·word puz·zle** /**kross**-wurd puhz-uhl/ (also **crossword**) *noun* a game where you write the word that answers a question into squares that go across or down on the paper. Each letter goes in one square: *The clue in the crossword puzzle was: "What is the fourth planet from the sun?" So I wrote "Mars" in the boxes.*

**crouch** /krowch/ *verb* to bend your knees and lean forward, so your body is close to the ground: *I crouched down behind the sofa and hoped they wouldn't see me.*

**crouch**

They are crouching down next to the wall.

**crow** /kroh/

● *noun* a large black bird that makes a loud sound ▶ see picture on page **A4**

● *verb*

**1** if a rooster crows, it makes a loud sound

**2** to boast about what you have done: *He was crowing about winning the game.*

**crowd** /krowd/

● *noun* a large group of people: *A huge crowd listened to the president's speech.*

● *verb* to come together in a large group: *A bunch of kids were crowded around the teacher's desk.*

**crowd·ed** /**krowd**-id/ *adjective* full of people: *The streets are crowded with people.*

**crown** /krown/

● *noun* something that a king or queen wears on his or her head. A crown is made of gold or silver and jewels: *The king wore a gold crown.* ▶ see picture at **queen**

● *verb* to put a crown on the head of a new king or queen in a special ceremony: *Elizabeth was crowned Queen of the United Kingdom in 1953.*

**cru·cial** /**kroosh**-uhl/ *adjective* very important: *Studying hard is crucial to success at school.*

**crude** /krood/ *adjective*

**1** rude: *He was telling crude jokes.*

**2** made in a simple way that is not very good: *People who lived thousands of years ago used crude stone tools.* (ANTONYM: **sophisticated**)

—**crudely** /**krood**-lee/ *adverb* in a crude way: *The village was full of crudely built huts.*

**cru·el** /**kroo**-uhl/ *adjective* someone who is cruel is mean and wants to upset or hurt people or animals: *The cruel witch tried to kill Snow White.* | *Not allowing someone to eat is a cruel punishment.*

—**cruelly** /**kroo**-uhl-lee/ *adverb* in a cruel way: *He was treated very cruelly and not given enough to eat.*

—**cruelty** /**kroo**-uhlt-ee/ *noun* cruel behavior: *The attack was an act of cruelty.*

**cruise** /krooz/
● *noun* a vacation on a large boat: *We went on a cruise around the Caribbean islands.*
● *verb* to move at a steady speed in a car, airplane, or boat: *The police car cruised slowly down the street.*

**crumb** /kruhm/ *noun* a very small piece of bread or cake: *After lunch, there were crumbs all over the table.*

**crum·ble** /**kruhm**-buhl/ *verb* if something very old or dry crumbles, it breaks into pieces: *The castle walls are starting to crumble.*

**crum·ple** /**kruhmp**-uhl/ *verb* to crush a piece of paper that you do not want: *He crumpled the letter and threw it in the wastebasket.*

**crunch** /kruhnch/
● *verb* to crush or chew something in a noisy way: *Rob crunched an apple.*
● *noun* the sound of something being crushed or chewed
—**crunchy** /**kruhnch**-ee/ *adjective* crunchy food is firm and makes a noise when you bite it: *a crunchy carrot*

**crush** /kruhsh/ *verb* to press very hard on something and break or damage it: *Be careful not to crush the strawberries.*

**crust** /kruhst/ *noun*
**1** the outer part of bread or a pie: *Will you cut the crust off my sandwiches?*
**2** the hard layer on the surface of the Earth: *the Earth's crust* ▶ see picture at **earth**

**crutch** /kruhch/ *noun* a stick that you put under your arm to help you walk: *He broke his leg and was on crutches.*

**cry** /krī/
● *verb* (**cries**, **crying**, **cried**)
**1** if you cry, tears come out of your eyes: *Katie was crying because she hurt her knee.* ▶ see **Thesaurus**
**2** to say something loudly: *"Stop!" she cried.* | *The boy cried out for help.*
● *noun* (plural **cries**)
**1** a loud shout or sound: *The boy gave a cry of fright.*
**2** a sound that some animals or birds make: *You could hear the cry of seagulls on the beach.*

**crys·tal** /**krist**-uhl/ *noun*
**1** a small shape with many flat surfaces, that forms when a liquid becomes solid: *Snowflakes, diamonds, and salt are all examples of crystals.*
**2** glass that is very good quality: *The best wine glasses are made of crystal.*

**cub** /kuhb/ *noun* the baby of some wild animals, for example a lion or bear: *Three tiger cubs were sitting with their mother.*

**cube** /kyoob/
● *noun*
**1** an object with six square sides: *I put an ice cube in my drink.*
**2** the number you get when you multiply a number by itself twice: *The cube of 2 is 8 (=2 x 2 x 2 = 8).*

cube

**cubed** /kyoobd/ *adjective* a number that is cubed is multiplied by itself twice: *3 cubed is 27 (3 x 3 x 3 = 27).*

**cu·bic** /**kyoob**-ik/ *adjective* a cubic measurement is one that measures the amount of space inside something. To get a cubic measurement, you multiply the length by the height by the width: *The box is 2 feet high by 3 feet long by 4 feet wide, so it measures 24 cubic feet.*

**cu·cum·ber** /**kyook**-uhm-bur/ *noun* a long round green vegetable. You eat a cucumber uncooked: *The salad had lettuce, tomato, and cucumber in it.* ▶ see picture on page **A7**

**cud·dle** /**kuhd**'l/ *verb* to hold someone close to you because you love them: *She was cuddling the baby.*
—**cuddly** /**kuhd**'l-ee/ *adjective* soft, warm, and nice to hold: *Puppies are very cuddly and children love holding them.*

**cue** /kyoo/ *noun* a signal that it is time for

someone to do something: *When I raise my hand, that is your cue to start singing.*

**cul·prit** /**kuhl**-prit/ *noun* someone who has done something wrong: *The police have arrested the culprits.*

**cult** /kuhlt/
● *noun* a small religious group with strange or extreme ideas: *Cult members are not allowed to speak to their families.*
● *adjective* very popular among a small group of people: *The movie became a cult favorite with students.*

**cul·ti·vate** /**kuhlt**-uh-vayl/ *verb* to grow crops and plants by preparing the land for them: *The land is used for cultivating wheat.*
—**cultivation** /kuhlt-uh-**vaysh**-uhn/ *noun* the act of cultivating crops and plants: *Spain has increased its cultivation of olive trees.*

**cul·ture** /**kuhlch**-ur/ *noun*
**1** the ideas and way of life of a society: *The story includes details about Native American cultures.*
**2** art, literature, music, etc.: *New York has always been a center of culture in America.*
—**cultural** /**kuhlch**-uhr-uhl/ *adjective* relating to culture: *There are big cultural differences between the U.S. and Japan.*

> **Word Family:** culture
>
> **culture** *noun* | **cultural** *adjective*

**cunn·ing** /**kuhn**-ing/ *adjective* good at tricking people: *a cunning plan*

**cup** /kuhp/ *noun*
**1** a small round container that you drink from: *Mom needs a cup of coffee as soon as she wakes up.*
**2** eight fluid ounces. You use a cup to measure foods in cooking: *Add a cup of flour.*
**3** a prize for winning a competition. A cup is shaped like a bowl and sometimes has two handles: *Who won the World Cup in soccer?*

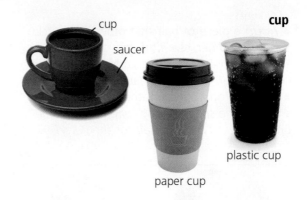

cup

cup

saucer

plastic cup

paper cup

**cup·board** /**kuhb**-urd/ *noun* a piece of furniture for keeping things in. Cupboards have a door and shelves: *He looked in the kitchen cupboard for a plate.* (SYNONYM: **cabinet**)

**cup·cake** /**kuhp**-kayk/ *noun* a small cake for one person: *Mom and I made some chocolate cupcakes.*

**curb** /kurb/ *noun* the edge of a sidewalk where it joins the road: *A big black car was parked at the curb.*

**cure** /kyoor/
● *verb*
**1** to make a sick person well: *The doctor says that she is now completely cured of her illness.*
**2** to find a way to stop something bad from happening: *I straightened the wheel on the bike, and that cured the problem.*
● *noun*
a way of making people well when they have an illness: *Scientists have found cures for some types of cancer.*

**cu·ri·ous** /**kyoor**-ee-uhss/ *adjective*
**1** wanting to know something, or learn about the world: *I'm curious to know who our new neighbors are.* | *Cats are naturally curious and they like to explore all of the house.*
**2** strange or unusual: *The flower has a curious name. It's called a "foxglove."*
—**curiously** /**kyoor**-ee-uhss-lee/ *adverb* in a curious way: *Sarah was watching me curiously.*
—**curiosity** /kyoor-ee-**ahss**-uht-ee/ *noun* the feeling of being curious: *He opened the box out of curiosity.*

**curl** /kurl/
● *noun* a piece of hair that grows in a circle: *She brushed her beautiful dark curls.*
—**curly** /**kurl**-ee/ *adjective* curly hair grows in circles: *I wish I had curly hair.*
● *verb* to form curves, rather than being straight: *The snake's body curled around the branch.* | *Let's curl our hair for the party!*

curl

curly hair                     straight hair

**cur·ren·cy** /**kur**-uhnss-ee/ *noun* (plural **currencies**) the type of money that a country uses: *The U.S. currency is the dollar.*

**cur·rent** /**kur**-uhnt/
● *adjective*
happening or existing now: *News programs tell us about current events.*
● *noun*
**1** a flow of water or air in a particular direction: *Be careful swimming on this beach. There is a strong current.*
**2** a flow of electricity through a wire: *An electric current passes through the wire and makes the light come on.*

**cur·rent·ly** /**kur**-uhnt-lee/ *adverb* at this time: *The president is currently visiting Europe.*
SYNONYM: **now**

**cur·ric·u·lum** /kuh-**rik**-yuhl-uhm/ *noun* (plural **curricula** /kuh-**rik**-yuhl-uh/ or **curriculums**) all the subjects that are taught at a school or college: *Music and art are part of the curriculum at school.*

**curse** /kurss/
● *verb* to say bad words that show you are angry: *Matt tore his pants and cursed loudly.*
SYNONYM: **swear**
● *noun* magic words that are used to bring someone bad luck: *The witch put a curse on the prince and he turned into a frog.*

**cur·sor** /**kurss**-ur/ *noun* a shape you can move on a computer screen, that shows where you are working: *Place the cursor at the beginning of the line.*

**cur·tain** /**kurt**'n/ *noun* a piece of cloth that you pull across a window or stage: *Sally opened her bedroom curtains and looked out.* ▶ see picture at **theater**

**curve** /kurv/
● *noun* a line that bends like part of circle: *The house is by a curve in the river.*
● *verb* to bend or move in a curve: *The road curves around the bottom of the hill.*
SYNONYM: **bend**
—**curved** /kurvd/ *adjective* bending in a curve: *Buffalos have curved horns.*

**cush·ion** /**kush**-uhn/ *noun* a bag filled with soft material that you sit on or rest against: *The chairs were hard so I got a cushion to sit on.*

**cus·to·di·an** /kuh-**stohd**-ee-uhn/ *noun* someone whose job is taking care of a public building: *The school custodian locks up when everyone has gone home.* SYNONYM: **janitor**

**cus·to·dy** /**kuhst**-uhd-ee/ *noun*
**1** the legal right to take care of a child: *The judge awarded custody to the children's mother.*
**2** if someone is in custody, they are in prison until they go to court: *The police are keeping him in custody until the trial.*

**cus·tom** /**kuhst**-uhm/ *noun* something traditional done by people in a society: *In Greece, it is the custom to give gifts on New Year's Day, instead of Christmas.*

**cus·tom·er** /**kuhst**-uhm-ur/ *noun* someone who buys things from a store or company: *The store is always full of customers.*

**cus·toms** /**kuhst**-uhmz/ *plural noun* a place where officials can search your bags when you enter or leave a country: *We passed through customs at Kennedy airport.*

**cut** /kuht/
● *verb* (**cutting**, **cut**)
**1** to divide something using a knife or scissors: *Maria cut the pizza into four pieces.* | *Cut off all the dead flowers.* | *The kids were cutting pictures out of magazines.* ▶ see **Thesaurus**

**2** to hurt yourself with a knife or something sharp: *He fell and cut his knee on a rock.*

**3** to make hair or grass shorter: *You need to get your hair cut.*

**4 cut and paste** to move writing or a picture in a computer document from one place to another

**5 cut back** to spend less money than you did before: *My dad lost his job and we're cutting back on things like clothes.*

**6 cut down** to eat, drink, or use less of something than before: *You should cut down on how much sugar you eat.*

**7 cut off** to stop the supply of electricity or water to a building: *The electricity was cut off because of a storm.*

**8 be cut off** a place that is cut off is very difficult to get to because of bad roads or weather: *In the winter, the ranch was cut off by snow.*

**9 cut it out!** used when telling someone to stop doing something: *You're making too much noise. Cut it out!*

● *noun*

**1** a small wound on your skin: *The cut on my finger was bleeding.*

**2** a hole that you make with scissors or a knife: *First, make a cut in the card.*

**3** a reduction in the price or amount of something: *The store is making big price cuts and you can buy a shirt for less than ten dollars.*

**cute** /kyoot/ *adjective* very pretty or attractive: *What a cute little kitten!*

**cut·ler·y** /**kuht**-luhr-ee/ *noun* knives, forks, and spoons

**cy·ber·space** /**sīb**-ur-spayss/ *noun* the imaginary place that information goes to when it travels between computers: *She didn't get my email so it must be lost in cyberspace.*

**Word Origin:** cyberspace

The word **cyberspace** was made up by a writer called William Gibson. He used the word in a science fiction story in 1982. People started using it about communication on the Internet in the 1990s.

**cycl-** /sīkl/

**Word Building**

**bicycle | cyclone | recycle**
These words all have the Greek word root **cycl** in them. **Cycl** means "circle" or "wheel." A *bicycle* has two wheels, and wheels are shaped like a circle. A *cyclone* is a very fast wind that goes around in a circle. If you *recycle* bottles, you make them into new bottles and use them again.

**cy·cle** /**sīk**-uhl/ *noun* a set of events that happen again and again in a pattern: *The seasons change in a never-ending cycle.*
—**cyclic** /**sīk**-lik/ (also **cy·cli·cal** /**sīk**-lik-uhl/) *adjective* happening again and again in a pattern: *The cyclic movement of the moon around the earth takes about 28 days.*

**cy·clist** /**sīk**-list/ *noun* someone who rides a bicycle: *Cyclists should always be careful when riding on busy roads.*

**cy·clone** /**sīk**-lohn/ *noun* a very strong wind that moves fast in a circle: *The cyclone destroyed many homes.* ( SYNONYM: **tornado** )

**cyl·in·der** /**sil**-uhnd-ur/ *noun*

**cylinder**

**1** a shape like a tube with flat circular ends: *A soup can is a cylinder.*

**2** a part in an engine that is shaped like a tube: *The engine has six cylinders.*
—**cylindrical** /suh-**lin**-drik-uhl/ *adjective* having a long round shape like a tube: *A pipe has a cylindrical shape.*

**cym·bal** /**sim**-buhl/ *noun* a brass musical instrument in the shape of a plate. You hit a cymbal with a stick or another cymbal to make a sound. ▶ see picture on page **A8**

**cyn·ical** /**sin**-ik-uhl/ *adjective* believing that people are not usually good or sincere: *I'm cynical about politicians. I think that all they want is to get power for themselves.*
—**cynic** /**sin**-ik/ *noun* someone who is cynical: *My dad's a cynic and thinks people only want to make money.*

a b c d e f g h i j k l m n o p q r s t u v w x y z

a b **d** e f g h i j k l m n o p q r s t u v w x y z

# Dd

**D** /dee/ *noun* a grade that you can get on a test or in a class. If you get a D, your work is not very good: *I didn't study and I got a D on the test.*

**dab** /dab/
● *verb* (**dabbing**, **dabbed**)
**1** to touch something gently several times with something soft: *Emily dabbed at her mouth with a napkin to wipe the ketchup off.*
**2** to put a small amount of something soft or liquid on something else: *Mom dabbed some antiseptic on the cut.*

**dachs·hund** /**dahkss**-hunt/ *noun* a small dog with short legs and a long body

**dad** /dad/ *noun* another word for father: *My dad works in an office.* | *Dad, can I go play outside?*

> ### Word Origin: dad
>
> **Dad** was first written down in English around 1500. It was probably used long before that. One of the first sounds a baby makes is "da da" and many languages have a word for father that sounds like this.

**dad·dy** /**dad**-ee/ *noun* (plural **daddies**) a word for father used by children: *Where's Daddy?*

**dad·dy long·legs** /dad-ee **long**-legz/ *noun* a creature that looks like a spider. It has a small round body and very long thin legs.

**daf·fo·dil** /**daf**-uh-dil/ *noun* a yellow flower that opens in the spring. Daffodils have a long stem and long leaves.

daffodil

**dai·ly** /**dayl**-ee/ *adverb*, *adjective* every day:

The library is open daily. | She's taking the dog for his daily walk.

**dair·y** /**dair**-ee/ *noun* (plural **dairies**)
**1** a place where milk is put into bottles, and where milk is made into other foods, such as butter and cheese: *The dairy sells milk to the supermarkets.*
**2** (also **dairy products**) foods made from milk, such as butter, cheese, and yogurt: *She doesn't eat dairy because she's allergic to milk.*

**dai·sy** /**dayz**-ee/ *noun* (plural **daisies**) a small flower with a yellow circle in the middle. Daisies often have white petals, but they can be yellow or pink: *The field was covered with little white daisies.*

daisy

**dal·ma·tian** /dal-**maysh**-uhn/ *noun* a large dog that is white with black or brown spots

**dam** /dam/ *noun* a big wall that is built to keep back the water in a river: *They built a dam across the river and made a big lake.*

dam

**dam·age** /**dam**-ij/
● *noun* if something causes damage, it breaks or destroys something: *The hurricane caused a lot of damage to buildings by blowing off roofs and doors.*

● *verb* to harm something: *Smoking damages your health by hurting your lungs.*
▶ see **Thesaurus**
—**damaging** /**dam**-ij-ing/ *adjective* something that is damaging causes damage: *Pollution in the water is damaging to fish. They can become sick or even die.*

**damp** /damp/ *adjective* a little wet: *Don't sit on the grass – it's damp.* ▶ see **Thesaurus**

**dance** /**danss**/
● *verb*
to move your body to music: *Everyone was dancing to loud music.*
● *noun*
**1** a set of movements that you do to music: *We did a dance in which everyone holds hands in a big circle.*
**2** a party where people dance: *There's going to be a dance at the end of term.*
▶ see **Thesaurus**
—**dancer** /**danss**-ur/ *noun* someone who dances: *The ballet dancers are wearing leotards and ballet shoes.*

**dan·de·li·on**
/**dand**-uh-lī-uhn/ *noun* a small weed with a bright yellow flower. The flower becomes round, soft, and white when it is time for the seeds to come off the flower.

**dandelion**

**dan·druff** /**dan**-druhf/ *noun* dry skin that comes off your head in very small white pieces: *This is a special shampoo for dandruff.*

**Dane** /dayn/ *noun* someone from Denmark

**dan·ger** /**daynj**-ur/ *noun*
**1** a dangerous situation: *The boy was in danger in the water because he couldn't swim.*
**2** something or someone that may harm you: *Cars are a danger to children – a car that is going fast could hit a child.*

**Word Family:** danger

danger *noun* | dangerous *adjective* |
dangerously *adverb* | endanger *verb*

**dan·ger·ous** /**daynj**-uhr-uhss/ *adjective* likely to harm someone: *Some snakes are dangerous because their bite is poisonous.*
▶ see **Thesaurus**
—**dangerously** /**daynj**-uhr-uhss-lee/ *adverb* in a way that is dangerous: *He was standing dangerously close to the edge of the cliff and we were scared he would fall.*

**dan·gle** /**dang**-guhl/ *verb* to hang down and swing from side to side: *I sat on a rock and let my feet dangle in the water.*

**Dan·ish** /**dayn**-ish/
● *adjective* from Denmark: *Hans Christian Andersen was a Danish writer.*
● *noun* the language spoken in Denmark

**dare** /dair/ *verb*
**1** to be brave enough to do something: *I didn't dare tell him he was wrong.*
**2** to say that someone must do something to show they are not afraid: *I dare you to jump off the roof!*

**dark** /dark/
● *adjective*
**1** without light: *The sun has gone down and the sky is getting dark.* ( ANTONYM: **light** )
▶ see **Thesaurus**
**2** not light in color: *Her hair is very dark, almost black.*
● *noun*
**1** somewhere with no light: *I'm scared of the dark and I always sleep with my light on.*
**2** the time in the evening when it stops being light: *Mom says we have to come home before dark.*

**dark·en** /**dark**-uhn/ *verb* to become dark: *The sky darkened as the clouds covered the sun, and rain began to fall.*

**dark·ness** /**dark**-niss/ *noun* if you are in darkness, there is no light: *Joe turned off the light, and I couldn't see anything in the darkness.*

**dar·ling** /**darl**-ing/
● *noun* used when talking to someone you love: *Thank you, darling.*
● *adjective* loved a lot: *Emma was his darling daughter.*

a b c **d** e f g h i j k l m n o p q r s t u v w x y z

**dart** /dart/
● *noun*
**1** the pointed object that you throw at the board in a game of darts
**2 darts** a game you play by throwing darts at a round board with numbers on it: *Let's play darts.*
● *verb*
to move somewhere suddenly and quickly: *The thief darted behind a wall as soon as he saw the police.*

**darts**

**dart·board** /**dart**-bord/ *noun* a round board used in the game of darts. The board has circles and numbers on it.

**dash** /dash/
● *verb*
to go somewhere very quickly: *Everyone dashed into the house as it began to rain.*
● *noun*
**1** a short fast run: *The phone rang and Anna made a dash to get it.*
**2** a short running race: *Lewis won the 50-yard dash.*
**3** a mark (–) used in writing to show a pause
**4** a small amount of something that gives food flavor: *Add a dash of lemon to the fish.*

**dash·board** /**dash**-bord/ *noun* the part of a car with the instruments and controls on it. The dashboard is in front of the driver: *The radio is next to the steering wheel on the dashboard.*

**da·ta** /**dayt**-uh/ *noun* information or facts: *We are collecting data for a report on birds in our neighborhood.*

**da·ta·base** /**dayt**-uh-bayss/ *noun* a large amount of information stored in a computer system: *They keep a database of all the students' addresses and telephone numbers.*

**date** /dayt/
● *noun*
**1** a day of the month or year. The date is shown by a number: *"What's today's date?" "It's August 11."* | *The date of the first moon landing was July 20, 1969.* | *My date of birth is July 22, 2003.*
**2** an arrangement to meet someone, especially a girlfriend or boyfriend: *My big sister has a date with Jordan. They're going to the movies.*
**3** a small sweet sticky brown fruit: *The cookies had dates in them.*

**IDIOMS with date**
**at a later date** at a time in the future: *You'll get your test scores at a later date.*
**to date** until now: *He has scored over 50 home runs to date.*
● *verb*
**1** to write today's date on something: *Don't forget to date your work.*
**2** to have a girlfriend or boyfriend: *Donna is dating a boy called Josh.*
**3** to have been built or made in a particular year, and still exist today: *The building dates from 1856.*

**dat·ed** /**dayt**-id/ *adjective* no longer fashionable: *The shoes look dated.*

**daugh·ter** /**dot**-ur/ *noun* someone's female child: *Mrs. Robinson's daughter is the same age as me.*

**daugh·ter-in-law** /**dot**-ur in lo/ *noun* (plural **daughters-in-law**) the wife of your son: *They spent Christmas with their son and daughter-in-law.*

**daw·dle** /**dod**'l/ *verb* to do something slowly, and waste time: *Stop dawdling and get dressed – you'll be late for school!*

**dawn** /don/ *noun*
**1** the time of day when light first appears as the Sun comes up: *I woke up at dawn and the sky outside my window was just starting to become light.* (SYNONYMS: **daybreak, sunrise**)
(ANTONYM: **dusk**)
**2** the time when something first began: *People have lived in Egypt since the dawn of civilization.*

dawn

**day** /day/ *noun*
**1** a period of 24 hours that starts at 12 o'clock at night. There are seven days in a week: *"What day is it today?" "Tuesday." | It's three days until my birthday.*
**2** the time when it is light, between morning and night: *In the summer, it gets very hot during the day.* (ANTONYM: **night**)
**3** the part of the day that you spend at school or at work: *The school day finishes at 3:00.*

**Word Family:** day

| **day** noun | **daily** adjective | **daily** adverb |

**day·break** /**day**-brayk/ *noun* the time of day when light first appears: *At daybreak the rooster started to crow.* (SYNONYMS: **dawn, sunrise**)
(ANTONYM: **dusk**)

**day·care** /**day**-kair/ *noun* a place where young children are taken care of during the day when their parents are at work: *My baby sister is in daycare while my mom is at work.*

**day·dream** /**day**-dreem/
● *verb* to think about nice things that you imagine happening: *She was looking out of the window, daydreaming about her party.*
—**daydreamer** /**day**-dreem-ur/ *noun* someone who daydreams
● *noun* thoughts about nice things that you imagine happening: *Carlos was in a daydream about being a famous football player.*

**day·light** /**day**-līt/ *noun*
**1** the light that comes from the Sun during the day: *The bright daylight hurt his eyes.*
**2** the time in the day when it is light and easy to see: *It's too dark to see now. We'll wait for daylight to look for your ball.*

**day·light-sav·ing time** /day-līt-**sayv**-ing tīm/ *noun* the time in spring when clocks are set one hour ahead of standard time

**day·time** /**day**-tīm/ *noun* the part of the day when it is light: *Owls sleep in the daytime and hunt for food at night.*
(ANTONYM: **nighttime**)

**day-to-day** /**day**-tuh-day/ *adjective* happening every day: *day-to-day events*

**daze** /dayz/ *noun* if you are in a daze, you cannot think clearly because you are surprised or hurt: *Mom was in a daze when she heard the bad news about Grandpa's car accident.*

**dazed** /dayzd/ *adjective* unable to think clearly because you are surprised or hurt: *He had fallen off his bike, and he looked a little dazed.*

**daz·zle** /**daz**-uhl/ *verb*
**1** to make you admire someone or something a lot: *He's a great baseball player and he dazzled everyone with his skill at the game.*
**2** to make someone unable to see clearly. A very bright light does this: *The car's headlights dazzled me.*

**daz·zling** /**daz**-ling/ *adjective*
**1** very attractive or impressive: *He gave her a dazzling smile.*
**2** very bright, so that you cannot see clearly for a short time: *The white snow was dazzling in the sun.*

**de-** /di/

**Word Building**

**de-** is a prefix.
**de**port | **de**scend | **de**crease | **de**cline | **de**tach
**de-** means "down" or "away." If the government *deports* people, it sends them away from this country back to their own country. If you *descend* a mountain, you go down it. If an amount *decreases*, it goes down or becomes less.

a b c **d** e f g h i j k l m n o p q r s t u v w x y z

**dead** /ded/
● *adjective*
**1** no longer alive: *Both his grandmothers are dead.* ► see **Thesaurus**
**2** not working because there is no power: *My cell phone is completely dead.*
**3** complete or exact: *There has to be dead silence during the test.* | *I hit the target dead center.*
**4** with nothing interesting happening: *The party was dead. No one was dancing or having fun.*
● *adverb*
**1** very: *I'm dead tired.*
**2** exactly: *We saw the island dead ahead.*
● *noun*
**the dead** people who are dead: *Let us pray for the dead and their families.* ( ANTONYM: **the living** )

**dead end** /ded **end**/ *noun* a street with no way out at one end: *Bridge Street is a dead end, so you have to turn around to get out.*

**dead·line** /**ded**-līn/ *noun* the latest date or time that you can do something: *The deadline for entering the competition is March 31.*

**dead·ly** /**ded**-lee/ *adjective* able or likely to kill you: *If the snake bites you, a deadly poison goes into your blood.*

**deaf** /def/ *adjective* not able to hear: *Grandpa doesn't always hear what I say because he's slightly deaf.*
—**deafness** /**def**-niss/ *noun* the state of not being able to hear: *Hearing aids can help with deafness.*

**deaf·en** /**def**-uhn/ *verb* if a loud noise deafens you, it makes it difficult for you to hear: *The music was so loud it deafened us.*
—**deafening** /**def**-uhn-ing/ *adjective* very loud: *The crowd was cheering and shouting and the noise was deafening.*

**deal** /deel/
● *noun*
**1** an agreement: *I made a deal with Jennifer. I would help her with math if she would help me with English.*
**2** if it is your deal, it is your turn to give out cards to players in a card game: *Whose deal is it now?*

IDIOMS with **deal**
**a great deal** a lot: *Mia has made a great deal of progress in reading this year.*
**make a big deal out of** to make something seem more important than it is: *I sat next to Emily at lunch instead of next to Jessie, and Jessie got really mad. She made a really big deal out of it.*
**no big deal** you say this about something that you do not think is very important: *So you lost one game. That's no big deal.*
● *verb* (**dealt** /delt/)
**1** to give cards to each player in a card game: *For this game you deal seven cards to each player.*
**2 deal in** to buy and sell a product: *That store deals in CDs and DVDs.*
**3 deal with** to do something to stop a problem: *How do you deal with bullying in your school?*
**4 deal with** to be about a subject: *The next chapter deals with the Civil War.*

**deal·er** /**deel**-ur/ *noun*
**1** the person who gives out the cards in a card game: *The dealer gives everyone five cards.*
**2** someone who buys and sells things: *His dad is a car dealer.*

**dealt** /delt/ *verb* the past tense and past participle of **deal**

**dear** /deer/
● *adjective*
**1** used to begin a letter, before someone's name: *Dear Aunt Linda, Thank you for the present.*
**2** a dear person is someone you like or love very much: *Michelle is a dear friend of my mother's.*
● *noun*
you say this to someone you like or love: *Thank you, dear.*
● *interjection*
**oh dear** you say this when something bad happens: *Oh dear! I spilled my milk.*

**death** /deth/ *noun* the end of someone's life: *I knew Grandpa was sick, but his death was still a shock.* ( ANTONYM: **birth** )

**death pen·al·ty** /**deth** pen'l-tee/ *noun* the legal punishment of killing someone who is guilty of a serious crime: *If he is found guilty of murder, he could get the death penalty.*

**de·bate** /di-**bayt**/
● *noun*
a discussion about a subject. In a debate, each

person says what they think about the subject, and other people find reasons to agree or disagree: *In class, we had a debate on whether TV was good for us or not.*
● *verb*
**1** to think about something carefully before you make a decision: *Katy's still debating what she wants to do for her birthday.*
**2** to discuss something in an official way: *Congress will debate the issue later this week.*

**de·bris** /di-**bree**/ *noun* the pieces of something that are left after an accident or explosion: *There was glass and other debris from the car wreck all over the road.*

**debt** /det/ *noun*
**1** money that you owe: *If I borrow money from a friend, I always repay my debt quickly.*
**2** if you are in debt, you owe money to people: *College is expensive and many students are in debt.*

**debt·or** /**det**-ur/ *noun* someone who owes money

**de·but** /day-**byoo**/ *noun* the first time that someone performs in public: *She made her debut on the stage in 2002.*

**dec-** /dek, dess/

## Word Building

**decade | decagon | decibel | decimal**
These words all have the Greek word root **dec** in them. **Dec** means "ten." A *decade* is ten years. A *decagon* is a flat shape with ten sides and ten angles. The *decimal* system of measuring is based on the number ten.

**dec·ade** /**dek**-ayd/ *noun* a period of ten years: *The world has changed a lot in the last decade.*

**de·caf·fein·at·ed** /dee-**kaf**-uh-nayt-id/ (also **de·caf** /**dee**-kaf/) *adjective* decaffeinated coffee or cola has had the caffeine taken out: *Mom only drinks decaffeinated coffee.*

**dec·a·gon** /**dek**-uh-gahn/ *noun* a flat shape with ten sides and ten angles

**de·cay** /di-**kay**/
● *verb*
**1** to become rotten and be slowly destroyed:

*When animals die, their bodies decay.*
**2** if a building or place decays, its condition becomes slowly worse: *Many of the houses here are old, dirty, and decaying.*
● *noun*
**1** a natural process in which something becomes rotten and is slowly destroyed: *Brushing your teeth helps prevent tooth decay.*
**2** a process in which the condition of something slowly becomes worse: *Parts of the city were in decay and many old buildings were falling down.*

**de·ceased** /di-**seest**/ *adjective* dead: *The house belonged to her deceased grandmother.*

**de·ceit** /di-**seet**/ *noun* behavior that is not honest, especially saying things that are not true: *He found out that she had lied, and he was upset by her deceit.*
—**deceitful** /di-**seet**-fuhl/ *adjective* not honest: *It was deceitful to pretend that you lost the money.*

**de·ceive** /di-**seev**/ *verb* to make someone believe something that is not true: *She deceived her parents. She said she was going to the store, when really she was meeting her friends.*

## Word Family: deceive

**deceive** *verb* | **deception** *noun* | **deceit** *noun* | **deceitful** *adjective* | **deceptive** *adjective*

**De·cem·ber** /di-**sem**-bur/ *noun*
(ABBREVIATION: **Dec.**) the 12th month of the year. December is between November and January: *It often snows in December.* | *Christmas is on December 25.*

## Word Origin: December

**December** comes from the Latin word **decem** which means "ten." The old Roman calendar had ten months. December was the tenth month. When the Romans started using a new calendar, they added two more months to the calendar. December became the 12th month, but it kept its old name.

**de·cen·cy** /**deess**-uhnss-ee/ *noun* good behavior that shows respect for other people: *The teacher treats the children with kindness and decency. She is fair and talks to them honestly.*

**de·cent** /**deess**-uhnt/ *adjective*
**1** good or satisfactory: *I got a B on the test – that's a decent grade.*
**2** decent people are good and honest: *He's a decent man and he always wants to help people.*

**de·cep·tion** /di-**sep**-shuhn/ *noun* dishonest behavior, especially saying things that are not true: *He used deception to get into the house. He said he was a salesman, but he wasn't.*

**de·cep·tive** /di-**sept**-iv/ *adjective* making you believe something that is not true: *The test is deceptive. The questions seem easy, but really they are very difficult.*
—**deceptively** /di-**sept**-iv-lee/ *adverb* in a deceptive way: *The game is deceptively packaged and looks like a box of candy.*

**dec·i·bel** /**dess**-uh-bel/ *noun* a unit for measuring how loud something is: *The music was being played at more than 100 decibels.*

**de·cide** /di-**sīd**/ *verb* to choose what you are going to do after thinking about it: *I decided to wear my blue shirt, not the white one.*
▶ see **Thesaurus**

**Word Family: decide**

**decide** *verb* | **decision** *noun* | **decisive** *adjective* | **indecisive** *adjective*

**de·cid·u·ous** /di-**sij**-oo-uhss/ *adjective* a deciduous tree loses its leaves in winter: *Maple trees are deciduous.*
(ANTONYMS: **coniferous, evergreen**)

**dec·i·mal** /**dess**-uhm-uhl/
● *noun* a number such as 0.8 or 2.63. A decimal can be a fraction, or a whole number and a fraction, written with a decimal point.
● *adjective* the decimal system is based on the number ten

**dec·i·mal point** /dess-uhm-uhl **poynt**/ *noun* a mark (.) used in decimal numbers. The numbers after this mark are tenths, hundredths, etc.

**dec·i·me·ter** /**dess**-uh-meet-ur/ *noun* one tenth of a meter: *There are ten decimeters in a meter.*

**de·ci·sion** /di-**sizh**-uhn/ *noun* a choice that you make: *His parents made a decision to move him to another school.*

**de·ci·sive** /di-**sīss**-iv/ *adjective*
**1** good at making decisions quickly: *The president is strong and decisive. He tries not to worry about making the wrong decision.*
(ANTONYM: **indecisive**)
**2** having a very definite and clear effect: *The army won a decisive victory and soon the war was over.*
—**decisively** /di-**sīss**-iv-lee/ *adverb* in a decisive way: *The team was decisively defeated by 15 goals to 2.*

**deck** /dek/ *noun*
**1** a set of playing cards that you play games with: *There are 52 cards in a deck.*
**2** a wooden floor built outside at the back of a house: *We eat on the deck in the summer.*
**3** one of the levels on a ship: *Let's go up on the top deck and look at the ocean.*

**deck**

deck

**dec·la·ra·tion** /dek-luh-**raysh**-uhn/ *noun* an important announcement that says you intend to do something: *The declaration of war was expected at any moment.*

**de·clare** /di-**klair**/ *verb* to announce or say something formally: *In court, the man declared that he was innocent.*

**de·cline** /di-**klīn**/
● *verb*
**1** to become fewer in number: *The number of tigers in the wild is declining and one day there will be no more tigers left.* (SYNONYM: **decrease**)
**2** to become worse: *His health has declined in the last year and he is very sick.*

**3** to politely say no to an invitation, offer, or request: *We had to decline their invitation to the wedding.*

● *noun*

a situation in which something becomes fewer, less, or worse: *There has been a decline in the number of bees and this is causing problems for farmers.* ( SYNONYM: **decrease** )

**de·com·pose** /dee-kuhm-**pohz**/ *verb* to be slowly destroyed by a natural process: *The animal was dead and its body had started to decompose.* ( SYNONYM: **decay** )

—**decomposition** /dee-kahmp-uh-**zish**-uhn/ *noun* the process of decomposing: *The decomposition of the leaves makes the soil richer and better for new plants.*

**de·com·pos·er** /dee-kuhm-**pohz**-ur/ *noun* a living thing such as bacteria, fungus, or an animal, that feeds on dead or decaying things and makes them decay

**de·con·tam·i·nate** /dee-kuhn-**tam**-uh-nayt/ *verb* to remove a dangerous substance from somewhere: *The river was full of chemicals from the factory, and the water had to be decontaminated.*

**dec·o·rate** /**dek**-uh-rayt/ *verb*

**1** to make something look nice by adding pretty things to it: *We decorated the room with balloons for his birthday.*

**2** to give someone a medal or badge because he or she has done something very good: *He was decorated for bravery in the war.*

decorate

—**decorative** /**dek**-uhr-uht-iv/ *adjective* used to make something look pretty: *The store sells jewelry, paintings, and other decorative objects.*

**dec·o·ra·tion** /dek-uh-**raysh**-uhn/ *noun*

**1** a pretty thing you put somewhere to look attractive, especially on special occasions: *The house was full of balloons and other birthday decorations.*

**2** a medal that is a sign of honor: *He received a decoration for bravery in the war.*

**de·crease** /di-**kreess**/

● *verb* to become fewer or less: *The number of students has decreased from 390 to 350.*

( ANTONYM: **increase** )

● *noun* /**dee**-kreess/ a situation in which there is less of something: *People are driving more slowly and there has been a decrease in the number of road accidents.* ( ANTONYM: **increase** )

**ded·i·cate** /**ded**-uh-kayt/ *verb*

**1** to say publicly that you wrote a book or song for someone you love or respect: *He dedicated the book to his wife.*

**2** if you dedicate yourself to something, you give it a lot of time and effort: *She dedicated her life to helping poor people.*

**ded·i·cat·ed** /**ded**-uh-kayt-id/ *adjective* working very hard at something because you believe it is important: *If you want to become a doctor, you need to be very dedicated and study hard.*

**ded·i·ca·tion** /ded-uh-**kaysh**-uhn/ *noun*

**1** hard work or effort that you give to something you care about: *It takes dedication to become a successful dancer.*

**2** the words used to dedicate a book or song to someone: *The dedication said "To my children."*

**de·duce** /di-**dooss**/ *verb* to decide that something is true, using the information you have: *From the fossil shells, you can deduce that these mountains were once under water.*

**de·duct** /di-**duhkt**/ *verb* to take an amount away from a bigger amount: *I owed dad $2 so he deducted it from my allowance.*

**de·duc·tion** /di-**duhk**-shuhn/ *noun*

**1** an amount that is taken away from a bigger amount: *There is a deduction of one point for every spelling mistake.*

**2** the process of finding the truth, using the information you have: *The story gives you all the clues to solve the mystery, but you have to use deduction to figure it out.*

**deed** /deed/ *noun*

**1** a good or bad action: *He was famous for his heroic deeds in battle.*

**2** a legal document that says who owns a house or land: *The deeds to the land show that it belongs to our family.*

a b c **d** e f g h i j k l m n o p q r s t u v w x y z

**deep** /deep/

● *adjective*

**1** something that is deep goes down a long way: *The snow was very deep – it went up to my waist.* (ANTONYM: **shallow**)

**2** used when saying the distance from the top to the bottom of something: *Dig a hole two feet deep.* | *They bought a four-foot-deep swimming pool.*

**3** a deep feeling is very strong: *I had a deep feeling of sadness after his death.*

**4** a deep sound is very low: *Men have deeper voices than women.*

**5** a deep color is dark and strong: *The wall was painted a deep blue, like the ocean.*
(ANTONYMS: **light, pale**)

**6** deep trouble is very bad or serious: *I will be in deep trouble if I'm late again.*

**7** if you are in a deep sleep, you are sleeping well and not easy to wake: *Sara was in a deep sleep and she did not hear her alarm clock.*

**8** if you take a deep breath, you breathe a lot of air into your body: *She took a deep breath and went under the water.*

● *adverb*

a long way down in something: *These fish live deep in the ocean.*

**deep**

**deep·en** /deep-uhn/ *verb*

**1** to become deeper: *The river deepens in the middle.* | *Boys' voices deepen when they get older.*

**2** if a serious situation deepens, it becomes worse: *Their troubles deepened when he lost his job.*

**deep·ly** /deep-lee/ *adverb* extremely: *Naomi was deeply upset by her parents' divorce.* | *His mother is deeply concerned about his illness.*

**deer** /deer/ *noun* (plural **deer**) a big wild animal with thin legs and a short tail. Deer live in forests, eat plants, and run fast: *Male deer have large horns called antlers.*

antlers  **deer**

hoof

**de·feat** /di-**feet**/

● *verb* to beat someone in a game, war, or election: *The Dolphins defeated the Jets 24–17.* (SYNONYM: **beat**) ▶ see **Thesaurus**

● *noun* a time when you do not win or succeed: *We lost 10–1, our worst defeat ever.*
(SYNONYM: **loss**) (ANTONYM: **victory**)

**de·fect**

● *noun* /**dee**-fekt/ a problem in the way something is made, that makes it not work or look wrong: *A defect in the car's engine caused the fire.*

● *verb* /di-**fekt**/ to leave your country or political group and join another one: *His parents defected to the U.S. from Cuba.*

**de·fec·tive** /di-**fekt**-iv/ *adjective* not made correctly, or not working correctly: *The software for the game was defective, so the game didn't work.*

**de·fend** /di-**fend**/ *verb*

**1** to protect someone or something from attack: *They built the fort to defend the island.*

**2** to say something to support an idea or action that other people do not like: *The school is defending its decision to make the children wear uniforms.*

**3** to try to stop the other team from scoring points: *Megan defended the goal well through the whole game.*

**Word Family:** **defend**

**defend** verb | **defense** noun | **defender** noun | **defendant** noun | **defenseless** adjective | **defensive** adjective

**de·fend·ant** /di-**fend**-uhnt/ *noun* the person in a court of law who has been accused of a crime: *The jury decided that the defendant was guilty of stealing the car.*

**de·fend·er** /di-**fend**-ur/ *noun* one of the players on a team whose job is to stop the other team from winning points: *Jake ran past the defenders and made a touchdown.*

**de·fense** *noun*
**1** /di-**fenss**/ something that protects something or someone: *A bee uses its sting as a defense against attackers.*
**2** /di-**fenss**/ the weapons and soldiers that a country uses to protect itself from attack: *The army and navy are important for our national defense.*
**3** /**dee**-fenss/ the players on a sports team who try to prevent the other team from scoring points: *We have a good defense and it will be difficult for anyone to beat us.*
**4** /di-**fenss**/ the lawyers in a court who try to show that someone is not guilty of a crime: *The defense is sure that they can prove he is innocent.*

**de·fense·less** /di-**fenss**-liss/ *adjective* unable to protect yourself: *He was arrested for kicking and hurting a defenseless animal.*

**de·fen·sive** /di-**fenss**-iv/ *adjective*
**1** trying to defend yourself because you think someone is criticizing you: *When the teacher talks to him about his behavior, he just gets defensive.*
**2** used for defending someone or something: *The ship took defensive action and moved away quickly.*

**de·fi·ant** /di-**fī**-uhnt/ *adjective* refusing to obey someone: *He never does what his mother asks him to. He's very defiant.*
—**defiantly** /di-**fī**-uhnt-lee/ *adverb* in a defiant way: *"I'm not going!" said Sam defiantly.*
—**defiance** /di-**fī**-uhnss/ *noun* behavior that shows you refuse to obey someone: *When the people in Boston threw the tea in the harbor in 1773, it was an act of defiance against the British government.*

**de·fi·cient** /di-**fish**-uhnt/ *adjective* not containing enough of something: *She doesn't eat meat or green vegetables, so her diet is deficient in iron.*
—**deficiency** /di-**fish**-uhnss-ee/ *noun* a lack of something you need: *A vitamin C deficiency can cause a disease called scurvy.*

**def·i·cit** /**def**-uhss-it/ *noun* the difference between the amount of money you have and the larger amount that you need: *The government has spent more money than it gets in taxes, so there is a big deficit.* ( ANTONYM: **surplus** )

**de·fine** /di-**fīn**/ *verb* to explain the meaning of a word: *This dictionary defines cat as "a small animal with soft fur and pointed ears."*

**def·i·nite** /**def**-uhn-it/ *adjective*
**1** certain and not likely to change: *I'm not sure if I can go to the party yet. I'll give you a definite answer tomorrow.*
**2** clear and noticeable: *She's been really sick, but the doctor says she shows definite signs of improvement.*

**def·i·nite ar·ti·cle** /**def**-uhn-it **art**-ik-uhl/ *noun* the word "the"

**def·i·nite·ly** /**def**-uhn-it-lee/ *adverb* certainly or without any doubt: *I'm definitely going to try again.*

**def·i·ni·tion** /def-uh-**nish**-uhn/ *noun* an explanation of what a word means: *In the dictionary, the definition of baby is "a very young child."*

**de·for·est** /dee-**for**-ist/ *verb* to cut or burn down all the trees in an area: *In Brazil, large areas of the jungle have been deforested.*

**de·frost** /dee-**frost**/ *verb* to put frozen food in a warmer place, until it is not frozen anymore: *The turkey was defrosting on the counter.*

**de·fy** /di-**fī**/ *verb* (**defies**, **defying**, **defied**) to refuse to obey someone or something: *People defied the rules, and they were punished.*

**de·grade** /di-**grayd**/ *verb* to treat people or animals very badly, in a way that shows no respect for them: *Keeping lions and tigers in small cages degrades them.*

**de·grad·ing** /di-**grayd**-ing/ *adjective* treating someone badly and making that person lose respect for himself or herself: *Slavery was degrading because slaves were treated as things that you could buy and sell.*

a
b
c
d
e
f
g
h
i
j
k
l
m
n
o
p
q
r
s
t
u
v
w
x
y
z

**de·gree** /di-**gree**/ *noun*
**1** a unit for measuring temperature. It is often shown by the sign (°): *Heat the oven to 400 degrees (400°).*
**2** a unit for measuring an angle. It is often shown by the sign (°): *The angles of a triangle add up to 180 degrees (180°).*
**3** a special statement that says you have successfully completed all your studies at a university or college: *He has a degree in law from Harvard University.*
**4** a level or amount of something: *Football involves a degree of risk, and players are sometimes hurt.*

**de·hy·drat·ed** /dee-**hī**-drayt-id/ *adjective* if you are dehydrated, you do not have enough water in your body: *Drink plenty of water to keep from getting dehydrated.*
—**dehydration** /dee-hī-**draysh**-uhn/ *noun* the state when you do not have enough water in your body: *In very hot weather, dehydration is a real risk.*

**de·lay** /di-**lay**/
● *verb*
**1** to make someone or something late: *We were late to school because the bus was delayed by heavy traffic.*
**2** to wait until a later time to do something: *Dad got sick and we had to delay our vacation until he was better.*
● *noun*
if there is a delay, something happens later than you planned or expected: *The snow caused delays at the airport when airplanes couldn't take off.*

**del·e·gate**
● *noun* /**del**-uhg-it/ someone who represents a country or group at a meeting: *Delegates from each class are on the school council.*
● *verb* /**del**-uh-gayt/ to give part of your work to someone else: *By voting, we delegate the job of making decisions about our country to our Senators and Congressmen.*

**de·lete** /di-**leet**/ *verb* to take out parts of a piece of writing, or to get rid of a whole computer document: *I deleted the last paragraph of my essay.* | *Don't delete the file – you might need it later.*
—**deletion** /di-**leesh**-uhn/ *noun* the act of deleting something

**del·i** /**del**-ee/ *noun* a small store that sells food such as cheese, cooked meat, and bread, and that often sells sandwiches
( SYNONYM: **delicatessen** )

**de·lib·er·ate**
● *adjective* /di-**libr**-it/ planned and intended: *Sorry – I didn't mean to bump into you. It wasn't deliberate.*
● *verb* /di-**lib**-uh-rayt/ to think carefully before you decide something: *The jury deliberated for six hours before deciding he was not guilty.*

**de·lib·er·ate·ly** /di-**libr**-it-lee/ *adverb* in a way that someone planned and intended: *The fire wasn't an accident – it was started deliberately.*
( SYNONYM: **on purpose** )

**del·i·cate** /**del**-ik-it/ *adjective*
**1** made of fine material and easy to damage: *Be careful with that china cup. It's very delicate.*
**2** needing great care in order not to upset people: *We want to get the two sides to agree without making anyone mad – it's a delicate job.*
**3** small and beautiful: *Louisa was pretty, with delicate features.*
**4** a delicate flavor is very pleasant and not strong: *The cheese had a delicate flavor.*

**del·i·ca·tes·sen** /del-ik-uh-**tess**-uhn/ *noun* a small store that sells food such as cheese, cooked meat, and bread, and that often sells sandwiches: *We bought some ham and bagels at the delicatessen.* ( SYNONYM: **deli** )

**de·li·cious** /di-**lish**-uhss/ *adjective* delicious food tastes very good: *The ice cream is delicious.*
▶ see **Thesaurus**

**de·light** /di-**līt**/
● *noun* great pleasure: *At the party, the kids were jumping up and down and laughing with delight.*
● *verb* to give someone great pleasure: *Lucy's singing delighted her grandma.*

**de·light·ed** /di-**līt**-id/ *adjective* very pleased: *Her parents were delighted with her grades.*

**de·light·ful** /di-**līt**-fuhl/ *adjective* very nice or pleasant: *His teacher says he is a delightful boy.*

**de·lin·quent** /di-**ling**-kwuhnt/
● *noun* a young person who does bad or illegal things: *The police arrested some delinquents who were stealing and causing fights.*

● *adjective* a delinquent young person does bad or illegal things: *The boys were involved in delinquent behavior such as burglaries.*

**de·liv·er** /di-**liv**-ur/ *verb*
**1** to take a letter or package to a particular place: *The mailman delivered a package to our house.*
**2** to make a speech: *The president delivered a speech to Congress.*
**3** to help a baby to be born: *The doctor who delivered my aunt's baby was really nice.*

**de·liv·er·y** /di-**liv**-uhr-ee/ *noun* (plural **deliveries**) the act of bringing something to a place or person: *If you buy two large pizzas, the delivery is free.*

**del·ta** /**delt**-uh/ *noun* an area where a big river spreads out near the ocean. The river often divides into smaller rivers. The river also leaves sand, mud, and small rocks in a delta.

**delta**

**del·uge** /**del**-yooj/
● *noun*
**1** very heavy rain, or a flood: *The river flooded and the deluge forced many people to leave their homes.*
**2** a lot of things that someone gets and has to deal with: *They received a deluge of complaints.*
● *verb*
to send a lot of things to someone, which they have to deal with: *She was deluged with cards and flowers on her birthday.*

**de·luxe** /di-**luhkss**/ *adjective* very good and expensive: *They stayed in a deluxe hotel.*

**de·mand** /di-**mand**/
● *noun*
**1** if there is a demand for something, people want to buy it: *There's a great demand for the toy – all the kids want it.*
**2** a strong request: *He made a demand for more money.*
**3** **demands** things that you need to do, that are difficult or take time: *The demands of school work increase as you get older.*
● *verb*
**1** to ask for something in a firm way: *My teacher demanded to see my homework.*
**2** to need a skill or quality: *Learning to play the piano demands effort.*

**de·mand·ing** /di-**mand**-ing/ *adjective* needing a lot of time, skill, or effort: *I had a big part in the play, which was demanding but fun.*

**de·mer·it** /di-**merr**-it/ *noun* a warning that you are given when you have behaved badly. If you get more demerits, you are usually given a punishment: *You can get a demerit for not staying in your seat on the school bus.*

**de·moc·ra·cy** /di-**mahk**-ruhss-ee/ *noun* (plural **democracies**)
**1** a system of governing a country in which the people choose their leaders by voting: *If there is democracy in a country, people can vote in elections.*
**2** a country that has this system: *The U.S.A. is a democracy.*

**Word Family:** democracy
**democracy** *noun* | **democrat** *noun* | **democratic** *adjective* | **democratically** *adverb*

**Word Origin:** democracy
**Democracy** comes from two Greek words that mean "ordinary people" and "rule." To rule means to control a country. In a country that has a democracy, ordinary people vote to choose their leaders. By voting, people control what their country does.

**Dem·o·crat** /**dem**-uh-krat/ *noun* a member of the Democratic Party: *The Democrats gained votes in nearly every state.*

**dem·o·crat·ic** /dem-uh-**krat**-ik/ *adjective*
**1** giving the people of a country the right to vote to choose the government: *In America, we have a democratic society.*
**2** relating to the Democratic Party. Democratic is written with a capital D: *He's the Democratic candidate for governor.*
—**democratically** /dem-uh-**krat**-ik-lee/ *adverb* in a democratic way: *Our president is democratically elected.*

**de·mol·ish** /di-**mahl**-ish/ *verb* to completely destroy something, especially a building: *The old houses were demolished and a hotel was built.*
—**demolition** /dem-uh-**lish**-uhn/ *noun* the act of demolishing something: *Demolition of the bridge will begin in May.*

**de·mon** /**deem**-uhn/ *noun* an evil spirit: *Some people believe that demons make us do bad things.*

**dem·on·strate** /**dem**-uhn-strayt/ *verb*
**1** to show someone how to do something: *Our teacher demonstrated how to solve the math problem on the board.*
**2** to show clearly that something is true: *The tests demonstrate that the children's reading has improved.*
**3** to protest about something in public with a lot of other people: *A crowd of people were demonstrating against the war.*
—**demonstrator** /**dem**-uhn-strayt-ur/ *noun* someone who is protesting about something in public: *Demonstrators stood outside the U.S. embassy to protest against the president's visit.*

**dem·on·stra·tion** /dem-uhn-**straysh**-uhn/ *noun*
**1** if you give a demonstration, you show people how to do something: *She gave us a demonstration of how to make pancakes.*
**2** an event at which a lot of people protest about something in public: *There were over a thousand people at the demonstration against the war.*

**den** /den/ *noun*
**1** a room in a house where you relax: *Dad was reading in the den.*
**2** the home of a wild animal such as a lion or fox

**den**

*a foxes' den*

**de·ni·al** /di-**nī**-uhl/ *noun* a statement saying that something is not true: *He said he had nothing to do with the crime, but nobody believed his denial.* ( ANTONYM: **admission** )

**den·im** /**den**-uhm/ *noun* a strong cotton cloth used to make jeans and other clothes: *I bought a blue denim jacket.*

**denim**

*a denim jacket*

## Word Origin: denim

The word **denim** comes from a French phrase, **serge de Nîmes**. Serge is a type of heavy cloth, and "de Nîmes" means that this cloth was made in the French city of Nîmes. In the 1850s, Americans pushed together "de Nîmes" to form **denim**. They started using the word denim to describe the thick cloth that jeans are made from.

**de·nom·i·na·tion** /di-nahm-uh-**naysh**-uhn/ *noun* a religious group that is part of one of the main world religions. Each denomination has slightly different beliefs: *The Catholic Church and the Baptist Church are both Christian denominations.*

**de·nom·i·na·tor** /di-**nahm**-uh-nayt-ur/ *noun* the number below the line in a fraction. It shows how many parts you are dividing the whole number into: *In the fraction 3/4, 4 is the denominator.*

**dense** /denss/ *adjective*
**1** with a lot of trees or plants growing close together, or a lot of people living close together: *The island is covered with a dense forest.*
**2** thick and difficult to see through: *Some flights were delayed because of dense fog.*
**3** not intelligent: *He didn't understand the joke at all. He's so dense!* ( SYNONYM: **stupid** )
—**densely** /denss-lee/ *adverb* in a way that has a lot of people or things close together: *Millions of people live in this densely populated city.*

**den·si·ty** /denss-uht-ee/ *noun*
**1** how heavy something is in relation to its size. You measure density by dividing an object's mass (=weight) by its volume (=size): *If you add salt to water, you increase its density because the water becomes heavier but its volume does not increase.*
**2** how many people or things there are in relation to the size of the area they are in: *The state of Wyoming has a low population density with only five people per square mile.*

**dent** /dent/
● *noun* a bent area in a surface, where something has hit it: *The truck had a big dent in the door, where the other car hit it.*
● *verb* to make a dent in something: *Dad hit a tree and dented the car.*

**den·tal** /dent'l/ *adjective* relating to your teeth: *If you brush your teeth regularly, you will have fewer dental problems.*

**den·tist** /dent-ist/ *noun* someone whose job is to examine and treat people's teeth: *The dentist took out one of my back teeth.*

**den·tures** /dench-urz/ *plural noun* a set of artificial teeth that you wear if you have no teeth

**de·ny** /di-nī/ *verb* (**denies, denying, denied**)
**1** to say that something is not true: *She denies that she stole the money.* ( ANTONYM: **admit** )
**2** to not let someone have something or do something: *The principal denied him permission to leave school early.*

**Word Family:** deny

**deny** *verb* | **denial** *noun*

**de·o·dor·ant** /dee-**ohd**-uhr-uhnt/ *noun* a substance that you put under your arms to prevent your body from smelling bad

**de·part** /di-**part**/ *verb* to leave a place: *The train for Denver will depart from track 9 at ten o'clock.* ( ANTONYM: **arrive** )

**de·part·ment** /di-**part**-muhnt/ *noun* a part of a large organization such as a business, college, or government: *He is a professor in the English Department at the university.*

**de·part·ment store** /di-**part**-muhnt stor/ *noun* a large store that sells many different kinds of things, such as clothes, furniture, and jewelry

**de·par·ture** /di-**parch**-ur/ *noun* the action of leaving a place: *The plane is now ready for departure.* ( ANTONYM: **arrival** )

**de·pend** /di-**pend**/ *verb*
**1** **depend on** to need the help or support of someone or something else: *Babies depend on their parents for everything.*
**2** **depend on** to be affected by something that is not certain: *We might go – it depends on the weather.*

**de·pend·a·ble** /di-**pend**-uhb-uhl/ *adjective* someone or something that is dependable will always do what you need: *My brother is very dependable. If he says he is coming at 6:30, he will be here at that time.* ( SYNONYM: **reliable** )

**de·pend·ent** /di-**pend**-uhnt/
● *adjective* needing someone or something in order to live or continue: *Bear cubs are totally dependent on their mother for food.*
( ANTONYM: **independent** )
—**dependence** /di-**pend**-uhnss/ *noun* a need for someone or something in order to live or continue: *Our dependence on computers is growing all the time.*
● *noun* a child or other person who is taken care of and given food, a place to live, and clothes by another person, such as parents or family members: *She is not married and has no dependents.*

## de·pend·ent var·i·a·ble /di-pend-uhnt vair-ee-uhb-uhl/ *noun*
something that changes because you have changed something else, for example in a science experiment: *We grew some plants in sunlight and others in darkness. In our experiment, the height of the plants was a dependent variable, and the independent variable was how much light they got.*

ANTONYM: **independent variable**

## de·port /di-port/ *verb*
to send someone back to his or her own country: *He was deported back to Guatemala because he was living in the U.S. illegally.*
—**deportation** /dee-por-**taysh**-uhn/ *noun* the act of deporting someone: *The president ordered the deportation of illegal immigrants.*

## de·pos·it /di-**pahz**-it/
● *noun*
**1** an amount of money that is put into a bank account: *I made a deposit of $25 into my bank account.* ANTONYM: **withdrawal**
**2** a small payment that you give a store when you arrange to buy something expensive. You pay the rest of the money when you get the thing you are buying: *Dad paid a deposit of $50 when he ordered our new computer.*
**3** money that you pay when you rent something such as an apartment or car. The deposit is given back to you if you do not cause any damage: *You can rent a car for $200 a week, plus a deposit of $500 which you get back when you return the car.*
● *verb*
to put money into a bank account: *She deposited all her birthday money into her savings account.* ANTONYM: **withdraw**

## de·press /di-**press**/ *verb*
to make you feel very unhappy: *It depresses me when people are mean to one another.*

## de·pressed /di-**prest**/ *adjective*
feeling very unhappy: *Lisa felt depressed about leaving all her friends when she moved to a new house.*

### Word Family: depressed
**depressed** *adjective* | **depressing** *adjective* | **depress** *verb* | **depression** *noun*

## de·press·ing /di-**press**-ing/ *adjective*
making you feel unhappy: *I don't like movies where somebody dies. They're too depressing.*

## de·pres·sion /di-**presh**-uhn/ *noun*
**1** a strong feeling of sadness that makes it difficult for someone to have a normal life: *He suffered from depression after his wife died.*
**2** a long period when the economy is doing badly and a lot of people do not have jobs: *During the Great Depression of the 1930s, many people lost their homes.*

## de·prive /di-**prīv**/ *verb*
to stop someone from having something that he or she should have: *In the past, unfair laws deprived many black people of their right to vote.*

## de·prived /di-**prīvd**/ *adjective*
not having the things that you need for a healthy, comfortable, or happy life: *He grew up in a deprived neighborhood, where few people had jobs or even enough food to eat.*
—**deprivation** /dep-ruh-**vaysh**-uhn/ *noun* a situation in which people do not have the things that they need for a healthy, comfortable, or happy life: *There is a lot of deprivation in parts of Africa.*

## depth /depth/ *noun*
**1** the distance from the top to the bottom of something that goes down into the ground: *The depth of the river is about 30 feet.*
**2** the distance from the front to the back of an object: *Measure the height, width, and depth of the box.*
**3 in depth** if you write or talk about something in depth, you give many details about it: *The book covers the Civil War in depth.*

## dep·u·ty /**dep**-yuht-ee/ (plural **deputies**) *noun*
**1** the person who has the second most important job in an organization: *I'm the deputy editor of the school newspaper.*
**2** a type of police officer who works for a sheriff

## de·rive /di-**rīv**/ *verb*
**1 derive from** to get an advantage or a good feeling from something: *Students derive a lot of pleasure from art classes.*
**2 derive from** to develop or come from something else: *The word "science" derives from the Latin word "scientia," which means "knowledge."*

**de·scend** /di-**send**/ *verb*
**1** to go down: *The elevator descended to the ground floor.* ( ANTONYM: **ascend** )
**2 be descended from** to be related to someone who lived a long time ago: *He is descended from a Native American chief.*

**de·scend·ant** /di-**send**-uhnt/ *noun* someone who is related to a person who lived a long time ago: *Her parents are descendants of the early settlers.*

**de·scent** /di-**sent**/ *noun*
**1** the action of going down to a lower place: *The plane began its descent to LaGuardia Airport.*
**2** used to describe where your family originally came from. For example, if you are of Mexican descent, your family originally came from Mexico: *Helena is of Polish descent, but she has never been to Poland.*

**de·scribe** /di-**skrīb**/ *verb* to say what someone or something is like: *Can you describe any of the animals we saw today?*

**Word Family:** describe

**describe** *verb* | **description** *noun*

**de·scrip·tion** /di-**skrip**-shuhn/ *noun* a statement that says what someone or something is like: *Students must write a description of the science experiment.* ▶ see **Thesaurus**

**de·seg·re·gate** /dee-**seg**-ruh-gayt/ *verb* to stop keeping people of different races separate in schools, restaurants, buses, and other places: *When the schools desegregated, black and white children started going to school together.*
—**desegregation** /dee-seg-ruh-**gaysh**-uhn/ *noun* the process of desegregating.

**des·ert**
● *noun* /**dez**-urt/
a large area of dry land in a hot place. A desert is usually covered in sand. Not many plants grow there: *The Mojave Desert is the biggest desert in the United States.*
● *verb* /di-**zurt**/
**1** to leave people who love you or need you: *He deserted his wife and children and moved to a different state.*
**2** to leave the army without permission: *Some soldiers desert because they do not want to fight.*

desert

**de·sert·ed** /di-**zurt**-id/ *adjective* empty after all the people have left: *It was late at night, and the streets were deserted.* ( SYNONYM: **empty** )

**de·serve** /di-**zurv**/ *verb* if you deserve something, you should get it because of what you have done: *If you hit someone, you deserve to be punished.*

**de·sign** /di-**zīn**/
● *noun*
**1** the shape or structure of something, and the way it looks: *The building is made of glass and steel, and the design is very modern.*
**2** a drawing of something new that will be made: *You draw the design first, before you make the dress.*

design

The vase has a floral design.

**3** a pattern for decorating something: *The T-shirt has a design of blue flowers on it.*
● *verb*
to draw or plan something that is going to be made: *She designs and makes all her own clothes.*
—**designer** /di-**zīn**-ur/ *noun* someone who designs new things: *The designers have made the software very easy to use.*

**de·sir·a·ble** /di-**zīr**-uhb-uhl/ *adjective* something that is desirable has good qualities that make people want it: *Manhattan is a very desirable place to live.*

**de·sire** /di-**zī**-ur/
● *noun* a strong feeling of wanting something: *She had a strong desire to go back to sleep.*
● *verb* to want something: *They sell every kind of ice cream you could desire.*

**desk** /desk/ *noun* a table that you sit at to write and work: *Our classroom has 30 desks in it.*

desk

desk

**des·pair** /di-**spair**/ *noun* a sad feeling of having no hope at all: *We watched in despair as the other team scored again.*

**des·per·ate** /**dess**-prit/ *adjective* wanting something very much, and willing to do anything in order to get it or do it: *I was desperate to find the cat and I looked everywhere for her.*
—**desperately** /**dess**-prit-lee/ *adverb* in a desperate way: *The doctors tried desperately to save her life.*
—**desperation** /desp-uh-**raysh**-uhn/ *noun* a desperate feeling: *In desperation, I asked my cousin for help.*

**de·spise** /di-**spīz**/ *verb* to hate someone or something very much: *He's a bully and I despise him.*

**de·spite** /di-**spīt**/ *preposition* although something happens or exists: *We enjoyed our picnic despite the cold weather.*
(SYNONYM: **in spite of**)

**des·sert** /di-**zurt**/ *noun* sweet food that you eat at the end of a meal: *For dessert, we are having apple pie with ice cream.*

dessert

apple pie

chocolate cake

ice cream sundae

strawberry shortcake

**des·ti·na·tion** /dest-uh-**naysh**-uhn/ *noun* the place that you are traveling to: *The plane will arrive at its destination, New York, at 5 p.m.*

**des·ti·ny** /**dest**-uhn-ee/ *noun* (plural **destinies**) the things that will happen to you in the future: *He believed it was his destiny to become president.* (SYNONYM: **fate**)

**de·stroy** /di-**stroy**/ *verb* to damage something so badly that it no longer exists or cannot be repaired: *The bomb destroyed the building.*
▶ see **Thesaurus**

**Word Family: destroy**

**destroy** *verb* | **destruction** *noun* | **destructive** *adjective*

**de·struc·tion** /di-**struhk**-shuhn/ *noun* the act of destroying something: *We must stop the destruction of the rain forests.*

**de·struc·tive** /di-**struhkt**-iv/ *adjective* causing a lot of damage: *A hurricane is a very destructive storm that causes floods and damages buildings.*

**de·tail** /di-**tayl**/ *noun* a small fact, feature, or piece of information: *I can remember every detail of what he was wearing, including the color of his socks.*

**de·tailed** /di-**tayld**/ *adjective* including a lot of details: *The map is very detailed and it shows every house on the street.*

**de·tect** /di-**tekt**/ *verb* to find or notice something that is not easy to notice: *The dogs are trained to detect the smell of bombs.*
—**detector** /di-**tekt**-ur/ *noun* a piece of equipment that detects something: *You should put smoke detectors in your home to warn you if there is a fire.*
—**detection** /di-**tek**-shuhn/ *noun* the act of detecting something: *The equipment is used for the detection of small earthquakes.*

**Word Family: detect**

**detect** *verb* | **detection** *noun* | **detector** *noun*

**de·tec·tive** /di-**tekt**-iv/ *noun* a police officer whose job is to find out who has committed a crime: *The detectives think they know who stole the money.*

**de·ten·tion** /di-**tensh**-uhn/ *noun* a punishment in which a student has to stay at school after the other students have gone home: *He got detention for throwing a ball during class and he had to stay at school until five o'clock.*

**de·ter** /di-**tur**/ *verb* (**deterred**, **deterring**) to stop someone from doing something by making it difficult: *The rain didn't deter them from playing outside.*

**de·ter·gent** /di-**turj**-uhnt/ *noun* a type of soap that is used for washing clothes or dishes: *I only use a little detergent when I'm washing the dishes.*

**de·te·ri·o·rate** /di-**teer**-ee-uh-rayt/ *verb* to become worse: *The weather is starting to deteriorate, and I think there will be a storm soon.*
—**deterioration** /di-teer-ee-uh-**raysh**-uhn/ *noun* the situation when something has become worse: *There has been a deterioration in your schoolwork. You were getting B's, but now you are getting C's and D's.*

**de·ter·mi·na·tion** /di-turm-uh-**naysh**-uhn/ *noun* a strong desire to do something, even when it will be difficult: *Maria shows great determination and works hard to improve her English.*

**de·ter·mine** /di-**turm**-in/ *verb*
**1** to find out the facts about something: *We had to determine whether the boys were telling the truth.*
**2** to directly influence or affect something: *Grades are determined by how good a student's work is.*

**de·ter·mined** /di-**turm**-ind/ *adjective* having a strong desire to do something, even when it will be difficult: *She was determined to win the contest.*

**det·o·nate** /**det**'n-ayt/ *verb* if someone detonates a bomb, it explodes: *The police safely detonated the bomb so that no one was hurt.*

**de·tour** /**dee**-toor/ *noun* a way of going from one place to another that is longer than the usual way: *The bridge is closed so we have to take a detour on our way to school.*

**dev·as·tate** /**dev**-uh-stayt/ *verb* to damage something very badly: *The earthquake devastated the city.*
—**devastation** /dev-uh-**staysh**-uhn/ *noun* great damage: *The floods caused widespread devastation.*

**dev·as·tat·ed** /**dev**-uh-stayt-id/ *adjective* very upset: *She was devastated when her grandfather died.*

**dev·as·tat·ing** /**dev**-uh-stayt-ing/ *adjective*
**1** causing a lot of damage: *Hurricane Katrina had a devastating effect on the city of New Orleans. Thousands of homes were flooded.*
**2** making someone feel very upset: *Her parents' divorce was devastating for Sonia.*

**de·vel·op** /di-**vel**-uhp/ *verb*
**1** to grow and change into something bigger, better, or more important: *The buds on the branches developed into leaves.* | *We can help you develop your computer skills.*
**2** to begin to have an illness, problem, or quality: *Soon after we left, the engine developed a problem.*
**3** to design and produce something new: *They are developing a new electric car.*

**de·vel·oped** /di-**vel**-uhpt/ *adjective*
**1** if something is developed, it has become as big or effective as it can be: *A 12-year-old's body is not yet fully developed.*
**2** a developed country has many businesses and factories, and most people have enough money to buy the things they need: *Most children in the developed world are able to go to school.*

**de·vel·op·ing** /di-**vel**-uhp-ing/ *adjective* a developing nation is a poor country that is starting to have more businesses and factories: *Developing nations need more and more electricity as their industries grow.*

**de·vel·op·ment** /di-**vel**-uhp-muhnt/ *noun*
**1** the process of growing: *The disease affects his physical development, so that he is smaller than other boys.*
**2** a new event that changes a situation: *Because of new developments in the war, the army sent more soldiers there.*
**3** a group of new buildings or the work of building them: *They are building a new housing development near the school.*

a
b
c
**d**
e
f
g
h
i
j
k
l
m
n
o
p
q
r
s
t
u
v
w
x
y
z

**de·vice** /di-**vīss**/ *noun* a small piece of equipment that is used to do a particular job: *This device can tell you how far you have walked.*

**dev·il** /**dev**-uhl/ *noun* the most powerful evil spirit in some religions, such as Christianity: *He said that the devil made him do all these wicked things.*

**de·vote** /di-**voht**/ *verb* to spend all your time doing something: *She devotes a lot of time to practicing her guitar.* ( SYNONYM: **dedicate** )

**Word Family:** devote

devote *verb* | devotion *noun* | devoted *adjective*

**de·vot·ed** /di-**voht**-id/ *adjective*
**1** caring about and loving someone a lot: *She is devoted to her brothers and sisters.*
**2** dealing with or used for only one thing: *This unit of the book is devoted to different types of trees.*

**de·vo·tion** /di-**vohsh**-uhn/ *noun* love and care that you show toward someone or something: *His devotion to his wife and family is easy to see.*

**dew** /doo/ *noun* small drops of water that form on things outdoors during the night: *In the morning, the grass is wet with dew.*

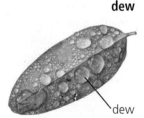

**dew**

dew

**di·a·be·tes** /dī-uh-**beet**-eez/ *noun* a medical condition that makes it difficult for someone's body to deal with sugar. The level of sugar in the person's blood becomes too high because the body cannot produce enough of a substance called insulin.
—**diabetic** /dī-uh-**bet**-ik/ *adjective* having diabetes: *My grandfather is diabetic.*
—**diabetic** /dī-uh-**bet**-ik/ *noun* someone with diabetes: *Diabetics should not eat lots of candy.*

**di·ag·nose** /dī-uhg-**nohss**/ *verb* to find out and say what illness someone has: *He was diagnosed with cancer by his doctor.*

**di·ag·no·sis** /dī-uhg-**nohss**-iss/ *noun* (plural **diagnoses** /dī-uhg-**nohss**-eez/) if a doctor makes a diagnosis, he or she says what illness someone has: *He got a diagnosis of flu, and the doctor told him to stay in bed and rest.*

**di·ag·o·nal** /dī-**ag**-uhn-uhl/
● *adjective* a diagonal line goes across a shape or area from one corner to the opposite corner: *Draw a diagonal line across the square.*
—**diagonally** /dī-**ag**-uhn-uhl-ee/ *adverb* from one corner to the opposite corner: *He walked diagonally from one corner of the room to the other.*
● *noun* a straight line that goes from one corner of a shape to the other: *Measure the length of the diagonal from one side of the rectangle to the other.*

**di·a·gram** /**dī**-uh-gram/ *noun* a drawing that explains something: *For homework, draw a diagram of a cell of a plant.*

**di·al** /**dī**-uhl/
● *verb*
to press the buttons on a telephone in order to make a call: *I dialed her number, but nobody answered.* ( SYNONYM: **call** )
● *noun*
**1** a round flat part with numbers on it, on a clock, telephone, or other machine: *The dial lights up so you can see the clock at night.*
**2** the part of a radio or other piece of equipment that you turn in order to change something: *I kept turning the dial, trying to find the station.*

**di·a·lect** /**dī**-uh-lekt/ *noun* a form of a language that is spoken in one area: *People in the South speak a dialect of English that uses some words that are not used in other parts of the United States.*

**di·a·logue**, dialog /**dī**-uh-log/ *noun* conversation in a book, play, or movie: *The movie has almost no dialogue: the story is told mostly through the pictures.*

**di·al tone** /**dī**-uhl tohn/ *noun* the sound you hear when you pick up a telephone before making a call

**di·am·e·ter** /dī-**am**-uht-ur/ *noun* a line or measurement from one side of a circle to the other, through the center: *The table is five feet in diameter.*

## dia·mond /**dīm**-uhnd/
*noun*

diamond

diamond

**1** a very hard stone that is clear in color. Diamonds cost a lot of money and are used in jewelry: *She has a diamond ring on her finger.*

*a diamond ring*

**2** a shape with four equal sides. A diamond has points at the top, bottom, and sides. It looks like this: (♦): *The cake is shaped like a diamond.*
**3** a card used in card games. The cards have diamond shapes on them: *I have the three of diamonds.*
**4** the area in a baseball field that is inside the four bases: *The bases are at the four corners of the diamond.*

## dia·per /**dīp**-ur/ *noun*
a piece of cloth or paper that is put around a baby's bottom to hold its waste: *The baby's diaper needs changing again.*

## di·a·phragm /**dī**-uh-fram/ *noun*
the muscle between your lungs and your stomach, which controls your breathing: *If you put your hand on your stomach, you can feel your diaphragm move when you breathe in and out.*

## di·ar·rhe·a /dī-uh-**ree**-uh/ *noun*
an illness that causes the solid waste from your body to become liquid and come out often: *The virus causes diarrhea and vomiting.*

## di·a·ry /**dī**-uhr-ee/ *noun* (plural **diaries**)
a book in which you write about the things that happen to you each day: *I started to keep a diary at the beginning of summer vacation.*

## dice /dīss/ *plural noun*
(singular **die** /dī/) small square objects with six sides. Each side has from one to six dots on it. Dice are used in games. One of these objects is called a "die," but many people say "dice" when there is only one: *I rolled the dice and got two sixes!*

dice

## dict- /dikt/

> ## Word Building
>
> **contradict** | **dictionary** | **predict** | **verdict**
> These words all have the Latin word root **dict** in them. **Dict** means "say." If you *contradict* someone, you say something that is the opposite of what that person said. A *dictionary* is a book that lists words and their meanings. If someone can *predict* the future, that person says what will happen in the future.

## dic·tate /**dik**-tayt/ *verb*
**1** to say words for someone else to write down: *The teacher dictated a poem to the class and the students all wrote it down in their books.*
**2** to tell people exactly what they must do: *Should parents dictate what their children can wear?*

## dic·ta·tion /dik-**taysh**-uhn/ *noun*
the act of speaking the words of something so that someone can write the words down: *We do dictation exercises to check our spelling and understanding.*

## dic·ta·tor /**dik**-tayt-ur/ *noun*
a leader of a country who has complete power: *The dictator put all his enemies in prison.*
—**dictatorship** /dik-**tayt**-ur-ship/ *noun* a country that is ruled by a dictator: *The country is a dictatorship and there is no political freedom.*
—**dictatorial** /dik-tuh-**tor**-ee-uhl/ *adjective* always telling people what to do, without listening to their opinions: *My father was very dictatorial and he never let the children do what they wanted.*

## dic·tion·ar·y /**dik**-shuh-nair-ee/ *noun* (plural **dictionaries**)
a book that contains a list of words in alphabetical order and explains what they mean: *If you don't know what a word means, look it up in the dictionary.*

## did /did/ *verb*
the past tense of **do**

## did·n't /**did**'nt/ *contraction*
short for "did not": *She didn't want to go to the movies.*

a b c **d** e f g h i j k l m n o p q r s t u v w x y z

**die** /dī/

● *verb* (**dies**, **dying**, **died**)

**1** to stop living: *My grandmother died last year.* | *The man died of a heart attack.*

▶ see Thesaurus

**2** to want to do something very much: *I'm dying to see my friends again.*

**3 die down** to become less strong: *We moved closer to the fire as the flames died down.*

**4 die out** if an animal or thing dies out, it no longer exists: *The dinosaurs died out about 65 million years ago.*

● *noun*

the singular of dice

**die·sel** /**deez**-uhl/ *noun* (also **die·sel fuel** /**deez**-uhl fyoo-uhl/) a type of fuel used in some engines: *The city's buses run on diesel.*

**di·et** /**dī**-uht/

● *noun*

**1** the type of food that you eat each day: *Do you have enough fruit and vegetables in your diet?*

**2** a plan to eat less food or eat a particular type of food: *I need to lose weight, so I'm going on a diet.*

● *verb*

to try to eat less food or eat a particular type of food: *His sister is always dieting to stay thin.*

**dif·fer** /**dif**-ur/ *verb* to be different from something else: *American schools differ from Japanese schools in many ways. Japanese schools often have bigger classes, and the students are better behaved.*

**dif·ference** /**dif**-ruhnss/ *noun*

**1** a way in which one thing is not the same as something else: *What is the difference between a square and a rectangle?* | *The twins are so alike I can't tell the difference.*

( ANTONYM: **similarity** )

**2** the difference between two numbers is how much more or less one number is than the other number: *The difference between 6 and 2 is 4 (6 − 2 = 4).*

**3 make a difference** to have a good effect on a situation: *A little extra effort can make a big difference to your grades.*

**4 make no difference** to not be important or to have no effect: *It makes no difference to me what beach we go to.*

**dif·ferent** /**dif**-ruhnt/ *adjective* not the same:

*My sister and I like different kinds of music. She likes classical and I like hip-hop.* | *This dog looks different because it has white spots and the other dogs are all black.* ( ANTONYM: **the same** )

▶ see Thesaurus

—**differently** /**dif**-ruhnt-lee/ *adverb* in a different way: *He behaves differently when his brother isn't around.*

**Word Family:** different

**different** *adjective* | **differently** *adverb* | **differ** *verb* | **difference** *noun*

**dif·fi·cult** /**dif**-uh-kuhlt/ *adjective* not easy to do or understand: *Learning to skate was difficult at first.* ( SYNONYM: **hard** ) ( ANTONYM: **easy** )

▶ see Thesaurus

**dif·fi·cul·ty** /**dif**-uh-kuhlt-ee/ *noun* (plural **difficulties**) a problem: *Some of the children have difficulty understanding English.*

**dig** /dig/ *verb* (**digging**, **dug** /duhg/)

**1** to make a hole in the ground by moving earth: *A man was digging a hole with a shovel so he could plant a tree.*

**2 dig up** to remove the dirt on top of something and take it out of the ground: *The dog digs up bones in the backyard.*

dig

**di·gest** /dī-**jest**/ *verb* when you digest food, the food changes in your stomach into a form that your body can use for energy and to keep healthy: *Some foods, like rice, are easier for your stomach to digest than other foods.*

**di·ges·tion** /dī-**jess**-chuhn/ *noun* the process of digesting food: *After digestion, food comes out of your body as waste.*

—**digestive** /dī-**jest**-iv/ *adjective* relating to digestion: *The food you eat passes through your digestive system.*

**dig·it** /**dij**-it/ *noun* any one of the numbers from 0 to 9: *Your password should be a four-digit number such as 9723.*

**dig·i·tal** /**dij**-it'l/ *adjective*
**1** storing sounds, pictures, or writing as a set of the numbers 1 and 0. For example, computers use digital systems: *I have a digital camera, so I can put all my pictures on my computer.*

**digital**

*a digital clock*

**2** showing information as a row of numbers: *The digital clock says that the time is 1:45.*

**dig·ni·fied** /**dig**-nuh-fīd/ *adjective* behaving in a calm and controlled way that people respect: *Mr. Bonnett is a tall dignified man who doesn't get angry easily.*

**dig·ni·ty** /**dig**-nuht-ee/ *noun* calm and controlled behavior that makes people respect you: *She walked with great dignity through the screaming crowd.*

**di·lem·ma** /dī-lem-uhr/ *noun* a situation in which you have to make a difficult choice between two things: *I faced a dilemma – I wanted to go to the concert, but I would have to use all my money to pay for the ticket.*

**dil·i·gent** /**dil**-uh-juhnt/ *adjective* working hard and carefully: *He is a diligent student and he always does his homework on time.*

**di·lute** /dī-**loot**/ *verb* to make a liquid weaker by adding water or another liquid: *I diluted the juice with some water.*

**dim** /dim/ *adjective* (**dimmer**, **dimmest**) not bright, so that you cannot see well: *The light was too dim to read.*

**dime** /dīm/ *noun* a coin that is worth ten cents

**dime**

**di·men·sions** /di-**mensh**-uhnz/ *noun* the height, depth, and length of an object: *The dimensions of the cube are six inches high, six inches deep, and six inches long.*

**dimension**

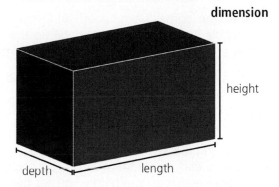

height
depth
length

**di·min·ish** /di-**min**-ish/ *verb* to become smaller, weaker, or less important: *She hoped her dog would come back, but as time passed, her hope diminished.*

**dim·ple** /**dimp**-uhl/ *noun* a small hollow place on your cheek or chin. Some dimples only show when you smile: *The baby smiled, and two dimples appeared on his cheeks.*

**din** /din/ *noun* a loud, continuous, and annoying noise: *There was such a din in the room I couldn't hear my cell phone.*

**dine** /dīn/ *verb* to have dinner: *They dined in an expensive restaurant.*

**din·er** /**dīn**-ur/ *noun*
**1** a small restaurant that serves cheap meals: *We had French fries in the diner after the movie.*
**2** someone who is eating in a restaurant: *The hotel restaurant was full of diners.*

**din·ing room** /**dīn**-ing room/ *noun* a room in a house where you sit down at a table to eat meals

**din·ner** /**din**-ur/ *noun* the main meal of the day, usually eaten in the evening: *We usually have dinner around 6:30. | What did you have for dinner?*

a
b
c
d
e
f
g
h
i
j
k
l
m
n
o
p
q
r
s
t
u
v
w
x
y
z

**di·no·saur** /**dīn**-uh-sor/ *noun* a very big type of animal that lived on Earth millions of years ago: *Tyrannosaurus was one of the biggest dinosaurs.*

### Word Origin: dinosaur

**Dinosaur** comes from Greek, and means "terrible lizard." A scientist made up the name dinosaur in the 1840s to describe the big bones people had found.

**dip** /dip/
- *verb* (**dipping**, **dipped**) to put something into a liquid and quickly take it out again
- *noun* a thick sauce that you can dip chips, raw vegetables, etc. into before you eat them: *We eat potato chips with a onion dip.*

**dip**

She is dipping the cookie in the milk.

**di·plod·o·cus** /di-**plahd**-uhk-uhss/ *noun* a large dinosaur with a long neck, long tail, and four strong legs. Diplodocus is the longest dinosaur that has been found. It probably ate leaves.

**di·plo·ma** /di-**plohm**-uh/ *noun* a document that you get when you have successfully completed high school or college

**dip·lo·mat** /**dip**-luh-mat/ *noun* someone who officially represents his or her government in a foreign country

**dip·lo·mat·ic** /dip-luh-**mat**-ik/ *adjective*
**1** relating to the work of a diplomat: *We would like to have a diplomatic solution to the disagreements between the two countries.*
**2** good at dealing with people politely and not upsetting them: *Try to be diplomatic if you have to criticize someone's work.*

**di·rect** /duh-**rekt**/
- *adjective*
**1** going straight from one place to another without stopping or changing direction: *We took the most direct route across the park, instead of going around it.*
**2** not involving any other person, thing, or event: *The flooding is a direct result of the storm.*
**3** saying what you mean in an honest and clear

**dinosaur**

Triassic Period

Plateosaurus

Coelophysis

Jurassic Period

Stegosaurus

Brachiosaurus

Apatosaurus

Cretaceous Period

Tyrannosaurus

Triceratops

Parasaurolophus

way: *If you ask her opinion, she is usually very direct.*

● *verb*

**1** to decide what the actors in a movie or play should do: *The movie was directed by Brad Bird.*
**2** to tell someone the way to a place: *You'll see signs directing you to the freeway.*

**di·rec·tion** /duh-**rek**-shuhn/ *noun*

**1** the way that someone or something is moving or pointing: *Todd saw us and ran away in the opposite direction.* | *He pointed in the direction of the kitchen.*
**2** **directions** information about how to get to a place, or how to do something: *Someone asked me for directions to the church.* | *Before taking any medicine, always read the directions on the label.*

**di·rect·ly** /duh-**rekt**-lee/ *adverb*

**1** with no other person, thing, or event involved: *If you click on the link, it takes you directly to the website, without making you look at any ads.*
**2** exactly in a particular position or direction: *I was sitting directly underneath the light.*

**di·rec·tor** /duh-**rekt**-ur/ *noun*

**1** the person who decides what the actors should do in a movie or play: *George Lucas was the director of "Star Wars."*
**2** someone who controls a company or organization: *She's one of the directors of the bank.*

**di·rec·to·ry** /duh-**rekt**-uhr-ee/ *noun* (plural **directories**)

**1** a book that has a list of people, stores, companies, etc., and their addresses or telephone numbers: *You can find our number in the telephone directory.*
**2** a sign in a building that tells you where to find someone or something: *If you're looking for a particular store, check the mall directory.*
**3** a place where a list of files are kept on a computer: *After you have saved your work, it will be listed in the directory.*

**dirt** /durt/ *noun* soil from the ground: *The dog keeps digging in the dirt.*

**dirt·y** /**durt**-ee/ *adjective* (**dirtier**, **dirtiest**)

**1** not clean: *My jeans are dirty because I was playing in the mud.* ▶ see **Thesaurus**
**2** unfair or not honest: *He lied to us – it was a really dirty trick.*

**3** a dirty word is a bad word that you should not say: *Anthony got in trouble for using a dirty word.*

dirty

dirty

clean

**dis-** /diss/

## Word Building

**dis-** is a prefix.

**dis**agree | **dis**connect | **dis**honest | **dis**respect | **dis**trust

**dis-** means "not." If you *disagree* with someone, you do not agree with that person. Someone who is *dishonest* is not honest. If you *distrust* someone, you do not trust that person.

**dis·a·bil·i·ty** /diss-uh-**bil**-uht-ee/ *noun* (plural **disabilities**) a physical or mental condition that makes it difficult for someone to do something that other people can do easily: *His disability makes it difficult for him to walk on his own.*

**dis·a·bled** /diss-**ayb**-uhld/ *adjective* someone who is disabled has a disability: *There are no steps at the entrance to the building, so disabled people in wheelchairs can get in easily.*

**dis·ad·van·tage** /diss-uhd-**vant**-ij/ *noun*

**1** something that may make you less successful than other people: *I was at a disadvantage because I had never played the game before.*
(ANTONYM: **advantage**)
**2** a bad feature of something: *The job's biggest disadvantage is you have to work Saturdays.*
(ANTONYM: **advantage**) ▶ see **Thesaurus**

**dis·ad·van·taged** /diss-uhd-**vant**-ijd/ *adjective* someone who is disadvantaged is poor and does not have the same chances as people with more money, making it more difficult for him or her to succeed: *The college gives scholarships to disadvantaged students.*

**dis·a·gree** /diss-uh-**gree**/ *verb* to have a different opinion from someone else: *My sister and I disagree about everything.* ( ANTONYM: **agree** )

**dis·a·gree·ment** /diss-uh-**gree**-muhnt/ *noun* a situation in which people disagree or argue: *We had a disagreement about whose turn it was to do the dishes.*

**dis·ap·pear** /diss-uh-**peer**/ *verb*
**1** to become impossible to see or find: *When I came back, Josh had disappeared. I don't know where he went.* ▶ see **Thesaurus**
**2** to stop existing: *The dinosaurs disappeared millions of years ago.*
—**disappearance** /diss-uh-**peer**-uhnss/ *noun* the act of disappearing: *Nobody could explain the disappearance of my bike.*

**dis·ap·point** /diss-uh-**poynt**/ *verb* to make someone feel sad because something does not happen or is not as good as expected: *I'm sorry to disappoint you, but the trip has been canceled.*
—**disappointed** /diss-uh-**poynt**-id/ *adjective* sad because something does not happen or is not as good as expected: *She was disappointed that Bella wasn't at the party.*
—**disappointing** /diss-uh-**poynt**-ing/ *adjective* making you feel disappointed: *My score on the test was a little disappointing.*

**dis·ap·point·ment** /diss-uh-**poynt**-muhnt/ *noun*
**1** a feeling of sadness because something has not happened or is not as good as you expected it to be: *She couldn't hide her disappointment when she opened the gift and it wasn't what she wanted.*
**2** someone or something that is not as good as you hoped or expected: *The party was a big disappointment. We didn't even play any games.*

**dis·ap·prov·al** /diss-uh-**proov**-uhl/ *noun* the opinion that someone or something is bad or wrong: *The crowd booed to show their disapproval when the band was late.*
( ANTONYM: **approval** )

**dis·ap·prove** /diss-uh-**proov**/ *verb* to think that someone or something is bad or wrong: *My parents disapprove of violent video games.*
( ANTONYM: **approve** )

**dis·as·ter** /di-**zast**-ur/ *noun*
**1** a sudden event that causes great harm or damage, such as an accident or flood: *The city has been hit by natural disasters, including floods and hurricanes.*
**2** a complete failure: *The meal was a disaster – I burned everything.*
—**disastrous** /di-**zass**-truhss/ *adjective* very bad: *He let the dog into the living room, with disastrous results. The dog made a mess on the carpet and chewed on the sofa.*

**dis·be·lief** /diss-buh-**leef**/ *noun* a feeling that something is not true or not possible: *They all stared in disbelief at my purple hair.*

**disc** /disk/ *noun* another spelling of disk

**dis·card** /di-**skard**/ *verb* to get rid of something because you do not need it: *Put the peanuts into a bowl and discard the shells.*
( SYNONYMS: **get rid of, throw out** )

**dis·charge** /diss-**charj**/ *verb*
**1** to officially allow someone to leave: *She was discharged from the hospital a day after having her baby.*
**2** to send out or let out a substance: *The water treatment center cleans dirty water then discharges it into the ocean.*

**dis·ci·ple** /di-**sīp**-uhl/ *noun* someone who believes in and supports a religious leader: *Peter was one of Jesus's 12 disciples.*
( SYNONYM: **follower** )

**dis·ci·pline** /diss-uh-plin/
● *noun* if there is discipline, people control their behavior and obey rules or orders: *The coach believes we need strict discipline on the team if we're going to win games.*
● *verb* to punish someone who has not obeyed a rule or order: *The school has a system for disciplining students who break the rules.*

**dis·co** /disk-oh/ *noun* a place where people dance to music on CDs or records

**dis·com·fort** /diss-**kuhmf**-urt/ *noun* slight pain or a feeling of not being relaxed: *The chairs are hard and cause some discomfort.*

**dis·con·nect** /diss-kuh-**nekt**/ *verb* to stop electricity or a signal from reaching a machine. You usually do this by unplugging the machine:

*Disconnect the computer from the power supply before moving it.* ( ANTONYM: **connect** )

**dis·count** /**diss**-kownt/ *noun* a lower price than usual: *Children get a discount on bus fares.*

**dis·cour·age** /diss-**kur**-ij/ *verb*
**1** to persuade someone not to do something: *My parents tried to discourage me from playing football because they think it is a dangerous sport.* ( ANTONYM: **encourage** )
**2** to make someone feel less confident: *Riding a bike is difficult at first, but don't let that discourage you.*
—**discouraged** /diss-**kur**-ijd/ *adjective* feeling less confident: *Don't get so discouraged. You'll do better next time!*
—**discouraging** /diss-**kur**-ij-ing/ *adjective* making you feel less confident: *Losing by 30 points was kind of discouraging.*

**dis·cov·er** /diss-**kuhv**-ur/ *verb*
**1** to find something that was hidden or not known about before: *Scientists have discovered a new star.* ▶ see **Thesaurus**
**2** to find out a fact: *The teacher discovered that they had been cheating.*

**dis·cov·ery** /diss-**kuhv**-ree/ *noun* (plural **discoveries**)
**1** a fact or answer to a question that people did not know before: *The scientists made an important discovery about how genes work.*
**2** the act of finding something that was hidden or not known about before: *The discovery of gold in California led to the gold rush.*

**dis·crim·i·nate** /di-**skrim**-uh-nayt/ *verb*
**1** to unfairly treat one person or group differently from another: *It is against the law to discriminate against someone because of their race.*
**2** to know that two things are different from each other: *People who are colorblind cannot discriminate between red and green.*
( SYNONYM: **differentiate** )
—**discrimination** /di-skrim-uh-**naysh**-uhn/ *noun* different and unfair treatment of people: *There are laws to prevent discrimination against women.*
—**discriminatory** /di-skrim-uhn-**uh**-tor-ee/ *adjective* treating people unfairly by treating them differently from each other: *The discriminatory treatment of older people is not acceptable.*

**dis·cuss** /di-**skuhss**/ *verb* to talk about

something in a serious way: *My parents went to discuss the bullying problem with my teacher.*

**dis·cus·sion** /di-**skuhsh**-uhn/ *noun* a talk in which people give their ideas about something: *We all read the book and then had a classroom discussion about it.* ▶ see **Thesaurus**

**dis·ease** /di-**zeez**/ *noun* an illness, especially one that spreads easily or that affects a particular part of your body: *Children often get diseases such as measles and chicken pox from other children at school.* | *My grandpa suffers from heart disease.* ▶ see **Thesaurus**

**dis·grace** /diss-**grayss**/ *noun*
**1** something or someone that is very bad and that people disapprove of: *The principal said my behavior was a disgrace.*
**2** if you are in disgrace, you have done something bad and people are ashamed of you: *He was sent to his room in disgrace after being rude to his grandma.*

**dis·grace·ful** /diss-**grayss**-fuhl/ *adjective* very bad or wrong: *It is disgraceful to treat your friends like that.*

**dis·guise** /diss-**gīz**/
● *verb*
**1** to make yourself look different because you want to hide who you are: *She disguised herself as a boy.*
**2** to hide your feelings or the truth about something: *He tried to disguise his surprise by pretending he knew about Rachel's plan.*
● *noun*
clothes or other things that you wear to hide who you are: *The singer wears a disguise to go shopping, so fans don't recognize her.*

**disguise**

*She disguised herself as a man.*

**dis·gust** /diss-**guhst**/
● *verb* if something disgusts you, you feel strongly that it is very bad, wrong, or unpleasant: *The thought of killing an animal disgusts me.*
● *noun* a strong feeling that something is very bad, wrong, or unpleasant: *The food was so awful that she pushed her plate away in disgust.*

**dis·gust·ed** /diss-**guhst**-id/ *adjective* feeling strongly that something is very bad, wrong, or unpleasant: *I was disgusted with them for cheating.*

**dis·gust·ing** /diss-**guhst**-ing/ *adjective* very bad or unpleasant: *This medicine tastes disgusting!*

**dish** /dish/ *noun*
**1** a container used for cooking or holding food: *He put a dish of ice cream on the table.*
**2 dishes** all the plates, cups, bowls, etc. that you use for a meal: *I'll help you wash the dishes.*
**3** food that is cooked in a particular way: *Mom brought a chicken dish to the picnic.*

**dish·cloth** /**dish**-kloth/ (also **dish·rag** /**dish**-rag/) *noun* a cloth used for washing dishes

**dis·hon·est** /diss-**ahn**-ist/ *adjective* not honest: *It's dishonest to copy someone else's work and say it is your own.* ▶ see **Thesaurus**
—**dishonestly** /diss-**ahn**-ist-lee/ *adverb* in a way that is not honest: *He dishonestly took something that did not belong to him.*
—**dishonesty** /diss-**ahn**-ist-ee/ *noun* dishonest behavior: *He lied to his mother and was punished for his dishonesty.*

**dish·tow·el** /**dish**-tow-uhl/ *noun* a cloth used for drying dishes

**dish·wash·er** /**dish**-wahsh-ur/ *noun* a machine that washes dishes: *Will you unload the dishwasher, please?*

**dis·in·fect** /diss-in-**fekt**/ *verb* to clean something with a chemical that kills bacteria: *Let me disinfect that cut with some iodine.*

**dis·in·fect·ant** /diss-in-**fekt**-uhnt/ *noun* a chemical that kills bacteria. Disinfectant is used for cleaning things: *He sprayed the kitchen counter with disinfectant.*

**disk** /disk/ *noun*
**1** a flat round piece of plastic or metal used for storing computer information, music, or a movie: *I saved my book report onto a disk.*
**2** a flat round shape or object: *A Frisbee is a plastic disk that you throw to another person.*

**disk drive** /**disk** drīv/ *noun* the part of a computer that you put a disk into: *There's no disk in the disk drive.*

**dis·like** /diss-**līk**/ *verb*
● *verb* to not like someone or something: *A lot of kids dislike vegetables.*
● *noun* a feeling of not liking someone or something: *I've always had a strong dislike of dogs.* (ANTONYM: **liking**)

**dis·lo·cate** /diss-**loh**-kayt/ *verb* if you dislocate a bone in your body, it moves out of its normal place: *Ellie dislocated her elbow playing hockey.*

**dis·loy·al** /diss-**loy**-uhl/ *adjective* doing or saying things that do not support your friends, your country, or the group you belong to: *It is disloyal to talk about your friends behind their backs.* (ANTONYM: **loyal**)
—**disloyalty** /diss-**loy**-uhl-tee/ *noun* disloyal behavior: *In an act of disloyalty, he gave secret information to the enemy.*

**dis·may** /diss-**may**/ *noun* disappointment or unhappiness that you feel when something bad happens: *She realized with dismay that she'd left her homework at home.*
—**dismayed** /diss-**mayd**/ *adjective* feeling worried or upset: *Ben's parents were dismayed at his grades.*

**dis·miss** /diss-**miss**/ *verb*
**1** to allow someone to leave a place: *Stay in your seats until I dismiss the class.*
**2** to make someone leave his or her job: *She was dismissed for taking too much time off.* (SYNONYM: **fire**)
**3** to refuse to think about an idea: *I said we should take the bus, but Tom dismissed the idea.*
—**dismissal** /diss-**miss**-uhl/ *noun* the act of making someone leave his or her job: *Stealing from work will result in dismissal.*

**dis·o·be·di·ent** /diss-uh-**beed**-ee-uhnt/ *adjective* refusing to obey someone: *How did teachers punish disobedient children in the past?* (ANTONYM: **obedient**)
—**disobedience** /diss-uh-**beed**-ee-uhnss/ *noun* disobedient behavior: *Her dog kept running away, and she didn't know what to do about its disobedience.*
—**disobediently** /diss-uh-**beed**-ee-uhnt-lee/ *adverb* in a disobedient way: *They disobediently sat on the grass when they had been told not to.*

**dis·o·bey** /diss-uh-**bay**/ *verb* to not obey a person or a rule: *The soldiers disobeyed orders by not wearing uniform.*

**dis·or·der** /diss-**ord**-ur/ *noun*
**1** if there is disorder in a place, things are not organized or neat: *The room was in a state of disorder and there were clothes all over the floor.* ( ANTONYM: **order** )
**2** an illness: *Her grandpa suffers from a heart disorder.*

**dis·or·der·ly** /diss-**ord**-ur-lee/ *adjective*
**1** not organized or neat: *There were disorderly piles of paper all over the room.* ( ANTONYM: **orderly** )
**2** behaving badly and making a lot of noise: *A group of disorderly drunks were yelling in the street.*

**dis·or·ga·nized** /diss-**org**-uh-nīzd/ *adjective* not arranged or planned very well: *His desk is totally disorganized – there are papers everywhere.* ( ANTONYM: **organized** )

**dis·pens·er** /di-**spenss**-ur/ *noun* a machine that gives you something when you push a button: *Press the soap dispenser to put soap on your hands.*

**dis·play** /di-**splay**/
● *noun* (plural **displays**)
**1** things that are put or shown somewhere so that people can see them: *There is a display of students' work in the hall. | Don't miss the fireworks display in the park!*
**2** a part of an electronic machine that shows you information: *The number you are calling is shown on the phone's display.*

> IDIOM with **display**
> **on display** in a public place for people to see: *The paintings will be on display until the end of the week.*

● *verb*
**1** to put things in a place where people can see them: *The list of people who are on the swim team will be displayed on the board.*
**2** to show a feeling: *The smile on her face displayed her happiness.*

**dis·pos·a·ble** /di-**spohz**-uhb-uhl/ *adjective* made to be used once and then thrown away: *Nurses use disposable gloves in order to avoid spreading diseases.*

**disposable**

*a disposable camera*

**dis·pos·al** /di-**spohz**-uhl/ *noun*
**1** a small machine in a sink that crushes food so that it can go down the pipes: *I turned on the disposal to get rid of the potato peelings.*
**2** the act of getting rid of something: *The garbage is taken away for disposal.*

**dis·pose** /di-**spohz**/ *verb* **dispose of** to throw away or destroy something: *We must dispose of waste carefully so that it does not harm the environment.* ( SYNONYM: **get rid of** )

> **Word Family:** dispose
> **dispose** *verb* | **disposal** *noun* | **disposable** *adjective*

**dis·prove** /diss-**proov**/ *verb* to show that something is not true: *In the 1500s, a scientist called Copernicus disproved the idea that the Sun goes around the Earth.* ( ANTONYM: **prove** )

**dis·qual·i·fy** /diss-**kwahl**-uh-fī/ *verb* (**disqualifies**, **disqualified**) to stop someone from taking part in a race, game, or competition because he or she has done something wrong: *He was disqualified from the race because he started running too soon.*

**dis·re·spect** /diss-ri-**spekt**/
● *noun* a lack of respect for someone or something: *Criminals show a disrespect for the law.*
● *verb* to show a lack of respect for someone or something: *Don't disrespect your mother by arguing with her all the time.*

**dis·re·spect·ful** /diss-ri-**spekt**-fuhl/ *adjective* showing no respect for someone or something: *It is disrespectful to talk while your teacher is talking.* ( ANTONYM: **respectful** )

**dis·rupt** /diss-**ruhpt**/ *verb* to stop something from happening in a normal way by causing problems: *He wouldn't be quiet, and that disrupted the class.*
—**disruption** /diss-**ruhp**-shuhn/ *noun* the action of stopping something from happening in a normal way by causing problems: *Heavy snow has caused a lot of disruption in our town this week.*
—**disruptive** /diss-**ruhpt**-iv/ *adjective* causing problems by behaving badly: *He was hitting other children and being very disruptive at school.*

**dis·sat·is·fied** /di-**sat**-iss-fīd/ *adjective* unhappy about something because it is not good enough: *The teacher was dissatisfied with Emily's work because she had not written enough.*
( ANTONYM: **satisfied** )
—**dissatisfaction** /di-sat-iss-**fak**-shuhn/ *noun* the feeling of being unhappy about something because it is not good enough: *The coach's dissatisfaction with the way the team played meant we had to practice more.*

**dis·sent** /di-**sent**/ *noun* an opinion that does not agree with an idea that most people accept: *In some countries you can be jailed for political dissent.*

**dis·sim·i·lar** /di-**sim**-uhl-ur/ *adjective* not the same: *The two brothers are dissimilar: one has red hair, and the other one has brown hair.*
( ANTONYM: **similar** )

**dis·solve** /di-**zahlv**/
*verb* if a substance dissolves in a liquid, it becomes part of the liquid and you cannot see it anymore: *The salt dissolves in the water.*

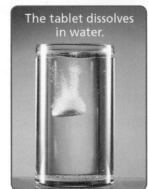
**dissolve**
The tablet dissolves in water.

**dis·tance** /**dist**-uhnss/
*noun* the amount of space between two places: *The school is only a short distance away from my house.*

IDIOMS with **distance**
**in the distance** far away: *I could see a bus coming in the distance.*
**keep your distance** to stay away from someone or something: *You'd better keep your distance from that dog – it looks dangerous.*

**dis·tant** /**dist**-uhnt/ *adjective*
**1** far away: *The story takes place on a distant planet.*
**2** a distant time is one that is a long time ago or a long time into the future: *In the distant past, dinosaurs lived on Earth.*
**3** a distant relative is a member of your family who is not closely related to you

**dis·tinct** /di-**stingkt**/ *adjective*
**1** very easy to see or hear: *Their voices got more distinct as they came closer.*
**2** clearly different or separate: *There are two distinct types of elephant – Asian elephants have smaller ears than African elephants.*
—**distinctly** /di-**stingkt**-lee/ very clearly: *Bees and wasps are distinctly different.*

**dis·tinc·tion** /di-**stingk**-shuhn/ *noun*
**1** a clear difference: *"What's the distinction between fiction and nonfiction?" "Fiction is about things that are not real. Nonfiction is about real things."*
**2** if you do something with distinction, you do it very well: *The soldier fought with distinction in the war.*

**dis·tinc·tive** /di-**stingkt**-iv/ *adjective* different from other things of the same type, and easy to recognize: *A panda has distinctive black marks around its eyes.*

**dis·tin·guish** /di-**sting**-gwish/ *verb*
**1** to see the difference between things: *The twins are so alike it's difficult to distinguish one from the other.*
**2** to show that someone or something is different: *The male bird's bright colors distinguish it from the female.*

**dis·tin·guished** /di-**sting**-gwisht/ *adjective* successful and admired by a lot of people: *She is one of the most distinguished writers in America.*

**dis·tort** /di-**stort**/ *verb* to change something and make it look or sound different from normal: *The funny mirrors distorted our bodies so we looked really tall and thin.*
—**distortion** /di-**storsh**-uhn/ *noun* a change in something that makes it look or sound different from normal: *The game lets you take a picture of someone and then produce a distortion, for example making the eyes very big.*

**distort**

The mirror distorts the shape of our bodies.

**dis·tract** /di-**strakt**/ *verb* to make someone stop paying attention to something: *The noise distracted us, and we looked away from our tests.*
—**distraction** /di-**strak**-shuhn/ *noun* something that makes you stop paying attention: *It's hard to study at home – there are too many distractions, like TV and video games.*

**dis·tress** /di-**stress**/
● *noun* a feeling of great sadness or worry: *Your dog can show signs of distress when you move to a new house.*

> IDIOM with **distress**
> **in distress** in a very difficult situation and needing help: *The police were called by a woman in distress, who said that her house had been broken into.*

● *verb* to make someone sad or worried: *It distresses me when people treat animals badly.*
—**distressed** /di-**strest**/ *adjective* feeling very sad or worried: *He was distressed about losing his watch.*
—**distressing** /di-**stress**-ing/ *adjective* making you feel very sad or worried: *He had distressing memories of his parents' divorce.*

**dis·trib·ute** /di-**strib**-yuht/ *verb*
**1** to give something to each person in a group: *The teacher distributed the books to the students.*
**2** to send things to stores and companies for them to sell: *The bakery makes cakes and distributes them to local stores.*

**Word Family: distribute**

**distribute** *verb* | **distribution** *noun* | **distributor** *noun*

**dis·tri·bu·tion** /dist-ruh-**byoosh**-uhn/ *noun*
**1** the act of giving things to people in a group: *The children helped with the distribution of pencils and paper.*
**2** the act of sending things to stores and companies for them to sell: *The fruit is put into cans and sent for distribution all over the United States.*

**dis·trib·u·tor** /di-**strib**-yuht-ur/ *noun*
**1** a company that sends things to stores or other companies for them to sell: *A computer game distributor agreed to market their game.*
**2** the part of a car's engine that sends electricity to the spark plugs. The spark plugs produce electric sparks that make the mixture of gas and air in the engine start burning.

**dis·trict** /**diss**-trikt/ *noun* an area of a city or a country: *My dad works downtown in the business district.*

**dis·trust** /**diss**-**truhst**/
● *noun* a feeling that you cannot trust someone: *She looked at him with distrust. He had lied to her before.*
● *verb* to not trust someone or something: *He has distrusted doctors ever since his wife died in the hospital.*

**dis·turb** /di-**sturb**/ *verb*
**1** to bother someone when he or she is doing something, for example by making a noise: *Dad's sleeping, so don't disturb him.*
**2** to worry or upset you: *I was disturbed by the way she kept staring at me.*
—**disturbing** /di-**sturb**-ing/ *adjective* making you feel worried or upset: *We have some disturbing news – a big storm may be coming this way.*

**dis·turb·ance** /di-**sturb**-uhnss/ *noun* something that bothers you when you are doing something, for example a loud noise: *The dogs keep barking and causing a disturbance at night.*

**ditch** /dich/ *noun* a long narrow hole that is dug in the ground for water to flow through. A ditch is usually at the side of a road or in a field: *He accidentally drove his car into a ditch.*

a b c **d** e f g h i j k l m n o p q r s t u v w x y z

**dive** /dīv/ *verb* (**dived** or **dove** /dohv/, **dived**)
**1** to jump into water with your arms and head first, not your feet: *Some boys were diving into the pool.*
**2** to go down suddenly toward the ground: *The plane suddenly dived down through the clouds.*

dive

**div·er** /**dīv**-ur/ *noun*
**1** someone who swims under water using equipment for breathing: *Deep sea divers went down to explore the wreck of the ship.*
**2** someone who dives into water as a sport: *We watched a diver jump off the high board into the pool.*

**di·verse** /duh-**vurss**/ *adjective* full of many different types of people or things: *Our school is very diverse, with students who speak many different languages.*

### Word Family: diverse

**diverse** *adjective* | **diversity** *noun*

**di·ver·si·ty** /duh-**vurss**-uht-ee/ *noun* many different people or things: *This forest is home for a huge diversity of animals and birds.*
SYNONYM: **variety**

**di·vert** /duh-**vurt**/ *verb* to make a vehicle, such as a car or an airplane, change direction: *They are diverting traffic on the freeway because of an accident.*

**di·vide** /duh-**vīd**/ *verb*
**1** to separate something into parts or groups: *Mom divided the cake into eight equal pieces. | The teacher divided up the class into two groups of students.*
**2** to share something: *The thieves divided the stolen money among themselves.*
**3** to find how many times a number will go into

a bigger number: *21 divided by 3 is 7.*
ANTONYM: **multiply**
**4** to make people disagree: *The plan to build a new road has divided local people: some support it, but many are against it.*

### Word Family: divide

**divide** *verb* | **dividend** *noun* | **divisible** *adjective* | **division** *noun* | **divisor** *noun*

**div·i·dend** /**div**-uh-dend/ *noun* in math, the number that you are dividing by another number: *In 15 ÷ 3 = 5, the dividend is 15.*

**di·vine** /duh-**vīn**/ *adjective* coming from God: *She had a strong feeling of divine love.*

**div·ing board** /**dīv**-ing bord/ *noun* a board for diving into water: *I dived off the diving board into the pool.*

**di·vis·i·ble** /duh-**viz**-uhb-uhl/ *adjective* if one number is divisible by another number, it can be divided by it: *The number 15 is divisible by 3.*

**di·vi·sion** /duh-**vizh**-uhn/ *noun*
**1** the process of finding out how many times one number goes into a bigger number: *We had to find the answer to the division problem 18 ÷ 3.*
ANTONYM: **multiplication**
**2** a part of a company, army, or organization: *Mom works in the sales division of a big company.*
**3** the act of separating something into two or more parts or groups: *We decided on a fair division of the work so that everyone had the same amount to do.*

**di·vi·sor** /duh-**vīz**-ur/ *noun* the number that you are using to divide another number: *In the problem 12 ÷ 4 = 3, the divisor is 4.*

**di·vorce** /duh-**vorss**/
● *noun* the end of a marriage by law: *After ten years of marriage, they decided to get a divorce.*
● *verb* to end a marriage by law: *His parents divorced when he was a baby.*

**di·vulge** /duh-**vuhlj**/ *verb* to give information about something secret: *The thief would not divulge where he had hidden the money.*
SYNONYMS: **disclose, reveal**

**Di·wa·li** /di-**wahl**-ee/ *noun* a Hindu festival that is celebrated in October or November. It is the

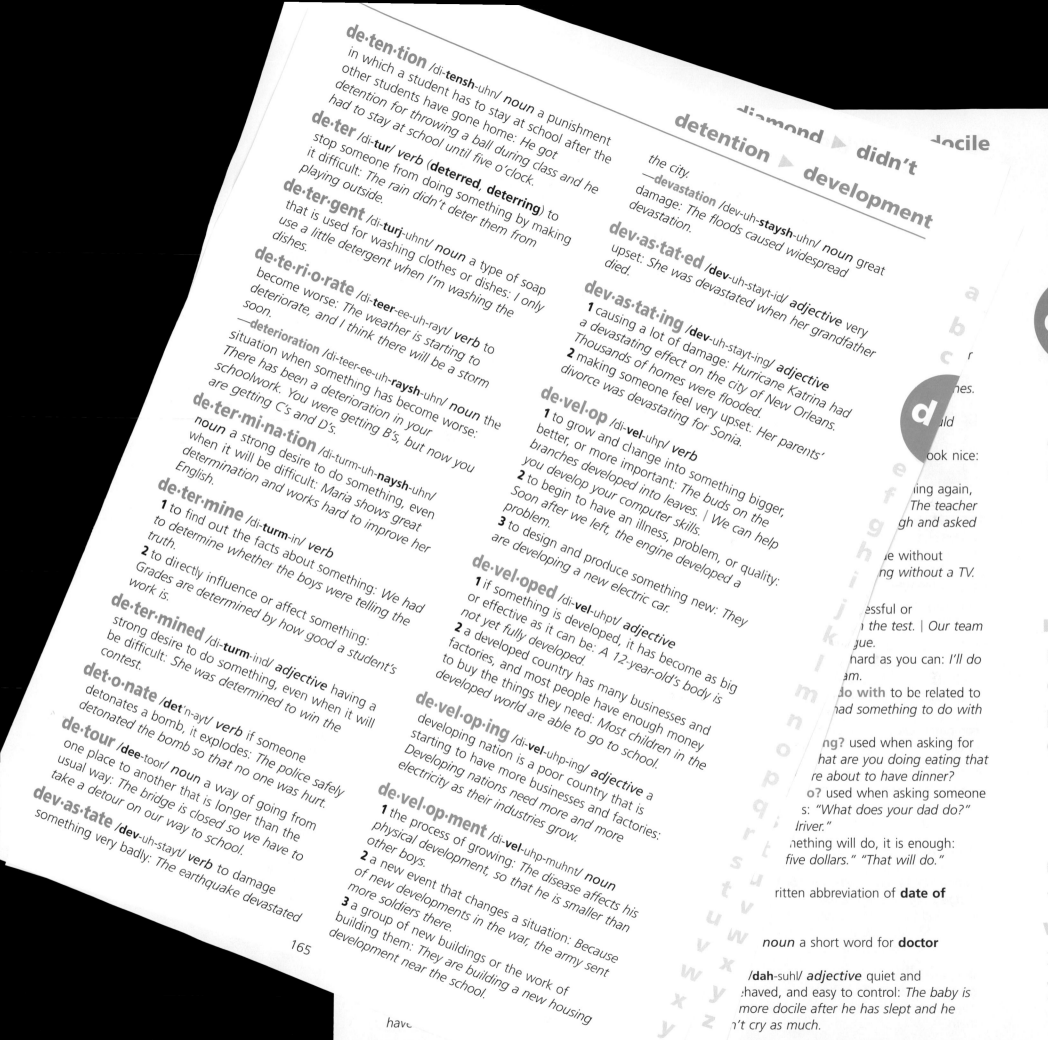

**de·ten·tion** /di-**tensh**-uhn/ **noun** a punishment in which a student has to stay at school after the other students have gone home: He got detention for throwing a ball during class and he had to stay at school until five o'clock.

**de·ter** /di-**tur**/ **verb** (**deterred, deterring**) to stop someone from doing something by making it difficult: The rain didn't deter them from playing outside.

**de·ter·gent** /di-**turj**-uhnt/ **noun** a type of soap that is used for washing clothes or dishes: I only use a little detergent when I'm washing the dishes.

**de·te·ri·o·rate** /di-**teer**-ee-uh-rayt/ **verb** to become worse: The weather is starting to deteriorate, and I think there will be a storm soon.

— **deterioration** /di-teer-ee-uh-**raysh**-uhn/ **noun** the situation when something has become worse: There has been a deterioration in your schoolwork. You were getting B's, but now you are getting C's and D's.

**de·ter·mi·na·tion** /di-turm-uh-**naysh**-uhn/ **noun** a strong desire to do something, even when it will be difficult: Maria shows great determination and works hard to improve her English.

**de·ter·mine** /di-**turm**-in/ **verb**
**1** to find out the facts about something: We had to determine whether the boys were telling the truth.
**2** to directly influence or affect something: Grades are determined by how good a student's work is.

**de·ter·mined** /di-**turm**-ind/ **adjective** having a strong desire to do something, even when it will be difficult: She was determined to win the contest.

**det·o·nate** /**det**'n-ayt/ **verb** if someone detonates a bomb, it explodes: The police safely detonated the bomb so that no one was hurt.

**de·tour** /**dee**-toor/ **noun** a way of going from one place to another that is longer than the usual way: The bridge is closed so we have to take a detour on our way to school.

**dev·as·tate** /**dev**-uh-stayt/ **verb** to damage something very badly: The earthquake devastated

165

the city.
— **devastation** /dev-uh-**staysh**-uhn/ **noun** great damage: The floods caused widespread devastation.

**dev·as·tat·ed** /**dev**-uh-stayt-id/ **adjective** very upset: She was devastated when her grandfather died.

**dev·as·tat·ing** /**dev**-uh-stayt-ing/ **adjective**
**1** causing a lot of damage: Hurricane Katrina had a devastating effect on the city of New Orleans. Thousands of homes were flooded.
**2** making someone feel very upset: Her parents' divorce was devastating for Sonia.

**de·vel·op** /di-**vel**-uhp/ **verb**
**1** to grow and change into something bigger, better, or more important: The buds on the branches developed into leaves. | We can help you develop your computer skills.
**2** to begin to have an illness, problem, or quality: Soon after we left, the engine developed a problem.
**3** to design and produce something new: They are developing a new electric car.

**de·vel·oped** /di-**vel**-uhpt/ **adjective**
**1** if something is developed, it has become as big or effective as it can be: A 12-year-old's body is not yet fully developed.
**2** a developed country has many businesses and factories, and most people have enough money to buy the things they need: Most children in the developed world are able to go to school.

**de·vel·op·ing** /di-**vel**-uhp-ing/ **adjective** a developing nation is a poor country that is starting to have more businesses and factories: Developing nations need more and more electricity as their industries grow.

**de·vel·op·ment** /di-**vel**-uhp-muhnt/ **noun**
**1** the process of growing: The disease affects his physical development, so that he is smaller than other boys.
**2** a new event that changes a situation: Because of new developments in the war, the army sent more soldiers there.
**3** a group of new buildings or the work of building them: They are building a new housing development near the school.

have

ook nice:

ing again,
The teacher
gh and asked

e without
ng without a TV.

essful or
n the test. | Our team
gue.
hard as you can: I'll do
am.

**do with** to be related to
had something to do with

ng? used when asking for
hat are you doing eating that
re about to have dinner?
o? used when asking someone
s: "What does your dad do?"
Iriver."
nething will do, it is enough:
five dollars." "That will do."

ritten abbreviation of **date of**

**noun** a short word for **doctor**

/**dah**-suhl/ **adjective** quiet and
:haved, and easy to control: The baby is
more docile after he has slept and he
n't cry as much.

**dock** /dahk/
- *noun* a place in a town where ships stop. Things are taken on or off the ship, or people get on or off: *The ship was waiting at the dock for the passengers to board.*
- *verb* if a ship docks, it sails into a dock: *The ship docked in Honolulu and started unloading its cargo.*

**dock**

The ship is waiting at the dock.

**doc·tor** /**dahkt**-ur/ *noun* ( ABBREVIATION: **Dr.** )
**1** someone whose job is treating people who are sick: *I had a rash all over my body so Mom took me to the doctor.* ▶ see **Thesaurus**
**2** someone who has a Ph.D., the highest type of university degree: *Dr. Ferrara is a biology professor.*

**doc·u·ment** /**dahk**-yuh-muhnt/ *noun*
**1** a piece of paper that has official information on it: *Your parents will need to bring documents such as your birth certificate.*
**2** a piece of work that you write and keep on a computer: *Click on the document you want to open.*

**doc·u·men·tary** /dahk-yuh-**men**-tree/ *noun*
(plural **documentaries**) a movie or television program that gives facts about something: *I watched a documentary about whales.*

**dodge** /dahj/ *verb*
**1** to move quickly in order to avoid someone or something: *When I was on my bike, I had to dodge a big hole in the road.*
**2** to avoid talking about something or doing something: *Mom dodged the question of whether we could have a dog.*

**dodge·ball** /**dahj**-bol/ *noun* a children's game in which two teams throw balls at each other. Players try to catch the balls or not be hit by them.

**doe** /doh/ *noun* a female deer

**does** /duhz/ *verb* the third person singular of the present tense of do

**does·n't** /**duhz**-uhnt/ *contraction* short for "does not": *She doesn't want to go.*

**dog** /dog/ *noun* an animal that people keep as a pet. There are many different kinds of dog. Some dogs are used for guarding buildings: *The dog barked all night.* ▶ see **Thesaurus**

### Word Origin: dog

**Dog** comes from an Old English word for a strong kind of dog. People began using dog to mean all kinds of dogs by the 1600s. Before the 1600s, the word used for dog was **hund**. We still use this word, but it is spelled "hound" now.

**dog**

paw

dog            puppy

**doll** /dahl/ *noun* a toy that looks like a baby or small person: *The little girl was playing with her dolls.*

**doll**

### Word Origin: doll

**Doll** started as a nickname for women called Dorothy. People then used it as a name for a female pet. In the 1700s, people started using it to mean a child's toy baby.

dig

**dol·lar** /**dahl**-ur/ *noun* the money used in the U.S. and some other countries. It is shown by the sign $: *Dad gave me five dollars for cleaning the car.* | *His sneakers cost almost a hundred dollars* (=$100).

### Word Origin: dollar

**Dollar** comes from a German word that means "valley." In Germany, there was a silver mine in a valley. The coins made from this silver mine were called **taler**, so they were "valley coins." This money was used all over Europe. After the Revolutionary War, the Americans did not want to use the British words for money, such as pounds and shillings. When the United States started making its own money, Congress decided to use the word dollar, which came from **taler**.

**dol·lar sign** /**dahl**-ur sīn/ *noun* the sign $, used to mean a dollar

**doll·house** /**dahl**-howss/ *noun* a small toy house with furniture inside: *My little sister Emma was playing with her dollhouse.*

**dol·lop** /**dahl**-uhp/ *noun* a small amount of soft food, usually served on a spoon: *Do you want another dollop of cream?*

**dol·phin** /**dahl**-fin/ *noun* a large gray animal that lives in the ocean. Dolphins look like large fish, but they are a kind of mammal. They breathe through a hole on top of their head. They are very smart: *The dolphins came right up to the side of the boat and swam around it.*

**dolphin**

**-dom** /duhm/

### Word Building

**-dom** is a suffix. It changes the root word into a noun.

bore**dom** | free**dom** | king**dom** | star**dom** | wis**dom**

**-dom** means that something has a particular quality. Someone who has *wisdom* is wise. *Freedom* is when you are free. A *kingdom* is a country that is ruled by a king.

**do·main** /doh-**mayn**/ *noun* an activity or area of land that is controlled by one person or group: *Cooking was traditionally a woman's domain.*

**do·main name** /doh-**mayn** naym/ *noun* domain name the address of a website: *They bought the domain name "books.com" for their website.*

**dome** /dohm/ *noun* a round curved roof: *The Capitol building in Washington is famous for its dome.*

**dome**

**do·mes·tic** /duh-**mest**-ik/ *adjective*
**1** relating to things that happen inside a country, rather than things that happen in other countries: *A domestic flight goes from one place to another inside the same country.*
**2** relating to life at home: *I help my parents with domestic chores such as cooking and cleaning our house.*
**3** a domestic animal lives on a farm or in someone's home: *Cats and dogs are domestic pets.*

**dom·i·nant** /**dahm**-uhn-uhnt/ *adjective* the most important or powerful: *English is the dominant language in the U.S.*
—**dominance** /**dahm**-uhn-uhnss/ *noun* the state of being the most important or powerful person or thing: *The team continued their dominance of the league with another easy victory.*

**dom·i·nate** /**dahm**-uh-nayt/ *verb* to be the most important or most noticeable person or thing: *Men still dominate in many types of job, such as firefighting.*
—**domination** /dahm-uh-**naysh**-uhn/ *noun* the position of being the most important or noticeable person or thing: *The American colonies fought against the domination of the British government.*

**Word Family: dominate**

**dominate** *verb* | **domination** *noun* | **dominant** *adjective* | **dominance** *noun*

**dom·i·no**
/**dahm**-uh-noh/ *noun* (plural **dominoes**)
**domino**
**1** a small flat piece of wood or plastic with dots on it. You use dominoes to play a game.
**2 dominoes** the game you play using dominoes. Players must put a domino next to one with the same number of dots on it.

**do·nate** /**doh**-nayt/ *verb*
**1** to give money to a group that needs help: *A rich businessman donated $10,000 to the charity for the homeless.*
**2** to give some of your blood or a part of your body to help someone who is sick: *Hospitals need more people to donate blood, which is used in operations.*
—**donation** /doh-**naysh**-uhn/ *noun* money that you give to help a group: *Please make a donation to buy food for people affected by the earthquake.*

**done** /duhn/
● *verb*
the past participle of do
● *adjective*
**1** finished: *My assignment is almost done – I just*

need to draw a picture.
**2** cooked enough to be eaten: *Those hamburgers are not done; they're still red in the middle.*
**3** if you are done with something, you have finished doing or using it: *Can I read your magazine when you're done with it?*

**don·key** /**dahngk**-ee/ *noun* an animal like a small horse with long ears. Donkeys are used to carry things or to do work on farms.

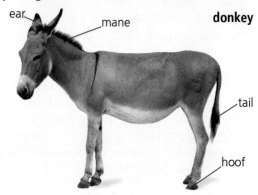

ear
mane
**donkey**
tail
hoof

**do·nor** /**dohn**-ur/ *noun*
**1** someone who gives blood or a part of his or her body to help someone who is sick: *Some people agree to be organ donors after they die. Their livers and hearts will help other people live.*
**2** someone who gives something, especially money, to an organization: *The museum got $10,000 from a generous donor.*

**don't** /dohnt/ *contraction* short for "do not": *I don't know.*

**do·nut** /**doh**-nuht/ *noun* another spelling of doughnut

**doo·dle** /**dood**'l/ *verb* to draw pictures, shapes, or patterns while you are thinking about something else: *He was doodling on a piece of paper while he talked on the phone.*

**doom** /doom/ *noun* something bad that is certain to happen: *I had a feeling of doom before the test.*

**doomed** /doomd/ *adjective* sure to fail: *Our trip was doomed when the car broke down after a few miles.*

**door** /dor/ *noun* the thing you open to get into a house, room, or car: *I opened the door and went inside.*

**door·bell** /**dor**-bel/ *noun* a button by a door of a house that you push to make a sound. The doorbell lets people inside know that you are there: *I rang the doorbell but nobody came to answer it.*

**door·knob** /**dor**-nahb/ *noun* a round handle that you turn to open a door: *I turned the doorknob and went inside the room.*

**door·mat** /**dor**-mat/ *noun* a thick piece of material beside a door for you to clean your shoes on: *Wipe your shoes on the doormat before you come in.*

**door·step** /**dor**-step/ *noun* a step in front of the door of a house: *A cat sat on the doorstep.*

**door·way** /**dor**-way/ *noun* the space where a door opens into a room: *Don't just stand there in the doorway – come in!*

**dope** /dohp/ *noun* someone who is stupid: *I spilled my milk all over the floor. I felt like such a dope!*

**dor·mi·to·ry** /**dorm**-uh-tor-ee/ (plural **dormitories**) (also **dorm** /dorm/) *noun* a large building where people live at a camp, school, or college: *There were six girls in the dormitory at camp.*

**dos·age** /**dohss**-ij/ *noun* the amount of medicine that you should take: *The correct dosage of this medicine is one tablet daily.*

**dose** /dohss/ *noun* an amount of medicine: *The doctor said I had to take three doses of the medicine every day.*

**dot** /daht/ *noun* a small round mark or spot: *My dress has red dots on it.*

> **IDIOM with dot**
> **on the dot** exactly at the right time: *The train left at ten o'clock on the dot.*

**doub·le** /**duhb**-uhl/
● *adjective*
**1** having two parts: *There are double doors at the front entrance of the school.*
**2** twice the usual amount or size: *He asked for a double cheeseburger.*
**3** for two people: *My parents' room has a double bed.*
**4** **double digits** the numbers from 10 to 99: *I was the only player to score in double digits.*
● *verb*
**1** to become twice as big: *The number of students in the drama club has doubled over the

last year.*
**2** to fold something in half so that it has two layers: *Take a sheet of paper and double it.*
● *noun*
**1** something that is twice as big as something else: *They get paid double if they work on weekends.*
**2** someone who looks like someone else: *Ben looks so much like his dad, he's almost his double.*
**3** a hit in baseball that allows the batter to reach second base

**doub·le bass**
/duhb-uhl **bayss**/ *noun* a very big musical instrument like a violin. It has four strings and makes very low sounds. You play it while you are standing up.
SYNONYM: **bass**

**double bass**

**doub·le-check**
/duhb-uhl **chek**/ *verb* to check something again so you are sure about it: *I double-checked that I had my ticket.*

**doub·les** /**duhb**-uhlz/ *noun* a game of tennis played between two pairs of players: *Andy and his brother won the men's doubles.*

**doubt** /dowt/
● *verb* to think that something may not happen or be true: *Many people doubted whether our team could win.* | *He says he is 16, but I doubt it.*
● *noun* a feeling that something is not right or true: *I have some serious doubts about Cory's plan.* | *The teacher said she had no doubt that I would do well.*

> **IDIOM with doubt**
> **beyond doubt** if information is beyond doubt, it is definitely correct: *The evidence proved beyond doubt that the man was guilty.*

**doubt·ful** /**dowt**-fuhl/ *adjective*
**1** probably not likely to happen or to be true: *It is doubtful that he'll pass the test.*
**2** not sure about something: *Everyone was doubtful that the idea would work.*

a b c **d** e f g h i j k l m n o p q r s t u v w x y z

**dough** /doh/ *noun* a soft mixture of flour and water that is baked to make bread and cookies: *Leave the dough to rise before you bake the bread.*

**dough·nut**, donut
/**doh**-nuht/ *noun* a small round cake that usually has a hole in the middle: *I want a doughnut with chocolate frosting.*

doughnut

**Word Origin:** doughnut

When the word **doughnut** was first written down, in 1809, it meant a ball of dough that had been fried. These balls of sweet dough looked a little like round nuts. It was probably in the middle 1800s that some kinds of doughnuts were made in a ring shape.

**dove**

● *noun* /duhv/ a medium-sized white bird that makes a soft sound. A dove is often used as a sign of peace.
● *verb* /dohv/ a past tense of **dive**

dove

**down** /down/

● *adverb, preposition*
**1** toward a lower place: *I ran down the hill.* | *Stop writing and put your pen down on the desk.* (ANTONYM: **up**)
**2** further along a street or path: *My friend lives just down the street.*
**3** toward a lower level: *Mom told me to turn the sound down on the TV.* (ANTONYM: **up**)
**4** toward the south: *We flew down to Arizona.*
(ANTONYM: **up**)
● *adjective*
**1** lower in amount than before: *The number of students at the school is down this year.*
(ANTONYM: **up**)
**2** sad: *She's been feeling a little down since her friend moved away.*
**3** a computer system that is down is not working: *All the school computers are down.*

● *noun*
**1** the soft feathers of a bird: *The bed had soft down pillows.*
**2** one of the four chances that a football team has to move forward at least ten yards in order to keep the ball

**down-** /down/

**Word Building**

**down-** is a prefix.
**down**hill | **down**pour | **down**size | **down**load | **down**stairs
**down-** means "toward a lower place or level." If you walk *downhill*, you are going toward the bottom of the hill. If you *download* something, you move it from a larger computer network to an individual computer. If a company *downsizes*, it stops having jobs for as many people, so that the number of employees goes down to a lower level.

**down·hill** /down-**hil**/ *adverb, adjective* toward the bottom of a hill or slope: *It's easier walking downhill.* (ANTONYM: **uphill**) ▶ see picture at **uphill**

**down·load** /**down**-lohd/ *verb* to move information or programs to your computer from the Internet or a computer network: *I downloaded some new songs today to put on my MP3 player.*

**down·pour** /**down**-por/ *noun* a lot of rain that falls in a short time: *I got really wet because I was caught in a downpour on the way home from school.*

**down·size** /**down**-sīz/ *verb* to make the number of people who work for a company a smaller number: *He lost his job when the company downsized.*

**down·stairs** /down-**stairz**/ *adverb, adjective* on or toward a lower level of a house: *He came downstairs to see what was happening.* | *Our house has a downstairs bathroom.*
(ANTONYM: **upstairs**)

**Down syn·drome** /**down** sin-drohm/ *noun* a medical condition that someone is born with, which can affect that person's physical and mental development

**down·town** /down-**town**/ *adverb, adjective* to or in the middle of a city, where there are a lot of stores and businesses: *Mom said that she has to go downtown to the library.* | *He works in a downtown restaurant.*

**down·ward** /**down**-wurd/ (also **downwards**) *adverb, adjective* toward a lower place or level: *Push the handle downward.* | *There has been a downward movement in prices.*

ANTONYM: **upward**

**doze** /dohz/ *verb*
**1** to sleep for a short time: *Grandpa was dozing in his chair.*
**2 doze off** to start sleeping when you do not intend to: *I was so tired that I dozed off in front of the TV.*

**doz·en** /**duhz**-uhn/ *number* a group of 12 things: *Mom bought a dozen eggs.*

**Dr.** /**dahkt**-ur/ the written abbreviation of **Doctor**

**draft** /draft/
● *noun*
**1** a piece of writing or a drawing that you will make changes to when you write or draw it again: *This is the first draft of my English assignment.*
**2** cold air blowing into a room: *Someone had left a window open and there was a draft.*
**3** a system in which people have to join the military: *During the Vietnam War, college students could avoid the draft.*
**4** a system in which professional teams choose players from colleges to join their teams: *He is the best player in the draft.*
● *verb*
**1** to write or draw something that you will make changes to later: *Our class drafted a letter to the fire station to ask if we could visit it.*
**2** to tell someone that he or she must join the military for a period of time: *My grandpa was drafted into the army when he was 18.*
● *adjective*
a draft piece of writing or a draft drawing is one that you will make changes to later: *Will you read a draft copy of my report and correct my mistakes?*

**draft·y** /**draft**-ee/ *adjective* a drafty room or building has cold air blowing through it: *They lived in a drafty old house.*

**drag** /drag/
● *verb* (**dragging**, **dragged**)
**1** to pull something heavy along the ground: *I had to drag a heavy suitcase up the stairs.*
**2** to pull a person or animal in a violent way: *Two men dragged him into a car and took him away.*
**3** if time drags, it passes slowly and in a boring way: *The movie was very long and it dragged toward the end.*
● *noun*
if something is a drag, it is boring or annoying: *"The trip takes eight hours." "What a drag!"*

**drag**

He is dragging the suitcase up the stairs.

**drag·on** /**drag**-uhn/ *noun* an animal that can fly and breathe out fire. Dragons are only found in stories: *The dragon was sleeping on a pile of treasure.*

**dragon**

**drag·on·fly** /**drag**-uhn-flī/ *noun* (plural **dragonflies**) a large flying insect. Dragonflies have a long body, big eyes, and two pairs of wings. They live near ponds and streams.

**dragonfly**

### drain /drayn/

● **noun** a pipe or hole that carries away dirty water: *The drain in the bathtub is blocked.*

● **verb** to make the liquid flow away from something: *I boiled the spaghetti and drained all the water.*

**drain**

> **IDIOM with drain**
> **go down the drain** if something goes down the drain, it is wasted or it is unsuccessful: *The new car broke right away, so all our money went down the drain.*

### dra·ma /**drahm**-uh/ *noun*

**1** a story that actors perform as a play in the theater, or on television or the radio: *The book was made into a TV drama.*
**2** the study of plays or acting in plays: *My drama teacher said that I was a good actor.*
**3** exciting things that happen: *There has been a lot of drama in this year's World Series.*
—**dramatist** /**dram**-uht-ist/ *noun* someone who writes plays: *William Shakespeare was a famous English dramatist who wrote "Romeo and Juliet."*

> **Word Family:** drama
>
> **drama** *noun* | **dramatic** *adjective* |
> **dramatically** *adverb* | **dramatize** *verb* |
> **dramatist** *noun* | **dramatization** *noun*

### dra·mat·ic /druh-**mat**-ik/ *adjective*

**1** very exciting: *The movie tells a dramatic story about a boy who defeats an evil wizard.*
**2** very noticeable or sudden: *There was a dramatic change in the weather. It went from sunny and warm to snowing!*
**3** relating to plays and the theater: *Mr. Davis is the author of several unpublished dramatic works.*
—**dramatically** /druh-**mat**-ik-lee/ *adverb* in a very exciting or extreme way: *Her appearance has changed dramatically.*

### dram·a·tize /**dram**-uh-tīz/ *verb* to write a play, movie, or TV program about a real event or story: *A TV writer decided to dramatize his life story.*

—**dramatization** /dram-uht-uh-**zaysh**-uhn/ *noun* a play, movie, or TV program that is based on a book or on a real event: *The movie is a dramatization of a true story that happened during the Iraq War.*

### drank /drangk/ *verb* the past tense of **drink**

### drape /drayp/ *verb* to put cloth over or around something: *I draped my coat over the back of a chair.*

### drapes /draypss/ (also **drap·e·ries** /**drayp**-uhr-eez/) *plural noun* heavy curtains

### dras·tic /**drast**-ik/ *adjective* drastic actions or changes have a big effect: *The coach has made some drastic changes. Now, if you don't come to practice, you don't get to play!*

—**drastically** /**drast**-ik-lee/ *adverb* in a drastic way: *Prices have drastically increased. A candy bar used to cost 60 cents, but now it costs 90 cents.*

### draw /dro/

● **verb** (**drew** /droo/, **drawn** /dron/)
**1** to make a picture of something using a pen or pencil: *Rick's very good at drawing animals.*
**2** to pull something or someone: *Mom drew him close and gave him a hug.*
**3** to attract people to come to see something: *The game drew a big crowd.*
**4 draw up** to write a list or plan: *I drew up a list of friends I wanted to invite.*

● **noun**
something that attracts people to see it: *The Statue of Liberty is always a big draw for tourists.*

**draw**

### draw·back /**dro**-bak/ *noun* a problem or disadvantage: *The main drawback of Mom's job is that she has to work on weekends.*

### draw·bridge /**dro**-brij/ *noun* a bridge that can be pulled up to let ships go under it, or to stop people from entering a castle

a b c **d** e f g h i j k l m n o p q r s t u v w x y z

**drawer** /dror/ *noun* a container that is part of a piece of furniture. You can pull it out and put things inside it: *The pens are in the top drawer of the desk.*

drawer

drawer

**draw·ing** /**dro**-ing/ *noun*
**1** a picture you make with a pen or pencil: *I did a drawing of a boat.*
**2** the art or skill of making pictures with a pen or pencil: *I am not very good at drawing.*

**drawn** /dron/ *verb* the past participle of draw

**dread** /dred/
● *verb* to feel very worried about something that is going to happen: *I'm really dreading the test.*
● *noun* a strong fear of something: *I felt a sense of dread as I walked into the principal's office.*

**dread·ful** /**dred**-fuhl/ *adjective* very bad or unpleasant: *Murder is a dreadful crime.*

**dream** /dreem/
● *noun*
**1** the images that you see in your mind when you are asleep: *I had a really strange dream last night.* ▶ see **Thesaurus**
**2** something that you hope will happen: *My dream is to become a professional basketball player.*
● *verb* (**dreamed** or **dreamt** /dremt/)
**1** to see images in your mind while you are asleep: *I dreamed about school last night.*
**2** to think about something that you hope will happen: *He dreamed of becoming a movie star.*

**dream·er** /**dreem**-ur/ *noun* someone who has ideas that are not likely to happen: *He's a dreamer: he has lots of ideas, but they're not very practical.*

**drench** /drench/ *verb* to make something completely wet: *He drenched his French fries in ketchup.*
—**drenched** /drencht/ *adjective* completely wet: *It rained so hard I got drenched on the way home from school.*

**dress** /dress/
● *verb*
**1** to put clothes on yourself or on another person: *I got out of bed and dressed quickly.* | *I sometimes help mom to dress the baby.*
**2 dress up** to wear your best clothes: *He dressed up in his best suit for church.*
**3 dress up** to wear special clothes that make you look like someone or something else: *I dressed up as a ghost for Halloween.*
● *noun*
a piece of clothing for a woman or girl, which covers her body and part of her legs: *Gina is wearing her new dress to the party.*
● *adjective*
a dress shirt or dress shoes are ones that you wear to a formal event such as a wedding, or that some people wear to work: *His dress shoes are black and shiny.*

dress

**dress code** /**dress** kohd/ *noun* a set of rules for what you should wear for a particular situation: *The school has a dress code, and you can't wear sandals.*

**dress·er** /**dress**-ur/ *noun* a piece of furniture with drawers. You keep clothes in a dresser: *Mom took a scarf out of her dresser drawer.*
( SYNONYM: **chest of drawers** )

**dress·ing** /**dress**-ing/ *noun*
**1** a mixture of oil and other things that you pour over salad: *Dad made a salad dressing from oil, vinegar, salt, and pepper.*
**2** a mixture of bread, onion, herbs, and other foods, that you put inside a chicken or turkey before cooking it: *My favorite part of a turkey dinner is the dressing.* ( SYNONYM: **stuffing** )
**3** a piece of material used for covering a wound: *The doctor put a dressing over the deep cut on my arm.*

**dress·y** /**dress**-ee/ *adjective* dressy clothes are ones you wear for special or formal occasions: *Those shoes are too dressy for school.*

**drew** /droo/ *verb* the past tense of **draw**

187

**drib·ble** /**drib**-uhl/ *verb*
**1** in soccer or basketball, to move a ball toward the goal or basket by bouncing or kicking it again and again
**2** to let liquid come out of your mouth: *The baby is dribbling on your shirt!* ( SYNONYM: **drool** )
**3** if a liquid dribbles, it flows in a slow thin stream: *Blood dribbled down from the cut on his lip.*

**dried** /drīd/ *verb* the past tense and past participle of **dry**

**dri·er** /**drī**-ur/ *noun* another spelling of dryer: *Mom asked me to put some laundry in the drier.*

**drift** /drift/
• *verb* to move along slowly in the air or water: *The clouds of smoke from the fire drifted over the city.*
• *noun* snow or sand that the wind has moved into a pile: *A big drift of snow covered the car.*

**drill** /dril/
• *noun*
a tool or machine for making holes in something hard: *You'll need an electric drill to make a hole in the wall.*
• *verb*
**1** to make a hole with a drill: *The carpenter drilled a hole in the wood.*
**2** to teach people something by making them repeat the same thing many times: *The teacher was drilling the students in pronunciation.*

**drill**

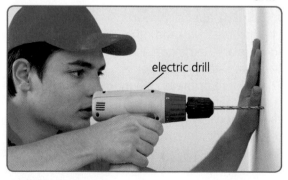
electric drill

**drink** /dringk/
• *verb* (**drank** /drangk/, **drunk** /druhngk/)
**1** to take liquid into your mouth and swallow it: *What do you want to drink?* | *I usually drink orange juice.* ▶ see **Thesaurus**
**2** to drink alcohol: *My parents don't drink.*

• *noun*
**1** a liquid such as water or juice that you can drink: *Can I have a drink of water, please?*
**2** an alcoholic drink: *The men had gone to the bar for a drink.*

**drink·ing foun·tain** /**dringk**-ing fownt-in/ *noun* a piece of equipment in a public place that gives you water to drink: *At recess, get a drink from the drinking fountain.*

**drip** /drip/ *verb*
(**dripping**, **dripped**) if a liquid drips, it falls in drops: *Water is dripping from the branches of the trees.*

**drip**

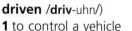

*The faucet is dripping.*

**drive** /drīv/
• *verb* (**drove** /drohv/, **driven** /**driv**-uhn/)
**1** to control a vehicle such as a car or bus: *She's learning to drive.* | *He was driving a red car.*
**2** if you drive someone somewhere, you take him or her there in a car: *Dad usually drives me to school.*
**3** to hit something hard: *She drove the nail into the wood.*

IDIOM with **drive**
**drive someone crazy/nuts** to make someone feel very annoyed or angry: *Stop making that noise! You're driving me crazy!*

• *noun*
**1** a trip in a car: *Dad took us for a drive in the new car.* | *It's a two-hour drive to the beach.*
**2** a part of a computer that can read or store information: *The files are stored on the C drive of my computer.*
**3** determination and energy to succeed: *He has the drive to become a successful athlete.*
**4** a planned attempt to achieve something: *We had a paper drive at school, to collect newspapers and magazines to sell to the recycling company.*
**5** a hard hit that sends a ball a long way: *He hit a line drive to center field.*

**driv·en** /**driv**-uhn/ *verb* the past participle of drive

**driv·er** /**drīv**-ur/ *noun* someone who drives: *The bus driver told us to sit down.*

**drive-through** /**drīv**-throo/ *noun* a restaurant

or bank that you can use without getting out of your car

**drive·way** /**drīv**-way/ *noun* the road for cars between a house and the street: *Dad parked the car in the driveway.*

**driz·zle** /**driz**-uhl/ *verb* if it is drizzling, it is raining very lightly: *It was only drizzling so I didn't take an umbrella.*

**drool** /drool/
● *verb* if you drool, liquid flows out of your mouth: *The dog drools whenever it sees food.*
● *noun* a flow of liquid that comes out of your mouth: *Mom wiped the drool from the baby's mouth.*

**droop** /droop/ *verb* if something droops, it hangs down because it is old or weak: *The flowers are drooping – you need to water them.*

**drop** /drahp/

**drop**

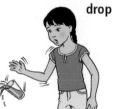

● *verb* (**dropping, dropped** )
**1** to let something fall from your hand: *I dropped a glass and it smashed on the floor.*
**2** to fall to the ground: *Some apples had dropped from the tree.*
**3** to become lower in level or amount: *The temperature dropped to below zero.* ( SYNONYMS: **fall, go down** )

She dropped the glass.

**4** to stop doing something or continuing with something: *He had to drop football because of a knee injury.*
**5** to not keep a player on a team: *If you don't play well, the coach will drop you from the team.*
**6 drop by** to visit someone who does not know you are coming: *I dropped by my aunt's house on my way home.*
**7 drop off** to take someone or something to a place in a car: *Mom drops me off at school on her way to work.*
**8 drop out** to leave school before you have finished: *My grandpa had to drop out of school at 14.*
● *noun*
**1** a very small amount of liquid: *Drops of rain splashed against the window.*

**2** a situation in which the amount or level of something becomes lower: *There was a sharp drop in temperature – from 20 degrees to 10 degrees.*
**3** a small piece of candy that you suck: *A cough drop will stop you from coughing so much.*

**drop·out** /**drahp**-owt/ *noun* someone who leaves school or college before they have finished their studies: *Many high school dropouts have trouble finding jobs.*

**drought** /drowt/ *noun* a long time when there is not enough rain: *All the grass has died because of the drought.*

**drove** /drohv/ *verb* the past tense of **drive**

**drown** /drown/ *verb*
**1** to die from being under water for too long: *He fell in the river and almost drowned.*
**2 drown out** to be so loud that something else cannot be heard: *The noise of the engine drowned out his voice.*

**drows·y** /**drowz**-ee/ *adjective* feeling that you want to sleep: *The room was very warm and I began to feel drowsy and my eyes started to close.* ( SYNONYM: **sleepy** )
—**drowsiness** /**drowz**-ee-niss/ *noun* a feeling that you want to sleep: *This medicine can cause drowsiness.*

**drudg·er·y** /**druhj**-uhr-ee/ *noun* boring and tiring work: *Washing machines helped to reduce the drudgery of housework.*

**drug** /druhg/
● *noun*
**1** an illegal substance that people smoke, swallow, or inject into their body: *He never drinks alcohol and he never takes drugs.*
**2** a medicine: *The drug is used to treat cancer.*
● *verb* (**drugging, drugged**)
to give someone drugs, usually in order to make him or her sleep: *The thieves drugged him and stole his money.*

**drug·store** /**druhg**-stor/ *noun* a store where you can buy medicine, soap, toothpaste, etc.: *Will you go to the drugstore and get me some tissues?*

### drum /druhm/

**drum**

● *noun*

**1** a round musical instrument that you hit with your hand or a stick: *Johnny plays the drums in a band.*

**2** a large round container for storing oil or chemicals: *The ship carried oil drums.*

—**drummer** /**druhm**-ur/ *noun* someone who plays a drum

drumstick

drum

● *verb* (**drumming**, **drummed**)

to hit something many times, making a sound like a drum: *He drummed his fingers on the table while he waited.*

### drum·stick /**druhm**-stik/ *noun*

**1** the leg of a chicken or turkey that you eat: *We had chicken drumsticks at the barbecue.*

**2** a stick that you use to hit a drum ▶ see picture at **drum**

### drunk /druhngk/

● *adjective*

if someone is drunk, he or she has drunk a lot of alcohol and cannot think or act normally: *People should never drive if they are drunk – it's too dangerous.*

● *noun* someone who often drinks too much alcohol

● *verb* the past participle of **drink**

### drunk·en /**druhngk**-uhn/ *adjective* drunk

### dry /drī/

● *adjective* (**drier, driest**)

**1** not wet: *When the paint is dry, we'll put your picture on the wall.* ( ANTONYM: **wet** )

**2** without any rain: *Tomorrow will be dry and sunny.*

( ANTONYM: **wet** )

**3** dry hair or skin does not have as much oil as normal hair or skin: *Put some lotion on your face if your skin is very dry.*

dry

dry

wet

● *verb* (**dries, drying, dried**)

**1** to make something dry: *Dry your hands on this towel.*

**2** to become dry: *Shirts were drying on the clothesline.*

**3** **dry up** if a lake or river dries up, there is no more water in it: *It was very hot in the summer and the rivers all dried up.*

### dry-clean /drī **kleen**/ *verb* to clean clothes with chemicals, not water: *Most suits have to be dry-cleaned or they will shrink.*

### dry clean·ers /drī **kleen**-urz/ (also **dry cleaner**) *noun* a place where you take clothes to be dry-cleaned: *We picked up Dad's shirts at the dry cleaners.*

### dry clean·ing /drī **kleen**-ing/ *noun* clothes that have just been dry-cleaned: *He went to pick up his dry cleaning.*

### dry·er, drier /**drī**-ur/ *noun* a machine that is used to dry clothes, hair, or hands: *Can you put the laundry in the dryer?*

### du·al /**doo**-uhl/ *adjective* having two of something, or having two parts: *My grandfather has dual citizenship – German and American.*

### du·bi·ous /**doob**-ee-uhss/ *adjective*

**1** not sure whether something is good or true: *I'm dubious about the idea and I'm not sure that it will work.* ( SYNONYM: **doubtful** )

**2** probably not real, true, good, or honest: *They say the changes will be good for everyone, but that seems dubious.*

### duck /duhk/

● *noun*

**1** a bird that swims on water. Ducks have short legs and a wide beak: *We went to the pond to feed the ducks.*

**2** the meat of a duck, which you eat: *We had roast duck for dinner.*

● *verb*

**1** to bend down quickly to avoid something: *Mike threw a pillow at me, but I ducked so it didn't hit me.*

**2** to avoid doing or dealing with something: *He tries to duck the question.*

**duck**

duck        duckling

**duck·ling** /**duhk**-ling/ *noun* a young duck

**duct** /duhkt/ *noun*
**1** a tube in a building for carrying air or electric wires: *Warm air was coming from the heating duct.*
**2** a narrow tube inside your body that liquid goes through: *Your tear ducts produce tears when you cry.*

**due** /doo/ *adjective*
**1** expected to happen, arrive, or be given to someone at a particular time: *Your homework is due on Friday.*
**2** happening because of something: *Her success was due to hard work.*

**du·el** /**doo**-uhl/ *noun* a fight in past times between two people with guns or swords: *He was hurt in a duel.*

**due pro·cess** /**doo**prahss-ess/ *noun* the correct legal way of doing something, which protects a person's rights: *No one can be put in prison without due process.*

**dues** /dooz/ *plural noun* money that you pay regularly to be a member of an organization: *The dues you pay at Girl Scouts are for activities, supplies, and snacks.*

**du·et** /doo-**et**/ *noun* a piece of music that is played or sung by two people: *Hannah sang a duet with her sister.*

**dug** /duhg/ *verb* the past tense and past participle of **dig**

**dull** /duhl/
 ● *adjective*
**1** not interesting or exciting: *The movie was so dull I fell asleep.* (SYNONYM: **boring**)
**2** a dull pain is not strong: *I have a dull ache in my back from sitting too long.*

**3** not bright or shiny: *The sky was dull and gray.*
**4** a dull sound is not clear or loud: *The book landed on the floor with a dull thud.*
 ● *verb*
to make a pain or feeling less strong: *She took some medicine to dull the pain.*

**dumb** /duhm/ *adjective* stupid: *It was kind of dumb to give her your toy when you knew she'd break it.* (ANTONYM: **smart**)

**dum·my** /**duhm**-ee/ *noun* (plural **dummies**)
**1** someone who is stupid: *You've done it wrong, you dummy!* (SYNONYM: **idiot**)
**2** a large model of a person: *They use crash dummies to test the safety of cars.*

**dump** /duhmp/
 ● *verb*
**1** to drop or put something somewhere in a careless way: *She dumped the magazines on the sofa.*
**2** to leave something somewhere because you do not want it: *You can't just dump your trash on the street.*
 ● *noun*
**1** a place where you can leave things you do not want: *We took the broken chair to the dump.*
**2** a place that is dirty or unpleasant: *The floors are really dirty and the whole place smells – it's a real dump.*

**dune** /doon/ *noun* a hill of sand near the ocean or in the desert. Sand dunes are made by the wind: *We walked over the sand dunes to the beach.*

**dune**

sand dunes

**dun·geon** /**duhnj**-uhn/ *noun* a prison under a building such as a castle. Dungeons were used in the past: *The king locked him in a dark dungeon.*

a b c **d** e f g h i j k l m n o p q r s t u v w x y z

**dunk** /duhngk/ *verb*
**1** in basketball, to jump up by the basket and throw the ball down through it
**2** to put something into a liquid for a very short time: *He dunked his cookie in his milk.*

**du·pli·cate**
● *noun* /**doop**-luhk-it/
an exact copy of something: *My parents made a duplicate of the front door key to give to my aunt.* ( SYNONYM: **copy** )
● *adjective*
exactly the same as something else: *I had two copies of my report saved on the computer, so I got rid of the duplicate file.*
● *verb* /**doop**-luh-kayt/
**1** to make an exact copy of something: *You can duplicate the photos and give copies to your friends.*
**2** to do the same thing as someone else: *Ben and I found out we were duplicating each other's work – we were both writing the introduction to our research paper.*
—**duplication** /doop-luh-**kaysh**-uhn/ *noun* the act of duplicating something: *The duplication of DVDs on your home computer is not legal.*

**dur·a·ble** /**door**-uhb-uhl/ *adjective* staying in good condition for a long time: *Expensive shoes should be more durable than cheap ones.*
—**durability** /door-uh-**bil**-uht-ee/ *noun* an ability to stay in good condition for a long time: *Steel is used in large buildings because of its strength and durability.*

**dur·ing** /**door**-ing/ *preposition*
**1** at some point in a period of time: *She fell asleep during class.*
**2** all through a period of time: *During the summer we go swimming almost every day.*

**dusk** /duhsk/ *noun* the time when it starts to become dark at the end of the day: *The street lights go on at dusk.* ( SYNONYM: **twilight** )
( ANTONYM: **dawn** )

**dust** /duhst/
● *noun* very small pieces of dirt that look like a powder: *The table had dust on it.*
● *verb* to clean the dust from something with a cloth: *I dusted the shelves in my bedroom.*

**dust·pan** /**duhst**-pan/
*noun* a flat container with a handle, that you sweep dirt from a floor into

dustpan

brush          dustpan

**dust·y** /**duhst**-ee/
*adjective* covered with dust: *I found some dusty old books that nobody had touched for years.*

**Dutch** /duhch/
● *adjective*
from or in the Netherlands: *The Dutch countryside is very flat.*
● *noun*
**1** the language used in the Netherlands: *His parents speak Dutch at home.*
**2 the Dutch** the people of the Netherlands: *The Dutch love soccer.*

**du·ty** /**doot**-ee/ *noun* (plural **duties**) something that you should do because it is right or it is part of your job: *We have a duty to deal with bullying in the playground.*

IDIOM with **duty**
**on duty** working: *There was no lifeguard on duty at the beach.*

**DVD** /dee vee **dee**/ *noun*
a disk that has movies, programs, music, or information recorded on it: *We made popcorn and watched a DVD.*

DVD

**dwarf** /dworf/ *noun*
**1** an imaginary creature that looks like a small man: *We read the story of "Snow White and the Seven Dwarfs".*
**2** a person who is much shorter than usual

DVD

DVD player

**dye** /dī/
● *noun* a substance you use to change the color of cloth or your hair: *She bought some black dye for her hair.*
● *verb* to change the color of something using a dye: *She dyed her hair red.*

**dy·nam·ic** /dī-**nam**-ik/ *adjective* full of energy and ideas: *A dynamic teacher can make any subject interesting.*

**dy·na·mite** /**dīn**-uh-mīt/ *noun* a substance that is used to make powerful explosions: *They blew up the building with dynamite.*

**Word Origin:** dynamite

The word **dynamite** was made up in 1867 by the Swedish inventor Alfred Nobel. He used a Greek word that means "power" to make a name for the explosive he invented.

**dys·lex·i·a** /diss-**lekss**-ee-uh/ *noun* if you have dyslexia, you have difficulty reading and writing because your brain cannot recognize written words correctly: *Some people with dyslexia see letters as upside-down or backward.*
—**dyslexic** /diss-**lekss**-ik/ *adjective* having dyslexia: *My brother is dyslexic so he has trouble spelling words.*

a
b
c
**d**
e
f
g
h
i
j
k
l
m
n
o
p
q
r
s
t
u
v
w
x
y
z

# Ee

**e-** /ee/

### Word Building

**e-** is a prefix.

**email | e-learning**

**e-** stands for "electronic." **e-** means that something is being done using a computer. *Email* is a way of sending letters to someone using your computer. *E-learning* means that you can learn about something by using a computer.

**each** /eech/ *adjective, pronoun, adverb* both or every one: *She had a bag in each hand. | The kids were given $5 each. | Each of the following sentences contains a mistake.*

### Grammar: each, every, all

**Each**, **every**, and **all** are all used to talk about every person or thing in a group.

When you are thinking about the people or things in the group separately, use **each** or **every**: *Each child has a math book. | Every child has a math book.*

When you are thinking about the whole group together, use **all**: *All the children have math books.*

**each oth·er** /eech **uh**th-ur/ *pronoun* if people do something to each other, each one does the same thing to the other person or people: *The boys started hitting each other.*

**ea·ger** /**eeg**-ur/ *adjective* wanting to do something very much: *Maria is eager to start school and make new friends.*
—**eagerly** /**eeg**-ur-lee/ *adverb* in an eager way: *The kids jumped eagerly off the bus.*

**ea·gle** /**eeg**-uhl/ *noun* a big bird with a beak like a hook. Eagles eat small animals and live in high places: *We saw an eagle flying above the mountain.*

eagle
beak
talon

**ear** /eer/ *noun* one of the two parts of your body that you hear with: *Mark whispered something in his sister's ear.*

**ear·ache** /**eer**-ayk/ *noun* pain inside your ear: *Mom took me to the doctor because I had an earache.*

**ear·drum** /**eer**-druhm/ *noun* a part inside your ear that moves when sound reaches it. The eardrum sends signals to your brain so that you hear the sound: *You should never put anything inside your ear because you could hurt your eardrum.*

**ear·ly** /**url**-ee/ (**earlier**, **earliest**)
● *adjective*
**1** happening before the usual time or before the right time: *You're early – the school bus doesn't leave for another 30 minutes.* ( ANTONYM: **late** )
**2** near the beginning of a period of time: *He spent the early part of his life in Florida. | The house was built in the early 1900s, probably about 1905.* ( ANTONYM: **late** )
● *adverb*
**1** before the usual time or before the right time: *I got to school 20 minutes early.* ( ANTONYM: **late** )
▶ see **Thesaurus**
**2** near the beginning of the day: *I woke up very early, when it was still dark.* ( ANTONYM: **late** )
**3** near the beginning of a period of time: *We moved here early last year, in January.*
( ANTONYM: **late** )

**earn** /urn/ *verb*
**1** to get money for the work you do: *My sister earns $7 an hour for babysitting.*
**2** to get or deserve something good because of what you have done: *You've worked really hard – you've earned a rest!*

**earn·ings** /**urn**-ingz/ *plural noun* money that you get for working: *I bought a new bike with my earnings from delivering newspapers.*

**ear·phones** /**eer**-fohnz/ *plural noun* a small piece of electrical equipment that you put in or over your ears. You connect the earphones to an MP3 player, radio, computer, etc. so you can listen to something but other people do not hear the sound.

earphones

**ear·ring** /**eer**-ing/ *noun* a piece of jewelry that you fasten to your ear: *She was wearing gold earrings.*

earring

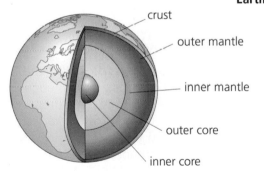
earring

**earth** /urth/ *noun*
**1** the planet that we live on. Earth is the third planet from the Sun. You often spell Earth with a capital letter: *Mount Everest is the highest mountain on Earth.*
**2** soil that plants grow in: *It hadn't rained, and the earth was hard and dry.*

Earth

crust
outer mantle
inner mantle
outer core
inner core

**earth·quake** /**urth**-kwayk/ *noun* a sudden shaking of the ground. Earthquakes happen when parts of the Earth's crust move: *The earthquake destroyed a lot of the city.*

**earth·worm** /**urth**-wurm/ *noun* a worm that digs through soil and eats dead leaves. Earthworms help to keep the soil fertile.

earthworm

**ease** /eez/
● *noun*
**1** if you do something with ease, you do it easily: *He won the race with ease.*
**2** if you are at ease, you feel calm and not worried: *I feel more at ease when I'm with people I know.*
● *verb*
**1** to become less bad: *The storm was easing.*
**2** to make something less bad: *The doctor gave me some medicine to ease the pain and I felt a lot better.*

**ea·sel** /**eez**-uhl/ *noun* a board that you put a painting on while you are painting it. The board is held up by legs and you stand in front of it to paint: *The artist put a new piece of paper on the easel and started to paint.*

**eas·i·ly** /**eez**-uhl-ee/ *adverb* without difficulty: *I found the house easily because it had a big number on the door. | She won the game easily 6-0.*

**east** /eest/
● *noun*
**1** the direction from which the Sun rises: *Which way is east?*
**2** the eastern part of a country or area: *We live in the east of the city.*
**3** **the East** the eastern part of the U.S., especially the states north of Washington D.C.: *She was born in the East but later moved to California when she was eight.*
**4** **the East** the countries in Asia, especially China, Korea, and Japan: *I would love to travel in the East and see the Great Wall of China.*
● *adjective*
**1** in or to the east: *Our hotel was on the east coast of the island.*
**2** an east wind comes from the east
● *adverb*
toward the east: *We drove east along Brooklyn Avenue.*

**East Coast** /eest **kohst**/ *noun* the part of the U.S. that is next to the Atlantic Ocean, especially the states north of Washington, D.C.

a b c d e f g h i j k l m n o p q r s t u v w x y z

195

**Eas·ter** /**eest**-ur/ *noun* a religious holiday in March or April. Easter is when Christians remember Jesus Christ being killed on the cross and returning to life.

## Word Origin: Easter

**Easter** comes from the name of an Old English goddess called **Eastre**. She was probably a goddess of the dawn because her name comes from an even older word that meant "light" or "sunrise." In the spring, there were celebrations for the goddess Eastre. When Christianity came to Britain, the church took the name Easter and used the celebrations for their own religious day.

**Eas·ter egg** /**eest**-ur eg/ *noun* an egg that has been colored and decorated for Easter: *There were Easter eggs hidden around the house.*

**Easter egg**

**east·ern** /**eest**-urn/ *adjective* in or from the east: *The town is on the eastern bank of the Mississippi River.*

**east·ern·er** /**eest**-urn-ur/ *noun* someone who comes from the eastern part of a country

**east·ward** /**eest**-wurd/ *adverb, adjective* toward the east: *The plane was traveling eastward, from Chicago to New York.*

**eas·y** /**eez**-ee/ (**easier, easiest**)
● *adjective*
**1** not difficult: *The test was easy.* | *The writing on the sign is easy to read.* (**ANTONYM: hard**)
▶ see **Thesaurus**
**2** without problems or hard work: *He doesn't care about money, he just wants an easy life.*
● *adverb*

**IDIOM with easy**
**take it easy**
**1** to relax and not do very much: *He hurt his leg, so he's going to take it easy for a few days.*
**2** used for telling someone to be less angry or upset: *Hey, take it easy! It was an accident!*

## Word Family: easy

**easy** *adjective* | **easily** *adverb* | **ease** *noun* | **ease** *verb*

**eas·y chair** /**eez**-ee chair/ *noun* a soft comfortable chair with soft sides: *Anya curled up in the easy chair with a book.*

**eas·y·go·ing** /eez-ee-**goh**-ing/ *adjective* not easily worried or annoyed: *Her parents are really easygoing – they never yell at her.*
(**ANTONYM: uptight**)

**eat** /eet/ *verb* (**ate** /ayt/, **eaten** /**eet**'n/)
**1** to put food in your mouth and swallow it: *She was eating an apple.* | *Hurry up and eat your breakfast – it's almost time to go to school.*
▶ see **Thesaurus**
**2** to have a meal: *We usually eat at around six.*
**3 eat up** to use too much of something: *Homework eats up a lot of my time.*

**eat·en** /**eet**'n/ *verb* the past participle of eat

**eaves·drop** /**eevz**-drahp/ *verb* (**eavesdropping, eavesdropped**) to listen secretly to people talking: *How do you know he said that? Were you eavesdropping?*

## Word Origin: eavesdrop

In Old English, the **eavesdrop** was the place where rain dropped off the edges of a roof. You were called an eavesdropper if you stood under this part of the roof and listened secretly to the people inside the house, or "eavesdropped" on them.

**ech·o** /**ek**-oh/
● *noun* (plural **echoes**) a sound that repeats another sound. An echo comes back off a surface such as a wall or mountain: *I heard the echoes of his footsteps on the stone floor.*
● *verb* (**echoes, echoing, echoed**) if a sound echoes, you hear it again because it comes back off a surface: *When he shouted, his voice echoed around the valley.*

**e·clipse** /i-**klipss**/ *noun*
**1** a time when the Moon is between the Earth and the Sun, so we cannot see the Sun: *There was a total eclipse of the Sun in 2009.*

**2** a time when the Earth is between the Sun and the Moon, and we cannot see the Moon because it is in the Earth's shadow

eclipse

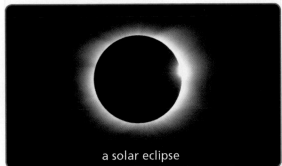
a solar eclipse

**eco-** /eek-oh/

## Word Building

ecology | ecosystem | economy

These words all have the Greek word root *eco* in them. *Eco* means "house" or "the place where you live." *Ecology* is the study of the environment and the plants, animals, and people that live there. An *ecosystem* is the environment in a place, and how all the animals and plants that live there are connected to each other and the environment. We use *economy* to talk about how a country earns and spends money to take care of the people who live in the country.

**e·col·o·gy** /i-**kahl**-uhj-ee/ *noun* the relationships between plants, animals, and people, and their environment: *Cutting down trees affects the ecology of the forest because the animals and insects who live there have to leave.*
—**ecologist** /i-**kahl**-uh-jist/ *noun* someone who studies ecology
—**ecological** /eek-uh-**lahj**-ik-uhl/ *adjective* relating to ecology: *Pollution has destroyed the ecological balance of the lake. Now the birds and frogs can't find fish and water insects to eat.*

**ec·o·nom·ic** /ek-uh-**nahm**-ik/ *adjective* relating to business, industry, and money in a country or area: *People hope that the economic situation will improve and they won't lose their jobs.*
—**economically** /ek-uh-**nahm**-ik-lee/ *adverb* in an economic way: *If people can start new businesses, the country will grow economically.*

**ec·o·nom·i·cal** /ek-uh-**nahm**-ik-uhl/ *adjective* not costing a lot of money to buy or use: *It's a very economical car – it doesn't use much gas.*

**ec·o·nom·ics** /ek-uh-**nahm**-ikss/ *noun* the study of business, industry, and money: *It's a basic rule of economics: if you lower the price, people buy more. If you raise the price, they buy less.*
—**economist** /i-**kahn**-uhm-ist/ *noun* someone who studies economics: *Economists say that the situation is going to improve soon and there will be more jobs.*

**e·con·o·my** /i-**kahn**-uhm-ee/ *noun*
**1** the business and industry in a country or area: *China's economy is growing rapidly.*
**2** the type of seats on an airplane that cost the least money: *We always fly economy in order to save money.* ( SYNONYM: **coach** )

## Word Family: economy

**economy** *noun* | **economist** *noun* | **economic** *adjective* | **economics** *noun*

**e·co·sys·tem** /**eek**-oh-sist-uhm/ *noun* the environment and all the plants and animals in a place, that are all connected with each other: *The chemicals kill the fish and damage the ecosystem in the river.*

**ec·ze·ma** /**ekss**-uhm-uh/ *noun* if you have eczema, your skin is dry, red, and itchy

**-ed** /id/

## Word Building

**-ed** is a suffix.
**1** chas**ed** | start**ed** | walk**ed**
**-ed** means that the verb is in the past tense. The past tense shows that an action happened in the past, not now.
**2** finish**ed** | bor**ed** | excit**ed**
**-ed** changes a verb into an adjective. If you are *bored* or *excited*, "bored" or "excited" describes how you feel. If the story you are writing is *finished*, "finished" describes the story by telling people that you are done writing it.

a
b
c
d
**e**
f
g
h
i
j
k
l
m
n
o
p
q
r
s
t
u
v
w
x
y
z

**edge** /ej/ *noun*
**1** the part of something that is farthest from the center: *Hold the edges of the CD so you don't get finger prints on it.* ► see **Thesaurus**
**2** the part of an area beside a steep slope: *Stay away from the edge of the cliff.*
**3** the thin sharp part of a tool used for cutting: *You need a knife with a sharp edge.*

**ed·i·ble** /**ed**-uhb-uhl/ *adjective* safe or good to eat: *How do you know if a mushroom is edible or poisonous?* (ANTONYM: **inedible**)

**ed·it** /**ed**-it/ *verb* to make a book, newspaper, magazine, or movie ready. When you edit something, you decide what to include and correct any mistakes: *The class wrote the stories for the newspaper, and their teacher edited it.*

**e·di·tion** /i-**dish**-uhn/ *noun* a copy of a book, newspaper, or magazine that is printed at the same time as other copies, and has the same information in it: *The old edition of the book had a black cover, but the new edition of the book has a picture from the movie on it.*

**ed·i·tor** /**ed**-uht-ur/ *noun* someone whose job is to decide what should be in a newspaper, magazine, book, or movie: *The editor wanted to include a story about healthy eating in the newspaper.*

**ed·i·to·ri·al** /ed-uh-**tor**-ee-uhl/
● *noun* a piece of writing in a newspaper that gives the opinion of the editor: *There was an editorial on the war in the paper yesterday.*
● *adjective* relating to editing: *She works with the editorial team on the magazine.*

**ed·u·cate** /**ej**-uh-kayt/ *verb* to teach someone: *We need to educate children to use the Internet safely.*
—**educator** /**ej**-uh-kayt-ur/ *noun* a teacher

**ed·u·cat·ed** /**ej**-uh-kayt-id/ *adjective* an educated person has a good education: *His mother is an educated woman who works as a lawyer.*

**ed·u·ca·tion** /ej-uh-**kaysh**-uhn/ *noun*
**1** the knowledge and skills that you get from going to school: *A good education teaches you to read, write, do math, and think carefully.*
**2** the process of teaching and learning information or skills: *She wants to work in education, probably as a teacher.*

**ed·u·ca·tion·al** /ej-uh-**kaysh**-uhn-uhl/ *adjective*
**1** relating to teaching and learning: *In the American educational system, first grade is for children who are six and seven years old.*
**2** teaching you something: *This game is very educational; you learn a lot about different countries of the world.*

**-ee** /ee/

## Word Building

**-ee** is a suffix. It is used in nouns.
**employee** | **nominee** | **refugee**
**-ee** is used in nouns that are people. An *employee* is someone who is employed by a company. A *nominee* is someone who has been nominated for an election or prize. A *refugee* is someone who is taking refuge in a different country.

**eel** /eel/ *noun* a long thin fish that looks like a snake

**eel**

**ef·fect** /i-**fekt**/ *noun* a change caused by something that happens: *Missing a lot of school has a bad effect on your grades because you don't learn all the things you should.*
► see **Thesaurus**

IDIOM with effect
**take effect** if something takes effect, it starts to work: *The medicine should take effect in about ten minutes, and then your head won't hurt so much.*

**ef·fec·tive** /i-**fekt**-iv/ *adjective* having the result that you want: *Reading every day is an effective way to improve your reading speed.*
(ANTONYM: **ineffective**)
—**effectively** /i-**fekt**-iv-lee/ *adverb* in an effective way: *The principal dealt with the problem*

*effectively because the bullying stopped.*
—**effectiveness** /i-**fekt**-iv-niss/ *noun* the quality of being effective: *Doctors are not sure about the effectiveness of this treatment. It seems to help some people, but not others.*

**ef·fi·cient** /i-**fish**-uhnt/ *adjective* doing something without wasting time, money, or energy: *Sending text messages or emails to parents is an efficient way for the school to contact them, since there are no papers that the children can lose.* ( ANTONYM: **inefficient** )
—**efficiently** /i-**fish**-uhnt-lee/ *adverb* in an efficient way: *The car runs very efficiently, so you do not have to fill the gas tank very often.*
—**efficiency** /i-**fish**-uhnss-ee/ *noun* the quality of being efficient: *This type of engine burns gasoline with greater efficiency.*

**ef·flu·ent** /**ef**-loo-uhnt/ *noun* liquid waste: *The factory was pouring effluent into the river and causing a lot of pollution.*

**ef·fort** /**ef**-urt/ *noun*
**1** hard work that you do when you are trying to achieve something: *If you put more effort into your schoolwork, your grades will improve.*
**2** an attempt to do something, especially something difficult: *My mom and I are making an effort to get more exercise.*

**ef·fort·less** /**ef**-urt-liss/ *adjective* done without trying hard: *She is so talented that her singing seems effortless.*
—**effortlessly** /**ef**-urt-liss-lee/ *adverb* in an effortless way: *The big man effortlessly picked up the heavy suitcase.*

**e.g.** the abbreviation of **for example**

**egg** /eg/ *noun*
**1** a round object that contains a baby bird, reptile, or fish before it is born. Eggs usually have a hard shell: *The turkey lays her eggs, and 28 days later the eggs hatch and the baby turkeys come out.*
**2** a cell made in the body of a woman or female animal. The egg grows into a baby or baby animal when it is fertilized.

**egg**
boiled eggs
fried egg
poached egg
scrambled eggs

**egg·plant** /**eg**-plant/ *noun* a large vegetable with a dark purple skin

**eggplant**

**egg·shell** /**eg**-shel/ *noun* the hard outside part of an egg: *He peeled the eggshell off the hard-boiled egg.*

**e·go** /**eeg**-oh/ *noun* the opinion that you have about yourself: *He has a very big ego and thinks he is the best at everything.*

**Eid ul-Fitr** /eed uhl **fit**-ur/ *noun* a Muslim religious holiday at the end of the month of Ramadan

**eight** /ayt/ *number*
**1** 8: *A cube has eight corners.*
**2** eight o'clock: *I woke up at eight.*
**3** eight years old: *Tina and I are both eight.*

**eight·een** /ay-**teen**/ *number*
**1** 18: *There are eighteen boys in our class.*
**2** eighteen years old: *I'm going to have a big party when I'm eighteen.*
—**eighteenth** /ay-**teenth**/ *number* 18th or 1/18

**eighth** /aytth/ *number*
**1** 8th
**2** 1/8

**eight·y** /**ayt**-ee/ *number*
**1** 80: *The candy bar costs eighty cents.*
**2** eighty years old: *He is almost eighty.*
**3** **the eighties** the years between 1980 and 1989: *His mom and dad met in the eighties.*
**4** **in your eighties** between 80 and 89 years old: *My grandfather is in his eighties.*
**5** **in the eighties** between 80 and 89 degrees in temperature: *The temperature was in the eighties all week.*
—**eightieth** /**ayt**-ee-ith/ *number* 80th or 1/80

**ei·ther** /**eeth**-ur/
● *conjunction*
**either ... or** used when there are two or more things that you can choose from: *You can either come with us or stay here.*
● *pronoun, adjective*
**1** one of two people or things: *Either team could win.* | *"Which one of these books do you want?" "I don't want either of them."*
**2 either side/end/hand etc.** both sides, ends, etc.: *There were trees on either side of the road.*
● *adverb*
also. This is used with negative words like "can't" and "won't": *"I can't swim." "I can't either."* | *My sister doesn't like bananas, and I don't either.*

**e·las·tic** /i-**last**-ik/ *noun* a rubber material that can stretch and then go back to its usual size: *Little kids have elastic at the top of their pants so they can pull them on and off.*

**el·bow** /**el**-boh/ *noun* the joint where your arm bends: *She put her elbows on the table.*
▶see picture on page **A13**

**el·der** /**eld**-ur/ *adjective* your elder sister or brother is older than you: *My elder sister is in high school.*

**el·der·ly** /**eld**-url-ee/ *adjective* old: *An elderly woman with gray hair walked slowly past.*

**el·dest** /**eld**-ist/ *adjective* the eldest son or daughter was born first: *Billy's eldest son is called Billy Jr.*

**elderly**

*an elderly woman*

**e·lect** /i-**lekt**/ *verb* to choose someone for a job by voting: *Barack Obama was elected president in 2008.*

**e·lec·tion** /i-**lek**-shuhn/ *noun* when there is an election, people vote to choose someone for a job: *She won the election for student-body president.*
—**electoral** /i-**lekt**-uhr-uhl/ *adjective* relating to elections: *The mayor was happy about his electoral victory.*

**e·lec·tor·al col·lege** /i-lekt-uhr-uhl **kahl**-ij/ *noun* the group of people who officially elect the U.S. president. The people in the state vote, and in most states the winner of the vote gets all the electoral college votes from that state.

**e·lec·tric** /i-**lek**-trik/ *adjective*
**1** needing electricity in order to work: *Electric guitars are loud because you can plug them in to a speaker.*
**2** relating to electricity: *If you pass an electric current through the wire, the light bulb goes on.*

> **Word Family:** electric
>
> **electric** *adjective* | **electricity** *noun* | **electrical** *adjective* | **electrician** *noun*

**e·lec·tri·cal** /i-**lek**-trik-uhl/ *adjective* using electricity to work or relating to electricity: *The store sells electrical goods like televisions and refrigerators.*

**e·lec·tri·cian** /i-lek-**trish**-uhn/ *noun* someone whose job is to put in electrical wires and repair electrical equipment

**e·lec·tric·i·ty** /i-lek-**triss**-uht-ee/ *noun* a type of energy that is used to make lights, televisions, computers, etc. work. Electricity can be carried by wires: *Turn off lights to save electricity.*

> **Word Origin:** electricity
>
> **Electricity** comes from Latin and Greek words that mean "amber." Amber is a stone that comes from a sticky fluid from trees. When you rub amber, it makes a kind of electricity – the same kind of electricity that makes a balloon stick to the wall after you have rubbed it. A scientist called William Gilbert experimented with amber and electricity in 1600. In his writing, he used the Latin word for amber, ***electrum***, to describe electricity, and the English word came from there.

**e·lec·tro·cute** /i-**lek**-truh-kyoot/ *verb* to kill someone with electricity: *Do not put anything metal into the wall socket because the electricity will go through the metal, and it could electrocute you.*

**e·lec·tro·mag·net** /i-lek-troh-**mag**-nit/ *noun* an object that becomes a magnet when electricity passes through it. A magnet is something that attracts metal objects: *When the electricity is on, the electromagnet will attract the paper clips.*
—**electromagnetic** /i-lekt-troh-mag-**net**-ik/ *adjective* relating to electromagnets: *We learned about electromagnetic forces in science class.*

**e·lec·tron** /i-**lek**-trahn/ *noun* a very small thing that moves around the middle part of an atom, the nucleus. Electrons have a negative electrical charge. ▶ see picture at **atom**

**e·lec·tron·ic** /i-lek-**trahn**-ik/ *adjective* electronic equipment has very small parts that control the electric current that the equipment uses to do complicated things. Computers, televisions, and cell phones are electronic: *Most people have a lot of electronic equipment in their homes today.*
—**electronically** /i-lek-**trahn**-ik-lee/ *adverb* in a way that involves electronic equipment: *You can send the document electronically, by attaching it to an email.*

**e·lec·tron·ics** /i-lek-**trahn**-ikss/ *noun* electronic equipment such as computers, televisions, and cell phones: *He works for a Japanese electronics company.*

**el·e·gant** /**el**-uhg-uhnt/ *adjective* very beautiful and graceful: *She wore an elegant dress to the wedding.*
—**elegance** /**el**-ugh-uhnss/ *noun* an elegant quality: *We admired the elegance of the dancers' movements.*

**el·e·ment** /**el**-uh-muhnt/ *noun*
**1** a chemical substance that is not made of other substances mixed together. Gold, iron, and oxygen are elements: *Oil is made of two elements – carbon and hydrogen.*
**2** one part of something: *The family is the most important element in a child's life.* | *When you are crossing the road, there is always an element of danger and you need to be careful.*

**el·e·men·ta·ry** /el-uh-**men**-tree/ *adjective* basic and simple: *The youngest students are learning elementary mathematics, such as counting, adding, and subtracting.*

**el·e·men·ta·ry school** /el-uh-**men**-tree skool/ *noun* a school that children go to for the first five to seven years of their education: *He is in*
second grade at the local elementary school.
SYNONYM: **grade school**

**el·e·phant** /**el**-uhf-uhnt/ *noun* a very large gray animal with big ears, a trunk (=long nose), and two tusks (=long teeth)

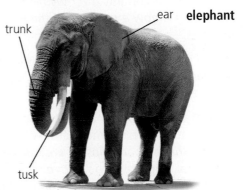

trunk · ear **elephant** · tusk

**el·e·va·tion** /el-uh-**vaysh**-uhn/ *noun* the height of a place above the level of the sea: *The city is at an elevation of 12,000 feet.*

**el·e·va·tor** /**el**-uh-vayt-ur/ *noun* a machine like a small room that takes people up and down in a building: *I took the elevator to the 12th floor.*

**e·lev·en** /i-**lev**-uhn/ *number*
**1** 11: *There are eleven players on a soccer team.*
**2** eleven o'clock: *I'll be back by eleven.*
**3** eleven years old: *My sister was eleven when I was born.*

**e·lev·enth** /i-**lev**-uhnth/ *number*
**1** 11th
**2** 1/11

**elf** /elf/ *noun* (plural **elves** /elvz/) a small imaginary person with pointed ears: *Santa's elves help him by making toys.*

**el·i·gi·ble** /**el**-uhj-uhb-uhl/ *adjective* officially allowed to do or have something, for example because you are old enough: *People are eligible to vote at the age of 18.*
—**eligibility** /el-uhj-uh-**bil**-uht-ee/ *noun* the right to do or have something: *Age will affect your eligibility to join the team, as we only take children above ten years old.*

**e·lim·i·nate** /i-**lim**-uh-nayt/ *verb*
**1** if you are eliminated in a competition, you can no longer take part in it because you have lost: *We were disappointed when our team was eliminated after the first game.*
**2** to get rid of something completely: *The school hopes to eliminate bullying.*

**e·lite** /ay-**leet**/
- *adjective* elite people are the very best: *Only elite runners can finish the race in under three hours.*
- *noun* a small group of people who are very powerful or important: *After winning an Oscar, the actress is now a member of the Hollywood elite.*

**elk** /elk/ *noun* a type of large deer. Male elks have large horns called antlers, that look like tree branches.

**el·lipse** /i-**lipss**/ *noun* a shape that is like a circle, but that is longer than it is wide: *The lake is in the shape of an ellipse.* ( SYNONYM: **oval** )
—**elliptical** /i-**lipt**-ik-uhl/ *adjective* shaped like an ellipse: *The planet Mercury has an elliptical orbit – it does not go around the sun in a circle.*

**elm** /elm/ *noun* a type of large tall tree

**elm**

**El Ni·ño** /el **neen**-yoh/ *noun* a rise in the temperature of the water in the Pacific Ocean near South America. El Niño has a large effect on the weather in many parts of the world. It causes storms in some places and very dry weather in other places: *El Niño can cause heavy rain in parts of North and South America.*

**else** /elss/ *adverb* another thing or person: *Here's your coat. Do you need anything else? | She told him she was in love with someone else.*

> IDIOM with **else**
> **or else** or: *Hurry up, or else you'll be late for school!*

**else·where** /**elss**-wair/ *adverb* in or to another place: *They didn't sell pens in the store, so we had to go elsewhere.*

**elves** /elvz/ *noun* the plural of **elf**

**e·mail** /**ee** mayl/
- *noun*
**1** a message you send from your computer to another computer: *I got an email from David yesterday.*
**2** a system for sending messages by computer: *We keep in touch by email. | What's your email address?*
- *verb*
to send someone an email: *I emailed Elizabeth to tell her the news.*

**e·man·ci·pate** /i-**manss**-uh-payt/ *verb* to make a group of people free: *Lincoln emancipated the slaves after the Civil War.*
—**emancipation** /i-manss-uh-**paysh**-uhn/ *noun* the act of emancipating people: *Women wanted emancipation and the right to vote.*

**em·bar·rass** /im-**barr**-uhss/ *verb* to make someone feel unhappy and worried that other people will have a bad opinion about him or her: *Her parents embarrassed her by arguing loudly in public.*
—**embarrassing** /im-**barr**-uhss-ing/ *adjective* making you feel embarrassed: *It was so embarrassing when I spilled orange juice all over my pants!*
—**embarrassment** /im-**barr**-uhss-muhnt/ *noun* the feeling of being embarrassed: *He turned red in the face with embarrassment when his mother kissed him in front of his friends.*

**em·bar·rassed** /im-**barr**-uhst/ *adjective* feeling unhappy and worried that people will have a bad opinion of you: *I was embarrassed because I had made a stupid mistake.* ▶ see **Thesaurus**

**em·bas·sy** /**em**-buhss-ee/ *noun* (plural **embassies**) the building where the ambassador and a group of officials from a foreign country work. People who work in an embassy help people from their own country and people who want to go to their country: *Because I'm from Mexico, I had to go to the Mexican embassy to get a new passport.*

**em·blem** /**em**-bluhm/ *noun* a picture or shape that represents something: *The team is called the Angels, and their emblem is a halo on a letter A.*

**em·brace** /im-**brayss**/
- *verb* to put your arms around someone and hold him or her in a caring way: *They embraced each other and said goodbye.* ( SYNONYM: **hug** )
- *noun* the action of embracing someone: *She gave her son a comforting embrace.*

**em·broi·der·y** /im-**broyd**-uhr-ee/ *noun*
**1** patterns or pictures that you sew on cloth as a decoration: *Her dress was white with silver embroidery.*
**2** the skill of sewing patterns on cloth as a decoration: *My grandmother taught me embroidery and I sewed a bookmark as a present.*

**em·bry·o** /**em**-bree-oh/ *noun* an animal or human that has just begun to develop inside its mother or inside an egg: *A human embryo develops into a fetus about 8 weeks after the egg is fertilized.*

**em·er·ald** /**em**-uhr-uhld/ *noun* a bright green jewel: *an emerald ring*

emerald

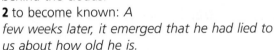

**e·merge** /i-**murj**/ *verb*
**1** to appear or come out after being hidden: *The sun emerged from behind the clouds.*
**2** to become known: *A few weeks later, it emerged that he had lied to us about how old he is.*

**e·mer·gen·cy** /i-**murj**-uhnss-ee/
● *noun* (plural **emergencies**) a very serious and dangerous situation that you must deal with immediately: *In an emergency such as a fire or traffic accident, call 911.*
● *adjective* relating to or used for emergencies: *If there is a fire, use the emergency exit to get out of the movie theater.*

**e·mer·gen·cy room** /i-**murj**-uhnss-ee room/ *noun* the part of a hospital that treats people who have been hurt or who have suddenly become very sick: *They took him to the emergency room after he was hit by a car.*

**em·er·y board** /**em**-uhr-ee bord/ *noun* a small rough object that you rub against your nails to shape them

**em·i·grate** /**em**-uh-grayt/ *verb* to leave your own country in order to live in another country: *He emigrated from Japan to the United States at the age of 25.*
—**emigration** /em-uh-**graysh**-uhn/ *noun* the act of emigrating

—**emigrant** /**em**-uhg-ruhnt/ *noun* someone who emigrates to another country: *Many emigrants left Europe for the United States in the late 1800s.*

**Word Choice: emigrant, immigrant**

An **emigrant** is someone who leaves his or her own country and goes to live in another country.

An **immigrant** is someone who comes into another country to live there.

For example, if you are Korean and you leave Korea to come to the United States, you are an **emigrant** from Korea and an **immigrant** to the United States.

**e·mis·sions** /i-**mish**-uhnz/ *plural noun* smoke, gases, and chemicals that are sent into the air by cars, planes, factories, etc.: *Emissions from cars pollute the air and cause a lot of damage to the environment.*

**e·mo·tion** /i-**mohsh**-uhn/ *noun* a strong feeling such as love, hate, or sadness: *His voice sounded full of emotion and he was obviously very unhappy about something.*

**Word Origin: emotion**

**Emotion** comes from an old French word meaning "to make someone have strong feelings." The French word comes from a Latin word that means "to move." Emotion may have meant a physical movement when it was first used in English, but it was used to mean "strong feelings" by the 1600s.

**e·mo·tion·al** /i-**mohsh**-uhn-uhl/ *adjective*
**1** showing strong feelings to other people, especially by crying: *He misses his dad a lot, and he always gets very emotional when he talks about him.*
**2** relating to your feelings: *If you listen to someone who is upset, you are helping to meet their emotional needs.*
—**emotionally** /i-**mohsh**-uhn-uhl-ee/ *adverb* in a way that relates to your feelings: *Children suffer emotionally when their parents fight.*

**em·pa·thize** /emp-uh-thīz/ *verb* to understand someone else's feelings and problems because you have been in the same situation yourself: *I empathize with her because I also used to have a problem with my weight.*

—**empathy** /**emp**-uhth-ee/ *noun* the ability to empathize: *Parents should remember what it was like to be little, and have empathy for their kids.*

**em·per·or** /**emp**-uhr-ur/ *noun* the ruler of an empire: *Augustus was a Roman emperor.*

**emperor**

a Roman emperor

**em·pha·sis** /**emf**-uhss-iss/ *noun*
**1** special importance and attention that is given to something: *On our soccer team, we work hard, but the emphasis is on having fun and playing as a team.*
**2** if there is emphasis on a word or part of a word, it is said louder or with more force: *In "hotel," the emphasis is on the second syllable.*
(SYNONYM: **stress**)

**Word Family:** emphasis
**emphasis** *noun* | **emphasize** *verb*

**em·pha·size** /**emf**-uh-sīz/ *verb* to say or show that something is important: *He emphasized that we must be back by five o'clock.*

**em·pire** /**emp**-ī-ur/ *noun* a group of countries that are controlled by the same ruler or government: *The Roman Empire included most of Europe and North Africa.*

**em·ploy** /im-**ploy**/ *verb*
**1** to pay someone to work for you: *The company employs over 5,000 people.*
**2** to use something: *Teachers employ different ways of teaching reading, such as phonics and looking at a whole word.*

**Word Family:** employ
**employ** *verb* | **employee** *noun* | **employer** *noun* | **employment** *noun*

**em·ploy·ee** /im-**ploy**-ee/ *noun* someone who is paid to work for a person, company, or organization: *The company has more than 200 employees.*

**em·ploy·er** /im-**ploy**-ur/ *noun* a person, company, or organization that pays someone for his or her work: *She has worked for the same employer for 30 years.*

**em·ploy·ment** /im-**ploy**-muhnt/ *noun* work that you do to earn money: *Many people who want to work can't find employment.*

**em·press** /**emp**-riss/ *noun* the female ruler of an empire, or the wife of an emperor: *The Empress Josephine was the wife of the French Emperor Napoleon.*

**emp·ty** /**emp**-tee/
● *adjective* (**emptier, emptiest**)
**1** something that is empty has nothing or no one inside it: *There is no soda left – the bottle is empty.* | *The theater is almost empty and most of the people have already gone home.*
(SYNONYM: **full**)
▶ see Thesaurus
**2** if your life is empty, nothing interesting happens and you feel unhappy: *When my sister isn't here, I always miss her and my life seems empty.*
● *verb* (**empties, emptying, emptied**)
**1** to take out everything that is in something: *I emptied my backpack and put all my stuff on the table.*
**2** if a place empties, the people inside it leave: *When the game was over, the stadium began to empty.*

**empty**

empty

full

**en·a·ble** /in-**ayb**-uhl/ *verb* to make it possible for someone or something to do something: *His bike enables him to go places without his mom having to drive him.*

**en·act** /in-**akt**/ *verb* to make a new law: *Laws are enacted by Congress.*

**e·nam·el** /i-**nam**-uhl/ *noun* the hard white material on the outside of your teeth: *Eating sugar damages the enamel on your teeth.*

**-ence** /uhnss/

### Word Building

**-ence** is a suffix. It is used in nouns.
**1** differ**ence** | intellig**ence** | pati**ence**
**-ence** means that something has a particular quality. If two things are not the same, they have the quality of *difference*. If someone is smart, that person has the quality of *intelligence*. If you can wait for things without becoming annoyed, you have the quality of *patience*.
**2** confer**ence** | experi**ence** | refer**ence**
**-ence** is a noun form that shows an action. It often changes a verb into a noun. A *conference* is a meeting where people talk to each other. Confer is a formal verb meaning to talk. A good or bad *experience* is something that has happened to you. A *reference* book is a book you use to look up information – you refer to it.

**en·chant** /in-**chant**/ *verb* to change something by magic: *The witch enchanted the prince, so that he became a frog.*
—**enchanted** /in-**chant**-id/ *adjective* changed by magic: *The Queen looked into the enchanted mirror to find Snow White.*

—**enchantment** /in-**chant**-muhnt/ *noun* magic that is used to change something: *The witch turned the giant to stone by an enchantment.*

**en·close** /in-**klohz**/ *verb*
**1** to put something inside an envelope with a letter: *I enclosed my school picture in my letter to Grandma.*
**2** if a wall or fence encloses something, the wall or fence goes all the way around it: *The yard was enclosed by a high wall.*

**en·coun·ter** /in-**kownt**-ur/
● *noun*
**1** a time when you meet a person or animal: *He had an encounter with a bear while he was hiking.*
**2** a time when you experience something, especially something bad: *My first encounter with bullying was in the park.*
● *verb*
**1** if you encounter problems, they happen and you have to do something about them: *Did you encounter any difficulties when you explained the math to your partner?*
**2** to meet, see, or hear something: *The children talked about the bugs they had encountered on their walk through the woods.*

**en·cour·age** /in-**kur**-ij/ *verb*
**1** to make someone feel more hopeful and confident: *The fans cheered to encourage the team.* (ANTONYM: **discourage**)
**2** to try to persuade someone to do something: *His parents encouraged him to go to college.* (ANTONYM: **discourage**)
—**encouraging** /in-**kur**-ij-ing/ *adjective* making you feel more hopeful and confident: *The coach's encouraging words made me feel I could play better.*
—**encouragement** /in-**kur**-ij-muhnt/ *noun* the act of encouraging someone: *Her piano teacher gave her lots of encouragement when she was learning the piece.*

**en·cy·clo·pe·di·a** /in-sīk-luh-**peed**-ee-uh/ *noun* a large book or a set of books that has a lot of facts about many subjects. The subjects are usually in alphabetical order, so that subjects starting with A are at the beginning: *If you don't know who George Washington is, look in an encyclopedia.*

**ex·haust·ed** /ig-**zost**-id/ *adjective* very tired: *I've been playing basketball for hours and I'm exhausted.*

**ex·haus·tion** /ig-**zoss**-chuhn/ *noun* the state of being very tired and weak: *Two runners were taken to the hospital suffering from exhaustion.*

**ex·hib·it** /ig-**zib**-it/
● *verb* to show something such as art in a place where everyone can see it: *Some of the student's artwork will be exhibited in the display cases in the hallway.*
—**exhibitor** /ig-**zib**-it-ur/ *noun* someone who is exhibiting something they have created
● *noun* (also **ex·hi·bi·tion** /ekss-uh-**bish**-uhn/) a public show of something such as art: *We went to see an exhibit of paintings by Picasso.*

> **Word Family:** exhibit
>
> **exhibit** *verb* | **exhibit** *noun* | **exhibition** *noun* | **exhibitor** *noun*

**ex·ist** /ig-**zist**/ *verb* if something exists, it is present in the world: *Dinosaurs existed millions of years ago.*

**ex·ist·ence** /ig-**zist**-uhnss/ *noun* the state of existing: *He believes in the existence of God.*

**ex·ist·ing** /ig-**zist**-ing/ *adjective* an existing thing is one that exists now or that you have now: *Two new classrooms will be added to the existing school building.*

**ex·it** /**egz**-it/
● *noun*
**1** a door that you go through to get out of a place: *There are two exits at the back of the plane.* (ANTONYM: **entrance**)
**2** a place where vehicles can leave a large road: *Leave the highway at the next exit.*
● *verb*
**1** to go out of a place: *Lucy exited through the back door.*
**2** to close a computer program or document: *Save your document before you exit.*

**ex·pand** /ik-**spand**/ *verb* to become larger: *The school has expanded from 1,000 students to over 3,000 students.* | *The metal expands as it gets hotter.* (ANTONYM: **contract**)
—**expansion** /ik-**spansh**-uhn/ *noun* the process of becoming larger

**ex·pect** /ik-**spekt**/ *verb*
**1** to think that something will happen: *Everyone expects the other team will win because they have a lot of good players.*
**2** to think that someone should do something: *My parents expect me to study hard.*
**3** to be waiting for someone or something to arrive: *Are you expecting visitors?*
**4** if a woman is expecting a baby, a baby is growing inside her: *My sister is expecting her first baby and it will be born in April.*
—**expectation** /ekss-pek-**taysh**-uhn/ *noun* a belief or strong hope that something will happen: *Dad has high expectations for me: he thinks I'm going to be a doctor some day.*

**ex·pe·di·tion** /ekss-puh-**dish**-uhn/ *noun* a long and carefully organized trip, often to a dangerous or unknown place: *Columbus led an expedition to find a new route from Europe to Asia, but he landed in America instead.*

**ex·pel** /ik-**spel**/ *verb* (**expelling, expelled**) to make someone leave a school, organization, or country, especially because of bad behavior: *He was expelled from school for never obeying the teacher.*

**ex·pense** /ik-**spenss**/ *noun* a lot of money that you have to spend on something: *When you get married, there's all the expense of the wedding and the wedding reception.*

**ex·pen·sive** /ik-**spenss**-iv/ *adjective* costing a lot of money: *I want a big expensive car like a Ferrari.* | *The jewelry is very expensive and most people can't afford it.*
(ANTONYMS: **cheap, inexpensive**)
▶ see Thesaurus
—**expensively** /ik-**spenss**-iv-lee/ *adverb* in a way that costs a lot of money: *The apartment was expensively furnished with gold mirrors and white leather chairs.*

> **Word Family:** expensive
>
> **expensive** *adjective* | **inexpensive** *adjective* | **expensively** *adverb* | **expense** *noun*

**ex·pe·ri·ence** /ik-**speer**-ee-uhnss/
● *noun*
**1** something that happens to you: *Seeing whales*

*in the ocean was an amazing experience.*
▶ see **Thesaurus**
**2** knowledge or skill that you get from doing a job or activity: *She has over 20 years of experience as a teacher and she's very good at her job.*
● *verb*
if you experience something, it happens to you: *He has experienced a few health problems.*

**ex·pe·ri·enced** /ik-**speer**-ee-uhnst/*adjective*
good at doing something because you have done it for a long time: *We felt safe flying with such an experienced pilot.*

( ANTONYM: **inexperienced** )

**ex·per·i·ment**
● *noun* /ik-**sperr**-uh-muhnt/ a scientific test you do to learn about something, or to show if an idea is true: *We did an experiment in class to see which materials float on water.*
● *verb* /ik-**sperr**-uh-ment/ to try several different things: *Janie likes to experiment with her hair and try lots of different hairstyles.*

experiment

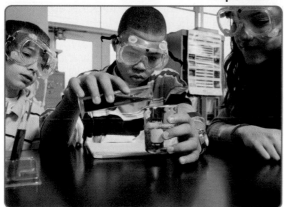

**ex·pert** /**ekss**-purt/
● *noun* someone who knows a lot about a subject: *Professor Jones is an expert on dinosaurs and she has written many books about them.*
● *adjective* done or given by someone who knows a lot about a subject: *My brother knows a lot about computers and he can give you expert advice about choosing the right one.*

**ex·per·tise** /ekss-pur-**teez**/ *noun* special skills or knowledge: *Dr. Zhang has great expertise in treating people with this type of illness.*

**ex·pire** /ik-**spī**-ur/ *verb* if a document expires, the period when you can use it has ended: *Her*

*visa expired in May, so she had to go back to her home country.*
—**expiration** /ekss-puh-**raysh**-uhn/ *noun* the end of the period when you can use a document: *The expiration date on my swim club membership card is November 30, 2011.*

**ex·plain** /ik-**splayn**/ *verb*
**1** to tell someone about something so that he or she can understand it: *She explained to us how to use the new computer system.* | *Jason explained why he was leaving the college.*
▶ see **Thesaurus**
**2** to be the reason for something: *The bus was late – that explains why he missed his first class.*

**Word Family:** explain

**explain** verb | **explanation** noun | **explanatory** adjective

**ex·pla·na·tion** /ekss-pluh-**naysh**-uhn/ *noun*
**1** a reason why something happened: *There is no explanation for his strange actions.*
**2** something you say or write to help someone understand something: *The teacher gave a quick explanation of what we had to do.*

**ex·plan·at·o·ry** /ik-**splan**-uht-uhr-ee/ *adjective* explaining about something: *an explanatory booklet*

**ex·plode** /ik-**splohd**/ *verb* to burst into small pieces with a loud noise and a lot of force: *A bomb exploded outside the hotel, injuring five people.* ▶ see **Thesaurus**

**Word Family:** explode

**explode** verb | **explosion** noun | **explosive** adjective | **explosive** noun

**ex·ploit** /ik-**sployt**/ *verb* to treat someone in an unfair way, in order to get advantages for yourself: *The company exploited its workers and paid them very badly.*
—**exploitation** /ekss-ploy-**taysh**-uhn/ *noun* unfair treatment of someone, in order to get advantages for your yourself: *The factory owners were accused of exploitation because they employed children as young as eight years old.*

**a b c d e f g h i j k l m n o p q r s t u v w x y z**

**ex·plore** /ik-**splor**/ *verb* to travel around a place so you can see what it is like: *We explored the narrow streets of the old town and looked at the houses.*
—**exploration** /ekss-pluh-**raysh**-uhn/ *noun* the activity of going to an unknown place, in order to find out more about it: *Hernando de Soto is famous for his exploration of the area that is now the southeastern United States.*
—**explorer** /ik-**splor**-ur/ *noun* someone who travels to unknown places to find out more about them: *I want to be a space explorer and go to the moon.*

**ex·plo·sion** /ik-**splohzh**-uhn/ *noun* if there is an explosion, something bursts into pieces with a loud noise and a lot of force: *The truck hit a gas station, causing a huge explosion.*

**ex·plo·sive** /ik-**splohss**-iv/
● *adjective*
**1** able or likely to explode: *Natural gas is highly explosive and it must be handled very carefully.*
**2** likely to become violent very quickly: *The situation in the country is very explosive, and there is a danger that fighting could start at any minute.*
● *noun*
a substance that can cause an explosion: *Dynamite is a type of explosive.*

**ex·po·nent** /ik-**spohn**-uhnt/ *noun* a number that shows how many times you should multiply a number by itself: *In 6², 2 is the exponent.*

**ex·port**
● *verb* /ik-**sport**/
to sell things to another country: *Saudi Arabia exports a lot of oil to the United States.*
( ANTONYM: **import** )
—**exporter** /ik-**sport**-ur/ *noun* a person, company, or country that exports things: *The U.S. is a major exporter of wheat.*
● *noun* /**ekss**-port/
**1** something that a country sells to another country: *Chile's main exports to the U.S. are fruit and vegetables.* ( ANTONYM: **import** )
**2** the business of selling and sending things to another country: *The export of wild animals is illegal.* ( ANTONYM: **import** )

**Word Family: export**
**export** *verb* | **export** *noun* | **exporter** *noun*

**ex·pose** /ik-**spohz**/ *verb*
**1** to show something that was covered or hidden: *He took off his shirt and exposed his chest.*
**2** to put someone in a situation where he or she may be affected by something harmful: *Parents should not expose their children to cigarette smoke because it is bad for the children's lungs.*

**ex·po·sure** /ik-**spohzh**-ur/ *noun*
**1** the state of being in a situation where you may be affected by something harmful: *The disease is caused by exposure to dangerous chemicals.*
**2** the harmful effect of very cold weather on someone's body: *The climbers were suffering from exposure because they had been outside in freezing temperatures.*

**ex·press** /ik-**spress**/
● *verb*
to tell other people about your feelings and opinions: *The protesters have a right to express their opinions.* | *The kids can express themselves by painting pictures and doing art.*
● *adjective*
**1** an express train or bus is quick because it does not stop very often: *Dad took the express train to Baltimore.*
**2** express mail arrives more quickly than normal: *Ethan sent the letter by express mail.*

**ex·pres·sion** /ik-**spresh**-uhn/ *noun*
**1** the look on someone's face: *He had a sad expression on his face as we said goodbye.*
**2** a group of words that has a special meaning: *The expression "all by myself" means "completely alone."* | *My grandfather sometimes uses old-fashioned expressions which I don't understand.*
**3** something you do which shows what you feel: *He gave her a ring as an expression of his love.*
**4** in math, a group of symbols and numbers that represents an amount or idea: *2y + 3 is a mathematical expression.*

**ex·press·way** /ik-**spress**-way/ *noun* a wide road that cars travel quickly on: *The truck was traveling north on the expressway through the city.*

**ex·pul·sion** /ik-**spuhlsh**-uhn/ *noun* the act of ordering someone to leave a school, an organization, or a country permanently:

*Expulsion from school is a very severe punishment.*

**ex·quis·ite** /ik-**skwiz**-it/ *adjective* very beautiful and delicate: *She paints exquisite pictures of flowers.*
—**exquisitely** /ik-**skwiz**-it-lee/ *adverb* in a very beautiful and delicate way: *The jewelry was exquisitely made from tiny pieces of gold.*

**ex·tend** /ik-**stend**/ *verb*
**1** to make something longer or bigger: *We decided to extend our visit to Mexico for another week.*
**2** to continue for a particular distance: *The line of people extended down the street because the pizza restaurant was offering free pizzas.*

**ex·tend·ed fam·ily** /ik-stend-id **fam**-lee/ *noun* your parents, grandparents, aunts, uncles, cousins, etc.: *She lives in a big house with her sisters, her parents, and her extended family.*

**ex·ten·sion** /ik-**stensh**-uhn/ *noun*
**1** more time that you are given to finish doing something: *If students are sick, they can ask for an extension to finish their work.*
**2** one of many telephones in a building: *Call the office and ask for extension 358.*
**3** the process of making something longer or bigger: *The extension of the railroad across the West took many years.*

**ex·ten·sive** /ik-**stenss**-iv/ *adjective*
**1** including a lot of things: *The restaurant has an extensive choice of different types of ice cream.*
**2** affecting a large area of something: *The accident caused extensive damage to both trucks.*
—**extensively** /ik-**stenss**-iv-lee/ *adverb* a lot: *He wrote extensively about the history of the United States.*

**ex·tent** /ik-**stent**/ *noun* how big or important something is: *This photo shows the extent of the damage caused by the storm.*

> **IDIOM with extent**
> **to some extent** partly: *I agree with him to some extent, but not completely.*

**exter-** /ekss-tur/, **extra** /ekss-truh/

**Word Building**

**exter**ior | **extr**act | **extra**ordinary
These words all have the Latin word root **exter** or **extra** in them. **Exter** means "outside of" or "beyond." The *exterior* of a building is the outside of it. If you *extract* oil from the ground, you take the oil out of the ground.

**ex·te·ri·or** /ik-**steer**-ee-ur/
● *noun* the outside of something: *The exterior of the house was made of wood.*
(ANTONYM: **interior**)
● *adjective* on the outside of something: *We painted the exterior walls white.*
(ANTONYM: **interior**)

**ex·ter·min·ate** /ik-**stuhr**-min-ayt/ *verb* to kill all of a group of animals or people

**ex·ter·nal** /ik-**sturn**'l/ *adjective* outside something: *Clams have a hard external shell that protects their bodies.* (ANTONYM: **internal**)

**ex·tinct** /ik-**stingkt**/ *adjective*
**1** an extinct type of animal or plant does not exist now: *Why did the dinosaurs become extinct?*
**2** an extinct volcano has stopped erupting
—**extinction** /ik-**stingk**-shuhn/ *noun* the situation in which a type of animal or plant stops existing completely: *The tiger is near to extinction, and could disappear completely if we don't protect it.*

**ex·tin·guish** /ik-**sting**-gwish/ *verb* to make a fire stop burning: *Firefighters extinguished the forest fire.* (SYNONYM: **put out**)

**ex·tin·guish·er** /ik-**sting**-gwish-ur/ *noun* a piece of equipment used for stopping small fires: *There was an extinguisher in the kitchen.*

**ex·tra** /**ekss**-truh/
● *adjective, adverb* more than the usual amount or price: *I ordered a cheeseburger with extra fries.* | *If you want a bigger room, you have to pay extra.*
● *noun* something that you can get in addition to the usual product or service: *The airline offers extras such as free food and drink.*

**ex·tract** /ik-**strakt**/ *verb* to take something out: *The dentist had to extract one of her teeth.*

**ex·traor·di·nar·y** /ik-**strord**'n-air-ee/ *adjective* very unusual or surprising: *He showed extraordinary bravery in rescuing the child from the burning house.*

**ex·tra·ter·res·tri·al** /ekss-truh-tuh-**ress**-tree-uhl/
● *adjective* from space or another planet: *Inside the spaceship were extraterrestrial beings from another galaxy.*
● *noun* a creature that may exist on another planet

**ex·trav·a·gant** /ik-**strav**-uhg-uhnt/ *adjective* spending too much money, or using too many things in a way that seems wasteful: *It seems very extravagant to order four pizzas for two people.*

**ex·treme** /ik-**streem**/ *adjective*
**1** very great: *Martha was in extreme pain.*
**2** very unusual and bad: *In extreme cases, an allergy can make you very sick.*
**3** extreme opinions are very unusual and not sensible: *She has very extreme views on religion.*
**4** extreme sports are dangerous and exciting: *She loves extreme sports like snowboarding and white water rafting.*

**ex·treme·ly** /ik-**streem**-lee/ *adverb* very: *Todd was extremely happy with his new bike.* | *It's extremely important to lock the door every time you go out of the house.*

**eye** /i/ *noun*
**1** one of the two things in your head that you see with: *Her eyes were big and blue.*
**2** the eye of a needle is the hole that you put the thread through
**3** the eye of a hurricane is the calm area at the center of a big storm

**IDIOMS with eye**
**catch someone's eye** to get someone's attention: *There was a beautiful red dress which caught my eye when I was in the store.*
**keep an eye on** to watch someone or something and make sure that he, she, or it is safe: *Our neighbor is keeping an eye on our house while we are on vacation.*

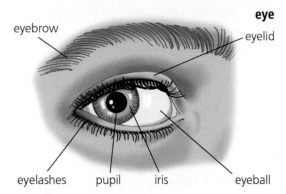

eye
eyebrow
eyelid
eyelashes    pupil    iris    eyeball

**eye·ball** /i-bol/ *noun* all of the eye, including the part inside your head

**eye·brow** /i-brow/ *noun* the line of short hairs on your forehead above your eye: *He had thick black eyebrows.*

**eye·lash** /i-lash/ *noun* one of the hairs that grow on the edge of your eyes: *She has beautiful long dark eyelashes.*

**eye·lid** /i-lid/ *noun* the piece of skin that covers your eye when it is closed: *Her eyelids gradually closed and she went to sleep.*

**eye·shad·ow** /i-shad-oh/ *noun* color that women put on their eyelids to make them look pretty: *Mom wears blue eyeshadow.*

**eye·sight** /i-sīt/ *noun* the ability to see: *My dad's eyesight is bad so he wears glasses.*

**eye·wit·ness** /i-**wit**-niss/ *noun* someone who sees a crime or an accident happen: *Eyewitnesses said the car was going very fast before it hit the tree.*

# Ff

**F** /ef/ *noun*

**1** a grade that you get when you fail a test or a class: *I got an F in English and I had to take the class again.*

**2** the written abbreviation of **Fahrenheit**, a scale used for measuring temperature: *The temperature outside dropped to 32°F.*

**fa·ble** /**fayb**-uhl/ *noun* a story that teaches us something. A fable often has animals in it: *He read the fable of the hare and the tortoise, in which the tortoise wins the race.*

**fab·ric** /**fab**-rik/ *noun* cloth: *The drapes were made of a heavy velvet fabric.*

SYNONYM: **material**

**fab·u·lous** /**fab**-yuhl-uhss/ *adjective* very good: *My mom is a fabulous cook.*

**face** /fayss/

● *noun*

**1** the front of your head. Your face has your eyes, nose, and mouth on it: *Edward has a very handsome face.*

**2** the expression on someone's face: *There were lots of happy faces when the team won the game.*

**3** the part of a clock or watch that you look at to see the time: *She looked at the clock face. It was five o'clock.* ▶ see pictures at **clock, watch**

**4** the side of a mountain, cliff, or tall building: *They climbed the north face of the mountain.*

**5** in math, one side of a 3-D shape such as a cube: *Each face of the cube has a different number of dots.*

● *verb*

**1** to look toward someone or something: *Mom turned to face me.* | *Their apartment faces the ocean.*

**2** to do something that you do not want to do because it seems difficult: *She couldn't face telling her mom what really happened.*

**3** to accept that something bad is true: *I just have to face the fact that I'm no good at sports.*

**fa·cil·i·tate** /fuh-**sil**-uh-tayt/ *verb* to make something happen more easily: *A quiet dark room facilitates sleep.*

**fa·cil·i·ty** /fuh-**sil**-uht-ee/ *noun* (plural **facilities**) a building or piece of equipment you can use for doing something: *Our school has great sports facilities.*

**fact** /fakt/ *noun* a piece of information that is true: *In class, we learned some interesting facts about China.*

—**factual** /**fak**-choo-uhl/ *adjective* containing facts: *The book is full of factual information about American history.*

⌜ **IDIOM with fact**
⌐ **in fact** used when adding more information to what you have just said: *Yes, I know Ryan. In fact, he's one of my best friends.*

**fact fam·ily** /**fakt** fam-lee/ *noun* a set of numbers that are related to each other by adding, subtracting, multiplying, or dividing: *7, 5, and 12 are a fact family because 5 + 7 = 12, 7 + 5 = 12, 12 − 5 = 7, 12 − 7 = 5.*

**fac·tor** /**fakt**-ur/ *noun*

**1** something that affects a situation: *Training was an important factor in the team's success.*

**2** a number that you can divide into another number exactly: *3 and 5 are factors of 15 because 15 ÷ 3 = 5.*

**fac·to·ry** /**fakt**-uhr-ee/ *noun* (plural **factories**) a building where things like clothes, cars, or chemicals are made, using machines: *The toys are produced in a factory in China.*

**factory**

a car factory

**fac·ul·ty** /**fak**-uhlt-ee/ *noun* (plural **faculties**) the teachers in a school, college, or university: *He joined the English faculty at Harvard.*

a b c d e f g h i j k l m n o p q r s t u v w x y z

**fad** /fad/ *noun* something that is popular for a short time: *These scooters are just a fad – next year no one will be using them.*

**fade** /fayd/ *verb*
**1** to become less bright in color
**2** to gradually disappear

**Fahr·en·heit** /farr-uhn-hīt/ *noun* a scale used to measure temperature. Water freezes at 32° Fahrenheit and boils at 212°. The short form of Fahrenheit is F: *In summer, the temperature reached 90 degrees Fahrenheit (90°F).*

**fail** /fayl/ *verb*
**1** to not succeed: *He tried to become an actor but failed.* ( ANTONYM: **succeed** )
**2** to not do something: *She failed to notice the step, and tripped.*
**3** to not pass a test: *I was upset because I failed my math test.* ( ANTONYM: **pass** )
**4** to not work correctly: *The car's brakes failed and it hit a tree.*

**Word Family:** fail

**fail** verb | **failure** noun

**fail·ure** /fayl-yur/ *noun*
**1** someone or something that is not successful: *The party was a complete failure – only three people came.* ( ANTONYM: **success** )
**2** a situation in which something stops working: *Engine failure caused the helicopter to crash.*
**3** a situation in which someone does not do something that he or she should do: *Mike's teacher called his parents about his failure to do his homework.*

**faint** /faynt/
● *adjective*
**1** difficult to see, hear, or smell: *There was a faint smell of coffee coming from the kitchen.*
**2** slight: *There is still a faint hope that someone will return the stolen bike.*
**3** feeling weak and unsteady: *He felt faint with hunger and tiredness.*
● *verb*
to fall to the ground because you become unconscious: *She fainted because she hadn't eaten anything all day.*

**fair** /fair/
● *adjective*
**1** dealing with people in an equal way: *Why do I*

have to go to bed before Dan? It's not fair!
( ANTONYM: **unfair** ) ▶ see **Thesaurus**
**2** fair hair or skin is light in color: *She has fair hair and blue eyes.* ( ANTONYM: **dark** )
**3** reasonable and right: *They got a good meal at a fair price.*
**4** quite good but not very good: *His test scores in science were fair but not great.*
( SYNONYM: **average** )
**5** fair weather is sunny: *Expect fair to cloudy weather tomorrow.*
—**fairness** /fair-niss/ *noun* the quality of being fair: *The students respected their teacher for her fairness.*
● *noun*
**1** an outdoor event where you can ride on exciting machines, and play games to win prizes: *He bought some cotton candy at the state fair.*
**2** an event at which people show or sell things: *She won a prize for her exhibit at the school science fair.*

**fair·ly** /fair-lee/ *adverb*
**1** quite but not very: *I did fairly well on the last test, but I hope I do better on the next one.*
**2** treating everyone in the same way: *The teacher always treats us fairly and lets everyone get a chance to speak.*

**fair·y** /fair-ee/ *noun* (plural **fairies**) a very small person with wings who can do magic. Fairies are not real and are only in stories.

**fair·y tale** /fair-ee tayl/ *noun* a story for children in which magic things happen

**faith** /fayth/ *noun*
**1** a strong belief that someone or something will succeed: *His parents have a lot of faith in him and they are sure he will do well in school.*
**2** belief in God: *Her faith in God helped her after her father died.*
**3** a religion: *We have students of many different faiths in our class.*

**faith·ful** /fayth-fuhl/ *adjective*
**1** loyal to someone or something: *The dog was her faithful companion and he followed her everywhere.*
**2** describing or showing something exactly, without changing it: *The movie is faithful to the book – the director has not changed the story at all.*

**faith·ful·ly** /**fayth**-fuhl-ee/ *adverb*
**1** in a loyal way: *He worked for the company faithfully for 20 years.*
**2** in an exact way, without changing anything: *She faithfully wrote down every word the teacher said.*

**fake** /fayk/
● *adjective* not real, but made to look real: *He used a fake I.D. to get into the building.*
● *noun* a copy of something, which is intended to deceive people: *The painting is a fake.*

**fall** /fol/
● *verb* (**fell** /fel/, **fallen** /**fol**-uhn/)
**1** to drop down onto the ground by accident: *He fell and hit his head on a rock.*
▶ see Thesaurus ▶ see picture on page **A15**
**2** to move down toward the ground: *The leaves on the trees were beginning to fall.*
**3** to become lower: *The temperature fell below zero last night.* ( ANTONYM: **rise** )

IDIOMS with **fall**
**fall apart** to become damaged and break: *My shoes were falling apart so Mom bought me some new ones.*
**fall asleep** to start to sleep: *I was so tired I fell asleep in class.*
**fall behind** to make less progress than other people: *He was falling behind with his schoolwork and his grades weren't very good.*
**fall in love** to begin to love someone: *My dad fell in love with my mom as soon as he saw her.*

● *noun*
**1** the season between summer and winter, when the weather becomes cooler and leaves fall from the trees: *My brother's starting college in the fall.*
▶ see picture at **season**
**2** an action in which you drop down onto the ground by accident: *My grandmother broke her hip in a fall.*
**3** if there is a fall in something, it becomes lower: *There was a fall in the number of students from 30 to 25.* ( SYNONYM: **drop** ) ( ANTONYM: **rise** )

**fall·en** /**fol**-uhn/ *verb* the past participle of fall

**false** /folss/ *adjective*
**1** not true: *He had given false information to the police.*
**2** not real, but made to look real: *Grandpa has false teeth.* ▶ see Thesaurus

**fame** /faym/ *noun* the state of being famous: *All they want is money and fame, but I think other things are more important.*

**fa·mil·iar** /fuh-**mil**-yur/ *adjective*
**1** to know something well: *I'm not familiar with the place because we just moved here.*
**2** a familiar person or thing is one that you recognize: *Her face is familiar, but I can't remember her name.*
—**familiarity** /fuh-mil-**yarr**-uht-ee/ *noun* knowledge of something: *Her familiarity with Spanish helped when she went to Mexico.*

**fam·ily** /**fam**-lee/ *noun* (plural **families**) your parents, brothers, sisters, etc.: *There are four people in my family – my mom, my dad, my sister, and me.* ▶ see Thesaurus

**Word Origin:** family

**Family** comes from a Latin word that means "servant." A servant is someone who does work in a house for someone else. When the word family was first used in English, it meant all the servants in a house. Family did not mean all the people who are related to you, such as your parents, until the 1600s.

**fam·ine** /**fam**-in/ *noun* a situation when a lot of people do not have enough food: *Thousands of people died in the famine.*

**fa·mous** /**faym**-uhss/ *adjective* known by a lot of people: *She's a famous actor.* | *San Francisco is famous for its great food.* ▶ see Thesaurus

**Word Family:** famous

**famous** adjective | **infamous** adjective | **fame** noun

**fan** /fan/ *noun*
**1** a person who likes someone or something very much: *He's a big music fan and has hundreds of CDs.* | *The stadium was full of Cowboys fans.*
**2** a machine or object that keeps you cool by making the air move: *It was hot, so I turned on the fan.*

fan

**fa·nat·ic** /fuh-**nat**-ik/ *noun* someone who likes something very much: *My brother's a fitness fanatic and he's always at the gym.*

**fan·cy** /**fanss**-ee/ *adjective* (**fancier, fanciest**)
**1** special and expensive: *Mom and Dad went to a fancy restaurant for their anniversary.*
**2** unusual or having a lot of decoration: *It was a plain blue dress – nothing fancy.*

**fang** /fang/ *noun* a long sharp tooth of an animal such as a dog or snake: *The dog growled, showing its sharp fangs.*

**fan·tas·tic** /fan-**tast**-ik/ *adjective*
**1** very good: *There was a fantastic fireworks display on July 4.*
**2** strange or imaginary: *The movie is about fantastic creatures from another world.*

**fan·ta·sy** /**fant**-uhss-ee/ *noun* (plural **fantasies**)
**1** something that you imagine happening, but that is not real: *She had a fantasy about becoming a movie star.*
**2** a story or movie about strange and imaginary events or creatures: *I like to read science fiction and fantasies.*

**far** /far/ (**farther** /**farth**-ur/ or **further** /**furth**-ur/, **farthest** /**farth**-ist/ or **furthest** /**furth**-ist/)
● *adverb*
**1** a long distance: *Did you have to travel far to get here? | I'll walk with you as far as the corner of the street.*
**2** much: *Esmeralda's a far better swimmer than I am.*

┌ **IDIOMS with far**
│ **as far as I know** used when saying that you
│ think something is true, but you are not sure:
│ *As far as I know, they still live in Washington,*
│ *but I could be wrong.*
│ **so far** until now: *I've only read five pages so*
└ *far.*
● *adjective*
a long distance away: *The beach isn't far from here – we can walk there.* (ANTONYM: **near**)
▶ see **Thesaurus**

**far·a·way** /**far**-uh-way/ *adjective* a long distance away: *The princess lived in a faraway land across the ocean.*

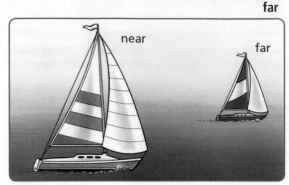
far

**fare** /fair/ *noun* the price you pay to travel by bus, train, or airplane: *Mom gave me some money for my bus fare.*

**Far East** /far **eest**/ *noun* the countries of east Asia, such as China, Korea, and Japan: *We've been learning about the Far East in our geography class.*

**farm** /farm/ *noun* an area of land and buildings where people grow crops or raise animals: *They grow wheat and barley on their farm.*
▶ see **Thesaurus**
—**farmer** /**farm**-ur/ *noun* a person who owns or manages a farm
—**farming** /**farm**-ing/ *noun* the work of growing crops or raising animals

**farm·yard** /**farm**-yard/ *noun* an area with farm buildings around it: *There were goats and chickens in the farmyard.*

**far·sight·ed** /**far**-sīt-id/ *adjective* unable to see things that are near to you: *I'm farsighted and wear glasses for reading.* (ANTONYM: **nearsighted**)

**far·ther** /**farth**-ur/ *adjective, adverb* the comparative of far: *The car was moving farther away.*

**far·thest** /**farth**-ist/ *adjective, adverb* the superlative of far: *The planet Neptune is the farthest from the sun.*

**fas·ci·nate** /**fass**-uh-nayt/ *verb* to interest someone very much: *Thunderstorms have always fascinated me and I really like watching big flashes of lightning.*
—**fascinated** /**fass**-uh-nayt-id/ *adjective* very interested: *I think people are fascinated by dinosaurs because they look so big and scary.*
—**fascinating** /**fass**-uh-nayt-ing/ *adjective* very

interesting: *We watched a fascinating TV program about monkeys.*

**fas·ci·na·tion** /fass-uh-**naysh**-uhn/ *noun* a very strong interest: *His fascination with planes started when he was a boy.*

**fash·ion** /**fash**-uhn/ *noun* something that is popular at a particular time: *There was a fashion for tight jeans.*

> IDIOMS with **fashion**
> **in fashion** liked or worn by a lot of people: *Long skirts are in fashion again.*
> ( SYNONYM: **fashionable** )
> **out of fashion** not liked or worn by a lot of people: *The band's music was out of fashion.*
> ( SYNONYM: **unfashionable** )

**fash·ion·a·ble** /**fash**-uhn-uhb-uhl/ *adjective*
**1** popular: *Short skirts were fashionable at the time.*
**2** expensive and for rich people: *She lived in a fashionable area of the city.*

**fast** /fast/
● *adjective*
**1** moving or doing something quickly: *Jake's a really fast runner – he can run 100 meters in under 14 seconds.* | *She's a fast learner and I'm sure her English will improve soon.*
( ANTONYM: **slow** )
**2** showing a time that is later than the real time: *My watch is fast – it says it's 5:30, but it's only 5:15.* ( ANTONYM: **slow** )
● *adverb*
quickly: *Ben was driving too fast.*
▶ see **Thesaurus**
● *verb*
to eat little or no food for a period of time, especially for religious reasons: *Muslims fast during the holy month of Ramadan.*

> IDIOM with **fast**
> **fast asleep** sleeping: *Dad was fast asleep in his chair.*

**fas·ten** /**fass**-uhn/ *verb*
**1** to join together the two sides of something: *Fasten your seat belts.* ▶ see **Thesaurus**
**2** to attach something to another thing: *I fastened the pin to my shirt.*

**fasten**
Fasten your seat belt.

**fas·ten·er** /**fass**-uhn-ur/ *noun* a button or pin used for attaching things to each other: *The fastener on my schoolbag is broken.*

**fast food** /**fast** food/ *noun* food from a restaurant which serves food very quickly: *We bought hamburgers and fries at a fast-food restaurant.*

**fat** /fat/
● *adjective*
having too much flesh on your body: *You'll get fat if you eat all that candy!* ( ANTONYM: **thin** )
▶ see **Thesaurus**
● *noun*
**1** an oily substance in food. Fat gives you energy, but eating a lot of it is bad for your health: *Pizzas and burgers contain a lot of fat.*
**2** the soft substance under people's skin: *Women have more fat on their bodies than men.*

**fa·tal** /**fayt**'l/ *adjective* causing someone to die: *There have been several fatal accidents on the freeway.*
—**fatally** /**fayt**'l-ee/ *adverb* in a way that makes someone die: *He was fatally injured in the accident.*

**fa·tal·i·ty** /fay-**tal**-uht-ee/ *noun* (plural **fatalities**) a death in an accident: *Several people were hurt, but there were no fatalities.*

**fate** /fayt/ *noun*
**1** a mysterious power that some people think controls what happens in your life: *She believes that fate brought her and Bob together and they are going to get married.* ( SYNONYM: **destiny** )
**2** the things that will happen to someone: *The results of this test will decide his fate; if he passes, he can finish high school.*

a b c d e **f** g h i j k l m n o p q r s t u v w x y z

**fa·ther** /**fah**th-ur/ *noun*
**1** someone's male parent: *My father is a teacher.*
( SYNONYM: **dad** )
**2** **Father** a priest in some Christian churches: *Do you know Father O'Donnell?*
—**fatherhood** /**fah**th-ur-hud/ *noun* the state of being a father: *He was enjoying fatherhood.*

**fa·ther-in-law** /**fah**th-ur in lo/ *noun* (plural **fathers-in-law**) the father of your husband or wife: *My grandpa is my mom's father-in-law.*

**Fa·ther's Day** /**fah**th-urz day/ *noun* a day when people give cards and gifts to their fathers. Father's Day is on the third Sunday in June.

**fa·tigue** /fuh-**teeg**/ *noun* tiredness: *Flu causes fatigue and makes you want to lie down.*
—**fatigued** /fuh-**teegd**/ *adjective* very tired: *She was too fatigued to run in the hot weather.*

**fat·ten** /**fat**'n/ *verb* to make a person or animal fatter: *My mom thinks I'm too thin, and she's always trying to fatten me up with cakes and cookies.*

**fat·ty** /**fat**-ee/ *adjective* containing a lot of fat: *Too much fatty food is bad for you.*

**fau·cet** /**foss**-it/ *noun* the thing you turn on and off to control the water coming from a pipe: *I turned on the faucet but the water was cold.*

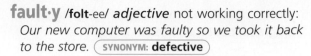
faucet

**fault** /folt/ *noun*
**1** a problem that stops something from working correctly: *The fire was caused by a fault in one of the plane's engines.* ( SYNONYM: **defect** )
**2** something that is bad about someone's character: *His worst fault is his laziness.*
**3** if something bad is your fault, you caused it to happen: *It was my brother's fault that we were late for school – he couldn't find his bag.*
**4** a large crack in the rocks that form the Earth: *The San Andreas Fault in California has caused many earthquakes.*

> IDIOM with **fault**
> **be at fault** to have caused something bad: *The report on the accident said the pilot was at fault, so he lost his job.*

**fault·y** /**folt**-ee/ *adjective* not working correctly: *Our new computer was faulty so we took it back to the store.* ( SYNONYM: **defective** )

**fa·vor** /**fayv**-ur/
● *noun* something helpful that you do for someone: *Can you do me a favor and save me a seat in class?*

> IDIOM with **favor**
> **be in favor of** to support or agree with something: *We were all in favor of getting some new sports equipment for the school.*
● *verb* to like one thing or person best and treat that person or thing differently from the others: *A good teacher never favors one student over the others.*

**fa·vor·a·ble** /**fayv**-uhr-uhb-uhl/ *adjective*
**1** showing that people think someone or something is good: *The movie had favorable reviews; all the critics liked it.*
**2** likely to make someone or something succeed: *The climate in this part of California is favorable for growing fruit trees.*
—**favorably** /**fayv**-uhr-uhb-lee/ *adverb* in a way that shows you think someone or something is good: *My parents reacted favorably to the idea and agreed to let me go.*

**fa·vor·ite** /**fayv**-rit/
● *adjective* your favorite person or thing is the one you like most: *My favorite color is red and I often wear red clothes.*
● *noun* the person or thing you like most: *I like all sports but baseball is my favorite.*

**fawn** /fon/ *noun* a young deer

**fax** /fakss/
● *noun* a copy of a document that is sent through a telephone line and then printed on paper: *After parents have signed the forms they can mail them to school or send a fax.*
● *verb* to send something using a fax: *The company faxed details of the vacation to my dad's office.*

**fear** /feer/
● *noun*
**1** the feeling you have when you are afraid: *He was shaking with fear when he saw the snake.*
► see **Thesaurus**
**2** something bad that you are worried could

happen: *My worst fear is that I will fail all my tests.*

● *verb*

**1** to feel worried: *His mother feared that something terrible must have happened to him.*
**2** to be afraid of someone or something: *His father was very strict and all the children feared him.*

**fear·ful** /**feer**-fuhl/ *adjective* afraid: *People left the area, fearful of more bombs.*

**fear·less** /**feer**-liss/ *adjective* not afraid: *He is totally fearless and loves dangerous sports.*

**feast** /feest/
● *noun* a big meal for a lot of people: *There were 200 guests at the wedding feast.*
● *verb* to eat a lot of good food with great enjoyment: *We feasted on pumpkin pie and vanilla ice cream.*

**feat** /feet/ *noun* an achievement that shows a lot of skill or strength: *Lifting the truck with his bare hands was an amazing feat of strength.*

**feath·er** /**feth**-ur/ *noun* one of the light soft things that cover a bird's body: *The parrot has beautiful blue and red feathers.*

**feather**

feathers

**fea·ture** /**feech**-ur/
● *noun*
**1** a part or quality of something: *The cell phone has a lot of useful features, such as a camera and calendar.*
**2** a part of someone's face, for example his or her mouth and nose: *He has similar features to his father and they both have the same nose.*
**3** an article or report about something in a newspaper or magazine, or on television: *There is a feature on my favorite baseball team in this week's magazine.*
● *verb*
if something features a person or thing, that person or thing has an important part in it: *The show featured paintings by American artists.*

**Feb·ru·ar·y** /**feb**-yoo-air-ee/ *noun*
( ABBREVIATION: **Feb.** ) the second month of the year. February is between January and March: *George*

Washington's birthday is on February 22. | We went to Florida in February.

**Word Origin:** February

The name **February** comes from a Latin word that means "purification." Purification means making something very clean. The Romans had a purification celebration in February.

**feces** /**feess**-eez/ *plural noun* the solid waste that comes out of someone's body

**fed** /fed/ *verb* the past tense and past participle of **feed**: *Have you fed the dog?*

**fed·er·al** /**fed**-uhr-uhl/ *adjective* relating to the central government of a country that consists of several states. In a federal system, each state also has its own government: *The U.S. has a federal government.*
—**federally** /**fed**-uhr-uhl-ee/ *adverb* in a way that involves the central government of a country: *Schools are paid for by the state but some education programs are federally funded.*

**fed up** /fed **uhp**/ *adjective* annoyed or bored: *I was fed up with waiting for my brother and I decided to go home.*

**fee** /fee/ *noun* an amount of money that you pay to do something: *The museum's entrance fee is $10.*

**feed** /feed/ *verb*
(**fed** /fed/)
**1** to give food to a person or animal: *Can you feed the cat?*
**2** if animals feed on something, they eat it: *Rabbits feed on grass and other plants.*
**3** to gradually put something into a machine, so the machine can use it: *Feed the paper into the printer.*

**feed**

**feed·back** /**feed**-bak/ *noun* opinions people give about how good something is or how well someone has done something: *The teacher gave me some feedback on my assignment.*

a b c d e f g h i j k l m n o p q r s t u v w x y z

## feel /feel/

● *verb* (**felt** /felt/)

**1** to have a particular feeling: *I felt tired so I went to bed. | Ellie felt very sad when her dog died.*

**2** if something feels hot, cold, etc., that is how it seems when you touch it or are in it: *It feels very hot in here. May I open a window?*

**3** to touch something with your fingers in order to find out about it: *Feel this cloth – it's so soft.*

**4** to notice something that is touching you: *She felt a bug crawling up her leg.*

**5** to think that something is true: *I like my school and I feel that it was a good decision to study here.*

**6** **feel like** to want to do something or have something: *It's very hot and I feel like a nice cool drink.*

● *noun*

**1** the way that something feels when you touch it: *I like the feel of this soft material.*

**2** an ability to do something well: *Susan seems to have a feel for tennis and she will be a good player one day. | Hitting the ball is easy, once you get the feel for it.*

## feel·ing /feel-ing/ *noun*

**1** an emotion that you have in your mind: *It was her birthday, and Alice woke up with a feeling of excitement.* ▶ see **Thesaurus**

**2** something you feel in your body such as pain or cold: *I hate being sick – it's a horrible feeling.*

**3** a belief or opinion: *My feeling is that we should wait to see what happens.*
( SYNONYM: **opinion** )

> **IDIOM with feeling**
> **hurt someone's feelings** to upset someone: *He said he didn't like her and it really hurt her feelings.*

## feet /feet/ *noun* the plural of **foot**

## feist·y /fist-ee/ *adjective* having a strong determined character and a lot of energy: *She's an old lady, but she's still very feisty.*

## fell /fel/ *verb*

**1** the past tense of **fall**

**2** to cut down a tree: *The men felled a big tree that was growing in the school yard.*

## fel·low /fel-oh/

● *adjective* belonging to the same class or group as you: *Her fellow students in the college were all much older than she was.*

● *noun* an old-fashioned word for a man

## fel·o·ny /fel-uhn-ee/ *noun* (plural **felonies**) a serious crime such as murder: *He was jailed for committing three felonies.*

## felt /felt/

● *verb* the past tense and past participle of **feel**

● *noun* a thick soft material made from threads that have been pressed together: *Felt is sometimes used in hats to make them feel softer.*

## felt tip pen /felt tip **pen**/ *noun* a pen with a hard piece of felt at the end that the ink comes through ▶ see picture on page **A9**

## fe·male /fee-mayl/

● *noun* an animal or person belonging to the sex that can have babies or produce eggs: *The female stays with her cubs for two or three months.* ( ANTONYM: **male** )

● *adjective* belonging to the sex that can have babies or produce eggs: *The female bird sits on the eggs in the nest.* ( ANTONYM: **male** )

## fem·i·nine /fem-uhn-in/ *adjective* having qualities that people think are typical of women: *Pink is a soft feminine color.*
( ANTONYM: **masculine** )

## fem·i·nism /fem-uh-niz-uhm/ *noun* the belief that women should have the same rights and opportunities as men

—**feminist** /fem-uh-nist/ *noun* someone who supports feminism

## fence /fenss/ *noun* a structure made of wood or wire that surrounds a piece of land: *The gate was locked so we climbed over the fence.*

**fence**

## fend·er /fend-ur/ *noun* the part of a car or bicycle that covers the wheels: *There's a scratch on the car's rear left fender.* ▶ see picture at **bicycle**

**fern** /furn/ *noun* a plant with green leaves that are like big feathers. Ferns have no flowers and grow in places where there is plenty of water.

fern

**fe·ro·cious** /fuh-**rohsh**-uhss/ *adjective* extremely violent or ready to attack: *There was a ferocious dog outside the house and I thought he was going to bite me.*
—**ferociously** /fuh-**rohsh**-uhss-lee/ *adverb* in a ferocious way

**Fer·ris wheel** /**ferr**-iss weel/ *noun* a big wheel with chairs that go up into the air, for people to ride on for fun ▶ see picture at **amusement park**

**fer·ry** /**ferr**-ee/ *noun* (plural **ferries**) a boat that regularly takes people across an area of water and back again: *We took the ferry to Staten Island.*

ferry

**fer·tile** /**furt**'l/ *adjective*
**1** able to produce good crops: *The land is very fertile and good for growing corn.*
**2** able to have babies: *Cows are fertile for about ten years.*
—**fertility** /fur-**til**-uht-ee/ *noun* the ability to have babies or produce good crops: *Farmers use manure from animals to improve the fertility of the soil.*

**fer·til·ize** /**furt**'l-īz/ *verb*
**1** to make a new animal or plant start to develop. This happens when the male sperm joins with the female egg, or when pollen lands on the stigma of a plant: *The female fish lays*

eggs, and the male fish fertilizes them.
**2** to add substances to the soil to help plants grow: *Vegetable scraps can be used to make compost to fertilize the soil.*

**fer·til·iz·er** /**furt**'l-īz-ur/ *noun* a substance that is put on the soil to help plants grow: *Farmers put fertilizer on the crops in the spring.*

**fes·ti·val** /**fest**-uhv-uhl/ *noun*
**1** a special occasion when people celebrate something: *There will be food, music, and dancing at the festival.*
**2** an event when there are many performances of movies, plays, or music. A festival often happens every year in the same place: *There will be lots of famous musicians at the jazz festival.*

**fes·tive** /**fest**-iv/ *adjective* happy because you are celebrating something: *It was the end of the school year and everyone was in a festive mood.*

**fetch** /fech/ *verb* to go and get something and bring it back: *The dog ran to fetch the stick.*

**fe·tus** /**feet**-uhss/ *noun* a baby that is developing inside its mother, before it is born: *The fetus is very small at first, and then after nine months it becomes a full size baby.*

**feud** /fyood/ *noun* an angry argument between two people or groups that continues for a long time: *For years there was a bitter feud between the two families and they refused to speak to each other.*

**fe·ver** /**feev**-ur/ *noun* If you have a fever, your body has a higher temperature than normal because you are sick. A fever is usually more than 98.6 degrees F: *I had a fever and I felt very hot and was sweating a lot.*
—**feverish** /**feev**-uhr-ish/ *adjective* affected by a fever: *The baby wouldn't eat and was feverish.*

**few** /fyoo/ *pronoun, adjective*
**1** a small number: *I've read a few of her books – maybe two or three of them.*
**2** not many, or almost none: *Few people knew her secret.*

**IDIOM with few**
**quite a few** a fairly large number of people or things: *She's invited quite a few friends to her birthday party.*

## Word Choice: fewer, less

You use **fewer** before nouns when you can count the number of things or people: *You have five pennies and I have three. I have fewer pennies.* | *There were fewer people at the park than yesterday.*

You use **less** before nouns that are things you cannot count: *There is less water in this cup than in that one.* | *I have less money than my brother.*

**fi·an·cé** /fee-ahn-**say**/ *noun* the man that a woman is going to marry: *Steve is my sister's fiancé and they are going to get married next year.*

**fi·an·cée** /fee-ahn-**say**/ *noun* the woman that a man is going to marry: *His fiancée was wearing a diamond ring.*

**fib** /fib/
● *noun* a small lie: *He didn't want to go to the party, so he told a fib and said he was feeling sick.*
● *verb* (**fibbing**, **fibbed**) to tell a fib to someone: *I believed her story, but later I found out that she was fibbing.*

**fi·ber** /**fib**-ur/ *noun*
**1** parts of plants that you eat but cannot digest. Fiber is good for you because it helps food to move through your body: *Fiber is found in fruits and vegetables.*
**2** a type of thread or cloth: *Cotton is a natural fiber; it grows on a plant.*

**fic·tion** /**fik**-shuhn/ *noun* books and stories about imaginary people and things: *My brother likes books about history and science, but I mainly read fiction.* ( ANTONYM: **nonfiction** )

**fid·dle** /**fid**'l/
● *noun* a violin: *My uncle plays the fiddle.*
● *verb* to keep moving and touching something because you are bored or nervous: *My mom told me to listen and stop fiddling with my pen.*

**fidg·et** /**fij**-it/ *verb* to keep moving your hands or feet because you are bored or nervous: *The children were bored by the movie and they started fidgeting.*

**field** /feeld/ *noun*
**1** an area of land for growing crops or feeding animals: *In North Carolina, there are a lot of cotton fields.*
**2** an area of ground where sports are played: *Our school has its own baseball field.*
**3** a subject that people study, or a type of work: *Professor Jones is an expert in the field of genetics and she has written many articles about it.*
**4** an area where there is oil, gas, or coal under the ground: *He worked in the Texas oil fields.*

**field·er** /**feeld**-ur/ *noun* one of the players in baseball who plays farthest away from the batter and tries to catch the ball after the batter has hit it: *The center fielder caught the ball and threw it to second base.*

**field goal** /**feeld** gohl/ *noun*
**1** in football, the act of kicking the ball over the bar of the goal. A field goal scores three points.
**2** in basketball, the act of putting the ball through the basket. A field goal scores two or three points.

**field trip** /**feeld** trip/ *noun* a trip that students go on to see and study something: *Our class went on a field trip to a pumpkin farm to see how the pumpkins are grown.*

**fierce** /feerss/ *adjective*
**1** angry, violent, and ready to attack: *The dog looked very fierce and I thought he was going to bite me.*
**2** involving a lot of energy and strong feelings: *There was fierce competition for first place because everyone wanted to win.*
**3** fierce weather has strong winds and a lot of rain or snow: *The storm was so fierce that it blew the roof off the house.*
—**fiercely** /**feerss**-lee/ *adverb* in a fierce way: *He is fiercely competitive and always tries to win.*
—**fierceness** /**feerss**-niss/ *noun* a fierce quality

**fierce**

**fi·er·y** /**fi**-uhr-ee/ *adjective*
**1** full of strong or angry emotion: *Patrick Henry made fiery speeches about American independence and he once famously said, "Give me liberty or give me death."*

**2** very bright in color, like a fire: *In the fall, the leaves turn a fiery red.*

**fi·es·ta** /fee-**est**-uh/ *noun* a party or religious holiday with dancing and music, especially in Spain and Central or Latin America: *At fiesta time, everyone is happy and there is dancing in the streets.*

**fif·teen** /fif-**teen**/ *number*
**1** 15: *It's only fifteen days until the summer vacation!*
**2** fifteen years old: *Her brother's fifteen.*
—**fifteenth** /fif-**teenth**/ *number* 15th or 1/15

**fifth** /fifth/ *number*
**1** 5th: *I was fifth in the race.*
**2** 1/5. You can say a fifth or one fifth: *There were five of us, so we had a fifth of the pizza each.*

**fif·ty** /**fift**-ee/ *number*
**1** 50: *Fifty people are in the room.*
**2** fifty years old: *He is almost fifty.*
**3** **the fifties** the years between 1950 and 1959: *She was born in the fifties.*
**4** **in your fifties** between 50 and 59 years old: *The principal is in his fifties.*
**5** **in the fifties** between 50 and 59 degrees in temperature: *The temperature yesterday was in the fifties.*
—**fiftieth** /**fift**-ee-ith/ *number* 50th or 1/50

**fig** /fig/ *noun* a soft sweet brown fruit with a lot of very small seeds. Figs are often dried before you eat them.

**fig**

**fight** /fīt/
● *verb* (**fought** /fot/)
**1** to use force or weapons to try to hurt someone: *Some boys were fighting in the school yard.* | *My grandfather fought in the Vietnam War.*
**2** to argue: *I always fight with my sister about what we watch on TV.*
**3** to try hard to do something: *They had to fight hard to win the game.*
● *noun*
**1** If there is a fight, people use force or weapons

to try to hurt each other: *Joe had been in a fight and had a cut on his face.*
**2** an argument: *My brother and I had a fight over which of us won the game.*
**3** the process of trying hard to do or to stop something: *We can all help in the fight against crime.*

**fight·er** /**fīt**-ur/ *noun*
**1** someone who always tries hard and does not give up: *Although she lost the first game, she's a real fighter and I'm sure she will win next time.*
**2** a boxer who fights as a sport: *He won a boxing match against a famous fighter.*
**3** a small fast military airplane that can destroy other airplanes: *His plane was attacked by three enemy fighters.*

**fig·ure** /**fig**-yur/
● *noun*
**1** a written number: *Add all these figures together to find out how much the meal cost.*
**2** a shape in mathematics: *A triangle is a three-sided figure.*
**3** the shape of a woman's body: *The actress has a great figure.*
**4** the shape of a person, when you do not know exactly who it is: *A figure was standing in the dark outside.*
**5** an important or famous person: *George Washington is a very important figure in American history.*
**6** a drawing in a book, with a number beside it: *Figure 2 shows how a plant takes energy from sunlight and turns it into food.*
● *verb*
**1** to think that something is probably true: *The lights were all switched off, so I figured everyone was in bed.*
**2** **figure out** to understand something, or find a way to do it: *I can't figure out how to solve this problem.*

**IDIOMS with figure**
**that figures** used when saying that something is not surprising: *"I missed the bus this morning." "Well you got up late so that figures!"*
**go figure** used when saying that something seems strange and you cannot understand it: *"He didn't say goodbye or anything." "Go figure."*

a b c d e **f** g h i j k l m n o p q r s t u v w x y z

### fig·ure skat·ing

/**fig**-yur skayt-ing/ *noun* a sport in which you skate on ice, and do jumps and spin in circles

figure skating

### file /fīl/

● *noun*

**1** information about someone or something that is kept somewhere. A file can be written on paper or on a computer: *There is a file on every student in the school office.*

**2** a box or paper cover for keeping loose papers together: *I keep all my drawings in a file.*

**3** a tool with a rough surface that you rub on something to make it smooth: *She was shaping her nails with a nail file.*

> IDIOM with **file**
>
> **in single file** moving in a line, with one person behind another: *The path is narrow so you had better walk in single file.*

● *verb*

**1** to store information somewhere, in sets of papers or on a computer: *I file my photos on my computer, under "My Pictures."*

**2** to walk in a line, with one person behind another: *The children filed out of the classroom.*

**3** to make something smooth by rubbing it with a special tool: *Mom filed her nails then painted them.*

### file cab·i·net /fīl kab-uhn-it/ *noun* a tall piece of furniture with big drawers that you keep papers in

### fill /fīl/ *verb*

**1** to put something in a container or space until it is full: *I filled a bottle with water.*

**2** to become full of something: *I know she was upset because her eyes filled with tears.*

**3** to use all the space in a place: *Our bags fill up the whole car – there's no space for us to sit.*

**4 fill in** to write something in a space, or to answer the questions on a form: *Try to fill in the gaps in the story.* | *Have you filled in the answer sheet?*

**5 fill out** to write information on a form: *Fill out the form with your name, address, and date of birth.* ( SYNONYM: **complete** )

fill

She is filling the bottle with water.

### fill·ing /fil-ing/ *noun*

**1** if you have a filling, a dentist puts a substance into a hole in your tooth: *The dentist said I needed to have two fillings.*

**2** the food inside something, for example a sandwich or a cake: *I made a cake with a chocolate cream filling.*

### film /film/

● *noun*

**1** the plastic material you put in older cameras to take pictures: *I put a new roll of film in my camera.*

**2** a very thin layer of something: *His shoes were covered with a film of dust.*

**3** a movie: *Did you see the film "Kung Fu Panda?"*

—**filmmaker** /**film**-mayk-ur/ *noun* someone who makes movies

● *verb*

to make a movie or a television program, using a camera: *They filmed the movie in Mexico.*

### fil·ter /**filt**-ur/

● *noun* a device that removes substances from liquid or gas. You pass liquid or gas through a filter: *When you're camping, you can use a water filter.*

● *verb* to use a filter to remove substances from something: *Filter the water until it is clear.*

### filth /filth/ *noun* a lot of dirt: *The wall behind the stove is covered in filth – I don't think anyone has ever cleaned it.*

### filth·y /**filth**-ee/ *adjective* (**filthier**, **filthiest**) very dirty: *The sidewalks were very muddy and my shoes were filthy by the time we arrived home.*

### fin /fin/ *noun*

**1** a thin part that sticks out from a fish's body.

Fins help fish to move through water: *They saw a shark's fin sticking up above the water.*
▶ see picture at **fish**
**2** a part on an airplane that sticks up and helps it to move along smoothly. The fin is at the back of the plane and is usually shaped like a triangle.

## fi·nal /**fin**'l/
● *adjective*
**1** last: *In the final chapter of the book, they find out who did the robbery.*
**2** a final decision or offer cannot be changed: *She hasn't made a final decision yet about which school she wants to go to.*
● *noun*
**1** the last game, race, or stage in a competition: *The team are in the finals and they have a good chance of winning the competition.*
**2** an important test that students take at the end of a semester: *She did well in her finals.*
—**finalist** /**fin**'l-ist/ *noun* someone who is in the final of a competition: *James was one of the five finalists but he didn't win.*

**Word Family:** final

**final** *adjective* | **final** *noun* | **finally** *adverb* | **finalist** *noun* | **semifinal** *noun*

## fi·nal·ly /**fin**'l-ee/ *adverb*
**1** after a long time: *The bus was late and there was a lot of traffic, so it was eight o'clock when we finally arrived home.*
**2** used before saying the last of a series of things: *Add the flour and the eggs, and finally a little milk.*

## fi·nance /fuh-**nanss**/
● *noun*
**1** the management of money: *My parents let me have my own bank account, so that I could understand a little about finance.*
**2** **finances** the amount of money that a person or organization has: *Mom went back to work to help the family finances.*
● *verb*
to provide the money to pay for something: *My parents offered to help finance my trip.*

**Word Family:** finance

**finance** *noun* | **finance** *verb* | **financial** *adjective* | **financially** *adverb*

## fi·nan·cial /fuh-**nansh**-uhl/ *adjective* relating to money: *They had financial problems and couldn't pay their bills.*
—**financially** /fuh-**nansh**-uhl-ee/ *adverb* in a way that relates to money: *A lot of people are struggling financially and can't afford to have a vacation.*

## find /fīnd/ *verb* (**found** /fownd/)
**1** to see or get something after looking for it, or by chance: *I can't find my ticket – I think I lost it. | Daniel found a dollar bill on the street.*
▶ see **Thesaurus**
**2** to learn new information, often using an experiment: *We found that the seeds grew best in a warm wet place.*
**3** to have an opinion about something: *Alice finds math really hard.*
**4** to officially decide that someone is guilty or not guilty of a crime: *The jury found him guilty and he was sent to prison.*
**5** if an animal or plant is found somewhere, it lives there: *Coyotes are mainly found in forests.*
**6** **find out** to get information that you need: *I'll find out what time the movie starts.*

## fine /fīn/
● *adjective*
**1** good enough: *Just a sandwich is fine for me – I'm not very hungry.* ( SYNONYMS: **okay, all right** )
**2** healthy and happy: *"How are you?" "Fine, thanks."*
**3** very thin or delicate: *The spider makes its web using very fine thread.*
**4** very good: *He's a fine player and we are lucky to have him on the team.*
**5** pleasant or sunny. Used about the weather: *The weather was fine so we went to the beach.*
—**fine** /fīn/ *adverb* in a good enough or normal way: *I had a few problems with my computer last week, but it's working fine now.*
—**finely** /**fīn**-lee/ *adverb* into very small pieces: *Chop the onions finely.*
● *noun*
money that you pay as a punishment for breaking a law: *You may have to pay a fine if you drop litter on the ground.*
● *verb*
to make someone pay money as a punishment: *The two boys were fined for breaking the window.*

**fin·ger** /**fing**-gur/ *noun* one of the long parts on your hand. You have four fingers and a thumb on each hand: *She has a wedding ring on the third finger of her left hand.*
▶ see picture at **hand**

> **IDIOM with finger**
> **keep your fingers crossed** to hope something will happen in the way that you want: *We're keeping our fingers crossed that we'll win.*

**fin·ger·nail** /**fing**-gur-nayl/ *noun* the hard flat part at the end of each finger: *Suzie has long fingernails and she paints them bright pink.*
▶ see picture at **hand**

**fin·ger·print**
/**fing**-gur-print/ *noun* a mark that a finger makes. Fingerprints have a pattern of lines, and every person's fingerprints are different: *The thief had left his fingerprints on the door.*

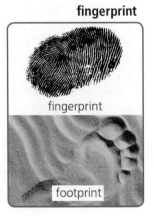
**fingerprint**
fingerprint
footprint

**fin·ger·tip** /**fing**-gur-tip/ *noun* the end of your finger: *You press your fingertips on the screen, to choose the numbers that you want.*

**fin·ish** /**fin**-ish/
● *verb*
**1** to come to the end of doing or making something: *You have to finish your homework before you can go out and play.*
(ANTONYMS: **start, begin**) ▶ see Thesaurus
**2** to eat or drink the rest of something: *Did you finish all the ice cream?*
● *noun*
**1** the end of an event, for example a race or game: *The race had a very exciting finish, as all the runners were close.*
**2** the way that the surface of an object looks: *This paint gives the wood a shiny finish.*

**fin·ish line** /**fin**-ish līn/ *noun* the line that you cross at the end of a race: *I crossed the finish line two seconds after him.*

**fir** /fur/ *noun* a tree with thin leaves like needles. Fir trees are evergreen, so their leaves do not fall off in the winter: *People bring fir trees into their houses at Christmas.*

**fir**

**fire** /**fī**-ur/
● *noun*
**1** flames that burn and destroy things: *Three people were killed in the fire.* ▶ see Thesaurus
**2** a pile of burning wood or coal used to provide heat: *We got some pieces of wood and made a fire on the beach to dry our clothes.*

> **IDIOM with fire**
> **be on fire** to be burning: *There's smoke coming out of the window – I think the house is on fire.*

● *verb*
**1** to make someone leave his or her job: *She was fired from her job for being late all the time.*
**2** to use a gun: *He aimed his gun at the target and fired.*

**fire a·larm** /**fī**-ur uh-larm/ *noun* a piece of equipment that warns people of a fire in a building. A fire alarm makes a loud noise if there is a fire: *If you hear the fire alarm, please leave the school at once.*

**fire·arm** /**fī**-ur-arm/ *noun* a gun: *The man had a firearm and was dangerous.*

**fire·crack·er** /**fī**-ur-krak-ur/ *noun* an object that explodes with a loud noise when you light it. Firecrackers are used at parties and special celebrations: *On Chinese New Year, people set off firecrackers in the street and they make a loud bang.*

**fire de·part·ment** /**fī**-ur di-part-muhnt/ *noun* an organization whose job is to stop fires: *If there is a fire, call the fire department.*

**fire drill** /**fī**-ur dril/ *noun* a time when people practice how to leave a building safely if there is a fire: *When we have a fire drill, we all have to leave the classroom and line up outside the building.*

**fire en·gine** /**fī**-ur en-jin/ *noun* a large truck with ladders and hoses that water can go through. Fire engines are used by firefighters to stop fires.

**fire engine**

**fire es·cape** /**fī**-ur i-skayp/ *noun* metal stairs on the outside of a building that people can use to escape from a fire: *They got out of the building safely by going down the fire escape.*

**fire ex·tin·guish·er** /**fī**-ur ik-sting-gwish-ur/ *noun* a container with water or chemicals in it that you use for stopping small fires: *There is a fire extinguisher in every classroom.*

**fire·fight·er** /**fī**-ur-fīt-ur/ *noun* someone whose job is to stop fires: *Nearly 80 firefighters rushed to the burning building.*

**fire·fly** /**fī**-ur-flī/ *noun* (plural **fireflies**) a small insect that flies at night. A firefly has a tail that shines in the dark. ▶ see picture on page **A15**

**fire·man** /**fī**-ur-muhn/ *noun* (plural **firemen** /**fī**-ur-muhn/) a man whose job is to stop fires

**fire·place** /**fī**-ur-playss/ *noun* a place in the wall of a room where you can light a fire: *A fire was burning in the fireplace.*

**fire·proof** /**fī**-ur-proof/ *adjective* made from material that cannot be damaged by fire: *The money is kept in a fireproof safe.*

**fire·wood** /**fī**-ur-wud/ *noun* wood for burning on a fire: *They went into the forest to collect firewood.*

**fire·works** /**fī**-ur-wurkss/ *plural noun* objects that explode and make bright colored lights in the sky. Fireworks are used to celebrate special days: *There is a big fireworks show every July 4.*

**firm** /furm/
● *adjective*
**1** not soft to touch or press: *The tomatoes are nice and firm.* | *The principal gave him a firm handshake and squeezed his hand tightly.*

( ANTONYM: **soft** )

**2** definite and not likely to change: *The teacher has not yet made a firm decision about who is going to be in the school play.*

**3** strong and in control: *His mother told him in a firm voice not to run across the road.*
—**firmly** /**furm**-lee/ *adverb* in a firm way: *"You need to do as I say," she said firmly.*
● *noun*
a business or small company: *He works for an advertising firm.*

**first** /furst/
● *number, adjective, pronoun*
coming before the other things or people. The number first is also written 1st: *It's the first of April (April 1).* | *I've read the first chapter of the book.* | *My name was the first on the list.*

⌈ IDIOM with **first**
| **at first** in the beginning, before there is a
| change: *At first, I didn't like her, but now I do.*
⌊ ● *adverb*
**1** before the other things or people: *Sara got on the bus first, and we all followed.*
**2** before doing something: *You can go out to play but clean up your room first.*

**first aid** /furst **ayd**/ *noun* simple medical treatment that you give quickly to someone who is injured or sick: *Our teacher knows how to give first aid if there is an accident.*

**first-class** /furst-**klass**/ *adjective* of the best kind: *It's a first-class hotel and very expensive.*
—**first class** /furst **klass**/ *adverb* if you travel first class, you travel in one of the best seats: *When she travels on business she usually flies first class.*

**first la·dy** /furst **layd**-ee/ *noun* the wife of the president of the U.S.: *The President and the First Lady visited Europe.*

**first·ly** /**furst**-lee/ *adverb* used before saying the first of several things: *There are a few things to remember about the trip. Firstly, it will probably be cold. Secondly, it might rain, so you need to take your umbrella.*

**first name** /**furst** naym/ *noun* the first of your names that your parents choose for you: *My first name is Maria and my last name is Gonzalez.*

**first per·son** /furst **purss**-uhn/ *noun* in grammar, the first person is "I" and "we", and the verb forms used with them: *Write the story in the first person, starting with the sentence: "I slowly opened the door."*

a b c d e **f** g h i j k l m n o p q r s t u v w x y z

237

**fish** /fish/
- *noun* (plural **fish** or **fishes**) an animal that lives in water. Fish swim and have fins but no legs. Fish breathe through the gills at the side of their heads: *We went to the river to catch some fish. | I'm having fish stew for dinner.*
- *verb* to try to catch fish: *You can fish in the river, but you have to throw the fish back after you catch them.*
—**fishing** /**fish**-ing/ *noun* the activity of trying to catch fish: *Dad and I went fishing.*

**fish**

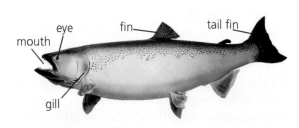

mouth · eye · fin · tail fin · gill

**fish·bowl** /**fish**-bohl/ *noun* a round glass container for keeping fish in as pets

**fishbowl**

**fish·er·man**
/**fish**-ur-muhn/ *noun* (plural **fishermen** /**fish**-ur-muhn/) a man who catches fish as a job or a sport: *In the mornings, the fishermen go out in their boats.*

**fish·ing rod** /**fish**-ing rahd/ *noun* a long stick that you catch fish with. A fishing rod has a long line with a hook at the end.

**fish stick** /**fish** stik/ *noun* a long piece of fish covered in little pieces of bread and fried or baked

**fist** /fist/ *noun* a hand with the fingers closed tightly together: *He banged on the table with his fist.*

**fit** /fit/
- *verb* (**fitting**, **fit**)
**1** to be the right size and shape: *These jeans fit me perfectly – they're just the right size.*
**2** if you can fit something into a space, it is not too big to go into the space: *I don't know if we can fit all the bags in the back of our car.*

**3** to be appropriate or right for something: *The punishment should fit the crime.*
**4 fit in** to be accepted by the other people in a group: *You'll soon fit in at your new school.*
- *adjective*
**1** healthy and strong: *Playing sports keeps you fit.*
**2** good for something: *The meat was tough and it wasn't fit to eat.*
- *noun*
a short time when you cannot control what you do: *Lisa and I had a sudden fit of the giggles – we couldn't stop laughing.*

**fit·ness** /**fit**-niss/ *noun* the condition of being healthy and strong: *You can improve your fitness by exercising a little every day.*

**five** /fīv/
- *number*
**1** 5: *We'll need five eggs.*
**2** five o'clock: *The movie starts at five.*
**3** five years old: *Laura is only five.*
- *noun*
a piece of paper money worth $5: *I paid with a five.*

**fix** /fikss/ *verb*
**1** to repair something: *Dad fixed your bike; you can ride it again now.*
**2** to prepare a meal or drink: *If you're hungry, I'll fix some lunch.* ( SYNONYM: **make** )
**3** to decide on a date or time for something: *Have they fixed a date for the school trip?*
**4 fix up** to decorate or repair a room or building: *We're going to fix up my bedroom in the summer.*

**fix·ture** /**fikss**-chur/ *noun* a piece of equipment that is attached inside a house. For example, an electric light or a faucet is a fixture: *There are new fixtures in the bathroom: a new bathtub, a new sink, and a new toilet.*

**flab** /flab/ *noun* soft fat on a person's body: *She has a lot of flab around her waist.*

**flab·by** /**flab**-ee/ *adjective* if part of your body is flabby, it is too fat and the skin feels soft and loose: *My mom says her arms are getting flabby and she needs to do some exercise.*

**flag** /flag/ *noun* a piece of cloth with a picture or pattern on it. Flags are used as a symbol of a country, or as a signal: *The American flag is red, white, and blue.*

flag

flagpole

**flag·pole** /**flag**-pohl/ *noun* a tall pole for a flag: *The flagpole above the White House flies the American flag.*

**flair** /flair/ *noun* a natural ability to do something well: *Tina has a real flair for art and she's very good at drawing people's faces.*

**flake** /flayk/ *noun* a small thin piece of something: *A few flakes of snow were falling down from the sky. | His hair was covered in flakes of paint.*

**flame** /flaym/ *noun*
**1** a hot bright light that you see when something is burning: *The candle burned with a bright yellow flame.*
**2** if something is in flames, a fire is destroying it: *The store was in flames and firefighters were trying to put out the fire.*

**fla·min·go**
/fluh-**ming**-goh/ *noun* (plural **flamingos** or **flamingoes**) a tall pink water bird with long thin legs and a long curved neck

**flam·ma·ble**
/**flam**-uhb-uhl/ *adjective* able to burn very easily: *In the science lab we need to be very careful with flammable gases such as hydrogen.*

**flan·nel** /**flan**'l/ *noun* a soft cloth for making warm clothes: *It was cold so he put on a thick flannel shirt.*

**flap** /flap/
● *verb* (**flapping**, **flapped**)
**1** if a bird flaps its wings, it moves them up and down: *The bird flapped its wings and flew away.*
**2** to move in one direction and then the other, especially because of the wind: *The flag above the school was flapping in the wind.*
● *noun*
a flat piece of paper or cloth that is attached to one side of something: *I opened the flap on the envelope and took out the letter.*

**flare** /flair/
● *verb*
**1** to suddenly begin to burn very brightly: *I put some new wood on the fire and the flames flared up the chimney.*
**2** if tempers flare, people suddenly become angry: *There was a big argument between the boys and tempers flared.*
● *noun*
an object that you use as a signal. You light a flare and it burns with a very bright light: *If you go walking in the mountains it's a good idea to take flares, in case you need help.*

**flash** /flash/
● *verb*
to shine brightly for a short time: *Lightning flashed in the sky. | The car flashed its headlights to warn the children.*
● *noun*
**1** a sudden quick bright light: *There was a sudden flash of lightning.*
**2** a bright light on a camera that you use when taking photographs inside a building: *It's fairly dark in here so you should use the flash.*

IDIOM with **flash**
**in a flash** very quickly: *The time passed in a flash.*

**flash card** /**flash** kard/ *noun* a card with a word, picture, or math problem on it. You use flash cards to practice and remember something you are trying to learn.

**flash·light** /**flash**-līt/ *noun* a small electric light that you carry in your hand: *Always take a flashlight when you're camping.*

flame

flame

flamingo

a b c d e **f** g h i j k l m n o p q r s t u v w x y z

**flat** /flat/
- *adjective* (**flatter**, **flattest**)

**1** smooth and level: *It's pretty flat around here – there are very few hills.* ▶ see **Thesaurus**

**2** a flat tire does not have enough air in it: *My bike has a flat tire.*

**3** E, B, etc. flat is a musical note that is a little lower than E, B, etc. It is shown by the symbol ♭: *Play an F flat.*

**4** very firm and definite: *Her answer was a flat "no" so she definitely doesn't want to come.*

- *adverb*

**1** with no parts raised off the surface: *He was lying flat on his back hiding under the bed.*

**2** after only a few seconds or minutes: *He's a very fast runner. He ran around the track in two minutes flat.*

**flat**

a flat tire

**flat·boat** /**flat**-boht/ *noun* a boat with a flat bottom. Flatboats are used for carrying heavy loads on rivers and lakes.

**flat·ly** /**flat**-lee/ *adverb* in a very firm way: *Mom flatly refused to let me go alone.*

**flat·ten** /**flat**'n/ *verb* to make something flat: *The heavy rain flattened the crops.*

**flat·ter** /**flat**-ur/ *verb*

**1** to say a lot of nice things to someone. When people flatter you, they do not always mean the things they say: *Everyone was flattering her, telling her she looked beautiful because they wanted to ride on her new bike.*

**2** if you are flattered, you feel happy because someone likes or admires you: *I was flattered when she asked me to her party.*

—**flattery** /**flat**-uhr-ee/ *noun* nice things you say to someone you flatter: *She tries to get what she wants by using flattery.*

**fla·vor** /**flayv**-ur/
- *noun* the taste of a food or drink: *Which*

flavor of ice cream do you like best: vanilla, chocolate, or strawberry?

—**flavorful** /**flayv**-ur-fuhl/ *adjective* having a strong good taste: *The fruit was ripe and flavorful.*

- *verb* to give food or drink taste: *The chicken was flavored with lemon and garlic.*

**fla·vor·ing** /**flayv**-uhr-ing/ *noun* a substance you use to give food or drink a taste: *I used some vanilla flavoring in the cake.*

**flaw** /flo/ *noun* a mark or weakness that stops something from being perfect: *There was one flaw in the plan: we needed a car, and we didn't have one.* (SYNONYM: **weakness**)

—**flawed** /flod/ *adjective* having one or more flaws: *The system is flawed because the best people don't always win.*

**flea** /flee/ *noun* a very small jumping insect. Fleas live on animals and they bite them and drink their blood: *Most cats have fleas.*

**flea mar·ket** /**flee** mark-it/ *noun* a market where old or used things are sold. Flea markets are often in the street: *I got this beautiful old necklace from the flea market.*

**flee** /flee/ *verb* (**fled** /fled/) to leave a place very quickly to escape from danger: *During the war, many people fled their homes to escape the bombing.*

**fleece** /fleess/ *noun*

**1** the woolly coat of a sheep

**2** a warm jacket made from an artificial material: *It will be cold at the top of the mountain, so take your fleece with you.*

**fleet** /fleet/ *noun*

**1** a group of ships: *Twenty-one ships in the U.S. fleet were damaged during the attack on Pearl Harbor.*

**2** a group of vehicles: *He owns a fleet of 50 taxis.*

**flesh** /flesh/ *noun*

**1** the soft part of a person's or animal's body. Flesh is made of fat and muscle: *He looks very thin and there is no flesh on his bones at all.*

**2** the soft part inside a fruit or vegetable: *The peach has sweet yellow flesh.*

**flew** /floo/ *verb* the past tense of **fly**

**flex·i·ble** /**flekss**-uhb-uhl/ *adjective*
**1** able to change easily: *The date of the picnic is flexible; we can change it if some people can't come.*
**2** able to bend easily: *Her body is very flexible and she can lift her foot above her shoulder.*
—**flexibility** /flekss-uh-**bil**-uht-ee/ *noun* the ability to change what you are doing depending on the situation

**flick** /flik/

**flick**

● *verb* to move something with a quick movement of your finger: *Adam flicked the dust off his shirt with his finger.*
● *noun* a quick movement of your finger or wrist: *With a flick of the wrist, he brushed the crumbs off the table.*

He flicked the ball of paper.

**flick·er** /**flik**-ur/
● *verb* to burn or shine with a light that is not steady: *The candle flickered and went out.*
● *noun* an unsteady light: *I could see a flicker of light from a flashlight in front of us.*

**fli·er** /**fli**-ur/ *noun* a piece of paper advertising something: *The man was handing fliers about the concert to people in the street.*

**flight** /flit/ *noun*
**1** a trip on an airplane: *Our flight leaves the airport at 2:30.*
**2** the act of flying through the air: *He looked up and watched the birds in flight.*
**3** a set of stairs between one floor and the next: *We went up a short flight of stairs to the principal's office.*

> IDIOM with **flight**
> **take flight** to run away: *The boys took flight when they saw the teacher coming.*

**flight at·tend·ant** /**flit** uh-tend-uhnt/ *noun* someone whose job is to help passengers and serve food and drinks on an airplane

**flim·sy** /**flimz**-ee/ *adjective* a flimsy object is not strong or thick and is easy to break: *The shelves are flimsy and you can't put a lot of books on them.*

**fling** /fling/ *verb* (**flung** /fluhng/) to throw or move something quickly with a lot of force: *She flung the door open and shouted "What are you doing in here?"*

**flip** /flip/ *verb* (**flipping, flipped**)
**1** if you flip a switch, you quickly change its position: *I flipped the switch and the light came on.*
**2** to turn over quickly: *The car flipped over and rolled down the side of the mountain. | Flip the hamburger after a few minutes and cook the other side.*
**3** **flip a coin** to make a coin turn over in the air. You flip a coin in order to choose something: *We flipped a coin to choose who would go first.*
**4** to suddenly become very angry or upset: *Dad flipped when he saw the damage to his car.*
**5** **flip through** to look quickly at the pages of a book or magazine: *I flipped through the book to see if it looked interesting.*

**flip·per** /**flip**-ur/ *noun*
**1** a part that some large sea animals use to swim: *Seals and turtles have flippers.*
▶ see picture at **seal**
**2** a large flat rubber shoe that you wear to help you swim faster

**flipper**

flipper

flipper

**flirt** /flurt/ *verb* to behave as if you are attracted to someone, but not in a serious way: *I don't think she loves me – she was just flirting with me and saying nice things.*

**float** /floht/ *verb*
**1** to stay or move on the surface of water without sinking: *The log floated down the river. | If you throw a ball into the water, it floats.*
(ANTONYM: **sink**) ▶ see picture at **sink**
**2** to move slowly through the air: *The balloon floated up into the sky.*

a
b
c
d
e
**f**
g
h
i
j
k
l
m
n
o
p
q
r
s
t
u
v
w
x
y
z

**flock** /flahk/ *noun* a group of sheep, goats, or birds: *The flock of sheep were grazing in the meadow.*

**flood** /fluhd/
● *noun*
a lot of water that covers land that is usually dry. Floods usually happen when there is so much rain that water comes out of the rivers: *There was a big flood and the water from the river went into people's houses.*
● *verb*
**1** if water floods a place, it causes a flood there: *If the level of the water gets any higher, the town will be flooded.*
**2** to receive so many letters or calls that you cannot deal with them all: *The TV station was flooded with complaints from people who were angry about the show.*
—**flooding** /fluhd-ing/ *noun* a situation in which a place is flooded: *The flooding was caused by heavy rain.*

**flood**

The road is flooded.

**flood·light** /fluhd-līt/ *noun* a very bright lamp used outdoors at night. Floodlights are used to light sports fields and the outside of buildings: *Floodlights light up the Washington Monument at night.*

**floodlight**

**floor** /flor/ *noun*
**1** the surface that you stand on in a building: *Mom told me to go get a mop and clean the kitchen floor.*

**2** one of the levels in a building: *My family lives in an apartment on the third floor.*

**flop** /flahp/
● *verb* (**flopping**, **flopped**)
**1** to sit or fall down in a loose heavy way: *When I get home I like to flop on the couch and watch TV.*
**2** if a play, movie, or product flops, it is very unsuccessful: *The show flopped and it was canceled after only one season.*
● *noun*
something that is not successful: *His first movie was a flop, but later he became extremely successful.* (ANTONYM: **hit**)

**flop·py** /flahp-ee/ *adjective* soft and hanging loosely down: *Rabbits have long floppy ears.*

**flo·ral** /flor-uhl/
*adjective* decorated with pictures of flowers, or made of flowers: *Her dress has a pretty floral pattern.*

**floral**

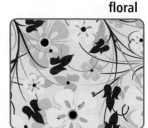

a floral pattern

**flo·rist** /flor-ist/ *noun* someone who works in a store that sells flowers

**floss** /floss/
● *noun* (also **den·tal floss** /dent'l floss/) special string that you use to clean between your teeth: *You should use floss after you brush your teeth.*
● *verb* to clean between your teeth with dental floss: *Dentists tell us we should floss regularly.*

**floun·der** /flownd-ur/ *noun* a flat ocean fish

**flounder**

**flour** /flow-ur/ *noun* a powder used for making bread and cakes. Flour is usually made from wheat: *Bread made from whole wheat flour is healthier for you.*

**Word Origin: flour**

**Flour** was spelled "flower" until about 1830. An old meaning of flower is "the finest part of something." To make flour, you use the best part of the wheat seed, and crush it to make it fine.

**flow** /floh/
- *verb* if a liquid flows, it moves along steadily: *The river flows all the way to the ocean.*
- *noun* a steady movement of liquid: *Doctors tried to stop the flow of blood from the wound.*

**flow chart** /**floh** chart/ *noun* a drawing that uses shapes and arrows to show how the parts of a process are connected to each other: *The flow chart shows how clouds, rain, and water on the Earth are connected.*

**flow·er** /**flow**-ur/
- *noun*
**1** a pretty colored part on a plant. Flowers are made up of petals, and they produce the plant's seeds or fruit: *This rose bush has pretty pink flowers.* ▶ see **Thesaurus**
**2** a small plant that produces flowers: *Let's plant some flowers in the yard.*
- *verb*
to produce flowers: *The apple tree flowers in the spring.*

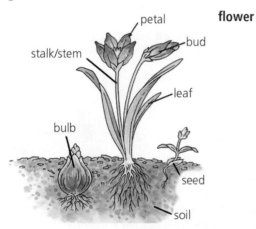

**flower**
- petal
- bud
- stalk/stem
- leaf
- bulb
- seed
- soil

**flow·ered** /**flow**-urd/ *adjective* covered in a flower pattern: *She wore a flowered dress.*

**flown** /flohn/ *verb* the past participle of fly

**flu** /floo/ *noun* an illness that is like a bad cold but can be very serious. Flu gives you a fever and makes your body ache: *She's at home in bed today – she has the flu.* (SYNONYM: **influenza**)

**flu·ent** /**floo**-uhnt/ *adjective* able to speak a language very well without thinking about it: *Miguel has lived in the U.S. for ten years and he speaks fluent English.*
—**fluently** /**floo**-unt-lee/ *adverb* in a fluent way: *She speaks Spanish fluently.*
—**fluency** /**floo**-uhnss-ee/ *noun* the ability to speak a language well without thinking about it: *Your grammar is good, but you need to improve your fluency.*

**fluff** /fluhf/ *noun* soft light pieces of thread that come off wool, fur, etc.: *The cushions are covered in fluff after the cat has been sitting on them.*

**fluff·y** /**fluhf**-ee/ *adjective*
**1** soft and light: *a fluffy new towel*
**2** having soft fur or feathers: *The duck has a lot of fluffy chicks.*

**fluffy**

a fluffy kitten

**flu·id** /**floo**-id/ *noun* a liquid: *Players need to drink plenty of fluids after a game.*

**flung** /fluhng/ *verb* the past tense and past participle of **fling**

**flunk** /fluhngk/ *verb*
**1** to fail a test or class: *I flunked my history test because I didn't study hard enough.*
**2** **flunk out** to have to leave a college because your work is not good enough: *He flunked out of law school.*

**fluo·res·cent** /flu-**ress**-uhnt/ *adjective*
**1** a fluorescent light is a very bright electric light. The light bulb is usually in the shape of a tube: *One of the fluorescent lights in the classroom went out.*
**2** fluorescent colors are very bright: *The workers wore fluorescent yellow jackets so that car drivers could see them easily.*

**fluor·ide** /**floor**-īd/ *noun* a chemical that helps stop your teeth from getting small holes in them. Fluoride is put in toothpaste and sometimes in water.

a b c d e **f** g h i j k l m n o p q r s t u v w x y z

a
b
c
d
e
**f**
g
h
i
j
k
l
m
n
o
p
q
r
s
t
u
v
w
x
y
z

**flur·ry** /**flur**-ee/ *noun* (plural **flurries**)
**1** a sudden short period of activity or excitement: *There was a flurry of activity in school today because we're getting ready for a visit from the mayor.*
**2** a small amount of snow that falls and blows around: *There was a sudden flurry of snow outside my window.*

**flush** /fluhsh/ *verb*
**1** if you flush a toilet, you make water go through it to clean it: *Remember to flush the toilet and wash your hands.*
**2** if you flush, your face becomes red because you feel embarrassed, angry, or excited: *The little boy's cheeks flushed with embarrassment because he knew he had done something wrong.*

**flushed** /fluhsht/ *adjective* if your face is flushed, it is red: *Mark's face was flushed and he was sweating nervously.*

**flute** /floot/ *noun* a metal musical instrument like a straight pipe. You play it by blowing air across a hole and opening and closing holes with your fingers. ▶ see picture at **woodwinds**
—**flutist** /**floot**-ist/ *noun* someone who plays the flute

**Word Origin: flute**

**Flute** comes from old French. The French word may have come from a Latin word that means "to blow," because you blow into a flute to play it.

flute

**flut·ter** /**fluht**-ur/ *verb*
**1** to make small movements in the air: *The flags fluttered in the wind.*
**2** if a small bird or an insect flutters somewhere, it flies there: *Butterflies fluttered over the fields.*

**fly** /flī/
● *verb* (**flies**, **flying**, **flew** /floo/, **flown** /flohn/)
**1** to move through the air: *I love to watch birds flying in the sky.* ▶ see **Thesaurus**
**2** to travel by airplane: *They are flying to Florida for their vacation.*
**3** to control an airplane: *When I'm older I want to learn to fly a plane.*
**4** if a flag is flying, it is being shown on a pole: *The American flag flies above the White House.*
**5** to suddenly move very quickly: *When she saw her father coming up the path she flew into his arms.*
● *noun* (plural **flies**)
**1** a common small flying insect: *There were flies all around the food and it smelled really bad.*
▶ see picture on page **A5**
**2** the part at the front of a pair of pants that you can open: *Your fly is unzipped.*

**fly·ing sau·cer** /flī-ing **soss**-ur/ *noun* a space vehicle shaped like a plate, which some people believe is from another planet (SYNONYM: **UFO**)

**foal** /fohl/ *noun* a very young horse

**foam** /fohm/ *noun*
**1** a lot of very small bubbles on the top of a liquid: *The soap bubbles made a white foam in the sink.*
**2** a very light solid substance that changes shape easily when it is pressed: *They put foam inside a football helmet to protect your head.*

foam

foam

**fo·cus** /**fohk**-uhss/
● *verb*
**1** to give your attention to something: *It's difficult to focus on my work when there is so much noise around me.*
**2** to move part of a camera or telescope so that you can see something clearly: *Hold up your camera and focus on the object you want to photograph.*
**3** if your eyes focus, you start seeing something clearly: *I tried to read, but my eyes would not focus right.*
—**focused** /**fohk**-uhst/ *adjective* giving all your attention to something: *If we stay focused, we can win this game.*

● *noun*
**1** the person or thing that gets the most attention: *The new girl in our class was the focus of everyone's attention.*
**2** if a photograph or image is in focus, it is clear. If it is out of focus, it is not clear: *Almost every picture she took was out of focus.*

**foe** /foh/ *noun* an enemy: *The king had many foes who wanted to kill him.*
( ANTONYMS: **ally, friend** )

**fog** /fahg/ *noun* cloudy air near the ground that is difficult to see through: *The fog was very thick and we couldn't see the end of the street.*
▶ see **Thesaurus**
—**foggy** /**fahg**-ee/ *adjective* not clear because of fog: *He switched on his headlights because it was very foggy.*

**foil** /foyl/ *noun* very thin metal, used for covering food: *Cover the turkey with foil before you put it in the oven.*

**fold** /fohld/
● *verb*
**1** to bend clothes or paper and make one part cover another part: *Fold the paper in half to make the card.*
**2** to make a table, chair, or bed smaller by bringing parts of it closer together: *You can fold the chairs up so that they are flat.*
**3** to bend your arms across your chest: *He folded his arms and looked at me angrily.*
● *noun*
a place on a piece of paper or cloth where it is bent: *Make a fold in the paper and cut along the fold.*

**fold**

fold a sheet of paper          fold your arms

**fold·er** /**fohld**-ur/ *noun*
**1** a large folded piece of strong paper, in which you keep letters or documents: *My homework is in a blue folder on my desk.*

**2** a group of computer files that are stored together on a computer: *She keeps all her digital pictures in a special folder on her computer.*

**fo·li·age** /**fohl**-ee-ij/ *noun* the leaves of a plant or tree: *The tree has dark green foliage.*

**folk** /fohk/ *adjective* traditional and made or done by the ordinary people who live in a country: *"I've Been Working on the Railroad" is a famous folk song.*

**folk·lore** /**fohk**-lor/ *noun* the stories, beliefs, and actions that the ordinary people in a country pass along to their children: *American folklore is full of stories about people who cross the wilderness to make a new life for themselves.*

**folks** /fohkss/ *plural noun*
**1** people in general: *Despite the rain, most folks had a good time.*
**2** your parents: *You should call your folks to tell them what time you'll be home.*

**folk tale** /**fohk** tayl/ *noun* an old story that people tell their children: *"The Little Red Hen" is a folk tale that teaches us about helping other people.*

**fol·low** /**fahl**-oh/ *verb*
**1** to move along behind someone: *Joe was in front and the others were following him.*
▶ see **Thesaurus**
**2** to do what orders or instructions tell you to do: *In any game, you have to follow the rules. | It's easy to make a cake if you follow the recipe.*
**3** to continue on a road: *Follow this road for around two miles.*
**4** to do the same thing as someone else: *When one person in a group starts to do something, the others usually follow.*
**5** to understand what someone says or a story: *I couldn't follow the teacher's explanation.*
**6** to happen immediately after something else: *It became dark and cloudy and rain soon followed.*
**7 follow through** to do what you have promised to do or started doing: *He followed through on his promise and got ice cream cones for the kids.*
**8 follow up** to find out more about something, or to do more about something: *The kids should follow up on what they have learned in class by looking on the Internet.*

a
b
c
d
e
**f**
g
h
i
j
k
l
m
n
o
p
q
r
s
t
u
v
w
x
y
z

**fol·low·er** /**fahl**-oh-ur/ *noun* someone who believes in someone's ideas or supports them: *Buddha told his followers to help others.*

**fol·low·ing** /**fahl**-oh-ing/
● *adjective* the following day, week, or year is the next day, week, or year: *I arrived on Tuesday, and Bobby arrived the following morning.*
● *preposition* immediately after something or as a result of something: *Following their victory, the team is feeling more confident.*

**fond** /fahnd/ *adjective* if you are fond of someone or something, you like that person or thing very much: *He's very fond of ice cream.*
—**fondly** /**fahnd**-lee/ *adverb* in a way that shows you like someone or something very much: *She looked fondly at her grandson.*
—**fondness** /**fahnd**-niss/ *noun* love for a person or thing: *She has always had a fondness for jigsaw puzzles.*

**food** /food/ *noun* things that people, animals, and plants eat: *We went to the grocery store to buy food.*

**food chain** /**food** chayn/ *noun* a food chain shows which animals eat other animals or plants. For example, a fox eats rabbits and rabbits eat grass, so the food chain is grass → rabbits → fox.

**food pro·ces·sor** /**food** prahss-ess-ur/ *noun* a piece of electrical equipment that cuts or mixes food very quickly

**food stamps** /**food** stampss/ *plural noun* special pieces of paper for buying food that the U.S. government gives to people who have very little money

**food web** /**food** web/ *noun* a food web shows how animals and plants are connected by what they eat. For example, a tree has seeds that mice, birds, and insects eat. The birds also eat the insects. Snakes and owls eat the mice.

**fool** /fool/
● *noun*
a stupid person: *I may not be as smart as you, but I'm not a fool.* (SYNONYM: **idiot**)

IDIOM with **fool**
**make a fool of yourself** to do something silly or embarrassing, which other people can see: *He made a fool of himself on national television because he did not know the answer to a simple question.*
● *verb*
**1** to make someone believe something that is not true: *The man tried to fool us into believing he was a doctor.*
**2 fool around** to behave in a silly way and

**food chain**

sun
grass
jackrabbit
hawk

waste time: *Stop fooling around and get on with your work!*

**fool·ish** /**fool**-ish/ *adjective* silly or not sensible: *It's foolish to worry about something that may never happen.* (SYNONYM: **stupid**)
—**foolishly** /**fool**-ish-lee/ *adverb* in a foolish way: *I foolishly agreed to help him with his work.*
—**foolishness** /**fool**-ish-niss/ *noun* foolish behavior: *I've had enough of your foolishness – settle down!*

**fool·proof** /**fool**-proof/ *adjective* certain to be successful: *There's no foolproof way to stop traffic accidents completely.*

**foot** /fut/ *noun*
**1** (plural **feet** /feet/) the part of your body at the end of your leg, which you stand on: *I need some new sneakers because my feet have grown.*
**2** (plural **feet** or **foot**) a length equal to 12 inches, used for measuring things: *Sarah is five feet tall.*
**3** the bottom part of something: *My cat sleeps at the foot of my bed.* | *The house was at the foot of the mountain.*

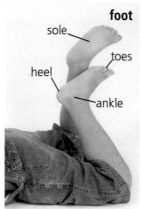
**foot**
sole
toes
heel
ankle

> **IDIOMS with foot**
> **on foot** if you go somewhere on foot, you walk there: *Sometimes I bike to school, sometimes I go on foot.*
> **put your foot down** to say very firmly that someone must or must not do something: *I really wanted to go to the party, but Mom put her foot down and said "no."*

**foot·ball** /**fut**-bol/ *noun*
**1** a game in which two teams of 11 players try to win points by kicking, carrying, or throwing a ball to the end of a field: *He plays football for the Chicago Bears.* ▶ see picture on page **A10**
**2** the ball that you use in this game: *I kicked the football over the wall.*

**foot·print** /**fut**-print/ *noun* a mark made by a foot or shoe: *There were fresh footprints in the snow.* ▶ see picture at **fingerprint**

**foot·step** /**fut**-step/ *noun* the sound of each step when someone is walking: *I heard footsteps coming toward the door.*

**foot·wear** /**fut**-wair/ *noun* things that you wear on your feet, such as shoes or boots: *You need special footwear for hiking.*

**for** /fur, for/ *preposition*
**1** used when you are saying who gets something or is helped by something: *I made cookies for you.* | *My grandma babysits for us when our mom goes out.*
**2** used when you are explaining the purpose or reason: *That knife is for cutting bread.* | *He got punished for breaking a window.*
**3** used when you are saying how long something continues: *They've lived here for ten years.* | *We waited for almost an hour.*
**4** used when saying where a person or vehicle is going: *What time do you usually leave for school?*
**5** used when talking about distance: *We walked for about six miles.*
**6** used when talking about the price of something: *I got these sneakers for $35.*
**7** used when saying what you eat at a meal: *What did you have for breakfast?*
**8** used when saying that someone is part of a company or team: *My mother works for a bank.* | *I play for the school basketball team.*
**9** used when saying that you support someone or something: *I voted for my friend in the student council election.* (ANTONYM: **against**)
**10** used when saying that a word has a particular meaning: *What's the Spanish word for oil?*

> **Word Choice:** for, since, ago
>
> **Ago**, **for**, and **since** are all used to talk about time.
>
> **For** is used to say how long something has lasted: *I have lived here for three years.* | *She waited for ten minutes.*
>
> **Since** is used to say when something started: *It's been raining since Monday.* | *I've been going to school here since 2010.*
>
> **Ago** is used to say how far back in the past something happened: *I moved here two years ago.* | *The movie started 15 minutes ago.*

**for·bid** /fur-**bid**/ *verb* (**forbade** /fur-**bad**/, **forbidden** /fur-**bid**'n/) to order someone not to do something: *Her parents have forbidden her from staying out late.* (ANTONYM: **permit**)
▶ see Thesaurus
—**forbidden** /fur-**bid**'n/ *adjective* not allowed: *Riding your bike on the grass is forbidden.*

**force** /forss/
● *verb*
**1** to make someone do something that he or she does not want to do: *The bad weather forced us to stay indoors.* | *He was innocent, but he was forced to sign a paper saying he was guilty.*
**2** to use your strength to move something: *The door was locked, but we managed to force it open.*
● *noun*
**1** a group of people who do military or police work: *Her dad served in the armed forces - he was an army captain.*
**2** physical violence that someone uses in order to achieve something: *The officers had to use force to arrest the man.*
**3** the strength or physical power that something has: *Big waves were hitting the rocks with great force.*
**4** an action that moves things or has a physical effect on them: *The force of gravity pulls everything downward.*

**ford** /ford/ *noun* a place where a river is not deep, so that you can cross it without a bridge: *The horses and wagons crossed the ford in the river.*

**fore-** /for/

## Word Building

**fore-** is a prefix.
**fore**cast | **fore**head | **fore**see
**fore-** means "before." The weather *forecast* tells you what the weather will be tomorrow or the next day, before it happens. Your *forehead* is in front of the rest of your head. If you *foresee* a problem, you see that the problem might happen before it does happen.

**fore·arm** /**for**-arm/ *noun* the part of your arm between your hand and your elbow: *She rested her forearms on the desk.* ▶ see picture on page **A13**

**fore·cast** /**for**-kast/ *noun* a description of what is likely to happen: *The weather forecast says it is going to snow tomorrow.*
—**forecast** /**for**-kast/ *verb* to say what is likely to happen: *They are forecasting rain this weekend.*

**fore·fa·thers** /**for** fahth-urz/ *plural noun* the members of your family who lived a long time ago: *Our forefathers came here hundreds of years ago.* (SYNONYM: **ancestors**)

**fore·head** /**for**-hed/ *noun* the part of your face above your eyes: *His hair covers his forehead.*
▶ see picture on page **A13**

**for·eign** /**far**-in/ *adjective* from or relating to a country that is not your own: *Can you speak any foreign languages?*

**for·eign·er** /**far**-uhn-ur/ *noun* someone who comes from a country that is not your country: *They live in a tiny village and they have never seen a foreigner before.* ▶ see Thesaurus

**fore·man** /**for**-muhn/ *noun* (plural **foremen** /**for**-muhn/)
**1** someone who is in charge of a group of workers: *Dad asked his foreman if he could leave work early.*
**2** the leader of a jury: *The judge asked the foreman if the jury had reached a decision.*

**fore·most** /**for**-mohst/ *adjective* the best or most important: *He is one of America's foremost artists.*

**fore·see** /for-**see**/ *verb* (**foresaw** /for-**sor**/, **foreseen** /for-**seen**/) to imagine that something will happen in the future: *Nobody could foresee that the accident would happen.*

**for·est** /**for**-ist/ *noun* a large area of land covered with trees: *It is easy to get lost in the forest because the trees grow very close together.* ▶ see picture on page **A11**
▶ see Thesaurus

**for·ev·er** /fuhr-**ev**-ur/ *adverb*
**1** for all of the time in the future: *I want to stay here forever.* | *Many of the world's forests have been cut down and are gone forever.*
**2** for a very long time: *The test seemed to go on forever.*

**fore·word** /**for**-wurd/ *noun* a short piece of writing at the beginning of a book that gives information about the book or the person who wrote it: *In the foreword the author explains why he wrote the book.*

**for·gave** /fur-**gayv**/ *verb* the past tense of **forgive**

**forge** /forj/ *verb* to make an illegal copy of something such as a painting or money to make people think it is real: *The man forged his mother's signature on the letter to make people think that she wrote it.*

**for·ger·y** /**forj**-uhr-ee/ *noun* (plural **forgeries**)
**1** a document, painting, or piece of paper money that someone has illegally copied: *The painting looks like the original one, but it's a forgery.*
SYNONYM: **fake**
**2** the crime of illegally copying something: *He made fake $100 bills and was sent to jail for forgery.*

**for·get** /fur-**get**/ *verb* (**forgetting**, **forgot** /fur-**gaht**/, **forgotten** /fur-**gaht**'n/)
**1** to not remember facts, information, or something that happened: *I'm sorry, I've forgotten your name.* | *I'll never forget about this wonderful day.*
**2** to not remember to do something that you should do: *Don't forget to lock the door.*
**3** to not remember to bring something with you: *Oh, no, I've forgotten my swimsuit.*

> ## Word Choice: forget, leave
>
> You can say "I forgot my homework."
>
> You cannot say "I forgot my homework at home."
>
> When you want to talk about the place where you left something by mistake, you must use "leave": *I left my homework at home.*

**for·get·ful** /fur-**get**-fuhl/ *adjective* often forgetting things that you should remember: *Lily is so forgetful – she never brings the right books to school.*

**for·give** /fur-**giv**/ *verb* (**forgave** /fur-**gayv**/, **forgiven** /fur-**giv**-uhn/) to stop being angry with someone who has done something wrong: *I will never forgive him for being so mean to me.*

▶ see **Thesaurus**
—**forgiveness** /fur-**giv**-niss/ *noun* the act of forgiving someone: *He said he was really sorry and begged for forgiveness.*

**fork** /fork/
● *noun*
**1** a small tool that you use for picking up food when you eat. A fork has three or four sharp points called prongs: *Can you put the knives and forks on the table?*
**2** a place where a road or river divides into two parts: *I came to a fork in the road and turned left.*
● *verb*
if a road or river forks, it divides into two parts: *The river forks and becomes two smaller rivers.*

**fork**

fork

a fork in the road

**forked** /forkt/ *adjective* divided at the end, in the shape of a letter "y": *The snake has a forked tongue.*

**form** /form/
● *noun*
**1** a type of something: *These days, people use many different forms of communication, including email, cell phones, and texting.*
SYNONYM: **kind**
**2** an official document with spaces where you have to write information: *If you want to join the sports club, you have to fill out this form.*
**3** a shape: *The hook is in the form of a letter "S."*
● *verb*
**1** to start to exist: *A line of students formed outside the school door.*
**2** to start a new organization or group: *My dad and my uncle formed a company.*
**3** to be something: *The river forms the border between the United States and Mexico.*

**for·mal** /**form**-uhl/ *adjective*
**1** formal clothes and language are suitable for important or official situations: *You need to wear formal clothes for a job interview - you shouldn't wear jeans.* | *"Purchase" is a formal word which means "buy."* ( ANTONYM: **informal** )
**2** a formal occasion is an important event, such as a wedding or a graduation ceremony: *The hall is used for formal occasions, for example graduation ceremonies.*
**3** a formal statement is made by someone who represents the government or an official organization: *The president will make a formal announcement later today.* ( ANTONYM: **informal** )
—**formally** /**form**-uhl-ee/ *adverb* in a formal way: *The winner will be formally announced this afternoon.*

**Word Family:** formal

**formal** *adjective* | **informal** *adjective* | **formally** *adverb* | **informally** *adverb* | **informality** *noun*

**for·mat** /**form**-at/ *noun*
**1** the size, shape, or design of a book or magazine: *The books are published in a large format to make them easy for young children to hold.*
**2** the way that something is organized or arranged: *We have changed the format of the class, so that every student can have a chance to speak.*

**for·ma·tion** /for-**maysh**-uhn/ *noun*
**1** the process of making a new organization: *The two schools were joined together, and this resulted in the formation of a new school.*
**2** something that has been formed into a particular shape: *The strange rock formations were created by the effect of the wind and water.*

**for·mer** /**form**-ur/
● *adjective* having a particular job or position in the past, but not now: *Her former students all say that she is a very good teacher.*
● *noun* the first of two people or things that are mentioned: *He visited London and Paris, spending two days in the former and one day in the latter.* ( ANTONYM: **latter** )

**for·mer·ly** /**form**-ur-lee/ *adverb* in the past, not now: *New York was formerly called New Amsterdam.*

**for·mi·da·ble** /for-**mid**-uh-buhl/ *adjective*
**1** very difficult to deal with: *The engineers faced formidable problems when building the bridge.*
**2** very powerful or impressive: *He is a player with formidable talents.*

**for·mu·la** /**form**-yuhl-uh/ *noun*
**1** a series of numbers or letters that represent a mathematical or scientific rule: *If the length of one side of a square is "X," the area of the square can be calculated using the formula $X^2$.*
**2** a liquid food for babies that is similar to a mother's milk: *The baby drinks formula.*

**fort** /fort/ *noun* a strong building used to defend an important place. The fort has soldiers in it: *Seven hundred Sioux warriors attacked the fort and forced the soldiers to surrender.*

fort

Fort Mandan

**forth** /forth/ *adverb* toward a place that is in front of you: *The soldiers went forth into battle.*

**for·tress** /**fort**-riss/ *noun* a large strong building that soldiers use for defending an important place

**for·tu·nate** /**forch**-uhn-it/ *adjective* in a good situation because of luck: *You're fortunate that you have such wonderful parents.*
( SYNONYM: **lucky** ) ( ANTONYM: **unfortunate** )

**for·tu·nate·ly** /**forch**-uhn-it-lee/ *adverb* happening because of good luck: *I fell off my bike, but fortunately I didn't hurt myself badly.*
( ANTONYM: **unfortunately** )

**for·tune** /**forch**-uhn/ *noun*
**1** a very large amount of money: *The house cost*

**fossil**

*a fortune – my dad paid over $1 million for it.*
**2** luck: *I have the good fortune to have Miss Lee as a teacher this year.*
**3** what will happen to you in the future: *A woman at the fair was telling people's fortunes.*

> ### Word Family: fortune
>
> **fortune** *noun* | **misfortune** *noun* | **fortunate** *adjective* | **unfortunate** *adjective* | **fortunately** *adverb* | **unfortunately** *adverb*

**for·ty** /**fort**-ee/ *number*
**1** 40: *I have forty dollars.*
**2** forty years old: *My dad is forty.*
**3** the forties the years between 1940 and 1949: *The college was built in the forties.*
**4** in your forties between 40 and 49 years old: *Mom and her friends are all in their forties.*
**5** in the forties between 40 and 49 degrees in temperature: *It was cold in the night, in the forties.*
—**fortieth** /**fort**-ee-ith/ *number* 40th or 1/40

**fo·rum** /**for**-uhm/ *noun* a place or meeting where people can discuss things: *There's a forum on the Internet where you can get advice about keeping fish.*

**for·ward** /**for**-wurd/
● *adverb* toward a place that is in front of you: *If you move forward you'll be able to see better.*
ANTONYM: **backward**
● *adjective* toward a place that is in front of you: *The cat made a sudden forward movement toward the door.*
● *verb* to send a letter or email that has been sent to you to another person: *Will you forward her email to me so I can read it?*
● *noun* a player on a basketball, hockey, or soccer team whose job is to score points or goals

**fos·sil** /**fahss**-uhl/ *noun* a rock that shows part of an animal or plant that lived thousands or millions of years ago. Fossils were made by parts of the animal or plant slowly turning into rock, or pressing against a rock: *Scientists have learned about dinosaurs from their fossils.*

**fos·sil fu·el** /**fahss**-uhl fyoo-uhl/ *noun* a substance such as coal, gas, or oil that can be burned for energy. Fossil fuels are formed from plants and animals that died millions of years ago.

**fos·ter** /**fahst**-ur/
● *verb* to take care of someone else's child for a period of time without becoming the child's legal parent: *The family fostered the boys for five years, until they were 18.*
● *adjective* relating to an arrangement in which a child is taken care of by someone who is not his or her parent: *He lived with foster parents while his mother was in the hospital.*

**fought** /fot/ *verb* the past tense and past participle of **fight**

**foul** /fowl/
● *adjective*
**1** tasting or smelling very bad: *There was a foul smell of rotten eggs.*
**2** rude and offensive: *Mom does not allow any foul language in the house.*
**3** stormy and windy, with a lot of rain or snow: *The foul weather continued for days, so we stayed indoors and played games.*
● *noun*
an action in a sport that is not allowed by the rules: *When you have five fouls you have to leave the game.*
● *verb*
to do something, especially to another player, that is not allowed by the rules of a sport: *If you foul another player, your team will get a penalty.*

**found** /fownd/ *verb*
**1** the past tense and past participle of **find**
**2** to start a business, organization, or school: *The Boys Choir of Harlem was founded in 1968.*

**foun·da·tion** /fown-**daysh**-uhn/ *noun*
**1** the solid base that supports a building. The foundation is below the ground and the building is built on top of it: *They discovered the foundations of an ancient temple under the ground.*
**2** an important basic idea, fact, or system that something is based on or develops from: *Reading, writing, and arithmetic provide the foundation for a child's education.*
**3** an organization that gives money to be used for particular purposes: *The foundation helps children from poor families.*

**found·er** /**fownd**-ur/ *noun* someone who starts a business, organization, or school: *There is a statue of the town's founder in the main square.*

**foun·tain** /**fownt**-uhn/ *noun*
**1** an object that makes water go up in the air or pour down its sides. Fountains are used to decorate places such as parks: *Water sprayed out of the fountain into the air.*
**2** an object that you drink from without using a cup. The water comes upward in a stream that you put your mouth over: *I got a drink from the water fountain.*

fountain

**four** /for/ *number*
**1** 4: *I have four brothers.*
**2** four o'clock: *I have swimming lessons at four.*
**3** four years old: *My sister will be four next week.*

**four·teen** /for-**teen**/ *number*
**1** 14: *It's 14 miles to the next town.*
**2** fourteen years old: *Grandma left school when she was only fourteen.*
—**fourteenth** /for-**teenth**/ *number* 14th or 1/14

**fourth** /forth/ *number*
**1** 4th
**2** 1/4 ( SYNONYM: **quarter** )

**Fourth of Ju·ly** /forth uhv joo-**lī**/ *noun* a national holiday in the U.S. to celebrate the time when the U.S. first became an independent nation ( SYNONYM: **Independence Day** )

**fowl** /fowl/ *noun* (plural **fowl** or **fowls**) a bird such as a chicken or a turkey that is kept for its meat and eggs

**fox** /fahkss/ *noun* a wild animal like a small dog with red-brown fur and a furry tail

fox

**frac·tion** /**frak**-shuhn/ *noun*
**1** a part of a whole number, for example 3/4 or 1/2: *Today, we are going to learn how to add fractions.*
**2** a very small amount of something: *His shot missed the target by just a fraction of an inch.*
—**fractional** /**frak**-shuhn-uhl/ *adjective* the fractional part of a number is the part that comes after the decimal point: *The fractional part of 5/2 (= 2.5) is 1/2 (= 0.5).*

**frac·ture** /**frak**-chur/
● *verb* to crack or break a bone in your body: *He fell off his bike and fractured his arm.*
● *noun* a crack or break in a bone: *The X-ray shows that Anthony has a fracture in his foot.*

**frag·ile** /**fraj**-uhl/ *adjective* easily broken or damaged: *Be careful when you pick the flowers because they are very fragile.* ( ANTONYM: **strong** )

**frag·ment** /**frag**-muhnt/ *noun* a small piece that has broken off a larger object: *Someone has broken a window and there are fragments of glass all over the sidewalk.*

**fra·grance** /**frayg**-ruhnss/ *noun*
**1** a nice smell: *The sweet fragrance of roses filled the room.* ( SYNONYM: **smell** )
**2** perfume: *I'm trying a new fragrance. Do you like the way it smells?*

**fra·grant** /**frayg**-ruhnt/ *adjective* having a nice smell: *The rose has beautiful fragrant flowers.*

**frame** /fraym/
● *noun*
**1** a structure that is around a picture, door, or window: *The photo is in a silver frame.*
**2** the main structure of a house, vehicle, or piece of furniture. The frame supports the other parts: *The frame of the house is made of wood.*
**3 frames** the part of a pair of glasses that holds the glass lens: *He is wearing dark glasses with black frames.*
● *verb*
**1** to put a picture in a frame: *That's a beautiful photograph – you should frame it and hang it on the wall.*
**2** to try to make someone seem guilty of a crime by deliberately giving false information: *He claims that the police tried to frame him for the murder.*

**frame**

frames

lens

frame

frame

**frame·work** /**fraym**-wurk/ *noun*
**1** the basic structure of a building or vehicle, that supports the rest of it: *The bridge is built on a strong steel framework.*
**2** a plan or system that other details can be added to: *The lesson plan gives the teacher a basic framework for what the students will do each day.*

**frank** /frangk/ *adjective* saying things in an honest and direct way: *The coach was frank with me and told me I was not good enough to play on the team.*
—**frankly** /**frangk**-lee/ *adverb* in an honest and direct way: *I hope you won't be offended if I speak frankly.*

**frank·fur·ter** /**frangk**-furt-ur/ *noun* a type of sausage ( SYNONYM: **hot dog** )

**fran·tic** /**frant**-ik/ *adjective* very worried or excited, so that you rush around: *My alarm clock didn't go off and I had to get ready for school in a frantic rush.*
—**frantically** /**frant**-ik-lee/ *adverb* in a frantic way: *He looked frantically for his house keys.*

**fraud** /frod/ *noun*
**1** the crime of deceiving people in order to get money or goods: *The man lied about how much money he earned, and he was arrested for fraud.*
**2** someone who pretends to be someone else in order to deceive people: *He isn't a real doctor – he's a fraud.*

**fray** /fray/ *verb* if a cloth or rope frays, its threads become loose at the edge because it is old or torn: *The shirt is old and the collar is beginning to fray.*
—**frayed** /frayd/ *adjective* with loose threads at the edge: *There was an old frayed blanket on the bed.*

**freak** /freek/
● *noun*
**1** someone who is very interested in a particular subject or activity: *My brother is a sports freak – when he's not playing sports, he's watching sports on TV.*
**2** someone who looks very strange or behaves in a very unusual way: *There were all sorts of freaks hanging around the bus station late at night.*
● *adjective*
a freak accident or storm is very unusual and strange: *Last summer there was a freak snowstorm and school was closed.*

**freck·le** /**frek**-uhl/ *noun* a small light brown spot on someone's skin, especially on the face: *He had red hair and a lot of freckles.*
—**freckled** /**frek**-uhld/ *adjective* having freckles: *She had a smiling freckled face.*

**freckle**

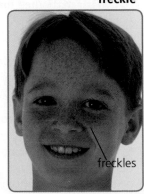

freckles

**free** /free/
- *adjective*

**1** if something is free, it does not cost any money: *I got free tickets to the concert because my aunt works at the theater.*
**2** allowed to do what you want and not controlled by other people: *At break time, the kids are free to play in the yard. | At last the slaves were free.*
**3** not busy doing other things: *If you're free this weekend, why don't you come over to my house?*
**4** not being used: *Excuse me, is this seat free?*
**5** not containing something: *The candy is free of artificial colors or flavors.*

- *adverb*

**1** without having to pay any money: *Entry to the museum is $2.50, but students can get in free.*
**2** able to move without being controlled or kept in one place: *I think wild animals should be allowed to run free, not kept in zoos.*

- *verb*

to let someone leave a place where he or she has been forced to stay: *The judge freed the men after they proved they were innocent.*
▶ see **Thesaurus**

**free·dom** /**freed**-uhm/ *noun*

**1** the state of being free and allowed to do what you want: *He believes that kids today have too much freedom. | This is his first day of freedom after ten years in jail.* ▶ see **Thesaurus**
**2** the legal right to do something, without the government stopping you: *People have the freedom to follow whatever religion they choose.*

**free·ly** /**free**-lee/ *adverb* without anyone or anything controlling or stopping something: *The wall has been taken down, and people can travel freely from one side of the city to the other.*

**free mar·ket** /free **mark**-it/ *noun* a system in which the government does not control prices, or control who can buy and sell things

**free·way** /**free**-way/ *noun* a very wide road on which cars can go very fast: *We took the freeway down to Los Angeles.*

**freeze** /freez/ *verb* (**froze** /frohz/, **frozen** /**frohz**-uhn/)

**1** if water freezes, it becomes solid and hard because it is very cold: *The temperature was below zero and the pond froze.* (ANTONYM: **thaw**)

**2** to put food in a freezer so you can keep it longer: *We'll freeze the rest of the fish and eat it later.* (ANTONYM: **defrost**)
**3** to suddenly stop moving and stay very still: *The cat froze when it saw the bird.*

**freez·er** /**freez**-ur/ *noun* a large piece of electrical equipment that freezes food so that you can keep it for a long time: *Put the ice cream in the freezer.*

**freez·ing** /**freez**-ing/
- *adjective* very cold: *Close the window – it's freezing in here. | I need a sweater. I'm freezing cold.*
- *noun* 32°F or 0°C, the temperature at which water freezes: *The temperature stayed below freezing all day.*

**freight** /frayt/ *noun* goods that trucks, airplanes, or ships take from one place to another: *A train passed, carrying freight.*

**French** /french/
- *adjective*
from France: *Do you like French food? | His mother is French.*
—**Frenchman** /**french**-muhn/ *noun* a man from France
—**Frenchwoman** /**french**-wum-uhn/ *noun* a woman from France
- *noun*
**1** the language spoken in France and in parts of Belgium, Switzerland, and Canada: *She speaks French.*
**2** the people of France: *The French are very proud of their cheeses.*

**French fries** /french **friz**/ *plural noun* long thin pieces of potato cooked in hot oil: *I'll have a cheeseburger and French fries.* (SYNONYM: **fries**)

**French horn** /french **horn**/ *noun* a metal instrument shaped like a circle, that you play by blowing into it and pressing keys ▶ see picture on page **A8**

**French toast** /french **tohst**/ *noun* bread covered with a mixture of eggs and milk and cooked in a pan: *I'll make French toast for breakfast.*

**fren·zy** /**frenz**-ee/ *noun* if people are in a frenzy, they are very excited or worried, and cannot control their behavior: *The team won and the fans went into a frenzy and started cheering.*

**fre·quen·cy** /**freek**-wuhnss-ee/ *noun*
**1** the number of times that something happens: *The frequency of accidents has increased because there are so many cars on the road.*
**2** the rate at which a sound or light wave is repeated. Frequency is used to talk about how high a sound is, or how strong a light is: *Dogs can hear high frequency sounds that humans cannot hear.*

**fre·quent** /**freek**-wuhnt/ *adjective* happening very often: *You should take frequent breaks from your computer – at least once every hour.*

ANTONYM: **infrequent**

—**frequently** /**freek**-wuhnt-lee/ *adverb* very often: *He goes to the gym frequently, sometimes every day.*

**Word Family:** frequent

**frequent** *adjective* | **infrequent** *adjective* | **frequently** *adverb* | **infrequently** *adverb* | **frequency** *noun*

**fresh** /fresh/ *adjective*
**1** fresh food has been picked or produced recently: *The bread is fresh – I made it this morning.* | *It's important to eat plenty of fresh fruit.*
**2** new or clean, and replacing what was used before: *The sheets are dirty and I need to put some fresh ones on the bed.*
**3** interesting and different from what has been done before: *The new teacher has lots of fresh ideas about teaching science and the students like her classes.*
**4** fresh air is clean air that you breathe when you are outdoors: *I've been sitting in the classroom all morning and I need some fresh air.*
**5** fresh water has no salt in it and comes from rivers and lakes: *The fish lives in fresh water.*
—**freshly** /**fresh**-lee/ *adverb* recently: *I love the smell of freshly baked bread.*
—**freshness** /**fresh**-niss/ *noun* a fresh quality: *Mom was impressed with the freshness of the fruit at the farmer's market.*

**fresh·man** /**fresh**-muhn/ *noun* (plural **freshmen** /**fresh**-muhn/) a student in the first year of high school or college

**fret** /fret/ *verb* (**fretting**, **fretted**) to worry about things that are not very important: *Keisha was fretting about being late for the party.*

**fric·tion** /**frik**-shuhn/ *noun*
**1** if there is friction between people, they disagree and argue: *Lydia was jealous of Donna's new friend, and this was causing friction between the girls.*
**2** a force that makes something move more slowly, because it is rubbing against another thing: *We oil the different parts of a bike so there is less friction when they move together.*

**Fri·day** /**frīd**-ee/ *noun*  ABBREVIATION: **Fri.**  the sixth day of the week. Friday is between Thursday and Saturday: *The party is on Friday.* | *Can you come over Friday morning?*

**Word Origin:** Friday

**Friday** is named for a goddess called Frige or Frigg in an old religion. Many people in northern Europe believed in this religion before Christianity. Frige was the most important goddess, and Friday was "Frige's day." She was the wife of the god Woden. Wednesday is named for Woden.

**fridge** /frij/ *noun* a piece of electrical equipment that you put food in to keep it cold and fresh: *Don't forget to put the milk back in the fridge.*
SYNONYM: **refrigerator**

**fried** /frīd/
● *verb* the past tense and past participle of **fry**
● *adjective* cooked in hot oil: *I like fried onions.*

**friend** /frend/ *noun* someone whom you like and enjoy spending time with: *Tony has been my best friend since second grade.* | *I've been friends with her for a long time.*
ANTONYM: **enemy** ▶ see Thesaurus
—**friendship** /**fren**-ship/ *noun* the relationship that friends have: *She hoped the argument wouldn't ruin their friendship.*

IDIOM with **friend**
**make friends** to start having someone as a friend: *I tried to make friends with him but he was very shy.*

**friend·ly** /fren-lee/ *adjective* (**friendlier, friendliest**)

**1** wanting to talk to and be nice to people you do not know: *Our new neighbors were very friendly, and they invited us over for a barbecue.*
▶ see Thesaurus

**2** if you are friendly with someone, the two of you are friends: *I used to be friendly with him, but we don't see each other now.*

—**friendliness** /fren-lee-niss/ *noun* a friendly quality: *I was surprised by the friendliness of the local people – they were very kind and helpful to me.*

**fries** /frīz/ *plural noun* long thin pieces of potato cooked in hot oil: *He ordered a hamburger and fries.* ( SYNONYM: **French fries** )

**fright** /frīt/ *noun* a sudden feeling of fear: *When he saw the man standing there it gave him a terrible fright.*

> **Word Family:** fright
>
> **fright** *noun* | **frighten** *verb* | **frightening** *adjective* | **frightened** *adjective*

**fright·en** /frīt'n/ *verb* to make someone feel afraid: *The loud noise frightened the horses.*
( SYNONYM: **scare** )

**fright·ened** /frīt'nd/ *adjective* afraid: *I am frightened of big dogs.* ( SYNONYM: **scared** )
▶ see Thesaurus

**fright·en·ing** /frīt'n-ing/ *adjective* making you feel afraid: *The movie is very frightening and it is not appropriate for young children.*
( SYNONYM: **scary** ) ▶ see Thesaurus

**fringe** /frinj/ *noun*

**1** a lot of threads that hang from the edge of a piece of clothing or a curtain. A fringe is used to decorate things: *He was wearing a cowboy jacket with a leather fringe.*

**fringe**

fringe

**2** the edge or border of something: *The airport is on the southern fringe of the town.*

**Fris·bee** /friz-bee/ *noun trademark* a piece of plastic shaped like a plate that people throw and catch as a game

**frisk** /frisk/ *verb* to move your hands over someone's clothes to see if he or she has a hidden weapon: *Security officers often frisk passengers before they get on an airplane to check for guns or knives.*

**frog** /frog/ *noun* a small green or brown animal with long legs that it uses for jumping. Frogs are amphibians, so they can live on land and in water: *A frog jumped out of the pond.*
▶ see picture on page **A1**

**from** /fruhm, frahm/ *preposition*

**1** used when saying where someone was born or lives: *I'm from Minneapolis – where are you from?*

**2** used when saying where something starts or used to be: *David ran all the way home from school.* | *Will you get me a chair from the kitchen?*

**3** used when saying what time something starts: *We worked from 2:30 to 4:00.*

**4** used when saying who has given or sent something: *The book was a gift from his father.*

**5** used when talking about the distance between two places: *I live about a mile from my school.*

**6** as a result of something: *He died from a heart attack.*

**7** used to say what is used to make something: *Butter is made from cream.*

**front** /fruhnt/

● *noun*

**1** the part of something that is farthest forward: *I sit in the front of the car, next to the driver.*
( ANTONYM: **back** )

**2** the side of something that you look at first: *The book had a picture of a lion on the front.*
( ANTONYM: **back** )

**3** the place where there is fighting in a war: *More soldiers were sent to fight on the front.*

**4** the edge of an area of warm or cold air, that makes the weather change: *A cold front is bringing more rain to the area.*

● *adjective*

at, on, or in the front of something: *She has a space between her front teeth.* ( ANTONYM: **back** )

**in front of**
**1** ahead of someone or something: *I couldn't see because a very tall man was standing in front of me.* (ANTONYM: **behind**)
**2** facing someone or something: *Can we have dinner in front of the TV?*
**3** when someone is with you: *Mom and Dad never argue in front of me. They wait until they are alone.*
**out front** in the area near the entrance of the building you are in: *Let's drive to their house and park the car out front.*

**fron·tier** /fruhn-**teer**/ *noun*
**1** the part of a country that is farthest away from the area where most people live: *Life on the frontier was very hard and there was no electricity or running water.*
**2** the place where two countries meet: *They crossed the frontier from Russia into China.*
(SYNONYM: **border**)

**frost** /frost/ *noun* white ice that covers things when it is very cold: *It was very cold and the trees were covered with frost.*
—**frosty** /**frost**-ee/ *adjective* very cold and with frost: *It was a frosty morning in January.*

**frost·bite** /**frost**-bīt/ *noun* if you get frostbite, parts of your body freeze and are badly damaged: *One of the climbers had frostbite and lost three of his toes.*

**frost·ing** /**frost**-ing/ *noun* a mixture made with sugar that you put on a cake: *I'm making chocolate frosting for the cake.* (SYNONYM: **icing**)

**frown** /frown/
● *verb* to move your eyebrows together and turn the corners of your mouth down when you are angry, unhappy, or thinking hard: *The man frowned at me and said he didn't understand my question.*
● *noun* the expression when you move your eyebrows together and turn the corners of your mouth down when you are angry, unhappy, or thinking hard: *There was a frown on the coach's face when his best player missed an easy goal.*

**froze** /frohz/ *verb* the past tense of **freeze**

**fro·zen** /**frohz**-uhn/
● *verb*
the past participle of **freeze**

● *adjective*
**1** frozen food has been made very cold so that it can be kept for a long time: *In the freezer we have frozen peas, frozen fish, and ice cream.*
**2** something that is frozen has become ice: *In the winter we skate on the frozen lake.*

**frozen**

a frozen pond

**fruit** /froot/ *noun*
**1** a type of food that grows on trees and plants and often tastes sweet. Apples and oranges are types of fruit: *Peaches are my favorite fruit.*
▶ see picture on page **A7**
**2** the part of a plant that contains the seed. The fruit develops from the flower: *The flowers produce fruit and seeds, and these grow into new plants.*

**fruit·ful** /**froot**-fuhl/ *adjective* having good and useful results: *We had a fruitful discussion about the future of the school, and people made a lot of good suggestions.*

**frus·trate** /**fruhss**-trayt/ *verb* to make you feel annoyed because you cannot do or have what you want: *It frustrates him when he can't explain what he means.*
—**frustrated** /**fruhss**-trayt-id/ *adjective* annoyed because you cannot do or have what you want: *I'm frustrated because I have to wait so long for the results of my exam.*
—**frustrating** /**fruhss**-trayt-ing/ *adjective* making you feel frustrated: *It's very frustrating when other people don't listen to me.*
—**frustration** /fruhss-**traysh**-uhn/ *noun* a frustrated feeling: *There is a lot of frustration because the team has not won any games this season.*

**fry** /frī/ *verb* (**fries**, **frying**, **fried**) to cook something in hot oil or butter: *I fried some eggs for breakfast.* ▶ see picture at **cook**

a b c d e **f** g h i j k l m n o p q r s t u v w x y z

**fry·ing pan** /**frī**-ing pan/ *noun* a round flat pan that you use to fry food. A frying pan has one long handle.
(SYNONYM: **skillet**)

frying pan

**ft.** the written abbreviation of **foot** or **feet**: *The swimming pool was 40 ft. long.*

**fudge** /fuhj/ *noun* a kind of candy, made with butter, sugar, milk, and usually chocolate: *I like eating fudge but it sticks to your teeth.*

**fu·el** /**fyoo**-uhl/ *noun* something such as coal, gas, or oil that you can burn to make heat or power: *The new planes use much less fuel than the old ones.*

**-ful** /fuhl/

## Word Building

**-ful** is a suffix. It is used in adjectives.
aw**ful** | beauti**ful** | help**ful** | joy**ful** | wonder**ful**
**-ful** means "full of." A *beautiful* woman is very pretty. She is full of beauty. A *helpful* boy helps a lot. He is full of help. A *joyful* day makes you feel very happy. It is full of joy.

**ful·fill** /ful-**fil**/ *verb* to do something you wanted or promised to do: *One year later, he fulfilled his promise and paid back the money.*
—**fulfillment** /ful-**fil**-muhnt/ *noun* the act of doing something you wanted or promised to do: *When she made her first record, it was the fulfillment of a dream for her.*

**full** /ful/ *adjective*
**1** containing so much, or so many things or people, that no more will fit in: *The refrigerator is full and there is no room for any more food.*
(ANTONYM: **empty**) ▶ see **Thesaurus**
**2** containing many things of the same kind: *His English is not very good and his essay is full of simple spelling mistakes.*
**3** complete or whole: *My full name is Jessica Anne Johnson.*
**4** as great as possible: *He was driving at full speed when he hit the tree.*

**full moon** /ful **moon**/ *noun* the Moon when it looks completely round: *There's a full moon tonight and it's really bright.*

**full time** /ful-**tīm**/ *adverb* for all the usual hours that people work or study in a week: *She worked full time until the kids were born.*
—**full-time** /**ful**-tīm/ *adjective* working or studying full time: *If you are a full-time student you don't have much time to work at a job.*

**ful·ly** /**ful**-ee/ *adverb* completely: *The kids are fully dressed and ready for school.*

**fum·ble** /**fuhm**-buhl/ *verb*
**1** to try to find or move something with your hands in an awkward way: *Gary fumbled for the light switch in the dark.*
**2** to drop a ball after catching it: *He fumbled the ball and I grabbed it.*
—**fumble** /**fuhm**-buhl/ *noun* the act of dropping a football: *Brian's fumble probably made us lose the game.*

**fumes** /fyoomz/ *plural noun* gas or smoke that smells bad: *The fumes from the traffic made her cough.*

**fun** /fuhn/
● *noun* something you enjoy doing: *Everyone was out having fun in the snow.* | *This game is a lot of fun.*

IDIOM with **fun**
**make fun of** to make unkind jokes about someone: *The other kids made fun of the way I talked.*

● *adjective* enjoyable: *There are lots of fun things to do at the beach.*

## Word Choice: fun, funny

You use **fun** to talk about situations or activities that you enjoy: *I have a lot of fun when I play with Brandon.* | *The art project was fun to do.*
You use **funny** to say that someone or something makes you laugh: *The movie was so funny we couldn't stop laughing.* | *Brandon is really funny. He's always telling jokes.*

**func·tion** /**fuhngk**-shuhn/
● *noun*
**1** the purpose or job of something: *The function*

of your heart is to pump blood around your body.
**2** a large party or social event: *She bought a new dress for a school function.*
**3** in mathematics, a number that changes as another number changes, or a relationship between two sets of numbers: *If y = 2x, then y is a function of x.*
● *verb*
**1** if something functions, it does what it should do: *The air conditioning isn't functioning correctly and it's very hot in our house.*
SYNONYM: **work**
**2** if something functions as something else, it is used like something else: *This phone can function as a camera.*

**Word Family: function**

**function** *noun* | **function** *verb* | **functional** *adjective*

**func·tion·al** /**fuhngk**-shuhn-uhl/ *adjective*
**1** designed to be useful, rather than to look nice: *The library is a functional ugly brick building.*
**2** something that is functional is able to do what it should do: *This computer is pretty old, but it's still functional.*

**fund** /fuhnd/
● *noun*
**1** an amount of money that is collected for a particular purpose: *They have put the money into a college fund for their grandson.*
**2** **funds** the money that an organization needs or has: *The hospital desperately needs more funds.*
● *verb*
to give the money that is needed for an activity or piece of work: *The company is funding research into treatments for cancer.*
SYNONYM: **pay for**

**fun·da·men·tal** /fuhnd-uh-**ment**'l/ *adjective*
relating to the most basic and important parts of something: *When my dad lost his job, there was a fundamental change in the way we lived because we suddenly had very little money.*
—**fundamentally** /fuhnd-uh-**ment**'l-ee/ *adverb* in the most basic and important way: *She doesn't believe that men's and women's personalities are fundamentally different.*

**fu·ner·al** /**fyoon**-uhr-uhl/ *noun* a ceremony for a dead person before his or body is buried or burned: *Over 250 people came to her funeral.*

**fun·gus** /**fuhng**-guhss/ *noun* (plural **fungi** /**fuhng**-gī/) a type of plant such as a mushroom or mold. Fungus often grows on decaying things or in damp places: *There was fungus growing on the fallen tree.*

**fun·nel** /**fuhn**'l/ *noun* a tube that you use to pour something into a container with a small opening. A funnel is wide at the top and narrow at the bottom.

**fun·ny** /**fuhn**-ee/ *adjective* (**funnier**, **funniest**)
**1** making you laugh: *His jokes are very funny and they always make me laugh* ▶ see **Thesaurus**
**2** strange: *The water has a funny taste – is it from the lake?*

funnel

funnel

**Word Choice: funny, fun**

You use **funny** to say that someone or something makes you laugh: *The movie was so funny we couldn't stop laughing.* | *Brandon is really funny. He's always telling jokes.*

You use **fun** to talk about situations or activities that you enjoy: *I have a lot of fun when I play with Brandon.* | *The art project was fun to do.*

**fur** /fur/
● *noun* the thick soft hair that covers an animal's body: *I stroked the dog's fur.*
▶ see picture at **polar bear**
● *adjective* made of fur: *a fur coat*

**fu·ri·ous** /**fyoor**-ee-uhss/ *adjective* very angry: *Dad was furious with me when he saw the mess.*
—**furiously** /**fyoor**-ee-uhss-lee/ *adverb* in a furious way: *"What are you doing?" she asked furiously.*

**fur·nace** /**furn**-iss/ *noun* a large container with a fire inside it, used to heat a building or to melt metal

**fur·nish** /**furn**-ish/ *verb* to put furniture and other things into a room or house: *They furnished the living room with comfortable chairs.*
—**furnished** /**furn**-isht/ *adjective* with furniture: *He rented a furnished apartment.*

**fur·ni·ture** /**furn**-i-chur/ *noun* things such as chairs, beds, tables, and cupboards: *The only piece of furniture in the room was an old sofa.*

**Grammar: furniture**

Do not say "furnitures." You can say **some furniture**, **any furniture**, or **pieces of furniture**. You can also say **the furniture** when you mean all of the sofas, chairs, and tables in a room: *Don't jump on the furniture! | They didn't have any furniture in their living room.*

**fur·ry** /**fur**-ee/ *adjective* a furry animal has fur: *My kitten is so furry and soft.*

**fur·ther** /**furth**-ur/
● *adverb*
**1** more: *I'll explain further when I see you tomorrow.*
**2** a greater distance: *I can't walk any further. | Things look smaller when they are further away.* ( SYNONYM: **farther** )
**3 go further/get further** to do more, or make more progress: *If you want to go further with your English, you will need to study a lot harder.*
● *adjective*
more or additional: *You can get further information from the tourist information center. | I gave him $20, but he asked for a further $20.*

**fur·ther·more** /**furth**-ur-mor/ *adverb* used when adding another piece of information: *He liked math. Furthermore, he was good at it.*

**fur·thest** /**furth**-ist/ *adjective*, *adverb* the greatest distance: *Who can throw a ball furthest?* ( SYNONYM: **farthest** )

**fu·ry** /**fyoor**-ee/ *noun* very great anger: *"How dare you?" she yelled, shaking with fury.* ( SYNONYM: **rage** )

**fuse** /fyooz/ *noun*
**1** a thin wire inside electrical equipment that breaks if too much electricity goes through it.

This stops the electricity from damaging the equipment: *When we turned on the heater a fuse blew, and all the lights went out.*
**2** a long string connected to a firework or explosive used to make it explode: *He lit the fuse and I watched the rocket shoot up into the sky.*

**fu·sion** /**fyoozh**-uhn/ *noun* a process in which different things become joined or mixed together: *The enormous heat and pressure causes the fusion of the hydrogen atoms.*

**fuss** /fuhss/
● *noun*
unnecessary attention, excitement, or activity: *I don't know why there was so much fuss about the test – it was easy.*

IDIOMS with fuss
**make a fuss** to complain loudly about something: *Just eat it and stop making a fuss!*
**make a fuss over** to give a lot of attention to someone: *Whenever my uncle visited us, my mother made a big fuss over him.*
● *verb*
**1** if a baby fusses, it cries a little: *The baby fussed for a while then fell asleep.*
**2 fuss over** to give a lot of attention to someone: *Everyone was fussing over the puppy.*

**fuss·y** /**fuhss**-ee/ *adjective* (**fussier**, **fussiest**)
**1** if you are fussy, you only accept a few particular things or things that are exactly right: *I'll eat anything – I'm not fussy.* ( SYNONYM: **picky** )
**2** a fussy baby cries a lot

**fu·ture** /**fyooch**-ur/
● *noun*
**1** the time after the present: *I hope we will meet again some time in the future.* ( ANTONYM: **past** )
**2** the things that will happen to someone or something: *Lots of people are worried about the future of our planet. | He is a young player with a lot of talent, and he has a great future ahead of him.*
**3** the future tense: *The future of "do" is "will do."*
● *adjective*
relating to or happening in the future: *He asked me about my future plans. | She met her future husband at school.* ( ANTONYM: **past** )

**fu·ture tense** /**fyooch**-ur tenss/ *noun* the form of a verb that you use when you are talking about the future. For example, "will go" is the future tense of "go."

**fuzz·y** /**fuhz**-ee/ *adjective*
**1** covered with or made of something that looks like fur: *The slippers are fuzzy and soft to touch.*
**2** not clear: *The photo was fuzzy and I couldn't recognize anyone in it.*

# Gg

g the written abbreviation of **gram**: *This sandwich contains 12g of fat.*

**gadg·et** /**gaj**-it/ *noun* a small tool or machine, especially a new one: *This is a useful little gadget for slicing apples.*

**gag** /gag/
● *noun*
**1** a joke: *The comedian told some funny gags and everyone laughed.*
**2** a piece of cloth that someone ties over your mouth so that you cannot speak
● *verb* (**gagging**, **gagged**)
**1** to tie a piece of cloth over someone's mouth: *The robbers tied him up and gagged him.*
**2** to almost bring up food from your stomach: *The smell from the garbage made me gag.*

**gain** /gayn/ *verb*
**1** to get something important or useful: *He gained the respect of the other players because he always tried very hard.* ( ANTONYM: **lose** )
**2** used when saying that someone or something becomes faster, heavier, etc.: *The bicycle gained speed as it went down the hill. | My dad is gaining weight because he doesn't do enough exercise.* ( ANTONYM: **lose** )

**gal·ax·y** /**gal**-uhkss-ee/ *noun* (plural **galaxies**) a very large group of stars. Our solar system is part of the Milky Way galaxy: *We do not know how many planets there are in other galaxies.*

### Word Origin: galaxy

In one area of the night sky, there are a lot of stars that form a white stripe. These stars make up our galaxy, which we call the Milky Way. The Greeks also thought these stars looked like milk, and the word **galaxy** comes from the Greek word for milk.

**gale** /gayl/ *noun* a very strong wind: *The fence was blown down in a gale.*

**gal·le·on** /**gal**-ee-uhn/ *noun* a large ship with sails. Galleons were used from the 15th to the early 18th century: *Spanish galleons took gold and silver from South America back to Spain.*

**gal·ler·y** /**gal**-uhr-ee/ *noun* (plural **galleries**) a building where people can look at or buy art: *She likes visiting museums and art galleries.*

**gal·lon** /**gal**-uhn/ *noun* a unit for measuring liquid, equal to 8 pints or 3.79 liters: *Dad put five gallons of gas in the car.*

**gal·lop** /**gal**-uhp/
● *verb* if a horse gallops, it runs very fast, and all four feet leave the ground together: *The racehorses are galloping toward the finish line.*
● *noun* the fastest speed a horse can run: *My horse was running at a gallop and I almost fell off the saddle.*

**gallop**

**gam·ble** /**gam**-buhl/
● *verb* to try to win money by playing cards, guessing the result of a race or game: *The men gambled all their money on card games.*
—**gambling** /**gam**-bling/ *noun* the activity of trying to win money by playing cards, or guessing the result of a race: *He lost a lot of money through gambling on horse races.*
—**gambler** /**gam**-blur/ *noun* someone who gambles: *Las Vegas has lots of casinos and is very popular with gamblers.*
● *noun* something you do that might not have the result you want: *Including such a young player on the team was a big gamble.* ( SYNONYM: **risk** )

**game** /gaym/ *noun*
**1** a sport or enjoyable activity in which you try to win or score points: *My favorite game is basketball. | My brother plays computer games all day.* ▶ see **Thesaurus**

**2** an occasion when people play a game: *Joe was watching a football game on TV.*
**3** wild animals and birds that people hunt: *They use their guns to hunt deer and other game in the mountains.*

**gang** /gang/ *noun*
**1** a group of young people living in a city who may be involved in crime: *Some of these kids are in gangs and they get into fights a lot.*
**2** a group of people who do something together: *He is skateboarding with his usual gang of friends in the park.*

**gang·ster** /**gang**-stur/ *noun* a member of a group of violent criminals

**gap** /gap/ *noun* a space between two things, or a space between two parts of something: *I climbed through a gap in the fence.*

**ga·rage** /guh-**rahzh**/ *noun*
**1** a building at your house where you can keep your car: *My dad is putting the car in the garage.*
**2** a place where cars are repaired: *The truck was making a strange noise, so we took it to the garage.*
**3** a building or underground area where people can park their cars: *The garage at the mall has enough spaces for 3,000 cars.*

**gar·bage** /**garb**-ij/ *noun*
**1** food, paper, and other things that you throw away: *One of my chores is to take out the garbage and put it in the yard to be collected.*
**2** something silly, untrue, or bad: *Why are you watching that show? It's garbage!*

## Word Origin: garbage

When the word **garbage** was first used, it meant the parts of a chicken or other bird that you throw away because you do not eat them. In the 1500s, people started to use garbage to mean anything that you throw away. The word garbage may come from an old French word.

**gar·bage can** /**garb**-ij kan/ *noun* a large container outside your home where you put your garbage: *My toy was completely broken so I put it in the garbage can.* ( SYNONYM: **trash can** )

**gar·bage truck** /**garb**-ij truhk/ *noun* a large truck that carries away things from garbage cans

**gar·den** /**gard**'n/ *noun* a piece of land where you grow flowers or vegetables: *We grow beans and lettuce in the garden.*

garden
a vegetable garden

**gar·den·ing** /**gard**'n-ing/ *noun* the work of caring for a garden and the plants that grow in it: *My mom likes gardening and she is always buying new plants.*
—**gardener** /**gard**'n-ur/ *noun* someone who works in a garden, especially as a job

**gar·lic** /**garl**-ik/ *noun* a small plant like an onion, used to give a strong taste to food. The garlic breaks into small pieces called cloves.

garlic

**gar·ment** /**garm**-uhnt/ *noun* a piece of clothing: *A poncho is a garment similar to a cloak, with a hole in the middle for your head.*

**gas** /gass/ *noun* (plural **gases**)
**1** a liquid that you put in a car to make it go: *We had to stop to put gas in the car.*
( SYNONYM: **gasoline** )
**2** a substance like air that is not a liquid or a solid: *Oxygen is a gas that you cannot see or smell.*
**3** a type of gas that people burn to heat their houses or cook food: *We cook on a gas stove.*
( SYNONYM: **natural gas** )

**IDIOM with gas**
**step on the gas** to make a car go faster, by pressing the accelerator: *He knew he was late, so he stepped on the gas and drove at full speed.*

**gash** /gash/
- *noun* a deep cut, usually in someone's body: *She had a big gash in her arm and there was blood coming out of it.*
- *verb* to make a deep cut in something: *He fell and gashed his knee.*

**gas·o·line** /gass-uh-**leen**/ *noun* a liquid that you put in a car to make it go: *We need to stop to get gasoline.* ( SYNONYM: **gas** )

**gasp** /gasp/
- *verb* to breathe in very quickly and loudly because you are very surprised or tired: *The audience gasped when the magician suddenly pulled a rabbit out of his hat. | By the time I got to the top of the hill, I was gasping for breath.*
- *noun* a quick noisy breath because you are surprised or tired: *He gave a gasp of surprise when he opened the door and saw her standing there.*

**gas sta·tion** /**gass** staysh-uhn/ *noun* a place where you can buy gas for your car: *The next gas station is another 20 miles away.*

**gate** /gayt/ *noun*
**1** a door in a fence or a wall around a place: *I opened the gate and walked up to the front door of the house.*
**2** a place where you leave an airport building to get on a plane: *Passengers for Flight 186 should go to Gate 7.*

**gath·er** /**gath**-ur/ *verb*
**1** to come together in a group: *The teacher asked the students to gather around and listen.*
**2** to bring things from different places together: *He gathered all his books and put them in his schoolbag.*
**3** to think something because of what you have heard: *I gather from his parents that he is often sick.*

**gath·er·ing** /**gath**-uhr-ing/ *noun* an event when people come together and talk to each other: *We are having a family gathering on Saturday to celebrate my grandma's birthday.*

**gauge** /gayj/
- *noun* an instrument that measures something: *The car's gas gauge was on empty – we had run out of gas.*
- *verb* to find out how great something is or

what it is really like: *It's difficult to gauge his feelings because his expression never changes.*

**gauze** /goz/ *noun* a type of very thin cloth. Gauze is often used for covering wounds: *She wrapped some gauze around his cut finger.*
▶ see picture at **kit**

**gave** /gayv/ *verb* the past tense of **give**

**gaze** /gayz/
- *verb* to look at someone or something for a long time: *We sat and gazed at the beautiful sunset.*
- *noun* the action of looking at someone or something for a long time: *Her gaze never left the TV, even when I was talking to her.*

**gear** /geer/ *noun*
**1** the parts in a car, truck, or bicycle that make it move well at different speeds: *I use the low gears for going up hills.* ▶ see picture at **bicycle**
**2** special equipment or clothes that you need for an activity: *We are going to take camping gear with us so we can camp if the weather's good.*

**GED** /jee ee **dee**/ *noun* an official piece of paper that shows you have passed a test in some subjects. This test is taken by people who did not finish high school. GED is short for General Equivalency Diploma.

**geese** /geess/ *noun* the plural of **goose**

**gel** /jel/ *noun* a thick clear wet substance: *He uses hair gel to make his hair stick up.*

**gem** /jem/ *noun*
**1** a valuable stone such as a diamond or ruby: *The precious gems in her necklace sparkled.* ( SYNONYM: **jewel** )
**2** something that is very good or special: *The last song on the record is a real gem.*

**gen·der** /**jend**-ur/ *noun*
**1** the sex of a person or animal: *The women feel that they are being treated unfairly because of their gender.*
**2** in grammar, the quality of being masculine, feminine, or neuter: *In Spanish, nouns have different genders.*

**gene** /jeen/ *noun* a part of each cell in a living thing. Genes control the basic size, shape, and color of living things. You get your genes from your parents: *The color of your eyes depends on the genes you get from your parents.*

**Word Origin:** gene

A German scientist gave the **gene** its name in the early 1900s. He used a Greek word that means "birth" or "kind" to make up the name because genes are passed from parent to child.

**gen·er·al** /**jen**-uhr-uhl/
● *adjective*
**1** relating to the whole of something or to the main parts: *Let's start with a few general comments about the book and then discuss the details.*
**2** including or relating to most or all people or things: *They treat all kinds of diseases at the General Hospital.*
● *noun*
an officer with a very high rank in the army, air force, or marines: *General Patton was a famous general in the U.S. army.*

> IDIOM with **general**
> **in general** used to talk about most parts of something without being specific about which: *I enjoy school in general, but there are some things I don't like.* ( SYNONYM: **overall** )

**Word Family:** general

**general** *adjective* | **generally** *adverb* | **generalize** *verb* | **generalization** *noun*

**gen·er·al·ize** /**jen**-uhr-uh-līz/ *verb* to say that something is true about all people or things of a particular kind: *You can't generalize about children – every child is different.*
—**generalization** /jen-uhr-uhl-uh-**zaysh**-uhn/ *noun* a statement that says that something is true about all people or things of a particular kind: *You shouldn't make generalizations about people based on where they come from.*

**gen·er·al·ly** /**jen**-uhr-uhl-ee/ *adverb*
**1** usually or mostly: *Her school work is generally very good, but she has a few problems with math.*
**2** by most people: *This is generally believed to be the writer's best book.*

**gen·er·ate** /**jen**-uh-rayt/ *verb*
**1** to make electricity: *Wind can be used to generate electricity.*
**2** to make something happen: *The ads for the new drink generated a lot of interest.*

**Word Family:** generate

**generate** *verb* | **generator** *noun*

**gen·er·a·tion** /jen-uh-**raysh**-uhn/ *noun*
**1** the people in a society or family who are about the same age: *People of my grandparents' generation grew up without computers.*
**2** a period of about 25 years, which is the time between two generations of a family: *Everyone there was at least a generation older than me.*

**gen·er·a·tor** /**jen**-uh-rayt-ur/ *noun* a machine that makes electricity: *If the power goes off, the hospital uses an emergency generator.*

**gen·er·os·i·ty** /jen-uh-**rahss**-uht-ee/ *noun* generous behavior: *Because of the generosity of the parents, we will be able to build a new gym at the school.*

**gen·er·ous** /**jen**-uhr-uhss/ *adjective* someone who is generous gives a lot of money or other things to people: *It is very generous of you to share your candy with me.*
—**generously** /**jen**-uhr-uhss-lee/ *adverb* in a way that seems kind because someone is giving a lot of money or other things: *He generously offered to pay for the whole dinner.*

**ge·net·ics** /juh-**net**-ikss/ *noun* the study of genes
—**genetic** /juh-**net**-ik/ *adjective* relating to or caused by genes: *She has a rare genetic disease that affects the way her bones grow.*

**ge·nie** /**jeen**-ee/ *noun* a magical creature in old Arab stories. Genies can make wishes come true: *When Aladdin rubbed the lamp, a genie appeared and asked him what he wished for.*

**ge·nius** /**jeen**-yuhss/ *noun* someone who is much more intelligent or much better at doing something than other people: *Einstein was a genius and his ideas changed the way we think about the universe.*

**gen·re** /**zhahn**-ruh/ *noun* a particular type of music, writing, art, or movie: *Her usual genre is writing detective stories, but this book is more of a love story.*

a
b
c
d
e
f
**g**
h
i
j
k
l
m
n
o
p
q
r
s
t
u
v
w
x
y
z

a
b
c
d
e
f

**g**

h
i
j
k
l
m
n
o
p
q
r
s
t
u
v
w
x
y
z

**gen·tle** /jent'l/ *adjective*
**1** careful not to hurt anyone or anything: *He was gentle with the little cat and picked her up very carefully.*
**2** not strong, loud, or extreme: *It was a perfect sunny day, with just a gentle breeze to cool us down.*
—**gently** /jent-lee/ *adverb* in a gentle way: *His mother gently wiped away his tears.*
—**gentleness** /jent'l-niss/ *noun* a gentle quality: *We admired his gentleness with his new baby sister.*

**gen·tle·man** /jent'l-muhn/ *noun* (plural **gentlemen** /jent'l-muhn/)
**1** a man. You use this to talk politely about a man you do not know: *A gentleman came into the store this morning to buy a suit. | Thank you, ladies and gentlemen.*
**2** a man who is polite and behaves well: *He was a perfect gentleman and held the door open for me.*

**gen·u·ine** /jen-yoo-in/ *adjective* real, not pretended or false: *Her surprise was genuine; she obviously wasn't expecting me to be there. | If the diamonds are genuine, they are worth a lot of money.*
—**genuinely** /jen-yoo-in-lee/ *adverb* in a genuine way: *He knows he hurt your feelings and he is genuinely sorry.*

**geo-** /jee-uh/

## Word Building

**geo**logy | **geo**metry | **geo**graphy

These words all have the Greek word root **geo-** in them. **Geo-** means "Earth." *Geology* is the scientific study of the Earth, for example the study of rocks or volcanoes. *Geometry* means "measuring the Earth." Geometry is a kind of math that measures shapes such as spheres (a ball shape) and triangles. *Geography* means "writing the Earth." In geography, you study maps and the way the Earth affects people.

**ge·og·ra·phy** /jee-ahg-ruhf-ee/ *noun* the study of the Earth's surface and the countries of the world: *In geography we have been studying the rain forests.*

—**geographical** /jee-uh-graf-ik-uhl/ (also **geographic**) *adjective* relating to the Earth's surface and the countries of the world: *The map shows geographical features such as mountains and rivers.*

**ge·ol·o·gy** /jee-ahl-uhj-ee/ *noun* the study of rocks and soil
—**geologist** /jee-ahl-uhj-ist/ *noun* someone who studies rocks and soil
—**geological** /jee-uh-lahj-ik-uhl/ *adjective* relating to rocks and soil: *These mountains were created by geological forces millions of years ago.*

**ge·om·e·try** /jee-ahm-uht-ree/ *noun* the study of shapes, lines, and angles: *In geometry we learned how to find the area of a triangle.*
—**geometric** /jee-uh-metr-ik/ *adjective* relating to or made of shapes or lines: *The curtains have a geometric pattern of squares and triangles.*

**ger·bil** /jurb-uhl/ *noun* a small furry animal with a long tail. Gerbils are often kept as pets.

**germ** /jurm/ *noun* a small living thing that spreads a disease from one person to another. Germs are too small to see: *When you sneeze or cough, you spread germs and other people can catch your cold.*

**Ger·man** /jurm-uhn/
● *noun*
**1** someone from Germany: *Germans love soccer.*
**2** the language spoken in Germany, Austria, and parts of Switzerland: *His grandmother only spoke German.*
● *adjective*
from or relating to Germany: *We bought some German sausage.*

**Ger·man meas·les** /jurm-uhn meez-uhlz/ *noun* a disease that gives you red spots on your body. German measles is not usually serious, but it can be dangerous for pregnant women and their babies. (SYNONYM: **rubella**)

**Ger·man shep·herd** /jurm-uhn shep-uhrd/ *noun* a large dog that looks like a wolf, used by police or for guarding buildings

**ger·mi·nate** /jurm-uh-nayt/ *verb* if a seed germinates, it begins to grow: *It takes about a week for the seeds to germinate.*

**ges·ture** /jess-chur/
● *noun*
**1** a movement of your hand or head that shows how you feel or what you mean: *She put her hand over her mouth in a gesture of shock.*
**2** something you do to show your feelings toward someone, usually friendly feelings: *It would be a nice gesture to invite him to your party.*
● *verb*
to move your hand or head in order to tell someone something: *He pointed at the chair, gesturing to me to sit down.*

**get** /get/ *verb* (**getting**, **got** /gaht/, **gotten** /**gaht**'n/)
**1** to receive something: *Did you get my text message?* | *I got a computer game for my birthday.* ▶ see **Thesaurus**
**2** to buy something: *I need to get some new clothes.*
**3** to bring something or someone from somewhere: *I'm thirsty. Could you get me a drink?*
**4** to arrive somewhere: *You can have something to eat when we get to Grandma's house.* | *Wait here until I get back.*
**5** to move somewhere: *A lot of people were waiting to get on the train.* | *He got out of bed.*
**6** to become: *It's getting late – I think I should go home.* | *She got sick and had to go to the hospital.*
**7** **get along** to be friendly with someone: *Andrew and Nick get along well and spend a lot of time together.*
**8** **get away** to escape: *The thief got away by jumping on someone's bicycle.*
**9** **get on with** to continue with something: *Stop thinking about what happened in the past and get on with your life.*
**10** **get over** to feel better after something bad has happened: *It's a big disappointment, but you'll get over it and one day you'll forget it happened.*
**11** **get up** to get out of bed: *What time do you get up in the morning?*
**12** **get up** to stand up: *You've been sitting at that computer all morning. Get up and go play outside.*

**Word Choice:** get, bring, take

You use **get** when you go to another place and come back with something or someone: *I'll get my soccer ball.*

You use **bring** when you take something or someone to a place: *Did you bring your homework to school?* | *Elise brought her friend with her to the party.*

You use **take** when you move something from one place to another, or help someone go from one place to another: *Mrs. Muñoz will take you home after school.* | *Don't forget to take your coat with you.*

**get·to·geth·er** /**get**-tuh-geth-ur/ *noun* a small party or informal meeting: *We had a family get-together to celebrate my grandpa's 70th birthday.*

**gey·ser** /**gīz**-ur/ *noun* a spring that sometimes sends hot water and steam up into the air: *The water from the geyser called Old Faithful erupts 100 feet into the air.*

geyser

**ghet·to** /**get**-oh/ *noun* (plural **ghettos**) a part of a city where poor people live in bad conditions, especially people who belong to the same group: *He was born in the ghetto in Harlem and he knew what it was like to be poor.*

**ghost** /gohst/ *noun* the spirit of a dead person that someone thinks is in a place: *Some people believe the old house is haunted by the ghost of a woman who used to live there.*
▶ see **Thesaurus**

**gi·ant** /**jī**-uhnt/
● *adjective* extremely big: *Help – there's a giant spider in the bathtub!* ( SYNONYM: **huge** )
● *noun* a very tall strong man, in children's stories

**gift** /gift/ *noun*
**1** a present: *I'm going to buy Sam a gift for his birthday.* ▶ see **Thesaurus**
**2** a natural ability to do something well: *He has a gift for writing and his stories are always really interesting.* ( SYNONYM: **talent** )

**gift·ed** /**gift**-id/ *adjective* having the natural ability to do something very well: *He is a gifted athlete – he is good at running, swimming, and basketball.* ( SYNONYM: **talented** )

**gig** /gig/ *noun* a pop concert or rock concert: *The band is going to play some gigs in Las Vegas next month.*

**gig·a·byte** /**gig**-uh-bīt/ *noun* a unit for measuring computer information, equal to 1,024 megabytes

**gi·gan·tic** /jī-**gant**-ik/ *adjective* extremely big: *The accident on the freeway caused a gigantic traffic jam which was over 20 miles long.*
( SYNONYM: **huge** )

**gig·gle** /**gig**-uhl/ *verb* to laugh quickly in a silly way: *The kids were giggling because he had ketchup all around his mouth.*

**gill** /gil/ *noun* one of the parts at the sides of a fish's head through which it breathes. As water goes from the fish's mouth out through its gills, oxygen from the water gets into its blood.
▶ see picture at **fish**

**gim·mick** /**gim**-ik/ *noun* something unusual that a company does to make you want to buy something: *The restaurant's latest gimmick is to give toys to all the children who visit.*

**gin·ger** /**jinj**-ur/ *noun* a light brown root with a strong taste. Ginger is used in cooking, especially in Chinese food.

ginger

**gin·ger·bread** /**jinj**-ur-bred/ *noun* a type of cookie or cake with ginger in it: *She was eating a gingerbread man.*

**ging·ham** /**ging**-uhm/ *noun* cotton cloth with a pattern of white and colored squares: *The restaurant has red and white gingham tablecloths.*

gingham

**gi·raffe** /juh-**raf**/ *noun* an African animal with a very long neck and long legs. Giraffes have dark spots on yellow-brown fur. Giraffes are the tallest animals in the world: *Giraffes have long necks so they can eat leaves off tall trees.*

giraffe

**girl** /gurl/ *noun* a female child: *The little girl's name was Jenny.* | *There are 12 boys and 18 girls in my class.*

**Word Origin:** girl

Until the 1300s, **girl** just meant "child," and it was used about boys and girls. In the 1300s, girl started to be used only for a female child. The word girl probably comes from Old English.

**girl·friend** /**gurl**-frend/ *noun*
**1** a girl or woman that someone is having a romantic relationship with: *My big brother has a girlfriend and they're always together.*
**2** a female friend of a girl or woman: *She likes to go shopping with her girlfriends.*

**give** /giv/ *verb* (**gave** /gayv/, **given** /**giv**-uhn/)
**1** to let someone have something: *My mom and dad gave me a bike for my birthday.* | *I'll give you $5 for that comic book.* ▶ see **Thesaurus**
**2** to put something in someone's hand: *She gave him the picture to look at.* | *Give the ball to Billy.*
( SYNONYMS: **hand, pass** )
**3** to tell someone something: *I gave her my phone number.* | *Let me give you a piece of advice.*
**4** to do something: *He gave her a big smile.* | *The band is giving a concert tonight.*

**5** to cause someone to have something: *Loud music gives me a headache.*
**6 give in** to finally agree to do something that you did not want to do: *He kept asking for a dog until his parents gave in and bought him a puppy.*
**7 give off** to produce a smell, gas, heat, or light: *The pond gave off a funny smell.*
**8 give up** to stop trying to do something because it is too difficult: *You may not succeed at first, but don't give up.*
**9 give up** to stop doing something that you have done a lot: *My dad gave up smoking about ten years ago.*

**giv·en** /**giv**-uhn/
● *verb* the past participle of give
● *adjective* particular: *On any given day, 10% of the students may be late for school.*
● *preposition* used when mentioning an important fact affecting something: *Given her family problems, it's not surprising she's sad sometimes.*

**giv·en name** /**giv**-uhn naym/ *noun* your first name: *His given name is Michael and his last name is Johnson.*

**gla·cier** /**glaysh**-ur/ *noun* a large amount of ice that moves very slowly over an area of land: *A glacier forms when snow falls in the same place again and again and becomes solid ice.*

glacier

**glad** /glad/ *adjective*
**1** happy about something: *I'm glad you like the present.* | *My parents were worried about me and they were glad to see that I was safe.*
**2** willing and happy to do something: *I will be glad to show you around the school.*
—**gladly** /**glad**-lee/ *adverb* in a way that shows you are pleased: *He gladly accepted her help.*

**glad·i·a·tor** /**glad**-ee-ayt-ur/ *noun* a man who fought with other men or animals, as an entertainment for people in ancient Rome

**glam·or·ize** /**glam**-uhr-iz/ *verb* to make something seem more attractive or exciting than it really is: *Some movies try to glamorize war.*

**glam·or·ous** /**glam**-uhr-uhss/ *adjective* attractive and exciting: *He had a glamorous career as a race car driver.*

**glam·our**, **glamor** /**glam**-ur/ *noun* the quality of being glamorous: *Some actors are attracted by the glamor of Hollywood.*

**glance** /glanss/
● *verb* to look at or read something quickly: *He glanced at his watch; it was time to go to school.*
● *noun* a quick look: *Karen took one glance at him and said "What's wrong?"* | *I could see at a glance that it was the wrong color.*

**gland** /gland/ *noun* a part of your body that produces something such as sweat or saliva: *You have thousands of sweat glands in your skin.*

**glare** /glair/
● *verb*
to look angrily at someone or something for a long time: *Dad glared at me and told me not to talk during the movie.*
● *noun*
**1** a very bright light that hurts your eyes: *You should wear sunglasses to protect your eyes from the glare of the sun.*
**2** a long angry look: *When he took the last cookie, she gave him an angry glare.*

**glar·ing** /**glair**-ing/ *adjective*
**1** too bright to look at: *Suddenly there was a glaring white light.*
**2** bad and very easy to notice: *There are some glaring mistakes on the menu – they've written "sandwitch" instead of "sandwich."*

a b c d e f **g** h i j k l m n o p q r s t u v w x y z

a b c d e f **g** h i j k l m n o p q r s t u v w x y z

**glass** /glass/ *noun*
**1** a hard clear material that is used for making windows and bottles: *The ball hit the window and broke the glass.* | *a glass jar*
**2** a container used for drinking. It is made of glass and has no handles: *I'd like a glass of orange juice.*
**3 glasses** something you wear in front of your eyes to help you see better. Glasses have a frame and two pieces of glass called lenses: *I need glasses because I'm nearsighted and I can't see things that are far away.* ▶ see **Thesaurus**

**glasses**

a glass of milk

**glass**
a glass jar

**gleam** /gleem/
● *verb*
**1** to look very shiny: *She polished her shoes until they gleamed.*
**2** if your eyes gleam, they are bright and show that you are excited: *His eyes gleamed when he saw the money.*
● *noun*
brightness: *There was an excited gleam in his eyes.*

**glide** /glīd/ *verb* to move smoothly and quietly: *The snake was gliding across the field, without making a sound.*

**gli·der** /**glīd**-ur/ *noun*
an airplane that flies without an engine: *A small airplane towed the glider up into the air, and then let it go.*

**glider**

**glimpse** /glimpss/
● *noun* if you catch a glimpse of something,

you are able to see it for a very short time: *We are hoping to catch a glimpse of a rare bird.*
● *verb* to see something for a very short time: *She glimpsed the robber's face as he ran off.*

**glitch** /glich/ *noun* a small problem in a computer, machine, or system: *The plane took off late because of a glitch in the computer system.*

**glit·ter** /**glit**-ur/
● *verb* to send back a lot of small flashes of light: *The diamond ring glittered in the light.*
SYNONYM: **sparkle**
● *noun* the brightness of something that reflects the light: *I saw the glitter of his gold teeth.*

**gloat** /gloht/ *verb* to show that you are happy that you have succeeded or that another person has failed, especially in a rather nasty way: *The fans were gloating because their team won easily.*

**glob·al** /**glohb**-uhl/ *adjective* including or affecting the whole world: *Climate change is a global problem; every country will be affected.*
SYNONYM: **worldwide**
—**globally** /**glohb**-uhl-ee/ *adverb* around the whole world: *They want to sell their products globally, not only in the U.S.*

**glob·al warm·ing** /glohb-uhl **worm**-ing/ *noun* an increase in world temperatures. Global warming is caused by gases such as carbon dioxide around the Earth which stop heat from leaving the Earth: *Scientists are discussing what we can do about the problem of global warming.*

**globe** /glohb/ *noun*
**1 the globe** the world: *Our company has offices all over the globe, not just in the U.S.*
**2** a round object that has a map of the Earth on it: *The teacher used a globe to show how the ships sailed from England to America.*
▶ see picture on page **A9**

**Word Family:** globe
**globe** *noun* | **global** *adjective* | **globally** *adverb*

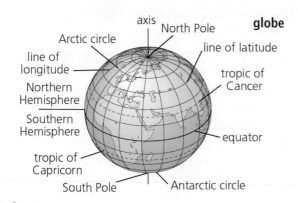

**globe**

axis
North Pole
Arctic circle
line of latitude
line of longitude
tropic of Cancer
Northern Hemisphere
Southern Hemisphere
equator
tropic of Capricorn
South Pole
Antarctic circle

**gloom·y** /**gloom**-ee/ *adjective* (**gloomier, gloomiest**)
**1** sad or with little hope: *He tried to cheer her up when she was gloomy.*
**2** dark: *The kitchen was a gloomy room with only one small window.*

**glo·ri·ous** /**glor**-ee-uhss/ *adjective*
**1** very beautiful or impressive: *There was a glorious sunrise this morning.*
**2** very good and deserving praise: *We have won a glorious victory.*

**glo·ry** /**glor**-ee/ *noun* (plural **glories**)
**1** praise and admiration that you get for succeeding: *My brother won first prize, so he got all the glory.*
**2** very great beauty: *These photographs show the glory of the natural world.*
**3** a very great achievement: *The painting is one of the glories of European art.*

**glos·sa·ry** /**glahss**-uhr-ee/ *noun* (plural **glossaries**) a list of difficult or technical words, with an explanation of their meaning: *There is a glossary of scientific words at the end of the book.*

**gloss·y** /**gloss**-ee/ *adjective* shiny and smooth: *She had beautiful glossy black hair.*

**glove** /gluhv/ *noun* a piece of clothing that you wear on your hand. Gloves have a separate part for each finger: *Put on your gloves if your hands are cold.*

**glove**

**glow** /gloh/
● *verb*
to shine with a soft steady light: *Heat the metal until it glows red.*

● *noun*
**1** a soft steady light: *The only light in the room is the glow of the computer screen.*
**2** if your face has a glow, it has a bright color and you look healthy, warm, or happy: *After her run, her face had a healthy glow.*
**3** a pleased feeling: *She felt a warm glow of satisfaction when she looked back at her work.*

**glow·ing** /**gloh**-ing/ *adjective* full of praise for someone: *His teacher liked his work and gave him a glowing report.*

**glow·worm** /**gloh**-wurm/ *noun* an insect that produces light from its body: *A glowworm is actually a type of beetle.*

**glu·cose** /**glook**-ohss/ *noun* a natural form of sugar that is found in fruits

**glue** /gloo/
● *noun* a sticky substance used for joining one thing to another: *Stick the two pieces of wood together with glue.* ▶ see picture on page **A9**
● *verb* to join things together using glue: *Glue the colored shapes to the paper.*

**glum** /gluhm/ *adjective* unhappy and quiet: *Anna looked glum when the teacher told her that she had failed her test.*

**glut** /gluht/ *noun* a situation in which you have much more of something than you need

**glut·ton** /**gluht**-uhn/ *noun* someone who eats too much food: *Our cat is a real glutton and he always wants more food*
—**gluttony** /**gluht**-uhn-ee/ *noun* the bad habit of eating too much food

**gm.** the written abbreviation of **gram**

**gnat** /nat/ *noun* a small flying insect that bites: *She squashed a gnat on her arm.*

**gnaw** /no/ *verb* to keep biting at something: *The dog loves to gnaw on a bone.* (SYNONYM: **chew**)

**gnome** /nohm/ *noun* a creature in children's stories like a little old man

**go** /goh/

• *verb* (**goes** /gohz/, **went** /went/, **gone** /gon/)

**1** to move or travel to a place: *I usually go to school by bus.* | *We went to Mexico last summer.*
▶ see **Thesaurus**

**2** to leave: *I have to go now.* | *Go away, and leave me alone!*

**3** to become: *The milk went bad so I threw it out.*

**4** to happen in a particular way: *I hope your concert goes well.*

**5** if something goes somewhere, it should be put there: *The dictionaries go on the bottom shelf.*

**6** to look good or taste good together: *That pink scarf doesn't go with that green coat.*

**7 be going to** used when talking about your intentions, or when saying that something will happen: *I'm going to take a bath.* | *I think it's going to rain.*

**8 go ahead** to do something you were planning to do: *Go ahead and ask him.*

**9 go by** if time goes by, it passes: *Another week went by, and still there was no news.*

**10 go off** to explode: *A bomb went off in the middle of the city.*

**11 go off** if an alarm goes off, it makes a loud noise: *My alarm clock went off at 6:30 this morning.*

**12 go off** if a light or the electricity goes off, it stops working: *There was a bang, and all the lights went off.*

**13 go on** to continue: *He went on walking down the road.* | *Just go on with the discussion – I'll be right back.*

**14 go on** to happen: *There's something funny going on, and I want to know what it is.*

**15 go out** if a light or fire goes out, it stops shining or burning: *The fire went out and it was really cold.*

**16 go through with** to do something you planned or promised to do: *He planned to ask her for her number, but he didn't go through with it.*

**17 go up** to become higher: *The price of gasoline has gone up so much that many people can't afford it.* (SYNONYM: **increase**)

**18 go out with** to have a romantic relationship with someone: *My sister is going out with a boy named Eric.*

• *noun* (plural **goes**)
if you give something a go, you try doing it: *We have never been surfing before, but this summer we decided to give it a go.*

> **Grammar:** gone, been
>
> **Gone** and **been** are past participles of **go**. A past participle is a form of a verb that shows an action happening in the past.
>
> **Has gone** is the usual way to say that someone has traveled to a place in the past: *Jordan has gone to Florida* (=Jordan has traveled to Florida and is there now).
>
> **Has been** is the way you say that someone has visited a place in the past: *Jordan has been to Florida* (=Jordan has visited Florida before, but he is not there now).

**goal** /gohl/ *noun*

**1** the place where you have to put the ball to score a point, in games such as soccer or hockey: *The ball just missed the goal.* ▶ see picture at **hockey**

**2** the action of making the ball go in an area so that you score a point in games such as soccer or hockey: *I scored two goals in soccer today.*

**3** something that you hope to achieve: *My goal is to win the race.*

**goal·ie** /**gohl**-ee/ *noun* a goalkeeper: *The goalie stopped the ball from going into the net.*

**goal·keep·er** /**gohl**-keep-ur/ *noun* the player who must stop the ball from going into the goal, in sports such as soccer or hockey: *He kicked the ball past the goalkeeper and scored a goal.*
▶ see picture on page **A10**

**goat** /goht/ *noun* a farm animal with horns on its head and long hair under its chin. People keep goats for their milk.

goat

**gob·ble** /**gahb**-uhl/ *verb* to eat something quickly: *I was so hungry I gobbled everything on my plate in about two minutes.*

**gob·lin** /**gahb**-lin/ *noun* a small ugly creature in children's stories. Goblins often trick people: *The goblins tricked him into going deep into the forest and he got completely lost.*

**go-cart** /**goh** kart/ *noun* a small low vehicle on four wheels, with an open top. People race go-carts for fun.

**god** /gahd/ *noun*
**1 God** the maker and ruler of the universe, in Christianity, Judaism, and Islam: *I believe in God.*
**2** one of many male spirits who has special powers, in some religions: *The Romans believed that Mars was the god of war.*

**god·dess** /**gahd**-iss/ *noun* one of many female spirits who has special powers, in some religions: *Venus was the Roman goddess of love.*

**gog·gles** /**gahg**-uhlz/ *plural noun* special glasses that fit close to your face. They stop things from going into your eyes: *He put on his swimming goggles.*

**goggles**

swimming goggles     safety goggles

**gold** /gohld/
● *noun* a valuable yellow metal. The symbol for gold is Au: *The ring is made of real gold so it is worth quite a lot of money.*
● *adjective* made of gold: *She was wearing gold earrings.*

**gold·en** /**gohld**-uhn/ *adjective*
**1** having a bright yellow color: *Lucy has golden hair.*
**2** made of gold: *The princess had a golden crown on her head.*

**gold·fish** /**gohld**-fish/ *noun* (plural **goldfish**) a small orange fish that people often keep as a pet: *The goldfish was swimming around in its bowl.*

**goldfish**

**golf** /gahlf/ *noun* a game you play by hitting a small white ball into 9 or 18 holes on a golf course. The stick you use for hitting the ball is called a club: *Dad plays golf almost every Saturday.* ▶ see picture on page **A10**
—**golfer** /**gahlf**-ur/ *noun* someone who plays golf

**gone** /gon/ *verb* the past participle of go

**good** /gud/
● *adjective* (**better**, **best**)
**1** of a high standard: *Your homework was very good.* (ANTONYM: **bad**) ▶ see **Thesaurus**
**2** if you are good at something, you can do it well: *He's good at baseball.*
**3** useful or appropriate: *That's a good idea.* (ANTONYM: **bad**)
**4** enjoyable and pleasant: *Did you have a good vacation?* (ANTONYM: **bad**)
**5** well and happy: *I feel really good because I've been exercising more.*
**6** behaving well: *If you're good, you can have an ice cream cone.*
**7** likely to make you healthy: *Apples and bananas are good for you.* (ANTONYM: **bad**)

**IDIOM with good**
**good luck!** used for saying that you hope someone will be successful: *Good luck on the test!*

● *noun*
behavior that is right and kind: *The story is about the fight between good and evil.*

**IDIOMS with good**
**for good** permanently: *He really likes California and he wants to stay there for good.*
**no good** not successful: *He thinks he's no good at math.* | *I tried to open the box, but it was no good – it was completely stuck.*

## Word Choice: good, well

You use **good** to talk about the quality of something or someone: *He's a good basketball player.* | *It's a really good book.*

You use **well** when someone does something in a good way: *He plays basketball really well.* | *She did well on the test.*

**good af·ter·noon** /gud aft-ur-**noon**/ *interjection* a formal way of saying "hello" to someone in the afternoon: *When the principal entered we all said "Good afternoon, Mr. Peterson."*

**a b c d e f**

**g**

**h i j k l m n o p q r s t u v w x y z**

**good·bye** /gud-**bī**/ *interjection* you say this when you are leaving, or when someone else is leaving: *Goodbye! Have a good trip! | We all said goodbye to Grandma, then got in the car and drove home.*

**good eve·ning** /gud **eev**-ning/ *interjection* a formal way of saying "hello" to someone in the evening: *Good evening, ladies and gentlemen.*

**Good Fri·day** /gud **frīd**-ee/ *noun* the Friday before Easter. Christians remember it as the day Jesus died on the cross.

**good-look·ing** /gud **luk**-ing/ *adjective* attractive: *All the girls like Jason and think he's good-looking.*

**good morn·ing** /gud **morn**-ing/ *interjection* a way of saying "hello" to someone in the morning: *Mrs. Jefferson came in and said "Good morning, class."*

**good·ness** /**gud**-niss/ *noun*
**1** the quality of being good and kind to other people: *She was loved and admired for her goodness.*
**2 my goodness** you say this when you are surprised about something: *My goodness, you've gotten so tall!*

**good night** /gud **nīt**/ *interjection* you say this when someone is leaving at night, or when someone is going to bed: *Mom said good night and turned out my light.*

**goods** /gudz/ *plural noun* things that are produced in order to be sold: *The store sells sporting goods such as golf balls and tennis rackets.*

**goo·ey** /**goo**-ee/ *adjective* sticky: *The fudge sauce was very gooey and it stuck to my fingers.*

**goof** /goof/
● *verb*
**1** to make a silly mistake: *I goofed on the test and made some stupid spelling mistakes.*
**2 goof around/off** to spend time doing silly or unimportant things: *The boys were goofing around in the yard.*
● *noun*
someone who is silly: *Of course he likes donuts. Don't be such a goof!*

**goof·y** /**goof**-ee/ *adjective* silly: *It was a really goofy idea.*

**goose** /gooss/ *noun* (plural **geese** /geess/) a large bird with a long neck and webbed feet. A goose looks like a duck, but is bigger.

goose

goose

gosling

**goose·bumps** /**gooss**-buhmpss/ *plural noun* small bumps on your skin that you get because you are cold or frightened: *The last part of the movie was very scary and it gave me goosebumps.*

**go·pher** /**gohf**-ur/ *noun* a light brown animal similar to a squirrel that lives in holes in the ground. Gophers have long teeth and tiny ears: *Gophers dug holes all over our lawn and ruined it.*

gopher

## Word Origin: gopher

**Gopher** is an American word that started being used in the early 1800s. No one knows for sure where the word came from. It may have come from the French word "gauffre" that means "waffle." Gophers live in holes under the ground, so maybe people thought that when gophers dig holes, they make the fields look like waffles.

**gorge** /gorj/ *noun* a narrow valley with high sides: *A small river ran along the bottom of the gorge.*

**gor·geous** /**gorj**-uhss/ *adjective* very beautiful: *You look gorgeous in that dress!*

**go·ril·la** /guh-**ril**-uh/ *noun* a large strong animal that looks like a monkey: *Gorillas are the largest type of ape and they live mainly in forests in Africa.*

**gorilla**

**gor·y** /**gor**-ee/ *adjective* involving a lot of violence: *The battle scene in the movie was too gory for me.*

**gos·ling** /**gahz**-ling/ *noun* a baby goose
▶ see picture at **goose**

**gos·pel** /**gahsp**-uhl/ *noun*
**1** one of the four books in the Christian Bible that tell the story of Jesus' life: *The Gospel of Mark.*
**2** the ideas that Jesus taught: *He wanted to spread the gospel.*
**3** something that is completely true: *Don't take what she says as gospel; it's just her opinion.*

**gos·sip** /**gahss**-uhp/
● *noun* things that people say about other people, sometimes things that may not be true: *I heard some gossip that they were now boyfriend and girlfriend, but I don't know if it's true.*
● *verb* to talk about what you think other people are doing, often by saying things that are not true: *Everyone was gossiping about them and saying that they were planning to get divorced.*

**Word Origin:** gossip

**Gossip** took a long time before it got the meaning it has today. It comes from a word in Old English that means "godparent." By the 1300s, people used gossip to mean a friend, especially a woman's friend. By the 1500s, gossip meant someone who talks about the unimportant things that happen each day. In the 1800s, gossip finally began to mean the things people say, rather than the person who says them.

**got** /gaht/ *verb* the past tense of **get**
**got·ten** /**gaht**'n/ *verb* the past participle of get

**gourd** /gord/ *noun* a round fruit with a hard shell: *People make bottles and bowls out of gourds.*

**gourd**

**gour·met** /goor-**may**/
● *adjective* relating to very good food and drink: *It's a gourmet restaurant and the food is really good.*
● *noun* someone who enjoys and knows about good food and drink: *My uncle's a gourmet and he loves cooking all kinds of foods.*

**gov·ern** /**guhv**-urn/ *verb* to control a country, state, or city: *The citizens vote to decide who will govern their country.*

**Word Family:** govern

**govern** *verb* | **government** *noun* | **governmental** *adjective* | **governor** *noun* | **governorship** *noun*

**gov·ern·ment** /**guhv**-ur-muhnt/ *noun*
**1** the group of people who are responsible for controlling a country or state: *The president is the head of the U.S. government.*
▶ see **Thesaurus**
**2** the process of governing a country: *We have a democratic form of government, where the people elect their leaders.*
—**governmental** /guhv-urn-**ment**'l/ *adjective*: *In a democracy, there are limits on governmental power.*

**gov·er·nor** /**guhv**-uhn-ur/ *noun* the person who is in charge of a state in the U.S.: *Who is the governor of Texas?*
—**governorship** /**guhv**-uhn-ur-ship/ *noun* the position of being governor: *He won the governorship of California.*

**gown** /gown/ *noun*
**1** a long evening dress: *The First Lady was wearing a beautiful white gown.*
**2** a piece of clothing like a long loose coat. People wear gowns for some formal ceremonies: *For the graduation ceremony, you have to wear a black gown.*

a
b
c
d
e
f

**g**

h
i
j
k
l
m
n
o
p
q
r
s
t
u
v
w
x
y
z

**GPA** /gee pee **ay**/ *noun* the average of all the grades that a student gets. GPA is short for grade point average: *He graduated with a GPA of 3.4, which is equivalent to a B+.*

**grab** /grab/ *verb* (**grabbing**, **grabbed**) to take hold of something suddenly and roughly: *Mom grabbed my arm to stop me from crossing the road.*

**grace** /grayss/ *noun*
**1** a smooth and attractive way of moving: *The dancers moved slowly and with a lot of grace.*
**2** polite behavior: *He accepted the award with grace, praising his opponents and thanking his team.*
**3** a short prayer said before a meal: *We sat at the table and Dad said grace before we began to eat.*

**grace·ful** /**grayss**-fuhl/ *adjective* moving in a way that is smooth and attractive: *The princess gave a graceful wave of her hand.*
—**gracefully** /**grayss**-fuhl-ee/ *adverb* in a graceful way: *The bird flew very gracefully from one tree to the other.*

**gra·cious** /**graysh**-uhss/ *adjective* behaving in a polite and kind way: *Our hosts were very gracious and they said we could stay as long as we wanted.*
—**graciously** /**graysh**-uhss-lee/ *adverb* in a gracious way: *"You played far better than I did," he said graciously.*

**grade** /grayd/
● *noun*
**1** a year in school in the U.S. There are 12 grades in addition to kindergarten: *My brother is in the third grade.*
**2** a number or letter that shows how good a student's work is: *Alvin studied hard and got good grades, all A's and B's.*

**IDIOM with grade**
**make the grade** to reach a good enough standard: *He wanted to be on the soccer team, but he didn't make the grade.*
● *verb*
to give a grade to a student's work: *My teacher is grading our tests tonight and we will get the results tomorrow.*

**grade point av·erage** /grayd poynt **av**-rij/ *noun* the average of all the grades that a student gets. People usually say GPA.

**grade school** /**grayd** skool/ *noun* a school that children go to for the first five to seven years of their education

**grad·u·al** /**graj**-oo-uhl/ *adjective* happening slowly over a long time: *Learning a language is a gradual process; it cannot be done in a few weeks.*
—**gradually** /**graj**-oo-uhl-ee/ *adverb* slowly over a long time: *Naomi's grades have gradually improved during the last two years.*

**grad·u·ate**
● *noun* /**graj**-oo-it/ someone who has finished studying at a school or college, and has a diploma or degree: *The lawyer is a graduate of Yale Law School. | My parents are both high school graduates.*
● *verb* /**graj**-oo-ayt/ to finish studying at a school or college and get a diploma or a degree: *When we graduate we're going to have a big party.*
● *adjective* /**graj**-oo-it/ relating to a student who is studying to get a master's degree or a Ph.D.: *After he finished his undergraduate degree, he went to graduate school in California.*

**grad·u·a·tion** /graj-oo-**aysh**-uhn/ *noun* a ceremony for students to receive their degree or diploma: *The whole family is coming to my sister's graduation.*

**graf·fi·ti** /gruh-**feet**-ee/ *noun* writing and pictures that people draw on the walls of buildings and trains, even though it is against the law: *The walls of the subway are covered in graffiti.*

graffiti

**grain** /grayn/ *noun*
**1** the seeds of crops, used as food: *The grain from wheat is used for making flour.*
**2** a very small piece of sand or salt: *The grains of sand slipped between my fingers.*

**gram** /gram/ *noun* (ABBREVIATION: **gm.**) a unit for measuring weight. There are 1,000 grams in a kilogram. Gram is sometimes written g: *You need 200 grams of sugar and 100 grams of butter.*

**gram·mar** /**gram**-ur/ *noun* the rules of a language: *He needs to be careful about* grammar, and make sure that he uses the right tense.

—**grammatical** /gruh-**mat**-ik-uhl/ *adjective* relating to grammar: *A common grammatical mistake is to say "Me and my friends are" instead of "My friends and I are."*

**grand** /grand/ *adjective*
**1** big and impressive: *The hotel is very grand and it has a big marble entrance hall.*
**2 grand total** the total from adding up several numbers or amounts: *I saved $5 a month for a year, so I had a grand total of $60.*

**grand·child** /**gran**-chīld/ *noun* (plural **grandchildren** /**gran**-chil-druhn/) someone's grandchild is the child of his or her son or daughter: *I am Grandpa's oldest grandchild.*

**grand·daugh·ter** /**gran**-dot-ur/ *noun* a grandchild who is a girl

**grand·fa·ther** /**gran**-fahth-ur/ *noun* the father of your mother or father: *My grandfather is 70.*

**grand·ma** /**gran**-mah/ *noun* another word for grandmother

**grand·moth·er** /**gran**-muhth-ur/ *noun* the mother of your mother or father: *We go see my grandmother every Sunday.*

**grand·pa** /**gran**-pah/ *noun* another word for grandfather

**grand·par·ent** /**gran**-pair-uhnt/ *noun* the parent of your mother or father: *My grandparents live a long way away.*

**grand·son** /**gran**-suhn/ *noun* a grandchild who is a boy

**grand·stand** /**grand**-stand/ *noun* rows of seats outdoors where people sit to watch sports: *We had seats for the race in the grandstand.*

**gran·ite** /**gran**-it/ *noun* a type of hard gray rock

**gra·no·la** /gruh-**nohl**-uh/ *noun* a breakfast food made of oats, nuts, seeds, and sometimes dried fruit

**grant** /grant/
● *noun* money that is given for a special purpose by an organization: *You may be able to get a grant to help pay for college.*

● *verb* to allow someone to do or have something: *In the story, Cinderella wishes she could go to the ball, and the fairy grants her wish.*

**IDIOM with grant**
**take something for granted** to not realize how important or useful something or someone is: *Dan's mother is always very kind to him, but Dan seems to take her for granted.*

**grape** /grayp/ *noun* a small round green or red fruit that you can eat. Grapes are used to make wine: *grape juice*
▶ see picture at **grapevine**

grape

**grape·fruit**
/**grayp**-froot/ *noun* a big round yellow or pink fruit with a thick skin. It looks like a large orange, but is not as sweet: *I usually have grapefruit juice for breakfast.*

grapefruit

**grape·vine** /**grayp**-vīn/ *noun* the plant that grapes grow on (SYNONYM: **vine**)

**IDIOM with grapevine**
**hear through the grapevine** to hear news that has been passed from one person to another: *I heard through the grapevine that we're going to get a new math teacher.*

grapevine

a b c d e f **g** h i j k l m n o p q r s t u v w x y z

**graph** /graf/ *noun* a picture that shows information about different numbers or amounts. A graph often uses bars, lines, or parts of a circle to compare the numbers or amounts: *You can see from the graph that July was the hottest month of the year.*

## Word Building

bio**graph**y | geo**graph**y | para**graph** | tele**graph**

These words all have the Greek word root **graph** in them. **Graph** means "writing" or "printing." A *biography* is a book that someone has written about another person's life. In *geography* you often make maps, which are a way of writing down what the Earth is like. You write a *paragraph* in a story or report.

**graph**

**line graph**

*(Speed (miles per hour))*

| | | | |
|---|---|---|---|
| 80 | | | |
| 70 | 70 | | |
| 60 | | | |
| 50 | 50 | | |
| 40 | | | 40 |
| 30 | | 30 | |
| 20 | | | |
| 10 | | | |
| 0 | | | |
| cheetah | lion | jackrabbit | coyote |

**picture graph**

| Home lunch | 🧍🧍🧍🧍🧍🧍 |
|---|---|
| School lunch | 🧍🧍🧍🧍🧍🧍🧍🧍 |
| Both home and school lunch | 🧍🧍🧍 |
| Key | 1 kid = 🧍 |

**graph·ic** /**graf**-ik/ *adjective*
**1** giving a lot of clear details, often in a way that is shocking: *The program showed how the heart works in graphic detail.*
**2** relating to drawing and design especially for books, magazines, etc.: *He's studying graphic art.*

**graph·ics** /**graf**-ikss/ *plural noun* pictures in books, or images on computers: *The graphics in some computer games are so good they almost look real.*

**grasp** /grasp/ *verb*
**1** to hold something firmly: *I grasped the rope with both hands and pulled the boat onto the beach.*
**2** to understand something: *She is smart and grasps new ideas really quickly.*

**grass** /grass/ *noun* a common plant with thin green leaves. Grass covers the ground in fields, parks, and yards: *She was sitting on the grass in front of the house.*

**grass·hop·per**
/**grass**-hahp-ur/ *noun* a green or brown insect with long back legs. It can jump very high.

**grasshopper**

**grass·land** /**grass**-land/ (also **grasslands**) *noun* a large area of land that is covered with wild grass and that has few trees: *Millions of bison lived on the prairie grassland.*

**gras·sy** /**grass**-ee/ *adjective* covered with grass: *We found a grassy area to have our picnic in.*

**grate** /grayt/
● *verb*
to break food into small thin pieces by rubbing it against a grater: *Grate some cheese on top of the pasta.*
● *noun*
**1** a metal frame with bars that cover a hole or window: *The coin fell through the grate and into the sewer.*

**grate**

**2** a metal frame that holds the wood in a fireplace: *A fire was burning in the grate.*

**grate·ful** /**grayt**-fuhl/ *adjective* wanting to thank someone who has been kind or helpful: *To show how grateful we are for your help, we got you a gift.*

—**gratefully** /**grayt**-fuhl-ee/ *adverb* in a grateful way: *He gratefully accepted their offer of help.*

> **Word Family:** grateful
>
> **grateful** *adjective* | **ungrateful** *adjective* | **gratefully** *adverb* | **gratitude** *noun* | **ungratefulness** *noun*

**grat·er** /**grayt**-ur/ *noun* a kitchen tool that has a flat metal surface with holes in it. You use it to cut or break food into thin or small pieces: *a cheese grater*

**grat·i·tude** /**grat**-uh-tood/ *noun* the feeling of being grateful for someone's kindness or help: *I'm going to write a letter to express my gratitude for his help.*

**grave** /grayv/
● *noun* the place where a dead person is buried: *I put some flowers on my grandmother's grave.*
● *adjective* very serious: *The ship was in grave danger of sinking.*
—**gravely** /**grayv**-lee/ *adverb* very seriously: *She is gravely ill and could die.*

**grav·el** /**grav**-uhl/ *noun* small stones used to make a surface for a path or road: *A car was parked on the gravel in the driveway.*

**grave·stone** /**grayv**-stohn/ *noun* a stone on a grave that shows the name of the person buried there

**grave·yard** /**grayv**-yard/ *noun* an area of land where dead people are buried: *My great-grandfather is buried in the graveyard next to the church.*

**grav·i·ty** /**grav**-uht-ee/ *noun* the force that makes things fall to the ground: *If you drop something, it falls downward because of the Earth's gravity.*

**gra·vy** /**grayv**-ee/ *noun* a sauce made from the juice of cooked meat: *When the chicken is cooked, use the juices in the roasting pan to make gravy.*

**gray** /gray/
● *adjective* having the color between black and white: *An old man with gray hair went past.*

● *noun* the color between black and white: *The door was painted in pale gray.*

**graze** /grayz/ *verb*
**1** if an animal grazes, it eats grass: *The cows were grazing in the field.*
**2** to damage the skin on part of your body, so that a little blood comes out: *I fell off my bike and I grazed my knee on the sidewalk.*

**grease** /greess/
● *noun*
**1** soft fat from animals, found in some meat: *After I cooked the sausages the pan was full of grease.*
**2** oil that you put on machines to help the parts move: *The mechanic's hands were covered in grease.*
● *verb*
to put fat or oil on something: *Grease the pan with butter first so the cake doesn't stick to it.*

**greas·y** /**greess**-ee/ *adjective*
**1** cooked in too much fat or oil: *I don't like greasy potato chips.*
**2** greasy hair has too much oil in it and it looks dirty: *My hair is so greasy. I really need to wash it.*

**great** /grayt/ *adjective*
**1** very good or enjoyable: *The pizza has a great taste!*
**2** very important or famous: *Dr. King was a great man and he worked hard to get equal rights for all Americans.*
**3** very big: *There's a great big bird in the yard.* | *the Great Barrier Reef*
**4** if something is greater than a number or amount, it is more than it: *The total cost is greater than we expected.*
**5** **great-grandmother/great-grandfather** the mother or father of one of your grandparents: *My great-grandmother and great-grandfather came to this country when my grandma was a little baby.*

**great·ly** /**grayt**-lee/ *adverb* very much: *Sara has greatly improved in math; she got a C on the last test but an A on this one.*

a b c d e f g h i j k l m n o p q r s t u v w x y z

**greed·y** /**greed**-ee/ *adjective* (**greedier**, **greediest**) wanting much more of something than you need: *He's very greedy and he won't help you unless you pay him.*
—**greed** /greed/ *noun* the desire to have much more of something than you need: *Did they steal the money because they really needed it, or was it just greed?*
—**greedily** /**greed**-uhl-ee/ *adverb* in a greedy way: *William greedily ate all the cookies.*

**Greek** /greek/
● *noun*
**1** someone from Greece: *We are learning about the ancient Greeks.*
**2** the language spoken in Greece: *His grandparents only speak Greek.*
● *adjective*
from Greece: *My friend Marina is Greek.*

**green** /green/
● *adjective*
**1** having the color of grass: *I chose the green T-shirt.*
**2** covered with grass and trees: *The city is full of parks and other green spaces.*
● *noun*
the color of grass: *Green is my favorite color.*

**green card** /green **kard**/ *noun* a card that allows people to live and work in the U.S., if they come from another country

**green·house** /**green**-howss/ *noun* a glass building for growing plants: *We keep the young tomato plants in the greenhouse to protect them from the cold.*

**green·house ef·fect** /**green**-howss i-fekt/ *noun* a gradual warming of the Earth's atmosphere. It is caused by gases that stop heat from escaping from the Earth: *Because of the greenhouse effect, the average temperature will rise during this century.*

**green·house gas** /**green**-howss gass/ *noun* a type of gas that stops heat from escaping from the Earth. Greenhouse gases are bad for the environment because they can change the Earth's climate: *Carbon dioxide and methane are both greenhouse gases which cause global warming.*

**greet** /greet/ *verb*
**1** to welcome or say hello to someone: *Karen greeted him at the door with a kiss on the cheek.*
**2** to react to something that happens: *The kids greeted the idea with excitement.*

**greet·ing** /**greet**-ing/ *noun*
**1** something you say or do when you meet someone: *"Hi" is a common greeting when two friends meet.*
**2** a message you send to someone on a special occasion: *We sent her a card with our birthday greetings.*

**gre·nade** /gruh-**nayd**/ *noun* a small bomb that you throw or fire from a gun: *The soldiers threw hand grenades into the building.*

**grew** /groo/ *verb* the past tense of **grow**

**grey** /gray/ *adjective*, *noun* another spelling of gray

**grey·hound** /**gray**-hownd/ *noun* a type of dog that can run very fast: *The greyhounds raced around the track.*

greyhound

**grid** /grid/ *noun* a pattern that crosses each other and form squares: *The puzzle consists of a grid of nine squares, and you have to fit the numbers into the grid.*

**grid·dle** /**grid**'l/ *noun* a flat pan for cooking food on top of a stove: *We usually fry burgers on a griddle.*

**grid·i·ron** /**grid**-ī-urn/ *noun* a football field

**grief** /greef/ *noun* great sadness: *We all feel grief when someone we love dies.*

**griev·ance** /**greev**-uhnss/ *noun* something you want to complain about because you think it is unfair: *If patients have any grievances about the treatment they received at the hospital, they can call this number.*

**grieve** /greev/ *verb* to feel very sad because someone you love has died: *Many people are still grieving for their friends and family members who died in the earthquake.*

**grill** /gril/
- *verb* to cook food on a frame over a fire: *Grill the sausages for around 15 minutes.*
- *noun* a metal frame over a fire. You cook food on it: *Cook the fish on the grill for a few minutes, until it starts to go brown.*

**grill**

**grim** /grim/ *adjective*
**1** very unpleasant or worrying: *I heard the grim news about the plans to close the school.*
**2** looking serious and sad: *Paula had a grim expression on her face and I knew she had failed her test.*
—**grimly** /**grim**-lee/ *adverb* in a very serious way: *"She's very sick," he said grimly.*

**grim·ace** /**grim**-uhss/
- *verb* to twist your face in a way that shows you do not like something: *Andy swallowed the bitter medicine and grimaced.*
- *noun* a look on your face that shows you do not like something: *"That hurts," she said with a grimace.*

**grin** /grin/
- *noun* a big smile: *He has a big grin on his face because he won the competition.*
- *verb* (**grinning, grinned**) to give a big smile: *She grinned at me in a friendly way and said "There's no need to worry."*

**grin**

**grind** /grīnd/ *verb* (**ground** /grownd/) to crush and break something into small pieces or powder: *This machine grinds the coffee beans.*

**grind·er** /**grīnd**-ur/ *noun* a machine that crushes something into small pieces or powder: *Put the beans in the coffee grinder.*

**grip** /grip/
- *noun* a strong hold on something: *I kept a grip on my camera because I didn't want to lose it.*
- *verb* (**gripping, gripped**) to hold something very firmly: *The little boy was frightened and he gripped his mother's arm tightly.*

**grit** /grit/ *noun* very small pieces of dirt or rock: *Wash the vegetables to remove the grit.*

**griz·zly bear** /**griz**-lee bair/ (also **grizzly**) *noun* a large brown bear that lives in parts of North America

**grizzly bear**

**groan** /grohn/
- *verb* to make a long deep sound because you are in pain or because you are not pleased about something: *My Dad told another terrible joke and everyone groaned.*
- *noun* a long deep sound that you make when you are in pain or not pleased: *"I have to go to the dentist tomorrow," she said with a groan.*

**gro·cer·ies** /**grohss**-uhr-eez/ *plural noun* food and other things for the home that you buy in a store: *I always help Mom carry the groceries.*

**groceries**

**gro·cer·y store** /**grohss**-uhr-ee stor/ *noun* a store that sells food and things you use in the home: *She went to the grocery store to get some bread and milk.*

**groom** /groom/
- *noun*
**1** a man who is getting married: *The picture shows the bride and groom outside the church after the wedding.*
SYNONYM: **bridegroom**
**2** someone whose job is taking care of horses
- *verb*
to brush and clean an animal such as a horse: *Linda was grooming her pony.*

**groove** /groov/ *noun* a line cut into the surface of something: *The closet door slides in a groove.*

**groove**

groove

**grope** /grohp/ *verb* to try to find something using your hands because it is difficult to see: *The light wasn't working, so I groped my way to the door.*

**gross** /grohss/ *adjective*
**1** very unpleasant: *That smell is gross!*
**2** very wrong: *You've made a gross mistake.*
**3** before tax or other amounts are taken away: *He has a gross income of $40,000.*

**gro·tesque** /groh-**tesk**/ *adjective* ugly and very strange: *The story is about a grotesque monster.*

**grouch·y** /**growch**-ee/ *adjective* becoming annoyed or angry easily: *Dad's a little grouchy because he has a headache.*

**ground** /grownd/
● *noun*
**1** the surface of the Earth: *The cat jumped down to the ground.* ► see **Thesaurus**
**2** an area of land or ocean used for an activity: *Boats sail to the fishing grounds to catch fish.*
**3 grounds** the land or gardens around a big building: *You cannot leave the school grounds without permission.*
**4 grounds** reasons for doing something: *If you lie to your boss, that is grounds for being fired.*
● *verb*
the past tense and past participle of **grind**
● *adjective*
**1** ground meat is cut into very small pieces: *You make hamburgers with ground beef.*
**2** ground coffee or pepper is a powder: *Add a little ground pepper.*

**ground floor** /**grownd** floor/ *noun* the part of a building that is on the same level as the

ground: *Her office is on the ground floor.*
( SYNONYM: **first floor** )

**ground·hog** /**grownd**-hog/ *noun* a small animal with thick brown fur and big front teeth: *Groundhogs live in holes in the ground.*
( SYNONYM: **woodchuck** )

**Ground·hog Day** /**grownd**-hog day/ *noun* February 2. In American stories, a groundhog comes out of its hole on this day. If it sees its shadow, there will be six more weeks of winter. If it does not see its shadow, good weather will come early.

**group** /groop/
● *noun*
**1** several people or things that are together in a place: *We walked toward a small group of trees.*
► see **Thesaurus**
**2** several people or things that are similar in some way: *Andrew has a nice group of friends.*
**3** several musicians who play and sing together: *Which is your favorite pop group?*
● *verb*
**1** to put people or things in a group: *All the kids are grouped according to their age.*
**2** to come together and make a group: *The sheep had grouped into a corner.*

**grove** /grohv/ *noun* a small group of trees: *an orange grove*

**grow** /groh/ *verb* (**grew** /groo/, **grown** /grohn/)
**1** to get bigger: *The tree has grown and it's now as tall as our house.* ► see **Thesaurus**
**2** to plant something and look after it: *We grow our own vegetables.*
**3** if a plant grows somewhere, it exists there: *The flowers grow next to the side of rivers.*
**4** to become: *It grew cold and we went indoors.*
**5 grow out of** if you grow out of clothes, you get bigger and they do not fit anymore: *Joe's grown out of his pants again.*
**6 grow up** to change from being a child to being an adult: *I want to be a doctor when I grow up.* | *All their kids have grown up now.*

**growl** /growl/
● *verb* if a dog or bear growls, it makes a deep angry sound: *Our dog always growls at cats.*
● *noun* a deep angry sound that a dog or bear makes: *The bear gave an angry growl.*

**grown** /grohn/
- *adjective* a grown man or woman is an adult and should behave like one: *Grown men aren't supposed to cry.*
- *verb* the past participle of grow

**grown-up** /**grohn** uhp/
- *adjective* someone who is grown-up is an adult: *Maria is 16, and she has two grown-up brothers.*
- *noun* an adult: *The grown-ups were talking and laughing downstairs.*

**growth** /grohth/ *noun*
**1** an increase: *There has been a growth in the number of students at the school.*
**2** the process of getting bigger in size, and stronger: *You can measure your growth on a chart on the wall.*

**grub·by** /**gruhb**-ee/ *adjective* dirty: *The boys were grubby after playing in the yard.*

**grudge** /gruhj/ *noun* an unfriendly feeling toward someone who has hurt or annoyed you in the past: *She holds a grudge against me because she thinks I stole her boyfriend.*

**gru·el·ing** /**groo**-uhl-ing/ *adjective* very difficult and tiring: *It was a grueling race and I was exhausted by the time I finished.*

**grue·some** /**grooss**-uhm/ *adjective* very shocking, and involving death or injury: *I saw some gruesome pictures of what happens to your lungs when you smoke cigarettes.*

**grum·ble** /**gruhm**-buhl/ *verb* to complain about something in a bad-tempered way, especially something that is not very important: *He's always grumbling about how much homework he has to do.*

**grump·y** /**gruhmp**-ee/ *adjective* (**grumpier**, **grumpiest**) feeling annoyed, or behaving in an annoyed way: *He's often grumpy when he gets up in the morning.*
—**grumpily** /**gruhmp**-uhl-ee/ *adverb* in an annoyed way: *"Go away," he said grumpily.*

**grunt** /gruhnt/
- *verb*
**1** if a pig grunts, it makes a low sound: *The pigs were grunting in the yard.*
**2** to make a short low sound instead of talking: *Instead of saying "yes," he just grunted.*

- *noun*
a short low sound that you make, or that a pig makes: *The pig gave a grunt and went back to his food.*

**gua·ca·mo·le** /gwahk-uh-**moh**-lay/ *noun* a food made with crushed avocado, tomatoes, and onions: *You can dip your chips in the guacamole.*

**guar·an·tee** /garr-uhn-**tee**/
- *verb*
to promise something: *It's a great movie – I can guarantee that you'll enjoy it!* ( SYNONYM: **promise** )
- *noun*
**1** if there is a guarantee of something, you can be sure that it will definitely happen: *There's no guarantee that the weather will be nice on the day of the picnic.*
**2** a promise by a company to repair or replace something if it breaks: *The computer has a two-year guarantee and the company will give you a new one if there's a problem.*
( SYNONYM: **warranty** )

**guard** /gard/
- *noun*
**1** someone whose job is to protect a person or place: *There were two security guards outside the bank.*
**2** someone whose job is to stop a person from escaping: *The prison guards took him down to his cell.*
**3** an object that protects part of your body: *Baseball catchers always wear shin guards to protect their legs.*
**4** in basketball, a player who moves the ball to help other team players gain points. There are two guards on each team.
**5** in football, a player who plays to the side of the center. There is a left and a right guard on each team.
- *verb*
**1** to protect a place or person from attack: *Their job is to guard the president and make sure that he is safe.*
**2** to prevent a prisoner from escaping: *Dangerous prisoners are guarded day and night.*
**3** **guard against** to try to stop something bad from happening: *You should use sunscreen to guard against sunburn.*

**guard dog** /**gard** dog/ *noun* a dog that protects someone's home or property: *A guard dog stood at the gate of the big house.*

**g**

h i j k l m n o p q r s t u v w x y z

**guard·i·an** /**gard**-ee-uhn/ *noun* someone who is responsible for a child by law, but is not the child's parent: *His guardian has agreed to allow him to go on the trip.*

**guer·ril·la** /guh-**ril**-uh/ *noun* a member of a group of fighters that is not the official army: *The guerrillas attacked government soldiers and tried to get control of the town.*

**guess** /gess/
● *verb*
**1** to give an answer, when you cannot be sure you are right: *I didn't know that the answer was 12 – I just guessed.* ▶ see **Thesaurus**
**2** to believe something is probably true: *His light isn't on, so I guess he has gone out.*
● *noun*
an attempt to give an answer when you cannot be sure you are right: *If you don't know the answer to the question, make a guess.*

**guest** /gest/ *noun*
**1** someone you invite to an event, or to stay in your home: *There were 100 guests at the wedding.*
**2** someone who is staying in a hotel: *The swimming pool is free to hotel guests.*

**guid·ance** /**gīd**'nss/ *noun* advice about what you should do: *I asked my teacher for guidance about which classes I should take next semester.*

**guide** /gīd/
● *noun*
**1** someone whose job is to show a place to tourists: *Our guide showed us around the old city and told us about its history.*
**2** a book which gives information about a subject: *The phone comes with a guide which tells you how to use it.*
● *verb*
**1** to help someone to go somewhere: *A nurse went with us and guided us to the room where my sister was in the hospital.*
**2** to help someone by showing him or her what to do: *The teacher guided us through the different parts of the test and explained what we had to do.*

**guide·book** /**gīd**-buk/ *noun* a book with information about a city, area, or country: *The guidebook tells you about all the things to see in Seattle.*

**guide dog** /**gīd** dog/ *noun* a dog that has been trained to guide blind people: *His guide dog can see the cars and knows when they can cross the road safely.*

SYNONYM: **Seeing Eye dog** *trademark*

**guide dog**

**guide·lines** /**gīd**-līnz/ *plural noun* rules or instructions about the best way to do something: *The guidelines say that your essay should be 500 words long.*

**guilt** /gilt/ *noun*
**1** a sad feeling you have when you have done something wrong: *He feels some guilt about accepting the prize because he doesn't think he deserves it.*
**2** the fact that someone has broken a law: *The thief admitted his guilt and said that he had stolen the money.* ANTONYM: **innocence**

**guilt·y** /**gilt**-ee/ *adjective*
**1** unhappy and ashamed because you have done something that you know is wrong: *I felt really guilty for cheating on the test.*
**2** if a court finds someone guilty, it decides that he or she committed a crime: *He was found guilty of murder, and he will spend the rest of his life in jail.* ANTONYM: **innocent**
—**guiltily** /**gilt**-uhl-ee/ *adverb* in an ashamed way because you have done something that you know is wrong: *She looked at me guiltily and said that she had broken the vase.*

**guin·ea pig** /**gin**-ee pig/ *noun*
**1** a small furry animal with no tail. Some people keep guinea pigs as pets: *My guinea pig lives in a cage in our yard.*

**guinea pig**

**2** someone who is used for testing something to see if it works or is good: *Mom uses us as guinea pigs when she tries out new recipes.*

**gui·tar** /gi-**tar**/ *noun* a wooden musical instrument with strings and a long neck. You play it by touching the strings: *He sings and plays the electric guitar.*
—**guitarist** /gi-**tar**-ist/ *noun* someone who plays the guitar: *My brother wants to be a guitarist in a band.*

> ## Word Origin: guitar
>
> **Guitar** comes from a Greek word for a musical instrument with strings. The word went from Greek to Arabic and then to Spanish, and English speakers took guitar from the Spanish word.

**guitar**

strings

**gulf** /guhlf/ *noun*
**1** a large area of ocean that is partly surrounded by land: *the Gulf of Mexico*
**2** a big difference between people: *There is a gulf between the way rich people and poor people live. Their lives are completely different.*

**gulf**

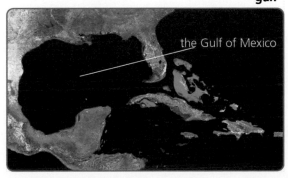

the Gulf of Mexico

**gull** /guhl/ *noun* a seagull

**gull**

**gul·li·ble** /**guhl**-uhb-uhl/ *adjective* a gullible person is easy to trick because he or she always believes what other people say: *"He said his mother needed the money and I believed him." "How could you be so gullible?"*

**gulp** /guhlp/
● *verb* (also **gulp down**) to swallow something quickly: *She gulped down her breakfast and ran for the bus.*
● *noun* the action of swallowing air or liquid quickly: *He took a deep gulp of air, and then dived into the pool.*

**gum** /guhm/ *noun*
**1** the pink parts inside your mouth that your teeth grow out of: *The dentist said my gums are healthy.*
**2** a sweet type of candy that you chew for a long time, but do not swallow: *We are not allowed to chew gum in class.*

**gun** /guhn/ *noun* a weapon that fires bullets: *Some soldiers started firing their guns.*

**gun·pow·der** /**guhn**-powd-ur/ *noun* an explosive substance used in bombs and fireworks

**gun·shot** /**guhn**-shaht/ *noun*
**1** the sound made by a gun: *We heard a gunshot and a loud scream.*
**2** the bullets that are fired from a gun: *He died from a gunshot wound.*

**gup·py** /**guhp**-ee/ *noun* (plural **guppies**) a very small brightly colored fish

**gush** /guhsh/ *verb* if liquid gushes somewhere, a large amount of it flows there: *Water was gushing out of a big hole in the pipe.*

**gust** /guhst/ *noun* a sudden strong wind: *The window was blown open by a gust of wind.*

a
b
c
d
e
f

**g**

h
i
j
k
l
m
n
o
p
q
r
s
t
u
v
w
x
y
z

**gut** /guht/ *adjective*
- *noun*

**1** (also **guts**) your stomach and the tubes in your body that food passes through: *He says that he has a pain in his gut.*
**2 guts** the courage and determination to do something difficult: *She didn't have the guts to tell him she was leaving.*
**3 gut feeling/reaction** a feeling or reaction that you are sure is right although you cannot say why: *I have a gut feeling that we are going to win this game.*
- *verb* (**gutting**, **gutted**)

to destroy the inside of a building completely: *Their beautiful house was gutted by fire.*

**gut·ter** /**guht**-ur/ *noun* an open pipe at the edge of a roof or a channel at the edge of a road. It carries away water: *Dad was cleaning leaves out of the gutter.*

**gutter**

gutter

**guy** /gī/ *noun* a man, especially a young man: *John's a really nice guy.*

**gym** /jim/ *noun* a building or room that has equipment for doing physical exercise: *She goes to the gym regularly to keep in shape.*

**gym·na·si·um** /jim-**nayz**-ee-uhm/ *noun* (plural **gymnasia** /jim-**nayz**-ee-uh/ or **gymnasiums**) a gym: *We play sports in the school gymnasium.*

**gym·nas·tics** /jim-**nast**-ikss/ *noun* a sport involving skillful physical exercises and movements: *In gymnastics we have to run and jump and turn over in the air.*
—**gymnast** /**jim**-nast/ *noun* someone who performs gymnastics: *The gymnasts ran across the mat and did somersaults through the air.*

**gyp·sy** /**jipss**-ee/ *noun* (plural **gypsies**) a member of a group of people who travel around rather than live in one place: *Gypsies used to live in beautiful wooden caravans that were pulled by horses.*

# Hh

**hab·it** /**hab**-it/ *noun* something that you do often or regularly: *Biting your nails is a bad habit.* | *Try to get into the habit of brushing your teeth after every meal.*

**hab·i·tat** /**hab**-uh-tat/ *noun* the particular area of land or water in which a plant or animal lives: *Water is the frog's natural habitat.*

**hack** /hak/ *verb*
**1** to cut something roughly or violently: *Tom hacked a branch off the tree.*
**2** to use your computer to secretly look at information on another person's computer, so that you can use it or change it: *Someone hacked into the school computer system and changed the students' grades.*

**hack·er** /**hak**-ur/ *noun* someone who secretly uses or changes the information in other people's computer systems: *Hackers were able to get into the system and download all the data.*

**had** /uhd, had/ *verb* the past tense and past participle of **have**

**had·n't** /**had**-n't/ *contraction* short for "had not": *I hadn't been to Los Angeles before.*

**hai·ku** /**hī**-koo/ *noun* (plural **haiku** or **haikus**) a short poem with three lines. The first line has five syllables, the second line has seven syllables, and the third line has five syllables. Haikus came from Japan.

**hail** /hayl/
● *verb*
**1** if it hails, small hard balls of frozen rain fall from the sky: *The weather was terrible; there was a strong wind and it was hailing.*
**2** to wave at a taxi in order to make it stop: *We hailed a cab and asked the driver to take us home.*
● *noun*
small hard balls of frozen rain that fall from the sky: *The hail destroyed the crops.*

**hair** /hair/ *noun*
**1** the covering of thin strands growing on your head: *Karen has long blonde hair.* | *Rob never brushes his hair.* ▶ see **Thesaurus**
**2** one of the many thin strands that grow on the skin of a person or animal: *There are cat hairs all over this chair.*

---

**Grammar:** hair

When you are talking about all of someone's hair, you use **hair** and it has no plural: *Tim has brown hair.*
You cannot say "Tim has brown hairs."
When you are talking about one or more pieces of hair, you can say **a hair** or **hairs**: *I found a hair in my soup!*

---

**hair·cut** /**hair**-kuht/ *noun*
**1** if you have a haircut, someone cuts your hair: *My dad keeps telling me my hair is too long and I should get a haircut.*
**2** the way your hair is cut: *I like your new haircut.*

**hair·do** /**hair**-doo/ *noun* (plural **hairdos**) a woman's hairstyle: *Lucy came home with a new hairdo – she cut it really short.*
( SYNONYM: **hairstyle** )

**hair·dress·er** /**hair**-dress-ur/ *noun* someone whose job is to cut people's hair: *I am going to the hairdresser this afternoon to have my hair cut.*

**hair·dry·er** /**hair**-drī-ur/ *noun* a machine that you use to dry your hair

**hair·spray** /**hair**-spray/ *noun* a liquid that you spray onto your hair. It makes your hair stay in the style you want.

hairdryer

hairdryer

**hair·style** /**hair**-stīl/ *noun* the style in which your hair is cut or arranged: *She's changed her hairstyle – she now has curly hair.*

**hair·y** /**hair**-ee/ *adjective* hairy arms, legs etc. have a lot of hair on them: *Monkeys have long hairy arms.*

**Haj**, **Hajj** /hahj/ *noun* a trip to the holy place Mecca that all Muslims should make, according to the Islamic religion
—**Haji** /**hahj**-ee/ *noun* a Muslim who has been to Mecca

**ha·lal** /huh-**lahl**/ *adjective* halal meat is from animals that were killed in a way that is approved by Muslim law

**half** /haf/ (plural **halves** /havz/)
● *noun*
**1** one of two equal parts of something: *Half of ten is five.* | *Break the chocolate bar in half* (=in two equal pieces). | *The trip takes half an hour* (=30 minutes). | *My brother is two and a half* (=two years and six months old).
▶ see picture at **quarter**
**2** one of two parts of a game in some sports: *The other team was leading at the end of the first half.*
● *adverb*
partly but not completely: *I can't concentrate on my work – I feel half asleep.* | *The plane was half empty.*

**half broth·er** /**haf** bruh*th*-ur/ *noun* a brother who has the same mother or father as you, but one different parent

**half dol·lar** /haf **dahl**-ur/ *noun* a coin worth 50 cents

**half-hour** /haf **ow**-uhr/ *noun* 30 minutes: *I got home a half-hour before my brother.*
—**half-hour** /**haf** ow-uhr/ *adjective* continuing for 30 minutes: *The lake is about a half-hour drive from here.*

**half-mast** /haf **mast**/ *adjective* if a flag is at half-mast, it is in the middle of the pole, not at the top. This is done to show respect for someone who has died: *Flags flew at half-mast across America after 9/11.*

**half sis·ter** /**haf** sist-ur/ *noun* a sister who has the same mother or father as you, but one different parent

**half·time** /**haf**-tīm/ *noun* the short period of rest between two parts of a game such as football or basketball: *The score at halftime was 34–7.*

**half·way** /haf-**way**/ *adjective, adverb*
**1** in the middle between two places or things: *Hartford, Connecticut, is halfway between New York City and Boston.*
**2** in the middle of a period of time or an event: *Dad fell asleep halfway through the movie and never saw the end.*

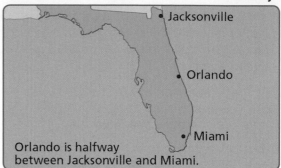
halfway

Orlando is halfway between Jacksonville and Miami.

**hall** /hol/ *noun*
**1** a narrow passage in a building, with doors that lead to other rooms: *Go down the hall and turn right, and you'll see the bathroom.*
( SYNONYM: **hallway** )
**2** an area that you go through when you enter a house, with doors that lead to other rooms: *You can hang your coats in the front hall.*
( SYNONYM: **hallway** )
**3** a big room or building that people use for public meetings, concerts, etc.: *The band will play at the concert hall downtown.*

**Hal·low·een** /hal-uh-**ween**/ *noun* October 31, when children dress as witches or ghosts and go to people's houses asking for candy by saying "trick or treat!": *We love dressing up in scary costumes for Halloween.*

**hal·lu·ci·nate** /huh-**looss**-uh-nayt/ *verb* to see or hear something that is not really there: *I thought I saw a ghost, but I was hallucinating because I had a fever.*
—**hallucination** /huh-looss-uh-**naysh**-uhn/ *noun* something someone sees or hears when it is not really there: *I wasn't sure if I really saw the ghost, or whether it was a hallucination.*

**hall·way** /**hol**-way/ *noun*
**1** a narrow passage in a building, with doors that lead to other rooms: *The bathroom is the last door on the right, at the end of the hallway.*
( SYNONYM: **hall** )

**2** a room that you go through when you enter a house, with doors that lead to other rooms: *I waited in the front hallway while my sister was getting ready for school.* ( SYNONYM: **hall** )

**ha·lo** /**hayl**-oh/ *noun* (plural **halos**) a bright circle drawn around the heads of angels and holy people in paintings

**halt** /holt/
● *verb* to stop: *Ice on the tracks halted the train.*
● *noun* a stop: *The elevator came to a halt and we got out.*

**halve** /hav/ *verb*
**1** to reduce something by a half: *The theater has halved the price of tickets on Wednesdays.*
**2** to cut or divide something into two equal parts: *She halved the sheet of paper and gave one half to me.*

**halves** /havz/ *noun* the plural of **half**

**ham** /ham/ *noun* the meat from a pig with salt added to it to keep it fresh. Ham is often eaten cold: *I had ham and eggs for breakfast.* | *a ham sandwich*

**ham·burg·er** /**ham**-burg-ur/ *noun*
**1** a flat circular piece of cooked beef, usually eaten inside a bun: *He was eating a hamburger and fries.*
**2** beef that is cut into very small pieces. It is used for making hamburgers and other dishes: *I bought a pound of hamburger to make chili.*

## Word Origin: hamburger

**Hamburger** is a word that started in the United States. Hamburger is short for Hamburg steak. Hamburg is a city in Germany, and many German people went through Hamburg when they left to come to the United States. But no one knows why a hamburger is named after this city in Germany!

**ham·mer** /**ham**-ur/
● *noun*
a tool you use for hitting nails into wood: *Dad was knocking nails in with a hammer.*
● *verb*
**1** to hit something with a hammer: *Hammer a nail into the wall and hang a picture on it.*

**2** to hit something repeatedly, making a loud noise: *I hammered on the front door, but he didn't hear me because he was asleep.* | *The rain was hammering on the roof of the bus.*

**hammer**

**ham·mock** /**ham**-uhk/ *noun* a long piece of material, that you hang between two trees or poles and lie on: *He was asleep in a hammock outside his beach hut.*

**hammock**

**ham·per** /**hamp**-ur/ *verb* to make it difficult to do something: *The bad weather hampered the rescue.*

**ham·ster** /**ham**-stur/ *noun* a small animal like a mouse with no tail. People often keep hamsters as pets: *You need to clean out the hamster's cage.*

**hamster**

a b c d e f g h i j k l m n o p q r s t u v w x y z

a
b
c
d
e
f
g
**h**
i
j
k
l
m
n
o
p
q
r
s
t
u
v
w
x
y
z

## hand /hand/

● *noun*

**1** the part of your body at the end of your arm. You use your hand to hold things: *I write with my left hand.* | *Wash your hands before dinner.*

**2** one of the parts on a clock that move to show the time: *The small hand on a clock shows the hours.*

▶ see pictures at **clock, watch**

**3** the cards that you are holding in a game: *Josh had a very good hand – he had three aces.*

● *verb*

**1** to give something to someone else using your hand: *Hand me the phone, please. I need to make a call.*

**2 hand down** to give something to a younger member of your family: *This necklace was handed down by my grandmother to me.*

**3 hand in** to give something to a teacher, the police, etc.: *I forgot to hand in my homework on Friday – can I give it to you now?*

**4 hand out** to give something to every person in a group: *The teacher handed out the tests, giving one to each student.*

> IDIOMS with **hand**
>
> **by hand** done or made by a person, not a machine: *This sweater needs to be washed by hand – don't put it in the washing machine.*
>
> **get out of hand** to become impossible to control: *The problem is getting out of hand – he spends all day playing computer games.*
>
> **give/lend someone a hand** to help someone: *If you need some help, I will give you a hand.*
>
> **on hand** near and ready if needed: *Make sure there is an adult on hand to help you.*

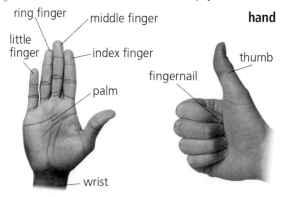

ring finger — middle finger — **hand**
little finger — index finger — thumb
— fingernail
— palm
— wrist

## hand·bag /**hand**-bag/ *noun* a bag in which a woman carries money, keys, and other small things: *She took her cell phone out of her handbag.* ( SYNONYM: **purse** )

## hand·ball /**hand**-bol/ *noun* a game in which players use their hands to hit a ball against a wall: *We played handball and Damon couldn't hit the ball before it bounced twice so he was out.*

## hand·book /**hand**-buk/ *noun* a small book with information or instructions about something: *The handbook says that students must wear school uniform.*

## hand·cuffs /**hand**-kuhfss/ *noun* two metal rings joined by a chain. Handcuffs are used to hold a prisoner's wrists together: *The police officers arrested him and put him in handcuffs.*
—**handcuff** /**hand**-kuhf/ *verb* to put handcuffs on someone: *Officers handcuffed him and took him to the police station.*

## hand·ful /**hand**-ful/ *noun*

**1** an amount that you can hold in your hand: *She took a handful of popcorn from the bowl.*

**2** a small number of people or things: *Only a handful of people know the truth.*

## hand·i·cap /**hand**-ee-kap/

● *noun*

**1** an inability to use part of your body or brain because it has been damaged: *Students with physical handicaps can come into the classroom in their wheelchairs.* ( SYNONYM: **disability** )

**2** something that makes it difficult for you to do something: *My shyness is a handicap when I meet new people.* ( SYNONYM: **disadvantage** )

● *verb* (**handicapping**, **handicapped**) to make it difficult for someone to do something: *Some students are handicapped by their poor English.*

## hand·i·capped /**hand**-ee-kapt/ *adjective* having a physical or mental handicap: *We provide transportation for handicapped children.*
( SYNONYM: **disabled** )

## han·dle /**hand**'l/

● *verb*

**1** to deal with something: *If I have a problem, I ask my parents' advice on how to handle it.*

**2** to pick up or touch something: *Always wash your hands before handling food.*

● *noun*

the part of something that you hold in your hand when you carry or use it: *The handle of my bag is broken.* | *She turned the door handle and slowly opened the door.* ▶ see picture at **bicycle**

**handle**

handle

handle

handle

handle

**han·dle·bars** /**hand**'l-barz/ *noun* the part of a bicycle or motorcycle that you hold with your hands to control the direction you go in

**hand·made** /han-**mayd**/ *adjective* made by a person and not a machine: *I gave her a handmade birthday card.*

**hand-me-downs** /**hand** me downz/ *noun* used clothing that someone gives to another person in his or her family: *I always have to wear my sister's hand-me-downs.*

**hand·out** /**hand**-owt/ *noun*
**1** a piece of paper with information on it that is given to people in a class or meeting: *The teacher gave us a handout that explained our math homework.*
**2** money or food that poor people receive because they need help: *My grandparents wouldn't accept handouts from the government.*

**hand·print** /**hand**-print/ *noun* a mark made by a hand: *Your dirty handprints are all over the window!*

**hand·shake** /**han**-shayk/ *noun* a greeting in which you take someone's hand in your hand and move it up and down. People often do this when they meet for the first time: *He greeted me with a handshake.*

**hand·some** /**hanss**-uhm/ *adjective* a handsome man is attractive: *He's a very handsome man – tall and tanned, with black hair.*
( SYNONYM: **good-looking** ) ( ANTONYM: **ugly** )

**hand·stand** /**han**-stand/ *noun* a movement in which you put your hands on the ground and hold your legs up in the air: *Cheryl can do a handstand, and even walk on her hands.*

**hand·writ·ing** /**hand**-rīt-ing/ *noun* the way someone writes with a pen or a pencil: *Her handwriting is very neat.*

**hand·y** /**hand**-ee/ *adjective* (**handier, handiest**)
**1** useful: *Email is a handy way of keeping in touch.*
**2** near and easy to reach: *I'm going to read out some useful phone numbers later, so make sure you have a pen handy.*

**hang** /hang/
● *verb*
**1** (**hung** /huhng/) to attach the top part of something onto something else, so that the top part does not move but the bottom is loose: *Hang up your coat in the closet – don't leave it on the floor.*

**hang**

She is hanging her jacket on the hook.

**2** (**hanged**) to kill someone by putting a rope around the person's neck and letting him or her drop down toward the ground. In the past, people were hanged as a punishment: *They put a rope around his neck and hanged him.*
**3 hang around** to stay in one place and not do much: *I'm just hanging around, waiting for Juan to come.*
**4 hang on** to hold something tightly in order to keep it or yourself safe: *He was hanging onto the branch of the tree and trying not to fall off it.* ( SYNONYM: **hold on** )
**5 hang on** used when you want someone to wait for you: *Don't leave yet – hang on a second. I want to talk to you!*
( SYNONYM: **hold on** )
**6 hang out** to spend a lot of time somewhere with friends and not do much: *"What did you do this morning?" – "Nothing much – just hung out with my friends."*
**7 hang up** to stop talking on the telephone by putting the telephone down: *She finished her phone call and hung up.*
● *noun*
**get the hang of** if you get the hang of something, you learn how to do it: *Skating is difficult at first but when you get the hang of it it's easy.*

a
b
c
d
e
f
g
**h**
i
j
k
l
m
n
o
p
q
r
s
t
u
v
w
x
y
z

**hang·er** /**hang**-ur/
*noun* an object you use for hanging clothes on. Hangers are made of metal, plastic, or wood and have a hook on top: *Put your coat on a hanger.*

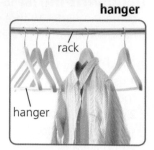
hanger

rack

hanger

**hang glid·er** /**hang** glīd-ur/ *noun* a flying machine with wings and no engine. It has a frame that you hang from in order to fly.

**Ha·nuk·kah**, **Chanukah** /**hahn**-uhk-uh/ *noun* a Jewish holiday in late November or early December that continues for eight days

**hap·pen** /**hap**-uhn/ *verb*
**1** to take place: *The accident happened outside my house.* | *Did anything interesting happen at school today?* ( SYNONYM: **occur** )
▶ see **Thesaurus**
**2** if you happen to do something, you do it by chance: *I happened to see Sean on my way home from school.*
**3** **happen to** to affect someone or something: *I'm really excited to get the prize – it's the best thing that has ever happened to me.* | *He's late – I hope nothing has happened to him.*

**hap·pi·ness** /**hap**-ee-niss/ *noun* the state of being happy: *Memories of his childhood filled him with happiness.*

**hap·py** /**hap**-ee/ *adjective* (**happier**, **happiest**)
**1** feeling pleased because your life is good or something good has happened: *Is Peter happy at his new school?* | *I'm really happy to be back home after being away for so long.*
( ANTONYM: **sad** ) ▶ see picture at **unhappy**
▶ see **Thesaurus**
**2** **Happy Birthday, Happy New Year, etc.** something you say to someone on a special occasion
—**happily** /**hap**-uhl-ee/ *adverb* in a happy way: *The children laughed happily at the clowns.*

**ha·rass** /huh-**rass**/ *verb* to keep offending or threatening someone: *The family said that their neighbors had harassed them by calling them names and damaging their car.*

—**harassment** /huh-**rass**-muhnt/ *noun* behavior that is threatening or offensive to other people

**har·bor** /**harb**-ur/ *noun* an area of water next to the land where ships can stay safely: *I watched the ship come into the harbor.*

harbor

**hard** /hard/
● *adjective*
**1** very firm and difficult to cut, break, or bend: *The chairs are hard and uncomfortable to sit on.* ( ANTONYM: **soft** ) ▶ see **Thesaurus**
**2** difficult to do or understand: *The math test was really hard – I couldn't answer most of the questions.* ( ANTONYM: **easy** )
**3** needing a lot of effort or work: *It was hard work clearing away the snow and I was very tired when I finished.* ( ANTONYM: **easy** )

IDIOM with **hard**
**be hard on** to criticize someone or be unfair to them: *He's very hard on his brother, and blames him when things go wrong.*
—**hardness** /**hard**-niss/ *noun* the quality of being firm and difficult to cut, break, or bend: *The hardness of the ice cream makes it difficult to get out of the container.*
● *adverb*
with a lot of effort or force: *The class has worked very hard so the teacher is very happy.* | *It was raining hard and we got very wet.*

**Grammar:** hard

Do not use **hardly** as an adverb meaning "with a lot of effort." The adverb of this sense of **hard** is also **hard**: *We worked very hard on our report.*
Do not say "we worked very hardly."

292

**hard**

hard

soft

**hard·back** /**hard**-bak/ (also **hardcover**) *noun* a book with a hard cover: *Hardback books are more expensive than paperbacks.*

**hard-boiled** /hard **boyld**/ *adjective* a hard-boiled egg has been cooked until it is solid inside

**hard·cov·er** /**hard**-kuhv-ur/ (also **hardback**)
● *noun* a book that has a strong stiff cover
● *adjective* having a strong stiff cover: *The hardcover edition costs $35.99.*

**hard drive** /**hard** drīv/ *noun* the part of a computer where information and programs are stored on a disk that you cannot take out of the computer: *The hard drive has 500 gigabytes of memory.*

**hard·en** /**hard**'n/ *verb* to become firm or stiff: *The glue takes about an hour to harden.*

**hard·ly** /**hard**-lee/ *adverb* almost none at all or almost not at all: *When we moved here, we hardly knew anyone.* | *I can hardly wait for my birthday.*

**Grammar: hardly**

Do not use **hardly** as an adverb meaning "with a lot of effort." The adverb of this sense of **hard** is also **hard**: *We worked very hard on our report.*
Do not say "We worked very hardly."

**hard·ship** /**hard**-ship/ *noun* something that makes your life difficult: *During those years of hardship, people did not have enough to eat.*

**hard·ware** /**hard**-wair/ *noun*
**1** computer equipment such as a monitor, keyboard, or printer: *The store sells computer hardware such as printers and cables.*
**2** tools you use to build and fix things: *I stopped by the hardware store to buy some nails.*

**hard-work·ing** /hard **wurk**-ing/ *adjective* putting a lot of effort into the work you do: *Dylan is a hard-working student and his teacher is very happy with him.* (ANTONYM: **lazy**)

**hare** /hair/ *noun* a wild animal that looks like a large rabbit but has longer ears and longer back legs: *Hares can run fast.*

**hare**

**harm** /harm/
● *noun* the damage, injury, or trouble caused by something: *Smoking can cause great harm to your health.*
● *verb* to hurt or damage something or someone: *Too much sun will harm your skin.*

**harm·ful** /**harm**-fuhl/ *adjective* causing harm: *Greenhouse gases are harmful to the Earth's atmosphere.*

**harm·less** /**harm**-liss/ *adjective* something that is harmless will not hurt someone or damage something: *Most North American spiders are completely harmless and do not bite.*

**har·mon·i·ca** /har-**mahn**-ik-uh/ *noun* a small musical instrument made of metal. It has holes along its side that you blow into to make sounds: *I can play country music on my harmonica.*

**harmonica**

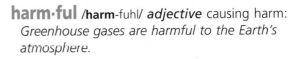

**har·mo·ny** /**harm**-uhn-ee/ *noun* (plural **harmonies**)
**1** a situation in which people do not argue with each other: *Why can't people live in peace and harmony?*
**2** a series of musical notes that sound good with other notes: *I sing the main tune and my sister sings the harmony.*

a
b
c
d
e
f
g
**h**
i
j
k
l
m
n
o
p
q
r
s
t
u
v
w
x
y
z

**har·ness** /**harn**-iss/ *verb*
● *verb* to control and use the energy from a natural force: *A dam harnesses the power of a river to produce electricity.*
● *noun* a set of leather bands that you put on a horse to control its movements

**harp** /harp/ *noun* a large triangular-shaped musical instrument that has lots of strings stretched across it from top to bottom. You play the strings with your hands.
—**harpist** /**harp**-ist/ *noun* someone who plays the harp

harp

**harsh** /harsh/ *adjective*
**1** severe or unpleasant: *If it's a harsh winter with very cold weather, many birds will die.*
**2** unkind or too strict: *I think that making him stay at home for two weeks is too harsh.*
—**harshly** /**harsh**-lee/ *adverb* in a harsh way: *You shouldn't speak to him so harshly – he didn't really do anything wrong.*

**har·vest** /**harv**-ist/
● *noun* the time when crops are collected from fields: *He helps out on the farm during the harvest.*
● *verb* to collect crops: *We harvest the corn at the end of the summer.*

**has** /uhz, haz/ *verb* the third person singular of the present tense of have: *Tina has brown eyes.*

**has·n't** /**haz**-uhnt/ *contraction* short for "has not": *He hasn't come home yet.*

**has·sle** /**hass**-uhl/
● *noun* something that is annoying to do or deal with: *I love my puppy, but cleaning up after him is a real hassle.*
● *verb* to argue with someone or to keep asking someone to do something: *He stood at the street corner, hassling people for money.*

**haste** /hayst/ *noun* if you do something in haste, you do it very quickly because you are in a hurry: He left the store in such haste that he forgot his bag of groceries.

**hast·y** /**hayst**-ee/ *adjective* done too quickly and without thinking carefully enough: *I made a hasty decision, and now I wish that I could change it.*
—**hastily** /**hayst**-uhl-ee/ *adverb* quickly: *Don't judge people too hastily before you know all the facts about the situation.* (SYNONYM: **quickly**)

**hat** /hat/ *noun* a piece of clothing that you wear on your head: *It's cold, so you should wear a hat on your head.* ▶ see **Thesaurus**

hat
sun hat
sombrero
wool hat
cowboy hat

**hatch** /hach/ *verb* if an egg hatches, a baby bird, fish, or insect comes out of it: *I saw the egg hatch and a baby chick come out.*

**hatch·back** /**hach**-bak/ *noun* a car with a door at the back that opens

hatch
The chick is hatching from the egg.

**hate** /hayt/
● *verb* to dislike someone or something very much: *I hate this town – it's so boring.*
(ANTONYM: **love**) ▶ see **Thesaurus**
● *noun* a very strong feeling of dislike: *Now that I'm older I don't feel hate for the kids who bullied me, I feel pity.* (SYNONYM: **hatred**)
(ANTONYM: **love**)

**ha·tred** /**hayt**-rid/ *noun* a very strong feeling of dislike: *She is full of hatred for the people who attacked her family.* (SYNONYM: **hate**)
(ANTONYM: **love**)

**haul** /hol/ *verb* to pull or carry something heavy: *They hauled the boat up onto the beach.*

**haunt** /hont/ *verb*
**1** if a ghost haunts a place, it appears there often: *People around here believe the old house is haunted by a ghost.*
**2** if something haunts you, you keep thinking and worrying about it: *The memory of the crash still haunts him.*
—**haunted** /**hont**-id/ *adjective* a haunted house is a place where ghosts are believed to appear: *Would you spend the night in a haunted house?*
—**haunting** /**hont**-ing/ *adjective* beautiful and a little sad, and staying in your thoughts for a long time: *The song has a haunting melody.*

**have** /hav/ *verb* (**has** /haz/, **had** /had/)
**1** to own or possess something: *Do you have a car? | He has a nice smile. | I don't have any brothers or sisters.*
**2** to eat or drink something: *We had chicken for dinner. | Can I have another donut?*
**3** to experience something: *Did you have a good time at the party?*
**4** to be sick or affected by an injury: *She has a cold. | The horse had a broken leg.*
**5** to be carrying something with you: *I don't have my cell phone with me.*
**6** to be allowed a particular amount of time to do something: *You have 30 minutes to finish the test.*
**7** if a woman has a baby, the baby is born: *My aunt had a baby girl.*
**8** (**have** /uhv/, **has** /uhz/, **had** /uhd/) used in front of other verbs to form the perfect tense when talking about the period of time up to the present: *She has been living in Boston for three years. | I have never been on a plane before.*

**have·n't** /**hav**-uhnt/ *contraction* short for "have not": *I haven't seen the movie yet.*

**have to** /**haft**-uh, **haft**-oo/ (also **have got to** /huhv **gaht** too/) *verb*
**1** if you have to do something, you must do it: *I have to get up early tomorrow. | We had to buy a new car because the old one broke down.*
**2** used when saying that you are sure that something is true or will happen: *It's nearly noon – it has to be lunchtime soon.*

**hawk** /hok/ *noun* a large bird that eats small birds and animals: *Hawks have very sharp claws.*

hawk

**hay** /hay/ *noun* dry grass that is given to farm animals to eat: *The farmer feeds the horses hay.*

**hay fe·ver** /**hay** feev-ur/ *noun* a condition like a bad cold that some people get from breathing in pollen from plants: *I get hay fever in June because of all the flowers, and it makes my eyes very sore.*

hay
The horse is eating hay.

**haz·ard** /**haz**-urd/ *noun* something that may be dangerous: *The old electrical wiring in the building is a hazard because it could cause a fire.*
—**hazardous** /**haz**-urd-uhss/ *adjective* dangerous: *Snow makes the roads hazardous.*

**haze** /hayz/ *noun* smoke, dust, or mist in the air that is difficult to see through: *After the fire, there was a haze of smoke over the town.*

**ha·zel·nut** /**hayz**-uhl-nuht/ *noun* a small round nut that tastes sweet

a b c d e f g **h** i j k l m n o p q r s t u v w x y z

**haz·y** /**hayz**-ee/ *adjective*
**1** hazy air has smoke, dust, or mist in it: *In the evening, the sky becomes hazy.* ( **ANTONYM: clear** )
**2** a hazy memory or idea is not clear: *My memory of the accident is a little hazy so I'm not sure what happened.*

**he** /ee, hee/ *pronoun* used when talking about a man, a boy, or a male animal: *He is the oldest boy in his class.* | *This is my dog Rex. He's a golden retriever.*

**head** /hed/
● *noun*
**1** the top part of your body, where your eyes, mouth, and ears are: *Emma rested her head on the pillow.* | *He gently patted the dog on the head.* ▶ see picture on page **A13**
**2** your mind: *In my head I have lots of good ideas but I find it hard to explain them.*
**3** the most important person in a company, organization, or group: *The principal is the head of the school.*
**4 heads** the side of a coin that has a picture of someone's head on it ( **ANTONYM: tails** )

  **IDIOM with head**
  **from head to toe** over all your body: *He was covered in mud from head to toe.*
● *verb*
to go in a particular direction: *It's getting dark – we'd better head home.* | *We were on a bus heading for the airport.*

**head·ache** /**hed**-ayk/ *noun* a pain in your head: *The loud noise of the music is giving me a headache.*

**head·ing** /**hed**-ing/ *noun* a word or words at the beginning of a piece of writing that tells what it is about: *At the top of the paper write your name, the date, and the heading "English Homework."*

**head·light** /**hed**-līt/ *noun* one of the two large lights on the front of a car: *It was getting dark so he turned on his headlights.*

**head·line** /**hed**-līn/ *noun* the title of a report in a newspaper: *The headline read: "Man arrested for murder."*

**head·phones**
/**hed**-fohnz/ *plural noun*
a piece of equipment
that you wear over your
ears to listen to music:
*Please put on your
headphones – I don't
want to listen to your
loud music!*

headphones

**head·quar·ters** /**hed**-kwort-urz/ *noun*
( **ABBREVIATION: HQ** ) the place from which people run a large organization or control military activities: *The company's headquarters are in Austin, Texas.*

**head start** /hed **start**/ *noun*
**1** an advantage that someone has in a race, by starting before the others: *I had a hundred-yard head start, and I still lost the race!*
**2** an advantage that helps you to be successful: *My dad taught me how to play baseball, and this gave me a head start when I started playing at school.*

**heal** /heel/ *verb* if a wound heals, the skin or flesh grows back together and becomes healthy again: *The scratch on her finger healed quickly.*

**health** /helth/ *noun* the condition of your body and your mind: *Smoking is very bad for your health.* | *My grandmother's 80, but she is in good health and walks to the store every day.*

**health care**, **healthcare** /**helth**-kair/ *noun* medical treatment and care: *Many people all over the world cannot afford to pay for health care.*

**health food** /**helth** food/ *noun* food that contains only natural substances that are good for you: *You can buy brown rice from the health food store.*

**health·y** /**helth**-ee/ *adjective*
**1** physically well and strong: *She gave birth to a healthy baby girl.* ( **ANTONYM: sick** )
▶ see **Thesaurus**
**2** good for your body and helping you to stay well: *I try to eat a healthy diet with plenty of fruit and vegetables.* ( **ANTONYM: unhealthy** )

**heap** /heep/
● *noun* a large messy pile of things: *There was a heap of clothes on the floor.*
● *verb* to put a lot of things on top of each

other in a messy way: *Her desk was heaped with books and papers so it was difficult to find the letter.*

**hear** /heer/ *verb* (**heard** /hurd/)
**1** to notice a sound with your ears: *I can hear people talking in the next apartment.* | *He heard the birds singing.* ▸ see **Thesaurus**
**2** to be told some information: *Have you heard the news? Jen had her baby.* | *I hear that you got a new job.*
**3 hear from** to get a letter, phone call, or email from someone: *Pat moved away, but we still hear from her every few months.*
**4 hear of** to know that someone or something exists: *I've heard of the book, but I haven't read it.*

**hear·ing** /**heer**-ing/ *noun*
**1** your ability to hear. Hearing is one of the five senses: *Grandpa's hearing is not very good, so you need to speak loudly and clearly.*
**2** a meeting at which people decide whether someone has done something wrong: *I know you think he is guilty, but he has the right to a fair hearing.*

**hear·ing aid** /**heer**-ing ayd/ *noun* a small piece of equipment that you put in or behind your ear to make sounds louder if you cannot hear well

**heart** /hart/ *noun*
**1** the organ that makes blood go around your body. Your heart is inside your chest: *Your heart beats faster when you run.* ▸ see picture at **anatomy**
**2** a shape that is used to mean love. It looks like this: ♥: *The Valentine's card was decorated with pink hearts.*
**3** the part of you that has strong feelings such as love: *The princess loved him with all her heart and she wanted to get married to him.*
**4** a card used in card games. The cards have red heart shapes on them: *The next card was the four of hearts.*
**5** the middle of an area or thing: *The hotel is in the heart of the city, close to all the stores and museums.*
**6** the most important part of something: *There is not enough water, and that is the heart of the problem.*

**IDIOMS with heart**
**know something by heart** to know a poem or song so well that you can say it or sing it without reading it: *I know all the words by heart – I don't need to read them.*
**break someone's heart** to make someone very unhappy: *It broke her heart when her dog died and she cried for days.*

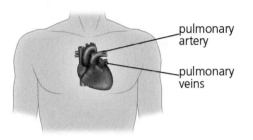

heart

pulmonary artery
pulmonary veins

**heart at·tack** /**hart** uh-tak/ *noun* a serious medical condition in which someone's heart suddenly stops working normally because it is not getting enough blood: *He had a heart attack and he almost died.*

**heart·beat** /**hart**-beet/ *noun* the movement or sound that your heart makes: *Your heartbeat increases when you exercise.*

**heart·break** /**hart**-brayk/ *noun* a strong feeling of sadness because something has happened: *Nothing can compare to the heartbreak I felt when my dog died.*

**heat** /heet/
● *noun*
**1** the warmth from something hot: *Sit a little closer so you can feel the heat from the fire.*
**2** very hot weather: *In the middle of the day we go indoors to escape the heat.*
**3** the system in a building or vehicle that keeps it warm: *It's getting cold in here – I'll turn the heat on.*
**4** one part of a race or competition. The winners of each heat compete against each other in the next round: *Taylor won his heat and will swim in the finals.*
● *verb* (also **heat up**)
to make something warm or hot: *I'll heat some soup for dinner.*

**heat·ed** /**heet**-id/ *adjective* kept warm by a heater: *They have a heated swimming pool in their yard.*

**heat·er** /**heet**-ur/ *noun* a machine for heating air or water: *The water heater is in the basement.*

**heat wave** /**heet** wayv/ *noun* a period of unusually hot weather: *The city is in the middle of a heat wave and the temperature is over 40°C.*

**heave** /heev/ *verb* to move something heavy with a lot of effort: *We heaved the old carpet into the corner of the room.*

**heav·en** /**hev**-uhn/ *noun* in some religions, the place where God is, and where good people go after they die: *She believes that if she says her prayers every night she will go to heaven.*
( ANTONYM: **hell** )

**heav·en·ly** /**hev**-uhn-lee/ *adjective*
**1** very nice, beautiful, or enjoyable: *The smell of the roses was heavenly.*
**2** relating to heaven: *We pray to God, our heavenly Father.*

**heav·i·ly** /**hev**-uhl-ee/ *adverb* a lot: *It was snowing heavily and the snow was thick on the ground.*

**heav·i·ness** /**hev**-ee-niss/ *noun* the feeling that something weighs a lot: *The heaviness of the table makes it difficult to lift.*

**heav·y** /**hev**-ee/ *adjective* (**heavier**, **heaviest**)
**1** weighing a lot: *I can't lift the box – it's too heavy.* ( ANTONYM: **light** )
**2** a lot of: *There was heavy traffic on the freeway, so it took longer to get home.* | *heavy rain* ( ANTONYM: **light** )
**3 a heavy sleeper** someone who is difficult to wake when he or she is sleeping: *He's a heavy sleeper and he didn't hear his mom telling him to get out of bed.*
**4 a heavy smoker** someone who smokes too many cigarettes: *Carlos is a heavy smoker. He smokes around 40 cigarettes every day.*
**5 a heavy drinker** someone who drinks too much alcohol

heavy

heavy          light

**heav·y-du·ty** /hev-ee **doot**-ee/ *adjective* strong and able to be used for hard work: *My mom wears heavy-duty gloves when she is cleaning the oven.*

**He·brew** /**heeb**-roo/
● *noun*
**1** a member of the Jewish people who lived long ago in the past
**2** the language spoken by some Jewish people living in Israel
● *adjective*
relating to Hebrews or their language: *Can anyone tell me the Hebrew word for God?*

**hec·tic** /**hekt**-ik/ *adjective* very busy, with a lot of different things happening: *Mom has a hectic life, with a job and three children to care for.*

**he'd** /eed, heed/ *contraction*
**1** short for "he had": *He'd never been to Washington before.*
**2** short for "he would": *Chris rang to say that he'd be late.*

**hedge** /hej/ *noun* a row of small bushes or trees growing close together. A hedge is used as a border around a yard.

**heel** /heel/ *noun*
**1** the round part in the back of your foot: *My heels were sore because my new sneakers don't fit right.* ▶ see picture at **foot**
**2** the part underneath the back of a shoe: *We don't allow shoes with high heels in school.*

**height** /hīt/ *noun*
**1** how tall someone or something is: *My brother is the same height as me.*
**2** a particular distance above the ground: *The waves can reach a height of 15 feet.*
**3** the time when something is busiest or most

successful: *July is the height of the tourist season, and the old town is very busy.*

**heir** /air/ *noun* someone who gets money or other things from a person who has died: *After the old farmer's death, his heirs decided to sell the farm.*

**held** /held/ *verb* the past tense and past participle of **hold**

**hel·i·cop·ter** /**hel**-uh-kahpt-ur/ *noun* an aircraft with long metal parts on top. These parts go around in a circle to make the helicopter fly: *A police helicopter landed on top of the building.*

### Word Origin: helicopter

**Helicopter** comes from a French word that was made up in the 1860s to describe a flying machine. That flying machine did not work, but when helicopters were invented in the 1920s, the word was borrowed to name them. The French made up the word helicopter from two Greek words. One Greek word means "spiral" and the other means "wing."

**helicopter**

**he·li·um** /**heel**-ee-uhm/ *noun* a gas that is lighter than air. Helium is often put inside balloons to make them float in the air. The symbol for helium is He.

**hell** /hel/ *noun* in some religions, the place where bad people go when they die ( ANTONYM: **heaven** )

**he'll** /eel, heel/ *contraction* short for "he will": *He'll be ten in April.*

**hel·lo** /huh-**loh**/ *interjection* a word you say when you meet someone, or talk on the telephone: *Hello Paul, how are you?*

**hel·met** /**helm**-it/ *noun* a hard hat that covers and protects your head: *Always wear a helmet when riding your bicycle.* ▶ see picture at **armor**

**helmet**

**help** /help/
● *verb*
**1** to do something that makes it easier for another person to do something: *Help Janice carry her bags to the car.* | *Mom, can you help me with my homework?* ▶ see **Thesaurus**
**2** to make a bad or unpleasant thing better: *If you take some aspirin for your headache, that will help.*
**3** if you cannot help doing something, you are unable to stop yourself doing it: *I couldn't help thinking about the test.*
**4 help yourself** used in order to tell someone to take as much food or drink as he or she wants to: *There's plenty of food, so help yourself.*
**5 help!** a word you shout when you are in danger, and you need someone to come
● *noun*
something that makes it easier for another person to do something: *If you need any help with making dinner, just ask.*
—**helper** /**help**-ur/ *noun* someone who helps another person: *The teacher asked for helpers because she had a lot of books to carry.*

**help·ful** /**help**-fuhl/ *adjective*
**1** useful: *The website is full of helpful information about taking care of your teeth.*
**2** willing to help: *The girls were very helpful and did a lot of the chores.*
—**helpfully** /**help**-fuhl-ee/ *adverb* in a helpful way: *"If you need anything, just ask me," he said helpfully.*

**help·ing** /**help**-ing/ *noun* an amount of food for one person: *I took a big helping of apple pie.*

**help·less** /**help**-liss/ *adjective* not able to take care of yourself: *When babies are born, they are totally helpless.*
—**helplessly** /**help**-liss-lee/ *adverb* without being able to do anything to help yourself: *People watched helplessly as the fire destroyed their homes.*

a b c d e f g **h** i j k l m n o p q r s t u v w x y z

**hem** /hem/ *noun* the bottom edge of clothes or curtains, that has been turned under and sewn down: *My skirt was so long that the hem touched the floor.*

**hem·i·sphere** /**hem**-uh-sfeer/ *noun* one half of something round. Hemisphere is often used to talk about half of the Earth: *The equator divides the Earth into the northern hemisphere and the southern hemisphere.* ▶ see picture at **globe**

**hen** /hen/ *noun* a female chicken: *Hens usually lay eggs in the same place every day.*

**hep·a·ti·tis** /hep-uh-**tīt**-iss/ *noun* a serious disease of the liver that can cause a fever and makes someone's skin yellow

**hep·ta·gon** /**hept**-uh-gahn/ *noun* a flat shape with seven sides

**her** /ur, hur/
● *pronoun* a woman or girl: *"Do you know Chantelle?" "Yes, I know her."*
● *adjective* belonging to a woman or girl: *Mary raised her hand.*

**herb** /urb/ *noun* a plant that you use for giving more taste to food, or for making medicine: *Cook the chicken with some fresh herbs such as parsley, thyme, or oregano.*

**herb·i·vore** /**hurb**-uh-vor/ *noun* an animal that only eats plants: *Cattle are herbivores and mainly eat grass.* ( ANTONYM: **carnivore** )

**herd** /hurd/
● *noun* a group of large animals that live together: *There was a herd of cows in the field.* | *a herd of elephants*
● *verb* to make a large group of people or animals move somewhere: *The guards herded the 100 prisoners into a large cell.*

**herd**

There is a herd of cows in the field.

**here** /heer/ *adverb*
**1** in or to the place where you are: *You need to be here by nine o'clock.* | *How far is Seattle from here?* | *It's cold in here.*
**2** if a period of time is here, it has begun: *Winter is gone and spring is here!*

**hemisphere**

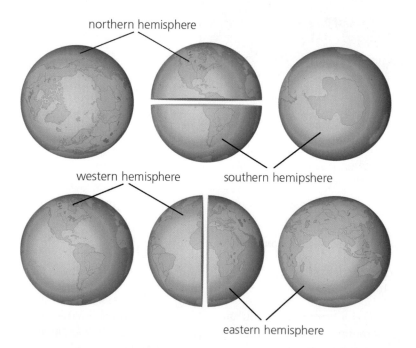
northern hemisphere
western hemisphere
southern hemipshere
eastern hemisphere

**3 here and there** in different places: *People were sitting here and there on the grass.*

**her·it·age** /**herr**-uht-ij/ *noun* the traditions and culture that are passed down over many years within a country, society, or family: *My family is Chinese-American, and we are proud of our Chinese heritage.*

**he·ro** /**heer**-oh/ *noun* (plural **heroes**)
**1** someone who you admire very much: *The firefighters who saved the boy's life are heroes.* | *His heroes are Martin Luther King and Michael Jordan.*
**2** a man who is the most important character in a book, play, or movie: *At the end of the movie, the hero catches the bad guy and saves the girl.*
—**heroism** /**herr**-oh-iz-uhm/ *noun* great courage: *The police officers received medals for their heroism.*

**he·ro·ic** /hi-**roh**-ik/ *adjective* very determined or brave: *They made heroic efforts to save her after she fell into the cold lake.*

**hers** /hurz/ *pronoun* something that belongs to a woman or girl: *My hair is brown and hers is blonde.*

**her·self** /ur-**self**, hur-**self**/ *pronoun*
**1** the woman or girl who you have just mentioned: *She hurt herself.* | *Amy bought some flowers for herself.*
**2** used with "she" or a woman's name to emphasize that you mean her and not other people: *She arranged the trip for everyone, but she herself had to stay at home.*

> **IDIOM with herself**
> **by herself** alone, without anyone else: *My grandmother lives by herself in a small house.* | *Sophie drew the picture all by herself, without anyone helping her.*

**he's** /eez, heez/ *contraction*
**1** short for "he is": *He's my brother.*
**2** short for "he has": *He's lost his keys again.*

**hes·i·tate** /**hez**-uh-tayt/ *verb* to wait for a moment before you do or say something: *She hesitated a moment and then said "Yes."*
—**hesitation** /hez-uh-**taysh**-uhn/ *noun* an act of waiting for a moment before you do or say something: *He answered the question without hesitation.*

**hex·a·gon** /**hekss**-uh-gahn/ *noun* a flat shape with six sides
—**hexagonal** /hek-**sag**-uhn-uhl/ *adjective* a hexagonal shape has six sides

hexagon

**hey** /hay/ *interjection* you say this to get someone's attention: *Hey, what are you doing with my jacket?*

**hi** /hī/ *interjection* another word for hello: *Hi! How are you?*

**hi·ber·nate** /**hīb**-ur-nayt/ *verb* if an animal hibernates, it sleeps all through the winter: *Some types of squirrel hibernate but some stay active all winter long.*
—**hibernation** /hīb-ur-**naysh**-uhn/ *noun* the state when an animal is sleeping because it is winter: *The animals eat a lot of food before they go into hibernation.*

**hic·cups** /**hik**-uhpss/ *plural noun* if you get the hiccups, you start making short sounds in your throat that you cannot control: *I laughed so much I got the hiccups.*

**hide** /hīd/
● *verb* (**hid** /hid/, **hidden** /**hid**'n/)
**1** to put something where people cannot see it or find it: *I always hide my candy in the closet so my sister can't find it.* ▶ see **Thesaurus**
**2** to go somewhere where people cannot see or find you: *You go hide and I'll come and find you.*
**3** to stop other people from knowing the truth, or seeing how you feel: *She couldn't hide her anger and started screaming and shouting.*
● *noun* the skin of an animal. People use it for leather: *Buffalo were killed for their hides, which were used to make floor coverings.*

**hide-and-seek** /hīd uhn **seek**/ *noun* a children's game. You shut your eyes while the other people hide in different places, and then you go and look for them.

**hid·e·ous** /**hid**-ee-uhss/ *adjective* very ugly: *That dress is hideous – choose another one.*

**hier·o·glyph·ics** /hīr-uh-**glif**-ikss/ *noun* a system of writing used by the ancient Egyptians in which pictures represent words

**high** /hī/

● *adjective*

**1** tall or a long way above the ground: *The wall is ten feet high.* | *We saw high mountains covered with snow.* | *The shelf is too high for me to reach.* ( ANTONYM: **low** ) ▶ see **Thesaurus**

**2** above the usual level or amount: *I got a really high score on my math test.*

**3** used to describe a very good quality or standard: *We only serve high-quality food in our restaurant.*

**4** a high sound is the opposite of a low one. Whistles and screams are examples of high sounds: *My dad can't sing the high notes because his voice is too deep.*

● *adverb*

a long way above the ground: *Throw the ball high into the air, and then see if you can catch it.*

**Word Choice: high, tall**

You use **high** to talk about mountains, walls, or fences: *Mount Whitney is the highest mountain in California.* | *The fence was too high for me to climb over.*

You use **high** to talk about how far something is from the ground: *The apples were high up in the tree.* | *There's a high diving board for the bigger kids, and a low diving board for the little ones.*

You use **tall** to talk about the height of people, trees, buildings, and other narrow objects: *She is five feet tall.* | *He is a tall man.* | *A redwood tree is very tall.* | *What is the tallest building in Chicago?* | *a tall flagpole*

**high·light** /hī-līt/

● *verb*

**1** to make people pay attention to something you think is important: *The president's speech highlighted the need to protect the environment.*

**2** to mark important words on paper or on a computer, using a color that is easy to see: *Highlight any words in the text that you do not know.*

● *noun*

the best, most important, or most exciting part of something: *The boat trip was the highlight of our vacation.*

**high·lights** /hī-lītss/ *noun*

**1** parts of someone's hair that have been made a lighter color than the rest: *My sister has blonde highlights in her hair.*

**2** the most exciting parts of a sports game that are shown on TV after the event has finished: *You can watch the game live on TV this afternoon, or see the highlights later this evening.*

**high·ly** /hī-lee/ *adverb* very or very much: *She is a highly successful singer and she has sold millions of records.* | *I highly recommend this book – it's excellent.*

**High·ness** /hī-niss/ *noun* a title for a king or queen, and some other royal people: *His Highness the Aga Khan is an important Muslim leader.*

**high pres·sure** /hī **presh**-ur/ *noun* an area of high air pressure in the sky. It usually brings warm weather.

**high school** /hī skool/ *noun* a school in the U.S. and Canada for students over the age of 14: *My sister goes to high school. She is in 10th grade.*

**high-tech**, **hi-tech** /hī **tek**/ *adjective* using very modern equipment and methods: *The classroom is very high-tech. Every student has a computer.*

**high·way** /hī-way/ *noun* (plural **highways**) a big fast road between cities: *Route 66 was a famous highway running from Chicago to Los Angeles.*

**hi·jack** /hī-jak/ *verb* to use force to take control of a plane or vehicle: *The plane was hijacked by terrorists who demanded money and weapons.*

—**hijacker** /hī-jak-ur/ *noun* someone who hijacks a plane or vehicle: *The hijackers told the pilot to fly to Rome.*

—**hijacking** /hī-jak-ing/ *noun* an act of hijacking a plane or vehicle: *The men used hijacking to steal trucks and the goods inside them.*

**hike** /hīk/ *noun* a long walk in the country: *On Sunday, we took a hike in the mountains.*

—**hike** /hīk/ *verb* to walk a long way in the country: *We hiked over the mountain into the next valley.*

**hik·ing** /hīk-ing/ *noun* the activity of taking long

walks in the mountains or in the country: *We're going to do some hiking this summer.*

**hi·lar·i·ous** /hi-**lair**-ee-uhss/ *adjective* very funny: *We couldn't stop laughing at his hilarious jokes.*

**hill** /hil/ *noun* an area of high land, like a small mountain: *From the top of the hill you can see the ocean.*
—**hilly** /**hil**-ee/ *adjective* having a lot of hills: *It's flat around here, but it gets hilly in the east.*

**hill**

hills

**him** /im, him/ *pronoun* a man or boy. You use "him" after a verb or preposition: *What did you say to him?*

**him·self** /im-**self**, him-**self**/ *pronoun*
**1** the man or boy who you have just mentioned: *Pete fell and hurt himself.*
**2** used with "he" or a man's name to emphasize that you mean him and not other people: *The president himself visited the school.*

> **IDIOM with himself**
> **by himself** alone, without anyone else: *He likes working by himself.* | *My baby brother can put his shoes on all by himself.*

**Hin·du·ism** /**hind**-oo-iz-uhm/ *noun* the main religion in India, which has many gods and teaches that people live another life on earth after they die
—**Hindu** /**hind**-oo/ *noun* someone whose religion is Hinduism
—**Hindu** /**hind**-oo/ *adjective* relating to Hinduism: *a Hindu temple*

**hinge** /hinj/ *noun* a piece of metal that is used to fix a door to its frame so that it can open and shut: *The hinge squeaks every time you open the door – put some oil on it.*

**hint** /hint/
● *noun*

**1** something you say that helps someone guess what you really want or mean: *She gave a few hints that she wanted a bicycle for her birthday.*
**2** useful advice: *The book has helpful hints on how to take care of your pet rabbit.*
**3** a small amount: *He said he was fine, but there was a hint of anger in his voice.*
● *verb*
to say something that helps someone guess what you really want or mean: *He didn't say anything directly, but he hinted that he knew a secret about Elena.*

**hip** /hip/ *noun* the part of your body where your legs join your body: *She stood with her hands on her hips.*

**hip·po·pot·a·mus** /hip-uh-**paht**-uhm-uhss/ (also **hip·po** /**hip**-oh/) *noun* (plural **hippopotamuses**) a large African animal with a fat body and thick gray skin. Hippopotamuses live in or near water.

**hippopotamus**

**hire** /hī-ur/ *verb* to pay someone to work for you: *The school is growing and plans to hire more teachers.* (SYNONYM: **employ**)

**his** /iz, hiz/
● *adjective* belonging to a man or boy: *Michael put on his baseball cap.*
● *pronoun* something that belongs to a man or boy: *Chris claimed that the phone was his.* | *Yes, I know Tommy. I'm a friend of his.*

**His·pan·ic** /hi-**span**-ik/ *noun* someone from a country where the people speak Spanish or Portuguese: *A lot of kids in my class are Hispanics. They come from Mexico and Guatemala.*
—**Hispanic** /hi-**span**-ik/ *adjective* from a country where the people speak Spanish or Portuguese: *A lot of Hispanic children speak Spanish at home and English at school.*

**hiss** /hiss/
● *verb*
**1** to make a noise that sounds like "ssss": *The snake hissed at me.*
**2** to make this noise when you do not like a performer or speaker: *The crowd began hissing at the band and telling them to get off the stage.*
**3** to say something quietly, but in an angry way: *"I hate you!" she hissed.*
● *noun*
a sound like "ssss": *The elevator doors opened with a hiss.* ▶ see picture on page **A16**

**hist·o·gram** /**hist**-uh-gram/ *noun* a type of bar graph in which the area of each bar represents how often a value appears in a set of data: *We made a histogram showing the birth months of everyone in the class.*

**his·to·ri·an** /hi-**stor**-ee-uhn/ *noun* someone who studies or writes about history: *She is a historian who wrote a book about the Civil War.*

**his·tor·ic** /hi-**stor**-ik/ *adjective* important in history: *It was a historic moment when man landed on the moon.*

**his·to·ry** /**hist**-uhr-ee/ *noun*
**1** the study of things that happened in the past: *I love history and really enjoyed learning about Christopher Columbus.*
**2** all the things that happened in the past: *Lincoln was one of the greatest U.S. presidents in history.*
—**historical** /hi-**stor**-ik-uhl/ *adjective* relating to things that have happened in the past: *I'm reading a historical novel about a child who was alive during the American Revolution.*

**Word Family: history**

**history** *noun* | **historic** *adjective* | **historical** *adjective* | **historian** *noun* | **prehistoric** *adjective*

**hit** /hit/
● *verb* (**hitting**, **hit**)
**1** to move your hand quickly, so that you touch something with a lot of force: *Sam was so angry that I thought he was going to hit me.* | *He swung the bat and hit the ball as hard as he could.* ▶ see **Thesaurus**
**2** to crash into something: *She fell and hit her head on the sidewalk.*

**3** to affect someone or something very badly: *The increase in prices will hit poor families.*

⌐ **IDIOM with hit**
**hit it off** if two people hit it off, they like each other as soon as they meet: *My dad and my friend's dad really hit it off because they both love football.*
● *noun*
**1** a movie, song, or play that is very successful: *I bought an album of Rhianna's greatest hits.*
**2** the act of hitting the ball in a game such as baseball

**HIV** /aych ī **vee**/ a virus that can cause the disease AIDS. HIV affects white blood cells that help the body to fight diseases. HIV is short for Human Immunodeficiency Virus.

**hive** /hīv/ *noun*
**1** (also **bee·hive** /**bee**-hīv/) a place where bees live: *The beekeeper took the honey out of the hive.*
**2** **hives** bumps on your skin that you want to scratch. You usually get hives when you are allergic to something: *Strawberries give me hives so my skin gets very uncomfortable when I eat them.*

hive

**hoard** /hord/
● *verb* (also **hoard up**) to collect or hide a lot of something you will use in the future: *Squirrels hoard food for the winter.*
—**hoarder** /**hord**-ur/ *noun* someone who hoards something: *He's a hoarder who never throws anything away, so his house is full of junk.*
● *noun* a large amount of something that someone has hidden: *The pirates had a secret hoard of buried treasure.*

**hoarse** /horss/ *adjective* if you are hoarse, your voice sounds low and is not clear: *She was hoarse from yelling.*
—**hoarsely** /**horss**-lee/ *adverb* if you speak hoarsely, your voice sounds hoarse: *"I have a sore throat," he said hoarsely.*

**hoax** /hohkss/ *noun* an unkind trick to make people think something that is not true: *Someone called the store and said there was a bomb inside, but it was just a hoax.*

**hob·by** /**hahb**-ee/ *noun* (plural **hobbies**) an activity that you enjoy doing in your free time: *My hobbies are reading and playing basketball.*

**hock·ey** /**hahk**-ee/ (also **ice hock·ey** /**iss** hahk-ee/) *noun* a game played on ice by two teams of six players. The players use special sticks to try to hit a puck (=small hard object) into a net at each end of the ice: *He plays hockey in a youth league.*

**hockey**

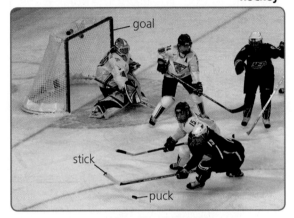

**hoe** /hoh/ *noun* a garden tool with a long handle, used for making the soil loose

**hog** /hog/
● *noun*
**1** a large pig: *They had a big party where they roasted a hog.*
**2** a greedy person who takes more than their share of something: *Don't be such a hog! You've already had two servings of pie!*
● *verb* (**hogging**, **hogged**)
to use something a lot, so it is difficult for other people to use it: *My brother always hogs the bathroom in the morning – he spends hours in there!*

**ho·gan** /**hohg**-uhn/ *noun* a traditional Navajo house made of branches covered with mud or soil

**hoist** /hoyst/
● *verb* to lift someone or something up to a higher place: *Dad hoisted me up onto his shoulders.* | *They hoisted the flag up the flagpole.*
● *noun* a piece of equipment used for lifting things and people: *He uses a special hoist to lift him into his wheelchair.*

**hold** /hohld/
● *verb* (**held** /held/)
**1** to have something in your hands or arms: *In the picture the girl is holding a flower in her hand.* | *Hold my books for a minute, will you?*
▶ see **Thesaurus** ▶ see picture on page **A15**
**2** to keep something in a position: *He held the door open for her and she walked in the room.* | *Hold up your hand if you think you know the right answer.*
**3** to have a meeting or a party: *The principal will hold a meeting for parents on Monday to tell them about the trip.*
**4** to have space for a number or amount of something: *The theater holds 800 people, but today it is only half full.*
**5** to have a particular position or job: *The president holds office for four years and then there is an election.*
**6 hold on** to wait for a short time: *Hold on a minute – let me just get my jacket.*
**7 hold out** to hold something in your hand and give it to someone: *She held the glass out to him and he took it.*
**8 hold up** to make someone or something late: *Sometimes the traffic holds us up and I'm late for school.*

IDIOMS with **hold**
**hold your breath** to stop breathing for a short time: *He held his breath and then jumped into the water.*
**hold it!** you say this when you are telling someone to wait or stop: *Hold it! You can't go in there!*
● *noun*
**1** the bottom part of a ship, where you store goods: *The boxes are all stored in the hold.*
**2** if you have a hold on something, you are holding it: *My dad had a firm hold on my arm, so that I wouldn't fall off my bike.* | *Take hold of my hand when we cross the street.*

IDIOM with **hold**
**get hold of** to find someone or something that you need or want: *If you need to get hold of me, call me on my cell phone.*

**hold·er** /**hohld**-ur/ *noun*
**1** someone who has or owns something: *Only ticket holders can go into the game.*
**2** something that holds or contains another thing: *a candle holder*

a
b
c
d
e
f
g

h

i
j
k
l
m
n
o
p
q
r
s
t
u
v
w
x
y
z

**hole** /hohl/ *noun*
**1** an empty space, especially where something is broken or torn: *I fell on the street and tore a hole in my jeans.* ▶ see **Thesaurus**
**2** a space in the ground where an animal lives: *a rabbit hole*

hole

hole

a rabbit hole

**hol·i·day** /hahl-uh-day/ *noun* (plural **holidays**)
an official day when people do not have to go to school or work: *Martin Luther King Day is a holiday in America.*

**Word Origin:** holiday

**Holiday** comes from an Old English word that means "holy day." At first, holidays were days that were important in the Christian religion, such as Christmas and Easter. Later, people started using holiday about any special day, especially if you do not have to work on that day.

**hol·low** /hahl-oh/
● *adjective* having an empty space inside: *The tree is hollow and you can hide inside it.*
( **ANTONYM: solid** )
● *noun* a hole that is not very deep: *A bird has made its nest in a hollow in the rocks.*

hollow

a hollow tree

**hol·ly** /hahl-ee/ *noun* a small tree with dark green pointed leaves and small red berries. The leaves and berries are used as decorations at Christmas.

holly

**ho·ly** /hohl-ee/ *adjective* (**holier, holiest**)
**1** relating to God or religion: *The Koran is the Islamic holy book.* ( **SYNONYM: sacred** )
**2** a holy person is very religious and good: *He is very holy and spends a lot of time praying.*
—**holiness** /hohl-ee-niss/ *noun* the quality of being good in a religious way

**home** /hohm/
● *noun*
**1** the place where you live: *I was at home watching TV.*
**2** a place where people live if they need someone to take care of them: *Grandpa lives in a home for the elderly.*
**3 at home** feeling happy and confident somewhere because you know it well: *I'm already feeling at home at my new school.*
● *adverb*
to or at the place where you live: *I walk home from school with my friends.* | *Is Dad home from work yet?*
● *adjective*
**1** done at home or for use at home: *We love Mom's home cooking.* | *Many families now have a home computer.*
**2** relating to the place where you live or were born: *What is your home address?* | *They met in their home town of Minneapolis.*
**3** playing on your team's sports field, not the field of another team: *Mom comes to watch all my home games but sometimes she can't come when we play away.* ( **ANTONYM: away** )

**home·land** /hohm-land/ *noun* the country where you were born: *My grandfather left his homeland and came to the U.S.*

**home·less** /hohm-liss/
● *adjective* without a place to live: *Recent floods have destroyed houses and left thousands of people homeless.*
● *noun* the homeless are people who do not

have a place to live: *He helps at a shelter, serving soup to the homeless.*

**home·made** /hohm-**mayd**/ *adjective* made at home rather than bought in a store: *I love Mom's homemade cookies.*

**home page**, homepage /hohm-payj/ *noun* the first page of a website that gives you general information about the website: *Click on this arrow to go back to the home page.*

**home plate** /hohm playt/ *noun* the place where you stand to hit the ball in baseball. The home plate is also the last place the player who is running must touch in order to get a point.

**home·room** /hohm-room/ *noun* a room where students go at the beginning of each school day to get information: *When the first bell rings, go to your homeroom.*

**home run** /hohm **ruhn**/ *noun* a good hit in baseball, that gives the player time to run all the way around, and get a point: *I was so happy when I hit a home run.*

**home·school** /hohm-skool/ *verb* to teach children at home instead of sending them to school: *Jessica lives on a farm a long way from town, so her mother homeschools her.*
—**homeschooling** /hohm-skool-ing/ (also **homeschool**) *noun* the process of teaching children at home

**home·sick** /hohm-sik/ *adjective* sad because you are away from your home: *For the first few days of summer camp you may feel a little homesick.*
—**homesickness** /hohm-sik-niss/ *noun* sadness because you are away from your home

**home·stead** /hohm-sted/ *noun*
**1** a farm and the area of land around it
**2** a piece of farming land that was given to people by the U.S. government under the Homestead Act, a law that was passed in 1862

**home·work** /hohm-wurk/ *noun* work for school that students do at home: *You have to do all your homework before you can go out and play.*

**hom·i·cide** /hahm-uh-sīd/ *noun* the crime of murder: *The police are investigating a homicide in which a young woman was killed.*

**homo-** /hohm-oh/

## Word Building

**homo**graph | **homo**phone | **homo**nym
These words all have the Greek word root *homo-* in them. *Homo-* means "same." A *homograph* is a word that is spelled the same as another word, but has a different meaning or part of speech. A *homophone* is a word that sounds the same as another word, but has a different meaning. A *homonym* is a word that is spelled the same and sounds the same as another word, but has a different meaning.

**hom·o·graph** /hahm-uh-grahf/ *noun* a word that is spelled the same way as another, but has a different meaning or part of speech. For example, the noun "record" is a homograph of the verb "record."

**hom·o·nym** /hahm-uh-nim/ *noun* a word that is spelled the same and sounds the same as another, but has a different meaning. For example, the noun "bear" and the verb "bear" are homonyms.

**hom·o·phone** /hahm-uh-fohn/ *noun* a word that sounds the same as another but has a different meaning. For example, the verb "knew" and the adjective "new" are homophones.

**hon·est** /ahn-ist/ *adjective* an honest person is good, and does not lie or steal: *He is very honest so I'm sure he will pay back the money.* | *Give me your honest opinion: do you really like my hair?* ( ANTONYM: **dishonest** ) ▶ see **Thesaurus**
—**honestly** /ahn-ist-lee/ *adverb* behaving in an honest way: *Please answer these questions honestly.*

**hon·es·ty** /ahn-uhst-ee/ *noun* the quality of being honest and not lying or stealing: *Thank you for telling me the truth – I admire your honesty.* ( ANTONYM: **dishonesty** )

**hon·ey** /huhn-ee/ *noun* a sweet sticky substance made by bees, which people eat: *I like to put honey on my toast.*

**hon·ey·moon** /huhn-ee-moon/ *noun* a trip that people take just after they get married: *My parents went to Italy on their honeymoon.*

a b c d e f g **h** i j k l m n o p q r s t u v w x y z

a
b
c
d
e
f
g
**h**
i
j
k
l
m
n
o
p
q
r
s
t
u
v
w
x
y
z

**honk** /hahngk/
● *verb*
to make a loud noise with a car horn: *Someone walked out in front of our car, and Dad honked his horn.*
● *noun*
**1** a loud noise made by a car horn: *I heard a honk and saw my friend pass by in his mom's car.*
**2** a loud noise made by a goose

**hon·or** /**ahn**-ur/
● *noun*
**1** something that makes you feel proud: *It is an honor to play for the school team.*
**2** the respect that someone or something receives from other people: *We wanted to win the game and defend the honor of the school.*
**3** something that is given to someone to show that people admire what they have done: *He was a brave soldier and he received his country's highest honor for bravery.*

> **IDIOM with honor**
> **in honor of** in order to show respect for someone or something important: *The stadium was named in honor of a famous player.*

● *verb*
**1** to give someone a special prize or title to show that they are admired: *The actor was honored with a Lifetime Achievement Award.*
**2** if you are honored, you feel very proud: *I felt honored to be asked to take part in the competition.*

**hon·or·a·ble** /**ahn**-uhr-uhb-uhl/ *adjective*
**1** an honorable person behaves in a way that people think is right: *He was an honorable man who always kept his promises.*
**2** an honorable action deserves respect and admiration: *The honorable thing to do is to admit you are wrong and apologize.*

**hood** /hud/ *noun*
**1** the part of a jacket or sweater that you pull up to cover your head: *My jacket has no hood, so my hair gets wet when it rains.*
**2** the metal cover over the engine of a car: *Dad stopped the car when smoke started coming out from under the hood.*

hood
**hood**

**-hood** /hud/

**hoof** /hoof/ *noun* (plural **hoofs** or **hooves** /hoovz/) the hard foot of an animal such as a horse or a cow: *I could hear the sound of horses' hoofs on the road.* ▶ see picture at **horse**

**hook** /huk/ *noun*
**1** a curved piece of metal, wood, or plastic that you hang things on: *Her coat was hanging on a hook on the door.*
**2** a thin curved piece of metal that you put on the end of a piece of thin string. You use hooks to catch fish: *a fishing hook*

**hook**
hook

> **IDIOM with hook**
> **off the hook** if a telephone is off the hook, the part that you speak into is not on its base, so nobody can call you: *I tried to call her, but she had taken the phone off the hook.*

**hooked** /hukt/ *adjective* if you are hooked on something, you like it so much that you want to do it or see it a lot: *My brother is hooked on computer games and he sometimes plays them all night.*

**hoop** /hoop/ *noun* a round piece of wood, metal, or plastic: *In basketball the players try to throw the ball through the hoop.*

**hoo·ray** /hu-**ray**/ you shout this when you are very happy about something: *Hooray! I won!*

**hoot** /hoot/
● *verb*
**1** to laugh loudly because you think something is

funny or stupid: *She hooted with laughter.*
**2** if an owl hoots, it makes a long "oo" sound
● *noun*
**1** a shout or laugh that shows you think something is funny or stupid: *Hoots of laughter came from the kitchen – it sounded like they were having fun.*
**2** a long "oo" sound that an owl makes

**hooves** /hoovz/ *noun* a plural of hoof

**hop** /hahp/
● *verb* (**hopping, hopped**)
**1** if a bird or animal hops, it moves with short quick jumps: *The bird hopped across the grass.*
**2** if people hop, they jump on one leg: *I could only find one shoe, so I hopped along the hallway.*
● *noun*
a short jump: *The little boy did three hops.*

**hop**

She is hopping along the path.

**hope** /hohp/
● *verb*
to want something to happen or be true: *I hope that everything is okay.* | *I am hoping to get an A.* | *We were hoping for good weather.*
● *noun*
**1** the feeling that something good may happen: *I am full of hope that things will get better.*
**2** a chance that you will succeed in doing something: *There is no hope that we will win the game now.*
**3** something that you hope will happen: *He talked about his hopes and dreams for his future.*

**hope·ful** /hohp-fuhl/ *adjective* believing that what you want will happen: *She is hopeful that she will pass the test.*

**hope·ful·ly** /hohp-fuhl-ee/ *adverb*
**1** you say this to show what you hope will happen: *Hopefully, the weather will be better tomorrow.*
**2** in a hopeful way: *"Can I come with you?" Andy asked hopefully.*

**hope·less** /hohp-liss/ *adjective*
**1** a situation that is hopeless is very bad and not likely to improve: *The explorers were lost in the desert, and the situation seemed hopeless.*
**2** someone who is hopeless at doing something is very bad at it: *I'm hopeless at basketball.*

**hop·scotch** /hahp-skahch/ *noun* a children's game in which each child has to jump from one numbered square to another in a pattern marked on the ground: *The children are playing hopscotch on the sidewalk.*

**Word Origin:** hopscotch

The word **hopscotch** was invented in the 1700s. In the game, you hop from square to square. The "scotch" part of the word comes from "scratch," because the squares were scratched into the ground with a stick (scratched means drawn or cut).

**ho·ri·zon** /huh-**rīz**-uhn/ *noun* the line where the land or ocean seems to meet the sky: *We looked out at the ocean and saw a ship on the horizon.*

**horizon**

A boat is on the horizon.

**hor·i·zon·tal** /hor-uh-**zahnt**'l/ *adjective* flat and going straight across from side to side: *The U.S. flag has horizontal red and white stripes.*
(ANTONYM: **vertical**)
—**horizontally** /hor-uh-**zahnt**'l-ee/ *adverb* in a horizontal way: *Cut the apples in half horizontally.*

**hor·mone** /**hor**-mohn/ *noun* a chemical that your body produces, and that makes your body grow and change: *When you are excited or afraid, your body releases a hormone called adrenaline.*

a b c d e f g **h** i j k l m n o p q r s t u v w x y z

### horn /horn/ noun

**1** a hard pointed part that grows on the heads of some animals: *One of the goat's horns was stuck in the fence.* ▶ see picture at **goat**

**2** the thing in a car, bus, or truck that you push to make a loud sound. You use it to make other drivers pay attention: *The driver behind us was honking his horn because he wanted to pass us.*

**3** (also **French horn**) a musical instrument that you play by blowing into it. The horn is made of a brass tube that is curved into a circle: *I'm learning to play the horn.*

**horn**

horn

horn

### hor·net /horn-it/ noun

a large flying insect that can sting you. Hornets are usually black and yellow or black and red: *My little brother got stung by a hornet.*

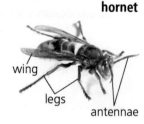

**hornet**

wing

legs

antennae

### hor·o·scope

/hor-uh-skohp/ noun a description of what someone says will happen to you, based on the position of the stars when you were born: *I'm a Libra and my horoscope says I will receive some good news today.*

### hor·ri·ble /hor-uhb-uhl/ adjective

**1** very bad: *Rotten eggs have a horrible smell.* | *The weather has been horrible this week.* ▶ see **Thesaurus**

**2** very frightening, worrying, or upsetting: *Four people were hurt in a horrible car accident on the freeway.*

—**horribly** /hor-uhb-lee/ adverb very badly: *He was horribly burned in the fire.*

### hor·ri·fied /hor-uh-fīd/ adjective feeling very

shocked or upset: *We were horrified to hear about the plane crash.*

—**horrify** /hor-uh-fī/ verb (**horrifies**, **horrified**) to make someone feel horrified: *The pictures horrified many people because they were so shocking.*

### hor·ror /hor-ur/ noun

**1** a feeling of great shock or fear: *I watched in horror as the car crashed into a tree.*

**2** a horror story or movie is one in which strange and frightening things happen: *I watched a horror movie about people who live in a house that has ghosts in it.*

### horse /horss/ noun a large animal that people

ride. Horses are often used in races: *I sometimes ride a horse on my uncle's farm.*

▶ see **Thesaurus**

IDIOM with **horse**

**hold your horses!** used when asking someone to wait or stop

**horse**

mane

neck    back

tail

knee

hoof

### horse·back /horss-bak/

● *noun* **on horseback** riding a horse: *We passed two girls on horseback.*

● *adverb* on a horse: *I learned to ride horseback.*

### horse·back rid·ing /horss-bak rīd-ing/ noun

the activity of riding horses: *I often go horseback riding.*

### horse·play /horss-play/ noun rough noisy

behavior in which children play by pushing or hitting each other for fun: *Horseplay on the school bus is not allowed.*

### horse·shoe /horsh-shoo/ noun a curved piece

of iron that is fixed to the bottom of a horse's foot

**hose** /hohz/ *noun* a long tube that water or air can travel through: *Mom was washing the car with the hose.*

hose

hose

**hos·pi·tal** /**hahss**-pit'l/ *noun* a building where doctors and nurses help people who are sick or hurt: *I hurt my arm and had to go to the hospital.*

**host** /hohst/ *noun*
**1** a person who organizes a party and invites people to it: *Our host greeted us at the door and took our coats.*
**2** someone who introduces the guests on a television or radio show: *He is the host of a very popular TV talk show.*

**hos·tage** /**hahst**-ij/ *noun* someone who is kept as a prisoner by an enemy, until other people do what the enemy asks: *The terrorists are holding five hostages and demanding money from the U.S.*

**host·ess** /**hohst**-iss/ *noun*
**1** a woman who organizes a party and invites people to it: *The hostess greeted the guests as they arrived.*
**2** the woman who introduces the guests on a television or radio show
**3** a woman who takes people to their table in a restaurant

**hos·tile** /**hahst**'l/ *adjective* very unfriendly: *You shouldn't be hostile to someone just because they are different from you.*
—**hostility** /hah-**stil**-uht-ee/ *noun* unfriendly feelings or behavior: *There is a lot of hostility between the two countries.*

**hot** /haht/ *adjective* (**hotter**, **hottest**)
**1** having a lot of heat: *I'm hot – can I take my sweater off? | a pot of hot water* ( ANTONYM: **cold** )
▶ see **Thesaurus**
**2** having a spicy taste: *I like pizza with hot peppers.* ( ANTONYM: **mild** )

**hot-air bal·loon** /haht-**air** buh-loon/ *noun* an aircraft that consists of a large bag filled with hot air or gas, with a basket under it that people can travel in: *The hot-air balloon went up into the sky.*

**hot dog**, **hotdog** /**haht**-dog/ *noun* a long sausage that you eat in a piece of bread: *You can get hot dogs from a stand on the street corner.*

**Word Origin:** hot dog

**Hot dogs** got their name in the 1890s. No one knows exactly why they are called hot dogs. The name may have started because some people believed that cheap sausages were made from dog meat.

**ho·tel** /hoh-**tel**/ *noun* a building where you pay to stay in a room, for example when you are on vacation: *We stayed in a hotel near the beach.*

**hour** /ow-ur/ *noun* a time period of 60 minutes: *I study for two hours every night. | I'll see you in an hour.*

**hour hand** /**ow**-ur hand/ *noun* the shorter of the two moving pieces on a clock or watch that show you what time it is: *The hour hand points to the hour of the day.*

**hour·ly** /**ow**-ur-lee/ *adjective*, *adverb* happening every hour: *There is an hourly bus service to the swimming pool from here.*

**hours** /**ow**-urz/ *noun* a very long time: *I waited for hours but nobody came.*

**house** /howss/ *noun* (plural **houses** /**how**-ziz/)
**1** a building that you live in, especially with your family: *I'm going to my friend's house after school today.* ▶ see **Thesaurus**
**2** all the people who live in a house: *Be quiet, you'll wake up the whole house!*

**house·hold** /**howss**-hohld/ *noun* all the people living together in a house or apartment: *Every member of the household helps with the cleaning.*
—**household** /**howss**-hohld/ *adjective* relating to a house and the people who live in it: *The store sells household appliances such as washing machines and dishwashers.*

**House of Rep·re·sent·a·tives** /howss uhv rep-ri-**zent**-uht-ivz/ *noun* the larger of the two sections of the government that makes laws in the U.S., Australia, and New Zealand

**house·wife** /**howss**-wīf/ *noun* (plural **housewives** /**howss**-wīvz/) a woman who works at home doing the cooking and cleaning for her family: *She is a busy housewife with two young children to take care of.*

**house·work** /**howss**-wurk/ *noun* work that you do at home such as washing and cleaning: *We always help our parents with the housework.*

**hous·ing** /**howz**-ing/ *noun* the houses and apartments that people live in: *New housing is going to be built on this land.*

**how** /how/ *adverb, conjunction*
**1** used for asking or talking about the way you do something: *How do you spell your name? | How are we going to explain this to Mom? | She showed me how to cook an omelet.*
**2** used for asking or talking about the amount of something: *How old are you? | I don't know how much it will cost.*
**3** used for asking someone for their opinion: *"How do I look in this dress?" "Great!" | "How's school?" "It's okay."*
**4** used for asking if someone is well: *Hello Tara, how are you? | How's your mom – is she better?*

**how·ev·er** /how-**ev**-ur/ *adverb*
**1** you use this to mean "but," before saying something a little surprising: *Our math homework was very hard. However, I managed to do it in the end.*
**2** **however long/however difficult, etc.** even if something is very long, difficult, etc.: *Most people make mistakes, however careful they are.*

**howl** /howl/
● *verb*
**1** if a dog or a wolf howls, it makes a long loud sound
**2** to make a loud sound because you are unhappy or in pain: *"Ow! That hurts!" he howled.*
**3** to laugh very loudly: *Everyone howled with laughter when they saw me covered in mud.*
● *noun*
**1** a long loud sound made by a dog or a wolf
**2** a loud sound made by someone who is unhappy or in pain: *She gave a howl as she hit her elbow hard on the corner of the desk.*
**3** a very loud laugh: *I could hear howls of laughter coming from the class next door.*

**hud·dle** /**huhd**′l/ (also **huddle together**) *verb* to

move very close to the other people in a small group: *It was freezing cold so we huddled together to keep warm.*

**hug** /huhg/
● *verb* to put your arms around someone to show love or friendship: *She put her arms around me and hugged me tightly.*
● *noun* the act of hugging someone: *Grandma gave me a hug.*

**huge** /hyooj/ *adjective* very big: *I had a huge cake for my birthday.*

**huge·ly** /**hyooj**-lee/ *adverb* very: *The movie was hugely successful and made millions of dollars.*

**hum** /huhm/ *verb* (**humming, hummed**)
**1** to sing a tune with your mouth closed: *She hummed along to a song on the radio.*
**2** to make a low steady sound like a bee: *My computer is making a humming sound.*

**hu·man** /**hyoom**-uhn/ *adjective* relating to people: *The human body is made up of a head, neck, torso, two arms and two legs.*

**hu·man be·ing** /hyoom-uhn **bee**-ing/ (also **human**) *noun* a person: *They have not tested the drug on human beings yet.*

**hu·mane** /hyoo-**mayn**/ *adjective* not cruel: *Farm animals should be kept in humane conditions, with enough space to move freely.*
—**humanely** /hyoo-**mayn**-lee/ *adverb* in a way that is not cruel: *The animals were killed humanely so they did not suffer.*

**hu·man·it·ies** /hyoo-**man**-uht-eez/ *noun* subjects of study such as literature, history, art, and philosophy, but not science

**hu·man·i·ty** /hyoo-**man**-uht-ee/ *noun*
**1** all the people in the world: *We want a clean safe world for all humanity.*
**2** kindness and respect toward other people: *Even in war we should treat prisoners with humanity.*

**hu·man race** /hyoom-uhn **rayss**/ *noun* **the human race** all people, rather than animals or other types of life: *Climate change could threaten the survival of the human race.*

**hu·man rights** /hyoom-uhn **rītss**/ *plural noun* the basic rights that everyone has to be free and to be treated well, especially by the government:

*She comes from a country that has a bad record on human rights; many people have been unfairly put in prison.*

**hum·ble** /**huhm**-buhl/ *adjective*

**1** someone who is humble does not think that he or she is special or important: *Despite her great achievements, she is still very humble.*

ANTONYM: **proud**

**2** poor and of a low social rank: *His parents were poor farmers, but he rose from these humble beginnings to become a senator.*

—**humbly** /**hum**-blee/ *adverb* in a humble way: *"It's such an honor to meet you," she said humbly.*

**hu·mid** /**hyoom**-id/ *adjective* if the weather is humid, the air feels warm and wet: *It was a hot humid afternoon and I wanted to take a shower.*

—**humidity** /hyoo-**mid**-uht-ee/ *noun* the amount of water in the air: *A warm bathroom is an ideal place for plants that need high humidity.*

**hu·mil·i·ate** /hyoo-**mil**-ee-ayt/ *verb* to make someone look stupid or weak, in an upsetting way: *You humiliated me in front of my friends by telling them my secret!*

—**humiliated** /hyoo-**mil**-ee-ayt-id/ *adjective* feeling upset because someone or something has made you look stupid or weak: *I was so humiliated when they all laughed at me.*

—**humiliating** /hyoo-**mil**-ee-ayt-ing/ *adjective* making you look stupid or weak: *Coming last in the race was a humiliating experience.*

—**humiliation** /hyoo-mil-ee-**aysh**-uhn/ *noun* a feeling of being upset because someone or something has made you look stupid or weak: *She suffered a lot of humiliation when she failed the test.*

**hum·ming·bird** /**huhm**-ing burd/ *noun* a very small, brightly colored bird whose wings move very quickly ▶ see picture on page **A4**

**hu·mor** /**hyoom**-ur/ *noun*

**1** funny things that someone says or writes: *I like her books because there is a lot of humor in them and I like to laugh.*

**2** **sense of humor** the ability to be funny and to understand things that are funny: *She doesn't get offended easily because she has a great sense of humor.*

**hu·mor·ous** /**hyoom**-uhr-uhss/ *adjective* funny:

*He is always telling humorous stories and making people laugh.*

—**humorously** /**hyoom**-uhr-uhss-lee/ *adverb* in a funny way

**hump** /huhmp/ *noun* a round part of something that is higher than the surface around it: *Camels have one or two humps on their backs.* ▶ see picture at **camel**

hump     **hump**

**hunch** /huhnch/ *noun* a feeling that something is true or will happen, which is not based on any facts: *I don't know why, but I had a hunch that something would go wrong.*

**hun·dred** /**huhn**-drid/ *number* 100: *The sneakers cost almost a hundred dollars!*

—**hundredth** /**huhn**-dridth/ *number* 100th or 1/100

**hun·dred thou·sand** /huhn-drid **thowz**-uhnd/ *number* 100,000

**hung** /huhng/ *verb* a past tense and past participle of **hang**

**Hun·ga·ri·an** /**huhng**-gehr-ee-uhn/ *noun*

● *noun*

**1** someone from Hungary

**2** the language spoken in Hungary

● *adjective*

from Hungary: *Hungarian food.*

**hun·ger** /**huhng**-gur/ *noun*

**1** the feeling you have when you want or need to eat: *At the end of the walk we were fine, apart from a few hunder pangs.*

**2** the state of not having enough food, especially for a long period of time: *The prisoners were weak from hunger.*

**hun·gry** /**huhng**-gree/ *adjective* (**hungrier, hungriest**) needing or wanting to eat something: *There's some cake in the kitchen if you get hungry.*

—**hungrily** /**huhng**-gree-lee/ *adverb* in a hungry way: *The cat looked hungrily at the fish on my plate.*

**hunk** /huhngk/ *noun* a thick piece of something, especially food: *He broke a hunk of bread off the loaf.*

a b c d e f g **h** i j k l m n o p q r s t u v w x y z

**hunt** /huhnt/
● *verb*
**1** to chase wild animals in order to kill them: *Some people hunt deer in these woods.*
**2** to look for something or someone very carefully: *We hunted for shells on the beach.*
( SYNONYM: **search** )
—**hunting** /huhnt-ing/ *noun* the activity of chasing wild animals in order to kill them: *He and his dad sometimes go hunting for rabbits.*
● *noun*
an attempt to catch or find someone or something: *The police started a hunt for the missing child.*

**hunt·er** /huhnt-ur/ *noun* someone who hunts wild animals: *Hunters kill animals for their skins or their meat.*

**hur·dle** /hurd'l/ *noun*
**1** a small fence that a person or a horse jumps over during a race: *Sally won the 100 meter hurdles race.*
**2** something difficult that you have to do: *Tests are a hurdle that everyone has to face.*

**hur·ri·cane** /hur-i-kayn/ *noun* a storm with very strong fast winds. Hurricanes start in the Atlantic Ocean or in the Caribbean Sea: *Hurricanes sometimes blow the roofs off buildings.*

**Word Origin:** hurricane

The word **hurricane** came into English through Spanish. Spanish explorers in the New World got the word for these big storms from the Indians who lived in the Caribbean islands.

**hur·ry** /hur-ee/
● *verb* (**hurries, hurrying, hurried**)
**1** to do something or go somewhere quickly: *We have to hurry or we'll miss the plane.*
( SYNONYM: **rush** )
**2 hurry up** to do something or move somewhere more quickly than before: *Hurry up! We're late!*
● *noun*
**in a hurry** more quickly than usual: *I was in a hurry to get to school on time.*

**hurt** /hurt/
● *verb* (**hurt**)
**1** to injure yourself or someone else: *I fell and*

hurt my knee. | *Was anyone hurt in the accident?* ▶ see **Thesaurus**
**2** if a part of your body hurts, it is painful: *My stomach hurts.*
**3** if something hurts, it makes you feel pain: *My throat hurts when I swallow.*
**4** to make someone feel upset: *I'm sorry. I didn't mean to hurt your feelings.*
● *adjective*
**1** injured: *Be careful with that knife or you could end up seriously hurt.*
**2** upset: *I was very hurt when she forgot my birthday.*

**hus·band** /huhz-buhnd/ *noun* the man that a woman is married to: *She lives in a small apartment with her husband and three children.*

**Word Origin:** husband

**Husband** comes from Old English and Old Norse. Old Norse was spoken in Sweden and Denmark. It comes from words that meant "house" and "live in." In Old English, a husband was the man who was in charge of a house and the people who lived in it.

**hush** /huhsh/
● *verb* you say this in order to tell someone, especially a child, to be quiet or stop crying: *Hush now. Try to get to sleep.*
● *noun* a peaceful silence: *Just before the play started, a hush fell over the audience.*

**hus·ky** /huhsk-ee/
● *adjective* a husky voice sounds low and a little rough: *I have a cold and that's why my voice is husky.*
● *noun* a strong dog with a thick coat that pulls sleds in cold parts of the world

**hut** /huht/ *noun* a small simple building with only one or two rooms: *In Africa, some people live in huts made from mud.*

**hy·brid** /hī-brid/ *noun*
**1** an animal or plant produced from parents that are genetically different: *The animal is a hybrid between a lion and a tiger.*
**2** a car that uses both gasoline and electricity

**hy·drant** /hīd-ruhnt/ *noun* a piece of equipment in the street that is used to get water for stopping fires. It is connected to a large water pipe under the ground.

**hy·dro·e·lec·tric** /hīdr-oh-i-**lek**-trik/ *adjective* using water power to produce electricity: *The Hoover Dam provided hydroelectric power to the city of Las Vegas.*

**hy·dro·gen** /**hīdr**-uhj-uhn/ *noun* a gas that has no color and is lighter than air. The symbol for hydrogen is H: *Hydrogen combines with oxygen to form water.*

**hy·giene** /**hīj**-een/ *noun* things you do to keep people and things clean in order to prevent diseases: *It is important to practice good personal hygiene, such as washing your hands before you eat.*
—**hygienic** /hī-**jen**-ik/ *adjective* clean, so that people will not get diseases: *Restaurants must have hygienic kitchens, so that people who eat in them do not get sick.*

**hy·gien·ist** /hī-**jeen**-ist/ *noun* someone who works with a dentist and cleans people's teeth or gives advice about how to care for teeth: *The hygienist told me I should use dental floss.*

**hymn** /him/ *noun* a song that people sing in Christian churches: *At church we sing hymns and pray.*

**hype** /hīp/ *noun* attempts to make people think something is good or important by talking about it a lot on television and on the radio: *I don't believe all this hype about the movie – it just looks boring.*

**hy·per·ac·tive** /hīp-ur-**akt**-iv/ *adjective* someone who is hyperactive is too active and is not able to keep quiet or be still for very long

### Word Origin: hyperactive

**Hyperactive** uses the Greek word root **hyper**, which means "too much" or "beyond measure." So someone who is hyperactive moves much more often than other people.

**hy·per·bo·le** /hī-**purb**-uhl-ee/ *noun* a way of describing something, in which you say that it is much bigger, better, worse, etc. than it really is: *Movie trailers are full of hyperbole like "the greatest film ever made!"*

**hy·phen** /**hīf**-uhn/ *noun* a mark (-) that you use to join two words or parts of a word: *The word "well-known" has a hyphen in it.*

**hyp·no·sis** /hip-**nohss**-iss/ *noun* a state like sleep during which another person can control or affect your thoughts: *Under hypnosis, he was able to remember things that had happened when he was a child.*
—**hypnotize** /**hip**-nuh-tīz/ *verb* to put someone in a state of hypnosis: *They hypnotized the witness, hoping she would remember more details of the robber's car.*

**hyp·no·tism** /**hip**-nuh-tiz-uhm/ *noun* the activity of putting someone in a state like sleep during which another person can control or affect his or her thoughts
—**hypnotist** /**hip**-nuht-ist/ *noun* a person who practices hypnotism: *He went to see a hypnotist who helped him to quit smoking.*

**hy·pot·e·nuse** /hī-**paht**'n-ooss/ *noun* the longest side in a right triangle, opposite the right angle

**hy·poth·e·sis** /hī-**pahth**-uhss-iss/ *noun* (plural **hypotheses** /hī-**pahth**-uhss-eez/) an idea that no one has proved to be true yet: *We did an experiment to test the hypothesis that girls can identify colors better than boys.*
SYNONYM: **theory**

**hys·ter·i·cal** /hi-**sterr**-ik-uhl/ *adjective*
**1** so upset or excited that you cannot control yourself: *When he saw the enormous spider, he became hysterical.*
**2** very funny: *The movie was hysterical – we laughed all the way through.*
—**hysteria** /hi-**sterr**-ee-uh/ *noun* a situation in which a lot of people feel fear, anger, or excitement: *There was hysteria when the band came on stage, with everybody screaming and jumping up and down.*

a b c d e f g **h** i j k l m n o p q r s t u v w x y z

# Ii

**I** /ī/ *pronoun* the person who is speaking: *I am ten years old.* | *If you don't want the cookie, I'll take it.*

**-ible** /uhb-uhl/

### Word Building

**-ible** is a suffix. It is used in adjectives.
aud**ible** | convert**ible** | divis**ible** | ed**ible** | invis**ible** | poss**ible**
**-ible** means "able." If a sound is *audible*, you are able to hear it. If a number is *divisible*, you are able to divide it. If a food is *edible*, you are able to eat it. If it is *possible* to do something, you are able to do it.

**-ic** /ik/

### Word Building

**-ic** is a suffix. It is used in adjectives.
allerg**ic** | athlet**ic** | histor**ic** | scientif**ic**
**-ic** means that something is related to a subject or person. Someone who is *allergic* has an allergy. Someone who is *athletic* is an athlete who is good at sports. A *historic* place is important in history. A *scientific* discovery is important in science.

**ice** /iss/ *noun* frozen water: *In winter, the water freezes, and the lake is covered in ice.* | *Do you want ice in your water?* ▶ see **Thesaurus**

**Ice Age** /iss ayj/ *noun* one of the long periods of time, thousands of years ago, when ice covered many northern countries

**ice·berg** /iss-burg/ *noun* a very large piece of ice floating in the ocean: *The ship sank after it hit an iceberg.*

### Word Origin: iceberg

**Iceberg** comes from a Dutch word that means "ice mountain." Many icebergs are as large as mountains.

**iceberg**

**ice cap** /iss kap/ *noun* an area of thick ice that covers the North and South Poles

**ice-cold** /iss-kohld/ *adjective* very cold: *She gave me an ice-cold drink from the refrigerator.*

**ice cream** /iss kreem/ *noun* a sweet frozen food made from milk or cream: *Chocolate ice cream is my favorite.*

**ice cream cone** /iss kreem kohn/ *noun* a type of cookie in the shape of a cone. You put ice cream inside it: *Do you want an ice cream cone?*

**ice cream cone**

cone

**ice cube** /iss kyoob/ *noun* a small square piece of ice that you put in a drink

**iced cof·fee** /ist kof-ee/ *noun* cold coffee served with ice, milk, and sugar

**iced tea** /ist tee/ *noun* cold tea served with ice and often lemon and sugar

**ice hock·ey** /iss hahk-ee/ *noun* a game played on ice in which two teams of players use sticks to hit a hard flat object into a goal

**ice skate** /ĭss skayt/
● *noun* a boot with a special blade on the bottom. You wear ice skates to move on ice.
▶ see picture at **skate**
● *verb* to move on ice wearing ice skates: *It's dangerous to go ice skating on frozen lakes.*
—**ice skater** /ĭss skayt-ur/ *noun* someone who ice skates

ice skate

**ice skat·ing** /ĭss skayt-ing/ *noun* the sport of sliding on ice wearing boots with metal parts on the bottom

**i·ci·cle** /ĭss-ik-uhl/ *noun* a long pointed piece of ice that hangs down from something: *It was freezing cold and there were icicles hanging from the roof.*

icicle
icicle

**ic·ing** /ĭss-ing/ *noun* a sweet substance that you put on cakes ( SYNONYM: **frosting** )

**i·con** /ĭk-ahn/ *noun*
**1** a small picture on a computer screen. You choose an icon with your mouse to make the computer do something: *Click on the printer icon to print out your work.*
**2** a famous person who a lot of people admire: *George Washington is an American icon.*

icon
icon

**ic·y** /ĭss-ee/ *adjective* (**icier**, **iciest**)
**1** very cold: *There was an icy wind so he buttoned his coat.*
**2** covered in ice: *Be careful – the sidewalk is icy.*

**I'd** /ĭd/ *contraction*
**1** short for "I had": *I'd just finished my homework when the phone rang.*
**2** short for "I would": *Thank you, I'd love to come to your party.*

**ID** /ī dee/ *noun* a document or card that shows your name, date of birth, and other personal information, usually with a photograph: *You need to show your ID when you go into the building.*

**i·de·a** /ī-dee-uh/ *noun* a plan, thought, or suggestion that you have: *Toni is very creative and has lots of good ideas.* | *I like the idea of going to the beach.* ▶ see **Thesaurus**

**i·de·al** /ī-dee-uhl/
● *adjective* the best possible: *The weather was ideal for a walk: sunny and dry, but not too hot.*
( SYNONYM: **perfect** )
● *noun* a standard or a way of behaving that is the very best and that you would like to achieve: *We support the American ideals of freedom and democracy.*

**i·de·al·ly** /ī-dee-uhl-ee/ *adverb*
**1** used to describe the way you would like things to be even if this is not possible: *Ideally, you need to do about 30 minutes of exercise every day.*
**2** in the best possible way: *The hotel was ideally located, close to the beach and the mountains.*

**i·den·ti·cal** /ī-dent-ik-uhl/ *adjective* exactly the same: *That cell phone is identical to my mom's.*

identical
identical twins

**i·den·ti·fi·ca·tion** /ī-dent-uhf-uh-**kaysh**-uhn/ *noun* official papers, such as your passport, that prove who you are: *You have to show identification before you are allowed into the building.* ( SYNONYM: **ID** )

**i·den·ti·fy** /i-**dent**-uh-fi/ *verb* (**identifies**, **identified**) to say who someone is or what something is: *Our biology teacher helped us identify all the plants we saw.*

**Word Family:** identify

identify *verb* | identification *noun* | identity *noun*

**i·den·ti·ty** /i-**dent**-uht-ee/ *noun* (plural **identities**)
**1** someone's name: *The police have discovered the identity of the thief.*
**2** the qualities that make one person or group different from others: *Maria lives in the U.S., but she still has a strong sense of her Mexican identity.*

**id·i·om** /**id**-ee-uhm/ *noun* a group of words which have a special meaning when they are used together: *"On top of the world" is an idiom meaning "extremely happy."*

**id·i·ot** /**id**-ee-uht/ *noun* a stupid person: *He's riding his bicycle with his eyes closed – what an idiot!*
—**idiotic** /id-ee-**aht**-ik/ *adjective* stupid: *They keep asking me idiotic questions like "Why are you reading?"*

**i·dle** /**id**'l/ *adjective*
**1** not working or being used: *The car has been sitting idle in the garage for years.*
**2** lazy: *Stop being so idle and clean your room!*

**i·dol** /**id**'l/ *noun*
**1** someone who you think is very good and you would like to be like them: *Miley Cyrus is my sister's idol.*
**2** a picture or statue that is worshipped as a god: *The temple was full of golden idols.*
—**idolize** /**id**'l-iz/ *verb* to admire someone very much: *He idolizes his father and wants to be a firefighter just like him.*

**if** /if/ *conjunction*
**1** used when talking about something that might happen or that might have happened: *If you're good, we'll go bowling. | He would have died if he hadn't been taken to the hospital.*
**2** whether: *I don't know if Jenny is home.*
**3** whenever: *If he eats nuts, he gets really sick.*

**IDIOM with if**
**if I were you** used when telling someone what you think he or she should do: *If I were you, I would choose the red sweater.*

**-ify** /uh-fi/

**Word Building**

**-ify** is a suffix.
simpl**ify** | clar**ify** | horr**ify** | magn**ify**
**-ify** changes the root word into a verb. Sometimes there is a spelling change in the root word. If you *clarify* something, you make it clear. If something *horrifies* you, it makes you feel horror. If you *simplify* something, you make it more simple.

**ig·loo** /**ig**-loo/ *noun* a round house made out of ice. Some Inuit people live in igloos.

**ig·ne·ous** /**ig**-nee-uhss/ *adjective* igneous rocks are formed when hot melted rock cools and becomes solid, especially after coming out of a volcano

**ig·nite** /ig-**nit**/ *verb* to make something start burning: *Someone dropped a cigarette, which ignited the dry grass.*

**ig·ni·tion** /ig-**nish**-uhn/ *noun* the part of a car where you put a key to start the engine: *He turned the key in the ignition and the engine started.*

**ig·no·rance** /**ig**-nuhr-uhnss/ *noun* the state of not knowing about something: *Fear is often caused by ignorance, so if you are scared of spiders, find out more about them.*

**ig·no·rant** /**ig**-nuhr-uhnt/ *adjective* not knowing something: *You may be ignorant of the law, but that does not excuse criminal behavior.*

**ig·nore** /ig-**nor**/ *verb* to act like someone or something is not there: *I said hello to her, but she just ignored me and kept walking.*

**il-** /il/ see note at in-

**ill** /il/ *adjective* sick: *Courtney wasn't in school today. She's ill.*

**I'll** /il/ *contraction* short for "I will": *I'll be back soon.*

**il·le·gal** /i-**leeg**-uhl/ *adjective* not allowed by the

law: *It's illegal to ride a bike without a helmet in this town.* (ANTONYM: **legal**)
—**illegally** /i-**leeg**-uhl-ee/ *adverb* in an illegal way: *He got the money illegally.*

**il·lit·er·ate** /i-**lit**-uhr-it/ *adjective* not able to read or write: *She teaches illiterate adults how to read and write.*

**ill·ness** /**il**-niss/ *noun* sickness: *She has missed a lot of school because of illness.* | *Cancer is a serious illness.*

**il·log·i·cal** /i-**lahj**-ik-uhl/ *adjective* not based on good thinking: *Why is she mean to me when she wants me to be her friend? It's illogical.* (ANTONYM: **logical**)

**il·lu·sion** /i-**loozh**-uhn/ *noun*
**1** something that seems to be real or true but is not: *One line looks longer than the other, but it's an optical illusion. They are the same length.*
**2** a belief that is wrong: *Some people have the illusion that he is very rich.*

**il·lus·trate** /**il**-uh-strayt/ *verb*
**1** to give or be an example that makes something clearer: *This story illustrates how important it is to be kind.*
**2** to draw pictures for a book: *She illustrates children's books.*
—**illustrator** /**il**-uh-strayt-ur/ *noun* someone who draws pictures for books

**Word Family: illustrate**

**illustrate** *verb* | **illustration** *noun* | **illustrator** *noun*

**il·lus·tra·tion** /il-uh-**straysh**-uhn/ *noun*
**1** a picture in a book: *There are color illustrations on every page.*
**2** an example that shows something: *The story is an illustration of how much you can achieve if you work hard.*

**im-** /im/ see note at **in-**

**IM** /ī **em**/ *verb* to send messages to someone using the Internet, using a program that lets him or her reply immediately. IM is short for "instant message": *IM me later.*

**I'm** /īm/ *contraction* short for "I am": *I'm hungry – are you?*

**im·age** /**im**-ij/ *noun*
**1** a picture that you can see on a television, in a mirror, or on a photograph: *Hold the camera steady to get a clear image.*
**2** the way that someone or something seems to people: *She decided to change her image, so she cut her hair and bought a lot of new clothes.*
**3** a picture that you have in your mind: *I have a clear image of the kind of house I want to live in.*

**im·age·ry** /**im**-ij-ree/ *noun* the things described or shown in poems, books, or movies: *The imagery in the poem is all about the ocean.*

**i·mag·i·nar·y** /i-**maj**-uh-nair-ee/ *adjective* not real and only existing in your mind: *My little sister has an imaginary friend who goes with her everywhere..*

**i·mag·i·na·tion** /i-maj-uh-**naysh**-uhn/ *noun* the ability to think of new ideas or make new pictures in your mind: *Use your imagination, and think about what it would be like to live in space.*

**i·mag·in·a·tive** /i-**maj**-uhn-uht-iv/ *adjective* having or showing a lot of imagination: *She's very imaginative and she has lots of ideas for stories.*

**i·mag·ine** /i-**maj**-in/ *verb*
**1** to use your mind to think of something: *Can you imagine having no food?*
**2** to think that something will probably happen or is probably true: *I imagine she was pretty upset.*

**Word Family: imagine**

**imagine** *verb* | **imagination** *noun* | **imaginative** *adjective* | **imaginary** *adjective*

**im·am** /**im**-ahm/ *noun* a Muslim religious leader: *The imam leads the prayers at the mosque.*

**im·i·tate** /**im**-uh-tayt/ *verb* to copy the way someone speaks or moves: *He imitated the sound of a chicken to make the kids laugh.*

## im·i·ta·tion

/im-uh-**taysh**-uhn/

● *noun* the act of copying the way someone speaks or moves: *I can do an imitation of a monkey.*

● *adjective* made to look like something real: *My jacket is made of imitation leather, not real leather.*

imitation

imitation pearls

## im·ma·ture

/im-uh-**choor**/ *adjective* behaving like someone much younger than you: *It's immature to laugh when you see two people kissing.*

( SYNONYM: **childish** ) ( ANTONYM: **mature** )

## im·me·di·ate /i-**meed**-ee-it/ *adjective*

**1** happening or coming very soon after something: *The medicine does not have an immediate effect – it takes a few hours to work.*

**2 immediate family** someone's parents, children, brothers, and sisters: *Only his immediate family was allowed to visit him in the hospital.*

## im·me·di·ate·ly /i-**meed**-ee-it-lee/ *adverb* very quickly and with no delay: *If you get ketchup on your clothes, clean it off immediately.*

( SYNONYM: **right away** ) ▶ see **Thesaurus**

## im·mense /i-**menss**/ *adjective* very large: *There was an immense amount of information to read before the trip.* ( SYNONYMS: **enormous, huge** )

## im·mense·ly /i-**menss**-lee/ *adverb* very much or very: *We enjoyed the movie immensely.*

## im·merse /i-**murss**/

*verb* to put something into a liquid so that it is completely covered: *Do not immerse electrical equipment in water.*

immerse

If you immerse a fresh egg in water, it will sink.

IDIOM with **immerse**
**immerse yourself in** to give all your attention to something: *She had immersed herself in a book and didn't notice the time.*

—**immersion** /i-**murzh**-uhn/ *noun* the act of putting something into a liquid so that it is completely covered

## im·mi·grant /im-uh-gruhnt/ *noun* someone who comes to live in a country: *His grandparents were Chinese immigrants who moved to the U.S.*

## im·mi·gra·tion /im-uh-**graysh**-uhn/ *noun* the act of coming to live in a country: *The government is trying to stop illegal immigration.*

—**immigrate** /**im**-uh-grayt/ *verb* to come to live in a country: *He immigrated to the United States from Poland.*

## im·mor·al /i-**mor**-uhl/ *adjective* bad and wrong: *Lying to your friends is immoral.*

—**immorality** /im-uh-**ral**-uht-ee/ *noun* immoral behavior: *He said that God would punish them for their immorality.*

## im·mor·tal /i-**mort**'l/ *adjective* living or continuing forever: *No one is immortal.*

( ANTONYM: **mortal** )

## im·mune /i-**myoon**/ *adjective*

**1** if you are immune to a disease, you cannot get it: *He had a test to see if he was immune to the disease.*

**2** if you are immune to something bad, it cannot affect you: *No country in the world is immune to the problem of global warming.*

—**immunity** /i-**myoon**-uht-ee/ *noun* the state of being immune to something: *Eating healthy food helps to strengthen your immunity to diseases.*

## im·mune sys·tem /i-**myoon** sist-im/ *noun* the system in your body that protects you from diseases. If your immune system is weak, you are likely to become sick: *When you are sick, your immune system works to make you well again.*

## im·mu·nize /**im**-yuh-nīz/ *verb* to protect someone from a disease by giving him or her a vaccine. The vaccine usually consists of a weak form of the disease: *Children are immunized against common diseases such as measles.*

—**immunization** /im-yuhn-uh-**zaysh**-uhn/ *noun* the act of immunizing someone: *We all had to see the nurse to get our immunizations.*

## im·pact

● *noun* /**im**-pakt/ the effect that something has: *Describe a person who has had a big impact on your life.*

● *verb* /im-**pakt**/ to affect something: *Too many late nights can impact your schoolwork.*

**im·par·tial** /im-**parsh**-uhl/ *adjective* not supporting any person or group: *When you're having problems with your friends, it can help to talk with someone impartial.*

**im·pa·tient** /im-**paysh**-uhnt/ *adjective*
**1** annoyed because something has not been done immediately: *We were getting impatient because our meals had still not arrived.*
**2** wanting to do something immediately: *I was impatient to see my new puppy.*
—**impatience** /im-**paysh**-uhnss/ *noun* the feeling of being impatient: *She was jumping up and down in her impatience to leave.*
—**impatiently** /im-**paysh**-uhnt-lee/ *adverb* in an impatient way: *"Hurry up!" he said impatiently.*

**im·peach** /im-**peech**/ *verb* to officially accuse an important public official of committing a serious crime: *They voted to impeach the president.*
—**impeachment** /im-**peech**-muhnt/ *noun* the act of impeaching a public official: *The accusations of lying led to impeachment of the president.*

**im·per·a·tive** /im-**perr**-uht-iv/
● *noun* the form of a verb that you use when you tell someone to do something: *In the sentence "Come here!" the verb "come" is in the imperative.*
● *adjective* something that is imperative is very important and you must do it: *It is imperative that you listen to the safety instructions.*

**im·per·fect** /im-**purf**-ikt/ *adjective* not perfect: *We live in an imperfect world, so you can't expect people to be perfect.*

**im·per·fection** /im-pur-**fek**-shuhn/ *noun* a defect or mark that stops something from being perfect: *Everyone has small imperfections on their skin.*

**im·pe·ri·al** /im-**peer**-ee-uhl/ *adjective* relating to an empire: *Ancient Rome was an imperial power, controlling many parts of the world.*

**im·per·son·al** /im-**purss**-uhn-uhl/ *adjective* not friendly or showing any interest in you: *Some people think emails are an impersonal way of communicating.*

**im·per·so·nate** /im-**purss**-uh-nayt/ *verb* to copy someone's voice and behavior in order to entertain or trick people: *He impersonates many famous people on his show.*
—**impersonation** /im-purss-uh-**naysh**-uhn/ *noun* an act of impersonating someone: *My dad does a funny impersonation of the president.*

**im·ple·ment**
● *verb* /**im**-pluh-ment/ to make a process or plan start happening: *We are going to implement a new system of working in groups.*
● *noun* /**im**-pluh-muhnt/ a simple tool: *A knife is a sharp implement for cutting.*

**im·pli·ca·tion** /im-pli-**kaysh**-uhn/ *noun* a possible result or effect of something: *Some people buy a dog without thinking about the implications. You need to buy him food and take him for walks every day.*

**im·ply** /im-**plī**/ *verb* (**implies, implying, implied**) to make someone think that something is true without saying it directly: *Are you implying that I'm not telling the truth?*

**im·po·lite** /im-puh-**līt**/ *adjective* not polite: *It's impolite to eat with your mouth open.*
SYNONYM: **rude**

**im·port**
● *verb* /im-**port**/
to bring things into a country to sell: *The U.S. imports most of its seafood from China.*
ANTONYM: **export**
● *noun* /**im**-port/
**1** something that is brought into a country to be sold: *The stores are full of cheap imports from other countries.* ANTONYM: **export**
**2** the action of bringing things into a country to sell: *We should stop the import of wild animals.*
ANTONYM: **export**

**im·por·tance** /im-**port**'nss/ *noun* the quality of being important: *He talked about the importance of always wearing a seat belt.*

**im·por·tant** /im-**port**'nt/ *adjective*
**1** if something is important, you care about it a lot or should care about it a lot: *It's important to brush your teeth every day.*
**2** an important person has power: *The principal is the most important person in the school.*
—**importantly** /im-**port**'nt-lee/ *adverb* used when mentioning something important: *The restaurant is beautiful and, more importantly, the food is excellent.*

**Word Family: important**

**important** *adjective* | **unimportant** *adjective* | **importance** *noun*

**im·pose** /im-**pohz**/ *verb* to force someone to accept something: *I'm not trying to impose my views on her; she can think what she likes.*

**im·pos·si·ble** /im-**pahss**-uhb-uhl/ *adjective* not able to be done or to happen: *In this computer game, nothing is impossible.*
—**impossibility** /im-pahss-uh-**bil**-uht-ee/ *noun* something that is not possible: *It would be an impossibility to build a house in one day.*

**im·pos·ter** /im-**pahst**-ur/ *noun* someone who pretends to be someone else in order to trick people: *He was not really a doctor – he was an imposter trying to steal money.*

**im·prac·ti·cal** /im-**prakt**-ik-uhl/ *adjective* an impractical plan or way of doing something is too difficult or too expensive: *It would be impractical to ask every person in school for his or her opinion before we change anything.*

**im·pre·cise** /im-pri-**sīss**/ *adjective* not exact: *The language is too imprecise for a legal document.*

**im·press** /im-**press**/ *verb* to make someone think you are good or special: *He likes to talk about his father's boat to impress his friends.*
—**impressed** /im-**prest**/ *adjective* thinking that someone or something is good or special: *The teacher said she was very impressed by my work.*

## Word Family: impress

**impress** *verb* | **impressed** *adjective* | **impressive** *adjective*

**im·pres·sion** /im-**presh**-uhn/ *noun*
**1** the opinion or feeling you have about someone or something: *I had the impression she was a little nervous.*
**2** the act of copying the voice or behavior of a famous person in order to entertain people: *He does a good impression of Barack Obama and he can talk just like him.* (SYNONYM: **imitation**)

**im·pres·sive** /im-**press**-iv/ *adjective* very good or special: *The White House is a very impressive building.*

**im·pris·on** /im-**priz**-uhn/ *verb* to put someone in prison: *He was imprisoned for causing a serious car accident.*
—**imprisonment** /im-**priz**-uhn-muhnt/ *noun* the state of being in prison: *He was sentenced to five years' imprisonment for robbing a bank.*

**im·prob·a·ble** /im-**prahb**-uhb-uhl/ *adjective* not likely to happen or to be true: *She says she has a pet lion, but that seems very improbable.*
(SYNONYM: **unlikely**) (ANTONYM: **probable**)

**im·prop·er** /im-**prahp**-ur/ *adjective* wrong or not acceptable: *He was sent off the tennis court for improper behavior, after he was very rude to his opponent.*
—**improperly** /im-**prahp**-ur-lee/ *adverb* in a way that is wrong: *Many people use the word "literally" improperly.*

**im·prop·er frac·tion** /im-prahp-ur **frak**-shuhn/ *noun* a fraction with the top number (the numerator) larger than the bottom number (the denominator): *4/3 is an improper fraction.*

**im·prove** /im-**proov**/ *verb* to become better, or to make something better: *Your English is really improving.* | *You could improve your writing by using more interesting adjectives.*

**im·prove·ment** /im-**proov**-muhnt/ *noun*
**1** when something becomes better: *We were waiting for an improvement in the weather before we went on our camping trip.*
**2** a change that makes something better: *Her new hairstyle is a great improvement.*

**im·pro·vise** /**im**-pruh-vīz/ *verb*
**1** to make something from the things you have available: *We didn't have a sled so we improvised and slid down the hill on a garbage bag.*
**2** to act or play music without preparing, making it up as you perform: *Jazz musicians often improvise.*
—**improvisation** /im-prahv-uh-**zaysh**-uhn/ *noun* the act of improvising: *The music was full of brilliant improvisation.*

**im·pulse** /**im**-puhlss/ *noun* a sudden desire to do something: *I had an impulse to laugh when she started speaking, but I stopped myself.*

**im·pul·sive** /im-**puhlss**-iv/ *adjective* doing things suddenly, without thinking about the results: *She's very impulsive, and bought the dress without trying it on.*
—**impulsively** /im-**puhlss**-iv-lee/ *adverb* in an impulsive way

**im·pure** /im-**pyoor**/ *adjective*
**1** containing a substance that should not be there: *Drinking impure water can make you very sick.* (ANTONYM: **pure**)

**2** bad, according to a religion: *The preacher told them they should put impure thoughts out of their heads.* ( ANTONYM: **pure** )
—**impurity** /im-**pyoor**-uht-ee/ *noun* an unwanted substance that another substance contains: *The air we breathe is full of impurities.*

**in** /in/ *preposition, adverb*
**1** inside something: *My keys are in my pocket.* | *Come in! The door's open.*
**2** during a month, year, or other long period of time: *We moved here in September.* | *I was born in 2001.*
**3** after a period of time: *I'm going out. I'll be back in 30 minutes.*
**4** using a particular language or way of speaking: *She was speaking in French.* | *They spoke in whispers so no one could hear them.*
**5** wearing: *A man in a black suit was at the door.*
**6** if you are in something, you are part of it or involved in it: *I talked to the other people in the group.* | *He has appeared in several movies.*

**in-** /in/, **im-** /im/, **il-** /il/, **ir-** /ir/

## Word Building

**in-**, **im-**, **il-**, and **ir-** are prefixes.
**1** **in**correct | **in**visible | **im**polite | **im**mature | **il**legal | **ir**responsible | **ir**regular
**in-**, **im-**, **il-** and **ir-** mean "not." If an answer is *incorrect*, it is not correct. Someone who is *impolite* is not polite. Something that is *illegal* is not legal. Someone who is *irresponsible* is not responsible.
**2** **in**hale | **im**migrant | **im**port
**in-** and **im-** mean "into." If you *inhale*, you breathe air into your lungs. An *immigrant* is someone who comes into a country to live and work there. *Imports* are goods that are brought into a country from other countries.

**in.** the written abbreviation of **inch**

**in·a·bil·i·ty** /in-uh-**bil**-uht-ee/ *noun* the fact of not being able to do something: *He was embarrassed about his inability to read.*
( ANTONYM: **ability** )

**in·ac·cu·rate** /in-**ak**-yuhr-it/ *adjective* not completely correct: *It's an old book and some of the information is inaccurate.* ( ANTONYM: **accurate** )
—**inaccuracy** /in-**ak**-yuhr-uhss-ee/ *noun* something that is not completely correct: *There are a few inaccuracies in your report – for example, you wrote that the town was founded in 1878, but it was 1858.*

**in·ac·tive** /in-**akt**-iv/ *adjective* not doing anything: *Most fish are inactive at night.*
( ANTONYM: **active** )
—**inactivity** /in-ak-**tiv**-uht-ee/ *noun* the state of not doing anything

**in·ad·e·quate** /in-**ad**-uh-kwit/ *adjective* not good enough: *Many health problems are caused by an inadequate diet.* ( ANTONYM: **adequate** )
—**inadequately** /in-**ad**-uh-kwit-lee/ *adverb* in a way that is not good enough: *The house was inadequately furnished for a family to live in.*

**in·an·i·mate** /in-**an**-uhm-it/ *adjective* something that is inanimate is not a living thing: *The car is only an inanimate object so I don't know why you love it so much.*

**in·ap·pro·pri·ate** /in-uh-**prohpr**-ee-it/ *adjective* not right for a particular situation or person: *The movie is inappropriate for children because it is very frightening.* ( ANTONYM: **appropriate** )
—**inappropriately** /in-uh-**prohpr**-ee-it-lee/ *adverb* in an inappropriate way: *She was inappropriately dressed for a funeral – she was wearing a pink dress!*

**in·au·di·ble** /in-**od**-uhb-uhl/ *adjective* too quiet to hear: *Her reply was almost inaudible, so I asked her to say it again.* ( ANTONYM: **audible** )

**in·au·gu·rate** /i-**nog**-yuh-rayt/ *verb* to have a ceremony when someone begins an important job: *Thousands of people traveled to Washington to see President Obama inaugurated.*
—**inaugural** /i-**nog**-yuhr-uhl/ *adjective* relating to an inauguration: *The Mayor gave his inaugural speech.*
—**inauguration** /i-nog-yuh-**raysh**-uhn/ *noun* when someone is inaugurated: *When is the president's inauguration?*

**Inc.** /ingk/ the written abbreviation of **incorporated**, used after the name of a big company: *General Motors, Inc.*

a b c d e f g h i j k l m n o p q r s t u v w x y z

a b c d e f g h **i** j k l m n o p q r s t u v w x y z

**in·ca·pa·ble** /in-**kayp**-uhb-uhl/ *adjective* not able to do something: *Since the accident, she has been incapable of moving her legs.*

**in·cen·tive** /in-**sent**-iv/ *noun* something that makes you want to do something: *As an incentive for you to work harder, there will be a prize for the best piece of work.*

**inch** /inch/ *noun* (plural **inches**) a unit for measuring length, equal to 2.54 centimeters. There are 12 inches in a foot.

**in·ci·dent** /**inss**-uhd-uhnt/ *noun* something unusual, serious, or violent that happens: *There was an incident in the park yesterday – a man stole someone's purse.*

**in·ci·den·tally** /inss-uh-**dent**'l-ee/ *adverb* used when giving more information or starting to talk about something new: *He's an excellent player. Incidentally, he's also my cousin.*

**in·cli·na·tion** /in-kluh-**naysh**-uhn/ *noun* a feeling that you want to do something: *I don't have the time or the inclination to write poetry.*

**in·clined** /in-**klīnd**/ *adjective*
**1** to have a particular opinion: *They think she's strange, and I'm inclined to agree.*
**2** to often do something in a particular situation: *He's inclined to get upset over small things.*

**in·clude** /in-**klood**/ *verb*
**1** if one thing includes another, the second thing is part of the first: *The trip includes a visit to the Grand Canyon.*
**2** to make someone or something part of a larger group: *Did you include my name on the list?* (ANTONYM: **exclude**)
—**inclusion** /in-**kloozh**-uhn/ *noun* the act of including something: *We want the inclusion of some new events in the school arts festival this year.*

**in·clud·ing** /in-**klood**-ing/ *preposition* used when saying that something is part of a group: *There are five people in my family, including Mom and Dad.* (ANTONYM: **excluding**)

**in·co·her·ent** /in-koh-**heer**-uhnt/ *adjective* speaking in a way that is not at all clear: *She was shouting and crying, incoherent with anger.*
—**incoherently** /in-koh-**heer**-uhnt-lee/ *adverb* in an incoherent way: *She was speaking incoherently because she was so tired.*

**in·come** /**in**-kuhm/ *noun* the money that you get for working: *Dad's income comes from working in a drugstore.*

**in·come tax** /**in**-kuhm takss/ *noun* money that you must give the government when you earn money: *You have to pay income tax on the money you earn.*

**in·com·pat·i·ble** /in-kuhm-**pat**-uhb-uhl/ *adjective*
**1** too different to be able to work together well: *The software is incompatible with my computer.* (ANTONYM: **compatible**)
**2** too different to have a good relationship: *They were incompatible and ended up getting a divorce.*

**in·com·pe·tent** /in-**kahmp**-uht-uhnt/ *adjective* not able to do your job well: *He lost his job because he was incompetent.* (ANTONYM: **competent**)
—**incompetence** /in-**kahmp**-uht-uhnss/ *noun* the quality of being incompetent

**in·com·plete** /in-kuhm-**pleet**/ *adjective* not finished, or not having all parts: *The list of students was incomplete. Several names were missing.* (ANTONYM: **complete**)

**incomplete**

The puzzle is incomplete.

**in·con·sid·er·ate** /in-kuhn-**sid**-uhr-it/ *adjective* not thinking or caring about what other people feel or need: *It was inconsiderate of you to drink all the juice without asking if anyone else wanted some.* (ANTONYM: **considerate**)

**in·con·sist·ent** /in-kuhn-**sist**-uhnt/ *adjective*
**1** not always the same: *His work is inconsistent. Sometimes it's good; sometimes it's terrible.*
**2** not the same as something else: *His story was inconsistent with what other witnesses told the police.*
—**inconsistently** /in-kuhn-**sist**-uhnt-lee/ *adverb* in

an inconsistent way: *If you are a top sports player, you can't play inconsistently. You must always play well.*

**in·con·ven·ient** /in-kuhn-**veen**-yuhnt/ *adjective* causing problems or difficulties: *You've called at an inconvenient time – I'm having my lunch.*
—**inconvenience** /in-kuhn-**veen**-yuhnss/ *noun* difficulties or problems that something causes: *We are sorry for the inconvenience caused by this delay.*

**in·cor·po·rate** /in-**korp**-uh-rayt/ *verb* to include something as part of something else: *Write a story in groups, and try to incorporate the ideas of everyone in the group.*

**in·cor·rect** /in-kuh-**rekt**/ *adjective* not right: *He said I was nine, which is incorrect – I'm ten.*
SYNONYM: **wrong**   ANTONYM: **correct**
—**incorrectly** /in-kuh-**rekt**-lee/ *adverb* in a way that is not right: *I didn't get the letter because it was incorrectly addressed.*

**in·crease**
● *verb* /in-**kreess**/ to get bigger or to make something bigger: *My parents increased my allowance from $3 to $4. | We measured the bean plants. They all had increased in size.*
ANTONYM: **decrease** ▶ see Thesaurus
● *noun* /**ing**-kreess/ a rise in the amount of something: *My doctor is worried about the big increase in my weight and says I should eat less food.* ANTONYM: **decrease**

**increase**

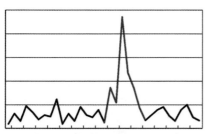

The graph shows an increase in temperature.

**in·creas·ing·ly** /in-**kreess**-ing-lee/ *adverb* more and more: *The questions get increasingly difficult as you work through the book.*

**in·cred·i·ble** /in-**kred**-uhb-uhl/ *adjective*
**1** very good: *The show was incredible – I loved it!*

**2** very large: *Building an airport takes an incredible amount of time.*
**3** very hard to believe: *It's incredible that no one was killed in such a major accident.*

**in·cred·i·bly** /in-**kred**-uhb-lee/ *adverb* very: *I am incredibly lucky to have such good friends.*

**in·cu·ba·tor** /**ing**-kyuh-bayt-ur/ *noun* a warm container with a bed for very small or sick babies. Incubators are used in a hospital to help keep the babies alive: *The baby was born weighing two pounds and was put in an incubator.*

**in·cur·a·ble** /in-**kyoor**-uhb-uhl/ *adjective* an incurable disease cannot be cured

**in·de·cent** /in-**deess**-uhnt/ *adjective* likely to shock people: *His father punished him for using indecent language.*
—**indecency** /in-**deess**-uhnss-ee/ *noun* indecent behavior

**in·de·ci·sive** /in-di-**siss**-iv/ *adjective* not able to make decisions quickly: *I'm so indecisive – I never know what to pick from the menu in a restaurant.* ANTONYM: **decisive**

**in·deed** /in-**deed**/ *adverb*
**1** used for emphasizing something: *The DNA tests showed that he was indeed the father of the child.*
**2** used for telling someone that what he or she says is right: *"Have you spoken to my teacher?" "I have indeed."*
**3** used when adding information: *He liked the book. Indeed, he said it was the best one he had ever read.*

**in·def·i·nite** /in-**def**-uhn-it/ *adjective* continuing for a period of time with no fixed end: *He is going to Europe for an indefinite period.*
—**indefinitely** /in-**def**-uhn-it-lee/ *adverb* for a period of time that has no fixed end: *You can't stay at home indefinitely – one day you will have to get a job and move out.*

**in·def·i·nite ar·ti·cle** /in-def-uhn-it **art**-ik-uhl/ *noun* "a" and "an": *You use the indefinite article before a noun when you are not talking about any particular thing or person.*

**in·dent** /in-**dent**/ *verb* to leave a space at the beginning of a line of writing: *Indent the first line of each paragraph.*

**in·de·pend·ence** /in-di-**pend**-uhnss/ *noun*
**1** the freedom to do what you want to do and take care of yourself: *She likes her independence so she prefers to live alone.*
**2** freedom from control by another country: *America fought for independence from Britain.*

**In·de·pend·ence Day** /in-di-**pend**-uhnss day/ *noun* a U.S. national holiday on July 4. It celebrates the day in 1776 when Americans signed the Declaration of Independence.
( SYNONYM: **Fourth of July** )

**in·de·pend·ent** /in-di-**pend**-uhnt/ *adjective*
**1** doing what you want to do and taking care of yourself: *She is only three but very independent, and likes to dress and feed herself.*
( ANTONYM: **dependent** )
**2** not controlled by another country or organization: *Mexico became independent in 1821.*
—**independently** /in-di-**pend**-uhnt-lee/ *adverb* in an independent way

**Word Family:** independent

> **independent** *adjective* | **dependent** *adjective* | **independence** *noun* | **dependence** *noun* | **independently** *adverb*

**in·de·pend·ent va·ri·a·ble** /in-di-pend-uhnt **vair**-ee-uhb-uhl/ *noun* something that you change in a way you can measure, to see how that change affects other things. You do this in a science experiment: *We wanted to see how fast an ice cube melts. The independent variable was the size of the ice cube, and the dependent variable was how fast the ice melted.*
( ANTONYM: **dependent variable** )

**in·depth** /in **depth**/ *adjective* having a lot of detail: *The local newspaper had an in-depth article about our school.*

**in·dex** /**ind**-ekss/ *noun* (plural **indexes** or **indices** /**ind**-uh-seez/) a list at the end of a book that tells you the page where each thing in the book is mentioned: *Use the index to help you find the section on horses.*

**Word Origin:** index

> **Index** comes from a Latin word that means "forefinger." The forefinger is the first finger. Because we often use our first finger to point at things, the Latin word also means "something that points out." An index in a book points out which pages you should read to find out the information you are looking for.

**in·dex fin·ger**
/**ind**-ekss fing-gur/ *noun* the finger next to your thumb: *People usually point with their index fingers.*

**index finger**

**In·di·an** /**ind**-ee-uhn/
● *noun*
**1** someone from India: *Fourteen million Indians live in Mumbai.*
**2** someone who belongs to one of the tribes that lived in North America before the Europeans arrived. People now usually say "Native American" instead of "Indian."
● *adjective*
**1** from India: *Bala is an Indian name.*
**2** relating to Native Americans. People now usually say "Native American" instead of "Indian."

**in·di·cate** /**ind**-uh-kayt/ *verb*
**1** to show that something is likely to be true: *The fact that she is smiling indicates that she is happy.*
**2** to say something in a way that is not direct: *The teacher nodded to indicate that she was happy with my work.*
—**indicator** /**ind**-uh-kayt-ur/ *noun* something that shows something else: *Your weight is an important indicator of how healthy you are.*

**Word Family:** indicate

> **indicate** *verb* | **indication** *noun* | **indicative** *adjective* | **indicator** *noun*

**in·di·ca·tion** /ind-uh-**kaysh**-uhn/ *noun* a sign that something exists or is likely to be true: *There are indications that the fire was started by a dropped cigarette.*

**in·di·ca·tive** /in-**dik**-uht-iv/ *adjective* showing something: *A sharp pain in your chest can be indicative of a broken rib.*

**in·di·ces** /**ind**-uh-seez/ *noun* a plural of index

**in·dif·fer·ent** /in-**dif**-ruhnt/ *adjective* not interested in something, or not caring about something: *I don't like her but I don't hate her. I'm indifferent toward her.*
—**indifference** /in-**dif**-ruhnss/ *noun* a feeling of not being interested in something or not caring about something: *Many young people feel complete indifference about politics.*

**in·di·ges·tion** /in-duh-**jess**-chuhn/ *noun* an uncomfortable feeling in your stomach or chest after eating. You get indigestion when your body is having problems digesting food: *I ate too much, and now I have indigestion.*

**in·di·rect** /in-duh-**rekt**/ *adjective*
**1** not directly caused by or relating to something: *The accident was an indirect result of the heavy rain, which had created a hole in the road.*
( ANTONYM: **direct** )
**2** not very clear: *His silence was an indirect way of showing his anger.* ( ANTONYM: **direct** )
**3** not going somewhere in a straight line: *We went home by an indirect route because we had to buy something from the store.*
( ANTONYM: **direct** )
—**indirectly** /in-duh-**rekt**-lee/ *adverb* in an indirect way

**in·di·rect ob·ject** /in-duh-rekt **ahb**-jikt/ *noun* a word or phrase that refers to the person or thing that receives something: *In the sentence "Karen sang me a song," "me" is the indirect object and "a song" is the direct object.*

**in·di·vid·u·al** /ind-uh-**vij**-oo-uhl/
● *adjective*
**1** used when talking about each person or thing, not the whole group: *He took a photograph of the whole class, then of each individual child.*
**2** for one person rather than a group: *The children had individual desks.*
—**individually** /ind-uh-**vij**-oo-uhl-ee/ *adverb* separately: *The teacher spoke to the students individually.*
● *noun*
a person, not a group: *Every individual is different.*

**Word Family:** individual

**individual** *adjective* | **individual** *noun* | **individually** *adverb* | **individualized** *adjective*

**in·di·vid·u·al·i·ty** /ind-uh-vij-oo-**al**-uht-ee/ *noun* the quality that makes someone different from other people: *Some young people like to show their individuality by wearing unusual clothes and strange hairstyles.*

**in·di·vid·u·al·ized** /ind-uh-**vij**-oo-uh-līzd/ *adjective* made for a particular person: *Each student will have his or her own individualized learning program.*

**in·di·vis·i·ble** /in-duh-**viz**-uhb-uhl/ *adjective* if something is indivisible, you cannot divide it or separate it into parts: *One is an indivisible number.*

**in·door** /**in**-dor/ *adjective* inside a building: *The gym has an indoor basketball court which we can use when it is raining.*
( ANTONYM: **outdoor** )

**indoor**

an indoor pool

an outdoor pool

**in·doors** /in-**dorz**/ *adverb* into or inside a building: *It's cold – let's go indoors. | Dad was indoors and he was cooking the meal.*
( SYNONYM: **inside** ) ( ANTONYM: **outdoors** )

a b c d e f g h i j k l m n o p q r s t u v w x y z

**in·dulge** /in-**duhlj**/ *verb*
**1** to do something that you enjoy, which you do not usually do or should not do: *I had a little extra time, so I indulged in an afternoon nap.*
**2** to let someone do or have whatever he or she wants, even if it is bad for him or her: *Our grandparents indulge us, bringing us gifts whenever they visit.*
—**indulgent** /in-**duhlj**-uhnt/ *adjective* indulging yourself or someone else: *Her parents are too indulgent; they let her have almost anything she wants.*
—**indulgence** /in-**duhlj**-uhnss/ *noun* something that you do for enjoyment, which you do not usually do, or you should not do: *I know it is an indulgence, but I bought us a big box of cookies to eat on the trip.*

**in·dus·tri·al** /in-**duhss**-tree-uhl/ *adjective*
**1** relating to industry: *There were a lot of factories and other industrial buildings.*
**2** having a lot of industry: *Detroit is an industrial city.*

**in·dus·tri·al·ize** /in-**duhss**-tree-uh-līz/ *verb* to start having a lot of industry: *America started to industrialize in the late 1800s.*

**in·dus·tri·al·ized** /in-**duhss**-tree-uh-līzd/ *adjective* an industrialized country has a lot of industries
—**industrialization** /in-duhss-tree-uhl-uh-**zaysh**-uhn/ *noun* the process of developing a lot of industries

**in·dus·tri·ous** /in-**duhss**-tree-uhss/ *adjective* an industrious person works hard
—**industriously** /in-**duhss**-tree-uhss-lee/ *adverb* in a way that involves working hard: *Taylor was working very industriously on her homework project.*

**in·dus·try** /**ind**-uhss-tree/ *noun* (plural **industries**)
**1** the making of things in factories: *Dad works in industry, making glass for windows.*
**2** all the businesses that make or do a particular type of thing: *Hollywood is the center of the film industry.*

**Word Family: industry**

**industry** *noun* | **industrial** *adjective* | **industrialized** *adjective* | **industrialization** *noun*

**in·ed·i·ble** /in-**ed**-uhb-uhl/ *adjective* dangerous to eat or tasting too bad to eat: *The bread was so old and hard it was inedible.* (ANTONYM: **edible**)

**in·ef·fec·tive** /in-uh-**fekt**-iv/ *adjective* not achieving what you want: *Fighting is an ineffective way of dealing with problems.* (ANTONYM: **effective**)

**in·ef·fi·cient** /in-uh-**fish**-uhnt/ *adjective* working or done in a way that wastes time, money, or energy: *The engine is inefficient and uses a lot of fuel.* (ANTONYM: **efficient**)
—**inefficiently** /in-uh-**fish**-uhnt-lee/ *adverb* in an inefficient way: *Our old heating system burns fuel very inefficiently.*
—**inefficiency** /in-uh-**fish**-uhnss-ee/ *noun* a way of doing something that wastes time, money, or energy: *Inefficiency at work wastes time and money.*

**in·e·qual·i·ty** /in-i-**kwahl**-uht-ee/ *noun* (plural **inequalities**) an unfair situation in which some people have the things they need or want and some people do not: *There is inequality because the women get paid less than the men for doing the same job.* (ANTONYM: **equality**)

**in·e·qual·i·ty sign** /in-i-**kwahl**-uht-ee sīn/ *noun* the sign > or < used in math. > means "greater than" and < means "less than."

**in·ev·i·ta·ble** /i-**nev**-uht-uhb-uhl/ *adjective* certain to happen and impossible to avoid: *She never brushes her teeth, so it is inevitable that she will have problems with them.*
—**inevitably** /i-**nev**-uht-uhb-lee/ *adverb* if something will inevitably happen, it will definitely happen: *If you have a lot of success, some people will inevitably be jealous.*

**in·ex·pen·sive** /in-ik-**spenss**-iv/ *adjective* costing only a small amount of money: *The food is simple and inexpensive.* (SYNONYM: **cheap**) (ANTONYM: **expensive**)

**in·ex·pe·ri·enced** /in-ik-**speer**-ee-uhnst/ *adjective* not having much knowledge about doing something because you have not done it very much before: *He's very young and inexperienced, and he has never played on a professional team before.* (ANTONYM: **experienced**)
—**inexperience** /in-ik-**speer**-ee-uhnss/ *noun* a lack of knowledge about doing something because you have not done it very much before: *Her*

*inexperience has led her to make a lot of mistakes at work.*

**in·fa·mous** /**in**-fuhm-uhss/ *adjective* well known for being bad or evil: *Adolf Hitler was the infamous Nazi leader of Germany during World War II.* (SYNONYM: **notorious**)

**in·fant** /**inf**-uhnt/ *noun* a baby: *The woman was holding an infant in her arms.*
—**infancy** /**inf**-uhnss-ee/ *noun* the period when someone is a baby: *Their son was born very weak and died in infancy.*

**in·fan·try** /**inf**-uhn-tree/ *noun* soldiers who fight on foot, not on horses or in vehicles: *The infantry marched into the city.*

**in·fect** /in-**fekt**/ *verb* to give someone a disease that you have: *If you have a cold, wash your hands often to avoid infecting other people.*
—**infected** /in-**fekt**-id/ *adjective* having harmful bacteria: *If you have your ears pierced, keep them clean or they will get infected.*

**Word Family: infect**

**infect** *verb* | **infection** *noun* | **infectious** *adjective* | **infected** *adjective*

**in·fec·tion** /in-**fek**-shuhn/ *noun* a disease that affects part of your body and is caused by bacteria or a virus: *Ear infections can be very painful.*

**in·fec·tious** /in-**fek**-shuhss/ *adjective* an infectious disease can be passed between people: *Flu is very infectious, so do not go to school if you have it.*

**in·fer** /in-**fur**/ *verb* (**inferring**, **inferred**) to decide that something is probably true because of what you see or hear: *If you do not reply to the invitation, they will infer that you do not want to go to the party.*

**in·fe·ri·or** /in-**feer**-ee-ur/ *adjective* not as good as someone or something else: *He thinks he's so smart and everyone is inferior to him.*
(ANTONYM: **superior**)
—**inferiority** /in-feer-ee-**or**-uht-ee/ *noun* the quality of not being as good as someone or something else: *He has a feeling of inferiority because his family is very poor.*

**in·field** /**in**-feeld/ *noun* the part of a baseball field that is inside the four bases: *The ball never left the infield.*

**in·field·er** /**in**-feeld-ur/ *noun* a baseball player who plays on the part of the field inside the four bases: *The infielders are the first, second, and third basemen and the shortstop.*

**in·fi·nite** /**in**-fuhn-it/ *adjective* without a limit or end: *We need to know how much the work will cost because we do not have an infinite amount of money.* (ANTONYM: **finite**)

**in·fi·nite·ly** /**in**-fuhn-it-lee/ *adverb* very much: *Their ice cream is infinitely better than any other ice cream – it tastes really delicious.*

**in·fin·i·tive** /in-**fin**-uht-iv/ *noun* the basic form of a verb, used with "to": *In the sentence "I want to go," "to go" is an infinitive.*

**in·fin·i·ty** /in-**fin**-uht-ee/ *noun*
**1** a space or distance without a limit or end: *The ocean seemed to stretch into infinity.*
**2** a number that is larger than all others: *It is impossible to count to infinity.*

**in·flamed** /in-**flaymd**/ *verb* red, swollen, and painful: *The skin around the cut had become very inflamed.*

**in·flam·ma·ble** /in-**flam**-uhb-uhl/ *adjective* burning very easily: *Never light a match near gasoline because it is very inflammable.*
(SYNONYM: **flammable**)

**in·flam·ma·tion** /in-fluh-**maysh**-uhn/ *noun* the state of being red, swollen, and painful: *Put this lotion on your skin to reduce the inflammation.*

**in·flate** /in-**flayt**/ *verb* to fill something with air so that it becomes bigger: *He blew into the balloon to inflate it.*
—**inflatable** /in-**flayt**-uhb-uhl/ *adjective* something that is inflatable must be filled with air before you use it: *An inflatable boat is made of rubber.*

**in·fla·tion** /in-**flaysh**-uhn/ *noun* a situation in which prices get higher and the value of money becomes less: *Because of inflation, a loaf of bread costs a lot more now than it did ten years ago.*

**in·flict** /in-**flikt**/ *verb* to make someone suffer something bad: *I don't understand how anyone could inflict pain on an animal.*

**in·flu·ence** /**in**-floo-uhnss/

● *noun*

**1** the effect that someone or something has, for example on someone's thinking or on the way that something works: *I love music and it has had a big influence on my life.*

**2** someone or something that affects what someone does or thinks: *Try to be a good influence for your little brother.*

—**influential** /in-floo-**ensh**-uhl/ *adjective* having a lot of influence: *She was a very influential painter and many people copied her style.*

● *verb*

to affect what someone does or thinks: *Companies use advertising to influence people and persuade them to buy their products.*

**in·fo·mer·cial** /in-foh-**mursh**-uhl/ *noun* a television program that gives information about something you can buy. An infomercial is a type of advertisement.

**in·form** /in-**form**/ *verb* to tell someone something: *Please inform the office if you are going to be late for school.*

**Word Family: inform**

**inform** *verb* | **information** *noun* | **informative** *adjective*

**in·for·mal** /in-**form**-uhl/ *adjective*

**1** relaxed, and not done in an official way or according to rules: *It's not a meeting – it's an informal discussion.* ( ANTONYM: **formal** )

**2** for ordinary situations, not formal ones: *"What's up?" is an informal way of saying "How are you?"* ( ANTONYM: **formal** )

—**informally** /in-**form**-uhl-ee/ *adverb* in an informal way: *He was dressed a little too informally for a job interview.*

—**informality** /in-for-**mal**-uht-ee/ *noun* the quality of being informal: *The informality of the waiting room is designed to make everyone feel comfortable.*

**in·for·ma·tion** /in-fur-**maysh**-uhn/ *noun* details about something: *Where can I get information about the ancient Romans?* ▶ see **Thesaurus**

**Grammar: information**

Do not say "an information" or "informations." Say, for example, **some information**, **any information**, **a lot of information**, or **a piece of information**: *You can find a lot of information on the Internet.* | *Some of the information was wrong.* | *I found a very interesting piece of information on page 3.*

**in·form·a·tive** /in-**form**-uht-iv/ *adjective* giving many facts: *It was a very informative program – I learned a lot.*

**in·fra·red** /in-fruh-**red**/ *adjective* infrared light produces heat but cannot be seen, because the light waves are longer than ordinary light waves: *Scientists use a special infrared telescope to look at stars that are a long distance away.*

**in·fre·quent** /in-**freek**-wuhnt/ *adjective* not happening often: *We enjoy her infrequent visits and wish she would come more often.*

( SYNONYM: **rare** )

—**infrequently** /in-**freek**-wuhnt-lee/ *adverb* not often: *Plane crashes happen very infrequently.*

**in·fu·ri·ate** /in-**fyoor**-ee-ayt/ *verb* to make someone very angry: *It infuriates me when she won't listen to me.*

—**infuriating** /in-**fyoor**-ee-ayt-ing/ *adjective* making you feel very angry: *He has an infuriating habit of leaving the front door open.*

**in·ge·nious** /in-**jeen**-yuhss/ *adjective*

**1** based on new and clever ideas: *They thought of some ingenious ways of saving money.*

**2** good at thinking of new plans or making new things: *He is an ingenious man and I'm sure he can find a solution to the problem.*

—**ingenuity** /inj-uh-**noo**-uht-ee/ *noun* the quality of being ingenious: *I admire the ingenuity of the game and it seems very well designed.*

**in·gre·di·ent** /in-**greed**-ee-uhnt/ *noun* one of the things that you use to make a particular food: *Stir the milk into the dry ingredients.*

ingredient

ingredients

**in·hab·it** /in-**hab**-it/ *verb* to live in a place: *Only 100 people inhabit the island.*
—**inhabited** /in-**hab**-it-id/ *adjective* if a place is inhabited, people live there: *Many of the islands are inhabited.* ( SYNONYM: **uninhabited** )

**in·hab·it·ant** /in-**hab**-uht-uhnt/ *noun* one of the people who live in a place: *The inhabitants of Los Angeles are called "Angelenos."*

**in·hale** /in-**hayl**/ *verb* to breathe in air, smoke, or gas: *Some of the people rescued from the fire had inhaled a lot of smoke.* ( ANTONYM: **exhale** )

inhale

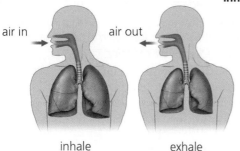

air in

air out

inhale

exhale

**in·hal·er** /in-**hayl**-ur/ *noun* an object that you use to breathe in medicine through your mouth. Inhalers are used by people who have problems with their breathing: *I have asthma, and I sometimes need my inhaler when I play sports.*

**in·her·it** /in-**herr**-it/ *verb*
**1** to get something from someone after he or she has died: *He will inherit a lot of money when his father dies.*
**2** to get a quality or feature from one of your parents: *Angela inherited her mother's blonde hair and blue eyes.*
—**inheritance** /in-**herr**-it-uhnss/ *noun* money or things that you get from someone after he or

she has died: *She wants her house to be her grandchildren's inheritance.*

**i·ni·tial** /i-**nish**-uhl/
● *noun* the first letter of a name: *His name is Jack Clark, so his initials are J. C.*
● *adjective* first: *My initial reaction was shock, but then I got angry.*

**i·ni·tial·ly** /i-**nish**-uhl-ee/ *adverb* at first: *Initially I didn't like school, but now I love it.*

**i·ni·ti·ate** /i-**nish**-ee-ayt/ *verb* to start something: *I initiated the conversation by asking him what his name was.*

**i·ni·ti·a·tion** /i-nish-ee-**aysh**-uhn/ *noun* the action of making someone a member of a group, usually with a ceremony: *The club has an initiation ceremony for new members.*

**i·ni·tia·tive** /i-**nish**-uht-iv/ *noun* the ability to do things without waiting for someone to tell you what to do: *He's 15 now – he can use his initiative and he doesn't need his mom to tell him what to do.*

**in·ject** /in-**jekt**/ *verb* to put a drug into someone's body using a special needle: *The nurse had to inject the drug into his arm.*
—**injection** /in-**jek**-shuhn/ *noun* if you have an injection, a drug is injected into your body

**in·jure** /**inj**-ur/ *verb* to damage someone's body: *She injured her back falling off a horse.*
—**injured** /**inj**-urd/ *adjective* having damage to part of your body: *an injured leg*

**Word Family:** injure

**injure** *verb* | **injured** *adjective* | **injury** *noun*

**in·ju·ry** /**inj**-uhr-ee/ *noun* (plural **injuries**) damage to someone's body: *He was taken to the hospital with serious head injuries.*
▶ see **Thesaurus**

**in·jus·tice** /in-**juhst**-iss/ *noun* a situation in which someone is treated unfairly: *She was put in jail for something she didn't do, which was a terrible injustice.* ( ANTONYM: **justice** )

**ink** /ingk/ *noun* a colored liquid used for writing or drawing. Ink is used inside a pen: *She wrote her name in red ink.*

a b c d e f g h **i** j k l m n o p q r s t u v w x y z

**in·laws** /**in**-loz/ *plural noun* the family of your husband or wife: *Tom is spending the holidays with his in-laws, his wife's family.*

**in·line skat·ing** /in līn

**in-line skating**

**skayt**-ing/ *noun* the activity of moving along wearing boots with a line of wheels under them: *Have you ever tried in-line skating?*
—**in-line skates** /in līn **skaytss**/ *plural noun* boots with a line of wheels under them

**in·mate** /**in**-mayt/ *noun* a prisoner in a prison: *The inmates go out into the yard to exercise once a day.*

**inn** /in/ *noun* a small hotel. Inns are usually not in cities: *They stayed at a country inn.*

**inn**

**in·ner** /**in**-ur/ *adjective*
**1** inside or near the middle of something: *The inner part of the earth is called the core.*
( ANTONYM: **outer** )
**2** relating to thoughts or feelings that you have deep inside you: *I believe in God, and that gives me an inner strength.*

**in·ner cit·y** /in-ur **sit**-ee/ *noun* an area close to the middle of a city, where many poor people live: *Kids in the inner city need more safe places to play.*
—**inner-city** /**in**-ur sit-ee/ *adjective* relating to the inner city: *The program aims to help people in inner-city neighborhoods.*

**in·ning** /**in**-ing/ *noun* one of the nine parts of a game of baseball. Each team bats in an inning: *Houston scored three times in the ninth inning.*

**in·no·cent** /**in**-uhss-uhnt/ *adjective*
**1** not guilty of a crime: *At his trial, he said he was innocent.* ( ANTONYM: **guilty** )
**2** not having much knowledge of the bad things in life: *I was young and innocent, and I trusted everyone.*
**3** used to describe an ordinary person who gets hurt in a war or during a crime: *The war has changed the lives of millions of innocent people.*
—**innocently** /**in**-uhss-uhnt-lee/ *adverb* in an innocent way: *The children were playing innocently in the yard, not doing any harm to anyone.*
—**innocence** /**in**-uhss-uhnss/ *noun* the quality of being innocent: *In a jury trial, the jury decides a person's innocence or guilt.*

**in·no·va·tion** /in-uh-**vaysh**-uhn/ *noun* a new invention or way of doing something: *Technological innovations like the cell phone have changed our lives.*
—**innovate** /**in**-uh-vayt/ *verb* to start making or doing something new: *The company had to innovate to compete with newer companies.*

**in·oc·u·late** /i-**nahk**-yuh-layt/ *verb* to protect someone against a disease by putting a weak form of the disease into his or her body using a needle: *All the children in the class have been inoculated against measles.*
—**inoculation** /i-nahk-yuh-**laysh**-uhn/ *noun* if you get an inoculation, a nurse or doctor inoculates you: *You have to go see the nurse to get an inoculation.*

**in·put** /**in**-put/ *noun*
**1** ideas from people about what should be done: *We would like to have students' input on the changes to the school.*
**2** information that is put into a computer
( ANTONYM: **output** )

**in·quire** /in-**kwī**-ur/ *verb* to ask someone for information: *The man inquired if I was Jack's son.*

**in·quir·y** /in-**kwī**-uhr-ee/ *noun* (plural **inquiries**)
**1** a question you ask in order to get information: *You should make inquiries about the area before you decide to move there.*
**2** if there is an inquiry, an official group tries to find out why something bad happened: *There was an inquiry into the accident, and they found*

*that it was caused by a defect in one of the plane's engines.*

**in·sane** /in-**sayn**/ *adjective*
**1** very stupid, and often dangerous: *It's insane to try to cross the ocean in such a small boat.*
**2** seriously mentally ill: *I thought I was going insane.*
—**insanity** /in-**san**-uht-ee/ *noun* serious mental illness

**in·sect** /**in**-sekt/ *noun* a small creature such as an ant or a fly. Insects have six legs and their bodies have three parts. Some insects also have wings: *We saw flies, bees, butterflies, and many other insects on our walk.* ▶ see picture on page **A15**

**Word Origin:** insect

Insect comes from a Latin word that means "an animal that is divided into sections." The body of an insect has three parts, or sections.

**in·sec·ti·cide** /in-**sekt**-uh-sīd/ *noun* a chemical used for killing insects: *We don't use insecticides on the vegetables we grow.*

**in·se·cure** /in-si-**kyoor**/ *adjective* not feeling confident: *She likes being praised a lot because she's very insecure.* (ANTONYM: **confident**)
—**insecurity** /in-si-**kyoor**-uht-ee/ *noun* the feeling of not being confident: *His insecurity made him want to stay with his parents.*

**in·sen·si·tive** /in-**senss**-uht-iv/ *adjective* not noticing or caring whether you upset someone: *It is really insensitive to ask her how much she weighs.*

**in·sert** /in-**surt**/ *verb* to put something into something else: *Jacob inserted the disk into the computer.*
—**insertion** /in-**sursh**-uhn/ *noun* the action of putting something into something else: *The insertion of the needle into his arm hurt a lot.*

**insert**

**in·side** /in-**sīd**/
• *adverb, preposition* in a container, building, car, etc.: *Inside the box there were some old*

photographs. | *It's raining – let's go inside.*
(ANTONYM: **outside**)
• *noun* the part of something that is nearer the middle, which is surrounded by walls or sides: *I had never seen the inside of his house, but I've often played in his yard.* | *the inside of a shell* (ANTONYM: **outside**)
• *adjective* on the inside of something: *Food was stuck to the inside surface of the saucepan.*

IDIOMS with **inside**
**inside out** if clothing is inside out, the part that is usually on the outside is on the inside: *She accidentally put her sweater on inside out and you can see all the stitching.*
**know something inside out** to know everything about a subject: *He had played basketball for years and he knew the game inside out.*

**in·sight** /**in**-sīt/ *noun* an understanding of something: *The TV program gave me an insight into how people live in the jungle.*

**in·sig·ni·a**
/in-**sig**-nee-uh/ *noun*
(plural **insignia**) a small design or symbol. An insignia shows someone's rank or the organization he or she belongs to: *The soldier's jacket had an insignia on the arm.*

insignia

insignia

**in·sig·nif·i·cant**
/in-sig-**nif**-uhk-uhnt/
*adjective* unimportant:
*The difference in the two measurements is so small it is insignificant.*
—**insignificance** /in-sig-**nif**-uhk-uhnss/ *noun* the quality of being unimportant

**in·sin·cere** /in-sin-**seer**/ *adjective* pretending to think or feel something: *He said he was sorry, but his apology sounded insincere.*
(ANTONYM: **genuine**)
—**insincerely** /in-sin-**seer**-lee/ *adverb* in an insincere way
—**insincerity** /in-sin-**serr**-uht-ee/ *noun* insincere feelings or behavior: *Not looking at someone when you speak to them can be a sign of insincerity.*

a b c d e f g h **i** j k l m n o p q r s t u v w x y z

**in·sist** /in-**sist**/ *verb*
**1** to say firmly that you will do something or that something must be done: *We wanted to go by ourselves, but my dad insisted on coming with us.*
**2** to keep saying firmly that something is true: *He insisted that he had not done anything wrong.*
—**insistent** /in-**sist**-uhnt/ *adjective* saying firmly that something must be done: *I didn't want to go on a diet, but the doctor was very insistent.*
—**insistence** /in-**sist**-uhnss/ *noun* the act of insisting: *At my mom's insistence, I wore my warm coat and my gloves.*

**in·som·ni·a** /in-**sahm**-nee-uh/ *noun* if you have insomnia, you are not able to sleep enough
—**insomniac** /in-**sahm**-nee-ak/ *noun* someone who is not able to sleep enough: *He is an insomniac so he often works at night.*

**in·spect** /in-**spekt**/ *verb* to look at something carefully to see if it is all right: *Our bags were inspected at the airport.*

**in·spec·tion** /in-**spek**-shuhn/ *noun* a careful look at something to see if it is all right: *All the equipment has passed a safety inspection.*

**in·spec·tor** /in-**spekt**-ur/ *noun*
**1** someone whose job is to check that something is being done correctly: *Health inspectors said the restaurant must be closed because the kitchens are very dirty.*
**2** a police officer with a fairly high rank

**in·spi·ra·tion** /in-spuh-**raysh**-uhn/ *noun*
**1** a person or thing that makes you want to achieve something: *Our grandfather was an inspiration to all of us because he worked very hard.*
**2** a good new idea: *The artist said he got inspiration from everything he saw.*
—**inspirational** /in-spuh-**raysh**-uhn-uhl/ *adjective* making you want to achieve something, or giving you a new idea: *He became a scientist because he had an inspirational science teacher.*

**in·spire** /in-**spī**-ur/ *verb*
**1** to make you feel that you want to achieve something or create something: *The mountains near his home inspired him to paint.*
**2** to make someone have a particular feeling: *The coach inspired confidence in the team.*

**in·stall** /in-**stol**/ *verb*
**1** to put a piece of equipment somewhere so that it is ready to be used: *The apartment gets very hot in the summer so we decided to install air conditioning.*
**2** to add new software to a computer: *I bought a new game and installed it on my computer.*

**in·stall·ment** /in-**stol**-muhnt/ *noun*
**1** one of a number of payments that you make to pay for something: *The computer costs $400, which you can pay in eight monthly installments of $50.*
**2** one part of a story or a television series: *I can't wait for the next installment to find out what happens to the hero!*

**in·stance** /**inst**-uhnss/ *noun*
**1** an example: *There have been several instances of bullying at the school.*
**2 for instance** for example: *Some birds, for instance penguins, can't fly.*

**in·stant** /**inst**-uhnt/
● *adjective*
**1** happening immediately: *She had instant success with her first book, which sold millions of copies.*
**2** instant coffee or food can be made very quickly by adding hot water: *Instant noodles are a good idea when you go camping.*
● *noun*
**1** a very short time: *He hesitated, just for an instant.* (SYNONYM: **moment**)
**2 the instant** as soon as: *I'll call you the instant I hear any news.*

**in·stant·ly** /**inst**-uhnt-lee/ *adverb* immediately: *When he told his dog to sit, it obeyed instantly.*

**in·stant mes·sag·ing** /inst-uhnt **mess**-ij-ing/ *noun* a system on the Internet that makes it possible to have conversations with people by sending and receiving written messages immediately

**in·stant re·play** /inst-uhnt **ree**-play/ *noun* when the action in a sports game on television is shown again, just after it happens: *We watched the instant replay, and you could clearly see that it was a goal.*

**in·stead** /in-**sted**/ *adverb* used when one thing replaces another, or when you do a different thing: *If you don't want pie, you can have ice* *cream instead.* | *Try to speak quietly instead of yelling.*

**in·stinct** /**in**-stingkt/ *noun* behavior that you have not learned or thought about: *When I saw the bear, my instinct was to run.*
—**instinctive** /in-**stingkt**-iv/ *adjective* based on instinct: *Most children have an instinctive fear of the dark.*
—**instinctively** /in-**stingkt**-iv-lee/ *adverb* in a way that is based on instinct: *She instinctively closed her eyes to keep the dust out of them.*

**in·sti·tute** /**inst**-uh-toot/ *noun* an organization where people study a subject: *The report was published by the Institute of Medicine.*

**in·sti·tu·tion** /inst-uh-**toosh**-uhn/ *noun*
**1** a large organization, such as a hospital or university or bank: *Schools, libraries, and other public institutions need more money.*
**2** something that people in a society or group have done for a very long time: *We still respect the institution of marriage.*

**in·struct** /in-**struhkt**/ *verb*
**1** to tell someone to do something: *We were instructed to arrive at the bus stop by 8:00.*
**2** to teach someone something: *He instructed them in drawing.*
—**instructor** /in-**struhkt**-ur/ *noun* someone who teaches a skill or activity: *The swimming instructor showed me how to swim on my back.*

**Word Family:** instruct

**instruct** *verb* | **instructor** *noun* | **instruction** *noun*

**in·struc·tion** /in-**struhk**-shuhn/ *noun*
**1 instructions** information that tells you how to do or use something: *Follow the instructions on the medicine bottle carefully.*
(SYNONYM: **directions**)
**2** if someone gives you instructions, he or she tells you what to do: *You have to obey the teacher's instructions.*
**3** lessons in a particular skill or subject: *The kids were given extra instruction in math to prepare them for the test.*

**in·stru·ment** /**inss**-truh-muhnt/ *noun*
**1** something such as a piano, guitar, or drum that you play in order to make music: *Can you play any musical instruments?* ▶ see picture on page **A8**
**2** a piece of scientific equipment or a medical tool: *A microscope is a scientific instrument.*

**in·stru·men·tal** /inss-truh-**ment**'l/ *adjective* instrumental music is played on instruments, without any singing

**in·suf·fi·cient** /in-suh-**fish**-uhnt/ *adjective* not enough: *We had insufficient time to do the experiment, so we did not finish it.*
(ANTONYM: **sufficient**)
—**insufficiently** /in-suh-**fish**-uhnt-lee/ *adverb* in a way that is not enough: *They were insufficiently careful so they made mistakes.*

**in·su·late** /**inss**-uh-layt/ *verb* to cover something with a material that stops heat, sound, or electricity from getting in or out: *Insulate your water pipes to stop them from freezing.*
—**insulation** /inss-uh-**laysh**-uhn/ *noun* material used to insulate something: *A roof contains a lot of insulation to keep heat in the house.*

**in·su·lin** /**inss**-uhl-uhn/ *noun* a substance in your body that is made by your pancreas. Insulin helps move sugar from your blood into cells where it can be used for energy. People with diabetes do not have enough insulin.

**in·sult**
● *verb* /in-**suhlt**/ to say or do something that is rude to someone: *He insulted me by calling me a liar.*
—**insulting** /in-**suhlt**-ing/ *adjective* rude to someone: *Calling someone dumb is pretty insulting.*
● *noun* /**in**-suhlt/ something rude that you say or do: *I won't let their insults upset me.*

**in·sur·ance** /in-**shoor**-uhnss/ *noun* if you have insurance, you pay a company, and the company pays you money if something bad happens to you or to something you own: *Her health insurance paid most of the doctor's bill.*

**in·sure** /in-**shoor**/ *verb*
**1** to buy or provide insurance for something or someone: *If a painting is insured for $5,000, the owner will be paid $5,000 if it gets stolen or damaged.*
**2** to make certain that something happens: *The teacher insures that all the students join in the activity.* (SYNONYM: **ensure**)

**in·tact** /in-**takt**/ *adjective* not damaged: *After the earthquake, only ten houses remained intact; the rest were damaged or destroyed.*

**in·te·ger** /**int**-ij-ur/ *noun* a whole number, not a fraction such as ¼ or ½: *6, –2, and 0 are all integers.*

**in·te·grate** /**int**-uh-grayt/ *verb*
**1** to become part of a group or society and be accepted by them: *The new immigrants soon integrated into American life.*
**2** to end the practice of separating people of different races, for example in schools: *During the 1960s people fought to integrate schools.*
—**integrated** /**int**-uh-grayt-id/ *adjective* containing people of different races: *We are proud of our integrated community.*
—**integration** /int-**uh-graysh**-uhn/ *noun* the act of integrating: *They campaigned for school integration.*

**in·teg·ri·ty** /in-**teg**-ruht-ee/ *noun* the quality of being honest and doing what you believe is right: *She wouldn't cheat on a test – she has too much integrity to do that.*

**in·tel·lect** /**int**'l-ekt/ *noun* the ability to think and understand things: *Professor Chang is a woman of great intellect.*

**in·tel·lec·tu·al** /int'l-**ek**-choo-uhl/
● *adjective*
**1** relating to your ability to think and understand: *These questions will test your intellectual abilities.*
**2** intelligent and liking to think about complicated things: *She is very intellectual and she likes talking about art.*
● *noun*
an intelligent person who likes thinking about complicated things: *Intellectuals admired his plays, but the general public didn't understand them.*

**in·tel·li·gence** /in-**tel**-uhj-uhnss/ *noun*
**1** the ability to learn, understand, and think about things: *He was of average intelligence, and got B's and C's at school.*
**2** information about the secret activities of foreign governments or terrorists: *They received intelligence reports that a terrorist attack was planned.*

**in·tel·li·gent** /in-**tel**-uhj-uhnt/ *adjective* able to learn and understand things quickly: *He's the most intelligent person in my class and gets the top score on every test.* (ANTONYM: **stupid**)
▶ see **Thesaurus**
—**intelligently** /in-**tel**-uhj-uhnt-lee/ *adverb* in an intelligent way: *Try to think intelligently about the problem.*

**in·tend** /in-**tend**/ *verb*
**1** to plan to do something: *I intended to wake up early, but I slept until ten!* (SYNONYM: **mean**)
**2** **be intended for** if something is intended for you, you are meant to have it or use it: *She accidentally sent me an email that was intended for someone else.*

**Word Family: intend**
**intend** *verb* | **intention** *noun* | **intentional** *adjective* | **intentionally** *adverb* | **intent** *noun*

**in·tense** /in-**tenss**/ *adjective*
**1** very great or strong: *The heat from the burning building was intense.*
**2** very serious and with very strong feelings: *He really loves music and he gets very intense when he talks about it.*
—**intensely** /in-**tenss**-lee/ *adverb* in an intense way: *I dislike her intensely.*
—**intensity** /in-**tenss**-uht-ee/ *noun* the quality of being intense: *You could clearly see the intensity of his feelings.*

**in·ten·si·fy** /in-**tenss**-uh-fi/ *verb* (**intensifies, intensified**) to become greater or stronger: *The pain intensified until it was unbearable.*

**in·tent** /in-**tent**/
● *noun* what you plan to do: *My intent is to win this competition.* (SYNONYM: **intention**)
● *adjective* **be intent on** to be determined to do something: *He was intent on solving the puzzle.*

**in·ten·tion** /in-**tensh**-uhn/ *noun* what you plan to do: *I have no intention of changing my mind.*

**in·ten·tion·al** /in-**tensh**-uhn-uhl/ *adjective* deliberate: *He broke the rules, but it wasn't intentional. It was a mistake.*
(ANTONYM: **accidental**)

—**intentionally** /in-**tensh**-uhn-uhl-ee/ *adverb* deliberately: *I didn't leave your name off the list intentionally.*

**inter-** /int-ur/, **intr-** /intr/

## Word Building

**inter**mission | **inter**rupt | **inter**national | **intr**oduce

These words all have the Latin word root *inter-* or *intr-* in them. *Inter-* means "between" or "among." The *intermission* is a break between the parts of a long movie, play, or show. If you *interrupt* someone, you say something while that person is talking. If you *introduce* people to each other, you stand between them and tell each one the other person's name.

**in·ter·act** /int-uhr-**akt**/ *verb* to talk or do things with someone: *Some people don't know how to interact with kids.*
—**interaction** /int-uhr-**ak**-shuhn/ *noun* behavior that involves talking or doing things with someone: *There is good interaction between students and teachers.*

**in·ter·ac·tive** /in-uhr-**akt**-iv/ *adjective* if a piece of equipment or software is interactive, you can make it perform actions: *The science museum has a lot of interactive exhibits and there are lots of buttons you can press to find out more information.*

**in·ter·cept** /int-ur-**sept**/ *verb* to stop something before it reaches the place where it is intended to go: *He threw the ball to a teammate, but a member of the other team intercepted it.*
—**interception** /int-ur-**sep**-shuhn/ *noun* the act of intercepting something: *Thanks to the interception of an email, the police knew what the men were planning.*

**in·ter·change·a·ble** /int-ur-**chaynj**-uhb-uhl/ *adjective* if things are interchangeable, they can be used instead of each other: *This toy monster has several interchangeable heads.*

**in·ter·com** /**int**-ur-kahm/ *noun* a system that lets people in different parts of a building, plane, or train speak to each other: *The pilot was telling us over the intercom that there will be a delay.*

**in·ter·de·pend·ent** /int-ur-di-**pend**-uhnt/ *adjective* if things or people are interdependent, they need each other in order to survive: *The plants and animals around the coral reef are interdependent.*
—**interdependence** /int-ur-di-**pend**-uhnss/ *noun* an interdependent situation: *We need to understand the economic interdependence of our country and other countries.*

**in·ter·est** /**in**-trist/
● *noun*
**1** the feeling that you want to know more about something: *My parents showed no interest in what I did. | She has an interest in medicine and would like to be a doctor.*
**2** something that you enjoy studying or doing: *My interests are music and swimming.*
**3** extra money that you pay to someone who lends you money: *You will have to pay interest on the money you borrow.*
● *verb*
if something interests you, you want to know more about it: *Space has always interested me and I want to be an astronaut one day.*

**in·ter·est·ed** /**in**-trist-id/ *adjective*
**1** if you are interested in something, you want to know more about it: *Donna reads the newspaper because she is interested in what's happening in the world.* ▶ see **Thesaurus**
**2** if you are interested in doing something, you want to do it: *Are you interested in joining a swimming club?*

**in·ter·est·ing** /**in**-trist-ing/ *adjective* if something is interesting, it keeps your attention because it seems exciting, or it tells you things you did not know about: *I saw an interesting TV program about dinosaurs.* ▶ see **Thesaurus**

**in·ter·fere** /int-ur-**feer**/ *verb*
**1** to try to affect a situation involving someone else, when that person does not want you to: *You have no right to interfere in my life.*
**2** **interfere with** to stop something from happening in the way that was planned: *Don't let anything interfere with your education.*
—**interference** /int-ur-**feer**-uhnss/ *noun* the act of interfering: *We are organizing the party our own way and we don't want any interference from anybody.*

**in·te·ri·or** /in-**teer**-ee-ur/
- *noun* the inside of something: *From the street we walked through the main doors into the interior of the hotel.* ( ANTONYM: **exterior** )
- *adjective* inside: *The interior walls of the house need to be painted but the paintwork on the outside is fine.* ( ANTONYM: **exterior** )

**in·ter·jec·tion** /int-ur-**jek**-shuhn/ *noun* a word or phrase that you say to show surprise, pain, anger, etc.: *"Ouch!" and "wow!" are interjections.*

**in·ter·me·di·ate** /int-ur-**meed**-ee-it/ *adjective* between two other levels or stages: *I was in the intermediate class, not the beginners' class or the advanced class.*

**in·term·in·a·ble** /in-**turm**-uhn-uhb-uhl/ *adjective* very long and boring: *If you don't enjoy a class, it can seem interminable.*

**in·ter·mis·sion** /int-ur-**mish**-uhn/ *noun* a short break in a play or concert: *There was a 20-minute intermission in the middle of the show.*

**in·tern** /**in**-turn/ *noun*
**1** someone who works without pay so that he or she can learn how to do a job: *She worked as an intern at a fashion magazine.*
**2** someone who has almost finished training as a doctor and is working in a hospital

**in·ter·nal** /in-**turn**'l/ *adjective*
**1** inside your body: *The scan lets the doctor see internal organs such as your heart, lungs, and stomach.* ( ANTONYM: **external** )
**2** inside an organization or country: *The price of the trip includes internal flights within Australia.*
—**internally** /in-**turn**'l-ee/ *adverb* in an internal way: *The medicine is not to be taken internally, which means it must be put on the skin, not swallowed.*

**in·ter·na·tion·al** /int-ur-**nash**-uhn-uhl/ *adjective* involving more than one country: *He won an international chess competition against players from Russia and China.*
—**internationally** /int-ur-**nash**-uhn-uhl-ee/ *adverb* involving more than one country

**In·ter·net** /**int**-ur-net/ *noun* a system that connects computers all over the world. You can use the Internet to look at information or send messages: *I found information about the Amazon rainforest on the Internet.*
( SYNONYMS: **the Net, the Web** )

**in·ter·pret** /in-**turp**-rit/ *verb*
**1** to translate spoken words from one language into another: *You know Spanish, so could you interpret for me?*
**2** to think that something has a particular meaning: *I interpreted his silence as a sign of guilt.*
**3** to explain the meaning of something: *The teacher interpreted the meaning of the poem for us.*
—**interpreter** /in-**turp**-ruht-ur/ *noun* someone who translates what someone says into another language
—**interpretation** /in-turp-ruh-**taysh**-uhn/ *noun* the meaning that someone thinks something has: *All the students had different interpretations of the poem.*

**in·ter·ro·gate** /in-**terr**-uh-gayt/ *verb* to ask someone questions for a long time in order to get information: *The police interrogated the men for more than three hours.*
—**interrogation** /in-terr-uh-**gaysh**-uhn/ *noun* the process of interrogating someone: *After a long interrogation, the man admitted he was guilty of the crime.*
—**interrogator** /in-**terr**-uh-gayt-ur/ *noun* a police officer or other official who asks someone questions in order to get information

**in·ter·rupt** /int-uh-**ruhpt**/ *verb*
**1** to speak while someone else is speaking: *Don't interrupt me when I'm talking!*
**2** to make something stop happening for a short time: *Rain interrupted the game for a while, but when it stopped we continued playing.*
—**interruption** /int-uh-**rup**-shuhn/ *noun* the act of interrupting someone: *I wanted to read my book without any interruptions.*

**in·ter·sect** /int-ur-**sekt**/ *verb* if roads or lines intersect, they meet or cross each other: *Where the two paths intersect, you should turn left.*

**in·ter·sec·tion** /**int**-ur-sek-shuhn/ *noun* a place where roads or lines meet or cross each other: *You should cross the street at the intersection, not in the middle of the block.*

**intersection**

**in·ter·state** /**int**-ur-stayt/
● *noun* a wide road that goes between states. Cars can travel very fast on interstates: *The accident happened on Interstate 84.*
● *adjective* between different states: *the interstate highway system*

**in·ter·val** /**int**-ur-vuhl/ *noun* a period of time or a space between two things: *He returned after an interval of a few minutes. | Plant the seeds at regular intervals, with five inches between each of them.*

**in·ter·vene** /int-ur-**veen**/ *verb* to try to stop an argument or problem involving other people: *If a teacher sees kids fighting, he or she should intervene.*
—**intervention** /int-ur-**vensh**-uhn/ *noun* an attempt to stop an argument or problem involving other people

**in·ter·view** /**int**-ur-vyoo/
● *noun*
**1** if a famous person gives an interview, he or she is asked questions by a reporter or a television host: *In the interview, the actor talked about his new movie.*
**2** a meeting in which you are asked questions by someone at a place where you want to work or study: *My brother has a job interview tomorrow.*
● *verb*
to ask someone questions during an interview: *Kelly was interviewed on the radio after the game.*
—**interviewer** /int-ur-**vyoo**-ur/ *noun* the person who asks someone questions during an interview: *The interviewer asked the singer whether she liked being famous.*

**in·tes·tine** /in-**test**-in/ *noun* the long tube in your body that food goes through after it leaves your stomach. Your intestines can be very long: *Liquids made by the body help digest food in the intestine.* ( SYNONYM: **bowel** ) ▶ see picture at **anatomy**

**in·ti·mate** /**itn**-uh-mit/ *adjective*
**1** having a very close relationship with someone: *He knows lots of people but he has few intimate friends.*
**2** relating to very private or personal things: *I told my sister my most intimate secrets.*

**in·tim·i·date** /in-**tim**-uh-dayt/ *verb*
**1** to make you feel worried or not confident: *I was intimidated by her because she was so much smarter than me.*
**2** to deliberately make someone feel frightened of you: *Bullies try to intimidate younger kids.*
—**intimidating** /in-**tim**-uh-dayt-ing/ *adjective* making you feel worried or not confident: *He found long books intimidating.*
—**intimidation** /in-tim-uh-**daysh**-uhn/ *noun* the use of threats to force someone to do something: *The gang used intimidation to get money from people.*

**in·to** /**int**-uh, **int**-oo/ *preposition*
**1** to the inside of something: *He went into the kitchen to get some juice. | Put some oil into a frying pan.*
**2** if you get into a situation, you are then involved in it: *Did you get into trouble? | She wants to go into teaching.*
**3** if one thing changes into another, it becomes a different thing: *Caterpillars turn into butterflies.*
**4** used to talk about hitting something, usually by accident: *The plane crashed into a mountain.*
**5** if you are into something, you like it and are interested in it: *Hannah is really into horses.*

**in·tol·er·a·ble** /in-**tahl**-uhr-uhb-uhl/ *adjective* if something is intolerable, it is so bad or extreme that you want to stop it or escape: *In summer, the heat is intolerable.*

**in·tol·er·ant** /in-**tahl**-uhr-uhnt/ *adjective* strongly disapproving of a way of behaving or a belief: *He is intolerant of lazy people.*
—**intolerance** /in-**tahl**-uhr-uhnss/ *noun* disapproval of a way of behaving or of a belief: *They had to leave their country because of the religious intolerance there.*

a b c d e f g h **i** j k l m n o p q r s t u v w x y z

**in·tri·cate** /**in**-trik-it/ *adjective* having many small parts or details: *The rug had an intricate pattern.*

**in·trigue** /in-**treeg**/ *verb* to seem mysterious and interesting to someone: *His message intrigued me – why did he need to talk to me?*

—**intriguing** /in-**treeg**-ing/ *adjective* mysterious and interesting: *The experiment produced some intriguing results.*

—**intrigued** /in-**treegd**/ *adjective* interested because something seems mysterious: *I was very intrigued to see a strange-shaped package on my doorstep.*

intricate

an intricate pattern

**in·tro·duce** /in-truh-**dooss**/ *verb*
**1** if you introduce someone, you tell people his or her name when they meet: *She introduced her new boyfriend to her parents.*
**2** to start selling or using something new: *Frozen yogurt was introduced in the 1970s.*
**3** to help someone experience or do something new: *Dad introduced me to classical music.*

**Word Family:** introduce

introduce *verb* | introduction *noun* | introductory *adjective*

**in·tro·duc·tion** /in-truh-**duhk**-shuhn/ *noun*
**1** the act of starting to sell or use something new: *The introduction of television meant fewer people went to the movies.*
**2** the act of telling people someone's name when they meet: *He is so famous he needs no introduction.*
**3** the part at the beginning of a book or speech: *In the introduction, the author explains why he wrote the book.*

—**introductory** /in-truh-**duhkt**-uhr-ee/ *adjective* done as an introduction: *Make the subject of your essay clear in the introductory paragraph.*

**in·trude** /in-**trood**/ *verb* to talk to or find out about someone when he or she does not want this: *I can see that you are having a private conversation – I won't intrude.*

—**intrusion** /in-**troozh**-uhn/ *noun* something that affects someone in a way that he or she does not want

**in·trud·er** /in-**trood**-ur/ *noun* someone who illegally goes into a building or area: *She saw an intruder, so she called the police.*

**in·tu·i·tion** /in-too-**ish**-uhn/ *noun* a feeling that you know something, which is not based on facts: *My intuition told me not to trust him.*

—**intuitive** /in-**too**-uht-iv/ *adjective* based on feelings, not facts: *She had an intuitive understanding of her baby's needs.*

**In·u·it** /**in**-oo-it/ *noun* a group of people who live in the very cold parts of North America and Greenland, or one person from this group: *In the past, the Inuit made all their clothes from animal skins.*

Inuit

**in·vade** /in-**vayd**/ *verb* to enter a country with an army in order to take control of it: *Iraqi troops invaded Kuwait in 1990.*

—**invader** /in-**vayd**-ur/ *noun* a country or soldier that invades another country

**in·va·lid**
● *noun* /**in**-vuhl-uhd/ someone who is sick or injured, and needs other people to do things for them: *I can tie my own shoelaces – I'm not an invalid!*
● *adjective* /in-**val**-id/ not acceptable, according to a law or rule: *This ticket is invalid because it does not have the right date on it.*
( ANTONYM: **valid** )

**in·val·ua·ble** /in-**val**-yuhb-uhl/ *adjective* very useful: *Thank you for your help – it has been invaluable.* ( SYNONYM: **valuable** )

**in·va·sion** /in-**vayzh**-uhn/ *noun* if there is an

invasion, an army enters a country in order to take control of it: *Iraq invaded Kuwait in 1990.*

**in·vent** /in-**vent**/ *verb*
**1** to think of something completely new, for example a new machine or game: *Alexander Graham Bell invented the telephone in 1876.*
▶ see **Thesaurus**
**2** to think of and tell people something that is not true: *I invented an excuse because I couldn't tell them the real reason why I was late.*
( SYNONYM: **make up** )

**Word Family:** invent

**invent** *verb* | **inventor** *noun* | **invention** *noun* | **inventive** *adjective*

**in·ven·tion** /in-**vensh**-uhn/ *noun*
**1** a machine, tool, or other thing that someone has made or thought of for the first time: *Television is a great invention.*
**2** the act of inventing something: *Books were rare before the invention of printing.*

**in·vent·ive** /in-**vent**-iv/ *adjective* good at thinking of new ideas: *She is an inventive cook who rarely uses recipes.*

**in·ven·tor** /in-**vent**-ur/ *noun* someone who makes or thinks of something completely new: *Bell was the inventor of the telephone.*

**in·ven·to·ry** /**in**-vuhn-tor-ee/ *noun* (plural **inventories**)
**1** a list of all the things in a place: *Make an inventory of all the equipment in the lab.*
**2** all the things that a store has for sale: *The store has a large inventory of computers.*

**in·ver·te·brate** /in-**vurt**-uh-brit/ *noun* a creature that does not have a backbone: *Worms are invertebrates.*

**invertebrate**

A frog is a vertebrate. | Worms are invertebrates.

**in·vest** /in-**vest**/ *verb* to buy something or to spend money in order to make a profit in the future: *He has invested a lot of money in art which he hopes will increase in value.*
—**investor** /in-**vest**-ur/ *noun* someone who invests money in something: *Investors rushed to buy stock in the company.*

**in·ves·ti·gate** /in-**vest**-uh-gayt/ *verb* to try to find out the truth about something: *Scientists are investigating how the drug works.*
—**investigator** /in-**vest**-uh-gayt-ur/ *noun* someone who investigates a crime or accident: *Investigators found traces of fingerprints on the bedroom wall.*

**Word Family:** investigate

**investigate** *verb* | **investigation** *noun* | **investigator** *noun*

**in·ves·ti·ga·tion** /in-vest-uh-**gaysh**-uhn/ *noun* an attempt to find out the truth about something: *The police are carrying out an investigation into what caused the fire.*

**in·vest·ment** /in-**vest**-muhnt/ *noun* if you make an investment, you spend or lend money in order to make a profit in the future: *Buying a house can be a good investment for the future.*

**in·vis·i·ble** /in-**viz**-uhb-uhl/ *adjective* something that is invisible cannot be seen: *The thread was so fine it was almost invisible.*
—**invisibility** /in-viz-uh-**bil**-uht-ee/ *noun* the quality of being impossible to see: *Black ice on roads is especially dangerous because of its invisibility.*

**in·vi·ta·tion** /in-vuh-**taysh**-uhn/ *noun* an offer to someone to come to your home or do something enjoyable with you: *We got an invitation to their New Year's party.*

**in·vite** /in-**vīt**/ *verb* to ask someone to come to your home or do something enjoyable with you: *I was invited to my cousin's wedding.*

**in·vit·ing** /in-**vīt**-ing/ *adjective* a place or thing that is inviting seems nice, so that you want to go there or try it: *The pool looked inviting and I really wanted to go for a swim.*

**in·voice** /in-voyss/
- *noun* a list that shows how much you must pay for things you have received or work that has been done: *The photographer sent them an invoice for the wedding photographs.*
( SYNONYM: **bill** )
- *verb* to send someone an invoice: *If you break anything in the apartment we will invoice you for the repair.* ( SYNONYM: **bill** )

**in·volve** /in-**vahlv**/ *verb*
**1** to affect or include someone or something: *The accident involved three cars.*
**2** to encourage someone to take part in something: *It's important to involve children in sports.*
**3** to have something as an important part: *His job involves a lot of travel.*

**in·volved** /in-**vahlvd**/ *adjective* if you are involved in something, you take part in it: *I didn't want to get involved in their argument.*

**in·volve·ment** /in-**vahlv**-muhnt/ *noun* the act of taking part in something: *He says he is innocent and that he had no involvement in the crime.*

**in·ward** /**in**-wurd/ (also **inwards**) *adverb* toward the inside or center of something: *Stand back because the door opens inward.*
( ANTONYM: **outward** )

**IOU** /ī oh **yoo**/ *noun* a piece of paper that you sign to say that you owe someone some money. IOU is short for "I owe you": *I don't have any money with me, so I'll give you an IOU.*

**IQ** /ī **kyoo**/ *noun* a number that is a test score showing how intelligent someone is. One hundred is the average score. IQ is short for "intelligence quotient.": *He has an IQ of 130 – he's really smart.*

**ir-** /ir/ see note at in-

**I·rish** /**ir**-ish/
- *adjective* from or in Ireland: *My dad is Irish – he was born in Dublin.*
- *noun* **the Irish** the people of Ireland: *The Irish are known for their love of music.*

**i·ron** /**ī**-urn/
- *noun*

**iron**

**1** a common hard metal that is used to make steel. There is also iron in your blood and some foods. The symbol for iron is Fe: *Pieces of iron will stick to a magnet.* | *Red meat has a lot of iron in it.*

iron

ironing board

**2** a piece of electrical equipment that heats up and is used for making clothes smooth: *Be careful – the iron is hot!*
- *verb*
to make clothes smooth using an iron: *You need to iron your shirt – it is very wrinkled.*
- *adjective*
made of iron: *The house has large iron gates.*

**i·ron·ic** /ī-**rahn**-ik/ *adjective*
**1** funny or sad because the opposite of what is expected happens: *It's ironic that such a great musician was deaf.*
**2** saying the opposite of what you really mean: *When he said "Good job!" he was being ironic.*
( SYNONYM: **sarcastic** )

**i·ron·ing** /**ī**-urn-ing/ *noun* the activity of making clothes smooth using an iron: *Mom was doing the ironing.*

**i·ron·ing board** /**ī**-urn-ing bord/ *noun* a narrow table used for ironing clothes

**i·ro·ny** /**ir**-uhn-ee/ *noun* (plural **ironies**)
**1** a situation that is funny or sad because the opposite of what is expected happens: *The irony is that his attempt to solve the problem made it worse.*
**2** a kind of humor in which you say the opposite of what you really mean: *"Thanks a lot," she said, with obvious irony. "You've ruined my week!"* ( SYNONYM: **sarcasm** )

**ir·ra·tion·al** /i-**rash**-uhn-uhl/ *adjective* not based on good reasons: *She has an irrational fear of birds.* ( ANTONYM: **rational** )

**ir·reg·u·lar** /i-**reg**-yuhl-ur/ *adjective*
**1** if things that happen are irregular, there are unequal periods of time between them: *The*

*patient's breathing was fast and irregular.*
**2** an irregular verb, noun, or adjective has forms that are not made in the normal way: *"Go" is an irregular verb. Its past tense is "went" and its past participle is "gone."* ( ANTONYM: **regular** )
**3** not even or smooth: *The surface of the field is too irregular for playing football.*
—**irregularly** /i-**reg**-yuhl-uhr-lee/ *adverb* in an irregular way: *She practices the piano very irregularly, so she doesn't really improve.*

**ir·reg·u·lar·i·ty** /i-reg-yuh-**larr**-uht-ee/ *noun*
(plural **irregularities**)
**1** something that has not been done according to the rules: *I can easily see if there have been any irregularities in the test, for example students copying each other's work.*
**2** a situation in which there are unequal periods of time between things: *The drug can cause irregularities in your heartbeat.*

**ir·rel·e·vant** /i-**rel**-uhv-uhnt/ *adjective* not connected with something, or not important in a particular situation: *Don't include irrelevant facts in your essay.* ( ANTONYM: **relevant** )

**ir·re·sist·i·ble** /irr-i-**zist**-uhb-uhl/ *adjective*
**1** if something is irresistible, it is so attractive or nice that it is impossible not to want it: *The cake looks irresistible. I can't wait to try it.*
**2** an irresistible feeling is so strong that you cannot stop yourself from doing something: *She felt an irresistible urge to cry.*
—**irresistibly** /irr-i-**zist**-uhb-lee/ *adverb* in an irresistible way: *The children were all irresistibly attracted to the plate of cookies.*

**ir·re·spon·si·ble** /irr-i-**spahnss**-uhb-uhl/ *adjective* behaving in a careless way, without thinking about the bad results that might happen: *It was irresponsible of you to let your little sister play near the road.*
—**irresponsibly** /irr-i-**spahnss**-uhb-lee/ *adverb* in an irresponsible way: *My parents let me go to the mall because they trust me not to behave irresponsibly.*
—**irresponsibility** /irr-i-spahnss-uh-**bil**-uht-ee/ *noun* irresponsible behavior: *I am shocked at people's irresponsibility in driving so fast near a school.*

**ir·ri·gate** /**irr**-uh-gayt/ *verb* to supply water to land or crops: *Water from the river is taken to irrigate the crops.*

—**irrigation** /irr-uh-**gaysh**-uhn/ *noun* the process of supplying land or crops with water

**ir·ri·ta·ble** /**irr**-uht-uhb-uhl/ *adjective* an irritable person gets annoyed very easily: *My mom sometimes gets irritable when she's tired, and she starts shouting at us.*
—**irritably** /**irr**-uht-uhb-lee/ *adverb* in an irritable way: *"Go away!" he said irritably.*

**ir·ri·tate** /**irr**-uh-tayt/ *verb*
**1** to make someone feel a little angry: *His stupid questions irritated me.* ( SYNONYM: **annoy** )
**2** to make a part of your body sore: *Smoke irritates my eyes.*
—**irritated** /**irr**-uh-tayt-id/ *adjective* a little angry: *I was irritated when I saw her sitting in my seat.*
—**irritating** /**irr**-uh-tayt-ing/ *adjective* making you feel a little angry: *He has a really irritating loud laugh.*
—**irritation** /irr-uh-**taysh**-uhn/ *noun* slight anger: *His refusal to apologize increased my irritation.*

**is** /z, iz/ *verb* the third person singular of the present tense of be: *Our house is very small.*

**-ish** /ish/

## Word Building

**-ish** is a suffix. It is used in adjectives.
**1** Jewish | Scottish | Polish
**-ish** means that a person or thing belongs to a country or group of people. The *Jewish* religion belongs to the Jews. Someone who is *Scottish* comes from Scotland. Someone who is *Polish* comes from Poland.
**2** yellowish | fortyish | tallish
**-ish** means that something has a little bit of a particular quality. If a dress is *yellowish*, it is yellow, but not a really good yellow. If someone is *fortyish*, that person is around forty in age, but is not exactly forty. Someone who is *tallish* is tall, but not very tall.

**Is·lam** /**iz**-lahm/ *noun* the religion which was started by Muhammad. People whose religion is Islam are called Muslims. Their holy book is the Koran.
—**Islamic** /iz-**lahm**-ik/ *adjective* relating to Islam: *Most Indonesians follow the Islamic faith.*

**is·land** /ī-uhnd/ *noun* a piece of land that is surrounded by water: *San Pedro is a small island off the coast of Washington State.* | *the Hawaiian islands*

island

**-ism** /iz-uhm/

## Word Building

**-ism** is a suffix. It is used in nouns.

**1** Commun**ism** | femin**ism** | Buddh**ism**

**-ism** is used to show a belief in a religion or idea. *Communism* is a political idea in which people believe goods should be shared equally among all the people in a country. *Feminism* is the idea that women have the same rights as men, and should be treated equally. *Buddhism* is a religion that is based on the teachings of Buddha.

**2** optim**ism** | hero**ism** | patriot**ism**

**-ism** is used to show a particular quality that something has. *Optimism* is the quality of believing that good things will happen. *Heroism* is the quality of being brave and acting like a hero. *Patriotism* is the quality of being loyal to your country.

**is·n't** /iz-uhnt/ *contraction* short for "is not": *That isn't true.*

**i·so·late** /īss-uh-layt/ *verb* to make one person or thing separate from others: *Isolate the sick child from the rest of the family.*

**i·so·lat·ed** /īss-uh-layt-id/ *adjective*
**1** far away from other things: *He grew up on an isolated farm.*
**2** feeling alone and without people to talk to: *When I first moved here, I felt very isolated.*
**3** having happened only once: *This is an isolated incident – he hasn't hit anyone before.*
—**isolation** /īss-uh-**laysh**-uhn/ *noun* the state of being isolated: *Living in isolation almost drove him crazy.*

**i·sos·ce·les** /ī-**sahss**-uh-leez/ *adjective* an isosceles triangle has two sides that are the same length and one side that is a different length
▶ see picture at **triangle**

**is·sue** /ish-oo/
● *noun*
**1** a subject or problem that people discuss: *The protection of the environment is a very important issue.* ( SYNONYM: **matter** )
**2** a magazine or newspaper that is printed for a particular day, week, or month: *The pictures are in the January issue of the magazine.*
( SYNONYM: **edition** )
● *verb*
**1** to make an official statement: *The Weather Service issued a tornado warning.*
**2** to give people the equipment, clothes, or documents they need for something: *They were issued coveralls to protect their clothes before they started work.*

**-ist** /ist/

## Word Building

**-ist** is a suffix. It is used in nouns.

art**ist** | Buddh**ist** | dent**ist** | guitar**ist** | novel**ist** | scient**ist**

**-ist** means that the noun is a person who does something. An *artist* makes art by painting or drawing. A *dentist* has the job of taking care of people's teeth. A *guitarist* plays the guitar. A *novelist* writes books.

**isth·mus** /iss-muhss/ *noun* a narrow piece of land, with water on both sides, that connects two larger pieces of land: *The Panama Canal cuts through the Isthmus of Panama to connect the Atlantic and Pacific Oceans.*

**it** /it/ *pronoun*
**1** a thing. You use "it" instead of the name of the thing when you have already talked about that thing: *He picked up a rock and threw it in the lake.*
**2** used to talk about an action or situation: *It's not fair!* | *It was nice seeing you.*
**3** used to talk about the weather or the time: *It's cold today.* | *It is six o'clock.*
**4** used to talk about a child or animal when you do not know the sex: *"Marilyn had a baby." "Is it a boy or a girl?"*

**i·tal·ics** /i-**tal**-ikss/ *plural noun* printed letters that lean to the right: *The examples in this dictionary are written in italics.*

**itch** /ich/
● *verb* if your skin itches, it feels unpleasant, so that you want to scratch it: *These wool socks make my feet itch.*
● *noun* an unpleasant feeling on your skin that makes you want to scratch it: *I have an itch in the middle of my back.*

**itch·y** /ich-ee/ *adjective* if your skin is itchy, it feels unpleasant, so that you want to scratch it: *The soap made my skin red and itchy.*

**it'd** /it-uhd/ *contraction*
**1** short for "it would": *It'd be easier if you helped us.*
**2** short for "it had": *I didn't know it'd been sold.*

**i·tem** /īt-uhm/ *noun* a thing: *The last item on the shopping list is bread.* | *Don't bring any valuable items such as cell phones on the school trip.*

**it'll** /it'l/ *contraction* short for "it will": *It'll be fun when we go to the park.*

**its** /itss/ *adjective* belonging to the thing or animal that has been mentioned: *The dog was barking and wagging its tail.* | *The hotel takes care of its guests very well.*

**it's** /itss/ *contraction*
**1** short for "it is": *It's snowing!*
**2** short for "it has": *It's been a long time since I saw Joe.*

**it·self** /it-**self**/ *pronoun*
**1** used when the same thing or animal does an action and receives the action: *The cat was licking itself.* | *The machine turns itself off when it has finished.*
**2** used to emphasize a particular thing: *The game itself is easy, but it takes a long time to be a good player.*

**-ity** /uht-ee/

## Word Building

**-ity** is a suffix.
simpli**city** | acti**vity** | creati**vity** | impossibil**ity**
**-ity** changes the root word into a noun. An *activity* is something you do to be active. The *simplicity* of a design or explanation is how simple it is. Your *creativity* is how creative you are.

**-ive** /iv/

## Word Building

**-ive** is a suffix. It is used in adjectives.
act**ive** | creat**ive** | expens**ive** | imaginat**ive** | sensit**ive** | talkat**ive**
**-ive** means that someone or something has a particular quality. Someone who is *active* moves a lot. If something is *expensive*, it costs a lot of money. Someone who is *talkative* talks a lot.

**I've** /īv/ *contraction* short for "I have": *I've finished my homework.*

**i·vo·ry** /ī**v**-uhr-ee/ *noun* the hard white substance that an elephant's long teeth is made of

ivory

an ivory statue

**i·vy** /īv-ee/ *noun* a plant with pointed leaves that grows up walls or spreads over the ground: *Ivy covered the old wall.*

ivy
ivy

a b c d e f g h i j k l m n o p q r s t u v w x y z

# Jj

### jab /jab/
- *verb* (**jabbing**, **jabbed**) to push someone with something pointed: *I jabbed him in the arm with my finger to make him wake up.*
- *noun* a sudden hard push with a pointed object or with your hand: *She gave him a friendly jab in the ribs.*

### jack /jak/ *noun*
**1** a tool used for lifting a car: *Dad got the jack out of the car so he could change the flat tire.*
**2** a card used in card games that has a picture of a young man on it: *I put down the jack of hearts.*

### jack·et /jak-it/ *noun* a short coat: *Dan was wearing a T-shirt and jeans jacket.*

> **Word Origin:** jacket
>
> **Jacket** comes from an Old French word that meant "a tight-fitting top." No one is sure exactly where the French word came from. It may have come from a man's name in French, Jacques. The word may also have come from Spanish and Arabic words that meant a kind of armor that covered your chest and back.

### jack·ham·mer /jak-ham-ur/ *noun* a powerful tool used for breaking up the surface of roads: *There is a man with a jackhammer making a lot of noise out in the street.*

### jack-in-the-box /jak in thuh bakss/ *noun* a toy box with a small model of a person inside. The person jumps up when you open the lid.

**jack-in-the-box**

### jack·knife /jak-nīf/ *noun* (plural **jackknives** /jak-nīvz/) a knife with a blade that folds into its handle

### jack-o'-lan·tern /jak uh **lant**-urn/ *noun* a pumpkin that you cut holes into so it looks like a face. You put a light inside, and use the jack-o'-lantern at Halloween.

**jack-o'-lantern**

### jack·rab·bit /jak-rab-it/ *noun* a large hare (=an animal like a rabbit). Jackrabbits have very long ears and are common in the western part of the U.S.

### jacks /jakss/ *noun* a game that involves bouncing a ball and picking up small metal or plastic pieces: *I like playing jacks.*

### Ja·cuz·zi /juh-**kooz**-ee/ *noun trademark* a large bathtub for several people. A Jacuzzi makes bubbles that help to relax your muscles.

### jade /jayd/ *noun* a green stone used in jewelry

**jade**
a jade necklace
a jade stone

### jag·ged /jag-id/ *adjective* having a sharp or uneven edge: *The waves crashed onto the jagged rocks of the coastline.*

### jag·uar /jag-war/ *noun* a large wild cat with yellow fur and black spots. Jaguars live in Central and South America.

**jaguar**

### jail /jayl/
- *noun* a place where criminals are sent as a punishment for a crime: *He was found guilty of fraud and sent to jail for five years.* (SYNONYM: **prison**)
- *verb* to put someone in prison: *The judge jailed him for two years for stealing cars.*

### jam /jam/
- *verb* (**jamming**, **jammed**)
**1** to push something into a small space: *I jammed my clothes into the suitcase and sat on it to make it close.*

**2** to make part of a machine stick and stop working correctly: *If the paper is too thick, it jams the copier.*

**3** if a lot of people or things jam a place, they completely fill it: *The freeway is jammed with cars – it will take hours to get home.*

● *noun*
**1** a thick sticky sweet food made from fruit and sugar. You put jam on bread: *Do you want strawberry jam on your toast?*

**2** a situation in which something is stuck somewhere: *There's a paper jam in the printer so it won't work.*

**jammed** /jamd/ *adjective* if something is jammed, you cannot move it or use it because it is stuck: *The car door is jammed and I can't open it.*

**jan·gle** /**jang**-guhl/ *verb* if metal things jangle, they make a noise when they hit each other: *The keys jangled in his pocket.*

**jan·i·tor** /**jan**-uht-ur/ *noun* someone whose job is to take care of a large building: *The school janitor locks the doors at the end of the day.*
( SYNONYM: **custodian** )

**Jan·u·ar·y** /**jan**-yoo-air-ee/ *noun*
( ABBREVIATION: **Jan.** ) the first month of the year. January is between December and February: *I was born on January 25, 2001.* | *It's very cold here in January.*

**Word Origin: January**

The ancient Romans named many of the months after one of their gods. **January** is named after the Roman god Janus. Janus was the god of doors and gates. The Romans saw January as the door that led into the new year. Janus was also the god of the beginning and end of things. January is the month that marks the end of the old year and the beginning of the new year.

**Jap·a·nese** /jap-uh-**neez**/
● *adjective*
from Japan: *We met some Japanese students.*

● *noun*
**1** the language used in Japan: *Tatsuya speaks Japanese and English.*
**2** the people of Japan: *The Japanese eat raw fish.*

**jar** /jar/ *noun* a glass container with a lid. You store food in a jar: *The cookie jar was full.* | *a jar of peanut butter*

**jar**
a jar of cookies

**jar·gon** /**jarg**-uhn/ *noun* words which people in a particular job use. Jargon is difficult for other people to understand: *We need someone to explain all the technical jargon in the instruction manual.*

**jaw** /jo/ *noun* the bottom part of your face with the bones that your teeth are in: *The dentist will give you an injection in your jaw, so you will not feel any pain.*

**jay** /jay/ *noun* a type of bird. Jays are noisy, and bright in color.

**jay·walk·ing** /**jay**-wok-ing/ *noun* the act of walking across a street at a place where it is dangerous to cross: *A cop stopped us for jaywalking.*
—**jaywalker** /**jay**-wok-ur/ *noun* someone who walks across a street at a place where it is dangerous to cross
—**jaywalk** /**jay**-wok/ *verb* to cross a street at a place where it is dangerous to cross

**jazz** /jaz/ *noun* a type of music. Jazz musicians often change the music or add notes as they play. Jazz was started in the early 1900s in New Orleans: *My dad likes listening to jazz.*

**jeal·ous** /**jel**-uhss/ *adjective*
**1** unhappy because you want what someone else has: *Hank was jealous because his friend had a new MP3 player.* ( SYNONYM: **envious** )
**2** angry and unhappy because someone you like or love is interested in someone else: *She was jealous when her friend talked to the new girl.*
—**jealousy** /**jel**-uhss-ee/ *noun* a feeling of being jealous: *There was a lot of jealousy between the brothers.*

**jeans** /jeenz/ *noun* pants made from denim (=a strong, usually blue, cotton cloth): *She was wearing a pair of jeans and a T-shirt.*

## Word Origin: jeans

**Jeans** probably comes from a French phrase, ***jean fustian***. Jean comes from the Old French name for Genoa, a city in Italy. Fustian is a type of strong cloth. People started using the word "jean" for the cloth. It is also possible that the cloth got the name "jean" because sailors from Genoa wore pants made from this strong cloth. In the 1800s, "jeans" started being used to describe the pants made from the cloth, and not just the cloth itself.

**-ject** /jekt/

## Word Building

**in*ject*** | **pro*ject*or** | **re*ject***

These words all have the Latin word root ***ject*** in them. ***Ject*** means "to throw." If a doctor *injects* you with a kind of medicine, he or she uses a special needle that pushes the medicine into your body. A *projector* throws a picture or words onto a screen. If you *reject* something, you say you do not want it, and "throw the offer back."

**jeer** /jeer/
- *verb* to shout or laugh at someone in a way that shows you dislike him or her: *The crowd became angry and started jeering at the speaker.*
- *noun* the sound of jeering

**Jell-O** /jel-oh/ *noun trademark* a soft sweet food that shakes when you move it: *For dessert we had strawberry Jell-O with whipped cream.*

**jel·ly** /jel-ee/ *noun* a sweet food that you spread on bread. Jelly is made from sugar and fruit: *Bart was eating a peanut butter and jelly sandwich.*

**jel·ly·bean** /jel-ee-been/ *noun* a small soft candy that is shaped like a bean. Jellybeans come in different colors and flavors.

**jel·ly·fish** /jel-ee-fish/ *noun* a sea animal with a round soft body. Jellyfish have long parts like string hanging down from their body. Jellyfish can sting you.

jellyfish

**jerk** /jurk/
- *verb* to move with a sudden quick movement: *The train jerked forward and I spilled my drink.* | *She quickly jerked her hand away from his.*
- *noun*
**1** a stupid or annoying person: *The guy's a real jerk – I'd stay away from him.*
**2** a sudden quick movement: *She pulled the curtains back with a jerk.*
—**jerky** /jurk-ee/ *adjective* stopping and starting suddenly and roughly: *I don't like the jerky way this elevator is moving.*

**jer·sey** /jurz-ee/ *noun* (plural **jerseys**) a shirt that sports players wear: *The team wear red and white jerseys.*

**Je·sus** /jeez-uhss/ (also **Jesus Christ** /jeez-uhss krīst/) the person whose life and ideas the Christian religion is based on. Christians believe that Jesus was the son of God.

**jet** /jet/ *noun*
**1** a fast airplane with a special type of engine that pushes out hot gases: *Military jets flew overhead.*
**2** a thin stream of liquid or gas that comes out of a small hole very quickly: *The fountain shoots jets of water into the air.*

**jew·el** /joo-uhl/ *noun* a small valuable stone, such as a diamond

**jew·el·er** /joo-uhl-ur/ *noun* someone who sells, makes, or repairs jewelry

**jew·el·ry** /joo-uhl-ree/ *noun* things such as rings and necklaces that you wear for decoration: *My mom wears lots of gold jewelry.*
▶ see **Thesaurus**

**jew·els** /joo-uhlz/ *plural noun* jewelry: *Someone had stolen the jewels.*

**Jew·ish** /joo-ish/ *adjective* relating to Judaism: *Hanukkah is a Jewish festival.*

348

—**Jew** /joo/ *noun* someone whose religion is Judaism: *Jews worship in a synagogue.*

**jig·saw puz·zle** /**jig**-so puhz-uhl/ (also **puzzle**) *noun* a set of small cardboard pieces with a picture on them. You put the pieces back together to make the whole picture: *This jigsaw puzzle has 220 pieces and makes a picture of a boat.*

**jin·gle** /**jing**-guhl/ *verb* if metal objects jingle, they shake and make a noise: *The bell on the cat's collar jingles when it runs.*

**jinx** /jingkss/
● *noun* someone or something that brings bad luck: *He is a jinx on the team. Every time he plays, we lose.*
● *verb* to make someone or something have bad luck: *If I say I'm going to win the competition, I'll jinx it.*
—**jinxed** /jingkst/ *adjective* having a lot of bad luck: *The trip was jinxed – Dad had his wallet stolen and Mom ended up in the hospital.*

**job** /jahb/ *noun*
**1** work that you do to earn money: *My mom got a job in a store.* ▶ see **Thesaurus**
**2** something that you are responsible for doing: *It's her job to produce reports.*
**3** something that you have to do without being paid: *Dad gave me some jobs to do, such as emptying the dishwasher.* ( SYNONYM: **task** )

> **Grammar: job**
>
> Do not say "What is your job?" or "What is your work?" Say "What do you do?" or "What kind of work do you do?"

**jock·ey** /**jahk**-ee/ *noun* someone who rides horses in races

**jog** /jahg/
● *verb* (**jogging**, **jogged**) to run at a slow steady speed for exercise: *Julie jogs in the park every morning.*
—**jogging** /**jahg**-ing/ *noun* the activity of running at a slow steady speed: *I went jogging around the neighborhood.*
—**jogger** /**jahg**-ur/ *noun* someone who jogs

jockey

jockey

● *noun* a slow steady run: *We went for a jog.*

**join** /joyn/ *verb*
**1** to become a member of an organization or group: *I want to join the tennis club.*
**2** to begin to take part in an activity that other people are involved in: *More police arrived to join the search for the missing boy.*
**3** to go somewhere in order to do something with someone else: *My aunt invited us to join her for tea.*
**4** to make things become connected together: *Join the pieces of wood with strong glue.*
▶ see **Thesaurus**
**5** to come together and become connected: *This is where the two rivers join to form the Ohio River.*

**joint** /joynt/
● *adjective* done or shared by two or more people: *This is a joint program run by two schools.*
—**jointly** /**joynt**-lee/ *adverb* in a way that involves two or more people: *The company is jointly owned by two big software makers.*
● *noun* a place where two bones meet: *Your knee, elbow, and hip are joints.*

**joke** /johk/
● *noun* something funny that you say or do to make people laugh: *Dad's always telling jokes.*
▶ see **Thesaurus**
● *verb* to say things that are intended to be funny: *He is always laughing and joking with his friends.*
—**joker** /**johk**-ur/ *noun* someone who likes to tell jokes and make people laugh

**jol·ly** /**jahl**-ee/ *adjective* (**jollier**, **jolliest**) happy and friendly: *Santa Claus is a jolly old man with a long white beard.*

**jolt** /johlt/
● *noun*
**1** a sudden shock or surprise: *He got a jolt when he read her letter.*
**2** a sudden rough movement: *The bus stopped with a jolt, and some people fell off their seats.*
● *verb*
**1** to make something move suddenly and roughly: *An earthquake jolted southern California.*
**2** to give someone a sudden shock: *She was jolted awake by a loud bang.*

a b c d e f g h i j k l m n o p q r s t u v w x y z

a b c d e f g h i **j** k l m n o p q r s t u v w x y z

**jot** /jaht/ *verb* (**jotting, jotted**) **jot down** to write something quickly on a piece of paper: *I grabbed some paper and jotted down her address.*

**jour·nal** /**jurn**'l/ *noun*
**1** a book where you write what you have done each day: *I wrote about the vacation in my journal.* (SYNONYM: **diary**)
**2** a magazine or newspaper for professional people, such as doctors: *People who work in banking usually read the "Wall Street Journal."*

**jour·nal·ist** /**jurn**'l-ist/ *noun* someone who writes reports for newspapers, magazines, television, or radio: *He's a journalist for the "New York Times."* (SYNONYM: **reporter**)
—**journalism** /**jurn**'l-iz-uhm/ *noun* the job or activity of writing reports for newspapers, magazines, television, or radio: *I think journalism would be a very interesting career.*

**jour·ney** /**jurn**-ee/ *noun* a long trip from one place to another: *The journey from New York to Florida takes about two days by car.*

**joy** /joy/ *noun*
**1** a feeling of great happiness: *Music brings great joy to many people.*
**2** something or someone that gives you happiness: *The baby is a joy to his parents and grandparents.*

**joy·ful** /**joy**-fuhl/ *adjective* very happy: *There were joyful celebrations in the city after the team won the competition.*

**joy·ous** /**joy**-uhss/ *adjective* very happy or likely to make people happy: *The wedding was a joyous occasion.*

**joy·stick** /**joy**-stik/ *noun* a handle that you use to control an aircraft or a computer game: *In the game you use a joystick to move the robots around.*

**Jr.** the written abbreviation of **Junior**

**Ju·da·ism** /**jood**-ee-iz-uhm/ *noun* the Jewish religion. Judaism is based on books called the Hebrew Scriptures, which include many of the books that are in the Old Testament of the Christian Bible.

**judge** /juhj/
● *noun*
**1** a person who makes decisions in a court of law, for example about how a criminal should be punished: *The judge sent him to jail for two years.* ▶ see **Thesaurus**
**2** someone who chooses the winner of a competition: *Her performance impressed the judges and she won the competition.*
● *verb*
**1** to form an opinion about someone or something: *You shouldn't judge people by the way they look.*
**2** to choose the winner of a competition: *My dad was asked to judge the school poetry competition.*

**judg·ment**, **judgement** /**juhj**-muhnt/ *noun*
**1** an opinion you have about someone or something: *In my judgment, he's wrong.*
**2** the ability to make good decisions: *If you use your judgment, I'm sure you can find the right answer.*
**3** a decision that a court or judge makes: *We're still waiting for the court to make a final judgment about the case.*

**ju·di·cial** /joo-**dish**-uhl/ *adjective*
**1** relating to courts or judges: *We have been learning about the U.S. judicial system.*
**2** **the judicial branch** the part of a government that consists of all the judges in a country

**judiciary** /joo-**dish**-ee-air-ee/ *noun* the judicial branch: *The federal judiciary consisted of about 800 judges.*

**ju·do** /**jood**-oh/ *noun* a sport from Japan. In judo, you try to throw another person to the ground: *If you are very good at judo, you can wear a special black belt.*

judo

**jug** /juhg/ *noun* a container for holding liquids. A jug has a small opening at the top and a small handle on the side: *She poured milk from the jug into all the cups.*

jug

**jug·gle** /**juhg**-uhl/ *verb*
**1** to keep balls or other objects moving in the air. You throw the balls up and catch them many times: *He took three oranges and started juggling.*
**2** to do two or more important jobs or activities at the same time: *Many mothers have to juggle work, home, and family.*
—**juggler** /**juhg**-lur/ *noun* someone who juggles objects in the air: *A juggler was doing an act in the street.*

juggle

**juice** /jooss/ *noun*
**1** the liquid from fruit and vegetables: *Can I have a glass of apple juice, please?*
**2** the liquid that comes out of meat when it is cooked: *You can use the meat juices to make gravy.*

**juic·y** /**jooss**-ee/ *adjective* (**juicier**, **juiciest**) full of juice: *The orange was very juicy and I got juice all over my chin.*

**juke·box** /**jook**-bahkss/ *noun* a machine that plays music when you put money in it: *The jukebox in the diner was playing her favorite song.*

**Ju·ly** /ju-**lī**/ *noun* (ABBREVIATION: **Jul.**) the seventh month of the year. July is between June and August: *Independence Day is on July 4. | We are going to Florida in July.*

**Word Origin:** July

The month of **July** is named after Julius Caesar. He was an important Roman leader who began the Roman empire. His birthday was in July.

**jum·ble** /**juhm**-buhl/ *noun* a group of things which looks messy: *He found a jumble of papers and photographs inside the desk.*

**jum·bo** /**juhm**-boh/ *adjective* very big: *Crowds watched the game on jumbo television screens.*

**jump** /juhmp/
● *verb*
**1** to push yourself up into the air or over something using your legs: *Her horse jumped over the fence easily. | Jumping on a trampoline is a lot of fun.* ▶ see **Thesaurus**
**2** to drop down from a place that is above the ground: *The cat jumped down from the wall.*
**3** to move somewhere quickly or suddenly: *Logan jumped up from his chair to help the teacher pass out the books.*
**4** to get bigger suddenly and by a large amount: *The number of children at the school has jumped from 175 to 230 this year.*
**5 jump at** to quickly accept the chance to do something: *Ashley loves dancing and jumped at the chance to go to dance classes.*

jump

IDIOM with **jump**
**make someone jump** if something makes you jump, it frightens you and your body makes a sudden movement: *A branch touched my arm in the dark and made me jump.*
● *noun*
**1** a movement into the air using your legs: *The boy was doing little jumps, pretending to be a frog.*
**2** a movement when you deliberately fall from a high place: *My dad did a parachute jump from a plane.*
**3** a sudden increase: *There has been a big jump in the number of students so they need more teachers.*

**jump·er** /**juhmp**-ur/ *noun* a dress with no sleeves. Girls usually wear it over a shirt.

**jump rope** /**juhmp** rohp/ *noun* a piece of rope that you turn and jump over as a game

a b c d e f g h i z

j

k l m n o p q r s t u v w x y z

**junc·tion** /**juhngk**-shuhn/ *noun* a place where roads join: *The school is at the junction of Latona Avenue and George Street.*
( SYNONYM: **intersection** )

**June** /joon/ *noun* ( ABBREVIATION: **Jun.** ) the sixth month of the year, between May and July: *Abby's birthday is on June 26.* | *We went to Seattle in June.*

**Word Origin:** June

The ancient Romans named many of the months after one of their gods. **June** is named after the Roman goddess Juno. Juno was the queen of the gods, and the wife of Jupiter, the king of the gods. She was the goddess of marriage, and people still like to get married in June.

**jun·gle** /**juhng**-guhl/ *noun* a tropical forest with a lot of trees and plants growing close together: *The snake lives in the jungles of South America.*

**jun·gle gym** /**juhng**-guhl jīm/ *noun* a metal or wooden structure that children climb and play on: *Joey climbed to the top of the jungle gym in the park.*

**jun·ior** /**joon**-yur/
● *noun*
a student in the third year of high school or college: *My brother is a junior at Center High School.*
● *adjective*
**1 Junior** (also **Jr.**) used after the name of a man who has the same name as his father: *Martin Luther King, Jr.*
**2** for younger people: *Ellie is only ten years old, so she is in the junior tennis team.*
( ANTONYM: **senior** )
**3** lower in rank: *Junior officials help more senior ones.* ( ANTONYM: **senior** )

**jun·ior col·lege** /**joon**-yur **kahl**-ij/ *noun* a college where students go for two years. They learn a skill or prepare to go to another college.
( SYNONYM: **community college** )

**jun·ior high school** /**joon**-yur **hī** skool/ (also **junior high**) *noun* a school in the U.S. and Canada for students who are between 12 and 14 or 15 years old: *My sister is in junior high school.*

**ju·ni·per** /**joon**-uhp-ur/ *noun* a plant that produces purple berries. You can use juniper berries in cooking.

**junk** /juhngk/ *noun* useless or broken things that you do not want: *Mom told me to get rid of the junk in my bedroom.*

**junk food** /**juhnk** food/ *noun* food that is not healthy because it has a lot of fat or sugar: *She eats too much junk food and she's always buying hamburgers and donuts.*

**junk mail** /**juhnk** mayl/ *noun* mail that companies send to people in order to advertise a product

**Ju·pi·ter** /**joop**-uht-ur/ *noun* the fifth planet from the Sun. Jupiter is the largest planet, and has many moons. ▶ see picture at **solar system**

**ju·ror** /**joor**-ur/ *noun* one of the 12 people in a court who decide whether someone is guilty of a crime: *The jurors decided he was innocent.*

**ju·ry** /**joor**-ee/ *noun* (plural **juries**) the 12 people in a court who decide whether someone is guilty of a crime: *The jury looked at all the evidence and decided that the man was innocent.*

**just** /juhst/
● *adverb*
**1** exactly: *His bike is just the same as mine.*
**2** only: *The team scored just three points in the whole competition.*
**3** a short time ago: *They have just arrived in the city and they don't know anybody.*
**4** a short time before or after something else: *He got home just before midnight.*
**5** if something just happens, it does happen, but it almost did not: *We just made it to the theater in time for the movie.*
**6** used for emphasizing something you are saying: *Just be quiet, will you?*

IDIOMS with just
**just about** almost: *Just about everyone in my class has seen the movie.*
**be just about to** to be going to do something soon: *The airplane was just about to take off.*
**just a minute/second/moment** used to tell someone to wait for a short time: *Just a second – I need to get my bag.*
● *adjective*
morally right and fair: *I think it was a just*

punishment and he deserved to lose his place on the team. ( **ANTONYM: unjust** )

**jus·tice** /**juhst**-iss/ *noun*

**1** fairness in the way people are treated: *They are working for justice and peace in their country.*
( **ANTONYM: injustice** )

**2** the laws of a country and the way they are used to punish people who have committed crimes: *The police and the courts are all part of the criminal justice system.*

**3** a judge in a court of law: *There are nine justices on the Supreme Court.*

**jus·ti·fi·ca·tion** /juhst-uhf-uh-**kaysh**-uhn/ *noun*

a good reason for doing something: *Even if he teased you, that is not a justification for hitting him.*

**jus·ti·fy** /**juhst**-uh-fī/ *verb* (**justifies**, **justified**) to give a good reason for something: *He tried to justify his behavior by saying his friends told him to do it.*

—**justifiable** /juhst-uh-**fī**-uhb-uhl/ *adjective* done for good reasons: *It is never justifiable to hit a child.*

**ju·ve·nile** /**joov**-uhn'l/

● *adjective* relating to children. Juvenile is used in legal language: *The number of juvenile offenders has increased.*

● *noun* a child, according to the law: *Two juveniles aged 10 and 15 pleaded guilty to the crime.*

a
b
c
d
e
f
g
h
i
**j**
k
l
m
n
o
p
q
r
s
t
u
v
w
x
y
z

# Kk

**K** /kay/

**1** 1,000: *He earns $50K (=$50,000) a year.*
**2** an abbreviation of **kilometer**: *We ran in a 5K race.*
**3** a written abbreviation of **kilobyte**

**ka·leid·o·scope** /kuh-**līd**-uh-skohp/ *noun* a tube with mirrors and pieces of colored glass in it. You look into the kaleidoscope and turn it to make different patterns.

## Word Origin: kaleidoscope

The **kaleidoscope** was invented in 1817. The person who invented it used three Greek words to make up the name. *Kalos* means "beautiful," *eidos* means "shape," and *scope* means "look at."

**kan·ga·roo**
/kang-guh-**roo**/ *noun* an Australian animal that jumps using its strong back legs. It has short front legs and a long tail. Mother kangaroos carry their babies in a pouch on their stomach after they are born.

kangaroo

**ka·ra·te** /kuh-**raht**-ee/ *noun* a sport from Japan. In karate, you use your hands and feet to hit and kick your opponent.

## Word Origin: karate

**Karate** comes from Japanese words that mean "empty hands." In karate, you fight with your hands and feet, and do not use weapons.

**kay·ak** /**kī**-ak/ *noun* a small boat for one or two people. It has pointed ends and the top is covered so that water does not get inside. You use a long paddle with two flat ends to move the kayak through the water.
—**kayaking** /**kī**-ak-ing/ *noun* the sport or activity of paddling a kayak: *We went kayaking on the river.*

kayak
paddle

## Word Origin: kayak

The word **kayak** comes from a language spoken by the Inuit people in Greenland. It means a small boat made of animal skins. It may also mean something like "man's boat" or "hunter's boat."

**ka·zoo** /kuh-**zoo**/ *noun* a musical instrument that you play by putting it to your lips and making sounds into it

**keep** /keep/ *verb* (**kept** /kept/)
**1** to continue to have something and not give it to anyone else: *You can keep that pen. I have another one.*
**2** to make someone or something continue to be in a place or situation: *Keep the door closed.* | *He put his coat on to keep warm.*
**3** (also **keep on**) to continue doing something: *Keep driving until you come to the next town.* | *She was tired but she kept on playing.*
**4** to store something in a place: *I keep my toys in my bedroom.* ▶ see **Thesaurus**
**5** to write down information regularly: *She keeps a diary of everything that happens.*
**6 keep your promise** to do what you have promised: *Mom said she'd take us to the concert and she kept her promise.*
**7 keep up** to do something as fast or as well as someone else: *The little boy had to run to keep up with his sisters.*

**keep·er** /**keep**-ur/ *noun* someone whose job is to take care of something: *The keepers at the zoo feed the penguins with fish.*

**kelp** /kelp/ *noun* a type of brown seaweed (=a plant that grows in the ocean)

**ken·nel** /ken'l/ *noun* a place where dogs are taken care of while their owners are away: *Our dog goes to a kennel when we are on vacation.*

**kept** /kept/ *verb* the past tense and past participle of **keep**

**ker·nel** /kurn'l/ *noun* a seed that you can eat: *Popcorn is made from kernels of corn.*

**ker·o·sene** /kerr-uh-seen/ *noun* a type of oil that people burn for heat and light: *The only light they had in the cabin was a kerosene lamp.*

**ketch·up** /kech-uhp/ *noun* a red sauce made from tomatoes, that you put on food: *Do you want ketchup on your fries?*

> ### Word Origin: ketchup
>
> **Ketchup** comes from a Malay word for fish sauce. The Malay probably borrowed the word from Chinese. In the 1800s, ketchup meant any sauce that was made using vinegar. Ketchup now only means a sauce made from tomatoes.

**ket·tle** /ket'l/ *noun* a metal container used for boiling and pouring water

**key** /kee/
* *noun*
**1** something used for locking something or for starting a car's engine: *Dad can't find his car keys. | I have a key to the back door of my house.* ▶ see picture at **padlock**
**2** one of the things you press on a computer keyboard: *Use the "Delete" or "Backspace" key to get rid of text.*
**3** one of the things that you press to make a sound on a musical instrument such as a piano: *Pianos have black and white keys.* ▶ see picture at **piano**
**4** a set of musical notes with a particular base note: *The piece was written in the key of C major.*
**5** the most important thing that will help you to achieve something: *Hard work is the key to success at school.*
* *adjective*
more important than other things: *I'm making a list of all the key points that I need to remember for the test.*

**key·board** /kee-bord/ *noun*

keyboard

**1** a piece of computer equipment with keys that you press to do work on the computer: *I sat at my computer keyboard and typed in my password.* ▶ see picture at **computer**

computer keyboard

electronic keyboard

**2** the row of keys on a piano or organ that you press to make musical sounds: *The keyboard of a piano has black and white keys.*
**3** a musical instrument like a small electric piano. A keyboard can also make the sounds of other instruments.

**key·hole** /kee-hohl/ *noun* the hole in a lock that you put a key in

**kg** the written abbreviation of **kilogram**

**kick** /kik/
* *verb*

kick

**1** to hit something with your foot: *The boys were kicking a ball around the yard.*
**2** to move your legs around in the air: *Andrea's baby was kicking his legs in the air.*
**3** **kick out** to make someone leave a place or job: *If you fight in school they might kick you out.*
* *noun*
a hit with your foot: *Give the ball a good kick with the side of your foot.*

**kick·ball** /kik-bol/ *noun* a children's game which is like baseball, but you kick the ball: *The kids were playing kickball.*

**kick·off** /kik-of/ *noun*
**1** the time when a game of football or soccer starts: *Kickoff is at 3:00.*
**2** the first kick in a game of football or soccer: *The coach asked me to take the kickoff.*

a
b
c
d
e
f
g
h
i
j
**k**
l
m
n
o
p
q
r
s
t
u
v
w
x
y
z

**kid** /kid/

● *noun*

**1** a child: *I like playing with the other kids in the neighborhood.*

**2** a young goat

● *verb* (**kidding, kidded**)

to say something as a joke: *"My dad won the lottery!" "You're kidding!"*

**kid·nap** /kid-nap/ *verb* (**kidnapping, kidnapped**) to take someone away using force: *The prince was kidnapped, and the kidnappers asked his family for money.*

—**kidnapper** /kid-nap-ur/ *noun* someone who kidnaps people

—**kidnapping** /kid-nap-ing/ *noun* the crime of kidnapping people

**kid·ney** /kid-nee/ *noun* (plural **kidneys**) an organ in your body that cleans waste from your blood and makes it into urine. You have two kidneys. ▶ see picture at **anatomy**

**kill** /kil/ *verb*

**1** to make a person, plant, or animal die: *The explosion killed 20 people.*

**2** to be very angry at someone: *My mom will kill you if you walk on the carpet in those muddy shoes.*

**kill·er** /kil-ur/ *noun* a person or thing that kills: *Police are searching for the killer of a young woman. | Smoking is one of the biggest killers.*

**ki·lo** /keel-oh/ *noun* (plural **kilos**) a kilogram

**Word Building**

**kilo**byte | **kilo**gram | **kilo**meter | **kilo**watt

These words all have the Greek word root **kilo** in them. **Kilo** means "thousand" (1,000). A *kilogram* is equal to 1,000 grams. A *kilometer* is equal to 1,000 meters.

**kil·o·byte** /kil-uh-bīt/ *noun*

(ABBREVIATION: **KB, kB, or K**) a unit for measuring computer information, which is around 1,000 bytes

**kil·o·gram** /kil-uh-gram/ (also **ki·lo** /keel-oh/) *noun* (ABBREVIATION: **kg**) a unit in the metric system for measuring weight, equal to 1,000 grams

**ki·lom·e·ter** /ki-**lahm**-uh-tur/ *noun*

(ABBREVIATION: **km, k**) a unit in the metric system for measuring length, equal to 1,000 meters

**kil·o·watt** /**kil**-uh-waht/ *noun* (ABBREVIATION: **kW**) a unit for measuring electrical power, equal to 1,000 watts

**kin** /kin/ *noun* your family: *People often like to spend the holidays with their kin.*

IDIOM with **kin**

**next of kin** your closest relative: *The police are trying to find the man's next of kin.*

**kind** /kīnd/

● *noun* a type of person or thing: *What kind of music do you like? | It looks like some kind of fruit.* (SYNONYMS: **sort, type**)

IDIOM with **kind**

**kind of** a little: *I felt kind of lonely when my brother went away to college.*

● *adjective* helpful, friendly, and nice: *Jenna was very kind to me and helped me with my homework.* ▶ see **Thesaurus**

—**kindly** /**kīnd**-lee/ *adverb* in a way that is kind: *Ann kindly lent me her umbrella.*

—**kindness** /**kīnd**-niss/ *noun* kind behavior toward someone: *She showed kindness to anyone who needed help.*

**kin·der·gar·ten** /**kind**-ur-gart'n/ *noun* a class in school for children who are about five years old. Children go to kindergarten before they start first grade: *Bella has been my best friend since we were in kindergarten.*

**Word Origin:** kindergarten

**Kindergarten** is a German word that is used in English. It means "children's garden." The word was invented by a German teacher who believed that young children learn best by playing.

**ki·net·ic** /ki-**net**-ik/ *adjective* caused by movement, or relating to movement: *Kinetic energy is the energy created by motion.*

**king** /king/ *noun*

**1** a man who is the ruler of a country because he is from a royal family: *King George III was king of England during the American Revolution.* ▶ see **Thesaurus**

**2** a card used in card games that has a picture of a king on it: *The first card was a king of clubs.*

**king·dom** /**king**-duhm/ *noun* a country that has a king or queen

**kiss** /kiss/
● *verb* to touch someone with your lips to show that you like them: *Grandma kissed me on the cheek.*
● *noun* a touch with your lips: *Come and give Mommy a kiss.*

**kit** /kit/ *noun*
**1** a set of tools or equipment that you use to do something: *The Scout leader has a first-aid kit in case someone gets hurt.*
**2** something that you buy as a set of parts and put together yourself: *a model airplane kit*

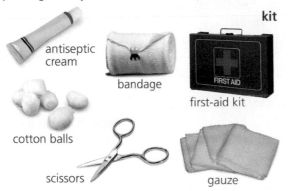

**kit**

antiseptic cream

bandage

first-aid kit

cotton balls

scissors

gauze

**kitch·en** /**kich**-uhn/ *noun* the room where you cook food: *Mom and Dad are in the kitchen making dinner.*

**kite** /kīt/ *noun* a toy that you fly in the air on the end of a long string. A kite is made of a frame covered in paper or cloth: *It was just windy enough to fly kites.*

**kite**

**kit·ten** /**kit**'n/ *noun* a young cat
▶ see picture at **cat**

**kit·ty** /**kit**-ee/ (also **kit·ty·cat** /**kit**-ee-kat/) *noun* (plural **kitties**) a cat: *Here, kitty kitty! Here's your food.*

**ki·wi** /**kee**-wee/ (also **ki·wi fruit** /**kee**-wee froot/) *noun* a green fruit with small black seeds and a hairy skin ▶ see picture on page **A7**

**klutz** /kluhtss/ *noun* someone who often drops things or falls: *I'm a total klutz at sports and I never get picked for the team.*

**Word Origin: klutz**

**Klutz** was first used in American English in the 1960s. It comes from a Yiddish word that means "a clumsy person."

**km** the written abbreviation of **kilometer**

**knack** /nak/ *noun* the ability to do something well: *He's a great player who has a knack for scoring goals.*

**knead** /need/ *verb* to press a bread mixture with your hands to make it ready to cook: *When you make bread, you knead the dough with your hands until it becomes soft.*

**knee** /nee/ *noun*
**1** the middle part of your leg, where it can bend: *Robbie fell and hurt his knee.*
**2** the part of your pants that covers your knee: *Billy's jeans had holes in both knees.*

**knee·cap** /**nee**-kap/ *noun* the bone at the front of your knee

**kneel** /neel/ *verb* (**knelt** /nelt/ or **kneeled**) to put your knees on the ground, so that they are supporting your body: *She knelt down to pray.*

**kneel**

**knew** /noo/ *verb* the past tense of **know**

**knife** /nīf/ *noun* (plural **knives** /nīvz/) a tool used for cutting things or as a weapon. It has a handle and a sharp metal part: *We use this knife for chopping vegetables.*

a b c d e f g h i j **k** l m n o p q r s t u v w x y z

**knight** /nīt/ *noun* a soldier who had a high position in society in the Middle Ages (500–1500 A.D.). Knights wore armor and fought while riding horses: *A knight in armor was riding on his horse toward the castle.*

knight

sword

helmet

armor

shield

**knit** /nit/ *verb* (**knitting, knit** or **knitted**) to make clothes out of thick thread using two long needles or a special machine: *My mother is knitting John a sweater.*
—**knitting** /nit-ing/ *noun* the activity of making clothes in this way: *My grandmother likes knitting and made me a really cool sweater.*

knit

knitting needle

yarn

**knob** /nahb/ *noun*
**1** a round handle on a door or drawer: *He turned the door knob and slowly opened the door.*
**2** a round button that you turn to control a machine: *You can twist the knob on the radio to change the station.*

**knock** /nahk/
● *verb*
**1** to hit a door or window with your hand so that the people inside can hear you: *Someone knocked on the door so I went to see who was there.*
**2** to hit or push something hard so that it moves or falls down: *The wind had knocked down several trees which were now lying on the ground.*
**3 knock out** to hit someone so hard that he or she becomes unconscious: *If a rock hits you on the head, it could knock you out.*
● *noun*
the sound that is made by hitting something hard: *There was a loud knock on the door – the police had arrived.*

knock

**knot** /naht/ *noun*
**1** the place where pieces of rope or string are tied together: *I learned how to tie knots in the Boy Scouts. | There's a knot in my shoelace.*
**2** a unit for measuring the speed of a ship or a plane. A knot is about 1,853 meters in an hour: *The ship was traveling at 20 knots.*
—**knot** /naht/ *verb* (**knotting, knotted**) to tie something in a knot: *Dad showed me how to knot a tie.*

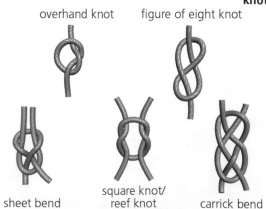

knot

overhand knot

figure of eight knot

sheet bend

square knot/ reef knot

carrick bend

**know** /noh/ *verb* (**knew** /noo/, **known** /nohn/)
**1** to have information about something: *Do you know what the capital city of France is? | "What*

*time is it?" "I don't know. I don't have a watch."*
▶ see **Thesaurus**
**2** to be able to do something: *My grandmother doesn't know how to use a computer.*
**3** to have met a person before, or to have been to a place before: *I know the McKenzies. They used to be our neighbors.*
**4** used to say that you agree with what someone is saying: *"Science was so boring today!" "I know."*

> **Word Family: know**
>
> **know** verb | **knowledge** noun | **knowledgeable** adjective | **known** adjective | **unknown** adjective

**know-how** /**noh**-how/ *noun* the knowledge or ability you need to do something: *The school needs someone with the technical know-how to create a website.*

**knowl·edge** /**nahl**-ij/ *noun*
**1** information, skills, and understanding: *He has a very good knowledge of computers so he can help you with your project.* ▶ see **Thesaurus**
**2** the fact of knowing about a situation or event: *He went to the party without his parents' knowledge.*
—**knowledgeable** /**nahl**-ij-uhb-uhl/ *adjective* knowing a lot about something: *Brad's very knowledgeable about music.*

**known** /nohn/
● *verb*
the past participle of know
● *adjective*
**1** if something is known, people know it: *It's a known fact that smoking can cause cancer.*
**2** famous: *The coast of Washington and Oregon is known for rain.*

**knuck·le** /**nuhk**-uhl/ *noun* one of the places where your fingers can bend: *I fell and scraped my knuckles.*

**ko·a·la** /koh-**ahl**-uh/
(also **ko·a·la bear** /koh-**ahl**-uh bair/) *noun* an Australian animal that looks like a small bear. Koalas live in trees and eat leaves.

koala

**Ko·ran** /kuh-**ran**/ *noun* the holy book of the Muslim religion

**Ko·re·an** /kuh-**ree**-uhn/
● *adjective*
from Korea: *Korean food is very spicy.*
● *noun*
**1** someone from Korea: *The people who live next door are Koreans.*
**2** the language spoken in Korea: *My mother can speak Korean and English.*

**ko·sher** /**kohsh**-ur/ *adjective* kosher food is prepared according to Jewish law

**kung fu** /kuhng-**foo**/ *noun* a sport from China. In kung fu, you fight using your hands and feet to hit and kick.

kung fu

**Kwan·zaa** /**kwahn**-zuh/ *noun* an African-American holiday between December 26 and January 1. Kwanzaa celebrates African-American culture, and each day celebrates a different idea, such as faith.

a b c d e f g h i j **k** l m n o p q r s t u v w x y z

359

a b c d e f g h i j k **l** m n o p q r s t u v w x y z

# Ll

**lab** /lab/ *noun* a laboratory: *We have been doing some experiments in the lab.*

**la·bel** /**layb**-uhl/
● *noun*
a piece of paper or cloth that is on something and shows information about it: *The label tells you how to wash the sweater.*
● *verb*
**1** to put a label on something or write information on it: *I labeled the box and wrote my address on it.*
**2** to always use a particular word to describe someone even if it is not a true or fair way to describe them: *I don't think it is fair to label him as a "lazy student" – he has had a lot of problems in his family life.*

**la·bor** /**layb**-ur/
● *noun*
**1** hard work that you do using your body and hands: *Working on a farm involves a lot of hard physical labor and it can be very tiring.*
**2** people who do a type of work: *Car companies need skilled labor to produce cars and trucks.*
**3** if a woman is in labor, she is pushing a baby out of her body
● *verb*
to work very hard: *The farm workers labored in the fields for ten hours a day.*

**lab·o·ra·to·ry** /**lab**-ruh-tor-ee/ (also **lab** /lab/) *noun* (plural **laboratories**) a room where scientists work and do experiments: *The blood is tested in a laboratory for signs of the disease.*

**La·bor Day** /**layb**-ur day/ *noun* a holiday on the first Monday in September. Labor Day shows respect for people who work.

**la·bor un·ion** /**layb**-ur yoon-yuhn/ *noun* an organization that helps workers get better pay, working conditions, health insurance, etc.: *Labor unions are asking for an increase in pay.*
SYNONYM: **union**

**lace** /layss/
● *noun*
**1** a type of cloth with a pattern of very small holes in it: *The tablecloth is made of white lace.*
**2** a string that you use to tie your shoes: *If you don't fasten your laces, you will trip over them.*
SYNONYM: **shoelace** ▶ see picture at **shoe**
● *verb* (also **lace up**)
to fasten something by tying a lace: *Paul put on his boots and laced them up.*

lace
lace

**lack** /lak/
● *verb* to not have enough of something: *Dan lacks confidence and he's too shy to answer questions in class.*
● *noun* a situation in which you do not have enough of something: *The baby is very noisy at night and the whole family is suffering from lack of sleep.*

**lad·der** /**lad**-ur/ *noun* a piece of equipment that you use to climb up to high places. It is made of two long pieces of metal or wood with bars between them that you step on: *He climbed up the ladder onto the roof.*

ladder
ladder
stepladder

**la·dies' room** /**layd**-eez room/ *noun* a room in a public building with toilets for women

**la·dle** /**layd**'l/
● *noun* a deep spoon with a long handle. You use a ladle for putting soup or stew into bowls.
● *verb* to use a ladle to put food into or onto something: *Mom ladled the stew into bowls.*

**la·dy** /**layd**-ee/ *noun* (plural **ladies**)
**1** a polite word for a woman: *Good evening ladies and gentlemen, and welcome to tonight's show.*
**2** a rude way of talking to a woman you do not know: *Hey, lady, hurry up!*

**la·dy·bug**
/**layd**-ee-buhg/ *noun* a small insect that has red or orange wings with black spots on them. Ladybugs eat insects that harm plants.

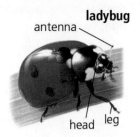
ladybug
antenna
head    leg

**lag** /lag/ *verb* (**lagging**, **lagged**) **lag behind** to be much slower than other people: *The boy lagged behind the other runners and he finished the race last.*

**la·goon** /luh-**goon**/ *noun* a pool of water that is separated from the ocean by a narrow piece of land

lagoon

lagoon

**laid** /layd/ *verb* the past tense and past participle of **lay**

**laid-back** /layd **bak**/ *adjective* relaxed and not worried about anything: *My mom is pretty laid-back. She doesn't mind if my friends stay for dinner.*

**lain** /layn/ *verb* a past participle of lie

**lake** /layk/ *noun* a large area of water with land all around it: *We went sailing on the lake.* | *Lake Michigan*

lake

**lamb** /lam/ *noun*
**1** a young sheep
**2** the meat of a young sheep: *We had lamb for dinner.*

**lame** /laym/ *adjective*
**1** silly or not very good: *The jokes were lame and no one laughed.*
**2** not able to walk easily because you have hurt your leg or foot: *My horse is lame and I can't ride him.*

**lamp** /lamp/ *noun* a type of light that you can put on a table or stand on the floor: *I turned on the lamp so I could read.*

**lamp·shade** /**lamp**-shayd/ *noun* a cover over the light of a lamp

**land** /land/
● *noun*
**1** an area of ground: *The land here is very flat and dry.* ▶ see **Thesaurus**
**2** the part of the Earth that is not covered by water: *Frogs live on land and in water.*
**3** a country: *He sailed around the world visiting faraway lands.*
● *verb*
to move down onto the ground: *The plane landed at the airport.*

land

land

take off

**land·fill** /**land**-fil/ *noun* a place where garbage is buried under the ground: *The trash is all taken to a landfill.*

**land·form** /**land**-form/ *noun* a natural feature on the Earth's surface, such as a mountain or a valley: *The rock landforms in the area were created by the wind and water.*

**land·ing** /**land**-ing/ *noun* the action of coming down onto the ground: *The plane made a safe landing.* (ANTONYM: **takeoff**)

**land·lord** /**land**-lord/ *noun* someone who owns a building and rents it to other people: *The landlord came to the apartment to collect the rent money.*

**land·mark** /**land**-mark/ *noun*
**1** an important building or place, that helps you know where you are: *The Empire State Building is a famous landmark in New York.*
**2** a very important event: *The signing of the Declaration of Independence was a landmark in the history of our country.*

**land·scape** /**land**-skayp/ *noun* the view across an area of land: *In the winter, the landscape looks very different.*

**land·slide** /**land**-slīd/ *noun*
**1** a sudden fall of dirt and rocks down the side of a mountain: *The house was destroyed by a landslide.*
**2** a victory in which someone wins an election by a lot of votes: *The president won the election in a landslide.*

**lane** /layn/ *noun*
**1** one of the parts that a road is divided into: *One lane of the highway is closed for road work.*
**2** one of the parts that a race track or swimming pool is divided into: *In the race I swam in lane four.*

**lan·guage** /**lang**-gwij/ *noun*
**1** the system of words and grammar that people living in a country or area use to speak and write to each other: *She can speak three languages – English, Spanish, and French.* ▶ see **Thesaurus**
**2** the type of words that someone uses: *The book is written in complicated scientific language which is difficult to understand.*
**3** a system that someone uses to give instructions to a computer: *We used a simple computer programming language to tell the robot to turn right or left.*

> ## Word Origin: language
>
> The word **language** comes from the Latin word **lingua** that means "tongue." Because we use our tongues to form the sounds of words, the Latin word also meant "speech."

**lan·guage arts** /**lang**-gwij artss/ *noun* a subject in school that includes reading, writing, spelling, and grammar: *In our class, we work on Language Arts every day.*

**lank·y** /**lank**-ee/ *adjective* tall and thin: *He is a lanky boy with long legs*

**lan·tern** /**lant**-urn/ *noun* a type of lamp that you can carry. It usually has a metal frame and glass sides: *We lit the lantern and hung it inside the tent.*

lantern

**lap** /lap/
● *noun*
**1** the flat area formed by the tops of your legs when you are sitting down: *Miguel sat on his dad's lap and listened to the story.*
**2** one trip around something such as a race track: *Everybody had to run two laps around the track.*
● *verb* (also **lap up**)
(**lapping**, **lapped**) if an animal laps a drink, it drinks it by touching it with its tongue: *The cat lapped up the milk.*

lap

The baby is sitting on her mother's lap.

**la·pel** /luh-**pel**/ *noun* the part of the collar of a coat or shirt that is folded back and goes over your chest: *He had a name tag on his lapel.*

**lap·top** /**lap**-tahp/ (also
**lap·top com·put·er**
/lap-tahp kuhm-**pyoot**-ur/)
*noun* a small computer
that you can carry with
you

laptop

( SYNONYM: **notebook** )

**larch** /larch/ *noun* a tree
with bright green leaves shaped like needles. The
leaves fall off in winter.

**lard** /lard/ *noun* a thick white fat from pigs, used
in cooking: *The beans were fried in lard.*

**large** /larj/ *adjective* big in size or amount: *I'm
very hungry – can we get a large pizza?* | *Their
house has four bedrooms, so it is larger than
ours.* ( ANTONYM: **small** )

**IDIOM with large**
**by and large** used when saying that
something is usually true: *By and large the kids
are well behaved.*

**large·ly** /**larj**-lee/
*adverb* mostly or
mainly: *By 3:00, our
work was largely
finished.*

lark

**lark** /lark/ *noun* a small
brown bird with long
pointed wings. Larks
have a beautiful song
and fly very high in the
sky.

**lar·va** /**larv**-uh/ *noun*
(plural **larvae** /**larv**-ee/)
a young insect at the
stage in its life when it
has a fat body and does
not look like the insect
that it will become later.
For example, a
caterpillar is a larva that
becomes a butterfly.

larva

butterfly

larva

**Word Origin:** larva

The name **larva** was given to young
animals that change their form by a
Swedish scientist named Carl Linnaeus. He
used a Latin word that means "ghost" or
"mask" for the name. He thought that the
larva stage was like a mask that hid what
the insect would become.

**lar·yn·gi·tis** /larr-uhn-**jīt**-iss/ *noun* an illness that
makes it difficult for you to speak because your
larynx is swollen and painful: *The singer cannot
sing because she has laryngitis.*

**lar·ynx** /**larr**-ingkss/ *noun* the part of your throat
where your voice is produced

**la·sa·gna** /luh-**zahn**-yuh/ *noun* a type of Italian
food that is made with layers of pasta, sauce,
cheese, and meat or vegetables: *The restaurant
serves Italian food like lasagna and spaghetti.*

**la·ser** /**layz**-ur/ *noun* a piece of equipment that
produces a powerful narrow beam of light: *A
laser is used to read the information on the disk
in the DVD player.*

**lash** /lash/
● *noun* an eyelash: *She has long dark lashes.*
● *verb* to tie something tightly to another
thing with a rope: *They lashed some logs
together to make a raft, so that they could cross
the river.*

**las·so** /**lass**-oh/
● *noun* (plural **lassos**)
a long length of rope
with one end tied in a
circle. You throw a lasso
over the head of an
animal to catch or
control it.
● *verb* (**lassoed**) to
catch an animal,
especially a cow or a
horse, using a lasso: *The
cowboys finally
managed to lasso the escaped cow.*

lasso

lasso

a b c d e f g h i j k l m n o p q r s t u v w x y z

**last** /last/
- *adjective*
**1** the last day or time is the most recent day or time: *I saw him last week. | Where were you last Saturday?*
**2** the last one is the only one that is left: *She ate the last cookie.*
**3** at the end, after everyone or everything else: *I am last in line. | On the last day of school we can bring in games to play.*
- *adverb*
**1** most recently: *Carrie was a little baby when we last saw her.*
**2** after everything or everyone else: *Everyone took a turn and I went last.*
- *verb*
**1** to happen for a particular amount of time: *Recess at our school lasts for 15 minutes.*
**2** to stay in good condition: *The shoes didn't last for very long – I had a hole in them after only a month.*
- *noun*
the person or thing that is after all the others: *Joe was the last to go to bed that night.*

> **IDIOM with last**
> **at last** after a long time: *It had rained all day, but at dinnertime the rain stopped at last.*

**last·ing** /**last**-ing/ *adjective* continuing for a long time: *The dog bite she got had a lasting effect; she was still afraid of dogs 20 years later.*

**last·ly** /**last**-lee/ *adverb* used when telling someone the last thing you want to say: *Lastly, I'd like to thank you all for coming.*

**last name** /**last** naym/ *noun* your family's name. In English this name comes after your other names: *Andrew's last name is Smith.*

**latch** /lach/ *noun* a small metal fastener or lock that is used to keep a door, gate, or window closed: *I saw the knob turn and then the latch clicked open.*

latch

**late** /layt/ *adjective, adverb*
**1** after the usual or expected time: *Maria is never late for school. | The bus was 20 minutes late.*

**2** near the end of a period of time: *In the winter, it gets dark in the late afternoon, around 4:30.*
**3** at night, or near the end of the day: *It's getting late. You'd better get ready for bed.*

**late·ly** /**layt**-lee/ *adverb* recently: *"Have you seen Matt lately?" "No, I haven't seen him for a couple of weeks."*

**lat·er** /**layt**-ur/
- *adverb* after the present time, or after the time you are talking about: *I'll see you later, after school. | Tom got there at one o'clock, and Sara arrived a few minutes later.*
- *adjective* coming in the future, or after something else: *You can finish the painting at a later time, maybe this afternoon.*

**lat·est** /**layt**-ist/ *adjective* most recent: *We get all the latest news from the school newsletter.*

**lath·er** /**lath**-ur/ *noun* a lot of small bubbles that are produced when you mix soap with water: *When you wash your hands, rub the soap and get a good lather.*

**La·tin** /**lat**'n/ *noun* an old language spoken by the ancient Romans. Some Latin words are still used in science, law, and medicine: *Many of the words we use today come from Latin, such as "college" and "educate."*

**La·ti·na** /luh-**teen**-uh/ *noun* a woman in the U.S. whose family came from a country in Latin America

**Lat·in A·mer·i·ca** /**lat**'n uh-**merr**-ik-uh/ *noun* the land including Mexico, Central America, and South America
—**Latin American** /**lat**'n uh-**merr**-ik-uhn/ *adjective* relating to Latin America

**La·ti·no** /luh-**teen**-oh/
- *noun* a man in the U.S. whose family came from a country in Latin America. In the plural, Latinos can mean a group of men and women: *Many Latinos live in the southwestern United States.*
- *adjective* belonging to or relating to Latinos: *He lives in a Latino neighborhood.*

**lat·i·tude** /**lat**-uh-tood/ *noun* the distance of a place north or south of the equator (=an imaginary line around the middle of the Earth):

*New York City is on the same latitude as Naples, Italy.* (ANTONYM: **longitude**) ► see picture at **globe**

## laugh /laf/

● *verb*

**1** to make a sound with your voice because you think something is funny: *I like Tony. He makes me laugh with all his jokes.* ► see **Thesaurus**
**2 laugh at** to make jokes about someone or laugh in a way that is not nice, so that he or she gets upset: *She tripped and fell down, and everyone laughed at her.*

● *noun*

the sound you make when you laugh: *"That's so funny!" she said, with a laugh.*

## laugh·ter /laft-ur/ *noun* the sound of people laughing: *We heard laughter from the other class as they tried on the costumes.*

## launch /lonch/ *verb*

**1** to send a space vehicle into space: *The spaceship will be launched on March 5.*
**2** to put a boat or ship into the water: *You can launch your boat anywhere on the beach.*
**3** to start something new: *The movie launched his acting career.*

## launch·pad /lonch-pad/ *noun* a special place from which a rocket or missile is sent up into the sky

## laun·dry /lond-ree/ *noun*

**1** clothes and sheets that you need to wash: *Put your dirty laundry in the hamper.*
**2** clothes and sheets that you have washed: *I folded and put away the laundry.*
**3 do the laundry** to wash clothes and sheets: *We do the laundry on Saturdays.*

## la·va /lahv-uh/ *noun* hot liquid rock that comes out of the top of a volcano: *Lava flowed out of the volcano.* ► see picture at **volcano**

## lav·a·to·ry /lav-uh-tor-ee/ *noun* (plural **lavatories**) a room with a toilet, in a public building or airplane: *The boys' lavatory is at the end of the hallway.*

## lav·en·der /lav-uhn-dur/ *noun* a plant with purple flowers that has a nice smell. It is used for making perfumes.

## law /lo/ *noun*

**1** a rule that everyone in a country must obey: *Stealing is against the law.* | *The law says that all*

children living in the United States must go to school.
**2** a statement in math or science that describes and explains how something works: *The law of gravity explains why things fall down to the Earth.*

## law-a·bid·ing /lo uh-bīd-ing/ *adjective* always obeying the law: *They are law-abiding citizens and they have never been in trouble with the police.*

## law·ful /lo-fuhl/ *adjective* allowed by the law: *If you find money on the street, is it lawful to keep it?* (SYNONYM: **legal**) (ANTONYM: **illegal**)

## lawn /lon/ *noun* an area of grass around a house or building: *My sister and I were playing on the front lawn.*

## lawn mow·er /lon moh-ur/ *noun* a machine for cutting grass: *He started the lawn mower and pushed it over the grass.*

## law·suit /lo-soot/ *noun* a problem that someone takes to a court of law to be solved: *He is involved in a lawsuit with a neighbor over who owns the land between their houses.*

## law·yer /lo-yur/ *noun* someone whose job is to advise people about the law, and speak for them in court: *When she got divorced, she got advice from her lawyer.* (SYNONYM: **attorney**)

## lay /lay/

● *verb* (**lays**, **laying**, **laid** /layd/)

**1** to put something in a particular place: *Mother laid the baby down for his nap.* | *Eileen laid her gloves on the table.*
**2** to put something in the correct place in the ground or on the floor: *The workers have to lay water pipes underground.*
**3** if a bird or insect lays eggs, eggs come out of its body: *The hen laid an egg.*
**4 lay off** to stop employing someone because there is not enough work for them: *The factory stopped making as many cars, so they had to lay off 150 workers.*

● *verb*

a past tense of **lie**, see Word Choice note on next page

a b c d e f g h i j k **l** m n o p q r s t u v w x y z

**Word Choice: lay, lie**

**Lay** means to put something down in a flat position: *Lay your books down on the table.*

The past tense for this is **laid**: *They laid their books down on the table.*

**Lie** has two different meanings:

1) to be or move into a flat position on the floor, a bed, or a sofa: *You should lie on the sofa and rest.*

The past tense for this meaning of **lie** is **lay**: *He lay on the sofa to rest.*

2) to say something that is not true: *Why did you lie to me about who broke the glass?*

The past tense for this meaning is **lied**: *She lied to her mother about who broke the glass.*

**lay·er** /**lay**-ur/ *noun* an amount of something that covers a surface or is between two surfaces: *There was a thick layer of dust on all the furniture.* | *It was cold, so we put on several layers of clothing before going outside.*

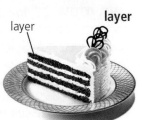

layer    **layer**

The cake has layers of chocolate and cream.

**lay·off** /**lay**-of/ *noun* the act of ending someone's job because there is not enough work to do: *The factory closed down, and there were about 100 layoffs.*

**la·zy** /**layz**-ee/ *adjective* (**lazier**, **laziest**)
**1** not wanting to work or make any effort: *Don't be so lazy – come and help me clean up.*
**2** a lazy time is a time when you can relax: *It was a hot lazy summer afternoon.* (ANTONYM: **busy**)
—**laziness** /**layz**-ee-niss/ *noun* a lazy attitude: *My mom doesn't like laziness so we have to do chores every day.*

**lb.** the written abbreviation of **pound**: *I weigh 75 lbs.*

**lead**
● *verb* /leed/ (**led** /led/)
**1** to show someone the way, by going in front of him or her: *We're going to the park. Paula, will you lead the way?* | *The teacher led the children back to the classroom.* (ANTONYM: **follow**)

**2** to be in charge of an activity or a group of people: *My dad leads a Cub Scout group.*
**3** to be winning a game or competition: *Our team was leading 2–0.*
**4** if a road or path leads to a place, it goes to that place: *This road leads to the lake.*
(SYNONYM: **go**)
**5 lead to** to cause something to happen: *Eating too much sugar can lead to health problems.*
● *noun*
**1** a position in front of everyone else in a competition or race: *She was in the lead from start to finish.*
**2** the amount by which one person is ahead of another during a competition or race: *Our team has a ten-point lead, but there are still five minutes left in the game.*
**3** a piece of information that may help you find out something: *The police are following all possible leads to find the robber.*
**4** /led/ a heavy gray metal: *Water pipes used to be made of lead, until scientists found out that lead is poisonous.*
**5** /led/ the gray substance in a pencil that makes marks when you write: *The lead broke when I pressed the pencil too hard into the paper.*

**lead·er** /**leed**-ur/ *noun*
**1** the person who is in charge of a country or group: *The president will join the leaders of other countries at the meeting.*
**2** the person or team that is winning a race or competition: *She was the leader for the first half of the race.*
—**leadership** /**leed**-ur-ship/ *noun* the quality of being good at leading people, or the position of being a leader: *Under the principal's leadership, the school has improved.*

**lead·ing** /**leed**-ing/ *adjective* best or most important: *Kevin has a leading role in the school play.*

**leaf** /leef/ *noun* (plural **leaves** /leevz/) one of the flat green parts of a plant or tree that grow out of the stem or branches: *By late October, most of the leaves had fallen.* ▶ see picture at **flower**

**leaf·let** /**leef**-lit/ *noun* a piece of paper with information or an advertisement printed on it: *He was handing out leaflets for a new restaurant.*

**league** /leeg/ *noun*
**1** a group of sports teams that play against each other: *Our soccer team finished second in the*

league this year.
**2** a group of people or countries that join together to try to achieve something: *The League of Nations was formed after World War I to help countries solve problems without going to war.*

## leak /leek/

● *verb*
**1** if something leaks, liquid or gas comes out of a hole in it: *The roof leaks when it rains.*
**2** to give secret information to a newspaper or television company: *Someone leaked information about the plan to close the school to a local newspaper.*
**—leaky /leek-ee/** *adjective* having a hole that a liquid or gas can come through: *The leaky faucet was dripping.*

● *noun*
**1** a hole that liquid or gas comes out of, where something is broken or damaged: *There is a leak in one of the pipes and there is water all over the floor.*
**2** a situation in which someone gives secret information to a newspaper or television company, so that people find out about something: *No one knew about the deal until there was a leak from the White House.*

## lean /leen/

● *verb*

lean

**1** to bend your body forward, backward, or to the side: *Ryan leaned over the desk to reach his pen.*
**2** to stand or sit with part of your body resting on something: *We leaned against the bridge and watched the sunset.*
**3** to put something in a sloping position against a wall or other surface: *Lean your bike against that tree.*

● *adjective*
**1** thin in a healthy way: *His body was lean and athletic – there was no fat on him.*
( ANTONYM: **fat** )
**2** lean meat does not have much fat on it
( ANTONYM: **fatty** )

## leap /leep/

● *verb* (**leaped** or **leapt** /lept/) to jump into the air or to jump over something: *The boys leaped from rock to rock.*
● *noun* a jump: *With one leap, she crossed the stream.*

leap

The boy is leaping from rock to rock.

## leap·frog /leep-frog/ *noun* a children's game in which one child bends down so that another child can jump over him or her

## leap year /leep yeer/ *noun* a year when February has 29 days instead of 28, which happens every four years

## learn /lurn/ *verb*
**1** to get knowledge or a skill especially by studying: *Sam is learning to read and write.* | *Today we learned about dinosaurs in science.*
► see **Thesaurus**
**2** to get to know something so well that you can easily remember it: *She learned a poem and said it in front of the class.*
**3** to find out information or news: *The next day, I learned that I had passed the test.*

### Word Choice: learn, teach

You **learn** a subject or skill when you study or practice it: *We learned about volcanoes in science.* | *My sister is learning to play the piano.*

If you **teach** someone a subject or skill, you help him or her learn it: *My teacher taught us about volcanoes in science.* | *Dad is teaching me to play the guitar.*

## learn·ing /lurn-ing/ *noun* the process of getting knowledge or skills: *The school has high standards of teaching and learning.*

367

**lease** /leess/

- **noun** a legal agreement that allows someone to live in or use a building for a period of time: *We have a one-year lease on our apartment.*
- **verb** to allow someone to use a building by paying rent: *The artists leased the rooms to show their artwork.*

**leash** /leesh/ **noun** a piece of rope, leather, or chain that you attach to a dog's collar. You hold the leash when you take the dog for a walk: *The sign said that dogs must be kept on a leash.*

leash

leash

**least** /leest/ **pronoun**, **adjective**, **adverb** the smallest amount: *This pencil costs 50¢ and this one costs 75¢. Which pencil costs the least? | He answered the least difficult questions.* ( **ANTONYM: most** )

> **IDIOM with least**
>
> **at least**
>
> **1** not less than a number or amount: *You need to write at least two paragraphs.*
> **2** used to say something good about a bad situation: *Well, at least you got your money back when it didn't work.*

**leath·er** /**leth**-ur/ **noun** a strong material made from animal skin. Leather is used for making shoes, bags, and other goods: *a leather jacket*

leather

a leather jacket

**leave** /leev/

- **verb** (**left** /left/)
**1** to go away from a place or person: *What time will we leave to get to the airport? | Danny left the house at 8:00 this morning.* ( **ANTONYM: arrive** )
▶ see **Thesaurus**
**2** to put something somewhere and go away without it: *Can I leave a note for Suzy? | I left my books in the library by mistake.*
**3** to let something stay the way it is: *Who left the door open? | Leave your shoes on – we're going out again.*
**4** to stop doing a job or going to school: *My*

father left school when he was 14 years old.
( **SYNONYM: quit** ) ( **ANTONYM: start** )
**5** if something is left, it is still there after everything else is gone: *Is there any cake left or did you eat it all?*
**6 leave someone alone** to not talk to or annoy someone: *Leave Kate alone – she's doing her homework.*
**7 leave something alone** to stop touching something: *Leave those glasses alone, or you'll break them.*
**8 leave behind** to not take someone or something with you when you go somewhere: *I left all my money behind at home and I had to go back and get it.*
**9 leave out** to not include someone or something: *She feels left out because the other children don't play with her.*

- **noun**
time that someone is allowed to spend away from a job: *Mrs. Griffin just had a baby, so she will be on leave until the spring.*

**leaves** /leevz/ **noun** the plural of **leaf**

**lec·ture** /**lek**-chur/

- **noun**
**1** a talk that someone gives in order to teach a group of people something: *He is giving a lecture on the history of Mexico.*
**2** a serious conversation in which someone tells you how you should behave: *Dad gave me a lecture about my schoolwork.*

- **verb**
**1** if someone lectures you, he or she talks to you in a serious way about how you should behave: *He was lecturing us about making too much noise.*
**2** to give a formal talk about a subject to a group of people: *Mrs. Davis will lecture about Japanese art at the museum.*

—**lecturer** /**lek**-chur-ur/ **noun** someone who gives lectures, especially in a university: *He is a college lecturer.*

**led** /led/ **verb** the past tense and past participle of **lead**

**ledge** /lej/ **noun** a narrow flat surface like a shelf that sticks out from the side of a building or cliff: *A bird landed on the window ledge.*

**left** /left/

- **verb** the past tense and past participle of **leave**

● *adjective* on the side where you start reading a line of writing in many languages such as English and Spanish. This arrow is pointing toward the left side of the page (←): *Hold the ball in your left hand. | My house is on the left side of the street.* ( ANTONYM: **right** )

● *adverb* toward the left side: *We turned left at the traffic lights.* ( ANTONYM: **right** )

● *noun* the left side or direction: *The school is up ahead on the left.* ( ANTONYM: **right** )

**Word Origin:** left

**Left** comes from the Old English word **lyft**, which means "weak" or "foolish." Around 1300 A.D., left started to mean the opposite of right, probably because your left hand is usually weaker than your right hand.

**left-hand·ed** /left **hand**-id/ *adjective* if you are left-handed, you use your left hand to do most things, for example to write: *I'm left-handed so I catch a ball with my left hand.*
( ANTONYM: **right-handed** )

**left·o·vers** /**left**-ohv-urz/ *noun* food that is left at the end of a meal, and that you can keep and eat later: *You can have the leftovers for lunch tomorrow.*

**leg** /leg/ *noun*
**1** one of the long parts of your body that you use for standing and walking: *She fell and hurt her leg. | A spider has eight legs.* ▶ see picture at **spider**, and on page **A13**
**2** one of the long parts that supports a piece of furniture: *One of the chair legs was broken.*
**3** the part of your pants that covers your leg: *There is a big hole in the left leg of my new jeans.*
**4** one of two sides of a triangle that meet and form an angle of 90°

**le·gal** /**leeg**-uhl/ *adjective*
**1** allowed by the law: *It is not legal to talk on a cell phone while driving.* ( ANTONYM: **illegal** )
**2** relating to laws: *You should go to a lawyer and get some legal advice.*
—**legally** /**leeg**-uhl-ee/ *adverb* according to the law: *To become a citizen, you must live in the U.S. legally for five years.*

**Word Family:** legal

**legal** *adjective* | **illegal** *adjective* | **legally** *adverb* | **illegally** *adverb*

**leg·end** /**lej**-uhnd/ *noun*
**1** an old story, especially about a famous person or a place. It sometimes has a part that is true: *According to the legend, King Arthur had a magical sword called Excalibur.*
**2** someone who is famous for being very good at something: *Elvis Presley is a rock and roll legend.*

**leg·end·ar·y** /**lej**-uhn-dair-ee/ *adjective* famous and admired for a long time: *Michael Jordan is a legendary basketball player.*

**leg·gings** /**leg**-ingz/ *noun* thin pants for girls or women that stretch and fit tightly on the legs: *Girls often wear leggings with long T-shirts.*

**leg·is·late** /**lej**-uh-slayt/ *verb* to make a law about something: *Congress will try to legislate new health care changes.*
—**legislator** /**lej**-uh-slayt-ur/ *noun* someone who has the power to make new laws: *State legislators decided to give more money to education.*

**leg·is·la·tion** /lej-uh-**slaysh**-uhn/ *noun* a law or set of laws: *The new legislation will protect the environment.*

**leg·is·la·ture** /**lej**-uh-slaych-ur/ *noun* a group of people who make or change laws in a government: *The legislature will vote on the bill tomorrow.*

**lei·sure** /**leezh**-ur/ *noun* the time when you are not at school or working and can do things that you enjoy: *I like to play outside during my leisure time.*

**lem·on** /**lem**-uhn/ *noun* a yellow fruit that tastes sour: *Do you want a slice of lemon with your drink?* ▶ see picture on page **A7**

**lem·on·ade** /lem-uh-**nayd**/ *noun* a drink made with lemon juice, sugar, and water: *Would you like a glass of lemonade?*

a b c d e f g h i j k **l** m n o p q r s t u v w x y z

**lend** /lend/ *verb* (**lent** /lent/)
**1** to let someone borrow money or something that belongs to you for a short time: *Could you lend me $5? | She lent her jacket to a friend.*
**2** if a bank lends you money, it gives it to you for a certain time. You must pay the money back with an additional amount called "interest": *Dad asked the bank to lend him money to start a business.*

## Word Choice: lend, borrow

If you **lend** something to someone, you give it to him or her so that he or she can use it for a short time: *I lent my book to Elena. | Mom, could you lend me some money?*

If you **borrow** something from someone, you take something that someone gives you for a short time, and then you give it back: *Can I borrow your bike?*

**length** /lengkth/ *noun*
**1** the distance from one end of something to the other end: *The length of the swimming pool is 25 yards. | This little fish will grow to be a foot in length.*
**2** the amount of time during which something happens: *The length of the class is ten weeks.*

**length·en** /**lengkth**-uhn/ *verb* to make something longer: *Mom lengthened the skirt for me.* ( ANTONYM: **shorten** )

**length·wise** /**lengkth**-wīz/ (also **length·ways** /**lengkth**-wayz/) *adverb* in the direction of the longest side: *Fold the cloth lengthwise.*

**length·y** /**lengkth**-ee/ *adjective* continuing for a long time: *The principal had a lengthy meeting with the boy's parents.*

**le·ni·ent** /**leen**-ee-uhnt/ *adjective* if you are lenient, you do not punish people very much when they break rules: *The teacher was lenient with him because it was the first time he'd been in trouble.*

**lens** /lenz/ *noun*
**1** a piece of curved glass or plastic. A lens makes things look bigger, smaller, or clearer when you look through it: *He wore glasses with thick lenses because his eyesight was very bad. | a camera lens* ▶ see picture at **frame**
**2** a part of the inside of your eye. The lens focuses the light that comes into your eye, so that you see things clearly.

## Word Origin: lens

**Lens** comes from the Latin word for lentils. Lentils are a kind of small round seed that has a curved surface. The curve of a lentil is similar to the curve of the lens of your eye.

**lent** /lent/ *verb* the past tense and past participle of **lend**

**Lent** /lent/ *noun* the 40 days before Easter

**len·til** /**lent**'l/ *noun* a small round seed like a bean: *I had lentil soup for lunch.*

**leop·ard** /**lep**-urd/ *noun* a large wild cat with yellow fur and black spots. Leopards live in Africa and southern Asia.

**leopard**

**le·o·tard** /**lee**-uh-tard/ *noun* a piece of clothing that fits the body tightly from the neck to the tops of the legs. Ballet dancers often wear leotards: *Stella was in a black leotard for her ballet class.*

**lep·re·chaun** /**lep**-ruh-kahn/ *noun* an imaginary creature in Irish stories who looks like a little man. A leprechaun will show hidden gold to anyone who can catch him.

**less** /less/
● *adverb* not as much: *The test was less difficult than I thought it would be. | You should enjoy yourself more and worry less.* ( ANTONYM: **more** )

● *adjective*, *pronoun* a smaller amount: *Last year, we had less homework.* | *If you eat less, you will lose weight.* | *The meal cost less than $10.* ( ANTONYM: **more** )

---

### Word Choice: less, fewer

You use **less** before nouns that are things you cannot count: *There is less water in this cup than in that one.* | *I have less money than my brother.*

You use **fewer** before nouns when you can count the number of things or people: *You have five pennies and I have three. I have fewer pennies.* | *There were fewer people at the park than there were last time.*

---

**-less** /liss/

---

### Word Building

**-less** is a suffix. It is used in adjectives.
breath**less** | care**less** | motion**less** | pain**less** | spot**less**

**-less** means "without." If you are *breathless*, you can't breathe normally because you have been running. You are without breath. If an operation is *painless*, the patient does not feel any pain. If a house is *spotless*, it is very clean. The house is without any spots of dirt.

---

**less·en** /**less**-uhn/ *verb* to make something become less: *He took medicine to lessen the pain.* ( SYNONYM: **reduce** ) ( ANTONYM: **increase** )

**les·son** /**less**-uhn/ *noun*
**1** a period of time when someone teaches you something: *I have a piano lesson after school.*
**2** an experience that you learn something from, or the thing that you learn: *I got a bad grade in my test. That taught me an important lesson: always study before an exam!*

**let** /let/ *verb* (**let**, **letting**)
**1** to allow someone to do something, or allow something to happen: *I wanted to go, but my mom wouldn't let me.* | *My sister lets her room get really messy.*

**2** to allow someone or something to come into or go out of a place: *They won't let us into the building.*
**3 let down** to make someone feel disappointed: *I had promised my friend that I would go to the party and I didn't want to let her down.*

> IDIOMS with **let**
> **let go** to stop holding someone or something: *Hold onto the rope and don't let go.*
> **let me know** used to say that someone should tell you something: *Let me know if you need any help.*

**let·down** /**let**-down/ *noun* something that makes you feel disappointed because it is not as good as you expected: *The movie was a real letdown and I didn't enjoy it at all.*

**le·thal** /**leeth**-uhl/ *adjective* if something is lethal, it can kill someone: *The drug is lethal if you take too much of it.*

**lethargic** /luh-**tharj**-ik/ *adjective* having no energy and feeling tired or lazy: *She's often lethargic in the mornings and she takes a long time to get out of bed.*

**let's** /letss/ *contraction* short for "let us": *Let's go for a walk.* | *Let's not talk about this right now.*

**let·ter** /**let**-ur/ *noun*
**1** one of the signs in writing that stands for a sound in speech. A, b, and c are all letters: *My name starts with the letter K.* | *There are 26 letters in the English alphabet.*
**2** a written message that you put into an envelope and send to someone by mail: *Julia is writing a letter to a friend.*

**let·tuce** /**let**-iss/ *noun* a green vegetable with large thin leaves that you eat raw in salads: *The salad had lettuce and tomatoes in it.*
▶ see picture on page A7

**leu·ke·mi·a** /loo-**keem**-ee-uh/ *noun* a serious disease that makes your body produce too many white blood cells. Leukemia is a type of cancer of the blood.

**lev·ee** /**lev**-ee/ *noun* a wall that is built to stop a river from flooding: *They built high levees to protect the town.*

a
b
c
d
e
f
g
h
i
j
k
**l**
m
n
o
p
q
r
s
t
u
v
w
x
y
z

**lev·el** /**lev**-uhl/
- *noun*

**1** the amount or degree of something: *The children had a high level of interest in the art project.*

**2** the height of something in relation to the ground or to another thing: *The water level of the lake was rising because of the heavy rain.*

**3** a standard of skill or ability: *The girls on the soccer team are all at the same level. There isn't anyone who plays a lot better or worse than anyone else.*

**4** a floor in a building that has several floors: *We parked the car on Level 2.*

- *adjective*

**1** flat, with no part higher than any other part: *The desk wasn't quite level, and my pencil kept rolling off it whenever I put it down.*

**2** at the same height as something else: *He bent down so that his face was level with the dog's face.*

- *verb*

to knock down or completely destroy a building or area: *An earthquake leveled several buildings.*

**lev·er** /**lev**-ur/ *noun*

**1** a long handle that you pull or push to make a machine work: *Pushing the red lever down starts the machine.*

**2** a long piece of metal or wood that is used for lifting something heavy. You put one end under the heavy object and push down on the other end.

**li·a·ble** /**lī**-uhb-uhl/ *adjective*

**1** likely to do something: *Remind me to call her because I'm liable to forget.*

**2** having to pay money for something because you are legally responsible: *The parents are liable for the damage their children caused.*

**li·ar** /**lī**-ur/ *noun* someone who tells lies: *You're a liar! I didn't say that.*

**li·bel** /**līb**-uhl/ *noun* the illegal act of writing or printing things about someone that are not true: *The magazine said the actor had been dishonest, so now he is suing the magazine for libel.*

**lib·er·al** /**libr**-uhl/

- *adjective* believing that the government should pay for the important things that people need and that business should not have too

much power: *The Democrats are a liberal political party.* (ANTONYM: **conservative**)

- *noun* someone with liberal opinions or ideas: *Political liberals want to spend more on education.* (ANTONYM: **conservative**)

—**liberalism** /**libr**-uhl-iz-uhm/ *noun* the attitude or behavior of liberals

**lib·er·ate** /**lib**-uh-rayt/ *verb* to make someone or something free: *The U.S. army liberated the town from the enemy.*

**lib·er·ty** /**lib**-urt-ee/ *noun* (plural **liberties**) the freedom to do what you want without too much control from a government or from someone who is in charge: *Americans have the liberty to live and work wherever they want to in the U.S.*

**li·brar·y** /**līb**-rair-ee/ *noun* (plural **libraries**) a room or building containing books and magazines that you can look at or borrow: *You need to take these books back to the library.*

—**librarian** /lī-**brair**-ee-uhn/ *noun* someone who works in a library

**lice** /līss/ *plural noun* (singular **louse**) very small insects that can live on the skin and hair of animals and people

**li·cense** /**līss**-uhnss/

- *noun* an official document that gives you permission to own something or do something: *My brother got his driver's license last week.*

- *verb* to give official permission for someone to own or do something: *Dr. Gordon is licensed to practice medicine in California.*

**li·cense plate** /**līss**-uhnss playt/ *noun* a sign with numbers and letters on it that is on the front and back of a car

**li·chen** /**līk**-uhn/ *noun* a small soft plant that grows on surfaces such as trees, rocks, and walls

**lichen**

The branch has lichen on it.

**lick** /lik/ *verb* to move your tongue across the surface of something: *The dog jumped up and licked her face.*

lick

The dog is licking the boy's face.

**lic·o·rice** /**lik**-uhr-ish/ *noun*
**1** a plant whose sweet roots are used to give a flavor to candy and some medicines
**2** a type of black or red candy that has licorice in it

licorice

**lid** /lid/ *noun* a cover for the top of a pot, box, or other container: *Take the lid off the pan and stir the sauce.* ▶ see picture at **glass**

lid

lid

**lie** /lī/
● *verb* (**lies**, **lay** /lay/, **lain** /layn/, **lying**)
**1** to be or to get into a position with your body flat on something: *Mia was lying on the sofa, reading a book.* | *Go lie down if you're not feeling well.*
**2** to be in a place without moving: *His clothes lay all over the floor.*
● *verb* (**lies**, **lying**, **lied** /līd/)
to deliberately tell someone something that is not true: *She lied about her age and said she was 18 when she was really 15.* | *Don't lie to me! I can tell if you're not telling the truth.*
● *noun*
something that you say which you know is not true: *She said she was okay, but it was a lie – she was very upset.* ▶ see **Thesaurus**

**Word Choice: lie, lay**

**Lie** has two different meanings:

1) to be or move into a flat position on the floor, a bed, or a sofa: *You should lie on the sofa and rest.*

The past tense for this meaning of **lie** is **lay**: *He lay on the sofa to rest.*

2) to say something that is not true: *Why did you lie to me about who broke the glass?*

The past tense for this meaning is **lied**: *She lied to her mother about who broke the glass.*

**Lay** means to put something down in a flat position: *Lay your books down on the table.*

The past tense for **lay** is **laid**: *They laid their books down on the table.*

lie

**lieu·ten·ant** /loo-**ten**-uhnt/ *noun* an officer who has a middle rank in the armed forces or in the police force: *Lieutenant Suarez is in charge of the investigation.*

**life** /līf/ *noun* (plural **lives** /līvz/)
**1** the period of time between birth and death: *My grandfather worked hard all his life.*
**2** the state of being alive: *Wearing a seat belt can save your life.*
**3** living things such as people, animals, or plants: *Do you think there is life on other planets?*
**4** the experiences or activities of someone: *Maya is popular and has a busy social life.*
**5** activity or movement: *My grandmother is 75, but she is still full of life.*
**6** **real life** things that really happen, rather than things that happen in a story or in your imagination: *Real life is not like the movies.*

a b c d e f g h i j k l m n o p q r s t u v w x y z

**life·boat** /līf-boht/ *noun* a small boat that can be used to save people if a big boat sinks: *The ship has enough lifeboats for everyone on board.*

**life cy·cle** /līf sīk-uhl/ *noun* all the stages in the life of an animal or plant, as it develops or changes into different forms: *We learned about the life cycle of the frog.*

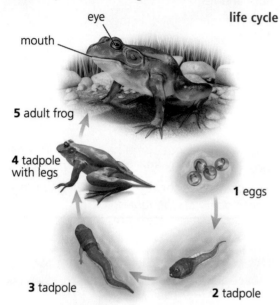

eye

mouth

**life cycle**

**5** adult frog

**4** tadpole with legs

**1** eggs

**3** tadpole

**2** tadpole

the life cycle of a frog

**life·guard** /līf-gard/ *noun* someone whose job is to help swimmers who are in danger: *The lifeguard pulled the child out of the water.*

**life jack·et** /līf jak-it/ *noun* a special jacket that stops you from sinking if you fall into water: *You must wear a life jacket if you're going in the boat.*

**life jacket**

life jacket

**life·long** /līf-long/ *adjective* continuing all through your life: *Mr. Bonnett and my father are lifelong friends: they have known each other since elementary school.*

**life pre·serv·er** /līf pri-zurv-ur/ *noun* a life jacket or a special ring filled with air that you can wear in water to stop yourself from sinking

**life raft** /līf raft/ *noun* a small rubber boat filled with air that can be used by passengers if their ship sinks: *The ship carries several life rafts.*

**life·style** /līf-stīl/ *noun* the way you live your life. Your lifestyle includes the things you own, the place where you live, and the activities you do: *We grew up on a ranch and had a very active outdoor lifestyle.*

**life·time** /līf-tīm/ *noun* the period of time during which someone is alive: *I've made a list of all the places I want to visit during my lifetime.*

**lift** /lift/
● *verb*
**1** to raise something or someone up: *I tried to lift the box but it was too heavy.* ▶ see picture on page **A15** ▶ see **Thesaurus**
**2** to move up from the ground: *The helicopter lifted into the air and flew away.*
● *noun*
**1** a ride in someone's car to a place you want to go: *I have a car. Do you want a lift home?*
( SYNONYM: **ride** )
**2** something that makes you feel happier: *Getting an A for science gave me a real lift.*
**3** a piece of equipment used to carry people or heavy objects: *We rode the ski lift to the top of the mountain.*

**lift·off** /lift of/ *noun* the moment when a spacecraft leaves the ground and rises up into the air: *The crew of the space shuttle is preparing for liftoff.*

**lig·a·ment** /lig-uhm-uhnt/ *noun* a band of strong white material in your body that holds your bones together at a joint: *He damaged a ligament in his knee, so he can't play football for a while.*

**light** /līt/
● *noun*
**1** the brightness from the Sun, a lamp, or a flame that allows you to see things: *I think she's awake because there is light coming from her bedroom window.* ( ANTONYM: **dark** )
**2** something such as an electric lamp that produces light: *Remember to turn off the lights before you go to bed.* ▶ see picture at **bicycle**
▶ see **Thesaurus**

**3** a set of red, green, and yellow lights used for controlling traffic: *Turn left at the light.*

● *adjective*

**1** a light color is not dark: *She wore a light blue dress.* (SYNONYM: **pale**) (ANTONYM: **dark**)

**2** not weighing very much: *The boxes were so light I could carry them all at once.* (ANTONYM: **heavy**) ▶ see picture at **heavy**

**3** if it gets light, the sky is no longer dark because the Sun is beginning to rise: *It gets light at about 5 a.m. in the summer.*

**4** light clothes are thin and not very warm: *Bring a light jacket because it may be cool in the evening.* (ANTONYM: **thick**)

**5** gentle or soft: *The sailboats moved slowly in the light breeze.* | *I felt a light tap on my arm.* (ANTONYM: **strong**)

—**lightness** /līt-niss/ *noun* the quality of being light

● *verb* (**lit** /lit/ or **lighted**)

**1** to make something start burning or producing light: *When it gets cold we'll light a fire.*

**2** to provide light in a place, or make a place become bright: *They only had candles to light the room.*

**light bulb** /līt buhlb/ *noun* the round glass part of an electric lamp: *We need a new light bulb in the bathroom.*

**light·en** /līt'n/ *verb*

**1** to become brighter: *The sky started to lighten and it stopped raining.* (ANTONYM: **darken**)

**2** to make something less heavy: *He lightened his backpack by taking out some books.*

**light·head·ed** /līt **hed**-id/ *adjective* unable to think clearly or move steadily: *I felt light-headed and had to sit down.* (SYNONYM: **dizzy**)

**light·house** /līt-howss/ *noun* a tall building near the ocean. A lighthouse has a bright light at the top. The light turns on and off to warn ships that they are near the coast or near rocks.

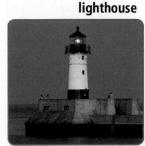
lighthouse

**light·ing** /līt-ing/ *noun* the lights in a building or street, or how bright the lights are: *It's difficult to read in here because the lighting is bad.*

**light·ly** /līt-lee/ *adverb* gently: *I knocked lightly on her bedroom door, not wanting to wake up everyone else.*

**light·ning** /līt-ning/ *noun* a bright flash of light in the sky during a storm. It is caused by the movement of electricity: *There was a flash of lightning, and then the sound of thunder.*

lightning

**light·weight** /līt-wayt/ *adjective* weighing less than other things of the same kind: *The flashlight is made of lightweight plastic, which makes it easy to carry.*

**light year** /līt yeer/ *noun* the distance that light travels in one year: *The star is millions of light years away from the Earth.*

**lik·a·ble**, **likeable** /līk-uhb-uhl/ *adjective* a likable person is nice and easy to like: *Luke's a likable guy, always helpful and friendly.*

**like** /līk/

● *verb*

**1** to think that someone or something is nice or good: *Mom doesn't like flying.* | *I like your new shoes.* | *I like people who make me laugh.* (ANTONYM: **dislike**) ▶ see **Thesaurus**

**2** to think that someone is nice or attractive: *She likes a boy in her class.*

**3** to want something or want to do something: *Would you like a drink?* | *I'd like to go with you.*

● *preposition, conjunction*

**1** similar to another person or thing: *You look a lot like your mom.* | *He flapped his arms up and down like a bird.*

**2** typical of a person or thing, or what they usually do: *It's not like Harry to say no to dessert.* (ANTONYM: **unlike**)

**like·a·ble** /līk-uhb-uhl/ *adjective* another spelling of likable

**like·ly** /līk-lee/ *adjective* if something is likely, it will probably happen or is probably true: *Snow is likely later tonight.*

—**likelihood** /līk-lee-hud/ *noun* how likely something is to happen: *There is a strong likelihood that they will win because they are so far ahead.*

**like·ness** /lῑk-niss/ *noun* a picture or image of someone, especially one that looks very like that person: *The coin has a likeness of President Lincoln on one side.*

**like·wise** /lῑk-wῑz/ *adverb* in the same way: *One little girl started crying and then the other children did likewise.*

**lik·ing** /lῑk-ing/ *noun* a feeling that someone is nice or that something is enjoyable to do: *If you have a liking for adventure, why not try snowboarding?*

**li·lac** /lῑl-uhk/ *noun* a small tree with purple or white flowers: *The lilac bush has a really nice smell.*

**lil·y** /lil-ee/ *noun* (plural **lilies**) a plant with big flowers shaped like trumpets. The flowers are usually white or yellow.

lily

**li·ma bean** /lῑm-uh been/ *noun* a flat bean that grows on plants in parts of South America

**limb** /lim/ *noun*

**1** an arm or leg: *Some people involved in the car crash lost limbs.*

**2** a large branch of a tree: *We threw a rope over one of the tree's lower limbs and climbed up.*

**lime** /lῑm/ *noun* a small round green fruit with a sour taste: *Use the juice of one lime.*

lime

**lim·er·ick** /lim-uhr-ik/ *noun* a short funny poem

**lim·it** /lim-it/

● *noun*

**1** the highest or lowest amount allowed: *The time limit for the test is one hour. | A police officer stopped him because he was driving faster than the speed limit.*

**2** the edge or border of something: *They live just outside the city limits.*

**IDIOM with limit**
**off limits** if a place is off limits, you are not allowed to go there: *The Oval Office is off limits to the public.*

● *verb*
to stop something from getting bigger than a particular amount: *Class size is limited to 30 students.*

—**limited** /lim-it-id/ *adjective* small in number or amount: *We had a limited amount of time to get the job finished.*

**lim·it·less** /lim-it-liss/ *adjective* without a limit or end: *There is an almost limitless number of books you could read.*

**lim·o** /lim-oh/ *noun* a limousine

**lim·ou·sine** /lim-uh-zeen/ *noun* a very large comfortable car that is driven by someone who is paid to drive

**limp** /limp/

● *verb* to walk with difficulty, because your leg or foot is hurt: *Why are you limping? Did you hurt your leg?*

● *noun* the way that you walk when your leg or foot is hurt: *She walks with a slight limp because she has a problem with her foot.*

● *adjective* not stiff or firm: *Mike's whole body went limp and he fell to the floor.*

—**limply** /limp-lee/ *adverb* in a limp way: *Her broken arm hung limply at her side.*

**line** /lῑn/

● *noun*

**1** a long thin mark on something, for example on a piece of paper: *Can you draw a straight line? | He crossed the finish line first, so he won the race. | the yellow lines on the street*

▶ see **Thesaurus**

**2** a row of people or things: *A long line of cars was waiting at the lights. | She stood in line to get her food.*

**3** a long piece of string or rope: *Mom hung the wet clothes on the line. | a fishing line*

**4** a single row of words in a poem, play, song, or book: *Has everyone in the play learned their lines?*

**5** a border between two states or countries: *We drove over the state line into Arizona.*

**6** an invisible straight path between two points: *Light travels in a straight line – it doesn't curve.*

**7** a wire or connection, for example for electricity or the telephone: *Strong winds can blow power lines down.*

**IDIOM with line**

**be out of line** to say or do something that is not acceptable in a situation: *Talking in class is out of line. You need to sit in the time-out chair.*

● *verb*

**1** to cover the inside of something with something: *Birds use leaves to line their nest.* | *Her jacket is lined with silk.*

**2** to form a line along the edge of something: *People lined the streets to watch the parade.* | *The shelves were lined with books.*

**3 line up** to form a line of people or things: *The fans were already lining up outside the stadium.*

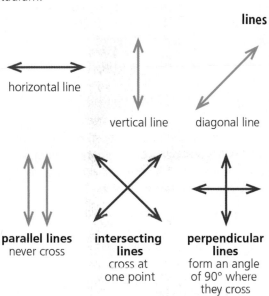

**lines**

horizontal line

vertical line    diagonal line

**parallel lines**
never cross

**intersecting lines**
cross at one point

**perpendicular lines**
form an angle of 90° where they cross

**line graph** /līn graf/ *noun* a graph that uses a line to show how amounts change over time: *The line graph showed the amount of rain in different months of the year.*

**lin·en** /lin-uhn/ *noun*

**1** cloth made from a plant called flax. Linen is used to make clothes, sheets, and tablecloths: *She is wearing a cool linen dress and sunglasses.*

**2** sheets or tablecloths. Sheets are called bed linen and tablecloths are called table linen: *I painted my bedroom and I'm getting new bed linen to match.*

**line of sym·me·try** /līn uhv **sim**-uhtr-ee/ *noun* a line that splits a shape into two halves that are both exactly equal or exactly the same: *If we fold the square along the line of symmetry, both halves will be exactly the same.*

**line plot** /līn plaht/ *noun* a simple graph showing how often one thing happens in relation to other things. It has a series of items along a straight line with a number of X's above each to show how many times it happens.

**line·up** /līn-uhp/ *noun*

**1** the players in a sports team who are playing in a particular game: *Eddie was in the starting lineup for the game but he came off the field at half-time.*

**2** a set of events or television programs that are arranged to happen one after the other: *The TV station has a great Wednesday night line-up with lots of good programs for people to watch.*

**lin·ger** /ling-gur/ *verb* to stay somewhere for a little longer: *The taste of the onions still lingered in my mouth after the meal.*

**lin·ge·rie** /lahnzh-uh-**ray**/ *noun* women's underwear

**lin·ing** /līn-ing/ *noun* something that covers the inside of something else: *The boots have a warm fur lining.*

lining    **lining**

The boots have a warm fur lining.

**link** /lingk/

● *verb*

**1** to show that one thing causes or affects another thing: *Smoking is linked to lung cancer.*

**2** to connect two things or places together: *The interstate links Portland and Seattle.*

● *noun*

**1** a connection between two or more things or people: *There is a definite link between poverty and crime.*

**2** one of the rings in a chain: *One of the links on my necklace is broken.*

**3** a connection between two websites that allows you to move from one site to the other: *Click the link in the top left-hand corner, to go back to the homepage.*

**lint** /lint/ *noun* soft small pieces of thread that come off cotton or woolen material: *I brushed the lint off my coat.*

a b c d e f g h i j k **l** m n o p q r s t u v w x y z

**li·on** /lī-uhn/ *noun* a big wild cat that lives in Africa and southern Asia. Male lions have long hair around their necks. This hair is called a mane.

mane

**lion**

tail

paw

**li·on·ess** /lī-uhn-iss/ *noun* a female lion

**lip** /lip/ *noun* your lips are the two outer parts of your mouth where the skin is redder: *He licked his lips when he saw the food.*

**lip·stick** /lip-stik/ *noun* a colored substance that women wear on their lips: *Mom usually puts on lipstick before we go out.*

**liq·uid** /**lik**-wid/
● *noun* a substance such as water that is not a solid or a gas: *She poured the liquid carefully back into the bottle.* ► see **Thesaurus**
● *adjective* in the form of a liquid, instead of being a gas or solid: *The medicine comes in liquid form and you drink it after a meal.*

**liq·uor** /**lik**-ur/ *noun* a strong alcoholic drink such as whiskey

**lisp** /lisp/ *noun* if someone has a lisp, he or she pronounces "s" sounds as "th" when speaking: *Cecilia speaks with a lisp, so she finds it hard to say her own name!*

**list** /list/
● *noun* a set of things that you write one below the other: *She made a list of all the groceries she needed.* ► see **Thesaurus**
● *verb* to write or say a list of things: *Their number is listed in the phone book.*

**lis·ten** /**liss**-uhn/ *verb* to pay attention to what someone is saying or to a sound that you can hear: *We listen to his radio show every morning.* | *If you listen very closely, you can hear a bird singing.*
► see **Thesaurus**

—**listener** /**liss**-uhn-ur/ *noun* someone who listens to something: *The radio station is popular with young listeners.*

**list·ing** /**list**-ing/ *noun* a list, or something that is on a list: *Let's check the TV listings to see if there is anything good on TV.*

**lit** /lit/ *verb* a past tense and past participle of **light**

**lite** /līt/ *adjective* used in the names of food and drink products that have less fat, sugar, or alcohol than normal: *My dad only drinks lite beer.*

**li·ter** /**leet**-ur/ *noun* ⟨ABBREVIATION: **l**⟩ a unit in the metric system for measuring liquids or gases. A liter is equal to 2.12 pints or 0.26 gallons: *The bottle holds a liter of water.*

**lit·er·a·cy** /**lit**-uhr-uhss-ee/ *noun* the ability to read and write: *Literacy skills are very important because you need to be able to read and write for most jobs.*

**lit·er·al** /**lit**-uhr-uhl/ *adjective* the literal meaning of a word is its basic or original meaning: *A price war is not a war in the literal sense of the word.*
⟨ANTONYM: **metaphorical**⟩

**lit·er·al·ly** /**lit**-uhr-uhl-ee/ *adverb*
**1** used to emphasize that something is really true: *There were literally hundreds of boats on the lake.*
**2** according to the original meaning of a word: *The word melodrama literally means a play with music.*

**lit·er·ar·y** /**lit**-uh-rair-ee/ *adjective* relating to literature: *He writes poems and other literary works such as novels and plays.*

**lit·er·a·ture** /**lit**-uhr-uhch-ur/ *noun* books, plays, or poems that people think are good or important: *We are learning about some of the great figures of American literature, such as Melville who wrote "Moby Dick."*

**lit·ter** /**lit**-ur/
● *noun*
**1** trash such as paper or cans that people leave on the ground: *We had to pick up litter on the playground because it was a real mess.*
**2** a group of baby animals born to one mother at the same time: *Our cat just had a litter of five kittens!*

● *verb*
**1** to drop trash on the ground and leave it there: *Don't litter – use the trash cans!*
**2** if things litter a place, they are there and make it look messy: *The floor was littered with toys – they were everywhere.*

## lit·tle /ˈlɪtˈl/
● *adjective*
**1** small in size: *We live in a little town about 40 miles south of Saint Paul.* | *She kissed her baby's tiny little fingers.*
**2** short in time or distance: *Grandma usually has a little nap in the afternoon.* | *The puppy followed us a little way down the road.*
**3** not very important: *Try not to get upset when little things go wrong.*
● *adjective, pronoun*
a small amount of something: *She put a little sugar in her coffee.* | *"Can you speak Spanish?" "A little."* | *We know very little about him.*
● *adverb*
**1** slightly: *I was a little surprised to see Joe at the party.*
**2** not much: *The town has changed very little since I was young.*

**Grammar: little, a little**

Use **little** when you mean "not much": *I have very little money left.* | *He knows little about dogs.*
Use **a little** when you mean "a small amount": *I got a little ice cream on my shirt.* | *"Do you have any water?" "I have a little."*
**Little** and **a little** are always used with nouns that are things that you cannot count, for example "water" or "information."

## live
● *verb* /lɪv/
**1** to be alive: *Plants can't live without water and sunlight.* | *My grandmother lived until she was 88.*
**2** to have your home in a particular place: *We live in Boston.* | *My friend Toby lives next door.*
▶ see **Thesaurus**
**3 live on** to have an amount of money to buy food and pay bills: *They live on $1,000 a month.*

● *adjective* /laɪv/
**1** live music is performed in a place where people are watching: *I love listening to music, but I've never been to see a live band.*
**2** if a television or radio show is live, people see or hear it as it happens: *You can watch live coverage of the Superbowl on NBC.*
**3** live animals are not dead: *The snake eats live mice.* (ANTONYM: **dead**)
● *adverb* /laɪv/
if something is broadcast live, it is on TV or radio at the same time as it happens: *The finals of the contest will be shown live on Saturday night.*

## live·li·hood /ˈlaɪv-lee-hud/ *noun* the work someone does to earn money in order to live: *People lost their livelihood when the factory closed down, and now they are having to look for new jobs.*

## live·ly /ˈlaɪv-lee/ *adjective* (**livelier**, **liveliest**) full of energy, activity, or excitement: *Ben is very lively and doesn't like to sit still.*

## liv·er /ˈlɪv-ur/ *noun*
**1** a large organ inside your body which cleans your blood ▶ see picture at **anatomy**
**2** the liver of an animal that is eaten as food

## lives /laɪvz/ *noun* the plural of **life**

## live·stock /ˈlaɪv-stahk/ *noun* animals that are kept on a farm: *The farmers keep livestock such as chickens and cattle.*

## liv·ing /ˈlɪv-ing/
● *adjective*
**1** alive: *The rainforest has a huge variety of living creatures.* (ANTONYM: **dead**)
**2** relating to where or how people live: *The miners' living conditions are very poor.*
● *noun*
the way that someone earns money, or the money he or she earns: *My dad drives a truck for a living.*

## liv·ing room /ˈlɪv-ing room/ *noun* the main room in a house where you can sit and relax: *I was sitting in the living room when the doorbell rang.*

**liz·ard** /**liz**-urd/ *noun* an animal that has rough skin, short legs, and a long tail. Lizards are reptiles: *Lizards are most common in hot countries.* ▶ see picture at **reptile**

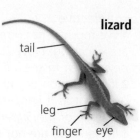

lizard

tail

leg

finger    eye

**load** /lohd/
- *noun*

**1** a large amount of something that is carried by a vehicle or person: *The horses have to carry very heavy loads.* ▶ see picture at **pulley**
**2** the amount of work that a person has to do or that a machine can do: *When her work load increased, Joanne had to work longer hours. | I've already done two loads of laundry today.*
**3** if you have a load of something, you have a lot of it: *She has loads of nice clothes – maybe I can borrow a dress from her.*
- *verb*

**1** (also **load up**) to put a lot of things into a vehicle: *Michael helped me load the bags into the car.*
**2** to put a program into a computer: *When the software has loaded, you can run the program. | I've loaded some new games onto my laptop.*
**3** to put bullets into a gun: *He loaded his gun and pulled the trigger.*

**loaf** /lohf/ *noun* (plural **loaves** /lohvz/) bread that has been cooked in one large piece: *He put a loaf of bread and some peanut butter on the table.*

**loan** /lohn/
- *noun*

an amount of money that you borrow, especially from a bank: *He is going to take out a loan to buy a new car.*
- *verb*

**1** to lend someone money: *I hope the bank will loan us the money to buy the house.*
( SYNONYM: **lend** )
**2** to let someone borrow something: *My sister loaned me her necklace to wear to the party.*
( SYNONYM: **lend** )

**loaves** /lohvz/ *noun* the plural of **loaf**

**lob·by** /**lahb**-ee/
- *noun* (plural **lobbies**)

**1** a large hall inside the entrance of a building: *The doorman carried her bags into the hotel lobby from the car.*
**2** a group of people who try to persuade the government to do something: *The tobacco lobby tried to stop the government from banning advertisements for cigarettes.*
- *verb* (**lobbies**, **lobbying**, **lobbied**)
to try to persuade the government to do something: *Labor unions have been lobbying for an increase in the minimum wage.*

**lob·ster** /**lahb**-stur/
*noun* a sea animal with a hard shell and ten legs. The front two legs are large claws. You can eat the meat of a lobster: *Lobsters turn red when they are cooked.*

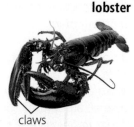

lobster

claws

**lo·cal** /**lohk**-uhl/
- *adjective* in or relating to the area where you live: *Donny goes to one of the local schools.*
—**locally** /**lohk**-uhl-ee/ *adverb* in a local area: *The family is well known locally because they run a store.*
- *noun* someone who lives in the place that you are talking about: *If you want to find a good restaurant, ask one of the locals.*

**lo·cate** /**loh**-kayt/ *verb*

**1** to be in a particular place: *The theater is located in the center of town.*
**2** to find the place where something is: *The Coast Guard located the crew of the missing boat.*

**lo·ca·tion** /loh-**kaysh**-uhn/ *noun* the place where something is, or where something happens: *The map shows the exact location of the treasure.*

**lock** /lahk/
- *noun*

a metal object that you open or close with a key. A lock prevents other people from opening a door, drawer, or container: *I turned the key in the lock and opened the door.*
- *verb*

**1** to close a door, drawer, etc. with a lock: *I tried to open the door but it was locked.*
( ANTONYM: **unlock** )
**2 lock up** to lock all the doors of a building:

*Don't forget to lock up when you leave the house.*
**3 lock up/away** to put someone in prison: *The prisoners will be locked up in the Cook County jail.*

**lock·er** /**lahk**-ur/ *noun* a small closet or cabinet that can be locked so that you can leave your books, clothes, etc. there while you do something else: *I put my books in my locker.*

**locker**

**lock·er room** /**lahk**-ur room/ *noun* a room with lockers in it where people change their clothes before playing sports

**lo·co·mo·tive** /lohk-uh-**moht**-iv/ *noun* the part of a train that pulls the other parts along
( SYNONYM: **engine** )

**lodge** /lahj/
● *verb*
**1** to become stuck somewhere: *A piece of food can lodge between your teeth.*
**2** to officially complain about something: *Some people lodged a complaint about how they had been treated by the airline.*
● *noun*
**1** a cabin or small hotel in the country where people stay for a short time: *We are going to spend the weekend in a lodge by the lake.*
**2** the home of a beaver

**log** /log/
● *noun*
**1** a thick piece of wood that has been cut off or fallen off a tree: *I put another log on the fire.*
▶ see picture at **tree**
**2** a book used for writing down things that have happened, especially on a ship or spacecraft: *The ship's captain wrote about the storm in his log.*
● *verb* (**logging**, **logged**)
**1 log in/on** to start using a computer by typing in your password: *When you log on you are asked for your password.*
**2 log off/out** to stop using a computer: *I logged off and turned off my computer.*

**Word Building**

dialogue | **log**ic | **log**o | mono**log**ue
These words all have the Latin word root *log* in them. *Log* means "thought" or "words." The *dialogue* in a movie or TV show is the words that people say to each other. *Logic* is a way of thinking about something very carefully. A *logo* is a word or picture that a company or team uses on its products or uniform.

**log·ic** /**lahj**-ik/ *noun* a way of thinking about or explaining something, using a series of reasons that are connected with each other in a sensible order: *I don't understand the logic behind their plans.*

**Word Family: logic**

**logic** *noun* | **logical** *adjective* | **illogical** *adjective* | **logically** *adverb*

**log·i·cal** /**lahj**-ik-uhl/ *adjective* sensible and reasonable: *It isn't logical to blame him when he wasn't even there.* ( ANTONYM: **illogical** )
—**logically** /**lahj**-ik-lee/ *adverb* in a logical way: *If we think about this logically, I'm sure we can figure out what went wrong.*

**lo·go** /**loh**-goh/ *noun* (plural **logos**) a small picture that is the official sign of a company or organization: *The company logo appears on all their products.*

**-logy** /luhj-ee/, **-ology** /ahl-uhj-ee/

**Word Building**

bio**logy** | etymo**logy** | geo**logy** | paleont**ology**
These words all have the Greek word root *logy* in them. *Logy* means "study of." *Biology* is the study of living things. *Etymology* is the study of how words change their form and meaning over many years. *Paleontology* is the study of fossils, and of animals and plants that lived millions of years ago.

**lol·li·pop**, **lollypop** /**lahl**-ee-pahp/ *noun* a piece of hard candy on the end of a stick

a b c d e f g h i j k l m n o p q r s t u v w x y z

a
b
c
d
e
f
g
h
i
j
k
**l**
m
n
o
p
q
r
s
t
u
v
w
x
y
z

**lone** /lohn/ *adjective* used to talk about the only person or thing in a place or the only one doing something: *The picture shows a lone figure walking along a beach.*

**lone·ly** /**lohn**-lee/ *adjective*
**1** unhappy because you are alone: *She felt so lonely without her best friend.*
► see **Thesaurus**
**2** a lonely place is a long way from where people live: *Our car broke down on a lonely stretch of highway and we thought we would never get help.*
—**loneliness** /**lohn**-lee-niss/ *noun* the feeling of being lonely: *After they left I had a terrible feeling of loneliness.*

**lone·some** /**lohn**-suhm/ *adjective* lonely: *Karen was lonesome when her sister went to college.*

**long** /long/
● *adjective*
**1** measuring a large distance from one end to the other: *She tied her long hair into a bun.* | *It's a long way from Houston to Denver.*
( ANTONYM: **short** ) ► see picture at **short**
**2** continuing for a large amount of time: *John's been gone a long time.* | *I'm glad it's spring and the days are getting longer.* ( ANTONYM: **short** )
► see **Thesaurus**
**3** used to talk about the length of something: *"How long was the flight?" "About two hours."* | *Their pool is over 20 feet long.*
● *adverb*
**1** for a long time: *Will it take long to get there?* | *We haven't been friends for very long.*
**2** much earlier or much later: *It all happened long ago, before I met you.*

IDIOM with **long**
**as long as** (also **so long as**) if: *You can go, as long as you're back by four o'clock.*
● *verb*
to want something very much: *Archie longed to be back in his own bed.*

**long-dis·tance** /long **dist**-uhnss/ *adjective*
**1** a long-distance telephone call is one you make to someone who lives far away: *Hiromi made a long-distance call to her brother in Japan.*
( ANTONYM: **local** )
**2** traveling between places that are far away from each other: *Her father is a long-distance truck driver, so he is often away from home.*

**long·house** /**long**-howss/ *noun* a type of house that was used by some Native American tribes: *A typical longhouse was about 80 feet long by 18 feet wide.*

**long·ing** /**long**-ing/ *noun* a feeling of wanting someone or something very much: *After years of working in a big city, Laura felt a longing to live somewhere quiet and peaceful.*
—**longingly** /**long**-ing-lee/ *adverb* in a longing way: *She looked longingly at her brother's ice cream because she had finished hers.*

**lon·gi·tude** /**lahnj**-uh-tood/ *noun* the distance east or west of a line going from the top of the Earth to the bottom. Longitude is used to show the position of a place, measured in degrees: *The island is at longitude 21° west.*
( ANTONYM: **latitude** ) ► see picture at **globe**

**long-term** /**long** turm/ *adjective* relating to what will happen a long time in the future: *My long-term goal is to become a doctor.*
( ANTONYM: **short-term** )

**look** /luk/
● *verb*
**1** to use your eyes so that you can see someone or something: *She looked at her husband and smiled.*
**2** to try to find someone or something: *I'm looking for my reading book – have you seen it?* | *My mom is looking for a new job.*
**3** to seem: *Mom looked tired – she was pale and moved slowly.* | *It looks like it might rain because there are dark clouds in the sky.*
**4** said when you are annoyed with someone: *Look, it's bedtime! No more TV!*
**5 look around** to look at what is in a building, store, or place while you are walking: *We'll have two hours to look around the museum.*
**6 look down on** to think that someone is not as good as you are: *The other children looked down on him because he came from a poor family.*
**7 look forward to** to be excited and happy about something that is going to happen: *We always look forward to Grandma's visits because she's a lot of fun.*
**8 look into** to try to find out about something: *In class, we looked into ways to save energy, like turning off lights.*
**9 look out!** you say this to tell someone to pay

attention because something dangerous is happening: *Look out! There's a car coming.*

**10 look up** to try to find information in a book: *I had to look the word up in the dictionary to find out what it means.*

**11 look up to** to like and respect someone, and want to be like him or her: *Your little brother looks up to you, so you need to show him how to be good.*

● *noun*

**1** an act of looking at something: *She took a good look at herself in the mirror.*

**2** an expression that you make with your eyes or face to show how you feel: *She gave her aunt an angry look.* | *There was a look of fear in her eyes.*

---

**Word Choice:** look, watch, see

You **look** at a picture, person, or thing because you want to. You usually **look** at things or people that are not moving: *Look at that car – it's pink!* | *Maria was looking at a picture book.* | *I looked out of the window.*

You **watch** TV, a game, or something that happens. You usually **watch** things or people that are moving: *They are watching TV.* | *I watched him drive away.*

You **see** someone or something accidentally, or because you are trying to find that person or thing: *I can see three people by the tree.* | *Josh saw a fire engine when he was walking to school.*

You can also say that you **saw** a movie, TV show, or game, or that you are going to **see** it in the future: *I saw a really good movie last week.* | *Do you want to see a movie on Saturday?*

---

**look·out** /**luk**-owt/ *noun* **be on the lookout** if you are on the lookout for something, you watch everything that is happening because you want to find something or to be prepared for problems: *He's always on the lookout for adventure.*

**looks** /lukss/ *plural noun* how attractive someone is: *He has the good looks to be a model.*

**loom** /loom/ *verb*

**1** to appear as a large unclear shape that seems dangerous or frightening: *The mountains loomed*

in the darkness.

**2** if something bad is looming, it is likely to happen very soon: *It's the end of the semester, and our tests are looming.*

**loop** /loop/

● *noun* a circle made in a piece of rope, string, or wire: *He tied a loop of wire around the gate to keep it closed.*

● *verb* to make a loop or to tie something in a loop: *I looped the leash around the dog's neck.*

**loose** /looss/ *adjective*

**1** not firmly attached to something: *I have a loose tooth – it's going to fall out soon!*

**2** loose clothes do not fit tightly on your body: *My jeans are loose around the waist so I need a belt.*

**3** free to move around, and not in a cage or prison: *She lets her dog run loose in the street and never puts it on a leash.*

—**loosely** /**looss**-lee/ *adverb* in a loose way: *The scarf was tied loosely around her neck.*

**loos·en** /**looss**-uhn/ *verb* to make something less tight: *I've eaten so much that I have to loosen my belt!*

**loot** /loot/

● *verb* to steal things from stores or houses during a war or riot: *Rioters looted stores and damaged cars.*

—**looting** /**loot**-ing/ *noun* the act of looting stores or houses: *There was looting and violence in the downtown area.*

—**looter** /**loot**-ur/ *noun* someone who loots stores or houses: *Looters stole from houses during the floods.*

● *noun* money or things that have been stolen: *The robbers hid the loot in the basement.*

**lop·sid·ed** /**lahp**-sīd-id/ *adjective*

**1** not equal or fair: *The Raiders beat the Redskins 38–9 in a lopsided victory.*

**2** having one side that is heavier, larger, or lower than the other side: *The cake looks a little lopsided – put more strawberries on this side.*

**lord**, **Lord** /lord/ *noun*

**1 Lord** a word meaning God or Jesus Christ that people use when they are praying: *We ask the Lord to help and guide us.*

**2** a man who belongs to the highest social class in Britain, and can use the word "Lord" before his name: *Lord Nelson*

**lose** /looz/ *verb* (**lost** /lost/)

**1** to stop having something that is important to you or that you need: *Many people will lose their jobs if the factory closes.* | *They lost their homes in the flood.*

**2** to be unable to find someone or something: *She always loses her gloves.* | *The package got lost in the mail.*

**3** to not win a game, war, or argument: *The British lost the American Revolutionary War.* | *The Steelers lost to the Raiders 27–7.*

**4** if you lose weight, you become thinner: *"Have you lost weight?" "Yes, I've lost about ten pounds."*

**5** to stop having a feeling, ability, or quality: *The younger kids began to lose interest in the movie.* | *He lost his memory after the accident.*

**los·er** /**looz**-ur/ *noun* someone who loses a competition or game: *In any game, there has to be a winner and a loser.* ( ANTONYM: **winner** )

**loss** /loss/ *noun*

**1** no longer having something: *Her son's loss of appetite began to worry her.* | *There have been a lot of job losses in this town.*

**2** an occasion when you do not win a game: *The team had three wins and four losses this season.*

**lost** /lost/

● *adjective*

**1** if you get lost, you do not know where you are or how to get somewhere: *We got lost walking around the city.* | *Are you okay? You look lost.*

**2** if something is lost, you cannot find it: *They put up pictures of their lost puppy.*

● *verb*

the past tense and past participle of **lose**

**lost-and-found** /lost uhnd **fownd**/ *noun* a place where things that people have lost are kept until someone comes to get them

**lot** /laht/ *noun*

**1** **a lot** (also **lots**) a large amount or number: *I ate a lot of chocolate and now I feel sick.* | *There were lots of people at the concert.*

**2** **a lot** (also **lots**) very much: *I like you a lot.* | *You'll feel better soon, lots better.*

**3** a small area of land in a city that is used for building on or for a purpose: *We left the car in the parking lot.*

---

**Word Choice: a lot of, much, many**

In sentences with "not," you can use **much** or **many** instead of **a lot of**.

**Much** is used with nouns that are things you cannot count: *There isn't much milk left.*

**Many** is used with nouns that show there is more than one thing or person: *There weren't many people in the room.*

**A lot of** can be used with both kinds of nouns: *There isn't a lot of milk left.* | *There weren't a lot of people in the room.*

---

**lo·tion** /**lohsh**-uhn/ *noun* a liquid that you put on your skin in order to make it soft or to protect it: *Put on some suntan lotion before you go outdoors.*

**lot·ter·y** /**laht**-uhr-ee/ *noun* (plural **lotteries**) a game in which you buy tickets with a series of numbers on them. If your number is picked, you win a lot of money: *If I win the lottery, I'll buy you a new car.*

**loud** /lowd/ *adjective* making a lot of noise: *The TV's too loud – please turn it down.* | *There was a loud cheer from the fans when we scored.* ( ANTONYM: **quiet** ) ▶ see **Thesaurus**
—**loudly** /**lowd**-lee/ *adverb* in a loud way: *Don't talk so loudly in the library.*

**loud·speak·er** /**lowd**-speek-ur/ *noun* a piece of equipment that makes sounds louder: *An announcement came from the loudspeaker, saying that the flight was delayed.*

**lounge** /lownj/

● *noun* a room in a public building where people can relax: *We'll meet you in the hotel lounge.*

● *verb* to sit or lie somewhere in a relaxed way without doing anything: *We spent most of the day lounging on the beach.*

**louse** /lowss/ *noun* (plural **lice** /līss/) a very small insect that can live on the skin and hair of animals and people

**lous·y** /**lowz**-ee/ *adjective* very bad: *I feel lousy because I hardly had any sleep last night.*

**lov·a·ble** /**luhv**-uhb-uhl/ *adjective* easy to love: *The puppies are so cute and very lovable.*

**love** /luhv/
● *verb*
**1** to care a lot about someone: *I love my Mom and Dad.* ▶ see **Thesaurus**
**2** to like something very much: *She loves chocolate chip cookies.* | *I love swimming.*
**3** to like someone very much, in a romantic way: *My brother loves Alice and they are going to get married.*
● *noun*
**1** a strong feeling of caring a lot about someone: *A mother's love for her children is always very strong.*
**2** a strong feeling of liking something: *She has a great love of animals.*
**3** if you are in love with someone, you like that person very much, in a romantic way: *When you are in love with someone you want to be with them all the time.*

**love·ly** /**luhv**-lee/ *adjective* (**lovelier**, **loveliest**)
**1** attractive: *What a lovely little kitten!*
**2** very enjoyable: *We had a lovely vacation and we didn't want to come home.*

**lov·er** /**luhv**-ur/ *noun* someone who likes something very much: *He's a real music lover and he often goes to concerts.*

**lov·ing** /**luhv**-ing/ *adjective* behaving in a gentle kind way toward the people you love: *They are a very loving family and they have a lot of fun together.*

**low** /loh/
● *adjective*
**1** not high: *The fence was low and it was easy to climb over it.* ( ANTONYM: **high** )
**2** below the usual amount: *The store has low prices so many people go to shop there.* ( ANTONYM: **high** )
**3** bad and below the usual standard: *He got a low grade in Spanish because he didn't work hard.* ( ANTONYM: **high** )
**4** not having much of something: *Fish is good for you because it is low in fat.*
**5** a low sound is quiet or deep: *They were talking in low voices and it was difficult to hear what they were saying.*
● *noun*
a very low level: *The temperature dropped to a low of 15 degrees below zero.* ( ANTONYM: **high** )

**low·er** /**loh**-ur/
● *verb*
**1** to reduce something: *They want to lower the number of students in each class from 30 to 25.* ( ANTONYM: **raise** )
**2** to move something down: *Billy lowered his head because he was ashamed of what he had done.* ( ANTONYM: **raise** )
**3** to make something less loud: *She lowered her voice so no one would hear.* ( ANTONYM: **raise** )
● *adjective*
**1** smaller in amount or level than something else: *Our score is still lower than theirs.* ( ANTONYM: **higher** )
**2** below something else of the same kind: *We looked through the lower windows of the house.* ( ANTONYM: **upper** )

**low·er·case** /**loh**-ur-kayss/ *noun* lowercase letters are written in their small form, for example a, b, or c: *In a name such as "Peter," the first letter is written in uppercase, and the other letters are written in lowercase.* ( ANTONYM: **uppercase** )

**low-fat** /**loh**-fat/ *adjective* low-fat food has very little fat: *I always drink low-fat milk.*

**low pres·sure** /loh **presh**-ur/ *noun* a type of pressure in the Earth's atmosphere that usually causes wind and rain

**loy·al** /**loy**-uhl/ *adjective* always giving support, or staying faithful: *You should always be loyal to your friends and help them when they are in trouble.*
—**loyalty** /**loy**-uhl-tee/ *noun* support and faithfulness: *Employees showed a lot of loyalty to the company even during its financial difficulties.*

**luck** /luhk/ *noun*
**1** good things that happen by chance: *I never have any luck when I play games.*
**2** **good luck/bad luck** good or bad things that happen by chance: *We had bad luck with the weather – it rained all week.*

> IDIOM with **luck**
> **Good luck!** you say this when you hope someone will be successful: *Good luck on your test!*

a b c d e f g h i j k **l** m n o p q r s t u v w x y z

a
b
c
d
e
f
g
h
i
j
k
l
m
n
o
p
q
r
s
t
u
v
w
x
y
z

**luck·y** /luhk-ee/ *adjective* (**luckier, luckiest**)
**1** if you are lucky, good things happen to you by chance: *I was lucky and guessed the right answer.* | *It was lucky you remembered to bring the map.* (SYNONYM: **fortunate**)
(ANTONYM: **unlucky**) ► see Thesaurus
**2** a lucky object makes you have good luck: *She wears that bracelet because she thinks it's lucky.*
—**luckily** /luhk-uhl-ee/ *adverb* used for saying that it is good that something has happened: *It rained, but luckily I had remembered to bring my umbrella.*

**lug** /luhg/ *verb* (**lugging, lugged**) to carry something heavy with difficulty: *The car broke down so we had to lug all our shopping home.*

**lug·gage** /luhg-ij/ *noun* the bags that you take with you when you are traveling: *You can carry one piece of luggage on the plane.*

**luke·warm** /look-**worm**/ *adjective* slightly warm: *The water in the shower was only lukewarm.*

**lul·la·by** /luhl-uh-bī/ *noun* (plural **lullabies**) a quiet song that you sing to small children to make them sleep: *Mom used to sing me a lullaby at bedtime.*

**Word Origin:** lullaby

**Lullaby** comes from a Middle English word that meant "to make someone quiet and ready for sleep." The word probably came from the kinds of sounds a mother makes when she is trying to make a baby sleepy. The "by" part of "lullaby" may come from the "bye" in "goodbye."

**lum·ber** /luhm-bur/ *noun* wood that is used for building: *The lumber is taken from the forest in big trucks.*

**lum·ber·jack** /luhm-bur-jak/ *noun* someone whose job is to cut down trees for wood

**lump** /luhmp/ *noun*
**1** a small piece of something, without a regular shape: *He took a lump of clay and made it into a pot.*
**2** a hard bump under the surface of your skin: *I fell off my bike and now I have a big lump on my head.*

**lump·y** /luhmp-ee/ *adjective* if something is lumpy, it contains a lot of small pieces, or it has a lot of bumps: *The mixture for the pancakes is all lumpy.*

**lu·nar** /loon-ur/ *adjective* relating to the Moon: *The first lunar landing was in 1969, when Neil Armstrong walked on the surface of the Moon.*

**lunch** /luhnch/ *noun* a meal that you eat in the middle of the day: *I often have a sandwich for lunch.*

**lunch·time** /luhnch-tīm/ *noun* the time when people eat lunch, in the middle of the day: *We get a one-hour break at lunchtime.*

**lung** /luhng/ *noun* one of the two parts inside your chest that you breathe with. Your lungs take in oxygen for your body to use. They also get rid of carbon dioxide: *Smoking is bad for your lungs.* ► see picture at **anatomy**

**lux·u·ry** /luhk-shuhr-ee/ *noun* (plural **luxuries**)
**1** the comfort that you get from expensive things: *They live in luxury, in a house with a big swimming pool.*
**2** something that you do not need, but that is nice to have or do: *We don't have much money for luxuries like meals in restaurants.*
—**luxurious** /luhg-**zhoor**-ee-uhss/ *adjective* very expensive and comfortable: *The hotel is very luxurious and the rooms are very big.*

**-ly** /lee/

**Word Building**

**-ly** is a suffix.
**carefully | correctly | quickly | slowly**
**-ly** changes the root word into an adverb. If you do something *carefully*, you do it in a careful way. If you run *quickly*, you run in a quick way. If you answer a question *correctly*, you answer it in the correct way.

**ly·ing** /lī-ing/ *verb* the present participle of lie

**lynx** /lingkss/ *noun* (plural **lynx** or **lynxes**) a big wild cat that has a short tail, long legs, and pointed ears: *Lynx live in mountains and forests.*

**lyr·ics** /lirr-ikss/ *plural noun* the words of a popular song: *Who wrote the lyrics to this song?*

# Mm

**m** the written abbreviation of **meter**

**ma'am** /mam/ *noun* used to speak politely to a woman, when you do not know her name: *May I help you, ma'am?*

**mac·a·ro·ni** /mak-uh-**rohn**-ee/ *noun* a type of pasta, in the shape of small tubes: *For dinner we had macaroni and cheese.*

## Word Origin: macaroni

**Macaroni** comes from the Italian word for this food. In the 1700s, many young English men traveled through Italy as part of their education. To them, macaroni was a new and stylish food. People started using the word macaroni to describe young men who liked to dress well and be stylish. This is where the word in the song "Yankee Doodle" comes from. When the song says that Yankees "stick a feather in their hat and call it macaroni," it is saying that Yankees think they are stylish when they are not really very well dressed.

**ma·chine** /muh-**sheen**/ *noun* a piece of equipment that you use to do a job. Machines use power to make them work: *Can you turn on the washing machine?*

## Word Family: machine

**machine** *noun* | **machinery** *noun* | **mechanical** *adjective*

**ma·chine gun** /muh-**sheen** guhn/ *noun* a gun that fires a lot of bullets very quickly

**ma·chin·er·y** /muh-**sheen**-uhr-ee/ *noun* large machines: *The company makes farm machinery such as tractors.*

**mad** /mad/ *adjective* (**madder**, **maddest**)
**1** angry: *Mom will be mad at me if I miss the bus and come home late.*

**2** mentally ill and unable to behave in a normal way: *She never left her house and people said that she was mad.* ( SYNONYMS: **crazy, insane** )

> **IDIOM with mad**
> **like mad** as quickly as you can: *I ran like mad to get help.*

**mad·am** /**mad**-uhm/ *noun* used when you do not know a woman's name, when you are speaking and writing: *I began my letter "Dear Sir or Madam."*

**made** /mayd/ *verb* the past tense and past participle of **make**

**mad·ness** /**mad**-niss/ *noun*
**1** very stupid behavior: *It was madness to go up the mountain in the dark.*
**2** mental illness ( SYNONYM: **insanity** )

**mag·a·zine** /mag-uh-**zeen**/ *noun* a big thin book with a paper cover that you can buy every week or month. Magazines have stories, pictures, games, or news in them: *The singer's picture was on the cover of the magazine.*

**mag·ic** /**maj**-ik/
● *noun*
**1** a special power that makes impossible things happen in stories: *The witch used magic to turn the prince into a frog.*
**2** tricks that someone does to entertain people: *He did some magic and produced white rabbits from a hat.*
**3** a special and exciting quality: *All kids love the magic of Christmas.*
● *adjective*
having special powers that make impossible things happen in stories: *In the book, the children go for a ride on a magic carpet.*

> **IDIOM with magic**
> **the magic word** a phrase that adults use when they want children to say "please": *"Mom, I want a piece of cake." "What's the magic word?" "Please, Mom."*

**mag·i·cal** /**maj**-ik-uhl/ *adjective*
**1** very special and exciting: *It's a magical feeling when you sleep outside under the stars.*
**2** relating to the use of special powers to make impossible things happen: *In her books she writes about a strange and magical world of wizards and witches.*

387

a b c d e f g h i j k l **m** n o p q r s t u v w x y z

### ma·gi·cian

/muh-**jish**-uhn/ *noun* someone who does magic tricks to entertain people who are watching: *The magician suddenly pulled a rabbit from a hat.*

magician

### mag·ma /**mag**-muh/

*noun* hot melted rock below the surface of the Earth: *When a volcano erupts, magma comes up from deep inside of the Earth.*

▶ see picture at **volcano**

### mag·ne·si·um /mag-**neez**-ee-uhm/ *noun* a

silver-white chemical element. It burns with a very bright white flame. The symbol for magnesium is Mg.

### mag·net /**mag**-nit/

*noun* a piece of iron or steel that makes other metal objects move toward it: *The magnet attracted the paper clips, but not the aluminum foil.*

magnet

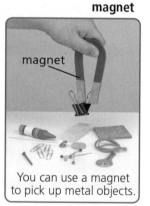

magnet

You can use a magnet to pick up metal objects.

### mag·net·ic /mag-**net**-ik/

*adjective* having the ability to be attracted by a magnet or to attract other metal objects like a magnet: *The iron is magnetic and it attracts other metal objects toward it.*

—**magnetism** /**mag**-nuht-iz-uhm/ *noun* the physical force that makes metal objects move toward each other

### mag·neti·c field /mag-net-ik **feeld**/ *noun*

**1** the area around a magnetic object, that can attract things made of iron
**2** the area around the Earth that has a magnetic force. It makes the needle on a compass point north.

### mag·nif·i·cent /mag-**nif**-uhss-uhnt/ *adjective*

very good or beautiful, and very impressive: *A lion is a magnificent animal.*

### mag·ni·fy /**mag**-nuh-fī/

*verb* (**magnifies**, **magnified**) to make something look larger: *The microscope magnifies the drop of water so that you can see the tiny living things in it.*

—**magnification** /mag-nuhf-uh-**kaysh**-uhn/ *noun* the process of magnifying something: *Magnification of the insect helps you to see it.*

magnify

### mag·ni·fy·ing glass /**mag**-nuh-fī-ing glass/

*noun* a round piece of glass that makes things look bigger: *I looked at the insect through a magnifying glass.*

### mag·ni·tude /**mag**-nuh-tood/ *noun*

**1** how big and important something is: *We soon began to realize the magnitude of the problem.*
**2** the force of an earthquake: *An earthquake with a magnitude of 6 can cause serious damage.*

### mag·pie /**mag**-pī/ *noun*

a bird with black and white feathers. Magpies make a loud sound.

### ma·hog·a·ny

/muh-**hahg**-uhn-ee/

● *noun* a hard dark wood used to make furniture: *Mahogany comes mainly from the rain forests.*
● *adjective* made of mahogany: *This is a mahogany table.*

magpie

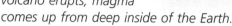

### maid /mayd/ *noun* a woman whose job is to

clean a house or the rooms in a hotel: *She got a job as a hotel maid.*

### maid·en /**mayd**'n/

● *noun* a girl or young woman who is not married: *In the story, the prince meets a beautiful maiden.*
● *adjective* a maiden voyage or flight is the first one that a ship or plane makes: *The ship was on its maiden voyage.*

**maid·en name** /**mayd**'n naym/ *noun* the family name that a woman has before she gets married: *My parents are George and Betty Aldridge, but Mom's maiden name was Betty Johnson.*

**maid of hon·or** /mayd uhv **ahn**-uhr/ *noun* the most important bridesmaid at a wedding: *She was maid of honor when her sister got married.*

**mail** /mayl/

● *noun*
**1** the system of delivering letters and packages: *On my birthday, a big package arrived in the mail.*
**2** the letters and packages that are delivered to your house or office: *"Was there any mail today?" "Yes, there's a letter from Grandma."*
**3** messages that you receive on a computer: *I want to check my mail to see if Jo has replied to my message.* (SYNONYM: **email**)

● *verb*
to send a letter or package to someone: *Sam bought a postcard and mailed it home.*

**mail·box** /**mayl**-bahkss/
*noun*
**1** a box outside your house where letters for you are put: *There was a postcard from Grandma in our mailbox.*

**mailbox**

**2** a box where you put letters you are sending. The box is on the sidewalk or at a post office: *She wrote a letter and took it to the mailbox on Severn Street.*
**3** the part of a computer where email messages arrive: *I checked my mailbox, but Ashley still hadn't replied to my email.*

**mail car·ri·er** /**mayl** karr-ee-uhr/ *noun* someone whose job is collecting and delivering mail

**mail·man** /**mayl**-man/ *noun* (plural **mailmen** /**mayl**-men/) a man whose job is collecting and delivering mail: *The mailman handed Mom some letters.*

**mail or·der** /mayl **ord**-ur/ *noun* a way of buying things. You order things at home and the company sends the things to you by mail: *Books are sometimes cheaper by mail order than if you buy them in a store.*

**main** /mayn/ *adjective* bigger or more important than other things of the same kind: *The main entrance to the school is at the front.* | *The main thing you need to remember is to check your spelling.*

**main clause** /mayn **kloz**/ *noun* a part of a sentence that has two or more parts. The main clause has a subject and a verb, and can be a sentence on its own: *In the sentence "On Friday, I saw Dan," "I saw Dan" is the main clause.*

**main·frame** /**mayn**-fraym/ *noun* a large powerful computer. A mainframe has a lot of smaller computers connected to it.

**main·land** /**mayn**-land/ *noun* the main area of land that forms a country, but not its islands: *The bridge connects the island to the mainland.*

**main·ly** /**mayn**-lee/ *adverb* mostly: *Racoons live mainly in North America, although a few are found in other areas.*

**main·stream** /**mayn**-streem/
● *noun* the usual ideas or ways of doing something: *His ideas were outside the mainstream, and a lot of people did not understand them.*
● *adjective* relating to mainstream ideas and ways of doing something: *Ed likes mainstream pop and rock, but he also likes some pretty strange music!*

**main·tain** /mayn-**tayn**/ *verb*
**1** to keep something in good condition: *My dad showed me how to maintain my bicycle and check the tire pressure.*
**2** to make something continue in the same way as before: *Your work is good, but you need to maintain the same high standard.*
**3** to say that something is true or correct: *Everyone disagreed with Kate, but she still maintained that she was right.*

**main·te·nance** /**maynt**-uhn-uhnss/ *noun* the work that is necessary to keep something in good condition: *Bicycle maintenance includes things like checking your tires and brakes.*

**ma·jes·tic** /muh-**jest**-ik/ *adjective* very big and impressive: *A lion is a majestic animal and is king of the jungle.*
—**majestically** /muh-**jest**-ik-lee/ *adverb* in a majestic way: *The Rocky Mountains rose majestically toward the sky.*

**maj·es·ty** /**maj**-uhst-ee/ *noun*
**1** the quality of being impressive or beautiful: *Tourists come to see the majesty of Niagara Falls.*
**2** **Her Majesty/His Majesty** the title of a queen or king: *Her Majesty Queen Elizabeth II is queen of England.*

**ma·jor** /**mayj**-ur/
● *adjective*
very big or important: *My dad has visited New York, Chicago, and all the other major cities in the U.S.* ( ANTONYM: **minor** )
● *noun*
**1** the main subject that you study in college: *Her major is chemistry, but she's also studying math.*
**2** an officer who has a middle rank in the army, air force, or Marines: *Mark used to be a captain, but he's a major now.*
● *verb*
**major in** to study something as your main subject in college: *My brother's majoring in biology because he wants to go to medical school.*

**ma·jor·ette** /mayj-uh-**ret**/ *noun* a girl who spins a baton (=a thin stick), while she is marching in a parade

**ma·jor·i·ty** /muh-**jor**-uht-ee/ *noun*
**1** most of the people or things in a group: *The majority of the class passed the test. Only three students failed it.* ( ANTONYM: **minority** )
**2** more votes than other people or groups in an election: *He's popular and people think he will win by a big majority.*

**ma·jor leagues** /mayj-ur **leegz**/ *noun* the best teams in professional baseball: *Chris was a player in the major leagues.*
—**major-league** /**mayj**-ur leeg / *adjective* belonging to the major leagues: *He's in a major-league baseball team.*

**make** /mayk/
● *verb* (**made** /mayd/)
**1** to produce or build something: *Mom made sandwiches for lunch. | The house is made of brick.* ► see **Thesaurus**
**2** to do something: *Oh no! I've made a mistake.*
**3** to cause something to happen, or someone to do something: *The smell was horrible and it made me feel sick. | Joshua hit her and made her cry.*

**4** to force someone to do something: *Don't make her come if she doesn't want to.*
**5** to equal a number or amount when you add things together: *Three and five make eight.*
**6** if you make the team, you win a place on it: *I'm practicing a lot because I want to make the school baseball team.*
**7** to earn money: *Movie stars make a lot of money.*
**8** to have the qualities that you need to become something: *My brother will make a good doctor because he's very intelligent and also very kind.*
**9** **make out** to be able to see, hear, or understand something: *I was sitting at the back and I couldn't make out what she was saying.*
**10** **make up** to think of a story that is not true, and tell it to someone: *Children have strong imaginations and sometimes they make up stories.*
**11** **make up** to become friends with someone again, after an argument: *I told the boys to stop fighting and make up.*
● *noun*
the make of a product is the name of the company that produces it: *What make is your dad's car?* ( SYNONYM: **brand** )

**make-be·lieve** /**mayk** buh-leev/ *noun* if something you do is make-believe, you pretend or imagine that it is real: *A lot of the games kids play are make-believe, like pretending to be superheroes.*

**make·up** /**mayk**-uhp/ *noun* colored powders and creams that women and actors put on their faces: *Mom is putting on her makeup because she's going out to a party.*

**mal-** /mal/

**Word Building**

**mal-** is a prefix.
**mal**nutrition | **mal**practice
**mal-** means "bad." If you suffer from *malnutrition*, you are not eating the right foods or not eating enough food. Your nutrition is bad. If a doctor is accused of *malpractice*, people say that the doctor has done something wrong.

**ma·lar·i·a** /muh-**lair**-ee-uh/ *noun* a serious disease that is spread by mosquitoes in tropical countries. Malaria causes fever and sometimes death: *He got malaria while he was working in Africa.*

**male** /mayl/
- *adjective* belonging to the sex that cannot have babies or lay eggs: *The male bird does most of the hunting, and the female bird stays on the nest.* ( ANTONYM: **female** )
- *noun* a person or animal that belongs to the sex that cannot have babies or lay eggs: *Three of the puppies were males and the other two were females.* ( ANTONYM: **female** )

**mall** /mol/ *noun* a very large building with a lot of stores in it: *I got some new jeans at one of the stores in the mall.* ( SYNONYM: **shopping mall** )

**Word Origin: mall**

The word **mall** comes from a game called *pall-mall* that used to be played in parks in England. The game needed a long flat grassy area, and this kind of area started to be called a mall. After a while, people thought of a mall as a place that was pleasant to walk in. In the 1960s, people started to use the word mall to mean a place with a lot of stores. Shopping malls were probably called malls because you walk from shop to shop.

**mal·le·a·ble** /**mal**-ee-uhb-uhl/ *adjective* easy to press or bend into a new shape: *Wet clay is very malleable and you can make any shape you want.*

**mal·nu·tri·tion** /mal-noo-**trish**-uhn/ *noun* a medical condition in which someone's body is weak and unhealthy because of lack of food, or lack of healthy food: *In some countries, children become sick from malnutrition because they do not have enough to eat.*

**mal·prac·tice** /mal-**prakt**-iss/ *noun* very careless or criminal behavior by a professional person, which could cause that person to lose his or her job: *The doctor was accused of malpractice after he gave someone the wrong medicine.*

**ma·ma**, momma /**mahm**-uh/ *noun* mother: *Mama met us at the school gate.*

**mam·mal** /**mam**-uhl/ *noun* an animal that drinks its mother's milk when it is young.

A mammal gives birth to baby animals, not eggs: *Cats, dogs, cows, and horses are all mammals.*
▶ see pictures on page **A2**

**mam·moth** /**mam**-uhth/
- *noun* an animal that lived on Earth thousands of years ago. A mammoth looked like a big hairy elephant with long tusks.
- *adjective* very big: *They've bought a new TV with a mammoth screen that covers the whole wall.* ( SYNONYM: **huge** )

**man** /man/
- *noun* (plural **men** /men/)
**1** a male person who is an adult: *Mr. Hall was a tall man of about 40.*
**2** all people, both men and women: *Diamond is the hardest substance known to man.*
- *verb* (**manning**, **manned**)
**1** to operate a machine or vehicle: *The ship was manned by 80 sailors.*
**2** to work at or guard a place: *Soldiers manned the fort and kept watch for the enemy.*

**man·age** /**man**-ij/ *verb*
**1** to succeed in doing something difficult: *I managed to answer all the questions correctly.*
**2** to be in charge of a business or store: *My uncle manages a hotel, so he is very busy during the summer vacation.*

**man·age·a·ble** /**man**-ij-uhb-uhl/ *adjective* possible to do: *The test was difficult but it was manageable.*

**man·age·ment** /**man**-ij-muhnt/ *noun*
**1** the job of controlling or organizing something: *Mr. Clarke has taken over the management of the soccer team.*
**2** the people who control the work of an organization or business: *The school has changed a lot because it has new management.*

**man·ag·er** /**man**-ij-ur/ *noun* someone who is in charge of a business, store, or group of people: *Mom wanted to complain about the food, so she asked to see the restaurant manager.*

**man·da·to·ry** /**mand**-uh-tor-ee/ *adjective* if something is mandatory, a law or rule says you must do it: *Attendance at school is mandatory for children aged 5 to 16.*

**mane** /mayn/ *noun* the long hair on the neck of a horse or male lion: *The horse shook its mane.*
▶ see picture at **lion**

**ma·neu·ver** /muh-**noov**-ur/
● *verb* to move something somewhere carefully and with skill: *Three men managed to maneuver the piano through the doorway.*
● *noun* a difficult movement that needs skill: *In each judo class, you will learn a new maneuver.*

**man·go** /**mang**-goh/
*noun* (plural **mangoes** or **mangos**) a fruit that is sweet, juicy, and orange inside. Mangoes grow in tropical places.

mango

**man·hole** /**man**-hohl/
*noun* a hole in a road with a cover on it. People go down manholes to check pipes or wires under the ground.

**ma·ni·ac** /**mayn**-ee-ak/ *noun* someone who is crazy or dangerous: *The man in front of us was driving like a maniac, and he nearly crashed his car.*

**man·i·cure** /**man**-i-kyoor/ *noun* if you have a manicure, someone shapes and paints your fingernails
—**manicurist** /**man**-i-kyoor-ist/ *noun* someone whose job is giving people a manicure

**ma·nip·u·late** /muh-**nip**-yuh-layt/ *verb*
**1** to move something into different shapes or positions: *The nurse was manipulating my arm into different positions, in order to stretch the muscles.*
**2** to secretly make someone do what you want, without that person realizing that you are doing this: *My sister is good at manipulating her friends and getting them to do all her work for her.*
—**manipulation** /muh-nip-yuh-**laysh**-uhn/ *noun* the act of manipulating people to do what you want: *Advertisements are a form of manipulation because they try to make you buy something.*

**man·kind** /man-**kīnd**/ *noun* all humans as a group: *When he walked on the moon, Neil Armstrong famously said that it was "one small step for man, one giant leap for mankind."*

**man·ly** /**man**-lee/ *adjective* having qualities that people think a man should have: *He was a good leader – strong, brave, and manly.*

**man-made** /**man** mayd/ *adjective* made by people, and not produced naturally: *Some lakes are natural and some are man-made.*

**man·ner** /**man**-ur/ *noun*
**1** the way you do something: *She always deals with problems in a sensible manner, without worrying about them.*
**2** the way you behave with other people: *I like Tom. He has a very friendly manner.*
**3** **manners** polite ways of behaving: *Their children all say "please" and "thank you" – they have very good manners.*

**man·sion** /**mansh**-uhn/ *noun* a very big house: *He's very rich and he lives in a mansion with 20 bedrooms and a pool.*

**man·slaugh·ter** /**man**-slot-ur/ *noun* the crime of killing someone when you did not plan to do it: *Two people died in the fire, and the man who started it was charged with manslaughter.*

**man·tel** /**mant**'l/ (also **man·tel·piece** /**mant**'l-peess/) *noun* the shelf above a fireplace: *There was a photo of her son on the mantel.*

mantel

mantel

**man·tle** /**mant**'l/ *noun* the part of the Earth below the surface, called the crust, and above the center part, called the core. The mantle is about 1,800 miles thick and is mostly solid rock.

**man·u·al** /**man**-yoo-uhl/
● *adjective*
**1** manual labor involves working with your hands and strength: *He earned a little money doing manual labor on a building site.*
**2** operated by hand: *The car windows are all manual and you have to turn a handle to make them go up and down.* ( ANTONYM: **automatic** )
—**manually** /**man**-yoo-uhl-ee/ *adverb* using your hands: *You can change the height of your seat manually.*
● *noun*
a book that tells you how to do something: *If*

*you have a problem with your computer, first check the manual.*

**man·u·fac·ture** /man-yuh-**fak**-chur/
● *verb* to make things in large amounts in order to sell them: *The company manufactures thousands of cars each year.*
● *noun* the process of making things in large amounts in order to sell them: *Aluminum is used in the manufacture of bikes.*
—**manufacturer** /man-yuh-**fak**-chuhr-ur/ *noun* a company that manufactures things: *Ford is a car manufacturer.*

**ma·nure** /muh-**noor**/ *noun* waste from animals. People put manure into the earth to make plants grow better: *I always put some manure on the soil around the vegetables, to make them grow big and strong.*

**man·u·script** /**man**-yuh-skript/ *noun*
**1** a piece of writing before it is printed: *When a writer finishes writing a book, he or she sends the manuscript to a publisher.*
**2** a very old book or document that was written by hand: *The original manuscript of the ancient book is now in a museum.*

**man·y** /**men**-ee/ *adjective, pronoun* (**more**, **most**) a large number of people or things: *There are many different flavors of ice cream.* | *Many of the children come to school by bus.*
( **ANTONYM: few** ) ▶ see **Thesaurus**

⎧ **IDIOM with many**
⎪ **how many** used to ask or talk about how big
⎪ a number is: *How many friends are coming to*
⎪ *your party?* | *I was surprised how many of the*
⎪ *students had never been on an airplane – it*
⎩ *was more than half the class.*

**Word Choice:** many, much, a lot of

In sentences with "not," you can use **many** or **much** instead of **a lot of**.

**Many** is used with nouns that show there is more than one thing or person: *There weren't many people in the room.*

**Much** is used with nouns that are things you cannot count: *There isn't much milk left.*

**A lot of** can be used with both kinds of nouns: *There isn't a lot of milk left.* | *There weren't a lot of people in the room.*

**map** /map/
● *noun* a drawing of an area that shows things such as the roads, cities, rivers, mountains, or countries: *You can see on the map that New York is north of Philadelphia.*
● *verb* to make a map of a place: *Scientists are mapping the surface of Mars.*

map

**ma·ple** /**mayp**-uhl/
*noun* a tree that grows in northern countries. A maple has leaves with five points that turn red and yellow in the fall: *The sap from maple trees is boiled to produce maple syrup.*

maple

**map-read·ing** /map **reed**-ing/ *noun* the activity of using a map to find out how to go somewhere

**mar** /mar/ *verb* (**marring**, **marred**) to spoil something and make it less attractive or enjoyable: *If they build a factory, it will mar the beauty of the forest.*

**mar·a·thon** /**marr**-uh-thahn/
● *noun* a very long race that people run. A marathon is 26 miles and 385 yards: *A lot of people run in the New York Marathon, but not everyone finishes the race.*
● *adjective* very long: *It was a marathon meeting and lasted over six hours.*

**Word Origin:** marathon

The **marathon** gets its name from an old Greek story. The Greeks were fighting the Persians in a town called Marathon. A Greek man ran 26 miles from Marathon to the city of Athens to tell them that the Greeks had won. No one knows if this story is really true, but it gave the race its name in the first modern Olympic Games.

a b c d e f g h i j k l **m** n o p q r s t u v w x y z

**mar·ble** /**marb**-uhl/ *noun*
**1** a type of hard rock that is often used to make floors, buildings, and statues. Marble can be made very smooth and shiny. Marble is often white, but it can be black or other colors: *The floor of the palace was made of marble.*
**2** a small colored glass ball that children roll along the ground in a game: *Does anyone want to play marbles?*

**Word Origin:** marble

The game of **marbles** is a very old game. It probably started being called marbles in the 1600s. At that time, the balls used in the game were made of marble. Now they are usually made of glass.

marble

marble                    marbles

**march** /march/
● *verb*
**1** to walk with regular steps like a soldier: *The girls in the parade march to military music.*
▶ see picture on page **A15**
**2** to walk quickly because you are angry or determined: *She marched out of the room and said that she was not coming back.*
**3** to walk somewhere in a large group to protest about something: *Thousands of people marched through the city to protest against the war.*
● *noun*
**1** an event when many people walk to protest about something: *There was a march to protest about the plans to close the factory.*
**2** an event when soldiers walk from one place to another: *The army began its long march south.*

**March** /march/ *noun* (ABBREVIATION: **Mar.**) the third month of the year. March is between February and April: *The weather begins to get warmer in March.* | *Dad's birthday is on March 11.*

**Word Origin:** March

The ancient Romans named many of the months for one of their gods. **March** comes from Mars, who was the god of war. The Romans believed that the spring was a good time to fight wars.

**mare** /mair/ *noun* a female horse or donkey

**mar·ga·rine** /**marj**-uh-rin/ *noun* a yellow food that is like butter. Margarine is usually made from vegetable oil: *To make a cake you will need margarine, sugar, flour, and eggs.*

**mar·gin** /**marj**-in/ *noun*
**1** the empty space at the side of a page of writing: *In the margin, my teacher had written "Good work."*
**2** the difference between two numbers or amounts, especially the numbers of points that people get in a game, or votes in an election: *They won the game by only a small margin. The final score was 82 to 84.*

**ma·rine** /muh-**reen**/ *adjective*
**1** relating to the ocean and the animals and plants that live there: *You can see all kinds of marine life at the New England Aquarium.*
**2** relating to ships or the navy: *The president visited a marine base in North Carolina.*

**Ma·rine** /muh-**reen**/ *noun* a soldier in the U.S. Marine Corps

**Mar·ine Corps** /muh-**reen** kor/ *noun* a part of the U.S. armed forces. The soldiers in the Marine Corps are trained to fight on land and on ships.

**mark** /mark/
● *verb*
**1** to write a word or draw a sign on something: *The price is marked on the bottom of the can.*
**2** to show where something is: *I have marked the way you need to go on the map.*
**3** to be a sign of an important event: *Mom and Dad are having a party to mark their wedding anniversary.*
**4** to make a scratch or dirty area on something: *Your muddy shoes have marked the carpet.*
● *noun*
**1** a scratch or dirty area on something: *Who*

made these black marks on the couch?
▶ see **Thesaurus**

**2** a sign that you write, print, or draw: *Don't forget to put a question mark after a question.*

### mar·ket /**mark**-it/ *noun*

**1** a place where people buy and sell food, clothes, or other things. Markets are often held outside on a particular day: *Mom stopped at the market to buy some milk.* | *The farmers' market sells fruit and vegetables that have been grown nearby.*

**2** all the people who want to buy something: *The market for computer games is still growing because more and more kids want to buy them.*

**market**

### mar·ket·place /**mark** it playss/ *noun*

**1** the situation in which companies are trying to sell goods to people: *The marketplace is changing all the time and people want new products.*

**2** a place in town, where a market is held: *Farmers come to sell meat, fruit, and vegetables in the marketplace.*

### ma·roon /muh-**roon**/

● *noun, adjective* a dark red-brown color: *He is wearing maroon socks.*

● *verb* if you are marooned somewhere, you are stuck there and you cannot leave: *They were marooned on an island after their boat sank.*

### mar·riage /**marr**-ij/ *noun*

**1** the relationship between two people who are married: *They have a very happy marriage and three great kids.*

**2** the ceremony that happens when two people get married: *The marriage will take place in a church.* ( SYNONYM: **wedding** )

### mar·ried /**marr**-eed/ *adjective* if you are married, you have a husband or a wife: *My sister*

is married now and she lives with her husband nearby. ▶ see **Thesaurus**

### mar·ry /**marr**-ee/ *verb* (**marries, marrying, married**)

**1** to become someone's husband or wife: *Charlie gave her a ring and asked her to marry him.*

**2** to perform the ceremony for two people to become husband and wife: *The priest agreed to marry us in our local church.*

> **Word Family:** marry
>
> **marry** *verb* | **married** *adjective* | **unmarried** *adjective* | **marriage** *noun*

### Mars /marz/ *noun* the fourth planet from the sun. Mars is the nearest planet to the Earth and it looks red in the sky. ▶ see picture at **solar system**

### marsh /marsh/ *noun* an area of ground that is soft and wet: *The plant grows in wet areas such as marshes and ponds.*

—**marshland** /**marsh**-land/ *noun* a large area of land that is soft and wet: *The bird usually lives in marshland areas.*

### mar·shal /**marsh**-uhl/

● *noun*

**1** a type of police officer in the U.S.: *Marshals wear uniforms and special badges.*

**2** the officer in charge of a city's fire department

● *verb*

to gather together the people or things you need so you are ready for something: *The general marshaled a large army and marched east.*

### marsh·mal·low

/**marsh**-mel-oh/ *noun* a very soft white or colored candy made of sugar. People sometimes toast marshmallows over a fire.

**marshmallow**

> **Word Origin:** marshmallow
>
> **Marshmallows** used to be made from the root of a plant called a mallow. Mallow plants grew in marshes. Even though marshmallows are not made from marsh mallow plants anymore, the name is still used.

**mar·su·pi·al** /mar-**soop**-ee-uhl/ *noun* a type of animal that carries its babies in a pocket on the front of its body. The pocket is called a pouch: *Kangaroos and koala bears are marsupials.*

**mar·tial arts** /marsh-uhl **arts**/ *plural noun* sports in which you use your hands and feet to fight, such as judo or karate. These sports began as a style of fighting in China and Japan: *Kung Fu is one of the Chinese martial arts.*

**Mar·tin Lu·ther King Day** /mart'n looth-ur **king** day/ *noun* a national holiday in the U.S., on the third Monday of January each year. The holiday honors the birthday of Dr. Martin Luther King, Jr. Dr. King achieved important progress on civil rights for African-Americans in the U.S. He was assassinated in 1968.

**mar·vel·ous** /**marv**-uhl-uhss/ *adjective* very good or enjoyable: *You should go and see the play – it's marvelous.*

**mas·car·a** /ma-**skarr**-uh/ *noun* a dark substance women put on their eyelashes to make them look longer and thicker

**mas·cot** /**mask**-aht/ *noun* something that people have because they think it will bring them good luck: *Our soccer team has a toy bear as a mascot.*

**mas·cu·line** /**mask**-yuhl-in/ *adjective*
**1** having qualities that are typical of a man: *Rob's older now and his voice is deep and masculine.*
**2** in grammar, relating to a man or boy: *"He" is a masculine pronoun.*

**mash** /mash/ *verb* to crush food until it is soft: *Mash the potatoes until they are smooth.*

**mask** /mask/ *noun* something you wear over your face to hide or protect it: *In class, we made masks for the Halloween party.* | *Hospital workers wear masks to prevent the spread of germs.*

**mash**

**mass** /mass/ *noun*
**1** a large amount of something: *The volcano sent a mass of ash and smoke into the air.*
**2** in science, the amount of matter that an object contains: *In science class we used a scale to find the mass of different objects.*
**3** the main religious ceremony in the Roman Catholic Church: *We go to mass in church on Sunday.*

**mas·sa·cre** /**mass**-uhk-ur/
● *verb* to kill a lot of people: *More than 100 people in the village were massacred.*
● *noun* the killing of a lot of people: *The guards shot over 50 people in the massacre.*

**mas·sage** /muh-**sahzh**/
● *noun* if you have a massage, someone presses and rubs your body to help you relax, or to make pain better: *If your back is painful, a massage can relax your muscles and make you feel better.*
● *verb* to give someone a massage

**mas·sive** /**mass**-iv/ *adjective* very big or powerful: *There was a massive earthquake and many houses were destroyed.*

**mast** /mast/ *noun*
**1** a tall pole that the sails of a ship hang from
**2** a tall pole that a flag hangs from

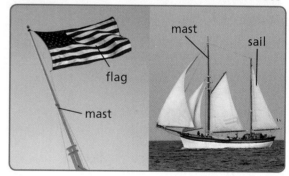

mast

mast

sail

flag

mast

**mas·ter** /**mast**-ur/
● *noun*
**1** a man who a person or animal must obey: *The dog came immediately when his master called.*
**2** someone who is very skilled at something: *All the kids love his books because he's a master of story telling.*
● *verb*
to learn and understand something well: *Japanese is a difficult language to master and it takes many years to learn.*
● *adjective*
most important or biggest: *The house has three smaller bedrooms, as well as the master bedroom.*

**mas·ter·piece** /**mast**-ur-peess/ *noun* a piece of art, literature, or music that is the best someone produced, or one of the best in the world: *He painted many great paintings, but I think this one is his masterpiece.*

**mat** /mat/ *noun*

mat

**1** a piece of thick material that protects something, for example a floor or a table: *Please wipe your feet on the mat when you come in.*
**2** a piece of thick soft material that you put on the floor to protect your body when you exercise or do some sports: *She did a roll on a gym mat.*

mat

**match** /mach/

● *noun*

match

**1** a small stick that you use to light a fire. A match makes a flame when you rub it against a surface: *She took a match from the box and lit the candle.*
**2** something that looks good or goes well with another thing: *The color of this T-shirt is a good match for your skirt.*

The hat and the scarf match.

**3** a game or competition, in some sports: *We're going to watch a soccer match.*
● *verb*
**1** if two things match, they look good or go well together: *The socks don't match.*
**2** to put two things together in a suitable way: *Match the words on the left with the pictures on the right.*
**3** to equal something: *The team played very well last week and they are hoping to match their performance and win again on Saturday.*

**mate** /mayt/
● *noun* a male or female partner for an animal or bird: *Male cats often fight to get a mate.*
● *verb* if animals or birds mate, the male and female come together to breed and make babies: *Birds mate in the spring.*

**ma·te·ri·al** /muh-**teer**-ee-uhl/ *noun*
**1** cloth for making things: *Mom bought some material to make a new dress.*
**2** a solid substance for making things: *Wood, brick, and stone are all building materials.*

**math** /math/ *noun* the short form of mathematics: *Billy's good with numbers so he really likes math.*

**mathe·ma·ti·cian** /math-muh-**tish**-uhn/ *noun* someone who studies or teaches mathematics

**mathe·mat·ics** /math-**mat**-ikss/ *noun* the study of numbers and shapes: *Her favorite subject is mathematics and she is good at doing calculations.* ( SYNONYM: **math** ) ▶ see Thesaurus
—**mathematical** /math-**mat**-ik-uhl/ *adjective* relating to mathematics: *The children are learning to multiply and do simple mathematical problems.*

**mat·i·née** /mat'n-**ay**/ *noun* a performance of a play or movie in the afternoon: *The matinée starts at 2:30 p.m.*

**mat·ter** /**mat**-ur/
● *noun*
**1** something that you need to deal with or discuss: *Your son will have to see the principal because skipping school is a serious matter.*
**2** the material that everything is made of. Matter can be solid, liquid, or gas: *Matter is made of tiny things called atoms.*
**3** reading matter is anything that people read: *There's plenty of good reading matter in the library.*

IDIOM with **matter**
**what's the matter?** what is the problem?: *"What's the matter?" Jo said kindly. "You look upset."*
● *verb*
to be important: *"I'm sorry, I broke a glass." "It doesn't matter."*

**mat·tress** /**mat**-riss/
*noun* the soft part of a bed that you lie on

mattress

mattress

397

a b c d e f g h i j k l **m** n o p q r s t u v w x y z

**ma·ture** /muh-**choor**/

● *adjective*

**1** behaving in a sensible way, like an adult: *Girls grow up faster than boys so they are often more mature.* ( **ANTONYM: immature** )

**2** a mature animal or plant has grown to its full size: *The park has many mature trees that have been here for hundreds of years.*

● *verb*

**1** to begin to behave in a sensible way, like an adult: *At 15, Anna had matured and she was more confident.*

**2** to grow and develop: *The plants mature to eight or ten feet in height.*

—**maturity** /muh-**choor**-uht-ee/ *noun* the state of being mature: *Baby rabbits reach maturity in only five weeks.*

**max·i·mum** /**makss**-uhm-uhm/

● *adjective* biggest or greatest: *The maximum speed this car can do is 130 miles per hour.*

● *noun* the largest number or amount: *You can have a maximum of six players in this game.*
( **ANTONYM: minimum** )

**may** /may/ *verb*

**1** used if something is possible but not certain: *Sara's feeling sick and she may need to see the doctor.*

**2** used for asking or giving permission: *May I use your phone?*

**May** /may/ *noun* the fifth month of the year. May is between April and June: *The field trip is in May. | My birthday is on May 9.*

> ## Word Origin: May
>
> The ancient Romans named many of the months for their gods. **May** is named after the Roman goddess Maia. Maia was the goddess of spring or of the Earth.

**may·be** /**may**-bee/ *adverb* used to say that something is possible but not sure: *"Can you come to my house later?" "Maybe – I'll have to ask Mom."*

**may·on·naise** /**may**-uh-nayz/ *noun* a thick sauce made from egg yolks and oil: *Do you want mayonnaise on your ham sandwich?*

**may·or** /**may**-ur/ *noun* the person who leads the government of a town or city: *He was elected mayor of Abilene.*

**maze** /mayz/ *noun*

**1** a puzzle made of a set of paths or lines that you have to find your way through. A maze can be built of walls or plants, or it can be printed on paper: *The book had mazes and other puzzles.*

**2** a place with many paths or streets that it is difficult to find your way through: *We got lost in the maze of tiny streets in the city.*

maze

**M.D.** /em **dee**/ used after a person's name, to show that he or she has a university degree in medicine. M.D. is short for "Doctor of Medicine": *The doctor's name badge said "Karen Johnson, M.D."*

**me** /mee/ *pronoun* the person who is speaking. You use "me" after a verb or preposition: *He kicked me. | Come and sit by me.*

**mead·ow** /**med**-oh/ *noun* a field with grass: *There were some cows eating grass in the meadow.*

**meal** /meel/ *noun* the food that you eat at regular times each day: *We have three meals a day: breakfast, lunch, and dinner.*

▶ see **Thesaurus**

**meal·time** /**meel**-tīm/ *noun* a time when you have a meal: *The whole family sits down together to eat at mealtimes.*

**mean** /meen/

● *verb* (**meant** /ment/)

**1** to have a meaning: *"Start" and "begin" mean the same thing. | A red light means "stop."*

**2** to want to do something: *Sorry, I didn't mean to step on your foot.* ( **SYNONYM: intend** )

**3** to make something necessary: *The car isn't*

398

*working, so that means we'll have to walk to school.*

● *adjective*

not kind or nice: *The other kids were mean to him and called him names.* ▶ see **Thesaurus**

● *noun*

the average of two or more numbers. You find out the mean by adding the numbers together, and dividing the result by how many numbers there are: *The mean of 3, 8, and 10 is 7 because 3 + 8 + 10 = 21, and 21 divided by 3 is 7.*

**mean·ing** /**meen**-ing/ *noun* the idea that someone wants to say, when using a word or sentence: *The word "bat" has two very different meanings – one is an animal and the other you use in baseball.*

**means** /meenz/ *noun* (plural **means**) a way of doing something: *Email is an important means of communication.*

**meant** /ment/ *verb* the past tense and past participle of **mean**

**mean·time** /**meen**-tīm/ *noun* **in the meantime** during the time when you are waiting for something to happen: *The movie starts in half an hour. In the meantime, let's get some popcorn.*

**mean·while** /**meen**-wīl/ *adverb* while something is happening, or before something happens: *I took the dog for a walk. Meanwhile, my sister fed the rabbits.*

**mea·sles** /**meez**-uhlz/ *noun* a disease that gives you small red spots on your body and a fever. Measles can be serious and children can easily catch it from each other: *He has measles and he has to stay home from school.*

**meas·ure** /**mezh**-ur/

● *verb*

**1** to find out the size or amount of something: *She measured my feet so I could get some new shoes.*
**2** to be a particular size: *My desk measures three feet by two feet.*
**3 measure up** to be good enough: *I wanted to play on the team, but I didn't measure up.*

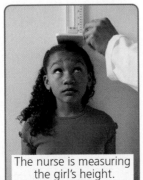

**measure**

The nurse is measuring the girl's height.

● *noun*

**1** an official action that someone does to deal with a problem: *Teachers have taken measures to stop bullying at school.*
**2** something that shows what the size or amount of something is: *Test scores are a measure of a student's progress.*

**meas·ure·ment** /**mezh**-ur-muhnt/ *noun* the length, width, or height of something: *The measurements of the room are 12 feet by 8 feet.*

**meat** /meet/ *noun* the flesh of animals and birds eaten as food: *I don't like beef, but I like other kinds of meat.*

**meat·ball** /**meet**-bol/ *noun* a small round ball made from very small pieces of meat: *We had spaghetti and meatballs for dinner.*

**Mec·ca** /**mek**-uh/ a city in Saudi Arabia that many Muslims visit because they believe it is very holy. The Prophet Muhammad was born in Mecca.

**me·chan·ic** /muh-**kan**-ik/ *noun* someone whose job is to fix vehicles and machines: *A mechanic fixed our car.*

**me·chan·i·cal** /muh-**kan**-ik-uhl/ *adjective* relating to machines: *The plane could not fly because of a mechanical problem.*

**mech·a·nism** /**mek**-uh-niz-uhm/ *noun* a part of a machine that does a specific job: *The car door has a special locking mechanism to stop children from opening it while the car is moving.*

**med·al** /**med**'l/ *noun* a flat piece of metal that someone gets as a prize, or gets for doing something brave: *He won a gold medal in the swimming competition.*
—**medalist** /**med**'l-ist/ *noun* someone who has won a medal: *He won several races and was a medalist at the Olympic Games.*

**medal**

medal

**me·di·a** /**meed**-ee-uh/ *plural noun* television, radio, and newspapers: *Celebrity scandals are always covered by the media.*

a b c d e f g h i j k l **m** n o p q r s t u v w x y z

**me·di·an** /**meed**-ee-uhn/ *noun*
**1** the middle number in a set of numbers that are arranged in order of size: *The median of 3, 9, 11, 13, and 14 is 11.*
**2** (also **me·di·an strip** /meed-ee-uhn **strip**/) a narrow piece of land or a fence that divides a road or highway

**med·ic** /**med**-ik/ *noun* someone in the army who is trained to give medical help

**med·i·cal** /**med**-ik-uhl/ *adjective* relating to illnesses and injuries, and ways of treating them: *She is hurt and needs medical care.*

**med·i·ca·tion** /med-i-**kaysh**-uhn/ *noun* medicine: *My dad takes medication for his heart.*

**med·i·cine** /**med**-uhss-uhn/ *noun*
**1** a pill or a liquid that you take when you are sick to help you get better: *The doctor gave me some medicine to make the pain go away.*
► see **Thesaurus**
**2** the study and treatment of illnesses and injuries: *She wants to study medicine and become a doctor.*

**me·die·val** /mi-**deev**-uhl/ *adjective* from the time between about 400 and 1500 A.D.: *This is a picture of a medieval castle.*

**medieval**

a medieval castle

**me·di·o·cre** /meed-ee-**ohk**-ur/ *adjective* not very good: *I got a C- on the test, which was a mediocre grade.*

**Med·i·ter·ra·ne·an** /med-it-uh-**rayn**-ee-uhn/
● *noun* the sea between northern Africa and southern Europe, and the land around it
● *adjective* in or relating to the area near the Mediterranean: *Mediterranean countries are hot in the summer.*

**me·di·um** /**meed**-ee-uhm/
● *adjective* not big or small, but a size in the middle: *"What size T-shirt do you wear?" "Medium."*
● *noun* (plural **media** /**meed**-ee-uh/) a way of communicating information and ideas to people: *The Internet is a very important medium of communication.*

**meet** /meet/
● *verb* (**met** /met/)
**1** to go to the same place as someone else because you have planned to see each other: *My mom will meet us in front of the school.*
**2** to see and talk to someone without planning to do this: *Guess who I met in the grocery store!*
**3** to see and talk to someone for the first time: *I want you to meet my sister's boyfriend.*
**4** if things meet, they join or touch: *There's a stop sign where the two roads meet.*
**5** to reach your goal: *I wanted to improve my English this semester and I have met my goal.*
**6** to give people what they need: *The school tries to meet the needs of all its students.*
**7 meet with** to have a meeting with someone to talk about something: *My parents met with my teacher to talk about my grades.*
● *noun*
a sports competition with races: *a swim meet*

**meet·ing** /**meet**-ing/ *noun* if people have a meeting, they come together to talk about something: *I have a Cub Scout meeting tonight.*
► see **Thesaurus**

**mega-** /**meg**-uh/

## Word Building

**mega-** is a prefix.
**megabyte**
**mega-** means "million." A *megabyte* is a million bytes, which is a way of saying how much information a computer can store. Sometimes people use **mega-** to mean "very." For example, someone might say that he is *"mega-busy"* or that a movie is *"mega-cool."*

**meg·a·byte** /**meg**-uh-bīt/ *noun*
(ABBREVIATION: **M.B.**) a unit for measuring computer information. A megabyte is equal to 1,024 kilobytes or about a million bytes.

**mel·low** /**mel**-oh/ *adjective* calm, friendly, and

relaxed: *He's very mellow and he doesn't get angry or upset.*

**mel·o·dy** /**mel**-uhd-ee/ *noun* (plural **melodies**) the main notes in a song or piece of music: *The song has a nice melody.* ( SYNONYM: **tune** )

**mel·on** /**mel**-uhn/ *noun* a large juicy fruit with a thick yellow or green skin and lots of flat seeds in the middle

**melon**

seeds

**melt** /melt/ *verb* if something frozen or solid melts, it changes to a liquid when it becomes warmer: *Ice cream starts to melt when you take it out of the refrigerator.* | *Melt some butter in a pan.*

**mem·ber** /**mem**-bur/ *noun* someone who belongs to a group or organization: *I'm a member of the tennis club.*

**mem·ber·ship** /**mem**-bur-ship/ *noun* if you have membership of a group or organization, you are a member: *When you join the tennis club, you get a membership card.*

**mem·o** /**mem**-oh/ (also **mem·o·ran·dum** /mem-uh-**rand**-uhm/) *noun* (plural **memos**) a short note to another person in the same organization: *The principal sent a memo to everyone who works at the school.*

**mem·o·ra·bil·i·a** /mem-uhr-uh-**bil**-ee-uh/ *noun* things that people collect because they are related to a famous person or event: *The museum has a big collection of Civil War memorabilia.*

**mem·ora·ble** /**mem**-ruhb-uhl/ *adjective* something memorable is likely to be remembered: *We wanted to make his birthday party a memorable event, so we made it a surprise.*

**me·mo·ri·al** /muh-**mor**-ee-uhl/
● *adjective* done to remind people of someone who has died: *A memorial service was held in the church for my grandfather, who died last year.*
● *noun* something that is built to remind people

of someone who has died: *The soldiers' names are carved on the war memorial.*

**Me·mo·ri·al Day** /muh-**mor**-ee-uhl day/ *noun* a U.S. national holiday on the last Monday in May. On Memorial Day, we remember soldiers who died in wars.

**mem·o·rize** /**mem**-uh-rīz/ *verb* to learn words, music, or facts so that you can remember them: *The teacher asked us to memorize the poem.*

**mem·ory** /**mem**-ree/ *noun* (plural **memories**)
**1** the ability to remember things: *She has a good memory and she can remember the name of every student in her school.*
**2** something in the past that you remember: *Grandma has many happy memories of her childhood.*
**3** the amount of space that a computer has for keeping information: *My computer has a lot of memory and it's good for playing computer games.*
**4** **in memory of** as a way of remembering someone who has died: *The statue was put up in memory of the soldiers who died.*

> **Word Family:** memory
>
> **memory** *noun* | **memorize** *verb* |
> **memorable** *adjective* | **memorial** *noun*

**men** /men/ *noun* the plural of **man**

**men·ace** /**men**-iss/ *noun* something or someone that is dangerous or frightening: *Drivers who speed are a menace on the roads.*

**mend** /mend/ *verb*
**1** to fix a hole in a piece of clothing: *Mom mended a hole in my jeans.*
**2** to heal: *It will take a few months for a broken arm to mend.*

**me·no·rah** /muh-**nor**-uh/ *noun* a special candlestick that holds seven candles, used in Jewish ceremonies

**men's room** /**menz** room/ *noun* a room in a public place with toilets for men

**men·stru·ate** /**menss**-troo-ayt/ *verb* if a woman menstruates, blood flows out of her body every month
—**menstruation** /menss-troo-**aysh**-uhn/ *noun* the time each month when blood flows out of a woman's body

**-ment** /muhnt/

> ### Word Building
>
> **-ment** is a suffix. It changes the root word into a noun.
>
> agree**ment** | disappoint**ment** | govern**ment** | move**ment** | pay**ment**
>
> **-ment** means "result of." An *agreement* is when people agree on something. A *movement* is what you do when you move. A *payment* is when someone pays you.

**men·tal** /**ment**'l/ *adjective* involving the mind: *Some children have mental problems and they suddenly become angry for no reason.*

**men·tal·ly ill** /**ment**'l-ee **il**/ *adjective* having an illness of the mind: *My dad works in a special hospital for people who are mentally ill.*
—**mental illness** /**ment**'l **il**-niss/ *noun* an illness of the mind that makes someone behave in strange ways: *She suffers from a mental illness that makes her feel very depressed.*

**men·tion** /**mensh**-uhn/
• *verb* to say something, usually without giving a lot of information: *She mentioned that it was her birthday next week.*

> **IDIOM with mention**
> **not to mention** used when you are adding something better, bigger, or more surprising: *He's really good at baseball, not to mention soccer and basketball.*

• *noun* the act of saying something, without giving a lot of information: *She made no mention of her brother's illness.*

**men·u** /**men**-yoo/ *noun*
**1** a list of the food that you can eat in a restaurant: *I looked at the menu and ordered a hamburger.*
**2** a list of things that you can ask your computer to do: *Go back to the main menu and click on print.*

**me·ow** /mee-**ow**/
• *verb* if a cat meows, it makes a crying sound: *The cat stood by the food dish and meowed.*
• *noun* the crying sound that a cat makes

**mer·chan·dise** /**murch**-uhn-dīz/ *noun* things that are being sold in a store: *The store sells a wide range of merchandise, including clothing and toys.*

**mer·chant** /**murch**-uhnt/ *noun* a person who buys and sells things: *Merchants set up stalls on the streets and sell postcards and souvenirs.*

**mer·ci·ful** /**murss**-i-fuhl/ *adjective* kind and forgiving: *The king was merciful and he did not punish the man for what he had done.*

**mer·cu·ry** /**murk**-yuhr-ee/ *noun* a silver-colored liquid metal that is used in thermometers. The symbol for mercury is Hg.

**Mer·cu·ry** /**murk**-yuhr-ee/ *noun* the first planet from the sun. Mercury is the smallest planet.
► see picture at **solar system**

**mer·cy** /**murss**-ee/ *noun* kindness and a willingness to forgive people: *He admitted that he was guilty, but he begged the judge for mercy.*

**merge** /murj/ *verb* to join together to form one thing: *The two companies will merge to form one big company.*

**me·rid·i·an**
/muh-**rid**-ee-uhn/ *noun* a line that goes from the North Pole to the South Pole on a map: *A meridian is about 20,000 kilometers long.*

**meridian**

meridian

**me·ringue** /muh-**rang**/ *noun* a light sweet food made by mixing sugar and the white part of eggs: *lemon meringue pie*

**mer·it** /**merr**-it/
• *noun* a good feature that something has: *We talked about the merits of the two schools, and decided that my school has the best sports facilities.*
• *verb* to deserve something: *The movie wasn't very good and didn't merit all the attention it got on TV.*

**mer·maid** /**mur**-mayd/ *noun* a woman in stories who has a fish's tail instead of legs

**mer·ry** /**merr**-ee/ *adjective* (**merrier**, **merriest**) happy: *Merry Christmas!*

**mer·ry-go-round** /**merr**-ee goh rownd/ *noun* a machine that turns around, that children ride on for fun. It often has wooden horses or vehicles on it that you sit on: *Anna rode a white horse on the merry-go-round.*

**merry-go-round**

**mess** /mess/
● *noun*
**1** if a place or a group of things is a mess, it is not neat or clean: *The room was a mess with toys and clothes everywhere.* | *My hair is a mess.*
**2** a situation in which there are a lot of problems: *Dave's life was a mess and he needed someone to help him sort out his problems.*
● *verb*
**1 mess around** to play or do silly things when you should be working or paying attention: *The teacher told him to stop messing around in class.*
**2 mess up** to do something badly or make a mistake: *I messed up the test and got a bad grade.*
**3 mess up** to make something dirty or messy: *The wind had messed her hair up.*
**4 mess with** to use something or change something in a way that causes problems: *Someone was messing with my computer and now it will not work right.*

**mes·sage** /**mess**-ij/ *noun* information that you send or give to another person: *My mother can't come to the phone. Can I take a message for her?*

**mes·sen·ger** /**mess**-uhnj-ur/ *noun* someone who takes packages or messages to other people

**Mes·si·ah** /muh-**sī**-uhr/ *noun* Jesus Christ in the Christian religion, or the leader sent by God to save the world in the Jewish religion

**mess·y** /**mess**-ee/ *adjective* (**messier**, **messiest**) dirty or not neat: *My room is very messy – there are toys and clothes all over the floor.*

**messy**

a messy room

**met** /met/ *verb* the past tense and past participle of **meet**

**me·tab·o·lism** /muh-**tab**-uh-liz-uhm/ *noun* the chemical process in your body that changes food into the energy that you need to do things: *Exercise helps to speed up your metabolism and helps you to lose weight.*

**met·al** /**met**'l/ *noun* a hard substance, such as iron, gold, or steel, that is good at conducting electricity and heat. Metals are found inside the Earth: *The bicycle frame is made of metal.* —**metallic** /muh-**tal**-ik/ *adjective* made of metal, or similar to metal: *metallic objects*

**met·al de·tec·tor** /**met**'l di-tekt-ur/ *noun* a machine used for finding metal. Metal detectors are used at airports to check if people are carrying weapons.

**met·al·loid** /**met**'l-oyd/ *noun* a chemical element that is not a metal but has some of the qualities of a metal. Silicon and arsenic are metalloids.

**met·a·morph·ic** /met-uh-**morf**-ik/ *adjective* metamorphic rocks are formed when heat and pressure are put on other types of rock. This happens deep inside the Earth. The heat or pressure changes the structure of the rock: *Marble is a metamorphic rock that forms from limestone.*

**met·a·morph·o·sis** /met-uh-**morf**-uhss-iss/ *noun* the changes that some types of animals go through as they develop. For example, a caterpillar goes through a metamorphosis when it changes into a butterfly.

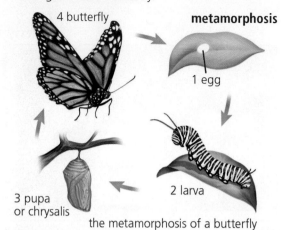

4 butterfly

**metamorphosis**

1 egg

3 pupa or chrysalis

2 larva

the metamorphosis of a butterfly

**met·a·phor** /**met**-uh-for/ *noun* a way of describing something in which you talk about a completely different thing that has the same qualities: *The sentence "She cried a river of tears" uses a metaphor. It tells you that she cried a lot because a river has a lot of water in it.*
—**metaphorical** /met-uh-**for**-ik-uhl/ *adjective* relating to or using a metaphor: *Poetry often uses metaphorical language.*

**me·te·or** /**meet**-ee-ur/ *noun* a piece of rock or metal that burns very brightly when it falls from space into the air around the Earth: *A meteor flashed across the night sky.*

**me·te·or·ite** /**meet**-ee-uh-rīt/ *noun* a small piece of a meteor that has landed on the Earth

**meteorite**

**me·te·or·ol·o·gy** /meet-ee-uh-**rahl**-uhj-ee/ *noun* the scientific study of the weather: *We're learning about meteorology and how some types of clouds make rain.*
—**meteorologist** /meet-ee-uh-**rahl**-uhj-ist/ *noun* someone whose job is to study the weather

**me·ter** /**meet**-ur/ *noun*
**1** ( ABBREVIATION: **m.** ) a unit in the metric system for measuring length, equal to 100 centimeters or 39.37 inches: *She is 1.68 meters tall.*

**2** a machine that measures the amount of something you have used: *A man came to read the gas meter.*

## Word Building

metric | diameter | geometry | thermometer

These words all have the Greek word root **meter** or **metr** in them. **Meter** means "measure." The *metric* system is used to measure weight, length, temperature, etc. *Geometry* is a kind of math that measures shapes and angles. A *thermometer* measures how hot or cold something is.

**meth·ane** /**meth**-ayn/ *noun* a gas with no color or smell, which can be burned to give heat. Rotting plants produce methane.

**meth·od** /**meth**-uhd/ *noun* a way of doing something: *We tried different methods for sticking the papers together: glue, tape, and staples.*

**me·thod·i·cal** /muh-**thahd**-ik-uhl/ *adjective* doing things in a careful and well organized way: *You should do your math problems in a methodical way, so that you don't make mistakes.*

**me·tic·u·lous** /muh-**tik**-yuhl-uhss/ *adjective* extremely careful to make sure that every small detail is right: *He's very meticulous about his appearance and he polishes his shoes every day.*
—**meticulously** /muh-**tik**-yuhl-uhss-lee/ *adverb* in a meticulous way: *The kitchen had been meticulously cleaned and there was no dirt anywhere.*

**met·ric sys·tem** /**metr**-ik sist-uhm/ *noun* the system of measuring that is based on meters, grams, and liters
—**metric** /**metr**-ik/ *adjective* using the metric system: *Centimeters and kilograms are metric units.*

**met·ric ton** /metr-ik **tuhn**/ *noun* a unit for measuring weight, equal to 1,000 kilograms or about 2,205 pounds

**met·ro·pol·i·tan** /metr-uh-**pahl**-uht'n/ *adjective* in or belonging to a big city: *The New York City metropolitan area includes Manhattan, Queens, Brooklyn, and the other boroughs.*

a b c d e f g h i j k l **m** n o p q r s t u v w x y z

**Mex·i·can** /**mekss**-ik-uhn/
● *adjective* from Mexico: *Mexican food* | *the Mexican government*
● *noun* someone from Mexico: *There are several Mexicans in my class.*

**mg** the written abbreviation of **milligram**

**mice** /mīss/ *noun* the plural of **mouse**

**micro-** /mīk-roh/

### Word Building

**micro**be | **micro**chip | **micro**phone | **micro**scope

These words all have the Greek word root *micro* in them. *Micro* means "small." A *microbe* is a living thing that is very small. A *microscope* is a piece of equipment that you look through. It lets you see very small things such as microbes. A *microphone* makes a small sound much bigger or louder.

**mi·crobe** /**mīk**-rohb/ *noun* a very small living thing that you cannot see without a microscope. Some microbes can cause disease. Other microbes help you to digest food.
( SYNONYM: **microorganism** )

**mi·cro·chip** /**mīk**-roh-chip/ *noun* a small part of a computer or a machine. It contains the electronic parts that control what the machine does. ( SYNONYM: **chip** )

**mi·cro·org·an·ism** /mīk-roh-**org**-uhn-iz-uhm/ *noun* a living thing that is so small that it cannot be seen without a microscope: *Germs and bacteria are microorganisms.* ( SYNONYM: **microbe** )

**mi·cro·phone**
/**mīk**-ruh-fohn/ *noun* a piece of equipment that you talk into. You use a microphone to make your voice sound louder, or to record your voice: *The singer held the microphone next to his mouth.*

microphone

microphone

**mi·cro·scope** /**mīk**-ruh-skohp/ *noun* a piece of equipment that makes very small things look bigger, so you can study them: *In class today we looked at some pond water under a microscope.*

microscope

**mi·cro·scop·ic** /**mīk**-ruh-skahp-ik/ *adjective* very small and difficult to see: *The air that we breathe contains microscopic particles of dust.*

**mi·cro·wave** /**mīk**-ruh-wayv/
● *noun* (also **mi·cro·wave ov·en** /mīk-ruh-wayv **uhv**-uhn/) a machine that cooks food very quickly: *I'll warm some milk up for you in the microwave.*
● *verb* to cook something in a microwave: *You can microwave the popcorn.*

**mid**, mid- /mid/

### Word Building

**mid-** is a prefix.
**mid**dle | **mid**night | **mid**way | **Mid**west
**Mid-** means "middle." *Midnight* (12 o'clock at night) is in the middle of the night. If you leave *midway* through a movie, you leave in the middle of the movie. The *Midwest* is the central part of the United States. **Mid-** is often used to mean the middle of a period of time, for example *mid-January* or *midafternoon*.

**mid·air** /mid-**air**/ *noun* in **midair** in the air or sky: *The balloon was floating in midair above the city.*

**mid·day** /**mid**-day/ *noun* the middle of the day, around 12:00: *At midday the sun is high in the sky and it feels very hot.*

**mid·dle** /**mid**′l/

● *noun*

**1** the part that is closest to the center of something: *David was standing in the middle of the room.*

SYNONYM: **center**

▶ see **Thesaurus**

**middle**

the middle drawer

**2** the part that is halfway between the beginning and the end: *I've reached the middle of the book – it's 300 pages long and I'm on page 150. | She heard a strange noise in the middle of the night.*

● *adjective*

closest to the center of something: *The middle drawer is the one between the top one and the bottom one.*

**mid·dle class** /mid′l **klass**/ *noun* **the middle class** the group of people in a country who are not rich but not poor either: *Most teachers and nurses belong to the middle class.*

—**middle-class** /**mid**′l klass/ *adjective* belonging to or involving the middle class: *He comes from a middle-class family and his parents are both teachers.*

**Mid·dle East** /mid′l **eest**/ *noun* the part of Asia that is between the Mediterranean Sea and the Arabian Sea, and includes countries such as Egypt and Iran

**mid·dle school** /**mid**′l skool/ *noun* a school in the U.S. for students between the ages of 10 and 14, or in grades 5 or 6 through 8

**midg·et** /**mij**-it/ *noun* a rude word for someone who is very short

**mid·night** /**mid**-nīt/ *noun* 12 o'clock at night: *We stayed up until midnight on New Year's Eve.*

**midst** /midst/ *noun* **in the midst of** in the middle of something: *We stood in the midst of the crowd.*

**mid·way** /mid-**way**/ *adjective, adverb*

**1** at the middle point between two places: *The town is midway between Joliet and Chicago.*

**2** in the middle of a period of time or an event: *Smith scored midway through the first quarter of the game.*

**Mid·west** /mid-**west**/ *noun* the central area of the U.S.: *Iowa and Minnesota are in the Midwest.*

—**Midwesterner** /mid-**west**-urn-ur/ *noun* someone from the Midwest

**might** /mīt/

● *verb*

**1** used for talking about what was or is possible: *They might have made a mistake. | I might be able to go to the party.*

**2** used for giving advice or making a suggestion: *You might try asking your brother for help. | You might not need a coat today.*

● *noun*

strength and power: *She tried with all her might to open the door.*

**might·y** /**mīt**-ee/ *adjective* strong and powerful: *The house was shaken by a mighty wind.*

**mi·graine** /**mī**-grayn/ *noun* a very bad headache: *People who suffer from migraines feel sick and have pain behind their eyes.*

**mi·grant** /**mīg**-ruhnt/ *noun* someone who goes to another area or country in order to find work: *Migrants come in the winter to pick oranges.*

**mi·grate** /**mī**-grayt/ *verb*

**1** if birds or animals migrate, they travel to a warmer part of the world in winter and return in spring: *The birds migrate south in the winter.*

**2** if people migrate, they move to another area or country in order to find work: *People migrated to the cities in search of work.*

—**migration** /mī-**graysh**-uhn/ *noun* the act of migrating somewhere: *The birds were returning from their winter migration.*

**Word Family:** migrate

**migrate** *verb* | **migration** *noun* | **migrant** *noun*

**mike** /mīk/ *noun* a microphone: *Shania held the mike and began to sing.*

**mild** /mīld/ *adjective*

**1** not very severe or serious: *She has a mild case of the flu, so she should be better soon.*

SYNONYM: **slight**

**2** having a taste that is not strong or spicy: *I like the mild salsa, not the really hot stuff.*

**3** mild weather is not too hot and not too cold:

*Usually it's pretty cold in March, but this year it has been mild.*

**mile** /mīl/ *noun* a unit for measuring distance, equal to 5,280 feet, 1,760 yards, or about 1,609 meters: *The school is three miles away, so I take the bus.*

**mile·age** /**mīl**-ij/ *noun*
**1** the number of miles that a car has traveled since it was new or since a certain time: *Mom drives a lot for work, so the mileage on our car is pretty high.*
**2** the number of miles a car can travel using one gallon of gasoline: *Dad's car gets pretty good mileage – 25 miles to the gallon.*

**mil·i·tar·y** /**mil**-uh-tair-ee/
● *adjective* relating to or used by the army, navy, or air force: *This military airplane flies faster than the speed of sound.*
● *noun* a country's army, navy, or air force: *My uncle is in the military – he is a captain in the army.*

**mi·li·tia** /muh-**lish**-uh/ *noun* a group of people who have weapons and can fight like soldiers, but who are not part of an army

**milk** /milk/
● *noun* a white liquid that female animals make to feed their babies. People drink the milk from cows: *I drank a glass of milk and ate some cookies. | The baby bear drinks its mother's milk.*
● *verb* to take milk from a cow or goat: *The farmer has to milk the cows every day.*

**milk·shake** /**milk**-shayk/ *noun* a cold drink made from milk, ice cream, and fruit or chocolate: *My favorite milkshake is strawberry.*

**Milk·y Way** /milk-ee **way**/ *noun* **the Milky Way** the pale white band of stars that you can see across the sky at night. The stars of the Milky Way form the galaxy that the Earth and Sun are part of.

**mill** /mil/ *noun*
**1** a factory where materials such as paper, steel, or cotton cloth are made: *In the mill, steel is made into flat sheets.*
**2** a building containing a large machine for crushing grain into a powder, or the machine itself: *They make flour in the mill.*
**3** a small machine for crushing coffee beans or pepper

**mil·let** /**mil**-uht/ *noun* a plant similar to grass, with small seeds that are used as food

**mil·li·gram** /**mil**-uh-gram/ *noun*
( ABBREVIATION: **mg** ) a unit for measuring weight. There are 1,000 milligrams in a gram.

**mil·li·li·ter** /**mil**-uh-leet-ur/ *noun*
( ABBREVIATION: **ml** ) a unit for measuring liquids. There are 1,000 milliliters in a liter.

**mil·li·me·ter** /**mil**-uh-meet-ur/ *noun*
( ABBREVIATION: **mm** ) a unit in the metric system for measuring length. There are 1,000 millimeters in a meter.

**mil·lion** /**mil**-yuhn/ *number*
**1** 1,000,000: *The company made $75 million last year. | Almost four million people now live in Los Angeles.*
**2** (also **millions**) a very large number of people or things: *I'm very busy and I have millions of things to do today.*

IDIOM with **million**
**not/never in a million years** used when saying that something is impossible: *I wouldn't have known the right answer in a million years.*
—**millionth** /**mil**-yuhnth/ *number* 1,000,000th or 1/1,000,000

**mil·lion·aire** /mil-yuh-**nair**/ *noun* someone who is very rich and has more than one million dollars: *He wants to become a millionaire before he's 30.*

**mim·ic** /**mim**-ik/ *verb* (**mimicking**, **mimicked**) to copy the way someone speaks or behaves, especially to make people laugh: *My sister is very good at mimicking other people's voices.*

**min-** /min/, **mini-** /min-ee/

**Word Building**
**min-** or **mini-** is a prefix.
**mini**ature | **min**imum | **mini**skirt | **min**ority | **min**us
**min-** or **mini-** means "small." A *miniature* camera is very small. A *miniskirt* is a very short skirt. A *minority* group is smaller than other groups of people.

**mind** /mīnd/

● *noun*

your thoughts, or the part of your brain you use for thinking and imagining things: *His mind was full of ideas for stories he wanted to write.*

▶ see **Thesaurus**

IDIOMS with **mind**

**change your mind** to change your opinion or decision about something: *I said I'd go to the park with them, but I changed my mind and didn't go.*

**make up your mind** to decide something: *I couldn't make up my mind what kind of ice cream to have.*

**be out of your mind** to be crazy: *When I said I wanted to climb the mountain, my friends all thought I was out of my mind.*

● *verb*

**1 do you mind/would you mind** used to ask politely if you can do something or if someone will do something: *Do you mind if I use your phone to call my dad?* | *Would you mind opening the window?*

**2 I wouldn't mind (doing) something** used when saying that you want to do something: *I wouldn't mind going to the beach today.*

**3 doesn't mind/don't mind** used when saying that someone is not annoyed or upset about something: *Are you sure your mom doesn't mind if I stay for dinner?*

**mine** /mīn/

● *pronoun*

the thing that belongs to the person who is speaking: *Can I borrow your pen? I lost mine.* | *A friend of mine gave me the book.*

● *noun*

**1** a deep hole in the ground from which people dig things such as coal and gold: *He worked in a mine, digging coal.*

**2** a type of bomb under the ground or in the ocean. It explodes when something touches it: *The ship hit a mine and sank.*

● *verb*

to dig something, such as gold or coal, out of the ground: *In the 1850s, thousands of people came to California to mine for gold.*

**min·er** /**mīn**-ur/ *noun* someone who digs into a hole in the ground for something such as coal or gold: *Coal miners work deep under the ground.*

**min·er·al** /**min**-uhr-uhl/ *noun* a natural

substance such as iron or salt that is found in the Earth and in some foods: *Water has minerals such as calcium in it.*

**min·er·al wa·ter** /**min**-uhr-uhl wot-ur/ *noun* water that you can buy in bottles. It comes from under the ground and has minerals in it

**min·gle** /**ming**-guhl/ *verb*

**1** if smells, sounds, or feelings mingle, they mix together: *My curiosity at seeing the snake was mingled with fear.*

**2** to meet and talk with a lot of different people, for example at a party: *The children from the different classes mingled at the dance.*

**min·i** /**min**-ee/ *noun* a very short skirt

SYNONYM: **miniskirt**

**min·i·a·ture** /**min**-ee-uhch-ur/ *adjective* smaller than other things of the same kind: *When we were learning about towns, we made miniature houses and stores.*

**min·i·mal** /**min**-uhm-uhl/ *adjective* very small in amount: *The accident caused minimal damage.*

**Word Family:** minimal

**minimum** *noun* | **minimum** *adjective* | **minimize** *verb* | **minimal** *adjective*

**min·i·mize** /**min**-uh-mīz/ *verb* to make the amount of something as small as possible: *Wash your hands often to minimize the risk of catching illnesses.*

**min·i·mum** /**min**-uhm-uhm/

● *adjective* smallest or lowest: *The minimum age for voting is 18.*

● *noun* the smallest number or amount: *You have to go to the airport a minimum of two hours before your flight.* ANTONYM: **maximum**

**min·i·mum wage** /min-uhm-uhm **wayj**/ *noun* the lowest amount of money that the person you work for can legally pay you for one hour of work: *The pizza restaurant pays its workers minimum wage.*

**min·ing** /**mīn**-ing/ *noun* the job or industry of digging something such as gold or coal out of the ground: *There is a lot of coal in this area and mining is an important industry.*

**min·i·skirt** /**min**-ee-skurt/ *noun* a very short skirt

**min·is·ter** /**min**-uhst-ur/ *noun*
**1** a religious leader in some Christian churches: *Pastor Green was the minister at my sister's wedding.*
**2** a politician who is in charge of a government department in some countries: *He is the Russian Foreign Minister.*

**min·is·try** /**min**-uhss-tree/ *noun* (plural **ministries**)
**1** the work of being a church leader: *My uncle joined the ministry and now has a church in Atlanta.*
**2** a government department in some countries

**mi·nor** /**min**-ur/
● *adjective*
small or not very important: *We've had a few minor problems with our car. For example, last month it needed a new front tire.*
( ANTONYM: **major** )
● *noun*
**1** someone who is younger than 18: *It's illegal to sell cigarettes to minors.* ( ANTONYM: **adult** )
**2** the second main subject that you study in college: *Her major is biology and her minor is psychology.*
● *verb*
**minor in** to study a second main subject in college: *She likes languages, so she majored in French and minored in Spanish.*

**mi·nor·i·ty** /muh-**nor**-uht-ee/ *noun* (plural **minorities**)
**1** a small part of a larger group of people or things: *Only a minority of students failed the test – 2 students out of 30.* ( ANTONYM: **majority** )
**2** a group of people whose race or religion is different from that of most people in a country: *The school has children from several minority groups, including Latinos and Asians.*

**mint** /mint/ *noun*
**1** a candy with a strong fresh taste: *Eating mints makes your breath smell fresh.*
**2** a plant with leaves that have a strong smell and taste. The leaves are used to give food a mint taste: *mint ice cream with chocolate chips* —**minty** /**mint**-ee/ *adjective* tasting like mint: *The chewing gum has a minty flavor.*

mint

**mi·nus** /**mīn**-uhss/
● *preposition*
used in math to show that you are subtracting one number from another: *Ten minus two equals eight (10 – 2 = 8).* ( ANTONYM: **plus** )
● *noun*
a minus sign ( ANTONYM: **plus** )
● *adjective*
**1 A minus, B minus, etc.** (also **A-, B-,** etc.) a grade for a piece of work that is slightly lower than a grade A, a grade B, etc.: *I got a B- on my history report.*
**2 minus 5, minus 20, etc.** (also **-5, -20,** etc.) 5, 20, etc. less than zero in temperature: *The temperature can go as low as minus 40 in the winter.*

**mi·nus sign** /**mīn**-uhss sīn/ *noun* the sign (-) that shows that you should subtract one number from another, or that a number is less than zero

**min·ute**
● *noun* /**min**-it/
**1** a measure of time equal to 60 seconds. There are 60 minutes in an hour: *It takes me about ten minutes to walk to school.*
**2** a very short period of time: *Wait there, I'll be back in a minute.* ( SYNONYM: **moment** )
**3 minutes** a written record of the things people say during a meeting: *I couldn't go to the meeting, so I read the minutes afterwards.*

IDIOMS with **minute**
**any minute (now)** very soon: *The movie will start any minute now.*
**at the last minute** at the latest possible time: *I was going to go to the party, but I changed my mind at the last minute*
● *adjective* /mī-**noot**/
very small: *The bacteria are minute and can only be seen through a microscope.* ( SYNONYM: **tiny** )

a
b
c
d
e
f
g
h
i
j
k
l

**m**

n
o
p
q
r
s
t
u
v
w
x
y
z

**min·ute hand** /**min**-it hand/ *noun* the long thin piece of metal that points to the minutes on a clock or watch: *The minute hand pointed to the three, and the hour hand pointed to the one, so it was 1:15.*

**min·ute·man** /**min**-it-man/ *noun* one of a group of men who were not soldiers but who were ready to fight at any time during the Revolutionary War in the U.S.

**mir·a·cle** /**mirr**-uhk-uhl/ *noun*
**1** something lucky that happens, which you did not think was possible: *It's a miracle that she wasn't killed in the accident.*
**2** an event that seems impossible and that people think was done by God: *The saint healed his blindness and performed many other miracles.*
—**miraculous** /mi-**rak**-yuhl-uhss/ *adjective* very good and very unexpected: *She made a miraculous recovery from her injuries and she is completely better now.*

**mi·rage** /mi-**rahzh**/ *noun* something that you think you can see, but is not really there. Mirages are caused by hot air, especially in the desert: *I thought I could see some trees in the distance, but it was actually a mirage.*

**mir·ror** /**mirr**-ur/ *noun* a piece of special glass that you look at when you want to see yourself: *Lauren was sitting in front of the mirror combing her hair.*

**Word Origin:** mirror

The word **mirror** comes from the Latin word **mirare**, which means "to look at."

**mirror**

She is looking at herself in the mirror.

**mis-** /miss/

**Word Building**

**mis-** is a prefix.
**mis**behave | **mis**lead | **mis**spell | **mis**take | **mis**understand
**mis-** means "wrong" or "bad." If you *misbehave*, you behave badly. A *misspelled* word is a word that is spelled wrong. If you *misunderstand* what I say, you do not understand me correctly.

**mis·be·have** /miss-bi-**hayv**/ *verb* to behave badly: *He misbehaves in class: he won't stay in his seat and he is always talking.*
—**misbehavior** /miss-bi-**hayv**-yuhr/ *noun* bad behavior: *Misbehavior such as fighting on the playground will be punished.*

**mis·cel·la·ne·ous** /miss-uh-**layn**-ee-uhss/ *adjective* of many different kinds: *There were a few miscellaneous books on the shelf: a book of poems, a dictionary, and a book about animals.*

**mis·chief** /**miss**-chif/ *noun* bad behavior by children that can be annoying or funny, but does not cause harm: *He's always getting into mischief. Yesterday he tied everyone's shoes together.*
—**mischievous** /**miss**-chuhv-uhss/ *adjective* a mischievous child behaves badly, but in a way that makes people laugh: *She had a mischievous grin on her face as she teased him.*

**mis·er·a·ble** /**miz**-uhr-uhb-uhl/ *adjective*
**1** very unhappy: *I felt miserable after getting a bad grade in the test.*
**2** very bad: *It's been cold and rainy and miserable all week.*
—**miserably** /**miz**-uhr-uhb-lee/ *adverb* in a miserable way: *She stared miserably at the rain outside the window.*

**mis·er·y** /**miz**-uhr-ee/ *noun* a lot of unhappiness: *The war caused a lot of misery as houses were bombed and food was hard to get.*

**mis·for·tune** /miss-**forch**-uhn/ *noun* bad luck, or something that happens because of bad luck: *He had the misfortune to break his leg when he fell off his bicycle.*

**mis·in·ter·pret** /miss-in-**turp**-rit/ *verb* to think

that what someone says or does means something different from what he or she really means: *She misinterpreted my joke and thought I was being serious.*

—**misinterpretation** /miss-in-turp-ruh-**taysh**-uhn/ *noun* the act of misinterpreting something: *A misinterpretation of the school rules has caused a lot of problems.*

**mis·lead** /mis-**leed**/ *verb* (**misled** /miss-**led**/) to make someone believe something that is not true, by not giving all the information or by giving wrong information: *He misled his mom by letting her think he was staying late at school when he was really going to the mall.*

—**misleading** /mis-**leed**-ing/ *adjective* likely to make someone believe something that is not true: *The sign is misleading – it makes you think the school is very close, when really it is on the other side of the town.*

**mis·place** /miss-**playss**/ *verb* to put something somewhere and then forget where you put it: *Grandpa is always misplacing his glasses.*
(SYNONYM: **lose**)

**mis·print** /**miss**-print/ *noun* a word in a book or magazine that is printed incorrectly: *There's a misprint here. It should read "He ate a mousse" not "He ate a mouse."*

**miss** /miss/
● *verb*
**1** to not do something because you forget about it or are doing something else: *I missed a whole week of school because I was sick.*
**2** to be too late for something: *We missed the beginning of the movie because we were late.*
**3** to feel sad because someone is not with you, or because you are away from a place where you feel happy: *I missed my sister when she was at camp.* | *He misses living in New York.*
**4** to not hit or catch something: *He missed the free throw.*
**5** to not see, hear, or understand something: *What did she say? I missed it.* | *He missed the point and and didn't understand what the teacher was telling him to do.*
**6 miss out** to not do something that you will enjoy: *Don't miss out on the fun! Come to the school fair tomorrow!*
● *noun*
**1 Miss** used in front of the family name of a girl

or a woman who is not married: *Miss Johnson is my teacher.*
**2** an action in which you try to hit or catch something but fail: *He hit ten balls without a miss.*

miss

He missed the bus.

He missed the goal.

**mis·sile** /**miss**-uhl/ *noun* a weapon that flies a long way and explodes when it hits something: *The planes fired missiles at the tanks and destroyed them.*

**miss·ing** /**miss**-ing/ *adjective* something or someone that is missing is not in the correct place and is hard to find: *Dad's keys are missing.* | *The police have found the missing child.*

**mis·sion** /**mish**-uhn/ *noun*
**1** an important job that someone has been given to do: *The soldiers' mission was to destroy the bridge.*
**2** a trip in a space vehicle: *The spacecraft went on a mission to Mars.*
**3** a church that was started by missionaries: *The California missions were begun by Spanish missionaries who wanted the Indians to become Christians.*

**mis·sion·ar·y** /**mish**-uh-nair-ee/ *noun* (plural **missionaries**) someone who goes to another country in order to teach people about his or her religion: *He went to Africa as a missionary to teach about Christianity.*

**mis·spell** /miss-**spel**/ *verb* to spell a word wrong: *It's easy to misspell "walk" because the "l" is silent.*

—**misspelling** /miss-**spel**-ing/ *noun* a word that is spelled wrong: *Go over your writing and correct your misspellings.*

**mist** /mist/ *noun* a thin cloud that is close to the ground, and that makes it difficult for you to see very far: *You can't see the mountain because of the early morning mist.*

**mis·take** /mi-**stayk**/
● *noun*

**1** something that is not correct: *I made two mistakes on the math test.* (SYNONYM: **error**)
▶ see **Thesaurus**

**2** something you do that you later find out was not the right thing to do: *It was a mistake to trust him; he lied to me.*

IDIOM with **mistake**
**by mistake** without intending to do something: *I opened your letter by mistake.*
(SYNONYM: **accidentally**)
(ANTONYMS: **on purpose, deliberately**)

● *verb* (**mistook** /mi-**stuk**/, **mistaken** /mi-**stayk**-uhn/)
to think that one thing is something else because the two things look, sound, or seem very similar: *She mistook the man for a police officer and asked him for help.*

**mis·tak·en** /mi-**stayk**-uhn/ *adjective* wrong about something: *He couldn't have been there. You must be mistaken.*

—**mistakenly** /mi-**stayk**-uhn-lee/ *adverb* because someone has made a mistake: *I mistakenly took the wrong bus.*

**mist·y** /**mist**-ee/ *adjective* if it is misty, there is a lot of mist in the air, making it hard to see very far: *It was misty, so we couldn't see across the lake.*

**mis·un·der·stand** /miss-und-ur-**stand**/ *verb* (**misunderstood** /miss-und-ur-**stud**/) to not understand something correctly: *I misunderstood what he said, and went to Jim's house at the wrong time.*

**mis·un·der·stand·ing** /miss-und-ur-**stand**-ing/ *noun*

**1** a problem caused by someone not understanding a question, situation, or instruction: *The teacher gave clear instructions so there wouldn't be any misunderstanding.*

**2** a disagreement that is not very serious: *My parents had a small misunderstanding about how much allowance I should get.*

**mitt** /mit/ *noun* a big leather glove that you use to catch a ball in baseball or softball

**mit·ten** /**mit**'n/ *noun* a piece of clothing that keeps your hand warm. Mittens have one part for your thumb and another part for all your other fingers together: *She pulled on a pair of mittens.*

**mitten**

**mix** /mikss/
● *verb*

**1** to put different things together to make one new thing: *You can make glue by mixing flour and water.* | *I mix red and blue paint together to make purple.*

**2 mix up** to make a mistake and think that someone or something is another person or thing: *I mixed up the dates. I thought your birthday was this Thursday, not next Thursday.*

**3 mix up** to put things in the wrong order: *I mixed up the letters and spelled "right" as "rihgt."*

● *noun*
different things or people together in a place: *There was a good mix of people at the party – young and old, girls and boys.*

**mixed num·ber** /mikst **nuhm**-bur/ *noun* a whole number and a fraction, for example 2¾

**mix·ture** /**mikss**-chur/ *noun*

**1** a substance you make by mixing different things together: *Stir the mixture in the pan until it is smooth.*

**2** several different things together: *He felt a mixture of fear and anger.*

**ml** the written abbreviation of **milliliter**

**mm** the written abbreviation of **millimeter**

**moan** /mohn/
● *verb*

**1** to make a long low sound because part of your body hurts or because you are unhappy: *Her leg was hurting her a lot and she was*

*moaning with pain.*
**2** to complain about something in an annoying way: *Sam's always moaning because he has to get up early to go to school.*
● *noun*
a long low sound that you make because part of your body hurts or because you are unhappy: *His leg hurt and he let out a moan.*

**moat** /moht/ *noun* a deep hole that was dug around a castle and filled with water. The moat helped protect the castle.

**mob** /mahb/ *noun* a large group of people who are noisy or angry: *A mob of people were pushing to get through the stadium gates.*

**mo·bile** /**mohb**-uhl/
● *adjective* able to move: *The mobile health clinic goes into different neighborhoods each week.*
—**mobility** /moh-**bil**-uht-ee/ *noun* the ability to move from place to place: *The invention of the car gave people more mobility.*
● *noun* a decoration that has objects hanging from wires or string, so that they move in the wind: *The mobile has lots of pretty paper fish hanging from wires.*

**mo·bile home** /mohb-uhl **hohm**/ *noun* a small metal house that can be moved on a truck
SYNONYM: **trailer**

**moc·ca·sin** /**mahk**-uhss-uhn/ *noun* a shoe with no heel that is made of soft leather. Native Americans wore moccasins.

**Word Origin: moccasin**

**Moccasin** comes from a Native American language. When English people came to America, they did not have a name for this kind of shoe. So they used the name the Native Americans used.

**mock** /mahk/
● *verb* to laugh at someone in a way that is not nice: *The other children mocked her because she spoke with a funny accent.*
● *adjective* not real: *The actors took part in a mock battle.*

**mock·ing·bird** /**mahk**-ing-burd/ *noun* a gray and white bird that copies the songs of other birds. Mockingbirds live in North and South America. ▶ see picture on page **A4**

**mo·dal verb** /mohd-uhl **vurb**/ (also **mo·dal aux·il·ia·ry** /mohd-uhl ok-**zil**-uhr-ee/) *noun* a word such as "can," "might," or "must" that usually comes before another verb: *In the sentence "I might go to the party," "might" is a modal verb.*

**mode** /mohd/ *noun* the most common number in a set of numbers: *The mode of 1, 2, 2, 2, 3, 3, 4, 4, and 5 is 2.*

**mod·el** /**mahd**'l/

**model**

● *noun*
**1** a small copy of something that you build or make: *He is making a clay model of a horse.*
**2** a beautiful person who wears new clothes in fashion shows and magazines: *Some fashion models are very thin.*

a model boat

**3** one type of car or machine that a company makes: *Dad is changing his car for a newer model.*
**4** someone who lets an artist paint, draw, or photograph him or her: *The teacher is looking for models for the art class.*
**5** a description that a scientist uses to explain how something works or show what will happen: *They created a computer model that showed how the world's population would grow.*
● *adjective*
**1** a model vehicle or building is a small copy of a vehicle or building that you put together from separate parts: *I'm making a model airplane and we're going to fly it in the park.*
**2** a model student, child, citizen, or employee works or behaves in the best way: *Ethan is a model student and works very hard.*
● *verb*
**1** to wear new clothes in fashion shows or magazines: *She models clothes for a fashion magazine.*
**2 model on** to copy the way another thing is done: *The new math book is modeled on one children use in Japan.*

**mo·dem** /**mohd**-uhm/ *noun* a piece of computer equipment. A modem sends information from one computer to another using telephone wires.

**mod·er·ate** /**mahd**-uhr-it/ *adjective* not extreme: *Run at a moderate speed – not too fast and not too slowly.* ( SYNONYM: **medium** )

**mod·ern** /**mahd**-urn/ *adjective*
**1** belonging to the present time: *The modern world is very different from the world that people lived in 100 years ago.*
**2** using the most recent designs, methods, and ideas: *The gym is very modern and they have all the latest sports equipment.*
( ANTONYMS: **old-fashioned, traditional** )
▶ see **Thesaurus**

**mod·ern·ize** /**mahd**-ur-nīz/ *verb* to change something and make it newer: *The school modernized the classrooms and put in new computers.*

**mod·est** /**mahd**-ist/ *adjective*
**1** not talking too proudly about your abilities or the things you have done: *She wins all her races, but she is modest and doesn't talk about it much.*
**2** not very big: *They live in a modest house with two bedrooms.*
—**modestly** /**mahd**-ist-lee/ *adverb* in a modest way: *"I was lucky to win," she said modestly.*
—**modesty** /**mahd**-uhst-ee/ *noun* the quality of being modest

**mod·i·fi·er** /**mahd**-uh-fī-ur/ *noun* a word that gives more information about another word in a sentence: *In the sentence "He walked slowly," "slowly" is a modifier. It gives more information about "walked."*

**mod·i·fy** /**mahd**-uh-fī/ *verb* (**modifies, modified**)
**1** to make small changes to something: *He modified his car to make it go faster.*
**2** if one word in a sentence modifies another, it gives more information about it: *In the sentence "I'm reading a good book," "good" modifies "book."*
—**modification** /mahd-uhf-uh-**kaysh**-uhn/ *noun* a small change that you make to something: *They made several modifications to improve the computer system.*

**moist** /moyst/ *adjective* a little wet: *It had rained a little, and the ground was moist.*
—**moisten** /**moyss**-uhn/ *verb* to make something moist: *She moistened her lips with her tongue.*

**mois·ture** /**moyss**-chur/ *noun* small amounts of water that make something a little wet: *There's always a lot of moisture on the bathroom windows after I have had a shower.*

**mois·tur·ize** /**moyss**-chuh-rīz/ *verb* to put a substance on your skin to make it soft: *My mom moisturizes her face every day.*
—**moisturizer** /**moyss**-chuh-rīz-ur/ *noun* a lotion that you use to make your skin soft

**mo·lar** /**mohl**-ur/ *noun* one of the large teeth in the back of your mouth

**mo·las·ses** /muh-**lass**-iz/ *noun* a thick sweet brown liquid that you use in cooking: *These cookies are made with molasses.*

**mold** /mohld/
● *noun*
**1** a fungus that grows on old food and on things that are warm and wet: *The old cheese was covered in mold.*
**2** a container that you pour liquid into. When the liquid becomes solid, it has the shape of the container: *She poured the Jell-O into the ring-shaped mold.*
—**moldy** /**mohld**-ee/ *adjective* covered in mold: *Bread becomes moldy after a few days.*
● *verb*
to give a substance a shape by pressing it or putting it in a mold: *Mold the clay into balls.*

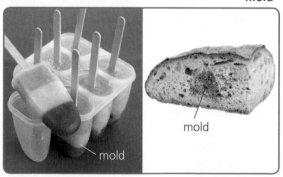

mold

mold

mold

**mole** /mohl/ *noun*
**1** a small dark brown spot on your skin: *He has a mole on his face.*
**2** a small animal with black fur. Moles live in holes in the ground: *Moles cannot see very well.*

mole

**mol·e·cule** /**mahl**-uh-kyool/ *noun* the smallest amount of a substance that can exist separately. Molecules are made of atoms: *A molecule of water has two hydrogen atoms and one oxygen atom.*
—**molecular** /muh-**lek**-yuhl-ur/ *adjective* relating to molecules: *The model shows the molecular structure of salt.*

**mol·lusk** /**mahl**-uhsk/ *noun* a creature with a soft body and no spine, which usually has a shell. A snail is a mollusk.

**molt** /mohlt/ *verb* if a bird or animal molts, its feathers, hair, or skin come off. New feathers, hair, or skin grow instead: *Moose molt after the winter and lose their thick coats.*

**mol·ten** /**mohlt**-uhn/ *adjective* molten metal or rock is liquid because it is very hot: *Molten rock flowed out of the volcano.*

**mom** /mahm/ *noun* mother: *My mom and dad were out.*

**Word Origin:** mom

**Mom** is an American word that started to be used in the late 1800s. It comes from "mama." One of the first sounds a baby makes is "ma ma ma," and many languages have a word for mother that sounds a little like this.

**mo·ment** /**mohm**-uhnt/ *noun*
**1** a very short period of time: *For a moment, I couldn't think of anything to say.* | *He'll be back in a moment.* (SYNONYM: **minute**)
**2** a particular point in time: *Just at that moment, Shelly came in.* (SYNONYM: **minute**)

IDIOMS with **moment**
**at the moment** now: *I'm not doing anything at the moment.*
**for the moment** now or for a short time: *The rain has stopped for the moment.*

**mo·men·tar·y** /**mohm**-uhn-tair-ee/ *adjective* lasting only a short time: *There was a momentary pause in the conversation, and then they started talking again.*
—**momentarily** /mohm-uhn-**tair**-uhl-ee/ *adverb* for a very short time, or very soon: *She will be here momentarily – she is in a meeting.*

**mo·men·tum** /moh-**ment**-uhm/ *noun* the force that makes something continue to move: *If you roll a ball down a hill, it goes faster as it gains momentum.*

**mom·my** /**mahm**-ee/ *noun* (plural **mommies**) mother: *I want my mommy!*

**mon·arch** /**mahn**-urk/ *noun* a king or queen: *Queen Elizabeth II is the British monarch.*
—**monarchy** /**mahn**-urk-ee/ *noun* the system of having a king or queen: *Britain has a monarchy and the official ruler is the queen.*

**mon·as·ter·y** /**mahn**-uhss-tair-ee/ *noun* (plural **monasteries**) a place where monks live

**Mon·day** /**muhnd**-ee/ *noun* (ABBREVIATION: **Mon.**) the second day of the week. Monday is between Sunday and Tuesday. Most people start school or work on a Monday: *I go back to school on Monday.* | *I have swimming lessons Monday afternoon.*

**Word Origin:** Monday

**Monday** comes from an Old English word that means "moon's day." Monday is the moon's day in many different languages.

**mon·ey** /**muhn**-ee/ *noun* coins and pieces of paper that you use to buy things: *He earns money by washing cars for his neighbors.*
► see **Thesaurus**

**mon·i·tor** /**mahn**-uht-ur/
● *noun*
**1** the part of a computer that shows words or pictures: *The computer has a big monitor, so it is good for watching movies.* (SYNONYM: **screen**)
► see picture at **computer**
**2** a machine that is used to see if something changes: *The patient is connected to a heart monitor that measures her heart rate.*
**3** a student who does a particular job at school: *The hall monitor told the other kids to get to class.*
● *verb*
to carefully watch or measure something to see if it changes: *Your teacher will monitor your work during the year and help you make progress.*

**monk** /muhngk/ *noun* a man who belongs to a religious group of men who live together. Monks live in buildings called monasteries.

**mon·key** /**muhngk**-ee/
*noun* an animal with a long tail. Monkeys have hands and feet that can hold onto things. Monkeys live in hot countries and climb trees: *I saw a monkey at the zoo.*

monkey

**mon·key bars**
/**muhngk**-ee barz/ *plural noun* a set of metal bars. Children hold onto a bar and swing from it to the next bar: *The boy is swinging from the monkey bars.*

**mon·key wrench** /**muhngk**-ee rench/ *noun* a tool for turning metal nuts. You can move part of a monkey wrench so that it will hold nuts of different widths: *The plumber used a monkey wrench to tighten the pipe.*

**mono-** /mahn-oh/

## Word Building

carbon **mono**xide | **mono**logue | **mono**tonous

These words all have the Greek word root **mono-** in them. **Mono-** means "one." *Carbon monoxide* is a type of gas. The molecule that the gas is made of has one oxygen atom. A *monologue* in a play or movie is a speech that one person says, when that person is not talking to anyone else. If something is *monotonous*, it is boring because you are only doing one thing for a long time.

**mon·o·logue** /**mahn**'l-og/ *noun* a long speech by one person in a play or movie: *The actor had a long monologue about why he loves Juliet.*

**mon·o·nu·cle·o·sis** /mahn-oh-nook-lee-**ohss**-iss/ *noun* a disease that makes you feel weak for a long time. It gives you a fever and a sore throat. Mononucleosis most often affects teenagers.

**mo·nop·o·ly** /muh-**nahp**-uhl-ee/ *noun* (plural **monopolies**) if a company has a monopoly, it is the only company that sells or does something: *It is the only company that makes the tools, and it has a monopoly.*

**mo·not·o·nous** /muh-**naht**'n-uhss/ *adjective* boring and always the same: *The monotonous sound of the engine made him fall asleep.* —**monotony** /muh-**naht**'n-ee/ *noun* a monotonous quality: *I hate the monotony of long car trips.*

**mon·soon** /mahn-**soon**/ *noun* the time when it rains a lot in India and other parts of Asia. Winds blowing from the ocean in the summer bring the rain.

**mon·ster** /**mahnst**-ur/
● *noun*
**1** a frightening creature in stories: *The monster had two heads and six legs.*
**2** a very bad person: *Only a monster would hurt a child.*
● *adjective*
very big: *I can see a monster fish behind the boat.*

## Word Origin: monster

The word **monster** comes from a Latin word that means both "monster" and "sign of something bad." From about 1000 to 1200 in English, monsters were very big animals or animals that had things wrong with them when they were born. People thought that these animals were a sign that bad things would happen. In the late 1300s, people started using the word monster about imaginary animals such as centaurs, which have the head of a person and the body of a horse. Now we use monster to mean a scary creature.

**month** /muhnth/ *noun*
**1** one of the 12 parts of a year: *January is the first month of the year.*
**2** about 30 days: *I haven't seen Michael for over a month.*

**month·ly** /**muhnth**-lee/ *adjective, adverb* happening every month: *It's a monthly magazine – you get 12 issues a year.*

**mon·u·ment** /**mahn**-yuh-muhnt/ *noun* something that is built so that people will remember an important event or person: *There is a monument to the people who died in the war.*

**moo** /moo/
● *noun* the sound that a cow makes

● *verb* to make the sound that a cow makes: *The cows mooed loudly.*

**mood** /mood/ *noun* the way you feel now, for example whether you are happy or sad: *Dad was in a good mood and bought us ice cream.*

**moody** /**mood**-ee/ *adjective* if you are moody, your feelings change often: *My sister is very moody. One minute she's happy and the next minute she's upset about something.*

**moon** /moon/ *noun*
**1** the round object in the sky that you see at night. The Moon moves around the Earth once each month and it reflects light from the Sun: *The Moon was shining brightly in the night sky.*
**2** a round object that moves around other planets: *Saturn has several moons.*

moon

new moon | waxing crescent | first quarter | waxing gibbous
full moon | waning gibbous | last quarter | waning crescent

the phases of the moon

**moon·light** /**moon**-līt/
● *noun* the light from the Moon: *The lake looked silver in the moonlight.*
● *verb* to do a second job: *He's a firefighter, but he moonlights as a mechanic.*

**moose** /mooss/ *noun*
(plural **moose**) a wild animal that looks like a very big brown deer. A moose has large flat antlers (=hard parts that grow from its head). Moose live in forests in cold areas: *The antlers of an adult moose may be more than five feet across.*

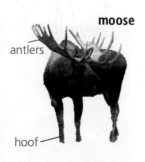
moose
antlers
hoof

**Word Origin:** moose

**Moose** comes from a Native American language. The word it comes from means something like "he pulls off," because moose pull the bark off trees and eat it.

**mop** /mahp/
● *noun*
a tool you use to wash floors. A mop is a long stick with soft material on the end: *He picked up the mop and a bucket of water and started washing the floor.*
● *verb* (**mopping, mopped**)
**1** to wash a floor with a mop: *Sweep the floor before you mop it.*
**2** to get liquid off something using a mop or cloth: *I need to mop up some juice. Can you pass a cloth?*

**mope** /mohp/ *verb* to be unhappy and bored, and not want to do anything: *Since his girlfriend left him, he's been moping around the house all day.*

**mor·al** /**mor**-uhl/
● *adjective*
**1** relating to what is right and wrong: *My parents have high moral standards and they expect me to always be honest.*
**2** a moral action is good and right: *The moral thing to do is to give back the money you took.*
(ANTONYM: **immoral**)
—**morally** /**mor**-uhl-ee/ *adverb* according to what is right and wrong: *Stealing from other people is morally wrong.*
● *noun*
**1 morals** someone's ideas about what is right and wrong: *He refuses to tell a lie – he says it's against his morals.*
**2** something that you learn from a story or from something that happens: *The moral of the story is: Never give up.*

**Word Family:** moral

**moral** *adjective* | **immoral** *adjective* | **morality** *noun*

**mo·rale** /muh-**ral**/ *noun* how happy and confident a group of people are: *The team's morale is low after losing several games.*

417

**mo·ral·i·ty** /muh-**ral**-uht-ee/ *noun* ideas about what is right and wrong: *Many people get their sense of morality from what their religion teaches them.*

**more** /mor/
● *adverb*
**1** having a larger amount of a quality: *The other book was much more interesting.* | *The test was more difficult than I expected.* (ANTONYM: **less**)
**2** a larger amount, a longer period, or a greater number of times: *I promise to help more with the housework.* (ANTONYM: **less**)

⌐ IDIOM with **more**
**more or less** about or almost: *The houses were all more or less the same.*
(SYNONYMS: **approximately, roughly**)

● *adjective, pronoun*
**1** an additional amount or number: *Can I have some more milk?* | *Mom gave him $5 but he wanted more.* | *More of the students are sick today.*
**2** a larger amount or number: *I have more money than my sister.* | *More than 400 people came to the school fair.* (ANTONYMS: **less, fewer**)

**more·o·ver** /mor-**ohv**-ur/ *adverb* used when you are giving more information: *You have worked hard this year. Moreover, you have made excellent progress.*
(SYNONYMS: **furthermore, in addition**)

**morn·ing** /**morn**-ing/ *noun*
**1** the part of the day before 12 noon: *She gets up at 7:00 every morning.* | *In the morning, I cleaned up my room.*
**2** (also **good morning**) you say this when you meet someone in the morning: *Morning, Mom. What's for breakfast?*

**Morse code** /morss **kohd**/ *noun* a way of sending messages using sounds or flashes of light. A group of short and long signals (dots and dashes) is used for each letter: *In Morse code, dot dot dot means S.*

**mort·gage** /**morg**-ij/ *noun* money that you borrow from a bank to buy a house: *They are paying off a big mortgage.*

**mo·sa·ic** /moh-**zay**-ik/ *noun* a pattern or picture made of small pieces of stone, glass, or pottery: *Some Roman houses had mosaics on the floors.*

**Mos·lem** /**mahz**-luhm/ *noun* another spelling of Muslim

**mosque** /mahsk/ *noun* a building where Muslims go to pray and learn about their religion: *We go to the mosque on Fridays to pray.*

mosque

**mos·qui·to** /muh-**skeet**-oh/ *noun* (plural **mosquitoes**) a small flying insect that bites people, drinks blood, and spreads disease: *A mosquito bit me on the leg.*

mosquito

**Word Origin:** mosquito

In Spanish, **mosquito** means "little fly." The word came into English in the 1500s, after the discovery of the New World. Before this, mosquitoes were called "gnats" in English, and we still use that word for some small flying insects that bite.

**moss** /moss/ *noun* a soft green plant that grows on trees and rocks: *The old stone wall was covered in moss.*

moss
moss
Moss is growing on the rocks.

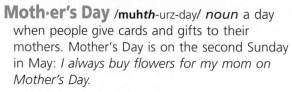

**most** /mohst/
● *adverb*
**1** having the largest amount of a quality: *I think Yosemite is the most beautiful place in the world. | Who is most likely to win?*
( ANTONYM: **least** )
**2** more than anything or anyone else: *Which poem do you like the most?* ( ANTONYM: **least** )
● *adjective, pronoun*
**1** almost all: *Most kids like animals. | Most of the children had finished the test.*
**2** the largest amount or number: *Miguel made the most baskets in the game. | Ten dollars is the most I can give you.*

> **IDIOMS with most**
> **at the most** not more than: *I'll be gone 20 minutes at the most.*
> **make the most of** to use a chance to do something in the best way you can: *You're lucky to go to volleyball camp; I hope you make the most of it.*

**most·ly** /**mohst**-lee/ *adverb*
**1** usually: *I mostly get up late on Sundays.*
**2** almost all: *My mother's relatives mostly live in Costa Rica.*

**mo·tel** /moh-**tel**/ *noun* a place you can stay in when you are traveling, that has a place for your car near your room: *We stopped at a motel for the night.*

**moth** /moth/ *noun* an insect with wings that flies at night: *Moths are flying around the light.*

moth

**moth·er** /**muhth**-ur/ *noun* your female parent: *He kissed his mother.*
—**motherhood** /**muhth**-ur-hud/ *noun* the state of being a mother: *She is 18 and she does not feel ready for motherhood.*

**moth·er-in-law** /**muhth**-ur in lo/ *noun* (plural **mothers-in-law**) the mother of someone's husband or wife

**moth·er-of-pearl** /**muhth**-ur uhv purl/ *noun* a pale shiny substance on the inside of some shells, used for making buttons and jewelry: *She is wearing a mother-of-pearl necklace.*

**Moth·er's Day** /**muhth**-urz-day/ *noun* a day when people give cards and gifts to their mothers. Mother's Day is on the second Sunday in May: *I always buy flowers for my mom on Mother's Day.*

**moth·er tongue** /**muhth**-ur tuhng/ *noun* the first language that you learn when you are a child. Your mother tongue is your main language: *He speaks English at school, but his mother tongue is Spanish.*

**mo·tion** /**mohsh**-uhn/ *noun* movement: *The motion of the boat made her feel sick.*

**mo·tion·less** /**mohsh**-uhn-liss/ *adjective* not moving: *The boy was lying motionless on the ground after he fell out of a tree.*

**mo·tion pic·ture** /**mohsh**-uhn **pik**-chur/ *noun* a movie: *The book is going to be made into a motion picture.*

**mo·ti·vate** /**moht**-uh-vayt/ *verb* to make you want to do something: *What motivated you to start learning to play the piano?*
—**motivation** /moht-uh-**vaysh**-uhn/ *noun* a reason for wanting to do something: *She wants to help her family, so her motivation is strong.*

**mo·tive** /**moht**-iv/ *noun* the reason why someone does something: *The motive for the crime was probably to get money.*

**mo·tor** /**moht**-ur/ *noun* the part of a machine that makes it work or move: *The boat's motor was very noisy.*

**mo·tor·boat** /**moht**-ur-boht/ *noun* a small boat with an engine

**motorboat**
seat — windshield — control panel
— light
— handrail
drainage hole
stern
bow
porthole
cabin
engine
propeller

a b c d e f g h i j k l **m** n o p q r s t u v w x y z

**mo·tor·cy·cle** /**moht**-ur-sīk-uhl/ *noun* a fast vehicle with two wheels and an engine: *My mom thinks that motorcycles are really dangerous.*

**mo·tor home** /**moht**-ur hohm/ *noun* a big vehicle with furniture and a kitchen in it. People drive and live in motor homes on vacation.

**mo·tor·ist** /**moht**-uhr-ist/ *noun* someone who drives a car: *Snow on the roads is causing problems for motorists.* (SYNONYM: **driver**)

**mot·to** /**maht**-oh/ *noun* (plural **mottoes**) a few words that show someone's main goal or rule: *The motto of the Boy Scouts is "Be Prepared."*

**mound** /mownd/ *noun*
**1** a pile of something: *There is a big mound of earth next to the hole.*
**2** in baseball, the small hill that you stand on to throw the ball toward the batter

**mount** /mownt/ *verb*
**1** to get on a horse or bicycle: *He mounted his horse and rode away.*
**2** to increase: *The fans' excitement is mounting as they wait for the game to begin.*
**3** to attach something to a wall, board, or piece of paper: *The teacher is going to mount the children's pictures on the wall.*

**Mount** /mownt/ *noun* used before the name of a mountain: *Mount Everest*

**moun·tain** /**mownt**-uhn/ *noun*
**1** a very high hill: *Mount McKinley is the highest mountain in North America.* | *We are going camping in the mountains.* ▶ see **Thesaurus**
**2** a large amount of something, especially work: *Mom still has a mountain of ironing to do.*
—**mountainous** /**mownt**-uhn-uhss/ *adjective* a mountainous place has many mountains

**mountain**

peak

**moun·tain bike** /**mownt**-uhn bīk/ *noun* a bicycle that you can ride over rough ground. A mountain bike has thick tires and a strong frame.

**moun·tain li·on** /**mownt**-uhn lī-uhn/ *noun* a large brown wild cat. Mountain lions live in the mountains of western North and South America.

**mourn** /morn/ *verb* to feel very sad because someone has died.

**motorcycle**

mirror

handlebars

seat/saddle

gas tank

fender

wheel

engine

exhaust pipe

**mouse** /mowss/ *noun*
**1** (plural **mice** /mīss/) a small animal with a long tail. Mice live in buildings or fields: *A little mouse ran across the kitchen floor.*
**2** (plural **mouses** or **mice** /mīss/) a small thing that you use to control a computer. You move the mouse with your hand: *Click the right button of your mouse.*
▶ see picture at **computer**

mouse

**mouse·trap** /**mowss**-trap/ *noun* a small trap that you use to catch mice in a house

**mousse** /mooss/ *noun*
**1** a cold sweet food made by mixing cream, eggs, and fruit or chocolate: *We had chocolate mousse for dessert.*
**2** a substance that you put in your hair to keep it in a particular style

**mouth** /mowth/ *noun* (plural **mouths** /mouthz/)
**1** the part of your face that you use for speaking and eating: *His mouth was full of cake.*
▶ see picture on page **A13**
**2** the part of a river where it joins the ocean: *New Orleans is at the mouth of the Mississippi, where it flows into the Gulf of Mexico.*
**3** the entrance to a cave, canyon, harbor, or tunnel: *He stepped into the mouth of the cave.*

**mouth·ful** /**mowth**-ful/ *noun* an amount of food or drink that you put in your mouth: *She drank another mouthful of soup.*

**mouth·wash** /**mowth**-wahsh/ *noun* a liquid you use to clean your mouth and make it smell good

**mov·a·ble** /**moov**-uhb-uhl/ *adjective* able to be moved: *The doll's arms and legs are movable.*

**move** /moov/
● *verb*
**1** to go from one place or position to another: *He moved toward the door.* | *The wind makes the clouds move across the sky.*
▶ see Thesaurus
**2** to go to live somewhere else: *We moved here from Boston.* | *Carla moved away, and I never saw her again.*
**3** to put something in a different place or position: *Move your chair over here.*

● *noun*
**1** a movement that someone makes: *Don't make a move! Stay where you are!*
**2** the action of moving an object in a game, for example in chess: *I've had my turn. It's your move now.*
**3** something that you do in order to achieve something: *Asking Dad to help us was a good move.*

**move·ment** /**moov**-muhnt/ *noun*
**1** the action of moving from one place or position to another: *In the game, you copy the movements of the leader. So, if she rubs her head, you rub your head.*
**2** a group of people who want to change something in society: *Dr. King was one of the leaders of the Civil Rights Movement and he worked hard to get equal rights for all Americans.*

**mov·ie** /**moov**-ee/ *noun*
**1** moving pictures that tell a story: *Have you seen the movie "The Wizard of Oz?"*
▶ see Thesaurus
**2 go to the movies** to go to a movie theater to see a movie: *Do you want to go the movies with me on Saturday?*

**mov·ing** /**moov**-ing/ *adjective* making you feel a strong emotion: *The book is the moving story of a young boy who has cancer.*

**mow** /moh/ *verb* (**mowed**, **mowed** or **mown** /mohn/) to cut grass with a machine: *Dad is mowing the lawn.*
—**mower** /**moh**-ur/ *noun* a machine that you use to cut grass: *The grass needs cutting but our lawn mower's broken.*

mow

**MP3** /em pee **three**/ *noun* a type of computer file that contains music. You can get MP3 files from the Internet: *He was listening to songs on his MP3 player.*

**mph** /em pee **aych**/ the abbreviation of **miles per hour**, used to say how fast something is moving: *The car was going at 60 mph.*

**Mr.** /**mist**-ur/ used before a man's family name: *This is Mr. Brown.*

**Mrs.** /**miss**-iz/ used before the family name of a married woman: *Our English teacher is named Mrs. Bell.*

**Ms.** /miz/ used before a woman's family name. This word does not show if the woman is married or not: *The letter was addressed to Ms. Garcia.*

**much** /muhch/
- *adverb*
a lot: *My brother is much taller and stronger than me.* | *I didn't like her much.* | *Thank you very much.*
- *adjective, pronoun*
**1** a lot of something: *Hurry up – we don't have much time.*
**2** **how much** used to ask about an amount or price: *How much cake do you want?*
**3** **too much** more than you need or want: *I ate too much ice cream.*

> ## Word Choice: much, many, a lot of
>
> In sentences with "not," you can use **much** or **many** instead of **a lot of**.
>
> **Much** is used with nouns that are things you cannot count: *There isn't much milk left.*
>
> **Many** is used with nouns that show there is more than one thing or person: *There weren't many people in the room.*
>
> **A lot of** can be used with both kinds of nouns: *There isn't a lot of milk left.* | *There weren't a lot of people in the room.*

**mud** /muhd/ *noun* wet earth: *Joe got mud all over his pants.*
—**muddy** /**muhd**-ee/ *adjective* covered with mud: *Take your muddy shoes off before stepping inside this house!*

mud

The boots are covered in mud.

**muf·fin** /**muhf**-uhn/ *noun* a small sweet type of cake with a round top. Muffins often have fruit in them: *I had a blueberry muffin for breakfast.*

muffin

**mug** /muhg/
- *noun* a large cup with straight sides and a handle. Mugs are used for hot drinks: *a coffee mug*
- *verb* (**mugging**, **mugged**) to attack and rob someone: *She was mugged outside her apartment by a man with a gun.*

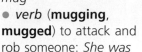

mug

—**mugging** /**muhg**-ing/ *noun* an attack in which someone is mugged: *There have been a lot of muggings in this area so be careful.*
—**mugger** /**muhg**-ur/ *noun* someone who attacks and robs people

**mug·gy** /**muhg**-ee/ *adjective* (**muggier**, **muggiest**) if it is muggy, it is hot and the air has a lot of water in it: *I can't sleep on muggy summer nights.*

**Mu·ham·mad** /mu-**ham**-uhd/ the man who started the religion of Islam in the 7th century A.D.

**mule** /myool/ *noun* an animal whose parents are a horse and a donkey: *We rode on mules to the bottom of the canyon.*

**multi-** /**muhlt**-ee/

> ## Word Building
>
> **multi-** is a prefix.
> **multi**cultural | **multi**media | **multi**ple | **multi**racial
> **multi-** means "many." A *multicultural* city is a city with people from many different cultures. A *multimedia* show uses many different things to give you information, for example pictures, sounds, and words. If something happens *multiple* times, it happens many times.

**mul·ti·cel·lu·lar or·gan·ism** /muhlt-i-sel-yuhl-ur **org**-uhn-iz-uhm/ *noun* a living thing which is made of many cells

**mul·ti·cul·tur·al** /muhlt-ee-**kuhl**-chuhr-uhl/ *adjective* including people or things from many different cultures: *We live in a multicultural society and people of all nationalities live together.*

**mul·ti·me·di·a** /muhlt-i-**meed**-ee-uh/ *adjective*
using pictures, video, and music as well as
words: *Modern computer games use multimedia
sound effects and videos to make the game
seem real.*

**mul·ti·ple** /**muhlt**-uhp-uhl/
• *adjective* many: *The school has multiple
copies of this book, at least five in every class.*
• *noun* a number that you can get by
multiplying a smaller number: *20 is a multiple of
5 because 4 x 5 = 20.*

**mul·ti·ple-choice** /muhlt-uhp-uhl **choyss**/
*adjective* a multiple-choice question on a test
shows you several answers. You must choose the
right answer: *It's a multiple-choice test, and
every question will have three answers to choose
from.*

**mul·ti·pli·ca·tion sen·tence**
/muhlt-uh-pluh-**kaysh**-uhn sent-uhnss/ *noun* the
numbers and signs that show a multiplication
problem and its answer: *5 x 2 = 10 is a
multiplication sentence.*

**mul·ti·pli·ca·tion ta·ble**
/muhlt-uh-pluh-**kaysh**-uhn tayb-uhl/ *noun* a list that
shows the results when you multiply a number
by a set of other numbers, usually the numbers 1
to 10. For example, the multiplication table for 3
is 1 x 3 = 3, 2 x 3 = 6, 3 x 3 = 9 etc.
( SYNONYM: **times table** )

**mul·ti·ply** /**muhlt**-uh-plī/ *verb* (**multiplies,
multiplied**)
**1** if you multiply a number, you add it to itself a
particular number of times: *4 multiplied by 5 is
20 (= 4 x 5 = 20).*
**2** if things multiply, there are then a lot more of
them: *Insects multiply in the summer.*
—**multiplication** /muhlt-uh-pluh-**kaysh**-uhn/ *noun*
the process of multiplying numbers: *The
multiplication problem was 3 x 6 = ?*

**mul·ti·ra·cial** /muhlt-i-**raysh**-uhl/ *adjective*
including people of many different races: *The
U.S. has a multiracial society that includes people
from all over the world.*

**mum·ble** /**muhm**-buhl/ *verb* to say something
quietly and not clearly: *The boy was mumbling
because he was nervous and I couldn't
understand what he was saying.*

**mum·my** /**muhm**-ee/ *noun* (plural **mummies**) a

dead body that is wrapped in cloth and treated
with special chemicals, in order to preserve it.
This method of preserving bodies was popular in
ancient Egypt.

**mumps** /muhmpss/ *noun* an illness that makes
your throat and neck swell and become painful.
You can catch the mumps from other people and
it can sometimes be dangerous: *When I had the
mumps I was off school for two weeks.*

**munch** /muhnch/ *verb* to eat something noisily
or steadily: *She was munching potato chips.*

**mu·nic·i·pal** /myoo-**niss**-uhp-uhl/ *adjective*
relating to the government of a town or city: *He
ran for mayor in the municipal elections.*

**mu·ral** /**myoor**-uhl/ *noun* a large painting on a
wall: *Our class painted a mural on one of the
school walls.*

mural

**mur·der** /**murd**-ur/
• *noun* the crime of killing someone on
purpose: *He went to prison for committing two
murders.*
• *verb* to kill someone deliberately: *Was she
murdered, or was it an accident?*

**mur·der·er** /**murd**-uhr-ur/ *noun* a person who
murders someone: *The murderer spent the rest
of his life in prison.* ( SYNONYM: **killer** )

**mur·mur** /**murm**-ur/
• *verb* to say something in a quiet gentle voice:
*"Goodnight. Sleep well," she murmured.*
• *noun* quiet talking or a quiet sound that
continues: *I could hear the murmur of the ocean
splashing against the beach.*

**a b c d e f g h i j k l m n o p q r s t u v w x y z**

**mus·cle** /**muhss**-uhl/ *noun* a part of your body that helps you to move. Some muscles move bones, and some move other parts such as your mouth: *Running will make your leg muscles stronger.*

### Word Origin: muscle

**Muscle** comes from a Latin word that means "little mouse." You can see the muscles in your arm move. People thought the movement looked like a little mouse moving under your skin.

**mus·cu·lar** /**muhsk**-yuhl-ur/ *adjective*
**1** having big strong muscles: *He has big muscular arms and he is good at lifting weights.*
**2** relating to your muscles: *It is a muscular disease that affects your ability to move.*

**mu·se·um** /myoo-**zee**-uhm/ *noun* a building where people can go and see art or other important or valuable objects: *There's a photography exhibit at the museum.*

**mush** /muhsh/ *noun* something that is soft and wet: *The apples had rotted and turned to mush.*

**mush·room** /**muhsh**-room/ *noun* a type of fungus with a stem and a round top. Some kinds of mushrooms can be eaten: *We had a ham and mushroom pizza.* ▶ see picture on page **A7**

**mu·sic** /**myooz**-ik/ *noun*
**1** the sounds that people make when they play instruments or sing: *Mom put on a CD so we could listen to music while we cleaned the house.* ▶ see **Thesaurus**
**2** the marks on paper that tell you what music to play or sing: *I'm learning to read music – this note is an E.*

**mu·si·cal** /**myooz**-ik-uhl/
● *adjective*
**1** relating to music: *His musical career started when he was just nine years old.*
**2** good at playing music or singing: *She's very musical and can play three instruments.*
● *noun*
a play or movie that has songs and dancing in it: *"High School Musical" helped make musicals popular with kids again.*

**mu·si·cal in·stru·ment** /myooz-ik-uhl **inss**-truh-muhnt/ *noun* something such as a piano or a guitar that you play in order to make nice sounds ▶ see pictures on page **A8**

**mu·si·cian** /myoo-**zish**-uhn/ *noun* someone who plays or sings music well, or as a job: *The musicians in the orchestra are all very good.*
▶ see **Thesaurus**

**Mus·lim** /**muhz**-luhm/
● *noun* someone whose religion is Islam: *Mecca is a holy city for Muslims.*
● *adjective* relating to Islam: *Saudi Arabia is a Muslim country.*

**mus·sel** /**muhss**-uhl/ *noun* a small sea animal with a black shell. Mussels have a soft body that you can eat: *You can find mussels both in the ocean and in rivers.*
▶ see picture on page **A3**

mussel

**must** /muhst/ *verb*
**1** if you must do something, it is very important that you do it: *You must feed your dog every day.*
**2** if you say that something must be true, you think that it is true because of the information you have: *The door's open, so she must be at home. | I must have fallen asleep.*

**mus·tache** /**muhst**-ash/ *noun* hair that grows above a man's mouth: *He has a beard and a mustache.*

**mus·tard** /**muhst**-urd/ *noun* a yellow sauce with a strong taste. Mustard is made from the seeds of a plant: *I put mustard on my hot dog.*

**mutt** /muht/ *noun* a dog whose parents were different types of dog: *Our dog is a mutt but he is very cute.*

**mut·ter** /**muht**-ur/ *verb* to say something quietly because you are angry or do not want people to hear: *"That's a lie," Lisa muttered, but Jess didn't hear her.*

**mu·tu·al** /**myooch**-oo-uhl/ *adjective*
**1** if a feeling is mutual, two people have the same feeling toward each other: *There was a mutual trust between the two men.*

**2** shared by two people: *Ava and I met through a mutual friend.*

**my** /mī/ *adjective* belonging to me: *I've hurt my leg.*

**my·self** /mī-**self**/ *pronoun*
**1** used instead of "me" after you have used "I": *I looked at myself in the mirror.*
**2** me and no one else: *I chose the gift myself.*

> IDIOM with **myself**
> **(all) by myself** alone or without help: *Look, Mommy – I tied my shoes all by myself!*

**mys·te·ri·ous** /mi-**steer**-ee-uhss/ *adjective* strange and difficult to explain or understand: *No one knows why the plane suddenly crashed – it's all very mysterious.*
—**mysteriously** /mi-**steer**-ee-uhss-lee/ *adverb* in a mysterious way: *The ship disappeared mysteriously in the Caribbean Sea.*

**mys·ter·y** /**mist**-uhr-ee/ *noun* (plural **mysteries**)
**1** something that is difficult to explain or understand: *The reason why the ship sank is still a mystery. There were no storms, and the ship was new.*
**2** a story about a murder or other crime. You do not know who committed the crime until the end: *In this mystery, the writer gives you the clues you need to solve the crime.*

**Word Origin:** mystery

When the word **mystery** was first used in English, it meant a religious experience. Mystery came from a Greek word that meant a secret religious ceremony or secret religious knowledge. Around 1300, mystery also began to mean something that was secret or hidden, that you could not understand. It was first used about detective stories in the early 1900's.

**myth** /mith/ *noun*
**1** an old story about gods, brave men, magical creatures, or the beginning of the world. Myths are part of ancient people's religious beliefs, and often try to explain things about the world: *There are lots of myths about how the world was created.*
**2** something that many people believe, but that is not true: *It's a myth that cats need to drink milk. They don't.*
—**mythical** /**mith**-ik-uhl/ *adjective* talked about in stories, but not real: *Dragons are mythical animals.*

**my·thol·o·gy** /mi-**thahl**-uhj-ee/ *noun* myths in general, especially all the myths of a particular culture: *Saturday is named for the god Saturn in Roman mythology.*

# Nn

**nag** /nag/ *verb* (**nagging**, **nagged**) to keep asking someone to do something, in an annoying way: *Mom's always nagging me to clean up my room.*

**nail** /nayl/
● *noun*
**1** the hard part on top of the end of each finger and toe: *She has long nails.*
**2** a small piece of metal with a sharp point. You can join pieces of wood together by hitting nails into them with a hammer.
● *verb*
to join things using nails: *Nail the pieces of wood together to make a box.*

**nail**

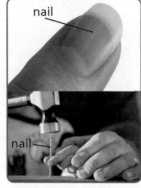

nail

nail

**nail pol·ish** /**nayl** pahl-ish/ *noun* paint that a woman puts on her nails: *She had red nail polish on her toenails.*

**na·ive**, **naïve** /nah-**eev**/ *adjective* believing that people are nicer and things are easier than they really are because you do not have much experience of life: *I was naive and I trusted him to look after my money, even though I had only just met him.*
—**naively** /nah-**eev**-lee/ *adverb* in a naive way: *She naively believes that no one cheats in sports.*

**na·ked** /**nayk**-id/ *adjective* not wearing any clothes: *I was naked because I had just taken a shower.* (SYNONYM: **nude**)

⌈ IDIOM with **naked**
| **the naked eye** if something can be seen with the naked eye, it can be seen without using a telescope or a microscope: *Germs can't be seen with the naked eye.*

**name** /naym/
● *noun*
**1** the word that someone or something is called:

*My name is Lisa.* | *What's the name of that song?* ▶ see **Thesaurus**
**2** the opinion that people have about someone or something: *The school has a good name because the children there do well.*
(SYNONYM: **reputation**)

⌈ IDIOM with **name**
| **call someone names** to be rude to someone by saying that he or she is something bad: *The other kids called him names.*
● *verb*
**1** to give a name to someone or something: *They named their son Jacob.*
**2** to say what the name of someone or something is: *"Name three kinds of fruit." "Apples, oranges, and pears."*

**nan·ny** /**nan**-ee/ *noun* (plural **nannies**) a woman who people pay to take care of their children in their home: *When I was a little girl, we had a nanny while Mom and Dad were at work.*

**nap** /nap/ *noun* a short sleep during the day: *My little sister takes a nap after lunch.*

**nap·kin** /**nap**-kin/ *noun* a piece of cloth or paper that you use to keep clean when you are eating: *He wiped his mouth with his napkin.*

**nar·cot·ic** /nar-**kaht**-ik/ *noun* a drug that stops pain and makes people sleep: *He was arrested for selling illegal narcotics.*

**nar·rate** /**narr**-ayt/ *verb* to describe what is happening in a movie, a television program, or a story: *The wildlife program was narrated by a famous actor.*
—**narration** /na-**raysh**-uhn/ *noun* a description in which someone says what is happening in a movie, a television program, or a story: *The teacher read the narration while the children acted out the story of the first Thanksgiving.*
—**narrator** /**narr**-ayt-ur/ *noun* someone who tells a story, or explains what is happening in a movie or a television program

**nar·ra·tive** /**narr**-uht-iv/ *noun* the description of events in a story: *The narrative is about Lewis and Clark's exploration of the West.*

**nar·row** /**narr**-oh/ *adjective* not wide: *The street* was very narrow and there was only room for one car. ( ANTONYM: **wide** )

IDIOM with **narrow**

**a narrow escape** an occasion when something bad almost happens to you: *The boy had a narrow escape when a car almost hit him as he crossed the street.*

**narrow**

a narrow path     a wide path

**nar·row·ly** /**narr**-oh-lee/ *adverb* only by a small amount: *Jordan narrowly avoided hitting the girl with his bike.*

**nar·row-mind·ed** /narr-oh **mīnd**-id/ *adjective* not willing to accept ideas that are new or different: *Some narrow-minded people do not like books about witches because they think that witches are bad.*

**na·sal** /**nayz**-uhl/ *adjective* relating to your nose: *He couldn't breathe because his nasal passages were blocked.*

**nas·ty** /**nast**-ee/ *adjective* (**nastier**, **nastiest**)
**1** not kind or nice: *Don't be so nasty to your sister!*
**2** very bad: *He had a nasty accident and broke his leg.*

**na·tion** /**naysh**-uhn/ *noun* a country, or the people in it: *We learned about the history of our nation.*

**Word Family:** nation

**nation** *noun* | **national** *adjective* |
**nationally** *adverb* | **nationality** *noun*

**Word Origin:** nation

**Nation** comes from a Latin word that means "to be born." When the word nation was first used, it meant a group of people who were born in the same area. The people of a nation shared a language and the people in it looked similar to one another. Nation gradually began to mean a country, and the people who belong to it.

**na·tion·al** /**nash**-uhn'l/ *adjective* relating to the whole of a nation: *July 4 is a national holiday, so no one has to go to work.*

**na·tion·al·i·ty** /nash-uh-**nal**-uht-ee/ *noun* (plural **nationalities**) the fact that you belong to a particular country: *"What nationality are you?" "I'm Canadian."*

**na·tion·al·ly** /**nash**-uhn'l-ee/ *adverb* in every part of a country: *The basketball game was broadcast nationally.*

**na·tion·al park** /**nash**-uhn'l **park**/ *noun* a large area of natural land that the government protects. National parks are usually very beautiful or special for a particular reason: *Have you ever been to Yellowstone National Park?*

**na·tion·wide** /naysh-uhn-**wīd**/ *adjective*, *adverb* in every part of a country: *The band went on a nationwide tour from California to Maine.*

**na·tive** /**nayt**-iv/
● *adjective*
**1** your native country is the place where you were born: *He was born in Peru, and he wanted to return to his native country.*
**2** your native language is the first language that you spoke: *She speaks English well, but her native language is Japanese.*
**3** native plants or animals grow or live naturally in a place: *The golden eagle is native to North America.*
● *noun*
someone who was born in a particular place: *Andrea is a native of Brazil.*

a b c d e f g h i j k l m **n** o p q r s t u v w x y z

**Na·tive A·mer·i·can** /nayt-iv uh-**merr**-ik-uhn/
● *noun* someone who belongs to one of the groups that lived in America before Europeans arrived: *Native Americans were the first people to live on this land.* ( SYNONYM: **Indian** )
● *adjective* relating to Native Americans: *Navajo is a Native American language.*

**Native American**

**nat·u·ral** /**nach**-uhr-uhl/ *adjective*
**1** part of nature, and not made by people: *The hurricane was one of the worst natural disasters to hit the United States.* ( ANTONYM: **man-made** )
▶ see Thesaurus
**2** normal or usual: *It's natural to feel nervous before you start at a new school.*
( ANTONYM: **unnatural** )
**3** used to say that someone was born with an ability: *He was a natural athlete and won most of the races.*

**nat·u·ral gas** /nach-uhr-uhl **gass**/ *noun* gas that is found under the Earth or the ocean, and is used for cooking or heating

**nat·u·ral·ize** /**nach**-uhr-uh-līz/ *verb* **be naturalized** if you are naturalized, you become a citizen of a different country
—**naturalized** /**nach**-uhr-uh-līzd/ *adjective* having become a citizen of a different country: *He was born in Poland and is a naturalized U.S. citizen.*
—**naturalization** /nach-uhr-uhl-uh-**zaysh**-uhn/ *noun* the process of being naturalized: *He's Costa Rican but is applying for U.S. naturalization.*

**nat·u·ral·ly** /**nach**-uhr-uhl-ee/ *adverb*
**1** happening on its own, without people doing

anything to make it happen: *My hair is naturally curly; I don't do anything to it to curl it.*
**2** in a way that is normal or not surprising: *Naturally, he was upset when he lost.*
( SYNONYM: **of course** )

**na·ture** /**naych**-ur/ *noun*
**1** everything in the world that people have not made, such as plants, mountains, or the weather: *We go hiking so we can spend time in nature, away from cities and cars.*
**2** what someone or something is like: *She has a quiet gentle nature, and she never shouts at anyone.* | *Scientists are still trying to understand the nature of the problem.*

**naugh·ty** /**not**-ee/ *adjective*
**1** a naughty child behaves badly, for example by being rude or not obeying a parent or teacher: *Ben was naughty today at school; he wouldn't stop talking when the teacher told him to.*
**2** a naughty word is a rude word that you should not say

**nau·se·a** /**noz**-ee-uh/ *noun* the feeling of needing to vomit: *Some people feel nausea when they travel on a boat because it keeps moving up and down.*

**na·val** /**nayv**-uhl/ *adjective* relating to the navy: *A naval officer showed the visitors around the ship.*

**na·vel** /**nayv**-uhl/ *noun* the small circle in the middle of your stomach: *She was wearing a short T-shirt that showed her navel.*
( SYNONYM: **belly button** )

**nav·i·gate** /**nav**-uh-gayt/ *verb*
**1** to decide which direction a car, ship, or plane should travel, using a map: *My mom usually navigates and she tells my dad which road to take.*
**2** to move around the Internet or a website: *The website is easy to navigate.*
—**navigator** /**nav**-uh-gayt-ur/ *noun* a person on a ship or airplane who decides which direction to travel
—**navigation** /nav-uh-**gaysh**-uhn/ *noun* the activity of finding how to go somewhere, usually by using a map: *Navigation is difficult in the desert because there are no roads or rivers that you can use to find the way.*

**na·vy** /**nayv**-ee/ *noun* (plural **navies**) the part of the military that uses ships: *My grandfather traveled all over the world when he was in the navy.*

**near** /neer/
● *adverb, preposition*
**1** close to someone or something: *My house is near the road and there is a lot of noise from cars.* | *Don't go near the fire.* ▶ see **Thesaurus**
**2** close to a time or event: *My birthday is near Christmas – it's on December 20.*
● *adjective*
**1** only a short distance from you: *I go to this school because it's the nearest one to my home.* ( ANTONYM: **far** ) ▶ see picture at **far**
**2** used for describing something bad that almost happens: *There was a near disaster in the kitchen when I almost dropped the turkey.*

IDIOM with **near**
**in the near future** soon: *We don't have any kids yet, but we hope to have some in the near future.*

**near·by** /neer-**bī**/
● *adjective* only a short distance from you or your home: *He was taken to a hospital in a nearby town.*
● *adverb* only a short distance from you or your home: *I walk to school with a friend who lives nearby.*

**near·ly** /**neer**-lee/ *adverb*
**1** almost: *Be careful – you nearly stepped on my foot!*
**2** **not nearly enough** much less than you need: *Fifty dollars is not nearly enough money to buy a computer.*

**near·sight·ed** /**neer**-sīt-id/ *adjective* unable to see things that are far away: *I'm nearsighted, so I wear glasses when I watch TV.*
( ANTONYM: **farsighted** )

**neat** /neet/ *adjective*
**1** clean and in good order: *I try to keep my bedroom neat and clean.*
**2** you use this to say that you like something or someone a lot: *The zoo is really neat.*
( SYNONYM: **great** )
—**neatly** /**neet**-lee/ *adverb* in a way that is clean and in good order: *Her clothes were neatly folded on her bed.*

**nec·es·sar·i·ly** /ness-uh-**sair**-uhl-ee/ *adverb* **not necessarily** used for saying that something may not always be true: *Expensive toys are not necessarily the best toys – you can have a lot of fun with just a ball and a piece of wood.*

**nec·es·sar·y** /**ness**-uh-sair-ee/ *adjective* if something is necessary, you need to have it or do it: *It's very cold here in winter, so warm clothes are necessary.* ▶ see **Thesaurus**

**ne·ces·si·ty** /nuh-**sess**-uht-ee/ *noun* (plural **necessities**) something you need to have or do: *Water is the most basic necessity of life.*

**neck** /nek/ *noun*
**1** the part of your body between your head and your shoulders: *She's wearing a red scarf around her neck.* | *A giraffe has a very long neck.*
**2** the part of a piece of clothing that goes around your neck: *They put a bug down the neck of his T-shirt!*

**neck**
neck

**neck·lace** /**nek**-liss/ *noun* a piece of jewelry that you wear around your neck: *Mom is wearing a gold necklace.*

**necklace**
necklace

**neck·tie** /**nek**-tī/ *noun* a long piece of cloth that a man ties in a special knot around his neck: *Dad was tying his necktie in front of the mirror.* ( SYNONYM: **tie** )

**nec·tar** /**nek**-tur/ *noun* the sweet liquid that bees collect from flowers: *The bees fly from flower to flower collecting nectar to make honey.*

**nec·ta·rine** /nekt-uh-**reen**/ *noun* a round yellow and red fruit. It has a smooth skin and a big seed inside, and it is sweet and juicy. ▶ see picture on page **A7**

**need** /need/
- *verb*
**1** if you need something, you must have it: *I'm thirsty – I need a drink.* ▶ see **Thesaurus**
**2** if you need to do something, you have to do it: *You need to try harder if you want to do well at school.*
- *noun*
**1** something that is necessary: *If something is working well, there is no need to change it.*
**2** something that you want to have or must have: *When it comes to learning, every child has different needs.*

> IDIOMS with **need**
> **in need** not having enough food or money: *We're collecting money for children in need.*
> **in need of** needing to have something: *We were tired and in need of a rest.*

**nee·dle** /need'l/ *noun*
**1** a small thin piece of metal with a sharp point. You use needles for sewing. A needle has a hole at one end that you put a thread through: *She used a needle and thread to sew the button back on my shirt.*
**2** a small thin hollow piece of metal with a sharp point at the end. A doctor uses a needle to put medicine into your body or to take blood out: *The doctor gave me a shot with a needle.*
**3** a thin pointed leaf on some kinds of trees, for example pine trees or fir trees: *The Christmas tree dropped needles everywhere when it got dry.*
**4** a long thin part on a piece of equipment. It points to measurements or directions: *The needle on the compass was pointing north.*
**5** a pointed stick used in knitting

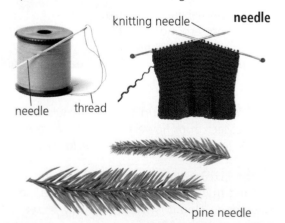

knitting needle · **needle**

needle · thread

pine needle

**need·less** /**need**-liss/ *adjective* not necessary: *I always switch off my computer when I'm not using it because I don't want any needless waste of electricity.*

**need·y** /**need**-ee/ *adjective* not having enough money or food: *They fill boxes with Christmas gifts for needy children.* ( SYNONYM: **poor** )

**neg·a·tive** /**neg**-uht-iv/ *adjective*
**1** bad: *Everyone knows the negative effects of smoking cigarettes.* | *My sister gets mad if I say anything negative about her friends.*
( ANTONYM: **positive** )
**2** meaning "no": *I asked if he agreed, and the reply was negative.*
**3** a negative number is lower than zero: *-1 is a negative number*
**4** having the type of electrical charge that is carried by electrons: *The negative terminal on a battery has a (-) symbol.*
—**negatively** /**neg**-uht-iv-lee/ *adverb* in a bad way: *People often react negatively to change because they like things to stay the same.*

**ne·glect** /ni-**glekt**/
- *verb* to not give something or someone enough care or attention: *If you neglect your plants by not watering them, they will die.*
—**neglected** /ni-**glekt**-id/ *adjective* not given enough care or attention: *The little boy felt neglected because his parents were too busy to give him any attention.*
- *noun* a lack of care or attention: *The dog is too thin and he is suffering from neglect.*

**ne·go·ti·ate** /ni-**gohsh**-ee-ayt/ *verb* to talk about something in order to get an agreement: *The two leaders will meet to negotiate an agreement to reduce the number of nuclear weapons.*
—**negotiator** /ni-**gohsh**-ee-ayt-ur/ *noun* someone who negotiates: *Negotiators from both sides are trying to reach an agreement.*
—**negotiation** /ni-gohsh-ee-**aysh**-uhn/ *noun* a discussion in which two groups or countries try to reach an agreement: *Negotiations are taking place to try to resolve the crisis.*

**Ne·gro** /**neeg**-roh/ *noun* (plural **Negroes**) a black person. This word was used in the past but people now think it is offensive.

**neigh** /nay/ *verb* if a horse neighs, it makes a long loud sound

a b c d e f g h i j k l m **n** o p q r s t u v w x y z

**neigh·bor** /**nayb**-ur/ *noun*
**1** someone who lives in the house next to your house, or very near you: *There is a low fence between our house and our neighbor's.*
**2** a country that is next to another country: *Canada is a neighbor of the U.S.*
**3** someone who is sitting or standing next to you: *You must not look at your neighbor's work during the test.*
—**neighboring** /**nayb**-uhr-ing/ *adjective* next to a place: *We went to Indiana and the neighboring states of Ohio and Illinois.*

**Word Origin: neighbor**

**Neighbor** comes from two Old English words that mean "near" and "someone who lives in a place." So a neighbor is someone who lives near you.

**neigh·bor·hood** /**nayb**-ur-hud/ *noun* a small area of a town: *He grew up in a poor neighborhood of Chicago.*

**nei·ther** /**neeth**-ur/
● *adjective*, *pronoun* not one and not the other of two people or things: *We don't have a car because neither of my parents can drive.*
● *adverb* you use this for agreeing with a negative statement: *"I don't have a bike." "Neither do I." | "I don't want to go home." "Me neither."*
● *conjunction* not one and not the other: *Neither John nor Mary can come to the party because they are both sick.*

**ne·on** /**nee**-ahn/ *noun* a gas that shines very brightly when electricity goes through it. Neon is used in lights and signs: *The restaurant has a neon sign outside.*

**neph·ew** /**nef**-yoo/ *noun*
**1** the son of your brother or sister: *Dad's sister says I am her favorite nephew.*
**2** the son of your wife's brother or sister or the son of your husband's brother or sister: *When Tom married Jane, he got five new nephews.*

**Nep·tune** /**nep**-toon/ *noun* the eighth planet from the Sun. Neptune is one of the largest planets in our solar system. ▶ see picture at **solar system**

**nerd** /nurd/ *noun* someone who is boring, and is interested only in boring things: *He thinks people who like reading books are nerds.*

**nerve** /nurv/ *noun*
**1** the ability to do something difficult or brave: *I don't have the nerve to go on stage and sing in front of people.*
**2** a thin fiber in your body that sends information between your brain and other parts of your body: *When you look at something, the nerves behind your eyes carry the information to your brain.*
**3** **nerves** the feeling of being nervous: *I felt sick on the morning of the school play, but it was just nerves.*

**IDIOM with nerve**
**get on someone's nerves** to annoy someone: *Stop kicking the ball around in the house. It's getting on my nerves!*

**nerv·ous** /**nurv**-uhss/ *adjective* worried or frightened: *It's normal to be nervous about starting a new school.* ▶ see **Thesaurus**
—**nervously** /**nurv**-uhss-lee/ *adverb* in a nervous way: *Students were waiting nervously outside the classroom before the test.*
—**nervousness** /**nurv**-uhss-niss/ *noun* a nervous feeling: *He couldn't hide his nervousness and was biting his nails.*

**ner·vous sys·tem** /**nurv**-uhss sist-uhm/ *noun* the system in your body that makes you feel pain and heat and that controls your movement. Your nervous system consists of your nerves, your brain, and your spinal cord: *She has a disease of the nervous system which sometimes makes her shake.*

**-ness** /niss/

**Word Building**

**-ness** is a suffix.
aware**ness** | blind**ness** | careless**ness** | fair**ness** | friendli**ness** | rude**ness** | sick**ness**
**-ness** changes an adjective into a noun. *Blindness* is when you are blind. *Rudeness* is when someone is rude. *Sickness* is when someone is sick. **-ness** can be added with another suffix, for example in *carelessness*.

**nest** /nest/ *noun*

**1** a home that a bird makes to lay its eggs in: *Most birds build their nests in trees.*
**2** a place where some small animals or insects live: *a wasp's nest | an ant's nest*

nest

**net** /net/ *noun*

**1** a bag or piece of loose material made of string or wire that is tied together. Nets have holes in them. You use nets to catch things: *We tried to catch fish in our nets. | a butterfly net*
**2** a thing you throw a basketball through. The net is made of string and hangs from a metal ring.
**3** a thing made of string that goes in the middle of a tennis or volleyball court: *He hit the ball over the net.*
**4 the Net** a system of computers that lets people around the world send messages and look at information: *I often look at the Net for information when I'm doing my homework.*

SYNONYM: **Internet, Web**

net

net

net

**net·work** /**net**-wurk/ *noun*

**1** a system of things that are connected to each other: *All the computers at school are part of a network.*
**2** a company that shows programs on TV: *ABC is an American television network.*

**neu·tral** /**noo**-truhl/ *adjective*

**1** not supporting any country in a war, or any person in an argument: *The judge in a court must be neutral and not support one side.*
**2** a neutral color is not strong or bright: *Gray is a neutral color.*

**neu·tral·ize** /**noo**-truh-līz/ *verb* to stop something from having an effect: *Lemon juice can be used to neutralize smells on your hands from chopping onions.*

**neu·tron** /**noo**-trahn/ *noun* a particle in the nucleus of an atom: *Neutrons have no electrical charge.* ▶ see picture at **atom**

**nev·er** /**nev**-ur/ *adverb* at no time: *I've never visited New York before, but I'd really like to go there.*

⎡ IDIOM with **never**
⎢ **never mind** you say this to tell someone that
⎢ something is not important and there is no
⎢ need to worry about it: *"I didn't win." "Never*
⎣ *mind. You can try again next year."*

**nev·er·the·less** /nev-ur-thuh-**less**/ *adverb*
used when giving a fact that is surprising: *She is only five years old. Nevertheless, she is a very good chess player.*

SYNONYMS: **however, nonetheless**

**new** /noo/ *adjective*

**1** if something is new, it has just been made or has just started being used: *They are planning to build some new houses on our street. | The store was full of shiny new bicycles.* ANTONYM: **old**
▶ see **Thesaurus**
**2** if something is new, people have only just discovered it: *Scientists have discovered a strange new fish at the bottom of the ocean.*
**3** a new person or thing is different from the one that you had before: *She has a new friend. | My chair is broken and I need a new one.*
ANTONYM: **old**
**4** if you are new to a place, you have never lived there before: *I'm new here and I don't have many friends.*
**5** if you are new to a subject, you have never done it or studied it before: *The book is very simple and for people who are new to science.*

new

a new bicycle  an old bicycle

newsstand

**new·born** /noo-**born**/ *adjective* born very recently: *She left the hospital carrying her newborn son.*

**new·ly** /**noo**-lee/ *adverb* recently: *The sheets smelled fresh and newly washed.*

**new·ly·wed** /**noo**-lee-wed/ *noun* a person who has recently got married: *The photograph was taken when Mom and Dad were newlyweds.*

**new moon** /noo **moon**/ *noun* the Moon when it first appears in the sky as a thin crescent: *There was a new moon, so the night was dark.*

**news** /nooz/ *noun*
**1** reports in the newspapers or on television or radio about things that are happening in the world: *Iraq is often in the news.*
**2** information about things that have happened in your life recently: *Is there any news about Maria? Her mother said she was in the hospital.*

**Grammar: news**

**News** is always followed by the form of the verb that shows there is only one thing: *The good news is that mom has a new job.*

You can say **some news**, **any news**, etc., or **a piece of news**: *Is there any news about the President?*

**news·pa·per** /**nooz**-payp-ur/ (also **paper**) *noun* pieces of thin paper containing news reports: *The story was on the front page of the newspaper.*

**news·stand** /**nooz**-stand/ *noun* a place on a street where you can buy newspapers and magazines: *I bought a comic book at the newsstand.*

**newt** /noot/ *noun* a small salamander that lives mainly on land but lays its eggs in water: *We went looking for frogs and newts in the stream.*
▶ see picture on page **A1**

**New Year's Day** /noo yeerz **day**/ *noun* January 1: *Most stores are closed on New Year's Day.*

**New Year's Eve** /noo yeerz **eev**/ *noun* December 31: *We're having a party on New Year's Eve!*

**next** /nekst/
● *adjective, pronoun*
**1** the next one is the one after this one: *He came back the next day. | Q is the next letter after P.*
**2** closest to where you are now: *I could hear voices in the next room.*
● *adverb*
**1 next to** close to someone or something, with no other person or thing in between: *Can I sit next to you?* ( SYNONYM: **beside** )
**2** after this: *I've finished coloring my picture. What do I do next?*

next

The boys are sitting next to each other.

**next door** /nekst **dor**/ *adverb* in the room or building that is next to another room or building: *You can see into the yard of the house next door from my bedroom window.*

a
b
c
d
e
f
g
h
i
j
k
l
m
**n**
o
p
q
r
s
t
u
v
w
x
y
z

**nib·ble** /**nib**-uhl/ *verb* to eat food by taking small bites: *The rabbit nibbled a piece of carrot.*

**nice** /nīss/ *adjective*
**1** pleasant, attractive, or enjoyable: *She looked nice in her new dress.* | *Did you have a nice time at the party?* ▶ see **Thesaurus**
**2** friendly or kind: *Be nice to your sister – she's only little.* | *He's a really nice guy.*

> **IDIOM with nice**
> **nice to meet you** used when you are meeting someone for the first time: *"Hi, I'm Cathy." "Hi, I'm Maria. Nice to meet you."*

—**nicely** /**nīss**-lee/ *adverb* in a nice way: *I'm sure he'll help you if you ask him nicely.*

> ## Word Origin: nice
>
> **Nice** has changed its meaning many many times. Nice comes from a Latin word that means "not knowing something."
>
> In the 1200s, if someone said that you were nice, you would be very upset. Then, nice meant "stupid." In the 1300s, you still might not like to be called nice. Then, it meant "fussy" – someone who is fussy wants every detail to be exactly right.
>
> In the 1400s, nice started to mean "delicate," so that something or someone nice seems pretty but not strong. In the 1500s, nice was still being used about details, and it meant "precise."
>
> By the 1700s, nice had started to be used about things that were pleasant and enjoyable. We still use this meaning today. Finally, in the 1800s, nice started to mean "kind and friendly." Now you would like someone to say you are nice!

**nick·el** /**nik**-uhl/ *noun*
**1** a coin used in the U.S. and Canada that is worth five cents: *A hundred years ago, it cost a nickel to ride the New York subway.*
**2** a hard silver-colored metal: *Nickel is used in making stainless steel.*

**nick·name** /**nik**-naym/
● *noun* a name that your friends or family use instead of your real name: *"Brownie" is his nickname. His real name is Michael Brown.*
● *verb* to give someone a nickname: *They*

nicknamed him "Trouble" because he was always getting into trouble.

> ## Word Origin: nickname
>
> **Nickname** comes from a Middle English phrase **an eke name**, which means "an extra name." People didn't pronounce "an eke name" clearly, and it started to sound like "a neke name." Later, people started saying "a nickname."

**nic·o·tine** /**nik**-uh-teen/ *noun* a dangerous substance in tobacco that makes it difficult for people to stop smoking: *Nicotine is the main drug in cigarettes.*

**niece** /neess/ *noun*
**1** the daughter of your brother or sister: *This is my niece, Maria. She's my sister's daughter.*
**2** the daughter of your wife's brother or sister or the daughter of your husband's brother or sister

**night** /nīt/ *noun*
**1** the part of the day when it is dark and most people are sleeping: *It gets very cold here at night.*
**2** the evening: *Every night after dinner, we play a game of chess.*

> **IDIOM with night**
> **night and day** (also **day and night**) all the time: *The nurses care for him night and day.*

**night·club** /**nīt**-kluhb/ *noun* a place where people go to drink and dance. Nightclubs are open late at night: *You're too young to go to nightclubs!*

**night·fall** /**nīt**-fol/ *noun* the time when it begins to get dark in the evening: *We walked until nightfall, then put up our tent.*
(**SYNONYM: dusk**)

**night·gown** /**nīt**-gown/ *noun* a piece of loose clothing, like a dress, that a woman wears in bed: *She put on her nightgown and went to bed.*

**night·life** /**nīt**-līf/ *noun* evening entertainment in places such as bars and nightclubs: *Las Vegas is famous for its nightlife: casinos, nightclubs, and shows.*

**night·ly** /**nīt**-lee/ *adjective, adverb* happening every night: *He appears nightly on TV.*

**night·mare** /nīt-mair/ *noun*
**1** a frightening dream: *Kids often have nightmares about monsters.*
**2** if something is a nightmare, it is very difficult and you have lots of problems: *The trip was a nightmare – there was a lot of traffic and someone drove into the back of Dad's car.*

**Word Origin: nightmare**

**Nightmare** comes from Old English. In the 1200s, people thought a nightmare was an evil creature. The nightmare would come to you while you were sleeping and sit on your chest, so that it was hard to breathe. In the 1700s and 1800s, people stopped believing in the evil spirit, and nightmare started to mean "a very bad dream."

**night school** /nīt skool/ *noun* a place where people can go to do classes in the evening: *After work, Juan goes to night school to study English.*

**night·time** /nīt-tīm/ *noun* the time during the night when the sky is dark: *It was nighttime when we arrived at our hotel, so we went straight to bed.* ( ANTONYM: **daytime** )

**nine** /nīn/ *number*
**1** 9: *Ten minus one is nine.*
**2** 9 o'clock: *School starts at nine.*
**3** nine years old: *I'll be nine next Tuesday.*
—**ninth** /nīnth/ *number* 9th or 1/9

**nine·teen** /nīn-**teen**/ *number*
**1** 19: *I counted nineteen cars in the parking lot.*
**2** nineteen years old: *He went to college when he was nineteen.*
—**nineteenth** /nīn-**teenth**/ *number* 19th or 1/19

**nine·ty** /nīn-tee/ *number*
**1** 90: *A soccer game lasts ninety minutes.*
**2** ninety years old: *Grandpa is ninety.*
**3** the nineties the years between 1990 and 1999: *Mom likes music from the nineties.*
**4** in your nineties between 90 and 99 years old: *My grandmother is in her nineties.*
**5** in the nineties between 90 and 99 degrees in temperature: *It was in the nineties and we were all very hot.*
—**ninetieth** /nīn-tee-ith/ *number* 90th or 1/90

**nip** /nip/ *verb* (**nipping**, **nipped**) to bite someone or something with small sharp bites: *The dog sometimes nips me when he gets excited.*

**nip·ple** /nip-uhl/ *noun*
**1** the dark circle in the center of someone's breast: *Babies suck milk from their mother's nipples.*
**2** the small piece of rubber on the end of a baby's bottle: *The baby bit a hole in the nipple of her bottle.*

**ni·tro·gen** /nītr-uhj-uhn/ *noun* a gas that is the main part of the Earth's air. Nitrogen has no color and no smell. The symbol for nitrogen is N: *The air contains about 78% nitrogen and 21% oxygen.*

**no** /noh/
● *adverb*
**1** used for saying something is not true or you do not want something: *"Are your parents home?" "No, they're at work."* | *"Would you like another piece of cake?" "No thanks, I'm full."*
( ANTONYM: **yes** )
**2** no parking used on signs for saying people cannot park their cars in a place
**3** no smoking used on signs for saying people cannot smoke cigarettes in a place
● *adjective*
not any: *There was no food – the refrigerator was empty.*

IDIOM with **no**
**no way** used for saying that you will not do something because you really do not want to do it: *They wanted Max to sing a song for them but he said "No way."*

**no·ble** /nohb-uhl/ *adjective*
**1** for the good of other people, not yourself: *He was noble and gave his seat to an old lady.*
**2** belonging to the richest or most respected social group: *He was born into a noble English family.*

**no·ble gas** /nohb-uhl **gass**/ *noun* a gas that is a chemical element and does not mix easily with other elements: *Neon and argon are noble gases.*

**no·bod·y** /nohb-uhd-ee/
● *pronoun* no person: *The room was silent – nobody spoke.* ( SYNONYM: **no one** )
● *noun* (plural **nobodies**) someone who is not important, successful, or famous: *I was just a nobody until I went on TV. Then suddenly everyone wanted to be my friend.*

**a b c d e f g h i j k l m n o p q r s t u v w x y z**

**noc·tur·nal** /nahk-**turn**'l/ *adjective* nocturnal animals sleep during the day and are awake at night: *Mice are nocturnal so you don't often see them in the daytime.*

**nod** /nahd/
- *verb* (**nodding, nodded**)
**1** to move your head up and down as a way of saying "yes": *When I asked him if he was OK, he nodded.*
**2 nod off** to begin to sleep when you do not plan to: *I was tired and bored and I almost nodded off.*
- *noun*
an up and down movement of your head: *He gave a nod toward the door, meaning that I should open it.*

**noise** /noyz/ *noun* a loud or annoying sound: *There's too much noise in this room – stop shouting!* ▶ see **Thesaurus**

**nois·y** /**noyz**-ee/ *adjective* (**noisier, noisiest**)
**1** making a lot of noise: *The old car has a noisy engine.*
**2** filled with noise: *It is always very noisy in the football stadium.*
—**noisily** /**noyz**-uhl-ee/ *adverb* in a noisy way: *Crowds were protesting noisily in the streets.*

**nom·i·nate** /**nahm**-uh-nayt/ *verb* to officially say that you think someone should get an important job or a prize. People can then vote for that person: *Each class has to nominate one person as its representative.*
—**nomination** /nahm-uh-**naysh**-uhn/ *noun* the act of nominating someone or something for a job or prize
—**nominee** /nahm-uh-**nee**/ *noun* someone who has been nominated

**non-** /nahn/

## Word Building

**non-** is a prefix.
**non**fiction | **non**-living | **non**sense | **non**stick | **non**stop
**non-** means "not." A *nonfiction* book is about real people, facts, or events, and is not a made-up story. A *nonstick* pan does not let food stick to it. If someone works *nonstop*, he or she works without stopping.

**non·a·gon** /**nahn**-uh-gahn/ *noun* a flat shape with nine sides

**none** /nuhn/ *pronoun*
**1** not any of something: *I wanted a piece of cake but there was none left.*
**2** not one person or thing: *None of my friends could come out to play because they all had homework.*

**none·the·less** /nuhn-thuh-**less**/ *adverb* used when saying something that is surprising, after what you have just said: *We were cold and tired, but we were happy nonetheless.*
SYNONYMS: **however, nevertheless**

**non-fat** /**nahn**-fat/ *adjective* non-fat milk or yogurt does not have any fat in it

**non·fic·tion** /nahn-**fik**-shuhn/ *noun* books or writing about real facts or events, not stories: *I am reading a nonfiction book about sharks.*
ANTONYM: **fiction**

**non-liv·ing** /nahn **liv**-ing/ *adjective* non-living things are not alive and can never be alive: *Books and cars are non-living things.*
SYNONYM: **inanimate**

**non·sense** /**nahn**-senss/ *noun*
**1** something false or stupid that someone says: *Mom says she's too old to learn to drive but that's nonsense – she's only 38.*
**2** bad behavior: *If there's any nonsense, you won't get any ice cream.*
**3** speech or writing that has no meaning: *I can't understand what you've written – it's just nonsense.*

**non-smok·ing** /nahn **smohk**-ing/ *adjective* a non-smoking area is a place where people are not allowed to smoke

**non·stick** /nahn-**stik**/ *adjective* a nonstick pan is one that food does not stick to when you use it for cooking: *Nonstick pans are easy to clean.*

**non·stop** /nahn-**stahp**/ *adjective*, *adverb* without stopping: *Ellen talks nonstop and it is difficult for other people to get a chance to speak.*

**noo·dles** /**nood**'lz/ *plural noun* a type of food made of flour, eggs, and water. Noodles are sold dry and in flat thin pieces. You cook them in boiling water: *I like chicken soup with lots of noodles.*

noodles

noodles

**noon** /noon/ *noun* 12 o'clock in the middle of the day: *We ate lunch at noon.*

**Word Origin:** noon

Noon comes from a Latin word that means "nine." Before the 1100s, noon was the ninth hour of daytime, when the priests always went into the church to pray. The ninth hour was probably about three o'clock. In the 1100s, the churches started to have prayers about 12 o'clock, but they kept the name "noon" for those prayers. So, noon now means 12 o'clock.

**no one** /**noh** wuhn/ *pronoun* not anyone: *No one knows how old she is. | I opened the door, but there was no one there.* ( SYNONYM: **nobody** )

**noose** /nooss/ *noun* a circle of rope that goes around something. When someone pulls the rope, the circle gets smaller and tighter: *He threw a noose around the man's neck.*

**nope** /nohp/ *adverb* no: *"Would you like some pizza?" "Nope, I'm not hungry."*

**nor** /nur, nor/ *conjunction*
**1 neither... nor** used when saying that two things are not true or possible: *Your story should be neither too long nor too short – three pages is just right.*
**2** and not: *I didn't have a key nor did my brother, so we had to wait for Mom to come home.*

**nor·mal** /**norm**-uhl/ *adjective* usual or expected: *It's normal to feel nervous when you start a new school.* ▶ see **Thesaurus**
—**normality** /nor-**mal**-uht-ee/ *noun* a situation in

which everything is normal: *It was nice to return to normality after being sick for so long.*

**Word Family:** normal

**normal** *adjective* | **abnormal** *adjective* | **normally** *adverb* | **normality** *noun*

**nor·mal·ly** /**norm**-uhl-ee/ *adverb* usually or in the expected way: *You're normally so happy – why are you crying?*

**north** /north/
● *noun*
**1** the direction toward the top of a map of the world: *The compass is pointing to the north.*
**2** the northern part of a country or area: *Michigan is in the north of the United States.*
**3 the North** the part of the U.S. that is east of the Mississippi River and north of Washington, D.C. The North is used as a name for the states that belonged to the Union during the Civil War.
● *adjective*
**1** in, to, or facing north: *Santa Barbara is 100 miles north of Los Angeles. | the north side of Chicago*
**2** a north wind comes from the north: *a cold north wind*
● *adverb*
toward the north: *Drive north on the highway.*

north

The compass is pointing to the north.

**north·east** /north-**eest**/
● *noun*
**1** the direction that is exactly between north and east: *Which state is to the northeast of Colorado?*
**2** the northeast part of a country or area: *Boston is the largest city in the Northeast.*
—**northeastern** /north-**eest**-urn/ *adjective* in or from the northeast: *The storm caused damage in the northeastern part of the U.S.*
● *adverb, adjective*
in, from, or toward the northeast: *A cold northeast wind was blowing.*

**north·ern** /**north**-urn/ *adjective* in or from the north: *Northern Alaska is covered with snow.*

**north·ern·er** /**north**-urn-ur/ *noun* someone who comes from the northern part of a country: *Northerners are used to snow in the winter.*

**North·ern Hem·is·phere** /north-urn **hem**-iss-feer/ *noun* the half of the world that is north of the Equator: *Europe is in the Northern Hemisphere.*

**North Pole** /north **pohl**/ *noun* the most northern place on the surface of the earth: *John Huston was the first American to ski to the North Pole.* ▶ see picture at **globe**

**north·ward** /**north**-wurd/ *adverb, adjective* toward the north: *We drove northward toward Canada.*

**north·west** /north-**west**/
● *noun*
**1** the direction that is exactly between north and west: *The rain is coming from the northwest.*
**2** the northwest part of a country or area: *The state of Washington is in the Northwest.*
—**northwestern** /north-**west**-urn/ *adjective* in or from the northwest: *the northwestern states of the U.S.*
● *adverb, adjective*
in, from, or toward the northwest: *Northwest California has a lot of beautiful forests.*

**nose** /nohz/ *noun*
**1** the part of your face used for breathing and smelling things: *My nose is stuffed up because I have a cold.* ▶ see picture on page **A13**
**2** the pointed front end of an airplane, boat, or rocket: *The plane crashed into the ocean, nose first.*

> **IDIOM with nose**
> **under your nose** if something is under your nose, it is very close and you should notice it, but you do not notice it: *The missing money was here all the time, right under our noses.*

**nose·bleed** /**nohz**-bleed/ *noun* if you have a nosebleed, blood starts coming out of your nose: *The ball hit him in the face and gave him a nosebleed.*

**nos·tril** /**nahss**-truhl/ *noun* one of the two holes in your nose. You breathe through your nostrils: *My little sister got a pea stuck in her left nostril.*

**nos·y** /**nohz**-ee/ *adjective* always trying to find out information about other people's lives: *"What are you writing in your journal?" "Don't be so nosy!"*

**not** /naht/ *adverb*
**1** used for showing the opposite of something: *If you're not ready, we'll wait for you.*
**2 not only** used for saying that someone has one quality and also another quality: *Not only is he good at basketball – he's also good at baseball and other sports.*

**note** /noht/
● *noun*
**1** a very short letter: *I'll leave a note on the table so Mom knows where we're going.*
**2** something that you write down to help you remember something: *Make a note of my cell phone number.*
**3** a musical sound, or the sign for that sound. Notes have names like e, f, a, and b: *I'll play a note on the piano and you try to sing it.*
**4 notes** information that students write down when they are in a class or reading a book. They make notes so they can remember what the teacher tells them or what they read: *If you forget something you learned in class, look in your notes.*

> **IDIOM with note**.
> **take note** to be careful to notice something: *The teacher always takes note of who is working hard.*
● *verb*
**1** to be careful to notice something: *Please note that the museum is closed on Mondays.*
**2** to write something on a piece of paper so that you will remember it: *I'll note your name and address.*

**note·book** /**noht**-buk/ *noun*
**1** a book in which you write notes: *I write all the new words I learn in my notebook so that I can remember them.*
**2** a small computer that you can carry
(SYNONYM: **laptop**)

notebook

**noth·ing** /**nuhth**-ing/ *pronoun*
**1** not anything or no thing: *There's nothing in my purse – it's empty.*
**2** zero: *If you take five away from five you get nothing.*

**IDIOMS with nothing**

**for nothing**

**1** without paying any money: *I didn't have to pay for my bike. I got it from my neighbor for nothing.*

**2** without getting what you expected or wanted: *I don't want to drive all the way to her house for nothing. Give her a call and see if she's home.*

**have nothing to do with** to not be about something: *Her problems have nothing to do with school. She's worried about her mom.*

**nothing but** only: *He drinks nothing but water because he doesn't like any other drinks.*

**nothing like someone** not at all similar to another person: *Emily is nothing like her sister. They look completely different.*

**no·tice** /**noht**-iss/

● *verb*

to see, feel, or hear something: *I noticed that Maria was crying and went to see if she was OK.*

▶ see **Thesaurus**

—**noticeable** /**noht**-iss-uhb-uhl/ *adjective* easy to notice: *There has been a noticeable improvement in his work.*

—**noticeably** /**noht**-iss-uhb-lee/ *adverb* in a way that is easy to see, feel, or hear: *If we leave after the rush hour, the journey will be noticeably quicker.*

● *noun*

**1** a piece of paper that someone has put up on a wall or door in a public place. The notice gives information about something: *The notice on the door says the library is closed.*

**2** if you give people notice of something, you tell them that it is going to happen so that they have enough time to prepare: *She only told me about the party the day before – that's not enough notice.*

**IDIOM with notice**

**take notice** to listen to what someone tells you and do what he or she wants: *His mother told him his lunch was ready, but he didn't take any notice and continued playing.*

**no·ti·fy** /**noht**-uh-fī/ *verb* (**notifies**, **notified**) to tell someone officially about something: *Please notify the school if you are sick.*

SYNONYM: **inform**

—**notification** /noht-uh-fee-**kaysh**-uhn/ *noun* the act of officially telling someone about something:

*He received official notification that he passed the test.*

**no·tion** /**nohsh**-uhn/ *noun* an idea, belief, or opinion about something, especially one that seems strange: *Daniel thinks I like him, but I don't know where he got that notion from.*

**no·to·ri·ous** /noh-**tor**-ee-uhss/ *adjective* famous for something bad: *In the story Snow White, the Queen is notorious for being wicked.*

**not·with·stand·ing** /**naht**-with-stand-ing/ *preposition* in spite of something else also being true: *He is doing well in school, notwithstanding the fact that he has been sick a lot.*

**noun** /nown/ *noun* a word that is the name of a person, place, or thing: *In the sentence "I like candy and chocolate," "candy" and "chocolate" are nouns.*

**nour·ish** /**nur**-ish/ *verb* to give someone or something the food they need to live and be healthy: *Water in the soil nourishes the plants.* —**nourishing** /**nur**-ish-ing/ *adjective* nourishing food makes you strong and healthy: *It's important to eat healthy nourishing food.*

**nour·ish·ment** /**nur**-ish-muhnt/ *noun* food that people or other living things need to live and be healthy: *If you eat plenty of different foods, you will get all the nourishment you need.*

**nov·el** /**nahv**-uhl/

● *noun* a book in which the story, characters, and events are not real: *"The Adventures of Huckleberry Finn" is a novel by Mark Twain.*

● *adjective* new and unusual: *Carrot ice cream sounds like a novel idea - I'm not sure that I want to eat it.*

—**novelist** /**nahv**-uhl-ist/ *noun* someone who writes novels

**Word Origin: novel**

A **novel** is about events and people that are not real, so they are new to you. The word novel comes from a Latin word that means "new." The Italians took the Latin word and made it into "novella," which meant "a new story." Novellas were always short stories. In the 1600s, people shortened the word novella to novel and started to use it to mean a long story. Before then, long stories were called "romances."

**nov·el·ty** /**nahv**-uhl-tee/ *noun* something that is new and unusual and attracts people's attention: *In those days, cars were still a novelty and most people used horses.*

**No·vem·ber** /noh-**vem**-bur/ *noun* (ABBREVIATION: **Nov.**) the 11th month of the year. November is between October and December: *Thanksgiving is in November. | My sister's birthday is on November 3.*

## Word Origin: November

**November** comes from the Latin word ***novem***, which means "nine." The old Roman calendar had ten months, and November was the ninth month. When the Romans started using a new calendar, they added two more months at the beginning of the year. November became the 11th month, but it kept its old name.

**nov·ice** /**nah**-viss/ *noun* someone who has only just learned how to do something

**now** /now/ *adverb*
**1** at the present time: *I used to live in Cuba, but now I live in the U.S.*
**2** immediately: *Come here now!* (ANTONYM: **later**)

IDIOMS with **now**
**now and then** sometimes, but not very often: *Now and then she asks me a question, but most of the time she doesn't speak.*

**now·a·days** /**now**-uh-dayz/ *adverb* now. You use nowadays when you are comparing now with a time in the past: *Nowadays, everybody carries a cell phone, but in the 1930s lots of people didn't even have a phone in the house!*

**no·where** /**noh**-wair/ *adverb*
**1** not any place: *There is nowhere to hang up your coat in this room.*
**2 get nowhere** to have no success: *You will get nowhere at school if you do not work hard.*

**nu·cle·ar** /**nook**-lee-ur/ *adjective*
**1** relating to nuclear energy: *France produces a lot of its electricity using nuclear power.*
**2** using nuclear weapons: *No one wants a nuclear war.*

**nu·cle·ar en·er·gy** /nook-lee-ur **en**-urj-ee/ *noun* the power produced by dividing an atom in two

or joining two atoms together: *Nuclear energy is used to make electricity.*

**nu·cle·ar fam·ily** /nook-lee-ur **fam**-lee/ *noun* a family that includes parents and children and no other people: *Not everyone lives in a nuclear family. Many people share a home with their cousins and grandparents.*

**nu·cle·ar weap·on** /nook-lee-ur **wep**-uhn/ *noun* a very powerful bomb or other weapon that uses nuclear energy

**nu·cle·us** /**nook**-lee-uhss/ *noun* (plural **nuclei** /**nook**-lee-ī/) the central part of an atom or cell: *There are electrons which are constantly moving around the nucleus of an atom.* ▶ see pictures at **atom, cell**

**nude** /nood/
● *adjective, adverb*
**1** not wearing any clothes, or showing someone without any clothes: *The movie has some nude scenes.*
**2 in the nude** not wearing any clothes: *He came out of the shower and stood there in the nude.*

**nudge** /nuhj/
● *verb* to push someone gently, especially with your elbow. You do this to get his or her attention: *Luis nudged me and said, "Did you see that?"*
● *noun* a gentle push: *Amy gave me a nudge and pointed.*

**nudge**

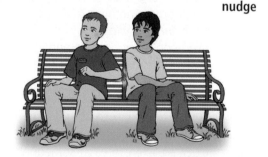

He nudged his friend in the arm.

**nug·get** /**nuhg**-it/ *noun* a small rough piece of gold or another valuable metal, that you find in the Earth

**nuisance**

**nug·get**

a gold nugget

**nui·sance** /**nooss**-uhnss/ *noun* someone or

something that annoys you or causes problems: *It's a nuisance when you forget your keys.*

**numb** /nuhm/ *adjective*
**1** if a part of your body is numb, you cannot feel anything in it: *It was very cold and my fingers were numb.*
**2** not able to react or show emotion in the normal way: *When my dad told me my dog had died, I felt numb.*

**num·ber** /**nuhm**-bur/
● *noun*
**1** a word or sign that shows a quantity: *Add the numbers 7, 4, and 3.* | *What is the answer to question number 8?* ▶ see **Thesaurus**
**2** a telephone number: *I'll call you later. What's your number?*
**3** an amount of something that you can count: *Daniel has a large number of friends.*
● *verb*
to give a number to something: *He numbered the pages of his essay.*

> ### Word Choice: number, amount
> Use **number** with nouns that are things you can count: *a small number of cookies* | *I talked to a number of people about the idea.*
>
> Use **amount** with nouns that are things you cannot count: *a small amount of food* | *Mom limits the amount of time I can watch TV.*

**num·ber line** /**nuhm**-bur līn/ *noun* a line with numbers written along it in order. Students can use a number line to help them add or take away numbers.

**num·ber one** /**nuhm**-bur wuhn/ *adjective* the best or most important: *Tiger Woods is the number one player in the world.*

**num·ber sen·tence** /**nuhm**-bur sent-uhnss/ *noun* a way of writing a calculation using numbers and signs such as +, -, and =: *1 + 2 = 3 is a number sentence.*

**nu·mer·al** /**noom**-uhr-uhl/ *noun* a number that is not written in words: *10, 89, and 323 are all numerals.*

**nu·me·ra·tor** /**noom**-uh-rayt-ur/ *noun* the number above the line in a fraction. The

numerator shows how many parts you have of the denominator (=the bottom number): *In the fraction 3/4, 3 is the numerator.*

**nu·mer·i·cal** /noo-**merr**-uhk-uhl/ *adjective* based on numbers: *I checked that the pages were all in numerical order.*

**num·er·ous** /**noom**-uhr-uhss/ *adjective* many: *There are numerous ways of cooking potatoes.*

**nun** /nuhn/ *noun* a woman who is a member of a group of religious women. Nuns live together in a convent: *Sister Agnes and the other nuns went into the church to pray.*

**nurse** /nurss/
● *noun* someone whose job is to take care of people who are sick or injured: *The nurses took care of him well when he was in the hospital.*
● *verb* to take care of someone who is sick or injured: *Mom had to return to Argentina to nurse her sick mother.*

nurse

**nurs·er·y** /**nurss**-uhr-ee/ *noun* (plural **nurseries**)
**1** a bedroom for a baby: *The baby was asleep in his crib in the nursery.*
**2** a place where you can buy trees and plants: *We bought a rose bush from a nursery.*

**nurs·er·y rhyme** /**nurss**-uhr-ee rīm/ *noun* a short poem or song for children that a lot of people know: *Her favorite nursery rhyme is "Humpty Dumpty."*

**nurs·er·y school** /**nurss**-uhr-ee skool/ *noun* a school for children from three to five years old: *My youngest sister is only four and she's still at nursery school.*

**nurs·ing** /**nurss**-ing/ *noun* the job of taking care of people who are sick, injured, or very old: *Nursing is a hard job but it is very rewarding.*

**nurs·ing home** /**nurss**-ing hohm/ *noun* a home for people who are too old or sick to take care of themselves: *Grandpa is in a nursing home.*

**nur·ture** /**nurch**-ur/ *verb* to help someone or something to grow and develop: *The coach tries to nurture the talents of the players and help them to improve their game.*

a b c d e f g h i j k l m **n** o p q r s t u v w x y z

**nut** /nuht/ *noun*
**1** a large seed that you can eat. It usually grows in a hard brown shell: *This cookie has nuts and raisins in it.*
**2** a small piece of metal with a hole in it. You use it with a bolt to fasten things together: *Dad used a wrench to tighten the nut.* ▶ see picture at **bolt**
**3** someone who is silly or crazy: *Some nut was running around the parking lot and yelling.*

nut

cashew nuts

pistachios

walnuts

peanuts

hazelnuts

pine nuts

chestnuts

coconuts

**nu·tri·ent** /**noo**-tree-uhnt/ *noun* a chemical or food that helps living things grow. Proteins, minerals, and vitamins are all nutrients: *Vegetables contain a lot of important nutrients.*

**nu·tri·tion** /noo-**trish**-uhn/ *noun* nutrition involves eating the right types of food to stay healthy and to grow: *Poor nutrition can make you very sick.*
— **nutritional** /noo-**trish**-uhn-uhl/ *adjective* relating to nutrition: *The website gives free recipes and nutritional advice.*

**nu·tri·tious** /noo-**trish**-uhss/ *adjective* nutritious food makes you stay healthy and grow well: *Peanuts are a nutritious snack.*

**nuts** /nuhtss/ *adjective*
**1** crazy: *Anyone who wants to jump out of an airplane is nuts!*
**2 go nuts** to become very angry: *Dad will go nuts if you break a window.*

**nut·ty** /**nuht**-ee/ *adjective*
**1** tasting like nuts: *Wild rice has a nutty flavor.*
**2** crazy: *He decided to walk backwards all the way to school. It was a nutty idea!*

**ny·lon** /**nīl**-ahn/ *noun* a strong material that is used for making plastic, cloth, and rope: *The tent is made from nylon.*

**ny·lons** /**nīl**-ahnz/ *plural noun* a thin piece of clothing that covers all of a woman's legs, feet, and lower body. Nylons are made of nylon.
SYNONYM: **pantyhose**

**-nym** /nim/

## Word Building

acro**nym** | anto**nym** | pseudo**nym** | syno**nym**

These words all have the Greek word root **nym** in them. **Nym** means "name" or "word." An *acronym* is a word that is made from the first letters of the name of something, such as N.A.S.A., which stands for National Aeronautics and Space Administration. A *pseudonym* is a name that an artist or writer uses instead of his or her real name. An *antonym* is a word that means the opposite of another word.

# Oo

**oak** /ohk/ *noun*
**1** a type of large tree. An oak's seeds are called acorns.
**2** the hard wood of an oak tree: *The heavy doors are made of oak.*

oak

**oar** /or/ *noun* a long pole with a wide flat part at one end. You use oars to row a boat.

oar

oar

**oath** /ohth/ *noun* (plural **oaths** /ohthz/) a serious promise: *Doctors have to take an oath to save people's lives if they can.* | *He is under oath and he has promised that he will tell the truth to the court.*

**oat·meal** /**oht**-meel/ *noun* a food made from cooked oats. You eat oatmeal for breakfast or use it in cooking: *We made some oatmeal cookies.*

**oats** /ohtss/ *plural noun* a grain that is used as food for people and animals: *Add a cup of oats to the cookie mixture.* | *The farmer gave the horse some oats.*
—**oat** /oht/ *adjective* made of oats: *oat cereal*

**o·be·di·ent** /uh-**beed**-ee-uhnt/ *adjective* always doing what a person or law tells you to do: *You must be obedient and do what your mother says.* ( ANTONYM: **disobedient** )
—**obediently** /uh-**beed**-ee-uhnt-lee/ *adverb* in an obedient way
—**obedience** /uh-**beed**-ee-uhnss/ *noun* obedient behavior

**o·bese** /oh-**beess**/ *adjective* very fat: *If you eat too much fried food you will become obese.*
—**obesity** /oh-**beess**-uht-ee/ *noun* the condition of being very fat: *Obesity can cause many health problems.*

**o·bey** /uh-**bay**/ *verb* to do what a person or law tells you to do: *If you do not obey the law, then you will be punished.* ( ANTONYM: **disobey** )

> ## Word Family: obey
> **obey** *verb* | **disobey** *verb* | **obedient** *adjective* | **disobedient** *adjective* | **obedience** *noun* | **disobedience** *noun*

**ob·ject**
● *noun* /**ahb**-jikt/
**1** a thing that you can see and touch: *Aircraft passengers are not allowed to carry sharp objects.*
**2** the purpose of a plan, action, or activity: *The object of the game is to score as many points as possible.*
**3** in grammar, the person or thing that is affected by the action of the verb: *"Apple" is the object in the sentence "I ate an apple."*
● *verb* /uhb-**jekt**/
to say that you do not agree with something: *My sister objected to the idea, and refused to help.*

**ob·jec·tion** /uhb-**jek**-shuhn/ *noun* the reason why someone does not agree with something: *My main objection to the plan is that it will cost too much money.*

**ob·jec·tive** /uhb-**jekt**-iv/ *noun* something that you are trying to achieve: *Our objective is to win the championship.*

**o·blig·a·to·ry** /uh-**blig**-uh-tor-ee/ *adjective* if something is obligatory, a law or rule says that you must do it: *The class is obligatory for all students and everyone must take it.*

a b c d e f g h i j k l m n **o** p q r s t u v w x y z

a b c d e f g h i j k l m n o p q r s t u v w x y z

**ob·long** /**ahb**-long/ *adjective* having a shape that is longer than it is wide: *The package was an oblong box which was 12 inches long by 8 inches wide.* (SYNONYM: **rectangular**)

**ob·nox·ious** /uhb-**nahk**-shuhss/ *adjective* very rude or unpleasant: *An obnoxious boy made rude gestures at them.*

**o·boe** /**ohb**-oh/ *noun* a long thin musical instrument made of wood. You play it by blowing into it and covering holes in it with your fingers: *My sister can play the oboe.*
▶ see picture at **woodwinds**

oboe

**ob·scene** /uhb-**seen**/ *adjective* offensive and shocking: *Students who use obscene language in class will be punished.*

**ob·scure** /uhb-**skyoor**/
● *adjective*
**1** not known by many people: *The book is by some obscure author that I have never heard of.*
**2** difficult to understand: *For some obscure reason, she likes Ryan. I don't like him at all.*
● *verb*
to make something difficult to see or hear: *Clouds obscured the top of the mountain.*

**ob·serv·ant** /uhb-**zurv**-uhnt/ *adjective* good at noticing things: *She's very observant and always notices what people are wearing.*

**ob·ser·va·tion** /ahbz-ur-**vaysh**-uhn/ *noun*
**1** the process of watching someone or something carefully for a long time: *Police observation of the man showed that he lived alone.*
**2** a remark about something that you have noticed: *She made some interesting observations about the dog's behavior.*

**ob·serv·a·to·ry** /uhb-**zurv**-uh-tor-ee/ *noun* (plural **observatories**) a special building with telescopes that scientists use to study the stars,

planets, and sky: *Observatories are usually built on mountains because the air is clearer for looking at the stars.*

**ob·serve** /uhb-**zurv**/ *verb*
**1** to notice something: *Mr. Davis observed the woman entering the building at 9:18.*
**2** to watch someone or something carefully: *Nurses carefully observed the patients for signs of the disease.*

**ob·sta·cle** /**ahb**-stik-uhl/ *noun*
**1** something that stops you doing something: *Lack of money was the main obstacle to the school's building plans.*
**2** something that blocks a road or path so that you must go around it: *They had to drive around branches and other obstacles in the road.*

**ob·sti·nate** /**ahb**-stuhn-it/ *adjective* refusing to change your opinions or behavior: *The little boy was obstinate and he refused to put on his shoes.*

**ob·tain** /uhb-**tayn**/ *verb* to get something: *You need to obtain permission from the principal if you want time off school.*

**ob·tuse an·gle** /uhb-tooss **ang**-guhl/ *noun* an angle between 90 and 180 degrees

**ob·tuse tri·an·gle** /uhb-tooss **trī**-ang-guhl/ *noun* a triangle that has one angle bigger than 90 degrees

**ob·vi·ous** /**ahb**-vee-uhss/ *adjective* easy to notice or understand: *It was obvious that Dan had been crying because his eyes were red.*
—**obviously** /**ahb**-vee-uhss-lee/ *adverb* if something is obviously true, it is easy to see that it is true: *She had a big house and was obviously very rich.*

**oc·ca·sion** /uh-**kayzh**-uhn/ *noun*
**1** a time when something happens: *We met each other on several occasions.*
**2** an important event: *I only wear this dress for weddings and other special occasions.*

**oc·ca·sion·al** /uh-**kayzh**-uhn'l/ *adjective* happening sometimes but not often: *I don't have candy every day, but Mom lets me have it as an occasional treat.*
—**occasionally** /uh-**kayzh**-uhn'l-ee/ *adverb* sometimes, but not often: *Mary has moved to another town, so now I only see her occasionally.*

**oc·cu·pant** /**ahk**-yuhp-uhnt/ *noun*
**1** someone who lives in a house, room, or building: *The burglar entered the house while the occupants were out.*
**2** someone who is in a vehicle or seat: *The two occupants of the car were seriously injured in the accident.*

**oc·cu·pa·tion** /ahk-yuh-**paysh**-uhn/ *noun*
**1** a job: *"What is your occupation?" "I'm a teacher."*
**2** a situation in which an army is in a place and has taken control of it: *The enemy's occupation of the city lasted several months.*

**oc·cu·py** /**ahk**-yuh-pī/ *verb* (**occupies**, **occupied**)
**1** to live in or use a building: *The company occupies the first floor of the office building.*
**2** to keep someone busy: *I occupied myself by playing with my toy soldiers.*
**3** to enter and get control of a place by force: *The soldiers occupied the city for several months.*
**4** to fill a space: *The piano was very big and it occupied most of the room.*

**oc·cur** /uh-**kur**/ *verb* (**occurring**, **occurred**)
**1** to happen: *The accident occurred on Monday night.*
**2** **occur to** if a thought or idea occurs to you, you suddenly think of it: *It suddenly occurred to him that he should tell his mom where he was going.*

**o·cean** /**ohsh**-uhn/ *noun*
**1** the large amount of salt water that covers most of the Earth's surface: *The ships sailed across the ocean. | We went swimming in the ocean.*
**2** one of the four large areas of salt water that make up the whole ocean: *Hawaii is in the Pacific Ocean.*

**o'clock** /uh-**klahk**/ *adverb* used when saying what the time is: *School starts at eight o'clock.*

**oct-** /ahkt/

## Word Building

**octagon | octopus**
These words have the Greek word root **oct-** in them. **Oct-** means eight. An *octagon* is a shape with eight sides and eight angles. An *octopus* is an ocean animal with eight arms.

**oc·ta·gon** /**ahkt**-uh-gahn/ *noun* a shape with eight sides and eight angles

octagon

**Oc·to·ber** /ahk-**tohb**-ur/ *noun* (ABBREVIATION: **Oct.**) the tenth month of the year. October is between September and November: *It's Matthew's birthday on October 20. | My sister will be two in October.*

## Word Origin: October

**October** comes from the Latin word **octo**, which means "eight." The old Roman calendar had ten months, and October was the eighth month. When the Romans started using a new calendar, they added two more months at the beginning of the year. October became the tenth month, but it kept its old name.

**oc·to·pus** /**ahkt**-uhp-uhss/ *noun* (plural **octopuses** or **octopi** /**ahkt**-uh-pī/) an ocean animal with a soft round body and eight arms

octopus

**odd** /ahd/ *adjective*
**1** strange or different from normal: *The tomato was an odd shape – a bit like a carrot.*
**2** an odd number cannot be divided by 2: *1, 3, 5, and 7 are all odd numbers.*

**odds** /ahdz/ *plural noun* how likely it is that something will happen: *The team's odds of winning are not very good.*

**o·dor** /**ohd**-ur/ *noun* a bad smell: *There was a bad odor coming from the trash can.*

a b c d e f g h i j k l m n **o** p q r s t u v w x y z

**of** /uhv, ahv/ *preposition*

**1** used when something has a feature or quality: *I like the color of your dress.* | *I was impressed by the size of the trees.*

**2** belonging to someone or something: *Jane is a friend of my mom.*

**3** containing something: *Do you want a glass of milk?*

**4** showing or describing someone or something: *He showed us a picture of his house.* | *It was a story of great bravery.*

**5** used when something is part of something: *I've read the first chapter of the book.*

**6** made or produced by someone: *the plays of Shakespeare*

**7** used about the members of a group: *A group of kids was playing in the park.*

**8** used when giving the time, to mean "before": *It's ten of five* (=ten minutes before 5:00).

(SYNONYM: **to**)

**9** because of something: *He died of a heart attack.*

**off** /of/ *adverb, preposition, adjective*

**1** not on something, or removed from something: *Keep off the grass!* | *He was too hot so he took his coat off.* (ANTONYM: **on**)

**2** away from a place: *She waved and drove off.*

**3** out of a bus, airplane, train, or boat: *We're getting off the bus at the next stop.*
(ANTONYM: **on**)

**4** if a machine or light is off, someone has made it stop working for a time: *He turned the TV off and went out.* (ANTONYM: **on**)

**5** a distance away, or in the future: *The school is just off Sunset Drive.* | *Summer is a long way off.*

**6** used when a price is reduced: *The jeans were 50% off, so I got them for $20 instead of $40.*

**7** not at work or school: *Dad's off tomorrow so he's taking us to the movies.*

**8** if a planned event is off, it will not now happen: *The school concert's off because the music teacher is sick.* (ANTONYM: **on**)

┌ **IDIOM with off**
│ **off and on** (also **on and off**) for short periods
│ of time during a longer period: *My sister's been
└ dating Brad off and on for five years.*

**of·fend** /uh-**fend**/ *verb* to make someone angry

and upset: *He was offended by her refusal to go to his party.*

┌─────────────────────────────────────────┐
│ **Word Family:** offend                  │
│                                          │
│ **offend** *verb* | **offense** *noun* | **offensive** │
│ *adjective*                              │
└─────────────────────────────────────────┘

**of·fend·er** /uh-**fend**-ur/ *noun* someone who is guilty of a crime: *Offenders face up to seven years in jail.*

**of·fense** /uh-**fenss**/ *noun*

**1** an action that is against the law: *The police stopped him for a speeding offense because he was driving much too fast.* | *The men are guilty of drugs offenses and they will go to prison.*
(SYNONYM: **crime**)

**2** /**of**-enss/ the group of players who try to score points in a sports game: *The offense has scored an average of 3.6 runs per game.*

**3** /**of**-enss/ the action of trying to score points in a sports game: *The Bears need to work on their offense this season.*

┌ **IDIOM with offense**
│ **take offense** to feel angry and upset because
│ of what someone has said or done: *She took
│ offense when I said I was too busy to go to her
└ house.*

**of·fen·sive** /uh-**fenss**-iv/ *adjective*

**1** very impolite and likely to upset people: *He had made offensive remarks about the color of her skin.* (SYNONYM: **rude**)

**2** used for attacking: *offensive weapons*
(ANTONYM: **defensive**)

**of·fer** /**of**-ur/

● *verb*

**1** to ask someone if he or she would like to have something: *I offered him a slice of my pizza.*

**2** to say that you will do something for someone: *Todd offered to help me with my homework.*

**3** to say that you are willing to pay a particular amount for something: *Dad offered him $40 for the bike.*

● *noun*

a statement that you are willing to do something for someone or give someone something: *He didn't receive any offers of help.*

**of·fice** /**of**-iss/ *noun*

**1** a room or building where people work at

desks: *My mom works in an office as a secretary.* | *I called the doctor's office for an appointment.*

**2** an important job, especially in government: *This is the president's first year in office.*

**of·fi·cer** /**of**-uhss-ur/ *noun*
**1** someone who has an important position in the army, navy, or air force: *The officer ordered his men to attack the enemy soldiers.*
**2** a police officer: *Officer Steele arrested him for stealing cars.*
**3** someone who has an important position in an organization: *O'Connor is the company's chief financial officer.*

**of·fi·cial** /uh-**fish**-uhl/
● *adjective* done or produced by someone who has an important position in an organization: *Official figures show that the crime rate is increasing.*
—**officially** /uh-**fish**-uhl-ee/ *adverb* in an official way: *They live together but they are not officially married.*
● *noun* someone who has an important position in an organization: *Federal officials raided the company's offices last week.*

**off·side** /of-**sīd**/ *adjective*, *adverb* if a soccer or hockey player is offside, he or she has broken a rule by being ahead of the ball: *Montella scored but he was ruled offside and the goal was not allowed.*

**off·spring** /**of**-spring/ *noun* (plural **offspring**)
**1** an animal's baby or babies: *The mother bird brings food to the nest for her offspring.*
**2** a person's child or children: *Mothers want to protect their offspring.*

**of·ten** /**of**-uhn/ *adverb* many times: *Ben's sometimes late for school, but not often.*
( ANTONYM: **rarely** ) ▸ see **Thesaurus**

IDIOM with **often**
**how often** used to ask how many times something happens: *"How often do you visit your grandmother?" "Three or four times a year."*

**o·gre** /**ohg**-ur/ *noun*
**1** a big person who eats people in children's stories: *A big ogre lived in the forest and everyone was afraid of him.*

**2** a cruel and frightening person: *We all thought that my uncle was an ogre because he was very strict.*

**oh** /oh/ said when you are surprised, happy, upset, or disappointed: *Oh, no! I forgot to bring my homework!*

**oil** /oyl/
● *noun*
**1** a thick liquid from under the ground, used for making gasoline: *Saudi Arabia is the world's biggest oil producer.*
**2** a thick liquid from a plant, which you use in cooking: *Fry the vegetables in olive oil.*
● *verb*
to put oil into or onto something: *He oiled the hinges of the door to stop them from making a squeaking noise.*

**oil rig** /**oyl** rig/ *noun* a structure with equipment for getting oil from under the ocean or under the ground

**oil slick** /**oyl** slik/ *noun* an area of oil floating on the water

**oil well** /**oyl** wel/ *noun* a deep hole that people dig so that they can get oil out from under the ground

**oil well**

**oil·y** /**oyl**-ee/ *adjective* covered with oil, or containing a lot of oil: *The car mechanic wiped his hands on an oily rag.*

**oink** /oynk/ *noun* the sound that a pig makes

**oint·ment** /**oynt**-muhnt/ *noun* a substance that you rub into your skin as a medicine: *He put some ointment on his sore skin.*

447

**o·kay**, OK /oh-**kay**/
● *adjective*
**1** used for saying yes: *"Can I come too?" "Okay."*
( SYNONYM: **all right** )
**2** used to get people's attention because you want to say something: *OK, is everyone ready?*
**3** acceptable: *"Sorry I'm late." "That's okay."*
( SYNONYM: **all right** )
**4** not sick, hurt, or unhappy: *You look very pale. Are you okay?* ( SYNONYM: **all right** )
**5** fairly good: *"Was the movie good?" "It was OK, but it was too long."* ( SYNONYM: **all right** )
● *adverb*
fairly well: *He's doing OK at school.*

## Word Origin: okay, OK

OK or **okay** is an American word that people around the world have started to use. No one is completely sure where the word okay comes from. This is the story that most people believe.

In the early 1800s, people thought it was funny to say or write things in a way that showed a strange pronunciation. Instead of "all correct," they would say "oll korrect." People also thought it was funny to use letters instead of saying whole words, a little bit like us writing LOL instead of "laugh out loud." So, people started saying "OK" instead of "oll korrect."

**old** /ohld/ *adjective*
**1** having lived for a long time: *My grandmother is very old – she's 98.* ( ANTONYM: **young** )
▶ see picture at **young** ▶ see Thesaurus
**2** having existed for a long time: *This old building is full of history.* ( ANTONYM: **new** ) ▶ see picture at **new**
**3** used for asking or talking about the age of someone or something: *"How old are you?" "I'm ten." | Our dog is three years old.*
**4** used for talking about the house, school, car, etc. that you had before but do not have now: *I preferred our old house – our new one is much smaller.*

**old age** /ohld **ayj**/ *noun* the time when you are old: *In old age, people's hair turns gray and they get wrinkles.*

**old-fash·ioned** /ohld **fash**-uhnd/ *adjective* not modern or popular now, but used in the past: *In the picture, the family are wearing old-fashioned clothes.*

**old-fashioned**

an old-fashioned phone

a modern phone

**ol·ive** /**ahl**-iv/ *noun* a small green or black fruit that you can eat or use for making oil: *olive oil*

**olive**

black olive

green olive

**O·lym·pic Games** /uh-limp-ik **gaymz**/ (also **Olympics**) *plural noun* a sports competition that happens every four years. People from many different countries take part: *The 2008 Olympic Games were held in Beijing.*
—**Olympic** /uh-**limp**-ik/ *adjective* relating to the Olympic Games: *Olympic athletes*

**ome·let**, omelette /**ahm**-lit/ *noun* a type of food made from eggs. You mix the eggs together and then cook them in a pan without stirring them. You usually put cheese or vegetables in an omelet and then fold it over: *a mushroom omelet*

**om·i·nous** /**ahm**-uh-nuhss/ *adjective* making you feel worried that something bad will happen: *There were some ominous black clouds and I thought it would rain soon.*

**o·mis·sion** /oh-**mish**-uhn/ *noun*
**1** the action of not including something or someone: *His omission from the team was a surprise because everyone expected him to be included.*
**2** something which has not been included: *There was one omission from the list. Tom's name was not on it.*

**o·mit** /oh-**mit**/ *verb* (**omitting**, **omitted**) to not include something: *They sang the song but omitted the last verse.* ( SYNONYM: **leave out** )

**om·ni·vore** /**ahm**-ni-vor/ *noun* an animal that eats meat and plants: *Pigs and humans are omnivores.*

**on** /on/ *preposition, adjective, adverb*
**1** supported by a surface, or covering part of a surface: *There is a book on the table.* | *You have paint on your face.* ( ANTONYM: **off** )
**2** wearing something: *It's cold outside. Put your coat on.* ( ANTONYM: **off** )
**3** in a particular place: *Look at the picture on page 4.* | *I live on a farm.* | *My house is the first house on the right.*
**4** in or into a bus, airplane, train, or boat: *I got on the school bus.* ( ANTONYM: **off** )
**5** at the side of a road, river, lake, or sea: *The toy store is on Market Street.*
**6** during a particular day: *Their next game is on March 12.* | *I'm going swimming on Tuesday.*
**7** if a machine or light is on, someone has made it start working: *All the lights were on.* | *Is your computer on?* ( ANTONYM: **off** )
**8** being broadcast by a television or radio station: *There's a good program on TV tonight.* | *My favorite show is on at five.*
**9** about a particular subject: *I'm reading a book on space.*
**10** using something: *Mom is talking on the phone.* | *I can play that song on the guitar.*
**11** taking part or included in something: *Are you on the basketball team?*

**on**

The lamp is on.

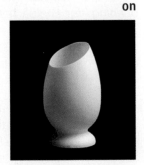

The lamp is off.

**once** /wuhnss/
● *adverb*
**1** one time: *I've only been to New York once.* | *I go swimming once a week – every Saturday.*
**2** at a time in the past: *This area was once just fields but there are now houses.*

IDIOMS with **once**
**at once**
**1** at the same time: *I can't hear when you're all talking at once.*
**2** immediately: *He knew at once that it was his sister's voice.*
**once again/more** one more time: *The team once again played very well.*
**once upon a time** a long time ago. This is used at the beginning of children's stories: *Once upon a time, there was a young princess who lived in a castle.*
● *conjunction*
after or when: *It's easy, once you learn how to do it.*

**one** /wuhn/
● *number*
**1** 1: *I have one brother and two sisters.* | *One of my teachers is French.*
**2** one o'clock: *We eat lunch at one.*
**3** one year old: *The little boy is one next week.*
**4** in math, a unit which is equal to 1: *In the number 346, the 6 is in the ones place.*

IDIOM with **one**
**one or two** a few: *I just bought one or two things.*
● *pronoun*
**1** used instead of a noun when it is clear which thing you mean: *"Do you have a bike?" "No, but I'm getting one for my birthday."* | *"Which cake do you want?" "That one, please."*
**2** people in general: *One does not usually ask adults how old they are.*
● *adjective*
**1** on a day, evening, etc. in the past: *I saw him out with his girlfriend one evening.*
**2** at some time in the future: *I'd like to visit England one day.*
**3** only: *My one goal is to do better in school.*

**one·self** /wuhn-**self**/ *pronoun* used when saying that people in general do something to themselves: *One should be honest with oneself.*

**one-way** /**wuhn** way/ *adjective*
**1** moving or allowing movement in only one direction: *He was driving the wrong direction on a one-way street.*
**2** a one-way ticket lets you travel to a place but not back again

**on·go·ing** /**on**-goh-ing/ *adjective* continuing: *The ongoing war is causing a lot of suffering.*

**on·ion** /**uhn**-yuhn/ *noun* a round vegetable with a strong smell and taste: *My eyes water when I chop onions.* ▶ see picture on page **A7**

**on·line** /on-**līn**/ *adjective, adverb* using the Internet: *If you have the Internet, you can buy your tickets online.* | *online shopping*

**on·ly** /**ohn**-lee/
● *adverb*
**1** used when a number or amount seems small: *There were only ten students in the class.*
**2** not anyone or anything else: *The movie is suitable for adults only.* ( SYNONYM: **just** )
**3** not in any other way or not in any other situation: *You can only get there by boat. There are no roads to the area.* ( SYNONYM: **just** )
**4** used for saying that something is not very important or serious: *Don't get upset – I was only joking.* ( SYNONYM: **just** )

> **IDIOM with only**
> **if only** used when you wish that something could happen or were true: *I miss my grandfather. If only I could see him again.*

● *adjective*
**1** used for saying that there is not more than one person or thing: *The only seat left is at the back of the class.*
**2** an only child has no brothers or sisters
● *conjunction*
but: *I'd come, only I must do my homework.*

**on·to** /**ont**-uh, **ont**-oo/ *preposition* to a place which is on something: *The cat jumped onto the table.*

**on·ward** /**on**-wurd/ (also **onwards**) *adverb*
**1** beginning at a particular time: *From the 1980s onward, the town got bigger.*
**2** forward: *They traveled onward to Auckland.*

**oops** /upss/ said when someone falls or makes a small mistake: *Oops! I've spelled your name wrong.*

**ooze** /ooz/ *verb* to flow slowly from something: *Blood oozed from the cut on his knee.*

**o·paque** /oh-**payk**/ *adjective* not letting light through: *Milk is opaque, so you can't see through it and it blocks light, but water is clear and lets light through.* ( ANTONYM: **clear, transparent** )

**open** /**ohp**-uhn/
● *adjective*
**1** not closed: *The door was open so the dog ran out.* ▶ see picture at **ajar** ▶ see **Thesaurus**
**2** if a store, museum, etc. is open, people can come in: *The store is open 8:30 through 5:30.*
**3** an open area is not surrounded by things or does not have many buildings or trees on it: *Seattle has a lot of parks and open spaces.*
**4** honest and not having secrets: *It is always best to be open with people and tell them about your true feelings.*
● *verb*
**1** to move something so that it is open: *I opened the window because I was too hot.* ( ANTONYMS: **close, shut** ) ▶ see **Thesaurus**
**2** to become open: *The door opened and a man came in.* ( ANTONYMS: **close, shut** )
**3** when a store, museum, etc. opens, people can come in: *The libary opens at 9 a.m.* ( ANTONYM: **close** )
**4** to start something: *She opened the meeting by welcoming everyone.* ( ANTONYM: **close** )

**o·pen·er** /**ohp**-uhn-ur/ *noun* a tool used for opening things: *a can opener*

**o·pen·ing** /**ohp**-uhn-ing/
● *noun*
**1** the time when a new store, museum, etc. is open for the first time: *Yesterday was the official opening of the new airport.*
**2** a hole in something: *She looked through a small opening in the front of the tent.*
**3** a chance, especially for a job: *There are many openings for English teachers in China.*
● *adjective*
coming at the start of something: *The opening chapter of the book introduces all of the main characters.*

**o·pen·ly** /**ohp**-uhn-lee/ *adverb* not trying to hide your feelings or things that you know about: *I trust my dad and I feel that I can talk openly about my problems with him.*

**op·era** /**ahp**-ruh/ *noun* a play in which the actors sing all the words: *Mozart wrote many famous operas.*

**op·er·ate** /**ahp**-uh-rayt/ *verb*
**1** to use a machine: *The camera is easy to operate.*

**2** to work: *The company operates in the U.S. and Europe.*
**3** to cut into someone's body to fix or remove a damaged part: *Doctors operated to fix the hole in his heart.*

**op·er·a·tion** /ahp-uh-**raysh**-uhn/ *noun*
**1** the process of cutting into someone's body to fix or remove a damaged part: *My dad was in the hospital for an operation on his knee.*
**2** something people do to achieve something: *The rescue operation was successful and all the people were saved.*

**op·er·a·tor** /**ahp**-uh-rayt-ur/ *noun*
**1** someone who connects telephone calls: *The hotel operator can connect your call.*
**2** someone whose job is to use a machine or piece of equipment: *the ship's radio operator*

**o·pin·ion** /uh-**pin**-yuhn/ *noun* your ideas about something, for example whether you think it is good or right: *What's your opinion about the death penalty?* | *In my opinion, it's a very good book.* ▶ see **Thesaurus**

**o·pos·sum** /uh-**pahss**-uhm/ *noun* an animal with thick fur and a long nose. An opossum looks like a large rat and it can climb trees. After its babies are born, an opossum carries them in a pouch on its stomach.

**Word Origin: opossum**

When English people came to North America, they had never seen an **opossum** before. They borrowed the word opossum from a Native American language. In that language, opossum means "white animal." Opossums are sometimes called "possums."

opossum

**op·po·nent** /uh-**pohn**-uhnt/ *noun*
**1** the person or team you are competing against in a game, competition, or election: *Venus Williams beat her opponent 6–2, 6–1.*
**2** someone who does not agree with a plan or action: *Opponents of the government protested outside government buildings.*

**op·por·tu·ni·ty** /ahp-ur-**toon**-uht-ee/ *noun* (plural **opportunities**) a chance to do something: *We had the opportunity to ask questions at the end of the class.*

**op·pose** /uh-**pohz**/ *verb* to disagree with a plan or action: *They oppose the plan because they think it will cost too much money.*

**op·posed** /uh-**pohzd**/ *adjective* disagreeing with a plan or action: *He was opposed to the war and joined the protest.*

**op·pos·ing** /uh-**pohz**-ing/ *adjective* opposing teams or groups are trying to defeat each other: *We won the game but the opposing team played well too.*

**op·po·site** /**ahp**-uh-zit/
● *noun*
someone or something that is completely different from someone or something else: *Fat is the opposite of thin.* | *The two boys are complete opposites – one is very talkative, and the other is very quiet.*
● *adjective*
**1** completely different: *Rich and poor have opposite meanings.* | *She was going in the opposite direction – I was going to the school and she was coming home.*
**2** on the other side of something: *He crossed to the opposite side of the street.*
● *preposition, adverb*
facing someone or something: *The art room is opposite our classroom.* | *They live in the house opposite ours.*

**op·po·si·tion** /ahp-uh-**zish**-uhn/ *noun*
**1** strong disagreement with something: *There was a lot of opposition to the plans to close the school.*
**2** the person or team you are competing against: *We won because the opposition played very badly.*

a
b
c
d
e
f
g
h
i
j
k
l
m
n
**o**
p
q
r
s
t
u
v
w
x
y
z

**op·press** /uh-**press**/ *verb* to treat people cruelly and not give them any rights: *The people are being oppressed by the military government and they are not allowed to have free speech.*
—**oppressed** /uh-**prest**/ *adjective* being cruelly treated and not having any rights: *The native people are an oppressed minority group.*
—**oppression** /uh-**presh**-uhn/ *noun* when people oppress other people: *Nelson Mandela fought against racial oppression in South Africa.*

**opt** /ahpt/ *verb* to choose to do something: *My sister opted to study English instead of Spanish.*

**op·ti·cal** /**ahpt**-ik-uhl/ *adjective* relating to seeing things: *The company makes optical equipment such as lenses and microscopes.*

**op·ti·cian** /ahp-**tish**-uhn/ *noun* someone who makes or sells glasses: *Mom took me to the optician because I failed a sight test.*

**op·ti·mism** /**ahpt**-uh-miz-uhm/ *noun* a belief that good things will happen: *Because of her optimism, she was sure that things would get better.* ( ANTONYM: **pessimism** )

**op·ti·mist** /**ahpt**-uhm-ist/ *noun* someone who believes that good things will happen: *An optimist would not worry about the future.*
( ANTONYM: **pessimist** )

**op·ti·mist·ic** /ahpt-uh-**mist**-ik/ *adjective* believing that good things will happen: *He was very optimistic and thought he would win the competition.* ( ANTONYM: **pessimistic** )

**op·tion** /**ahp**-shuhn/ *noun* something that you can choose to do or have: *She has the option to take the test again if she fails.*

**op·tion·al** /**ahp**-shuhn'l/ *adjective* if something is optional, you can choose if you want to have it or do it: *The French class is optional but we have to study English.* ( ANTONYM: **mandatory** )

**op·tom·e·trist** /ahp-**tahm**-uh-trist/ *noun* someone who tests people's eyes and orders glasses for them: *The optometrist said I need to wear glasses.*

**or** /ur, or/ *conjunction*
**1** used when mentioning another possible thing: *Would you like milk or cola?*
**2** used when mentioning another thing after "not," "never," etc.: *I don't like apples or pears.*
**3** used when mentioning something bad that will happen if someone does not do something: *Clean up the mess or Mom will be mad.*

**-or** /ur/

**Word Building**

**-or** is a suffix. It is used in nouns.
act**or** | doct**or** | profess**or** | sail**or** | sculpt**or**
**-or** means that a person does something. An *actor* acts in movies and TV shows. A *doctor* helps people who are sick or hurt. A *sculptor* is a kind of artist who makes things out of clay, wood, or metal.

**o·ral** /**or**-uhl/ *adjective*
**1** spoken, not written: *We did an oral history project and recorded people talking about their lives.*
**2** relating to the mouth: *oral cancer*

**or·ange** /**or**-inj/
● *noun*
**1** a fruit that is round and very juicy. An orange has thick skin that is orange in color: *Eduardo peeled the orange and ate it.* | *He was drinking a glass of orange juice.* ▶ see picture on page **A7**
**2** a color that is a mix of red and yellow
● *adjective*
having a color that is a mix of red and yellow: *Carrots are orange.*

**Word Origin:** orange

You might think that **oranges** are named for their color, but it is the other way around! The word orange comes from Sanskrit, a language of India. As oranges started to be grown and sold in different countries, the name moved into different languages. The word for the fruit came into English first, in the 1300s. It was almost 200 years before people started calling the color orange in the 1500s.

**o·rang·u·tan** /uh-**rang**-uh-tan/ *noun* a large ape that has long arms and orange-brown hair: *Orangutans live in trees in Borneo and Sumatra.* ▶ see picture at **ape**

**or·bit** /**orb**-it/
● *noun* the path of an object that is moving

around another object in space: *The picture shows the Moon's orbit around the Earth.*
● *verb* to move around an object in space: *Many satellites now orbit the Earth.*

**or·chard** /**orch**-urd/ *noun* a place where fruit trees are growing: *The orchard is full of apple trees.*

**or·ches·tra** /**ork**-iss-truh/ *noun* a large group of musicians who play together. The musicians play different instruments, such as violins, flutes, and drums. Orchestras usually play classical music: *Ryan plays the violin in the school orchestra.*

orchestra

**or·deal** /or-**deel**/ *noun* a very bad experience: *The woman had a terrifying ordeal when she got locked in the basement.*

**or·der** /**ord**-ur/
● *noun*
**1** the way that you arrange things: *The names were written in alphabetical order so Andrew was before Ben.*
**2** something that you ask for in a restaurant: *The waiter came to the table and took our order.*
**3** something that you ask a company to send you: *Orders made before 12:00 will be delivered the next day.*
**4** something that someone tells you to do: *Soldiers must obey orders.* ( SYNONYM: **command** )
**5** a situation in which people obey rules and do not behave violently: *When there were riots, the police soon restored order.*

⎰ **IDIOMS with order**
**in order to** so that you can do something: *Mom came to school in order to speak to the principal.*
**out of order** if a machine is out of order, it is not working: *The candy machine was out of order so I couldn't get a candy bar.*

● *verb*
**1** to ask for something in a restaurant: *I ordered a burger and fries.*
**2** to ask a business to send you something: *Mom and Dad have ordered a new sofa.*
**3** to tell someone to do something: *The teacher ordered him to sit down.*

**or·dered pair** /ord-urd **pair**/ *noun* a set of two numbers in a fixed order. An ordered pair can show you the position of a point on a grid.

**or·der·ly** /**ord**-ur-lee/ *adjective*
**1** arranged or organized in a neat way: *The tools were arranged in orderly rows so they were easy to find.*
**2** sensible and calm: *If there's a fire, students should leave the building in an orderly way.*

**or·di·nal num·ber** /ord'n-uhl **nuhm**-bur/ *noun* a word that shows the position of something in a series of things: *"First," "second," "third," etc. are ordinal numbers.*

**or·di·nar·i·ly** /ord'n-**air**-uhl-ee/ *adverb* usually: *Ordinarily, Dad takes us swimming on weekends.*

**or·di·nar·y** /**ord**'n-air-ee/ *adjective* not different or special: *He liked reading about ordinary people, not famous people.*

**ore** /or/ *noun* rock or earth that contains metal: *The country exports iron ore.*

**or·gan** /**org**-uhn/ *noun*
**1** a part of your body that does a particular job: *The heart is the organ that makes blood move around your body.*
**2** a musical instrument like a piano but with long pipes: *She plays the organ for the church.*

organ

pipes

keyboard

**or·gan·ic** /or-**gan**-ik/ *adjective*
**1** grown or produced without using chemicals: *The restaurant uses only organic meat and vegetables.*
**2** relating to living things: *You can improve soil by adding organic matter such as leaves and grass.*
—**organically** /or-**gan**-ik-lee/ *adverb* without using chemicals: *The vegetables are grown organically.*

a b c d e f g h i j k l m n **o** p q r s t u v w x y z

**or·ga·nism** /org-uh-niz-uhm/ *noun* a living thing, especially a very small one: *Viruses and bacteria are organisms.*

**or·ga·ni·za·tion** /org-uh-nuh-**zaysh**-uhn/ *noun*
**1** a group such as a club or business: *The organization works to help homeless people.*
▶ see **Thesaurus**
**2** the way in which something is organized: *The political organization of the city has changed.*
**3** the job of organizing something: *Maria was responsible for the organization of the school play.*

**or·ga·nize** /org-uh-nīz/ *verb*
**1** to plan an activity or event: *My parents are organizing a party for my birthday.*
**2** to put people or things into an order or system: *She organized the letters and put the most recent ones on top.*

**Word Family:** organize

organize *verb* | organized *adjective* | disorganized *adjective* | organization *noun*

**or·ga·nized** /**org**-uh-nīzd/ *adjective*
**1** planned or arranged carefully: *The book is well organized – it's easy to find the information you need.* ( ANTONYM: **disorganized** )
**2** an organized person plans and arranges things carefully: *Diego is very organized and always finishes his work on time.*
( ANTONYM: **disorganized** )

**or·ga·nized list** /org-uh-nīzd **list**/ *noun* a list of important information that you write to help you solve a math problem

**or·i·gin** /**or**-uhj-in/ *noun*
**1** the start of something: *There are different ideas about the origin of the universe, but no one knows for sure how it started.*
**2** the place or group of people that someone comes from: *Many of the students are of Hispanic origin and speak Spanish at home.*

**Word Family:** origin

origin *noun* | original *adjective* | originally *adverb*

**o·rig·i·nal** /uh-**rij**-uhn'l/ *adjective*
**1** first: *These are the original tiles that were on the floor when the house was built.*

**2** new and different: *The book is full of original ideas for unusual birthday parties.*
**3** not copied: *The original painting is in the museum but you can buy copies.*

**o·rig·i·nal·ly** /uh-**rij**-uhn'l-ee/ *adverb* in the beginning: *My family is originally from Mexico but we've been living in the U.S. for ten years.*

**or·i·ole** /**or**-ee-ohl/ *noun* a bird that is black with a red and yellow stripe on its wings

**or·na·ment**
/**orn**-uh-muhnt/ *noun* a beautiful object that you show in your home, or use to decorate something: *We hung the ornaments on the Christmas tree.*

ornament
ornament

**or·phan** /**orf**-uhn/ *noun* a child whose parents are dead

**or·phan·age** /**orf**-uhn-ij/ *noun* a home for children whose parents are dead: *He lived in an orphanage after his parents were killed in a road accident.*

**orth·o·don·tist** /orth-uh-**dahnt**-ist/ *noun* someone whose job is to make people's teeth straight: *The orthodontist said I needed braces.*

**os·trich** /**ahss**-trich/ *noun* a very large African bird with long legs and a long neck. Ostriches run fast but cannot fly.

ostrich

**oth·er** /**uhth**-ur/ *adjective, pronoun*
**1** the second of two things: *I have one glove but I don't know where the other is.*
**2** the rest of a group: *John is here, but the other children are still at school.*
**3** different or extra: *Does anyone have any other questions? | Some computers are better than others.* ( SYNONYM: **additional** )

IDIOMS with **other**
**other than** except for: *He had no money with him other than a dime.* ( SYNONYM: **besides** )
**the other day/week** recently: *I saw Mario the other week.*

**oth·er·wise** /**uh**_th_-ur-wīz/ *adverb*
**1** used when mentioning something bad that will happen if someone does not do something: *You should leave now otherwise you'll be late.*
( SYNONYM: **or else** )
**2** if the situation had been different: *He had to have an operation. Otherwise, he would have died.*
**3** except for what has just been mentioned: *The plane was delayed, but otherwise the trip was good.*

**ot·ter** /**aht**-ur/ *noun* a small animal with thick brown fur. Otters live near water and eat fish.

**otter**

**ouch** /owch/
*interjection* said when you suddenly feel pain: *Ouch! That hurt!*

**ought to** /**ot**-uh, ot-oo/ *verb*
**1** used when saying that someone should do something: *New York's a great place – you ought to go there.* ( SYNONYM: **should** )
**2** used when saying what you expect to happen: *You ought to get a seat. The bus is never full.*
( SYNONYM: **should** )

**ounce** /ownss/ *noun* ( ABBREVIATION: **oz.** ) a unit for measuring weight. An ounce is equal to 28.35 grams: *There are 16 ounces in a pound.*

**our** /ar, ow-ur/ *adjective* belonging to us: *Our dog is called "Bouncer."*

**ours** /ow-urz/ *pronoun* something that belongs to us: *"Whose car is that?" "It's ours."*

**our·selves** /ow-ur-**selvz**/ *pronoun*
**1** the people, including yourself, that you have just mentioned: *It was strange seeing ourselves on television.*
**2** used with "we" to emphasize that we did something: *We started the school choir ourselves.*

IDIOM with ourselves
**by ourselves** alone or without help: *Amy and I made supper all by ourselves – Mom didn't help us.*

**-ous** /uhss/

## Word Building

**-ous** is a suffix. It is used in adjectives.
**adventur**ous | **anx**ious | **courte**ous | **danger**ous | **marvel**ous | **religi**ous
**-ous** means that someone or something has a particular quality. Someone who is *adventurous* has the quality of liking adventure. A *dangerous* situation has the quality of danger. A *religious* person has the quality of believing in a religion.

**out** /owt/ *adverb, adjective*
**1** away from the inside of a place: *It's cold today so take your jacket if you're going out.*
( ANTONYM: **in** )
**2** not at home, or not in your office: *Dad's out but I'll tell him you called when he gets home.*
( ANTONYM: **in** )
**3** if a player is out, he or she cannot play in the game anymore: *If you hit the ball and someone catches it, you are out.*
**4** not shining or burning: *Turn the light out and go to sleep.* | *She blew out all the candles on the cake.*
**5** away from the main part or center of something: *Paths lead out from the farm into the countryside.* | *Everybody spread out so that you have space around you.*
**6** able to be seen in the sky: *The clouds disappeared and the sun came out.*
**7** available to buy: *Her new book will be out next month.*
**8** aloud: *He read out the names of the winners.*
**9** if you are out of something, you do not have any because you have used it all: *We're out of milk – I'll go get some from the store.*

## Word Building

**out-** is a prefix.
**out**dated | **out**doors | **out**field | **out**going | **out**standing
**out-** means "away from." If you go *outdoors*, you go away from a building and its doors. People who are *outgoing* like to meet and talk to people. If your work is *outstanding*, it is very good and much better than other people's work.

a
b
c
d
e
f
g
h
i
j
k
l
m
n

**o**

p
q
r
s
t
u
v
w
x
y
z

**out·break** /owt-brayk/ *noun* the start of something bad such as war or disease: *At the outbreak of war, many people left the country.*

**out·burst** /owt-burst/ *noun* a short time when someone is very angry or emotional: *He started yelling in class, but later he was really embarrassed about his outburst.*

**out·come** /owt-kuhm/ *noun* the final result: *You can never be sure of the outcome of a game until it is finished.*

**out·dat·ed** /owt-**dayt**-id/ *adjective* old and not useful anymore: *This map is outdated – there are a lot of new roads that are not on it.*

**out·door** /owt-dor/ *adjective* outside: *When the weather's good, the kids do outdoor activities such as hiking and climbing.* ( ANTONYM: **indoor** )

**out·doors** /owt-**dorz**/ *adverb* outside: *I'm bored with watching TV – let's go play outdoors.* ( ANTONYM: **indoors** )

**out·er** /owt-ur/ *adjective* on the outside of something: *A coconut has a brown outer shell, and white flesh inside.* ( ANTONYM: **inner** )

**out·er space** /owt-ur **spayss**/ *noun* the area where the stars and planets are. Outer space is outside the Earth's atmosphere: *The movie is about aliens from outer space who visit the Earth.*

**out·field** /owt-feeld/ *noun*
**1** the part of a baseball field that is farthest from the player who is batting
**2** the players in this part of the field

**out·fit** /owt-fit/ *noun* a set of clothes: *He came to the party in a cowboy outfit.*

**out·go·ing** /owt-goh-ing/ *adjective* someone who is outgoing enjoys meeting people: *Everyone likes him because he's so outgoing and friendly.* ( SYNONYM: **friendly** )

**out·grow** /owt-**groh**/ *verb* (**outgrew** /owt-**groo**/, **outgrown** /owt-**grohn**/) to grow too big for your clothes: *Jason's outgrown his sneakers again – we'll have to buy a bigger pair.*

**out·ing** /owt-ing/ *noun* a short trip for fun: *This weekend we're going on an outing to the beach.*

**out·law** /owt-lo/
• *noun* a criminal who is hiding from the police: *The movie is about two outlaws who rob banks.*
• *verb* to make something illegal: *Congress outlawed cigarette commercials on television.*

**out·let** /owt-let/ *noun*
**1** a place on a wall where you connect things to the electricity supply: *The kitchen has a lot of electrical outlets for kitchen equipment.*
**2** a store or organization that sells things to the public: *The company has 375 sales outlets.*
**3** a way of using your energy or expressing your feelings: *Sports are a good outlet for your energy.*

**out·li·er** /owt-lī-ur/ *noun* in math, a number that is a lot higher or lower than the other numbers in a group: *In the set {3, 5, 4, 6, 2, 25, 5, 6}, 25 is an outlier.*

**out·line** /owt-līn/ *noun*
**1** the main ideas or facts: *First, write down an outline for your story, and then add more details.*
**2** a line that shows the shape of something: *I could see the outline of the island, but I couldn't see if it was rocky or covered with trees.*

**out·look** /owt-luk/ *noun*
**1** the general way you think about life: *His outlook changed after she died and he became less cheerful.*
**2** the situation that people expect in the future: *The school is doing very well and the outlook for the future is good.*

**out·num·ber** /owt-**nuhm**-buhr/ *verb* to be more in number than another group: *There are 25 girls and 5 boys, so the girls outnumber the boys by 5:1.*

**out of bounds** /owt uhv **bowndz**/ *adjective* not inside the official playing area in a sports game: *The referee said that the ball was out of bounds.*

**out·pa·tient** /owt-paysh-uhnt/
• *noun* someone who goes for treatment in a hospital, but does not stay there at night: *People with minor injuries are treated as outpatients.*

● *adjective* relating to outpatients: *The hospital has built a new outpatient clinic.*

**out·put** /**owt**-put/ *noun* the amount of goods or work that something or someone produces: *The new machines are faster and have increased our output.* ( SYNONYM: **production** )

**out·rage** /**owt**-rayj/ *noun*
**1** great anger or shock: *The closing of the hospital caused outrage in the neighborhood.*
**2** something that makes you very angry or shocked: *It is an outrage that some people treat their animals so badly.*

**out·ra·geous** /owt-**rayj**-uhss/ *adjective* very wrong or shocking: *His behavior was outrageous – he didn't need to yell at us like that.*

**out·right** /**owt**-rīt/
● *adjective* clear and definite: *He says that he is 16, but that is an outright lie – I know he's only 13.*
● *adverb* clearly and immediately: *She told him outright that she didn't want to go to the party.*

**out·set** /**owt**-set/ *noun* the beginning of something that happens: *We had planned the trip carefully, but it went wrong from the outset.*

**out·side** /owt-**sīd**/
● *adverb*, *preposition*
**1** not inside a building or room: *It's cold outside – can I come in?* | *I'll meet you outside the movie theater.* ( ANTONYM: **inside** )
**2** not in a city or area, but near it: *Great Falls National Park is just outside Washington.*
● *adjective*
not inside a building: *We turn on the outside light if we are going out when it's dark.* ( ANTONYM: **inside** )
● *noun*
the outer part or surface of something: *The outside of the house needs painting but the inside is fine.* ( ANTONYM: **inside** )

**out·sid·er** /owt-**sīd**-ur/ *noun* someone who does not belong to a particular group: *All the other kids knew each other, and I felt like an outsider.*

**out·skirts** /**owt**-skurtss/ *plural noun* the areas that are on the edge of a town: *They live on the outskirts of town, close to the countryside.*

**out·spo·ken** /owt-**spohk**-uhn/ *adjective* always saying exactly what you think: *She is an*

outspoken woman, and she is not afraid to criticize her boss.

**out·stand·ing** /owt-**stand**-ing/ *adjective* extremely good: *Her performance on the test was outstanding – she got every question right.* ( SYNONYM: **excellent** )

**out·stretched** /owt-**strecht**/ *adjective* reaching out as far as possible: *With my outstretched hand I managed to pick one of the apples.*

**out·ward** /**owt**-wurd/
● *adjective*
**1** relating to how someone seems: *Most people feel nervous before a test, even if they don't show any outward sign of nerves.* ( ANTONYM: **inward** )
**2** going away from a place: *The outward flight was delayed, but the trip back home was fine.*
● *adverb*
toward the outside, or away from the middle: *All the windows open outward.* | *Light from the sun spreads outward.* ( ANTONYM: **inward** )

**out·weigh** /owt-**way**/ *verb* to be more important that something else: *The advantages outweigh the disadvantages.*

**o·val** /**ohv**-uhl/
● *noun* a shape like a circle, but that is longer than it is wide: *The racetrack is shaped like an oval.*
● *adjective* in the shape of an oval: *She has an oval face.*

oval

**O·val Of·fice** /**ohv**-uhl **of**-iss/ *noun* the office where the president of the U.S. works. The Oval Office is in the White House in Washington D.C.

**o·va·ry** /**ohv**-uhr-ee/ *noun* (plural **ovaries**)
**1** the part of a female plant that produces seeds
**2** the part of a female person or animal that produces eggs

**ov·en** /**uhv**-uhn/ *noun* a piece of equipment that you cook food in. An oven is like a metal box with a door: *Bake the cake in the oven for 30 minutes.*

**o·ver** /**ohv**-ur/

● *preposition*

**1** above: *There was a mirror over the fireplace.*
ANTONYM: **under**

**2** from one side to the other: *I went over the bridge.* SYNONYM: **across**

**3** covering something: *Sprinkle some cheese over the top of the pasta.* ANTONYM: **under**

**4** more than: *His jacket cost over $100.*
ANTONYM: **under**

**5** during: *What did you do over the summer?*

**6** if you are over something, you feel better after you have been sick or upset: *I was really disappointed when I lost, but I'm over it now. | It can take a few weeks to get over the flu.*

● *adverb*

**1** down from an upright position: *She fell over and cut her knee.*

**2** to a place: *Come over to my house later and we'll play.*

**3** again: *I decided to throw the drawing away and start over.*

● *adjective*

finished: *The game was over and we all went home.* SYNONYM: **done**

## Word Building

**over-** is a prefix.

**1 over**crowded | **over**do | **over**eat | **over**population | **over**time

**over-** means "too much." If you *overeat*, you eat too much food. *Overpopulation* is when there are too many people living in an area.

**2 over**alls | **over**cast | **over**coat | **over**lap

**Over-** means "covering." *Overalls* are a piece of clothing that covers your chest and your legs. If the sky is *overcast*, clouds cover the sky.

**3 over**board | **over**flow | **over**hand | **over**head

**Over-** means "above" or "higher than." If you fall *overboard*, you fall out of a boat by going above one of the sides and falling down. If you throw a ball *overhand*, you move your hand above your head before letting go of the ball.

**o·ver·all** /**ohv**-ur-ol/ *adjective* including or considering everything: *The overall cost of the trip is $500, including food, hotel, and transportation.*

**o·ver·alls** /**ohv**-ur-olz/ *plural noun* pants with a square piece that covers your chest. Two straps go over your shoulders: *The mechanic was wearing dirty blue overalls.*

overalls

**o·ver·board** /**ohv**-ur-bord/ *adverb* over the side of a boat into the water: *Sit down or you will fall overboard!*

> IDIOM with overboard
> **go overboard** to do something too much, or more than necessary: *Try not to go overboard and spend all your money in the first store you visit!*

**o·ver·cast** /**ohv**-ur-kast/ *adjective* if the sky is overcast, it is full of dark clouds: *The sky is overcast and it looks like it is going to rain.*

**o·ver·coat** /**ohv**-ur-koht/ *noun* a long warm coat: *If it's very cold, Dad wears an overcoat to work.*

**o·ver·come** /**ohv**-ur-**kuhm**/ *verb* (**overcame** /**ohv**-ur-**kaym**/, **overcome**)

**1** to control a feeling, or deal with a problem: *She has tried very hard to overcome her fear of spiders.*

**2** if you are overcome by a feeling, you feel it very strongly: *The woman asked us for money and I was overcome by pity for her.*

**o·ver·crowd·ed** /**ohv**-ur-**krowd**-id/ *adjective* if a place is overcrowded, there are too many people there: *The beaches near the city are overcrowded in the summer.*

**o·ver·do** /**ohv**-ur-**doo**/ *verb* (**overdoes** /**ohv**-ur-**duhz**/, **overdid** /**ohv**-ur-**did**/, **overdone** /**ohv**-ur-**duhn**/) to do or use something too much: *You can put a little salt on your food, but don't overdo it – it's not good for you.*

**o·ver·dose** /**ohv**-ur-dohss/ *noun* too much of a drug, taken at one time: *An overdose of any kind of medicine can be dangerous.*

**o·ver·due** /ohv-ur-**doo**/ *adjective* something that is overdue is late: *My science project is overdue – I should have handed it in yesterday.*

( SYNONYM: **late** )

**o·ver·eat** /ohv-ur-**eet**/ *verb* (**overate** /ohv-ur-**ayt**/, **overeaten** /ohv-ur-**eet'n**/) to eat too much: *A lot of people overeat at Christmas and then they feel fat.*

**o·ver·flow** /ohv-ur-**floh**/ *verb* if something overflows, liquids or objects fill it completely and come over the edge: *There was so much rain the river overflowed its banks.* | *The wastepaper basket was overflowing with paper.*

overflow

The glass is overflowing.

**o·ver·grown** /ohv-ur-**grohn**/ *adjective* full of plants that you do not want, or that need cutting: *The yard is overgrown with weeds.*

**o·ver·hand** /**ohv**-ur-hand/ *adjective*, *adverb* an overhand throw is when you throw a ball with your arm above your shoulder: *In baseball, you do an overhand throw.*

**o·ver·head** /ohv-ur-**hed**/ *adjective*, *adverb* above your head: *A plane flew overhead.* | *I turned on the overhead light so I could see better.*

**o·ver·hear** /ohv-ur-**heer**/ *verb* (**overheard** /ohv-ur-**hurd**/) to hear what other people are saying by accident: *Tammy and Karen were talking about me and I overheard what they said.*

**o·ver·lap** /ohv-ur-**lap**/ *verb* (**overlapping**, **overlapped**) if two things overlap, part of one thing covers part of the other: *Draw two circles that overlap each other.*

**o·ver·look** /ohv-ur-**luk**/ *verb*
**1** to have a view of something: *Most of the hotel rooms overlook the lake.*
**2** to not notice something: *The police overlooked one important piece of information in the case.*

**o·ver·night** /ohv-ur-**nīt**/ *adverb*, *adjective*
**1** for or during the night: *I stayed overnight at Rosy's house after the party.* | *We took an overnight train because the trip took ten hours.*

**2** very quickly or suddenly: *Dad lost his job and everything changed overnight.* | *The play was an overnight success.*
**3** an overnight bag is one you use on short trips: *I packed my toothbrush and some clean clothes in an overnight bag.*

**o·ver·pass** /**ohv**-ur-pass/ *noun* a part of a road that crosses over another road or a railroad: *The street went under the freeway overpass.*

overpass

**o·ver·pop·u·la·tion** /ohv-ur-pahp-yuh-**laysh**-uhn/ *noun* too many people living in an area: *Overpopulation is a problem because there are not enough houses for everyone to live in.*

**o·ver·seas** /ohv-ur-**seez**/ *adjective*, *adverb* to or in a country that is across the ocean: *A lot of people travel overseas if they can't find work in their own country.* | *My first overseas trip will be to Europe.*

**o·ver·sleep** /ohv-ur-**sleep**/ *verb* (**overslept** /ohv-ur-**slept**/) to sleep for longer than you planned: *I overslept and missed the bus to school.*

**o·ver-the-coun·ter** /ohv-ur thuh **kownt**-ur/ *adjective* over-the-counter medicines are available for people to buy in a store, without needing to see a doctor first: *If you have a cold, there are many over-the-counter medicines that you can buy.*

**o·ver·throw** /ohv-ur-**throh**/ *verb* (**overthrew** /ohv-ur-**throo**/, **overthrown** /ohv-ur-**throhn**/) to remove a leader or government from power by force: *The country's army tried to overthrow the government.*

**o·ver·time** /**ohv**-ur-tīm/ *noun* time that you spend doing your job that is more than your normal working hours: *He got home late because he was doing overtime at work.*

**o·ver·turn** /ohv-ur-**turn**/ *verb*
**1** to turn upside down or onto one side: *The boat overturned and we all fell out.*
**2** to change an official decision: *A judge overturned the court's decision and the man was freed from jail.*

**o·ver·view** /**ohv**-ur-vyoo/ *noun* a short description that gives the main ideas but not the details: *The teacher gave us an overview of the story before we started to read the book.*

**o·ver·weight** /ohv-ur-**wayt**/ *adjective* too fat: *If you are overweight, you should eat less and get more exercise.*

**o·ver·whelmed** /ohv-ur-**welmd**/ *adjective* if you are overwhelmed by something, it has a very strong effect on you: *I was so overwhelmed by their kindness that I cried.*

**o·ver·whelm·ing** /ohv-ur-**welm**-ing/ *adjective*
**1** an overwhelming feeling is very strong: *When she left, I was filled with overwhelming sadness.*
**2** very big in amount or number: *The president has overwhelming support and is sure to win the election.*

**owe** /oh/ *verb*
**1** to have to give someone money because you borrowed it from him or her: *I still owe Daniel $6 that I borrowed from him last week.*
**2** to feel that someone has helped you, so you want to help him or her in return: *Thanks for helping me – I owe you a favor.*

**owl** /owl/ *noun* a bird that flies at night to hunt mice and other small animals. An owl has large eyes and a round head: *In the middle of the night I heard an owl make a hooting sound.*

owl

**own** /ohn/
● *adjective*, *pronoun*
belonging to you and no one else: *I have my own bedroom but my brothers share a room.*

**IDIOM with own**
**on your own**
**1** with no one helping you: *This is very good work. Did you do it on your own?*
**2** alone: *Lucy was sitting on her own, with no one to talk to.*
● *verb*
**1** if you own something, it belongs to you: *My uncle owns a ranch near Santa Fe.*
**2** **own up** to admit that you did something wrong: *In the end, Paul owned up to breaking the window.*

**own·er** /**ohn**-ur/ *noun* someone who owns something: *My grandfather is the owner of the land.*

**ox** /ahkss/ *noun* (plural **oxen** /**ahkss**-uhn/) a male cow that farmers use for farm work: *In some countries, oxen are still used to plow the fields.*

**ox·y·gen** /**ahkss**-ij-uhn/ *noun* a gas in the air that has no color. People, animals, and plants need oxygen to live. The symbol for oxygen is O: *The oxygen we breathe goes to our lungs and then into our blood.*

**oys·ter** /**oyst**-ur/ *noun* a flat shellfish. You can eat the meat inside. Oysters sometimes make pearls inside their shells. ▶ see picture on page **A3**

oyster

**oz.** the written abbreviation of **ounce** or **ounces**: *Add 2 oz. sugar.*

**o·zone lay·er** /**oh**-zohn lay-ur/ *noun* a layer of gases around the Earth. The ozone layer stops harmful heat from the Sun from reaching the Earth: *Pollution has damaged the ozone layer, and that has resulted in more people getting skin cancer.*

# Pp

## pace /payss/

● *noun*

**1** the speed at which you do something: *He walks at a slow pace.*

**2** a step that you make when you are walking: *Mark took eight paces away from me and then turned around.*

● *verb*

to walk in one direction and then another, in a nervous way: *She was pacing the room, waiting for the phone to ring.*

## Pa·cif·ic O·cean /puh-sif-ik **ohsh**-uhn/ *noun* the ocean that is between Asia and Australia in the west and North and South America in the east: *Hawaii is in the Pacific Ocean.*

## pac·i·fi·er /**pass**-uh-fī-ur/ *noun* an object that a baby sucks on. A pacifier stops the baby from crying.

## pack /pak/

● *verb*

**1** to put things into boxes, bags, or suitcases, ready to take somewhere: *I have to pack my bag because we're going on vacation in the morning.*

**2** to fill a building or space: *A crowd of students packed the hall.*

—**packing** /**pak**-ing/ *noun* if you do your packing, you put things into boxes or bags: *Mom helped me with my packing for the school trip.*

● *noun*

**1** a paper container: *There are little packs of sugar on the table.* ( SYNONYM: **packet** )

**2** a set of things that you buy or use together: *We bought a six-pack of sodas.*

**3** a group of wild animals that live and hunt together: *The story is about a pack of wolves.*

**4** a strong bag for carrying things on your back ( SYNONYM: **backpack** )

## pack·age /**pak**-ij/ *noun*

**1** something sent by mail, wrapped in paper or in a box: *A package came for me in the mail on my birthday.*

**2** a box or bag that holds things that are for sale: *I bought a package of cookies.*

—**package** /**pak**-ij/ *verb* to put something into a container, ready to sell or send somewhere: *A lot of food is packaged in cans.*

## pack·ag·ing /**pak**-ij-ing/ *noun* the box or paper that something is sold in: *Don't throw away paper packaging – you can recycle it.*

## packed /pakt/ *adjective* full of people: *The stadium is packed for tonight's game.*

## pack·et /**pak**-it/ *noun* a small paper container or envelope: *He poured a packet of sugar into his coffee.*

## pact /pakt/ *noun* an agreement between people or countries: *Let's make a pact that we will always be best friends.*

## pad /pad/

● *noun*

**1** a lot of sheets of paper fastened together at one edge: *I wrote down the message on a pad of paper.*

**2** a thick piece of soft material. A pad is used to protect something or to make something more comfortable: *Skateboarders should wear knee pads and elbow pads.*

**3** a platform from which a space rocket is fired: *The rocket will leave the launch pad in Florida at 8 a.m.*

● *verb* (**padding**, **padded**)

to walk around quietly: *She was padding around with no shoes on.*

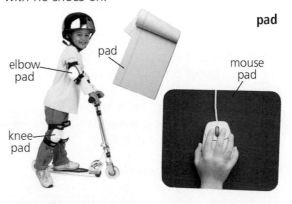

pad

elbow pad

pad

knee pad

mouse pad

## pad·ded /**pad**-id/ *adjective* covered or filled with soft material: *This bicycle helmet is padded, so it's very comfortable.*

a b c d e f g h i j k l m n o p q r s t u v w x y z

### pad·dle /**pad**'l/

● *noun*

**1** a short pole with a wide flat end, for moving a boat across water ▶ see picture at **kayak**

**2** a small round board with a short handle, for hitting the ball in ping-pong

● *verb*

to move a boat across water, using a paddle: *The kids learned how to paddle a canoe.*

### pad·lock /**pad**-lahk/

*noun* a metal lock you put on something. It has a curved bar that you put through a chain or opening. Then you press the bar into the main part of the lock: *Emily used a chain and padlock to lock her bike to the rack.*

**padlock**

key     padlock

### page /payj/ *noun*

**1** one side of a sheet of paper in a book, magazine, or newspaper: *Look at the picture on page 37 in your books.*

**2** the writing and pictures that you see on a computer screen when you visit a website: *Click on this arrow if you want to go to the next page.*

### paid /payd/ *verb* the past tense and past participle of **pay**

### pail /payl/ *noun* a bucket: *She went to get a pail of water.*

### pain /payn/ *noun*

**1** the feeling you have when part of your body hurts: *If you have a pain in your chest, you should visit the doctor.* ▶ see **Thesaurus**

**2** unhappiness: *He has had a lot of pain in his life – his mother died when he was only 12 years old.*

**3** if someone is a pain, he or she is very annoying: *My brother is a real pain sometimes – he keeps asking stupid questions.*

### pain·ful /**payn**-fuhl/ *adjective*

**1** making part of your body hurt: *It was very painful when I broke my arm.* ( **ANTONYM: painless** )
▶ see **Thesaurus**

**2** making you feel unhappy: *Lisa tried to forget her painful memories of that day.*

—**painfully** /**payn**-fuhl-ee/ *adverb* in a way that is very bad and very noticeable: *Robbie is painfully shy and he finds it very difficult to talk to people.*

### pain·kill·er /**payn**-kil-ur/ *noun* a medicine that stops pain: *If you have a bad headache, take a painkiller.*

### pain·less /**payn**-liss/ *adjective* causing no pain: *Most treatment you get at the dentist is completely painless.* ( **ANTONYM: painful** )

### paint /paynt/

● *noun*

a liquid that you use to color surfaces or make pictures: *We bought a can of yellow paint for my bedroom walls.* ▶ see picture on page **A9**

● *verb*

**1** to put paint on a surface: *Dad's going to paint the window frames.*

**2** to make a picture using paint: *Sally loves to paint and draw.*

### paint·brush /**paynt**-bruhsh/ *noun* a brush you use for painting ▶ see picture on page **A9**

### paint·er /**paynt**-ur/ *noun*

**1** someone who paints pictures: *Leonardo da Vinci was an Italian painter who is famous for his picture of the Mona Lisa.* ( **SYNONYM: artist** )

**2** someone whose job is painting houses and rooms

### paint·ing /**paynt**-ing/

*noun* a picture that someone has painted: *There was a painting of a bunch of flowers on the wall.*

**painting**

### pair /pair/ *noun*

**1** two things that are the same and that you use together: *I need a clean pair of socks.*

**2** something made of two parts that are joined together: *Do you have a pair of scissors?* | *a pair of jeans*

**3** if people do something in pairs, they do it in groups of two: *The teacher asked us to work in pairs with the person next to us.*

pair

a pair of socks

a pair of jeans

a pair of scissors

**pa·ja·mas** /puh-**jahm**-uhz/ *plural noun* pants and a shirt that you wear in bed: *Go and put on your pajamas. It's time for bed.*

**Word Origin:** pajamas

**Pajamas** comes from Hindi, a language of India. From the 1700s to the 1900s, British people lived and worked in India. The British saw that men and women in India wore loose pants that tied around their waist. The Hindi word for these pants comes from a Persian word, ***paejamah***, that means "leg clothes." In the 1800s, the British started wearing these pants to bed, and used the Hindi word for them. Over time, pajamas came to mean the pants and top that you wear to bed.

**pal** /pal/ *noun* a friend: *Tommy and Dean are good pals – they do everything together.*

**pal·ace** /**pal**-iss/ *noun* a large house for a king, queen, or other ruler: *The princess lived in a beautiful palace.*

**pal·ate** /**pal**-it/ *noun*
**1** the top part inside your mouth
**2** your sense of taste: *Mexican food tastes spicy to an American palate.*

**pale** /payl/ *adjective*
**1** if you are pale, you look white because you are sick or frightened: *You look pale – do you feel all right?*
**2** a pale color is very light: *I like this pale yellow dress.* (ANTONYM: **dark**)

**pa·le·on·tol·o·gy** /payl-ee-uhn-**tahl**-uhj-ee/ *noun* the study of fossils. Fossils are animals and plants from a very long time ago that have been preserved in rock.

**pal·ette** /**pal**-uht/ *noun*
**1** the curved board that an artist uses for mixing colors
**2** the set of colors that an artist uses: *In his paintings he often uses a palette of greens and browns.*

**palm** /pahm/ *noun*
**1** the flat part on the inside of your hand: *The woman put out the palm of her hand, asking for money.* ▶ see picture at **hand**
**2** another word for a palm tree

**palm tree** *noun*
/**pahm** tree/ a tall tree that grows in warm places. It has a very straight trunk and big pointed leaves at the top: *Palm trees mainly grow in hot dry countries.*

palm tree

**pam·phlet** /**pamf**-lit/ *noun* a thin book with a paper cover. A pamphlet gives information about something: *We were given a pamphlet about the dangers of alcohol.*

**pan** /pan/
● *noun*
a metal container that you cook food in: *Mom was cooking sausages in a frying pan.*
● *verb* (**panning**, **panned**)
**1** to criticize something very strongly: *All the newspapers panned the movie but lots of people still went to see it and said that it was terrible.*
**2** to look for gold by washing small stones and sand: *In 1917, miners were panning for gold in this area.*

**pan·cake** /**pan**-kayk/ *noun* a flat round food made from flour, milk, and eggs. You cook pancakes in a pan on the stove: *I love pancakes with syrup for breakfast.*

**pan·cre·as** /**pangk**-ree-uhss/ *noun* a gland in your body near your stomach. The pancreas produces a liquid that helps your body digest food. It also produces insulin, a hormone that helps your body use sugar for energy.
▶ see picture at **anatomy**

463

a b c d e f g h i j k l m n o **p** q r s t u v w x y z

**pan·da** /**pand**-uh/ (also **giant panda**) *noun* a large black and white animal that looks like a bear. Pandas live in China: *Pandas mainly eat bamboo.*

panda

**pane** /payn/ *noun* a piece of glass in a window or door: *The ball hit the window and broke one of the panes.*

**pan·el** /**pan**'l/ *noun*
**1** a flat piece of wood or other hard material. A panel forms part of a door or wall: *The doors are made of four wood panels.*
**2** a group of people who are chosen to decide or discuss something: *A panel of judges will decide who wins the poetry competition.*
**3** the place in a vehicle that has the controls on it: *The pilot looked at the control panel to check the aircraft's speed.*

**pan·ic** /**pan**-ik/
● *noun* a sudden strong feeling of fear and worry: *There was a moment of panic when I couldn't find my parents.*
● *verb* (**panicked**, **panicking**) to suddenly feel very frightened and worried: *If there is a fire, don't panic – walk calmly out of the building.*

**pan·o·ram·a** /pan-uh-**ram**-uh/ *noun* a view over a wide area: *From here, there is a fantastic panorama of Niagara Falls.*
—**panoramic** /pan-uh-**ram**-ik/ *adjective* giving a view over a wide area: *The hotel has a panoramic view of the bay.*

**pan·sy** /**panz**-ee/ *noun* (plural **pansies**) a small brightly colored flower that people grow in their gardens

**pant** /pant/ *verb* to breathe quickly with short breaths: *I had been running fast so I was panting.*

**pan·ther** /**panth**-ur/ *noun*
**1** a large black leopard
**2** another word for a cougar or a jaguar

**pant·ies** /**pant**-eez/ *plural noun* a piece of underwear that girls and women wear on their bottoms

**pan·try** /**pan**-tree/ *noun* (plural **pantries**) a small room or a big cupboard in a kitchen. You keep food and dishes in a pantry.

**pants** /pantss/ *plural noun* a piece of clothing with two legs. Pants cover you from your waist to your feet: *You'll need to wear some nice pants and a shirt.*

**pan·ty·hose** /**pant**-ee-hohz/ *noun* a very thin tight piece of clothing that covers your legs from your feet to your waist.

**pa·pa** /**pahp**-uh/ *noun* father: *Goodnight, Papa.*

**pa·pa·ya** /puh-**pī**-uh/ *noun* a big sweet tropical fruit. A papaya is yellow-green with orange flesh and it has a lot of small black seeds inside. ▶ see picture on page **A7**

**pa·per** /**payp**-ur/ *noun*
**1** thin material that you write or draw on, or wrap things in. Paper is made from trees: *I used three pieces of paper for my story.*
**2** a newspaper: *Dad likes to read the paper at breakfast time.*
**3** a piece of writing on a subject that people study: *The professor wrote a paper for a scientific journal.*
**4 papers** important documents or letters: *The president gave all his official papers to the library.*

**pa·per·back** /**payp**-ur-bak/ *noun* a book with a soft paper cover: *I took a paperback to read on the trip.*

**pa·per clip** /**payp**-ur klip/ *noun* a small piece of curved wire that you use to hold sheets of paper together: *I held the pages together with a paper clip.*

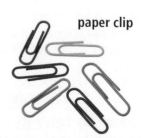

paper clip

**pa·per·work** /**payp**-ur-wurk/ *noun* work such as writing reports and filling in forms:

*As well as teaching their class, teachers have a lot of paperwork to do.*

**pap·ier-mâ·ché** /payp-ur muh-**shay**/ *noun* a mixture of paper, water, and glue that becomes hard when it dries. You use papier-mâché for making things: *We made papier-mâché masks for Halloween.*

**para-** /parr-uh/

### Word Building

**para**graph | **para**llel | **para**medic | **para**site

These words all have the Greek word root **para-** in them. ***Para-*** means "beside." A *paragraph* is a part of a piece of writing that starts on a new line. The paragraph is written beside other paragraphs. *Parallel* lines are beside each other but never cross. A *parasite* is a plant or animal that lives on or in another plant or animal.

**par·a·chute**

/**parr**-uh-shoot/ *noun* a large piece of cloth attached to ropes. You use a parachute so you can jump from an airplane and fall slowly to the ground: *The man jumped out of the plane and opened his parachute.*

parachute

### Word Origin: parachute

The word **parachute** was invented by a French man who used them to jump from hot-air balloons that were damaged. He used **para** in the meaning of "defense against" and **chute**, a French word meaning "a fall."

**pa·rade** /puh-**rayd**/

● *noun* a celebration with a long line of musical bands and trucks that move along a street: *The school band is going to march in the Fourth of July parade.*

● *verb* to walk or march together to celebrate or protest something: *At Mardi Gras people parade through the streets wearing brightly colored clothes.*

**par·a·dise** /**parr**-uh-dīss/ *noun*

**1** a place that is very beautiful and enjoyable: *The island is a paradise, with white sandy beaches and clear blue water.*

**2** heaven: *He hoped that one day he would meet his friend again in paradise.*

### Word Origin: paradise

The word **paradise** comes from an ancient Persian word that meant "garden." Persia was where Iran is today. The Persian word went into Greek, Latin, and Old French before it came into English. It was used in the Bible in the 1100s to describe the Garden of Eden. In the 1200s people used it to mean heaven.

**par·a·dox** /**parr**-uh-dokss/ *noun* a statement or situation that seems strange because it contains two very different things that are both true: *It's a paradox that in a rich country there are so many poor people.*

**par·a·graph** /**parr**-uh-graf/ *noun* a group of sentences in a piece of writing that is about one fact or idea. Each paragraph starts on a new line: *In the first paragraph of my essay I explain what the essay is about.*

**par·a·keet**

/**parr**-uh-keet/ *noun* a small bird with brightly colored feathers and a long tail. Some people keep parakeets as pets.

parakeet

**par·al·lel** /**parr**-uh-lel/

● *adjective* parallel lines stay the same distance apart and never meet: *Draw two parallel lines across the page.* | *The street runs parallel to the railroad for about a mile.*

● *noun* an imaginary line on a map of the Earth. A parallel shows the position of a place north or south of the Equator: *U.S. troops crossed the 38th parallel.*

**par·al·lel cir·cuit** /parr-uh-lel **surk**-it/ *noun* a type of electrical circuit. The parts are connected so that each part receives power separately and can work when the other parts are not working.

a b c d e f g h i j k l m n o p q r s t u v w x y z

## par·al·lel·o·gram

/parr-uh-**lel**-uh-gram/
*noun* a flat shape with four straight sides. Each side is the same length as the side parallel to it: *Rectangles and squares are parallelograms.*

**parallelogram**

## pa·ral·y·sis

/puh-**ral**-uhss-iss/ *noun* the loss of ability to move or feel part of your body: *The accident caused paralysis of his legs, so he was unable to walk.*

## par·a·lyze /**parr**-uh-līz/ *verb*

**1** to make someone lose the ability to move or feel part of his or her body: *He was paralyzed in a horse-riding accident.*
**2** if you are paralyzed by fear, you are so frightened that you cannot move: *Lucy saw the spider on her leg and she was paralyzed by fear.*
**3** to make something unable to work normally: *The snow has paralyzed all roads out of the city.*
—**paralyzed** /**parr**-uh-līzd/ *adjective* unable to move part of your body

## par·a·med·ic /parr-uh-**med**-ik/ *noun* someone whose job is to help sick or injured people until they get to a hospital: *Paramedics arrived in an ambulance and took the woman to the hospital.*

## par·a·phrase /**parr**-uh-frayz/

● *verb* to say or write something using different words: *For your homework, I want you to paraphrase the story and put it in your own words.*
● *noun* something that is said or written using different words: *In his speech he uses a paraphrase of a line from the Bible.*

## par·a·site /**parr**-uh-sīt/ *noun* a plant or animal that gets food by living on or in another plant or animal: *Fleas are parasites; they bite the skin of animals and drink their blood.*

## par·cel /**parss**-uhl/ *noun* something wrapped in paper and sent by mail: *The mailman left a parcel for you – I wonder what it is.*

SYNONYM: **package**

## par·don /**pard**′n/

● *verb* to allow someone who is guilty of a crime to go free: *After three years in jail, he was pardoned by the governor.*

IDIOM with pardon
**pardon me**
**1** used as a polite way of saying you are sorry, for example when you touch or interrupt someone: *Pardon me, I didn't mean to step on your foot.* SYNONYM: **excuse me**
**2** used to politely ask someone to say something again: *"The correct answer is 25." "Pardon me?" "The answer is 25."*
SYNONYM: **excuse me?**

● *noun* an official order that allows someone who is guilty of a crime to go free: *The governor gave Davis a pardon and he walked free from jail.*

## par·ent /**pair**-uhnt/ *noun* a father or mother: *I live with my parents and my two brothers.*
—**parental** /puh-**rent**′l/ *adjective* of or by a parent: *Children are happiest when they have parental love and care.*
—**parenthood** /**pair**-uhnt-hud/ *noun* the time when someone is a parent: *Sally has a baby now and she's really enjoying parenthood.*

## pa·ren·the·ses /puh-**renth**-uh-seez/ *plural noun* the symbols ( ). You use parentheses when adding extra information after something. You also put parentheses around numbers and symbols in mathematics: *After the name of each student on the list, she wrote the student's age in parentheses.*

## park /park/
● *noun*
**1** a large area with grass and trees in a town: *After school, we went to play ball in the park.*
**2** a large area of land that is kept natural to protect the plants and animals there: *In Yellowstone National Park there is a wide variety of wildlife.*
● *verb*
to put your car somewhere and leave it for some time: *We parked in front of the store.*

## par·ka /**park**-uh/ *noun* a thick warm coat with a hood: *It was freezing so we put on parkas and boots.*

## park·ing /**park**-ing/ *noun*
**1** putting your car somewhere and leaving it for some time: *There's no charge for parking here – it's completely free.*
**2** **parking space/parking area** a space or area where you can leave a car: *The town was full*

of tourists and it was hard to find a parking space.

**park·ing lot** /**park**-ing laht/ *noun* a large area where you can leave your car: *The supermarket has its own parking lot.*

**park·ing me·ter** /**park**-ing meet-ur/ *noun* a machine beside a space where you can park your car. You put money in the meter for the amount of time you want to park: *Dad put 50 cents in the parking meter so we could park for an hour.*

**par·lia·ment** /**parl**-uh-muhnt/ *noun* a group of people who are elected to make laws in some countries: *The British Parliament passed a law against fox hunting.*

**par·lor** /**parl**-ur/ *noun*
**1** a store that sells ice cream or pizzas: *Mom took us to the pizza parlor.*
**2** a business that provides a service: *She went to have her hair done at the beauty parlor.*

**par·o·dy** /**parr**-uhd-ee/ *noun* (plural **parodies**) a piece of writing or acting that copies something in a funny way: *The show was a very funny parody of "Star Wars."*

**pa·role** /puh-**rohl**/
● *noun* permission for a prisoner to leave prison early: *He was sentenced to ten years, but if he behaves well he may get parole after six years.*
● *verb* to give someone permission to leave prison early: *He behaved well and was paroled last year.*

**par·rot** /**parr**-uht/ *noun* a bird with colored feathers and a curved beak. Parrots live in warm places. Some people keep parrots as pets. You can teach some parrots to say words.

parrot

**pars·ley** /**parss**-lee/ *noun* a plant with curly green leaves. You use parsley to give flavor in cooking or to decorate food.

**part** /part/
● *noun*
**1** one of the pieces or areas that form the whole of something: *I liked the last part of the story best.* ▶ see **Thesaurus**
**2** a character that an actor plays: *I got the part of Annie in the school play, which is the biggest part!*
**3** something that you do in an activity that people share: *Everyone on the team plays a part in the team's success.*
**4** a piece used to make a machine or vehicle: *He works in a factory making car parts.*

> **IDIOM with part**
> **take part** to do an activity with other people: *If you want to take part in the trip, tell your teacher.* ( SYNONYM: **participate** )

● *verb*
**1** if you part your hair, you divide it so that there is a line on your head: *She parts her hair in the middle.*
**2** to say goodbye and go to different places: *It's hard to part from the people we love.*
**3** **part with** to give or sell something to someone, when you do not want to: *I liked my old bicycle, and I didn't want to part with it.*
● *adverb*
partly one thing and partly another: *The drawing showed an animal that was part man and part horse.*

**par·tial** /**parsh**-uhl/ *adjective*
**1** not complete: *This is only a partial list of who is coming. Some people have not replied yet.*
( ANTONYM: **full** )
**2** if you are partial to something, you like it very much: *Dad is very partial to apple pie.*
—**partially** /**parsh**-uhl-ee/ *adverb* partly, not completely: *What he said is only partially true – he got some of the facts wrong.*

**par·tial prod·uct** /parsh-uhl **prahd**-uhkt/ *noun* a number that you get when you multiply one number by part of another number that has two or more digits: *I am going to multiply 2 by 23: 2 x 3 = 6. The result 6 is a partial product. 2 x 20 = 40. The result 40 is also a partial product. Add them together and the answer is 46.*

**par·tic·i·pant** /par-**tiss**-uhp-uhnt/ *noun* someone who does an activity with other people: *There are only six participants left in the tennis tournament.*

a
b
c
d
e
f
g
h
i
j
k
l
m
n
o
**p**
q
r
s
t
u
v
w
x
y
z

**par·tic·i·pate** /par-**tiss**-uh-payt/ *verb* to do an activity with other people: *Many children at school participate in a team sport.*

( SYNONYM: **take part** )

**par·ti·ci·ple** /**part**-uh-sip-uhl/ *noun* a form of a verb that you use to make verb tenses. You can sometimes use a participle as an adjective: *The past participle of "annoy" is "annoyed." The present participle is "annoying."*

**par·ti·cle** /**part**-ik-uhl/ *noun* a very small piece of something. A particle is often too small to see: *The air is full of particles of dust.*

**par·tic·u·lar** /pur-**tik**-yuhl-ur/ *adjective*
**1** special, or more than usual: *Pay particular attention to your spelling on the test.*
**2** used to mean the thing you are talking about, and not another one: *I can't come on that particular Saturday, but most Saturdays are fine.*
**3** very definite about what you want or like: *Joey's very particular about his food – there are a lot of things he won't eat.* ( SYNONYM: **picky** )

IDIOM with **particular**
**in particular** especially: *I like all kinds of books, but I like adventure stories in particular.*

**par·tic·u·lar·ly** /pur-**tik**-yuhl-ur-lee/ *adverb*
**1** especially: *Is there anything you particularly want for your birthday?*
**2 not particularly** not very: *I like math, but I'm not particularly good at it.*

**part·ly** /**part**-lee/ *adverb* a little, but not completely: *The sun was partly hidden by clouds.*

**part·ner** /**part**-nur/ *noun*
**1** someone that you do an activity with: *We each had to choose a partner to practice throwing and catching the ball.*
**2** one of the people who owns a business: *The two women are business partners.*
**3** your husband or wife, or your girlfriend or boyfriend: *I hope you can come to the party – and bring your partner.*
—**partnership** /**part**-nur-ship/ *noun* a relationship between people or organizations who work together: *The company formed a partnership with the Department of Education.*

**part of speech** /part uhv **speech**/ *noun* (plural **parts of speech**) in grammar, one of the groups that words belong to: *Nouns, verbs, and adjectives are all parts of speech.*

**part-time** /part-**tīm**/ *adjective, adverb* for only part of each day or week: *Mom has a part-time job and works very hard at home too.*

( ANTONYM: **full-time** )

**par·ty** /**part**-ee/ *noun* (plural **parties**)
**1** an event when people get together and enjoy themselves, usually with food and drinks: *Will you come to my birthday party?*
▶ see **Thesaurus**
**2** an organization of people with the same political ideas. People vote for a party in elections: *In the U.S., most people vote for the Democratic party or the Republican party.*

**pass** /pass/
● *verb*
**1** to go past someone or something: *I pass Ethan's house on the way to school every day.*
**2** to take something and put it in someone's hand: *Can you pass me the sugar?*
**3** to kick, throw, or hit a ball to someone on your team in a game: *Pass the ball to me!*
**4** to succeed on a test or in class: *I passed the reading test so I moved up into the next group.*
( ANTONYM: **fail** )
**5** to go through a place, or to go over a place in an airplane: *We will pass through Texas on our way to Mexico. | A plane passed over our house.*
( SYNONYM: **go** )
**6** to accept a law by voting on it: *Congress passed a new law giving more money for education programs.*
**7** if time passes, it happens and ends: *The weekends are fun and they always pass quickly.*
**8 pass away** to die: *Her grandfather passed away last week and she's going to the funeral.*
**9 pass out** to suddenly become unconscious: *It was so hot that she passed out.* ( SYNONYM: **faint** )
**10 pass up** to not use a chance to do something: *I'm not going to pass up the chance to play on the team if I get it.*
● *noun*
**1** a pass in a game is when you kick, throw, or hit a ball to someone on your team: *Andy threw a great pass to Neil.*
**2** a piece of paper that allows you to do something: *You can buy a special pass to get on all the rides in the amusement park.*
**3** a road or path high up in the mountains: *They walked along a mountain pass to get to the other side of the mountain.*

**pas·sage** /**pass**-ij/ *noun*
**1** a short piece of writing or music: *He read a passage from the Bible.*
**2** a long narrow area in a building: *The library is at the end of that passage.* ( SYNONYM: **corridor** )

**pas·sen·ger** /**pass**-uhnj-ur/ *noun* someone who is traveling in a vehicle, boat, or airplane, but is not driving it: *The bus stopped and two passengers got off.*

**pas·sion** /**pash**-uhn/ *noun*
**1** a very strong feeling such as love, hate, or anger: *The coach spoke with passion about the importance of winning the game.*
**2** a strong feeling of liking something: *Dad has a passion for golf and plays three times a week.*

**pas·sion·ate** /**pash**-uhn-it/ *adjective* showing very strong feelings such as love, hate, or anger: *He gave a passionate speech and was almost crying.*
—**passionately** /**pash**-uhn-uht-lee/ *adverb* in a passionate way: *They fell passionately in love.*

**pas·sive** /**pass**-iv/
● *adjective*
**1** in a passive sentence, the form of the verb shows that someone else did the action: *In the sentence "The cake was eaten by Jim," "was eaten" is a passive verb.* ( ANTONYM: **active** )
**2** a passive person accepts things as they are and does not try to change them: *Her husband is very passive and he lets his wife make all the decisions.*
—**passively** /**pass**-iv-lee/ *adverb* without trying to change what is happening
● *noun*
the passive form of a verb: *In the sentence "The ball was kicked by John," "was kicked" is in the passive.*

**Pass·o·ver** /**pass**-ohv-ur/ *noun* an important Jewish religious holiday when people remember the escape of the Jews from Egypt

**pass·port** /**pass**-port/ *noun* a small official book with your photograph inside that you need when you travel to a foreign country: *He was born in Madrid and has a Spanish passport.*

**pass·word** /**pass**-wurd/ *noun* a secret word that you need to get into a computer system or enter a place: *I've forgotten my password so I can't log onto the computer.*

**past** /past/
● *noun*
**1** the time before now, especially a long time ago: *In the past, people used horses instead of cars.* ( ANTONYM: **future** )
**2** someone's life before now: *The newspapers revealed some embarrassing secrets about the pop star's past.*
**3** (also **past tense**) the form of a verb that is used to talk about things that happened in the time before now: *Put these sentences into the past; for example, "He is hungry" becomes "He was hungry."*
● *adjective*
**1** used when talking about an earlier time that has been happening until now: *I've been studying hard over the past few weeks and I need to have a rest.* ( SYNONYM: **last** )
**2** past events happened before now: *The problems we have now are the result of past mistakes.* ( ANTONYM: **future** )
● *adverb, preposition*
**1** up to and beyond someone or something: *He walked right past me as if he hadn't seen me. | I watched the cars going past.*
**2** after a particular time: *It's half past three in the morning.*
**3** further than a particular place: *There's a movie theater just past the bank.* ( SYNONYM: **beyond** )

**pas·ta** /**pahst**-uh/ *noun* an Italian food that is made from flour and water, and sometimes eggs. You cook it in boiling water. Spaghetti and lasagne are types of pasta: *My favorite kind of pasta is spaghetti.*

**paste** /payst/
● *noun*
**1** thick glue: *We stuck the paper onto the walls with wallpaper paste.*
**2** a soft wet mixture made from crushed food that you can spread easily: *We need tomato paste for this recipe.*
● *verb*
**1** to put words in a new place on a computer screen after moving or copying them from another place: *I copied his name and pasted it onto the list.*
**2** to stick one thing to another using thick glue: *Cut the pictures out and paste them on the chart.*

a b c d e f g h i j k l m n o **p** q r s t u v w x y z

**pas·tel** /pa-**stel**/
● *noun*
**1** a pale color such as pale blue or pale pink: *Dad painted the baby's room in pastels.*
**2** a small colored stick used for drawing pictures, similar to chalk
● *adjective*
pastel colors are pale: *I'm wearing a pastel blue dress.*

**pas·time** /**pass**-tīm/ *noun* something that you enjoy doing when you are not working: *Playing computer games is my favorite pastime.*
( SYNONYM: **hobby** )

**pas·tor** /**past**-ur/ *noun* a Christian religious leader in some Protestant churches: *He is a pastor in a Baptist church.*

**past par·ti·ci·ple** /past **part**-uh-sip-uhl/ *noun* the form of a verb that shows an action happening in the past: *"Gotten" is the past participle of the verb "get."*

**pas·tra·mi** /pa-**strah**-mee/ *noun* smoked beef that contains a lot of spices and is usually eaten in sandwiches

**pas·try** /**payss**-tree/ *noun* (plural **pastries**)
**1** a mixture of flour, butter, and water, which you use to make the outer part of a pie: *I helped Mom to roll out the pastry.*
**2** a small sweet cake: *On Saturdays we buy pastries from the bakery for breakfast.*

**past tense** /past **tenss**/ *noun* the past tense the form of a verb that shows past time: *The past tense of the verb "go" is "went."*

**pas·ture** /**pass**-chur/ *noun* land covered with grass for cows and sheep to eat: *There are some cows in the pasture.*

**pat** /pat/
● *verb* (**patting**, **patted**) to touch something gently several times, with your hand flat: *He patted the dog on the head.*
● *noun* a gentle touch: *She gave the little boy a pat on the head.*

**IDIOM with pat**
**a pat on the back** praise for something you have done well: *He deserves a pat on the back for all his hard work.*

**patch** /pach/

patch

● *noun*
**1** a small area of something that looks different from the rest: *Our dog is white with a black patch over one eye.*
**2** a small piece of material that covers a hole in clothes: *Both knees of his jeans have patches on them.*
**3** a small area of ground for growing vegetables or fruit: *Behind the house there is a small vegetable patch.*
● *verb*
to put a small piece of material over a hole to cover it: *Mom patched my pants because they were full of holes.*

**pat·ent** /**pat**'nt/
● *noun* if you have a patent on something, only you have the legal right to make it or sell it: *The company has a patent for a new type of medicine.*
● *verb* to get a patent on something: *He patented his invention.*

**path** /path/ *noun* (plural **paths** /pathz/)
**1** a narrow road for walking on: *We walked along the path that goes through the forest.*
**2** the direction in which something is moving: *The tornado destroyed everything in its path.*

**pa·thet·ic** /puh-**thet**-ik/ *adjective* very bad, useless, or weak: *He gave a pathetic excuse for not doing his homework.*
—**pathetically** /puh-**thet**-ik-lee/ *adverb* in a pathetic way: *"I can't do it," he said pathetically.*

**pa·tience** /**paysh**-uhnss/ *noun* the ability to deal with a problem or wait for something without becoming angry or upset: *You need a lot of patience to be a teacher.* ( ANTONYM: **impatience** )

**pa·tient** /**paysh**-uhnt/
● *noun* someone who is getting medical treatment from a doctor or hospital: *We can treat up to 500 patients in this hospital.*
● *adjective* able to deal with a problem or wait for something without getting angry or upset: *Be patient, the bus will be here soon.*
( ANTONYM: **impatient** )

—**patiently** /**paysh**-uhnt-lee/ *adverb* in a patient way: *She waited patiently for her father to arrive.*

**pat·i·o** /**pat**-ee-oh/ *noun* (plural **patios**) a hard flat area next to a house, where you can sit outside: *She's outside on the patio, eating her breakfast.*

**pa·tri·ot** /**pay**-tree-uht/ *noun* someone who loves his or her country and is proud of it: *He is a patriot who became a soldier to defend his country.*

**pa·tri·ot·ic** /pay-tree-**aht**-ik/ *adjective* someone who is patriotic loves his or her country and is proud of it: *She is a very patriotic woman who has the American flag outside her house.*

**pa·tri·ot·ism** /**pay**-tree-uh-tiz-uhm/ *noun* great pride in your country: *The politician is well known for his patriotism.*

**pat·rol** /puh-**trohl**/
● *verb* (**patrolling**, **patrolled**) if police or soldiers patrol a place, they go regularly around it checking for problems or crime: *Guards patrol the prison 24 hours a day.*
● *noun* a group of police officers or soldiers who go regularly around an area checking for problems or crime: *The California Highway Patrol stopped a man who was driving too fast.*

> **IDIOM with patrol**
> **on patrol** going around a place checking for problems or crime: *Sometimes you see police officers on patrol in the town.*

**pa·tron·iz·ing** /**pay**-truh-nīz-ing/ *adjective* talking to someone in a way that shows you think they are less important or intelligent than you: *Teachers should avoid being patronizing toward their students.*

**pat·tern** /**pat**-urn/
*noun*
**1** an arrangement of shapes, lines, or colors, used as a decoration: *The flag has a pattern of red and white stripes.*
**2** the way that things come in a particular order, so that you can

**pattern**

The cushion has a pattern on it.

say what will come next: *The set of numbers 3, 6, 9 has a pattern, and you can see that the next number is 12.*

**pat·ty** /**pat**-ee/ *noun* (plural **patties**) a round flat piece of meat or other food: *I'm cooking a hamburger patty.*

**paunch** /ponch/ *noun* a man's fat stomach

**pause** /poz/
● *verb*
**1** to stop speaking or doing something for a short time: *The teacher paused to check her watch.*
**2** to push a button on a CD player or a DVD player to make a CD or DVD stop playing for a short time: *I paused the movie so that I could answer the phone.*
● *noun*
a short time when you stop speaking or doing something: *There was a pause in the game while one of the players was being treated for an injury.*

**pave** /payv/ *verb* to cover a road with a hard surface such as concrete: *They are going to pave the trail that leads through the valley.*

> **IDIOM with pave**
> **pave the way for** to do something that will make something else possible in the future: *All his hard work at college paved the way for a successful career.*

**pave·ment** /**payv**-muhnt/ *noun* the hard surface of a road: *She fell off her bike and hit her head on the pavement.*

**pa·vil·ion** /puh-**vil**-yuhn/ *noun* a building in a park or fair, used for entertainment or exhibitions: *The zoo has an educational pavilion where you can find out about the animals that live in the rainforest.*

**paw** /po/
● *noun* the foot of an animal such as a dog or cat: *The cat is licking its paws.* ▶ see picture at **dog**
● *verb* if an animals paws something, it touches the thing with its paw: *The dog was pawing at the door and asking to go out.*

a b c d e f g h i j k l m n o **p** q r s t u v w x y z

**pay** /pay/
● *verb* (**pays, paying, paid** /payd/)
**1** to give money to someone when you buy something or when someone has done work for you: *How much did you pay for that DVD? | My brother gets paid $15 an hour. | Dad pays me to wash his car.*
**2** if something pays, it has a good result for you: *It pays to listen when the teacher is explaining what to do. | Crime doesn't pay.*
**3** if you pay for something bad you have done, someone punishes you for it: *You're going to pay for being mean to my sister!*
**4 pay attention** to listen or watch something carefully: *You need to pay attention to the teacher's instructions.*
**5 pay a compliment** to say something nice about someone: *It makes you feel good when someone pays you a compliment.*
**6 pay a visit** to visit a person or place: *Why don't we pay a visit to Grandpa?*
**7 pay back** to give someone the money that you owe him or her: *Can I borrow $10? I'll pay you back tomorrow.* ( SYNONYM: **repay** )
**8 pay off** to have a good result: *All my hard work paid off because I got a good grade in the test.*
● *noun*
money you get for work you have done: *The pay is around $8 an hour. | The workers are asking their boss for a pay raise.*

**pay·check** /**pay**-chek/ *noun* a check that you get as payment for your job: *Dad gets a weekly paycheck.*

**pay·day** /**pay**-day/ *noun* the day when you get your money for work you have done: *Could you lend me some money, just until payday?*

**pay·ment** /**pay**-muhnt/ *noun*
**1** an amount of money that you pay to someone, often one of many amounts in a series: *You can make payments by cash or credit card.*
**2** the act of paying: *Late payment of this bill will result in a $10 fine.*

**pay-per-view** /pay pur **vyoo**/ *adjective* a pay-per-view television channel makes people pay for each program they watch

**pay phone** /**pay** fohn/ *noun* a telephone you can use by putting coins or a card into it: *I called Mom from a pay phone.*

**PC** /pee **see**/
● *noun* (**personal computer**) a type of computer that people have at home: *I play games on my PC.*
● *adjective* (**politically correct**) using language in a careful way, in order to avoid offending or upsetting a group of people: *It's not PC to call a woman "baby."*

**P.E.** /pee **ee**/ *noun* (**physical education**) sports and exercise taught as a school subject

**pea** /pee/ *noun* a very small round green vegetable: *For dinner we had chicken, potatoes, and peas.* ► see picture on page **A7**

**peace** /peess/ *noun*
**1** a time when there is no war or fighting: *All the people of the world want to live together in peace.*
**2** a situation that is quiet and calm: *I went to my room for some peace and quiet.*

**Word Family:** peace

peace *noun* | peaceful *adjective* | peacefully *adverb*

**peace·ful** /**peess**-fuhl/ *adjective*
**1** quiet and calm: *Life in the country is more peaceful than in the city.*
**2** without fighting or violence: *The group organized a peaceful protest against the new law.*
—**peacefully** /**peess**-fuhl-ee/ *adverb* in a peaceful way: *The baby is sleeping peacefully.*

**peace·time** /**peess**-tīm/ *noun* a period of time when a country is not fighting a war: *In peacetime the country does not need a big army.*

**peach** /peech/ *noun* a juicy yellow and red fruit with a soft skin and one large seed in the middle ► see picture on page **A7**

**pea·cock** /**pee**-kahk/ *noun* a large bird with a long neck. The male has long blue and green tail feathers. The bird can lift up these feathers and spread them out in the shape of half a circle. The female is often called a peahen.

peacock

**peak** /peek/ *noun*
**1** the pointed top of a mountain: *I could see the mountain peaks above the clouds.* ▶ see picture at **mountain**
**2** the time when something is best, biggest, or most successful: *She is at the peak of her career and she will win the game easily.*

**pea·nut** /**pee**-nuht/ *noun*
**1** a small light brown nut with a soft shell that people eat: *Peanut butter is a spread made out of peanuts.* ▶ see picture at **nut**
**2** peanuts a very small amount of money: *They get paid $4 an hour, which is peanuts.*

**pea·nut but·ter** /**pee**-nuht buht-ur/ *noun* a soft food made from crushed peanuts, which you eat on bread: *I'm eating a peanut butter sandwich.*

**pear** /pair/ *noun* a sweet juicy fruit, usually green or yellow, that is round and wide at the bottom and thin at the top ▶ see picture on page **A7**

**pearl** /purl/ *noun* a small round white object used in jewelry. A pearl forms inside an oyster shell, when sand gets into the shell. The oyster covers the sand with a hard shiny substance to form the pearl: *She was wearing pearl earrings.*

pearl
pearl

**peas·ant** /**pez**-uhnt/ *noun* a poor person who worked on the land in past times: *Her parents were poor peasants and they could not afford to send her to school.*

**peb·ble** /**peb**-uhl/ *noun* a small smooth round stone: *The boys were throwing pebbles into the water.*

pebble

**pe·can** /pi-**kahn**/ *noun* a long brown sweet nut: *Would you like some pecan pie?*

**peck** /pek/ *verb* if a bird pecks at something, it moves its head forward quickly to eat or attack that thing: *The chickens are pecking at their food with their beaks.*

peck

The hen is pecking at the seeds.

**pe·cu·liar** /pi-**kyool**-yur/ *adjective* strange and surprising: *The bird makes a peculiar noise – it sounds like a telephone.*
—**peculiarly** /pi-**kyool**-yur-lee/ *adverb* in a strange or unusual way: *She's been behaving peculiarly recently and I wonder if she is worried about something.*
—**peculiarity** /pi-kyool-ee-**arr**-uht-ee/ *noun* something that is strange or unusual. *One of the peculiarities of tennis is that you say "love" instead of "zero" when you give the score.*

**ped·al** /**ped**'l/
● *noun*
**1** the part of a bicycle that you push with your foot in order to make it move forward: *I lowered the bicycle seat so that my feet could touch the pedals.* ▶ see picture at **bicycle**
**2** the part of a car or machine that you press with your foot to control its movements: *You press on the gas pedal to make the car go faster.*
● *verb*
to ride a bicycle by pushing the pedals with your feet: *You have to pedal hard to get up the hill.*

**pe·des·tri·an** /puh-**dess**-tree-uhn/ *noun* someone who is walking in the streets, rather than driving a car or riding a bicycle: *The driver almost hit a pedestrian.*

**pe·di·a·tri·cian** /peed-ee-uh-**trish**-uhn/ *noun* a doctor who deals with children and their illnesses

a b c d e f g h i j k l m n o **p** q r s t u v w x y z

*a b c d e f g h i j k l m n o p q r s t u v w x y z*

**peek** /peek/
- *verb* to quickly look at something: *He opened her bag and peeked inside.*
- *noun* a quick look: *Take a peek in the oven and see if the cake's done.*

**peel** /peel/
- *verb* to take the skin off a fruit or vegetable: *Will you peel the potatoes, please?*
- *noun* the skin of a fruit or vegetable: *He took off the peel and started eating the orange.*

peel

**peep** /peep/ *verb* to look at something quickly and secretly: *He was peeping at me from behind the curtain.*

**peer** /peer/
- *noun* your peers are people who are the same age as you: *Teenagers prefer to spend time with their peers.*
- *verb* to look very carefully because it is dark or you cannot see well: *He peered through the window but it was too dark to see inside.*

**peg** /peg/ *noun*
**1** a piece of wood or metal on a wall that you hang things on: *The students each have a peg to hang their coats on.*
**2** (also **tent peg**) a pointed piece of wood or metal that you push into the ground to keep a tent in the right place ▶ see picture at **tent**

**pel·i·can** /**pel**-ik-uhn/ *noun* a big bird with a bag of skin under its beak. Pelicans catch fish and keep them in the bag before eating them. Pelicans live near the ocean.

pelican

**pelt** /pelt/
- *verb* to throw a lot of things at someone: *They pelted us with snowballs.*
- *noun* the skin of a dead animal with the fur on it: *Hunters killed the animals and sold their pelts.*

**pel·vis** /**pel**-viss/ *noun* the wide curved bones at the base of your spine that are connected to the top of your legs
—**pelvic** /**pel**-vik/ *adjective* relating to the pelvis

**pen** /pen/ *noun*
**1** something you use for writing and drawing in ink: *I need to write his number down – can I borrow your pen?* ▶ see picture on page **A9**
**2** a small area with a fence around it where a farmer keeps animals: *The pigs are kept in a pen.*

**pe·nal·ize** /**peen**'l-īz/ *verb*
**1** to punish someone for not obeying a rule or law: *People who pay their bills late are sometimes penalized with a fine.*
**2** to punish a player or team in sports by giving an advantage to the other team: *The referee can penalize a player for wasting time.*

**pen·al·ty** /**pen**'l-tee/ *noun* (plural **penalties**)
**1** a punishment for not obeying a law or rule: *The penalty for riding the bus without a ticket is a $50 fine.*
**2** a disadvantage that a player or team in sports gets for not obeying the rules: *A ten-yard penalty was given to the offense.*

**pen·cil** /**penss**-uhl/ *noun* a wooden stick you use for writing and drawing, with a black or colored substance inside: *First, I drew the picture in pencil.* ▶ see picture on page **A9**

**pen·e·trate** /**pen**-uh-trayt/ *verb* to enter something or pass through it: *This type of bullet can penetrate metal.*
—**penetration** /pen-uh-**traysh**-uhn/ *noun* the act of penetrating something

**pen·guin** /**peng**-gwin/ *noun* a big black and white sea bird. Penguins can swim under water but cannot fly. Penguins live in the Antarctic and other cold places and eat fish.

penguin

**pen·i·cil·lin** /pen-uh-**sil**-uhn/ *noun* a medicine that cures illnesses by destroying bacteria

**pe·nin·su·la** /puh-**ninss**-uh-luh/ *noun* a large area of land that is mostly surrounded by water. A peninsula is joined at one end to a bigger area of land: *The state of Florida is a peninsula which goes out into the Atlantic Ocean.*

**pen·i·ten·tia·ry** /pen-uh-**tensh**-uhr-ee/ *noun* (plural **penitentiaries**) a prison: *The judge sent him to the state penitentiary for five years.*

**pen name** /**pen** naym/ *noun* a name a writer uses instead of his or her real name: *Samuel Clemens wrote his books using the pen name of "Mark Twain."* ( SYNONYM: **pseudonym** )

**pen·ny** /**pen**-ee/ *noun* (plural **pennies**) a coin that is worth one cent: *Do you have three pennies?*

**pen pal** /**pen** pal/ *noun* someone in another country that you write letters to, as a way of becoming friends: *I have a pen pal in Mexico. We write to each other once a month.*

**pen·sion** /**pensh**-uhn/ *noun* the money that a company pays regularly to someone after he or she gets old and stops working: *He gets a yearly pension of $30,000.*

**pent·a·gon**
/**pent**-uh-gahn/ *noun* a flat shape with five sides

**Pent·a·gon**
/**pent**-uh-guhn/ *noun* the government building in Washington, D.C. from which the army, navy, etc. are controlled, or the people who work in this building

pentagon

**peo·ple** /**peep**-uhl/ *noun*
**1** the plural of person: *I met lots of new people at the party.* ▶ see **Thesaurus**
**2 the people** all the ordinary people in a country or a state: *In a democracy, the government is chosen by the people.*
**3** a race or nation: *The French people are very proud of their wine.*

**pep·per** /**pep**-ur/ *noun*
**1** a black powder that tastes a little hot. You put it on food to give it more flavor: *Add some salt and pepper.*
**2** a red, green, or yellow vegetable that is hollow

pepper

inside. Some peppers taste hot: *I had a pizza with mushrooms and red peppers.*

**pep·per·mint** /**pep**-ur-mint/ *noun*
**1** a plant with a strong sweet taste and smell. People use it for making tea and candy: *This toothpaste tastes of peppermint.*
**2** a candy that tastes like peppermint: *Would you like a peppermint?*

**per** /pur/ *preposition* for each or during each: *Tickets are $10 per person. | He works six days per week.*

**per·ceive** /pur-**seev**/ *verb*
**1** to consider something in a particular way: *People get angry when they perceive a decision as unfair.*
**2** to see or hear something: *Cats cannot perceive color.*

**per·cent** /pur-**sent**/ *noun* **five percent (5%)/ ten percent (10%), etc.** five, ten, etc. in every hundred: *Thirty percent of people think that taxes should be reduced. | 60% of the students are boys and 40% are girls.*

**per·cent·age** /pur-**sent**-ij/ *noun* an amount that you express as part of one hundred: *"What percentage of teenagers play computer games?" "Probably about 90 percent."*

**per·cep·tion** /pur-**sep**-shuhn/ *noun* your opinion of what something is like: *Our perception of what life is like in other countries is often wrong.*

**per·cep·tive** /pur-**sept**-iv/ *adjective* good at noticing and understanding things: *She is very perceptive about how other people are feeling.*

**perch** /purch/
● *noun* a branch or stick where a bird sits: *The parrot is in a cage, sitting on its perch.*
● *verb* to be on the top or edge of something: *Birds like to perch on the branches of that tree.*

**per·cus·sion** /pur-**kuhsh**-uhn/ *noun* drums and other musical instruments which you play by hitting them

a
b
c
d
e
f
g
h
i
j
k
l
m
n
o
**p**
q
r
s
t
u
v
w
x
y
z

## per·fect

● *adjective* /**purf**-ikt/

**1** if something is perfect, it is so good that it cannot be better: *Michiko speaks perfect English.* | *The car is in perfect condition.*

▶ see Thesaurus

**2** exactly right for a particular purpose: *The weather is perfect for sailing.*

● *verb* /pur-**fekt**/

to make something very good and without any mistakes: *I'm trying to perfect my skills at table tennis.*

## per·fec·tion /pur-**fek**-shuhn/ *noun*

**1** the state of being perfect and without any mistakes: *Dan's piano teacher expected perfection from him; she stopped him every time he made a mistake.*

**2 to perfection** if something is done to perfection, it is done in the best possible way: *The food was delicious, and it was cooked to perfection.*

## per·fect·ly /**purf**-ikt-lee/ *adverb*

**1** without any mistakes or problems: *He speaks Spanish perfectly.*

**2** completely: *She is sick and so has a perfectly good excuse to miss school.*

## per·form /pur-**form**/ *verb*

**1** to entertain people, for example by being in a play, singing, or dancing: *Many students will be performing in the school play.*

**2** to do a job or piece of work: *Scientists perform experiments to find out more about the world.*

## per·form·ance /pur-**form**-uhnss/ *noun*

**1** an occasion when a person or a group of people entertains people, for example by acting or singing: *We watched a performance of a new play at the theater.*

**2** how well someone or something does something: *His teacher is very pleased with his performance this semester: he got an A.*

## per·form·er /pur-**form**-ur/ *noun* someone, such as an actor or singer, who entertains people: *Everyone cheered as the performers came on stage.*

## per·fume /**pur**-fyoom/ *noun*

**1** a liquid with a pleasant smell that women put on their skin: *I like that perfume you're wearing.*

**2** a pleasant sweet smell: *The air was full of the perfume of flowers.*

## per·haps /pur-**hapss**/ *adverb*

**1** possibly: *Tom is late – perhaps he missed his bus.* ( SYNONYM: **maybe** )

**2** used when politely suggesting something: *Perhaps you should sit down.* ( SYNONYM: **maybe** )

## per·il /**perr**-uhl/ *noun* great danger: *Their lives were in peril when the enemy attacked.*

—**perilous** /**perr**-uhl-uhss/ *adjective* very dangerous: *The storm put the sailors in a perilous situation.*

## pe·rim·e·ter /puh-**rim**-uht-ur/ *noun* the length around the edge of an area or shape: *The perimeter of the triangle is the total length of its sides.*

## pe·ri·od /**peer**-ee-uhd/ *noun*

**1** a length of time: *Julio has lived here for only a short period of time.*

**2** the mark (.) that you use in writing at the end of a sentence, or after an abbreviation

**3** one of the equal times that divide the school day: *We have math second period.*

**4** one part of a game in some sports: *The captain of our hockey team scored a goal in the second period.*

**5** the time when blood comes out of a woman's body once a month

## pe·ri·od·ic /peer-ee-**ahd**-ik/ *adjective* happening at different times again and again: *The weather report says there will be periodic showers.*

—**periodically** /peer-ee-**ahd**-ik-lee/ *adverb* in a periodic way: *The river floods periodically – usually every two or three years.*

## pe·ri·od·i·cal /peer-ee-**ahd**-ik-uhl/ *noun* a magazine, especially one about a serious or technical subject. A periodical comes out at regular times such as once a month.

## pe·ri·od·ic ta·ble /peer-ee-ahd-ik **tayb**'l/ *noun* **the periodic table** a list of the chemical elements in order

## per·i·scope /**perr**-uh-skohp/ *noun* a long tube with mirrors in it that you use for looking over the top of something, especially in a submarine: *The submarine captain looked in the periscope to see if there were any enemy ships nearby.*

## per·ish /**perr**-ish/ *verb* to die: *Many soldiers perished during the battle.*

## per·ju·ry /**purj**-uhr-ee/ *noun* the crime of telling

a lie in a court of law: *He was sent to jail for perjury.*

**perm** /purm/ *noun* a treatment for hair that makes it curly: *Mom got a new perm.*
( SYNONYM: **permanent** )

**per·ma·nent** /**purm**-uhn-uhnt/
● *adjective* continuing for a long time or for always: *He suffered some permanent injuries in the car crash.* ( ANTONYM: **temporary** )
—**permanently** /**purm**-uhn-uhnt-lee/ *adverb* for always: *Grandma now lives with us permanently.*
—**permanence** /**purm**-uhn-uhnss/ *noun* the state of being permanent
● *noun* a treatment for hair that makes it curly
( SYNONYM: **perm** )

**per·mis·sion** /pur-**mish**-uhn/ *noun* if you have permission to do something, someone allows you to do it: *I asked Dad for permission to use the phone.*

**per·mit**
● *verb* /pur-**mit**/ (**permitting**, **permitted**)
**1** to allow someone to do something: *You are permitted to use a calculator on the math test.* | *Ball games are not permitted in the yard.*
**2** to make it possible for something to happen: *Weather permitting, we're going to the beach this weekend.*
● *noun* /**purm**-it/
an official piece of paper that allows you to do something: *You can't park here without a permit.*

**Word Family: permit**

**permit** *verb* | **permit** *noun* | **permission** *noun*

**per·pen·dic·u·lar** /purp-uhn-**dik**-yuhl-ur/
● *adjective* if two lines are perpendicular to each other, they form an angle of 90 degrees where they cross: *The flagpole is perpendicular to the ground.*
● *noun* an exactly upright position or line: *Draw a line 15 degrees from the perpendicular.*

**per·se·vere** /purss-uh-**veer**/ *verb* to continue trying to do something difficult: *Climbing the hill was hard, but we persevered until we reached the top.*

**per·sist** /pur-**sist**/ *verb* to continue to do

something or to happen: *If the rain persists, we won't be able to play tennis.*
—**persistent** /pur-**sist**-uhnt/ *adjective* continuing to do something or to happen: *He's very persistent. He's called me four times today.*
—**persistence** /pur-**sist**-uhnss/ *noun* determination to succeed in doing something, by trying many times: *Eventually, because of her persistence, she passed her test after failing six times.*

**per·son** /**purss**-uhn/ *noun* (plural **people** /**peep**-uhl/) a man, woman, or child: *Tim is a nice person.* | *What kind of person is she?*

IDIOM with **person**
**in person** if you do something in person, you do it by going to a place, not by writing or using the telephone: *He came to my house to thank me in person.*

**per·son·al** /**purss**-uhn-uhl/ *adjective*
**1** belonging or relating to you: *He packed all his personal belongings in a small suitcase.*
**2** if something is personal, it concerns your private life and you do not want to talk about it with other people: *She's had some personal problems recently – her mom has been very sick.*
**3** doing something yourself, instead of asking someone else to do it: *The president made a personal visit to the scene of the accident.*

**per·son·al com·put·er** /purss-uhn-uhl kuhm-**pyoot**-ur/ *noun* ( ABBREVIATION: **PC** ) a type of computer that people have at home: *I do my homework on a personal computer.*

**per·son·al·i·ty** /purss-uh-**nal**-uht-ee/ *noun* (plural **personalities**)
**1** the type of person someone is, and how he or she behaves toward other people: *She has a very friendly personality and is very popular.*
**2** a famous person, especially in sports or on television: *He's a well-known TV personality.*

**per·son·al·ize** /**purss**-uhn-uh-līz/ *verb*
**1** to decorate something in the way you like: *She personalized her notebook with pictures of her rabbit.*
**2** to put your name or the first letters of your name on something: *Harry has a personalized license plate on his car, which reads HARRY.*

**per·son·al·ly** /**purss**-uhn-uhl-ee/ *adverb*
**1** used when saying what you think about something, not what anyone else thinks: *Many people like spicy food. Personally, I hate it.*
**2** if you do something personally, you do it and no one else does it for you: *I know she has the letter because I gave it to her personally.*
**3** if you know someone personally, you have met and talked to him or her: *I don't know her personally, but I've seen her at school.*

┌ **IDIOM with personally**
**take something personally** to get upset by things people say because you think they are saying them because they do not like you: *If the teacher criticizes your work, you shouldn't take it personally.*

**per·son·i·fi·ca·tion**
/pur-sahn-uhf-uh-**kaysh**-uhn/ *noun*
**1** someone who is a perfect example of a particular quality – used especially when saying that someone is a very good or very bad person: *The newspapers said that he was a very bad man, who was the personification of evil.*
**2** the representation of a thing or quality as a person: *Uncle Sam, with his red, white, and blue hat, is a personification of the United States.*

**per·son·nel** /purss-uh-**nel**/ *noun* people who work in an organization: *There is a meeting for all company personnel tomorrow.*

**per·spec·tive** /pur-**spekt**-iv/ *noun*
**1** a way of thinking about something: *Travel to foreign countries gives you a new perspective on life.* ( SYNONYM: **viewpoint** )
**2** the ability to think about something sensibly, so that it does not seem worse than it is: *You got a bad grade, but keep things in perspective. You can always do better next time.*

**per·spire** /pur-**spī**-ur/ *verb* if you perspire, water comes out of your skin because you are hot
( SYNONYM: **sweat** )
—**perspiration** /pursp-uh-**raysh**-uhn/ *noun* water from your skin when you perspire: *After the race his forehead was covered with perspiration.*
( SYNONYM: **sweat** )

**per·suade** /pur-**swayd**/ *verb* to make someone decide to do something by giving him or her good reasons: *She says she doesn't like parties,*

but I'll try to persuade her to come.
▶ see **Thesaurus**

**Word Family: persuade**

**persuade** *verb* | **persuasion** *noun* |
**persuasive** *adjective* | **persuasively** *adverb*

**per·sua·sion** /pur-**swayzh**-uhn/ *noun* the act of persuading someone to do something: *After a little persuasion, Alex joined in the game.*

**per·sua·sive** /pur-**swayss**-iv/ *adjective* able to persuade people to do things: *She is very persuasive and I'm sure that she can make him change his mind.*

**pes·si·mism** /**pess**-uh-miz-uhm/ *noun* the feeling that bad things will happen: *The team lost their last three games, and there was a mood of pessimism among the players.*
( ANTONYM: **optimism** )

**pes·si·mist** /**pess**-uh-mist/ *noun* someone who always expects bad things to happen: *Steve's such a pessimist. He thinks he will fail the test.*
( ANTONYM: **optimist** )

**pes·si·mis·tic** /pess-uh-**mist**-ik/ *adjective* someone who is pessimistic always expects that bad things will happen ( ANTONYM: **optimistic** )

**pest** /pest/ *noun*
**1** an animal or insect that harms plants growing on farms or damages places where people live: *Farmers use chemicals to kill pests that attack their crops.*
**2** someone who annoys you

**pes·ter** /**pest**-ur/ *verb* to ask for something many times in an annoying way: *The cats are always pestering me for food.*

**pes·ti·cide** /**pest**-uh-sīd/ *noun* a chemical that kills insects that destroy crops: *Farmers spray pesticides on their crops to kill insects.*

**pet** /pet/
● *noun* an animal that you keep at home: *Do you have any pets?* | *I have a pet rabbit.*
● *verb* (**petting**, **petted**) to move your hand over an animal's fur to show that you like it: *She was petting a cat on her knee.*
▶ see picture on page **A14**

**pet**

hamster

cat

dog

rabbit

**pet·al** /**pet**'l/ *noun* one of the brightly colored parts of a flower: *The rose is dropping its petals.*
▶ see picture at **flower**

**pe·tite** /puh-**teet**/ *adjective* a woman who is petite is short and thin in an attractive way
SYNONYM: **small**

**pe·ti·tion** /puh-**tish**-uhn/ *noun* a piece of paper that a lot of people sign in order to ask for something or complain about something: *Five hundred parents signed a petition asking for a crossing guard outside the school.*

**pet·ri·fied** /**pet**-ruh-fīd/ *adjective* very frightened: *I'm petrified of spiders.*
SYNONYM: **terrified**

**pe·tro·le·um** /puh-**trohl**-ee-uhm/ *noun* oil from beneath the ground for making gasoline

**pet·ty** /**pet**-ee/ *adjective*
**1** petty things are not important: *The two girls are having a petty argument about who should wash the dishes.*
**2** if someone is petty, they care too much about small unimportant things: *"You owe me five cents." "Don't be so petty!"*

**pew** /pyoo/ *noun* a long wooden seat in a church

**phan·tom** /**fant**-uhm/ *noun* the spirit of a dead person that some people believe you can see
SYNONYM: **ghost**

**pha·raoh** /**fair**-oh/ *noun* a ruler of ancient Egypt

**phar·ma·cist** /**farm**-uh-sist/ *noun* someone whose job is to prepare and sell medicines: *If you want medicine for a cold, you can ask the pharmacist at the drugstore.*

**phar·ma·cy** /**farm**-uhss-ee/ *noun* (plural **pharmacies**) a store that sells medicines: *Mom wants to buy some aspirin from the pharmacy.*

**phase** /fayz/
● *noun*
**1** one part of a process in which something develops: *The first phase of building the new library will be to clear the ground.*
SYNONYM: **stage**
**2** one of the changes in the shape of the Moon in each month, as seen from the Earth
▶ see picture at **moon**
● *verb*
**phase in** to gradually start using a new way of doing something: *The school will phase in the new technology over the next six months.*

**Ph.D.** /pee aych **dee**/ *noun* the highest university degree, that someone studies for after getting a bachelor's or a master's degree: *She has a Ph.D. in history.* SYNONYM: **doctorate**

**phe·nom·e·nal** /fi-**nahm**-uhn-'l/ *adjective* extremely impressive or surprising: *The movie has been a phenomenal success.*
—**phenomenally** /fi-**nahm**-uhn-'l-ee/ *adverb* very: *Diamonds are phenomenally expensive.*

**phe·nom·e·non** /fi-**nahm**-uhn-uhn/ *noun* (plural **phenomena** /fi-**nahm**-uhn-uh/) something that happens or exists, especially something unusual: *Earthquakes are natural phenomena.*

**phi·los·o·pher** /fi-**lahss**-uhf-ur/ *noun* someone who studies or teaches philosophy: *Philosophers think about ideas like why people choose to do good or bad things.*

**phi·los·o·phy** /fi-**lahss**-uhf-ee/ *noun* (plural **philosophies**)
**1** the study of ideas about the meaning of life, and how we know that something is true or real
**2** your ideas about what you should do in your life: *My philosophy is that you should always help other people because you never know when you will need another person to help you.*
—**philosophical** /fil-uh-**sahf**-ik-uhl/ *adjective* relating to philosophy: *They are having a philosophical discussion about the meaning of life.*

**Word Family:** philosophy
**philosophy** *noun* | **philosopher** *noun* | **philosophical** *adjective*

a b c d e f g h i j k l m n o **p** q r s t u v w x y z

**phlo·em** /**floh**-em/ *noun* the tissue in plants that carries food substances from the leaves to all parts of the plant

**pho·bi·a** /**fohb**-ee-uh/ *noun* a strong fear of something: *She has a phobia about spiders – she panics if she sees one.*

**phone** /fohn/
● *noun* a piece of equipment you use to speak to someone in another place: *Can I use your phone? | The phone rang and I answered it.* ( SYNONYM: **telephone** )
● *verb* to talk to someone using a phone: *I'll phone you tomorrow.* ( SYNONYM: **call** )

**-phone** /fohn/, **phon-** /fahn/

## Word Building

**ear**phone**s** | homo**phone** | micro**phone** | **phon**ics | tele**phone**

These words all have the Greek word root **-phone** or **-phon** in them. **Phone** means "sound." You wear *earphones* to hear sounds from an MP3-player, radio, or CD player. A *homophone* is a word that sounds the same as another word, but is spelled or means something different. For example, "one" and "won" are homophones. When you learn *phonics*, you learn the sounds that go with letters.

**phone booth** /fohn booth/ *noun* a small structure with a telephone that you pay to use: *My cell phone wasn't working so I had to use a phone booth.*

phone booth

**phone num·ber** /**fohn** nuhm-bur/ *noun* a set of numbers that you press on a telephone when you call someone: *I'll call you if you give me your phone number.*

**pho·net·ic** /fuh-**net**-ik/ *adjective* relating to the sounds you make when you speak: *She used a phonetic writing system to record the sounds of the language.*

**phon·ics** /**fahn**-ikss/ *noun* a way of teaching people to read. In phonics, you are taught the sounds that the letters make: *Phonics helps you sound out the words as you are reading.*

**pho·ny** /**fohn**-ee/ *adjective* false or not real: *The police arrested him for having a phony driver's license.* ( SYNONYM: **fake** )

**phos·pho·rus** /**fahs**-fuhr-uhss/ *noun* a chemical substance that starts to burn when it is in contact with the air. The symbol for phosphorus is P.

**pho·to** /**foht**-oh/ *noun* (plural **photos**) a photograph: *I took some photos of my brother in the backyard. | Who's the girl in this photo?* ( SYNONYM: **picture** )

## Word Building

**photo**copier | **photo**graph | **photo**synthesis

These words all have the Greek word root **photo** in them. **Photo** means "light." A *photocopier* uses light to copy a piece of paper or a picture. A *photograph* is made by light going into a camera. *Photosynthesis* is how plants use light to change other substances into food.

**pho·to·cop·i·er** /**foht**-uh-kahp-ee-ur/ *noun* a machine for copying pieces of writing or pictures: *Dad has a photocopier in his office.* ( SYNONYM: **copier** )

**pho·to·cop·y** /**foht**-uh-kahp-ee/
● *noun* (plural **photocopies**) a copy of a piece of writing or picture that you make on a photocopier: *I made a photocopy of my homework in case I lost it.* ( SYNONYM: **copy** )
● *verb* (**photocopies, photocopying, photocopied**) to make a copy of a piece of writing or picture on a photocopier: *I photocopied an interesting story I found in the newspaper.* ( SYNONYM: **copy** )

**pho·to·gen·ic** /foht-oh-**jen**-ik/ *adjective* a photogenic person looks good in photographs: *My sister is very photogenic and her picture has appeared in magazines.*

**pho·to·graph** /**foht**-uh-graf/
● *noun* a picture you take using a camera: *I often take photographs of our cat. | The man*

*in this photograph is my grandfather.*

$(SYNONYM: **picture**)$

● *verb* to take a picture of someone or something using a camera: *He photographed the movie star coming out of a night club.*

**pho·tog·ra·pher** /fuh-**tahg**-ruhf-ur/ *noun* someone whose job is to take pictures using a camera: *She's a fashion photographer and her pictures are often in magazines.*

**pho·tog·ra·phy** /fuh-**tahg**-ruhf-ee/ *noun* the activity of taking pictures with a camera: *My brother is very interested in photography and he likes taking pictures of people.*

—**photographic** /foht-uh-**graf**-ik/ *adjective* relating to photography: *The store sells cameras and other photographic equipment.*

**pho·ton** /**foht**-ahn/ *noun* the smallest particle of light or radiation. A photon has energy but no electrical charge or mass.

**pho·to·syn·the·sis** /foht-oh-**sinth**-uhss-iss/ *noun* the process by which plants use light to change carbon dioxide and water into carbohydrates. The plant uses the carbohydrates as food.

**phras·al verb** /frayz-uhl **vurb**/ *noun* a two- or three part verb made of a verb and one or more words such as "off," "up," or "down": *"Take off" and "give up" are phrasal verbs.*

**phrase** /frayz/ *noun* a group of words that is not a complete sentence: *In the sentence "Maria was wearing a red dress," "a red dress" is a phrase.*

▶ see **Thesaurus**

**phys·i·cal** /**fiz**-ik-uhl/

● *adjective*

**1** relating to your body, not your mind or soul: *My dad is very healthy and he does a lot of physical activity.*

**2** relating to things that you can see, touch, smell, or taste: *Scientists are looking for signs of physical damage to the environment caused by climate change.*

—**physically** /**fiz**-ik-lee/ *adverb* in a physical way: *His job is difficult both physically and mentally.*

● *noun*

a medical examination by a doctor to check that you are healthy: *Pilots have to take a physical every six months to make sure that they are healthy enough to fly a plane.*

**phy·si·cian** /fi-**zish**-uhn/ *noun* a doctor

**phys·ics** /**fiz**-ikss/ *noun* the study of natural forces, such as heat, light, and movement: *In physics we learned about magnets.*

—**physicist** /**fiz**-uhss-ist/ *noun* someone who studies or teaches physics

**phys·i·ol·o·gy** /fiz-ee-**ahl**-uhj-ee/ *noun* the study of how the bodies of living things work

**phy·sique** /fi-**zeek**/ *noun* the shape and size of someone's body: *He is a tall man with a powerful physique.*

**pi** /pī/ *noun* a number that is equal to the distance around a circle divided by its width. Pi is represented by the Greek letter (π) and is about 3.1416.

**pi·an·ist** /pee-**an**-ist/ *noun* someone who plays the piano

**pi·an·o** /pee-**an**-oh/ *noun* (plural **pianos**) a large musical instrument that you play by pressing black and white keys. The keys move little soft hammers inside the piano. The hammers hit strings to make the sound: *Sarah's learning to play the piano.*

## Word Origin: piano

The Italian man who invented the **piano** in the 1700s gave it a very long name. He called it "the harpsichord that can play soft and loud." A harpsichord is like a piano, but you cannot change how loudly it plays. In Italian, "soft and loud" is ***piano e forte***, and at first people called the instrument a "pianoforte." Later this was shortened to just piano.

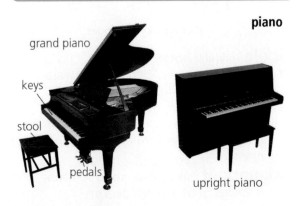

**piano**

grand piano

keys

stool

pedals

upright piano

a
b
c
d
e
f
g
h
i
j
k
l
m
n
o
**p**
q
r
s
t
u
v
w
x
y
z

**pick** /pik/
● *verb*
**1** to choose something or someone: *I hope the coach picks me for the basketball team.*
**2** to pull a flower or fruit from a plant or tree: *We usually pick the tomatoes in July and August.*
**3** to remove small things from something: *Stop picking your nose – use a tissue!*
**4 pick on** to treat someone in an unfair or mean way: *The other girls were always picking on her and calling her names because she had big ears.*
**5 pick up** to lift something up in your hand from a surface: *I picked up a stick that was lying on the grass.* ► see picture on page **A15**
**6 pick up** to go somewhere and get someone or something: *Mom comes to pick me up from school in her car.*
**7 pick up** to learn something quickly: *I picked up some Spanish when I was on vacation in Mexico.*

> **IDIOM with pick**
> **pick a fight/an argument** to behave in an unpleasant way toward someone so that they will fight you or argue with you: *Jerry's always trying to pick a fight but I don't like arguing with him.*

● *noun*
**take your pick** used when telling someone to choose anything from a group of things: *You can have orange juice, lemonade, or cola – take your pick.*

pick
Rick is picking oranges.

**pick·le** /**pik**-uhl/ *noun*
**1** a cucumber kept in vinegar or salt water: *I don't want pickles on my burger.*
**2** a difficult situation, in which you have problems: *I'm in a pickle because I forgot to bring my house keys with me, and I can't reach my mom.*

**pick·pock·et** /**pik**-pahk-it/ *noun* someone who steals things from people's pockets

**pick·up** /**pik**-uhp/ *noun* a small truck with a part with no roof in the back. It is used for carrying large things: *Dad put all his tools in the back of his pickup.* ► see picture at **truck**

**pick·y** /**pik**-ee/ *adjective* (**pickier, pickiest**) someone who is picky is difficult to make happy because there are a lot of things he or she does not like: *She's a picky eater – the only vegetable she likes is corn.*

**pic·nic** /**pik**-nik/ *noun* an occasion when you go somewhere and take food to eat outdoors: *If it's sunny, let's have a picnic on the beach.*

picnic
The family is having a picnic.

**pic·to·graph** /**pikt**-uh-graf/ (also **pic·to·gram** /**pikt**-uh-gram/) *noun* a picture, symbol, or sign that represents a word or idea: *Some languages, such as ancient Egyptian, are written using pictographs.*

**pic·ture** /**pik**-chur/
● *noun*
**1** a drawing, painting, or photograph: *I'm drawing a picture of a horse.* | *Can I take a picture of you with my camera?*
► see **Thesaurus**
**2** an idea or image in your mind of what someone or something is like: *My mom often talked about my uncle, and I had a picture of him in my mind.*
**3** the image that you see on a television or in a movie: *The picture's not very clear on this TV set.*
● *verb*
**1** to imagine something: *I pictured myself swimming in a warm ocean.*
**2** to show something or someone in a photograph, painting, or drawing: *She was pictured in a magazine with a famous movie star.*

**pic·ture graph** /**pik**-chur graf/ *noun* a graph that uses pictures to represent information

**pic·tur·esque** /**pik**-chuhr-esk/ *adjective* a picturesque place is pretty to look at: *Monterey is a picturesque town.*

**pie** /pī/ *noun*
**1** a sweet food made with fruit baked inside a pastry covering: *For dessert we had apple pie.*
▶ see picture at **dessert**
**2** a food made of meat or vegetables baked inside a pastry covering: *Mom used the rest of the chicken to make a chicken pie.*

**piece** /peess/ *noun*

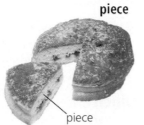
piece

piece

**1** a part of something that has been cut or broken from the rest: *Would you like a piece of cake?* | *The glass fell and broke into pieces.*
▶ see **Thesaurus**
**2** something that someone has written, drawn, or made: *Jessica was at the piano practicing a piece of music.*
**3** a small object or figure used in board games such as chess: *In chess, each player has 16 pieces.* ▶ see picture at **chess**
**4** some advice, information, news, or luck: *Let me give you a piece of advice – always listen to your mother.*
**5** a coin with a particular value: *I only had a 50-cent piece in my pocket.*

**pie chart** /pī chart/ (also **pie graph** /pī graf/) *noun* a circle divided into different parts by lines coming from the center. Pie charts are used to show the sizes of different amounts compared with each other. ( SYNONYM: **circle graph** )

**pier** /peer/ *noun* a long structure you can walk along that goes from the land over the ocean: *A fishing boat was tied up to the pier.*

pier
pier

**pierce** /peerss/ *verb* to make a hole in something with a sharp object: *She had her ears pierced so that she could wear earrings.*

**pig** /pig/ *noun*
**1** a fat pink farm animal: *Bacon and pork come from pigs.*
**2** someone who eats too much: *Don't be such a pig – save some pizza for me!*

**pi·geon** /**pij**-uhn/ *noun* a gray bird that you often see in cities: *There were pigeons eating crumbs on the sidewalk.* ▶ see picture on page **A4**

**pig·gy** /**pig**-ee/ *noun* a word for a pig, used by children

**pig·gy·back** /**pig**-ee-bak/ *adverb* riding on someone's back as he or she walks along: *My older brother carried me piggyback.*

**pig·gy bank** /**pig**-ee bangk/ *noun* a container that children use for saving coins. It is often in the shape of a pig.

piggy bank

**pig·let** /**pig**-lit/ *noun* a young pig

**pig·sty** /**pig**-stī/ *noun* (plural **pigsties**)
**1** a place on a farm where pigs are kept
**2** if a place is a pigsty, it is very dirty and messy: *Your room is a pigsty – go and clean it up!*

**pig·tail** /**pig**-tayl/ *noun* if a girl has pigtails, she has pulled her hair into two pieces, one on each side of her head. Sometimes the hair is braided: *The little girl had her hair in pigtails.*

pigtail

**pile** /pīl/
● *noun* a lot of things on top of each other: *There was a pile of books on the table.* | *I fell in a pile of dirt.* ( SYNONYMS: **heap, stack** )
● *verb* to make a pile: *Let's pile all these boxes in the corner of the room.*

a b c d e f g h i j k l m n o **p** q r s t u v w x y z

**pil·grim** /**pil**-gruhm/ *noun*
**1** someone who travels a long way to reach a holy place for religious reasons: *Many pilgrims visit Jerusalem each year.*
**2 the Pilgrims** a group of people who left England and came to America in 1620. They left England because of religious disagreements. They sailed on the "Mayflower" and landed at Plymouth Rock in what is now the state of Massachusetts.
—**pilgrimage** /**pil**-gruhm-ij/ *noun* a trip by pilgrims: *They went on a pilgrimage to Mecca.*

**the Pilgrims**

the Pilgrims landing
at Plymouth Rock

**pill** /pil/ *noun* a small hard piece of medicine: *I find it very hard to swallow pills.*
(SYNONYM: **tablet**)

**pil·lar** /**pil**-ur/ *noun* a tall piece of stone that supports part of a building: *The roof is held up with big stone pillars.* (SYNONYM: **column**)

**pil·low** /**pil**-oh/ *noun* a soft square thing that you put your head on in bed

**pil·low·case** /**pil**-oh-kayss/ *noun* a cover for a pillow: *She put clean pillowcases on all the pillows.*

**pi·lot** /**pī**-luht/ *noun* someone who flies a plane: *The pilot managed to land the plane safely.*

**pim·ple** /**pimp**-uhl/ *noun* a small raised spot on your skin, where oil is blocking an opening: *Teenagers often get pimples on their faces.*
(SYNONYM: **zit**)

**pin** /pin/
● *noun*
**1** a thin piece of metal with a sharp point. You use pins to fasten pieces of material together before sewing them: *I stuck a pin into the balloon, and it made a loud bang!*
**2** a piece of jewelry or a small sign that you fasten to your clothes: *She is wearing a diamond pin on her jacket.*
**3** one of the things you try to knock down in a game of bowling: *He knocked down all ten pins.*
● *verb* (**pinning**, **pinned**)
to attach something with a pin or a thumbtack: *Does anyone have a thumbtack? I need to pin this list of names on the board.*

**pi·ña·ta** /pi-**nyaht**-uh/ *noun* a decorated paper container filled with candy or toys. A piñata is hung up and children try to break it open with sticks.

**pinch** /pinch/
● *verb*
to press someone's skin between your finger and thumb: *Ouch! Justin pinched me!* ▶ see picture on page **A14**
● *noun*
**1** if you give someone a pinch, you pinch him or her: *She gave him a little pinch to wake him up.*
**2** the amount of a powder that you can hold between your finger and thumb: *Add a pinch of salt.*

**pine** /pīn/ *noun*
**1** a tree with thin leaves like needles. Pines do not lose their leaves in the winter. The seeds of a pine are in hard brown objects called pine cones: *The sides of the mountains are covered with pines.*
**2** a soft light-colored wood from pine trees: *a pine table*

**pine**

**pine·ap·ple** /**pīn**-ap-uhl/ *noun* a large fruit that is yellow inside and has pointed leaves on top. Pineapples grow in hot places. ▶ see picture on page **A7**

**pine cone** /**pīn** kohn/ *noun* a hard brown object that contains the seeds of a pine tree

**Ping-Pong** /**ping** pahng/ *noun trademark* a game that two people play by hitting a small light ball across a net on a special table. The thing used to hit the ball is called a paddle.

SYNONYM: **table tennis**

**pink** /pingk/ *noun, adjective* a color that is a mixture of red and white: *She is wearing pink lipstick.*

**pink·ie** /**pingk**-ee/ *noun* the smallest finger on your hand

**pint** /pīnt/ *noun* a unit for measuring liquid, equal to 0.47 liters: *The recipe uses a pint of cream.*

**pi·o·neer** /pī-uh-**neer**/ *noun*
**1** one of the first people to go to a new place and start living there: *The pioneers traveled across America in covered wagons.*
**2** one of the first people to do something that later has a big effect on people's lives: *The Wright Brothers were aviation pioneers, and Orville Wright made the first powered flight at Kitty Hawk in 1903.*

**pioneer**

covered wagon

**pipe** /pīp/
● *noun*
**1** a tube for carrying water or gas: *There is water on the floor because a pipe under the sink is leaking.*
**2** an object for smoking tobacco. It is a thin tube with a small bowl at the end: *Grandpa Ray smoked a pipe.*
● *verb*
to send a liquid or gas through a pipe: *Oil is piped across hundreds of miles of desert.*

**pipe**

**pipe·line** /**pīp**-līn/ *noun* a set of pipes that carry oil or gas over long distances: *A new 100-mile oil pipeline has just been built.*

**pi·rate** /**pīr**-it/
● *noun* someone who sails on the ocean and attacks other boats to steal from them: *Their ship was seized by pirates who stole the cargo.*
● *verb* to illegally copy and sell movies, music, or software: *The DVD they were watching had been pirated and the picture quality was really bad.*
—**piracy** /**pīr**-uhss-ee/ *noun* the act of illegally pirating movies, music, or software: *Software piracy is a crime.*

**pirate**

hat
eye patch
shirt
coat
belt
sword
boots

**pis·tol** /**pist**'l/ *noun* a small gun: *He fired his pistol at the target.*

**pit** /pit/ *noun*
**1** a large hole in the ground: *We'll dig a pit and bury the box.*
**2** a large hard seed in a fruit: *Remove the pits from the peaches.*
**3 the pits** something that is very bad: *"Life is the pits," he said miserably.*

a b c d e f g h i j k l m n o p q r s t u v w x y z

**pitch** /pich/
● *verb*
**1** to throw the ball for a player to hit in baseball: *He pitches for his baseball team.*
**2** to put up a tent so that you can use it: *We pitched our tent near the river.*
**3 pitch in** to help other people with a job: *If everyone pitches in, we'll be finished soon.*
● *noun*
**1** a throw of the ball for a player to hit in baseball: *His next pitch was high.*
**2** how high or low a musical note is: *Press the guitar string to change the pitch of the note.*

**pitch·er** /**pich**-ur/ *noun*
**1** the baseball player who throws the ball for other players to hit
**2** a container used for holding and pouring liquids: *She was carrying a pitcher of water.*
( SYNONYM: **jug** )

**pit·y** /**pit**-ee/
● *noun* the sadness you feel when someone is in a bad situation: *I don't feel any pity for them because their problems are all their own fault.*

IDIOMS with pity
**it's a pity/what a pity** used to say you wish a situation was different: *It's a pity you missed the party.*
**take/have pity on** to help someone who is in a bad situation: *When she said she had no money, he took pity on her and gave her $50.*
● *verb* (**pities**, **pitying**, **pitied**) to feel sorry for someone: *I pity people who have no friends.*

**pix·el** /**pikss**-uhl/ *noun* one of the small areas of light that cover a TV or computer screen: *Each picture and word on the screen is formed from many pixels.*

**piz·za** /**peetss**-uh/ *noun* a round flat piece of special bread, with tomato, cheese, and other things on top: *We ordered a mushroom pizza.*

**place** /playss/
● *noun*
**1** an area, building, city, or country: *This town is a really nice place.* | *Where is your favorite place to go on vacation?* ▶ see **Thesaurus**
**2** a space for something or someone: *That's not the right place for that book.* | *He sat down at his place at the table.*
**3** someone's position in a race or competition: *Joe finished the race in third place.*

IDIOMS with place
**all over the place** everywhere: *He spilled paint all over the place.*
**in place of** instead of: *You can use mushrooms in place of meat in this recipe.*
**out of place** if something is out of place, it does not belong: *She looked out of place at the wedding because she was wearing jeans.*
**take place** to happen: *The wedding will take place on Saturday.*
**take someone's place** to do something instead of someone else: *David was sick and couldn't play, so I took his place.*
● *verb*
to put something somewhere carefully: *Rachel placed the box on the table.*

**place val·ue** /**playss** val-yoo/ *noun* the value of the position that a figure has in a number: *In the number 467, the digit 4 is in the hundred place value, so it is equal to 400.*

**pla·gia·rism** /**playj**-uh-riz-uhm/ *noun* the act of copying someone else's work and pretending that it is yours: *If you copy your essay from the Internet, that's plagiarism.*
—**plagiarize** /**playj**-uh-rīz/ *verb* to copy someone else's work and pretend that it is yours: *He was accused of plagiarizing someone else's novel.*

**plague** /playg/ *noun* a disease that kills people and spreads quickly: *In medieval times, many people in Europe died of the plague.*

**plaid** /plad/ *noun* a pattern on cloth of squares and lines that cross each other: *She was wearing a red plaid skirt.*

plaid

**plain** /playn/
● *adjective*
**1** without a pattern or any extra things: *I'm wearing a plain white T-shirt.* | *I like plain yogurt, without any fruit in it.*
( ANTONYM: **fancy** )
**2** easy to see, hear, or understand: *It was plain that she didn't like me.* ( SYNONYM: **clear** )
● *noun*
a large area of flat land: *We looked down across the plain from the mountain.* ▶ see picture at **hill**

486

**plain·ly** /**playn**-lee/ *adverb*
**1** in a way that is easy to see, hear, or understand: *She was plainly nervous and kept biting her nails.* | *The price is marked plainly on the tag.* ( SYNONYMS: **clearly, obviously** )
**2** in a simple way: *The room was small and plainly decorated.*

**plan** /plan/
● *noun*
**1** an idea for how you can do something: *The prisoners made an escape plan.*
**2** something you have decided to do: *Do you have any plans for Friday night?*
**3** a drawing showing all the parts of a building or machine: *All the doors of the school are marked on the plan.*
● *verb* (**planning, planned**)
**1** to think about how you will do something, and make all the arrangements: *My mother planned our trip very carefully and booked all the plane tickets.*
**2** to intend to do something: *She was planning to study Spanish in college.* | *I'm planning on leaving at 5:00.*

**plane** /playn/ *noun*
**1** a vehicle with wings that flies: *We watched the planes taking off and landing at the airport.*
( SYNONYM: **airplane** )
**2** a tool that you push along wood to make it smooth. A plane has a flat bottom with a blade in it.

**plane fig·ure** /**playn** fig-yur/ (also **plane shape** /**playn**-shayp/) *noun* a flat shape such as a triangle or a circle

**plan·et** /**plan**-it/ *noun* a large round object in space that moves around a sun. There are eight planets moving around our Sun: *Earth is the third planet from the sun.*
—**planetary** /**plan**-uh-tair-ee/ *adjective* relating to the planets: *The Sun is at the heart of our planetary system.*

**planet**

**Word Origin:** planet

**Planet** comes from a Greek word that means "moving star." The Greeks noticed that stars did not move in the sky from night to night, but that planets did. In the 1600s, scientists began to understand that planets move around the sun.

**plan·e·tar·i·um** /plan-uh-**tair**-ee-uhm/ *noun* a building that has a special curved ceiling with lights that show the stars and the movement of the planets

**plank** /plangk/ *noun* a long flat piece of wood: *The deck of the ship was made of wooden planks.*

**plank·ton** /**plangk**-tuhn/ *noun* very small plants and animals that float in the ocean and lakes: *Fish eat plankton.*

**plant** /plant/
● *noun*
**1** a living thing that has leaves and roots: *You can grow plants in pots on your windowsill.*
▶ see **Thesaurus**
**2** a factory: *The car plant makes cars that are sold all over the world.*
● *verb*
to put plants or seeds in soil so they will grow: *We planted some pumpkin seeds in the yard.*

**plan·ta·tion** /plan-**taysh**-uhn/ *noun* a large farm in a hot place. Crops such as tea, cotton, and sugar are grown on plantations: *There were many sugar plantations on Caribbean islands.*

**plaque** /plak/ *noun*
**1** a piece of flat metal or stone with writing on it: *A plaque on the wall tells you when the hospital was opened.*
**2** a substance that forms on your teeth and causes decay: *Brushing your teeth every day helps to stop plaque.*

**plaque**

**plas·ter** /**plast**-ur/

● *noun*

a substance that a builder puts on walls and ceilings to give them a smooth surface. Plaster is a soft mixture that becomes hard when it dries.

● *verb*

**1** to cover a surface with a lot of something: *He has plastered the walls of his bedroom with posters of his favorite singers.*

**2** to cover a wall or ceiling with plaster: *First Dad plastered the room, then he painted it.*

**plas·tic** /**plast**-ik/ *noun* a light strong substance made from chemicals: *Many toys are made of plastic. | You can recycle plastic bottles.*

**plas·tic sur·ger·y** /plast-ik **surj**-uhr-ee/ *noun* medical operations to change or repair the appearance of someone's face or body: *He had plastic surgery after a car accident.*

**plate** /playt/ *noun*

**1** a flat dish that you put food on: *She put some more potatoes on my plate.*

**2** in baseball, the place where you stand to hit the ball: *He picked up his bat, and walked up to the plate.* ( SYNONYM: **home plate** )

**3** a flat piece of metal: *The name of the company is on a brass plate by the door.*

**pla·teau** /pla-**toh**/ *noun* (plural **plateaus** or **plateaux**) an area of flat high land

**plat·form** /**plat**-form/ *noun*

**1** a raised structure like a stage for people to stand or work on: *He is standing on a platform and he is ready to give his speech.*

**2** the place in a railroad station where you get on and off a train: *She stepped off the train onto the platform.*

platform

platform

**plat·i·num** /**plat**'n-uhm/ *noun* an expensive silver-white metal that is used for making jewelry

**plat·ter** /**plat**-ur/ *noun* a large plate that is used for serving food: *Put the vegetables on a serving platter.*

**play** /play/

● *verb*

**1** to take part in a game or sport: *Do you want to play chess? | We're playing against a team from another school.*

**2** to enjoy yourself with toys and games: *Let's play with the train set. | The kids were playing outside in the yard.*

**3** to make music on an instrument: *I'm learning to play the guitar.*

**4** to act the part of a character in a movie or play: *I have been chosen to play the part of Oliver.*

**5 play with** to keep touching or moving something: *She looks nervous because she keeps playing with her hair.*

● *noun*

**1** a story that actors perform in a theater: *There are only three characters in the play.*

**2** an action or set of actions in a game or sport: *The first play of the game was very exciting.*

**3** the things that children do for fun, such as using toys or playing games: *Children need to have time in the evenings for play, as well as doing schoolwork.*

play

They are playing basketball.   He is playing the guitar.

**play·er** /**play**-ur/ *noun*

**1** someone who plays a game or sport: *He's a good basketball player.* ▶ see picture on page **A10**

**2** someone who plays a musical instrument: *We listened to the piano player.*

**3** a machine that plays recorded music or movies: *Put another CD in the CD player.* ▶ see picture at **DVD**

**play·ful** /**play**-fuhl/ *adjective*

**1** active and wanting to have fun: *Puppies are very playful and they like chasing after things.*

**2** intended to be fun or friendly rather than serious: *She gave him a playful slap on* *the shoulder.*

—**playfully** /**play**-fuhl-ee/ *adverb* in a playful way: *She hit him playfully with a sock.*

**play·ground** /**play**-grownd/ *noun* an outdoor area where children can play. Playgrounds often have special equipment to play on: *We played on the swings and the slide at the playground.*

**play·ing card** /**play**-ing kard/ *noun* one of a set of 52 cards that you use for playing games: *Playing cards are divided into four suits: clubs, diamonds, hearts, and spades.* ( SYNONYM: **card** )

**play·mate** /**play**-mayt/ *noun* someone you play with: *The girls who live next door are my playmates.*

**play·pen** /**play**-pen/ *noun* a structure that a very young child can play in safely: *The baby always throws her teddy bear out of her playpen.*

**play·wright** /**play**-rīt/ *noun* someone who writes plays: *Shakespeare was a famous English playwright.*

**pla·za** /**plahz**-uh/ *noun*
**1** a place in a town with a lot of stores: *Let's go shopping at the plaza.*
**2** a wide public area in a town: *There is a fountain in the middle of the plaza.*

**plea** /plee/ *noun*
**1** a strong emotional request: *Nobody answered her plea for help.*
**2** a statement by someone on trial that he or she is guilty or not guilty: *When he saw the evidence against him he changed his plea from "not guilty" to "guilty."*

**plead** /pleed/ *verb*
**1** to ask for something in a strong emotional way: *I pleaded with him not to go.*
( SYNONYM: **beg** )
**2** to officially say to a court of law whether you are guilty of a crime: *If she pleads guilty she may not get such a harsh punishment.*

**pleas·ant** /**plez**-uhnt/ *adjective*
**1** enjoyable: *We had a pleasant walk in the woods.* ( SYNONYM: **nice** ) ( ANTONYM: **unpleasant** )
**2** polite and friendly: *He was pleasant to all his neighbors, and they all liked him.* ( SYNONYM: **nice** )
( ANTONYM: **unpleasant** )
—**pleasantly** /**plez**-uhnt-lee/ *adverb* in a pleasant way

**please** /pleez/
● *interjection*
**1** used when politely asking someone to do something or give you something: *Can I have that towel, please?*
**2** used when politely accepting something: *"Do you want some more orange juice?" "Yes, please."*
● *verb*
to make someone feel happy by doing what he or she likes: *It's hard to please everyone because everyone likes different things.*

**Word Family:** please

**please** *verb* | **pleased** *adjective* | **pleasing** *adjective* | **pleasant** *adjective* | **pleasure** *noun*

**pleased** /pleezd/ *adjective* happy about something: *My parents are always pleased when I get good grades.*

**pleas·ing** /**pleez**-ing/ *adjective* making you feel happy: *The teacher says it is very pleasing that my grades have improved.*

**pleas·ur·a·ble** /**plezh**-uhr-uhb-uhl/ *adjective* enjoyable: *For me, reading is a pleasurable activity.*

**pleas·ure** /**plezh**-ur/ *noun*
**1** a happy feeling you get when you do something enjoyable: *Helping people gives her a lot of pleasure.*
**2** something enjoyable: *It was a pleasure to meet you.*

**pleat·ed** /**pleet**-id/ *adjective* a pleated piece of cloth has folds made in it: *The girl was wearing a pleated blue skirt.*

**pledge** /plej/
● *noun*
**1** a formal promise: *She made a pledge to do her very best for the team.*
**2** the **Pledge of Allegiance** a formal promise by Americans to be loyal to the flag of America. American children usually make this promise each morning at school.
● *verb*
to make a formal promise: *He pledged to help her in any way he could.*

**plen·ti·ful** /**plent**-i-fuhl/ *adjective* if something is plentiful, there is a large amount of it: *The town grew up here because food and water were plentiful.*

**plen·ty** /**plent**-ee/ *pronoun* more than enough: *There's plenty of food here for everyone.*

**pli·ers** /**plī**-urz/ *plural noun* a tool used for bending or cutting wire: *Use a pair of pliers to twist the wire into the shape you want.*

**plod** /plahd/ *verb* (**plodding**, **plodded**) to walk very slowly especially because you are tired: *We plodded up the hill to the top.*

**plot** /plaht/
● *noun*
**1** the story told in a book, movie, or play: *I didn't really understand the plot of the movie because it was very complicated. | The plot in a story works with the other story elements such as the characters and the setting where the story happens.*
**2** a secret plan to do something bad: *The plot to kidnap the boy failed.*
**3** a small piece of land for building or growing things on: *He wants to buy a plot of land and build a house on it.*
● *verb* (**plotting**, **plotted**)
**1** to make a secret plan to do something bad: *Terrorists were plotting to put a bomb in the building.*
**2** to mark a point or draw a line on a graph: *Plot a line connecting the points on the graph.*

**plow** /plow/
● *noun*
**1** a piece of farm equipment that cuts the ground so that seeds can be planted. It is pulled by an animal or a tractor: *The tractor is pulling the plow up and down the field.*
**2** a large vehicle that pushes snow off the roads: *It snowed in the night and today the plows are out clearing the highways.*
(SYNONYM: **snowplow**)
● *verb*
to use a plow to cut the ground so that seeds can be planted: *The farmer plowed the fields and prepared the soil for planting wheat.*

plow

plow

**pluck** /pluhk/ *verb*
**1** to pull something quickly in order to remove it: *She plucked an apple from the tree.*
**2** to pull the feathers off a bird before cooking it: *The chicken had been plucked and was ready for cooking in the oven.*

**plug** /pluhg/
● *noun*
**1** an object that you push into a wall to get electricity for a piece of equipment: *Put the plug in the socket and turn the lamp on.*
**2** an object that you put into the hole of a bathtub or sink, to stop the water from going out: *I pulled the plug out and all the water ran down the drain.*
● *verb* (**plugging**, **plugged**)
**1** to fill a hole so that something cannot get in or out: *We plugged the hole in the side of the boat by pushing a soda can in it.*
**2** **plug in** to push a plug into a wall, so that a piece of equipment is connected to the electricity supply: *Your computer won't work because you haven't plugged it in!* (ANTONYM: **unplug**)

plug

plug

electric plug

**plum** /pluhm/ *noun* a round fruit with a red or purple skin. A plum has one large seed.
► see picture on page **A7**

**plumb·er** /**pluhm**-ur/ *noun* someone whose job is to put in and repair water pipes, sinks, toilets, etc.

**plumb·ing** /**pluhm**-ing/ *noun*
**1** the system of water pipes in a building: *The plumbing is very old and the pipes make a noise*

a b c d e f g h i j k l m n o **p** q r s t u v w x y z

when you turn on the radiators.
**2** the job that a plumber does: *My dad does all our plumbing and he knows how to fix taps.*

**plump** /pluhmp/ *adjective* large and round in an attractive way: *The baby had plump cheeks.*

**plunge** /pluhnj/ *verb*
**1** to jump into water: *She plunged into the lake from the high rocks.*
**2** to fall quickly from a high place: *The car plunged off the bridge.*
**3** if an amount plunges, it suddenly becomes much lower: *The temperature plunged to 20 below zero.*
**4** to quickly push something deep into something else: *He plunged his hand into the bag and pulled out a piece of paper.*

**plu·ral** /**ploor**-uhl/ *noun* the form of a word that you use when talking about more than one person or thing: *"Dogs" is the plural of "dog."*

**plu·ral·ism** /**ploor**-uhl-iz-uhm/ *noun* a situation in which people of many different races, religions, and beliefs live together freely: *I want to live in a country where there is religious pluralism and people are free to belong to any religion they want.*

**plus** /pluhss/
● *preposition*
**1** used in math when one number is added to another: *Three plus six equals nine is written as 3 + 6 = 9.* ( ANTONYM: **minus** )
**2** and: *I have lots of chores to do. Plus I have to do my homework.*
● *noun*
a plus sign (+) ( ANTONYM: **minus** )
● *adjective*
**A plus, B plus, etc.** (also **A+, B+, etc.**) a grade that is slightly higher than an A, a B, etc.: *I was hoping for an A, but I got a B plus.*

**plus sign** /**pluhss** sīn/ *noun* the sign (+) that is used to show that numbers are being added

**Plu·to** /**ploot**-oh/ *noun* a dwarf planet (=a very small planet) that is further away from the Sun than Neptune

**plu·to·ni·um** /ploo-**tohn**-ee-uhm/ *noun* a metal that is used for making nuclear power and nuclear bombs. Plutonium is radioactive.

**ply·wood** /**plī**-wud/ *noun* a type of board.

Plywood is made from thin pieces of wood that have been stuck together: *They covered the floor with sheets of plywood.*

**p.m.** /pee **em**/ used to show that a time is in the afternoon or evening. The letters stand for "post meridiem." In Latin, that means "after midday": *The grocery store closes at 8 p.m.*

**pneu·mo·nia** /nu-**mohn**-yuh/ *noun* a serious illness that affects the lungs. Pneumonia can cause a fever and a cough, and make it difficult to breathe.

**poach** /pohch/ *verb*
**1** to cook food in a small amount of boiling liquid: *I poached the eggs in a little hot water with some salt.*
**2** to catch animals illegally: *Park rangers caught two men poaching deer.*

**pock·et** /**pahk**-it/ *noun* the part of a coat, skirt, or pair of pants that you can put things in: *I had no gloves so I kept my hands in my coat pockets.*

pocket

pocket

**pod** /pahd/ *noun* the long case that beans and peas grow in: *You can take the peas out of the pod and eat them without cooking them.*

**po·em** /**poh**-uhm/ *noun* a piece of writing with short lines that describes something or tells a story. Sometimes the lines of a poem rhyme: *There's a famous poem that has the lines, "The woods are lovely, dark and deep. But I have promises to keep, And miles to go before I sleep."*

**Word Family:** poem

poem *noun* | poet *noun* | poetry *noun* | poetic *adjective*

**po·et** /**poh**-it/ *noun* someone who writes poems: *Robert Frost was a famous American poet.*

**po·et·ic** /poh-**et**-ik/ *adjective* relating to poetry or like poetry: *Her description of the desert is very poetic and the language is very beautiful.*

**po·et·ry** /**poh**-uh-tree/ *noun* poems: *Have you read any of her poetry?*

**point** /poynt/

● *noun*

**1** the sharp end of something: *Make sure your pencil has a sharp point.*

point

**2** an idea or opinion in a discussion: *Rebecca made some interesting points in her talk.* | *"But Jay hates sports." "That's a good point."*

He is pointing upward.

**3** something useful that you will achieve by doing something: *There's no point in crying – it won't change anything.* | *I don't see the point of taking tests.*

**4** something that you score in a game or sport: *Our team lost by 14 points.*

**5** the most important thing: *The point is I don't have enough money.*

**6** a quality that someone or something has: *He isn't all bad – he has his good points.*

**7** a particular time: *At one point, I thought the boat was going to sink.*

**8** the way you say the mark (.) before a decimal: *You say 4.5 as "four point five."*

**9** an exact position: *The two paths meet at this point.* | *a point on a graph*

● *verb*

**1** to show someone something by holding your finger out toward it: *She pointed to a building and said, "That's my school."*

**2** to aim something toward a person or thing: *The teacher pointed his pencil at me and asked me for an answer.*

**3** **point out** to tell someone something that he or she does not already know: *My mom pointed out that some kids do not have enough food to eat.*

**point·ed** /**poynt**-id/ *adjective* having a point at the end: *Cats have pointed ears.*

**point·less** /**poynt**-liss/ *adjective* not likely to achieve anything useful: *She realized it was pointless to argue with him.*

**point of view** /poynt uhv **vyoo**/ *noun* (plural **points of view**)

**1** an opinion: *I don't agree with his point of view.*

**2** a particular way of thinking about or judging something: *The movie was successful from a financial point of view.*

**poi·son** /**poyz**-uhn/

● *noun* a substance that can kill you or make you sick: *Some people use poison to kill rats.*

● *verb* to kill or harm someone by using poison: *They tried to poison the king, by putting something in his drink.*

**poi·son i·vy** /poyz-uhn **ī**v-ee/ *noun* a plant that makes your skin red and painful when you touch it

**poi·son oak** /poyz-uhn **ohk**/ *noun* a plant similar to poison ivy, that makes your skin red and painful when you touch it

**poi·son·ous** /**poyz**-uhn-uhss/ *adjective* containing poison: *The berries of this plant are poisonous and you must not eat them.*

**poke** /pohk/ *verb* to push something or someone with your finger or a pointed object: *I poked the snake with a stick.*

poke

**pok·er** /**pohk**-ur/ *noun*

**1** a card game that people play for money

**2** a metal stick used for moving coal or wood on a fire to make it burn better

**po·lar** /**pohl**-ur/ *adjective* relating to the North Pole or the South Pole: *Polar explorers have to wear warm clothing.*

**po·lar bear** /**pohl**-ur bair/ *noun* a large white bear that lives near the North Pole: *Polar bears can swim.*

fur

**polar bear**

paw

**pole** /pole/ *noun*
**1** a long post made of wood or metal: *There was a flag flying from a pole.* ▶ see picture at **flag**
**2** the most northern or southern point of the Earth: *The South Pole is in Antarctica.*
**3** one of the two ends of a battery or a magnet

**Pole** /pohl/ *noun* someone from Poland

**pole vault** /**pohl** volt/ *noun* a sport in which you jump over a high bar using a long pole. You put one end of the pole on the ground and swing up holding the other end.

**po·lice** /puh-**leess**/ *plural noun* the people whose job is to catch criminals and make sure that people obey the law: *The police soon caught the thief.* | *a police car*

**po·lice force** /puh-**leess** forss/ *noun* the organization of police somewhere: *He wants to join the Miami police force.*

**po·lice·man** /puh-**leess**-muhn/ *noun* (plural **policemen** /puh-**leess**-muhn/) a male police officer

**po·lice of·fi·cer** /puh-**leess** of-uhss-ur/ *noun* a member of the police: *Police officers arrested the man for selling drugs.*

**po·lice·wom·an** /puh-**leess**-wum-uhn/ *noun* (plural **policewomen** /puh-**leess**-wim-in/) a female police officer

**pol·i·cy** /**pahl**-uhss-ee/ *noun* (plural **policies**)
**1** the way of doing things that has been decided by an organization: *The school has a strict policy on jewelry, and students are not allowed to wear rings or bracelets in school.*
**2** an agreement with an insurance company: *The policy protects you if you lose any of your belongings on vacation.*

**po·li·o** /**pohl**-ee-oh/ *noun* a serious disease that can affect the spinal cord and make it impossible to move some muscles: *Children were given a vaccine to stop them from getting polio.*

**pol·ish** /**pahl**-ish/
● *verb* to make something shiny by rubbing it: *Mom dusted and polished the furniture.*
—**polished** /**pahl**-isht/ *adjective* shiny as a result of polishing: *polished shoes*
● *noun* a substance that you rub on something to make it shiny: *Put a little polish on a cloth and shine your shoes with it.*

**Po·lish** /**pohl**-ish/
● *adjective* from Poland: *Our neighbors are Polish – they come from Krakow.*
● *noun* the language spoken in Poland: *His grandparents speak to each other in Polish.*

**po·lite** /puh-**līt**/ *adjective* behaving well, in a way that shows you respect other people: *It's not polite to laugh at people.*
( ANTONYMS: impolite, rude ) ▶ see **Thesaurus**
—**politely** /puh-**līt**-lee/ *adverb* in a way that is polite: *He politely let other people get on the bus first.*

**po·lit·i·cal** /puh-**lit**-ik-uhl/ *adjective* relating to politics: *The U.S. has two main political parties: the Republicans and the Democrats.*
—**politically** /puh-**lit**-ik-lee/ *adverb* in a way that relates to politics

**pol·i·ti·cian** /pahl-uh-**tish**-uhn/ *noun* someone who was elected as a member of a government, or who wants to be: *Politicians make a lot of promises to voters.* ▶ see **Thesaurus**

**pol·i·tics** /**pahl**-uht-ikss/ *noun* what politicians do: *He got involved in politics because he wanted to change things.*

**Word Family:** politics

**politics** *noun* | **politician** *noun* | **political** *adjective*

**pol·ka dot** /**pohl**-kuh daht/ *noun* one of a number of round spots on cloth: *The dress was blue with white polka dots.*

a
b
c
d
e
f
g
h
i
j
k
l
m
n
o
**p**
q
r
s
t
u
v
w
x
y
z

a
b
c
d
e
f
g
h
i
j
k
l
m
n
o

**p**

q
r
s
t
u
v
w
x
y
z

**poll** /pohl/

● *noun*

**1** if an organization does a poll, it asks people questions to find out what they think about something: *Opinion polls showed that the president was very popular.*

**2 polls** if people go to the polls, they vote in an election: *We want to encourage more young voters to go to the polls.*

● *verb*

to do a poll: *The school polled parents on the issue of school uniform, and most parents supported it.*

**pol·len** /**pahl**-uhn/ *noun* a powder that flowers produce. Pollen contains male cells, and is carried by the wind or insects to other flowers so they can make seeds: *Bees fly around from one flower to another collecting the pollen to make honey.*

**pol·li·nate** /**pahl**-uh-nayt/ *verb* to make a flower produce seeds by giving it pollen from another flower: *The flowers are pollinated by insects.*
—**pollination** /pahl-uh-**naysh**-uhn/ *noun* the process of pollinating a flower

**pollinate**

The bee is pollinating the flower.

**pol·lute** /puh-**loot**/ *verb* to make air, water, or soil dirty and dangerous to people: *Smoke from factories pollutes the air and makes it unsafe to breathe.*
—**polluted** /puh-**loot**-id/ *adjective* polluted air, water, or soil is dirty: *They got sick after drinking polluted water.*
—**pollutant** /puh-**loot**-uhnt/ *noun* something that pollutes air, water, or soil: *Cars and trucks produce pollutants.*

**pol·lu·tion** /puh-**loosh**-uhn/ *noun*

**1** substances that make air, water, or soil dirty and dangerous to people: *Pollution in the river is killing all the fish.*

**2** the process of making air, water, or soil dangerously dirty: *We must stop the pollution of the planet by planes and cars.*

**poly-** /pahl-ee/

### Word Building

**poly**ester | **poly**gon

These words all have the Greek word root **poly-** in them. **Poly-** means "many." A *polygon* is a shape with many sides. *Polyester* is a type of cloth made from many molecules joined together in a chain.

**pol·y·es·ter** /**pahl**-ee-est-ur/ *noun* an artificial type of cloth: *The employees at the store wear blue polyester uniforms.*

**pol·y·gon**
/**pahl**-ee-gahn/ *noun* a closed flat shape with three or more straight sides: *Squares and hexagons are polygons.*

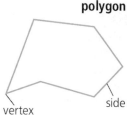

**polygon**

vertex

side

**pom·e·gran·ate**
/**pahm**-uh-gran-it/ *noun* a round fruit with a thick red skin and many small red seeds inside it that you eat ▶ see picture on page **A7**

**pon·cho** /**pahnch**-oh/ *noun* a coat made of a piece of thick cloth or waterproof cloth. Ponchos are square and have a hole in the middle for your head, but no sleeves. Ponchos were originally worn in South America: *There was a picture of a Peruvian man wearing a poncho.*

**poncho**

poncho

**pond** /pahnd/ *noun* a small area of water in the countryside or a yard: *There's a little pond in their back yard with goldfish in it.*

**po·ny** /**pohn**-ee/ *noun* (plural **ponies**) a small horse: *The children were riding ponies.*

## po·ny·tail

/**pohn**-ee-tayl/ *noun* long hair that you tie together at the back of your head: *She wears her hair in a ponytail when she plays soccer.*

ponytail

ponytail

## poo·dle /**pood**'l/ *noun*
a dog with thick curly hair. Poodles often have their hair cut into special shapes.

## pool /pool/ *noun*

**1** a large container that is filled with water for people to swim in: *I have swimming lessons at the pool.*

**2** a small area of a liquid on a surface: *There was a pool of dirty water on the floor.*

**3** a game in which you use a long stick to hit balls into holes at the sides and corners of a table. The balls are different colors and have different numbers on them: *Two men were playing pool.*

## poor /poor/ *adjective*

**1** having very little money: *Her family was very poor and they didn't have enough money to buy new clothes.* ( ANTONYM: **rich** )

**2** used for showing that you feel sorry for someone: *The poor girl looked very scared.*

**3** not very good: *His English is poor and he can't spell simple words.* ( ANTONYM: **good** )

## poor·ly /**poor**-lee/ *adverb* badly: *The dress was poorly made and started to come apart the first time I wore it.*

## pop /pahp/

● *noun*

**1** (also **pop mu·sic** /**pahp**-myooz-ik/) modern music that is popular with young people: *I like listening to pop music.*

**2** a sweet drink with bubbles that does not contain alcohol: *She is drinking a can of pop.*
( SYNONYM: **soda** )

**3** a sudden short sound like a small explosion: *The cork came out of the bottle with a loud pop.*

● *verb* (**popping**, **popped**)

**1** to make a short loud sound, for example by bursting: *David accidentally sat on a balloon and it popped.*

**2** to go somewhere quickly or suddenly: *I just popped in to say hello.*

## pop·corn /**pahp**-korn/ *noun* a type of corn that gets bigger and bursts open when you heat it: *Let's buy some popcorn to eat while we watch the movie.*

## Pope /pohp/ *noun* the leader of the Roman Catholic Church: *The Pope lives in Vatican City, within the city of Rome.*

## pop·u·lar /**pahp**-yuhl-ur/ *adjective* liked by a lot of people: *She's a very popular girl and has lots of friends.* ( ANTONYM: **unpopular** )

## pop·u·lar·i·ty /pahp-yuh-**larr**-uht-ee/ *noun* the quality of being liked by a lot of people: *The popularity of soccer has grown and now almost every school plays it.*

## pop·u·lat·ed /**pahp**-yuh-layt-id/ *adjective* a populated area has people living in it: *The desert is the least populated part of the country.*

## pop·u·la·tion /pahp-yuh-**laysh**-uhn/ *noun* the number of people who live in a place: *Chicago has a population of nearly three million.*

## porch /porch/ *noun* a structure with a roof and a floor, that is built onto a house. People often sit on the porch: *As I walked up the path I saw Mr. Smith sitting on his front porch.*

## por·cu·pine

/**pork**-yuh-pīn/ *noun* an animal with quills (=long sharp hairs) all over its back and sides. The quills point up when the porcupine thinks another animal is going to hurt it.

porcupine

## pore /por/

● *noun* one of the small holes in your skin that sweat comes through

● *verb* **pore over** to read or look at something carefully for a long time: *She pored over her school books for hours, trying to remember everything for the test.*

## pork /pork/ *noun* the meat from pigs: *Most sausages are made from pork.*

## por·poise /**porp**-uhss/ *noun* a large gray animal that lives in the ocean. Porpoises are mammals. They look like dolphins, but have shorter heads.

## por·ridge /**por**-ij/ *noun* oatmeal cooked in hot water or milk: *I have porridge for breakfast.*

a b c d e f g h i j k l m n o **p** q r s t u v w x y z

**port** /port/ *noun* an area or city where ships can be loaded and unloaded: *The ship called at several ports.*

---

## Word Building

**ex**port | **port**able | sup**port** | trans**port**

These words all have the Latin word root **port** in them. **Port** means "to carry." If a company *exports* something, it sells it to another country. A *portable* television is small enough that you can carry it. If you stand on a chair and it *supports* your weight, you are on top of it and it does not break.

---

**port·a·ble** /**port**-uhb-uhl/ *adjective* light and easy to move or carry: *We took a portable DVD player with us on vacation.*

**por·tion** /**porsh**-uhn/ *noun*
**1** a part of something: *I've read a large portion of the book, but not all of it.*
**2** an amount of food for one person: *She gave me a huge portion of spaghetti.*

**por·trait** /**por**-trit/
*noun* a painting, drawing, or photograph of someone: *The artist painted a portrait of his wife.*

**portrait**

**por·tray** /por-**tray**/ *verb*
**1** to describe someone or something, or show someone or something in a picture: *In the book, he portrays his brother as a hero.*
**2** to pretend to be someone, in a movie or play: *Cleopatra has been portrayed by many actresses.*
( SYNONYM: **play** )
—**portrayal** /por-**tray**-uhl/ *noun* the action of portraying someone: *He won an Oscar for his portrayal of a detective.*

**Por·tu·guese** /porch-uh-**geez**/
● *adjective*
from Portugal: *Vasco da Gama was a great Portuguese explorer.*
● *noun*
**1** the language spoken in Portugal and Brazil: *At home they speak Portuguese.*

**2** the Portuguese people from Portugal: *The Portuguese eat a lot of fish.*

**pose** /pohz/
● *verb*
**1** to cause a problem or danger: *Getting down the cliff might pose a problem.*
**2** to ask a question: *The teacher posed some questions about the experiment.*
**3** to sit or stand so that someone can do a picture or photograph of you: *The winning team will pose for a photograph.*
**4** to pretend to be someone in order to deceive people: *The thief posed as a police officer to get into the house.*
● *noun*
the position that you stand or sit in, especially for a photograph or picture: *The painting shows her in a relaxed pose.*

**po·si·tion** /puh-**zish**-uhn/
● *noun*
**1** the place where someone or something is, in relation to other things: *He moved the table to a different position.*
**2** the way someone stands, sits, or lies: *I moved so that I was sitting in a more comfortable position.*
**3** the situation that someone is in: *I'm in a difficult position because I don't want to upset either of my friends.* ( SYNONYM: **situation** )
**4** a job: *After the interview, they offered him the position of sales manager.*
**5** someone's official opinion about something: *The school's position on bullying is clear: we will not tolerate it.*
● *verb*
to put something in a particular place: *They positioned the TV in the corner of the room.*

**pos·i·tive** /**pahz**-uht-iv/ *adjective*
**1** very sure that something is true: *I'm positive that this is the right way home.*
**2** good or useful: *There are lots of positive things you can do to lose weight and get in shape.*
( ANTONYM: **negative** )
**3** expressing agreement or approval: *So far, we've had very positive reactions to the new show: everyone seems to like it.*
( ANTONYM: **negative** )
**4** greater than zero: *When you multiply two positive numbers, the product is always positive.*
( ANTONYM: **negative** )

**5** a medical test that is positive shows that someone has a disease or condition: *Six children at the school tested positive for the flu.*

(ANTONYM: **negative**)

—**pos·i·tive·ly** /**pahz**-uht-iv-lee/ *adverb* in a way that expresses agreement or approval: *Everyone responded positively to the teacher's suggestion that we take a break.*

**pos·i·tive in·te·ger** /**pahz**-uht-iv **int**-uhj-ur/ *noun* a whole number that is greater than zero. 1, 2, and 3 are the first three positive integers.

**pos·sess** /puh-**zess**/ *verb* to own or have something: *Joe possesses a natural talent for music.*

**pos·ses·sion** /puh-**zesh**-uhn/ *noun* something that you own: *I keep all my favorite possessions in this box.* (SYNONYM: **belongings**)

**pos·ses·sive** /puh-**zess**-iv/ *adjective*
**1** not wanting to share someone or something: *She is so possessive about her toys.*
**2** in grammar, a possessive word shows who something belongs to: *In the sentence "My shoes are red," "my" is a possessive adjective.*

**pos·si·bil·i·ty** /pahss-uh-**bil**-uht-ee/ *noun* (plural **possibilities**) something that might happen or be true: *There's a possibility that I'll go to a different school next year.*

**pos·si·ble** /**pahss**-uhb-uhl/ *adjective*
**1** something that is possible may happen or be true: *It's possible that he is not telling the truth.* | *There are several possible solutions to the problem.*
**2** if something is possible, you can do it: *It will soon be possible to travel to other planets.*
(ANTONYM: **impossible**)

**pos·si·bly** /**pahss**-uhb-lee/ *adverb* maybe: *"Are you going to the beach tomorrow?" "Possibly. It depends on the weather."*
(SYNONYMS: **perhaps, maybe**)

**pos·sum** /**pahss**-uhm/ *noun* another word for an opossum. A possum is an animal that looks like a large rat and carries its babies in a pouch on its stomach.

**post** /pohst/
● *noun*
**1** a wooden or metal pole that you put into the ground to support something: *Before we build the fence, we have to put wooden posts into the ground.*
**2** a job, especially an important one: *The school offered him the post of head coach.*
● *verb* /pohst/
to put a notice about something on a wall or bulletin board: *The school rules are posted on the bulletin board in each classroom.*

**post-** /pohst/

## Word Building

**post-** is a prefix.
**post**pone | **post**-World War II | **post**-1990
**post-** means "after." If you *postpone* a meeting, you say that you want to have the meeting at a later time. If something happened *post-World War II*, it happened after World War II.

**post·age** /**pohst**-ij/ *noun* the money that you pay for sending something by mail: *How much was the postage for that package you sent to Dan?*

**post·al** /**pohst**'l/ *adjective* relating to the organization that takes letters from one place to another: *A postal worker took my package and weighed it.*

**post·card** /**pohst**-kard/ *noun* a card that has a picture on one side. You can send a postcard to someone without an envelope: *I sent my friend a postcard from San Francisco.*

**post·er** /**pohst**-ur/ *noun* a large sign or picture that you use as a decoration, or that advertises something: *Nick's bedroom walls are covered with posters of football players.* | *a poster for the school play*

**post·mark** /**pohst**-mark/
● *noun* a mark on a letter or package that shows the place and time it was sent: *Do you know who this letter could be from? The envelope has a Chicago postmark.*
● *verb* to put a postmark on a letter or package: *The letter was postmarked December 21.*

**post·mas·ter** /**pohst**-mast-ur/ *noun* the person in charge of a post office

**post of·fice** /**pohst** of-iss/ *noun* a place where you can buy stamps and send letters and packages: *Mom asked me to take a package to the post office for her.*

**post·pone** /pohst-**pohn**/ *verb* to change the time of an event to a later time or date: *The game was postponed because of rain.*

**pos·ture** /**pahss**-chur/ *noun* the way you hold your body when you sit or stand: *You need to improve your posture and sit up straight.*

**pot** /paht/ *noun*
**1** a round container that you cook things in: *Mom made a big pot of chicken soup for supper.*
**2** a container that you make coffee or tea in. It has a handle and a lid: *Is the coffee in the pot still hot?*
**3** a container that you grow plants in: *Plant the seeds in a pot.*

pot

pot

flowerpot

coffee pot

teapot

**po·tas·si·um** /puh-**tass**-ee-uhm/ *noun* a silver-white soft metal. Potassium is used to make fertilizers and soap and is in some foods, such as bananas. The symbol for potassium is K: *It's important to get enough potassium in your diet.*

**po·ta·to** /puh-**tayt**-oh/ *noun* (plural **potatoes**) a round white or yellow vegetable that grows under the ground. Potatoes can have brown, red, or yellow skin: *I'll peel the potatoes.* | *Can I have more mashed potatoes?* ▶ see picture on page **A7**

**Word Origin:** potato

**Potato** comes from a language called Carib that was spoken on the island of Haiti. Spanish explorers first saw and ate sweet potatoes in the 1500s, when they came to the Caribbean islands. The Spanish used the same word for the white potatoes they saw a few years later in Peru. Soon potatoes were being grown all over the world.

**po·ta·to chip** /puh-**tayt**-oh chip/ *noun* a thin hard piece of potato that has been cooked in oil: *I got a sandwich and some potato chips for lunch.*

**po·ten·tial** /puh-**tensh**-uhl/
● *noun* a quality or an ability that has not developed completely yet: *She has only just started learning the piano, but she has the potential to be a great player.*
● *adjective* possible, but not yet completely developed: *We need to be ready for any potential problems.*
—**potentially** /puh-**tensh**-uhl-ee/ *adverb* possibly in some situations or in the future: *Fireworks are potentially dangerous and you need to be very careful with them.*

**pot·hole** /**paht**-hohl/ *noun* a hole in the surface of a road: *He tried to drive around the potholes in the street.*

**pot·luck** /paht-**luhk**/ *adjective* a potluck meal is one where everyone brings food to share: *Our class is having a potluck picnic next month and we all have to bring some food.*

**pot·ter·y** /**paht**-uhr-ee/
*noun*
**1** the activity of making objects out of clay. These objects are then heated in a special oven to make them hard: *I made this bowl in my pottery class.*
**2** plates, cups, and other objects that are made out of clay: *The scientists found broken pottery where the Indians had lived.*

pottery

**poul·try** /**pohl**-tree/ *noun* birds such as chickens and ducks that are kept on farms for their eggs and meat: *We buy poultry at the supermarket.*

**pounce** /pownss/ *verb* to suddenly jump on and catch a person or animal: *The cat pounced on a bird.*

pounce

The cat pounced on a bird.

**pound** /pownd/
● *noun*
**1** ( ABBREVIATION: **lb.** ) a unit for measuring weight, equal to 16 ounces or 453.6 grams: *Tammy weighs 70 pounds.* | *The apples cost 65 cents a pound.*
**2** the standard unit of money in Great Britain and some other countries
● *verb*
**1** to hit something many times: *I was pounding on the door, but no one answered.*
**2** if your heart pounds, it beats very quickly: *I was scared, and my heart was pounding.*

**pour** /por/ *verb*
**1** to make a liquid flow out of a container: *Pour the water into the bowl.*
**2** to flow somewhere quickly and in large amounts: *Sweat was pouring down my face when I finished the race.*
**3** to rain a lot: *It was pouring outside, so we stayed indoors.*
**4** to move somewhere quickly and in large numbers: *People from all over the U.S. poured into Washington to see Obama.*

pour

**pov·er·ty** /**pahv**-urt-ee/ *noun* the state of being poor: *Many people around the world are living in poverty.*

**pow·der** /**powd**-ur/ *noun* a soft dry substance in the form of very small grains: *Baking powder is a substance you put in cakes to help them rise.*

**pow·er** /**pow**-ur/ *noun*
**1** the ability to control people or events: *The president has a lot of power – he is the most important man in the U.S.*
**2** electricity or other kinds of energy: *During the storm last night we lost all electrical power.*
**3** force or strength: *The power of the explosion blew out all the windows.*

IDIOM with **power**
**to the power of** if a number is increased to the power of 3, 4, 5, etc., it is multiplied by itself three, four, five, etc. times: *3 to the power of 4 means 3 x 3 x 3 x 3.*

**pow·er·ful** /**pow**-ur-fuhl/ *adjective*
**1** a powerful person or country is important and has a lot of control over people or events: *The United States is a rich and powerful nation.*
**2** something that is powerful is very strong or has a strong effect: *Television has a powerful influence on our lives.*
—**powerfully** /**pow**-ur-fuhl-ee/ *adverb* in a powerful way: *He was powerfully affected by his mother's death.*

**pow·er·less** /**pow**-ur-liss/ *adjective* not having strength or control: *The small group of soldiers was powerless to stop the attack.*

**pow·er plant** /**pow**-ur plant/ (also **pow·er sta·tion** /**pow**-ur staysh-uhn/) *noun* a building where electricity is made

**prac·ti·cal** /**prakt**-ik-uhl/ *adjective*
**1** sensible and likely to work correctly or do something in a way that works well: *The shoes are pretty, but they are not very practical.*
**2** relating to doing things rather than thinking or talking about them: *The teacher is new – he doesn't have a lot of practical experience yet.*

**prac·ti·cal joke** /prakt-ik-uhl **johk**/ *noun* a trick that surprises someone and makes other people laugh: *He put a toy mouse in her desk drawer as a practical joke.*

**prac·ti·cally** /**prakt**-ik-lee/ *adverb* almost: *The two girls eat lunch together practically every day.*

**prac·tice** /**prakt**-iss/

● *noun*

**1** the activity of doing something regularly so that you can do it better: *It takes a lot of practice to be a good piano player.*

**2** the place where a doctor or lawyer works: *Dr. Anderson works at a small medical practice in the neighborhood.*

● *verb*

**1** to do something regularly in order to improve your skill at it: *He practiced hitting the golf ball every day until he could hit it perfectly.*

▶ see **Thesaurus**

**2** to work as a doctor or lawyer: *She practices law in Boston.*

**prai·rie** /**prair**-ee/ *noun* a large area of land that is covered in grass and does not have many trees. In the past, the middle part of North America was covered in prairies: *In the 1860s, they moved to a small farm on the Iowa prairie.*

**prairie**

**prai·rie dog** /**prair**-ee dog/ *noun* an animal that is related to the squirrel. Prairie dogs live in holes on the prairies of North America.

**praise** /prayz/

● *verb* to say that someone has done something well, or that something is good: *Mrs. Harris praised all the children for working so hard.*

▶ see **Thesaurus**

● *noun* things you say to praise someone or something: *The police officers deserve praise for their bravery.*

**prank** /prangk/ *noun* a joke in which you play a trick on someone in order to make him or her look silly: *We played a prank on my grandpa and hid his hat under his chair.*

**pray** /pray/ *verb* to speak to God in order to ask for help or give thanks: *We prayed for Nancy when she was in the hospital.*

**prayer** /prair/ *noun* the words that you say when you pray: *I said my prayers and went to sleep.*

**pre-** /pri/

## Word Building

**pre-** is a prefix.

**pre**dict | **pre**fix | **pre**pare | **pre**school | **pre**vent | **pre**-1990

**pre-** means "before." If you *predict* an event, you say that it will happen before it does happen. A *preschool* is a school children can go to before they start kindergarten. If you *prevent* a problem, you do something that stops the problem before it happens. If something happened *pre-1990*, it happened before 1990.

**preach** /preech/ *verb* to talk about a religious subject in church: *The minister preaches at the church every Sunday.*

**preach·er** /**preech**-ur/ *noun* someone who talks about religious subjects in a church
( SYNONYM: **minister** )

**pre·cau·tion** /pri-**kosh**-uhn/ *noun* something that you do to stop something bad or dangerous from happening: *I was feeling a little sick, so Mom kept me home from school as a precaution.*

**pre·cede** /pri-**seed**/ *verb* to come before something else: *In English, the subject of a sentence usually precedes the verb.*

**pre·cinct** /**pree**-singkt/ *noun* one of the parts that a city is divided into: *How many precincts are there in the city of Chicago?*

**pre·cious** /**presh**-uhss/ *adjective*

**1** valuable and rare: *In the past, coins contained precious metals like gold and silver.*

**2** very important or special to you: *The doll is precious to me because it belonged to my grandmother.*

**pre·cip·i·ta·tion** /pri-sip-uh-**taysh**-uhn/ *noun* rain or snow: *This area of the U.S. has a lot of precipitation and there are many floods.*

**pre·cise** /pri-**sīss**/ *adjective* exact and correct: *They were trying to find the precise location of* the sunken ship.

—**precisely** /pri-**sīss**-lee/ *adverb* exactly: *He arrived at 4:00 precisely.*

**pre·ci·sion** /pri-**sizh**-uhn/ *noun* the quality of being very exact and correct: *She explained the idea with great precision.*

**pre-Co·lum·bi·an** /pree kuh-**luhm**-bee-uhn/ *adjective* relating to the time before 1492, when Christopher Columbus came to the Americas: *The museum has a large collection of pre-Columbian art.*

**pred·a·tor** /**pred**-uht-ur/ *noun* an animal that kills and eats other animals: *The mouse has many predators such as birds, cats, and snakes.*

( ANTONYM: **prey** )

**pred·i·cate** /**pred**-ik-it/ *noun* in grammar, the part of a sentence that includes the main verb, and that tells you what the subject is doing or describes the subject. In the sentence "He ran out of the house," "ran out of the house" is the predicate. In the sentence "Jasmine is very smart," "is very smart" is the predicate.

**pre·dict** /pri-**dikt**/ *verb* to say that something is going to happen: *They are predicting that it will rain tomorrow.*

—**predictable** /pri-**dikt**-uhb-uhl/ *adjective* happening in the way that you expect, and not different or interesting: *The ending of the movie is very predictable and I wasn't surprised when they got married.*

---

**Word Family: predict**

**predict** *verb* | **prediction** *noun* | **predictable** *adjective*

---

**pre·dic·tion** /pri-**dik**-shuhn/ *noun* something that you say will happen in the future: *My prediction is that Scott will win.*

**pref·ace** /**pref**-iss/ *noun* an introduction at the beginning of a book: *The novel has a preface that tells us about the author's life.*

**pre·fer** /pri-**fur**/ *verb* (**preferring**, **preferred**) to like someone or something better than someone or something else: *Would you prefer a hot drink or a cold drink?*

**pref·erence** /**pref**-ruhnss/ *noun* if someone has a preference for something, he or she likes it

better than another thing: *We could get pizza or Chinese food. Do you have any preference?*

**pre·fix** /**pree**-fikss/ *noun* a group of letters that you add to the beginning of a word in order to make a new word: *If we add the prefix "un" to the word "happy," we make the word "unhappy."*

**preg·nan·cy** /**preg**-nuhnss-ee/ *noun* (plural **pregnancies**) the condition of being pregnant: *A woman's body changes and becomes bigger during pregnancy.*

**preg·nant** /**preg**-nuhnt/ *adjective* if a woman is pregnant, she has a baby growing in her body: *I stood up on the bus so that a pregnant woman could sit down.*

**pre·his·tor·ic** /**pree**-hi-**stor**-ik/ *adjective* relating to the time thousands of years ago, before anything was written down: *In prehistoric times, people hunted animals for food.*

**prej·u·dice** /**prej**-uhd-iss/ *noun* an unfair opinion about someone that is not based on facts or reason: *There's still a lot of prejudice against disabled people.* ▸ see **Thesaurus**

**prej·u·diced** /**prej**-uhd-ist/ *adjective* having an unfair opinion about someone that is not based on facts or reason: *Some men are prejudiced against women and don't want to have a woman as their boss.*

**pre·ma·ture** /**pree**-muh-**choor**/ *adjective* happening too early: *The baby was born six weeks premature and was very small.*

**pre·mier** /pri-**meer**/
● *noun* (also **Premier**) the leader of the government in some countries: *The president met with the Chinese premier.*
● *adjective* best or most important: *The Superbowl is football's premier event.*

**pre·mi·um** /**preem**-ee-uhm/
● *noun* money that you pay for insurance every month or year: *My parents pay $1,200 in car insurance premiums every year.*
● *adjective* higher quality or more expensive: *The premium service costs more than the standard service.*

a b c d e f g h i j k l m n o **p** q r s t u v w x y z

**pre·oc·cu·pied** /pree-**ahk**-yuh-pīd/ *adjective* thinking about something a lot, so that you do not pay attention to other things: *I was so preoccupied, I didn't realize the teacher was asking me a question.*

**prep·a·ra·tion** /prep-uh-**raysh**-uhn/ *noun* the act of getting something or someone ready: *She spent hours on the preparation of the meal.*

**pre·pare** /pri-**pair**/ *verb*
**1** to make something ready to be used: *Carol went upstairs to prepare a room for the guests.*
**2** to make yourself or another person ready to do something: *Our teacher is helping us prepare for the test.*

**pre·pared** /pri-**paird**/ *adjective* ready to do something or to be used: *He wasn't prepared for their questions and didn't know how to answer them.*

**prep·o·si·tion** /prep-uh-**zish**-uhn/ *noun* a word such as "to," "on," or "by" which is put in front of a noun to show place, time, or direction: *In the sentence "The book is on the desk," "on" is a preposition.*
—**prepositional** /prep-uh-**zish**-uhn'l/ *adjective* relating to a preposition: *In the sentence "The book is on the desk," "on the desk" is a prepositional phrase.*

**pre·school** /**pree**-skool/
● *noun* a nursery school or daycare center. A preschool is for children who are between the ages of two and five years old: *My little sister goes to preschool three days a week.*
● *adjective* relating to children who are younger than five years old: *The library has many books for preschool children.*

**pre·scribe** /pri-**skrīb**/ *verb* to say what medicine or treatment a sick person should have: *Sophie had an ear infection, so the doctor prescribed antibiotics.*

**pre·scrip·tion** /pri-**skrip**-shuhn/ *noun* a note that a doctor writes that allows someone to get a particular medicine at a pharmacy: *You need a prescription for this medication.*

**pres·ence** /**prez**-uhnss/ *noun* the state of being in a particular place at a particular time: *The test showed the presence of dangerous chemicals in the water.* ( ANTONYM: **absence** )

**pres·ent**
● *adjective* /**prez**-uhnt/
**1** to be in a place or at an event: *All 28 children were present in class.* ( ANTONYM: **absent** )
**2** happening or existing now: *Our present situation is difficult, but we hope things will get better soon.*
● *noun* /**prez**-uhnt/
**1** something that you give someone: *I need to get a birthday present for my dad.*
( SYNONYM: **gift** )
**2** the time that is happening now: *The book tells you about the history of the United States from 1776 to the present.*
● *verb* /pri-**zent**/
**1** to give something to someone: *She presented flowers to all of the dancers at the end of the show.*
**2** to give or show information: *The teacher tries to present grammar in an interesting way.*

**pre·sen·ta·tion** /preez-uhn-**taysh**-uhn/ *noun*
**1** the act of giving someone something in a formal ceremony: *The presentation of the awards will take place after dinner.*
**2** a formal talk about a particular subject: *I'm going to ask everyone to make a short presentation to the class.*

**pres·ent par·ti·ci·ple** /prez-uhnt **part**-uh-sip-uhl/ *noun* the form of a verb that ends in "-ing": *In the sentence "Kristen is reading a book," "reading" is a present participle.*

**pres·ent per·fect** /prez-uhnt **purf**-ikt/ *noun* in grammar, the tense of a verb that is formed by adding the verb "have" to the past participle of the verb. The present perfect is often used to talk about an action that started in the past and continues to the present time: *In the sentence "I have lived here since 2005," "have lived" is in the present perfect.*

**pres·ent tense** /prez-uhnt **tenss**/ *noun* in grammar, the form of a verb that you use to talk about what exists or what happens regularly: *In the sentence "I do my homework every night," "do" is in the present tense.*

**pre·serv·a·tive** /pri-**zurv**-uht-iv/ *noun* a chemical that is added to food to keep it in good condition: *The juice contains no artificial preservatives.*

**pre·serve** /pri-**zurv**/
● *verb*
to keep something from being harmed, destroyed, or changed too much: *Many Native Americans have worked hard to preserve their cultures.*
—**preservation** /prez-ur-**vaysh**-uhn/ *noun* the act of preserving something: *The organization is dedicated to the preservation of rainforests.*
● *noun*
**1** an area of land or water in which the government protects animals, fish, or trees: *We went for a walk in the nature preserve.*
**2** a sweet food such as jam, made from large pieces of fruit boiled with sugar: *strawberry preserve*

**pres·i·den·cy** /**prez**-uhd-uhnss-ee/ *noun* (plural **presidencies**) the job or time of being a president: *I am reading a book about the presidency of Abraham Lincoln.*

**pres·i·dent** /**prez**-uhd-uhnt/ *noun*
**1** the official leader of a country that does not have a king or queen: *Barack Obama was elected president in 2008.* | *Who is the president of Mexico?*
**2** someone who is in charge of an organization: *Kim is president of the drama club.*
—**presidential** /prez-uh-**densh**-uhl/ *adjective* relating to a president: *The U.S. presidential election is in November.*

**Pres·i·dents' Day** /**prez**-uhd-uhntss day/ *noun* a U.S. holiday that is on the third Monday in February. On Presidents' Day people remember the presidents George Washington and Abraham Lincoln, who were both born in February.

**press** /press/
● *verb*
**1** to push something with your finger: *What happens when you press this button?*
( SYNONYM: **push** )
▶ see **Thesaurus**
**2** to push something hard against something else: *She pressed her face against the window and felt the cold glass on her skin.*
( SYNONYM: **push** )
**3** to make clothes smooth using an iron: *Dad was pressing a shirt for work when the iron broke.* ( SYNONYM: **iron** )
● *noun*
newspapers and magazines and the people who work for them: *Members of the press were outside the building, waiting to ask the singer questions.*

**press**

**pres·sure** /**presh**-ur/
● *noun*
**1** the act of trying to persuade or force someone to do something: *Her father puts a lot of pressure on her to play sports, even though she doesn't really want to.*
**2** a feeling of worry that you have because you have too much to do or because people expect a lot from you: *We have to take a lot of tests, and it can be hard to deal with the pressure.*
**3** the force that something causes when it pushes on another thing: *If you apply pressure to the cut, it will stop bleeding.*
● *verb*
to make someone feel that he or she must do something, when he or she does not really want to: *Don't let your friends pressure you into doing something that you think is wrong.*

**pres·tige** /pre-**steezh**/ *noun* if you have prestige, people respect and admire you because of your job or something that you have achieved: *The college has a lot of prestige and a lot of students want to go there.*
—**prestigious** /pre-**stij**-uhss/ *adjective* admired as being one of the best or most important: *I am very proud that I have won such a prestigious award.*

**pre·sum·a·bly** /pri-**zoom**-uhb-lee/ *adverb* probably: *The lights in his house are all off, so presumably he has gone out.*

**pre·sume** /pri-**zoom**/ *verb* to think that something is probably true: *The house looks empty, so I presume that they are away on vacation.* ( SYNONYM: **assume** )
—**presumption** /pri-**zuhmp**-shuhn/ *noun* the belief that something is probably true: *You should not make the presumption that someone is guilty before a trial.*

**pre·tend** /pri-**tend**/ *verb* to behave as if something is true or real, when it is not: *She closed her eyes and pretended to be asleep.*

a b c d e f g h i j k l m n o **p** q r s t u v w x y z

**pret·ty** /**prit**-ee/
• *adjective* (**prettier**, **prettiest**) nice to look at: *Your dress is very pretty – I really like the color! | Who is the pretty girl with the long brown hair?*
• *adverb* partly, but not completely: *The movie was pretty good, but it wasn't great. | Dad was pretty angry, but he didn't yell or anything.*
SYNONYM: **fairly**

**pret·zel** /**pretss**-uhl/
*noun* a type of bread in the shape of a loose knot and covered with salt. Pretzels can be large and soft or small and hard: *You can buy pretzels, chips, and other snacks.*

pretzel

**pre·vent** /pri-**vent**/ *verb* to stop something from happening, or stop someone from doing something: *To prevent arguments, Mom made us divide the candy equally.*
—**preventable** /pri-**vent**-uhb-uhl/ *adjective* able to be prevented: *Many accidents are preventable.*
—**preventive** /pri-**vent**-iv/ *adjective* done in order to prevent something: *Vaccines are an example of preventive health care.*

**pre·ven·tion** /pri-**vensh**-uhn/ *noun* the things you do in order to stop something from happening: *Today at school we learned about fire prevention.*

**pre·view** /**pree**-vyoo/ *noun* an advertisement for a movie or television program. A preview usually consists of short parts from the movie or television program: *I saw a preview of the movie – it looks very good.*

**pre·vi·ous** /**preev**-ee-uhss/ *adjective* happening before or earlier: *Our house had only one previous owner.*

**pre·vi·ous·ly** /**preev**-ee-uhss-lee/ *adverb* before now: *We live in a house now. Previously, we lived in an apartment.*

**prey** /pray/ *noun* an animal that is hunted and eaten by another animal: *Lions hunt in groups for antelope and other prey.* ANTONYM: **predator**

**price** /priss/
• *noun* the amount of money that you have to pay in order to buy something: *The prices are too high at this restaurant – let's go eat somewhere else.*
• *verb* to give a price to something that is for sale: *The shoes were priced at $60.*

**price·less** /**priss**-liss/ *adjective* very valuable: *The museum has many priceless works of art.*

**prick** /prik/ *verb* to make a small hole in something with a sharp point: *She pricked her finger on the needle.*

**pride** /prīd/ *noun* a feeling of satisfaction and pleasure in what you have done: *Margo's parents watched with pride as she accepted the award.*

**priest** /preest/ *noun* in some religions, a person who leads religious services and performs religious ceremonies: *The priest gave a sermon about treating people as we would like to be treated.*

**pri·mar·i·ly** /prī-**mair**-uh-lee/ *adverb* mainly: *Anne enjoys many subjects, but she is primarily interested in art.*

**pri·mar·y** /**prī**-mair-ee/ *adjective* most important: *The primary aim of this class is to improve your spoken English.* SYNONYM: **main**

**pri·mar·y col·or** /prī-mair-ee **kuhl**-ur/ *noun* one of the three colors that you can mix together to make any other color. The primary colors are red, yellow, and blue.

**prime** /prīm/ *adjective*
**1** most important: *Our prime concern is for the children's safety.* SYNONYMS: **primary, main**
**2** very good: *The house is in a prime location and it has a great view of the ocean.*

**prime fac·tor·i·za·tion** /prīm fakt-uhr-i-**zaysh**-uhn/ *noun* in math, a way of describing a number as the product of prime numbers: *The prime factorization of 36 is 2 x 2 x 3 x 3.*

**prime num·ber** /prīm **nuhm**-bur/ *noun* a number that can only be divided by itself and the number one: *2, 3, 5, 7, and 11 are all prime numbers.*

**prim·i·tive** /**prim**-uht-iv/ *adjective*
**1** belonging to an early stage in the development of human beings or animals: *Primitive people used stones as tools.* ANTONYM: **modern**
**2** very simple and without anything modern: *The houses were primitive, with no electricity.*

**prince** /prinss/ *noun* the son of a king or queen: *In the story, the prince falls in love with Cinderella.*

**prin·cess** /**prinss**-iss/ *noun* the daughter of a king or queen, or the wife of a prince: *The princess got married to a handsome prince.*

**prin·ci·pal** /**prinss**-uhp-uhl/
● *noun* someone who is in charge of a school: *Our school is small, so the principal knows everyone.*
● *adjective* most important: *The principal character in the story is a girl.* ( SYNONYM: **main** )

**prin·ci·ple** /**prinss**-uhp-uhl/ *noun* an idea that you believe is right, and that helps you to decide how to behave: *It's against my principles to tell a lie to my friends.*

**print** /print/
● *verb*
**1** to put words, numbers, or pictures on paper, using a machine: *I am printing the document right now.*
**2** to write words without joining the letters together: *Print your name in big capital letters, so that people can read it easily.*
● *noun*
**1** a mark that something makes on a surface or in something soft: *Don't touch the window – you'll leave prints.*
**2** the letters that are printed in books, newspapers, and magazines: *My father can't read small print without his glasses.*
**3** a photograph or a printed copy of a painting: *I'll order two prints of this picture, and you can have one of them.*

**print·er** /**print**-ur/ *noun* a machine that prints a document from a computer onto paper: *We have a computer and printer at home.*

**print·ing** /**print**-ing/ *noun* the process of making a book or magazine, using a machine: *His new book is ready for printing.*

**pri·or** /**prī**-ur/ *adjective* happening or existing before: *She had no prior knowledge of English before she started the course.*

**pri·or·i·ty** /prī-**or**-uht-ee/ *noun* the thing that you think is most important and that needs your attention first: *The governor said that education is his top priority.*

—**prioritize** /prī-**or**-uh-tīz/ *verb* to decide in what order you should do things, based on how important they are: *You should make a list of all your homework assignments and prioritize them.*

**prism** /**priz**-uhm/ *noun*
**1** a block of glass that separates light into different colors. The ends of the prism are usually shaped like a triangle: *If you shine white light through a prism, it will split into the colors of the rainbow.*
**2** a solid figure with ends that are the same size and shape, and sides that are parallelograms
▶ see picture on page **A12**

**pris·on** /**priz**-uhn/ *noun* a building where people must stay as a punishment for a crime: *The police arrested him for stealing, and he was sent to prison for two years.* ( SYNONYM: **jail** )

**pris·on·er** /**priz**-uhn-ur/ *noun* someone who must stay in a prison as a punishment for a crime: *The prisoner was released after many years.* ( SYNONYM: **convict** )

**pri·va·cy** /**prīv**-uhss-ee/ *noun* the state of being alone and not seen or heard by other people: *I shut my bedroom door because I wanted some privacy.*

**pri·vate** /**prīv**-it/ *adjective*
**1** secret and not for other people to know about: *She wrote all her private thoughts in her journal.*
**2** for one person or group, and not for everyone: *We can't go through that field – it's private property.*
**3** not owned or paid for by the government: *A private company is going to open a restaurant in the park.* ( ANTONYM: **public** )

IDIOM with **private**
**in private** without other people listening or watching: *Kevin waited after class, so he could speak to the teacher in private.*

**pri·vate school** /**prīv**-it skool/ *noun* a school where parents pay for their children's education

**priv·i·lege** /**priv**-uhl-ij/ *noun* a special right or advantage that only one person or group has: *My older sister gets special privileges, like being allowed to stay up later.*
—**privileged** /**priv**-uhl-ijd/ *adjective* having advantages that other people do not have: *He had a privileged childhood, and his parents lived in a big house in a wealthy part of town.*

**priv·y** /**priv**-ee/ *adjective* knowing about something that is a secret: *We only told our best friends; no one else was privy to our plans.*

**prize** /prīz/ *noun* something that you win in a game, competition, or race: *She won first prize in the poetry competition.* ▶ see **Thesaurus**

**pro** /proh/ *noun* someone who earns money by playing a sport: *He explained how to hit the ball like a pro.* ( SYNONYM: **professional** )
( ANTONYM: **amateur** )

> **IDIOM with pro**
> **pros and cons** the advantages and disadvantages of something: *What are the pros and cons of having a dog as a pet?*

**prob·a·bil·i·ty** /prahb-uh-**bil**-uht-ee/ *noun* how likely it is that something will happen: *There is a high probability of rain.*

**prob·a·ble** /**prahb**-uhb-uhl/ *adjective* likely to happen or be true: *It's probable that he will be late because there is a big traffic jam on the freeway.*

**prob·a·bly** /**prahb**-uhb-lee/ *adverb* likely to happen or be true: *We will probably go to Florida this summer, but we are not completely sure.*

**probe** /prohb/
● *verb* to ask questions in order to get information: *She does not want anyone to probe into her past because she is embarrassed about it.*
● *noun* a space vehicle that is sent into space to get information. A probe does not have people in it: *They sent a space probe to Mars.*

**probe**

**prob·lem** /**prahb**-luhm/ *noun*
**1** a difficult situation: *She is having some problems in school because some other girls are being mean to her.* ▶ see **Thesaurus**

**2** a question that you must answer using numbers or other information: *The teacher wrote some problems on the board for us to solve.*

**pro·ce·dure** /pruh-**seej**-ur/ *noun* the correct or normal way of doing something: *The teacher explained the procedure for moving from elementary to middle school.*

**pro·ceed** /pruh-**seed**/ *verb*
**1** to continue: | *The school will proceed with plans to build a new library.*
**2** to go in a direction: *Passengers for New York should proceed to Gate 5.*

**pro·cess** /**prahss**-ess/
● *noun* something that happens over a period of time: *Learning a new language is a long process.*
● *verb* to deal with information by putting it through a system or computer: *Your application has not been processed yet.*

**pro·ces·sor** /**prahss**-ess-ur/ *noun* the part of a computer that deals with information: *Processors are much faster today than they used to be.*

**pro·cras·ti·nate** /pruh-**krast**-uh-nayt/ *verb* to delay doing something that you should do: *Just do your homework and stop procrastinating.*
—**procrastination** /pruh-krast-uh-**naysh**-uhn/ *noun* delay in doing something that you should do: *After a lot of procrastination, he finally started to write the essay.*

**pro·duce**
● *verb* /pruh-**dooss**/
**1** to make or grow something: *The company produced 30,000 cars last year.*
**2** to control the making of a movie or show: *The movie "Shrek" was produced by DreamWorks Animation.*
● *noun* /**prahd**-ooss/
food that people grow to sell, especially fruits and vegetables: *You can buy all kinds of produce at the farmers' market.*

**pro·duc·er** /pruh-**dooss**-ur/ *noun*
**1** a person, company, or country that makes or grows something to sell: *Brazil is one of the largest producers of coffee.*
**2** someone whose job is to plan and control how a movie or television program is made and paid for: *The producer can fire the director, but the director actually makes the movie.*

**prod·uct** /**prahd**-uhkt/ *noun*
**1** something that people make or grow in order to sell: *The store sells a wide range of different products.*
**2** the number you get when you multiply numbers: *The product of 3 x 3 is 9.*

**pro·duc·tion** /pruh-**duhk**-shuhn/ *noun*
**1** the process of making or growing things in order to sell them: *We learned about the production of cheese at the farm.*
**2** a movie, play, or other form of entertainment: *We are going to see a new production of the ballet "Swan Lake."*

**pro·duc·tive** /pruh-**duhkt**-iv/ *adjective*
producing or achieving a lot: *The principal and teachers had a very productive meeting in which they made a lot of important decisions.*

**pro·fes·sion** /pruh-**fesh**-uhn/ *noun* a job that needs special education and training: *She wants to go into a profession such as medicine, law, or teaching.*

**pro·fes·sion·al** /pruh-**fesh**-uhn'l/
● *adjective*
doing a sport or activity for money, as a job: *She became a professional tennis player at the age of 16.* ( ANTONYM: **amateur** )
● *noun*
**1** someone who works in a job that needs a lot of education or training: *Mostly doctors, lawyers, and other professionals live in this part of town.*
**2** someone who earns money by playing a sport
( SYNONYM: **pro** ) ( ANTONYM: **amateur** )

**pro·fes·sor** /pruh-**fess**-ur/ *noun* a teacher at a university: *Cameron is a professor of history.* | *Professor Alvarez teaches Spanish.*

**pro·file** /**proh**-fil/ *noun*
**1** a short piece of writing that gives important details about what something is like: *We had to write a profile of our favorite author.*
**2** a view or picture of someone's head from the side: *The picture shows a woman's face in profile.*

profile

**prof·it** /**prahf**-it/
● *noun* money that you make when you sell

something for more than it cost you: *He bought candy bars for $1.50 and sold them for $2, making a 50 cent profit on each one.*
● *verb* to get something good or useful from a situation: *You would profit from studying a little harder.*

**prof·it·a·ble** /**prahf**-it-uhb-uhl/ *adjective*
producing a profit: *The company had a profitable year, making $250,000.*

**pro·found** /pruh-**fownd**/ *adjective* having a very great effect: *Her uncle had a profound influence on her and made her want to become a doctor.*

**pro·gram** /**proh**-gram/
● *noun*
**1** a show on television or radio: *There's a program on TV tonight about whales.*
▶ see **Thesaurus**
**2** a set of instructions for a computer that makes it do something: *There is something wrong with the program and my computer keeps crashing.*
**3** a set of organized activities: *The museum has programs for families every Saturday.*
**4** a thin book or piece of paper that gives you information about an event or performance: *When I was in the school play I loved seeing my name in the program.*
● *verb* (**programming**, **programmed**)
to set a machine to work in a particular way: *The lights are programmed to come on as soon as it gets dark outside.*

**pro·gram·mer** /**proh**-gram-ur/ *noun* someone whose job is writing programs for computers: *Valerie works as a computer programmer.*
—**programming** /**proh**-gram-ing/ *noun* the activity of writing programs for computers: *We are studying computer programming.*

**prog·ress**
● *noun* /**prahg**-ruhss/ if you make progress, you get better or get closer to achieving something: *She has worked hard and made a lot of progress in English this semester.*
● *verb* /pruh-**gress**/ to move forward: *As Sarah's career progressed, she earned more money.*

**pro·gres·sion** /pruh-**gresh**-uhn/ *noun* in math, a sequence of numbers where the difference between the numbers is the same each time: *The sequence 3, 6, 9, 12, 15 is a progression with the common difference 3.*

a b c d e f g h i j k l m n o **p** q r s t u v w x y z

**pro·gres·sive** /pruh-**gress**-iv/
● *adjective*
**1** using modern ideas and ways of doing things: *The school uses progressive teaching methods.*
**2** moving forward or happening gradually over a period of time: *Laura's homework has shown progressive improvement and she is getting much better.*
● *noun*
**1** someone who believes in changing society to improve it
**2** a form of the verb that shows that an action was, is, or will be continuing to happen at a particular time. In the sentence "She is reading," "is reading" is a progressive form.
( SYNONYM: **continuous** )

**pro·hib·it** /proh-**hib**-it/ *verb* if something is prohibited, it is not allowed: *Selling alcohol to people under 21 is prohibited.* ( ANTONYM: **permit** )
—**prohibition** /proh-uh-**bish**-uhn/ *noun* the act of not allowing people to do something

**proj·ect**
● *noun* /**prahj**-ekt/
a piece of work that you plan carefully, and that often takes a long time: *I'm still working on my school science project.* | *A big project to make the city more attractive has just started.*
● *verb* /pruh-**jekt**/
**1** to calculate what the amount or cost of something will be in the future: *The company is projecting a 5% rise in sales over the next month.*
**2** to show a movie or photograph on a screen or wall, using a machine: *Dad projected the slides onto the wall.*

**pro·jec·tion** /pruh-**jek**-shuhn/ *noun* a statement that says what is likely to happen in the future: *Some projections of future weather show that the ice at the North Pole will melt.*

**pro·jec·tor** /pruh-**jekt**-ur/ *noun* a machine that shows a movie or photograph on a screen or wall: *The teacher used a projector to show the class a short film.*

**pro·long** /pruh-**long**/ *verb* to make something continue for longer: *Modern drugs can prolong the lives of sick people.*

**prom** /prahm/ *noun* a dance party for students in high school: *Dan invited Annie as his date for the high school prom.*

**prom·i·nent** /**prahm**-uhn-uhnt/ *adjective* famous or important: *My uncle has many businesses, and is a prominent businessman in our town.*

**prom·ise** /**prahm**-iss/
● *verb*
**1** to say that you will definitely do something: *I promised mom that I would clean my bedroom.* ▶ see **Thesaurus**
**2** to seem likely to be good, exciting, etc.: *Tomorrow's baseball game promises to be exciting.*
● *noun*
if you make a promise, you say that you will definitely do something: *Dad made a promise that he would take us out for a meal.*

**prom·is·ing** /**prahm**-iss-ing/ *adjective* likely to be successful or good in the future: *a promising young tennis player*

**pro·mote** /pruh-**moht**/ *verb*
**1** to give someone a more important job at work: *Bill was promoted to sales manager.*
**2** to tell people about something so that they want to buy it or do it: *The actor appeared on a talk show to promote his new movie.*
**3** to help something to develop or increase: *The meetings are intended to promote communication between parents and teachers.*

**pro·mo·tion** /pruh-**mohsh**-uhn/ *noun*
**1** if you get a promotion, you get a more important job at work: *After his promotion, the company gave him his own office.*
**2** something that someone does to make people want to buy or do something: *The store is having a promotion – you get two shirts for the price of one.*

**prompt** /prahmpt/ *adjective* quick and without a delay: *I sent him an email and received a very prompt answer just a few minutes later.*
—**promptly** /**prahmpt**-lee/ *adverb* quickly and without a delay: *The firefighters arrived promptly and put the fire out before much damage was done.*

**prone** /prohn/ *adjective* if you are prone to something bad, you are likely to do it or suffer from it: *People who are overweight are more prone to heart disease.*

**pro·noun** /**proh**-nown/ *noun* a word that you use instead of a noun. "He," "she," and "it" are pronouns.

**pro·nounce** /pruh-**nownss**/ *verb* to say a word or letter: *I don't know how to pronounce her name.*

**pro·nun·ci·a·tion** /pruh-nuhnss-ee-**aysh**-uhn/ *noun* the way that you say a word: *The pronunciation of "tomato" is different in the U.S. and in England.*

**proof** /proof/ *noun* facts that prove something is true: *The police don't have any proof that he stole the money.*

**-proof** /proof/

### Word Building

**-proof** is a suffix.
fire**proof** | fool**proof** | water**proof**
**-proof** means "not able or allowed to do something." If something is *fireproof*, fire cannot destroy it. If a plan is *foolproof*, it cannot fail even if someone does something stupid. If a coat is *waterproof*, it does not let rain in.

**prop** /prahp/
● *verb* (**propping**, **propped**) to make something stay in a position, by using something to support it: *The builder propped his ladder against the wall.*
● *noun* an object used by actors in a play or movie: *We're looking for props for the school play as we need a wooden sword.*

**prop·a·gan·da** /prahp-uh-**gand**-uh/ *noun* false information that political organizations use. They use propaganda to try to make people agree with them: *Political parties use propaganda to make people vote for them.*

**pro·pane** /**proh**-payn/ *noun* a gas used for cooking and heating

**pro·pel·ler** /pruh-**pel**-ur/ *noun* a piece of equipment with parts that turn around in a circle. A propeller makes an airplane or ship move: *The boat has two underwater propellers.*

**propeller**
propeller

**prop·er** /**prahp**-ur/ *adjective* right for a situation: *You need the proper equipment if you want to go climbing.*

**prop·er·ly** /**prahp**-ur-lee/ *adverb* in the right way: *My computer isn't working properly. I'll ask Dad if he can fix it.* ( SYNONYM: **correctly** )

**prop·er noun** /prahp-ur **nown**/ (also **prop·er name** /prahp-ur **naym**/) *noun* a noun that is the name of a person, place, or thing. A proper noun begins with a capital letter: *"Tom," "Boston,"* and *"Christmas"* are proper nouns.

**prop·er·ty** /**prahp**-urt-ee/ *noun*
**1** something that someone owns: *The police arrested the thief and returned the stolen property to its owner.*
**2** land or buildings: *He owns several properties including a large house near the beach.*
**3** a quality that something has: *Different metals have different properties – steel is very hard, but aluminum is much softer and easier to bend.*

**proph·e·cy** /**prahf**-uhss-ee/ *noun* (plural **prophecies**) a statement that says what will happen in the future: *In the story, an old man with magical powers makes a prophecy that the girl will become a princess.*

**proph·et** /**prahf**-it/ *noun*
**1** a man who people believe was sent by God to be their leader and teach them about their religion
**2** **the Prophet** Muhammad, who began the religion of Islam: *The Koran teaches Muslims to follow the Prophet.*
**3** someone who tells people what will happen in the future

509

a
b
c
d
e
f
g
h
i
j
k
l
m
n
o
**p**
q
r
s
t
u
v
w
x
y
z

**pro·por·tion** /pruh-**porsh**-uhn/ *noun*
**1** a part of a group of people or things: *A large proportion of the students have a computer at home.*
**2** the relationship between the amount of two different things or groups: *The proportion of girls to boys at the school has increased.*
**3 proportions** the size or shape of something: *Your room has about the same proportions as mine – they are both about 10 feet by 8 feet.*

**pro·pos·al** /pruh-**pohz**-uhl/ *noun*
**1** a plan or suggestion: *The principal made several proposals for improving the school.*
**2** the act of asking someone to marry you: *Jennifer accepted Ben's proposal, and they will get married in the summer.*

**pro·pose** /pruh-**pohz**/ *verb*
**1** to suggest something: *One of the teachers proposed having a school sports competition.*
**2** to intend to do something: *The mayor is proposing to build a new swimming pool in the town.*
**3** to ask someone to marry you: *Bob has bought a ring and is going to propose to Jane.*

**prop·o·si·tion** /prahp-uh-**zish**-uhn/ *noun*
**1** a statement that expresses an opinion or belief: *In class, we discussed the proposition that everyone should have an equal chance to succeed in life.*
**2** an offer or suggestion: *Jim accepted a business proposition from his brother to open a restaurant together.*
**3** a suggestion for a new law that people in a state vote on: *If the voters accept the proposition, there will be more money for building new schools.*

**pro·pri·e·tor** /pruh-**prī**-uht-ur/ *noun* the owner of a business: *The hotel's proprietor is in charge of making business decisions.*

**prose** /prohz/ *noun* writing that is not poetry: *Novels are written in prose.*

**pros·e·cute** /**prahss**-uh-kyoot/ *verb* to say officially that you think someone is guilty of a crime and must be judged in a court: *The police caught the man stealing from a store and prosecuted him for theft.*
—**prosecutor** /**prahss**-uh-kyoot-ur/ *noun* a lawyer who is trying to show that someone is guilty of a

crime: *The prosecutor said that Smith stole over $100,000.*

**pros·e·cu·tion** /prahss-uh-**kyoosh**-uhn/ *noun* the lawyers in a court who are trying to show that someone is guilty of a crime: *The prosecution must prove that he robbed the bank.*

**pros·pect** /**prahss**-pekt/ *noun* the thought of something that will probably happen in the future: *The prospect of making a speech in front of the whole school is terrifying.*

**pros·per** /**prahss**-pur/ *verb* to be successful, especially by making a lot of money: *His business prospered and he now owns several stores.*
—**prosperity** /prah-**sperr**-uht-ee/ *noun* the state of having plenty of money and being successful: *The country is going through a time of prosperity.*

**pros·per·ous** /**prahss**-puhr-uhss/ *adjective* rich and successful: *The town became prosperous because of money from the steel industry.*

**pro·tect** /pruh-**tekt**/ *verb* to stop someone or something from being damaged: *Wear a hat to protect your head from the sun.*
▶ see **Thesaurus**
—**protection** /pruh-**tek**-shuhn/ *noun* something that protects someone or something: *Take your umbrella. It will give you some protection from the rain.*

**pro·tein** /**proht**-een/ *noun* a substance in food such as meat or eggs that helps your body to grow and be healthy: *Fish is high in protein.*

**pro·test**
● *noun* /**proht**-est/
**1** an action or words that show you do not agree with something: *Dad didn't let us stay up late despite our protests.*
**2** an event when a group of people show in public that they do not agree with something: *A local peace group organized a street protest against the war.*
● *verb* /pruh-**test**/
if a group of people protest, they show in public that they do not agree with something: *People are protesting about the increase in taxes.*
—**protester, protestor** /**proht**-est-ur/ *noun* someone who protests about something in public, with a group of other people: *The police*

arrested a small number of protesters for violent behavior.

**Prot·es·tant** /**praht**-uhst-uhnt/
● *adjective* relating to a part of the Christian church that separated from the Catholic church in the 1500s: *Our neighbors go to the Protestant church every Sunday.*
● *noun* someone who belongs to a Protestant church

**pro·tist** /**proht**-ist/ *noun* any living thing with a cell or cells inside an enclosed nucleus, but that is not a plant or an animal: *Some bacteria are protists.*

**pro·ton** /**proht**-ahn/ *noun* a particle in the nucleus of an atom: *Protons have a positive electrical charge.* ▶ see picture at **atom**

**pro·trac·tor** /proh-**trakt**-ur/ *noun* something that you use for measuring and drawing angles. A protractor is in the shape of a half-circle.

**proud** /prowd/ *adjective*
**1** pleased because you or someone in your family has done something good: *I was proud to be picked for the basketball team.*
▶ see **Thesaurus**
**2** not wanting other people to help you because you do not want to seem weak: *The old man was too proud to ask for help with fixing his meals.*
—**proudly** /**prowd**-lee/ *adverb* in a way that shows you feel pleased about something you or your family have done: *He proudly showed me the medal he had won.*

**prove** /proov/ *verb* (**proved**, **proved** or **proven** /**proov**-uhn/)
**1** to show that something is true: *Tests proved that he was the baby's father.*
**2** to have a specific result: *Not taking an umbrella proved to be a big mistake. It started raining and we got wet.*

**prov·en** /**proov**-uhn/ *adjective* shown to be good or true: *He's a basketball player of proven ability who has been captain of his team for many years.*

**prov·erb** /**prahv**-urb/ *noun* a short well-known statement that gives advice about life: *"An apple a day keeps the doctor away" is a proverb which means that eating apples is good for your health.*

**pro·vide** /pruh-**vīd**/ *verb*
**1** to give something that someone needs: *This dictionary provides information about words.*
**2** **provide for** to buy the food, clothes, and other things that someone needs: *People need jobs so that they can provide for their families.*

**pro·vid·ed** /pruh-**vīd**-id/ (also **pro·vid·ing** /pruh-**vīd**-ing/) *conjunction* if something happens: *You'll get a good grade, provided that you work hard.*

**pro·voke** /pruh-**vohk**/ *verb* to deliberately make someone angry: *One boy provoked another boy into a fight by calling him bad names.*

**prow** /prow/ *noun* the front part of a ship or boat

**prowl** /prowl/ *verb* to move around quietly, especially to hunt: *At night, cats prowl around the streets.*

**pru·dent** /**prood**'nt/ *adjective* sensible and careful: *It is prudent to save some money.*

**prune** /proon/ *noun* a dried plum

**prune**

**pry** /prī/ *verb* (**pries, prying, pried**)
**1** to open or remove something using force: *I used a spoon handle to pry the lid off the can.*
**2** to try to find out about someone's private life when the person does not want you to: *She was prying, and asking him all about his girlfriend.*

**P.S.** /pee **ess**/ you write P.S. when you want to add something at the end of a letter. P.S. is short for "postscript": *P.S. See you in December!*

**psalm** /sahm/ *noun* a song or poem that praises God: *In church we sang a psalm from the Bible.*

**pseu·do·nym** /**sood**'n-im/ *noun* a name that a writer or artist uses instead of his or her real name: *Her real name was Mary Ann Evans, but she used the pseudonym "George Eliot" when she was writing her books.*

a b c d e f g h i j k l m n o **p** q r s t u v w x y z

a b c d e f g h i j k l m n o **p** q r s t u v w x y z

**psy·chi·a·try** /sī-**kī**-uh-tree/ *noun* the study and treatment of mental illness: *He's studying psychiatry because he wants to get a job helping people with mental illnesses.*
—**psychiatrist** /sī-**kī**-uh-trist/ *noun* a doctor who treats people who have a mental illness

**psy·chic** /**sīk**-ik/
● *adjective* having strange and unusual abilities, for example knowing what other people are thinking, or what will happen in the future: *He claims to have psychic powers, and that he predicted that there would be an attack on the city in 2008.*
● *noun* someone who has strange mental abilities, for example knowing what other people are thinking, or what will happen in the future

**psy·chol·o·gy** /sī-**kahl**-uhj-ee/ *noun* the study of the mind: *She's studying psychology because she's interested in how the human mind works.*
—**psychologist** /sī-**kahl**-uhj-ist/ *noun* someone who has studied psychology
—**psychological** /sīk-uh-**lahj**-ik-uhl/ *adjective* relating to the mind: *Children can suffer psychological problems if their parents divorce.*

**PTA** /pee tee **ay**/ *noun* (**Parent-Teacher Association**) an organization of the teachers and parents at a school: *The PTA organizes events to raise money for our school.*

**pter·o·dac·tyl** /terr-uh-**dakt**-uhl/ *noun* a type of large flying reptile that lived many millions of years ago

**Word Origin: pterodactyl**

When the bones of **pterodactyls** were first discovered, scientists thought that the animal may have lived in water. In 1809, a scientist said that the animal probably flew, and named it "pterodactyl." The name comes from a Greek word that means "fingers on wings," because pterodactyls have three fingers on each wing, and the wing is attached to a very long fourth finger.

**pu·ber·ty** /**pyoob**-urt-ee/ *noun* the time when your body changes from a child to an adult: *Puberty usually takes place from about ages 10 to 15.*

**pub·lic** /**puhb**-lik/
● *adjective*
**1** for anyone to use: *This is a public beach which everybody is allowed to use.* (ANTONYM: **private**)
**2** relating to all the people in an area or country: *New laws to protect the environment have a lot of public support.*
**3** relating to the government: *The government wants to reduce public spending by providing less money for services such as health and education.*
● *noun*
all the people in an area or country: *All the city's parks are open to the public.*

IDIOM with **public**
**in public** in a place where anyone can see or hear: *She was nervous because she had never sung in public before.*

—**publicly** /**puhb**-lik-lee/ *adverb* in a way or place that other people can see or hear: *I didn't think she was right but I didn't say that publicly.*

**pub·li·ca·tion** /puhb-luh-**kaysh**-uhn/ *noun*
**1** the process of printing a book, newspaper, or magazine and sending it to stores: *The publication of the writer's first book was in 2008.*
**2** a book, magazine, or newspaper: *"Sports Illustrated" is a weekly publication.*

**pub·lic·i·ty** /puh-**bliss**-uht-ee/ *noun* attention that someone or something gets in newspapers, on television, or on the radio: *The movie is getting a lot of publicity and you often see commercials for it on the television.*
—**publicize** /**puhb**-luh-sīz/ *verb* to give information about something to as many people as possible: *We put up posters to publicize the school fair.*

**pub·lic school** /**puhb**-lik **skool**/ *noun* a free local school that any child can go to. The government pays for and controls it.

**pub·lish** /**puhb**-lish/ *verb* to print a book, magazine, or newspaper for people to buy: *The company publishes a monthly children's magazine.*

**pub·lish·er** /**puhb**-lish-ur/ *noun* a person or company that produces and sells books, newspapers, or magazines

**puck** /puhk/ *noun* the thing you hit in a game of

hockey. A puck is flat and round. ▶ see picture at **hockey**

**pud·ding** /**pud**-ing/ *noun* a thick sweet food that you make with milk, eggs, and sugar: *Mom is making chocolate pudding.*

**pud·dle** /**puhd**'l/ *noun* a small pool of water on the ground: *It was raining and there were puddles all over the street.*

puddle

**pueb·lo** /**pweb**-loh/ *noun*
**1** a small town of Native American homes in the southwest U.S. The homes are made of stone or earth and straw and are built next to and on top of each other.
**2** a small town, especially in the southwest U.S. near Mexico

**puff** /puhf/
● *verb* to breathe quickly and with difficulty: *Sally was puffing after running for the bus.*
● *noun* a small amount of air, smoke, or wind: *Puffs of smoke came from the chimney.*

**puff·y** /**puhf**-ee/ *adjective* puffy eyes, cheeks, or faces are swollen: *Her eyes were puffy from crying.*

**pull** /pul/
● *verb*
**1** to move something toward you, using your hands: *He pulled the door toward him until it was closed.* (ANTONYM: **push**)
▶ see **Thesaurus**
**2** to make something move behind you in the direction you are moving: *The train is pulling 20 boxcars.* (ANTONYM: **push**)
**3** to remove something from its place: *The dentist pulled out the tooth.*
**4** if you pull a muscle, you hurt it by using it too much: *If you're lifting something heavy, you must be careful not to pull a muscle.*
**5** to move somewhere in a vehicle: *Wait for the car in front to pull away from the curb.*
**6 pull off** to succeed in doing something

difficult: *The team pulled off a win in Saturday's game.*
**7 pull through** to stay alive after a serious injury or illness: *He is very sick and we don't know if he will pull through.*
**8 pull up** if a car pulls up, it stops: *The car pulled up at the stop lights.*

IDIOM with **pull**
**pull someone's leg** to tell someone something that is not true, as a joke: *I didn't mean it – I was only pulling your leg.*
● *noun*
the action of holding something and moving it toward you: *He gave the handle a pull and succeeded in opening the door.* (ANTONYM: **push**)

**pul·ley** /**pul**-ee/ *noun* a piece of equipment made of a wheel that a rope goes around. You use it to lift heavy things: *They use a pulley to raise the flag up the pole.*

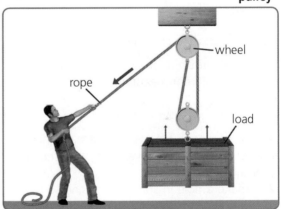
**pulley**
wheel
rope
load

**pul·mo·nar·y** /**pul**-muh-nair-ee/ *adjective* relating to the lungs: *The pulmonary artery carries the blood from your heart to your lungs.*

**pul·pit** /**pul**-pit/ *noun* a high place where a priest or minister stands to speak to people in a church

**pulse** /puhlss/ *noun* the regular beat that you can feel as your heart moves blood around your body: *The nurse held my wrist and checked my pulse to see if it was normal.*

**pu·ma** /**poom**-uh/ *noun* a large brown wild cat. Pumas live in the mountains in North and South America. (SYNONYM: **cougar**)

**pump** /puhmp/
● *noun* a machine that makes liquid or gas go into or out of something: *You use a gas pump to put gas in a car. | I have a special pump for filling my bicycle tires with air.*
● *verb* to make liquid or gas go into or out of something by using a pump: *Firefighters pumped the water out of the flooded basement.*

pump

**pump·kin** /**puhmp**-kin/
*noun* a very large orange fruit that grows on the ground. People often cut faces in pumpkins to make jack-o'-lanterns at Halloween: *We cut open the top of the pumpkin and scooped out the seeds inside.*

pumpkin

**pun** /puhn/ *noun* a joke using a word that has two very different meanings

**punch** /puhnch/
● *verb*
**1** to hit someone hard with your hand closed: *Boxers wear special gloves and punch each other.*
**2** to make a hole in something using something sharp: *The bus driver will punch your ticket.*
● *noun*
**1** a hard hit with your hand closed: *He gave me a punch on the arm.*
**2** a drink made from fruit juice, sugar, and water: *We made a bowl of punch for the party.*

**punc·tu·al** /**puhngk**-choo-uhl/ *adjective* arriving at the right time: *He's always punctual for his classes and he is never late.*
—**punctuality** /puhngk-choo-**al**-uht-ee/ *noun* the quality of being punctual: *The principal thinks punctuality is important and doesn't like students being late for school.*

**punc·tu·ate** /**puhngk**-choo-ayt/ *verb* to use punctuation marks in your writing: *In our English class, the teacher is showing us how to punctuate sentences correctly.*

**punc·tu·a·tion** /puhngk-choo-**aysh**-uhn/ *noun* the use of punctuation marks in your writing: *It is important to use the right punctuation and to put a period at the end of every sentence.*

**punc·tu·a·tion mark** /puhnk-choo-**aysh**-uhn mark/ *noun* a symbol, such as a comma (,) or a question mark (?), that you use in your writing to make sentences clearer: *A question mark is the punctuation mark that you use at the end of a question.*

**punc·ture** /**puhngk**-chur/
● *noun* a small hole made by something sharp: *There's a puncture in my bike tire.*
● *verb* to make a small hole in something, so that air or liquid comes out: *He punctured the balloon with a pin.*

**pun·ish** /**puhn**-ish/ *verb* to make someone suffer because he or she has done something wrong: *Dad punished me for breaking the window by not letting me watch TV.*

**pun·ish·ment** /**puhn**-ish-muhnt/ *noun* something bad that someone makes you suffer when you have done something wrong: *Mom sent Sally to bed early as a punishment for being naughty.* ▶ see **Thesaurus**

**pu·pa** /**pyoop**-uh/ *noun* (plural **pupae** /**pyoop**-ee/) a young insect at a stage when it is protected inside a cover before it becomes an adult: *The pupae develop into adult ants.*
▶ see picture at **metamorphosis**

**pu·pil** /**pyoop**-uhl/ *noun*
**1** a child in school: *There are 30 pupils in my class.*
**2** the black part in the middle of your eye: *In bright light, your pupils get smaller.*
▶ see picture at **eye**

**pup·pet** /**puhp**-it/ *noun* a toy in the shape of a person or animal. You move it by putting your hand inside it or by pulling the strings on it: *We made puppets out of old socks and put on a show.*
—**puppeteer** /puhp-uh-**teer**/ *noun* someone who makes and uses puppets

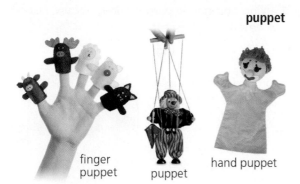

**puppet**

finger
puppet

puppet

hand puppet

**pup·py** /**puhp**-ee/ *noun* (plural **puppies**) a young dog ▶ see picture at **dog**

**pur·chase** /**purch**-uhss/
● *verb*
to buy something: *He purchased the house for $500,000.*
● *noun*
**1** the act of buying something: *She made several purchases with her credit card.*
**2** something you bought: *She paid for her purchases and left the store.*

**pure** /pyoor/ *adjective*
**1** not mixed with anything else: *This shirt is made of pure silk.*
**2** pure water or air does not contain anything harmful: *The water in the mountain streams is so pure that you can drink it.* (ANTONYM: **impure**)
**3** complete and total: *There was a look of pure joy on her face, when she found out that she had passed her test.*
—**purity** /**pyoor**-uht-ee/ *noun* the quality of being pure: *I love the purity of the air in the countryside.*

**pu·rée** /pyu-**ray**/ *noun* food that is boiled or crushed until it is almost liquid: *I usually put tomato purée in the spaghetti sauce.*

**pure·ly** /**pyoor**-lee/ *adverb* in every way: *I met Jim purely by chance on the street this morning.*
(SYNONYMS: **completely, totally**)

**pur·ple** /**purp**-uhl/ *noun, adjective* a dark color that is a mixture of red and blue: *I'm wearing a purple shirt.*

**pur·pose** /**purp**-uhss/ *noun* the thing you are trying to achieve by doing something: *The purpose of exercise is to improve your health.*
▶ see **Thesaurus**

IDIOM with **purpose**
**on purpose** if you do something on purpose, you intend to do it and it is not an accident: *Police think that someone started the fire at the factory on purpose.*
(SYNONYMS: **deliberately, purposely**)
(ANTONYM: **accidentally**)

**pur·pose·ly** /**purp**-uhss-lee/ *adverb* if you purposely do something, you plan to do it and it is not an accident: *I purposely did not invite Tom to the party because I knew he would be away on vacation.*
(SYNONYMS: **deliberately, on purpose**)
(ANTONYM: **accidentally**)

**purr** /pur/
● *verb* if a cat purrs, it makes a soft low sound because it is happy: *The cat was purring because Mary was stroking it.*
● *noun* the sound a cat makes when it is happy

**purse** /purss/ *noun* a bag that women use to carry money and other things: *Mom keeps her cell phone in her purse.*

**pur·sue** /pur-**soo**/ *verb*
**1** to chase someone in order to catch him or her: *The police pursued the bank robbers through the streets.* (SYNONYM: **follow**)
**2** to work hard in order to achieve something: *He wants to pursue a career in medicine so he's studying to become a doctor.*

**pur·suit** /pur-**soot**/ *noun*
**1** the act of chasing someone in order to catch him or her: *Two police cars were in pursuit of the criminals.*
**2** an activity that you spend a lot of time doing: *My father's favorite outdoor pursuit is playing golf.*
**3** the act of trying to get something: *The athlete spent his life in pursuit of winning a gold medal.*

**pus** /puhss/ *noun* a yellow liquid that comes out of an infected part of your body: *The spot was full of pus.*

a b c d e f g h i j k l m n o **p** q r s t u v w x y z

## push /push/

● *verb*

**1** to move something away from you by putting your hands or feet on it and moving them: *He pushed the door open.* ( ANTONYM: **pull** )

▶ see **Thesaurus**

**2** to press a button to make a machine start or stop working: *Push the button to turn on the computer.* ( SYNONYM: **press** )

**3** to move somewhere by pressing your body against other people as you move: *We pushed our way to the front of the crowd.* ( SYNONYM: **shove** )

**4** to try hard to make someone decide to do something: *I tried to push Mom into buying me an ice cream cone.*

**5** to make someone work very hard: *Some parents push their children to do well in school.*

● *noun*

**1** the act of pushing someone or something: *The door was stuck so I gave it a good push.* ( ANTONYM: **pull** )

**2** a situation in which someone works very hard to get something: *The team is making a big push to try to win the game.*

**push**

He is pushing the skateboard.

## push-up /**push**-uhp/ *noun* an exercise in which you lie on the floor, and push yourself up with your arms: *In P.E. class we do push-ups to make our arms stronger.*

## push·y /**push**-ee/ *adjective* trying hard to get what you want, in a rude way: *The salesman was pushy, and wouldn't go away when I said I didn't want to buy anything.*

## puss·y·cat /**puss**-ee-kat/ *noun*

**1** a cat: *Come here, pussycat!*

**2** a kind and gentle person: *He looks very tough, but he's a real pussycat.*

## put /put/ *verb* (**putting, put**)

**1** to move something into a place or position: *I'll put the books back on the shelf.* | *Dad put his hand on my shoulder.* | *Put down your pencils.*

▶ see **Thesaurus**

**put**

He's putting on his T-shirt.

**2** to write or print something: *Put your name at the top of the paper.*

**3** to make someone be in a situation or make someone have a feeling: *I had a fight with my sister, which put me in a bad mood.*

**4** to say something using a particular set of words: *The teacher tries to put everything very simply so we can understand it.*

**5 put away** to put something where it belongs: *When you have finished, put your toys away in the toy box.*

**6 put off** to decide not to do something right now, but to do it later instead: *We have put off our trip until next year.* ( SYNONYM: **delay** )

**7 put someone off** to make someone not like or want to do something: *The movie is very long and that puts some people off.*

**8 put on** to put a piece of clothing on your body: *Mom told me to get dressed so I put on my clothes.* ( ANTONYM: **take off** )

**9 put out** to make something stop burning or shining: *We put out the fire with a bucket of water.*

**10 put up with** to accept something bad without trying to stop it: *Our teacher does not put up with any bad behavior and she punishes us if we talk in class.*

## puz·zle /**puhz**-uhl/

● *noun*

**1** a game that is made of a picture that has been cut into pieces. You have to put the pieces together again: *This puzzle has 100 pieces.* ( SYNONYM: **jigsaw** )

**2** a game in which you have to think hard to solve a problem: *Dad likes doing the crossword puzzle in the newspaper.*

**3** something that is difficult to understand or explain: *It's a puzzle why she wasn't at the party even though she said she wanted to come.*

● *verb*

**1** if something puzzles you, it confuses you because you cannot understand it: *It puzzled me why Tim didn't want to go to the game even though he loves football.*

**2 puzzle over** to think for a long time about something because you do not understand it: *He was puzzling over the questions on his English test.*

—**puzzled** /**puhz**-uhld/ *adjective* confused because you cannot understand something: *Students are often puzzled by English spelling – it doesn't seem to make sense.*

—**puzzling** /**puhz**-ling/ *adjective* making you puzzled: *I found it puzzling that Bill was wearing a thick coat, even though the weather was very hot.*

puzzle

**py·lon** /**pīl**-ahn/ *noun*

**1** a plastic orange cone that is used on the road to direct traffic or warn of danger: *There were orange pylons in the road to mark the pothole.*

**2** a tall metal structure that supports wires carrying electricity

**pyr·a·mid** /**pirr**-uh-mid/ *noun*

**1** a solid shape with a flat base and four sides that form a point at the top: *The sides of a pyramid are triangles.* ▶ see picture on page **A12**

**2** a very large building in the shape of a pyramid. There are some famous pyramids in Mexico and Egypt: *The Egyptians buried kings and queens in pyramids.*

pyramid

**py·thon** /**pīth**-ahn/ *noun* a large snake. Pythons kill animals for food by curling around them and pressing them. Pythons live in Africa, Asia, and Australia. ▶ see picture on page **A1**

a
b
c
d
e
f
g
h
i
j
k
l
m
n
o
**p**
q
r
s
t
u
v
w
x
y
z

# Qq

### quack /kwak/
- *verb* if a duck quacks, it makes a short loud sound
- *noun* the sound a duck makes

### quad·rant /**kwahd**-ruhnt/ *noun* a quarter of a circle

### quad·ri·lat·er·al
/kwahd-ruh-**lat**-uhr-uhl/
- *noun* a flat shape with four straight sides
- *adjective* having four straight sides

quadrilateral

### quaint /kwaynt/
*adjective* a quaint place is pretty, in an old-fashioned way: *The rooms were quaint, with antique furniture and pretty lace curtains.*

### quake /kwayk/
- *verb* to shake: *She was quaking with fear when she saw the snake.* (SYNONYM: **tremble**)
- *noun* a strong and sudden shaking of the ground: *The quake destroyed many houses.* (SYNONYM: **earthquake**)

### qual·i·fi·ca·tion /kwahl-uhf-uh-**kaysh**-uhn/
*noun* a skill, training, or experience that makes you able to do a job: *You need to have special qualifications to be a doctor.*

### qual·i·fied /**kwahl**-uh-fīd/ *adjective* having the right knowledge or skills to do something: *My uncle is a qualified car mechanic.*

### qual·i·fi·er /**kwahl**-uh-fī-ur/ *noun*
**1** someone who has proved that he or she is good enough to be in a race or competition: *Johnson was the fastest qualifier in the race, and will go on to the semifinals.*
**2** a word or phrase that tells you more about another word or phrase: *In the phrase "red bike," "red" is a qualifier of "bike."*

### qual·i·fy /**kwahl**-uh-fī/ *verb* (**qualifies, qualified**)
**1** to have the education or skills that you need to do a particular job: *It takes a long time to qualify as a doctor.*
**2** to be able to have or do something because of something you have done or because you are in a particular situation: *Children from poor families qualify for free school lunches.*

> **Word Family:** qualify
> **qualify** verb | **qualification** noun | **qualified** adjective | **disqualify** verb

### qual·i·ta·tive ob·ser·va·tion
/kwahl-uh-tayt-iv ahbz-ur-**vaysh**-uhn/ *noun* a statement about the quality or standard of something, and not about its amount or number: *"The weather is hot" is a qualitative observation, but "The temperature is 90 degrees" is a quantitative observation.*

### qual·i·ty /**kwahl**-uht-ee/ *noun* (plural **qualities**)
**1** how good or bad something is: *The teacher said that the quality of my work was excellent.* | *The air quality today is poor. There is a lot of smog.*
**2** something that is part of someone's character: *The qualities that make you a good learner are curiosity and willingness to work hard.*
**3** something that is typical of a thing and makes it different from other things: *The hot dry quality of the air is typical of a desert environment.*

### quan·ti·ta·tive ob·ser·va·tion
/kwahnt-uh-tayt-iv ahb-zur-**vaysh**-uhn/ *noun* a statement about the amount or number of something or about a measurement: *"The temperature is 0 degrees" is a quantitative observation, but "The weather is cold" is a qualitative observation.*

### quan·ti·ty /**kwahnt**-uht-ee/ *noun* (plural **quantities**) an amount: *Gold was found in small quantities in the rocks at the bottom of the stream.*

### quar·an·tine /**kwor**-uhn-teen/
- *noun* a place where a person or animal is kept away from other people or animals, so that they do not pass on a dangerous disease: *People with the flu were put in quarantine.*
- *verb* to put a person or animal in quarantine:

*The pigs were quarantined to try to stop the spread of the disease.*

### quar·rel /**kwor**-uhl/

● *noun* an angry argument: *I had a quarrel with my brother about whose turn it was on the computer.*

● *verb* to have an angry argument: *The girls quarreled over the last piece of cake.*

### quart /kwort/ *noun* a unit for measuring liquid. A quart is equal to 0.95 liters: *There are two pints in one quart.*

## Word Building

**quart | quarter | quadrant | quadrilateral**

These words all have the Latin word root **quart** or **quad** in them. **Quart-** or **quad-** means "four." A *quart* is used to measure liquids. There are four quarts in a gallon. A *quarter* is one of four equal parts of something. The quarter coin gets its name because there are four quarters in a dollar. A *quadrilateral* is a shape with four straight sides.

### quar·ter /**kwort**-ur/ *noun*

**1** one of four equal parts of something. In math, one quarter is written ¼: *2 is a quarter of 8.* | *I cut the sandwiches into quarters.* | *Add a quarter of a cup of sugar.*

**2** a coin worth 25 cents, which is ¼ of a dollar: *I had 60 cents in my pocket – two quarters and a dime.*

**3** 15 minutes: *I'll meet you at a quarter after 8* (=15 minutes after 8).

**4** one of the four equal periods in a basketball or football game. A quarter is usually 15 minutes long: *The score was 66—58 in the third quarter.*

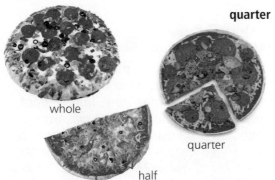

**quarter**

whole

quarter

half

### quar·ter·back /**kwort**-ur-bak/ *noun* the player in football who throws the ball or tries to move the ball forward toward the goal

### quar·ter·hour /kwort-ur **ow**-ur/ *noun* 15 minutes

### quar·ter moon /kwort-ur **moon**/ *noun* the Moon when you can only see half of it because it is one quarter or three quarters of the way through its cycle

### quartz /kwortss/ *noun* a hard rock that is usually clear or white in color. Quartz is used in electronic clocks.

**quartz**

### quea·sy /**kweez**-ee/ *adjective* feeling that you are going to throw up: *The boat was moving a lot and making me feel queasy.*

### queen /kween/ *noun*

**1** a woman from a royal family who is the ruler of a country: *Victoria became Queen of England in 1837.*

**2** the wife of a king: *The king and queen wanted their daughter to marry a prince.*

**3** a card used in card games that has a picture of a queen on it

**4** a female bee, wasp, or ant that lays eggs: *The queen is bigger than the other bees.*

**queen**

crown

robe

**queer** /kweer/ *adjective* strange: *The light was queer – it was a strange pink color.*
(SYNONYMS: **peculiar, odd**)

**que·ry** /**kweer**-ee/
● *noun* (plural **queries**) a question: *Ask your teacher if you have any queries about the work.*
● *verb* (**queries, querying, queried**) to ask a question about something: *"How is Patricia?" he queried.*

**ques·tion** /**kwess**-chuhn/
● *noun*
**1** something you say or write to ask something: *Raise your hand if you want to ask a question about the homework.* (ANTONYM: **answer**)
▶ see Thesaurus
**2** a part of a test that asks you to give information: *I didn't understand one of the questions on the test.*
**3** a problem that people need to talk about and deal with: *We discussed the question of where we should have the party.* (SYNONYM: **issue**)
● *verb*
to ask someone about something: *Police questioned two men about the robbery.*

**ques·tion mark** /**kwess**-chuhn mark/ *noun* the symbol (?) used in writing at the end of a question

**ques·tion·naire** /kwess-chuh-**nair**/ *noun* a written set of questions that someone gives to a lot of people in order to get information: *The principal gave the students questionnaires to find out what they did and didn't like about the school.*

**quiche** /keesh/ *noun* a type of food made with eggs, milk, and cheese baked in a pie crust

**quick** /kwik/ *adjective*
**1** taking only a short time: *Mom took a quick look at my homework.* (SYNONYM: **brief**)
(ANTONYM: **long**) ▶ see Thesaurus
**2** moving fast or doing things fast: *He's a very quick runner.* (SYNONYM: **fast**) (ANTONYM: **slow**)

**Word Origin:** quick

**Quick** comes from an old English word that meant "alive." By the 1300s, it had also started to mean "lively" and "fast," because people who are alive and full of life often do things fast. Now, people only use quick to mean "fast."

**quick·ly** /**kwik**-lee/ *adverb* fast: *He ate his food quickly and went back outside to play.*

**qui·et** /**kwī**-uht/
● *adjective*
**1** not loud: *Be quiet because the baby is sleeping.* (ANTONYMS: **noisy, loud**)
▶ see Thesaurus
**2** someone who is quiet does not talk very much: *Mary is a quiet shy girl.*
**3** without a lot of activity: *We live in a quiet neighborhood with a lot of older people.*
(ANTONYM: **busy**)
—**quietly** /**kwī**-uht-lee/ *adverb* without making a lot of noise: *We all sat quietly reading our books.*
● *noun*
the state of being quiet: *He worked on his report in the quiet of his room.* (ANTONYM: **noise**)

**quilt** /kwilt/ *noun* a thick bed cover made from many pieces of cloth sewn together: *The bed was covered with a patchwork quilt.*

**quit** /kwit/ *verb* (**quitting, quit**)
**1** to stop doing something: *The doctor told my mom to quit smoking because it was bad for her health.* (ANTONYM: **start**) ▶ see Thesaurus
**2** to leave your job or school: *My grandfather had to quit school and work to help his family.*

**quite** /kwīt/ *adverb* very, but not extremely: *I'm quite good at math, but Jenny is better.*
(SYNONYM: **pretty**)
IDIOM with **quite**
**not quite** not completely: *"Are you ready?" "Not quite. I still have to put on my shoes."*

**quiz** /kwiz/ *noun* (plural **quizzes**)
**1** a short test: *We had a spelling quiz.*
**2** a set of questions you answer for fun: *The magazine had a quiz called "Are you a good friend?"*

**Word Origin:** quiz

No one is sure where the word **quiz** comes from. It was first used to mean "test" in the 1800s. Quiz may come from a word meaning "to question" that was used in one part of England. It may also have come from Latin because students in the past were asked *qui es?* which means "who are you?" before they took a test.

**quo·ta·tion** /kwoh-**taysh**-uhn/ *noun* words from a book or speech that you repeat in your own speech or writing: *"To be or not to be" is a famous quotation from Shakespeare.*

SYNONYM: **quote**

**quo·ta·tion marks** /kwoh-**taysh**-uhn markss/ *plural noun* the symbols (" "), which you write before and after what someone says

**quote** /kwoht/
- *verb* to say or write exactly what someone else has said or written: *She quoted the Declaration of Independence, "All men are created equal."*
- *noun* another word for a quotation

**quo·tient** /**kwohsh**-uhnt/ *noun* the number you get when you divide one number by another number: *If you divide 15 by 3, the quotient is 5.*

**Qur·'an** /kuh-**ran**/ *noun* another spelling of the Koran, the holy book of the Muslim religion

a
b
c
d
e
f
g
h
i
j
k
l
m
n
o
p
**q**
r
s
t
u
v
w
x
y
z

521

a
b
c
d
e
f
g
h
i
j
k
l
m
n
o
p
q
**r**
s
t
u
v
w
x
y
z

# Rr

**rab·bi** /**rab**-ī/ *noun* (plural **rabbis**) a Jewish religious leader

**rab·bit** /**rab**-it/ *noun* a small animal with long ears and soft fur. Rabbits usually live in holes in the ground. People also keep them as pets.

rabbit

**rac·coon** /ra-**koon**/ *noun* an animal with black fur around its eyes and black and white lines around its tail. A raccoon is about the size of a dog. Raccoons live in North America: *A raccoon was looking for food in the trash can.*

## Word Origin: raccoon

When English people first came to New England, they had never seen a **raccoon**. They borrowed the word raccoon from a Native American language called Algonquian. In Algonquian, raccoon means "he scratches with his hands." Raccoons use their front paws like hands.

raccoon

**race** /rayss/
● *noun*
**1** a competition to find out who can do something fastest, for example running, driving, or swimming: *She is a good runner and I think she will win the race.*
**2** a large group of people who look the same in some ways, for example in the color of their skin or hair: *There are students from many different races in our class. Some are Latino, some are Asian, and one boy is African.*
● *verb*
**1** to compete in a race: *I watched the cars racing each other around the racetrack.*
**2** to go somewhere very quickly: *A police car raced past us.*

**race car** /**rayss** kar/ *noun* a special car for racing

**race·track** /**rayss**-trak/ *noun* a place where horses, cars, or people compete in races: *Dad sometimes goes to the racetrack to watch the horse racing.* (SYNONYM: **track**)

**ra·cial** /**raysh**-uhl/ *adjective* relating to someone's race: *I believe in racial equality – everyone should be treated in the same way, whatever his or her race.*

**rac·ism** /**rayss**-iz-uhm/ *noun* unfair treatment of people because they belong to a different race: *Racism is unacceptable and any racist behavior will be severely punished.*

**rac·ist** /**rayss**-ist/
● *noun* someone who believes that his or her own race of people is better than any other: *He is a racist and he doesn't believe that black people have the same rights as white people.*
● *adjective* treating people badly because you believe that your race is better than theirs: *There have been several racist attacks against Jewish businesses.*

**rack** /rak/ *noun* an object used for holding things or hanging things on: *I put my coat on the rack.*
▶ see picture at **hanger**

**rack·et** /**rak**-it/ *noun*
**1** an object you use to hit the ball in games such as tennis: *My tennis racket has a broken string.*
**2** a loud noise: *Be quiet – stop making such a racket!*

racket
racket
ball

## Word Origin: racket

**Racket** comes from an Arabic word that means "the palm of your hand." When a game like tennis was first played, people probably used their hands to hit the ball. The Arabic word went into Spanish, Italian, and French before it came into English.

**rack·et·ball** /**rak**-it-bol/ *noun* an indoor game played by two people. They use rackets to hit a ball against the walls of a special room: *Will you play racketball with me?*

racketball

**ra·dar** /**rayd**-ar/ *noun* a system that uses radio waves to find out where ships and planes are: *The captain looked at the radar screen to see if any enemy ships were nearby.*

**ra·di·a·tion** /rayd-ee-**aysh**-uhn/ *noun*
**1** a form of energy that is dangerous to living things if there is too much of it: *People were exposed to radiation when the nuclear power station exploded.*
**2** energy that is sent out as waves of light or heat: *Radiation from the sun can damage your skin.*

**ra·di·a·tor** /**rayd**-ee-ayt-ur/ *noun*
**1** a flat metal object on a wall that heats a room: *Hot water passes through a radiator.*
**2** the part of a car that keeps the engine cool: *A radiator sends a special liquid around the engine to keep it from becoming too hot.*

**rad·i·cal** /**rad**-ik-uhl/ *adjective*
**1** a radical change is very big and makes something very different: *There have been some radical changes in our life since we moved from the city to the farm.*
**2** wanting to change a political system

completely: *His political opinions are very radical and he wants to get rid of all taxes.*

**ANTONYM: moderate**

—**radically** /**rad**-ik-lee/ *adverb* extremely or completely: *Many African countries are radically different from the U.S.A.*

**ra·di·o** /**rayd**-ee-oh/
*noun*

radio

**1** a piece of electrical equipment that you use to listen to music, news, and other programs: *I was listening to the news on the car radio.*
**2** a way of sending and receiving messages through the air: *Ships send messages to each other by radio.*

**ra·di·o·ac·tive** /rayd-ee-oh-**akt**-iv/ *adjective* containing a very harmful form of energy, which is produced during a nuclear reaction: *Plutonium is a highly radioactive chemical and needs to be handled with great care.*

—**radioactivity** /rayd-ee-oh-ak-**tiv**-uht-ee/ *noun* a form of energy that can be very harmful and is produced by radioactive substances: *There was a high level of radioactivity in the soil for many years after the nuclear explosion.*

**rad·ish** /**rad**-ish/ *noun* a small red or white vegetable with a hot taste. It grows in the ground. You eat it without cooking it: *Radishes are great in salads.*

radish

**ra·di·us** /**ray**-dee-uhss/
*noun* (plural **radii** /**rayd**-ee-ī/)
**1** the distance from the center of a circle to the edge: *If you know the radius of a circle, you can calculate its area using the formula ($\pi r^2$).*
**2** an area of a particular distance around a place: *All our students live within a 15-mile radius of the school.*

**raf·fle** /**raf**-uhl/ *noun* a competition in which people buy tickets with numbers on them in order to try to win prizes: *The winning ticket in the raffle was 3789. The person with this ticket won a vacation to Florida.*

**a b c d e f g h i j k l m n o p q r s t u v w x y z**

**raft** /raft/ *noun*
**1** a flat boat that you make by tying pieces of wood together: *They made a raft out of logs and sailed away from the island.*
**2** a small boat that you fill with air before you use it: *The rafts take people down the Colorado River.*

raft

**rag** /rag/ *noun* a piece of old cloth: *I use an old rag to clean my bicycle.*

> **IDIOM with rag**
> **in rags** wearing old torn clothes: *The children were very poor and were dressed in rags.*

**rage** /rayj/ *noun* very strong anger: *She hit him in a fit of rage.* ( SYNONYM: **fury** )

**raid** /rayd/
● *noun*
**1** a sudden visit by police who are looking for something: *Police found stolen guns during a raid on an apartment.*
**2** a sudden attack on a place during a war: *Enemy planes destroyed several buildings during a bombing raid.*
● *verb*
**1** if the police raid a place, they go there suddenly to search for something: *Police found drugs when they raided the house.*
**2** to attack a place suddenly during a war: *Soldiers raided the village.*
—**raider** /raider/ *noun* someone who raids a place: *Raiders seized bomb-making materials from the house.*

**rail** /rayl/ *noun*
**1** a wooden or metal bar that stops you from falling: *Hold on to the rail as you walk up the stairs.*
**2** one of the two long metal bars that a train moves on: *The train hit a rock and came off the rails.* ( SYNONYM: **track** )
**3** railroad: *the Amtrak rail system*

**rail·ing** /**rayl**-ing/ *noun* a low fence made of wooden or metal bars that stops you from falling over an edge: *There were railings all the way along the bridge.*

**rail·road** /**rayl**-rohd/ *noun* the system of tracks

and equipment that trains use: *Dad took us to the railroad station so that we could catch the train. | The train is moving along the railroad tracks.*

**rail·way** /**rayl**-way/ *noun* another word for railroad

**rain** /rayn/
● *noun* water that falls from clouds in the sky: *There has been a lot of heavy rain and the fields are flooded.* ▶ see **Thesaurus**
● *verb* if it rains, drops of water fall from the sky: *Take your umbrella because it is still raining outside.*

**rain·bow** /**rayn**-boh/ *noun* a large curve of different colors in the sky. You see rainbows after it has rained. When the light from the Sun hits the water in the sky, the light bends a little bit. This makes you see colors instead of white light: *Do you know all the colors of the rainbow?*

rainbow

**rain·coat** /**rayn**-koht/ *noun* a coat that keeps you dry in the rain: *She was wearing a raincoat so she didn't get wet.*

raincoat
raincoat

**rain·drop** /**rayn**-drahp/ *noun* a single drop of rain: *I can hear the raindrops landing on the roof.*

**rain·fall** /**rayn**-fol/ *noun* the amount of rain that falls somewhere: *Our geography teacher told us that rainfall in the Amazon is around 2 meters a year.*

**rain·for·est** /**rayn**-for-ist/ *noun* a thick forest in a part of the world that is hot and wet: *Some amazing birds live in the rainforests of South America.*

**rain·y** /**rayn**-ee/ *adjective* a rainy day is a day when there is a lot of rain: *It was a rainy day and we couldn't play outside.*

**raise** /rayz/
- *verb*

**1** to move something to a higher position: *She raised her hand to get the teacher's attention.*
( SYNONYM: **lift** ) ( ANTONYM: **lower** )

**2** to increase something: *The supermarket has raised the price of this bread from $1.10 to $1.30.* ( ANTONYM: **lower** )

**3** to take care of children, animals, or crops until they are grown: *She was raised by her grandparents. | My aunt raises horses and cattle on her farm.*

**4** to collect money to help people: *The class raised $400 for charity by washing cars.*

**5** to begin to talk or write about something that you want people to think about: *The students raised several interesting questions during the discussion.*

- *noun*

an increase in the money you earn: *She asked her boss for a raise.*

**rai·sin** /**rayz**-uhn/ *noun*
a dried grape: *The cookies have raisins in them.*

raisin

**rake** /rayk/
- *noun* a garden tool that you use for gathering dead leaves together or for making the soil level: *I used the rake to sweep up the leaves off on the grass.*
- *verb* to use a rake to gather dead leaves together or to make the soil level: *He is raking the lawn because it is covered with leaves.*

rake

rake

**ral·ly** /**ral**-ee/
- *noun* (plural **rallies**)

**1** a large public meeting to support a political idea or a sports team: *The students are holding a big rally to protest against the war.*

**2** a car race on public roads

- *verb* (**rallies, rallying, rallied**)
to come together to support someone or something: *Many politicians rallied around the president and said they supported what he was doing.*

**ram** /ram/
- *verb* (**ramming, rammed**) to hit something with a lot of force: *The driver lost control of his truck and rammed into a tree.*
- *noun* a male sheep

**Ram·a·dan** /**rahm**-uh-dahn/ *noun* a month each year when Muslims do not eat or drink between sunrise and sunset. They pray and give special attention to God: *The holy month of Ramadan is a time of great religious importance to Muslims all over the world.*

**ramp** /ramp/ *noun*

**1** a road for driving onto or off a main road: *There was a line of cars on the exit ramp.*

**2** a slope that connects two levels of a building: *There are three steps up to the front door and a ramp for wheelchair users.*

ramp

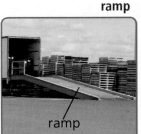

ramp

**ran** /ran/ *verb* the past tense of run

**ranch** /ranch/ *noun* a large farm with cows, horses, or sheep: *My uncle owns a ranch and raises cattle.*

—**rancher** /**ranch**-ur/ *noun* someone who owns or works on a ranch: *Ed likes being outdoors and he wants to become a cattle rancher.*

**Word Origin: ranch**

**Ranch** comes from the Spanish word *rancho*. Ranchos were large farms for raising cows and sheep. The Spanish and Mexican governments gave ranchos to people to get them to settle in California. When Americans in the West started raising cows, horses, and sheep on large farms, they made the word rancho shorter, and called the farm "ranch."

**ranch·o** /**ranch**-oh/ *noun* a ranch

a
b
c
d
e
f
g
h
i
j
k
l
m
n
o
p
q
r
s
t
u
v
w
x
y
z

**ran·dom** /**rand**-uhm/ *adjective* without any plan or pattern: *The books were arranged in a random order so it was difficult to find what I wanted.*
—**randomly** /**rand**-uhm-lee/ *adverb* in a random way: *You can scatter the seeds randomly – you don't need to plant them in rows.*

**rang** /rang/ *verb* the past tense of **ring**

**range** /raynj/
● *noun*
**1** a variety of things of the same type: *We have a wide range of ice cream – there are about 20 flavors to choose from.*
**2** the numbers between two limits: *In elementary school, the age range is 5 to 11.*
**3** a line of mountains or hills: *The Andes is a big mountain range in South America.*
**4** the distance that something can reach or travel: *The city is safe because it is outside the range of enemy missiles.*
**5** an area where you can practice shooting: *I learned to shoot at a rifle range.*
● *verb*
**1** to include the numbers or amounts you say, and others between them: *Tickets range from $23 to $36.*
**2** to wander over a large area: *In past centuries, bison ranged freely across the state.*

**rang·er** /**raynj**-ur/ *noun* someone whose job is to take care of a forest or park: *He's a Yellowstone park ranger.*

**rank** /rangk/
● *noun* a position or level in an organization: *In the army, he reached the rank of major.*
● *verb* to have a position in a list that shows how good you are: *The team ranks 13th in the nation this year.*

**ran·som** /**ranss**-uhm/ *noun* money paid to criminals who are keeping someone prisoner. The criminals agree to let that person go when they get the ransom: *The kidnappers want a $200,000 ransom for the businessman.*

**rap** /rap/
● *noun* a type of popular music. You speak the words very quickly rather than sing them: *Loud rap music was coming from the car stereo.*
● *verb* (**rapping**, **rapped**) to knock on something quickly several times: *Someone rapped on the door so he went to open it.*
—**rapper** /**rap**-ur/ *noun* someone who speaks the words in rap songs

**rap·id** /**rap**-id/
● *adjective* very quick: *Katy's making rapid progress at the piano – she's already playing simple songs.* (SYNONYM: **fast**) (ANTONYM: **slow**)
—**rapidly** /**rap**-id-lee/ *adverb* very quickly: *The disease can spread rapidly.*
● *plural noun* **rapids** a place in a river where the water is moving very fast: *The rapids are dangerous for canoes because the water is flowing very fast and there are a lot of rocks.*

**rap·tor** /**rapt**-ur/ *noun*
**1** a type of dinosaur. Raptors moved fast on two feet, had long stiff tails, and ate other animals.
**2** a bird, such as an eagle, that kills other birds and animals for food

**rare** /rair/ *adjective*
**1** not happening often: *He was a calm person and it was rare for him to get angry.*
(ANTONYM: **frequent**)
**2** if something is rare, there are very few of them in the world: *The plant is very rare and it only grows in a few small areas of the United States.*
(ANTONYM: **common**)
**3** rare meat is only cooked for a short time: *I like a rare steak that's still pink in the middle.*

**rare·ly** /**rair**-lee/ *adverb* not often: *It rarely snows in Texas – a lot of kids have never seen snow.* (ANTONYM: **frequently**)

**rash** /rash/
● *noun* an area of red spots on your skin: *If you have a fever and a rash, it could be a disease such as measles.*
● *adjective* done too quickly and without thinking carefully: *Don't make any rash decisions that you will regret later.*

**rasp·ber·ry**
/**raz**-berr-ee/ *noun*
(plural **raspberries**) a soft sweet red berry. It is the fruit of a raspberry bush.

**raspberry**

**rat** /rat/ *noun* an animal like a large mouse with a long tail

a b c d e f g h i j k l m n o p q **r** s t u v w x y z

**rate** /rayt/

● *noun*

**1** the speed at which something happens: *Kids between 8–13 grow at a very fast rate, so they are always needing new clothes.*

**2** the number of times that something happens: *New drugs have reduced the death rate from the disease.*

**3** the amount of money that someone charges for something: *$20 is the usual rate for a haircut.*

● *verb*

to decide how good, bad, or important something or someone is when compared to others: *He was rated the best player on the team.*

**rath·er** /**rath**-ur/ *adverb*

**1** a little: *Shelley was rather hungry so she bought a sandwich.* ( SYNONYM: **fairly** )

**2** instead of: *I chose to learn the trumpet rather than the saxophone.*

**3** used when correcting something you've just said: *My brother's six years old, or rather he's nearly six.*

> IDIOM with **rather**
> **would rather** if you would rather do or have something, you would prefer it: *I'd rather have ice cream than fruit.*

**ra·ti·o** /**raysh**-ee-oh/ *noun* (plural **ratios**) a relationship between two amounts. You use two numbers to show the difference between the amounts: *There are 30 boys and 10 girls, so the ratio of boys to girls is 3:1.*

**ra·tion** /**rash**-uhn/

● *noun* a limited amount of something that you are allowed to have: *Each family is given a ration of food, and they have to make it last for a week.*

● *verb* to limit the amount of something that people are allowed to have: *There was not enough gasoline, and so it was rationed.*

**ra·tion·al** /**rash**-uhn-uhl/ *adjective* based on sensible ideas and not feelings: *I know that being afraid of tiny spiders is not rational.*

( ANTONYM: **irrational** )

—**rationally** /**rash**-uhn-uhl-ee/ *adverb* in a rational way: *Luke was shocked and he couldn't think rationally.*

**rat·tle** /**rat**'l/

● *verb*

**1** to shake and make a knocking sound: *The*

strong wind made the windows rattle.

**2 rattle off** to say something very quickly, especially something you have learned and remembered: *I was impressed by the way he could rattle off all the teams' scores.*

● *noun*

**1** a baby's toy that makes a noise when you shake it

**2** the noise made by things knocking against each other: *I can hear the rattle of cups – I think Mom is bringing us a drink.* ▶ see picture on page **A16**

**rat·tle·snake** /**rat**'l-snayk/ *noun* a poisonous American snake that makes a noise like a rattle with its tail

rattlesnake

**ra·ven** /**rayv**-uhn/ *noun* a large shiny black bird with a black beak and a loud cry

raven

**ra·vine** /ruh-**veen**/ *noun* a deep narrow valley with steep sides: *There's a stream at the bottom of the ravine.*

**raw** /ro/ *adjective* raw food has not been cooked: *In Japan, people sometimes eat fish raw, without cooking it.*

raw

cooked

**raw ma·te·ri·als** /ro muh-**teer**-ee-uhlz/ *noun* substances such as coal, oil, or iron that are in their natural state, before they are changed so that they can be used

raw

**ray** /ray/ *noun*

**1** a narrow beam of light from the Sun or a lamp: *A ray of sunshine is coming down through the trees.*
**2** a large flat ocean fish. It has wide fins that look like wings, and a long pointed tail.

ray

ray

**3** a small amount of something: *There is a small ray of hope, and scientists believe that they will find a cure for the disease one day soon.*

**ray·on** /**ray**-ahn/ *noun* a smooth artificial cloth used for making clothes: *This skirt is made from rayon.*

**ra·zor** /**rayz**-ur/ *noun* a sharp tool for removing hair from your face or body: *He shaved off his beard with a razor.* ▶ see picture at **shave**

**Rd.** the written abbreviation of **road**. You can use it when you are writing someone's address: *My address is 223, Branch Rd.*

**re-** /ree/

## Word Building

**re-** is a prefix.
**recycle** | **reelect** | **reflect** | **remember** | **repeat** | **retreat**
**re-** means "again" or "back." If you *recycle* newspapers, you make it so that they can be used again. If people *reelect* the mayor, they elect the same mayor again. If an army *retreats*, it goes back to a safer place.

**reach** /reech/

● *verb*

**1** to arrive somewhere: *What time do you think you'll reach New York?*
**2** to be able to touch or get something by stretching out your arm: *Can you reach that jar on the top shelf? It's too high for me.*
**3** to get to a level or

reach

stage: *Tomorrow will be hot and the temperature will reach 95°.*
**4** to be able to talk to someone on the telephone: *You can reach me on my cell phone any time.*
**5** to decide something: *It took me a long time to reach a decision.*
**6** to go as far as something: *The cabinet is very big and it reaches all the way to the ceiling.*

● *noun*

**1** **out of reach** if something is out of reach, it is too far away for you to touch or get: *I stood on a ladder but the cat was still out of reach.*
**2** **within reach** if something is within reach, it is near enough for you to touch or get: *Medicines should not be kept within reach of small children.*

**re·act** /ree-**akt**/ *verb*

**1** to do something because another thing has happened: *You need to react quickly if the ball comes your way.*
**2** if a substance reacts with another substance, it changes when they are mixed: *Hydrogen reacts with sodium and forms sodium hydride.*

**re·ac·tant** /ree-**akt**-uhnt/ *noun* a substance that changes when you mix it with another substance. This happens because of a chemical reaction.

**re·ac·tion** /ree-**ak**-shuhn/ *noun*

**1** something someone does or feels because of something that happens: *I want to see Mom's reaction when I tell her I got the highest score in the class.*
**2** a chemical change that happens when you mix substances together: *If you mix baking soda and vinegar together, they start to bubble because of a chemical reaction.*

**read** /reed/ *verb* (**read** /red/)

**1** to look at words and understand them: *I'm reading a book about space travel.*
▶ see **Thesaurus**
**2** to say written words, so that other people can hear them: *Mom usually reads me a story at bedtime.*

**read·er** /**reed**-ur/ *noun*

**1** someone who reads: *Matthew's a good reader – he finishes books really quickly.*
**2** someone who reads a particular newspaper or

magazine: *The magazine's readers are girls from about 13 to 20.*

**3** a book for people who are learning to read, or learning another language: *The teacher gives us a new reader each week.*

**read·i·ly** /**red**'l-ee/ *adverb* quickly and easily: *Information is readily available on the Internet.*

**read·i·ness** /**red**-ee-niss/ *noun* the state of being ready to deal with something: *Firefighters are waiting in readiness, in case there is another big forest fire.*

**read·ing** /**reed**-ing/ *noun* looking at words and understanding them: *Reading, writing, and numbers are the first things you learn at school.*

**read·y** /**red**-ee/ *adjective*
**1** prepared: *Are you ready to go yet? | Supper's ready!* ▶ see **Thesaurus**
**2** willing: *Dad's usually ready to play baseball if I ask him to.*

**real** /reel/ *adjective*
**1** something that is real exists, and it is not imaginary: *Witches and wizards are not real – they only exist in stories.*
**2** true: *My friends call me Lisa, but my real name is Elizabeth.* ▶ see **Thesaurus**
**3** not artificial: *Her bracelet is real gold and it must be very expensive.* ( ANTONYM: **fake** )
**4** used for emphasizing something: *Clean up your room. It's a real mess!*

**real es·tate** /**reel** i-stayt/ *noun* houses or land: *He made a lot of money buying and selling real estate.*

**re·al·is·tic** /ree-uh-**list**-ik/ *adjective*
**1** accepting the facts and understanding what is possible: *Let's be realistic. We can't do that trip in one day.*
**2** showing things as they are in real life: *This model of a horse is very realistic – it looks as if it's almost alive.*
—**realistically** /ree-uh-**list**-ik-lee/ *adverb* in a realistic way: *Realistically, I know I'm not good at singing but I still enjoy it.*

**re·al·i·ty** /ree-**al**-uht-ee/ *noun* (plural **realities**) the true situation, not what you imagine or would like: *Our team has a small chance of winning, but the reality is that we might lose.*

**re·al·i·za·tion** /ree-uhl-uh-**zaysh**-uhn/ *noun* the

process of understanding that something is true, when you did not know it before: *There was a sudden realization in my mind that the store would be closed by now.*

**re·al·ize** /**ree**-uh-līz/ *verb*
**1** to know or understand something that you did not know before: *I thought for a few minutes and then I realized what the answer was.*
**2** to achieve something that you want: *When he grew up, Nicolas realized his dream of becoming an actor.*

**real·ly** /**reel**-ee/ *adverb*
**1** very or very much: *I think Craig's really nice. | My stomach really hurts.*
**2** definitely: *They really are the best team. | Are you really sure that you are OK?*

**realm** /relm/ *noun*
**1** an area of knowledge, experience, or thought: *In the realm of science, new discoveries are always being made*
**2** a country ruled by a king or queen

**real num·ber** /reel **nuhm**-bur/ *noun* any number that is not the square root of a negative number

**Real·tor** /**reel**-tur/ *noun trademark* someone whose job is to sell houses and land

**rear** /reer/
• *noun*
**1** the back part of something: *The rear of the car was damaged when he reversed into a tree.*
**2** the part of your body that you sit on: *She kicked him in the rear.* ( SYNONYM: **bottom** )
• *adjective*
relating to the back of something: *They just ran out the rear door into the yard.* ( ANTONYM: **front** )

**re·ar·range** /ree-uh-**raynj**/ *verb*
**1** to put things in a different place: *If we rearrange the furniture, we can fit another chair in here.*
**2** to change the time or day when something will happen: *Mom had to rearrange my doctor's appointment so it's tomorrow instead of today.*

**rear·view mir·ror** /reer-vyoo **mirr**-ur/ *noun* the mirror in a car that you use to see what is behind you

a b c d e f g h i j k l m n o p q **r** s t u v w x y z

**rea·son** /**reez**-uhn/
- *noun*

**1** a fact that explains why something happens, or why you do something: *The reason he was late was that he missed the bus.* ► see Thesaurus
**2** something that makes it right or fair to do something: *There is reason to believe that he is not telling the truth.*
**3** the ability to think in a clear logical way and make sensible decisions: *Your argument should be based on reason, not just on your feelings.*
- *verb*

**1** to decide that something is true by thinking about the facts: *I reasoned that if I told my parents now, it would save a lot of trouble later.*
**2 reason with** to try to persuade someone to be more sensible: *You can't reason with him when he's angry – he won't listen to you.*

**rea·son·a·ble** /**reez**-uhn-uhb-uhl/ *adjective*
**1** fair and sensible: *Let's share the cost. Is that reasonable? | Chris will understand. He's very reasonable.*
**2** not too much: *$12 is a reasonable price.*

**rea·son·a·bly** /**reez**-uhn-uhb-lee/ *adverb*
**1** fairly but not very: *I did reasonably well on the test – I got a B.* (SYNONYM: **fairly**)
**2** in a way that is fair and sensible: *If you don't agree, let's talk about it reasonably and find an answer.*

**rea·son·ing** /**reez**-uhn-ing/ *noun* the ability to think very carefully and find answers to problems: *The questions are designed to test the student's reasoning.*

**re·as·sure** /ree-uh-**shoor**/ *verb* to make someone feel less worried: *The bus was late so I called mom and dad to reassure them that I was fine.*
—**reassurance** /ree-uh-**shoor**-uhnss/ *noun* things you say or do to make someone feel less worried: *Children need plenty of reassurance that they are doing well at school.*

**reb·el**
- *noun* /**reb**-uhl/ someone who fights against a leader or government: *The rebels entered the city and attacked government buildings.*
- *verb* /ri-**bel**/ (**rebelling**, **rebelled**) to disobey or argue with someone who has authority: *Teenagers have their own ideas and sometimes they rebel against their parents.*

**re·bel·lion** /ri-**bel**-yuhn/ *noun* an attempt to remove a government or leader by using violence: *The army moved in to stop the rebellion.*

**re·bel·lious** /ri-**bel**-yuhss/ *adjective* refusing to do what your parents, teachers, etc. tell you to do: *At 15, Anne is becoming rebellious and she never does what her parents ask her to do.*

**re·call** /ri-**kol**/ *verb* to remember something: *We stayed there a long time ago and I don't recall the name of the hotel.*

**re·ceipt** /ri-**seet**/ *noun* a piece of paper that shows you have paid for something: *When you buy something, you should keep the receipt in case you want to take back what you bought.*

**re·ceive** /ri-**seev**/ *verb* to get or be given something: *Naomi received a prize for writing the best story.* (SYNONYM: **get**)

**re·ceiv·er** /ri-**seev**-ur/ *noun*
**1** the part of a telephone that you hold next to your mouth and ear: *The phone was ringing, so he picked up the receiver and said "Hello?"*
**2** a piece of equipment that receives radio or television signals. The receiver changes the signals into sounds or pictures: *Satellite receivers receive television programs from satellites in space.*

**re·cent** /**reess**-uhnt/ *adjective* happening or done a short time ago: *You'll need a recent photograph in order to get a passport.*

**re·cent·ly** /**reess**-uhnt-lee/ *adverb* not long ago: *The school recently got a new principal but she hasn't changed anything yet.* ► see Thesaurus

**re·cep·tion** /ri-**sep**-shuhn/ *noun*
**1** a big formal party: *Around 100 people were at their wedding reception.*
**2** the place where visitors to a hotel or business go first: *We checked into the hotel at the reception desk and they took our bags up to our room.*
**3** the quality of radio, television, or other electronic signals, which affects the sounds or pictures: *The reception is very bad and my cell phone doesn't work.*

**re·cep·tion·ist** /ri-**sep**-shuhn-ist/ *noun* someone whose job is to welcome people when they arrive at a hotel or an office: *The hotel receptionist gave us the keys to our rooms.*

**re·cess** /**reess**-ess/ *noun*
**1** a time in the school day when children go outside to play: *Normally Tony plays with Sam at recess.*
**2** a time in the year when a government or law court does not work: *Congress returns from its Christmas recess next week.*

**Word Origin:** recess

Recess comes from a Latin word that means "to go back." The members of the British government used to go back to their private rooms to take a break from discussing government business. By the 1600s, recess started to mean "the time when you take a break," rather than "to go back." Schools use the word recess because it is a time when children take a break from their work.

**re·ces·sion** /ri-**sesh**-uhn/ *noun* a time when businesses are not very successful: *During the recession, a lot of people lost their jobs.*

**rec·i·pe** /**ress**-uhp-ee/ *noun* the instructions for how to cook something: *Do you have a recipe for apple pie? I'd like to try and make one.*

**re·cip·ro·cal** /ri-**sip**-ruhk-uhl/ *noun* a number that produces the answer 1 when you use it to multiply another number: *The reciprocal of 2 is ½ because 2 x ½ = 1.*

**re·cite** /ri-**sīt**/ *verb* to say aloud something you have learned, without reading it: *He recited the poem in front of the whole school, and he didn't make any mistakes.*

**reck·less** /**rek**-liss/ *adjective* doing things in a careless and dangerous way: *Reckless driving causes a lot of accidents.*
—**recklessness** /**rek**-liss-niss/ *noun* careless and dangerous behavior: *I worry about his recklessness – he doesn't look before he crosses the road.*

**re·claim** /ri-**klaym**/ *verb*
**1** to ask for something to be given back to you: *You can reclaim the money that you paid for the tickets.*
**2** to make land able to be used for farming or building when it could not be used before: *The land for the airport was reclaimed from the ocean.*

**rec·la·ma·tion** /rek-luh-**maysh**-uhn/ *noun* the process of making land suitable for farming or building: *Land reclamation work is taking place so that they can build a new airport next to the ocean.*

**rec·og·ni·tion** /rek-uhg-**nish**-uhn/ *noun*
**1** the ability to know who someone is, when you see that person: *The actress was wearing dark glasses to try and avoid recognition.*
**2** public praise for what someone has done: *He was given the medal in recognition of his bravery.*

**rec·og·nize** /**rek**-uhg-nīz/ *verb*
**1** to know someone when you see him or her: *I didn't recognize Emma because she's grown up a lot.*
**2** to know a sound, smell, or taste because you have heard, smelled, or tasted it before: *I picked up the phone and I recognized my cousin's voice immediately.*
**3** to realize that something is true: *Everyone recognizes that Matt has a real talent for baseball.*
—**recognizable** /rek-uhg-**nīz**-uhb-uhl/ *adjective* easy to recognize: *Lemon has a very strong and recognizable smell.*

**rec·ol·lect** /rek-uh-lekt/ *verb* to remember something: *I cannot recollect his name.*
—**recollection** /rek-uh-**lek**-shuhn/ *noun* something that you remember

**rec·om·mend** /rek-uh-**mend**/ *verb*
**1** to advise something: *My piano teacher recommends that I practice for half an hour each day.*
**2** to say that you think something is good: *One of my friends recommended the movie to me and I went to see it.*

**rec·om·men·da·tion** /rek-uhm-uhn-**daysh**-uhn/ *noun* a statement saying that someone should do or get something because it is good: *I decided to buy the computer game because of a recommendation from a friend – he said that it was really good.*

**re·con·sid·er** /ree-kuhn-**sid**-ur/ *verb* to think again about your decision or opinion in order to decide if you should change it: *The referee said the ball did not cross the line, but then he reconsidered his decision and allowed the goal.*

a
b
c
d
e
f
g
h
i
j
k
l
m
n
o
p
q
**r**
s
t
u
v
w
x
y
z

## re·cord

● *noun* /**rek**-urd/

**1** information about something that is written down or stored on a computer: *In our science class, we keep a record of what happens in our experiments.*

**2** the best result that anyone has ever achieved: *Usain Bolt holds the world record for the 100 meters and he is the fastest runner in the world.*

**3** a round flat piece of black plastic that music is stored on: *You can still buy old records, but most people listen to music on CDs or computers now.*

**4** the facts about how good or bad something or someone has been in the past: *Nathan has a good attendance record at school – he hasn't missed any days this year.*

● *verb* /ri-**kord**/

**1** to write down information or store it on a computer: *Mom told me to check how much I spend by recording it in a notebook.*

**2** to store music, sound, or pictures on tape or disks: *Press this button if you want to record a program and watch it later.*

## re·cord·er /ri-**kord**-ur/ noun

**1** another word for a tape recorder

**2** a musical instrument made of wood or plastic that you play by blowing. You cover holes with your fingers to make different notes.

recorder

## re·cord·ing /ri-**kord**-ing/ *noun* sounds or pictures that are recorded on a tape or disk: *The class sang a song and made a recording of it to give to their parents.*

## re·cov·er /ri-**kuhv**-ur/ *verb*

**1** to get better after an illness or injury: *Stay at home until you have fully recovered from the flu.*

**2** to get back something that you lost or that someone stole: *The paintings were stolen from the museum and they were never recovered.*

## re·cov·er·y /ri-**kuhv**-uhr-ee/ *noun* your recovery from an illness or injury is when you get better from it: *She injured her knee and the doctor said her recovery could take three to four weeks.*

## rec·re·a·tion /rek-ree-**aysh**-uhn/ *noun* things that you do for fun: *There are lots of recreation activities at summer camp, and you can play games and go swimming in the lake.*

## re·cruit /ri-**kroot**/

● *verb* to find new people to join an organization or company: *We recruited 15 parents to help at the school fair.*

● *noun* someone who has recently joined an organization or company: *The new army recruits do training exercises to improve their fitness.*

## rec·tan·gle

/**rek**-tang-guhl/ *noun* a shape with four straight sides. Two of the sides are longer than the other two. A rectangle has four angles of 90 degrees.

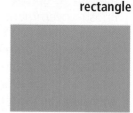
rectangle

## rec·tan·gu·lar

/rek-**tang**-gyuhl-ur/ *adjective* in the shape of a rectangle: *Draw a rectangular shape, 6 cm wide and 4 cm high.*

## rec·tan·gu·lar prism

/rek-tang-gyuhl-ur **priz**-uhm/ *noun* a solid shape or object with six sides that are rectangles

rectangular prism

## rec·tan·gu·lar pyr·a·mid

/rek-tang-gyuhl-ur **pirr**-uh-mid/ *noun* a solid shape with a base that is a rectangle. A rectangular pyramid has four triangular sides that meet in a point at the top.

## re·cy·cle /ree-**sīk**-uhl/

*verb* to put old paper, glass, or other materials through a special process so that they can be used again: *We keep all our old newspapers so that they can be recycled and used for making new paper.*

recycle

He is recycling the trash.

—**recycled** /ree-**sīk**-uhld/ *adjective* recycled objects or materials have been put through a process and used again: *The bags are made from 100% recycled cotton.*

**re·cy·cling** /ree-**sīk**-ling/ *noun* the system of putting things through a special process so they can be used again: *Recycling is important because we waste less and this helps to protect the environment.*

**red** /red/ *noun, adjective*
**1** the color of blood: *The sky is sometimes red when the sun goes down. | Her face is bright red because she is embarrassed.*
**2** red hair is an orange-brown color: *He has red hair and pale skin.*

**red·coat** /**red**-koht/ *noun* a British soldier in the wars of the 1700s and 1800s. The soldiers wore bright red coats.

**red-hand·ed** /red **hand**-id/ *adjective* if you catch someone red-handed, you see him or her doing something bad: *The boy was caught red-handed stealing from the store.*

**re·do** /ree-**doo**/ *verb* (**redoes** /ree-**duhz**/, **redid** /ree-**did**/, **redone** /ree-**duhn**/) to do something again: *I got questions 4 and 5 wrong and I had to redo them.*

**re·duce** /ri-**dooss**/ *verb* to make something less or smaller: *The school plans to reduce the number of children in the class from 25 to 20.*
▶ see Thesaurus
—**reduction** /ri-**duhk**-shuhn/ *noun* if there is a reduction, the amount of something becomes less or smaller: *There has been a big reduction in the number of accidents on the roads.*

**red·wood** /**red**-wud/ *noun* a very tall tree that grows in forests next to the coast of northern California and southern Oregon. Redwoods can be over 100 meters tall and live for over 2,000 years: *There are ancient redwood forests along the Pacific Coast.*
( SYNONYM: **sequoia** )

redwood

**reed** /reed/ *noun*
**1** a tall plant that looks like grass and grows near water
**2** a thin piece of wood on a musical instrument such as a saxophone, oboe, or clarinet that you blow over. The reed vibrates when you blow and makes a sound.

**reef** /reef/ *noun* a long line of sharp rocks, coral, or sand close to the surface of the ocean: *There is a coral reef around the island where you can see some amazing fish.*

**re·e·lect** /ree-uh-**lekt**/ *verb* to choose the same person again to do a job, by voting: *The president is very popular and he is sure to be reelected.*

**ref** /ref/ *noun* short for "referee"

**re·fer** /ri-**fur**/ *verb* (**referring, referred**)
**1** to mention someone or something: *He referred to the subject of world peace several times in his speech.*
**2** to look at a book or map in order to get information: *If you are not sure what a word means, you should refer to a dictionary.*

**ref·er·ee** /ref-uh-**ree**/ *noun* someone who makes sure that players obey the rules in sports such as football, basketball, and boxing: *The referee called a foul.*

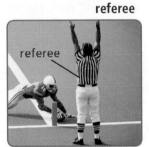
referee

**ref·er·ence** /**ref**-ruhnss/ *noun*
**1** if you use a book or map for reference, you use it for finding information: *There are plenty of encyclopedias in the library that you can use for reference.*
**2** something you say or write that mentions another person or thing: *He made no reference to my new haircut and I don't think he noticed it.*
**3** someone who knows you and can say what your character and abilities are: *You should list three references when you apply for the job.*

**ref·er·ence book** /**ref**-ruhnss buk/ *noun* a book that you look at to find information: *Dictionaries and encyclopedias are reference books.*

**re·fill**
● *verb* /ree-**fil**/ to fill something again: *I drank all the water and refilled the bottle.*
● *noun* /**ree**-fil/ another drink to fill your cup or glass again: *Patty finished her lemonade and asked for a refill.*

**re·fine** /ri-**fīn**/ *verb* to remove things from a substance such as oil or sugar by using an industrial process: *After it comes out of the ground, the oil is refined and turned into gasoline.*

**re·fined** /ri-**fīnd**/ *adjective* a refined product such as oil or sugar has had things removed from it by an industrial process: *Refined sugar is not very good for you because it contains almost no vitamins or minerals.*

**re·fin·er·y** /ri-**fīn**-uhr-ee/ *noun* (plural **refineries**) a factory where things are removed from substances such as oil or sugar: *An oil refinery turns crude oil into a whole range of useful substances.*

**re·flect** /ri-**flekt**/ *verb*
**1** to show the image of something in a mirror or in water: *The trees are reflected in the clear water of the river.*
**2** to send back the light, heat, or sound that reaches a surface: *The tiles behind the stove are designed to reflect the heat, so that the wall does not become too hot.*
**3** to be a sign of something: *Your good grade reflects how hard you have worked.*
**4** to think carefully: *I reflected on his advice and decided he was right.*

**re·flec·tion**
/ri-**flek**-shuhn/ *noun*
**1** the image that you see when you look in a mirror, glass, or water: *When I looked at my reflection in the mirror, I was surprised by how tired I looked.*

**reflection**

**2** the process of thinking carefully about something: *After some reflection, I felt sorry for what I had done.*
**3** a sign of what something is really like: *Their behavior is a bad reflection on the school.*
**4** the process of light, heat, or sound being sent back from a surface after hitting it

**re·form** /ri-**form**/
● *verb* to change a law, system, or organization in order to make it better: *He wants to reform the education system, so that more people can go to college.*
● *noun* a change that improves a law, system,

or organization: *The reforms will make it easier for people to vote.*

**re·fresh** /ri-**fresh**/ *verb* to make someone feel less tired or hot: *Have a cool drink – it will refresh you.*
—**refreshed** /ri-**fresht**/ *adjective* less tired or hot: *Suzy woke up in the morning feeling refreshed.*

**re·fresh·ing** /ri-**fresh**-ing/ *adjective*
**1** making you feel less tired or less hot: *It is very hot, so we are going for a refreshing swim in the pool.*
**2** different from usual, in a good way: *After living in the city, it is a refreshing change to be in the country.*

**re·fresh·ments** /ri-**fresh**-muhntss/ *plural noun* food and drinks that you get at a meeting, show, sports game, etc.: *Refreshments will be available during the day on the sports field.*

**re·frig·er·ate** /ri-**frij**-uh-rayt/ *verb* to put food into a refrigerator to keep it cold and fresh: *Always refrigerate meat until you are ready to cook it.*
—**refrigeration** /ri-frij-uh-**raysh**-uhn/ *noun* the state or process of refrigerating something: *The milk is treated so that it does not need refrigeration.*

**re·frig·er·a·tor** /ri-**frij**-uh-rayt-ur/ *noun* a piece of kitchen equipment that you put food in to keep it cold and fresh: *The milk is in the refrigerator.* ( SYNONYM: **fridge** )

**ref·uge** /**ref**-yooj/ *noun*
**1** a place where you feel safe: *For most children, home is a refuge from the world outside.*
**2** a place that provides protection for animals and birds: *You can see the birds at the wildlife refuge in Montana.*

> **IDIOM with refuge**
> **take refuge** to go somewhere to be safe from bad weather or danger: *When the storm started, we took refuge in a cave.*

**ref·u·gee** /ref-yu-**jee**/ *noun* someone who leaves his or her country because it is dangerous to be there: *Many people came to the U.S. as refugees from countries where there was a war or the people were very poor.*

**re·fund**
● *verb* /ri-**fuhnd**/ to give money back to the

person who paid it: *If you have any problems with the watch, bring it back and we will refund the money that you paid for it.*
● *noun* /ree-fuhnd/ if you get a refund, you get back the money that you paid for something: *He took the sweater back to the store and asked for a refund because it had a hole in it.*

**re·fus·al** /ri-**fyooz**-uhl/ *noun* a statement saying that you will not do something or will not allow something: *My sister was upset by Dad's refusal to let her go to the party.*

**re·fuse**
● *verb* /ri-**fyooz**/ to say that you will not do something or will not allow something: *I asked him to help me, but he refused and said he was busy.* ( ANTONYM: **agree** )
● *noun* /**ref**-yooss/ things that people throw away, such as old food and paper: *On Wednesday, the truck comes along the street collecting refuse.* ( SYNONYM: **garbage** )

**re·gard** /ri-**gard**/
● *verb*
**1** to have an opinion about someone: *People regard her as very intelligent.*
**2** to look at someone or something: *I said what I thought and he regarded me with amusement.*
● *noun*
**1** respect for someone or something: *The students have a high regard for their teachers and think they are really good.*
**2 regards** good wishes: *Give my regards to your parents.*

⌐ IDIOM with **regard**
**with regard to** used for saying what you are writing or talking about: *I am writing to you with regard to your son's behavior at school.*
( SYNONYM: **regarding** )

**re·gard·ing** /ri-**gard**-ing/ *preposition* used for saying what you are writing or talking about: *There will be a meeting on May 23 regarding the class trip in June.* ( SYNONYM: **about** )

**re·gard·less** /ri-**gard**-liss/ *adverb* without being affected or influenced by something: *We decided to go to the beach regardless of the bad weather.*

**re·gime** /ray-**zheem**/ *noun* a government, especially a strict or unfair one that was not

elected: *The regime put many people in prison and refused to allow any demonstrations.*

**reg·i·ment** /**rej**-uh-muhnt/ *noun* a large group of soldiers in an army

**re·gion** /**reej**-uhn/ *noun* a large part of a country: *This region of the country has a lot of mountains and it gets very cold in the winter.*
—**regional** /**reej**-uhn'l/ *adjective* relating to a region: *a regional competition*

**reg·is·ter** /**rej**-uhst-ur/
● *noun*
**1** an official list or record of something: *Voters are listed on the register, and they must sign it before they vote.*
**2** a machine in a store that shows how much you must pay, and is used to keep the money in: *The robbers took all the money from the register and ran out of the door.* ( SYNONYM: **cash register** )
● *verb*
**1** to put a name or details on an official list: *700 new students registered at the school.*
**2** if an instrument registers an amount, it shows that amount: *The thermometer registered 74°F.*

**reg·is·tered nurse** /**rej**-uhst-urd **nurss**/ *noun*
( ABBREVIATION: **R.N.** ) a nurse who has a college degree and has worked in a hospital as part of the training

**reg·is·tra·tion** /rej-uh-**straysh**-uhn/ *noun*
**1** the act of putting names or details on an official list: *Registration for elementary school will take place between April 2 and April 6.*
**2** a piece of paper that shows you have registered something on an official list: *The police officer wanted to see his car registration.*

**re·gret** /ri-**gret**/
● *verb* (**regretting**, **regretted**) to wish that you had not done something: *Dan started crying, and I regretted the unkind things I had said.*
● *noun* sadness you feel because you wish you had not done something

**re·group** /ree-**groop**/ *verb* to form new groups, or to form a group again: *Both teams have regrouped, with a number of new players.*

a b c d e f g h i j k l m n o p q **r** s t u v w x y z

**reg·u·lar** /**reg**-yuhl-ur/ *adjective*
**1** always happening at the same time: *Children need regular meals each day.* ( ANTONYM: **irregular** )
**2** doing something often: *Mary is a regular churchgoer. She's there every Sunday.*
**3** normal or usual: *I know he's famous, but he just seems like a regular guy.*
**4** of a standard size: *"Can I get a lemonade?" "Large or regular?"*
**5** a regular verb or noun changes its form in the same way as most other verbs or nouns: *"Finish" and "play" are regular verbs because their past tenses are "finished" and "played." "Do" is not a regular verb because its past tense is "did."*
( ANTONYM: **irregular** )

**reg·u·lar·ly** /**reg**-yuhl-ur-lee/ *adverb*
**1** at the same time every day, every week, etc.: *My family goes to church regularly on Sundays.*
**2** often: *We like to see my grandparents regularly.*

**reg·u·late** /**reg**-yuh-layt/ *verb*
**1** to control something by having rules: *There are rules regulating the sale of alcohol.*
**2** to keep something at the same level: *People sweat to regulate their body heat, so they don't get too hot.*

**reg·u·la·tion** /reg-yuh-**laysh**-uhn/ *noun*
**1** an official rule: *The school regulations say what kind of clothes the students are allowed to wear.*
**2** control of something, using rules: *People want more regulation of pollution from cars and factories, in order to protect the environment.*

**re·hears·al** /ri-**hurss**-uhl/ *noun* a practice of a play or other performance before people come to see it: *There will be another rehearsal for the school play on Friday afternoon.*

**re·hearse** /ri-**hurss**/ *verb* to practice for a play or other performance before people come to see it: *You have to rehearse a lot if you are in the school band.*

**reign** /rayn/
● *noun* the time when a king or queen rules a country: *Queen Victoria's reign lasted for 63 years.*
● *verb* to be the king or queen of a country: *King Henry reigned from 1509 to 1547.*

**rein·deer** /**rayn**-deer/
*noun* (plural **reindeer**)
a large deer with antlers that look like the branches on a tree. Reindeer live in the very cold northern parts of the world.
( SYNONYM: **caribou** )

reindeer

**re·in·force**
/ree-in-**forss**/ *verb*
**1** to make a part of a building or a piece of clothing stronger: *The ceiling is reinforced with steel bars.* ( SYNONYM: **strengthen** )
**2** to make someone's idea, opinion, or attitude stronger and more definite: *When you praise children, it reinforces their good behavior.*

**reins** /raynz/ *plural noun* long pieces of leather that you hold to control a horse when you are riding: *You can stop the horse by pulling on the reins.*

**re·ject** /ri-**jekt**/ *verb* to refuse to accept something or someone: *He tried to get several jobs, but he was rejected each time.* | *I was disappointed when they rejected my suggestion.*
( ANTONYM: **accept** )

**re·jec·tion** /ri-**jek**-shuhn/ *noun* the act of saying or showing that you do not want something or someone: *The college sent her a letter of rejection because her grades weren't good enough.*

**re·late** /ri-**layt**/ *verb*
**1** if things relate to each other, there is a connection between them: *Your health relates to the type of food you eat because fresh food helps you stay healthy.*
**2** to tell someone about something that happened: *Suzy saw the accident and was able to relate what happened.*
**3** if people relate to each other, they like and understand each other: *A team plays best when its members relate to each other.*

**re·lat·ed** /ri-**layt**-id/ *adjective*
**1** if people are related, they belong to the same family: *The boys look like each other so I thought they were related.*
**2** if events or situations are related, there is a connection between them: *The disease is related to drinking dirty water.* ( SYNONYM: **connected** )

**re·lat·ed facts** /ri-layt-id **faktss**/ *plural noun* number sentences that are like each other because they add or subtract using the same numbers: *7 + 5 = 12 and 12 − 7 = 5 are related facts.*

**re·la·tion** /ri-**laysh**-uhn/ *noun*
**1** a connection between things: *There is a relation between the weather in an area and the type of plants that grow there.*
( SYNONYM: **relationship** )
**2** a member of your family: *He's Mexican, and most of his relations live in Mexico.*
( SYNONYM: **relative** )
**3 relations** the way people or countries behave toward each other: *Relations between students and teachers at the school are very good.*

**re·la·tion·ship** /ri-**laysh**-uhn-ship/ *noun*
**1** the way two people or groups feel and behave toward each other: *The brothers have a good relationship and they like spending time with each other.*
**2** the way two events or situations are connected: *There is a clear relationship between practicing a sport and playing well.*
**3** a situation in which two people love each other: *Elena and Gary have been in a relationship for more than two years now.*

**rel·a·tive** /**rel**-uht-iv/
● *noun* a member of your family: *I have five uncles and aunts, seven cousins, and a few other relatives.*
● *adjective* having a particular quality when compared with something else: *Relative to little Rhode Island, the state of California is huge.*

**rel·a·tive lo·ca·tion** /rel-uht-iv loh-**kaysh**-uhn/ *noun* the position of a place in relation to another place: *The relative location of Florida is south of Georgia.*

**rel·a·tive·ly** /**rel**-uht-iv-lee/ *adverb* when compared with something else: *Some jeans are very expensive, but these are relatively cheap.*

**re·lax** /ri-**lakss**/ *verb*
**1** to rest and not do very much: *Some evenings I just want to relax in front of the TV.*
**2** to become less worried: *Try to relax. I'm sure the test won't be so bad.*
**3** if your muscles relax, they become less tight or stiff: *The P.E. teacher told us to lie on the floor and relax all our muscles.*

**re·lax·a·tion** /ree-lak-**saysh**-uhn/ *noun* a way of resting and enjoying yourself: *I read for relaxation.*

**re·laxed** /ri-**lakst**/ *adjective* calm and not worried: *On Saturdays I always wake up feeling relaxed because there's nothing I have to do.*
( ANTONYM: **tense** )

**re·lax·ing** /ri-**lakss**-ing/ *adjective* making you feel calm and not worried: *I like listening to music because it's very relaxing.*

**re·lay** /**ree**-lay/
● *verb* to send information from one person or place to another: *Satellites can relay news all over the world as soon as something happens.*
● *noun* a race between teams. All the members of each team run or swim part of the distance: *The U.S. won a gold medal in the relay.*

**re·lease** /ri-**leess**/
● *verb*
**1** to let a person or animal go free: *I kept the mouse for a few days and then I released it in a field.*
**2** to make a movie, song, or CD available for people to buy or see: *The band's new album will be released next week.*
● *noun*
**1** the time when someone is allowed to go free: *He spent five years in jail, waiting for his release.*
**2** a new movie, song, or CD that is available for people to see or buy: *The website tells you about all the new releases this week, and which songs they think are best.*

**rel·e·vant** /**rel**-uhv-uhnt/ *adjective* something that is relevant relates to what you are discussing or doing: *Only write about things that are relevant to the subject of your essay.*
( ANTONYM: **irrelevant** )

**re·li·a·ble** /ri-**lī**-uhb-uhl/ *adjective*
**1** always doing what you say you will do: *David's a good friend and I trust him because he's very reliable.* ( SYNONYM: **dependable** )
**2** something that is reliable always works well, or comes at the right time: *The school bus is always on time – it's very reliable.*
—**reliably** /ri-**lī**-uhb-lee/ *adverb* in a reliable way: *Dad's car doesn't always start reliably so we're sometimes late.*

a
b
c
d
e
f
g
h
i
j
k
l
m
n
o
p
q
**r**
s
t
u
v
w
x
y
z

**re·lief** /ri-**leef**/ *noun*

**1** a good feeling that you have because something bad did not happen or because something bad has finished: *Our dog was lost for three days so it was a big relief when we found her again.*

**2** the reduction of pain or an unpleasant feeling: *If you have a bad headache, one of these pills is good for pain relief.*

**3** food, clothes, and money that organizations give to people who are suffering because of a flood, earthquake, war, etc.: *The Red Cross is an organization that brings relief to people who have lost their homes or have no food.*

**re·lieve** /ri-**leev**/ *verb*

**1** to make pain or a problem less bad: *She hurt her back, and takes pills to relieve the pain.*

**2** to do a duty that someone else has been doing: *Another guard will come at 12 o'clock to relieve this guard.*

**re·lieved** /ri-**leevd**/ *adjective* happy and less worried than before: *I'll be relieved when the tests are over.*

**re·li·gion** /ri-**lij**-uhn/ *noun*

**1** a set of beliefs about God or gods: *Christianity, Islam, Judaism, Hinduism, and Buddhism are all important religions.*

**2** belief in God or gods: *My family goes to church because religion is important to us.*

**re·li·gious** /ri-**lij**-uhss/ *adjective*

**1** relating to religion: *Christmas is a religious holiday to celebrate Jesus Christ's birth.*

**2** believing in God or gods and obeying the rules of a religion: *She's very religious and she prays every day.*

**re·luc·tant** /ri-**luhkt**-uhnt/ *adjective* not wanting to do something: *I was reluctant to tell Mom what had happened because I knew she would be angry.* (ANTONYM: **eager**)

—**reluctantly** /ri-**luhkt**-uhnt-lee/ *adverb* in a reluctant way: *Joshua reluctantly went upstairs to bed.*

—**reluctance** /ri-**luhkt**-uhnss/ *noun* the feeling of not wanting to do something: *He is very shy, and I worry about his reluctance to play with the other children.*

**re·ly** /ri-**lī**/ *verb* (**relies**, **relying**, **relied**)

**1 rely on** to need someone to help you or do something: *Young birds rely on their parents for*

food. (SYNONYM: **depend on**)

**2 can rely on** to know that someone will help you or do something: *I can always rely on Anne when I need someone to talk to.*

**Word Family:** rely

**rely** *verb* | **reliable** *adjective* | **unreliable** *adjective*

**re·main** /ri-**mayn**/ *verb*

**1** to continue being something: *They remained friends for years after going to kindergarten together.* | *Try to remain calm during the fire drill.*

**2** to stay in the same place: *He told me to remain in the car.*

**3** to still exist, after other things or parts have gone: *Not much of the building remained after it was destroyed in the earthquake.*

—**remaining** /ri-**mayn**-ing/ *adjective* still present when all the others are gone: *The remaining two teams will play each other in the finals.*

**re·main·der** /ri-**maynd**-ur/ *noun*

**1** the part of something that is still there after the other parts have gone: *Add half the milk and stir the mixture. Then add the remainder of the milk.* (SYNONYM: **rest**)

**2** the number that is left when one number cannot be divided exactly by another number: *When you divide 20 by 6, the remainder is 2 (20 ÷ 6 = 3 remainder 2).*

**re·mains** /ri-**maynz**/ *plural noun*

**1** the parts of something that are left after the rest has been destroyed or eaten: *They found the remains of an ancient city in the jungle.*

**2** the body of a dead person or animal: *His remains are buried in the graveyard.*

**re·mark** /ri-**mark**/

● *noun* something that you say about a person or thing: *He keeps making rude remarks about my clothes.* (SYNONYM: **comment**)

● *verb* to say something about a person or thing: *Mom remarked that I looked tired.*

**re·mark·a·ble** /ri-**mark**-uhb-uhl/ *adjective* very unusual or surprising, especially in a good way: *The team won the championship five times, which was a remarkable achievement.*

—**remarkably** /ri-**mark**-uhb-lee/ *adverb* in an unusual or surprising way, especially because it is good: *Steven is only eight, but he plays chess remarkably well.*

**re·mar·ry** /ree-**marr**-ee/ *verb* (**remarries, remarried**) to get married again: *My aunt never remarried after her husband died.*

**re·me·di·al** /ri-**meed**-ee-uhl/ *adjective* remedial work or classes are for students who need more help to learn something: *My math wasn't very good and so I had to go in the remedial class for a year.*

**rem·e·dy** /**rem**-uhd-ee/ *noun* (plural **remedies**)
**1** a medicine or drink that you use to make an illness better: *Mom gave me a cold remedy to help me breathe.*
**2** a successful way of dealing with a problem: *The Bears finally found the remedy for their losing streak and won their next five games.*
( SYNONYM: **cure** )

**re·mem·ber** /ri-**mem**-bur/ *verb*
**1** if you remember something, it is in your mind or comes into your mind: *I remember my first day at school.* | *He suddenly remembered where he had left his reading book.* ( ANTONYM: **forget** )
► see **Thesaurus**
**2** to not forget to do something you need to do: *Did you remember to feed the cat this morning?*
( ANTONYM: **forget** )

**re·mem·brance** /ri-**mem**-bruhnss/ *noun* the act of remembering and showing respect to someone who has died: *She planted a tree in remembrance of her grandfather.*

**re·mind** /ri-**mīnd**/ *verb*
**1** to make someone remember something: *Remind me to clean the fish tank tomorrow.*
**2** to make you think of someone or something that is like another person or thing: *Dan reminds me of a boy I used to know at my last school.*

**re·mind·er** /ri-**mīnd**-ur/ *noun* something that makes you remember something else: *The scar on his leg was a reminder of the accident.*

**rem·i·nisce** /rem-uh-**niss**/ *verb* to think or talk about nice things that happened in the past: *My grandpa was reminiscing about life on the farm and working with horses.*

**re·morse** /ri-**morss**/ *noun* a feeling that you are sorry for doing something very bad: *The thief showed no remorse at his trial.*

**re·mote** /ri-**moht**/ *adjective*
**1** far away from other places: *They went hiking in a remote mountain area, a long way from any towns or cities.*
**2** a remote chance or possibility is very unlikely to happen: *There is only a remote chance that we will be able to get tickets for the game.*

**re·mote con·trol** /ri-moht kuhn-**trohl**/ (also **remote**) *noun* a small box with buttons that you press to turn a television or a DVD player on or off, or change the sound, without touching the TV or player itself: *I found the remote control and turned up the sound on the TV.*

**re·move** /ri-**moov**/ *verb* to take something away, off, or out: *Remove the pie from the oven.* | *She removed her coat.*
► see **Thesaurus**
—**removal** /ri-**moov**-uhl/ *noun* the act of removing something: *The airport is closed until snow removal can begin.*
—**removable** /ri-**moov**-uhb-uhl/ *adjective* designed to be easy to remove: *The toy car has a removable roof.*

**Ren·ais·sance** /**ren**-uh-sanss/ *noun* the period in Europe between the 14th and 17th centuries, when there was a lot of new art and scientific progress: *Many of the greatest artists of the Renaissance lived in Italy.*

**re·new** /ri-**noo**/ *verb*
**1** to do something so that something else will continue for a longer time: *I renewed the magazine subscription so I would get it for another year.*
**2** to begin doing something again: *The police will renew their search for the missing boy in the morning.* ( SYNONYM: **resume** )

**re·new·a·ble** /ri-**noo**-uhb-uhl/ *adjective* if something is renewable, you will always be able to get more of it because it continues to be produced all the time: *We get renewable energy from the wind and the sun.*

**ren·o·vate** /**ren**-uh-vayt/ *verb* to repair something so that it is in good condition and can be used again: *They are renovating the old church and putting on a new roof.*

## rent /rent/

● *verb*

**1** to pay money to live in a place: *They rented a house for six months.*

**2** to pay money to use something for a short time: *We rented a DVD to watch on Saturday.*

**3** to get money from someone for letting them use something: *They rented the apartment to a family with two kids.*

—**renter** /**rent**-ur/ *noun* someone who pays money to live in a place: *New renters have moved into the apartment.*

● *noun*

money that you pay to live in a place or use something for a time: *She didn't have enough money to pay the rent.*

> IDIOM with **rent**
> **for rent** available to be rented: *There are lots of apartments for rent in our building.*

## rent·al /**rent**'l/

● *noun* an arrangement to rent something: *The bike rental costs $5 an hour.*

● *adjective* relating to renting something: *There is a small rental fee for using the bicycles.*

## re·paid /ree-**payd**/ *verb* the past tense and past participle of repay

## re·pair /ri-**pair**/

● *verb* to fix something that is damaged or not working: *A man came to repair the washing machine because it wasn't working properly.* SYNONYM: **fix**

▶ see Thesaurus

● *noun* something that you do to fix something: *The roof is in need of repair – it has a big hole in it.*

**repair**

She is repairing the bicycle.

## re·pair·man /ri-**pair**-man/ *noun* someone whose job is to fix things that are damaged or not working correctly: *The repairman came to fix our TV.*

## re·pay /ree-**pay**/ *verb* (**repays**, **repaying**, **repaid** /ree-**payd**/)

**1** to give money back to the person you borrowed it from: *I borrowed $5 from him, and I'll repay him next week.*

**2** to do something nice for someone who helped you: *How can I repay my parents for what they*

have done for me?

—**repayment** /ree-**pay**-muhnt/ *noun* the act of giving money back to the person you borrowed it from: *Repayment of the loan should be completed within three years.*

## re·peal /ri-**peel**/ *verb* to officially end a law

## re·peat /ri-**peet**/

● *verb*

to say or do something again: *Could you repeat what you just said?* | *Repeat the experiment, and see if you get the same result.*

● *noun*

**1** something that is exactly like something that happened before: *We lost to them last year, and we don't want a repeat.*

**2** a television program that is being shown again: *I'm sure I've seen this before; it must be a repeat.* SYNONYM: **rerun**

> **Word Family:** repeat
> **repeat** verb | **repeat** noun | **repetition** noun | **repeated** adjective | **repeatedly** adverb | **repetitive** adjective

## re·peat·ed /ri-**peet**-id/ *adjective* repeated actions are done several times: *He made repeated attempts to call her, but she never answered the phone.*

—**repeatedly** /ri-**peet**-id-lee/ *adverb* again and again: *They asked him repeatedly to leave, but he wouldn't go.*

## re·pel /ri-**pel**/ *verb* (**repelling**, **repelled**) to make something move away: *This end of the magnet will repel another magnet, so that you cannot make them stay together.*

## rep·e·ti·tion /rep-uh-**tish**-uhn/ *noun*

**1** the act of saying or doing the same thing many times: *Repetition can help you learn your multiplication tables.*

**2** something that is exactly like something that happened before: *They are afraid of a repetition of the floods that destroyed their town.*

SYNONYM: **repeat**

## re·pet·i·tive /ri-**pet**-uht-iv/ (also **rep·e·ti·tious** /rep-uh-**tish**-uhss/) *adjective* doing or saying the same thing many times: *The children kept jumping up and down, and the repetitive movement made her legs hurt.*

**re·place** /ri-**playss**/ *verb*
**1** to get or use a new thing or person instead of the one you had before: *When the TV stopped working, we replaced it with a bigger one.* | *The new teacher will replace Miss Johnson.*
**2** to put something back: *After looking at the book, he replaced it on the shelf.*

**re·place·ment** /ri-**playss**-muhnt/ *noun* a new thing or person that you use instead of the one you had before: *The coach is leaving, so we need to find a replacement for him.*

**re·play**
● *noun* /**ree**-play/ an action in a sports game that is shown again on television, usually just after it happens: *You can see on the replay that the player dropped the ball.*
● *verb* /ree-**play**/ to show an action in a game again on television: *The touchdown was replayed several times.*

**re·ply** /ri-**plī**/
● *verb* (**replies**, **replying**, **replied**) to answer: *"Can I come too?" I asked. "Yes," she replied.* | *He didn't reply to my email.*
● *noun* (plural **replies**) an answer to what someone says or writes: *I am still waiting for a reply to my letter.* | *What did she say in reply to your question?*

**re·port** /ri-**port**/
● *noun*
a written or spoken account that gives information about something: *You will each write a report on our visit to the museum.*
● *verb*
**1** to tell people about something that has happened: *The newspaper reported that the missing child had been found.*
**2** to tell the police that a crime or accident has happened: *Did you report the theft to the police?*

**re·port card** /ri-**port** kard/ *noun* a piece of paper with your grades on it, and statements from your teachers: *He had A's and B's on his report card.*

**re·port·er** /ri-**port**-ur/ *noun* someone who finds out and tells people news, in newspapers or on television or radio: *The president answered the reporters' questions.*

**rep·re·sent** /rep-ri-**zent**/ *verb*
**1** to show or mean something: *The blue line on the map represents the river.*
**2** to officially speak for someone: *He hired a lawyer to represent him in court.* | *The Congressman's job is to represent the people who voted for him.*
—**representation** /rep-ri-zen-**taysh**-uhn/ *noun* the act of representing someone or something: *The American colonies said "No taxation without representation!" This means that they did not want to pay taxes without having anyone to speak for them in the British government.*

**Word Family:** **represent**

**represent** *verb* | **representation** *noun* | **representative** *noun*

**rep·re·sent·a·tive** /rep-ri-**zent**-uht-iv/ *noun*
**1** someone who people have chosen to speak for them: *The class representatives were asked to come to the meeting.*
**2** a member of the House of Representatives in the U.S. Congress: *She is one of California's Representatives.*

**rep·ri·mand** /**rep**-ruh-mand/
● *verb* to tell someone in an angry way that he or she has done something wrong: *The teacher reprimanded him for being late.* (SYNONYM: **scold**)
● *noun* if someone gives you a reprimand, he or she tells you in an angry way that you have done something wrong: *The girl who was rude to the teacher got a reprimand from the principal.*

**re·pro·duce** /ree-pruh-**dooss**/ *verb*
**1** if animals or plants reproduce, they make more animals or plants: *People reproduce by having babies.*
**2** to make a copy of something such as a picture: *The painting of George Washington is reproduced in the history book.*

**re·pro·duc·tion** /ree-pruh-**duhk**-shuhn/ *noun*
**1** the act of producing young animals or plants of the same type. People do this by having babies, animals produce young animals or eggs, and plants produce seeds.
**2** a copy of something such as a picture: *The picture is a reproduction of a painting of Abraham Lincoln.*

a b c d e f g h i j k l m n o p q **r** s t u v w x y z

**rep·tile** /**rep**-tīl/ *noun* an animal such as a snake or lizard whose body is covered in scales. Reptiles are cold-blooded and most reptiles lay eggs containing their babies.

**reptile**

lizard

alligator

snake

crocodile

**re·pub·lic** /ri-**puhb**-lik/ *noun* a country that elects its government and does not have a king or queen: *The United States is a republic.*

**Re·pub·li·can** /ri-**puhb**-lik-uhn/
● *noun* a member of the Republican Party: *Is he a Democrat or a Republican?*
● *adjective* relating to the Republican Party: *Abraham Lincoln was the first Republican president.*

**rep·u·ta·tion** /rep-yuh-**taysh**-uhn/ *noun* the opinion that people have of someone or something: *This school has a very good reputation and many parents want to send their children here.*

**re·quest** /ri-**kwest**/
● *noun* if you make a request, you ask for something politely or formally: *She made a request for more time to write her essay.*
● *verb* to ask for something politely or formally: *The librarian requested that we be a little quieter.*

**re·quire** /ri-**kwī**-ur/ *verb*
**1** to need something: *Dogs require a lot of care. You need to feed them and take them on walks.*
**2** to say officially that someone must do something: *All students are required to take the test.*

**re·quire·ment** /ri-**kwī**-ur-muhnt/ *noun*
**1** something that you need: *The school must meet the requirements of children in wheelchairs by having ramps to the classrooms.*
**2** something that you must do or have because of a rule: *He did not meet the height requirement for the roller coaster ride, so he couldn't go on it.*

**re·run** /**ree**-ruhn/ *noun* a television program that is being shown again: *I think I've seen this before; it must be a rerun.* ( SYNONYM: **repeat** )

**res·cue** /**resk**-yoo/
● *verb* to save someone who is in danger: *He rescued two people from the wrecked car.*
—**rescuer** /**resk**-yoo-ur/ *noun* someone who rescues someone else: *The rescuer pulled him out of the freezing water.*
● *noun* the act of saving someone from danger: *He was given a medal for his rescue of the passengers on the boat.*

┌ **IDIOM with rescue**
│ **come to someone's rescue** to come and save someone from danger: *Firefighters came to the rescue of the people in the burning building.*
└

**re·search**
● *noun* /**ree**-surch/ the work of finding out facts about something, for example by doing experiments or reading books: *Scientists are doing research into the causes of cancer.*
● *verb* /ri-**surch**/ to find out facts about a subject, for example by doing experiments or reading books: *He began researching his family's history.*
—**researcher** /ri-**surch**-ur/ *noun* someone who does research: *The researchers were trying to find out if this medicine would help people with the disease.*

**re·sem·blance** /ri-**zem**-bluhnss/ *noun* if there is a resemblance between two things or people, they are like each other: *I noticed the resemblance between Jacob and his father.*

**re·sem·ble** /ri-**zem**-buhl/ *verb* to be like someone or something else: *The taste of the meat resembled chicken.*

**re·sent** /ri-**zent**/ *verb* to feel angry and upset about something unfair: *He resents having to do more chores than his brother.*
—**resentful** /ri-**zent**-fuhl/ *adjective* angry and upset about something unfair: *She was resentful that her baby sister got more attention than she did.*

**re·sent·ment** /ri-**zent**-muhnt/ *noun* a feeling of anger about something that you think is unfair:

*There is a lot of resentment toward her because she always wins.*

**res·er·va·tion** /rez-ur-**vaysh**-uhn/ *noun*
**1** if you make a reservation, you ask for something such as a seat or a room to be kept for you: *Dad made reservations at the restaurant for Saturday night.*
**2** an area of land that is kept separate for Native Americans to live on: *He was born on a Navajo reservation.*

**re·serve** /ri-**zurv**/
● *verb*
**1** to make an arrangement so that something such as a seat or a room will be kept for you to use: *We reserved seats by the window on the airplane.*
**2** to keep something for a special purpose: *This area is reserved for buses, so you can't park your car here.*
● *noun*
**1** an amount of something that you keep so that you can use it if you need to: *Keep a reserve of food and water in case there is an emergency such as an earthquake.*
**2** an area of land where wild animals and plants are protected: *Many rare animals and birds live in the reserve.*

**re·served** /ri-**zurvd**/ *adjective* not liking to talk about or show your feelings: *Her father was a reserved man, but she knew he was proud of her even if he didn't say much.*

**res·er·voir** /**rez**-ur-vwar/ *noun* a lake that people have made for storing water: *The water we use comes from a reservoir.*

**re·side** /ri-**zīd**/ *verb* to live somewhere: *She resides in New York.*

**res·i·dence** /**rez**-uhd-uhnss/ *noun* the house or other building where someone lives: *The White House is the president's residence.*

**res·i·dent** /**rez**-uhd-uhnt/ *noun* someone who lives in a place: *He has been a resident of this town for 30 years.*

**res·i·den·tial** /rez-uh-**densh**-uhl/ *adjective* a residential area or building is one where people live: *This residential neighborhood is not far from schools or stores.*

**re·sign** /ri-**zīn**/ *verb* to say officially that you are going to leave your job: *She resigned from her old job when she got another job that paid better.*

**res·ig·na·tion** /rez-ig-**naysh**-uhn/ *noun* a statement or letter in which you say that you are going to leave your job: *He handed in his resignation because he wants to go back to college.*

**re·sist** /ri-**zist**/ *verb*
**1** to stop yourself from doing or having something that you like: *I can't resist chocolate!*
**2** to not want to accept something and try to stop it: *In 1773, the Americans resisted the British taxes on tea that they thought were unfair.*

**re·sist·ance** /ri-**zist**-uhnss/ *noun*
**1** if there is resistance to something, people do not want to accept it and try to stop it: *There was resistance to the idea of school uniforms.*
**2** the quality of not being easily harmed by something: *If you eat good food and exercise, your body's resistance to illnesses gets stronger.*
**3** the way a substance slows down something that is moving through it or over it: *A feather falls slowly because of air resistance.*
**4** the ability of a substance to slow down electricity that is going through it: *Most metals have a low resistance and electricity flows through them easily.*

**res·o·lu·tion** /rez-uh-**loosh**-uhn/ *noun*
**1** a promise that you make to yourself to do something: *I made a New Year's resolution to be nicer to my sister.*
**2** the ending of a problem or argument: *We hope there will soon be a resolution to the war.*

**re·solve** /ri-**zahlv**/ *verb*
**1** to end a problem or argument: *Let's try to resolve this disagreement by talking about it.*
**2** to decide to do something difficult or important: *He resolved to work harder.*

**re·sort** /ri-**zort**/
● *noun* a place where a lot of people go for a vacation: *We went to a ski resort for our vacation.*
● *verb* **resort to** to do something extreme in order to achieve something because no other way will be successful: *When he still wouldn't stop shouting, his mother resorted to punishing him.*

a
b
c
d
e
f
g
h
i
j
k
l
m
n
o
p
q
**r**
s
t
u
v
w
x
y
z

**re·source** /**ree**-sorss/ *noun*

**1** something that people can use to do other things: *The Internet is a useful resource if you want information about something.*

**2** something that a country has, for example oil, minerals, or land, which it can use to increase its wealth: *Canada is rich in natural resources and has a lot of oil and gas.*

**re·spect** /ri-**spekt**/

● *noun*

**1** a good opinion of someone: *He is a very good teacher and I have a lot of respect for him.*

**2** a polite way of behaving toward other people: *You can show respect for older people by opening a door for them or giving them your seat on a bus.*

⎧ **IDIOM with respect**
⎪ **in many respects** in many ways: *The two boys*
⎨ *are the same in many respects. They both like*
⎪ *sports, and they both are tall.*
⎩

● *verb*

**1** to have a high opinion of someone: *She respected him for his honesty.*

**2** to behave in a polite way to other people: *Please respect the other children in the class, for example by not talking while they are talking.*

**3** if you respect a law or rule, you obey it: *When you are riding your bike, you need to respect the rules of the road.*

**re·spect·ful** /ri-**spekt**-fuhl/ *adjective* showing respect: *She is quiet and respectful toward the teacher.*

—**respectfully** /ri-**spekt**-fuhl-ee/ *adverb* in a respectful way: *He waited respectfully for her to finish talking.*

**res·pi·ra·tion** /resp-uh-**raysh**-uhn/ *noun* breathing: *When you sleep, your respiration becomes slow and regular.*

**re·spond** /ri-**spahnd**/ *verb*

**1** to answer: *When I asked her who she was, she responded in Spanish.* ( SYNONYM: **reply** )

**2** to do something because of something that has happened: *The team responded by hitting six home runs.* ( SYNONYM: **react** )

**Word Family:** respond

**respond** *verb* | **response** *noun*

**re·sponse** /ri-**spahnss**/ *noun*

**1** an answer to what someone says or writes: *She called out his name, but there was no response.* ( SYNONYM: **reply** )

**2** something you do or feel because of something that has happened: *When I heard him talk in that funny voice, my first response was to laugh.*

**re·spon·si·bil·i·ty** /ri-spahnss-uh-**bil**-uht-ee/ *noun* (plural **responsibilities**)

**1** something that you must do: *It's your responsibility to feed the rabbit.* ( SYNONYM: **duty** )

**2** blame for something bad that has happened: *The accident was John's fault, and he took full responsibility for it.*

**re·spon·si·ble** /ri-**spahnss**-uhb-uhl/ *adjective*

**1** if you are responsible for doing something, it is your job to do it: *You are responsible for making your bed every morning.*

**2** if you are responsible for doing something bad, you caused the bad thing to happen: *The person who is responsible for breaking the window will be punished.*

**3** sensible and able to be trusted: *My older sister is very responsible, so my mother lets her babysit us.*

—**responsibly** /ri-**spahnss**-uhb-lee/ *adverb* in a responsible way: *You must act responsibly on the playground, and not push or hit the other students.*

**Word Family:** responsible

**responsible** *adjective* | **responsibly** *adverb* | **responsibility** *noun*

**rest** /rest/

● *noun*

**1** the other part of a group or thing: *One of the students failed the test, but the rest passed.*

**2** a time when you relax or sleep: *We have a busy day tomorrow. You'd better get some rest.*

● *verb*

**1** to relax or sleep: *Run for ten minutes and then rest for a few minutes.*

**2** to put something on or against something that will support it: *She rested her head on a pillow.*

**res·tau·rant** /**rest**-uh-rahnt/ *noun* a place where

you can buy and eat a meal: *They had lunch at an Italian restaurant.*

**Word Origin:** restaurant

**Restaurant** comes from French. In French, restaurant originally meant "food that restores," or "food that gives you energy again." Later, restaurant started to be used more about the place that serves food than about the food itself. Restaurant started to be used in English in the 1800s.

**rest·less** /**rest**-liss/ *adjective* unable to keep still because you are bored or nervous: *The kids got restless when they were waiting for the movie to begin.*

**re·store** /ri-**stor**/ *verb*
**1** to make something be the way it was before: *The boys started yelling, but the teacher quickly stopped them and restored order.*
**2** to repair something so that it looks new again: *They bought an old house and restored it.*

**re·strain** /ri-**strayn**/ *verb* to stop someone or something from moving or from doing something: *The boy wasn't strong enough to restrain the big dog and it ran away from him.*

**re·strained** /ri-**straynd**/ *adjective* calm and controlled: *He answered in a restrained voice, but I knew he was mad.*

**re·straint** /ri-**straynt**/ *noun* calm and controlled behavior: *She was very angry, but she showed restraint and didn't yell at him.*

**re·strict** /ri-**strikt**/ *verb* to limit something or say what is allowed and what is not allowed: *Some parents restrict their children's use of computers.*
( SYNONYM: **limit** )
—**restricted** /ri-**strikt**-id/ *adjective* limited, or having rules about what is allowed: *This is a restricted area; only soldiers are allowed in.*

**Word Family:** restrict

**restrict** *verb* | **restricted** *adjective* | **restriction** *noun*

**re·stric·tion** /ri-**strik**-shuhn/ *noun* a rule that says what is allowed: *Nuts make him sick, so there are restrictions on what he can eat.*

**rest·room** /**rest**-room/ *noun* a room with a toilet, in a public building: *I need to use the restroom.*

**re·sult** /ri-**zuhlt**/
● *noun*
**1** something that happens because of something else: *He hurt his leg as a result of the accident.*
▶ see **Thesaurus**
**2** information that you get by testing or examining something: *We are waiting for the results of your blood test.*
**3** the answer you get when you add, subtract, multiply, or divide numbers: *When you multiply 4 and 7, the result is 28.*
**4** the points or votes at the end of an election, fight, or competition, that tells you who won: *The election results will be announced today.*
● *verb*
**1** to happen or exist because of something: *The fires resulted from a campfire that burned out of control.*
**2 result in** to make something happen: *Reading in bad light may result in headaches.*
( SYNONYM: **cause** )

**re·sume** /ri-**zoom**/ *verb* to start again after stopping: *We'll resume the discussion after lunch.*

**ré·su·mé** /**rez**-uh-may/ *noun* a list showing your education and the jobs you have done. You send it to employers when you are looking for a job.

**re·tail** /**ree**-tayl/
● *noun* the business of selling things to people in stores: *He works in retail.*
● *verb* **retail for/at** to sell at a specific price in a store: *The toy car retails for $30.*

**re·tail·er** /**ree**-tayl-ur/ *noun* a person or business that sells things to people in a store: *It's a clothing retailer that sells kids clothes.*

**re·tain** /ri-**tayn**/ *verb* to keep something: *Pine trees retain their leaves all year.*

**ret·i·na** /**ret**'n-uh/ *noun* the area at the back of your eye. When light reaches the retina, the retina sends information about what you are seeing to your brain.

**re·tire** /ri-**ti**-ur/ *verb* to stop working at the end of your working life: *I retired when I was 65.*

**re·tire·ment** /ri-**tī**-ur-muhnt/ *noun* the time after you have retired: *My grandpa is enjoying his retirement.*

**re·treat** /ri-**treet**/

● *verb*

**1** if an army retreats, it moves away from the enemy: *The soldiers retreated when they were attacked by a much larger army.*

( ANTONYM: **advance** )

**2** to move away to a safer or quieter place: *When Joe heard his parents arguing, he retreated to his room.*

● *noun*

if an army makes a retreat, it moves away from the enemy: *The general ordered a retreat because he saw that his men could not win the battle.*

**re·trieve** /ri-**treev**/ *verb* to get something back from the place where it is: *He went next door to retrieve the lost ball.*

**re·turn** /ri-**turn**/

● *verb*

**1** to go back to a place: *He returned home after midnight.*

**2** to give something back to someone: *I need to return these books to the library.*

**3** to start happening again: *I had a headache yesterday, and now it's returned.*

( SYNONYM: **come back** )

**4 return someone's call** to call someone after he or she has tried to speak to you on the phone: *She left a message, but he didn't return her call.*

● *noun*

**1** the act of going or coming back to a place: *We were looking forward to Mom's return from her trip.*

**2** the act of giving something back: *She offered a reward for the return of her stolen necklace.*

⌐ IDIOM with **return**

**in return** if you do something in return, you do something as a payment or thanks for what someone has done for you: *He didn't ask for anything in return for helping us.*

**re·un·ion** /ree-**yoon**-yuhn/ *noun* a meeting of people who have not met for a long time: *He saw a lot of old friends at his high school reunion.*

**re·u·nite** /ree-yoo-**nīt**/ *verb* to bring people together again: *The little girl who was lost was found and reunited with her mother.*

**re·use** /ree-**yooz**/ *verb* to use something again, instead of throwing it away: *Reuse plastic bags when you go shopping.*

**Rev.** the written abbreviation of **Reverend**

**re·veal** /ri-**veel**/ *verb*

**1** to tell people something that was secret or not known before: *The thief would not reveal the names of the other men who had robbed the bank.*

**2** to show something that could not be seen before: *He opened the lid of the box and revealed a birthday cake.*

**Word Family: reveal**

**reveal** *verb* | **revealing** *adjective*

**re·veal·ing** /ri-**veel**-ing/ *adjective*

**1** showing or telling new things about someone or something: *In this revealing book, the actress talks about her childhood for the first time.*

**2** revealing clothes show parts of your body that you usually keep covered: *The dress had a low neck and was very revealing.*

**re·venge** /ri-**venj**/ *noun* something bad you do to someone who did something bad to you: *She took revenge on the girls who had laughed at her by telling lies about them.*

**rev·e·nue** /**rev**-uh-noo/ *noun* money that a company earns or that a government gets from taxes: *Magazines get a lot of their revenue from advertisements.*

**Rev·erend** /**rev**-ruhnd/ *noun* ( ABBREVIATION: **Rev.** ) used before the name of a Christian minister: *The new minister is Reverend Stephen Dyer.*

**re·verse** /ri-**vurss**/

● *verb*

to change something to the opposite: *The principal said we couldn't bring cell phones to school, but then she reversed her decision and let us.*

—**reversal** /ri-**vurss**-uhl/ *noun* a change to the opposite thing: *There has been a reversal of opinion – people used to hate him and now they like him.*

—**reversible** /ri-**vurss**-uhb-uhl/ *adjective* able to

be reversed: *They hope that the damage to the forest will be reversible and not permanent.*

● *noun*

**1** the control in a vehicle that makes it go backward: *He put the car in reverse and backed out of the driveway.*

**2** the opposite: *She thinks she's good at singing, but the reverse is true – she's terrible!*

● *adjective*

opposite: *He was trying to help, but his advice had the reverse effect and made things worse.*

## re·view /ri-**vyoo**/

● *noun*

**1** a piece of writing that says what someone thinks of a new book, play, movie, etc.: *The movie got very good reviews, so I really want to see it.*

**2** the process of thinking carefully about something, to see if it needs to be changed: *The safety rules are under review because there was an accident on the playground.*

● *verb*

**1** to write a report telling people your opinion about a book, play, movie, etc.: *When he reviewed the book, he said it was very interesting.*

**2** to prepare for a test by reading and practicing things again: *Review your spelling words before the test.*

**3** to think about something again, so that you can decide if it needs to be changed: *The Scout leader is reviewing the way we have our meetings.*

—**reviewer** /ri-**vyoo**-ur/ *noun* someone whose job is reviewing new books, plays, movies, etc.: *Reviewers loved the movie.* ( SYNONYM: **critic** )

## re·vise /ri-**vīz**/ *verb*

**1** to change and improve a piece of writing: *Revise your book report before you turn it in.*

**2** to change your opinion or plans: *We were going to the beach, but we had to revise our plans when Ashley got sick.* ( SYNONYM: **change** )

—**revision** /ri-**vizh**-uhn/ *noun* the process of changing something, especially in order to improve it

## re·volt /ri-**vohlt**/

● *verb*

**1** to fight against a government or someone who is in charge: *Even before the Civil War, many*

slaves revolted against their owners.
( SYNONYM: **rebel** )

**2** to make you feel sick and shocked: *The idea of eating a snail revolted me.*

● *noun*

if there is a revolt, people fight against a government or people who are in charge: *The Americans started a revolt against the British government, so that they could have their own country.*

## rev·o·lu·tion /rev-uh-**loosh**-uhn/ *noun*

**1** if there is a revolution, people change their ruler or political system using violence: *During the American Revolution, Americans fought against the British rulers.*

**2** a complete change in the way people do something: *Because of computers, there has been a revolution in the way children learn.*

**3** a movement in a circle around something: *The Earth makes one revolution around the Sun each year.*

## rev·o·lu·tion·ar·y /rev-uh-**loosh**-uhn-air-ee/ *adjective*

**1** completely new and different, and usually much better than before: *The revolutionary new cancer medicine could save thousands of lives every year.*

**2** relating to or involved in a political revolution: *The Revolutionary War began in Lexington, Massachusetts.*

**re·volve** /ri-**vahlv**/ *verb* to move in a circle around a point in the middle: *The Earth revolves around the Sun.*

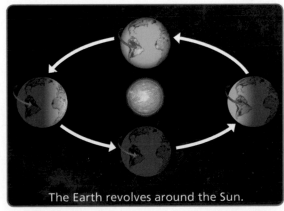

**revolve**

The Earth revolves around the Sun.

**re·volv·er** /ri-**vahlv**-ur/ *noun* a small gun. A revolver has a part containing bullets that moves around.

a b c d e f g h i j k l m n o p q **r** s t u v w x y z

**re·ward** /ri-**word**/
● *noun* something that you are given for doing something good: *His parents will buy him a new game as a reward for getting good grades.*
● *verb* to give something to someone because he or she has done something good: *When we behaved well, we were rewarded with extra time to play.*

**re·ward·ing** /ri-**word**-ing/ *adjective* a rewarding activity makes you feel happy and satisfied: *Learning to play the piano is hard, but it is rewarding too.*

**re·wind** /ree-**wīnd**/ *verb* (**rewound** /ree-**wownd**/) to make a tape go back to the beginning: *Rewind the videotape when you're done watching it.*

**re·write** /ree-**rīt**/ *verb* (**rewrote** /ree-**roht**/, **rewritten** /ree-**rit**'n/) to do a piece of writing again: *I rewrote my story to make it clearer.*

**rhi·noc·er·os** /rī-**nahss**-uhr-uhss/ (also **rhi·no** /**rīn**-oh/) *noun* a large heavy animal with one or two horns on its nose and thick rough skin. It lives in Africa and southern Asia.

**Word Origin:** rhinoceros

The **rhinoceros** has a name that describes how it looks. Rhino comes from the Greek word that means "nose," and ceros comes from the Greek word that means "horn." So a rhinoceros is an animal that has a horn on its nose.

rhinoceros

**rhom·bus** /**rahm**-buhss/ *noun* a shape with four straight sides that are the same length and four angles that are not 90°

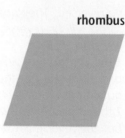
rhombus

**rhu·barb** /**roob**-arb/ *noun* a plant with long thick red stems that can be cooked and eaten: *a rhubarb pie*

rhubarb

**rhyme** /rīm/
● *verb* if words rhyme, they end with the same sound: *"Door" rhymes with "floor."*
● *noun*
**1** a short children's poem or song that uses words that rhyme: *We sang the nursery rhyme "Twinkle, Twinkle, Little Star."*
**2** words that end with the same sound: *"Dog" and "fog" and "hog" are rhymes.*

**rhythm** /**rith**-uhm/ *noun* a regular pattern of sounds or movements: *Your heart beats in a regular rhythm.*
—**rhythmic** /**rith**-mik/ *adjective* having a rhythm: *The rhythmic sound of the drums made her want to dance.*

**rib** /rib/ *noun* one of the curved bones in your chest. You have 12 pairs of ribs: *She was so thin you could see her ribs under her skin.*

**rib·bon** /**rib**-uhn/ *noun*
**1** a long narrow piece of cloth for tying things and making them look pretty: *Her braids were tied with small red ribbons.*
**2** a decoration made of colored ribbon. It is given as a prize in a competition: *Kelli's pony won the blue ribbon at the state fair.*

ribbon
ribbon
ribbon

**rib cage** /**rib** kayj/ *noun* your ribs and the bones they are joined to. Your rib cage protects your lungs and heart.

**rice** /rīss/ *noun* a white or brown grain that you boil in water until it becomes soft enough to eat. Rice grows on plants that are grown in very wet fields: *The tacos came with rice and beans.*

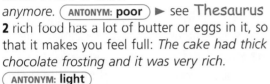

rice
rice plant
rice

**rich** /rich/ *adjective*
**1** having a lot of money: *He's so rich that he doesn't have to work anymore.* ( ANTONYM: **poor** ) ▶ see Thesaurus
**2** rich food has a lot of butter or eggs in it, so that it makes you feel full: *The cake had thick chocolate frosting and it was very rich.* ( ANTONYM: **light** )
**3** if something is rich in something good, it has a lot of it: *Oranges are rich in Vitamin C.*

**rich·es** /**rich**-iz/ *plural noun* a lot of money or expensive things: *His success as an actor earned him riches and fame.*

**rich·ly** /**rich**-lee/ *adverb* in a beautiful or expensive way: *The women were richly dressed in expensive clothes.*

**Rich·ter scale** /**rik**-tur skayl/ *noun* a scale that shows how powerful an earthquake is. 1 is a very gentle earthquake and 10 is the most powerful earthquake: *The earthquake measured 6.8 on the Richter scale.*

**ric·o·chet** /**rik**-uh-shay/ *verb* if something such as a bullet or ball ricochets, it hits a surface and moves away again in a different direction: *The ball ricocheted off the edge of the basket, and Sam caught it.* ( SYNONYM: **bounce** )

**rid** /rid/ *adjective*

> IDIOM with rid
> **get rid of** to throw away or remove something you do not want: *I got rid of a lot of old toys I didn't play with anymore.*

**rid·den** /**rid**'n/ *verb* the past participle of ride

**rid·dle** /**rid**'l/ *noun* a joke or funny question that you guess the answer to: *Here's a riddle: What keys have fur? The answer is "Monkeys."*

**ride** /rīd/
● *verb* (**rode** /rohd/, **ridden** /**rid**'n/)
**1** to sit on a bicycle, motorcycle, or horse and make it move forward: *She rides her bicycle to school.*
**2** to travel in a car, truck, or bus: *We rode the bus into New York City.*
● *noun*
**1** a trip in a vehicle or on an animal: *He took me for a ride in his new car.*
**2** something such as a roller coaster that people ride on for fun: *The best ride was the log ride because we got really wet.*

ride
He is riding his bicycle.

**rid·er** /**rīd**-ur/ *noun* someone who rides a horse, motorcycle, or bicycle: *Bike riders should wear helmets.*

**ridge** /rij/ *noun*
**1** a long narrow area of high land along the top of hills or mountains: *The road went along the ridge of the mountains before going down into the valley.*
**2** a long narrow raised stripe on something: *These potato chips have ridges instead of being smooth.*

**rid·i·cule** /**rid**-uh-kyool/
● *verb* to make jokes that show you think someone or something is silly: *The other kids ridiculed the way I talked. They said I had a funny accent.*
● *noun* jokes that show you think someone or something is silly: *He didn't tell anyone his idea because he was afraid of ridicule.*

**ri·dic·u·lous** /ri-**dik**-yuhl-uhss/ *adjective* very silly: *$150 is a ridiculous price for a pair of sneakers!*

**rid·ing** /**rīd**-ing/ *noun* the sport of riding horses: *We went horseback riding when we stayed at the ranch.*

**ri·fle** /**rīf**-uhl/ *noun* a long gun that you hold up to your shoulder to shoot: *He went hunting with his rifle.* ▶ see picture at **soldier**

a b c d e f g h i j k l m n o p q **r** s t u v w x y z

**rift val·ley** /rift val-ee/ *noun* a valley with very steep sides, formed by the cracking and moving of the Earth's surface

**rig** /rig/
● *noun*
a large structure that is used when getting oil out of the ground: *The oil rig is used to drill for oil and then pump it out of the ground.*
● *verb* (**rigging**, **rigged**)
**1** to dishonestly make a competition or election have the winner you want: *They rigged the election by letting some people vote twice.*
**2 rig up** to make something using the things that you find around you: *We rigged up a shower using an old bucket.*

**rig·ging** /rig-ing/ *noun* the ropes and sails on the masts of a sailing ship: *The sailor climbed up the rigging to see if there were any other ships.*

**right** /rīt/
● *adjective*
**1** correct: *Did you get the right answer?* | *I thought it would rain, and I was right.*
( ANTONYM: **wrong** ) ▶ see **Thesaurus**
**2** on or toward the side of your body that has the hand most people write with: *Put your right hand over your heart when you say the Pledge of Allegiance.* | *The school is on the right side of the street.* ( ANTONYM: **left** )
**3** if something is right, people should do it because it is good or fair: *It's not right to steal things.* ( ANTONYM: **wrong** )
● *adverb*
**1** exactly in a place, or exactly at a time: *We parked right in front of the store.* | *He got there right at eight o'clock.* | *I don't have time to talk to you right now.*
**2** toward the right side: *Turn right at the lights.*
( ANTONYM: **left** )
**3** immediately or very soon: *She knew right away that something was wrong.* | *I'm going to the store – I'll be right back.*
**4** correctly: *I hope I pronounced your name right.*
( ANTONYM: **wrong** )
● *noun*
**1** something that the law says you can do: *In 1920, women got the right to vote.*
**2** the right side or direction: *When you go along the street, the library is on the right.*
( ANTONYM: **left** )

**Word Origin:** right

**Right** comes from an Old English word that meant "good," "correct," or "straight." Right still often means those things. But, in Old English, people didn't use the word "right" about the right side of your body. They called your right hand "the stronger hand" instead. Over time, people began thinking of the right hand as the "good" or "correct" hand, so they started using the word "right" instead of "stronger."

**right an·gle** /rīt ang-guhl / *noun* an angle of 90 degrees, like the angle at a corner of a square

**right-hand·ed** /rīt **hand**-id/ *adjective* if you are right-handed, you use your right hand to write or throw a ball: *Dan is a right-handed pitcher on the baseball team.*

**right tri·an·gle** /rīt **trī**-ang-guhl/ *noun* a triangle that has one right angle

**rig·id** /rij-id/ *adjective*
**1** not easy to bend or move: *The blocks are made of rigid plastic that does not bend or break easily.* ( ANTONYM: **flexible** )
**2** strict and difficult to change: *My parents set rigid rules about homework. It has to be done before we can play.* ( ANTONYM: **flexible** )

**rim** /rim/ *noun* the top edge of something round: *He filled the glass to the rim, so when he picked it up, it spilled.*

**rind** /rīnd/ *noun* the hard outer skin of fruits such as oranges, lemons, or melons
( SYNONYM: **peel** )

rind
**rind**

**ring** /ring/
● *noun*
**1** a piece of jewelry that you wear on your finger: *She wears a gold ring on her finger.*
**2** a line, mark, or object shaped like a circle: *The hot cup had left a ring on the table.*
**3** the area where a boxing or wrestling match takes place: *The two fighters went into the ring.*
**4** a group of criminals who work together to do something illegal: *The police arrested members of a drug smuggling ring.*

● *verb* (**rang** /rang/, **rung** /ruhng/)
**1** if a bell or a telephone rings, it makes a sound: *When the telephone rings, I answer it.*
**2** to make a bell make a sound: *Ring the doorbell and see if anyone's home.*

**rink** /ringk/ *noun*
**1** an area of ice that has been specially prepared for skating and ice hockey
**2** an area with a smooth surface where you can go around on rollerskates

rink

**rinse** /rinss/ *verb* to use water to wash soap or dirt off something: *Brett rinsed the shampoo out of his hair.*

**ri·ot** /rī-uht/
● *noun* violent behavior by a crowd of people who are protesting about something: *During the riot, people threw bottles and stones at the police officers.*
● *verb* if people riot, they behave in a violent way as a protest: *Hundreds of people rioted to protest about high food prices.*

**rip** /rip/
● *verb* (**ripping, ripped**) to tear something: *He ripped his shirt on a nail. | She ripped up the letter and put it in the garbage can.*
● *noun* a tear in material or paper: *She was sewing up a rip in her dress.*

**ripe** /rīp/ *adjective* ripe fruit is ready to be eaten: *Bananas turn yellow when they are ripe.*

**rip·en** /rīp-uhn/ *verb* if fruit ripens, it becomes softer and ready to eat: *The tomatoes were ripening and turning red.*

**rise** /rīz/
● *verb* (**rose** /rohz/, **risen** /riz-uhn/)
**1** to increase: *The number of students in the*

school rose from 250 to 310.
SYNONYMS: **increase, go up** ANTONYM: **fall**
**2** to go up: *Smoke rose from the chimney.*
ANTONYM: **fall**
**3** when the Sun or Moon rises, you start to see it in the sky: *The sun will rise at 5:45 tomorrow morning.* ANTONYM: **set**
**4** to stand up: *Everyone must rise when the judge enters the court.*
● *noun*
an increase: *There has been a rise in sales so the company is doing very well.* SYNONYM: **increase**
ANTONYM: **fall**

**ris·en** /riz-uhn/ *verb* the past participle of rise

**risk** /risk/
● *noun* the chance that something bad might happen: *Most sports involve some risk of getting hurt.*

> IDIOM with **risk**
> **take a risk** to do something even though there is a chance that something bad will happen: *She was taking a risk by driving so fast on wet roads.*

● *verb* to do something that could make something bad happen to you: *Frank risked his life by going into the burning building to save a child.*

**risk·y** /risk-ee/ *adjective* if an action is risky, something bad might happen when you do it: *Biking on busy roads is risky.*
SYNONYM: **dangerous** ANTONYM: **safe**

**rit·u·al** /rich-oo-uhl/ *noun* something that people always do at an important event or time of year: *Part of the ritual of Christmas is giving presents.*

**ri·val** /rīv-uhl/ *noun* a person, group, or company that tries to be more successful than another one: *The two schools are football rivals.*
SYNONYM: **competitor**

**Word Origin: rival**

**Rival** comes from a Latin word that means "people who are sharing the same river." In ancient times, people always tried to settle near streams and rivers so that they would have water. Sometimes groups of people might end up having to fight to use the water.

**a b c d e f g h i j k l m n o p q r s t u v w x y z**

**ri·val·ry** /**rīv**-uhl-ree/ *noun* (plural **rivalries**) a situation in which two people, groups, or companies are trying to be more successful than each other: *There is a lot of rivalry between the boys because they both want to be top of the class.*

**riv·er** /**riv**-ur/ *noun* a long wide flow of water that goes into an ocean or lake: *The Mississippi River flows through or along the borders of ten states.* ▶ see Thesaurus

**riv·er·bank** /**riv**-ur-bangk/ *noun* the land at the edge of a river: *We sat on the riverbank and watched the boats.*

**R.N.** /ar **en**/ *noun* a nurse. R.N. is short for "registered nurse": *She's an R.N. at Harborview Medical Center.*

**roach** /rohch/ *noun* a large insect that lives in places where people keep food: *The roaches ran across the kitchen floor.* (SYNONYM: **cockroach**)

**road** /rohd/ *noun* the surface that cars and trucks drive on: *There were no cars coming so we crossed the road.* ▶ see Thesaurus

**roam** /rohm/ *verb* to walk or travel in a place freely: *Bears and other wild animals roam the woods.*

**roar** /ror/
● *verb* to make a deep loud sound, like a lion or machine: *The plane's engines roared as it prepared to take off.*
● *noun* a deep loud noise: *We could hear the roar of traffic on the freeway. | a lion's roar*

**roast** /rohst/
● *verb* to cook meat or vegetables in an oven: *Roast the chicken for 90 minutes.* ▶ see picture at **cook**
● *noun* meat that you cook in an oven: *Mom made a pork roast for dinner.*
● *adjective* roast meat or vegetables have been cooked in an oven: *We had roast beef on Sunday.*

**rob** /rahb/ *verb* (**robbing**, **robbed**) to take something that is not yours from a person or place: *Two men robbed a bank and stole $500,000.*

**rob·ber** /**rahb**-ur/ *noun* someone who goes to a place and takes something that does not belong

to him or her: *The robbers took jewelry and money from the house.* (SYNONYMS: **thief, burglar**)

**rob·ber·y** /**rahb**-uhr-ee/ *noun* (plural **robberies**) a crime in which someone goes to a place and takes something that does not belong to him or her: *My CD player was stolen in the robbery.* (SYNONYM: **burglary**)

**robe** /rohb/ *noun* a long loose piece of clothing that covers most of your body: *The judge was wearing a black robe.*

**rob·in** /**rahb**-in/ *noun* a common bird with a red chest and a gray back

robin

**ro·bot** /**rohb**-aht/ *noun*
**1** a machine that can move and do work. Robots are used in factories: *A line of robots assemble the cars.*
**2** in movies and stories, a machine that can talk, walk, and think like a real person

## Word Origin: robot

In the 1920s, a Czech man called Karel Čapek wrote a play about machines that looked like people. His brother said that he should call these artificial people **robotnik**, which is the Czech word for "worker" or "slave." When Čapek's play was translated into English, the word **robotnik** became **robot**.

**rock** /rahk/
● *noun*
**1** the stone that forms part of the Earth's surface: *You can see the different layers of rock in the Grand Canyon.*
**2** a large piece of stone lying on the ground: *The heavy rain caused mud and rocks to fall down the mountains.* (SYNONYM: **stone**)
**3** a type of loud pop music: *My brother likes rock and he plays the electric guitar in a rock band.* (SYNONYM: **rock 'n' roll**)
● *verb*
to move gently from one side to another: *The boat was rocking on the waves.*

**rock**

layers of rock

**rock climb·ing** /rahk klīm-ing/ *noun* the sport of climbing up big rocks or the side of a mountain. You use ropes and other equipment: *We went hiking and did a little rock climbing.*

**rock cy·cle** /rahk sīk-uhl/ *noun* the way in which the Earth's three main rock types change from one type to another over a long period of time: *New environments cause rock types to change from sedimentary to metamorphic to igneous.*

**rock·er** /rahk-ur/ *noun* a chair that moves backward and forward on two curved pieces of wood ( SYNONYM: **rocking chair** )

**rock·et** /rahk-it/ *noun*
**1** a tall vehicle that travels into space: *The rocket carried a satellite into space.*
**2** a long thin object that is fired from a weapon. The rocket explodes when it lands: *The soldiers were firing rockets at the enemy.*

**rocket**

**rock·ing chair**
/rahk-ing chair/ *noun* a chair that moves backward and forward on two curved pieces of wood ( SYNONYM: **rocker** )

**rock·ing horse** /rahk-ing horss/ *noun* a toy that looks like a horse. A child sits on it and moves it backward and forward.

**rock 'n' roll**, **rock and roll** /rahk uhn **rohl**/ *noun* a type of pop music with a strong loud beat. Rock 'n' roll became popular in the 1950s.
( SYNONYM: **rock** )

**rock·y** /rahk-ee/ *adjective* ground that is rocky has a lot of rocks on it: *The beach was rocky, so I kept my shoes on.*

**rod** /rahd/ *noun* a long thin piece of metal or wood: *The fishermen were using rods to catch fish.*

**rode** /rohd/ *verb* the past tense of **ride**

**ro·dent** /rohd'nt/ *noun* a type of animal with long sharp front teeth: *Mice, rats, and squirrels are rodents.*

**ro·de·o** /rohd-ee-oh/ *noun* a competition in which people ride wild horses and catch cows with ropes: *At the rodeo, one cowboy stayed on a bucking horse for six seconds.*

**role** /rohl/ *noun*
**1** the job or purpose someone has in a situation or activity: *The teacher's role is to help children to learn.*
**2** a character in a play or movie: *He played the role of the king in the movie.* ( SYNONYM: **part** )

**role mod·el** /rohl mahd-uhl/ *noun* someone whose behavior people copy because they think he or she is good: *The singer is a good role model because he doesn't smoke or swear.*

**roll** /rohl/
● *verb*
**1** to move by turning over and over: *The ball rolled under the couch.* | *My pencil rolled off the desk.*
**2** to make something into the shape of a tube or ball: *We rolled up our sleeping bags.*
**3** to make something flat on a surface: *Roll out the dough into a circle.*
**4** to move on wheels: *The car rolled backward down the hill.*
**5** if you roll dice, you throw them as part of a game: *I rolled the dice and got a six.*
● *noun*
**1** a long amount of something that is curled into a tube: *Here's a new roll of toilet paper.*
**2** a small round piece of bread
**3** a list of names of everyone in a class: *When I call the roll, say "here" as I say your name.*

**Roll·er·blade** /rohl-ur-blayd/ *noun trademark* a boot with a row of wheels on the bottom
—**rollerblading** /rohl-ur-blayd-ing/ *noun* the sport of moving wearing Rollerblades: *We went rollerblading in the park.*

**roll·er coast·er** /**rohl**-ur kohst-ur/ *noun* a ride at a fair or amusement park. A roller coaster is like a train that moves very fast on a track that goes up and down: *People on the roller coaster screamed as they went around in a circle.*
▶ see picture at **amusement park**

**roll·er·skate** /**rohl**-ur-skayt/ *noun* a boot with four wheels on the bottom: *I put on my rollerskates and skated on the sidewalk.*
▶ see picture at **skate**
—**rollerskating** /**rohl**-ur-skayt-ing/ *noun* the sport of moving wearing rollerskates: *You can go rollerskating on the path around the park.*

**roll·ing pin** /**rohl**-ing pin/ *noun* a wooden tool that you roll over dough to make it flat. A rolling pin is shaped like a long solid tube: *We rolled out the playdough with a rolling pin and then used cookie cutters to make shapes.*

**ROM** /rahm/ *noun* a type of computer memory that lets you see information but not change it. ROM is short for "Read Only Memory."

**Ro·man** /**rohm**-uhn/
● *noun* someone who lived in ancient Rome: *The Romans started an empire that lasted a 1,000 years.*
● *adjective* from or relating to ancient Rome: *a Roman soldier*

Roman

sandals

a Roman citizen

**Ro·man Cath·olic** /rohm-uhn **kath**-lik/ *adjective* relating to the church whose leader is the Pope: *Roman Catholic priests are not allowed to marry.* ( SYNONYM: **Catholic** )

**ro·mance** /**rohm**-anss/ *noun*
**1** an exciting relationship between two people who love each other: *His first romance was with a girl in high school.*
**2** a story about love between two people: *My mom is reading a romance about a woman who falls in love with a soldier.*

**Word Origin: romance**

When **romance** was first used in English, it meant a popular story that was written and told in French. French is called a Romance language because it developed from Latin, the language of the Romans. Stories that were written in French were called romances for this reason. Usually, romances were long stories about a knight and his adventures. Of course, some of the stories were about how the knights fell in love and what they did to prove their love, such as fighting dragons. By the 1600s, if you read a romance, you were reading a love story.

**Ro·man nu·mer·al** /rohm-uhn **noom**-uhr-uhl/ *noun* a number that is written as a letter. People in ancient Rome used these numbers: *X is the Roman numeral for 10.*

**ro·man·tic** /roh-**mant**-ik/ *adjective* showing strong feelings of love: *Her boyfriend is very romantic and often buys flowers for her.*

**roof** /roof/ *noun*
**1** the part of a building or vehicle that covers the top: *Rain was coming into the house from a hole in the roof.*
**2** the top part of the inside of your mouth: *The peanut butter stuck to the roof of my mouth.*

roof

roof

**rook·ie** /**ruk**-ee/ *noun* someone who has just started doing a job or playing a sport: *He won the Rookie of the Year award because he played so well during his first season in baseball.*

**room** /room/ *noun*
**1** one of the areas inside a building. A room has

a door and walls: *The apartment has four rooms – a kitchen, a bedroom, a bathroom, and a living room.*
**2** enough space: *My bedroom is very small. There isn't room for a desk.*

**room·mate** /**room**-mayt/ *noun* someone you share a room or house with: *My sister and her roommate live in the college dorms.*

**room·y** /**room**-ee/ *adjective* big and with plenty of space inside: *The car is roomy enough for six people.* ( SYNONYM: **spacious** )

**roost** /roost/ *noun* a place where birds rest and sleep: *Birds use the tree as a roost.*

**roost·er** /**roost**-ur/ *noun* a male chicken: *The rooster woke us up early in the morning.*

**root** /root/ *noun*
**1** the part of a plant or tree that grows under the ground: *Plants take in water through their roots.* ▶ see picture at **tree**
**2** the bottom or beginning part of something, for example a hair or a tooth: *Her hair was dyed brown, but the roots were gray.*
**3** the most basic part of a word, that you can add a prefix or a suffix to: *"Happiness" is formed from the root "happy" and the suffix "-ness."*
**4** **roots** your roots are your family and where they come from: *She wanted to find out about her roots, so she asked her grandpa about his parents.*
**5** the root of a number is a smaller number which, when it is multiplied by itself a particular number of times, equals that number: *2 is the fourth root of 16 (2 x 2 x 2 x 2 = 16).*

**root**

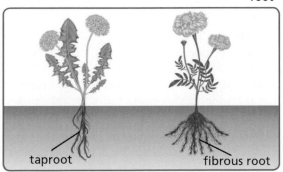

taproot   fibrous root

**root beer** /**root** beer/ *noun* a sweet drink made from the roots of some plants

**rope** /rohp/ *noun* thick strong string. It is made by twisting together many thinner pieces of string or other material: *They tied ropes around the fallen tree, and pulled it out of the road.*

**rope**

**rose** /rohz/
● *noun* a flower that has a pleasant smell. Roses are usually red, pink, white, or yellow: *My Dad gave my Mom 12 red roses on Valentine's Day.* | *a rose bush*
● *verb* the past tense of **rise**

**rose**

**Rosh Ha·sha·na** /rahsh huh-**shahn**-uh/ *noun* the Jewish New Year, which is celebrated in September or October

**rot** /raht/ *verb* (**rotting, rotted**)
**1** to slowly become bad or soft because of natural chemical changes: *After a week, the fish was starting to rot and smell.* ( SYNONYM: **decay** )
**2** to make something become bad or soft: *Sugar rots your teeth.* ( SYNONYM: **decay** )

**ro·tate** /**roh**-tayt/ *verb*
**1** to turn around a fixed central point: *The Earth rotates completely around its axis every 24 hours.*
**2** to change who does something or which things you use. You change them in an order: *Mom rotates our chores, so I set the table one week, and my sister sets it the next.*
—**rotation** /roh-**taysh**-uhn/ movement in which something turns around a fixed central point: *The rotation of the planet Venus is very slow.*

**ro·ta·tion sym·me·try** /roh-taysh-uhn **sim**-uht-ree/ (also **ro·ta·tion·al sym·me·try** /roh-taysh-uhn-uhl **sim**-uht-ree/) *noun* a shape has rotation symmetry if it looks exactly the same after you have turned it less than 360° one or more times

**rot·ten** /**raht**'n/ *adjective*

**1** rotten food or wood is bad because it is old and starting to decay: *Meat turns rotten very quickly if you do not keep it in the refrigerator.* ( ANTONYM: **fresh** )

**2** very bad: *The weather was rotten. It was cold and rainy.* ( SYNONYMS: **terrible, awful** ) ( ANTONYM: **great** )

**rough** /ruhf/ *adjective*

**1** not even or not smooth: *Pine trees have rough bark with a lot of bumps and holes in it.*
▶ see **Thesaurus**

**2** using force or violence: *He was very rough and dragged me by the arm.* ( ANTONYM: **gentle** )

**3** not exact: *I have a rough idea where John lives but I don't know the exact house.*

**4** difficult to deal with: *I had a rough time when my parents divorced – it was very hard for me.* ( SYNONYM: **hard** )

**rough draft** /ruhf **draft**/ *noun* a piece of writing or a drawing that you do first and plan to improve later: *Write a rough draft of your report first, and then rewrite any parts that you are not happy with.*

**rough·ly** /**ruhf**-lee/ *adverb*

**1** used when giving a number that is not exact: *I'm not sure how far it is, but it's roughly 200 miles.* ( SYNONYMS: **approximately, about** ) ( ANTONYM: **exactly** )

**2** not gently or carefully: *He hurt my arm when he roughly pulled me away.*

**round** /rownd/

● *adjective*
like a circle or ball in shape: *Peaches are round and juicy.* | *We sat at a round table.*
▶ see **Thesaurus**

● *noun*

**1** one of the parts of a competition that you must finish or win to get to the next part: *The winners of this round will play each other tomorrow.*

**2** one in a series of events that are connected: *The second round of peace talks will take place in Washington.*

**3** a song that people start singing at different times, so that different parts of the song are being sung at the same time: *We sang "Row, Row, Row Your Boat" as a round.*

**4** a round of applause a time when you clap for someone: *The audience gave the singer a round of applause.*

**5** a complete game of golf: *Dad played a round of golf at the club.*

● *verb*

**1** to go around a bend or the corner of a building: *The car rounded the bend too quickly and hit a tree.*

**2** if you round a number to the next whole number, next ten, next hundred, etc., you change the number to the nearest whole number or the nearest multiple of ten, hundred, etc.: *Round the following numbers to the nearest ten: 13, 27, 136 (answer: 10, 30, 140).*

**3** round up to find and bring together a group of people or animals: *The cowboys are rounding up the cattle.* | *The gang members were rounded up and put in prison.*

**round-trip** /**rownd** trip/ *adjective* a round-trip ticket is for a trip to a place and back again: *Can I have a round-trip ticket to San Diego, leaving today and returning tomorrow?* ( ANTONYM: **one-way** )

**route** /root/ *noun* a way from one place to another: *The quickest route to school is through the park.*

**rou·tine** /roo-**teen**/

● *noun* the usual things that someone does: *Mom always reads me a story when I'm in bed – it's part of my bedtime routine.*

● *adjective* happening regularly, not for any special reason or problem: *I have a routine check-up at the dentist every six months.*

**row** /roh/

● *noun* a line of things or people next to each other: *The kids sat in a row on a bench.* | *The front row in the movie theater was full.*

IDIOM with **row**
**in a row** one after another: *The team has lost three games in a row.*

● *verb* to make a boat move through water using two long sticks with flat ends called oars: *We rowed to the middle of the lake and started fishing.*

—**rowing** /**roh**-ing/ *noun* the activity of rowing a boat ▶ see picture on page **A10**

**row·boat** /**roh**-boht/
*noun* a small boat that you move through water using oars

rowboat

**row·dy** /**rowd**-ee/
*adjective* a rowdy group of people is making a lot of noise: *Rowdy fans shouted and screamed at the players.*

**roy·al** /**roy**-uhl/ *adjective* relating to or belonging to a king or queen: *Cinderella went to the royal palace for the dance.*

**roy·al·ty** /**roy**-uhl-tee/ *noun* a king or queen and his or her family: *The grand palace was built for royalty.*

**RSVP** /ar ess vee **pee**/ used on an invitation to ask the person you invited to tell you if he or she can come to the party. RSVP stands for French words that mean "respond please": *Please come to my party on August 24 at 3:00 at Lexington Avenue. RSVP.*

**rub** /ruhb/ *verb* (**rubbing**, **rubbed**) to move your hand or a cloth backward and forward over something: *He kept rubbing his eyes so I knew he was tired.*

**rub·ber** /**ruhb**-ur/ *noun* a strong substance that bends easily. Rubber is used for making tires and in making boots, gloves, etc. that water cannot get through: *The ground is very wet and you'll need to wear rubber boots.*
—**rubbery** /**ruhb**-ur-ee/ *adjective* like rubber: *The chicken was all rubbery and I didn't want to eat it.*

rubber

rubber boots

**rub·ber band** /**ruhb**-ur band/ *noun* a thin piece of rubber in the shape of a circle. You put a rubber band around things to hold them together: *She put a rubber band around the letters to keep them together.*

**rub·ble** /**ruhb**-uhl/ *noun* broken stones or bricks from a building or wall that was destroyed: *There was a big earthquake and many houses were now just a pile of rubble.*

**ru·by** /**roob**-ee/ *noun* (plural **rubies**) a dark red jewel: *The ring had a ruby on it.*

ruby

**rud·der** /**ruhd**-ur/ *noun* the part of a boat that you move to change the boat's direction. A rudder is flat and is at the back of the boat.

**rude** /rood/ *adjective* not polite: *It's rude not to say thank you when someone gives you something.* ▶ see **Thesaurus**
—**rudely** /**rood**-lee/ *adverb* in a rude way: *He rudely interrupted me.*
—**rudeness** /**rood**-niss/ *noun* behavior or speech that is not polite: *The teacher won't put up with any rudeness, like talking when she is talking.*

**ruf·fle** /**ruhf**-uhl/ *noun* a decoration on clothes or other things made of cloth. A ruffle is made by sewing a thin piece of cloth in folds along the edge of another piece of cloth: *She was wearing a party dress with lots of ruffles on it.*

**rug** /ruhg/ *noun* a thick piece of cloth that covers part of a floor: *The cat was sitting on a rug in front of the fire.*

**rug·ged** /**ruhg**-id/ *adjective* rough, uneven, and with a lot of rocks: *It was hard to get the covered wagons through the rugged mountains.*

**ru·in** /**roo**-in/ *verb* to spoil something completely: *The rain ruined our camping trip because we had to go home early.*

**ru·ins** /**roo**-inz/ *plural noun* the part of a building that is left when the rest has been destroyed: *We visited the ruins of a castle.*

| **IDIOM with ruins**
| **in ruins** very badly damaged: *After the bombing, the buildings were in ruins.*

a b c d e f g h i j k l m n o p q **r** s t u v w x y z

**rule** /rool/

● *noun*

**1** a statement of what you can or cannot do: *It's against school rules to bully other children.*
▶ see Thesaurus

**2** a situation in which a particular group of people control a country: *Vietnam was under French rule before World War II.*
( SYNONYM: **control** )

● *verb*

**1** to control a country: *Britain was ruled by Queen Victoria between 1837 and 1901.*

**2** to make an official decision about something: *The judge ruled that the trees had been cut down illegally.* ( SYNONYM: **decide** )

**rul·er** /**rool**-ur/ *noun*

**ruler**

**1** a flat straight piece of wood, plastic, or metal that you use for measuring or for drawing straight lines: *Use a ruler to draw a line under the title.*

**2** someone such as a king or queen who controls a country: *King Tutankhamun became the ruler of ancient Egypt when he was only nine years old.*

**rum·ble** /**ruhm**-buhl/ *verb* to make a long low sound: *Trucks rumbled past the house all day.*

**ru·mor** /**room**-ur/ *noun* something that people tell each other but that may not be true: *I heard a rumor that our teacher is going to have a baby – do you think it's true?*

**run** /ruhn/

● *verb* (**running**, **ran** /ran/, **run**)

**1** to move very quickly using your legs: *I ran to school because I was late.* ▶ see Thesaurus

**2** to be in charge of a business or organization: *My dad runs a restaurant, and he gave Tom a job as a cook.*

**3** if a machine runs, it works or operates: *Some cars run on electricity.* ( SYNONYM: **operate** )

**4** to go somewhere quickly, either walking or in a car: *Mom needed to run to the store for some milk.*

**5** if a path, road, wall, etc. runs somewhere, it goes there: *Interstate 80 runs from California to New Jersey.*

**6** to use a computer program: *You can run this software on any computer.*

**7** to try to get a job or position by winning an election: *Obama ran for president in 2008 and won.*

**8** if liquid runs somewhere, it goes there in a steady stream: *Sweat was running down his face because he was so hot.* ( SYNONYM: **flow** )

**9** if your nose runs, liquid comes out of it: *Do you have a tissue? My nose is running.*

**10 run after** to chase someone or something: *He ran after his brother but couldn't catch him.*

**11 run away** to leave home because you are unhappy: *My sister ran away after she had a fight with Mom, but she came back later.*

**12 run into** to hit someone or something with a car, truck, etc.: *The car skidded on ice and ran into a tree.*

**13 run into** to meet someone when you were not expecting to: *I ran into Eduardo at the park.*

**14 run out** to use all of something, so that there is none left: *We ran out of bread so Dad went to buy some more.*

● *noun*

**1** a period of time you spend running: *She goes for a run every day to keep in shape.*

**2** a point in a baseball game: *The other team scored three runs in the first inning.*

**run**

The children are running.

**rung** /ruhng/

● *verb* the past participle of ring

● *noun* one of the steps on a ladder that you put your foot on: *Dad put his foot on the bottom rung and started to climb the ladder.*

**run·ner** /**ruhn**-ur/ *noun* someone who runs as a sport: *There are 25 runners in today's race.*

**run·ner-up** /ruhn-ur **uhp**/ *noun* (plural **runners-up**) the person or team that finishes second in a race or competition: *Clayton won the race and Damien was the runner-up.*

**run·ning** /**ruhn**-ing/ *noun* the activity of running

as a sport: *Dad goes running every day for exercise.*

**run·ning mate** /**ruhn**-ing mayt/ *noun* the person that a candidate for president chooses to become the vice president if they win the election. In some states, candidates for governor also choose running mates: *Joe Biden was Barack Obama's running mate.*

**run·ny** /**ruhn**-ee/ *adjective* if you have a runny nose, liquid is coming out of it: *I have a cold and my nose is runny.*

**run·way** /**ruhn**-way/ *noun*
**1** the long flat road at an airport where planes take off and land: *The airplane landed on the runway.*
**2** a long narrow part of a stage that goes out into the area where the audience sits: *The models were walking up and down the runway.*

**rup·ture** /**ruhp**-chur/ *verb* to burst or tear suddenly: *The gas tank ruptured and spilled fuel.*

**ru·ral** /**roor**-uhl/ *adjective* relating to the country, not the city: *He moved from a farm in a rural area into a town.* ( **ANTONYM: urban** )

**rush** /ruhsh/
● *verb*
**1** to move or do something quickly because you do not have much time: *We were rushing so we wouldn't miss the school bus.*
**2 rush into** to do something without thinking carefully about it first: *Don't rush into buying the first computer game you see.*
● *noun*
**1** a situation in which you need to do things quickly because you do not have much time: *We were in a rush to get to our swimming lessons on time.* | *Take your time to answer the question. There's no rush.*
**2** a sudden fast movement somewhere by a group of people: *There was a rush for the door when the school bell rang.*
**3** a sudden fast movement of air or water: *I felt a rush of cold air when the door opened.*

**rush hour** /**ruhsh** ow-ur/ *noun* the time of day when there are a lot of cars on the road because people are going to or from work: *It was rush hour, so it took us a long time to get home.*

**Rus·sian** /**ruhsh**-uhn/
● *adjective*
from Russia: *He's visited two Russian cities – Moscow and St. Petersburg.*
● *noun*
**1** someone from Russia
**2** the language spoken in Russia: *She can speak Russian and Spanish.*

**rust** /ruhst/
● *noun* the brown-red substance that can form on iron and steel when it has been wet: *The old car has a lot of rust on it.*
● *verb* to become covered with rust: *He painted the gates to stop them from rusting.*

**rus·tle** /**ruhss**-uhl/
● *verb* if something such as dry leaves or papers rustle, they make a noise as they move: *Leaves rustled in the wind.*
● *noun* the sound of something rustling: *I heard the rustle of his newspaper as he tried to fold it up.* ▶ see picture on page **A16**

**rust·y** /**ruhst**-ee/
*adjective*
**1** metal that is rusty is covered with rust: *I left my bike outside in the rain and it got rusty.*
**2** not as good at something as you used to be because you have not practiced for a long time: *I used to be good at playing the piano, but I'm a little rusty now.*

**rusty**

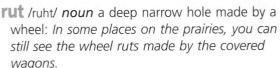
rusty nails

**rut** /ruht/ *noun* a deep narrow hole made by a wheel: *In some places on the prairies, you can still see the wheel ruts made by the covered wagons.*

> **IDIOM with rut**
> **in a rut** if you are in a rut, you are doing the same boring things all the time: *My dad felt he was in a rut and wanted to get a new job.*

**ruth·less** /**rooth**-liss/ *adjective* cruel and not caring if you harm other people to get what you want: *The judge said the man was a ruthless killer.*

**rye** /rī/ *noun*
**1** a type of grain that is used to make flour and whiskey
**2** a dark bread made from rye flour: *I had a tuna sandwich on rye.*

a
b
c
d
e
f
g
h
i
j
k
l
m
n
o
p
q
r
**s**
t
u
v
w
x
y
z

# Ss

**-s** /ss, z/, **-es**, **-ies**

## Word Building

**-s**, **-es**, or **-ies** is a suffix.

**1** pens | planets | times | glasses | boxes | heroes | days | ladies | puppies

**-s**, **-es**, or **-ies** makes a noun into a plural, to show that there is more than one thing. Most nouns just add **-s** to form the plural, for example *pen → pens*. You add **-es** if the word ends in an "s", "sh," "ch," "x," or "o," for example *glass → glasses* and *hero → heroes*. If the word ends in a "y," you add **-s** if the word has a vowel before the "y", for example *day → days*. If the word has a consonant before the "y," you add **-ies**, for example *puppy → puppies*.

**2** hits | catches | flies

**-s**, **-es**, or **-ies** form the third person singular of a verb. So, they are used with "he," "she," and "it" – he *hits* the ball, she *catches* the ball, the plane *flies* high in the sky. The spelling rules are the same as the rules you use when you add these suffixes to a noun.

**Sab·bath** /**sab**-uhth/ *noun* the day of the week when Christians or Jews rest and pray: *Saturday is the Sabbath for Jewish people.*

**sa·ber-toothed ti·ger** /**sayb**-ur tootht **tīg**-ur/ *noun* a large animal of the cat family that lived a very long time ago. Saber-toothed tigers had very long curved teeth.

**sab·o·tage** /**sab**-uh-tahzh/
● *verb* to secretly damage or spoil something: *He sabotaged my bike! He let the air out of my tires so he'd win the race.*
● *noun* an act of secretly damaging or spoiling something: *The soldiers checked to see if sabotage had caused the damage to the bridge.*

**sack** /sak/ *noun* a large bag made of strong material. Sacks are used for storing or carrying food: *I carried the grocery sacks into the house.*

sack

**sa·cred** /**sayk**-rid/ *adjective* relating to a god or religion: *A mosque is a sacred building.*
( SYNONYM: **holy** )

**sac·ri·fice** /**sak**-ruh-fīss/
● *noun*
**1** something that you decide not to have or do so that you can have something more important: *My parents made a big sacrifice. They didn't take vacations so that they could pay for my brother to go to college.*
**2** something that you offer to a god: *They killed a sheep as a sacrifice to God.*
● *verb*
to stop having or doing something so that you can have something more important: *Mom sacrificed her job to stay home and look after us.*

**sad** /sad/ *adjective* (**sadder**, **saddest**) unhappy: *She's sad because her dog died.*
( ANTONYM: **happy** ) ▶ see Thesaurus

**sad·den** /**sad**'n/ *verb* to make someone sad: *He was saddened by her death.*

**sad·dle** /**sad**'l/ *noun*
**1** a leather seat that you sit on when riding a horse
**2** a seat on a bicycle or motorcycle ▶ see picture at **bicycle**

saddle

saddle

**sad·ly** /**sad**-lee/ *adverb*
**1** in a way that shows you are sad: *"I miss Maria," he said sadly.* ( SYNONYM: **unhappily** )
( ANTONYM: **happily** )

**2** used when talking about something that you wish were not true: *Sadly, Jason's mother died when he was a baby.* ( SYNONYM: **unfortunately** ) ( ANTONYM: **happily** )

**sad·ness** /**sad**-niss/ *noun* an unhappy feeling: *He felt great sadness at leaving his family and friends behind.* ( SYNONYM: **unhappiness** ) ( ANTONYM: **happiness** )

**sa·fa·ri** /suh-**far**-ee/ *noun* a trip through a place to watch wild animals, especially in Africa: *On safari in Kenya, you can see elephants and lions.*

**safe** /sayf/
● *adjective*
**1** not likely to be harmed or damaged: *I feel very safe in this neighborhood. There aren't many crimes.* | *Keep your money in a safe place.*
**2** not likely to harm you: *The water is clean and safe to drink.* ( ANTONYM: **dangerous** )
**3** in baseball, a runner is safe if he or she gets to a base before a player on the other team can touch the base while holding the ball: *"Safe!" the umpire shouted as Juan slid into home plate.* ( ANTONYM: **out** )
—**safely** /**sayf**-lee/ *adverb* so that something is safe: *He put the money safely in his pocket.*
● *noun*
a strong metal box with a lock. You keep money, jewelry, and important papers in a safe: *Keep your passport and birth certificate in a safe.*

**safe·guard** /**sayf**-gard/
● *noun* a rule or system that protects someone or something: *The school has safeguards to stop the children from seeing websites they shouldn't see.*
● *verb* to do something that protects someone or something: *We need to stop pollution in order to safeguard the planet.*

**safe·ty** /**sayf**-tee/ *noun* the state of being safe from danger or harm: *Carry the scissors with the points down, for safety reasons.*

**safe·ty pin** /**sayf**-tee pin/ *noun* a metal pin for fastening things together. The point of the pin fits into a cover so that it does not hurt you.

**safety pin**

**said** /sed/ *verb* the past tense and past participle of **say**

**sail** /sayl/
● *verb* to travel on water in a boat: *Columbus sailed across the ocean and found the islands.*
▶ see picture on page **A10**
—**sailing** /**sayl**-ing/ *noun* the activity of sailing in boats: *We went sailing on the lake.*
● *noun* a large cloth that makes a boat move when the wind blows it ▶ see picture at **mast**

**sail·boat** /**sayl**-boht/ *noun* a small boat with one or more sails: *A lot of sailboats were out on the lake.*

**sailboat**

**sail·or** /**sayl**-ur/ *noun* someone who works on a ship

**saint** /saynt/ *noun* ( ABBREVIATION: **St.** ) a good person who lived a religious life. The Christian church decides who will be a saint after he or she has died: *St. Paul helped spread the Christian religion.*

**sake** /sayk/ *noun*

IDIOMS with **sake**
**for the sake of** in order to try to achieve or improve something: *He began to exercise for the sake of his health.*
**for someone's sake** in order to help or please someone: *I tried to be brave for my mom's sake because I didn't want her to be upset.*

**sal·ad** /**sal**-uhd/ *noun* a mixture of raw vegetables that you eat cold: *She made a salad with lettuce, cucumber, and tomatoes.*

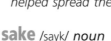
**Word Origin:** salad

**Salad** comes from a Latin word for salt. Vegetables with salt water on them were popular in Roman times. The vegetables were often called by their short name, *salata*, which means "salted." The Latin word passed into French, and then into English, and began to mean the vegetables instead of the salt.

a b c d e f g h i j k l m n o p q r **s** t u v w x y z

**sal·a·man·der** /**sal**-uh-mand-ur/ *noun* a small animal that looks like a lizard. Salamanders can live on land or in water. ▶ see picture on page **A1**

**sal·a·ry** /**sal**-uhr-ee/ *noun* (plural **salaries**) money that you get for doing your job: *Most lawyers make a high salary.* ▶ see **Thesaurus**

### Word Origin: salary

The word **salary** comes from a Latin word that means "a soldier's payment for salt." Salt was very important and valuable in the past because it was used to stop food from spoiling. Salt was also sometimes used as money. Roman soldiers may have been given salt as payment for their work, or they may have been given extra money to buy salt with. They may also have been paid a salary to protect the roads that people used when they carried salt to sell in other places.

**sale** /sayl/ *noun*
**1** the act of selling something: *The sale of cigarettes to children is not legal.*
**2** a time when stores sell things at lower prices than usual: *You can get things cheaper if you shop when stores are having sales.*
**3** the total number of products that are sold: *Sales of cars have gone down from 16 million to 10 million.*

> **IDIOMS with sale**
> **for sale** if something you own is for sale, you want to sell it: *Their house is for sale because they are moving to Miami.*
> **be on sale** available for people to buy at a lower price than usual: *The dress was on sale for $30. It used to cost $75.*
> **go on sale** to become available for people to buy in stores: *Tickets for the concert go on sale next week.*

**sales·per·son** /**saylz**-purss-uhn/ *noun* (plural **salespeople** /**saylz**-peep'l/) someone whose job is to sell things to people: *The salesperson showed Mom a couple of different cars.*
—**salesman** /**saylz**-muhn/ *noun* (plural **salesmen** /**saylz**-muhn/) a man whose job is to sell things to people
—**saleswoman** /**saylz**-wum-uhn/ *noun* (plural **saleswomen** /**saylz**-wim-in/) a woman whose job is to sell things to people

**sales tax** /**saylz** takss/ *noun* a tax that is added to the cost of something you are buying: *The jeans cost $25, plus sales tax. So they were $27.75 altogether.*

**sa·li·va** /suh-**līv**-uh/ *noun* the liquid that your mouth produces, which helps you to swallow food: *The smell of food made her mouth fill with saliva.*

**salm·on** /**sam**-uhn/ *noun* (plural **salmon**) a large fish with pink flesh that you can eat. Salmon live in the ocean but swim up a river to lay their eggs.

**salmon**

**sa·lon** /suh-**lahn**/ *noun* a place where you get your hair cut or have special treatments for your skin or your nails: *Mom went to the salon to get her hair cut.*

**sal·sa** /**salss**-uh/ *noun*
**1** a sauce with a strong taste. Salsa is usually made from tomatoes, onions, and peppers: *She was eating chips and salsa.*
**2** a type of music or dance from Latin America

**salt** /solt/ *noun* a white substance that you put on food to make it taste better, or to preserve it. Salt is found in sea water or under the ground.

**salt**

salt

**salt·y** /**solt**-ee/ *adjective* having the taste of salt: *The chips were very salty and made me thirsty.*

**sa·lute** /suh-**loot**/ *verb* to lift your hand to your head to show respect to a military officer: *The soldier saluted his captain.*

**sal·vage** /**salv**-ij/
● *verb* to save something after an accident or a situation when things have been damaged or destroyed: *People were trying to salvage their furniture from the flooded houses.*
● *noun* the act of saving something after an accident or after something has been damaged: *A salvage team is looking for the wreckage of the crashed plane.*

**same** /saym/
● *adjective*
**1** used when you mean one person or thing, not two or more different ones: *My brother and I go to the same school. | We both started to talk at the same time, so I stopped and let him speak.*
( ANTONYM: **different** )
**2** exactly like another person or thing: *Ben and John were both wearing the same T-shirt.*
( ANTONYM: **different** ) ▶ see Thesaurus
● *pronoun*
**1** someone or something that is exactly like another person or thing: *She wants to have a salad and I'll have the same.*
**2** if someone or something is the same, he, she, or it has not changed: *I hadn't seen my uncle for three years, but he was just the same as I remembered.* ( ANTONYM: **different** )
● *adverb*
in the same way: *Mom treats me and my sister the same.*

**sam·ple** /**samp**-uhl/
● *noun* a small amount of something that shows you what the rest is like: *The blood sample showed that he did not have the disease.*
● *verb* to taste food or drink to see what it is like: *We sampled four kinds of ice cream before we chose the one we wanted.* ( SYNONYM: **try** )

**sanc·tu·ar·y** /**sangk**-choo-air-ee/ *noun* (plural **sanctuaries**)
**1** a safe area for birds or animals where people cannot hunt them: *The injured bird was taken to a wildlife sanctuary.*
**2** a part of a religious building that is the most holy part: *The church service is held in the sanctuary.*

**sand** /sand/ *noun* the very small grains of rock that form beaches and deserts: *We went to the beach and made castles in the sand.*

sand
sand

**san·dal** /**sand**'l/ *noun* a shoe that does not cover your whole foot, which you wear in warm weather: *It was hot so I wore shorts and sandals.*
▶ see picture at **Roman**

**sand·box** /**sand**-bahkss/ *noun* a large box with sand in it, for children to play in: *The kids were making sandcastles in the sandbox.*

**sand·pa·per** /**sand**-payp-ur/ *noun* paper with very small pieces of sand glued on one side. You rub sandpaper on wood to make the wood smooth.

**sand·stone** /**sand**-stohn/ *noun* a yellow or red rock made from sand: *Sandstone is a soft sedimentary rock that is made when grains of sand are pressed tightly together.*

**sand·wich** /**sand**-wich/ *noun* two pieces of bread with cheese, meat, etc. between them: *I had a peanut butter sandwich for lunch.*

**Word Origin: sandwich**

The **sandwich** is named after John Montagu, the fourth Earl of Sandwich. Sandwich is a place in England. The Earl was a rich man who loved to play cards and gamble. When he didn't want to stop gambling to eat, he would eat meat between two pieces of bread. He made it fashionable to eat meat and bread together, so people started calling them sandwiches after him.

**sand·y** /**sand**-ee/ *adjective* covered with sand: *a sandy beach*

**sane** /sayn/ *adjective* mentally healthy and able to think in a normal way: *He thinks he's a dog. That's not sane!* ( ANTONYM: **insane** )

a b c d e f g h i j k l m n o p q r s t u v w x y z

a b c d e f g h i j k l m n o p q r **s** t u v w x y z

**sang** /sang/ *verb* the past tense of **sing**

**san·i·tar·y** /san-uh-tair-ee/ *adjective* clean and not likely to cause anyone to get sick: *The bathroom didn't look sanitary to me – the sink was dirty and it smelled.*
—**sanitation** /san-uh-**taysh**-uhn/ *noun* the process of keeping places clean: *The Department of Sanitation is responsible for taking away the garbage.*

**san·i·ty** /san-uht-ee/ *noun* the state of having a normal healthy mind: *He was behaving strangely, and I wondered about his sanity.*
( ANTONYM: **insanity** )

**sank** /sangk/ *verb* the past tense of **sink**

**sap** /sap/ *noun* the liquid that carries food through a plant: *The part of a tree that carries sap to the leaves and branches is called the xylem.*

**sap·phire** /saf-ī-ur/ *noun* a bright blue jewel: *The ring had sapphires and diamonds on it.*

sapphire

**sar·casm** /sark-az-uhm/ *noun* a way of speaking in which you say the opposite of what you mean. People use sarcasm to be mean or to show that they are annoyed: *"This is fun,"  said Emily with sarcasm, as she cleaned her bedroom.*
—**sarcastic** /sar-**kast**-ik/ *adjective* using sarcasm: *"That's a lot of money, Dad," she said in a sarcastic voice when he gave her a dime.*

**sar·dine** /sar-**deen**/ *noun* a small fish that you can eat. Sardines are often sold in cans.

**sat** /sat/ *verb* the past tense and past participle of **sit**

**sat·el·lite** /sat'l-īt/ *noun*
**1** a machine that is put into space to receive and send radio and television signals. A satellite goes around the Earth: *The satellite was launched last year. | Television shows can be sent by satellite to anywhere in the world.*
**2** a moon or other object that moves around a planet: *The planet Jupiter has four satellites.*

**sat·el·lite dish** /sat'l-it dish/ *noun* a piece of equipment that receives radio and television signals sent from a satellite. A satellite dish is round and is attached to the outside of a building: *We have a satellite dish so we can see all the basketball games, even when they're not on local TV.*

**sat·in** /sat'n/ *noun* a type of cloth that is very smooth and shiny: *The dancer's dress was made of pink satin.*

**sat·is·fac·tion** /sat-iss-**fak**-shuhn/ *noun* the feeling you get when you are pleased because you have achieved something: *Rachel finished writing and looked at her work with satisfaction – it was a good story.*

**sat·is·fac·to·ry** /sat-iss-**fakt**-uhr-ee/ *adjective* good enough, but not very good: *My grades are satisfactory, but I can do better if I work harder.*

**sat·is·fied** /sat-iss-fīd/ *adjective* pleased because something is good or because you have achieved something: *I am very satisfied with my grades – I got all A's and B's.* ( ANTONYM: **dissatisfied** )

**sat·is·fy** /sat-iss-fī/ *verb* (**satisfies**, **satisfied**) to make someone feel happy, by doing what he or she wants: *I did my homework before I went out, to satisfy my parents.*
—**satisfying** /sat-iss-fī-ing/ *adjective* making you feel happy because you have done something or gotten something you want: *We won 5–0, which was very satisfying.*

**Word Family:** satisfy

**satisfy** verb | **satisfied** adjective | **satisfying** adjective | **satisfactory** adjective | **satisfaction** noun

**sat·u·rat·ed fat** /sach-uh-rayt-id **fat**/ *noun* fat that comes from meat and milk: *Too much saturated fat is not good for your body.*

**Sat·ur·day** /sat-ur-dee/ *noun*
( ABBREVIATION: **Sat.** ) the seventh day of the week. Saturday is between Friday and Sunday: *We're going swimming on Saturday. | I'll see you Saturday morning.*

a
b
c
d
e
f
g
h
i
j
k
l
m
n
o
p
q
r
**s**
t
u
v
w
x
y
z

## Word Origin: Saturday

**Saturday** was named for the planet Saturn by the ancient Romans because they thought the planet Saturn controlled the first hour of that day. The planet itself was named for Saturn, the god of farming. Saturday is the only day of the week that is named after a Roman god.

**Sat·urn** /sat-urn/ *noun* the sixth planet from the Sun. Saturn is the second largest planet. Saturn has rings around it and many moons.
▶ see picture at **solar system**

**sauce** /soss/ *noun* a thick liquid that you serve with food to give it a good taste: *Mom cooked meatballs with tomato sauce.*

**sauce·pan** /soss-pan/ *noun* a metal container with a handle, that you use for cooking: *Heat the soup in a saucepan.*

**sau·cer** /soss-ur/ *noun* a small round plate that you put a cup on: *The tea spilled over the edge of the cup onto the saucer.* ▶ see picture at **cup**

**sau·sage** /soss-ij/ *noun* meat and spices that are put inside a skin shaped like a tube: *We had sausages and eggs for breakfast.*

**sav·age** /sav-ij/ *adjective* very violent and cruel: *The dog bit his arm in a savage attack.*

**save** /sayv/ *verb*
**1** to make someone or something safe from danger or harm: *Firefighters saved three children from the fire.*
**2** to keep money instead of spending it, so that you can use it later: *I'm saving up to buy a new bike.*
**3** to use less of something, and not waste it: *We saved electricity by turning the lights off.*
**4** to keep something, and not throw it away: *Mom saved my baby shoes.*
**5** to make a computer keep the work that you have done on it: *Don't forget to save your work before you turn the computer off.*

**sav·ings** /sayv-ingz/ *plural noun* all the money you have saved: *She spends all the money she earns so she has no savings.*

**Sav·ior** /sayv-yur/ *noun* used as a name for Jesus Christ, who Christians believe saves people from evil

**saw** /so/
● *verb* the past tense of **see**
● *noun* a tool that you use for cutting wood. A saw has a flat blade and a row of sharp points: *Cut the branch off the tree with a saw.*
● *verb* (**sawed**, **sawed** or **sawn** /son/) to cut something using a saw: *He sawed the wood into three pieces.*

**saw·dust** /so-duhst/ *noun* very small pieces of wood that fall to the ground when you cut wood

**saw·mill** /so-mil/ *noun* a factory where machines cut trees into pieces for boards and lumber

**sax·o·phone** /sakss-uh-fohn/ *noun* a metal musical instrument that is usually curved. You play a saxophone by blowing into it and pressing buttons.

saxophone

**say** /say/
● *verb* (**says** /sez/, **saying**, **said** /sed/)
**1** to speak words: *"I'm going now," she said.* | *She says she doesn't like him.* ▶ see **Thesaurus**
**2** to give information in writing, pictures, or numbers: *The clock said 6:45.* | *What does the letter say?*
● *noun* the chance to give an opinion and help decide something: *The teacher lets us have a say about what games we play in P.E.*

## Word Choice: say, tell, talk

You **say** words to someone. You cannot say "say me": *The teacher said to us that plants need sunlight to grow.* | *She said "plants need sunlight to grow."*

You **tell** someone facts or information: *The teacher told us that plants need sunlight to grow.*

You **talk** about a particular subject: *The teacher talked about how plants grow.*

**say·ing** /**say**-ing/ *noun* a well-known phrase that gives advice or information about life: *My dad's favorite saying is "be prepared."*

**scab** /skab/ *noun* a hard layer of dry blood that forms over a cut on your skin: *The girl had a scab on her knee where she had scraped it.*

**scald** /skold/ *verb* to burn yourself with hot liquid or steam: *He scalded his hand when he spilled a pan of boiling water.*
—**scalding** /**skold**-ing/ *adjective* extremely hot: *The bath water was scalding.*

**scale** /skayl/ *noun*
**1** a piece of equipment for weighing people or objects: *Our bathroom scale says I weigh 65 pounds.*
**2** a system for measuring something: *The earthquake measured 7.0 on the Richter scale.*
**3** the relationship between a map and the size of the place it represents: *This map has a scale of 1 inch to 1 mile.*
**4** a series of musical notes that you play in a set order. The notes gradually become higher or lower in sound: *She was playing the C major scale.*
**5** one of the small pieces of hard skin that cover the body of a fish, snake, or other reptile: *An alligator is covered with scales.*
**6** how big or important something is: *People don't understand the scale of the problem – it is very serious.*

**scale draw·ing** /**skayl** dro-ing/ *noun* a drawing of an object or area. Each part has been made smaller or larger by the same amount, so the relation between them is the same as the real object or area.

**sca·lene tri·an·gle** /skayl-een **trī**-ang-guhl/ *noun* a triangle with sides that are all different lengths

**scalp** /skalp/ *noun* the skin on your head, under your hair: *This shampoo is good for your hair and scalp.*

**scal·pel** /**skalp**-uhl/ *noun* a small sharp knife that a doctor uses for doing an operation: *The doctor cut open the patient's stomach with a scalpel.*

**scan** /skan/
● *verb* (**scanning**, **scanned**)
**1** to read something quickly to find important information: *She scanned the list to see if her name was on it.*
**2** to use a machine to check something, for example to see what the price is or to see what is inside something: *They scan your bags at the airport to check if there are any weapons inside.*
**3** to copy a picture or piece of writing onto a computer using a special machine: *She scanned the letter and emailed it to me.*
● *noun*
a medical test that uses a machine to make a picture of something inside your body: *The doctors gave him a scan to make sure that his heart was OK.*

**scan·dal** /**skand**'l/ *noun* something very bad or shocking that a famous or important person does: *There was a big scandal when a politician took money that didn't belong to him.*

**Scan·di·na·vi·an** /skand-uh-**nayv**-ee-uhn/
● *noun* someone from Norway, Sweden, Denmark, Finland, or Iceland: *A lot of Scandinavians moved from northern Europe to the U.S. many years ago.*
● *adjective* from Norway, Sweden, Denmark, Finland, or Iceland: *My father is Scandinavian – he was born in Sweden.*

**scan·ner** /**skan**-ur/ *noun*
**1** a machine that copies a picture or a page of writing. The scanner is connected to a computer, so you can see the copy on the computer screen: *If you have a scanner, you can put your favorite photographs onto your computer.*
**2** a machine that makes a picture of what is inside an object or inside a part of your body: *The scanner can take pictures of people's brains.*

**scar** /skar/ *noun* a mark on your skin from a cut or wound. A scar stays on your skin forever: *I fell off my bike when I was six years old and I still have a scar on my leg.*

**scarce** /skairss/ *adjective* if something is scarce, there is not much of it and it is difficult to get: *Food was scarce and we were always hungry.*
—**scarcity** /**skairss**-uht-ee/ *noun* a situation when something is scarce: *There is a scarcity of clean water in some poor countries.*

**scarce·ly** /**skairss**-lee/ *adverb* almost not at all, or almost none at all: *Scarcely anybody in my class has been to Canada – in fact, only one person has.* ( SYNONYMS: **barely, hardly** )

**scare** /skair/
- *verb*
to make someone feel afraid: *Movies about monsters scare me.* ( SYNONYM: **frighten** )
- *noun*
**1** a sudden feeling of fear: *Carlos jumped out of the closet and gave me a scare.*
**2** a situation that frightens or worries people because they think something bad will happen: *The flu caused a health scare because people didn't know how bad it might be.*

**scare·crow** /**skair**-kroh/
*noun* a person made of straw and dressed in old clothes. A farmer puts a scarecrow in a field to keep birds away, so that the birds do not eat seeds or the crop.

scarecrow

**scared** /skaird/ *adjective* afraid or nervous about something: *Are you scared of ghosts?* | *I'm scared about having to give a report to the class.*
( SYNONYMS: **afraid, frightened** )

**scarf** /skarf/ *noun* (plural **scarves** /skarvz/ or **scarfs**) something you wear around your neck to keep you warm or to make you look nice: *It's cold outside. Put on your scarves and gloves.*
▶ see picture at **match**

**scar·let** /**skarl**-it/ *noun, adjective* a bright red color: *She is wearing a scarlet coat.*

**scar·let fe·ver** /skarl-it **feev**-ur/ *noun* a disease that gives you a sore throat, a red tongue, and red spots on your skin. Scarlet fever mainly affects children.

**scar·y** /**skair**-ee/ *adjective* making you feel afraid: *Some of the rides at the fair are very scary because they go so fast.*
( ANTONYM: **frightening** )

**scat·ter** /**skat**-ur/ *verb*
**1** to throw things over a big area: *We scattered the seeds over the ground.*
**2** to move away quickly in different directions: *The birds scattered when they saw the cat.*

scatter

**scene** /seen/ *noun*
**1** a short part of a play or movie. The events in one scene happen in the same place: *I like the scene where Annie goes to live with Mr. Warbucks.*
**2** the place where an accident or crime happened: *They found a gun at the scene of the crime.*
**3** a view or picture of a place: *He paints beautiful scenes of mountains and lakes.*

**sce·ner·y** /**seen**-uhr-ee/ *noun*
**1** the natural things you can see in a place, for example mountains, forests, and fields: *The scenery in Yosemite National Park is beautiful. I like the waterfalls best.*
**2** the background and furniture on a theater stage: *The scenery is simple – just a chair and a desk, and a window painted on the background.*

**sce·nic** /**seen**-ik/ *adjective* a scenic place has beautiful views of natural things such as mountains, forests, and oceans: *The road is very scenic, with views of the ocean and cliffs.*

**scent** /sent/ *noun*
**1** a pleasant smell: *The flowers growing by the back door have a beautiful scent.*
**2** the smell that a person or animal leaves on things it walks on or touches: *The dogs follow the scent of the rabbit until they find it.*

**sched·ule** /**skej**-uhl/ *noun*
**1** a plan of what you will do and when you will do it: *Mom made a schedule for watching TV, so we could see our favorite shows but not watch too much.*
**2** a list showing the times that buses, trains, etc. arrive at and leave a place: *The schedule says the next train will arrive in 15 minutes.*

**scheme** /skeem/ *noun* a plan, especially to do something bad or illegal: *The men thought of a scheme to get money. They tricked people into buying things that the men would never deliver.*

a b c d e f g h i j k l m n o p q r **s** t u v w x y z

**schol·ar** /**skahl**-ur/ *noun* someone who studies a subject and knows a lot about it: *Some scholars think that the temple is over 1,000 years old.*

**schol·ar·ship** /**skahl**-ur-ship/ *noun* money that an organization gives someone to help pay for his or her education: *He did really well in school and he got a scholarship to the University of Washington.*

**scho·las·tic** /skoh-**last**-ik/ *adjective* relating to schools and studying: *He received a prize for his scholastic achievements.*

**school** /skool/ *noun*

**1** a place where children go to learn: *My school is very close to my house.*
**2** the time you spend at school: *Do you want to play soccer after school?*
**3** all the people in a school: *She played the piano in front of the whole school.*
**4** a university, or a university department that teaches a particular subject: *My sister wants to go to law school and study to become a lawyer.*
**5** a group of fish: *We saw a school of fish swim by.*

### Word Origin: school

**School** comes from a Greek word that originally meant "leisure." Leisure is your spare time, when you can do things that you enjoy. The Greeks must have enjoyed discussing ideas because the Greek word started to mean a discussion. Soon, it also meant a place where you discussed things in order to learn about them. From that idea, the word came to mean a place to learn.

**sci·ence** /**sī**-uhnss/ *noun* the study of how things in the world grow, behave, or work. Science is based on testing things and showing that ideas are true: *We are doing a science experiment to see what floats in water and what doesn't.*

### Word Family: science

**science** *noun* | **scientist** *noun* | **scientific** *adjective*

**sci·ence fic·tion** /**sī**-uhnss **fik**-shuhn/ *noun* books and stories about the future or about life on other planets: *I'm reading a science fiction book about a boy living on Mars.*

**sci·en·tif·ic** /**sī**-uhn-**tif**-ik/ *adjective* relating to science: *We did a scientific experiment to find out what plants need in order to grow.*

**sci·en·tist** /**sī**-uhnt-ist/ *noun* someone who works in science: *Scientists think that there may be water on the Moon.*

**sci-fi** /**sī**-**fī**/ *noun* another word for science fiction: *I watched a sci-fi movie about a boy who goes into the future.*

**scis·sors** /**siz**-urz/ *plural noun* a tool for cutting paper or cloth. It has two sharp blades and handles with holes for your finger and thumb: *I cut a circle out of the paper with a pair of scissors.*

scissors

**scold** /skohld/ *verb* to tell someone in an angry way that he or she has done something wrong: *Dad scolded him for breaking the window.*

**scoop** /skoop/
● *noun*
**1** a deep spoon for serving food
**2** an amount of food that a scoop holds: *I had two scoops of ice cream on my cone.*
● *verb*
to remove something using a spoon or your hand: *She scooped the seeds out of the pumpkin.*

**scoot·er** /**skoot**-ur/ *noun*

scooter

**1** a children's vehicle with a tall handle on a board with two wheels. You stand on the board with one foot and move by pushing against the ground with your other foot.
**2** a small motorcycle

scooter

568

**scope** /skohp/ *noun* the range of things that a book, job, subject, etc. deals with: *The scope of the book is very wide and it tries to cover all of American history.*

**-scope** /skohp/

## Word Building

kaleido**scope** | micro**scope** | peri**scope** | tele**scope**

These words all have the Greek word root **-scope** in them. **Scope** means "see" or "watch." If you look through a *kaleidoscope*, you see pretty patterns. A *periscope* in a submarine lets you see what is above you in the water. A *telescope* lets you see things that are far away.

**scorch** /skorch/ *verb* to burn the surface of something and make it change color: *The hot pan scorched the table.*

**score** /skor/
● *noun*
the number of points that you get in a game or on a test: *I got a score of ten out of ten on the spelling test.* | *The final score was 1–0.*

> **IDIOM with score**
> **keep score** to write down how many points each person or team has in a game: *Someone has to keep score so we know who is winning!*

● *verb*
**1** to get points in a game or on a test: *Did you score a goal?*
**2** to give someone a particular number of points in a game, competition, or test: *The tests are scored by a computer.*

**score·board** /skor-bord/ *noun* a sign that shows the latest score in a game, while it is being played

**scorn** /skorn/
● *noun* a way of behaving that shows you do not like someone because you think he or she is not important or good: *"That's a stupid idea,"* she said with scorn.
● *verb* to treat someone as if he or she is stupid and not good enough or important enough: *In the past, people scorned women's intelligence, and women were not even allowed to vote.*

**scor·pi·on**
/skorp-ee-uhn/ *noun* a small animal that can use its tail to sting people. It has eight legs. The two front legs have pincers on them, which the scorpion can use for holding onto things: *Most scorpions live in the desert, but they are also found in other places.*

scorpion

**Scot·tish** /skaht-ish/ *adjective* from Scotland: *McKenzie is a Scottish name.*

**scout** /skowt/
● *noun*
**1** a member of the Girl Scouts or Boy Scouts: *A group of Scouts went on a hike together.*
**2** someone who goes to an area to find out information about it, and who brings the information back to tell other people: *A scout said that enemy soldiers were hiding in the forest.*
**3** someone whose job is to find good sports players in order to employ them: *A baseball scout is watching the high school game today.*
● *verb*
to look for something in a particular area: *I'll scout around for a good picnic spot.*

**scowl** /skowl/
● *verb* to look at someone in an angry way: *He scowled at me and didn't say anything.*
● *noun* an angry look: *"I'm not eating this,"* she said with a scowl.

**scram·ble** /skram-buhl/ *verb* to climb up or over something quickly, using your hands to help you: *We scrambled over the rocks on our hands and knees.*

**scram·bled eggs** /skram-buhld egz/ *plural noun* eggs that have the white and yellow parts mixed together while you cook them: *We had scrambled eggs for breakfast.*

**scrap** /skrap/ *noun* a small piece of paper, cloth, or food: *I wrote his phone number on a scrap of paper.*

**scrap·book** /skrap-buk/ *noun* a book in which you can stick pictures, newspaper articles, or other things you want to keep: *He collects postcards and sticks them in his scrapbook.*

a
b
c
d
e
f
g
h
i
j
k
l
m
n
o
p
q
r
**s**
t
u
v
w
x
y
z

**scrape** /skrayp/
- *verb*
**1** to damage something by rubbing it against a rough surface: *She scraped both her knees when she fell down.*
**2** to remove something using an object with a sharp edge: *Melissa was scraping the last little bit of ice cream out of the carton with a spoon.*
- *noun*
a mark made when something scrapes someone's skin or an object: *He had a lot of scrapes and bruises on his legs from falling off his bike.*

**scratch** /skrach/
- *verb*
**1** to rub your skin with your fingernails: *I keep scratching this mosquito bite on my leg because it really itches.* ▶ see picture on page **A14**
**2** to damage a surface or to slightly cut someone's skin by pulling something sharp across it: *The cat sometimes scratches me with his paw when he wants attention.*
- *noun*
a long thin cut or mark on the surface of something or on someone's skin: *Dad noticed a scratch on the car door.*

**scratch·y** /skrach-ee/ *adjective* scratchy clothes or materials have a rough surface and are uncomfortable to wear or touch: *I don't like wearing thick wool sweaters – they're too scratchy.*

**scream** /skreem/
- *verb* to make a loud high noise with your voice because you are afraid, hurt, or excited: *A girl fell off the slide and started screaming.*
- *noun* a loud high noise that you make when you are afraid, hurt, or excited: *There were screams of excitement as the kids opened their gifts.*

**screech** /skreech/
- *verb*
**1** to make a loud high noise: *The car's tires screeched as it came to a stop.*
**2** to say something in a loud high voice, especially when you are angry: *"Come here now!" she screeched.*
- *noun* a loud high noise: *One of the big birds gave a horrible screech.*

**screen** /skreen/ *noun*
**1** the flat glass part of a television or a computer: *An email appeared on the screen.*
**2** a large flat white surface that movies are shown on in a movie theater: *We sat in the front row, closest to the screen.*
**3** a wire net that covers an open door or window. Screens let air get into a house but stop insects getting in: *A big moth flew onto the window screen.*

screen
a flatscreen TV

**screw** /skroo/
- *noun* a thin pointed piece of metal you use to fasten pieces of wood or metal together. It looks like a nail with a round pattern around it. You turn the screw around with a screwdriver to put it into place: *The bookcase is held together by a few screws.*
- *verb* to fasten one thing to another, using a screw: *Dad screwed the shelf to the wall.*

**screw·driv·er** /**skroo**-drīv-ur/ *noun* a tool that you use to turn screws: *She used a screwdriver to put the furniture together.*

**-scrib-** /skrib/ (also **-scrip-** /skrip/)

> ## Word Building
>
> **describe | prescrip**tion **| scrib**ble **| scrip**ture
>
> These words all have the Latin word root **-scrib-** or **-scrip-** in them. *Scrib* and *scrip* mean "write." If you *describe* someone, you use words to say what that person is like. If you get a *prescription* from a doctor, the doctor writes down the medicine that you need to have. If someone reads the *scriptures*, he or she reads religious teachings that have been written down, for example in the Bible or the Koran.

**scrib·ble** /**skrib**-uhl/ *verb* to write or draw something quickly in a messy way: *She started to scribble down her address.*

**scrim·mage** /**skrim**-ij/ *noun* a game played for practice in sports such as football and basketball: *The team played a few scrimmages to prepare for the big game on Friday night.*

**script** /skript/ *noun* the written words of a movie, play, or speech: *She read her lines from the script.*

**scrip·ture** /**skrip**-chur/ *noun*
**1** the Bible: *Scripture says that you should love your enemies.*
**2** the holy books of any religion: *The box contains Jewish scriptures.*

**scroll** /skrohl/
● *verb* to move information up or down a computer screen so that you can read it: *You can scroll up and down using the arrows at the right of the screen.*
● *noun* a long piece of paper that can be written on and rolled up: *The Roman soldier read from a scroll.*

**scrub** /skruhb/ *verb* (**scrubbing**, **scrubbed**) to clean something by rubbing it very hard: *I had to really scrub the bathtub to get it clean.*

**scu·ba div·ing** /**skoob**-uh dīv-ing/ *noun* the sport of swimming under water and breathing from a container of air on your back: *When you go scuba diving you see some amazing fish.*

**scuba diving**

**sculp·tor** /**skuhlpt**-ur/ *noun* an artist who makes objects from stone, wood, or metal: *The sculptor made a statue of a horse.*

**sculp·ture** /**skuhlp**-chur/ *noun*
**1** a work of art that someone has made from stone, wood, or metal: *There is a sculpture of a lion in front of the library.*
**2** the art of making objects out of stone, wood, or metal: *We did some sculpture in art class.*

**scum** /skuhm/ *noun* a dirty substance that forms on the top of a liquid: *There was soap scum on the bathtub.*

**sea** /see/ *noun*
**1** a part of an ocean that is partly surrounded by land: *Sardinia is an island in the Mediterranean Sea.*
**2** the ocean: *The ship sailed out to sea.*

**sea·food** /**see**-food/ *noun* fish and shellfish that you can eat: *I didn't eat the fish because I don't like seafood.*

**sea·gull** /**see**-guhl/ *noun* a common gray and white bird that lives near the sea and makes a loud sound

seagull

**seal** /seel/
● *noun*
**1** a large animal that lives near the ocean. Seals swim, have smooth fur, and eat fish: *Sometimes you can see seals here, swimming in the ocean or lying on the rocks.*
**2** a piece of plastic or paper that you have to break to open something: *If the seal on the jar is broken, you know the jar has already been opened.*
**3** a mark that is put on documents to prove that they are official: *There was a government seal on the letter.*
● *verb*
to close something so that nothing can get in or out: *She put the letter in the envelope and sealed it.*

seal

**sea lev·el** /**see** lev-uhl/ *noun* the height of the surface of the ocean. Sea level is used when talking about how high or low places are compared to the surface of the ocean: *Mexico City is 7,300 feet above sea level.* | *Sea levels are rising because of global warming.*

s

**sea li·on** /see lī-uhn/ *noun* a large seal with ears that stick out and long flippers that it can use to walk on land. Sea lions live mainly in the Pacific Ocean: *At the zoo, we saw a sea lion balance a ball on its nose.*

**seam** /seem/ *noun* the line where two pieces of cloth have been sewn together: *My old shirt was starting to come apart at the seams.*

**search** /surch/
- *noun*
**1** an attempt to find someone or something by looking very carefully: *My friends and I all went out on a search for our missing dog.*
**2** an attempt to find information or an answer: *Do a search on the Internet to see if you can find out when Lincoln was born.*
- *verb*
**1** to try to find someone or something by looking very carefully: *I searched through my backpack but I couldn't find my book report.*
**2** to try to find information or an answer to a problem: *She's searching the Internet for information about the Pilgrims.*

**search en·gine** /surch enj-in/ *noun* a computer program that helps you find information on the Internet

**sea·shell** /see-shel/
*noun* an empty shell of a small sea animal such as a clam: *The beach was covered with seashells.*

**seashell**

**sea·shore** /see-shor/ *noun* the land along the edge of the ocean: *I like looking for shells on the seashore.*

**sea·sick** /see-sik/ *adjective* feeling sick because of the movement of a boat: *The ocean was very rough and everyone on the ship felt seasick.*
—**seasickness** /see-sik-niss/ *noun* the feeling of being seasick: *Mom doesn't like boats because she suffers from seasickness.*

**sea·son** /seez-uhn/ *noun*
**1** one of the four time periods in the year, which each have a different type of weather. The seasons are winter, spring, summer, and fall:

*Spring is my favorite season because there are so many flowers.*
**2** a part of a year when an activity or event usually happens: *Football season is in the fall.*
—**seasonal** /seez-uhn-uhl/ *adjective* relating to the seasons of the year: *There are seasonal changes in the colors of the leaves. They are green in the summer, and red or yellow in the fall.*

**season**

spring | summer

fall | winter

**seat** /seet/ *noun* something you can sit on, for example a chair: *After recess, go back to your seats quietly.* ▶ see picture at **motorcycle**

> **IDIOM with seat**
> **take/have a seat** to sit down: *Take a seat in the waiting room.*

**seat belt** /seet belt/ *noun* a belt that holds you in your seat in a car or airplane if there is an accident: *Get in the car and fasten your seat belts.*

**sea·weed** /see-weed/ *noun* a plant that grows in the ocean. Seaweed has no roots, stems, or leaves. It produces oxygen and people can eat it: *Seaweed is an algae and there are thousands of different kinds.*

**se·cede** /si-seed/ *verb* to stop being part of a country or group: *The Southern states seceded from the rest of the U.S., and the Civil War began.*

**se·clud·ed** /si-klood-id/ *adjective* a secluded

place is very private and quiet: *Not many people know about this beach. It's very secluded.*

**sec·ond** /**sek**-uhnd/
● *number, pronoun*
someone or something that comes next after the first one: *Joe won the race and I came in second.*
● *noun*
**1** a unit for measuring time. There are 60 seconds in a minute: *Hold the button down for ten seconds and then let go.*
**2** a very short period of time: *Just let me finish my homework – it will only take a second.*

**sec·ond·ar·y** /**sek**-uhn-dair-ee/ *adjective* not as important as something else: *My dad says his job is always secondary to his family because family is the most important thing.*

**sec·ond·ar·y source** /**sek**-uhn-dair-ee **sorss**/ *noun* a piece of writing that discusses an event, person, or period of time, but is written by someone who did not experience these things himself: *A textbook is an example of a secondary source.* ( **ANTONYM: primary source** )

**sec·ond·hand** /**sek**-uhnd-**hand**/ *adjective* used by someone else before you: *Some of these secondhand clothes look like new.*

**sec·ond per·son** /**sek**-uhnd **purss**-uhn/ *noun* "you," and the verb forms you use with "you": *The poem is written mostly in the second person – "your eyes are like stars."*

**se·cre·cy** /**seek**-ruhss-ee/ *noun* if there is secrecy about something, people keep it a secret: *You can tell everyone about this. There is no need for secrecy.*

**se·cret** /**seek**-rit/
● *adjective*
if something is secret, only you or only a few people know about it: *My brother and I have a secret place to keep candy that only we know about.* ▶ see **Thesaurus**
—**secretly** /**seek**-rit-lee/ *adverb* without other people knowing: *I secretly put Mom's birthday present under my bed.*
● *noun*
**1** an idea, plan, or information that you do not tell other people about: *Don't tell anyone about the party. It's a secret.*
**2 in secret** without other people knowing: *I hid*

behind the sofa and listened in secret to what Mom and Dad were saying.

**se·cret a·gent** /**seek**-rit **ayj**-uhnt/ *noun* someone whose job is to get secrets about other countries' governments: *James Bond is a secret agent who works for the British government.*
( **SYNONYM: spy** )

**sec·re·tar·y** /**sek**-ruh-tair-ee/ *noun* (plural **secretaries**)
**1** someone who works in an office answering the telephone, writing letters, and arranging meetings: *When I called Dad at work, his secretary said he was in a meeting.*
**2** an official who is in charge of a large U.S. government department: *Robert Gates was appointed as the Secretary of Defense.*

**se·cret serv·ice** /**seek**-rit **surv**-iss/ *noun* the U.S. government department whose job is to protect the president: *Members of the secret service go with the president wherever he goes.*

**sec·tion** /**sek**-shuhn/ *noun* a part of something: *The children's section of the library has lots of good books to read.*

**se·cure** /si-**kyoor**/ *adjective*
**1** likely to stay the same, and not change or be lost: *Dad's job is not secure because the company he works for is losing money.*
**2** a secure person feels safe and confident: *The school tries hard to make the children feel secure.*
**3** safe from damage or attack: *People tried to make their houses secure before the storm hit.*
( **SYNONYM: safe** )
**4** fastened or closed carefully: *Make sure the windows are secure so small children can't open them.*
—**securely** /si-**kyoor**-lee/ *adverb* in a way that is secure: *Close the gate and lock it securely.*

**se·cu·ri·ty** /si-**kyoor**-uht-ee/ *noun*
**1** things that a government or organization does to protect people from crime or attack: *They increased security at the airport. They check everyone's bags before they get on planes.*
**2** the state of being safe from damage or attack: *The locks on the windows give extra security.*

**se·dan** /si-**dan**/ *noun* a car that has seats for four or more people. Sedans have a metal roof and have a trunk at the back: *The president arrived in a black sedan.*

a b c d e f g h i j k l m n o p q r s t u v w x y z

**sed·a·tive** /**sed**-uht-iv/ *noun* a drug that makes someone calm or makes them want to sleep: *The doctor gave him a sedative after the accident so he could sleep.*

**sed·i·ment** /**sed**-uh-muhnt/ *noun* small solid pieces that go to the bottom of a liquid: *Small pieces of sand and rock form layers of sediment at the bottom of the lake.*
—**sedimentary** /sed-uh-**men**-tree/ *adjective* sedimentary rock is formed from small pieces of sand, rock, mud, etc. that are left by water or ice, and pressed together to become solid

**se·di·tion** /suh-**di**-shuhn/ *noun* words and actions that encourage people to oppose the government

**see** /see/ *verb* (**saw** /so/, **seen** /seen/)
**1** to notice something with your eyes: *I can see the train coming.* | *It was so dark we couldn't see at all.* ▶ see **Thesaurus**
**2** to understand or realize something: *Don't you see, she's crying because you shouted at her.* | *"I see what you mean."*
**3** to meet or visit someone: *We're going to see my grandparents.*
**4** to find out information or a fact: *Let's see if Mike wants to come too.*
**5** to watch a television program, play, or movie – used when talking about the past, or the future: *I've already seen that movie.* | *We're going to see the baseball game on Saturday.*

> **IDIOM with see**
> **see you later** used for saying goodbye to someone: *I'm going now – see you later!*

**seed** /seed/ *noun* a small hard object from which a new plant will grow: *The spring is the best time for planting seeds.* ▶ see picture at **flower**

seed

**See·ing Eye dog** /see-ing ī **dog**/ *noun* **trademark** a dog that has been trained to guide blind people

**seek** /seek/ *verb* (**sought** /sot/) to try to find or get something: *She sought my help with her math homework.*

**seem** /seem/ *verb* to appear to be something: *You seem sad – what's the matter?*

**seen** /seen/ *verb* the past participle of see

**see·saw** /**see**-so/ *noun* a piece of play equipment. A seesaw is made of a long board with a support in the middle. A child sits on each end of the board. When one end of the board goes up, the other end goes down: *We played on the seesaw at the park.*

seesaw

**seg·ment** /**seg**-muhnt/ *noun* a part of something: *The worm's body has over 100 segments.*

**seg·re·gate** /**seg**-ruh-gayt/ *verb* to separate people from different races, sexes, or religions: *In the church, the men and women were segregated. The men sat on one side of the church and the women on the other.*
—**segregated** /**seg**-ruh-gayt-id/ *adjective* if a place is segregated, people of different races, sexes, or religions are not allowed to be together: *In the past, black and white children went to segregated schools.*
—**segregation** /seg-ruh-**gaysh**-uhn/ *noun* the practice of segregating people in places such as schools and restaurants: *Racial segregation in schools, or any other public place, is not allowed.*

**seize** /seez/ *verb*
**1** to take hold of something quickly and roughly: *She seized my hand and pulled me away from the road.* (SYNONYM: **grab**)
**2** to take control of something using force: *The soldiers seized control of the city.*
**3** to take something away from someone: *Police seized his car because they thought it was stolen.*

**sei·zure** /**seezh**-ur/ *noun*
**1** if someone has a seizure, he or she suddenly becomes unconscious and his or her body may shake: *She has a disease called epilepsy, which sometimes makes her have seizures.*
(SYNONYM: **fit**)
**2** the act of seizing something or someone: *The information led to the seizure of illegal drugs by the police.*

**sel·dom** /**seld**-uhm/ *adverb* not often: *It seldom rains here so the ground is very dry.*
( SYNONYM: **rarely** )

**se·lect** /si-**lekt**/ *verb* to choose something or someone: *The coach selects who will be on the team.* ( SYNONYMS: **choose, pick** )

**se·lec·tion** /si-**lek**-shuhn/ *noun*
**1** the action of choosing someone or something: *There are 50 books to choose from. Make a selection and read that book in the next two weeks.* ( SYNONYM: **choice** )
**2** a group of things that you can choose from: *The store has a large selection of chocolate and other candy.* ( SYNONYMS: **choice, range** )

**self** /self/ *noun* (plural **selves** /selvz/) the type of person you are, including what you feel and think and how you behave: *When I'm dancing I feel like my true self.*

**self-cen·tered** /self **sent**-urd/ *adjective* only interested in yourself and not thinking about other people: *Stop being so self-centered and think about how your mother feels!*
( SYNONYM: **selfish** )

**self-con·fi·dent** /self **kahn**-fuhd-uhnt/ *adjective* feeling sure that you can do things well and that people like you: *Mario is very self-confident and wasn't nervous about singing in front of the whole school.* ( SYNONYM: **confident** )
( ANTONYM: **shy** )
—**self-confidence** /self **kahn**-fuhd-uhnss/ *noun* a self-confident feeling: *She didn't have much self-confidence and was afraid to say what she thought.*

**self-con·scious** /self **kahnsh**-uhss/ *adjective* worried and embarrassed about what you look like or what other people think of you: *At first I was a little self-conscious about wearing glasses.*

**self-con·trol** /self kuhn-**trohl**/ *noun* the ability to control your feelings and behavior even when you are angry, excited, or upset: *It takes great self-control not to hit back when someone is mean to you.*

**self-de·fense** /self di-**fenss**/ *noun* the use of force to protect yourself when someone attacks you: *I go to karate classes to learn self-defense.*

**self-es·teem** /self i-**steem**/ *noun* the feeling that you are a good person and that people

should like you: *Your self-esteem will improve if you work hard at things.*

**self-gov·ern·ment** /self **guhv**-ur-muhnt/ *noun* the situation when a country is controlled by its own people, not a foreign government: *The American colonies wanted self-government, instead of being ruled by Britain.*

**self·ish** /**self**-ish/ *adjective* caring only about yourself and not about other people: *Don't be selfish – let me have a piece of your candy.*
( ANTONYM: **unselfish** )
—**selfishness** /**self**-ish-niss/ *noun* a selfish quality
—**selfishly** /**self**-ish-lee/ *adverb* in a selfish way: *Rob selfishly took the biggest piece of cake.*

**self-res·pect** /self ri-**spekt**/ *noun* the feeling that you are a good person and that people should respect you: *Working hard and doing the best you can helps to build your self-respect.*
( SYNONYM: **self-esteem** )

**self-serv·ice** /self **surv**-iss/ *adjective* if a store or restaurant is self-service, you get things for yourself, rather than being served by someone else: *She got gas at a self-service gas station.*

**sell** /sel/ *verb* (**sold** /sohld/)
**1** to give something to someone when they give you money for it: *I sold my old bike to my neighbor for $50.* ( ANTONYM: **buy** )
**2 sell out** if something sells out, there is none of it left to buy because it has all been sold: *The tickets to the game sold out quickly.*

**sell·er** /**sel**-ur/ *noun* a person or company that sells something: *The seller and the buyer agree a fair price between them.* ( ANTONYM: **buyer** )

**se·mes·ter** /suh-**mest**-ur/ *noun* one of the two time periods that a school year is divided into: *The fall semester starts in September.*

**semi-** /**sem**-ee/

**Word Building**

**semi**circle | **semi**colon | **semi**final | **semi**-metal

These words all have the Latin word root *semi-* in them. *Semi* means half. A *semicircle* is half of a circle. A *semifinal* is one of two games that are played before a final game, so one semifinal is half of the two games. A *semi-metal* is like a metal in some ways, and not like a metal in others.

**sem·i·cir·cle** /**sem**-ee-surk-uhl/ *noun* half a circle: *The class sat in a semicircle in front of the teacher.*

**sem·i·co·lon** /**sem**-ee-kohl-uhn/ *noun* the symbol (;) that is used in writing to separate different parts of a sentence or list

**sem·i·fi·nal** /**sem**-ee-fīn'l/ *noun* one of the two sports games that are played in a competition before the final game. The winners of the two semifinals play each other in the last game to decide who wins the competition: *We won our semifinal and got through to the final.*

**sem·i·met·al** /**sem**-ee met'l/ *noun* a chemical element that is like a metal in some ways and not like a metal in other ways: *Tin is a semi-metal.*

**sen·ate** /**sen**-it/ *noun* the smaller of the two government groups that make laws. The U.S., Canada, Australia, and some other countries have senates: *Members of the senate are called senators.*

**Word Origin:** senate

Ancient Rome had a **senate** as part of its government, and the American senate gets its name from the Roman one. The word senate is from the Latin word for "old." The Roman senate was given its name because it was a council made up of wise old men.

**sen·a·tor** /**sen**-uht-ur/ *noun* a member of a senate: *Each state has two senators.*

**send** /send/ *verb* (**sent** /sent/)
**1** to arrange for something to go to another place: *You should send a letter to your aunt to say thank you for the present.*
**2** to make someone go somewhere: *When I've behaved really badly, Mom sends me to my room.*
**3 send for** to ask someone to come to you: *He was very sick, so his wife sent for the doctor.*

**se·nile** /**seen**-īl/ *adjective* a senile person is often confused and cannot remember things easily because he or she is old: *I don't want to go senile and forget the names of my grandchildren.*
**—senility** /si-**nil**-uht-ee/ *noun* the fact of being

senile: *Forgetting what day it is could be a sign of senility.*

**se·nior** /**seen**-yur/
● *noun*
**1** a student in the last year of high school or college: *The high school seniors are graduating soon.*
**2** someone who is over 60 years old: *The Internet is not just for young people – seniors can use it too.* (SYNONYM: **senior citizen**)
● *adjective*
**1** having an important position in an organization: *The principal is the most senior person in the school.*
**2 Senior** (ABBREVIATION: **Sr.**) used after the name of a man who has the same name as his son: *George Bush Senior is the father of George W. Bush.*

**se·nior cit·i·zen** /seen-yur **sit**-uhz-uhn/ *noun* someone who is over 60 years old: *Senior citizens can get into the museum for free.*

**sen·sa·tion** /sen-**saysh**-uhn/ *noun*
**1** a feeling that you get in your body: *When I walk I get a painful sensation in my foot.*
**2** something that makes people feel very excited or interested: *The movie caused a big sensation and everyone wanted to see it.*

**sen·sa·tion·al** /sen-**saysh**-uhn'l/ *adjective*
**1** very good, interesting, or exciting: *It's a great movie and the acting is sensational.*
**2** causing a lot of excitement or interest: *Magazines are full of sensational stories about famous people.*

**sense** /senss/
● *noun*
**1** one of the five natural abilities that people and animals have. The senses are sight, hearing, touch, taste, and smell: *We had to use our sense of touch to decide what was in the box. We weren't allowed to look.*
**2** the ability to make good decisions about what you should do: *She had the sense to look for cars before she crossed the street.*
**3** a feeling: *All the kids have a sense of excitement on the last day of school.*
**4** the meaning of a word: *You can look up the sense of the word in your dictionary.*
**5 sense of humor** the ability to understand things that are funny, or the ability to make

people laugh: *She didn't like my joke because she has no sense of humor.*

**IDIOM with sense**

**make sense**

**1** to have a clear meaning and be easy to understand: *Stand the box backwards? That doesn't make any sense.*

**2** if it makes sense to do something, there is a good reason to do it: *It would make sense to talk to the teacher first.*

● *verb*

to feel or know that something is true without being told or having proof: *I could sense that something was wrong – she just didn't seem happy.*

**sense·less** /**senss**-liss/ *adjective* happening or done for no good reason or with no purpose: *The violence was senseless – it achieved nothing.*

**sen·si·ble** /**senss**-uhb-uhl/ *adjective*

**1** having good judgment and making good decisions: *Mom trusts me to take care of my little sister because I'm sensible.*

**2** good for a particular purpose, but not always fashionable: *It's a long walk, so wear sensible shoes.*

—**sensibly** /**senss**-uhb-lee/ *adverb* in a way that shows you have good judgment and make good decisions: *Children are expected to behave sensibly at school.*

**sen·si·tive** /**senss**-uht-iv/ *adjective*

**1** able to understand other people's feelings and problems: *Ethan is very sensitive – he knew Chloe was upset about being teased.*

( ANTONYM: **insensitive** )

**2** easily upset by the things that people do or say: *He's very sensitive about the way he looks, so don't mention his big ears!*

**3** easily hurt or damaged by something: *I have sensitive skin, so I have to use a special soap.*

**sent** /sent/ *verb* the past tense and past participle of **send**

**sen·tence** /**sent**-uhnss/

● *noun*

**1** a group of words that makes a statement or asks a question. A sentence has a subject and a verb. In writing, a sentence starts with a capital letter and ends with a period, a question mark, or an exclamation point: *Please write your*

answers in complete sentences. For example, do not just write "Mark Twain." Instead, write "The book was written by Mark Twain."

**2** a punishment that a judge gives to someone who is guilty of a crime: *He was given a jail sentence for robbery.*

● *verb*

if a judge sentences someone, he or she gives the person an official punishment: *The thief was sentenced to seven years in prison.*

**sen·ti·men·tal** /sent-uh-**ment**'l/ *adjective* making people feel emotions such as love or sadness: *He wrote a sentimental love song about his wife.*

**sep·a·rate**

● *adjective* /**sep**-rit/

**1** different: *We do art in a separate room.*

**2** not close to or touching something: *Keep raw meat separate from other foods in the fridge.*

● *verb* /**sep**-uh-rayt/

**1** to divide something into two or more parts: *Mrs. Barker separated the class into four groups.*

**2** to be between two things and keep them apart: *A high wall separates the two houses.*

**3** to stop living with your husband, wife, or partner: *Her parents have separated and they are going to get divorced.*

—**separation** /sep-uh-**raysh**-uhn/ *noun* the act of separating something or being separated: *Small children don't like separation from their mothers.*

**sep·a·rate·ly** /**sep**-rit-lee/ *adverb* not together with other people or things: *You can wear the skirt and top separately or together.*

**Sep·tem·ber** /sep-**tem**-bur/ *noun*

( ABBREVIATION: **Sept.** ) the ninth month of the year. September is between August and October: *School starts in September. | Labor Day was on September 7.*

**Word Origin: September**

**September** comes from the Latin word *sept*, which means "seven." The old Roman calendar had ten months, and September was the seventh month. When the Romans started using a new calendar, they added two more months at the beginning of the year. September became the ninth month, but it kept its old name.

a b c d e f g h i j k l m n o p q r **s** t u v w x y z

**se·quel** /**seek**-wuhl/ *noun* a movie or book that continues the story of an earlier one: *"Heidi Grows Up" and "Heidi's Children" are sequels to "Heidi."*

**se·quence** /**seek**-wuhnss/ *noun* events or actions that happen in a particular order: *8 is the next number in the sequence 2, 4, 6.*

**se·quin** /**seek**-win/ *noun* a very small shiny circle that is sewn on clothes for decoration: *The dancers' dresses are covered in sequins.*

**se·quoi·a** /si-**kwoy**-uh/ *noun* a very tall tree with thick red-brown bark. The trunk is very big. Sequoias do not lose their leaves in the winter. Some sequoia trees are more than 1,000 years old. Sequoias grow in California and Oregon. They are often called redwoods: *Sequoias are the tallest trees on Earth.* ▶ see picture on page **A6**

**Word Origin:** sequoia

A scientist gave **sequoia** trees their name. He wanted to honor a Cherokee Indian called Sequoya. Sequoya invented a way to write down the Cherokee language.

**ser·geant** /**sarj**-uhnt/ *noun* (ABBREVIATION: **Sgt.**) someone who has a position in the army, air force, or police: *Dad is a police sergeant.*

**se·ri·al** /**seer**-ee-uhl/ *noun* a story that is shown or printed in several separate parts: *The story was printed in the newspaper as a serial over several weeks.*

**se·ries** /**seer**-eez/ *noun* (plural **series**)
**1** several events, actions, or things that happen one after the other: *The test has a series of questions that get more and more difficult.*
**2** a set of television programs or books with the same characters or on the same subject: *What is your favorite TV series?*
**3** a set of sports games played between the same two teams: *There are seven games in baseball's World Series, so a team has to win four games to win the series.*

**se·ries cir·cuit** /**seer**-eez surk-it/ *noun* a type of electrical circuit. In a series circuit, the parts are connected one after the other, so the same electric current flows through all of them.
(ANTONYM: **parallel circuit**)

**se·ri·ous** /**seer**-ee-uhss/ *adjective*
**1** a serious problem or situation is very bad or important: *I have a serious problem – my computer crashed and I lost all my work.*
**2** saying what you really mean, and not joking or pretending: *Juan says his favorite color is pink. Do you think he's serious?*
—**seriously** /**seer**-ee-uhss-lee/ *adverb* in a way that is serious: *He is seriously ill and might die.*

**ser·mon** /**surm**-uhn/ *noun* a talk about a religious subject. Priests or ministers give sermons in church: *Sunday's sermon was about "loving your neighbor."*

**serv·ant** /**surv**-uhnt/ *noun* someone who works in a rich person's house doing cleaning, cooking, or other jobs: *One of the king's servants brings him his clothes in the morning.*

**serve** /surv/
● *verb*
**1** to give someone food or drink as part of a meal: *Mom served the meat onto our plates.*
**2** to be used for a particular purpose: *His home also serves as his office.*
**3** to work in the army or another government organization: *He served in the army for three years.*
**4** to hit a ball over a net to start a game such as tennis or volleyball: *It's your turn to serve.*

┌ **IDIOM with serve**
│ **it serves you right** used when you think it is right that something bad happens to someone because he or she did something bad: *"I can't find my ball." "It serves you right for not taking care of it."*
└

● *noun*
an act of serving the ball in games such as tennis or volleyball: *It was a good serve, and the other player couldn't hit it.*

**serv·er** /**surv**-ur/ *noun* a computer that all the computers in a network get information from: *I can't connect to the server, so I can't read my emails.*

**serv·ice** /**surv**-iss/ *noun*
**1** the help that people who work in a restaurant, hotel, or store give you: *The service in the store was terrible – I had to wait 20 minutes before someone came to help me.*
**2** the work that you do for a person or

organization over a long period of time: *He left the army after 20 years of service.*

**3** a religious ceremony: *At the beginning of the service, the preacher asks us to say a prayer.*

**4** a system or way of doing something that helps people or does jobs for people: *The company has a home delivery service.*

**serv·ice sta·tion** /**surv**-iss staysh-uhn/ *noun* a place that sells gas for cars: *We stopped at a service station to fill up with gas.*

( SYNONYM: **gas station** )

**ses·sion** /**sesh**-uhn/ *noun* a period of time when people work or do a particular activity: *The soccer team has two practice sessions each week.*

**set** /set/

● *verb* (**setting**, **set**)

**1** to put something somewhere carefully: *I set the vase of flowers on the table.*

**2** if a movie or story is set in a place or time, the events take place there or at that time: *The story is set on the Mississippi River.*

set

a chess set

**3** to change the controls on a clock or a machine so that it will do something at a particular time: *I set my alarm clock for 7 a.m.*

**4** when the Sun or Moon sets, it moves lower in the sky and disappears: *It's really beautiful when the sun sets at the end of the day.*

( ANTONYM: **rise** )

**5** if a substance sets, it becomes hard: *Someone walked in the concrete before it had set and made footprints.*

**6 set the table** to put knives, forks, and plates on a table so that you can eat a meal: *It's my job to set the table before dinner.*

**7 set off** to make something start happening or start doing something: *Someone got into the house and set off the burglar alarm.*

**8 set up** to build or put something somewhere in order to get ready for something: *The band members are setting up their equipment.*

( IDIOM with **set**

**set fire to** to make something start burning: *A candle set fire to the tablecloth.*

● *noun*

**1** a group of similar things that belong together:

Mom bought a new set of dishes. | *I got a chess set for my birthday.*

**2** a television: *Everyone was watching the TV set.*

**3** the place where a movie or television program is filmed: *The actor hurt his back on the set of his new movie.*

**4** in math, a group of numbers or shapes that are similar in one or more ways: *This is a drawing of a circle, square, triangle, and rectangle. Which shape does not belong to the set?*

**5** one part of a game such as tennis or volleyball: *Matthew won the first set 6–2.*

● *adjective*

**1** decided and not changing: *The date for the party is set now – it's on July 31.*

**2** ready: *We're all set, so let's go!*

**set·back** /**set**-bak/ *noun* a problem that makes success less likely: *Our best player hurt his leg, which was a setback for the team.*

**set·ting** /**set**-ing/ *noun* the place where something is, or the time when something happens: *The house is in a beautiful setting by a lake.*

**set·tle** /**set**'l/ *verb*

**1** to end an argument: *Dad settled the argument over which channel to watch by turning off the TV.*

**2** to decide or choose something: *She tried out several colors of paint, and finally settled on blue.*

**3** to begin to live permanently in a place: *They left their homes in Europe and settled in America.*

**4** to move into a comfortable position: *Danny settled back on the sofa and turned on the TV.*

**5** if snow or dust settles, it falls onto something and stays there: *Snowflakes were settling on the grass.*

**6 settle down** to become quiet and calm: *Settle down! There's no need to get so excited!*

**7 settle for** to accept something that is not as good as the thing you wanted: *I wanted a puppy for my birthday but I had to settle for a goldfish.*

**8 settle in** to become happy and comfortable in a new place: *She soon settled in at her new school and made some friends.*

**set·tled** /**set**'ld/ *adjective* feeling comfortable in your home or job, and unlikely to move: *I've been at my new school for a month and I'm starting to feel settled.*

**set·tle·ment** /**set**'l-muhnt/ *noun*
**1** an official decision that ends a disagreement: *Elena's parents have finally reached a divorce settlement.*
**2** a group of buildings where people live, when they first come to a new country or area: *Jamestown was the first permanent English settlement in America. It started in 1607.*

**set·tler** /**set**'l-ur/ *noun* someone who goes to live in a new country or area: *The settlers came to Texas in covered wagons, and they had to bring everything they needed with them.*

**sev·en** /**sev**-uhn/ *number*
**1** 7: *There are seven days in a week.*
**2** seven o'clock: *The movie starts at seven.*
**3** seven years old: *My brother is seven.*

**sev·en·teen** /sev-uhn-**teen**/ *number*
**1** 17: *They invited seventeen people to the party.*
**2** seventeen years old: *Her brother is seventeen.*
—**seventeenth** /sev-uhn-**teenth**/ *number* 17th or 1/17

**sev·enth** /**sev**-uhnth/ *number*
**1** 7th: *I didn't do very well in the race – I came in seventh out of eight people.*
**2** 1/7: *There were seven people, so we cut the pie into sevenths.*

**sev·en·ty** /**sev**-uhnt-ee/ *number*
**1** 70: *Seventy people are coming to the party.*
**2** seventy years old: *Grandpa is almost seventy.*
**3 the seventies** the years between 1970 and 1979: *My dad grew up in the seventies.*
**4 in your seventies** between 70 and 79 years old: *Grandma's in her early seventies.*
**5 in the seventies** between 70 and 79 degrees in temperature: *Temperatures will be in the seventies tomorrow.*
—**seventieth** /**sev**-uhnt-ee-ith/ *number* 70th or 1/70

**sev·eral** /**sev**-ruhl/ *adjective*, *pronoun* some, but not many: *I've seen several of his movies.* | *Several people said her dress was very pretty.*

**se·vere** /suh-**veer**/ *adjective*
**1** very bad or serious: *His injuries were severe, so he was taken to the hospital.*
**2** very strict and extreme: *She got a severe punishment for hurting the other girl.*

—**severity** /suh-**verr**-uht-ee/ *noun* how bad something is: *He committed murder. Because of the severity of his crime, he will go to prison for a long time.*

**se·vere·ly** /suh-**veer**-lee/ *adverb*
**1** very badly or very much: *His car was severely damaged in the accident, and couldn't be fixed.*
**2** in a very strict and extreme way: *Players who cheat will be severely punished, and will not be allowed to play again.*

**sew** /soh/ *verb* (**sewed**, **sewn** /sohn/ or **sewed**) to use a needle and thread to make or fix clothes: *Do you know how to sew a button on your shirt?*

sew

**sew·age** /**soo**-ij/ *noun* dirty water and waste from toilets that is carried away from buildings by pipes: *The sewage is treated with chemicals before it goes into the ocean.*

**sew·er** /**soo**-ur/ *noun* a pipe or passage under the ground that carries away dirty water and waste from toilets

**sew·ing** /**soh**-ing/ *noun*
**1** the activity of using a needle and thread to make or fix clothes: *Mom is good at sewing, so she can fix the rip in your dress.*
**2** something that you are making or fixing by using a needle and thread: *Grandma picked up her sewing; she is making a quilt.*

**sew·ing ma·chine** /**soh**-ing muh-sheen/ *noun* a machine used for making or fixing clothes

**sex** /sekss/ *noun*
**1** the fact of being male or female: *They don't know what sex the baby will be.*
**2** the group of males or females: *The male bird shows off its brightly colored feathers to impress the opposite sex.*

**sex·ism** /**sekss**-iz-uhm/ *noun* unfairness to one sex, especially women: *It's sexism to say that women can't be astronauts.*
—**sexist** /**sekss**-ist/ *adjective* unfair to one sex, especially women: *He made a sexist comment. He said that girls are no good at sports.*

**Sgt.** the written abbreviation of **Sergeant**: *He was arrested by Sgt. John Robertson.*

**shab·by** /**shab**-ee/ *adjective* old and needing to be repaired: *The apartment was very shabby and needed painting.*

**shack** /shak/ *noun* a small building that has not been built very well: *They are very poor, and live in shacks made out of pieces of wood and metal.*

**shade** /shayd/

● *noun*
**1** an area that is cooler and darker because the light of the Sun does not reach it: *It was very hot, so we sat in the shade under a tree.*
**2** a particular form of a color: *Her T-shirt had stripes in different shades of blue.*
**3** a cover for a window that blocks light: *She walked to the window and pulled down the shade so the sun wouldn't come in.*
**4** a cover over the light on a lamp: *The lamp has a pink-colored shade.*

● *verb*
to stop the light of the Sun from reaching something: *She raised her hand to shade her eyes from the sun.*

shade

shade
He is standing in the shade.

**shad·ow** /**shad**-oh/

*noun* a dark shape on a surface, made when someone or something blocks the light: *At school, we measured our shadows in the morning, at noon, and in the afternoon.*

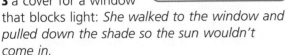
shadow
shadow

IDIOMS with **shadow**
**cast a shadow** to make something seem less good or enjoyable: *The bad news cast a shadow over the evening.*
**without/beyond a shadow of a doubt** definitely: *Our team will win, without a shadow of a doubt.*

**shad·y** /**shayd**-ee/ *adjective* protected from the sun: *Let's find a nice shady spot under the trees for our picnic.*

**shaft** /shaft/ *noun*
**1** a long narrow passage that goes up through a building or down into the ground: *There are two elevator shafts in the center of the building.*
**2** a long thin part of a tool, weapon, or machine: *The shaft of the spear is made of wood.*
**3** a narrow beam of light: *A shaft of sunlight came through the small window.*

**shag·gy** /**shag**-ee/ *adjective* having long rough hair: *The shaggy dog shook itself dry after going in the pond.*

**shake** /shayk/

● *verb* (**shook** /shuk/, **shaken** /**shayk**-uhn/)
**1** to move up and down or from side to side quickly: *She was so scared her hands were shaking.* | *He shook the dice and rolled them.* | *The house shook in the earthquake.*
**2** if you shake your head, you move it from side to side as a way of saying no: *She offered James a cookie, but James shook his head.*
**3** if you shake someone's hand, you hold it and move it up and down. You do this as a greeting or to show that you agree to something: *Don't forget to shake his hand when you meet him.*
**4** if your voice shakes, it sounds unsteady because you are upset, nervous, or angry: *Mom was upset and her voice was shaking.*

● *noun*
**1** a cold drink made from milk, ice cream, and fruit or chocolate: *He ordered a hamburger and a chocolate shake.* ( SYNONYM: **milkshake** )
**2** if you give something a shake, you shake it: *Put the mixture in a bottle and give it a good shake.*

shake
The two boys are shaking hands.

### shak·y /**shayk**-ee/ adjective

**1** weak and unsteady because of illness, old age, or fear: *She is still feeling shaky after falling off her bike.*

**2** not very good: *The team looked a little shaky at the start of the game, but in the second half they improved.*

### shall /shuhl, shal/ verb

**1** used to make a suggestion or ask someone what to do: *Shall I open a window?* | *What shall we do today?*

**2** used to say in a formal way that something must or will happen: *All bullying shall be reported to the principal.*

### shal·low /**shal**-oh/ adjective

**1** not deep from top to bottom: *The water was shallow and only reached my knees.*

( ANTONYM: **deep** ) ► see picture at **deep**

**2** not interested in important or serious things: *She's very shallow and is only interested in clothes and makeup.*

### sha·man /**shay**-muhn/ noun someone who people believe has the power to talk to spirits and cure illnesses

### shame /shaym/ noun

**1** the bad feeling you have after doing something that is wrong: *She felt a deep sense of shame for stealing from her mother.*

**2** a loss of respect or honor: *You all need to behave well on the field trip, so that you do not bring shame on the school.*

**3** something that you feel sad or disappointed about: *It's a shame it rained, but we still had a good day.*

> IDIOM with **shame**
>
> **shame on you!** used to tell someone that he or she should feel bad for doing something: *You kicked the dog? Shame on you!*

### sham·poo /sham-**poo**/

● *noun* a liquid soap used for washing your hair: *She rubbed the shampoo into her wet hair.*

● *verb* to wash your hair with shampoo

### shape /shayp/

● *noun*

**1** the form of an object, for example round, square, or triangular: *A triangle is a shape with three sides.* | *My birthday cake was in the shape of a car.*

**2** if you are in shape, your body is healthy and you can exercise easily: *Running every day keeps you in shape.* | *My dad is so out of shape! He gets out of breath when we play basketball.*

**3** condition: *Your old coat is in pretty good shape. We don't need to buy you a new one.*

● *verb*

to give something a shape: *Shape the dough into small balls.*

—**shaped** /shaypt/ *adjective* having a particular shape: *The stone was shaped like a heart.*

### share /shair/

● *verb*

**1** to use something with someone else: *There are 10 books and 16 people, so some of you will have to share.*

**2** to let someone have part of something or use something that belongs to you: *Matthew shared his fries with me.*

**3** to give part of an amount or thing to each person in a group: *Mom shared out the cake so that everyone got a piece.*

**4** to tell someone else what you think, know, or did: *I didn't want to share my secret with anyone.*

**5** to have the same interest, opinion, name, etc. as someone else: *They share a love of baseball, and often go to games together.*

● *noun*

**1** one part of something that has been divided between people: *Mom paid us $5 to wash the car, and my share of the money was $2.50.*

**2** one of the equal parts that the ownership of a company is divided into. The price of shares changes, and people buy and sell shares to make money: *He sold his shares in the company because he thought it was going to fail.*

### share·ware /**shair**-wair/ noun computer software that you can use for a short time without paying for it

### shark /shark/ noun a large ocean fish with very sharp teeth: *There are many kinds of sharks, but Great White Sharks are the most dangerous.*

**shark**

## sharp /sharp/ *adjective*

**1** having a thin edge or point that can cut things easily: *Be careful – that knife is sharp. | A shark has very sharp teeth.* ( ANTONYM: **dull** )
▶ see Thesaurus

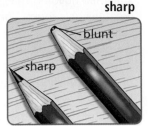
sharp

blunt

sharp

sharp

**2** a sharp pain is sudden and very bad: *The sharp pain in her stomach made her cry.* ( ANTONYM: **dull** )

**3** a sharp turn or bend turns a lot: *There's a sharp bend in the road ahead – you can't see the cars coming.*

**4** a sharp change or increase is large and sudden: *There has been a sharp increase in the price of milk. It has gone from $1.35 a quart to $1.60.*

**5** very clear: *We get a really sharp picture on our new TV. | Look at the sharp outline of the mountain against the sky.*

**6** exactly: *School starts at eight o'clock sharp.*

**7** good at noticing things or thinking quickly: *He's a sharp guy – he will know if you try to trick him.*

**8** **F sharp, C sharp, etc.** a musical note that is a half tone higher than F, C, etc. It is shown by the sign (#). ( ANTONYM: **flat** )

—**sharply** /**sharp**-lee/ *adverb* in a sharp way: *He turned sharply left.*

## sharp·en /**sharp**-uhn/ *verb* to make something sharper: *She sharpened her pencil.*

## sharp·en·er /**sharp**-uhn-ur/ *noun* a tool that you use to make pencils sharper ▶ see picture on page **A9**

## shat·ter /**shat**-ur/ *verb*

**1** to break suddenly into very small pieces: *The ball hit the window and the glass shattered.*

**2** to end someone's hopes, beliefs, or confidence: *A car accident shattered her dreams of becoming a professional athlete. She never ran again.*

## shave /shayv/

● *verb* to cut off hair from your skin using a special sharp tool called a razor: *Dad shaves every morning before work.*

● *noun* an act of shaving: *He needs a shave.*

shave

## shav·ing cream /**shayv**-ing kreem/ *noun* a thick liquid that a man puts on his face to make shaving easier ▶ see picture at **shave**

## shawl /shol/ *noun* a piece of cloth that a woman wears around her shoulders or head: *She wrapped her shawl around herself to keep warm.*

## she /shee/ *pronoun* a woman or girl, or a female animal. You use "she" instead of a name when you have already talked about that person: *Mom sat down because she was tired.*

## shears /sheerz/ *noun* a tool like a large pair of scissors: *He cut the hedge with shears.*

## shed /shed/

● *noun*
a small building used for storing things: *He keeps his tools in the shed.*

● *verb* (**shedding**, **shed**)

**1** if a plant sheds its leaves, its leaves come off. If an animal sheds its hair or skin, its hair or skin comes off: *The cat has shed hair all over the couch.*

**2** **shed tears** to cry: *She shed a few tears when she said goodbye to her daughter.*

## she'd /sheed/ *contraction*

**1** short for "she had": *She knew she'd seen the man before.*

**2** short for "she would": *I thought she'd like the gift.*

## sheep /sheep/ *noun*
(plural **sheep**) a farm animal that is kept for its wool and its meat: *Some sheep were eating grass in the field.*

sheep

## sheer /sheer/ *adjective*

**1** pure or complete, with nothing else mixed in: *When he won, there was a look of sheer joy on his face.*

**2** very big: *Look at the sheer size of the dinosaurs. Many of them were bigger than elephants.*

**3** a sheer cliff is very steep or vertical: *He climbed down the sheer cliff on a rope.*

**4** sheer material is very thin, so that you can almost see through it: *The sheer curtains did not keep out the light.*

a b c d e f g h i j k l m n o p q r **s** t u v w x y z

**sheet** /sheet/ *noun*
**1** a large piece of thin cloth that you put on a bed to lie on or under: *It was too hot for blankets, so we only had sheets.*
**2** a thin flat piece of paper, metal, or glass: *I asked the teacher for another sheet of paper.*

sheet

a sheet of paper

**shelf** /shelf/ *noun* (plural **shelves** /shelvz/) a board to keep things on, on a wall or in a cupboard or bookcase: *The dictionary is on the bottom shelf of the bookcase.*

**shell** /shel/ *noun*
**1** the hard outside part of a nut or egg: *A coconut has a hard hairy brown shell.*
**2** the hard part that protects the body of some animals, such as a crab or a snail: *A turtle has a shell on its back.*
**3** a bomb that is fired from a large gun: *Shells fell on the city and exploded.*
**4** a metal case containing a bullet and some explosive that is fired from a gun: *The police found empty shotgun shells on the ground.*

**she'll** /sheel/ *contraction* short for "she will": *She'll never forgive me.*

**shell·fish** /shel-fish/ *noun* (plural **shellfish**) a small sea or water animal that has a shell: *Crabs, clams, and shrimp are shellfish.*

**shellfish**
clams
mussel
lobster
oysters
shrimp

**shel·ter** /shelt-ur/
● *noun*
**1** protection from bad weather or danger: *It's starting to rain, so we'd better find shelter quickly.*

**2** a small building that protects you from bad weather or danger: *They built a shelter out of branches.*
**3** a place for people or pets who have no homes or are in danger: *Dogs stay at the animal shelter until we can find new owners for them.*
● *verb*
to protect someone or something from bad weather or danger: *A row of trees sheltered the house from the wind.*

**shelves** /shelvz/ *noun* the plural of **shelf**

**shep·herd** /shep-urd/ *noun* someone whose job is to take care of sheep

**sher·bet** /shurb-uht/ *noun* a frozen food made from water, fruit, sugar, and milk: *For dessert we had lime sherbet.*

**sher·iff** /sherr-if/ *noun* the chief police officer in a county

**she's** /sheez/ *contraction*
**1** short for "she is": *She's really smart.*
**2** short for "she has": *She's seen the movie already.*

**shh** /sh/ *interjection* used when telling people to be quiet: *Shh! You'll wake the baby!*

**shield** /sheeld/
● *noun* a strong piece of plastic, wood, or metal that someone holds and uses to protect his or her body in a fight: *He used his shield to protect his head from his enemy's sword.*
▶ see picture at **armor**
● *verb* to protect someone or something: *Parents want to shield their children from websites that have inappropriate information or pictures.*

**shift** /shift/
● *verb*
**1** to move from one position to another: *He was uncomfortable and kept shifting around in his chair.*
**2** to change: *His attitude to his school work has shifted; he is more interested now.*
**3** to change the gears when you are driving: *When you slow down, you need to shift into a lower gear.*
● *noun*
**1** a period in the day when people work, for example when one group works at night and another group works in the day: *Her dad*

*is a police officer and he has to work night shifts.*
**2** a change in what people think or do: *There was a shift in the boys' attitude toward school and they seem much happier.*

**shim·mer** /**shim**-ur/ *verb* to shine with a soft unsteady light: *The lake shimmered in the moonlight.*

**shin** /shin/ *noun* the hard front part of your leg between your knee and your foot: *He kicked me in the shin.*

**shine** /shīn/ *verb*
**1** (**shone** /shohn/ or **shined**) to produce light or look bright: *The sun is shining.* | *She polished the table until it shone.* ▶ see **Thesaurus**
**2** (**shined** or **shone** /shohn/) to point a light in a particular direction: *Don't shine the flashlight in my eyes!*
**3** (**shined**) to make shoes bright by rubbing them: *I need to shine my shoes before the party.*

**shin·gle** /**shing**-guhl/ *noun* one of many thin flat pieces of wood or another material which cover the roof or wall of a house: *The wind blew a few shingles off the roof.*

**shin·y** /**shīn**-ee/ *adjective* looking bright and smooth: *The car was clean and shiny.*

**ship** /ship/
● *noun* a large boat that carries people and things on the ocean: *The ship was crossing the Atlantic Ocean.*
● *verb* (**shipping**, **shipped**) to send something to a customer: *The company will ship the books to us today.*

ship

**-ship** /ship/

## Word Building

**-ship** is a suffix. It is used in nouns.
champion**ship** | citizen**ship** | friend**ship** | leader**ship** | member**ship** | sportsman**ship**
**-ship** shows that someone or something has a particular quality or position. If a team wins a *championship*, they are the champions. Your *citizenship* of a country is the fact that you are a citizen. If you show good *sportsmanship* when you are playing a game, you have the qualities of being fair and honest when you are playing sports.

**ship·mate** /**ship**-mayt/ *noun* a sailor who works with the other sailors on a ship: *One of his shipmates jumped into the water and rescued him.*

**ship·ment** /**ship**-muhnt/ *noun* an amount of things that are sent somewhere: *We received a shipment of art supplies this morning.*

**ship·ping** /**ship**-ing/ *noun*
**1** the action or cost of sending something to a customer: *The price does not include shipping.*
**2** ships: *The port was closed to shipping because of the storm.*

**ship·wreck** /**ship**-rek/
● *noun* an accident in which a ship is destroyed: *The boy survived the shipwreck and was able to swim to an island.*
● *verb* if people are shipwrecked, the ship they are traveling on is destroyed in an accident: *The ship and its crew were hit by a storm and shipwrecked.*

**ship·yard** /**ship**-yard/ *noun* a place where ships are built or repaired

**shirt** /shurt/ *noun* a piece of clothing for the top half of your body. A shirt usually has a collar, sleeves, and buttons: *He always wears a suit, a shirt, and a tie to work.*

**shiv·er** /**shiv**-ur/ *verb* to shake because you are cold or frightened: *I started to shiver because I was cold and wet.*

shiver

He is shivering with cold.

**shock** /shahk/

● *noun*

**1** something that you did not expect, which makes you very upset: *It was a big shock to our family when Dad lost his job.*

**2** the feeling of surprise you have when something very bad happens that you did not expect: *I was in shock when I saw how thin and sick she was.*

**3** if you are suffering from shock, your body is not working correctly because you have been hurt, frightened, or upset: *After the bus crashed, many of the people on it were treated for shock.*

**4** a sudden painful feeling caused by electricity going through your body: *She got an electric shock when she touched the wire.*

● *verb*

to make someone feel very surprised and upset: *The principal's sudden decision to leave shocked the whole school.*

—**shocked** /shahkt/ *adjective* feeling shock: *I was shocked to find out that she had lied to me.*

**shock·ing** /**shahk**-ing/ *adjective* very upsetting: *He showed us shocking pictures of animals kept in tiny cages.*

**shoe** /shoo/ *noun* something that you wear to cover your feet. Shoes are made of leather or another strong material: *Do you need a new pair of shoes for school?*

shoe

**shoe·lace** /**shoo**-layss/ *noun* a string that you use to tie your shoes: *He bent down to tie his shoelace.* ( SYNONYM: **lace** )

**shone** /shohn/ *verb* a past tense and past participle of **shine**

**shook** /shuk/ *verb* the past tense of **shake**

**shoot** /shoot/

● *verb* (**shot** /shaht/)

**1** to hurt or kill someone with a gun: *The soldier was shot in the leg.*

**2** to make a bullet come out of a gun: *They practiced shooting at a target.*

**3** to throw, kick, or hit a ball toward the goal or basket: *The crowd cheered as they saw him shoot and score.*

**4** to take photographs or make a movie: *The movie was shot in New Zealand.*

● *noun*

a new part of a plant: *New shoots appear on the bush in spring.*

**shop** /shahp/

● *noun*

**1** a small store: *He works at a sandwich shop.*

**2** a place where people make or fix things: *The car is in the repair shop for a week.*

● *verb* (**shopping**, **shopped**)

to go to one or more stores to buy things: *We shopped all day for Christmas presents.*

**shop·lift·ing** /**shahp**-lift-ing/ *noun* the crime of stealing things from a store: *When she took a magazine without paying for it, she was arrested for shoplifting.*

—**shoplifter** /**shahp**-lift-ur/ *noun* someone who steals things from stores

**shop·per** /**shahp**-ur/ *noun* someone who is shopping: *The mall was full of shoppers.*

**shop·ping** /**shahp**-ing/ *noun* the activity of going to stores to buy things: *We went shopping and bought some clothes.*

**shore** /shor/ *noun* the land along the edge of an ocean, lake, or river: *We rowed the boat to the shore and got out.*

**short** /short/ *adjective*

**1** not long in length, time, or distance: *His hair is very short. | The school is only a short walk away, about five minutes. | The book was short, only 50 pages.* ( ANTONYM: **long** )

**2** not tall: *Short people stand at the front and tall people at the back, so everyone can see.* ( ANTONYM: **tall** )

**3** **short for** if a word is short for a longer word, part of the longer word is used instead of the full word: *Kilo is short for kilogram.*

**4** if you are short of breath, you cannot breathe

easily: *I had been running so fast that I was short of breath.*

**short**

short hair | long hair

**short·age** /**short**-ij/ *noun* if there is a shortage of something that people need, there is not enough of it: *There is a shortage of food and many people are hungry.*

**short cir·cuit** /short **surk**-it/ *noun* a problem in a piece of electrical equipment that makes it stop working correctly. A short circuit is an electrical connection where there should not be a connection: *The lights went out because of a short circuit.*

**short·com·ing** /**short**-kuhm-ing/ *noun* something that is not very good about a person or thing: *He knows he has shortcomings as a football player. He needs to run faster.*
( SYNONYM: **fault** )

**short·cut** /**short**-kuht/ *noun* a quicker way of getting to a place or doing something: *We took a shortcut across the field, rather than going around it.*

**short·en** /**short**'n/ *verb* to make something shorter: *Mom shortened the legs of my pants by folding them under and sewing them.*
( ANTONYM: **lengthen** )

**short·en·ing** /**short**'n-ing/ *noun* a fat made from vegetable oil that you use to make pastry or cakes

**short·ly** /**short**-lee/ *adverb* very soon: *You just missed him – he left shortly before you got here.*

**shorts** /shortss/ *plural noun*
**1** short pants that only cover the top parts of your legs: *We wear shorts and T-shirts to play soccer.*
**2** underwear for men or boys that looks like short pants

**short·stop** /**short**-stahp/ *noun* the baseball player whose position is between second base and third base

**short sto·ry** /short **stor**-ee/ *noun* a short written story: *She has written two novels and a book of short stories.*

**short-term** /short-**turm**/ *adjective* continuing for only a short time: *The change in times is a short-term arrangement – things will be back to normal next week.* ( ANTONYM: **long-term** )

**shot** /shaht/
● *verb*
the past tense and past participle of **shoot**
● *noun*
**1** if someone fires a shot, he or she makes a bullet come out of a gun: *She heard two shots and a scream.*
**2** the action of throwing, kicking, or hitting a ball toward a goal in sports: *Tyler blocked the shot and stopped Elliot from scoring.*
**3** a photograph, or a view of something in a movie or a television program: *I got a good shot of Andrew falling in the pool.*
**4** if you have a shot, medicine is put into your body with a needle: *People get flu shots if they don't want to get sick.* ( SYNONYM: **injection** )
**5** an attempt to do something: *I've never tried snowboarding before, but I'll give it a shot.*

**shot·gun** /**shaht**-guhn/ *noun* a long gun that fires a lot of small metal balls: *He uses his shotgun to hunt birds.*

**should** /shuhd, shud/ *verb*
**1** used to say what is or was the right thing to do: *You should brush your teeth every day.* | *They should have waited for us.*
**2** used to say what you expect to happen or be true: *My homework should take about an hour to finish.*

**shoul·der** /**shohld**-ur/ *noun*
**1** one of the two round parts where your arm joins your body. Your shoulders are on each side of your neck: *Her hair comes down to her shoulders.* ▶ see picture on page **A13**
**2** an area of ground beside a road where drivers can stop their cars if they are having trouble: *He drove the car onto the shoulder to change the tire.*

**shoul·der blade** /**should**-ur blayd/ *noun* one of the flat bones on each side near the top of your back

**should·n't** /**shud**'nt/ *contraction* short for "should not": *You shouldn't tease your sister!*

**should've** /**shud**-uhv/ *contraction* short for "should have": *You should've told me you were going to be late.*

**shout** /showt/
● *verb* to say something very loudly: *He shouted angrily at the kids.* ( SYNONYM: **yell** )
▶ see **Thesaurus**
● *noun* words that someone shouts: *There were shouts of "No!" from the crowd.*

**shove** /shuhv/
● *verb* to push something or someone hard with your hands or shoulders: *He shoved her, and she fell over.*
● *noun* a hard push with your hands or shoulders: *The door wouldn't open, so he gave it a shove.*

**shov·el** /**shuhv**-uhl/
● *noun* a tool you use for digging or moving earth or snow. It has a long handle and a wide piece of metal at the bottom: *He picked up his shovel and began to dig a hole.*
● *verb* to dig or move earth or snow using a shovel: *Dad was outside shoveling snow from the driveway.*

**show** /shoh/
● *verb* (**showed**, **shown** /shohn/)
**1** to let someone see something: *She showed me a picture of her cat.* | *Show your model of a bridge to the rest of the class.*
**2** to teach someone how to do something: *Can you show me how to make these cookies?*
**3** to take someone to a place, when he or she does not know the way: *I showed the visitor to the principal's office.*
**4** to make something clear: *"He smiled at me." "That shows that he likes you."*
**5** to be able to be seen: *She wore long skirts because she didn't want the scar on her leg to show.*
**6** if a picture shows something, that thing is in the picture: *The picture shows two women outside a house.*
**7** **show off** to do things to make people think

you are smart, funny, or attractive: *The boys were telling jokes and showing off in front of the girls.*
**8** **show up** to arrive somewhere, especially when other people are waiting for you: *Lauren showed up an hour late.*
● *noun*
**1** a play, a performance, or a program on television or radio: *Mom was watching her favorite TV show.*
**2** an event when things are put together for people to see: *We saw paintings by all the students at the art show.*

**show busi·ness** /**shoh** biz-niss/ *noun* the business of doing plays, movies, and performances: *The actor's career in show business lasted 50 years.*

**show·er** /**show**-ur/
● *noun*
**1** a piece of bathroom equipment that you stand under to wash yourself: *He turned the shower on and started washing his hair.* | *Sarah's in the shower.*
**2** if you take a shower, you wash yourself by standing under a shower: *I'm going to take a shower and get changed.*
**3** a short period of rain: *Today will be mainly sunny, with some showers possible.*
**4** a party at which people give presents to a woman who is going to get married or have a baby: *My aunt's friends gave her lots of baby clothes at her baby shower.*
● *verb*
to wash yourself by standing under a shower: *He showers every morning.*

**shown** /shohn/ *verb* the past participle of show

**show-off** /**shoh**-of/ *noun* someone who tries in an annoying way to show how smart, funny, or attractive he or she is: *He's a good player, but he always wants people to notice him when he's playing – he's such a show-off!*

**show·room** /**shoh**-room/ *noun* a large room where you can look at things that are for sale: *They looked at every car in the showroom.*

**shrank** /shrangk/ *verb* the past tense of **shrink**

**shrap·nel** /**shrap**-nuhl/ *noun* pieces of metal from a bomb that has exploded: *When the* *bomb exploded, a piece of shrapnel went into his leg.*

**shred** /shred/
- *noun* a thin piece that is torn from something: *I was so angry I wanted to tear the letter to shreds.*
- *verb* (**shredding**, **shredded**) to cut or tear something into thin pieces: *Chop the tomatoes and shred the lettuce.*

**shred·der** /**shred**-uh/ *noun* a machine that cuts documents into pieces so that no one can read them

**shrewd** /shrood/ *adjective* good at judging situations and people, and knowing what decisions to make: *A shrewd teacher knows when she can get her students to work harder.*

**shriek** /shreek/
- *verb* to shout in a high voice because you are frightened, excited, or angry: *"I can't swim," she shrieked.* ( SYNONYM: **scream** )
- *noun* a shout in a high voice: *When his mother saw him, she let out a shriek of joy.* ( SYNONYM: **scream** )

**shrill** /shril/ *adjective* high and loud, and not nice to listen to: *"There's a spider in my room!" Lucy cried in a shrill voice.*

**shrimp** /shrimp/ *noun* a small shellfish with a soft shell. You can eat the meat from a shrimp.
▶ see picture at **shellfish**

**shrine** /shrīn/ *noun* a holy place: *People traveled for miles to visit the shrine of the saint.*

**shrimp**

**shrink** /shringk/ *verb* (**shrank** /shrangk/, **shrunk** /shruhngk/) to become smaller: *Wool clothes sometimes shrink when you wash them.* | *The number of students has shrunk from 900 to 550.*

**shriv·el** /**shriv**-uhl/ *verb* if something shrivels, it becomes smaller because it is dry or old: *The plants shriveled up in the sun and died.*
—**shriveled** /**shriv**-uhld/ *adjective* small and dry: *The grapes were too old and shriveled to eat.*

**shroud** /shrowd/
- *verb* **be shrouded in** to be covered and hidden by something such as fog: *The top of the mountain was shrouded in clouds, so we could not see it.*
- *noun* a cloth that is used to wrap a dead body

**shrub** /shruhb/ *noun* a bush: *Some of the shrubs in the garden have beautiful flowers.*

**shrub·be·ry** /**shruhb**-uhr-ee/ *noun* bushes that grow close together: *Billy hid in the shrubbery around the house.*

**shrug** /shruhg/
- *verb* (**shrugging**, **shrugged**) to move your shoulders up and down. You shrug to show that you do not know something, or do not care about it: *I asked Dan if he knew the answer, but he just shrugged.*
- *noun* a movement of the shoulders to show that you do not know or do not care

**shrug**

**shrunk** /shruhngk/ *verb* the past participle of shrink

**shud·der** /**shuhd**-ur/ *verb*
- *verb* to shake a lot because you are very frightened, upset, or cold: *She shuddered when she saw the dead rat.*
- *noun* a shaking movement, because you are frightened, upset, or cold

**shuf·fle** /**shuhf**-uhl/ *verb*
**1** to move things around, especially playing cards, so they are in a different order: *I'll shuffle the cards before we start playing.*
**2** to walk without lifting your feet off the ground: *The old lady shuffled into the kitchen.*

**shun** /shuhn/ *verb* (**shunning**, **shunned**) to avoid someone or something deliberately: *He shuns elevators and uses the stairs instead.*

**shush** /shuhsh/ *interjection* used when telling someone to be quiet: *Shush! We don't want to wake the baby.*

a b c d e f g h i j k l m n o p q r **s** t u v w x y z

a b c d e f g h i j k l m n o p q r **s** t u v w x y z

**shut** /shuht/
- *verb* (**shutting**, **shut**)

**1** to close something: *Shut the door and lock it.*

(ANTONYM: **open**)

**2 shut down** to make a computer stop working: *Shut the computer down when you're not using it.*

**3 shut down** to make a factory or business stop working for ever: *The company shut the factory down because it was losing money.*

**4 shut off** to make a machine or piece of equipment stop working: *Tom shut off the dishwasher and took out the clean plates.*

(SYNONYM: **turn off**)

**5 shut up** used to tell someone rudely to stop talking: *My sister started shouting so I told her to shut up.*

- *adjective*

closed: *Make sure the door is shut, so the rabbit can't get out.* (ANTONYM: **open**)

**shut·ter** /shuht-ur/ *noun* a wood or metal cover that you can move over a window: *She closed the shutters to keep the room cool.*

**shut·tle** /shuht'l/ *noun*

**1** a vehicle that can carry people into space and come back to Earth more than once: *The shuttle will return to Earth tonight.*

(SYNONYM: **space shuttle**)

**2** an airplane, bus, or train that makes regular short trips between two places: *There is a shuttle from the hotel to the airport.*

**shy** /shī/ *adjective* nervous about meeting people and talking to them: *She is very shy and finds it hard to make new friends.*

—**shyness** /shī-niss/ *noun* a shy quality: *Shyness is very common in children.*

**sib·ling** /sib-ling/ *noun* a brother or sister: *My mom has a brother and a sister, but my dad doesn't have any siblings.*

**Word Origin: sibling**

**Sibling** comes from an Old English word that meant "relatives" or "family." The word sibling was not used in English for 400 years. Then, in 1903, a scientist needed a word for "brothers and sisters." He started to use the Old English word for this meaning.

**sick** /sik/ *adjective*

**1** having a disease or illness: *David didn't go to school because he was sick with a sore throat.*

(ANTONYM: **well**) ► see **Thesaurus**

**2** feeling like you are going to vomit: *Stop the car – I think I'm going to be sick.*

**3** feeling unhappy or bored with something: *Can we have something else for dinner? I'm sick of pasta.*

**sick·en** /sik-uhn/ *verb* to make you feel angry and shocked: *We are sickened by the crime in our neighborhood.*

—**sickening** /sik-uhn-ing/ *adjective* making you feel angry and shocked: *It's sickening to see people wasting so much food, when other people don't have enough.*

**sick·ness** /sik-niss/ *noun* the state or feeling of being sick: *He missed a lot of school because of sickness.*

**side** /sīd/
- *noun*

**1** a part of something that is not the front, back, top, or bottom: *Your ears are on the sides of your head.*

**2** one of the flat surfaces of an object, or one of the edges of a flat shape: *A cube has six sides. | A triangle has three sides. | There was writing on both sides of the paper.*

**3** the part of something that is at the edge, not in the middle: *She pushed herself off from the side of the pool and started swimming.*

**4** the left or right part of your body, not the front or back: *She sleeps on her side.*

**5** one half of something: *You go on that side of the tennis court, and I'll go on this side.*

**6** one of the people, groups, or countries in an argument or fight: *Mom said I couldn't go, but Dad was on my side and said I could.*

**7** one side of your family is all the people who are related to one of your parents: *My mother's side of the family all live in Arizona.*

- *adjective*

in or on the side of something: *He left the hotel through a side entrance.*

**IDIOM with side**

**side by side** next to each other: *The two girls were sitting side by side, Ava on the left and Emily on the right.*

side

They are sitting side by side.

**side·burns** /**sīd**-burnz/ *plural noun* hair that grows on the sides of a man's face in front of his ears, and that he does not shave off: *He had brown hair and sideburns.*

sideburns

sideburns

**side ef·fect** /**sīd** i-fekt/ *noun* an effect that a medicine has on your body that you did not want: *Headaches are a common side effect of the medication.*

**side·walk** /**sīd**-wok/ *noun* a path with a hard surface, next to a street: *She was standing on the sidewalk, waiting for the light to change.*

**side·ways** /**sīd**-wayz/ *adverb* toward one side: *He stepped sideways to let me pass.*

**siege** /seej/ *noun* a situation in which an army surrounds a place, and stops food and weapons from getting to it: *The siege lasted for six months.*

**sift** /sift/ *verb* to remove large pieces or lumps from a substance such as flour: *Sift the flour and add it to the butter and sugar in the bowl.*

**sigh** /sī/
● *verb* to breathe out loudly and slowly to express a feeling such as relief or disappointment: *I sighed with relief as I finished the test.*
● *noun* an act of sighing: *"We're home at last,"* she said with a sigh.

**sight** /sīt/ *noun*
**1** the ability to see. Sight is one of the five senses: *He has very good sight and doesn't need glasses.*
**2** the act of seeing something: *Maria can't stand the sight of blood.*

**3** the area within which you can see: *Mom told me not to let my little sister out of my sight.*

**sight·see·ing** /**sīt**-see-ing/ *noun* the activity of visiting famous or interesting places: *During our trip to New York City, we did a lot of sightseeing.*
—**sightseer** /**sīt**-see-ur/ *noun* someone who is visiting a famous or interesting place: *A group of sightseers visited the White House in Washington, D.C.*

**sign** /sīn/
● *noun*
**1** something with words or pictures on it. A sign can be a board or paper that gives information in a public place: *I followed the signs to the restrooms.*
**2** a symbol that has a particular meaning: *In math "+" is a plus sign.* | *Put a dollar sign in front of the price: $1.75.* (SYNONYM: **symbol**)
**3** a fact that shows that something is true or is starting to happen: *Headaches can be a sign that you need glasses.*
● *verb*
**1** to write your name, for example at the end of a letter: *He signed his name as K. Ortega.*
**2 sign up** to put your name on a list because you want to do something: *A lot of kids are signing up for the after-school sports program.*

**sig·nal** /**sig**-nuhl/
● *noun* a sound or action that tells someone to do something: *The whistle is the signal for everyone to start running.*
● *verb* to make a movement or sound that tells someone to do something: *Tom signaled to the boys to be quiet, by putting his finger to his lips.*

**sig·na·ture** /**sig**-nuhch-ur/ *noun* your usual way of writing your name, for example at the end of a letter: *My father's signature was at the bottom of the letter.*

**sig·nif·i·cance** /sig-**nif**-uhk-uhnss/ *noun* the importance or meaning of something: *The teacher explained the significance of the poem to us. She said the poem is about making choices.*

a b c d e f g h i j k l m n o p q r **s** t u v w x y z

**sig·nif·i·cant** /sig-**nif**-uhk-uhnt/ *adjective*
**1** important: *There has been a significant improvement in your work. You have gone from getting C's to getting B's.* ( ANTONYM: **insignificant** )
**2** a significant number or amount is fairly large: *Beef has a significant amount of fat, much more than chicken.*

**sign lan·guage** /**sīn** lang-gwij/ *noun* a language that uses hand, face, and body movements and not words. Sign language is used by people who cannot hear well.

**sign language**

Aa Bb Cc Dd Ee Ff Gg Hh Ii
Jj Kk Ll Mm Nn Oo Pp Qq Rr
Ss Tt Uu Vv Ww Xx Yy Zz

**Sikh** /seek/ *noun* someone who belongs to a religious group from India that follows the teachings of Guru Nanak: *Sikhs believe that there is only one God and that all people are equal.*
—**Sikhism** /**seek**-iz-uhm/ *noun* the religion of Sikhs

**si·lence** /**sīl**-uhnss/ *noun* complete quiet: *There must be silence during the test.*

**si·lent** /**sīl**-uhnt/ *adjective*
**1** completely quiet: *The house was dark and silent because everyone was asleep.*
**2** a silent letter is not pronounced: *In the word "know," the "k" is silent.*
—**silently** /**sīl**-uhnt-lee/ *adverb* in a silent way: *The students were listening silently to the story.*

**sil·i·con** /**sil**-i-kahn/ *noun* a chemical element in sand and rocks that is used for making glass, bricks, and parts for computers. The symbol for silicon is Si.

**silk** /silk/ *noun* a soft shiny cloth. Silk is made from the threads that a type of caterpillar produces: *She was wearing a red silk scarf around her neck.*

**silk·y** /**silk**-ee/ *adjective* soft and smooth like silk: *Sally had silky blond hair.*

**sill** /sil/ *noun* the narrow flat piece of wood at the bottom of a window frame
( SYNONYM: **windowsill** )

**sil·ly** /**sil**-ee/ *adjective*
**1** stupid or not sensible: *Of course I'm not mad at you – don't be silly!*
**2** funny and not serious or sensible: *Dad put on a silly hat to make me laugh.*

**silt** /silt/ *noun* sand or mud that is carried along by a river: *There is a lot of silt at the bottom of the river.*

**sil·ver** /**silv**-ur/ *noun, adjective*
**1** a shiny white metal that people use for making jewelry and other valuable things: *The box had gold and silver coins in it.* | *a silver necklace*
**2** the color of this metal: *She is wearing a party dress and some silver shoes.*

**sil·ver·ware** /**silv**-ur-wair/ *noun* knives, forks, and spoons that are made of silver or a similar metal: *The table looked pretty, with bright silverware.*

**sim·i·lar** /**sim**-uhl-ur/ *adjective* almost the same, but not exactly: *The house next door is very similar to ours. They are built the same way, but their house is white and our house is yellow.*
—**similarly** /**sim**-uhl-ur-lee/ *adverb* in a similar way: *The two girls were dressed similarly – they both wore pink dresses.*

**Word Family:** similar

similar *adjective* | **dissimilar** *adjective* |
**similarly** *adverb* | **similarity** *noun*

**sim·i·lar·i·ty** /sim-uh-**larr**-uht-ee/ *noun* (plural **similarities**) something that is the same about two people or things: *Both these leaves are small, so that is one similarity between them.*

**sim·i·le** /**sim**-uhl-ee/ *noun* a way of describing something by comparing it to something else, using the words "like" or "as": *The sentence "Her hair is as white as snow" uses a simile.*

**sim·mer** /**sim**-ur/ *verb* to boil very gently: *Let the sauce simmer for 20 minutes.*

**sim·ple** /**simp**-uhl/ *adjective*
**1** not difficult or complicated: *The camera is very simple to use – just turn it on and press the button.* ( SYNONYM: **easy** )

**2** plain and without a lot of decoration: *She wore a simple white dress.*

**3** a tense of a verb in English that is formed without an auxiliary verb such as "have" or "be": *In the sentence "I walked to school yesterday," the verb "walked" is in the simple past.*

—**simplicity** /sim-**pliss**-uht-ee/ *noun* the quality of being simple: *I liked the simplicity of the room. It was very plain, with no decorations, but it felt calm.*

**Word Family: simple**

**simple** *adjective* | **simply** *adverb* | **simplicity** *noun* | **simplify** *verb*

**sim·plest form** /simp-list **form**/ *noun* a fraction is in simplest form when the numerator and denominator have no common factors except 1: *The simplest form of 6/9 is 2/3.*

**sim·pli·fy** /**simp**-luh-fī/ *verb* (**simplifies,** **simplified**) to make something easier to do or understand: *I simplified the recipe by using a jar of tomato sauce instead of making my own.*

**sim·ply** /**simp**-lee/ *adverb*
**1** only: *I made mistakes simply because I was in a hurry.* (SYNONYM: **just**)
**2** in a way that is easy to understand or do: *My teacher's good at explaining things simply.*
**3** in a simple way, without a lot of extra things that are not needed: *She was dressed simply, in a plain T-shirt and jeans.*

**sim·u·late** /**sim**-yuh-layt/ *verb* to make or do something that seems real, but is not real: *The astronauts are trained in a machine that simulates being in space.*

—**simulation** /sim-yuh-**laysh**-uhn/ *noun* an activity that seems real, but is not real: *The computer game is a simulation that lets you drive 100 miles per hour.*

**sim·u·la·tor** /**sim**-yuh-layt-ur/ *noun* a machine that allows you to do something that seems real, but is not real: *When he was learning how to fly airplanes, he used the flight simulator.*

**si·mul·ta·ne·ous** /sīm-uhl-**tayn**-ee-uhss/ *adjective* happening at the same time: *During the war, the army fought simultaneous battles in different places.*

—**simultaneously** /sīm-uhl-**tayn**-ee-uhss-lee/ *adverb*

at the same time: *The game is being broadcast simultaneously on TV and radio.*

**sin** /sin/ *noun* something you do that religious rules do not allow: *It is a sin to lie.*

**since** /sinss/ *preposition, conjunction, adverb*
**1** from a time in the past until now: *Mrs. Brown has been a teacher at our school since 2005. | The girls have been best friends since they were five years old.*
**2** because: *You'll have to get up early, since the bus leaves at 6:00 a.m.* (SYNONYM: **as**)

**Word Choice: since, ago, for**

**Since**, **ago**, and **for** are all used to talk about time.

**Since** is used to say when something started. You say the word **since** and then say the day, date, or time after it: *It's been raining since Monday. | I've been going to school here since last year.*

**Ago** is used to say how far back in the past something happened. You say the amount of time, and then the word **ago**: *I moved here two years ago. | The movie started 15 minutes ago.*

**For** is used to say how long something has lasted. You say the word **for** and then the amount of time: *I have lived here for three years. | She waited for ten minutes.*

**sin·cere** /sin-**seer**/ *adjective* honest and meaning what you say: *She sounded very sincere when she thanked us.* (ANTONYM: **insincere**)

—**sincerity** /sin-**serr**-uht-ee/ *noun* the quality of being sincere: *"I am so sorry," she said with sincerity.*

**sin·cere·ly** /sin-**seer**-lee/ *adverb*
**1** in an honest way, and meaning what you say: *I sincerely hope that you succeed.*
**2** something you write at the end of a formal letter, before you write your name: *Sincerely, Hilary Walsh.*

**sing** /sing/ *verb* (**sang** /sang/, **sung** /suhng/) to make musical sounds with your voice: *They sang a beautiful song. | The mother was singing to her baby.*

**sing·er** /**sing**-ur/ *noun* someone who sings: *He's a singer in a band.*

a b c d e f g h i j k l m n o p q r **s** t u v w x y z

**sin·gle** /**sing**-guhl/

● *adjective*

**1** only one: *We lost the game by a single point.*

**2** not married: *Is Jessica married or single?*

**3** for one person: *The room has two single beds.*

● *noun*

**1** one song, which you can buy on a record or CD, or which you can download: *The band's latest single sold three million copies.*

**2** a one-dollar bill: *Can you give me a single for four quarters?*

● *verb*

**single out** to give special attention to one person or thing from a group: *Our class was singled out for praise because we worked really hard.*

**sin·gle file** /sing-guhl **fīl**/ *noun* a line with one person behind the other: *Our teacher told us to walk in single file.*

**sin·gu·lar** /**sing**-gyuhl-ur/ *noun* the form of a word for only one person or thing: *"Child" is the singular, and "children" is the plural.*

**sin·is·ter** /**sin**-ist-ur/ *adjective* frightening, and making you feel that something bad will happen to you: *The house was dark and full of shadows that seemed sinister.*

**sink** /singk/

● *verb* (**sank** /sangk/ or **sunk** /suhngk/)

**1** to go down below the surface of water: *If you throw a stone in water it sinks.* ( ANTONYM: **float** )

**2** to move down to a lower level: *I watched the sun sinking in the sky at the end of the day.*

● *noun*

the container in a kitchen or bathroom that you fill with water to wash dishes or your hands: *There were some dirty dishes in the sink.*

**sink**

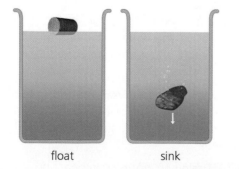

float        sink

**sin·ner** /**sin**-ur/ *noun* someone who does bad

things that religious rules do not allow: *He asked God to forgive him because he was a sinner.*

**-sion** /zhuhn/

### Word Building

**-sion** is a suffix. It is used in nouns.

admis**sion** | confu**sion** | deci**sion** | discus**sion** | permis**sion** | supervi**sion**

**-sion** means "the act of doing something." If there is *confusion* about something, people are confused. If a class has a *discussion*, they talk about something. If someone gives you *permission* to do something, he or she lets you do it.

**sip** /sip/ *verb*

● *verb* (**sipping**, **sipped**) to drink something slowly in small amounts: *She sat down and sipped her hot chocolate.*

● *noun* a very small amount of a drink: *Stacy took a sip of the lemonade to see if she liked it.*

**sir** /sur/ *noun*

**1** used in order to speak politely to a man when you do not know his name: *Can I help you, sir?*

**2** used at the beginning of a formal letter to a man, when you do not know his name: *Dear Sir*

**si·ren** /**sīr**-uhn/ *noun* a piece of equipment that is on a police car, ambulance, or fire truck. Sirens make a loud warning sound: *We heard ambulance and police sirens outside.*

**sis·ter** /**sist**-ur/ *noun*

**1** a girl or woman who has the same parents as you: *Joey has two sisters. | My older sister is in tenth grade.*

**2** a nun: *Sister Mary Boyle is a teacher at the Catholic school down the street*

### Word Origin: sister

**Sister** comes from Old English. The word for sister in many other languages sounds a little like the English word for sister. This is because all these words for sister come from a language that people used many thousands of years ago. English, Greek, Latin, Hindi, and many other languages developed from this very old language.

**sis·ter-in-law** /**sist**-ur in lo/ (plural **sisters-in-law**) *noun*
  **1** the wife of someone's brother: *My brother and sister-in-law invited me for Thanksgiving.*
  **2** the sister of someone's husband or wife

**sit** /sit/ *verb* (**sitting**, **sat** /sat/)
  **1** to put your bottom on a chair or the ground, with your body upright: *I usually sit at the front of the class.* | *Mrs. Morton told me to sit down and be quiet.*
  **2** to be in a place or on a surface: *A photograph sat on his desk.*
  **3** to stay in one place for a long time without doing anything useful or interesting: *It was raining so we just sat around at home all day.*
  **4** to take care of someone else's children: *My sister sometimes sits the neighbors' kids.*
  SYNONYM: **babysit**

sit

The children are sitting at their desks.

**sit·com** /**sit**-kahm/ *noun* a funny television program that has the same people in different situations each week. Sitcom is short for "situation comedy": *"Everybody Loves Raymond" was a popular sitcom that started in 1996.*

**site** /sīt/ *noun*
  **1** a place where something important or interesting happened: *This field is the site of a famous Civil War battle.*
  **2** an area where people build something: *Only people who are working on the houses are allowed to go into the construction site.*
  **3** a website: *This is a really good site for information about American history.*

**sit·ter** /**sit**-ur/ *noun* a babysitter: *Mom and Dad are going out, so the sitter is coming.*

**sit·u·at·ed** /**sich**-oo-ayt-id/ *adjective* to be in a particular place: *The house is situated next to a busy road.*

**sit·u·a·tion** /sich-oo-**aysh**-uhn/ *noun* the things that are happening at a particular time, or the things that are happening in someone's life: *Her dad just lost his job, and the family is in a very difficult situation.*

**sit-up** /**sit** up/ *noun* an exercise that makes your stomach muscles strong. To do a sit-up, you lie on your back and raise the top part of your body to a sitting position: *How many sit-ups can you do?*

**six** /sikss/ *number*
  **1** 6: *There were six apples in the bowl.*
  **2** six o'clock: *We eat dinner at six.*
  **3** six years old: *My younger brother is six.*

**six·teen** /sikss-**teen**/ *number*
  **1** 16: *There are sixteen girls on the soccer team.*
  **2** sixteen years old: *John just turned sixteen.*
  —**sixteenth** /sikss-**teenth**/ *number* 16th or 1/16: *She is having a big party for her sixteenth birthday.*

**sixth** /siksth/ *number*
  **1** 6th: *Next year, I'll be in the sixth grade.*
  **2** 1/6: *Five kids out of thirty, which is one sixth of the class, speak Spanish.*

**six·ty** /**sikst**-ee/ *number*
  **1** 60
  **2** sixty years old: *He is almost sixty.*
  **3** the sixties the years between 1960 and 1969: *A lot of great music is from the sixties.*
  **4** in your sixties between 60 and 69 years old: *Grandpa is in his sixties.*
  **5** in the sixties between 60 and 69 degrees in temperature: *The temperature was in the low sixties, so it felt cool outside.*
  —**sixtieth** /**sikst**-ee-ith/ *number* 60th or 1/60

**size** /sīz/ *noun*
  **1** how big or small something is: *My sister's room is the same size as mine.*
  **2** one in a series of measurements that shows how big something is: *I wear size 2 shoes.*

**siz·zle** /**siz**-uhl/ *verb* to make the sound of food cooking in hot oil: *Bacon was sizzling in the pan.*

a b c d e f g h i j k l m n o p q r **s** t u v w x y z

**skate** /skayt/
● *noun* a boot with wheels or a single piece of thin metal attached to the bottom: *You can rent skates at the rink for $5.*

SYNONYMS: **roller skate, ice skate**

● *verb* to move over ice or the ground on skates: *You have to skate very well to play ice hockey.*

**skates**

ice skates

roller skates

**skate·board** /skayt-bord/ *noun* a short board with wheels under it, which you stand on to move along the ground: *Do you want to ride skateboards after school?*
—**skateboarding** /skayt-bord-ing/ *noun* the activity of riding on a skateboard: *Let's go skateboarding in the park.*

**skat·ing** /skayt-ing/ *noun* the activity or sport of moving over ice or over the ground wearing skates: *We went skating at the ice rink.*

**skel·e·ton** /skel-uht'n/ *noun* all the bones in a person or animal, which form the shape of the person or animal: *The museum has the skeleton of a dinosaur.*

**skep·ti·cal** /skept-ik-uhl/ *adjective* not believing that something is true or right: *Jane said that she saw a shark in the water, but we were all skeptical.*
—**skeptic** /skept-ik/ *noun* someone who is skeptical: *He has to convince skeptics that his plan will work.*

**sketch** /skech/
● *noun* a quick drawing that does not have a lot of details: *I did a sketch of the bird before it flew away.*
● *verb* to draw a picture quickly and without a lot of details: *I sketched a little map to show my friend how to get to my house.*

**ski** /skee/
● *noun* (plural **skis**) a long narrow piece of wood or plastic that you fasten to boots. You use skis for moving on snow or over water: *It is much better to use shorter skis when you are learning how to ski.*

**ski**

● *verb* (**skied**) to move over snow on skis: *Tony skied down the mountain.*
—**skier** /skee-ur/ *noun* someone who skis: *He's a good skier.*

**skid** /skid/ *verb* (**skidding, skidded**) if a vehicle skids, it suddenly slides sideways: *A car skidded on the ice.*

**ski·ing** /skee-ing/ *noun* the activity or sport of moving over snow on skis: *We're going skiing in the mountains.*

**skill** /skil/ *noun* an ability to do something very well because you have learned it: *The workbook will help you improve your reading skills.*

**skilled** /skild/ *adjective* having the training and ability to do a job well: *Ken will be able to fix the car. He's a very skilled mechanic.*

ANTONYM: **unskilled**

**skil·let** /skil-it/ *noun* a frying pan: *I cooked the eggs in a skillet.*

**skill·ful** /skil-fuhl/ *adjective* good at doing something: *She is a skillful painter.*

**skim** /skim/ *verb* (**skimming, skimmed**)
**1** to read something very quickly: *Skim the test questions first. Then, go back and read each part carefully.*
**2** to remove something that is floating on top of a liquid: *Skim the oil off the soup.*

**skim milk** /skim milk/ *noun* milk without much fat in it: *Cereal with fruit and skim milk is a healthy breakfast.*

**skin** /skin/
● *noun*
**1** the outer covering of a person's or animal's body: *Babies have very soft skin.* | *She had a red mark on her skin where she'd burned herself.*

**2** the outer layer of some fruits and vegetables: *Bananas have yellow skins.*
● *verb* (**skinning, skinned**)
**1** to hurt your skin by rubbing it against something rough, so that you bleed: *I fell down and skinned my knees.* ( SYNONYM: **scrape** )
**2** to remove the skin from an animal or vegetable

**skin·ny** /**skin**-ee/ *adjective* (**skinnier, skinniest**) very thin: *He was a tall skinny kid.*

**skip** /skip/ *verb* (**skipping, skipped**)
**1** to move forward with quick jumps from one foot to the other: *The girls were skipping down the street.*
**2** to avoid something or not do something: *You shouldn't skip breakfast. If you don't eat, you won't have enough energy for the day.*

**skirt** /skurt/ *noun* a piece of clothing for girls or women that fits around the waist and hangs down: *She was wearing a white shirt and a blue skirt.*

**skull** /skuhl/ *noun* the bones of a person's or animal's head: *We saw the skulls of different animals at the science museum.*

**skunk** /skuhngk/ *noun* a small black and white animal with a long furry tail. Skunks spray liquid that has a very bad smell when they are afraid.

skunk

## Word Origin: skunk

When English people came to North America, they had never seen a **skunk** before. They borrowed the word skunk from a Native American language called Algonquian. In Algonquian, skunk means something like "the fox that urinates." When skunk was first written in English, people spelled it "squuncke."

**sky** /skī/ *noun* (plural **skies**) the space above the Earth where the Sun, clouds, and stars are: *Today, the sky is blue and the sun is shining.*

**sky·div·ing** /**skī**-dīv-ing/ *noun* the sport of jumping from an airplane. You fall through the sky and then open a parachute .
—**skydiver** /**skī**-dīv-ur/ *noun* someone who does skydiving

skydiving

**sky·line** /**skī**-līn/ *noun* the shape that tall buildings or hills make against the sky: *From the boat we could see the New York City skyline.*

skyline

skyline

**sky·scrap·er** /**skī**-skrayp-ur/ *noun* a very tall building in a city: *The skyscraper is 80 stories tall!*

**slab** /slab/ *noun* a thick flat piece of something: *The house was built on a slab of concrete.*

**slack** /slak/ *adjective* loose and not pulled tight: *The fishing line went slack, so I knew I'd lost the fish.*

slack

The rope is slack.

**slacks** /slakss/ *plural noun* nice-looking pants

597

**slam** /slam/
- *verb* (**slammed**, **slamming**)

**1** to shut something with a loud noise, usually because you are angry: *She ran up to her bedroom and slammed the door.*

**2** to put something somewhere quickly and with a lot of force: *He slammed his fist on the desk.*
- *noun*

the noise or action of something slamming: *The door closed with a slam.* ▶ see picture on page **A16**

**slang** /slang/ *noun* very informal spoken words: *"Wicked" is a slang word that means "good."*

**slant** /slant/
- *verb* to be at an angle, rather than straight up and down or flat: *The writing in this example slants a little to the right.*
- *noun* an angle, not straight up and down or flat: *As it sets, the Sun's rays hit the earth at a slant.*

**slap** /slap/
- *verb* (**slapping**, **slapped**) to hit someone quickly with the flat part of your hand: *She was so angry that she slapped his face.*
- *noun* a quick hit with the flat part of your hand: *He gave me a slap on the back to help me stop coughing.*

**slash** /slash/ *verb* to cut something in a violent way: *Someone slashed the tires on our car. We had to buy new ones.*

**slaugh·ter** /**slot**-ur/
- *verb*

**1** to kill an animal for food: *The cows are slaughtered for their meat.*

**2** to kill a lot of people in a violent way: *Many innocent people were slaughtered during the war.*
- *noun*

the act of slaughtering people or animals: *The animals were raised for slaughter.*

**slave** /slayv/
- *noun* someone who is owned by another person and is forced to work for no money: *In the 1700s, many Africans were captured and forced to work as slaves in America.*
- *verb* to work very hard: *I've been slaving away in the kitchen all day!*

**Word Origin:** slave

In the Middle Ages, an emperor called Otto the Great took control of areas in Eastern Europe. The people who lived in those areas were Slavs. The word **slave** comes from the medieval Latin word for Slav, because the Slavs were taken to become slaves in Otto the Great's empire.

**slav·er·y** /**slayv**-uhr-ee/ *noun* the system of having slaves: *Slavery existed in the United States until 1865.*

**slave trade** /**slayv** trayd/ *noun* the business of buying and selling slaves, especially Africans who were taken to America in the 18th and 19th centuries.

**sled** /sled/ *noun*
something you sit or lie on to slide over snow: *When it snows we like to play on our sled.*

sled

**sleek** /sleek/ *adjective* smooth and shiny: *The cat had sleek black fur.*

**sleep** /sleep/
- *verb* (**slept** /slept/)

**1** to lie down with your eyes closed and your mind and body not active: *Did you sleep well?* | *Try to be quiet – dad is sleeping.*

▶ see **Thesaurus**

**2 sleep in** to sleep later than usual in the morning: *On Saturday morning, I usually sleep in and get up late.*

**3 sleep over** to sleep at someone's house for a night: *I'm going to sleep over at my friend's house this weekend.*

**IDIOM with sleep**

**sleep tight** used to tell a child that you hope he or she sleeps well: *Goodnight, Rick. Sleep tight.*
- *noun*

a time when you are sleeping: *I didn't get much sleep last night because of the noise.*

**IDIOM with sleep**

**go to sleep** to start sleeping: *Be quiet and go to sleep!*

## Word Choice: sleep

You use **sleep** when you are talking about how long someone sleeps, or where she or he sleeps: *Cats sleep a lot during the day.* | *We slept in a tent.*

Do not use **sleep** to talk about starting to sleep. Use **fall asleep** or **go to sleep**: *I fell asleep as soon as I lay down in bed.* | *Ben and Adam, stop talking and go to sleep!*

**sleep·ing bag** /**sleep**-ing bag/ *noun* a large warm bag for sleeping in: *When we go camping, we sleep in sleeping bags in a tent.*

**sleep·walk·er** /**sleep**-wok-ur/ *noun* someone who walks around while he or she is sleeping

**sleep·y** /**sleep**-ee/ *adjective* tired and wanting to sleep: *You look sleepy – why don't you go to bed?*

**sleet** /sleet/ *noun* a mixture of rain and snow: *The weather became colder and the rain turned to sleet.*

**sleeve** /sleev/ *noun* the part of a piece of clothing that covers your arm: *It's warm, so wear a shirt with short sleeves.*

**sleigh** /slay/ *noun* a vehicle that horses pull over snow. A sleigh has metal bars instead of wheels under it: *Santa's sleigh was full of toys.*

**slen·der** /**slend**-ur/ *adjective* thin in a way that looks good: *She is tall, slender, and beautiful.*
( SYNONYM: **slim** )

**slept** /slept/ *verb* the past tense and past participle of **sleep**

**slice** /slīss/
● *noun* a flat piece of food that you have cut from a whole thing: *He usually has two slices of toast for breakfast.* | *Would you like a slice of pizza?*
● *verb* to cut something into thin flat pieces: *I sliced the tomato and put it in the salad.*

slice

slice

slice

**slick** /slik/
● *adjective*
**1** smooth and wet or shiny: *His hands were slick with sweat.* ( SYNONYM: **slippery** )
**2** good at persuading people, often in a way that does not seem honest: *A slick car salesman tried to convince Mom and Dad to buy an expensive car.*
● *verb*
**slick back/down** to make your hair smooth and shiny by putting oil or water on it: *His hair was slicked back behind his ears.*

**slide** /slīd/
● *verb* (**slid** /slid/) to move smoothly over a surface: *He slid the window open.* | *We slid down the hill on our sleds.*
● *noun* something for children to play on which has a slope that they slide down: *I went down the slide in the playground.*

**slight** /slīt/ *adjective* small and not serious or important: *There is one slight change – the game will start at 7:30 instead of 7:00.*

**slight·ly** /**slīt**-lee/ *adverb* a little: *My father is slightly older than my mother.* | *This test is harder than the last one, but only slightly.*

**slim** /slim/
● *adjective*
**1** thin in a way that looks good: *Most ballet dancers are very slim.* ( SYNONYM: **slender** )
( ANTONYM: **fat** )
**2** very small in amount: *We have only a slim chance of winning because they are much better than us.*
● *verb* (**slimming**, **slimmed**)
**slim down** to become thinner by eating less and exercising more: *The doctor said that I am overweight and need to slim down.*

**slime** /slīm/ *noun* a thick, wet, unpleasant substance that covers something: *The pond was covered with green slime.*
—**slimy** /**slīm**-ee/ *adjective* covered with slime: *The rocks at the beach were wet and slimy.*

**sling** /sling/ *noun* a piece of cloth tied around your neck to support your arm or hand when it is hurt: *Emily's arm is in a sling because she has broken it.*

**slip** /slip/
- *verb* (**slipping**, **slipped**)
**1** to slide on a smooth surface and lose your balance or fall: *Diane slipped on the ice and hurt her ankle.*
**2** to move or slide out of a place: *The ball slipped out of my hands as I tried to catch it.*
**3** to go somewhere or put something somewhere quickly and quietly: *While everyone was talking, we slipped outside.*
- *noun*
**1** a small piece of paper: *He wrote the message on a slip of paper.*
**2** a small mistake: *One little slip made us lose the game.*

slip

She slipped on the ice.

**slip·per** /**slip**-ur/ *noun* a soft shoe that you wear in your house: *The floor was cold, so I put on a pair of slippers.*

**slip·per·y** /**slip**-uhr-ee/ *adjective* something that is slippery is difficult to walk on or hold because it is wet, oily, or covered with ice: *Don't run beside the pool – it is very slippery.*

**slit** /slit/
- *noun* a narrow cut or opening in something: *Her skirt is tight, so it has a slit in the back at the bottom so that she can walk.*
- *verb* (**slitting**, **slit**) to make a narrow cut in something: *He slit the envelope open.*

**slith·er** /**slith**-ur/ *verb* to slide somewhere in a smooth way, close to the ground: *The snake slithered away as we came closer.*

**slob** /slahb/ *noun* someone who is lazy and messy: *Don't be such a slob – clean up your room.*

**slo·gan** /**slohg**-uhn/ *noun* a short phrase that is easy to remember, used in advertisements and politics: *"Yes we can" was the slogan Barack*

Obama used when he was running for president.

**slope** /slohp/
- *noun* a piece of ground or a surface that is higher at one end than the other: *She walked slowly up the steep slope.*
- *verb* if a surface or piece of ground slopes, it is higher at one end than the other: *The field sloped down to the lake.*

**slop·py** /**slahp**-ee/ *adjective* not done neatly or carefully: *Your homework was very sloppy. You need to write carefully so it is easier to read.*
—**sloppily** /**slahp**-uhl-ee/ *adverb* in a sloppy way: *He was dressed sloppily in a baggy T-shirt and old jeans.*

**slot** /slaht/ *noun* a narrow hole in something, for example a hole in a machine where you put money: *I put the coins in the slot and got a candy bar out of the machine.*

**slouch** /slowch/ *verb* to stand, sit, or walk with your shoulders bent forward: *Sit up straight! Don't slouch.*

**slow** /sloh/
- *adjective*
**1** not moving or happening quickly: *I'm a very slow runner so I never win races.* | *My computer seems really slow today – it's taking so long to save things.* (ANTONYM: **fast**)
**2** if a clock or watch is slow, it shows a time that is earlier than the true time: *This clock is ten minutes slow; it says 2:30 but the real time is 2:40.* (ANTONYM: **fast**)
—**slowness** /**sloh**-niss/ *noun* the quality of being slow: *People complain about the slowness of the traffic on the freeways.*
- *verb*
**slow down** to go less fast than before: *It's not healthy to eat so fast. Slow down!*

**slow·ly** /**sloh**-lee/ *adverb* at a slow speed: *I don't understand you. Can you speak more slowly?* (ANTONYM: **quickly**) ▶ see Thesaurus

**slug** /sluhg/ *noun* a small soft creature with no legs that moves very slowly. A slug is a type of snail that has no shell: *Slugs eat garden plants.*

slug

**slum** /sluhm/ *noun* an area of a city where the houses are in bad condition and many poor people live: *There was a lot of crime and poverty in the slum where he grew up.*

**slum·ber par·ty** /**sluhm**-bur part-ee/ *noun* a party at which a group of children sleep at one child's house: *I'm having a slumber party for my birthday.*

**slump** /sluhmp/ *verb* to sit with the top part of your body leaning forward and down: *He slumped in the chair, tired after a long day.*

**slur** /slur/ *verb* (**slurring, slurred**) to speak in a way that is not clear, for example because you are sick: *It was difficult to understand her because she was slurring her words.*

**slush** /sluhsh/ *noun* snow on the ground that has started to melt: *The snow did not last very long – it became slush within a few hours.*

**sly** /slī/ *adjective* good at getting what you want by tricking people or doing unfair things: *In the story, a sly fox tries to steal the hen's eggs.*

**smack** /smak/ *verb* to hit someone or something in a way that makes a noise: *The kids were smacking balls against a wall outside.*

**small** /smol/ *adjective*
**1** not large in size or amount: *We live in a small house. | My class is small this year – only 20 students.* (ANTONYM: **big**) ▶ see **Thesaurus**
**2** not important or easy to deal with: *There were a few small mistakes on his math homework.*
(SYNONYM: **minor**) (ANTONYM: **big**)

**small·pox** /**smol**-pahkss/ *noun* a serious disease that causes spots on the skin. In the past, many people died of smallpox, but no one has had it for many years: *In the 1800s, many Native Americans died of measles and smallpox.*

**smart** /smart/ *adjective* intelligent: *Troy is very smart and he learns really fast.* (ANTONYM: **stupid**)

**smart·y-pants** /**smart**-ee pantss/ *noun* someone who tries to seem intelligent or funny in a way that other people think is annoying: *OK, smarty-pants, if you know all the answers, why are you asking me?*

**smash** /smash/ *verb*
**1** to break into many small pieces: *The plates fell onto the floor and smashed. | The ball smashed our neighbor's window.*
**2** to hit something in a violent way: *He was killed when his car smashed into a tree.*

smash

Someone has smashed the plate.

**smear** /smeer/
● *verb* to spread a liquid or soft substance on a surface: *His face was smeared with mud.*
● *noun* a dirty mark: *There were smears of paint on his face.*

**smell** /smel/
● *noun*
**1** the quality you notice by using your nose. Smell is one of the five senses: *The smell of paint in the classroom was really strong.*
▶ see **Thesaurus**
**2** a bad smell: *What's that smell? Is it the garbage?*
**3** the ability to notice smells: *Dogs have a very good sense of smell.*
● *verb*
**1** to have a bad smell: *His feet smelled because he'd been wearing sneakers without socks.*
(SYNONYM: **stink**)
**2** to use your nose to notice something: *I can smell something burning.*

**smell·y** /**smel**-ee/ *adjective* having a bad smell: *Put those smelly socks in the washing machine.*

**smile** /smīl/
● *verb* if you smile, you have a happy expression on your face and your mouth curves up: *Mom smiled at me and said "Hi, honey."*
▶ see **Thesaurus**
● *noun* a happy expression on your face, with your mouth curved up: *The teacher looked at us with a smile.*

**smog** /smahg/ *noun* dirty air in cities that is a mixture of smoke, gases, and chemicals: *As we drove into Los Angeles, we could see a layer of smog over the city.*

a b c d e f g h i j k l m n o p q r **s** t u v w x y z

**smoke** /smohk/

● *noun* the white, gray, or black gas that comes from something that is burning: *Clouds of smoke came from the chimney.*

● *verb* to breathe in smoke from a cigarette or pipe: *Nobody in my family smokes cigarettes.*

smoke

smoke

**smok·er** /**smohk**-ur/ *noun* someone who smokes: *Smokers have to leave the building and go outside if they want to smoke.*

**smok·ing** /**smohk**-ing/ *noun* the habit of smoking cigarettes or pipes: *Smoking is very bad for your health.*

**smok·y** /**smohk**-ee/ *adjective* filled with smoke: *The room was still smoky even after the fire was put out.*

**smol·der** /**smohld**-ur/ *verb* to burn slowly with smoke but no flame: *The factory is still smoldering after last night's fire.*

**smooth** /smooth/ *adjective*

**1** without any lumps or rough areas: *Babies have beautiful smooth skin. | Mix the powdered paint with water until it is smooth.* (ANTONYM: **rough**)
**2** happening in the way you want, without problems or sudden changes: *We want the move to your new school to be as smooth as possible.*
—**smoothness** /**smooth**-niss/ *noun* a smooth quality: *I liked the smoothness of the polished stone.*

**smooth·ie** /**smooth**-ee/ *noun* a thick drink that is a mixture of fruit and juice or milk: *My smoothie has strawberries and yogurt in it.*

**smooth·ly** /**smooth**-lee/ *adverb* if something happens smoothly, it happens without any problems: *I was nervous before I had to sing, but everything went smoothly.*

**smoth·er** /**smuhth**-ur/ *verb*

**1** to cover someone's face so that the person cannot breathe and dies
**2** to cover the whole surface of something with something else: *He always smothers his French fries in ketchup.*

**smudge** /smuhj/

● *noun* a dirty mark: *There was a smudge of mud on his face.*

● *verb* to put a dirty mark on a clean surface: *The mirror was smudged with dirty fingerprints.*

**smug** /smuhg/ *adjective* very pleased with yourself, in a way that annoys other people: *She looked a little smug about knowing the answer before anyone else.*
—**smugly** /**smuhg**-lee/ *adverb* in a smug way: *"My story won first prize," she said smugly.*

**smug·gle** /**smuhg**-uhl/ *verb* to take someone or something illegally from one place to another: *They were trying to smuggle guns into the country.*
—**smuggling** /**smuhg**-ling/ *noun* the crime of taking someone or something illegally from one place to another: *He was sent to prison for drug smuggling.*

**smug·gler** /**smuhg**-lur/ *noun* someone who takes something illegally from one place to another: *The smugglers were hiding jewels in suitcases.*

**snack** /snak/

● *noun* something that you eat between meals: *We try to eat healthy snacks like fruit and yogurt.*

● *verb* to eat food between meals: *After school, they snacked on cheese and crackers.*

**snack bar** /**snak** bar/ *noun* a place where you can buy drinks, snacks, and small meals: *We got sandwiches at the snack bar in the museum.*

**snag** /snag/ *noun* a small problem: *I want to come to the party, but there's just one snag – I need someone to drive me home.*

**snail** /snayl/ *noun* a small soft creature with no legs that moves very slowly. Snails have a hard curved shell covering their body. Some kinds of snails live in water, and some kinds live on land.

snail

**snake** /snayk/ *noun* a long thin animal with no legs, which slides along the ground. Snakes are a type of reptile. Some snakes are small, but other types are very large: *She was bitten by a poisonous snake.* ▶ see picture at **reptile**

snake

**snap** /snap/
● *verb* (**snapping**, **snapped**)

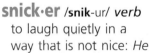
snap

**1** to break with a short loud noise: *A branch snapped off the tree during the storm.*
**2** to open, close, or join together with a short loud noise: *The lid on the box snapped shut.*
**3** to suddenly speak to someone in an angry way: *"You are not listening to me," she snapped at her son.*
**4 snap your fingers** to move two of your fingers together to make a noise: *The teacher snapped her fingers to get our attention.*
● *noun* a sudden short loud noise of something breaking: *I heard the snap of a twig behind me so I knew someone was there.*

**snap·shot** /**snap**-shaht/ *noun* a photograph that you take quickly: *He showed us some snapshots of his friends.*

**snare** /snair/
● *noun* a trap for catching an animal: *They catch rabbits in snares.*
● *verb* to catch an animal using a snare: *He snared a squirrel.*

**snarl** /snarl/ *verb*
**1** if an animal snarls, it makes a low angry sound and shows its teeth: *The two dogs snarled at each other and started fighting.*
**2** to say something in an angry way: *"Get out of here!" he snarled.*

**snatch** /snach/
● *verb* to take something from someone very quickly: *Someone snatched her purse and ran away.* ( SYNONYM: **grab** )

● *noun* a short part of something that you hear: *We could hear snatches of conversation from the other room.*

**sneak** /sneek/ *verb* (**sneaked** or **snuck** /snuhk/) to go somewhere quietly because you do not want people to see or hear you: *Sometimes I sneak into the kitchen to get a cookie when my parents are watching TV.*

**sneak·er** /**sneek**-ur/ *noun* a soft shoe that you wear for playing sports: *The girl was wearing shorts and white sneakers.*

**sneak·y** /**sneek**-ee/ *adjective* doing things secretly in an unfair or dishonest way: *"I told Mom I needed to do my homework with you, so I could come over and play." "That was sneaky."*

**sneer** /sneer/ *verb* to smile or speak in an unpleasant way that shows you have no respect for someone: *One of the girls sneered at her for wearing the wrong clothes.*

**sneeze** /sneez/ *verb* to make air suddenly come out of your nose and mouth, for example because you have a cold: *The dust made her sneeze.*

sneeze

**snick·er** /**snik**-ur/ *verb* to laugh quietly in a way that is not nice: *He snickered when his sister fell over and got mud on her new dress.*

**sniff** /snif/ *verb*
**1** to breathe in through your nose in order to smell something: *I sniffed the milk to see if it was still fresh.*
**2** to breathe air into your nose with a loud sound, for example when you are crying or when you have a cold: *Stop sniffing and blow your nose!*

**snob** /snahb/ *noun* someone who thinks that he or she is better than other people: *She's kind of a snob. She'll only be friends with you if you wear the right kind of clothes.*

**snoop** /snoop/ *verb* to try to find out about someone's life or activities by secretly looking at his or her things: *I caught my brother snooping around in my bedroom, looking at my diary.*

a b c d e f g h i j k l m n o p q r **s** t u v w x y z

**snooze** /snooz/
- *verb* to sleep for a short time: *The cat was snoozing in front of the fire when a loud noise woke him up.* ( SYNONYM: **doze** )
- *noun* a short sleep: *Grandpa gets tired after lunch and likes to have a snooze.* ( SYNONYM: **nap** )

**snore** /snor/
- *verb* to make a loud noise each time you breathe when you are sleeping: *I couldn't sleep because my brother was snoring so loudly.*
- *noun* the sound you make when you snore: *Loud snores were coming from the bedroom.*

**snor·kel** /**snork**-uhl/ *noun* a tube that a swimmer uses to breathe air through when his or her face is under water

**snort** /snort/ *verb* to make a sudden loud noise through your nose, for example because you are angry or laughing: *Dad told a joke, and my brother snorted with laughter.*

**snout** /snowt/ *noun* the long nose of a pig or similar animal

**snow** /snoh/
- *noun*
soft white pieces of frozen water that fall from the sky when it is very cold: *We made a snowman in the snow.* ▶ see **Thesaurus**
- *verb*
**1** if it snows, snow falls from the sky: *It's very cold here in the winter and it often snows.*
**2** **be snowed in** to not be able to leave a place because so much snow has fallen: *It snowed for a week and we got snowed in.*

**snow·ball** /**snoh**-bol/ *noun* a ball that children make from snow and throw at each other: *Pete threw a snowball at him and knocked his hat off.*

**snow·board** /**snoh**-bord/ *noun* a large board that you stand on with both feet and use to slide down a hill that is covered in snow
—**snowboarding** /**snoh**-bord-ing/ *noun* the activity of using a snowboard: *We went snowboarding.*

**snow·fall** /**snoh**-fol/ *noun* an amount of snow that falls in a particular period of time: *A heavy snowfall has blocked the road.*

**snow·flake** /**snoh**-flayk/ *noun* a small piece of snow that falls from the sky

**snow·man** /**snoh**-man/ *noun* (plural **snowmen** /**snoh**-men/) an object shaped like a person made of snow. You make a snowman by putting two or three large balls of snow on top of each other: *The kids were in the yard building a snowman.*

snowman

**snow·plow** /**snoh**-plow/ *noun* a vehicle used for pushing snow off roads

**snow·shoe** /**snoh**-shoo/ *noun* something that you attach under your shoe so that you can walk on snow: *The snow was deep, so we used snowshoes on our walk.*

**snow·storm** /**snoh**-storm/ *noun* a storm with strong winds and a lot of snow: *The snowstorm left four feet of snow on the ground.*

**snow·y** /**snoh**-ee/ *adjective* having a lot of snow or covered with snow: *The cars moved slowly through the snowy streets.*

**snuck** /snuhk/ *verb* a past tense and past participle of **sneak**

**snug** /snuhg/ *adjective* warm and comfortable: *I felt safe and snug in my bed.*

**snug·gle** /**snuhg**-uhl/ *verb* to get into a warm comfortable position: *The cat likes to snuggle up against me on the couch.*

**so** /soh/
- *adverb*
**1** very: *I felt so sick yesterday.*
**2** used in place of what someone has just said, to avoid repeating it: *"Is it raining outside?" "I don't think so."* | *You have to turn the TV off, because Mom said so.*
**3** used for saying that something is also true about someone else: *Ruth is very tall and so is her sister.* | *"I like playing computer games." "So do I."*
**4** used for getting someone's attention or before you ask him or her a question: *So, Lisa, what are you doing after school today?*

**IDIOMS with so**
**and so on** used after a list to show that there are other similar things that you have not mentioned: *We share jobs around the house, such as setting the table, cleaning, and so on.*
**or so** used when you are not giving an exact number or amount: *It takes 20 minutes or so to drive home.*
**so long!** used for saying goodbye: *So long, George, and good luck!*
● *conjunction*
**1** used for showing why something happens: *I got thirsty, so I drank some water.*
**2** in order to do something or make something happen: *I put the ice cream in the refrigerator so that it wouldn't melt.*

**soak** /sohk/ *verb*
**1** to leave something in water for a time: *The dishes were very dirty so I left them to soak in the sink.*
**2** to make something completely wet: *The rain soaked our clothes.*
**3** if something soaks up a liquid, it takes the liquid into itself: *A sponge soaks up water.*
( SYNONYM: **absorb** )

**soaked** /sohkt/ *adjective* very wet: *We got soaked when it started to rain.*

**soak·ing** /**sohk**-ing/ (also **soak·ing wet** /sokh-ing **wet**/) *adjective* very wet: *I dropped my hat in the pool and now it's soaking wet.*

**soap** /sohp/ *noun*
**1** a substance that you use with water to wash yourself: *Wash your hands with soap and water.*
**2** (also **soap op·era** /sohp ahp-ruh/) a story on television about the lives of a group of people: *My aunt's favorite soap is "Days of Our Lives."*

**soar** /sor/ *verb*
**1** to go up quickly to a high level: *Gas prices soared to their highest level in five years.*
**2** to fly high in the air: *The birds soared into the sky.*

**sob** /sahb/
● *verb* (**sobbing**, **sobbed**) to cry with quick noisy breaths: *She was sobbing because her favorite toy was broken.*
● *noun* a quick noisy breath that someone makes when he or she is crying: *I knew she was crying because I could hear her sobs.*

**so·ber** /**sohb**-ur/ *adjective* not having drunk too much alcohol: *I thought he was drunk but he was totally sober.* ( ANTONYM: **drunk** )

**soc·cer** /**sahk**-ur/ *noun* a game played by two teams of 11 players. They try to kick a ball into a large net at each end of a field and are not allowed to touch the ball with their hands: *She plays for the school's soccer team.* ▶ see picture on page **A10**

**Word Origin:** soccer

**Soccer** is a game that was invented in Britain. The name soccer comes from a short form of Association Football, the official name for soccer. Association was shortened to "assoc," and people soon changed the letters arround to "socca." Later, the spelling became "soccer." Most people in Britain now call the game "football," but Americans use soccer because we have a different game that we call football.

**so·cia·ble** /**sohsh**-uhb-uhl/ *adjective* someone who is sociable is friendly and enjoys being with other people: *She is a very sociable person and has a lot of friends.*

**so·cial** /**sohsh**-uhl/ *adjective*
**1** relating to the people in a society and the way they live: *Crime is a serious social problem.*
**2** relating to spending time with people for fun: *He has a busy social life and is always going out with friends.*
—**socially** /**sohsh**-uhl-ee/ *adverb* in a way that relates to society or to spending time with people for fun: *She wanted a socially useful job such as nursing or teaching.*

**so·cial·ize** /**sohsh**-uh-līz/ *verb* to spend time with people for fun: *We often socialize with other families from the church.*

**So·cial Se·cu·ri·ty** /sohsh-uhl si-**kyoor**-uht-ee/ *noun* money that the government pays to people who are old or cannot work: *Our neighbor is 75 years old and lives on Social Security.*

a
b
c
d
e
f
g
h
i
j
k
l
m
n
o
p
q
r
**s**
t
u
v
w
x
y
z

**so·cial stud·ies** /**sohsh**-uhl stuhd-eez/ *noun* a subject that you study at school. Social studies includes history, geography, and government: *The class is learning about the state's history in social studies.*

**so·ci·e·ty** /suh-**sī**-uht-ee/ *noun* (plural **societies**)
**1** all the people who live in a country, and the way they live: *Our society includes people from many different races and religions.*
**2** an organization of people with the same interest or purpose: *The book on the early settlers is published by the Montana Historical Society.*

> **Word Family:** society
>
> **society** *noun* | **social** *adjective* | **socially** *adverb*

**sock** /sahk/ *noun* a piece of clothing that you wear on your foot inside your shoe: *When he took his shoes off you could see the hole in his sock.*

**sock·et** /**sahk**-it/ *noun*
**1** a place in a wall where you can connect a piece of equipment to the supply of electricity: *I put the plug in the socket and then switched the lamp on.* ( SYNONYM: **outlet** )
**2** the place where one thing fits into another: *The bone in your upper arm fits into a hollow space in your shoulder bone called an arm socket.*

**sod** /sahd/ *noun* the top layer of dirt that has grass growing in it

**so·da** /**sohd**-uh/ *noun* a sweet drink with bubbles: *"Do you want a soda?" "Yeah, do you have any cola?"* ( SYNONYM: **pop** )

**so·di·um** /**sohd**-ee-uhm/ *noun* a silver-white chemical element. Its symbol is Na: *Salt contains sodium and chlorine.*

**so·fa** /**sohf**-uh/ *noun* a comfortable seat that is wide enough for two or three people: *Mom and Dad were sitting on the sofa and watching TV.*
( SYNONYM: **couch** )

**soft** /soft/ *adjective*
**1** not hard or firm, but easy to press: *The bed was very soft and comfortable.* ( ANTONYM: **hard** )
▶ see **Thesaurus**

**2** smooth and nice to touch: *She petted the cat's soft fur.* ( ANTONYM: **rough** )
**3** a soft sound is quiet: *"Goodnight, sweetheart," she said in a soft voice.* ( ANTONYM: **loud** )
**4** soft colors or lights are not too bright: *The baby blanket was a soft blue.* ( ANTONYM: **bright** )
—**softness** /**soft**-niss/ *noun* a soft quality: *She felt the softness of the baby's skin.*

**soft·ball** /**soft**-bol/ *noun* a game similar to baseball, but played with a larger and softer ball: *The girls are on a softball team.* ▶ see picture on page **A10**

**soft drink** /**soft** dringk/ *noun* a sweet drink with bubbles. Soft drinks do not contain alcohol.

**soft·en** /**sof**-uhn/ *verb*
**1** to become less hard: *Rub oil onto your baseball glove to soften the leather.* ( ANTONYM: **harden** )
**2** to become more gentle or kind: *She looked at her baby and her face softened.*

**soft·ly** /**soft**-lee/ *adverb* quietly: *She spoke softly so she wouldn't wake up the baby.*

**soft·ware** /**soft**-wair/ *noun* a set of programs that tells a computer to do something: *This software has lots of math games you can play.*

**sog·gy** /**sahg**-ee/ *adjective* too wet and soft: *Don't put the milk on my cereal yet; I don't like soggy cereal.*

**soil** /soyl/ *noun* the substance on the ground in which plants grow: *Cover the seeds with soil.*
( SYNONYMS: **dirt, earth** ) ▶ see picture at **flower**

soil

soil

**so·lar** /**sohl**-ur/ *adjective* relating to the Sun: *Solar heating uses energy from the Sun to heat air or water.*

**so·lar en·er·gy** /sohl-ur **en**-urj-ee/ *noun* energy from the Sun: *Scientists have found ways to use solar energy to make electricity.*

**so·lar sys·tem** /**sohl**-ur sist-uhm/ *noun* a sun and the planets that move around it. The solar system also includes moons, comets, and asteroids: *There are eight planets in our solar system.*

**sold** /sohld/ *verb* the past tense and past participle of **sell**

**sol·dier** /**sohl**-jur/ *noun* someone in the army: *The soldiers fought bravely in the war.*

**soldier**

helmet

rifle

camouflage gear

**sole** /sohl/
● *adjective* only: *When we first moved, I didn't know anyone. My sole friend was my dog.*
● *noun* the bottom of your foot or shoe: *I got gum stuck to the sole of my shoe.* ▶ see picture at **foot**

**sole·ly** /**sohl**-lee/ *adverb* only: *Students must use the computers solely for school work, not for games.*

**sol·emn** /**sahl**-uhm/ *adjective* serious or formal: *I gave a solemn promise that I would take care of my sister.*
—**solemnly** /**sahl**-uhm-lee/ *adverb* in a solemn way: *"I have some bad news for you," he said solemnly.*

**sol·id** /**sahl**-id/
● *adjective*
**1** hard or firm, and not a liquid or gas: *When water freezes, it becomes solid and turns into ice.*
**2** having no space or holes inside: *The door is strong because it is solid wood.*
( ANTONYM: **hollow** )
**3** not mixed with anything else: *The necklace is solid gold.*
● *noun*
a substance that is not a liquid or gas: *Wax is a solid at room temperature.*

**solar system**

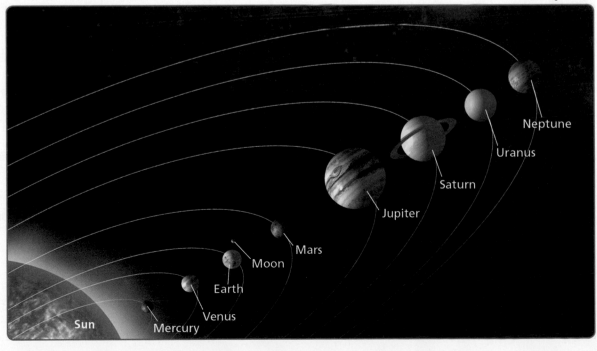

Neptune

Uranus

Saturn

Jupiter

Mars

Moon

Earth

Venus

Sun

Mercury

**sol·id fig·ure** /sahl-id **fig**-yur/ *noun* an object that has length, depth, and height rather than being a flat shape: *A ball is a solid figure, but a circle is not.*

**sol·i·tar·y** /sahl-uh-tair-ee/ *adjective*
**1** a solitary person or thing is the only one you can see in a place: *The street was empty except for a solitary person waiting at the bus stop.*
**2** done or experienced alone: *Reading to yourself is a solitary activity.*

**sol·i·tude** /sahl-uh-tood/ *noun* the state of being alone: *I had a few hours of solitude before the rest of the family got home.*

**so·lo** /sohl-oh/
● *adjective* done alone, without anyone else helping you: *After the singer left the band, he made a solo CD.*
● *noun* a piece of music performed by one person: *He plays a violin solo before the rest of the orchestra joins in.*

**sol·u·bil·i·ty** /sahl-yuh-**bil**-uht-ee/ *noun* the ability of a solid substance to dissolve in a liquid: *We put salt, sand, and flour in water to test their solubility.*

**sol·u·ble** /sahl-yuhb-uhl/ *adjective* a soluble substance can be mixed with a liquid until it disolves and becomes part of the liquid: *Salt is soluble in water.*

**so·lu·tion** /suh-**loosh**-uhn/ *noun*
**1** a way of stopping a problem: *Our house was too small for us and the only solution was to find a bigger one.*
**2** the right answer to a puzzle or a difficult question: *The solution to the math problem is in the back of the book.*
**3** a liquid that has a substance mixed completely into it: *We made a solution of sugar and water.*

**solve** /sahlv/ *verb*
**1** to find a successful way to deal with a problem: *Instead of arguing, maybe we could solve the problem by having a chart that says whose turn it is to do the dishes.*
**2** to find the correct answer to a puzzle or a difficult question: *The first one to solve all the math problems will get a prize.*

**some** /suhm/ *adjective, pronoun, adverb*
**1** an amount of something, or a number of people or things: *Do you want some ice cream?* |

*There were some books on the table.*
**2** part of a group or thing: *Some of my friends don't know how to ride a bike, but most of us do.*
**3** used instead of "a" when you do not know who someone is or what something is: *Some guy called while you were out.*

**some·bod·y** /**suhm**-bahd-ee/ *pronoun* another word for someone

**some·day** /**suhm**-day/ *adverb* at some time in the future: *Someday I'm going be rich.*

**some·how** /**suhm**-how/ *adverb*
**1** in some way, although you do not know how: *Somehow we have to get Mom to let us go to the game.*
**2** for a reason that you cannot explain clearly: *I don't know why, but somehow I don't trust him.*

**some·one** /**suhm**-wuhn/ *pronoun* a person: *Someone broke the window, but we don't know who.* | *"Did you bring this book to school?" "No, someone else did."* ( SYNONYM: **somebody** )

**Grammar:** someone, anyone

In questions and sentences with "not" in them, we usually use **anyone**: *Did you ask anyone to help you?* | *I didn't see anyone there.*
In other sentences, we use **someone**: *There's someone knocking on the door.*

**some·place** /**suhm**-playss/ *adverb* another word for somewhere

**som·er·sault** /**suhm**-ur-solt/ *noun* a movement in which you roll or jump forward, so that your feet go over your head: *I learned how to do a somersault on the trampoline.*

**some·thing** /**suhm**-thing/ *pronoun* a thing: *Do you want something to drink?* | *Can we watch something else? This is boring.*

**IDIOM with something**
**or something** said when you cannot remember or are not sure: *I'm not sure where Jennifer is. She might be out shopping or something.*

## Grammar: anything, something

In questions and sentences with "not" in them, we usually use **anything**: *Mrs. Hogan did not say anything.* | *Do you know anything about dinosaurs?*

In other sentences, we use **something**: *There's something on the table for you.*

**some·time** /**suhm**-tīm/ *adverb* at some time in the past or future: *Do you want to play at my house sometime?*

**some·times** /**suhm**-tīmz/ *adverb* on some occasions, but not always: *Sometimes we go to Grandma's for dinner.*

**some·what** /**suhm**-wuht/ *adverb* slightly: *I did somewhat better on the spelling test this week.*

**some·where** /**suhm**-wair/ *adverb*
**1** in or to some place: *I left my watch somewhere, but I can't remember where I put it.* | *It's too noisy here. Let's go somewhere else.*
**2** a little more or less than a particular number, time, or amount: *It will take somewhere between three and four hours to get there.*

## Grammar: somewhere, anywhere

In questions and sentences with "not" in them, we usually use **anywhere**: *I couldn't find my hairbrush anywhere.* | *Have you seen my keys anywhere?*

In other sentences, we use **somewhere**: *You all need to find somewhere to sit.*

**son** /suhn/ *noun* someone's male child: *She has two daughters and one son.*

**song** /song/ *noun* a short piece of music with words: *I sang the song and my sister played the guitar.*

**son-in-law** /**suhn** in lo/ *noun* the husband of your daughter

**son·net** /**sahn**-it/ *noun* a poem that has 14 lines with a pattern of rhymes

**soon** /soon/ *adverb* after a short time: *I hope he comes soon – I'm tired of waiting.* | *I met Sam soon after we moved to our new house.*

IDIOMS with **soon**
**as soon as** immediately after something has happened: *I'll call you as soon as we get there.*
**sooner or later** used for saying that something will definitely happen, but you are not sure when: *Mom's going to find out sooner or later that you lost her key.*

**soot** /sut/ *noun* the black powder that is left on things by smoke: *After the fire, the walls were covered in soot.*

**soothe** /sooth/ *verb*
**1** to make someone feel less worried, angry, or upset: *Her mother held her close, talking quietly to her and soothing her.*
**2** to make something less painful: *A warm bath will soothe your sore muscles.*
—**soothing** /**sooth**-ing/ *adjective* making you feel less worried, or making something less painful: *Blue is a soothing color that makes you feel calmer.*

**so·phis·ti·cat·ed** /suh-**fist**-uh-kayt-id/ *adjective*
**1** complicated, and needing a lot of intelligence and skill to make: *The airport now has sophisticated security equipment to check your bags.*
**2** confident and knowing a lot about art, fashion, food, etc.: *He was a sophisticated man who had traveled all over the world.*
—**sophistication** /suh-fist-uh-**kaysh**-uhn/ *noun* the quality of being sophisticated: *I was impressed by the sophistication of the design.*

**sopho·more** /**sahf**-mor/ *noun* a student in the second year of high school or college

**sore** /sor/
● *adjective* painful: *I have a sore throat.*
—**soreness** /**sor**-niss/ *noun* the feeling of being sore
● *noun* a place where your skin is painful or infected: *He had a sore on his hand where he burned himself.*

**sor·row** /**sar**-oh/ *noun* great sadness: *We all felt great sorrow when Grandpa died.* ( ANTONYM: **joy** )

a b c d e f g h i j k l m n o p q r **s** t u v w x y z

**sor·ry** /**sar**-ee/ *adjective*

**1 sorry/I'm sorry** used for telling someone that you feel bad about doing something: *Oh, sorry, I didn't mean to spill my milk!* | *I'm sorry to keep you waiting.*

**2** disappointed or sad about something: *I'm sorry that you can't come to the party.* ( **ANTONYM: glad** )

> **IDIOM with sorry**
>
> **feel sorry for** to feel sad for someone because he or she is in a bad situation: *He looked unhappy and I felt sorry for him.*

**sort** /sort/

● *noun* a type of person or thing: *What sort of ice cream do you like?* ( **SYNONYMS: type, kind** )

> **IDIOM with sort**
>
> **sort of** used for saying that something is partly true but not totally true: *"Have you finished your homework?" "Sort of – I just need to check one or two things."*

● *verb* to put things in an order or into groups: *The books were sorted into two boxes, one box for children and the other for adults.*

**SOS** /ess oh **ess**/ *noun* a signal or message that a ship or airplane is in danger and needs help: *The ship was in danger of sinking so the captain sent out an SOS.*

**so-so** /**soh** soh/ *adjective, adverb* neither very good nor very bad: *"How are you feeling?" "Oh, so-so."*

**sought** /sot/ *verb* the past tense and past participle of **seek**

**soul** /sohl/ *noun* the part of you that is not your body but contains your most important thoughts and feelings: *Some people believe that when you die, your soul goes to heaven.*

**sound** /sownd/

● *noun*

something that you hear: *I could hear the sound of voices outside the house.* | *What sound does the letter "d" make?* ▶ see picture on page **A16**

▶ see **Thesaurus**

● *verb*

**1** if someone or something sounds good, bad, etc., they seem good, bad, etc. to you when you hear or read about them: *That new computer game sounds pretty good. Jake really likes it.*

**2** to be pronounced in a particular way: *"Bite" and "byte" sound the same.*

**3** to make a noise: *The bell sounds at the end of the school day.*

● *adjective*

sensible and likely to produce good results: *The teacher gave the class some sound advice about how to prepare for the test.*

● *adverb*

**sound asleep** completely asleep: *I tried to wake him but he was sound asleep.*

**sound·ly** /**sownd**-lee/ *adverb* if you sleep soundly, you sleep well and peacefully: *After yesterday's soccer game, I was very tired and slept soundly.*

**sound·track** /**sownd**-trak/ *noun* the music that is played during a movie

**soup** /soop/ *noun* a hot liquid food that usually has pieces of meat or vegetables in it: *We had tomato soup for lunch.*

**sour** /**sow**-ur/ *adjective*

**1** having a strong taste like the taste of a lemon: *I don't like this apple. It's too sour.*

**2** sour milk is not fresh and has a bad taste and smell: *I forgot to put the milk in the refrigerator and it went sour.*

**source** /sorss/ *noun*

**1** the place that something comes from: *The mechanic found the source of the problem – the car battery wasn't working.*

**2** a place or person that you get information from: *The Internet is a good source of information.*

**sour·dough** /**sow**-ur-doh/ *noun* uncooked dough that has time to turn a little sour before you use some of it to make bread: *I had ham and cheese on sourdough bread.*

**south** /sowth/

● *noun*

**1** the direction toward the bottom of a map of the world: *Mexico is to the south of California.*

**2** the southern part of a country or area: *In the south, Utah has some amazing national parks.*

**3 the South** the southeastern part of the U.S.: *My uncle comes from the South. He was born in Alabama.*

a b c d e f g h i j k l m n o p q r s t u v w x y z

● *adjective*

**1** in, to, or facing south: *New Jersey is south of New York.*

**2** a south wind comes from the south

● *adverb*

toward the south: *Birds fly south in the winter.*

## south·east /sowth-**eest**/

● *noun*

**1** the direction that is exactly between south and east

**2** the southeast part of a country or area: *Florida is in the Southeast.*

—**southeastern** /sowth-**eest**-urn/ *adjective* in or from the southeast: *the hills of southeastern Ohio*

● *adverb, adjective*

in, from, or toward the southeast: *We drove southeast till we reached the ocean.*

## south·ern /**suhth**-urn/ *adjective* in or from the south: *South Carolina is in the southern part of the U.S.A.*

## south·ern·er /**suhth**-urn-ur/ *noun* someone who comes from the southern part of a country: *Southerners are used to hot summers.*

## South·ern Hem·i·sphere /**suhth**-urn **hem**-iss-feer/ *noun* the half of the world that is south of the Equator

## South Pole /sowth **pohl**/ *noun* the most southern point on the surface of the Earth

▶ see picture at **globe**

## south·ward /**sowth**-wurd/ *adverb, adjective* toward the south: *The ship sailed southward.*

## south·west /sowth-**west**/

● *noun*

**1** the direction that is exactly between south and west

**2** the southwest part of a country or area: *Arizona is in the Southwest.*

—**southwestern** /sowth-**west**-urn/ *adjective* in or from the southwest: *There are deserts in the southwestern states.*

● *adverb, adjective*

in, from, or toward the southwest: *We drove southwest toward Texas.*

## sou·ve·nir /soov-uh-**neer**/ *noun* an object that you buy in order to remember a special occasion

or a place that you have visited: *I bought a T-shirt as a souvenir of our vacation in Florida.*

### Word Origin: souvenir

**Souvenir** comes from a French word that means "to remember." So, a souvenir is something that helps you remember a special event.

## sov·er·eign /**sav**-rin/

● *noun* a king or queen

● *adjective* a sovereign country is independent and governs itself

## sow

● *verb* /soh/ (**sowed**, **sown** /sohn/ or **sowed**) to put seeds into the ground so that they will grow into plants: *In March, the farmer sows the seeds in the field.*

● *noun* /sow/ a female pig

## soy·bean /**soy**-been/ *noun* a bean used in many things we eat. People make oil and other foods, for example tofu or soy sauce, from soybeans.

## soy sauce /soy **sorss**/ *noun* a dark brown liquid made from soybeans, used in Chinese and Japanese cooking

## space /spayss/

● *noun*

**1** an area that is empty: *Is there enough space in your suitcase for all your clothes?* | *Mom found a parking space near the supermarket.*

**2** the area beyond the Earth where the stars and planets are: *The astronauts will spend two weeks in space.* ( SYNONYM: **outer space** )

**3** the empty area between two things: *The dog got out by squeezing through the space under the fence.*

● *verb*

to put objects somewhere with a particular amount of space between them: *Space the plants two feet apart so they have room to grow.*

## space·craft /**spayss**-kraft/ *noun* (plural **spacecraft**) a vehicle that can travel in space

## space·ship /**spayss**-ship/ *noun* a vehicle in stories that can carry people through space

a b c d e f g h i j k l m n o p q r **s** t u v w x y z

### space shut·tle

/**spayss** shuht'l/ *noun* a vehicle that can carry people into space and come back to Earth more than once. A space shuttle looks like a special kind of airplane. A rocket helps it get into space.

**space shuttle**

### space sta·tion

/**spayss** staysh-uhn/ *noun* a place or vehicle in space where people can stay: *The astronauts are living in the space station for three weeks.*

**space·suit** /**spayss**-soot/ *noun* a special piece of clothing that astronauts wear in space. A spacesuit protects your whole body and has air for you to breathe.

**space·walk** /**spayss**-wok/ *noun* if astronauts do a spacewalk, they move around in space outside their spaceship

**spa·cious** /**spaysh**-uhss/ *adjective* a place that is spacious is large and has a lot of space: *Our new apartment is very spacious and there is plenty of room for the whole family.*

### spade /spayd/ *noun*

**1** a tool you use for digging. A spade has a long handle and a flat metal end.
**2** a card used in card games. The cards have pictures on them that look like this: (♠): *The next card I picked up was the king of spades.*

**spade**

**spa·ghet·ti** /spuh-**get**-ee/ *noun* long thin pieces of pasta that look like strings: *We're having spaghetti with meatballs for dinner.*

**spam** /spam/ *noun* email messages and advertisements that you receive but do not want to read: *My email inbox is always full of spam.*

### span /span/

● *noun*
**1** a length of time: *Some butterflies have a life span of just a week.*

**2** the distance from one side of something to the other: *The plane has a wing span of 40 feet.*
● *verb* (**spanning**, **spanned**)
**1** to include all of a length of time: *The actor's movie career spanned 25 years.*
**2** to go from one side of something to the other: *The bridge spans the river.*

### Span·ish /**span**-ish/

● *adjective*
from Spain: *Maria is Spanish. She was born in Madrid.*
● *noun*
**1** the language spoken in Spain, Mexico, and South America: *Do you speak Spanish?*
**2** the people of Spain: *I like the Spanish. They are very friendly people.*

**spank** /spangk/ *verb* to hit a child on the buttocks with your open hand: *Some parents spank their children as a punishment if they are bad.*
—**spanking** /**spangk**-ing/ *noun* the action of spanking someone

### spare /spair/

● *adjective*
**1** a spare key, bedroom, tire, etc. is an extra one that is available for someone to use: *It's a good idea to have a spare pen in case yours stops working.* | *If we have visitors, they sleep in the spare bedroom.*
**2** spare time is time when you are not working or at school: *I like playing football and baseball in my spare time.*
● *verb*
**1** to be able to give or lend someone something: *"Could you spare me a dollar?" "Sure, as long as you pay it back."*
**2** if you have something to spare, you have more of it than you need: *We had a few cupcakes to spare after the party, so I took them over to Jay's house.*
**3** to not harm or kill someone: *The king spared the prisoners' lives and set them free.*

**spark** /spark/ *noun* a very small piece of burning material that comes from a fire: *A spark from the fire landed on the rug and set it on fire.*

### spar·kle /**spark**-uhl/

● *verb* to shine in small bright lights: *People like diamond rings because they sparkle and look beautiful.*

● *noun* a bright shiny appearance that something has: *I love the sparkle of the ocean when the sun shines on it.*

**spar·row** /**sparr**-oh/ *noun* a small brown or gray bird with a short tail.

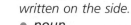
sparrow

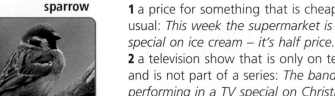

**spat** /spat/ *verb* a past tense and the past participle of **spit**

**speak** /speek/ *verb* (**spoke** /spohk/, **spoken** /**spohk**-uhn/)
**1** to talk to someone about something: *Can I speak with you about your homework for a moment?* ▶ see **Thesaurus**
**2** to use your voice to say words: *Speak quietly so we don't wake up the baby.*
**3** to be able to talk in a particular language: *Can you speak Italian?*
**4 speak out** to say publicly what you think about something: *She didn't agree with the new rules so she decided to speak out.*
**5 speak up** to speak more loudly: *Could you speak up please – I can't hear you.*

**speak·er** /**speek**-ur/ *noun*

speaker

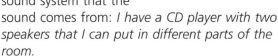

speaker

**1** someone who makes a speech: *One of the speakers at the party made some very funny jokes in his speech.*
**2** the part of a radio or sound system that the sound comes from: *I have a CD player with two speakers that I can put in different parts of the room.*

**spear** /speer/ *noun* a pole with a sharp pointed blade at one end, used as a weapon: *The people use spears for hunting animals.*

**spe·cial** /**spesh**-uhl/
● *adjective*
**1** different from ordinary things, and better in some way: *I want to do something special for Mom's birthday – maybe we could have a surprise party.*
**2** very important and deserving your love or attention: *There are lots of people I like, but Helen's my special friend.*

**3** used by one person or animal and no one else: *The dog has its own special bowl, with DOG written on the side.*
● *noun*
**1** a price for something that is cheaper than usual: *This week the supermarket is having a special on ice cream – it's half price.*
**2** a television show that is only on television once and is not part of a series: *The band will be performing in a TV special on Christmas Eve.*

**spe·cial ef·fects** /spesh-uhl i-**fektss**/ *noun* images or sounds that have been produced artificially for a movie

**spe·cial·ist** /**spesh**-uhl-ist/ *noun* someone who knows a lot about a subject: *He works at the hospital where he's a specialist in heart problems.*

**spe·cial·ize** /**spesh**-uh-līz/ *verb* to only sell, study, or deal with a particular kind of thing, so that you know a lot about it: *The store specializes in clothes for big people.*

**spe·cial·ly** /**spesh**-uhl-ee/ *adverb* for one particular purpose: *These boots are specially made for climbing.*

**spe·cial·ty** /**spesh**-uhl-tee/ *noun* (plural **specialties**) a subject that you know a lot about, or an activity that you are skilled at doing: *He writes books, but his specialty is short stories.*

**spe·cies** /**speesh**-eez/ *noun* (plural **species**) a group of animals or plants of the same kind that breed together to produce young animals or plants: *There are eight species of bear. The North American black bear and the brown bear are two of these.*

**spe·cif·ic** /spi-**sif**-ik/ *adjective*
**1** detailed or exact: *It will be easy to find his house because he's given me specific instructions about how to get there.*
**2** used when talking about one particular thing, person, time, etc.: *This puzzle is for a specific age group. It's for people between eight and ten years old.*

**spe·cif·i·cally** /spi-**sif**-ik-lee/ *adverb* for a particular type of person or thing: *The program is specifically for children.*

a b c d e f g h i j k l m n o p q r **s** t u v w x y z

**spe·ci·fy** /**spess**-uh-fi/ *verb* (**specifies**, **specified**) to give exact details about something: *You must specify the kind of computer that you are using.*

**spec·i·men** /**spess**-uh-muhn/ *noun* a small amount of something that is tested or examined: *The doctors took a blood specimen from the patient to find out what was wrong with her.*

SYNONYM: **sample**

**speck** /spek/ *noun* a very small piece of something: *She brushed some specks of dust from her jacket.*

**spec·ta·cle** /**spekt**-uhk-uhl/ *noun* a very impressive or unusual thing that you see: *The show is an amazing spectacle, with lots of fireworks and loud music.*

**spec·tac·u·lar** /spek-**tak**-yuhl-ur/ *adjective* very impressive or exciting: *The movie has some spectacular battle scenes.*

**spec·ta·tor** /spek-**tayt**-ur/ *noun* someone who watches an event or game: *There are over 50,000 spectators at the game.*

**spec·trum** /**spek**-truhm/ *noun* (plural **spectra** /**spek**-truh/)
**1** the different colors that light separates into when it passes through a clear block of glass: *The colors of the spectrum are red, orange, yellow, green, blue, indigo, and violet.*
**2** a wide range of things or people: *There is a wide spectrum of entertainment available on TV these days.*

**sped** /sped/ *verb* a past tense and past participle of **speed**

**speech** /speech/ *noun*
**1** a formal talk about a subject that you give to a group of people: *The principal will make a speech at the graduation ceremony.*
**2** the act of speaking or the ability to speak: *Humans are different from other animals because they are capable of speech.*

**speech·less** /**speech**-liss/ *adjective* unable to speak because you are too surprised: *When my sister told me she was getting married, I was speechless and I didn't know what to say.*

**speed** /speed/
● *noun*
**1** how fast something moves: *A cheetah can run at a speed of 70 miles per hour.*

**2** how quickly something happens: *I was amazed at the speed with which he learned to speak English.*
● *verb* (**sped** /sped/ or **speeded**)
**1** to move or happen quickly: *An ambulance sped past us with its lights flashing.* | *The weeks were speeding by and soon it was the end of the semester.*
**2** if you are speeding, you are driving faster than the legal limit: *The police officer said my aunt was speeding and gave her a ticket.*
**3 speed up** to move or do something more quickly: *The train moved slowly out of the station and then began to speed up.*
—**speeding** /**speed**-ing/ *noun* the crime of driving too fast: *He was given a fine for speeding because he was going 50 mph in a 35 mph zone.*

**speed·boat** /**speed**-boht/ *noun* a small boat with a powerful engine that can go very fast

**speedboat**

**speed·om·e·ter** /spi-**dahm**-uht-ur/ *noun* an instrument in a vehicle that shows how fast it is going

**speed·y** /**speed**-ee/ *adjective* happening or doing something quickly: *I hope Jack makes a speedy recovery from his illness.*

**spell** /spel/
● *verb*
to say or write the letters of a word in the correct order: *"How do you spell your name?" "G-A-R-C-I-A."*
● *noun*
**1** words or actions that make magic things happen: *In the story, the witch uses a spell to change the prince into a frog.*
**2** a short time when there is a particular kind of weather: *The weather will be cloudy with sunny spells.*

**spell·ing** /**spel**-ing/ *noun*
**1** the ability to spell words correctly: *My spelling is terrible and I often make mistakes.*
**2** the way that a word is spelled: *Many people do not know the correct spelling of "Mississippi."*

**spend** /spend/ *verb* (**spent** /spent/)
**1** to use money to buy or pay for something: *Here's $2 – don't spend it all on candy!*
**2** to pass time doing something or staying somewhere: *I often spend the evening looking at websites on the Internet.* | *We spent our last vacation in Florida.*

**spent** /spent/ *verb* the past tense and past participle of **spend**

**sperm** /spurm/ *noun* (plural **sperm**) a male cell that can join with a female egg. When this happens, a baby or young animal starts to develop.

**sphere** /sfeer/ *noun* something that has the shape of a ball: *We know that the earth is a sphere, but in the past people thought it was flat.* ▶ see picture on page **A12**
—**spherical** /**sfeer**-ik-uhl/ *adjective* in the shape of a sphere: *An orange is a spherical object.*

**spice** /spīss/ *noun* a seed or powder from plants that you put into food to give it a special taste: *Mexican food uses a lot of strong spices such as chili.*
—**spicy** /**spīss**-ee/ *adjective* containing a lot of spices: *People from India love eating spicy food.*

**spi·der** /**spīd**-ur/ *noun* a small creature with eight legs. Spiders make webs to catch insects that they eat. There are many different kinds of spider: *A big spider was crawling up my leg.*

spider

**spied** /spīd/ *verb* the past tense and past participle of **spy**

**spike** /spīk/ *noun*
**1** a thin piece of metal with a sharp point: *The prison walls are covered with spikes to stop prisoners from escaping.*
**2** a sharp metal or plastic point on the bottom of a sports shoe: *Spikes are good for running because they stop you from slipping.*

**spill** /spil/ *verb* if you spill a liquid, it comes out of a container by accident: *Tomás spilled some juice on the table and I had to clean it up.*

spill

The milk spilled all over the table.

**spin** /spin/ *verb* (**spinning**, **spun** /spuhn/)
**1** to turn around and around very quickly: *The dancers were spinning around on their toes.*
**2** to make a web or cocoon: *Spiders spin webs to catch insects.*
**3** to make cotton or wool into thread by twisting it together: *A woman on the farm showed the kids how to spin wool from sheep.*

**spin·ach** /**spin**-ich/ *noun* a vegetable with large dark green leaves: *Spinach and other dark green vegetables are very good for you.* ▶ see picture on page **A7**

**spine** /spīn/ *noun*
**1** the long row of bones down the center of your back: *He damaged a bone at the bottom of his spine and had a very sore back.*
**2** a stiff sharp point on an animal or plant: *Porcupines are covered with spines that protect them from other animals.*

**spi·ral** /**spīr**-uhl/ *noun*
**1** a curved line that goes around a central point many times, for example on a screw: *I got a straight piece of wire and twisted it around into a spiral.*
**2** a spiral staircase curves upward around a central point

**spir·it** /**spirr**-it/ *noun*
**1** the part of you that is your character, thoughts, and feelings. Many people think that your spirit continues to live after you die: *Grandma is 80 but she's still young in spirit.*
**2** a creature such as a ghost or an angel that does not have a physical body: *People are scared to go to the old house now because they think there are evil spirits there.*
**3** courage and determination: *The team played with great spirit, although it was clear they could not win.*
**4** **spirits** how you feel, and whether you are happy or sad: *My aunt was in good spirits and she was laughing and joking.*

a b c d e f g h i j k l m n o p q r **s** t u v w x y z

**spir·it·u·al** /**spirr**-ich-oo-uhl/ *adjective*
**1** relating to religion: *The priest is a kind of spiritual leader.*
**2** relating to your soul and how you feel about yourself, rather than about money, success, or physical things: *People's spiritual needs are important – you can be very rich and still be very unhappy.*

**spit** /spit/
● *verb* (**spitting**, **spit** or **spat** /spat/)
to force a small amount of liquid or food from your mouth: *The food tasted disgusting and he spit it out.*
● *noun*
**1** a long thin stick that you put through meat so you can turn the meat while it is cooking: *They were cooking a whole pig on a spit over a fire.*
**2** the liquid that is produced in your mouth
( SYNONYM: **saliva** )

**spite** /spīt/ *noun* a nasty feeling of wanting to upset or hurt someone: *She said some mean things to me out of spite because I got a better grade than her on the test.*

> **IDIOM** with **spite**
> **in spite of** even though something happens or is true: *Everyone had a great time, in spite of the rain.* ( SYNONYM: **despite** )

**splash** /splash/
● *verb*
**1** if a liquid splashes, it falls on something and makes it wet: *The bottle burst and soda splashed all over the floor.*
**2** to make water move through the air: *The kids were having fun splashing around in the pool.*
● *noun*
the sound that water makes when something hits it: *There was a loud splash and I saw that the girl had fallen into the water.* ▶ see picture on page **A16**

**splen·did** /**splend**-id/ *adjective* very good or impressive: *The White House is a splendid building.*

**splin·ter** /**splint**-ur/ *noun* a small sharp piece of wood, glass, or metal: *There's a splinter in my finger and it hurts. Can you get it out?*

**split** /split/
● *verb* (**splitting**, **split**)
**1** to divide something into groups or parts: *The*

teacher split the class into three groups, with eight children in each.
**2** to break or tear: *My jeans split so I had to go home and change my clothes.*
**3** **split up** to end your marriage or relationship: *They used to argue all the time and in the end they split up.*
● *noun*
a situation in which people disagree and separate into two groups: *There was a split in the class over which was the best way to solve the problem.*

**spoil** /spoyl/ *verb*
**1** to make something less good or enjoyable: *I had an argument with my friend and it really spoiled my day.*
**2** to let a child have or do everything he or she wants. If you spoil a child, it has a bad effect on the child's behavior: *His parents have spoiled him and now he cries every time they say "no" to him.*
—**spoiled** /spoyld/ *adjective* a spoiled child behaves badly because he or she has been allowed to have or do too many things

**spoke** /spohk/
● *verb* the past tense of **speak**
● *noun* one of the thin pieces of metal or wood that connect the edge of a wheel to the center
▶ see picture at **bicycle**

**spok·en** /**spohk**-uhn/ *verb* the past participle of speak

**spokes·per·son** /**spohkss**-purss-uhn/ *noun* someone who speaks officially for a group or organization: *A club spokesperson said that the player's injury will mean he is out of the game.*
—**spokesman** /**spohkss**-muhn/ *noun* a man who speaks for a group or organization
—**spokeswoman** /**spohkss**-wum-uhn/ *noun* a woman who speaks for a group or organization

**sponge** /spuhnj/ *noun*
**1** a soft object you use for washing or cleaning things. It is made of a substance full of small holes: *I have a yellow sponge that I wash with in the shower.*
**2** an animal that lives in the ocean. Sponges have a soft skeleton with many holes in it. These skeletons were used in the past for cleaning.

**sponge**

sponge

sponge

**spon·sor** /**spahnss**-ur/
● *noun* a person or company that provides money for a public event or a sports team: *The company is a sponsor of the Sugar Bowl, a college football game that takes place every year.*
● *verb* to provide money for something: *The study was sponsored by Ohio State University.*

**spon·ta·ne·ous** /spahn-**tayn**-ee-uhss/ *adjective* doing something suddenly, without planning or thinking about what you are going to do: *There was spontaneous cheering and clapping from the crowd.*
—**spontaneously** /spahn-**tayn**-ee-uhss-lee/ *adverb* suddenly and without planning: *They spontaneously decided to go out for a meal.*

**spook·y** /**spook**-ee/ *adjective* strange and frightening: *The old house looked dark and spooky, and I didn't want to go inside.*

**spool** /spool/ *noun* an object like a wheel that you wind wire, thread, or film around: *I need a needle and a spool of white thread.*

**spoon** /spoon/ *noun* a tool for eating that is made of a small bowl with a handle on the end. You use a spoon to eat food like soup or ice cream, or to stir things: *Can you put the knives, forks, and spoons out on the table?*

**spoon·ful** /**spoon**-ful/ *noun* the amount that a spoon can hold: *Dad has two spoonfuls of sugar in his coffee.*

**sport** /sport/ *noun* a physical game with rules. People or teams compete against each other in a sport: *My favorite sport is basketball.*

**sports car** /**sportss** kar/ *noun* a low fast car

**sports·man·ship** /**sportss**-muhn-ship/ *noun* behavior that is fair and respectful in a sport or game: *It's good sportsmanship to shake hands with the opposing team after a game.*

**spot** /spaht/
● *noun*
**1** a place: *The cat was asleep in a sunny spot in the yard.*
**2** a small round area that is a different color from the area around it: *Our dog is white with black spots.*
**3** a small mark on something: *She cut her finger and there were a few spots of blood on her T-shirt.*
● *verb* (**spotting**, **spotted**)
to see or recognize someone or something: *We tried to spot Dad among the people coming off the plane.*

**spot·less** /**spaht**-liss/ *adjective* completely clean: *She cleans her house every day so it is always spotless.*

**spot·light** /**spaht**-līt/ *noun* a powerful light that is pointed at someone or something: *They use spotlights at the theater so that you can see the actors' faces clearly.*

**spot·ted** /**spaht**-id/ *adjective* covered in round colored marks: *The snakes are a spotted brown color.*

**spotted**

a spotted dog

**spouse** /spowss/ *noun* a husband or wife

**spout** /spowt/ *noun* a pipe on the side of a container that you pour liquid through: *Hot coffee came out of the spout of the coffee pot.*

**sprain** /sprayn/
● *verb* to injure a joint in your body by suddenly twisting it: *Paul fell and sprained his ankle so he can't play football this week.*
● *noun* an injury you get in a joint by suddenly twisting it: *The doctor says Sam has a knee sprain and should rest his leg.*

**sprang** /sprang/ *verb* a past tense of **spring**

**sprawl** /sprol/ *verb* to lie or sit with your arms or legs stretched out: *He was sprawled on the ground, looking up at the stars in the sky.*

a b c d e f g h i j k l m n o p q r **s** t u v w x y z

**spray** /spray/
- *verb* to make a liquid come out of a container in very small drops: *She sprayed a little perfume on her neck.*
- *noun* liquid that comes out of a container in a stream of very small drops: *I use a spray to clean the windows.*

spray

**spread** /spred/ *verb* (**spread**)
**1** to open something so that it is not folded: *Mom spread the tablecloth over the table. | The bird spread its wings and flew up into the air.*
**2** to affect more people or things: *The disease spreads very easily from one person to another. | The fire started in one house and quickly spread to others.*
**3** to cover something with a soft substance: *She spread some butter on the bread.*
**4** if news spreads, more people hear about it: *News of the accident spread and soon everyone was talking about it.*
**5 spread out** if the people in a group spread out, they move farther apart from each other: *Spread out so you all have enough space to raise your arms to your shoulders.*

**spread·sheet** /spred-sheet/ *noun* a record of information that is arranged in rows and columns. You usually make a spreadsheet using a computer: *The spreadsheet shows the grades of all the students throughout the year.*

**spree** /spree/ *noun* if you go on a spree, you buy lots of things, or you do something too much because you enjoy doing it: *She went on a shopping spree and bought lots of clothes.*

**spring** /spring/
- *noun*
**1** the season between winter and summer, when plants and flowers begin to grow: *The days get warmer in spring and the leaves appear on trees again.* ▶ see picture at **season**
**2** a place where water comes up from the ground and becomes a stream: *They get all their water from a spring in the mountains.*
**3** a small strong piece of metal that is twisted

around in a circle several times. Springs go back to their original shape after you press down on them: *The mattress on the bed has a lot of springs in it and it's very comfortable.*
- *verb* (**sprang** /sprang/ also **sprung** /spruhng/, **sprung**)
**1** to jump or move suddenly: *The cat sprang on to the table and started eating my food.*
**2 spring up** to suddenly appear: *Weeds are springing up everywhere.*

**spring·time** /spring-tīm/ *noun* the time of year when it is spring: *In springtime the fields are covered in flowers.*

**sprinkle** /springk-uhl/
- *verb*
**1** to drop small amounts of liquid or small pieces of something over an area: *I sprinkled the plants with water, to stop them from getting too dry.*
**2** if it is sprinkling, it is raining a little: *It is sprinkling a little, but it's not raining very hard.*

sprinkle

- *noun*
**1** a few small pieces or drops of something, especially food: *Cover the cake with a sprinkle of chocolate chips.*
**2** a short period of light rain: *There was only a sprinkle of rain today so we still played baseball.*

**sprin·kler** /springk-lur/ *noun* a piece of equipment used for covering grass with small drops of water

**sprint** /sprint/
- *noun* a fast race that you run over a short distance: *She is running in the 50 meter sprint.*
- *verb* to run fast for a short distance: *I sprinted down the road to catch the bus.*
—**sprinter** /sprint-ur/ *noun* someone who takes part in a short fast race

**sprout** /sprowt/
- *verb*
**1** to start to grow and produce new leaves or shoots: *If you soak the seeds in water, it will help them to sprout and produce shoots.*
**2** to appear suddenly in large numbers: *New*

a b c d e f g h i j k l m n o p q r **s** t u v w x y z

*coffee shops are always sprouting up all over town.*

● *noun*

**1** a new growth on a plant: *The plant looks healthy and there are one or two little sprouts on the stem.*

**2 sprouts** the young shoots of some plants, which people eat: *We made a salad with lots of bean sprouts.*

**spruce** /sprooss/ *noun* a tree with short leaves shaped like needles: *A spruce is an evergreen tree, so it does not lose its leaves in winter.*

spruce

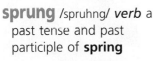

**sprung** /spruhng/ *verb* a past tense and past participle of **spring**

**spun** /spuhn/ *verb* the past tense and past participle of **spin**

**spy** /spī/

● *noun* (plural **spies**)

someone who secretly tries to find out information about another country or group: *The spy was giving top secret military information to the enemies of the U.S.*

● *verb* (**spies**, **spying**, **spied**)

**1** to watch people secretly, or collect information about them: *A neighbor was spying on the boys through an upstairs window.*

**2** to see something: *In the distance, they spied another ship.*

**squad** /skwahd/ *noun*

**1** the group of people that a sports team is chosen from: *Brandon's a member of the football squad and he often plays on the varsity team.*

**2** a team of officers or soldiers who do a particular job: *The bomb squad is a special team of officers who deal with bombs.*

**square** /skwair/

● *noun*

**1** a shape with four straight sides of the same length. A square has four angles of 90 degrees: *Draw a square with sides 5 inches long.*

square

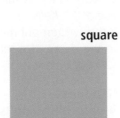

**2** the number that is the result when you multiply a number by itself: *The square of 5 is 25 (5 x 5 = 25).*

**3** an open area with buildings around it on four sides: *Times Square is a famous square in New York.*

● *adjective*

**1** having four straight sides of the same length and four angles of 90 degrees: *a square table*

**2** a square inch, foot, yard, etc. is the measurement of an area that is square. You find the measurement by multiplying the length of the area by its width: *The room is 12 feet long and 8 feet wide, so it measures 96 square feet.*

● *verb*

to multiply a number by itself: *2 squared is 4.*

**square num·ber** /skwair **nuhm**-bur/ *noun* a number that you get if you multiply another number by itself: *3 x 3 = 9, so 9 is a square number.*

**square pyr·a·mid** /skwair **pirr**-uh-mid/ *noun* a solid figure that has a square base and four triangular sides

**square root** /skwair **root**/ *noun* the square root of a number is a smaller number that you must multiply by itself to equal the bigger number: *The square root of 9 is 3 because 3 x 3 = 9.*

**squash** /skwahsh/

● *verb* to press something so that it becomes flat: *The tomatoes will get squashed if you put them at the bottom of the bag.*

● *noun* a large vegetable with solid flesh and a hard skin. A pumpkin is a type of squash.

▶ see picture on page **A7**

**Word Origin: squash**

The English people who came to North America had never seen **squash** before. They borrowed part of an Indian word to use as a name for this new food. Squash comes from a Native American language called Algonquian. The word it comes from means "the green things that can be eaten raw."

**squat** /skwaht/ *verb*
(**squatting**, **squatted**)
to bend your knees so
that your body is near
the ground, resting on
the backs of your legs:
*He squatted down and
looked under the table.*

squat

**squat·ter** /**skwaht**-ur/
*noun* someone who
lives in a place without
the owner's permission
and without paying rent: *The land was
occupied by squatters who had no legal right to
live there.*

**squawk** /skwok/
● *verb* if a bird squawks, it makes a loud and
angry noise: *The ducks started squawking as
soon as I went near them.*
● *noun* a loud angry noise made by a bird

**squeak** /skweek/
● *verb* to make a short high sound: *The door
squeaks when you open it – it needs a little oil.*
● *noun* a short high sound: *The mouse gave a
frightened squeak.* ▶ see picture on page **A16**
—**squeaky** /**skweek**-ee/ *adjective* making short
high sounds: *Your voice sounds all squeaky.*

**squeal** /skweel/
● *verb* to make a long high sound or cry: *The
kids were jumping around in the water and
laughing and squealing with pleasure.*
● *noun* a long high sound or cry: *I accidentally
walked on the dog's foot and he gave a loud
squeal.*

**squeeze** /skweez/ *verb*
**1** to press something with your fingers or hands:
*Squeeze the orange until you have half a cup of
juice.* | *He squeezed her hand and smiled.*
**2** to go into or through a small space: *There was
a tiny gap in the fence and I managed to
squeeze through it into the park.*

**squid** /skwid/ *noun* a sea animal with a long soft
body and ten long arms around its mouth.
People eat the meat from squid.

**squint** /skwint/ *verb* to look at something with
your eyes partly closed in order to see better:

The light was very bright and I had to squint to
read the writing on my computer screen.

**squirm** /skwurm/ *verb*
**1** to feel embarrassed or uncomfortable because
of something that you see or hear: *I squirmed
when I saw the doctor getting the needle ready.*
**2** to twist your body around because you are
uncomfortable: *The baby was crying and
squirming in my arms and I almost dropped her.*

**squir·rel** /**skwur**-uhl/
*noun* a small animal
with a long furry tail.
Squirrels are usually
gray or brown. Squirrels
live in trees and eat
nuts.

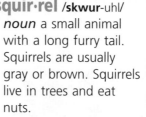

squirrel

**squirt** /skwurt/ *verb* if
liquid squirts, it comes
out of a narrow hole
very quickly: *The juice squirted all over his shirt.* |
*He squirted water at me with his water pistol.*

squirt

**squish·y** /**skwish**-ee/ *adjective* very soft, easy to
press, and usually wet: *I left an apple in my bag
and it got all brown and squishy.*

**St.**
**1** the written abbreviation of **street**. You use St.
when you are writing someone's address: *They
live at 22 Kelly St.*
**2** the written abbreviation of **Saint**. You use St.
in the name of a saint: *St. Patrick is the patron
saint of Ireland.*

**stab** /stab/
● *verb* (**stabbing**, **stabbed**) to push a sharp
object into someone or something: *The other
man tried to stab him with a knife.*
● *noun* a sudden strong and unpleasant feeling:

*I felt a stab of pain and I saw that I had stepped on a nail.*

**IDIOM with stab**
**take a stab at** to try to do something: *If you don't know the answer, take a stab at it anyway. You might get it right.*

**sta·bi·lize** /**stayb**-uh-līz/ *verb* to become steady and stop changing: *Lucy had a fever but after two days her temperature stabilized and she started to get better.*

**stable** /**stayb**-uhl/
● *adjective*
**1** staying in the same position and not moving: *Make sure the ladder is stable before you start climbing it.* ( **ANTONYM: unstable** )
**2** staying the same, with no big changes or problems: *He was very ill, but the doctor says his condition is now stable.* ( **ANTONYM: unstable** )
—**stability** /stuh-**bil**-uht-ee/ *noun* conditions in which there is no sudden change: *Children need stability in their lives and they don't like a lot of big changes.*
● *noun*
a building where horses are kept: *She led the horses back into the stable.*

**stack** /stak/
● *noun* a pile of things on top of each other: *The teacher has a big stack of books on her desk.*
● *verb* to put things into a pile: *Just stack the dirty dishes on the counter and I'll wash them later.*

**stack**
a stack of books

**sta·di·um** /**stayd**-ee-uhm/ *noun* a building used for sports games or concerts. A stadium is a field surrounded by rows of seats: *The new baseball stadium in New York has seats for around 51,000 fans.*

**staff** /staf/
● *noun*
**1** the people who work for an organization: *The school has a staff of 30 teachers.*
**2** a big stick that you carry to help you walk. People used staffs in past times: *The old shepherd had a staff.*
**3** the set of five lines that music is written on

● *verb*
to provide an organization with workers: *The college cafe is staffed by students.*

**stage** /stayj/
● *noun*
**1** the raised floor in a theater, where people perform: *I had a big part in the play so I was on stage most of the time.* ▶ see picture at **theater**
**2** a time in the development of something or someone: *At this stage, the baby birds are almost ready to fly.*
● *verb*
to organize a performance or public event: *The high school is staging a performance of "Grease."*

**stage·coach** /**stayj**-kohch/ *noun* a covered vehicle pulled by horses. A stagecoach carried passengers and mail over long distances in the past.

**stag·ger** /**stag**-ur/ *verb* to walk or move in an unsteady way, almost falling over: *The man was drunk and he was staggering along the road.*

**stag·nant** /**stag**-nuhnt/ *adjective* stagnant water does not move and often smells bad: *The water in the pond was stagnant and it was not suitable for drinking.*

**stain** /stayn/
● *noun*
**1** a mark that is difficult to remove: *I've washed your shirt but I can't get the ink stains out.*
**2** a liquid you use to change the color of wood: *You can use a stain to make the wood a darker color.*
● *verb*
to make a mark on something, which is difficult to remove: *I spilled some juice and I think I've stained the carpet.*

**stain·less steel** /stayn-liss **steel**/ *noun* a type of steel that does not get stains or rust on it: *These knives and forks are made of stainless steel so they always look clean and shiny.*

**stair** /stair/ *noun*
**1** **stairs** a set of steps that you use for going from one level of a building to another: *Shall we go up the stairs or take the elevator?*
**2** one of the steps in a set of stairs: *Lisa was sitting on the top stair waiting for the rest of us to get there.* ( **SYNONYM: step** ) ▶ see picture at **staircase**

a
b
c
d
e
f
g
h
i
j
k
l
m
n
o
p
q
r
**s**
t
u
v
w
x
y
z

**stair·case** /**stair**-kayss/
*noun* a set of stairs inside a building: *I climbed the staircase to the third floor.*

staircase

banister

stair/step

**stair·way** /**stair**-way/
*noun* a set of stairs and the structure that supports it: *There's a bucket in the closet under the stairway.*

**stake** /stayk/
● *noun*
**1** a pointed post that you push into the ground: *We pushed wooden stakes in the ground and made a fence with them.*
**2** if you have a stake in a business or plan, you have a part or a share in it and you want it to succeed: *The company has a big stake in the project and they have spent over $20 million.*

> IDIOM with **stake**
> **at stake** if something important is at stake, you could lose it, if you are unsuccessful: *In a war, thousands of people's lives are at stake.*

● *verb*
**1** to bet on the result of a competition or situation: *He lost $500 because he staked it on a horse that didn't win.* ( SYNONYM: **bet** )
**2 stake a claim** to say that you have a right to have or own something: *He has already staked his claim to the land and he says that it is his.*

**stale** /stayl/ *adjective* not fresh: *This bread is hard and stale – we need to buy some fresh bread.* ( ANTONYM: **fresh** )

**stalk** /stok/
● *noun* the long thin part of a plant that comes up from the ground. The leaves or flowers grow from the stalk. ▶ see picture at **flower**
● *verb* to follow a person or animal secretly or quietly in order to attack him, her, or it: *The man was arrested by the police for stalking the famous actress for two months.*

**stall** /stol/
● *noun*
**1** a table or a small store with an open front, where goods are sold: *At the farmer's market there are a lot of stalls that sell fruit and vegetables.*

**2** a small enclosed area in a room, for washing or using the toilet: *There is a guest room in the house, with a shower stall.*
**3** an enclosed area in a building for an animal such as a horse: *Each horse has a stall where it is kept during the winter.*
● *verb*
**1** if a car stalls, its engine suddenly stops working: *The car stalled in the center of town and there was a long line of traffic behind it.*
**2** to delay doing something and make someone wait because you need to have more time: *He kept stalling and he never answered my question.*

**stal·lion** /**stal**-yuhn/ *noun* an adult male horse

**stam·i·na** /**stam**-uhn-uh/ *noun* the strength to continue doing something for a long time and not get tired: *You need a lot of stamina to run for 20 miles.*

**stam·mer** /**stam**-ur/
● *verb* to speak in an uncertain way, pausing a lot or repeating sounds: *Kids sometimes stammer when they are nervous or very excited.*
( SYNONYM: **stutter** )
● *noun* if you have a stammer, you stammer when you speak: *"I'm s-s-sorry," he said with a slight stammer.* ( SYNONYM: **stutter** )

**stamp** /stamp/
● *noun*
**1** a small piece of paper that you stick onto an envelope or package to show you have paid to send it: *How much is a stamp for a letter to Mexico?* ▶ see picture at **envelope**
**2** an official mark that is put on something: *They put a stamp in your passport to show you have crossed the border.*
**3** a special tool for making a mark on something, using ink
● *verb*
**1** to put your foot down very hard: *"I don't want to go," he shouted, stamping his foot angrily.*
**2** to put an official mark on a piece of paper using a special tool: *The officer looked at my photograph and stamped my passport.*

**stam·pede** /stam-**peed**/
● *noun* a situation in which a lot of people or animals suddenly start running together: *When the fire started, there was a stampede toward*

the door of the building and everyone rushed outside.

● *verb* if a lot of people or animals stampede, they all run together: *The buffaloes stampeded across the plain.*

## stand /stand/

**stand**

a music stand

● *verb* (**stood** /stud/)

**1** to be on your feet, in an upright position: *We had to stand in a line for 45 minutes and I was really tired.*

**2** to move so that you are on your feet: *Please stand up when the principal comes in the room.*

**3 stand on your head/hands** to support yourself on your head or hands with your feet in the air

**4** if a building stands somewhere, it is in that place: *The school stands on a hill.*

**5** if you can't stand something, it is so bad that you cannot accept it: *She was crying because she couldn't stand the pain.* (SYNONYM: **tolerate**)

**6** if you can't stand something, you hate it: *I can't stand cabbage – it makes me feel sick.*

**7** to put something in a place or position: *Stand the lamp in the corner over there.*

**8 be standing by** to be waiting, ready to do something: *An ambulance was standing by outside the stadium, ready to take any injured players to the hospital.*

**9 stand for** to represent something: *DVD stands for "digital video disc."*

**10 stand out** to be very easy to see or notice: *The words on the sign are written in red so they really stand out.*

**11 stand up for** to defend someone or something that other people are criticizing: *The other boys were teasing George, but I stood up for him and told them to stop.*

● *noun*

**1** an object that you put something on: *She put the sheet of music on the music stand and started to play.*

**2** a table or cart used for selling things to people: *We got some lunch at a hot dog stand.*

**3 stands** the seats where you sit to watch a

baseball or football game: *There were 1,400 people in the stands at the game.*

> **IDIOM with stand**
> **take a stand** to show very firmly and publicly what your opinion is about something: *Many people took a stand against the war by marching in the streets.*

## stan·dard /stand-urd/

● *noun* a level that measures how good something is: *The standard of Patsy's school work is always very high and she is often at the top of her class.*

● *adjective* normal or usual: *$12.50 is the standard price, but you sometimes can get the tickets for a lower price.*

## stan·dard form /stand-urd **form**/ *noun* if a number is written in standard form, it is written in numbers in the usual way: *Two thousand five hundred eighty-three is written in the standard form 2,583.*

## stan·dard of liv·ing /stand-urd uhv **liv**-ing/ *noun* the amount of wealth that people have: *The standard of living in the U.S. is very high compared to other countries.*

## stand·still /stand-stil/ *noun* if something is at a standstill, it is not moving or not making progress: *There has been an accident on the highway and the traffic is at a standstill.*

## stank /stangk/ *verb* a past tense of **stink**

## sta·ple /stayp-uhl/

● *noun*

**1** a small thin piece of metal used for fastening pieces of paper together: *I wrote on two pages and clipped them together with a staple.*

**2** a food or other product that people often use or make: *Tortillas are a staple in Mexican cooking.*

● *verb*

to fasten pieces of paper together with a staple

## sta·pler /stayp-lur/
*noun* a small tool you use for putting staples into paper

**stapler**

a b c d e f g h i j k l m n o p q r **s** t u v w x y z

**star** /star/

● *noun*

**1** a large ball of burning gas in space. You see a star as a point of light in the night sky: *On a clear night you can see thousands of stars in the sky.* ▶ see **Thesaurus**

**2** a famous actor, musician, or sports player: *Tom Cruise is a famous Hollywood movie star.*

**3** a shape with five or six points: *There are 50 stars on the U.S. flag.*

● *verb* (**starring**, **starred**)

to be the main character in a movie, TV program, or play: *Johnny Depp stars in the movie.*

**starch** /starch/

● *noun*

**1** a substance in foods such as bread, rice, and potatoes: *Starch is an important part of your diet because your body uses it for energy.*

**2** a substance used for making cloth stiff

● *verb*

to make cloth stiff by using starch: *Some people starch shirt collars to make them look neat.*

**star·dom** /**star**-duhm/ *noun* the situation of being a famous actor, singer, or sports player: *Michael Jackson's rise to stardom began when he was a child.*

**stare** /stair/

● *verb* to look at someone or something for a long time without moving your eyes, especially because you are surprised or angry: *Don't stare at people – it's rude.*

● *noun* the action of looking at someone for a long time, without moving your eyes: *I gave him an angry stare to try to make him stop talking.*

**star·fish** /**star**-fish/

*noun* a flat sea animal that is shaped like a star

**starfish**

starfish

**start** /start/

● *verb*

**1** to begin happening: *The party starts at three o'clock.* (ANTONYM: **end**)

▶ see **Thesaurus**

**2** to begin doing something: *Kids in the U.S. start school when they are five years old.*

**3** to make a new organization or company: *The company was started in 1986.*

**4** if a car or an engine starts, it begins to work: *The car wouldn't start, so we had to catch the bus.*

● *noun*

**1** the beginning of something: *Next week is the start of the vacation.* (ANTONYM: **end**)

**2** an advantage that allows you to begin a race before the other people: *Because he was the youngest, they gave him a 30 yard start in the race.*

**start·le** /**start**'l/ *verb* to surprise or frighten someone: *The loud noise startled her and she dropped the glass.*

—**startled** /**start**'ld/ *adjective* surprised because something unexpected has happened: *The man was looking at us with a startled expression on his face.*

—**startling** /**start**'l-ing/ *adjective* very unusual or surprising: *Scientists have made a startling new discovery.*

**star·va·tion** /star-**vaysh**-uhn/ *noun* a situation in which people do not have enough food to eat so they die or become sick: *There is very little food and people are dying of starvation.*

**starve** /starv/ *verb* to become sick or die because you do not have enough to eat: *If they don't eat soon, they will starve to death.*

**starv·ing** /**starv**-ing/ *adjective*

**1** someone who is starving has not had enough food for a long time and is sick or dying: *The U.S. sends large quantities of food to help starving people all over the world.*

**2** very hungry: *I'm starving! What's for supper?*

**state** /stayt/

● *noun*

**1** one of the parts that the U.S. and some other countries are divided into. Each state has its own government: *There are 50 states in the U.S. | Yosemite is in the state of California.*

**2** the condition of someone or something: *His room is in a terrible state and he hasn't cleaned it for a long time.*

**3** a country that has its own government: *Ghana became an independent state in 1957.*

● *verb*

to say something publicly or officially: *In court,*

the man stated that he was not guilty of the crime.

**state·hood** /**stayt**-hud/ *noun*
**1** if an area achieves statehood, it becomes one of the states that make up a nation such as the U.S.: *Kansas achieved statehood in 1861.*
**2** if a country achieves statehood, it becomes an independent nation: *Slovakia achieved independent statehood in 1992.*

**state·ment** /**stayt**-muhnt/ *noun* something that you say or write publicly and officially: *The president will make a statement to the nation later today.*

**states·man** /**staytss**-muhn/ *noun* (plural **statesmen** /**staytss**-muhn/) a politician with a lot of experience, who people respect: *He was a great leader of his country and a fine statesman.*

**states·wom·an** /**staytss**-wum-uhn/ (plural **stateswomen** /**staytss**-wim-in/) *noun* a female politician with a lot of experience, who people respect

**stat·ic** /**stat**-ik/ *noun* the noise that you hear when electricity in the air spoils the sound from a radio or TV: *I tried to listen to the radio, but there was too much static.*

**stat·ic e·lec·tric·i·ty** /**stat**-ik i-lek-**triss**-uht-ee/ *noun* electricity that collects on an object, and is not flowing in a current: *When you rub a balloon, it produces static electricity, and you can get a tiny electric shock.*

**sta·tion** /**staysh**-uhn/
● *noun*
**1** a building where trains or buses stop and people can get on and off them: *My mom will meet me at the station.*
**2** a company that broadcasts on radio or television: *I usually listen to the local radio station in the morning.*
● *verb*
to send someone to a place to do a job or military duty: *My dad was in the navy and he was stationed in Japan for three years.*

**sta·tion·a·ry** /**staysh**-uh-nair-ee/ *adjective* not moving: *Wait until the bus is stationary before you get off.*

**sta·tion·er·y** /**staysh**-uh-nair-ee/ *noun* things that you use for writing such as paper and envelopes: *If you want to write a letter, there's some stationery in the drawer.*

**sta·tion wag·on** /**staysh**-uhn wag-uhn/ *noun* a large car with a lot of space at the back for carrying things

**sta·tis·tic** /stuh-**tist**-ik/ *noun*
**1** a number that gives a fact or measurement. Statistics are collected by finding out how many or how much of something there is: *Statistics show that traveling by plane is much safer than traveling by car.*
**2 statistics** /stuh-**tist**-ikss/ the study of numbers that give facts or measurements: *If you major in math at college, you will probably study statistics.*

**stat·ue** /**stach**-oo/ *noun* a model of a person or animal made from metal or stone: *The Statue of Liberty stands on an island in New York Harbor.*

statue

**sta·tus** /**stayt**-uhss/ *noun* someone's position, especially in a society: *Doctors have high social status and are paid a lot of money.*

**stay** /stay/
● *verb*
**1** to continue to be in the same place: *Can you stay here while I get the car out of the garage?*
**2** to continue to be in the same condition: *Fresh fruit and vegetables help you to stay healthy.*
**3** to spend a short time in a place: *We stayed at Grandpa's house for a week.*
**4 stay up** to go to bed later than usual: *During summer vacation, Mom and Dad sometimes let me stay up late because there's no school in the morning.*
● *noun*
the period of time when you are visiting a place: *The kids really enjoyed their stay in Florida.*

**stead·fast** /**sted**-fast/ *adjective* refusing to change your opinion or actions, especially because you are very loyal to someone: *He was a steadfast supporter of the president and he worked with him for many years.*

a b c d e f g h i j k l m n o p q r **s** t u v w x y z

**stead·i·ly** /sted-uhl-ee/ *adverb* at a speed or level that stays the same and does not change much: *It had been raining steadily all day so we didn't go out.*

**stead·y** /sted-ee/
● *adjective*
**1** staying firm and not moving or shaking: *Make sure that you hold the camera steady when you take the picture.*
**2** continuing at the same speed or level and not stopping: *Paul's teacher says that he is making steady progress at school.*
**3** a steady girlfriend or steady boyfriend is one that you have been dating for a long time: *Jonas has a steady girlfriend who he's been with for around nine months.*
**4** a steady job is a good job that you are likely to continue doing: *My brother left college and got a steady job in a bank.*
● *verb*
to stop something from shaking or falling: *Can you steady the ladder for me while I climb up it?*

**steak** /stayk/ *noun* a thick flat piece of meat or fish, especially beef: *I ordered my steak well done.*

**steal** /steel/ *verb* (**stole** /stohl/, **stolen** /stohl-uhn/)
**1** to take something that belongs to someone else: *Mom can't find her wallet and she thinks that someone has stolen it.* ► see **Thesaurus**
**2** to get to the next base in baseball before someone hits the ball: *He tried to steal second base, but he was thrown out.*

**steam** /steem/
● *noun*
the gas that forms when water boils. It looks a little like fog: *She left a pan of boiling water on the stove and the kitchen was full of steam.*

⌐ IDIOM with **steam**
**let off steam/blow off steam** to get rid of your energy or angry feelings by doing something: *The kids have been indoors all day so they need to run around and let off steam.*
● *verb*
**1** to cook something using steam: *You can steam the vegetables over a pan of boiling water.* ► see picture at **cook**
**2** to produce steam: *The water in the bathtub was steaming because it was very hot.*

**steam**

**steel** /steel/ *noun* a strong metal made from iron and carbon: *Steel is used for making cars and machines.*

**steep** /steep/ *adjective*
**1** a steep road or hill goes up or down very quickly: *The mountain is very steep and difficult to climb.*
**2** a steep increase or decrease is large and sudden: *There was a steep rise in the price of gasoline, from two dollars a gallon to almost three dollars.*

**steer** /steer/
● *verb* to control the way a vehicle goes: *You need both hands on the wheel when you are steering a car.*
● *noun* a young male cow that is raised for its beef

**steer·ing wheel** /steer-ing weel/ *noun* the round object that the driver of a vehicle turns to make the vehicle go right or left

**steg·o·sau·rus** /steg-uh-**sor**-uhss/ *noun* a big dinosaur with an arched back, short front legs, and a long stiff tail. A stegosaurus ate plants and had a line of spikes and bony structures on its back. ► see picture at **dinosaur**

**stem** /stem/
● *noun*
the long thin part of a plant that the leaves or flowers grow from: *I cut the stems and put the flowers in a vase of water.* ► see picture at **flower**
● *verb* (**stemming**, **stemmed**)
**1** to stop something from flowing or increasing: *The nurse put a bandage around my arm to stem the flow of blood.*

**2 stem from** to happen as a result of something: *The fight stemmed from a disagreement over a girl.*

**stem and leaf plot** /stem uhnd **leaf** plaht/ *noun* a way of showing mathematical information. You write the different parts of a number in separate columns. The first digit of a number (the stem) is written in the first column. The other digits (the leaves) are written next to it in the second column.

**sten·cil** /stenss-uhl/
● *noun* a piece of stiff paper or plastic with a design cut out of it. You color over the stencil to make the design appear on something: *I made a pattern of leaves on the wall using a stencil.*
● *verb* to paint a design on something using a stencil

**step** /step/
● *noun*
**1** the movement of lifting one foot and putting it down in front of the other: *I took another step toward the door.*
**2** one of the things that you do, in order to achieve or make something: *When you are drawing a picture of someone, the first step is to draw the shape of the person's face.*
**3** a surface that you put your foot on to go up or down to another level: *There are 20 steps that lead down to the basement.* (SYNONYM: **stair**)
▶ see picture at **staircase**

IDIOMS with **step**
**step by step** in a way that explains clearly each thing that you have to do: *The book tells you step by step how to build your own model airplanes.*
**watch your step** said to tell someone to be careful about what they do or say: *You'd better watch your step or you will get into trouble.*
● *verb* (**stepping**, **stepped**)
**1** to move somewhere by lifting one foot and putting it down again: *The actress stepped onto the stage to receive the prize.*
**2 step out** to go out for a short time: *Dad just stepped out – he should be back soon.*

**step·broth·er** /step-bruhth-ur/ *noun* the son of someone who has married one of your parents

**step·child** /step-chīld/ *noun* (plural **stepchildren** /step-chil-druhn/) a stepdaughter or stepson

**step·daugh·ter** /step-dot-ur/ *noun* a daughter that someone's husband or wife has from another marriage

**step·fa·ther** /step-fahth-ur/ *noun* a man who is married to your mother but who is not your father: *Steve is my stepfather. Mom married him after Dad died.*

**step·lad·der** /step-lad-ur/ *noun* a ladder with two parts that lean toward each other and join at the top: *I had to use a stepladder to reach the top shelf.* ▶ see picture at **ladder**

stepladder

**step·moth·er** /step-muhth-ur/ *noun* a woman who is married to your father but who is not your mother

**step·par·ent** /step-pair-uhnt/ *noun* a stepfather or stepmother

**step·sis·ter** /step-sist-ur/ *noun* the daughter of someone who has married one of your parents: *I have a stepsister named Lily. Dad married Lily's mom.*

**step·son** /step-suhn/ *noun* a son that someone's husband or wife has from another marriage

**ster·e·o** /sterr-ee-oh/ *noun* a machine or system that produces music or sounds from two speakers: *The music sounds much better if you listen to it on a stereo.*

**ster·e·o·type** /sterr-ee-uh-tīp/
● *noun* a common idea of what a type of person is like. A stereotype is often not correct: *The stereotype of a Texan is someone who wears a big cowboy hat and boots.*
● *verb* to think that some people have specific qualities because of their race, sex, or social class: *Girls used to be stereotyped as not being as smart as boys, but that doesn't happen much anymore.*

**ster·ile** /sterr-uhl/ *adjective* completely clean and not containing any bacteria: *Babies' bottles need to be sterile to prevent the babies from getting infections.*

a b c d e f g h i j k l m n o p q r **s** t u v w x y z

**stern** /sturn/
- *adjective* very serious or strict: *The teacher gave me a stern warning not to be late again.*
—**sternly** /**sturn**-lee/ *adverb* in a stern way: *"Where have you been?" his mother asked sternly.*
- *noun* the back part of a ship

**steth·o·scope** /**steth**-uh-skohp/ *noun* an instrument that a doctor uses to listen to your heart or breathing: *The doctor listened to my chest through his stethoscope and said that my breathing was fine.*

**stew** /stoo/
- *noun* a meal made of pieces of meat or fish and vegetables that you cook slowly in liquid: *We had beef stew for lunch today.*
- *verb* to cook meat or fish and vegetables slowly in liquid: *The meat was stewed in a thick sauce.*

**stew·ard** /**stoo**-urd/ *noun* a man whose job is to serve food and drinks to people on a ship or plane: *I asked the steward on the plane for a glass of water.*

**stew·ard·ess** /**stoo**-urd-iss/ *noun* a woman whose job is to serve food and drinks to people on a ship or an airplane

**stick** /stik/
- *verb* (**stuck** /stuhk/)
**1** to join or fasten one thing to another, often using glue: *I stuck a stamp on the envelope.*
**2** if something sticks to a surface, it stays there because it is wet or there is glue on it: *The mud in the field sticks to your boots.*
**3** to push a pointed object into something: *He stuck a knife in the cake and cut it into pieces.*
**4** **stick out** to come out from the surface of something, or the main part of something: *I hit my head on a branch that was sticking out across the path.*
**5** **stick to** to continue doing something in the way you planned: *It was raining, but we stuck to our plan and went for a walk.*
**6** **stick up for** to defend someone who other people are criticizing: *Joe's my friend and we always stick up for each other if there is an argument.*
- *noun*
**1** a long thin piece of wood from a tree: *I picked up a stick and put it on the fire.*

**2** something that is a long thin shape: *Do you want a stick of gum?*

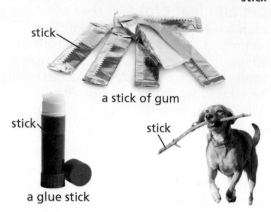

stick

stick

a stick of gum

stick

stick

a glue stick

**stick·er** /**stik**-ur/ *noun* a small piece of paper or plastic that you can stick onto something: *Carrie put colored stickers all over her notebook so it looks really pretty.*

**stick·y** /**stik**-ee/ *adjective* (**stickier**, **stickiest**) made of or covered with a substance that sticks to things: *His hands are sticky because they have honey on them.*

**stiff** /stif/
- *adjective*
**1** if you are stiff, your muscles or joints hurt and it is difficult to move: *My arm feels stiff because I was playing tennis yesterday.*
**2** difficult to bend or press: *You can make a birthday card using a piece of stiff paper.*
**3** a stiff punishment is very severe: *There should be stiffer sentences for criminals who use guns.*
**4** difficult to deal with or defeat: *There was stiff competition in the race, and he came in third.*
- *adverb*
**scared stiff/bored stiff/worried stiff** very scared, bored, or worried: *I was scared stiff when I saw the snake.*

**stiff·en** /**stif**-uhn/ *verb*
**1** if you stiffen, your body suddenly becomes firm or still because you are angry, frightened, or worried: *The dog suddenly stiffened when he saw the snake.*
**2** to become stiffer: *Her back has stiffened up and it is difficult for her to bend.*

**still** /stil/
- *adverb*
**1** used for saying that a situation has not

628

changed and is continuing: *I had a sandwich but I'm still hungry.*

**2** not moving: *You have to sit still when I'm cutting your hair.*

**3** in spite of what has just been said or done: *I studied hard, but I still failed the test.*

● *adjective*

quiet and calm: *In the early morning, the town was still.*

**stim·u·late** /**stim**-yuh-layt/ *verb*

**1** to make someone excited and interested in something: *The pictures help to stimulate the reader's imagination.*

**2** to make something start to happen or happen more: *The warm sun stimulates the plants to grow.*

—**stimulating** /**stim**-yuh-layt-ing/ *adjective* making someone interested or excited: *The classes are always very stimulating and the students find them interesting.*

—**stimulation** /stim-yuh-**laysh**-uhn/ *noun* things that make you interested or excited: *Little cats need lots of stimulation and they like to play.*

**stim·u·lus** /**stim**-yuhl-uhss/ *noun* (plural **stimuli** /**stim**-yuhl-ī/) a thing that makes someone or something do something: *Tests are a useful stimulus to make people study harder.*

**sting** /sting/

● *verb* (**stung** /stuhng/)

**1** if an insect, jellyfish, or plant stings you, it puts poison into your skin and causes a sharp pain: *Don't touch that wasp – it might sting you.*

**2** to make you feel a sharp pain on your skin or in your eyes: *Antiseptic stings when you put it on a cut.*

● *noun*

a wound made when an insect, jellyfish, or plant stings you: *A bee sting can be very painful.*

**stin·gy** /**stinj**-ee/ *adjective* not liking to spend money or give things: *He was so stingy that he didn't even buy his mother a Christmas present.*

**stink** /stingk/

● *verb* (**stunk** /stuhngk/ or **stank** /stangk/, **stunk**)

**1** to have a very strong bad smell: *The house stinks of cigarette smoke.*

**2** to be very bad or unfair: *It stinks that I have to do all the work.*

● *noun*

a very strong bad smell: *She held her nose because of the stink.*

**stir** /stur/ *verb* (**stirring**, **stirred**) to mix a liquid or food by moving a spoon around in it: *Stir the chocolate powder into the milk.*

stir

**stitch** /stich/

● *noun*

**1** a line of thread that you make by putting a needle up and down through cloth once: *She sewed the edge of the tablecloth with tiny stitches.*

**2** a line of thread that a doctor uses to sew two sides of a wound together: *Jacob had to have five stitches in his head after he fell off his bicycle.*

**3** one of the small circles of wool you make around a needle when you are knitting: *A stitch slipped off her knitting needle by mistake.*

● *verb*

to make a line of stitches, especially to join something together: *Mom, can you stitch this hole in my pants?*

**stock** /stahk/

● *noun*

**1** if you have stocks in a company, you own part of the company. Stocks are bought and sold on the stock market: *If you have stock in a company, that means you own a very small part of that company.*

**2** an amount of something that is kept to be sold or used: *They did not know how long their stock of food would last.* ( SYNONYM: **supply** )

**3** a liquid made by boiling meat, bones, or vegetables: *Make the soup using chicken stock.*

**4** animals that are kept on a farm: *His stock includes 10 cows and 100 sheep.*

> **IDIOM with stock**
>
> **in stock** if something is in stock, a store has it and you can buy it there now: *We don't have that book in stock, but we can order it for you.*

● *verb*

**1** to have an amount of something available to be sold or used: *The store stocks a lot of video games.*

**2 stock up** to buy or get a lot of something, so that you can use it later: *We're stocking up on wood for the winter.*

a
b
c
d
e
f
g
h
i
j
k
l
m
n
o
p
q
r
**s**
t
u
v
w
x
y
z

a
b
c
d
e
f
g
h
i
j
k
l
m
n
o
p
q
r

**s**

t
u
v
w
x
y
z

**stock·brok·er** /**stahk**-brohk-ur/ *noun* someone whose job is buying and selling stocks in companies for other people

**stock ex·change** /**stahk** ikss-chaynj/ *noun* a place where people buy and sell stocks in companies: *The New York Stock Exchange is on Wall Street.*

**stock·ing** /**stahk**-ing/ *noun*
**1** a very thin piece of clothing that covers a woman's foot and leg: *She put on black stockings and black shoes.*
**2** a large sock that people hang up before Christmas to be filled with presents: *We hang our stockings by the fireplace on Christmas Eve.*

**stock mar·ket** /**stahk** mark-it/ *noun* the business of buying and selling stocks in companies: *He works on the stock market, buying and selling stock.*

**stock·y** /**stahk**-ee/ *adjective* having a short heavy body that looks strong

**stole** /stohl/ *verb* the past tense of **steal**

**sto·len** /**stohl**-uhn/ *verb* the past participle of steal

**stom·ach** /**stuhm**-uhk/ *noun*
**1** the organ in your body where your food is digested: *My stomach feels full after eating so much food.* ▶ see picture at **anatomy**
**2** the front part of your body, below your chest: *He patted his stomach to show he had enjoyed the meal.*

**stom·ach·ache** /**stuhm**-uhk-ayk/ *noun* a pain in your stomach: *I've eaten too much ice cream and now I have a stomachache.*

**stomp** /stahmp/ *verb* to walk by putting your feet down firmly and noisily, especially because you are angry: *She stomped out of the room and slammed the door behind her.*

**stone** /stohn/ *noun*
**1** a hard solid substance found in the Earth, used for making things such as floors and walls: *The first tools that humans used were made of stone.* | *a large stone building*
**2** a small rock: *Some boys were throwing stones at an old can.* (SYNONYM: **rock**)
**3** a jewel: *Diamonds are very hard precious stones.*

**Stone Age** /**stohn**ayj/ *noun* a very early period in human history, when people used stone for making tools and weapons: *In the Stone Age people made arrows from pieces of stone and wood, and used them for hunting animals.*

**stood** /stud/ *verb* the past tense and past participle of **stand**

**stool** /stool/ *noun* a seat that has three or four legs. A stool has no back or arms: *I usually have breakfast on a stool at the counter in the kitchen.* ▶ see picture at **piano**

**stool**

**stoop** /stoop/ *verb* to bend forward and down: *Tom stooped to pick up his pencil.*

**stop** /stahp/
● *verb* (**stopping**, **stopped**)
**1** to not continue doing something or moving: *The baby won't stop crying. I think he must be hungry.* | *Every time the bus stops, a few people get on or off it.* ▶ see **Thesaurus**
**2** to end: *I wish that awful noise would stop.* | *The teacher stopped the fight by pulling the two boys apart.*
**3** to make someone or something not move any farther: *I'm feeling sick – can you stop the car?*
**4** to prevent someone from doing something: *He held her arm to stop her from leaving.*
**5 stop by** to make a short visit to a person or place, especially when you are going somewhere else: *I'll stop by Grandma's house on my way home.*
● *noun*
**1** if something comes to a stop, it stops: *The taxi came to a stop outside the hotel.*
**2** a place where you stop during a trip, or the short time you spend at that place: *Memphis will be the first stop on our trip.*
**3** a place where a bus or train regularly stops: *I'm going to get off the bus at the next stop.*

**stop·light** /**stahp**-līt/ *noun* a set of red, yellow, and green lights used for controlling traffic: *The stoplight changed from red to green and the cars started moving.* (SYNONYM: **traffic light**)

**stop·watch** /**stahp**-wahch/ *noun* a watch used for measuring the exact time it needs to do something, for example run a race

**stor·age** /**stor**-ij/ *noun*
**1** the action of keeping something somewhere until you need it: *We use the attic for storage for old furniture, clothes, and toys.*
**2** if something is in storage, it is being kept in a place where people pay to store things: *He sold his house and all his furniture is in storage while he looks for another house to buy.*

**store** /stor/
● *noun*
**1** a building where things are sold: *Mom's gone to the grocery store to buy some food.*
**2** an amount of something that you keep to use later: *Squirrels keep stores of nuts for the winter.*

⌐ **IDIOM with store**
**in store** if something is in store for someone, it is going to happen to them soon: *There is trouble in store for him if he doesn't start behaving better.*

● *verb*
**1** to put things away and keep them until you need them: *We store our camping gear in the garage.*
**2** to put or keep information on a computer, CD, etc.: *All the information about the students is stored on computer.*

**stork** /stork/ *noun* a tall white bird with long legs and a long beak

**storm** /storm/
● *noun*
if there is a storm, there is a lot of wind and rain or snow: *There was thunder and lightning during the storm.* ▶ see **Thesaurus**
—**stormy** /**storm**-ee/ *adjective* with a lot of wind and rain or snow: *It was a stormy night, and the wind kept me awake.*
● *verb*
**1** to go somewhere quickly in an angry way: *Sarah got mad and stormed out of the room.*
**2** to attack a place and enter it using force: *Police officers stormed the building and arrested the men inside.*

**sto·ry** /**stor**-ee/ *noun* (plural **stories**)
**1** a description of a set of events. The events can

be real or imaginary: *Grandma told us stories about her childhood.* | *I'm reading a book of science fiction stories.* ▶ see **Thesaurus**
**2** a report in a newspaper or news program: *There was a story about the new school in our local newspaper.*
**3** an excuse, explanation, or lie: *I don't believe his story about where he was last night.*
**4** a level of a building: *Our apartment is on the sixth story.* ( SYNONYM: **floor** )

> ## Word Origin: story
>
> **Story** and **history** come from the same Latin word. In Middle English, both words were used about descriptions of real events. In the late 1400s, people started using history to mean only "a description of real events that happened in the past." In the 1500s, the word story was still used about real events, but it also started to be used about descriptions of imaginary events. We still use it about both things today.

**sto·ry·board** /**stor**-ee-bord/ *noun* a set of drawings that show a series of events, especially drawings that show what will happen in a movie: *The students are doing a storyboard first, to plan what will happen in the video.*

**stove** /stohv/ *noun*
**1** a large piece of kitchen equipment that you use to cook food. It has a place to cook food on top and an oven inside: *You can fry the eggs on the stove.*
**2** a piece of equipment for heating a room. You burn wood or coal inside it: *An old wood stove keeps the cabin warm.*

stove
oven

**St. Pat·rick's Day** /saynt **patr**-ikss day/ *noun* the day on which people celebrate St. Patrick, the patron saint of Ireland. St. Patrick's Day is on March 17. It is a holiday in Ireland and a special day with parties and parades in the U.S. and some other countries.

a b c d e f g h i j k l m n o p q r **s** t u v w x y z

**straight** /strayt/

● *adjective*

**1** not bent or curved: *Draw a straight line using your ruler.* | *Is her hair straight or curly?*

**2** level or upright, and not leaning: *The picture on that wall is not straight – you need to move the left side down a little.* | *The braces will make your teeth straight.*

**3** honest and saying exactly what you mean: *Come on, just give me a straight answer – yes or no?*

**4** one after the other: *The team had three straight wins and then lost the fourth game.*

**5** if you get straight A's, you get an A in all of your school subjects: *Kim studies hard and always gets straight A's.*

● *adverb*

**1** not leaning or bending: *Stand up straight and take your hands out of your pockets!*

**2** directly, or not to one side: *The library is straight ahead of you.*

**3** immediately: *I got into bed and went straight to sleep.*

**4** happening one after the other: *We continued driving for five hours straight, without stopping.*

> **IDIOM with straight**
> **not think straight** to be unable to think clearly: *It was so noisy that I couldn't think straight.*

straight

straight          crooked

**straight an·gle** /**strayt** ang-guhl/ *noun* an angle of 180 degrees

**straight·en** /**strayt**'n/ *verb*

**1** to make something straight: *She had to wear braces to straighten her teeth.*

**2** **straighten out** to deal with a problem or a bad situation successfully: *He had a lot of problems, but now he's straightened them out and he seems really happy.*

**3** **straighten up** to make a messy room neat and clean: *"Go straighten up your room," said Mom.*

**4** **straighten up** to stand or sit up with your body straight: *I can't measure you if you're bending your knees – straighten up.*

**straight·for·ward** /strayt-**for**-wurd/ *adjective*

**1** simple or easy to understand: *The instructions are straightforward and you shouldn't have any problems.*

**2** honest and not hiding what you think: *I always try to be straightforward with people and tell them if I think they are wrong.*

**strain** /strayn/

● *verb*

**1** to damage part of your body by stretching it or using it too much: *Rob strained his back when he was lifting a heavy box.*

**2** to try very hard to do something: *She put her ear next to the door and strained to hear what they were saying.*

**3** to separate solid things from a liquid by pouring the liquid through a container with holes: *Strain the sauce to remove any lumps.*

● *noun*

**1** the state of having too much to worry about or deal with: *She's under a lot of strain because she has important college exams.*

**2** an injury to part of your body, caused by stretching it or using it too much: *Lee can't play in the game because of a muscle strain.*

**strained** /straynd/ *adjective*

**1** a strained relationship is unfriendly and not relaxed: *They had a really bad argument and since then their relationship has been strained.*

**2** looking or sounding worried and tired: *His voice sounded strained, so I asked him what was wrong.*

**strain·er** /**strayn**-uhr/ *noun* an object that you use to separate solid things from a liquid. A strainer usually looks like a bowl with holes in it: *Press the berries through a strainer to remove the juice.*

**strait** /strayt/ *noun* a narrow area of water that joins two larger areas of water: *The Bering Strait connects the Arctic Ocean with the Pacific Ocean.*

**strand** /strand/ *noun* a piece of thread, hair, or wire: *She brushed a strand of hair from her face.*

**strand·ed** /strand-id/ *adjective* not able to leave a place, for example because of bad weather: *We were stranded at the airport because of the snow.*

**strange** /straynj/ *adjective*
**1** unusual or surprising: *The engine was making a very strange noise.* | *"He said he didn't want any chocolate." "That's strange – is he sick?"*
SYNONYMS: **odd, weird** ▶ see Thesaurus
**2** not familiar: *It can be hard when you move to a strange neighborhood and you don't know anyone.*
—**strangely** /straynj-lee/ *adverb* in a strange way

**strang·er** /straynj-ur/ *noun* someone you do not know: *If a stranger stops and offers you a ride, always say no.*

**stran·gle** /strang-guhl/ *verb* to kill someone by pressing his or her throat: *She tried to strangle him with a piece of rope.*

**strap** /strap/
● *noun* a band of cloth or leather. For example, a watch has a strap, and some shoes are fastened with a strap: *His camera is hanging from a strap around his neck.* ▶ see picture at **watch**
● *verb* (**strapping**, **strapped**) to fasten something or someone in place with a band of cloth or leather: *In a car, you must strap yourself in with a seat belt.*

**strat·e·gy** /strat-uhj-ee/ *noun* (plural **strategies**) a planned way of achieving something: *The team's strategy is to try to stop the other team from scoring any points.*
—**strategic** /struh-teej-ik/ *adjective* done as part of a plan to achieve something

**straw** /stro/ *noun*
**1** a thin tube of plastic used for sucking a drink out of a glass: *I usually drink lemonade with a straw.*
**2** the dried stems of wheat or other plants like wheat. Straw is used for animals to sleep on, or for making things: *There is a big pile of straw in the barn.* | *a straw hat*

**straw**

**straw·ber·ry**
/**stro**-berr-ee/ *noun*
(plural **strawberries**) a soft sweet red fruit that grows on plants close to the ground: *For dessert, there is strawberries and ice cream.*

**strawberry**

**stray** /stray/
● *verb*
to move away from the place where you should be: *Don't stray from the path because you might get lost.*
● *adjective*
**1** a stray animal is lost or has no home: *We found a stray dog, so we put up a sign to try to find its owner.*
**2** stray parts of something are separate from the main part: *I tried to stop the stray hairs from getting into my eyes.*
● *noun*
a dog or cat that is lost or has no home: *Our cat was a stray – we found him on the street.*

**streak** /streek/
● *noun*
**1** a long thin mark or line of color: *Mrs. Brooks has brown hair with gray streaks in it.*
**2** a quality in your character that affects your behaviour: *Matt has a stubborn streak and he refuses to admit that he is wrong.*
**3** a period of time when you always succeed or always fail: *The team is on a winning streak and they have won their last four games.*
● *verb*
**1** to move very quickly: *The cat streaked out of the door.*
**2** **be streaked** to have long thin marks or lines of color: *Her hair was streaked with gray.*

**stream** /streem/

● *noun*

**1** a very small river: *Streams flow down the mountains into the valleys and lakes.*
**2** a flow of air, smoke, or water: *I opened the door and a stream of icy air came in.*
**3** a line of people or things that are moving in the same direction: *There was a steady stream of traffic on the street.*

● *verb*

**1** to move quickly and steadily, in large numbers or amounts: *Hundreds of people were streaming out of the movie theater.*
**2** to flow steadily: *Tears streamed down her face as she told her sad story.*

**stream**

**stream·er** /**streem**-uhr/ *noun* a long thin piece of colored paper or cloth, used as a decoration: *They decorated the room with streamers and balloons for his birthday.*

**street** /street/ *noun* a road in a town or city with houses, stores, or offices along it: *Julia lives on the same street as me.*

**strength** /strengkth/ *noun*

**1** the physical power to lift, move, or do things: *I don't have the strength to lift up the table.*
( ANTONYM: **weakness** )
**2** the ability to do something in a determined way, even though it is difficult: *He has great strength of character and he doesn't give up easily.*
**3** something that is good about someone or something: *His ability to hit the ball is one of his greatest strengths as a player.*
( ANTONYM: **weakness** )
**4** how strong a feeling, belief, or relationship is: *Her actions showed the strength of her love for her son.*

**5** the power of a country or leader: *The country's military strength helped it win the war.*

**strength·en** /**strengkth**-uhn/ *verb* to make something stronger: *You need to strengthen your arms so you can lift heavier weights.* | *If you praise children, it strengthens their confidence and makes them try harder.* ( ANTONYM: **weaken** )

**stren·u·ous** /**stren**-yoo-uhss/ *adjective* needing or using a lot of effort: *His doctor told him to rest and not do any strenuous exercise.*

**stress** /stress/

● *noun*

**1** worry that you feel all the time because of the situation you are in: *Students are under a lot of stress before tests.*
**2** if there is stress on a particular word or part of a word, it is said louder or with more force: *When you say the word "after," the stress is on the first syllable.* ( SYNONYM: **emphasis** )
**3** a force that affects or damages something: *Running puts stress on the joints in your legs, so it's important to wear the right shoes.*
**4** special attention or importance that is given to something: *Mom always put stress on having good manners.* ( SYNONYM: **emphasis** )

● *verb*

**1** to make it very clear that something is true or important: *Doctors always stress the importance of eating fresh fruit and vegetables.*
( SYNONYM: **emphasize** )
**2** to say a word or part of a word louder or with more force: *"Don't tell anyone," she said, stressing the word "anyone."*
**3** **stress out** to make someone feel worried and not relaxed: *Visiting the dentist used to stress me out, but now I'm much more relaxed about it.*

**Word Family: stress**

**stress** *noun* | **stress** *verb* | **stressful** *adjective*

**stressed** /strest/ (also **stressed out** /strest-**owt**/) *adjective* worried and unable to relax: *Suzie is very stressed about her math test.*

**stress·ful** /**stress**-fuhl/ *adjective* making you worry a lot: *Dad's job is very stressful so he needs to find time to relax.*

**stretch** /strech/

● *verb*

**1** if clothes or materials stretch, they become bigger or looser: *These pants stretch so they're easy to pull on.*
**2** to spread out your arms, legs, or body as far as possible: *If I stretch, I can just reach that shelf.*
**3** to spread out over a large area: *Yellowstone National Park stretches over 3,400 square miles.*
**4** to pull something so it is tight: *They stretched a rope between two trees.*
**5 stretch out** to lie down to rest or sleep with your body straight: *The dog stretched out on the floor and went to sleep.*

IDIOM with **stretch**
**stretch your legs** to stand up and move around, after you have been sitting for a long time: *After the long flight we needed to stretch our legs.*

● *noun*

**1** an area of land or water, especially a long one: *We walked on to find a quieter stretch of beach.*
**2** a period of time: *Don't use the computer for a long stretch of time without a break.*
**3** if you do a stretch, you move a part of your body as far as possible: *It's good to do a few stretches before you exercise.*

**stretch**

**stretch·er** /strech-ur/ *noun* something that is used to carry someone who is injured or sick. A stretcher is usually a large piece of cloth fixed between two poles: *The injured player was taken away on a stretcher.*

**strict** /strikt/ *adjective*

**1** making people obey rules and do what you say: *Her parents are very strict and she has to be in bed by 8 o'clock every night.*
**2** a strict rule, law, or order must be obeyed exactly: *There is a strict rule that only children under 12 can use the playground.*

**strict·ly** /strikt-lee/ *adverb*

**1** in a way that people must obey: *Smoking is strictly forbidden.*
**2** only: *This book deals strictly with butterflies, not with other insects.*
**3 not strictly** not completely: *It isn't strictly true that I'm ten – I'll be ten next week.* | *Milk isn't strictly necessary for the recipe – you can use water too.*

**stride** /strīd/

● *verb* (**strode** /strohd/, **stridden** /strid-uhn/) to walk with quick long steps: *He strode confidently across the room to greet her.*
● *noun* a long step: *I can reach the door in three long strides.*

IDIOM with **stride**
**take something in stride** to not be upset by something bad that happens: *She takes everything in stride – nothing seems to bother her.*

**strike** /strīk/

● *verb* (**struck** /struhk/)

**1** to hit or attack someone or something: *The snake lifts up its head when it is ready to strike.* | *The tree was struck by lightning.*
**2** if an idea strikes you, you suddenly realize it or think of it: *A thought struck me: perhaps he hadn't gotten my message.*
**3** when a clock strikes, its bell makes sounds to show the time: *Cinderella had to leave the party before the clock struck 12.*
**4** if workers strike, they stop working for a while because they want more money or better working conditions: *The bus drivers are striking for higher pay.*
**5** to seem to be a particular kind of person or thing: *She strikes me as a sensible person.*
● *noun*

**1** if there is a strike, the workers stop working because they want more money or better working conditions: *The trains aren't running because the railroad workers are on strike.*
**2** an unsuccessful attempt to hit the ball in baseball
**3** a military attack: *Several people were killed in an air strike.*

**strik·er** /strīk-ur/ *noun* someone who has stopped working as a protest

**strik·ing** /strīk-ing/ *adjective* unusual or interesting, in a way that attracts your attention: *There is a striking similarity between the two girls and I think they must be twins.*

**string** /string/

● *noun*

**1** strong thread used for tying things: *I put string around the newspapers and tied them together.*

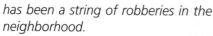

string

**string**

**2** a group of similar events that happen one after the other: *There has been a string of robberies in the neighborhood.*

**3** a line of similar things: *We sailed around a string of islands. | The little girl was wearing a string of pink beads around her neck.*

**4** a long thin piece of wire on a musical instrument, which produces a sound when you touch it: *One of the strings on her guitar broke.* ▶ see picture at **guitar**

**5** **the strings** the people in an orchestra who play instruments such as the violin or cello

● *verb* (**strung** /struhng/)

to put things on a string or wire: *Make holes in the shells and string them together.*

**strip** /strip/

● *verb* (**stripping**, **stripped**)

**1** to take off your clothes: *He stripped and got into the shower.*

**2** to remove something that is covering something else: *Strip off the old wallpaper.*

● *noun*

a long narrow piece or area: *She tore off a strip of cloth to use as a bandage. | You can camp on a strip of land near the beach.*

**stripe** /strīp/ *noun* a straight line of color: *The U.S. flag has red and white stripes on it.*

**striped** /strīpt/

*adjective* having a pattern of stripes: *A zebra is a black and white striped animal.*

**striped**

**stroke** /strohk/

● *verb*

to move your hand gently over something:

*I like stroking the cat because her fur is so soft.* (SYNONYM: **pet**) ▶ see picture on page **A14**

● *noun*

**1** a short movement or line, made by a brush or pen: *If you look closely at the painting, you can see the artist's brush strokes.*

**2** a way of swimming: *We are learning the back stroke in our swimming lessons today.*

**3** if someone has a stroke, a blood vessel in his or her brain bursts or becomes blocked. A stroke may damage the brain: *After Grandma had a stroke, she couldn't move her left arm.*

IDIOMS with **stroke**

**a stroke of luck** something good that happens by chance: *There are two tickets left. What a stroke of luck!*

**at the stroke of midnight/six/nine, etc.** at exactly 12 o'clock, 6 o'clock, 9 o'clock, etc.: *At the stroke of midnight, the bells began to ring.*

**stroll** /strohl/

● *verb* to walk in a slow relaxed way: *People are strolling through the park in the sunshine.*

● *noun* a slow relaxed walk: *Let's go for a stroll along the beach.*

**stroll·er** /strohl-ur/

*noun* a chair on wheels that a baby or small child sits in. You push the stroller along, by holding the handles: *A young mother was pushing a baby in a stroller.*

**stroller**

**strong** /strong/

*adjective*

**1** having a lot of physical strength, so that you can lift heavy things, or use a lot of effort: *My dad is very strong and he can lift me up on his shoulders.* (ANTONYM: **weak**) ▶ see **Thesaurus**

**2** not easily broken or damaged: *Tents are made of a strong material that won't tear easily. | Our friendship is strong and will last.*

**3** determined, and not getting too upset about problems: *You need to be strong and not take any notice of what other people say about you.* (SYNONYM: **tough**)

**4** a strong smell or taste is very easy to notice: *The smell of her perfume was so strong it made me feel sick.* (ANTONYMS: **faint, slight**)

**5** a strong liquid or medicine has a lot of a

substance in it: *This lemonade is very strong – how many lemons did you use?* ( ANTONYM: **weak** )

**6** a strong wind blows quickly and with a lot of force: *The wind is strong and it is blowing the leaves off the trees.* ( ANTONYM: **gentle** )

**7** having a lot of power, influence, or ability: *We need a strong leader who people will listen to.* ( ANTONYM: **weak** )

**8** a strong feeling or idea is one that you feel or believe a lot: *She has a strong belief in God and she goes to church every Sunday.* ( ANTONYM: **weak** )

**9** strong sun or sunshine is very bright and hot: *Strong sun can damage your skin so always wear sunscreen.*

**Word Family: strong**

**strong** adjective | **strongly** adverb | **strength** noun | **strengthen** verb

**strong·ly** /**strong**-lee/ *adverb* a lot: *I disagree very strongly with his decision – it's totally wrong.* | *The soup tasted strongly of onions.*

**struck** /struhk/ *verb* the past tense and past participle of **strike**

**struc·ture** /**struhk**-chur/
● *noun*
**1** something that people have built: *The museum is a huge structure of steel and glass.*
**2** the way that the parts of something are arranged: *The diagram shows the structure of the eye.*
● *verb*
to plan and put together the different parts of something: *Structure your essay so that there is a clear introduction followed by clear arguments.*
—**structural** /**struhk**-chuhr-uhl/ *adjective* relating to the structure of something: *The main structural parts of a house are the walls and the roof.*

**strug·gle** /**struhg**-uhl/
● *verb*
**1** to try very hard to do something difficult: *Martin Luther King struggled to create an equal society for all Americans.* | *It is very late and I am struggling to stay awake.*
**2** to fight someone who is attacking you or holding you: *The boys were on the bedroom floor yelling and struggling with each other.*

● *noun*
**1** an attempt to do something that is difficult to do: *The test is hard and it is a struggle to finish it in time.*
**2** a fight: *There was a struggle and one of the boys broke his glasses.*

**strut** /struht/
● *verb* (**strutting**, **strutted**) to walk in a very proud and confident way, which other people think is annoying: *He struts around the place and thinks he is more important than anyone else.*
● *noun* a long piece of metal or wood, used for supporting part of a bridge, aircraft, etc.

**stub** /stuhb/
● *noun* the short part of something that is left after the rest has been used or torn off: *He tore off the main part of the ticket, and gave me the stub.*
● *verb* (**stubbing**, **stubbed**) if you stub your toe, you hurt your toe by hitting it against something: *I stubbed my toe on the table and hurt my toe.*

**stub·born** /**stuhb**-urn/ *adjective* determined not to do something or to change your ideas: *My brother is very stubborn and he won't do what other people tell him.*

**stuck** /stuhk/
● *verb*
the past tense and past participle of **stick**
● *adjective*
**1** not able to move: *The drawer is stuck – when I pull it, I can't make it open.*
**2** not able to continue working on something because it is too difficult: *Can you help me with my homework? I'm stuck on question 7.*

**stu·dent** /**stood**'nt/ *noun* someone who is studying at school or college: *How many students are there in your class?* ▶ see picture on page **A9**

**stu·di·o** /**stood**-ee-oh/ *noun*
**1** a room where a painter or photographer works: *He does his paintings in his studio.*
**2** a place where movies, records, or television or radio programs are made: *My brother's jazz band went to a recording studio to record their song.*
**3** an apartment with one room: *She rents a small studio in an apartment block.*

**stud·y** /stuhd-ee/

● *verb* (**studies**, **studying**, **studied**)

**1** to spend time learning about a subject: *She's studying history in college.* | *If you study hard, you'll get good grades.*

**2** to look at something carefully in order to find out something: *He studied the map to see which route to take.* | *We learn about animals by studying their habits.*

● *noun* (plural **studies**)

**1** a piece of work that is done to find out more about something: *The scientists are doing a study on changes in our climate.*

**2** the activity of learning about a subject: *Biology is the study of living things.*

**3** a room in a house that is used for work or study: *Dad has his own study, with a desk and a computer.*

**stuff** /stuhf/

● *noun*

**1** a substance or material: *The brown stuff on the table is peanut butter.*

**2** a number of different things: *Where's the tent and the other camping stuff?* | *You can leave your stuff here.*

**3** things that someone says, believes, or does: *I don't believe all that stuff about witches and wizards.*

● *verb*

**1** to push something into a space quickly: *When he heard the others coming, he stuffed the money in his pocket.*

**2** to fill something with things, or with a soft substance: *Stuff the doll's body with cotton.*

**stuff·ing** /stuhf-ing/ *noun*

**1** a mixture of food that you put inside a chicken, vegetable, etc. before cooking it: *You can make a stuffing for chicken using pieces of bread and onions.*

**2** material that is used for filling something such as a pillow: *The sofa is torn and the stuffing's coming out.*

**stuff·y** /stuhf-ee/ *adjective* if a place is stuffy, there is not enough fresh air in it: *Can you open the window? It's very stuffy in here.*

**stum·ble** /stuhm-buhl/ *verb*

**1** to fall or almost fall while you are walking, especially because you hit something with your foot: *I stumbled on a piece of rock and I almost fell down onto the ground.*

**2** to make a mistake when you are reading or speaking to people: *Please read the poem aloud slowly so you don't stumble.*

**3 stumble on/across** to find something by chance: *I stumbled across some old pictures while I was cleaning my room.*

**stump** /stuhmp/

● *noun*

**1** the part of a tree that is left when the tree has been cut down: *The tree had been cut down and all that was left was a stump.*

**2** the part of an arm or leg that is left when the rest has been cut off

● *verb*

if a question or puzzle stumps you, you cannot think of the right answer: *Everyone was stumped by the question, so the teacher had to give them the answer.*

**stun** /stuhn/ *verb* (**stunning**, **stunned**) to hit someone's head and make him or her almost unconscious for a short time: *The ball hit him on his head and stunned him for a few moments.*

**stung** /stuhng/ *verb* the past tense and past participle of **sting**

**stunk** /stuhngk/ *verb* a past tense and past participle of **stink**

**stunned** /stuhnd/ *adjective* very surprised or impressed: *I am stunned by the size of the trees – they are the biggest I have ever seen.*

**stun·ning** /stuhn-ing/ *adjective*

**1** extremely beautiful: *I had never seen anyone so beautiful – she was stunning.*

**2** very good or surprising: *The U.S. team won 2–0 in a stunning victory against Spain.*

SYNONYM: **amazing**

**stunt** /stuhnt/ *noun*

**1** something dangerous that someone does in a movie or for an audience: *The actor did a stunt in which he jumped from a high window onto a horse.*

**2** something unusual that someone does to get people's attention: *The soft drink company filled a swimming pool with its new soda as a publicity stunt.*

**stu·pid** /stoop-id/ *adjective* not intelligent or not sensible: *It was a stupid idea to have the fire*

*next to the house.* (SYNONYM: **dumb**)
(ANTONYM: **smart**) ▶ see Thesaurus
—**stupidity** /stoo-**pid**-uht-ee/ *noun* stupid behavior

**stur·dy** /**sturd**-ee/ *adjective* strong and not likely to break: *You need to wear sturdy shoes when you are hiking over rough ground.*
(ANTONYMS: **fragile, delicate**)

**stut·ter** /**stuht**-ur/
● *verb* to repeat the first sound of words because you are nervous or have a speech problem: *"My n-n-n-name is Joe," he stuttered.*
(SYNONYM: **stammer**)
● *noun* a way of talking in which you stutter: *He doesn't like speaking in public because he has a stutter.* (SYNONYM: **stammer**)

**style** /stīl/ *noun*
**1** the way of doing or making something: *The girls wear their hair in all kinds of different styles.* | *This style of architecture was popular during the 1960s.*
**2** if you have style, you dress or do things in a way that people admire: *Ethan has a lot of style and he always wears nice clothes.*

**styl·ish** /**stīl**-ish/ *adjective* looking fashionable: *He is wearing a very stylish shirt with a narrow collar.*

**Sty·ro·foam** /**stīr**-uh-fohm/ *noun trademark* a light plastic material with air in it. Styrofoam is used for making containers.

**sub-** /suhb/

## Word Building

**sub**dued | **sub**marine | **sub**merge | **sub**way

These words all have the Latin word root **sub-** in them. *Sub* means "below" or "under." If people are *subdued*, they are quieter than usual. In a way, they are below their usual level of noise or activity. A *submarine* goes under the water. A *subway* is a train that goes under the ground.

**sub·dued** /suhb-**dood**/ *adjective* if someone is subdued, he or she is quieter than usual: *Is Ella worried about something? She seems very subdued today.* (ANTONYM: **talkative**)

**sub·ject**
● *noun* /**suhb**-jikt/
**1** something that you talk or write about: *Can we talk about a different subject?* | *She has written a book on the subject of party games.*
**2** something that you study at school: *My favorite subject is math.*
**3** the word or words referring to the main person or thing that a sentence is about. The subject usually comes before the verb: *In the sentence "The bird ate the worm," "The bird" is the subject.*
● *verb* /suhb-**jekt**/
**subject someone to** to make someone experience something bad: *The doctors had to subject him to a lot of painful tests.*

**sub·jec·tive** /suhb-**jekt**-iv/ *adjective* involving your feelings or opinions, not facts: *Beauty is a subjective thing – people think different things are beautiful.* (ANTONYM: **objective**)

**sub·li·ma·tion** /suhb-luh-**maysh**-uhn/ *noun* the process in which a substance changes from a solid to a gas, without becoming a liquid. Carbon dioxide does this and changes from dry ice into a gas.

**sub·ma·rine** /**suhb**-muh-reen/ *noun* a ship that can travel under water

**submarine**

**sub·merge** /suhb-**murj**/ *verb* to go under water: *The seal put its head out of the water and then submerged again.* (SYNONYM: **sink**)

**sub·mit** /suhb-**mit**/ *verb* (**submitting, submitted**)
**1** to give an essay, plan, etc. to someone so that he or she can make a decision about it: *You must submit your homework by Friday.*
**2** to accept that someone has power or control over you: *The people refused to submit to the enemy.*

**sub·scribe** /suhb-**skrīb**/ *verb* to pay money so that you will get a magazine, newspaper, or service regularly: *I subscribe to a monthly computer magazine.*
—**subscription** /suhb-**skrip**-shuhn/ *noun* an arrangement to get a magazine, newspaper, or service regularly: *He has a subscription to a science magazine and they send him a new magazine every week.*

**sub·se·quent** /**suhb**-suh-kwuhnt/ *adjective* coming after something: *Subsequent experiments had the same results as the first experiment.*
( SYNONYM: **later** ) ( ANTONYM: **earlier** )
—**subsequently** /**suhb**-suh-kwuhnt-lee/ *adverb* later: *He went to college and subsequently became a teacher.*

**sub·stance** /**suhb**-stuhnss/ *noun* any type of solid or liquid: *Honey is a sweet substance made by bees.* ( SYNONYM: **stuff** )

**sub·stan·tial** /suhb-**stansh**-uhl/ *adjective* large in amount or number: *$100,000 is a substantial amount of money.*

**sub·sti·tute** /**suhb**-stuh-toot/
• *noun* someone or something that replaces another person or thing: *Our teacher was sick, so we had a substitute.* ( SYNONYM: **replacement** )
• *verb* to use something instead of something else: *You can substitute margarine for butter in this recipe.*
—**substitution** /suhb-stuh-**toosh**-uhn/ *noun* the act of substituting people or things: *One of the players was injured so the coach had to make a substitution.*

**sub·ti·tles** /**suhb**-tīt'lz/ *plural noun* words at the bottom of a movie screen or television screen that tell you what the actors are saying in another language: *We watched a French movie with English subtitles.*

**sub·tle** /**suht**'l/ *adjective* not easy to notice: *There's a subtle difference between the two drinks – one is slightly sweeter than the other.*
( SYNONYM: **small** ) ( ANTONYM: **obvious** )

**sub·tract** /suhb-**trakt**/ *verb* to take one number away from another number: *If you subtract 3 from 5, you get 2.* ( SYNONYM: **take away** )
( ANTONYM: **add** )

**sub·trac·tion** /suhb-**trak**-shuhn/ *noun* the act of taking one number away from another: *Here is a*

subtraction question: what is 200 – 150?
( ANTONYM: **addition** )

**sub·trac·tion sign** /suhb-**trak**-shuhn sīn/ *noun* a symbol (-) showing that one number should be taken away from another ( SYNONYM: **minus sign** )

**sub·urb** /**suhb**-urb/ *noun* an area away from the center of a city, where people live: *People travel into the city every day from the suburbs.*
—**suburban** /suh-**burb**-uhn/ *adjective* in a suburb or relating to a suburb: *Suburban areas are less crowded than the center of the city, and there is more space for children to play.*

**sub·way** /**suhb**-way/ *noun* a railroad that is under the ground in cities: *We took the subway home to avoid the traffic delays on a bus.* | *a subway station*

subway

**suc·ceed** /suhk-**seed**/ *verb* to do something that you tried or aimed to do: *He succeeded in passing all his tests.* ( ANTONYM: **fail** )

**suc·cess** /suhk-**sess**/ *noun*
**1** if you have success, you do what you tried or aimed to do: *The team has had a lot of success this year and they have won every game.*
( ANTONYM: **failure** )
**2** something or someone that is successful: *The party was a big success, and everyone had a good time.* ( ANTONYM: **failure** )

**suc·cess·ful** /suhk-**sess**-fuhl/ *adjective*
**1** someone who is successful has done what he or she wanted or tried to do: *She is a successful actor, with her own TV show.*
( ANTONYM: **unsuccessful** ) ▶ see Thesaurus
**2** having the result or effect that you want: *If the operation on his leg is successful, he will be able to walk again soon.* ( ANTONYM: **unsuccessful** )
—**successfully** /suhk-**sess**-fuhl-ee/ *adverb* in a

successful way: *You will get a certificate if you successfully complete the course.*

**such** /suhch/ *adverb, adjective*
**1** used when saying that something is very good, very big, very bad etc.: *We had such a good time at the beach! | I ate such a big piece of cake that I felt sick.*
**2** like the thing that you have been talking about: *"Mom, how do clouds make rain?" "Your dad knows about such things – ask him."*

> **IDIOM with such**
> **such as** used when giving an example of something: *In the San Diego zoo there are lots of large animals, such as bears and lions.*
> SYNONYM: **for example**

**suck** /suhk/ *verb*
**1** to pull liquid into your mouth with your lips: *I sucked the milkshake with a straw.*
**2** to hold something in your mouth and pull on it with your lips and tongue: *The baby was sucking on her pacifier.*
**3** to pull air, liquid, or dust somewhere: *The vacuum cleaner sucks up all the dust from the carpet.*

**suck·er** /**suhk**-ur/ *noun* a part of an animal's or insect's body that it uses to stick to a surface: *The suckers on the end of the frog's feet help it to climb trees.*

**sud·den** /**suhd**'n/ *adjective* something that is sudden happens quickly, when you are not expecting it: *There was a sudden flash of light in the sky.*

> **IDIOM with sudden**
> **all of a sudden** suddenly: *We were driving along, when all of a sudden the traffic came to a stop.*

**sud·den·ly** /**suhd**'n-lee/ *adverb* if something happens suddenly, it happens quickly, when you are not expecting it: *The door suddenly opened and two police officers came in.*

**sue** /soo/ *verb* to go to a court of law to try to make someone pay you money because he or she is responsible for something bad that has happened to you: *If a dog bites you, you can sue the owner.*

**suede** /swayd/ *noun* soft leather with a slightly rough surface: *Suede shoes feel nice and soft.*

**suf·fer** /**suhf**-ur/ *verb*
**1** to feel pain or unhappiness: *She suffered a lot when she broke her leg. | When parents have big arguments, it's often the kids who suffer.*
**2** **suffer from** to have an illness: *My grandma suffers from heart disease and she can't walk very far.*
**3** to have something bad happen to you: *The team suffered another bad defeat.*
**4** to become worse in quality: *Tom's grades are suffering because he is not working hard enough.*

**suf·fer·ing** /**suhf**-uhr-ing/ *noun* serious physical or mental pain: *The photograph showed the suffering of families who had lost everything in the earthquake.*

**suf·fi·cient** /suh-**fish**-uhnt/ *adjective* enough: *Try to leave sufficient time to check that you have answered all the questions.*
ANTONYM: **insufficient**
—**sufficiently** /suh-**fish**-uhnt-lee/ *adverb* enough: *She seemed sufficiently pleased with the work I had done.*

**suf·fix** /**suhf**-ikss/ *noun* letters that you add to the end of a word to make a new word: *You can add the suffix "-ness" to the adjective "kind" to make the noun "kindness."*

**suf·fo·cate** /**suhf**-uh-kayt/ *verb* to die because there is not enough air to breathe: *We were stuck in an elevator for an hour and I thought I was going to suffocate.*
—**suffocation** /suhf-uh-**kaysh**-uhn/ *noun* death from suffocating

**suf·frage** /**suhf**-rij/ *noun* the right to vote in national elections: *The struggle for women's suffrage in America began in the 1820s and lasted until the 1920s.*

**sug·ar** /**shug**-ur/ *noun* a sweet white or brown substance used to make food or drinks sweet: *He puts two spoonfuls of sugar in his coffee.*
—**sugary** /**shug**-uhr-ee/ *adjective* containing a lot of sugar: *Sugary drinks can harm your teeth.*

**sug·gest** /suhg-**jest**/ *verb* to tell someone you think he or she should do something: *I suggest that you take the subway – it will be quicker than driving.* ► see **Thesaurus**

**sug·ges·tion** /suhg-**jess**-chuhn/ *noun* an idea that someone suggests: *Does anyone have any suggestions for a good place for a party?*

**suit** /soot/
● *noun*
**1** a set of clothes made of the same material. A suit includes a jacket and pants, or a jacket and a skirt: *I want to look good so I've bought a new suit for the wedding.*
**2** one of the four types of cards in a set of playing cards. The suits are called diamonds, hearts, spades, and clubs. There are 13 cards in each suit.
**3** a claim or complaint that someone brings to a court of law so that a judge can make a decision about it: *The state is filing a suit against the company for not paying its taxes.*
( SYNONYM: **lawsuit** )
● *verb*
**1** if something suits you, it is acceptable and does not cause you problems: *"I can meet you at the mall." "That suits me fine."*
**2** clothes or colors that suit you make you look attractive: *Your new hairstyle really suits you.*

**suit·able** /**soot**-uhb-uhl/ *adjective* right for a person or situation: *The two-bedroom apartment is suitable for a small family.*
( SYNONYM: **appropriate** ) ( ANTONYM: **unsuitable** )

**suit·case** /**soot**-kayss/
*noun* a large bag with a handle. You carry clothes in a suitcase when you travel: *I put all my clothes for my vacation in a big suitcase.*

**suitcase**
handle

**sul·fur** /**suhlf**-ur/ *noun*
a yellow chemical substance that has a strong smell

**sulk** /suhlk/ *verb* to show that you are annoyed about something by not speaking and looking unhappy: *She is sulking because her mom won't let her go to the party.*

**sum** /suhm/
● *noun*
**1** an amount of money: *The house sold for $1.5 million, which is a huge sum of money.*

**2** the amount you get when you add two numbers together: *The sum of 4 and 5 is 9.*
● *verb* (**summing**, **summed**)
**sum up** to repeat the main points mentioned in a speech, document, etc. in a short statement at the end: *At the end of her speech, the principal summed up by saying that she was very proud of the students' achievements.*

**sum·ma·rize** /**suhm**-uh-rīz/ *verb* to give the main information about something, not all the details: *The results of the experiment are summarized at the end of this chapter.*

**sum·ma·ry** /**suhm**-uhr-ee/ *noun* (plural **summaries**) a short statement that gives the main information about something, not all the details: *For homework, write a brief summary of what happens in Chapter 5.*

**sum·mer** /**suhm**-ur/ *noun* the season between spring and fall, when the weather is hottest: *The summer is my favorite time of year because we are outside most of the time.* ▶ see picture at **season**

**sum·mer·time** /**suhm**-ur-tīm/ *noun* the time of year when it is summer: *It gets really hot here in summertime.*

**sum·mit** /**suhm**-it/ *noun*
**1** the top of a mountain: *After a long climb, he reached the summit of the mountain.*
▶ see picture on page **A11**
**2** an important meeting between the leaders of two or more countries: *Japan and the United States will hold a summit to discuss trade.*

**sum·mon** /**suhm**-uhn/ *verb*
**1** to order someone to come to a place: *The principal summoned the boys to her office.*
( SYNONYM: **call** )
**2** to make a great effort to be brave or strong: *He tried to summon the courage to dive off the high board.*

**sun** /suhn/ *noun*
**1** the star in the sky that gives us light and heat. The Earth and other planets move around the Sun: *The sky was blue and the sun was shining.*
▶ see picture at **solar system**

**2** the heat and light that come from the Sun: *At noon, it's too hot to sit in the sun.*
**3** any bright star that has planets going around it

**sun·bathe** /**suhn**-bayth/ *verb* to lie in the sun so that your skin becomes brown: *You'll burn your skin if you sunbathe for too long.*

**sun·block** /**suhn**-blahk/ *noun* a cream that you put on your skin to stop the Sun from burning you ( SYNONYM: **sunscreen** )

**sun·burn** /**suhn**-burn/ *noun* red and sore skin caused by spending too much time in the sun: *Wearing a hat protects your face from sunburn.* —**sunburned** /**suhn**-burnd/ (also **sunburnt** /**suhn**-burnt/) *adjective* having red sore skin caused by spending too much time in the sun: *He was sunburned after a day on the beach.*

**sun·dae** /**suhnd**-ee/ *noun* ice cream covered with nuts, cream, and sweet sauce: *She is eating a chocolate sundae.* ▶ see picture at **dessert**

**Sun·day** /**suhnd**-ee/ *noun* ( ABBREVIATION: **Sun.** ) the first day of the week. Sunday is between Saturday and Monday: *Mike is coming for dinner Sunday night. | We go to church on Sundays.*

**Word Origin: Sunday**

**Sunday** comes from an Old English word that means "day of the sun."

**sun·down** /**suhn**-down/ *noun* the time in the evening when the Sun goes very low in the sky and then disappears: *They work all day from sunrise to sundown.* ( SYNONYM: **sunset** )

**sun·flow·er**

/**suhn**-flow-ur/ *noun* a tall plant with a large yellow flower and a brown center. A sunflower has seeds that you can eat.

sunflower

**sung** /suhng/ *verb* the past participle of sing

**sun·glass·es** /**suhn**-glass-iz/ *plural noun* dark glasses that you wear to protect your eyes when the sun is bright

**sunk** /suhngk/ *verb* the past participle of sink

**sun·light** /**suhn**-līt/ *noun* light from the Sun: *Mary shaded her eyes in the bright sunlight.*

**sun·ny** /**suhn**-ee/ *adjective* if it is sunny, the sun is bright and there are few clouds: *It was a warm sunny morning, with hardly a cloud in the sky.* ( ANTONYM: **cloudy** )

**sun·rise** /**suhn**-rīz/ *noun* the time in the morning when the Sun first appears: *When we are camping, we often get up at sunrise before other people are awake.*

**sun·screen** /**suhn**-skreen/ *noun* a cream that you put on your skin to stop the sun from burning you ( SYNONYM: **sunblock** )

**sun·set** /**suhn**-set/ *noun* the time in the evening when the Sun goes very low in the sky and then disappears: *The sunset turned the sky a deep red.*

sunset

**sun·shine** /**suhn**-shīn/ *noun* the light and heat from the sun: *The sunshine will help the clothes to dry.*

**sun·tan** /**suhn**-tan/ *noun* brown skin that someone with pale skin gets after they have spent time in the sun: *After a few days at the beach, I started to get a suntan.* ( SYNONYM: **tan** )

**su·per** /**soop**-ur/ *adjective* very good: *You guys have done a super job cleaning the house – it looks great.* ( SYNONYM: **great** )

**Word Building**

**superb** | **superhero** | **superior** | **supervisor**
These words all have the Latin word root *super* in them. *Super* means "over" or "above." A *superb* meal is very good, so it is above other meals in quality. A *superhero* has special abilities, for example the ability to fly, that make him even better than other heroes. A *supervisor* makes sure that other people do their jobs correctly, so he or she is above them in rank.

a b c d e f g h i j k l m n o p q r **s** t u v w x y z

**su·perb** /su-**purb**/ *adjective* very good: *The food at that restaurant is superb.* ( SYNONYM: **excellent** )
( ANTONYM: **terrible** )

**su·per·fi·cial** /soop-ur-**fish**-uhl/ *adjective*
**1** not serious and only affecting the outside part of something: *The damage to the car is superficial – it only has a few scratches.*
( SYNONYM: **minor** )
**2** not thorough or complete: *I only have a superficial knowledge of golf – I've watched it on television, but I've never actually played it.*

**su·per·in·tend·ent** /soop-ur-in-**tend**-uhnt/ *noun*
**1** the person who is in charge of all the schools in an area
**2** someone who takes care of an apartment building

**su·pe·ri·or** /suh-**peer**-ee-ur/
● *adjective* better than other people or things: *This hotel is far superior to the place we stayed last year.* ( ANTONYM: **inferior** )
—**superiority** /suh-peer-ee-**or**-uht-ee/ *noun* the quality of being superior: *The team showed its superiority and won the game.*
● *noun* someone who has a higher position than you in your job: *Maria's a math teacher, and Steve is her superior because he's head of the math department.*

**su·per·la·tive** /suh-**purl**-uht-iv/ *noun* a form of a word that shows that something is the best, worst, biggest, smallest, etc.: *The superlative of "big" is "biggest."*

**su·per·mar·ket** /**soop**-ur-mark-it/ *noun* a large store that sells food and things that people need for the house: *Once a week, we do a lot of shopping at the supermarket.*

**su·per·nat·u·ral** /soop-ur-**nach**-uhr-uhl/ *adjective* supernatural things are not possible to explain using science and the laws of nature: *I don't believe that supernatural beings like ghosts and spirits really exist.*

**su·per·sti·tion** /soop-ur-**stish**-uhn/ *noun* a belief that some things are lucky and some are not: *Black cats aren't unlucky – that's just silly superstition.*
—**superstitious** /soop-ur-**stish**-uhss/ *adjective* having many superstitions: *Betsy was very*

superstitious and thought that walking under a ladder would bring bad luck.

**su·per·vise** /**soop**-ur-vīz/ *verb* to be in charge of an activity or person and make sure that the activity is done correctly or that someone behaves correctly: *The teachers always supervise the students when they are in the playground during recess.*

**su·per·vi·sion** /soop-ur-**vizh**-uhn/ *noun* the activity of supervising someone or something: *The children receive constant supervision when they go on a field trip.*

**su·per·vis·or** /**soop**-ur-vīz-ur/ *noun* someone who is in charge of a place, activity, or group of people: *You should tell your supervisor at work if you're going to be late.*

**sup·per** /**suhp**-ur/ *noun* an evening meal: *We usually have supper around seven. | For supper, we had chicken and a salad.* ( SYNONYM: **dinner** )

**sup·pli·er** /suh-**plī**-ur/ *noun* a company that provides products for a business or organization to buy: *The school has found a new supplier for paper.*

**sup·ply** /suh-**plī**/
● *noun* (plural **supplies**)
**1** an amount of something that is available to use: *We took a week's supply of food with us when we went camping.* ( SYNONYM: **store** )
**2 supplies** food and other things that people need: *During the heavy snow, supplies had to be taken to some areas by helicopter.*
● *verb* (**supplies**, **supplying**, **supplied**)
to give or sell something to someone who needs it: *The farmers supply milk and vegetables to people in the town.* ( SYNONYM: **provide** )

**sup·port** /suh-**port**/
● *verb*
**1** to hold something so that it does not fall: *The bridge is supported by a tower at each end.*
**2** to say that you agree with a person, group, or idea: *Most parents support the principal's plan to change the school uniform.*
**3** to provide the money for you to buy the things you need in order to live: *He works hard to support his family.*
**4** to help a person by being kind to them during a difficult time in their life: *Friends should support each other when things go wrong.*

● *noun*
if you give someone or something your support, you help them or say that you hope they will be successful: *Please show your support for our charity by donating money.*

**sup·port·er** /suh-**port**-ur/ *noun* someone who supports a person, group, or plan: *His supporters hope he wins the election.* ( SYNONYM: **fan** )

**sup·port·ive** /suh-**port**-iv/ *adjective* a supportive person gives you help and advice when you have a problem: *When Mom was sick, all the neighbors were very supportive and helped us.*

**sup·pose** /suh-**pohz**/ *verb*
**1** if you are supposed to do something, you should do it: *You're supposed to call the school if you're sick and staying at home.*
**2** if something is supposed to happen, it should happen: *The game was supposed to start at 10:00, but it didn't start until 10:30.*
**3** if something is supposed to be good or bad, a lot of people say that it is good or bad: *I've never been to Boston, but it's supposed to be a nice city.*
**4 I suppose** used when you think that something is probably true: *His car isn't here, so I suppose he has gone out.*
**5 suppose ...** used when talking about what might happen: *Suppose you won the lottery, what would you spend the money on?*
( SYNONYM: **supposing** )

**sup·pos·ed·ly** /suh-**pohz**-id-lee/ *adverb* if something is supposedly true, a lot of people say that it is true, but it may not be true: *Supposedly, it rains almost every day in Seattle, but when I went there it was sunny.*

**sup·pos·ing** /suh-**pohz**-ing/ *conjunction* used to talk about what might happen or be true: *Supposing we win the next two games, then we will be in the finals.*

**su·preme** /suh-**preem**/ *adjective* highest, best, or most important: *The president is the supreme commander of the armed forces.*

**Su·preme Court** /suh-preem **kort**/ *noun* the highest and most important court in the United States

**sure** /shoor/
● *adjective*
**1** certain about something: *I'm sure he said to meet at six.* | *"How long will it take us to drive there?" "I'm not sure."* ▶ see **Thesaurus**
**2** certain to happen: *If you lie to her, she's sure to find out.*

**IDIOMS with sure**
**for sure** certainly or definitely: *The boy disappeared and no one knows for sure what happened to him.*
**make sure** to check that something is true or that something has been done: *I checked the back door to make sure that it was locked.*
● *adverb*
**1** used to say "yes" to someone: *"Can I get a ride to the mall with you?" "Sure."*
**2** used when emphasizing something you are saying: *It sure is hot in here.* ( SYNONYM: **certainly** )

**sure·ly** /**shoor**-lee/ *adverb* used when you are surprised about something: *Surely you're not going to walk to Pete's house – it's at least five miles.*

**surf** /surf/
● *verb*
**1** to ride on ocean waves while standing on a board: *When you're learning to surf, you fall in the water a lot.* ▶ see picture on page **A10**
**2** to look quickly at different pages on the Internet: *I surfed the Internet looking for information about the movie.*
—**surfing** /**surf**-ing/ *noun* the activity of surfing: *Did you go surfing when you were in California?*
● *noun*
the white substance that forms on waves as they reach the shore: *We walked along the beach and let the surf wash over our feet.*

surf

a b c d e f g h i j k l m n o p q r **s** t u v w x y z

**sur·face** /**surf**-uhss/
● *noun*
**1** the outside or top part of something: *Over 70% of the Earth's surface is covered with water. | There were cracks in the surface of the road.*
**2** the qualities that someone or something appears to have, when the other qualities are hidden or not easy to notice: *On the surface, Ted appeared calm but inside he was feeling really nervous.*
**3** one of the sides of a solid object: *A cube has six surfaces.*
● *verb*
to rise up to the surface of water: *Suddenly a whale surfaced right beside our boat.*
( SYNONYM: **come up** ) ( ANTONYM: **sink** )

**surf·board** /**surf**-bord/ *noun* a board that you stand on to ride along ocean waves for fun
▶ see picture on page **A10**

**surge** /surj/
● *verb* to suddenly move forward very quickly: *He hit the gas pedal and the car surged forward.*
● *noun* a sudden large increase in something: *There was a sudden surge of interest in the game, and all the kids wanted to play it.*

**sur·geon** /**surj**-uhn/ *noun* a doctor who cuts open someone's body to fix or replace something inside: *Surgeons will perform an operation to remove the bullet.*

**sur·ger·y** /**surj**-uhr-ee/ *noun* the act of cutting open someone's body to fix or replace something inside: *She needs surgery to fix her broken leg.*

**sur·name** /**sur**-naym/ *noun* your family's name. In English, this name comes after your other names: *Roberto's surname is Bolano.*
( SYNONYM: **last name** )

**sur·plus** /**surp**-luhss/
● *noun* more of something than you need or can use: *The U.S. produces a surplus of corn and sells a lot to other countries.* ( ANTONYM: **shortage** )
● *adjective* surplus things are ones that are more than you need: *She gives the surplus vegetables from her garden to her neighbors.*

**sur·prise** /sur-**prīz**/
● *noun*
**1** the feeling you have when something happens

that you do not expect: *She looked at me with surprise when I said I didn't agree with her.*
**2** something that you do not expect to happen: *It was a surprise when Tom failed his math test, because he's really smart.*
● *adjective*
not expected: *We're having a surprise birthday party for him – you must not tell him about it.*
● *verb*
to make someone have a feeling of surprise: *It surprised me when he shouted, because he never usually gets angry with anyone.*
—**surprised** /sur-**prīzd**/ *adjective* having a feeling of surprise: *I'm surprised you went to the game – I didn't think you liked baseball.*
▶ see **Thesaurus**
—**surprising** /sur-**prīz**-ing/ *adjective* if something is surprising, you do not expect it to happen: *He ran up the hill with surprising ease, when you know he isn't in good shape.* ▶ see **Thesaurus**

**Word Family: surprise**
**surprise** *noun* | **surprise** *verb* | **surprise** *adjective* | **surprised** *adjective* | **surprising** *adjective*

**sur·ren·der** /suh-**rend**-ur/
● *verb* to stop fighting because you know that you cannot win: *The police ordered him to drop his gun and surrender.*
● *noun* the act of surrendering: *The General announced his army's surrender.*

**sur·round** /suh-**rownd**/ *verb* to be all around something or someone: *The yard is surrounded by a wall. | He scored a goal and his teammates surrounded him, slapping his back.*

**surround**

The house is surrounded by a fence.

**sur·round·ings** /suh-**rownd**-ingz/ *plural noun* the things that are around you in the place where you are: *I was glad to be back home in familiar surroundings.*

### sur·vey

● *noun* /**sur**-vay/ a set of questions that you ask a large number of people to find out about their opinions and behavior: *The survey showed that most students were happy at school.*

● *verb* /sur-**vay**/ to ask a large number of people a set of questions to find out about their opinions or behavior: *We surveyed 100 students to find out what kind of foods they eat.*

### sur·viv·al /sur-**vīv**-uhl/ *noun* the state of continuing to live after a difficult or dangerous time: *When people get lost in the desert, their chances of survival are not very good.*

### sur·vive /sur-**vīv**/ *verb* to continue to live after an accident, illness, or war: *When the plane crashed, only 12 of the 100 passengers survived.* —**survivor** /sur-**vīv**-ur/ *noun* someone who survives: *The boat sank in the ocean and there were no survivors.*

**Word Family: survive**

**survive** *verb* | **survival** *noun* | **survivor** *noun*

### sus·pect

● *verb* /suh-**spekt**/
**1** to think that someone may be guilty of a crime: *We suspect him of stealing the money, but we can't prove it.*
**2** to think that something is probably true, especially something bad: *From the sound of his voice, I suspect that there's something wrong.*
SYNONYM: **think**

● *noun* /**suhss**-pekt/
someone who the police think may have committed a crime: *Police have arrested a suspect in the murder case.*

**Word Family: suspect**

**suspect** *verb* | **suspect** *noun* | **suspicion** *noun* | **suspicious** *adjective*

### sus·pend /suh-**spend**/ *verb*
**1** to stop someone from going to a school, being on a team, or working for an organization for a period of time, as a punishment: *She was*

suspended from school for cheating on a test.
**2** to officially stop something from continuing for a short time: *The company will have to suspend the construction work because it does not have enough money.*
**3** if something is suspended somewhere, it hangs there: *The stage lights are suspended from a platform above the stage.*

### sus·pense /suh-**spenss**/ *noun* a nervous and excited feeling that you get when you do not know what is going to happen next: *The book keeps readers in suspense until the very last page.*

### sus·pen·sion /suh-**spensh**-uhn/ *noun*
**1** a punishment in which someone is stopped from going to a school, being on a team, or working for an organization for a period of time: *He got a three-day suspension from school for fighting.*
**2** the part of a vehicle that makes it more comfortable to drive on roads that are not smooth: *My dad's truck has good suspension and you don't feel the bumps on the road.*

### sus·pi·cion /suh-**spish**-uhn/ *noun*
**1** a feeling that something bad is probably true: *I had a suspicion that she was lying, but I could not prove it.*
**2** a feeling that you do not trust someone: *Strangers are treated with suspicion by the local people.*

### sus·pi·cious /suh-**spish**-uhss/ *adjective*
**1** not trusting someone or something: *She is suspicious of anybody she doesn't know.*
**2** likely to be dishonest or illegal: *If you see any suspicious behavior, such as people hanging around the house late at night, report it to the police.*

### sus·tain /suh-**stayn**/ *verb*
**1** to make something continue to exist or happen: *They have sustained their friendship for 20 years.* SYNONYM: **maintain**
**2** to experience something bad, for example damage or injury: *She fell from a horse and sustained a serious head injury.* SYNONYM: **suffer**

### sus·tain·a·ble /suh-**stayn**-uhb-uhl/ *adjective* sustainable methods and forms of energy do not harm the environment: *The school uses a wind turbine to produce sustainable energy.*

**swal·low** /**swahl**-oh/
● *verb*
to make food or drink go down your throat:
*I swallowed the last bite of my sandwich and got up to leave.*

> **IDIOM with swallow**
> **swallow your pride** to do something even though it embarrasses you: *You should swallow your pride and say you're sorry.*

● *noun*
**1** an act of making food or drink go down your throat: *Mikey drank his milk in one swallow.*
**2** a small bird with a tail that has two points
▶ see picture on page **A4**

**swam** /swam/ *verb* the past tense of **swim**

**swamp** /swahmp/ *noun* a large area of land that is always very wet: *The swamp is full of mosquitoes.* ▶ see picture on page **A10**
—**swampy** /**swahmp**-ee/ *adjective* like a swamp: *The land around the pond was a swampy marsh.*

**swan** /swahn/ *noun* a large white bird with a long neck. Swans swim on rivers and lakes.

swan

**swap** /swahp/
● *verb* (**swapping**, **swapped**) to exchange something you have for something someone else has: *My sister and I are the same size and we often swap clothes.*
( SYNONYM: **trade** )

● *noun* an act of swapping things: *Let's make a swap – you can have my T-shirt, and I'll take yours.*

**swarm** /sworm/
● *noun*
a large group of insects that move together: *The swarm of locusts destroyed crops as it moved across the state.*
● *verb*
**1** to move somewhere in a large group: *Hundreds of fans began swarming into the stadium.*
**2 be swarming with** if a place is swarming with people, it is full of people moving around: *The mall was swarming with people.*

swarm

hive

a swarm of bees

**sway** /sway/ *verb* to move slowly from one side to the other: *The palm trees sway in the wind.*

**swear** /swair/ *verb* (**swore** /swor/, **sworn** /sworn/)
**1** to say very rude words: *I want you to apologize for swearing at your sister, and you must never use words like that again.*
**2** to make a promise to do something: *When Juan became a citizen, he swore to support the U.S.*
**3** to say firmly that what you are saying is true: *I swear I didn't take your pen.*

**sweat** /swet/
● *verb* to have water come out of your skin because you are hot or doing exercise: *I always sweat a lot when I play basketball.*
( SYNONYM: **perspire** )
● *noun* water that comes out of your skin when you are hot: *After the race, my shirt was covered in sweat.* ( SYNONYM: **perspiration** )
—**sweaty** /**swet**-ee/ *adjective* covered in sweat: *Sam was nervous, which made the palms of his hands sweaty.*

**sweat·er** /**swet**-ur/ *noun* a piece of warm clothing for the top part of your body: *Take a sweater with you in case it gets cold.*

**sweat·shirt** /**swet**-shurt/ *noun* a soft thick piece of clothing for the top part of your body: *I put on a sweatshirt and shorts and went jogging.*

**sweat·suit** /**swet**-soot/ (also **sweats** /swetss/) *noun* a set of clothes made of thick soft cotton that you wear when you play sports

**sweep** /sweep/ *verb* (**swept** /swept/)
**1** to clean the dirt from something using a brush: *I sweep the kitchen floor with a broom.*
**2** to move quickly: *The president's car swept past the crowd of people outside the White House.*

**sweet** /sweet/ *adjective*
**1** containing sugar or tasting like sugar: *Chocolate drinks are very sweet.* (ANTONYM: **sour**)
**2** pleasant, kind, and friendly: *It is very sweet of you to remember my birthday.* (SYNONYM: **nice**)
—**sweeten** /**sweet**'n/ *verb* to make something sweet: *She sweetened the pancakes with maple syrup.*

**sweet·heart** /**sweet**-hart/ *noun*
**1** used when talking to someone you love: *I love you too, sweetheart.*
**2** the person that you love: *Juanita married her high school sweetheart.*

**sweet po·ta·to** /sweet puh-**tayt**-oh/ *noun* a sweet-tasting vegetable that looks like a red potato ▶ see picture on page **A7**

**swell** /swel/ (also **swell up**) *verb* (**swelled, swollen** /**swohl**-uhn/) to get bigger and rounder, especially because of being hurt: *My finger began to swell up where the bee had stung me.*
—**swelling** /**swel**-ing/ *noun* an area on your body that becomes larger than usual because of injury or sickness: *He put ice on his ankle to help the swelling go down.*

**swept** /swept/ *verb* the past tense and past participle of **sweep**

**swerve** /swurv/ *verb* to move suddenly to the left or right: *The car swerved to avoid hitting the dog.*

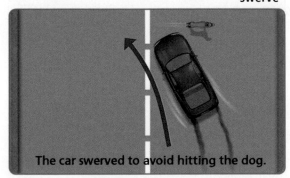
swerve
**The car swerved to avoid hitting the dog.**

**swift** /swift/ *adjective* happening or moving very quickly: *He had a swift look at his watch.*
—**swiftly** /**swift**-lee/ *adverb* in a swift way: *The bird moved swiftly through the air.*

**swim** /swim/
● *verb* (**swimming, swam** /swam/, **swum** /swuhm/) to move through the water using your

arms and legs: *Let's swim to the island and back again.*
● *noun* if you go for a swim, you swim in some water for enjoyment: *On vacation, I went for a swim in the pool every morning.*
—**swimming** /**swim**-ing/ *noun* the activity of moving through the water using your arms and legs: *I love going swimming in the ocean.*
—**swimmer** /**swim**-ur/ *noun* someone who swims: *Sally is a strong swimmer – she can swim 50 laps of the pool.*

swim

breaststroke

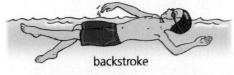
backstroke

crawl

**swim·suit** /**swim**-soot/ *noun* a piece of clothing worn for swimming (SYNONYM: **bathing suit**)

**swin·dle** /**swind**-uhl/
● *verb* to get money or things from someone by doing something dishonest: *He swindled the company out of thousands of dollars.*
● *noun* a dishonest plan to get money from people

**swing** /swing/
● *verb* (**swung** /swuhng/) to move backward and forward: *The monkeys swing from branch to branch in the trees.* | *The bathroom door swung open.*
● *noun* a seat hanging

swing

from ropes or chains that you sit on. The seat moves backward and forward in the air: *The park has swings and slides for kids to play on.*

**Swiss** /swiss/
- *adjective* relating to or coming from Switzerland: *He bought an expensive Swiss watch.*
- *plural noun* **the Swiss** people from Switzerland: *Most of the Swiss speak German.*

**switch** /swich/

**switch**

- *verb*
**1** to change from doing one thing to doing another: *I played soccer for a while but then I switched to baseball.*
**2** to take what someone else has, while they take what you have: *Do you want to switch seats with me so you can see out of the window?* ( SYNONYMS: **exchange, trade** )
**3 switch off** to make a light or machine stop working by pressing a switch: *She said good night and switched off the light.*
( SYNONYM: **turn off** )
**4 switch on** to make a light or machine start working by pressing a switch: *Could you switch the TV on? There's a show I want to watch.*
( SYNONYM: **turn on** )
- *noun*
**1** a thing that you press to make a light or machine start or stop working: *I flicked the switch and the light came on.*
**2** a change from one thing to another: *A lot of people weren't ready to make the switch to digital TV.*

**swol·len** /swohl-uhn/
- *verb* the past participle of swell
- *adjective* a part of your body that is swollen is bigger than usual because of injury or sickness: *I twisted my ankle playing football and now it's really swollen.*

**swoop** /swoop/ *verb* to move quickly down through the air: *The eagle swooped down and grabbed a rabbit.*

**sword** /sord/ *noun* a weapon with a long sharp blade and a handle: *The Roman soldiers marched forward with their swords in their hands.*
▶ see picture at **armor**

**swore** /swor/ *verb* the past tense of **swear**

**sworn** /sworn/ *verb* the past participle of swear

**swum** /swuhm/ *verb* the past participle of **swim**

**swung** /swuhng/ *verb* the past tense and past participle of **swing**

**syc·a·more** /**sik**-uh-mor/ *noun* a tree with broad leaves. The old bark of a sycamore tree comes off in layers as the new bark is growing.

**syl·la·ble** /**sil**-uhb-uhl/ *noun* a section that a word can be divided into. Each syllable has a single vowel sound: *"Dog" has one syllable, "butter" has two syllables, and "computer" has three syllables.*

**sym·bol** /**sim**-buhl/ *noun* a sign, picture, object, etc. that represents something else: *The cross is a symbol of the Christian Church.*
—**symbolize** /**sim**-buh-līz/ *verb* to be the symbol of something: *The children stood in a circle and held hands to symbolize peace.*

**sym·bol·ism** /**sim**-buh-liz-uhm/ *noun* the use of pictures, shapes, colors, or words to represent an idea: *The picture is full of religious symbolism – for example, the shepherd taking care of his sheep represents Jesus.*

**sym·met·ri·cal** /suh-**metr**-ik-uhl/ *adjective* having two sides that are exactly the same size and shape: *A perfect circle is a symmetrical shape.*

**symmetrical**

*A butterfly's wings are symmetrical.*

**sym·me·try** /**sim**-uht-ree/ *noun* the quality of having two sides that are exactly the same size and shape: *Can you see the symmetry in the picture of the butterfly? | When you fold the square in half along the line of symmetry, both sides match.*

**sym·pa·thet·ic** /simp-uh-**thet**-ik/ *adjective* showing that you care about and understand how someone feels: *The teachers are sympathetic to children who find school work hard, and they will do a lot to help the students.*
( ANTONYM: **unsympathetic** )

**sym·pa·thize** /simp-uh-**thīz**/ *verb* to show that you care about and understand someone's problems: *I can sympathize with kids who are bullied because it happened to me.*

**sym·pa·thy** /**simp**-uhth-ee/ *noun* (plural **sympathies**)
**1** the feeling of caring about and understanding someone's problems: *The president expressed his sympathy for the flood victims and promised to help them.*
**2** belief in or support for an idea, plan, or opinion: *I have a lot of sympathy with the idea that smoking should be completely banned in public places.*

**Word Family: sympathy**

**sympathy** *noun* | **sympathetic** *adjective* | **sympathize** *verb*

**sym·pho·ny** /**simf**-uhn-ee/ *noun* (plural **symphonies**) a long piece of music that is played by an orchestra

**symp·tom** /**simpt**-uhm/ *noun* something that shows you may have a particular illness: *A sore throat is often the first symptom of a cold.*

**syn·a·gogue**
/**sin**-uh-gahg/ *noun* a building where Jewish people go to pray, worship, and study religion

**syn·o·nym** /**sin**-uhn-im/ *noun* a word with the same meaning as another word: *"Big" is a synonym of "large."*

( ANTONYM: **antonym** )

synagogue

**syn·thet·ic** /sin-**thet**-ik/ *adjective* a synthetic substance is not natural. It is made by people in a factory: *The shoes were made from some kind of synthetic material, not leather.*

**sy·ringe** /suh-**rinj**/ *noun* a hollow tube attached to a needle, which is used for giving medicine or taking out liquids through the skin

**syr·up** /**sur**-uhp/ *noun* a thick sweet liquid made from sugar: *She put some syrup on her pancakes.*

**sys·tem** /**sist**-uhm/ *noun*
**1** a way of organizing or doing something: *In our political system, every citizen has the right to vote.*
**2** a group of computers that are connected to each other: *Information about students is held on the school's computer system.*
**3** a group of things or parts that work together for one particular purpose: *The city's transportation system is very good.*

**sys·tem·at·ic** /sist-uh-**mat**-ik/ *adjective* done in a carefully organized way: *They did a systematic check of all of the electrical equipment in the school.*
—**systematically** /sist-uh-**mat**-ik-lee/ *adverb* in a carefully organized way: *She arranged the books systematically according to subject.*

a
b
c
d
e
f
g
h
i
j
k
l
m
n
o
p
q
r
s
**t**
u
v
w
x
y
z

# Tt

**tab** /tab/ *noun*
**1** a bill that shows how much you need to pay for your food or drink: *He ordered a drink at the hotel bar and put it on his tab.*
**2** a small piece of metal or plastic that you pull to open a container: *The label says "pull tab to open."*

**ta·ble** /**tayb**-uhl/ *noun*
**1** a piece of furniture with a flat top on legs: *We eat our breakfast at the kitchen table.*
**2** a list of numbers or other information. A table is arranged in rows on the page: *The table shows the number of children in each grade for the past five years.*

**ta·ble·cloth** /**tayb**-uhl-kloth/ *noun* a large piece of cloth used for covering a table

**ta·ble of con·tents** /tayb-uhl uhv **kahn**-tentss/ *noun* a list at the beginning of a book that tells you the order and the page numbers of the chapters

**ta·ble·spoon** /**tayb**-uhl-spoon/ *noun* a large spoon used for measuring or serving food: *Melt two tablespoons of butter and add a tablespoon of flour.*

**tab·let** /**tab**-lit/ *noun*
**1** a small round piece of medicine that you swallow: *The doctor will give you some tablets to stop the pain.* ( SYNONYM: **pill** )
**2** a set of pieces of paper for writing on that are glued together at the top ( SYNONYM: **pad** )
**3** a flat piece of stone with words cut into it: *The names of the soldiers are written on stone tablets.*

**ta·ble ten·nis** /**tayb**-uhl ten-iss/ *noun* a game played on a table by two or four players who hit a small plastic ball to each other across a net ( SYNONYM: **Ping-Pong** )

**tack** /tak/ *noun* a short pin or nail with a large round flat top: *She attached the notice to the board with some tacks.* ( SYNONYM: **thumbtack** )

**tack·le** /**tak**-uhl/
● *verb*
**1** to deal with a difficult problem: *What do you think is the best way to tackle the problem of bullying on the playground?*
**2** to make a player fall to the ground in football, so that he or she cannot carry the ball forward: *Before he could reach the line, he was tackled by two players from the other team.*
● *noun*
the act of tackling someone in football

**tackle**

**ta·co** /**tahk**-oh/ *noun* (plural **tacos**) a type of Mexican food consisting of a corn tortilla that is folded in half and filled with meat, beans, or other food

**tact** /takt/ *noun* the ability to say or do things carefully and politely so that you do not upset someone: *The teacher showed a lot of tact and he was careful not to mention my mother's illness.*

**tact·ful** /**takt**-fuhl/ *adjective* careful not to say or do something that will upset someone: *I will try to tell him in a tactful way that he hasn't been chosen for the team.* ( ANTONYM: **tactless** )
—**tactfully** /**takt**-fuhl-ee/ *adverb* in a tactful way

**tac·tic** /**takt**-ik/ *noun* a plan for doing or achieving something: *Next time we changed our tactics and we won the game.*

**tact·less** /**takt**-liss/ *adjective* saying or doing things that will upset someone because you do not think carefully enough about what you say: *It was tactless to tell her that she needs to lose weight.* ( ANTONYM: **tactful** )
—**tactlessly** /**takt**-liss-lee/ in a tactless way

**tad·pole** /**tad**-pohl/
*noun* a small animal that grows to become a frog or toad. A tadpole lives in water and has a large head and a long tail. As it grows, it stops having a tail and starts to grow legs. ▶ see picture at **life cycle**

tadpole

**taf·fy** /**taf**-ee/ *noun* a type of soft chewy candy

**tag** /tag/ *noun*
**1** a small piece of paper, plastic, etc. that is attached to something and gives information about it: *The hotel employees all wear name tags on their coats, so that you know their names.*
**2** a children's game in which one player chases the others: *Let's play tag – you try to catch me first.*

**tail** /tayl/ *noun*
**1** a part of an animal that sticks out from its bottom. The tail is often long and thin, and the animal can move it: *A dog wags its tail when it is happy.* ▶ see picture at **horse**
**2** the back part of an aircraft: *We were sitting at the back of the plane, in the tail.* ▶ see picture at **airplane**
**3 tails** the side of a coin that does not have a picture of someone's head on it: *I'll flip the coin and you tell me "heads" or "tails."*
( ANTONYM: **tails** )

**tail·light** /**tayl**-līt/ *noun* one of the two red lights at the back of a car

**tai·lor** /**tayl**-ur/ *noun* someone whose job is to make clothes, especially men's suits

**Tai·wan·ese** /tī-wah-**neez**/
● *adjective* relating to or coming from Taiwan: *Have you ever eaten Taiwanese food?*
● *noun* the **Taiwanese** people from Taiwan

**take** /tayk/ *verb* (**took** /tuk/, **taken** /**tayk**-uhn/)
**1** to move someone or something from one place to another: *Dad takes me to school in the morning.* | *The waitress took away our plates.* ▶ see **Thesaurus**
**2** to do a particular action: *I took a deep breath and dived into the water.* | *Mom is taking a bath.*
**3** to need an amount of time, money, effort, etc.: *It takes about seven hours to fly from London to*

New York. | *The party took a lot of effort to organize.*
**4** to steal or borrow something without asking someone's permission: *I left my cell phone on the table and someone took it.*
**5** to accept something that has been offered to you: *Larry decided not to take the job.* | *I took her advice and went to see a doctor.*
**6** to get hold of something in your hands: *She took a knife and began to chop the onions.*
**7** to use a car, bus, train, etc.: *We can take the bus to Grandma's house.*
**8** to study a subject: *What classes are you taking next semester?*
**9** to do a test: *Sandy's taking her driving test tomorrow.*
**10** to drink or swallow some medicine or a drug: *If you've got a headache, take an aspirin.*
**11 take after** to look or behave like another person in your family: *Karen is very good at sports – she takes after her mom.*
**12 take back** to return something to the store where you bought it: *If the dress doesn't fit properly, you can take it back.*
**13 take off** to remove clothing from your body: *Take your shoes off when you come into the house.*
**14 take off** if an airplane takes off, it leaves the ground and goes up into the air: *The plane took off right on time.* ▶ see picture at **land**

---

**Word Choice:** take, bring

**Take** means to move something to another place, or go with someone to another place: *Don't forget to take your coat with you.* | *Mrs. Gomez will take you home after school.*

**Bring** means to take someone or something to the place where you are now, or a place you are going to with other people: *Did you bring your homework?* | *Elise brought her friend with her to the party.*

---

**tak·en** /**tayk**-uhn/ *verb* the past participle of take

**take·out** /**tayk**-owt/ *noun* food that you buy at a restaurant to eat at home: *Mom didn't feel like cooking so we got a takeout.*

**tale** /tayl/ *noun* a story: *The book tells the tale of a princess who lives alone in a big castle.*
( SYNONYM: **story** )

**tal·ent** /**tal**-uhnt/ *noun* an ability to do something well: *Todd has a real talent for music – he plays the violin and the piano really well.* —**talented** /**tal**-uhnt-id/ *adjective* very good at something: *She's a very talented artist and has won a lot of competitions.*

**talk** /tok/

● *verb*

**1** to say things to someone: *She's talking to Emma on the phone.*
▶ see **Thesaurus**

**talk**

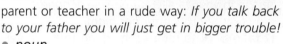

She is talking on her cell phone.

**2** to discuss something: *Let's talk about where to go on our vacation.* | *Why don't you talk it over with your teacher before you decide?*

**3 talk back** to answer a parent or teacher in a rude way: *If you talk back to your father you will just get in bigger trouble!*

● *noun*

**1** a conversation: *I need to have a talk with Suzanne about the way she's been behaving.*

**2** a speech to a group of people: *Ms. Mason will be giving a talk on starting middle school.*

**Word Choice: talk, tell, say**

You **talk** about a subject: *The teacher talked about how plants grow.*

You **tell** someone facts or information: *The teacher told us that plants need sunlight to grow.*

You **say** words: *The teacher said that plants need sunlight to grow.* | *She said, "Plants need sunlight to grow."*

**Word Family: talk**

talk *verb* | talk *noun* | talkative *adjective*

**talk·a·tive** /**tok**-uht-iv/ *adjective* someone who is talkative talks a lot: *He's very talkative and the teacher is always telling him to be quiet in class.*

**talk show** /**tok** shoh/ *noun* a television show in which famous people answer questions about themselves: *The star was on the talk show to talk about his latest movie.*

**tall** /tol/ *adjective*

**tall**

He is taller than his brother.

**1** higher than most other people or things: *William is very tall – he's 6 foot and he's only 13 years old.* | *There were some tall trees behind the house.*
( **ANTONYM: short** )

**2** having a particular height: *I'm almost five feet tall.*

**Word Choice: tall, high**

You use **tall** to talk about the height of people and trees: *She is five feet tall.* | *He is a tall man.* | *A redwood tree is very tall.*

You use **tall** to talk about buildings: *What is the tallest building in Chicago?*

You use **tall** to talk about other narrow objects: *a tall flagpole*

You use **high** to talk about mountains, buildings, walls, or fences: *Mount Whitney is the highest mountain in California.* | *The fence was too high for me to climb over.*

You use **high** to talk about how far something is from the ground: *The apples were high up in the tree.* | *There's a high diving board for the bigger kids.*

**tal·low** /**tal**-oh/ *noun* animal fat used for making candles

**tall tale** /tol **tayl**/ *noun* a story that is difficult to believe: *She told us a tall tale about Paul Bunyan, the biggest man who ever lived.*

**tal·ly** /**tal**-ee/ *noun* (plural **tallies**) a record you keep when you are counting something: *Keep a tally of each player's score.*

**tal·ly chart** /**tal**-ee chart/ *noun* a math drawing which shows how many things there are. In a tally chart, you write the mark (I) for every thing there is. You usually write the marks in groups of five.

**tal·ly mark** /**tal**-ee mark/ *noun* a mark (I) that you write to keep a record when you are counting something. If you have counted four things, you would write IIII.

**Tal·mud** /**tahl**-mud/ *noun* the set of Jewish laws

**tam·bou·rine**
/tam-buh-**reen**/ *noun* a round musical instrument that you shake or hit with your hand. It looks like a small drum with flat round metal pieces around the edge.

**tambourine**
tambourine

**tame** /taym/
● *adjective* a tame animal is one that is not afraid of people because it has been with people a lot: *The bird is very tame, and it will eat from your hand.*
ANTONYM: **wild**
● *verb* to train a wild animal so that it is not frightened of people: *In zoos, wild animals are tamed so they do not attack their keepers.*

**tan** /tan/ *noun*
**1** dark skin that you get after you have been in the sun: *She is sunbathing because she wants to get a tan.* SYNONYM: **suntan**
**2** a pale yellow-brown color

**tan·ger·ine** /tanj-uh-**reen**/ *noun* a fruit that looks like a small orange ▶ see picture on page **A7**

**tan·gle** /**tang**-guhl/ *verb* to twist hair, wire, or threads together into messy knots: *The wind had tangled her long hair and she needed to brush it.*
—**tangled** /**tang**-guhld/ *adjective* twisted in a messy knot: *The wires were all tangled.*

**tangle**
tangled Christmas lights

**tan·go** /**tang**-goh/ *noun* a South American dance, or the music for this dance: *Do you know how to dance the tango?*

**tank** /tangk/ *noun*
**1** a large container that holds liquid or gas: *She filled up the car's gas tank.* ▶ see picture at **motorcycle**
**2** a military vehicle with guns on it and metal belts over its wheels: *The U.S. attacked Iraq using tanks and missiles.*

**tank·er** /**tangk**-ur/ *noun* a large ship or truck that carries liquids: *an oil tanker*

**tanned** /tand/ *adjective* having darker skin than usual because you have been in the sun: *Jimmy looked tanned and relaxed after his vacation in Hawaii.*

**tan·trum** /**tan**-truhm/ *noun* a time when a young child suddenly becomes angry and starts shouting and crying: *My brother had a tantrum and started screaming because Mom wouldn't buy him any candy.*

**tap** /tap/
● *verb* (**tapping**, **tapped**) to gently hit your fingers or foot against something: *He tapped me on the shoulder to get my attention.*
● *noun*
**1** a gentle hit: *I heard a tap on the window and went to see who was there.*
**2** an object that starts and stops the flow of liquid from a pipe or container: *He turned off the water tap to stop the flow of water.*
SYNONYM: **faucet**

**tap**
She tapped him on the shoulder.

**tap danc·ing** /**tap** danss-ing/ *noun* a type of dancing that you do wearing special shoes. The shoes have metal parts on the bottom so that they make a sound when you dance.

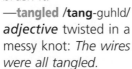

## tape /tayp/

● *noun*

**1** a long band of sticky plastic that you use for sticking things together: *If you tear a page, fix it with tape.* ▶ see picture on page **A9**

**2** something used for recording sounds or pictures. A tape is a long thin band in a plastic case: *Put the tape in the VCR and press the "play" button.*

● *verb*

**1** to record sounds or pictures onto a tape: *Dad taped the movie so we could watch it later.*

**2** to stick something onto something else using tape: *Wrap up the package, then tape or glue an address label on it.*

## tape meas·ure /tayp

mezh-ur/ *noun* a long band of cloth or metal with inches or centimeters marked on it. You use it to measure things: *Dad used a tape measure to measure the room.*

**tape measure**

## tape re·cord·er /tayp ri-kord-ur/ *noun* a

machine that records and plays music and talking: *Police used a tape recorder to record the interview.*

## tar /tar/ *noun* a thick black substance used for

making roads: *The tar on the road is very hot and sticky because it hasn't dried yet.*

## ta·ran·tu·la /tuh-**ranch**-uhl-uh/ *noun* a big hairy

spider that lives in hot countries. Tarantulas can bite people.

### Word Origin: tarantula

When explorers in the New World saw **tarantulas**, they named them after a town in Italy called Taranto. Taranto was in an area where big spiders were common. So, tarantula means something like "from Taranto."

## tar·get /**targ**-it/ *noun*

**1** the aim or result that you try to achieve: *We're raising money for our school, and our target is $5,000.* ( SYNONYM: **goal** )

**2** an object that you aim at if you are shooting: *His first shot missed the target by an inch.*

**3** an object, person, or place that someone chooses to attack: *The building was the target of a bomb.*

## tart /tart/ *adjective* having a sharp sour taste:

*The blackberries were very tart so I added some sugar.*

## task /task/ *noun* a thing that you have to do:

*I faced the difficult task of cleaning my bedroom.*

## taste /tayst/

● *noun*

**1** the feeling that you get when your tongue touches a food or drink. Taste is one of the five senses: *Most people like the taste of chocolate.* ▶ see **Thesaurus**

**2** the type of clothes, music, etc. that someone likes: *Ben and I have the same taste in music so I know which CDs he will like.*

**3** a small amount of a food or drink that you have to find out what it is like: *Can I have a taste of your dessert to see if I like it?*

● *verb*

**1** to have a particular type of taste: *The pizza tasted really good so I had some more.*

**2** to put a small amount of food or drink in your mouth in order to find out what it is like: *I asked Lisa if I could taste some of her ice cream.*

## taste bud /**tayst** buhd/ *noun* one of the parts

on your tongue that help you to taste things: *Your taste buds sense whether a food is sweet, salty, sour, or bitter.*

## tast·y /**tayst**-ee/ *adjective* having a very good

taste: *Mom is a great cook – everything she makes is very tasty.*

## tat·tle·tale /**tat**'l-tayl/ *noun* someone who tells

a teacher or parent that another child has done something bad

## tat·too /ta-**too**/ *noun* (plural **tattoos**) a picture

or word on your skin, made using a needle and ink: *My dad has a tattoo of an eagle on his arm.*

### Word Origin: tattoo

On the islands of Polynesia, such as Tahiti and Samoa, the native people often drew **tattoos** on their bodies. When Captain James Cook of Britain explored the Polynesian islands in the 1700s, he saw the tattoos and borrowed the word to describe the pictures on their skin.

**taught** /tot/ *verb* the past tense and past participle of **teach**

**tax** /takss/
- *noun* money that people must pay to the government: *Almost everyone pays taxes on the money they earn.*
- *verb* to make people pay tax: *The government taxes people to pay for schools, roads, and other things.*

**tax·a·tion** /tak-**saysh**-uhn/ *noun*
**1** the system of having taxes: *Taxation is necessary to pay for things such as schools and parks.*
**2** the money a government gets from taxes: *When taxation increases, people pay more money in taxes and have less money to spend.*

**tax·i** /**takss**-ee/ *noun* a car with a driver that you pay to take you somewhere: *We can take a taxi to the airport.* ( SYNONYM: **cab** )

**T-ball** /**tee** bol/ *noun* a children's game that is like baseball: *The kids are playing T-ball in the park.*

**tea** /tee/ *noun* a hot drink that you make by pouring boiling water onto dried leaves: *Would you like a cup of tea or coffee?*

**teach** /teech/ *verb* (**taught** /tot/)
**1** to give someone lessons in a school or college: *She teaches English at Keene High School.*
**2** to tell or show someone how to do something: *My dad taught me how to ride a bike.*

**Word Choice: teach, learn**

If you **teach** someone a subject or skill, you help him or her learn it: *My teacher taught us about volcanoes in science. | Dad is teaching me to play the guitar.*

You **learn** a subject or skill when you study or practice it: *We learned about volcanoes in science. | My sister is learning to play the piano.*

**teach·er** /**teech**-ur/ *noun* someone whose job is to teach: *My mom is a teacher in an elementary school.* ▶ see **Thesaurus**

**teach·er's pet** /teech-urz **pet**/ *noun* a child who everyone thinks is the teacher's favorite student: *The other school children didn't like Danny because they thought he was teacher's pet.*

**teach·ing** /**teech**-ing/ *noun* the job of being a teacher: *Maria enjoys teaching and is a very popular teacher.*

**team** /teem/ *noun*
**1** a group of people who compete against another group in a sport or game: *Tyler is on the school basketball team.*
**2** a group of people who work together: *His life was saved by a team of doctors and nurses.*

**team·mate** /**teem**-mayt/ *noun* someone who plays or works on the same team as you: *He passed the ball to his teammate, who scored.*

**team·work** /**teem**-wurk/ *noun* the ability of a group of people to work well together: *You all worked together to put up the tent – that was great teamwork.*

**tea·pot** /**tee**-paht/ *noun* a container for serving tea ▶ see picture at **pot**

**tear**
- *verb* /tair/ (**tore** /tor/, **torn** /torn/)
**1** to make a hole in paper or cloth or pull it into pieces: *My shirt tore on a nail. | He tore up the letter.* ( SYNONYM: **rip** )
**2** to pull something away from a person or place, using force: *The wind tore branches off the trees.*
**3** to move very quickly: *Some boys were tearing across the playground.*
**4 tear down** to deliberately destroy a building: *The old store had to be torn down.*
- *noun* /tair/
**1** a hole in a piece of paper or cloth where someone or something has torn it: *I offered to sew up the tear in his shirt.*
**2** /teer/ a drop of liquid that comes out of your eyes when you cry: *I had tears in my eyes when we said goodbye.*

**tease** /teez/ *verb* to make jokes about someone in order to embarrass or annoy him or her: *Other children teased her about her weight.*

**tea·spoon** /**tee**-spoon/ *noun*
**1** a small spoon used for eating or putting sugar in drinks: *She was eating some yogurt with a teaspoon.*
**2** a small spoon used for measuring food

**tech·ni·cal** /**tek**-nik-uhl/ *adjective* relating to machines or science: *We had to get technical support because my computer wasn't working.* | *My brother knows a lot about technical things and he is good at fixing computers.*

**tech·ni·cian** /**tek**-nish-uhn/ *noun* someone whose job is to check equipment or machines and make sure that they are working correctly: *a laboratory technician*

**tech·nique** /tek-**neek**/ *noun* a special way of doing something: *Doctors are using a new technique for treating heart problems.*

**tech·nol·o·gy** /tek-**nahl**-uhj-ee/ *noun* (plural **technologies**) scientific knowledge that is used for practical purposes, for example for making machines: *New technology has meant that cell phones are much smaller than they used to be.* —**technological** /tek-nuh-**lahj**-ik-uhl/ *adjective* relating to technology: *There have been enormous technological advances in recent years, with the development of computers and the Internet.*

**ted·dy bear** /**ted**-ee bair/ *noun* a soft toy that looks like a bear: *I always sleep with my teddy bear.*

**Word Origin:** teddy bear

**Teddy bears** are named after President Theodore Roosevelt. His nickname was "Teddy." Roosevelt liked to hunt. Once when he was hunting, the people with him caught a bear and tied it to a tree. Roosevelt would not kill the bear because he felt it was not fair. A newspaper printed a drawing of Roosevelt and the bear, and a man who made soft animal toys saw the drawing. He decided to make a bear. President Roosevelt allowed him to sell the bear as "Teddy's bear." The bears were very popular, and so we still call them teddy bears today.

**te·di·ous** /**teed**-ee-uhss/ *adjective* boring, and continuing for a long time: *Writing the report was a slow and tedious job.*

**teen** /teen/ *noun*
**1** a teenager: *There is nothing for teens to do in our neighborhood.*

**2 teens** the period of time when you are between 13 and 19 years old: *My sister is in her teens.*

**teen·age** /**teen**-ayj/ *adjective* between 13 and 19 years old: *The magazine is intended for teenage girls.*

**teen·ag·er** /**teen**-ayj-ur/ *noun* someone who is between 13 and 19 years old: *Two teenagers aged 15 and 18 were slightly injured in the accident.*

**tee·pee** /**tee**-pee/ *noun* another spelling of tepee

**teeth** /teeth/ *noun* the plural of **tooth**

**teethe** /teeth/ *verb* if a baby is teething, its first teeth are growing

**tele-** /tel-uh/

**Word Building**

**tele**graph | **tele**phone | **tele**scope | **tele**vision

These words all have the Greek word root *tele-* in them. *Tele-* means "distance" or "from far away." A *telephone* lets you talk to people who are far away from you. A *telescope* lets you see things like stars that are far away. A *television* receives shows from a place that is far away, so that you can see them.

**tel·e·graph** /**tel**-uh-graf/ *noun* an old way of sending messages through wires, using electronic signals.

**tel·e·phone** /**tel**-uh-fohn/
● *noun* a phone: *Can you answer the telephone if it rings?*
● *verb* to call someone using a phone: *He saw the robbery and telephoned the police.*

**tel·e·scope** /**tel**-uh-skohp/ *noun* a piece of equipment that makes things that are far away look bigger and closer. A telescope is made of a long tube with special lenses in it. You use a telescope to look at the stars: *We looked at the moon through the telescope.*

**telescope**

**tel·e·vi·sion** /**tel**-uh-vizh-uhn/ *noun*
**1** (also **television set** /tel-uh-**vizh**-uhn set/)
a piece of equipment with a screen that you watch programs on: *I turned on the television to watch the baseball game.*
( SYNONYM: **TV** )
**2** the programs that you can watch on a television: *Mom doesn't like me watching too much television.* ( SYNONYM: **TV** )

**tell** /tel/ *verb* (**told** /tohld/)
**1** to give someone information by talking or writing to them: *Diego told me that the party was next Saturday.* ▶ see **Thesaurus**
**2** to say that someone should do something: *Dad told me to clean my bedroom.*
**3 tell off** to talk to someone in an angry way because he or she has done something bad: *The teacher told him off for talking in class.*

**Word Choice: tell, talk, say**

You **tell** someone facts or information: *The teacher told us that plants need sunlight to grow.*

You **talk** about a subject: *The teacher talked about how plants grow.*

You **say** words: *The teacher said that plants need sunlight to grow.* | *She said, "Plants need sunlight to grow."*

**tell·er** /**tel**-ur/ *noun* someone whose job is to take and pay out money in a bank: *The bank teller counted out the money and gave it to the customer.*

**tem·per** /**temp**-ur/ *noun* someone who has a temper gets angry easily or suddenly: *Michael has a temper and shouts a lot.*

IDIOM with **temper**
**lose your temper** to suddenly become very angry: *My dad is very calm and never loses his temper.*

**tem·pera·ment** /**tem**-pruh-muhnt/ *noun* the type of character you have, for example whether you are usually happy, sad, or friendly: *The little boy has a very cheerful temperament and always seems happy.*

**tem·pera·men·tal** /tem-pruh-**ment**'l/ *adjective* suddenly changing from being happy to being angry or sad: *My brother is very temperamental and his mood changes very quickly.*

**tem·pera·ture** /**tem**-pruhch-ur/ *noun*
**1** how hot or cold something is. You measure temperature in degrees Fahrenheit (°F) or Centigrade (°C): *The temperature at night can drop to as low as 10°F.*
**2** if you have a temperature, you feel very hot because you are sick: *I had a temperature, so I stayed home from school.*

**tem·ple** /**temp**-uhl/ *noun*
**1** a building used for worship in some religions, for example Buddhism: *In ancient Greece, the temple of Zeus was very famous.*
**2** the area on the side of your head, between your ear and your eye: *His hair is gray at the temples.*

**temple**

**tem·po·rar·y** /**temp**-uh-rair-ee/ *adjective* existing or happening for a short time only: *She got a temporary job during the summer before she went back to college.* ( ANTONYM: **permanent** )

**tempt** /tempt/ *verb* to make someone want to do or have something, especially when this will have a bad effect: *Banks are always trying to tempt people into borrowing more money, even though they cannot pay it back.*

a b c d e f g h i j k l m n o p q r s **t** u v w x y z

**temp·ta·tion** /temp-**taysh**-uhn/ *noun* a strong feeling of wanting to have or do something that you should not: *I couldn't resist the temptation, so I took another cookie.*

**tempt·ing** /**tempt**-ing/ *adjective* something that is tempting seems good and you would like to have it: *The chocolate cake looked very tempting.*

**ten** /ten/
● *number*
**1** 10: *Dad gave me ten dollars.*
**2** ten o'clock: *My swimming lesson is at ten.*
**3** ten years old: *His sister is ten.*
● *noun*
a piece of paper money worth $10: *I paid with a ten.*

**ten·ant** /**ten**-uhnt/ *noun* someone who pays rent to live in a room or house: *The tenants pay rent to my parents.*

**tend** /tend/ *verb* to be likely to do or have something: *Children tend to have more colds than adults.*

**tend·en·cy** /**tend**-uhnss-ee/ *noun* (plural **tendencies**) if you have a tendency to do something, you often do it: *My grandmother is very old and has a tendency to forget things.*

**ten·der** /**tend**-ur/ *adjective*
**1** tender food is soft and easy to cut and eat: *Cook the potatoes until they are tender.*
( ANTONYM: **tough** )
**2** painful when touched: *My arm is still tender where I hurt it when I fell off my bicycle.*
**3** gentle and showing love: *He gave her a tender smile.*
—**tenderly** /**tend**-ur-lee/ *adverb* in a gentle way that shows love: *She stroked his hair tenderly.*

**ten·don** /**tend**-uhn/ *noun* the part that connects the muscles to the bone

**ten·nis** /**ten**-iss/ *noun* a game in which two or four people use rackets to hit a ball to each other across a net: *My racket broke when I was playing tennis.* ▶ see picture on page **A10**

**tense** /tenss/
● *adjective*
**1** nervous and worried: *He felt very tense before the test, and he couldn't sleep.* ( ANTONYM: **calm** )

**2** making people feel nervous or worried: *There were some tense moments when the other team almost scored.*
**3** tense muscles feel tight and stiff: *If your muscles are tense, it helps to have a massage.*
● *noun*
a form of a verb that shows whether you are talking about the past, the present, or the future: *"She played" is in the past tense, and "She plays" is in the present tense.*

**Word Family: tense**

**tense** *adjective* | **tension** *noun*

**ten·sion** /**tensh**-uhn/ *noun* a nervous feeling because you do not know what is going to happen: *There was a lot of tension while we waited for the competition results to be announced.*

**tent** /tent/ *noun* a cloth house you sleep in when you are camping. The cloth is held up by poles and ropes: *We are trying to find a campsite where we can put up our tent.*

tent
dome tent
A-frame tent
rope
peg

**ten·ta·cle** /**tent**-uhk-uhl/ *noun* one of the long thin parts like arms on an octopus: *An octopus has eight tentacles.*

**ten·ta·tive** /**tent**-uht-iv/ *adjective* not definite or certain: *We've made tentative plans to go to Hawaii, but we don't know if we have enough money.*

**tenth** /tenth/ *number*
**1** 10th
**2** 1/10

**ten thou·sand** /ten **thowz**-uhnd/ *number* 10,000

**te·pee** /**tee**-pee/ *noun* a large tent that is round at the bottom and has a pointed top. It was used in past times by Native Americans who lived on the plains.

**tepee**

poles

opening for smoke

door

**ter·mite** /**tur**-mīt/ *noun*
an insect like an ant that eats wood. Termites damage trees and buildings. Termites live in large groups in big nests made of earth and wood.

**termite**

**-terr-** /terr/

## Word Building

**extra**terr**estrial** | **terr**ain | **terr**itory

These words all have the Latin word root *terr* in them. *Terr* means "earth." An *extraterrestrial* is a creature that comes from a different planet than Earth. The *terrain* of a place is what the land is like, for example whether it has mountains or is very dry. A country's *territory* is the part of the Earth that belongs to that country.

**ter·rain** /tuh-**rayn**/ *noun* a particular type of land: *Military vehicles can drive on rough terrain.*

**ter·ra·pin** /**terr**-uh-pin/ *noun* a turtle that lives in water

**ter·ri·ble** /**terr**-uhb-uhl/ *adjective* very bad: *It was a terrible accident and many people were hurt.* ( SYNONYM: **awful** )

**ter·ri·bly** /**terr**-uhb-lee/ *adverb*
**1** very badly: *The team is playing terribly and they deserve to lose.*
**2** very: *She is terribly busy and she doesn't have time to talk to me.*

**ter·rif·ic** /tuh-**rif**-ik/ *adjective* very good: *That's a terrific idea! Let's get started! | You look terrific in that dress.* ( SYNONYM: **wonderful** )

**ter·ri·fy** /**terr**-uh-fī/ *verb* (**terrifies**, **terrified**) to make someone very frightened: *The idea of holding a snake terrifies me.*
—**terrified** /**terr**-uh-fīd/ *adjective* very frightened: *My sister's terrified of the dark and she always sleeps with her light on.*
—**terrifying** /**terr**-uh-fī-ing/ *adjective* making someone very frightened: *He had a terrifying experience when he was attacked by a big dog.*

**term** /turm/ *noun*
**1** a word or phrase: *There were a lot of legal terms in the document that I couldn't understand.*
**2** a period of time when someone does a job: *The president has a four-year term.*
**3** one of the periods that the school or college year is divided into: *She'll graduate after spring term.*
**4 terms** the things that are part of a legal agreement: *The terms of the contract say that the work must be finished within six months.*

**ter·min·al** /**turm**-uhn-uhl/
● *noun*
**1** a building where people get on airplanes, buses, or ships: *The plane leaves from Terminal 4.*
**2** a screen and keyboard that are connected to a computer: *The classroom has computer terminals for students to use.*
● *adjective*
a terminal disease cannot be cured, and causes death: *He is very sick with terminal cancer.*

**ter·mi·nate** /**turm**-uh-nayt/ *verb* to end something: *They decided to terminate their agreement.*

**ter·min·us** /**turm**-uhn-uhss/ *noun* the place where a train line or bus service ends

a
b
c
d
e
f
g
h
i
j
k
l
m
n
o
p
q
r
s
**t**
u
v
w
x
y
z

**ter·ri·to·ry** /terr-uh-tor-ee/ *noun* (plural **territories**)
**1** land that a country controls: *Hong Kong became Chinese territory in 1997.*
**2** an area of land: *Asia is a vast territory.*

**ter·ror** /terr-ur/ *noun*
**1** great fear: *She was shaking in terror when she saw the gun.*
**2** violent attacks for political reasons: *The World Trade Center was destroyed in the September 11 terror attacks.* ( SYNONYM: **terrorism** )

**ter·ror·ism** /terr-uh-riz-uhm/ *noun* violent attacks for political reasons: *The bombing was an act of terrorism.* ( SYNONYM: **terror** )

**ter·ror·ist** /terr-uhr-ist/ *noun* someone who uses violent actions for political reasons: *Terrorists often use bombs to kill people.*

**test** /test/
● *noun*
**1** a set of questions or activities to measure your knowledge or skill: *I passed my math test with a B.* | *Mom is taking her driving test next week.*
( SYNONYM: **exam** ) ▶ see **Thesaurus**
**2** a medical check on part of your body: *Children should have an eye test every year.*
( SYNONYM: **exam** )
**3** something that scientists do to examine a substance: *Scientists are doing tests on the water to see if there are any bacteria in it.*
● *verb*
**1** to measure someone's knowledge or skill by asking questions or making him or her do things: *The teacher tests us on spellings every week.*
**2** to use something to find out whether it works: *The company is testing its new computer software to make sure that there are no problems with it.*
**3** to do a medical check on part of someone's body: *You should have your eyes tested if you can't read that sign.*
**4** to check a substance to see what is in it: *They test the water to see if it contains any lead.*

**tes·ti·fy** /test-uh-fi/ *verb* (**testifies**, **testified**) to say what you know in a law court: *She testified that her son was home at the time of the murder.*

**tes·ti·mo·ny** /test-uh-mohn-ee/ *noun* (plural **testimonies**) the things you say in a law court about what you know about a crime: *Because of his testimony, the two men were sent to prison.*

**test tube** /test toob/ *noun* a narrow glass container used in scientific tests: *When you heat the liquid in a test tube, it turns blue.*

**test tube**

**tet·a·nus** /tet'n-uhss/ *noun* a serious disease that is caused by an infection in a cut on your skin. Tetanus makes the jaw muscles and other muscles stiff.

**teth·er** /teth-ur/
● *noun* a rope or chain that is used to tie an animal to something, so that it does not move away
● *verb* to tie an animal to a post or tree so that it does not move away: *The goat was tethered to a tree.*

**text** /tekst/
● *noun*
**1** a written message that you send using a cell phone: *I'll send you a text when I get home.*
( SYNONYM: **text message** )
**2** the writing in a book, magazine, etc.: *The website has both pictures and text.*
**3** a book that students use when they are studying a subject: *The novel is one of the texts that we have to read for our English class.*
( SYNONYM: **textbook** )
● *verb*
to send someone a written message using a cell phone: *I'll text you to let you know what time the movie starts.*

**text·book** /tekst-buk/ *noun* a book about a subject, that students use: *Chapter One of the math textbook is about adding numbers.*

**tex·tile** /tekss-til/ *noun* a material that is made by weaving. Textiles are used to make things such as clothes or carpets.

**text mes·sage** /tekst mess-ij/ *noun* a written message that you send using a cell phone: *I use my cell phone mainly for sending text messages.*

**tex·ture** /tekss-chur/ *noun* the way that something feels when you touch it: *Sandpaper has a very rough texture.*

**than** /thuhn, than/ *preposition, conjunction*

used when comparing people or things: *My friend is taller than me.*

**thank** /thangk/ *verb* to tell someone that you are pleased about something he or she has done for you or given to you: *I thanked my grandmother for the birthday present.*

**thank·ful** /**thangk**-fuhl/ *adjective* glad about something: *We're thankful that nobody was hurt in the accident.*
—**thankfully** /**thangk**-fuhl-ee/ *adverb* used for saying that you are glad about something: *Thankfully, the weather was good for our camping trip.*

**thanks** /thangkss/ *plural noun*
**1** you say this to thank someone: *Thanks for the Christmas present, Joe.* | *"Would you like something to drink?" "No, thanks."*
**2** something that you say or do to thank someone: *I bought him some candy as thanks for helping me with my homework.*

> IDIOM with **thanks**
> **thanks to** because of: *I was late for school, thanks to my sister.*

**Thanks·giv·ing** /thangkss-**giv**-ing/ *noun* a holiday in the U.S. and Canada in the fall. Families have a large meal together to show their thanks for food, families, health, etc.

**thank you** /**thangk** yoo/ *interjection* used when someone does something kind for you: *Thank you for helping me.* | *"Here's your drink." "Thank you."*

**thank you note** /**thangk** yoo noht/ *noun* a letter that you write to thank someone: *I have to write thank you notes to all the people who gave me birthday presents.*

**that**
● *adjective, pronoun* /that/ (plural **those** /thohz/)
**1** used when talking about someone or something that is farther away from you, often in a place you are pointing at: *Who is that girl over there?*
**2** used when saying something about the thing you are already talking about: *Have you seen the movie "Little Miss Sunshine?" "No, I've never seen that movie."*
**3** /thuht/ used instead of "who" or "which":

*He's the boy that gave me some candy.* | *There are lots of things that I need to do.*
● *conjunction* /thuht/
**1** used when joining two parts of a sentence: *Mark's brother said that he wanted to come with us.*
**2** used after a phrase with "so" or "such" to say what the result of something is: *He was so rich that he owned ten houses.*
● *adverb* /that/
**1** so or very: *It won't cost all that much.* | *I didn't realize he was that tall.*
**2** used when showing an amount or size with your hands: *The little kitten was only that big.*

**thaw** /tho/ *verb* if something frozen thaws, it stops being frozen: *The snow began to thaw in the warmer weather.* (ANTONYM: **freeze**)

**the** /thuh, thee/ *definite article*
**1** used before a noun to show that you are talking about a particular person or thing: *The room is very small.* | *He's the man I told you about.* | *Today is the fifth of May.*
**2** used before the names of rivers, oceans, groups of mountains, and some countries: *the Mississippi River* | *the Alps* | *the U.S.*
**3** used when talking about all of a group of people: *He gave all his money to the poor.* | *The British often talk about the weather.*
**4** /thee/ used when saying that something is the best or most famous one: *This is the movie to see this year.*

---

**Grammar: the**

Do not use **the** when you are talking about all of something or about every one of something: *I like chocolate.* | *Dogs bark at other dogs.*

Use **the** when you are talking about a particular thing or group of things: *I like the chocolate they sell.* | *The dogs next door bark a lot.*

Do not use **the** before the names of airports, train stations, or streets: *The plane left from LaGuardia Airport.* | *She lives on Wilson Street.*

Use **the** when you are talking about a particular airport, train station, or street but are not using its name: *We got to the airport just in time.* | *They live on the same street.*

---

**the·a·ter** /**thee**-uht-ur/ *noun*
**1** a building where actors perform plays on a stage: *I'm going to see a play at our local theater.*
**2** a building where you go to see movies: *There's a good movie showing at the theater.*
**3** the work of performing or writing plays: *Some actors prefer theater to movies because they like performing to a live audience.*

**theft** /theft/ *noun* the crime of stealing something: *There have been a number of thefts at the mall and two women had their purses stolen.*

**their** /thur, thair/ *adjective* belonging to particular people: *The children are eating their candy bars.*

**theirs** /thairz/ *pronoun* something that belongs to particular people: *Our house has a blue door and theirs has a white door.*

**them** /thuhm, them/ *pronoun* the people or things that have already been mentioned. You use "them" after a verb or preposition: *She bought some flowers and gave them to Ann.*

**theme** /theem/ *noun* the main subject or idea in a book, movie, speech, etc.: *Love is the main theme of the book.*

**them·selves** /thuhm-**selvz**/ *pronoun* used when the same people or animals that you have just mentioned do an action: *The elephants were washing themselves in the river.*

**then** /then/ *adverb*
**1** after that: *I did my homework, and then I went out to play.*
**2** at a time in the past: *My dad worked in Arizona back then.*
**3** used for saying what the result of a situation is: *"I'm not ready yet." "Then you're going to be late!"*

**the·o·ry** /**thee**-uhr-ee/ *noun* (plural **theories**) an idea or set of ideas that tries to explain why something happens: *Charles Darwin had a theory that only the best and fittest animals survived.*

**ther·a·py** /**therr**-uhp-ee/ *noun* (plural **therapies**) treatment for mental or physical problems: *After her son died, she had therapy for depression.*
—**therapist** /**therr**-uhp-ist/ *noun* someone whose job is treating mental or physical problems: *The therapist gave me a program of exercises to do, to make my leg muscles stronger.*

**there** /thair/
● *pronoun* **there is/there are, etc.** used for

theater

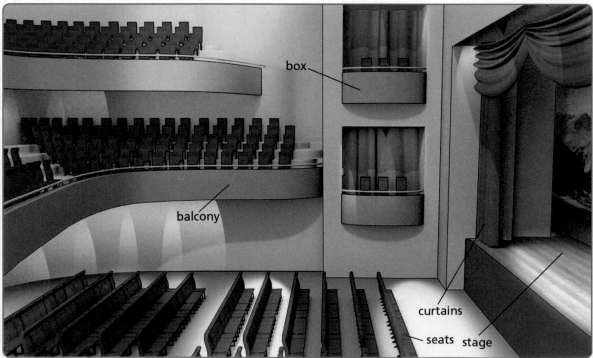

box

balcony

curtains

seats   stage

describing what is in a place, or what happens: *There's a library next to our school. | There are 30 children in the class.*
● *adverb* in, to, or at that place: *We're going to London. Have you ever been there?*

**there·by** /thair-**bī**/ *adverb* with the result that something happens: *Cars produce poisonous gas, thereby polluting the air.*

**there·fore** /**thair**-for/ *adverb* for the reason that you have mentioned: *This phone has more features and is therefore more expensive.*

**therm-** /thurm/

> ## Word Building
>
> **therm**al | **therm**ometer | **therm**ostat
> These words all have the Greek word root **therm** in them. **Therm** means "heat" or "warm." *Thermal* energy is the heat produced by the sun. A *thermometer* measures how hot your body or the air is.

**ther·mal** /**thurm**-uhl/ *adjective* relating to or caused by heat: *The water is heated using thermal energy from the sun.*

**ther·mal con·duc·tiv·i·ty** /**thurm**-uhl kahn-duhk-**tiv**-uht-ee/ *noun* the ability of a material or substance to allow heat to go through it

**ther·mom·e·ter**
/thur-**mahm**-uht-ur/ *noun* an instrument that measures the temperature of something or someone: *When I was sick, the nurse took my temperature with a thermometer.*

**thermometer**

thermometer

**ther·mo·stat** /**thurm**-uh-stat/ *noun* an instrument that controls how hot or cold a room or machine is: *I turned down the thermostat to 65° to save energy.*

**the·sau·rus** /thi-**sor**-uhss/ *noun* (plural **thesauruses** or **thesauri** /thi-**sor**-ī/) a book that lists groups of words that have similar meanings

**these** /theez/ *adjective*, *pronoun* the plural form of this: *Do you like these shoes?*

**the·sis** /**theess**-iss/ *noun* (plural **theses** /**theess**-eez/) a long piece of writing that you do in college, especially for a master's degree: *She wrote her thesis on 19th century American history.*

**they** /thay/ *pronoun* people or things. You use "they" instead of names when you have already talked about those people or things: *I asked Eduardo and Pedro if they wanted to come too. | Have some of these cookies – they are delicious.*

**thick** /thik/ *adjective*
**1** a thick object or material has a large distance between its sides: *It's cold – you'll need a thick sweater. | Dad cut a thick slice of bread.* (ANTONYM: **thin**)
**2** thick hair grows closely together: *Her thick hair seems to protect her head from the sun.* (ANTONYM: **thin**)
**3** thick forest has trees growing closely together: *The chimpanzees live in thick forests in central Africa.*
**4** thick liquid does not have much water in it: *If the paint is too thick, add a little water.*
(ANTONYM: **thin**)

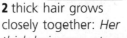
**thick**
thin    thick

**thick·en** /**thik**-uhn/ *verb* if a liquid thickens, it becomes more solid and has less water: *Stir the sauce until it thickens.*

**thick·ly** /**thik**-lee/ *adverb*
**1** in thick pieces: *He sliced the bread thickly.* (ANTONYM: **thinly**)
**2** in a thick layer: *She spread the cream thickly on the cake.* (ANTONYM: **thinly**)

**thick·ness** /**thik**-niss/ *noun* how thick and solid something is: *Choose the screws according to the thickness of the wood.*

**thief** /theef/ *noun* (plural **thieves** /theevz/) someone who steals things: *A thief stole all her jewelry.*

**thigh** /thī/ *noun* the top part of your leg above your knee ▶ see picture on page **A13**

a b c d e f g h i j k l m n o p q r s t u v w x y z

**thin** /thin/ *adjective* (**thinner**, **thinnest**)
**1** not having much fat on your body: *Mom says I'm too thin and should eat more.* | *His body is weak and his legs are very thin.* ( ANTONYM: **fat** )
▶ see Thesaurus
**2** not very wide or not very thick: *The ground is covered by a thin layer of snow.* | *Cut the lemon into thin slices.* ( ANTONYM: **thick** ) ▶ see picture at **thick**
**3** if you have thin hair, you do not have a lot of hair: *He is getting old and his hair is becoming thin at the back of his head.* ( ANTONYM: **thick** )
**4** a liquid that is thin has a lot of water in it: *This soup's too thin – it looks like red water.*
( ANTONYM: **thick** )

**thing** /thing/ *noun*
**1** an object: *What's that thing on the table?*
**2** an event, or something that someone says or does: *A strange thing happened to me yesterday.* | *People say some funny things.*
**3** **things** the events that are happening in your life, and how they affect you: *I hope things will get better soon.*
**4** **things** the objects that you own: *I put all my things in the bag.*

**think** /thingk/ *verb* (**thought** /thot/)
**1** to use your mind to have ideas or solve problems: *I was thinking about our vacation and what we should do.* ▶ see Thesaurus
**2** to have an opinion or belief: *I think Mr. Morley is the best teacher.*
**3** to consider the idea of doing something in the future: *My brother is thinking about becoming a firefighter.*

**thin·ly** /**thin**-lee/ *adverb*
**1** in thin pieces: *Slice the bread thinly – I don't like it too thick.* ( ANTONYM: **thickly** )
**2** in a thin layer: *You don't need much butter, so spread it thinly.* ( ANTONYM: **thickly** )

**third** /thurd/ *number*
**1** 3rd: *James finished third in the race.*
**2** 1/3. You can say a third or one third.

**third per·son** /thurd **purss**-uhn/ *noun* the pronouns "he," "she," "it," and "they," and the forms of the verbs you use with them: *The verb "speaks" is in the third person singular.*

**Third World** /thurd **wurld**/ *noun* the poor countries in the world that do not have a lot of industry

**thirst** /thurst/ *noun*
**1** the feeling of wanting a drink: *It was very hot and I thought I was going to die of thirst.*
**2** the feeling of wanting to get something: *Kids have a thirst for knowledge.*

**thirst·y** /**thurst**-ee/ *adjective* (**thirstier**, **thirstiest**) feeling that you want a drink: *I was thirsty so I drank some water.*
—**thirstily** /**thurst**-uhl-ee/ *adverb* in a way that shows that you are thirsty: *Evie drank the water thirstily.*

**thir·teen** /thur-**teen**/ *number*
**1** 13: *The flight takes thirteen hours.*
**2** thirteen years old: *My big sister is thirteen.*
—**thirteenth** /thur-**teenth**/ *number* 13th or 1/13

**thir·ty** /**thurt**-ee/ *number*
**1** 30: *I got thirty dollars for my birthday.*
**2** thirty years old: *Our teacher is thirty next week and we're having a special party for her.*
**3** **the thirties** the years from 1930 to 1939: *The house was built in the thirties.*
**4** **in your thirties** between 30 and 39 years old: *Mom and Dad are in their thirties.*
**5** **in the thirties** between 30 and 39 degrees in temperature: *It was a very cold night with temperatures in the thirties.*
—**thirtieth** /**thurt**-ee-ith/ *number* 30th or 1/30

**this** /thiss/
● *adjective*, *pronoun* (plural **these** /theez/)
**1** the one that is close to you, or that you are holding: *This is my book, and that's yours.*
**2** used when talking about the day, week, etc. that is closest to today: *I'm going swimming this Friday.* | *We have a school trip this week.*
**3** used when talking about something that someone has just mentioned: *Where is this store you were talking about?*
● *adverb*
as big, tall, etc. as the one you are talking about: *I've never seen an apple this big before.*

**thongs** /thongz/ *plural noun* a pair of flat shoes that are open on top. Thongs are held on your feet by a band of material that goes between your toes: *Some people wear*

thongs

*thongs on their feet before they get in the swimming pool.*

**tho·rax** /**thor**-akss/ *noun* the part of an insect's body between its head and its abdomen

**thorn** /thorn/ *noun* a sharp point that grows on a plant such as a rose or a cactus: *I pricked my finger on a thorn when I was picking a rose.*

**thor·ough** /**thur**-oh/ *adjective* careful to do things correctly without any mistakes: *The dentist makes a thorough examination of your teeth and gums.*

**thor·ough·ly** /**thur**-oh-lee/ *adverb*
**1** very much: *I thoroughly enjoyed my vacation.*
**2** carefully, so that you make sure that you do not miss anything: *Check your answers thoroughly before handing in your test.*

**those** /thohz/ *adjective, pronoun* the plural of that: *Who are those people over there?* | *"Are these your shoes?" "No, those are mine."*

**though** /thoh/ *conjunction*
**1** used when you say a fact that makes the other part of your sentence seem surprising: *The ground was still very dry, though it had rained during the night.* (SYNONYM: **although**)
**2** but: *She's pretty, though not as pretty as her sister.*
**3 as though** as if: *It looked as though he knew what he was doing, but he didn't.*

**thought** /thot/
● *verb*
the past tense and past participle of think
● *noun*
**1** an idea that you think of: *Just the thought of flying makes me nervous.*
**2** the act of thinking about something: *Mike stared out of the window, lost in thought.*
**3** careful and serious consideration: *I've given your idea some thought, and I'm going to do what you suggest.*

**thought·ful** /**thot**-fuhl/ *adjective*
**1** serious and quiet because you are thinking about something: *Laura gave me a thoughtful look, before she answered my question.*
**2** kind and thinking how to make other people happy: *It was very thoughtful of you to send me a get-well card.*

**thought·less** /**thot**-liss/ *adjective* not kind and not thinking about the feelings of other people: *It was thoughtless of you to talk about the party in front of Tom, when you knew he hadn't been invited.*

**thou·sand** /**thowz**-uhnd/ *number* 1,000
—**thousandth** /**thowz**-uhndth/ *number* 1,000th or 1/1,000

**thread** /thred/
● *noun* a long thin string of cotton used for sewing cloth: *Mom sewed on my button with a needle and thread.*
● *verb* to put thread through a hole: *Take a piece of cotton and thread the needle.*

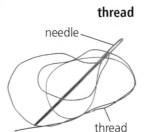

**thread**
needle
thread

**threat** /thret/ *noun* a statement in which someone says that they will hurt you if you do not do what they want: *The robbers used threats of violence to force people to give them money.*

**threat·en** /**thret**'n/ *verb* to say that you will do something bad to someone if he or she does not do what you want: *My parents have threatened to ground me if I get home late again.*
—**threatening** /**thret**'n-ing/ *adjective* seeming to threaten someone: *She received several threatening phone calls telling her to leave town.*

**three** /three/ *number*
**1** 3: *I have three older sisters.*
**2** three o'clock: *I will be home by three.*
**3** three years old: *My little sister is going to be three tomorrow.*

**three-di·men·sion·al** /three di-**mensh**-uhn-uhl/ (also **3-D** /three **dee**/) *adjective* having or appearing to have length, depth, and height: *The class built a three-dimensional model of the bridge.* | *3-D movies make you feel that the people and animals in the movie are really there with you.*

**threw** /throo/ *verb* the past tense of **throw**

**thrift store** /**thrift** stor/ *noun* a store that sells used things and old clothes at low prices

**thrif·ty** /**thrift**-ee/ *adjective* using money carefully and not wasting any: *He's very thrifty and makes all his own meals.*

a
b
c
d
e
f
g
h
i
j
k
l
m
n
o
p
q
r
s
t
u
v
w
x
y
z

**thrill** /thril/
- *noun* a strong feeling of excitement and pleasure: *Winning the race was a great thrill.*
- *verb* to make someone feel great excitement and pleasure: *The movie has thrilled audiences around the world.*

**thrilled** /thrild/ *adjective* very excited, pleased, or happy: *He was thrilled with his new bike.*

**thrill·er** /**thril**-ur/ *noun* a movie or book that tells an exciting story about murder or crime: *Nick likes reading spy thrillers.*

**thrill·ing** /**thril**-ing/ *adjective* exciting and interesting: *The Red Sox beat the Yankees 10–9 in a thrilling game last night.*

**thrive** /thrīv/ *verb* (**thrived**) to become successful, strong, or healthy: *Plants thrive in the hot wet environment of the tropical rainforest.*

**throat** /throht/ *noun*
**1** the passage at the back of your mouth, where you swallow: *The soda tasted good as it went down his throat.*
**2** the front part of your neck: *She was lying in the bath with the water up to her throat.*

**throb** /thrahb/ *verb* (**throbbing**, **throbbed**) if part of your body throbs, you keep getting a regular feeling of pain in it: *I have a bad headache and my head is throbbing.*

**throne** /throhn/ *noun* the special chair on which a king or queen sits

throne

**through** /throo/ *preposition, adverb*
**1** in one side of a passage or hole, and out the other side: *The train went through a tunnel. | He opened the window and climbed through.*
**2** across an area to another area: *We traveled through Texas to Mexico.*
**3** because of someone or something: *Our team won through skill and determination.*
**4** during and to the end of a period of time: *The show opens today and runs through April.*

**through·out** /throo-**owt**/ *adverb, preposition*
**1** in every part of a place: *The movie is showing in theaters throughout the country.*
**2** during all of a period of time, from the beginning to the end: *Southern California has mild sunny weather throughout the year.*

**throw** /throh/
- *verb* (**threw** /throo/, **thrown** /throhn/)
**1** to make something go through the air, by moving your arm and letting it go out of your hand: *He threw the ball to me, and I caught it.*
▶ see **Thesaurus** ▶ see picture on page **A15**
**2 throw away/out** to get rid of things by putting them in the garbage: *Just throw away the paper plates when you've finished using them. | I threw out a lot of old magazines because I had already read them.*
**3 throw up** if you throw up, food comes back up from your stomach and out through your mouth: *If you eat too many donuts you will throw up!* (SYNONYM: **vomit**)
- *noun* the action of throwing something such as a ball: *That was a good throw – the ball came right to me!*

**thrown** /throhn/ *verb* the past participle of throw

**thrust** /thruhst/ *verb* (**thrust**) to push something somewhere quickly and suddenly, often with a lot of force: *She thrust some money into my hand.*

**thumb** /thuhm/ *noun* the short thick finger on your hand that helps you hold things: *She held the dirty cloth carefully between her thumb and fingers.* ▶ see picture at **hand**

**Word Origin: thumb**

**Thumb** comes from an Old English word which meant "the thick finger."

**thumb·tack**
/**thuhm**-tak/ *noun* a short pin with a round flat top. You use a thumbtack to attach papers to walls: *You'll need thumbtacks to put the sign on the bulletin board.*

thumbtack

**thump** /thuhmp/
● *verb*
**1** to hit something in a way that makes a low sound: *The child was screaming and thumping the table with her fist.*
**2** if your heart thumps, it beats very quickly because you are frightened or excited: *He heard footsteps on the stairs and his heart began to thump.*
● *noun*
the low sound made when something hits a surface: *She fell and hit the floor with a loud thump.*

**thun·der** /**thuhnd**-ur/ *noun* the loud noise that you hear in the sky during a storm: *I could hear the rumble of thunder in the distance as the storm got closer.*

**thun·der·storm** /**thuhnd**-ur-storm/ *noun* a storm with thunder and lightning: *We walked home in a thunderstorm, with lightning flashing all around us.*

**Thurs·day** /**thurzd**-ee/ *noun*
( ABBREVIATION: **Thurs.** ) the fifth day of the week, between Wednesday and Friday: *Today is Thursday, so it's almost the weekend.* | *I go to dance classes on Thursday.*

> ## Word Origin: **Thursday**
>
> **Thursday** is named for a god called Thor in an old religion. Many people in northern Europe believed in this religion before Christianity. Thor was the god of thunder, and he was the son of the god Odin, or Woden. Wednesday is named after Woden.

**thus** /thuhss/ *adverb*
**1** as a result of what you have just said: *He owns the land, and thus he owns any oil that people find on his land.* ( SYNONYM: **so** )
**2** **thus far** until now: *The team has failed to win thus far this season.* ( SYNONYM: **so far** )

**thy·roid** /**thī**-royd/ (also **thyroid gland** /**thī**-royd gland/) *noun* a gland in your neck that produces hormones. Hormones are substances that affect how your body grows and how you behave.

**ti·a·ra** /tee-**ar**-uh/ *noun* a piece of jewelry like a small crown. A tiara is worn by a woman on formal occasions.

**tick** /tik/
● *noun*
**1** a small creature like an insect that lives on the skin of other animals and sucks their blood: *If you walk in long grass, you may get bitten by a tick.*
**2** the short sound that a clock or watch makes: *The only sound was the tick of my watch.*
▶ see picture on page **A16**
● *verb*
if a clock or watch ticks, it makes a short sound every second: *I lay awake, listening to the clock ticking.*

**tick·et** /**tik**-it/ *noun*
**1** a small piece of paper that shows that you have paid to see a movie, travel on a bus, etc.: *I can get you a ticket for the concert on Friday.*
**2** a legal note saying that you must pay money because you drove or parked your car illegally: *He got a ticket for driving too fast.*
**3** a list of the people supported by a particular political party in an election: *He is running for governor on the Republican ticket.*

**tick·le** /**tik**-uhl/ *verb*
**1** to move your fingers lightly on parts of someone's body to try and make him or her laugh: *Dad tickles my feet to make me laugh.*
▶ see picture on page **A14**
**2** if something tickles, it makes you want to scratch your body: *I don't like this sweater, it tickles.*
—**ticklish** /**tik**-lish/ *adjective* if you are ticklish, it is easy to make you laugh when someone tickles you: *Don't touch my feet – I'm ticklish!*

**tic-tac-toe** /tik tak **toh**/ *noun* a children's game for two players. You take turns drawing X's and O's in nine squares. You try to get three of the same letter in a row.

tic-tac-toe

She is playing tic-tac-toe.

**ti·dal wave** /**tī**-duhl wayv/ *noun* a very big wave that causes a lot of damage when it comes onto the land: *The village was destroyed by a tidal wave, after a big earthquake.*

a b c d e f g h i j k l m n o p q r s **t** u v w x y z

**tide** /tīd/ *noun* the change in the level of the ocean against the land. Tides are caused by the gravity of the Sun and Moon pulling on the oceans: *The ocean covers the whole beach at high tide.*

tide

low tide

high tide

**ti·dy** /tīd-ee/ *adjective* clean and neat, with everything in the right places: *My sister's room is always neat and tidy – mine is always a mess.*

**tie** /tī/

● *verb* (**ties**, **tying**, **tied**)

**1** to fasten something using rope or string to make a knot: *Your shoelaces are undone – you need to tie them.* | *The robbers tied him up with a rope.* | *The dog was tied to a tree.*
(ANTONYM: **untie**)

**2** to have the same number of points in a game, or to finish at the same time at the end of a race: *The two teams tied. The score was 3–3.*

**3 be tied up** to be very busy: *I'm tied up at the moment. Can I help you with your homework later?*

● *noun*

**1** a narrow piece of cloth that men tie around their neck and wear outside their shirts: *He wears a suit and tie in the office.*

**2** a relationship between two people, groups, or countries: *Their family ties are strong, and they see their grandparents every week.*

**3** the result of a game in which two people or teams get the same number of points: *The race was a tie because two runners crossed the line at the same time.*

**tied** /tīd/ *adjective* having the same number of points in a game: *At halftime, the score was tied 22–22.*

**ti·ger** /tīg-ur/ *noun* a large wild cat that has orange fur with black lines: *Tigers live in India and other parts of Asia.*

tiger

**tight** /tīt/

● *adjective*

**1** tight clothes fit your body very closely: *These shoes are too tight – I need a bigger size.* | *She was wearing tight jeans.* (ANTONYM: **loose**)

**2** string, wire, or rope that is tight has been pulled or stretched firmly so that it is straight or cannot move: *He tied the rope around a fence post and pulled it tight.* (ANTONYM: **loose**)

**3** firmly fastened and difficult to move: *If the lid isn't tight enough, the jar will leak.*

● *adverb*

very firmly: *On the roller coaster, she grabbed his hand and held on tight.* (SYNONYM: **tightly**)

**tight·en** /tīt'n/ *verb* to fasten something firmly so that it is not loose: *Make sure the shelf is in the right position, before you tighten all the screws.*

**tight·ly** /tīt-lee/ *adverb* very firmly: *She held the reins tightly so that the horse couldn't run away.* (SYNONYM: **tight**)

**tights** /tītss/ *noun* a piece of clothing for girls or women that fits closely over the feet and legs and goes up to the waist

**tile** /tīl/ *noun* a thin square piece of baked clay that you use for covering floors or walls: *Some of the floor tiles are cracked and need replacing.*

**till** /til/

● *preposition, conjunction* until: *I studied till about 8:00.* | *Wait there till I get back.*

● *noun* a machine in a store that shows how

much you must pay, and is used to keep the money in: *There was a long line of people waiting to pay at the till.* ( SYNONYM: **cash register** )

**tilt** /tilt/ *verb* to move something so that its position is not straight or upright: *She tilted the mirror slightly so that she could see over her shoulder.*

**tim·ber** /**tim**-bur/ *noun* trees that people cut down and use for building things: *Most of the timber was used to build ships.*
( SYNONYM: **lumber** )

**time** /tīm/
● *noun*
**1** the thing that is measured in minutes, hours, years, etc.: *Frank spends a lot of time in the library studying. | I wasted so much time trying to fix my computer.*
**2** the exact hour and minute in a day that you can see on a clock: *"What time is it?" "It's quarter after five."*
**3** a period of time: *I haven't seen my brother for a long time, maybe three years.*
**4** an occasion when something happens or someone does something: *This is the first time she has ever been to New York. | I'll tell you all about it the next time I see you. | I've seen the movie at least four times.*
**5** a good, bad, enjoyable, etc. experience: *We had a great time at the beach.*

**IDIOMS with time**
**in time** early enough to do something: *Make sure you're home in time for dinner.*
**on time** at the right time, and not early or late: *The train arrived on time.*

● *verb*
**1** to arrange for something to happen at a particular time: *The fireworks are timed to go off at the end of the show.*
**2** to measure how long it takes someone to do something: *Our coach timed us running 100 meters, and I was the fastest.*

**time·line** /**tīm**-līn/ *noun* a line next to which you write different events to show the order in which they happened: *On the classroom wall, we have a timeline of the 20th century showing all the important historical events.*

**time out** /tīm **owt**/ *noun* a short break during a sports game when players rest or receive instructions from their coach: *Denver's coach called a time out.*

**tim·er** /**tīm**-ur/ *noun* a part of a machine or system that you use to make it stop or start at a particular time: *We set the timer to switch the heating on an hour before we get home.*

**times** /tīmz/ *preposition* multiplied by: *Two times two equals four (2 x 2 = 4).*

**times ta·ble** /tīmz **tayb**-uhl/ *noun* a list that shows the results when you multiply a number by a set of other numbers, usually the numbers 1 to 10. For example, the times table for 3 is 1 x 3 = 3, 2 x 3 = 6, 3 x 3 = 9, etc.
( SYNONYM: **multiplication table** )

**time zone** /tīm zohn/ *noun* one of the 24 areas that the world is divided into, each of which has its own time: *When you fly from New York to Los Angeles, you cross four time zones: Eastern Time, Central Time, Mountain Time, and Pacific Time.*

**tim·id** /**tim**-id/ *adjective* shy and nervous: *Ruth was too timid to tell Freddie that she liked him.*

**tin** /tin/ *noun* a soft silver-white metal. Tin is used for making cans. It is often mixed with other metals, for example copper and tin make bronze. Tin is a chemical element.

**ti·ny** /**tīn**-ee/ *adjective* (**tinier**, **tiniest**) very small: *She lives in a tiny one-bedroom apartment.*

**-tion** /shuhn/

## Word Building

**-tion** is a suffix. It is used in nouns.
aboli**tion** | admira**tion** | celebra**tion** | discrimina**tion** | mo**tion** | separa**tion**
**-tion** means "the act of doing something." *Abolition* means "the act of abolishing something." *Celebration* means "the act of celebrating something," for example someone's birthday. *Motion* means "the act of moving."

a b c d e f g h i j k l m n o p q r s **t** u v w x y z

**tip** /tip/
- *noun*

**1** the end of something long, narrow, and pointed: *His glasses had slipped down to the tip of his nose.*

**2** a useful piece of advice: *The guidebook contains some useful tips on places to visit.*

**3** an additional amount of money that you give to someone who has done a job for you, as a way of thanking him or her: *You should leave a tip for the waiter.*

- *verb* (**tipping**, **tipped**)

**1** to move something so that one side of it is higher than the other: *Joel tipped his chair back and put his feet on the desk.*

**2** to give an additional amount of money to someone such as a waiter or a cab driver as a way of thanking them: *I tipped the driver $5.*

**3 tip over** to fall over after leaning forward or backward: *The candle tipped over and set fire to the rug. | A large wave tipped the boat over.*

**tip·toe** /tip-toh/
- *noun* if you stand or walk on tiptoe, you stand or walk on your toes in order to make yourself taller or to walk quietly: *I had to stand on tiptoe to see over the girl in front of me.*

- *verb* to walk quietly and carefully on your toes: *His mother tiptoed into the bedroom and turned off the lamp.* ▶ see picture on page **A15**

**on tiptoe**

She is standing on tiptoe.

**tire** /tī-ur/ *noun* a thick round piece of rubber that fits around the wheel of a car, bicycle, etc.: *My bike has a flat tire, so I will have to walk to school today.*

**tired** /tī-urd/ *adjective*

**1** if you are tired, you feel that you want to sleep or rest: *After finishing my homework, I was too tired to go out.* ▶ see **Thesaurus**

**2** if you are tired of something, you are bored with it: *I'm tired of watching TV – let's go for a bike ride.*

—**tiredness** /tī-urd-niss/ *noun* the feeling you have when you are tired

**tire·some** /tī-uhr-suhm/ *adjective* annoying and boring: *If you eat the same food every day, it can become tiresome.*

**tir·ing** /tī-uhr-ing/ *adjective* making you feel tired: *Hiking through the mountains is very tiring.*

**tis·sue** /tish-oo/ *noun*

**1** a piece of soft thin paper that you use to blow your nose: *Pass me a tissue – I'm going to sneeze.*

**2** a group of cells that form part of an animal or plant: *The doctor took a sample of tissue from his skin, in order to do some tests.*

**ti·tle** /tīt'l/ *noun*

**1** the name given to a book, painting, play, etc.: *The title of his most famous novel is "Charlie and the Chocolate Factory."*

**2** a word such as "Mr.," "Mrs.," or "Dr." that you use before someone's name: *Many women use the title "Ms."*

**3** the position of being the winner of an important sports competition: *He won the world title last year.*

**4** the name that describes someone's job: *His title is Senior Vice President.*

**to** /tuh, tu/
used with verbs to make the infinitive: *She started to cry. | It's nice to meet you.*

- *preposition*

**1** used when saying where someone or something goes: *He walks to school every day. | I'm going to the mall with Hannah.*

**2** used when saying who receives something: *My aunt sends presents to us at Christmas. | The principal made a phone call to my parents.*

**3** used when saying who or what is affected by an action: *I like talking to my friends. | Don't be so mean to your sister.*

**4** used when saying when something ends: *The ticket office is open from 9:30 to 5:00.*

**5** used when saying the place where something is attached: *Some gum had stuck to my shoe.*

**6** used when saying who has an idea or opinion: *That seems stupid to me.*

**7** used to say how much time there is before an event: *It's only two weeks to summer vacation.*

**8** used when saying that the time is a certain number of minutes before the hour: *"It's ten to four" means that it's ten minutes before four o'clock.* (SYNONYM: **of**)

**toad** /tohd/ *noun* an animal that looks like a large frog with bumpy skin. Toads live mainly on land. A toad is an amphibian (=an animal that lives on land and in water).

toad

**toast** /tohst/
● *noun*
**1** bread that has been heated until it is brown: *For breakfast, I have a piece of toast and honey.*
**2** the action of drinking a glass of wine, beer, etc. in order to thank someone, wish someone luck, or celebrate something: *At a wedding, the guests often drink a toast to the bride and groom.*
● *verb*
**1** to drink a glass of wine, beer, etc. in order to thank someone, wish someone luck, or celebrate something: *We toasted Jack's graduation with champagne.*
**2** to heat bread or other food until it is brown: *I toasted the cheese sandwich under the grill.*

**toast·er** /**tohst**-ur/ *noun* a machine used for making toast: *You can put bread or waffles into the toaster.*

**to·bac·co** /tuh-**bak**-oh/ *noun* dried brown leaves that people smoke in cigarettes and pipes: *Tobacco smoke is bad for your health.*

**to·bog·gan** /tuh-**bahg**-uhn/
● *noun* a light sled with a curved front, used for sliding down hills covered in snow
● *verb* to slide down a hill on a toboggan
—**tobogganing** /tuh-**bahg**-uhn-ing/ *noun* the activity of sliding down a hill on a toboggan: *It was snowing so we went tobogganing.*

**Word Origin: toboggan**

**Toboggan** comes from a Native American language called Algonquian. It means "a sled with a flat bottom."

**to·day** /tuh-**day**/
● *adverb*
**1** on this day: *I'm going swimming today.*
**2** at the present period of time: *People today would find it hard to live without electricity.*

● *noun*
**1** this day: *Today's date is August 24.* | *Today is my birthday.*
**2** the present period of time: *Today's cell phones are much smaller than the first models.*

**tod·dler** /**tahd**-lur/ *noun* a very young child who is just learning to walk: *A group of toddlers were playing happily in the sandbox.*

**toe** /toh/ *noun* one of the five parts at the end of your foot: *I banged my foot against the bed and hurt my big toe.* ▶ see picture at **foot**

**toe·nail** /**toh**-nayl/ *noun* the hard flat part at the end of your toe: *She paints her toenails red.*

**tof·fee** /**tof**-ee/ *noun* a sticky brown candy: *I like the toffees that are covered in chocolate.*

**to·fu** /**toh**-foo/ *noun* a soft white food made from soya beans, which originally came from China. People often eat tofu instead of meat.

**to·geth·er** /tuh-**geth**-ur/ *adverb*
**1** if two or more people do something together, they do it as a group, not alone: *The children were playing together on the swings.*
**2** if you put two or more things together, you join them so that they form a single thing: *Mix the eggs and milk together.*
**3** all in one place: *I keep all my books together on a shelf in my bedroom.*
**4** at the same time: *I mailed the two packages at the same time so they should arrive together.*
**5** against each other: *Rub your hands together to keep them warm.*

**toi·let** /**toyl**-it/ *noun* a large bowl that you sit on to get rid of waste substances from your body

**to·ken** /**tohk**-uhn/ *noun*
**1** a round piece of metal that you use instead of money in some machines: *a subway token*
**2** something that you do or give which represents your feelings towards someone: *We'd like to thank you for your help, and give you this gift as a token of our gratitude.*

**told** /tohld/ *verb* the past tense and past participle of **tell**

**tol·er·ance** /**tahl**-uhr-uhnss/ *noun* willingness to let people do, say, or believe what they want, even if you do not agree with them: *You should show more tolerance for other people's opinions.*

t

**tol·er·ant** /**tahl**-uhr-uhnt/ *adjective* letting other people do or say what they want, even if you do not approve of it: *We live in a tolerant country where people are free to have their own religious beliefs.*

**tol·er·ate** /**tahl**-uh-rayt/ *verb* to accept behavior or a situation that you do not like, and not do anything about it: *The teachers will not tolerate bad behavior in class.*

**toll** /tohl/
● *noun*
**1** the number of people that have been killed by something: *The death toll from the earthquake is almost 200.*
**2** money that you pay to use a road, bridge, or tunnel: *If we take the tunnel under the river, we'll have to pay a toll.*
● *verb*
if a large bell tolls, or you toll it, it keeps ringing slowly: *The bells of St. Luke's Church were tolling for Sunday Mass.*

**to·ma·to** /tuh-**mayt**-oh/ *noun* (plural **tomatoes**) a soft round red fruit, that is eaten as a vegetable. You eat tomatoes in salads, soups, and sauces: *I sliced some tomatoes and put them into the salad.* ▶ see picture on page **A7**

> ## Word Origin: tomato
>
> **Tomato** comes from the Aztec language, Nahuatl. The word it comes from means "swelling fruit." The Spanish explorers had never seen a tomato before, and they borrowed the word from the Aztecs. When tomatoes were first grown in England, people would not eat them because they thought they were poisonous.

**tomb** /toom/ *noun* a large grave or room where a dead person is buried: *George Washington's tomb at Mount Vernon contains the bodies of the former president and his wife.*

**to·mor·row** /tuh-**mar**-oh/
● *noun* the day after today: *If today is Sunday, tomorrow is Monday.* | *The team doesn't have a catcher for tomorrow's game.*
● *adverb* on or during the day after today: *Let's go bowling tomorrow.*

**ton** /tuhn/ *noun* a unit for measuring weight. A ton is equal to 2,000 pounds: *Big trucks weigh several tons.*

**tone** /tohn/ *noun*
**1** the way that your voice sounds, which shows how you are feeling: *He spoke in an angry tone.*
**2** the general feeling or quality that something has: *The tone of the letter was very friendly.*
**3** one of the sounds that you hear on the telephone: *I knew the phone line was dead because I couldn't hear a dial tone.*
**4** how firm and strong your muscles or skin are: *Swimming improves your muscle tone.*
**5** the difference in pitch between two musical notes that are separated by one key on the piano

**tongs** /tahngz/ *plural noun* a tool you use for picking things up. Tongs have two thin pieces that are joined together at the top: *She used tongs to turn the hotdogs over on the barbecue.*

tongs

**tongue** /tuhng/ *noun*
**1** the soft part inside your mouth that moves when you eat and speak: *Don't stick your tongue out – it's rude.*
**2** a language: *Her native tongue is Spanish.*

**tongue twist·er** /**tuhng** twist-ur/ *noun* a word or phrase with many similar sounds that is difficult to say quickly: *"She sells sea shells by the sea shore" is a well-known tongue twister.*

**to·night** /tuh-**nīt**/
● *adverb* during the night of this day: *We're going to see a movie tonight.*
● *noun* the night of this day: *Do you have any plans for tonight?* | *Tonight is the first night of our school play.*

**ton·sil·li·tis** /tahnss-uh-**līt**-iss/ *noun* an infection of the tonsils that causes a sore throat and a fever: *Lisa is in bed because she has tonsillitis.*

**ton·sils** /**tahnss**-uhlz/ *plural noun* the two small round pieces of flesh at the sides of your throat, near the back of your tongue

**too** /too/ *adverb*
**1** used when you want to say that another thing is also true: *She can play the violin, and the piano too.* ( SYNONYMS: **also, as well** )
**2** used when saying that something is true about another person or thing: *"I love playing baseball." "Me too."*
**3** more than you like, want, or need: *It's too hot to play outside.* | *There is too much food for one person to eat.*

**took** /tuk/ *verb* the past tense of **take**

**tool** /tool/ *noun* a thing such as a hammer or screwdriver that you use for making or doing something. You usually hold the tool in your hands.

**tool**
tools

**tool·bar** /**tool**-bar/
*noun* a row of small pictures on a computer screen. You choose one of the pictures and click on it, in order to make a computer program do things.

**tooth** /tooth/ *noun* (plural **teeth** /teeth/) one of the hard white things in your mouth that you use for biting food: *I always brush my teeth before I go to bed.*

**tooth**

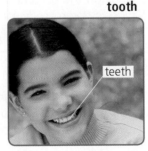

teeth

**tooth·ache** /**tooth**-ayk/ *noun* a pain in a tooth: *I had a toothache, so I went to see the dentist.*

**tooth·brush** /**tooth**-bruhsh/ *noun* a small brush for cleaning your teeth ▶ see picture at **brush**

**tooth·paste** /**tooth**-payst/ *noun* a substance that you use for cleaning your teeth: *Put some toothpaste on your brush and brush your teeth.*

**tooth·pick** /**tooth**-pik/ *noun* a very small pointed stick for removing pieces of food from between your teeth

**top** /tahp/
● *noun*
**1** the highest part of something: *You can see a long way from the top of the hill.* | *Jack climbed up and stood on top of the rock.*
( ANTONYM: **bottom** )
**2** a piece of clothing that covers your shoulders, chest, and back: *I don't have a top to wear with these pants.*
**3** the lid or cover for a container or pen: *I can't get the top off this jar.*
**4** if you are at the top of a group, you are the best or most important in that group: *He is very smart and near the top of the class.*
● *adjective*
**1** highest: *There was a big pile of books but I could only see the title of the top one.*
( ANTONYM: **bottom** )
**2** best or most successful: *The top score is 100 percent.*

**top**

He is standing on top of a rock.

**top·ic** /**tahp**-ik/ *noun* the subject that you speak or write about: *The topic for our discussion is "What can we do to save our planet?"*

**top-se·cret** /tahp-**seek**-rit/ *adjective* top-secret documents or information must be completely secret: *Don't tell anyone else about that – it's top-secret.*

**To·rah** /**tor**-uh/ *noun* the holy writings of the Jewish religion. The Torah is written in Hebrew and contains the first five books of the Jewish Bible.

**torch** /torch/ *noun* a long stick that you burn at one end. A torch is used for light or as a symbol: *At Easter, the people light torches and carry them through the streets of the town.*

**tore** /tor/ *verb* the past tense of **tear**

**torn** /torn/ *verb* the past participle of tear

**tor·na·do** /tor-**nayd**-oh/ *noun* (plural **tornadoes**) a violent storm with strong winds that spin around: *The tornado destroyed several buildings in the town.*

**tor·pe·do** /tor-**peed**-oh/ *noun* (plural **torpedoes**) a type of bomb that travels under water. A torpedo is fired from a ship or submarine: *The ship sank after it was hit by a torpedo.*

**tor·ti·lla** /tor-**tee**-yuh/ *noun* a type of thin round Mexican bread made from corn or wheat flour: *For lunch, we had beans rolled in tortillas.*

**tor·toise** /**tort**-uhss/ *noun* an animal like a turtle, which lives on land and moves very slowly. It has a thick curved shell that covers its body. A tortoise can hide its head and legs inside its shell. It is a kind of reptile.

**tor·ture** /**torch**-ur/ *verb* to hurt someone deliberately in a very cruel way: *The enemy tortured their prisoners by making them stand for days and refusing to let them sleep.*

**toss** /toss/ *verb* to throw something in a careless way: *Chris came in and tossed his jacket on the sofa.*

**to·tal** /**toht**'l/
● *adjective*
**1** complete: *No one said anything. There was total silence in the room.*
**2** including all the amounts or points: *At the end of the game, my total score was 68.*
● *noun*
the number that you get when you add all the amounts or points together: *I spent a total of $25 at the store.*
● *verb*
to be a specific amount when you add everything together: *I've added all the numbers together and they total 548.*

**to·tal·ly** /**toht**'l-ee/ *adverb* completely: *Sam and David are brothers but they like totally different things.*

**to·tem pole** /**toht**-uhm pohl/ *noun* a tall wooden pole with images of animals or plants on it. Totem poles are made by Native Americans.

**tou·can** /**took**-uhn/ *noun* a tropical bird with brightly colored feathers and a large curved beak

**touch** /tuhch/
● *verb*
**1** to put your finger or hand on something or someone: *Don't touch that pan – it's hot.*
▶ see **Thesaurus**

**2** if things touch, they come together so that there is no space between them: *We were sitting so close together that our shoulders were touching.*
● *noun*
**1** the sense that you use when you feel something with your fingers. Touch is one of the five senses: *Babies pick up things because they learn about the world through the sense of touch.*
**2** the action of putting your finger or hand on someone or something: *I felt her touch on my shoulder.*
**3** a small amount of something: *The soup needs a touch more salt.*

> **IDIOM with touch**
> **keep/stay in touch** to regularly speak or write to someone who you do not see often: *I go to a new school now but I keep in touch with my old friends.*

**touch·down** /**tuhch**-down/ *noun*
**1** if someone scores a touchdown, he or she moves the ball over the other team's line in football: *Everyone cheered when Daniel scored the winning touchdown.*
**2** the moment when an airplane or spacecraft lands on the ground: *The pilot puts the airplane's wheels down ready for touchdown.*

**touch·ing** /**tuhch**-ing/ *adjective* making you feel sympathy or sadness: *The movie is a touching story about a little boy and his dog.*

**touch·y** /**tuhch**-ee/ *adjective* easily offended or annoyed: *She is very touchy about her work and you must be careful not to criticize her.*

**tough** /tuhf/ *adjective*
**1** difficult to do or deal with: *She asked me a lot of tough questions and I wasn't sure what to say.* (SYNONYM: **hard**) (ANTONYM: **easy**)
**2** strong and determined: *People admire him because he's tough and he gets what he wants.*
**3** strong and difficult to damage: *The tent is made from a tough cotton material called canvas.*
**4** very strict: *The school is pretty tough on kids who break the rules.*
**5** difficult to cut or bite: *Some of this meat is too tough to eat.* (ANTONYM: **tender**)

**tough·en** /**tuhf**-uhn/ *verb*
**1** to make a rule or law more strict: *Some of the*

children were behaving badly so the school has toughened its rules.

**2 toughen up** to make someone stronger: *In the army they do a lot of training to toughen the men up.*

**tour** /toor/

● *noun*

**1** a trip to different places in a country or area: *We want to go on a tour of California to Los Angeles, San Francisco, and San Diego.*

**2** a short trip around a building or city: *A guide took us on a tour of the museum.*

**3** a trip to different places to give concerts or plays: *The band is on tour performing songs from their new album.*

● *verb*

to travel around an area and visit different places: *Before she goes to college, she's spending a few months touring Australia.*

**tour·ism** /**toor**-iz-uhm/ *noun* the business of providing tourists with places to stay and things to do: *The country makes most of its money through tourism.*

**tour·ist** /**toor**-ist/ *noun* someone who visits a place for pleasure: *The beach is very popular with tourists.*

**tour·na·ment** /**toorn**-uh-muhnt/ *noun* a competition between many players or teams. The players or teams compete against each other until there is one winner: *Our school team won the girls' basketball tournament.*

**tow** /toh/ *verb* if one vehicle tows another one, it pulls the other vehicle along behind it: *If you park in the wrong place, your car might get towed away!*

tow

The truck is towing a car.

**to·ward** /tord/ (also **towards**) *preposition*

**1** in the direction of: *Harvey was walking toward the bus stop.*

**2** just before a time: *Toward noon the rain stopped.*

**3** showing how you behave to someone: *Be very gentle toward her – she's only a baby.*

**tow·el** /**tow**-uhl/ *noun* a piece of cloth for drying something: *If you're going swimming, remember to take a towel.*

**tow·er** /**tow**-ur/ *noun* a tall narrow building or part of a building: *The castle has two towers on the outside wall.*

**town** /town/ *noun* a place that has many houses, stores, and offices but is smaller than a city: *We live in a town called La Porte.*

▶ see **Thesaurus**

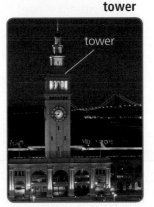

tower

tower

**town meet·ing** /town **meet**-ing/ *noun* a meeting where people who live in a town discuss problems that affect their town

**tox·ic** /**tahkss**-ik/ *adjective* poisonous: *Toxic chemicals leaked into the river and killed the fish.*

**toy** /toy/ *noun* a thing for children to play with: *My brother's favorite toy is a red plastic car he can ride on.*

**trace** /trayss/

● *verb*

**1** to copy a picture by drawing on a thin piece of paper that you put over the picture: *Use tracing paper and trace the map.*

**2** to find someone or something that has disappeared: *Police are trying to trace the owner of a car that has been left outside the school.*

**3** to find out when something began or where it came from: *My family can trace its history back to Peru, where my grandfather came from.*

● *noun*

**1** if there is no trace of something, you cannot find it anywhere: *She looked for her rabbit everywhere but there was no trace of him.*

**2** a very small amount of something that is difficult to notice: *In the morning there were a few traces of snow on the ground.*

a b c d e f g h i j k l m n o p q r s **t** u v w x y z

## track /trak/

● *noun*

**1** a course on which people, cars, or horses race: *The cars raced around the track.*

**2** the two metal lines that a train travels on: *Don't cross the train tracks when the lights are flashing.*

**3 tracks** marks on the ground that were made by someone or something moving along: *A fox had left tracks in the snow.*

**4** the sport of running races on a track: *He ran track in high school.*

**5** a group of sports including running, jumping, and throwing: *She's on the track team – her sport is the high jump.*

track

tracks

IDIOMS with **track**

**keep track** to pay attention so that you know what is happening to someone or something: *There are so many students that it is difficult to keep track of them all.*

**lose track** to forget to pay attention to someone or something, so that you do not know what is happening: *I enjoyed the game so much that I lost track of time, and I arrived home late.*

● *verb*

**track down** to find someone or something by searching or asking questions: *I finally tracked down the book I wanted at the library on Maple Street.*

## track and field /trak uhn **feeld**/ *noun* sports that involve running races, jumping, and throwing things

## trac·tor /**trakt**-ur/ *noun*

a powerful vehicle with large wheels that is used to pull machinery on farms: *The tractor was pulling a load of hay.*

tractor

## trade /trayd/

● *noun*

**1** the business of buying and selling goods: *The U.S. does a lot of trade with China.*

**2** if you make a trade, you exchange something you have for something that another person has: *Let's make a trade – my baseball cap for your soccer ball.*

**3** a job that involves work with your hands: *Chris is an electrician by trade.*

● *verb*

**1** to exchange one thing for another: *Do you want to trade your cheese sandwich for my tuna sandwich?*

**2** to buy and sell goods: *We trade with many countries all over the world.*

## trade·mark /**trayd**-mark/ *noun* a word or picture on a product that shows the product is made by a particular company: *"Coca-Cola" and "Google" are trademarks, so no other company can call their product by those names.*

## trade-off /**trayd**-of/ *noun* a balance between two opposing things, in which one may have a bad effect on the other: *There's a trade-off – this computer is much cheaper, but it's not very good quality.*

## trade wind /**trayd** wind/ *noun* a wind that blows continuously toward the equator from the northeast or the southeast: *A trade wind took their boat toward land.*

## tra·di·tion /truh-**dish**-uhn/ *noun* something that people have done for a long time, and continue to do: *It's a tradition to give gifts on someone's birthday.*

## tra·di·tion·al /truh-**dish**-uhn'l/ *adjective* based on ideas and ways of doing things that have existed for a long time: *The dancers were wearing the colorful traditional costumes of Mexico.*

## traf·fic /**traf**-ik/ *noun* the vehicles moving along a road: *There's a lot of traffic on the roads in the morning when people are going to work.*

## traf·fic jam /**traf**-ik jam/ *noun* a long line of vehicles on the road that are not moving or are moving very slowly: *We got stuck in a traffic jam on the freeway and it took us an hour to go five miles.*

## traf·fic light /**traf**-ik līt/ (also traf·fic sig·nal /**traf**-ik sig-nuhl/) *noun* a set of colored lights at the side of the road that show when cars are

allowed to move: *The driver stopped because the traffic light turned red.*

**trag·e·dy** /**traj**-uhd-ee/ *noun* (plural **tragedies**)
**1** a very sad event: *The football game ended in tragedy when one of the boys broke his leg when he was tackled.*
**2** a serious play with a sad ending: *The play "Romeo and Juliet" is a tragedy because both the main characters die.*

**tra·gic** /**traj**-ik/ *adjective* very sad: *After the tragic death of President Kennedy, Johnson became president.*
—**tragically** /**traj**-ik-lee/ *adverb* in a very sad way: *Tragically, many houses were destroyed in the fire.*

**trail** /trayl/ *noun*
**1** a dirt path that you walk on through a forest, in the mountains, etc.: *We hiked on the trail up Deer Mountain.*
**2** a long line or a series of marks that has been left by someone or something: *A trail of animal tracks led across the snow.*

**trail·blaz·er** /**trayl**-blayz-ur/ *noun* someone who is the first person to do something

**trail·er** /**trayl**-ur/ *noun*
**1** (also **trailer home**) a small metal house that can be moved on a truck. A trailer home is shaped like a long box: *After the hurricane destroyed their houses, people were given trailers to live in.* (SYNONYM: **mobile home**)
**2** a vehicle that can be pulled behind a car, that has beds and a kitchen in it and is used for vacations: *A car with a trailer pulled into the campsite.*
**3** a vehicle that can be pulled behind a car or truck, used for carrying something heavy: *They loaded the boat onto the trailer.*

**train** /trayn/
● *noun*
a vehicle that runs on metal tracks. A train has many railroad cars that can carry people or things: *I took the train from Grand Central Station.* | *There were no flights so we decided to go by train.*
● *verb*
**1** to teach someone the skills they need to do something difficult: *We trained the dog to roll over and sit.*

**2** to prepare for a sports competition by exercising and practicing: *He has been running a lot to train for a marathon.*

**train**

**train·ing** /**trayn**-ing/ *noun* activities that help you learn how to do a job or play a sport: *He finished his training and became a pilot in the air force.*

**trai·tor** /**trayt**-ur/ *noun* someone who helps the enemies of his or her country or group: *He was a traitor who gave secret information to the enemy during the war.*

**tramp** /tramp/
● *noun* someone poor who has no home or job and moves from place to place: *Sometimes you see tramps sleeping on the sidewalk.*
● *verb* to walk somewhere with heavy steps: *The soldiers tramped through the muddy fields.*

**tram·po·line**
/tramp-uh-**leen**/ *noun* a piece of sports equipment that you jump up and down on. A trampoline is made of a large piece of material attached with springs to a metal frame: *Watch me do a somersault on the trampoline!*

**trampoline**

trampoline

**trance** /transs/ *noun* a state in which you seem to be asleep, but you are still able to hear and understand things: *I saw a magician on TV who put a woman into a trance and then got her to do silly things.*

**trans-** /transs, tranz/

> ### Word Building
>
> **trans**continental | **trans**late | **trans**parent | **trans**portation
>
> These words all have the Latin word root **trans-** in them. ***Trans-*** means "across" or "beyond." The *transcontinental* railroad went across the North American continent. If a radio *transmits* a signal, it sends it across an area to another radio. *Transportation* is things like trains or cars that take you across a city or state.

**trans·ac·tion** /tran-**zak**-shuhn/ *noun* an action in which you buy or sell something: *The cash register wasn't working, so the salesman had to write down each transaction on a piece of paper.*

**trans·at·lan·tic** /tranz-uht-**lant**-ik/ *adjective* crossing the Atlantic Ocean: *We took a transatlantic flight from New York to London.*

**trans·con·ti·nen·tal** /transs-kahnt-uhn-**ent**'l/ *adjective* crossing a continent: *The transcontinental railroad that linked the western states to the east was finished in 1869.*

**trans·fer** /**transs**-fur/
• *verb* (**transferring**, **transferred**) to move someone or something from one place to another: *Dad's company is transferring him from San Francisco to New York.* | *She transferred the money into her savings account.*
• *noun*
**1** the process of moving someone or something from one place to another: *There is a transfer of power from one president to the next.*
**2** a ticket that allows a passenger to change from one bus, train, etc. to another without paying more money: *Ask the bus driver for a transfer because you need to change buses.*

**trans·form** /transs-**form**/ *verb* to change someone or something completely: *The Internet has transformed our lives. You can find lots of information quickly instead of spending hours in a library.*
—**transformation** /transs-fur-**maysh**-uhn/ *noun* a complete change in someone or something: *The transformation of a caterpillar into a butterfly takes several weeks.*

**tran·sit** /**tranz**-it/ *noun*
**1** a system for moving people or goods from one place to another, using buses, trains, etc.: *In New York, many people use public transit, especially the subway and buses, to get to work.*
**2 in transit** when someone or something is being taken from one place to another: *The package was lost in transit.*

**tran·si·tion** /tran-**zish**-uhn/ *noun* a change from one situation or condition to another: *The school tries to make the transition from kindergarten to first grade easy for the children.*

**trans·late** /**tranz**-layt/ *verb* to change speech or writing from one language to another: *I translated the sentence from Spanish into English.*
—**translator** /**tranz**-layt-ur/ *noun* someone who translates things from one language into another

**trans·la·tion** /tranz-**laysh**-uhn/ *noun*
**1** something that has been changed from one language into another: *I read an English translation of the Spanish story.*
**2** the process of changing the words of one language into another: *The computer program does translation, but it doesn't always get the meaning right.*

**trans·mis·sion** /tranz-**mish**-uhn/ *noun* a set of gears in a car that makes power from the engine go to turn the wheels

**trans·mit** /tranz-**mit**/ *verb* (**transmitting**, **transmitted**)
**1** to send out radio, television, or computer signals from one place to another: *Over the Internet, computers transmit data at very high speeds.*
**2** to pass a disease from one person to another: *The flu virus is transmitted through the air by coughing or sneezing.*
—**transmitter** /tranz-**mit**-ur/ *noun* a machine that sends out radio or television signals: *Scientists put small radio transmitters on the bears so that they can find out where the bears go.*

**trans·par·ent** /transs-**parr**-uhnt/ *adjective* if something is transparent, you can see through it: *The plastic cover is transparent.*

**trans·plant** /transs-**plant**/ *verb*
**1** to remove an organ from someone's body and put it in the body of a sick person who needs it:

*The man died in a car accident, and doctors transplanted his liver into a patient whose liver had failed.*
**2** to move a plant from one place to another: *We grew the beans in pots and then transplanted them into the vegetable garden.*
● *noun*
an operation to transplant an organ: *He had a kidney transplant and is now very healthy.*

**trans·port** /transs-**port**/ *verb* to move things or people from one place to another in a vehicle: *The trucks transport fruit and vegetables to the supermarkets.*

**trans·por·ta·tion** /transs-pur-**taysh**-uhn/ *noun*
**1** vehicles that people use to travel from one place to another: *Bicycles are a good form of transportation. They don't cause pollution and they give you exercise.*
**2** the activity of moving people or things from one place to another: *The company uses planes for the transportation of goods from the U.S. to Europe.*

**trap** /trap/
● *noun*
**1** a piece of equipment for catching animals: *a mouse trap*
**2** a trick that is used to catch or harm someone: *The police set a trap for the thieves.*
● *verb* (**trapping**, **trapped**)
**1 be trapped** to not be able to escape from a bad place or situation: *Three people were trapped in the burning building.*
**2** to catch an animal in a trap

**tra·peze** /tra-**peez**/ *noun* a short bar hanging from two ropes above the ground: *A circus acrobat was swinging on the trapeze high above the ground.*

**trap·e·zoid**
/**trap**-uh-zoyd/ *noun* a shape with four sides. Two of the sides are parallel (=the same distance apart) and two sides are not parallel.

**trapezoid**

**trash** /trash/ *noun*
**1** things that you do not want and throw away, for example food, paper, or plastic: *Don't just drop your trash on the ground, put it in a trash can. | It's my job to take out the trash from the kitchen.*
〔SYNONYM: **garbage**〕
**2** something that is of very bad quality: *There is a lot of trash on TV and I can't understand why people watch it.*

**trash can** /**trash** kan/ *noun* a large container outside your house in which you put things such as old food and paper that you do not want: *We always put old food wrappers in the trash can.*
〔SYNONYM: **garbage can**〕

**trau·ma** /**trom**-uh/ *noun* a very upsetting experience that has a strong effect on someone: *Some soldiers have a hard time dealing with the trauma of their war experiences.*

**trau·mat·ic** /truh-**mat**-ik/ *adjective* very upsetting: *Sara's parents' divorce was traumatic for her, especially because her dad moved so far away afterwards.*

**trav·el** /**trav**-uhl/
● *verb*
**1** to go from one place to another: *The pioneers traveled across the Great Plains in covered wagons.* ▶ see **Thesaurus**
**2** to move a particular distance or at a particular speed: *Lewis and Clark traveled over 5,000 miles.*
**3** in basketball, to walk or run without bouncing the ball on the floor. You are not allowed to travel: *The referee saw her traveling with the ball and blew his whistle.*
● *noun*
the activity of traveling: *Dad's job involves a lot of travel. This week he's in Atlanta. Next week he'll be in Minneapolis.*

**Word Origin:** travel

**Travel** came into English from Old French in the 1300s. The Old French word meant "to work hard." Travel today can be a lot of fun, but in the Middle Ages it was hard work. People had to walk, ride a horse, or go on a ship to go anywhere.

a b c d e f g h i j k l m n o p q r s t u v w x y z

**trav·el a·gen·cy** /**trav**-uhl ayj-uhnss-ee/ *noun* a business that arranges travel and vacations for people

**trav·el·er** /**trav**-uhl-ur/ *noun* someone who goes on a trip: *He is a frequent traveler between New York and Los Angeles because of his job.*

**tra·vois** /tra-**voy**/ *noun* a wooden frame used for pulling things or people along the ground. A travois consisted of two poles and a platform or net. It was used by Native Americans.

**trawl·er** /**trol**-ur/ *noun* a fishing boat. The trawler catches fish by pulling a big net along the bottom of the ocean.

**tray** /tray/ *noun* a flat object that is used for carrying things such as plates and glasses: *Mom was carrying three glasses of orange juice on a tray.*

tray

tray

**treach·er·ous** /**trech**-uhr-uhss/ *adjective*
**1** dangerous: *Ice makes the roads treacherous and there are often car accidents in the winter.*
**2** someone who is treacherous secretly intends to harm his or her friends: *In the story "Hansel and Gretel," the stepmother is a treacherous woman who wants to get rid of the two children.*
—**treachery** /**trech**-uhr-ee/ *noun* the actions of a treacherous person

**tread** /tred/ *noun* the lines in the surface of a tire or the bottom of a shoe: *The tread on a car tire helps it to grip the road.*

**tread·mill** /**tred**-mil/ *noun* a piece of exercise equipment that you walk or run on. A treadmill has a large flat surface that moves: *He ran a mile on the treadmill at the gym.*

**trea·son** /**treez**-uhn/ *noun* the crime of helping your country's enemies: *Benedict Arnold was an American general who committed treason by trying to help the British during the Revolutionary War.*

**treas·ure** /**trezh**-ur/
● *noun* a group of valuable things, especially gold, silver, or jewels: *The pirates stole the treasure and hid it on an island.*
● *verb* to feel that something is very important to you and keep it very carefully: *I treasure the watch that my grandfather gave me.*

**treas·ur·er** /**trezh**-uhr-ur/ *noun* the person who takes care of an organization's money: *Please send your membership fees to the treasurer of the baseball league.*

**treas·ur·y** /**trezh**-uhr-ee/ *noun* (plural **treasuries**) the government office that controls a country's money: *The U.S. Treasury collects taxes and prints money.*

**treat** /treet/
● *verb*
**1** to behave toward someone in a particular way: *You should treat your teachers with respect.*
**2** to do something to make a sick or injured person better: *Forty people were treated for injuries after the accident.*
**3** to deal with something in a particular way: *The school treats bullying very seriously.*
**4** to buy something special for someone: *We're going to treat Mom to dinner for her birthday.*
● *noun*
something nice and special: *Homemade brownies are my favorite treat.*

**Word Family: treat**

**treat** *verb* | **treat** *noun* | **treatment** *noun*

**treat·ment** /**treet**-muhnt/ *noun*
**1** a way of making a sick or injured person better: *This new drug is a treatment for heart disease.*
**2** a way of behaving toward someone: *The school's treatment of new students must make them feel welcome.*

**trea·ty** /**treet**-ee/ *noun* (plural **treaties**) a written agreement between two or more countries: *The two countries signed a peace treaty to end the war between them.*

**tree** /tree/ *noun* a tall plant that has branches, leaves, a trunk, and roots: *an apple tree*

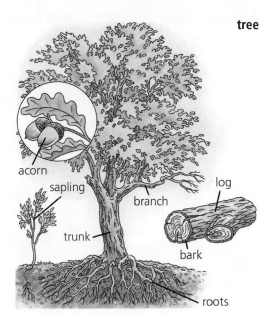

**tree**

acorn
sapling
branch
log
trunk
bark
roots

**tree di·a·gram** /**tree** dī-uh-gram/ *noun* a drawing that shows how likely a particular result is when many results are possible: *If you have six balls of different colors in a bag, a tree diagram can help you figure out the probability of taking one green ball and one red ball out of the bag.*

**trem·ble** /**trem**-buhl/ *verb* to shake: *She began to tremble with fear when she saw the gun in his hand.*

**tre·men·dous** /tri-**mend**-uhss/ *adjective*
**1** very large in size, amount, or power: *A motorcycle went past at tremendous speed.*
**2** very good: *He's a tremendous basketball player.*

**trem·or** /**trem**-ur/ *noun* a small earthquake in which the ground shakes slightly

**trench** /trench/ *noun* a long narrow hole that is dug in the ground: *The workmen are digging a trench for a new gas pipe.*

**trend** /trend/ *noun* the way that a situation is changing or developing: *There is a trend toward driving cars that use less gas.*

**trend·y** /**trend**-ee/ *adjective* (**trendier**, **trendiest**) relating to things that are popular or stylish now: *She wears trendy clothes and the other girls try to copy her style.*
( SYNONYM: **fashionable** )

**tres·pass** /**tress**-pass/ *verb* to go onto someone's land without permission: *They have dogs that might attack anyone who trespasses on their land.*

**tri-** /trī/

**Word Building**

**tri-** is a prefix.
**tri**angle | **tri**athlon | **tri**ceratops |
**tri**cycle | **tri**o | **tri**ple
**tri-** means "three." A *triangle* is a shape with three angles. A *tricycle* is a bike with three wheels. A *trio* is a group of three people.

**tri·al** /**trī**-uhl/ *noun*
**1** an event in which the people in a court of law listen to information about a crime and then decide whether someone is guilty: *The trial of the bank robber ended, and he was sent to prison.*
**2** a test to find out if someone or something is good or effective: *Scientists are doing trials of the new medicine to see if it really works.*

**tri·an·gle** /**trī**-ang-guhl/ *noun*
**1** a flat shape with three straight sides that meet at three angles: *She cut the sandwich into two triangles.*
**2** a musical instrument shaped like a triangle. It is made of metal. You hit it with a metal stick to make a ringing sound.
—**triangular** /trī-**ang**-gyuhl-ur/ *adjective* in the shape of a triangle: *The napkin was folded in a triangular shape.*

**triangle**

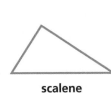

**equilateral triangle**
all three sides are the same length

**isosceles triangle**
at least two sides are the same length

**scalene triangle**
all three sides are of different lengths

**tri·an·gu·lar pyr·a·mid** /trī-ang-gyuhl-ur **pirr**-uh-mid/ *noun* a shape that has a triangle as a base and three triangles as sides

**tri·ath·lon** /trī-**ath**-lahn/ *noun* a sports competition in which you run, swim, and ride a bicycle

**trib·al** /**trīb**-uhl/ *adjective* relating to a tribe: *The Navajo tribal council meets four times a year in the reservation's capital, Window Rock, Arizona.*

683

a b c d e f g h i j k l m n o p q r s **t** u v w x y z

**tribe** /trīb/ *noun* a group of people who have their own language and ways of living: *The Native American tribes on the plains hunted buffalo for food.*

**trib·u·ta·ry** /**trib**-yuh-tair-ee/ *noun* (plural **tributaries**) a river or stream that flows into a larger river

**tri·cer·a·tops** /trī-**serr**-uh-tahpss/ *noun* a dinosaur with three horns on its head
▶ see picture at **dinosaur**

**Word Origin: triceratops**

**Triceratops** comes from Greek words that mean "three-horned face." Many dinosaurs have names that describe the way they look.

**trick** /trik/
● *noun*
**1** an action you do to make someone believe something that is not true, or a joke that you do to make someone mad: *I played a trick on my sister by putting a plastic spider in her bed.*
**2** an action that entertains people because they cannot see how you do it: *The magician did a trick where he pulled a rabbit out of an empty hat.*
● *verb*
to make someone believe something that is not true: *My friend tried to trick me into going with him to the park by saying my mother said it was okay, when she never did.*

**trick·le** /**trik**-uhl/
● *verb* to flow slowly in a thin line: *Sweat trickled down his face.*
● *noun* a small amount of liquid that is flowing slowly: *There was only a trickle of water in the stream.*

trickle

**trick or treat** /trik or **treet**/ *interjection* said by children when they dress in costumes on Halloween and go from house to house. The children will play a trick on someone if they are not given some candy.

**trick·y** /**trik**-ee/ *adjective* difficult and needing to be thought about carefully: *This math question is tricky and I can't figure out the answer.*

**tri·cy·cle** /**trīss**-ik-uhl/ *noun* a vehicle for small children. A tricycle has one wheel at the front and two wheels at the back. You sit on it and push the pedals with your feet to make it move: *My little sister likes riding her tricycle.*

tricycle

**tried** /trīd/ *verb* the past tense and past participle of **try**

**trig·ger** /**trig**-ur/
● *noun* the part of a gun that you move with your finger to fire it: *The soldier aimed his gun and pulled the trigger.*
● *verb* to make something happen: *One of the boys said something during the game that triggered a fight.*

**tril·lion** /**tril**-yuhn/ *number* 1,000,000,000,000

**trim** /trim/ *verb* (**trimming**, **trimmed**) to cut a small amount off something to make it look neater: *Your hair needs trimming – when are you going to get it cut?*

**tri·o** /**tree**-oh/ *noun* a group of three people, especially musicians: *A trio came to play at the school. There was a piano player, a violin player, and a cello player.*

**trip** /trip/
● *noun*
a visit to a place that you travel to: *Julia's going on a trip to Hawaii! | a camping trip*
▶ see **Thesaurus**
● *verb* (**tripping**, **tripped**)
**1** to hit your foot against something so that you fall or almost fall: *I tripped on a rock and fell.*
▶ see picture on page **A15**
**2** to make someone fall by putting something in front of his or her foot: *Brian stuck out his foot and tripped Joe.*

**tri·ple** /**trip**-uhl/
● *adjective* involving three similar things: *He is a triple gold medal winner. That means he has three gold medals!*
● *verb* to become three times as big: *The tree*

*quickly tripled in size. It went from two feet tall to six feet tall in just two years.*

**tri·umph** /**trī**-uhmf/ *noun* an important win or success: *His triumph in the race was followed by a second win in the long jump.*

SYNONYMS: **victory, win**   ANTONYM: **defeat**

—**triumphant** /trī-**uhmf**-uhnt/ *adjective* very happy and proud because you have won or succeeded: *She had a triumphant smile on her face after winning the race.*

**triv·i·a** /**triv**-ee-uh/ *noun* facts that are not important: *The magazine was full of trivia about famous actors and actresses.*

**triv·i·al** /**triv**-ee-uhl/ *adjective* not important: *Why are you crying over something as trivial as breaking a plate?*

**troll** /trohl/ *noun* an imaginary creature in fairy tales, who is sometimes big and frightening or sometimes like a magic person: *In the story, the troll under the bridge wanted to eat the goats.*

**trol·ley** /**trahl**-ee/ *noun* an electric vehicle like a bus that runs on metal tracks: *We took the trolley downtown.*

**trom·bone** /trahm-**bohn**/ *noun* a metal musical instrument that you play by blowing into it and moving a long sliding part

—**trombonist** /trahm-**bohn**-ist/ *noun* someone who plays the trombone

**trombone**

**troop** /troop/ *noun*

**1 troops** soldiers: *More troops will go to fight in the area.*

**2** a group of people or animals: *Our Girl Scout troop meets on Fridays.*

**troop·er** /**troop**-ur/ *noun* a member of a state police force in the U.S.: *A state trooper pulled the car over for speeding.*

**tro·phy** /**trohf**-ee/ *noun* (plural **trophies**) a metal cup or other object that someone gets for winning a game or race: *She was a great swimmer and won a lot of trophies.*

**trophy**

**trop·i·cal** /**trahp**-ik-uhl/ *adjective* in or from the hottest and wettest parts of the world: *Birds such as macaws and toucans live in tropical jungles in South America.*

**trop·ics** /**trahp**-ikss/ *noun* **the tropics** the hottest and wettest parts of the world, near the equator: *Bananas grow in the tropics.*

**trot** /traht/ *verb* (**trotting**, **trotted**) to run with quick short steps: *The horse was trotting around the field.*

**trou·ble** /**truhb**-uhl/

● *noun*

**1** problems or difficulty: *I had trouble sleeping because it was so noisy.* | *The trouble is that I can't get there on time.*

**2** an effort that you must make to do something: *Mom went to a lot of trouble to get everything ready so we could go camping.*

**IDIOM with trouble**

**in trouble**

**1** if you are in trouble, you have done something wrong and someone in charge knows about it: *He got into trouble for stealing a bicycle.*

**2** having a lot of problems: *The soup kitchen gives people food when they are in trouble and don't have money to buy food themselves.*

● *verb*

to make someone feel worried: *Is something troubling you? You don't seem very happy.*

SYNONYM: **bother**

—**troubling** /**truhb**-ling/ *adjective* making someone feel worried: *He is a smart boy, so his low grades are troubling.*

**trou·bled** /**truhb**-uhld/ *adjective*

**1** worried: *Sylvia looked troubled when I said that the boys chased me.*

**2** having a lot of problems: *Her father was violent and mean, and she had a troubled childhood.*

**trou·ble·mak·er** /**truhb**-uhl-mayk-ur/ *noun*
someone who deliberately causes problems: *The police arrested the troublemakers who were setting fires in the park.*

**trough** /trof/ *noun* a long open box that holds water or food for animals: *The farmer put food in the trough for the pigs to eat.*

**trou·sers** /**trowz**-urz/ *plural noun* another word for pants: *She's wearing a pair of pink trousers.*

**trout** /trowt/ *noun* a common river fish that is good to eat

trout

**truant** /**troo**-uhnt/ *adjective* not going to school when you do not have permission to stay away and you are not sick: *If you are truant and miss school a lot, you don't get the education you need.*

**truce** /trooss/ *noun* an agreement between two enemies to stop fighting or arguing for a period of time: *The Seminole Indians asked for a truce with the U.S. soldiers, but it was soon broken.*

**truck** /truhk/ *noun* a large vehicle that you drive on roads. People use trucks for carrying things: *They loaded the furniture into the truck.*

truck

towtruck

pickup truck

forklift truck

fire truck

truck

**true** /troo/ *adjective*
**1** correct and based on facts: *"Is it true that Miss Egan is getting married?" "Yes, next month." |*
*The movie is based on a true story.*
⟨ANTONYM: **false**⟩
**2** real: *She has been a true friend to me, and has helped me whenever I've had problems.*

**IDIOM with true**
**come true** if a dream or wish comes true, what you hope for happens: *Her dream of becoming an actress came true when she was given a part in a play.*

**Word Family: true**
**true** adjective | **untrue** adjective | **truth** noun | **truthful** adjective | **truthfully** adverb

**tru·ly** /**trool**-ee/ *adverb* used to show that you strongly believe something is correct or real: *He was truly a great man who did lots of good things during his life.* ⟨SYNONYM: **really**⟩

**trum·pet** /**truhm**-pit/ *noun* a metal musical instrument that you play by blowing into it and pressing three buttons
—**trumpeter** /**truhm**-pit-ur/ *noun* someone who plays the trumpet

trumpet

**trunk** /truhngk/ *noun*
**1** the thick main stem of a tree: *A big redwood tree can have a trunk that is over 50 feet around.* ▶ see picture at **tree**
**2** a covered place in the back of a car where you can carry things: *They put their suitcases in the trunk.*
**3** the long nose of an elephant ▶ see picture at **elephant**
**4** **trunks** short pants that men wear when they swim: *I bought a new pair of swimming trunks.*

**trust** /truhst/
● *verb* to believe that someone is good and will

do what they say or what is right: *I don't trust her because she has lied to me before.*

● *noun* the belief that you can trust someone or something: *She has a lot of trust in him because he always does what he says he'll do.*

ANTONYM: **distrust**

**Word Family:** trust

**trust** *noun* | **trust** *verb* | **trustworthy** *adjective* | **distrust** *verb*

**trust·wor·thy** /**truhst**-wurth-ee/ *adjective* someone who is trustworthy is honest, and you can trust him or her to do something: *Peter is trustworthy. I know he'll pay me back if I lend him some money.*

**truth** /trooth/ *noun* the true facts about something: *He was telling the truth when he said he didn't steal the money. Someone else did it.*

**truth·ful** /**trooth**-fuhl/ *adjective* giving the true facts about something: *He gave a truthful answer and said that he had broken the window accidentally.* SYNONYM: **honest**

—**truthfully** /**trooth**-fuhl-ee/ *adverb* in a truthful way: *I want you to answer truthfully.*

**try** /trī/
● *verb* (**tries**, **trying**, **tried**)
**1** to make an effort to do something: *I tried to do the math homework, but I didn't understand it.* SYNONYM: **attempt** ▶ see **Thesaurus**
**2** to do, use, or taste something, in order to find out if it is good or successful: *Try some of this cake. Do you like it?*
**3** if someone is tried for a crime, people in a court of law listen to information about the crime and then decide whether the person is guilty: *He was tried for robbery and found guilty.*
**4 try on** to put on a piece of clothing to find out if it fits or makes you look nice: *I tried on a yellow dress, but it was too big.*
**5 try out** to use something in order to find out if it works or is good: *Have you had a chance to try out your new computer game yet?*
● *noun* (plural **tries**)
an attempt to do something: *How about giving golf a try? You might like playing it.*

**try·out** /**trī**-owt/ *noun* a time when people who want to be on a sports team are tested so that

the best players can be chosen: *My brother is going to the baseball tryouts. He's a good player so maybe he'll make the team.*

**T-shirt** /**tee** shurt/ *noun* a soft cotton shirt, with short sleeves: *He was wearing a T-shirt and jeans.*

**Word Origin:** T-shirt

The word **T-shirt** was invented in the 1920s. When you lay a T-shirt flat, it is shaped like the letter T.

**tsu·na·mi** /tsu-**nahm**-ee/ *noun* a very large ocean wave that destroys buildings and kills people. It is caused by an earthquake or volcano under the water.

**tub** /tuhb/ *noun*
**1** a long container that you fill with water and sit in to wash yourself: *She ran some more hot water into the tub then got in.*
SYNONYM: **bathtub**
**2** a round plastic or paper container that food is sold in: *I put the tub of margarine on the table.*

tub

a tub of popcorn

**tu·ba** /**toob**-uh/ *noun* a large metal musical instrument that you play by blowing into it. Tubas make very low sounds.

tuba

**Word Origin:** tuba

**Tuba** came into English from French in the 1800s. The French word came from a Latin word for a trumpet that was used in wars to give signals to soldiers. The Latin word comes from the word for "tube."

a b c d e f g h i j k l m n o p q r s **t** u v w x y z

**tube** /toob/ *noun*

**1** a container for something such as toothpaste, paint, or food. You press or twist the tube to get the toothpaste out. A tube is usually round at one or both ends: *Squeeze the substance out of the tube.* | *a tube of lipstick*

**2** a narrow pipe that a liquid or gas can flow through: *Let some water flow out of the fish tank through a plastic tube.*

**3** an object that has ends shaped like circles and solid sides, and is hollow in the middle: *The toilet paper is wrapped around a cardboard tube.*

**tube**

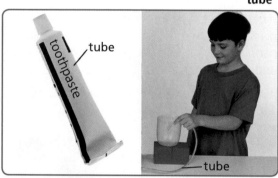

tube

toothpaste

tube

tube

**tu·ber·cu·lo·sis** /tu-burk-yuh-**lohss**-iss/ *noun* a serious disease that harms your lungs. Tuberculosis can spread from one person to another when someone who is sick with the disease coughs or sneezes into the air.

SYNONYM: **TB**

**tu·bu·lar** /**toob**-yuhl-ur/ *adjective* shaped like a tube: *The chair has tubular steel legs.*

**tuck** /tuhk/ *verb*

**1** to push the edge of a cloth or piece of clothing into something else: *He tucked his shirt into his pants.*

**2** to put something in a small space or a safe place: *He tucked the newspaper under his arm.*

**3** **tuck in** to make a child feel comfortable in bed by arranging the covers around him or her: *Mom pulled up the blankets and tucked me in.*

**Tues·day** /**toozd**-ee/ *noun* ( ABBREVIATION: **Tues.** )
the third day of the week. Tuesday is between Monday and Wednesday: *He'll be back Tuesday morning.* | *Martha is going to St. Louis on Tuesday.*

**Word Origin: Tuesday**

**Tuesday** is named for the god Tiw or Tyr in an old religion. Many people in northern Europe believed in this religion before Christianity. Tiw was the god of the sky and the god of war, and Tuesday was Tiw's day.

**tug** /tuhg/

● *verb* (**tugging**, **tugged**)
to pull something suddenly and hard: *I tugged at the door, but it wouldn't open.*

● *noun*
**1** (also **tug boat** /**tuhg** boht/) a small strong boat used for pulling ships
**2** a sudden strong pull: *She grabbed the door handle and gave it a tug.*

**tu·i·tion** /too-**ish**-uhn/ *noun* the money you pay for someone to teach you: *Tuition at a private university costs more than tuition at a state college.*

**tu·lip** /**tool**-ip/ *noun* a garden flower that is brightly colored and shaped like a cup. A tulip has a long stem and large smooth leaves. Tulips grow from bulbs.

**tulip**

**tum·ble** /**tuhm**-buhl/
*verb* to fall with a rolling movement: *All the toys inside the cupboard tumbled out when I opened the door.*

**tum·ble·weed** /**tuhm**-buhl-weed/ *noun* a plant with a round shape that grows in the desert areas of North America. When tumbleweeds die and get dry, they are blown from place to place by the wind.

**tum·my** /**tuhm**-ee/ *noun* (plural **tummies**) your stomach: *I ate too much and now my tummy hurts.*

**tu·mor** /**toom**-ur/ *noun* a group of cells in someone's body that grows too quickly. Some tumors are caused by cancer: *The doctors operated to remove a brain tumor.*

**tu·na** /**toon**-uh/ *noun* a large fish that lives in the ocean. You can eat tuna: *a can of tuna*

tuna

**tun·dra** /**tuhn**-druh/ *noun* the large flat areas of land where it is very cold and there are no trees, in places such as the north of Canada and Russia

**tune** /toon/
● *noun*
a series of musical notes that are nice to listen to: *Everyone knows the tune to "Happy Birthday to You."*
● *verb*
**1** to make small changes to a musical instrument so that it makes the correct sounds: *The music teacher showed me how to tune a guitar.*
**2 tune in** to watch or listen to a particular television or radio program: *Millions of people tuned in to watch the game on TV.*

**tun·nel** /**tuhn**'l/ *noun* a passage through a mountain or under the ground: *They built a railroad tunnel through the mountain.*

tunnel

tunnel

**turf** /turf/ *noun* short grass and the soil under it: *The trucks left muddy tracks on the soft turf of the football field.*

**tur·key** /**turk**-ee/ *noun* a large bird that you can eat. It has a large tail that it can spread out. Turkeys are a North American bird: *It is traditional to eat turkey at Thanksgiving.*

turkey

**turn** /turn/
● *verb*
**1** to move your body or an object to face a different direction: *She turned and looked at me.* | *Turn your chair around to face the wall.*
**2** to start going in a different direction: *Turn right at the next light.*
**3** to move around in a circle: *The wheels of the car began to turn.* | *She turned the key and opened the door.* ▶ see **Thesaurus**
**4** to change and become different from before: *The weather turned colder.* | *The witch turned the prince into a frog.*
**5** to move a page in a book or magazine so that you can see another one: *Turn to page 32.*
**6** to become a particular age: *My brother turned four yesterday.*
**7 turn down** to make a machine less loud or less hot: *Turn the TV down; it's too loud.*
**8 turn in** to give work that you have done to your teacher: *I'm doing my homework tonight because I have to turn it in tomorrow.*
**9 turn off** to make a machine or light stop working: *I turned off the light and the room went dark.*
**10 turn on** to make a machine or light start working: *Dad turned on the TV to watch the news.*
**11 turn out** to happen in a particular way, or have a particular result: *It turned out that Miguel was wrong.*
**12 turn up** to make a machine louder or hotter: *Can you turn up the radio? I can't hear it.*
● *noun*
**1** the time when one person does something, when different people do it, one after another: *We took turns on the bike, first me and then Sam.*
**2** a change in direction: *Make a right turn.*

turn

turn on
turn off

**tur·nip** /**turn**-ip/ *noun* a large round pale yellow or white vegetable that grows under the ground
▶ see picture on page **A7**

a b c d e f g h i j k l m n o p q r s t u v w x y z

**turn·pike** /**turn**-pik/ *noun* a large road for fast traffic that drivers have to pay to use

**turn sig·nal** /**turn** sig-nuhl/ *noun* one of the lights on a car that flash to show that the car is going to turn left or right

**tur·quoise** /**tur**-kwoyz/ *noun*
**1** a type of stone with a blue-green color, used in jewelry: *I bought a turquoise ring.*
**2** a bright blue-green color: *Her top was turquoise.*

**tur·tle** /**turt**'l/ *noun* an animal with a thick curved shell that covers its body. Turtles can hide their heads and legs inside their shell. A turtle can live on land or in water. Turtles are reptiles.

turtle

**tur·tle·neck** /**turt**'l-nek/ *noun* a type of sweater or shirt with a high collar that folds over and covers most of your neck: *It was cold, so I wore a turtleneck.*

**tusk** /tuhsk/ *noun* one of the two very long teeth that stick out of the mouth of an animal such as an elephant ▶ see picture at **elephant**

**tu·tor** /**toot**-ur/
● *noun* someone who teaches a subject to one student or only a few students: *I have a math tutor because I want my grades to get better.*
● *verb* to teach a subject to one student or only a few students: *We tutor students after school if they need extra help in one of their subjects.*

**tu·tu** /**too**-too/ *noun* a short skirt that ballet dancers wear. A tutu is made of many folds of stiff material, so that it sticks out from the dancer's body.

**tux·e·do** /tuhk-**seed**-oh/ *noun* (plural **tuxedos**) a suit that a man wears at formal events. Tuxedos are usually black and a man wears a bow tie with them: *The boys wear tuxedos to the prom.*

**TV** /tee-**vee**/ *noun* television: *The kids are watching TV. | I saw that movie on TV. | They don't have a TV.* ▶ see picture at **screen**

**TV set** /tee-**vee** set/ *noun* a television: *He watched the game on a big-screen TV set.*

**tweez·ers** /**tweez**-urz/ *plural noun* a small tool made from two thin metal pieces that are joined at one end. You use it for holding or pulling very small things: *She used tweezers to pull the splinter out of my finger.*

**twelfth** /twelfth/ *number*
**1** 12th: *Her birthday is on December the twelfth.*
**2** 1/12: *A twelfth of 240 is 20.*

**twelve** /twelv/ *number*
**1** 12: *There are twelve people in my judo class.*
**2** twelve o'clock: *The train leaves at twelve.*
**3** twelve years old: *He's twelve.*

**twen·ty** /**twent**-ee/
● *number*
**1** 20
**2** twenty years old: *My older sister is almost twenty.*
**3** **the twenties** the years between 1920 and 1929: *The painter lived in Paris in the twenties.*
**4** **in your twenties** between 20 and 29 years old: *I'd say he's in his late twenties, maybe 28 or 29 years old.*
**5** **in the twenties** between 20 and 29 degrees in temperature: *The temperature is likely to reach the low twenties today.*
—**twentieth** /**twent**-ee-ith/ *number* 20th or 1/20
● *noun*
a piece of paper money worth $20: *Do you have two ten-dollar bills for a twenty?*

**twen·ty-first** /twent-ee **furst**/ *noun, adjective*
21st: *My birthday is on the twenty-first of December.*

**twen·ty-one** /twent-ee **wuhn**/ *number*
**1** 21: *There are only twenty-one more days until summer vacation!*
**2** twenty-one years old: *Gina is going to be twenty-one, so we're going to have a party for her.*

**twice** /twīss/ *adverb* two times: *I play tennis twice a week. | This computer game is $25, but that one costs $50, so it is twice as expensive!*

**twig** /twig/ *noun* a very thin branch that grows on a larger branch of a tree: *The birds build their nests out of twigs.*

**twi·light** /**twī**-līt/ *noun* the time between day and night when the sky starts to become dark: *At twilight, the sun went down and the streetlights came on.*

**twin** /twin/ *noun*
● *noun* one of two children who are born at the same time to the same mother: *Jenny and Julie are identical twins. They look exactly like each other.*
● *adjective* one of two similar things: *The plane has twin engines.* | *My brother and I sleep in twin beds.*

**Word Origin:** twin

**Twin** comes from an Old English word that meant "two" or "double."

**twin·kle** /**twingk**-uhl/ *verb*
**1** if a star or light twinkles, it shines with a light that keeps changing from bright to less bright: *The stars are twinkling in the sky.*
**2** if someone's eyes twinkle, they shine because the person is happy: *The old lady's eyes twinkled when she saw her new baby granddaughter.*

**twirl** /twurl/ *verb* to turn around several times very quickly: *The cheerleader was twirling a silver baton between her hands.*

**twist** /twist/
● *verb*
**1** to bend or wind something around something else several times: *Hannah twisted her hair around her finger nervously.*
**2** to turn something so that it moves around in a circle: *To open the bottle, you have to twist the lid off.*
**3** to change the position of your body by turning: *Mom stopped the car and twisted around in her seat to look at me.*
**4** if you twist a part of your body, such as your knee, you injure it by bending it too much or bending it the wrong way: *While I was running to catch the bus, I fell and twisted my ankle.*
**5** if a road or river twists, it has a lot of curves in it: *The road twisted between the mountains.*
● *noun*
**1** an unexpected change in a story or situation: *The book has a lot of plot twists that make you want to keep reading.*
**2** a movement in which you turn something in a circle: *A twist of the handle changes the bicycle's gears.*

**twit·ter** /**twit**-ur/ *verb* if a bird twitters it makes a lot of short high sounds: *I can hear the birds twittering outside my window.*

**two** /too/ *number*
**1** 2: *He has two brothers.*
**2** two o'clock: *The movie begins at two.*
**3** two years old: *My younger sister will be two in April.*

**ty·coon** /**tī**-koon/ *noun* someone who is very successful in business and has a lot of money and power: *The tycoon owns three newspapers and a TV station.*

**ty·ing** /**tī**-ing/ *verb* the present participle of tie

**type** /tīp/
● *noun* a group of people or things that are similar to each other in some way: *My favorite type of music is rap.* | *"What type of cake do you want for your birthday?" "Chocolate."*
► see **Thesaurus**
● *verb* to write something using a computer or typewriter: *Type your password into the computer.*

**type·writ·er** /**tīp**-rīt-ur/ *noun* a machine that prints letters and numbers onto paper when you press the buttons on it

**ty·phoid** /**tī**-foyd/ (also **ty·phoid fe·ver** /**tī**-foyd **feev**-ur/) *noun* a serious disease that people get from dirty food or water. It causes a high fever and diarrhea, and sometimes death.

**ty·phoon** /tī-**foon**/ *noun* a very strong tropical storm that happens in the western part of the Pacific Ocean. In a typhoon, the wind moves in circles at very high speed: *The typhoon hit the island and snapped off the tops of trees and destroyed houses.*

**Word Origin:** typhoon

**Typhoon** may come from a Chinese word that means "big wind." It may also come from the Greek god Typhon, who was the god of the winds.

**typ·i·cal** /**tip**-ik-uhl/ *adjective* having the usual qualities of a particular person, group, or thing: *On a typical day, I watch about three hours of TV.*

**ty·ran·no·saur·us** /tuh-ran-uh-**sor**-uhss/ (also **ty·ran·no·saur·us rex** /tuh-ran-uh-sor-uhss **rekss**/) *noun* a very large dinosaur that ate other animals ▶ see picture at **dinosaur**

**Word Origin:** tyrannosaurus rex

**Tyrannosaurus rex** comes from Greek words that mean "tyrant," "lizard," and "king." A tyrant is a cruel ruler. So the name tyrannosaurus means the cruel king of the lizards. Many scientists believe that tyrannosaurus was a very strong dinosaur that ate other dinosaurs.

**tyr·an·ny** /**tirr**-uhn-ee/ *noun* government by a cruel ruler who has complete power: *People suffered because of the tyranny of the king.* —**tyrant** /**tīr**-uhnt/ *noun* a cruel ruler who has complete power: *He was a tyrant who put anybody who disagreed with him in jail.*

# Uu

**UFO** /yoo ef **oh**/ *noun* a strange moving object in the sky. Some people believe that some UFOs are spaceships from another planet. UFO stands for "unidentified flying object": *There was a big light in the sky and someone thought it was a UFO.*

**ugh** /uhg/ *interjection* said when you dislike something very much: *Ugh! I hate fish!*

**ug·ly** /**uhg**-lee/ *adjective* (**uglier**, **ugliest**) not nice to look at: *The witch was an ugly old woman with a long bent nose.*

ANTONYM: **beautiful**

## Word Origin: ugly

**Ugly** comes from an Old Norse word that meant "causing fear." Old Norse was spoken in Sweden and Denmark. When it was first used in English, ugly was much stronger than it is now. Someone ugly was horrible to look at, and made you feel afraid. In the late 1300s, ugly became not quite so strong, and started to mean "not nice to look at."

**ul·cer** /**uhlss**-ur/ *noun* a sore area on your skin or inside your body: *My uncle has a stomach ulcer and he has to take special tablets.*

**ul·te·ri·or** /uhl-**teer**-ee-ur/ *adjective* an ulterior motive is a reason for doing something, which someone deliberately tries to hide: *He said that he was trying to help me, but I think he had an ulterior motive.*

**ul·ti·mate** /**uhlt**-uhm-it/ *adjective*
**1** greatest, best, or most important: *The ultimate challenge for a climber is to reach the top of Mount Everest, the world's highest mountain.*
**2** last in a series of things: *Her ultimate goal is to become a doctor, so she's working hard at school.*
—**ultimately** /**uhlt**-uhm-it-lee/ *adverb* finally, after

everything else: *Ultimately, people will be able to travel to other planets.*

**ul·ti·ma·tum** /uhlt-uh-**mayt**-uhm/ *noun* a statement saying that if someone does not do what you want, he or she will be punished: *Mom gave me an ultimatum. I have to finish my homework, or I won't be allowed to watch TV.*

**ul·tra·vi·o·let** /uhl-truh-**vī**-uhl-it/ *adjective* ultraviolet light cannot be seen, because the light waves are very short. Ultraviolet light from the Sun or a lamp makes your skin become darker.

**um·brel·la**
/uhm-**brel**-uh/ *noun* an object you hold over your head so that you do not get wet in the rain. An umbrella is made of a circle of cloth stretched on a metal frame: *It looks like rain, so you had better take your umbrella with you.*

umbrella  **umbrella**

## Word Origin: umbrella

English got the word for **umbrella** from Italian in the late 1600s, but umbrellas were used for different reasons in Britain and Italy. The Italian word came from a Latin word that means "shade." In Italy, it is often sunny and you use an umbrella to give you shade from the sun. In Britain, it rains a lot, and you need an umbrella to stop the rain from making you wet.

**um·pire** /**uhm**-pī-ur/ *noun* the person who makes sure that a sport such as tennis or baseball is played correctly: *The umpire at first base said the runner was out.*

## Word Origin: umpire

**Umpire** comes from an Old French word that meant "an uneven number." The idea was that you need a third person to judge when two people do not agree, and three is not an even number. When the word was first used in English, umpires worked in legal cases. In the 1700s, umpires began to be used in sports.

u

**un-** /uhn/

> ## Word Building
>
> **un-** is a prefix.
> **1 un**clear | **un**healthy | **un**able
> **un-** means "not." If something is *unclear*, it is not clear. Food that is *unhealthy* is not good for you. If you are *unable* to do something, you cannot do it.
> **2 un**dress | **un**cover | **un**fasten
> **un-** means "the opposite of." *Undress* means the opposite of *dress*. If you *undress*, you take your clothes off. *Unfasten* means the opposite of *fasten*. If you *unfasten* your seat belt, you take it off.

**un·a·ble** /uhn-**ayb**-uhl/ *adjective* not able to do something: *I'm unable to come to your birthday party because we'll be on vacation.*
ANTONYM: **able**

**un·ac·cept·a·ble** /uhn-uhk-**sept**-uhb-uhl/ *adjective* something that is unacceptable is wrong or bad and should not be allowed to continue: *Swearing in class is unacceptable.*
ANTONYM: **acceptable**

**un·a·fraid** /un-uh-**frayd**/ *adjective* not afraid: *She loves all animals, and is even unafraid of snakes and spiders.* ANTONYMS: **afraid, scared**

**u·nan·i·mous** /yoo-**nan**-uhm-uhss/ *adjective* agreed on by everyone: *Everyone thought Maria should be class president, so she won a unanimous vote.*
—**unanimously** /yoo-**nan**-uhm-uhss-lee/ *adverb* in a unanimous way: *The students unanimously agreed that the book was really good.*

**un·armed** /uhn-**armd**/ *adjective* not carrying any weapons: *Don't shoot! I'm unarmed!*
ANTONYM: **armed**

**un·at·trac·tive** /uhn-uh-**trakt**-iv/ *adjective* not nice to look at: *He was very unattractive, with his long greasy hair.* SYNONYM: **ugly**
ANTONYM: **attractive**

**un·a·void·a·ble** /uhn-uh-**voyd**-uhb-uhl/ *adjective* impossible to prevent: *Lots of people drive to work in the morning so traffic delays are unavoidable.*

**un·a·ware** /uhn-uh-**wair**/ *adjective* not knowing or seeing what is happening: *I was unaware that Karen had an older brother. She never talks about him.* ANTONYM: **aware**

**un·bear·a·ble** /uhn-**bair**-uhb-uhl/ *adjective* very unpleasant or painful: *The music was so loud it was unbearable.*
—**unbearably** /uhn-**bair**-uhb-lee/ *adverb* in a way that is very unpleasant or painful: *The temperature can get unbearably hot in the summer.*

**un·be·liev·a·ble** /uhn-bi-**leev**-uhb-uhl/ *adjective*
**1** very difficult to believe and probably not true: *Yvonne's excuse was totally unbelievable. She said her dog ate her homework!*
**2** used when saying that something is very good, bad, etc., in a surprising way: *The game's special effects are unbelievable and I was really impressed.*
—**unbelievably** /uhn-bi-**leev**-uhb-lee/ *adverb* used when saying that something is very good, bad, etc., in a surprising way: *My computer is unbelievably slow today.*

**un·bi·ased** /uhn-**bī**-uhst/ *adjective* fair and not influenced by someone else's opinions: *Teachers must be unbiased and treat all their students equally.* SYNONYM: **impartial** ANTONYM: **biased**

**un·but·ton**
/uhn-**buht**'n/ *verb* to unfasten a piece of clothing that is closed with a button: *He unbuttoned his shirt and took it off.*
ANTONYM: **button**

**unbutton**

**un·cer·tain** /uhn-**surt**'n/ *adjective* not sure about something: *I was uncertain about who I should invite to my birthday party.* ANTONYM: **certain**
—**uncertainty** /uhn-**surt**'n-tee/ *noun* the quality of being uncertain: *There is uncertainty about how much the trip will cost.*
—**uncertainly** /uhn-**surt**'n-lee/ *adverb* in an uncertain way: *"I could come with you," said Rosa uncertainly.*

**un·cle** /**uhngk**-uhl/ *noun* the brother of your

mother or father, or the husband of your aunt: *My aunt and uncle live in Iowa.*

### Word Origin: uncle

**Uncle** comes from a Latin word that meant "little grandfather." It was used about your mother's brothers, who were littler, or younger, than your grandfather. Old French got uncle from Latin, and it came into English from Old French.

**un·clean** /uhn-**kleen**/ *adjective* dirty: *The water is unclean and not suitable for drinking.*

**un·clear** /uhn-**kleer**/ *adjective* difficult to understand or know about: *Ryan gave us directions to his house, but they were unclear and we got lost.* ( ANTONYM: **clear** )

**Un·cle Sam** /uhngk-uhl **sam**/ *noun* a picture of a man with a white beard and a tall hat with stars and stripes on it. Uncle Sam represents the United States, or the government of the United States.

**un·com·fort·a·ble** /uhn-**kuhmft**-uhb-uhl/ *adjective*
**1** not nice to wear, sit on, or lie in: *My new shoes are uncomfortable. They're too tight and hurt my feet.* ( ANTONYM: **comfortable** )
**2** feeling a little bit worried or embarrassed: *Josh's mom was really mad at him, and I felt uncomfortable being there.*
—**uncomfortably** /uhn-**kuhmft**-uhb-lee/ *adverb* in a way that does not feel pleasant: *The room was uncomfortably hot.*

**un·com·mon** /uhn-**kahm**-uhn/ *adjective* rare or unusual: *This kind of accident is very uncommon.*

**un·con·scious** /uhn-**kahnsh**-uhss/ *adjective* not able to see, move, feel, or hear because you are not awake and aware of what is happening: *The baseball hit Bill hard on the head and knocked him unconscious.* ( ANTONYM: **conscious** )

**un·con·sti·tu·tion·al** /uhn-kahnst-uh-**toosh**-uhn-uhl/ *adjective* not allowed by the rules of a country or organization: *The Supreme Court can decide whether a new law is unconstitutional.*
( ANTONYM: **constitutional** )

**un·con·trol·la·ble** /uhn-kuhn-**trohl**-uhb-uhl/ *adjective* impossible to control or stop: *Alice told a joke and Sara started shaking with uncontrollable laughter.*

**un·cooked** /uhn-**kukt**/ *adjective* not cooked: *The meat was uncooked in the middle and it had a pink color.* ( SYNONYM: **raw** )

**un·co·op·era·tive** /uhn-koh-**ahp**-ruht-iv/ *adjective* not willing to help people or not willing to do what they ask: *Sue wouldn't sit still while Mom cut her hair. She was being really uncooperative.*

**un·cov·er** /uhn-**kuhv**-ur/ *verb*
**1** to discover something that was secret or hidden: *The police uncovered the truth about what had really happened that night.*
**2** to remove the cover from something: *Uncover the chicken for the last 15 minutes of cooking.*
( ANTONYM: **cover** )

**un·de·cid·ed** /uhn-di-**sīd**-id/ *adjective* if you are undecided, you have not made a decision yet: *We're still undecided about where to go for our next vacation.*

**un·der** /**uhnd**-ur/ *preposition, adverb*
**1** below something or covered by it: *We sat under a tree.* ( ANTONYM: **over** )
**2** less than a number, age, or amount: *The game is for children under eight. Tom is seven, so it will be fine for him.* ( ANTONYM: **over** )
**3** affected by a situation or action: *The city is under attack. | I had everything under control.*
**4** in a situation when there is a particular leader or government: *Will things be better under the new president?*

**under**

She is sitting under a tree.

**under-** /uhnd-ur/

### Word Building

**under-** is a prefix.

**1 under**arm | **under**line | **under**neath | **under**wear | **under**water

**under-** means "below." If you *underline* a word, you put a line below the word. If you stand *underneath* a tree, you stand below it. You wear *underwear* below your other clothes.

**2 under**estimate | **under**nourished | **under**privileged

**under-** means "too little." If you *underestimate* how much something costs, you think it costs less money than it really does. If someone is *undernourished*, that person does not eat enough food. If someone is *underprivileged*, that person has less money and fewer chances to get things like a good education or health care.

**un·der·arm** /**uhnd**-ur-arm/ *plural noun* the area under your arm where it joins your body
( SYNONYM: **armpit** )

**un·der·clothes** /**uhnd**-ur-klohz/ *plural noun* clothes that you wear next to your body, under your other clothes ( SYNONYM: **underwear** )

**un·der·cov·er** /uhnd-ur-**kuhv**-ur/ *adjective*, *adverb* working secretly, in order to find out information for the police: *Undercover police officers bought drugs to catch the drug dealers.*

**un·der·dog** /**uhnd**-ur-dog/ *plural noun* the person or team in a competition that is not expected to win: *Our team is the underdog – no one thinks that we can win the game.*

**un·der·es·ti·mate** /uhnd-ur-**est**-uh-mayt/ *verb*
**1** to guess that something is smaller than it really is: *I thought the dog weighed about 25 pounds, but I underestimated it. He weighs almost 45 pounds.* ( ANTONYM: **overestimate** )
**2** to think that someone is less strong or intelligent than he or she really is: *Don't underestimate him. He'll know you're lying.*

**un·der·go** /uhnd-ur-**goh**/ *verb* (**undergoes**, **underwent** /uhnd-ur-**went**/, **undergone** /uhnd-ur-**gon**/) if you undergo something, it is

done to you or it happens to you: *She will undergo surgery on her leg next week.*

**un·der·grad·u·ate** /uhnd-ur-**graj**-oo-it/ *noun* a student in college, who is working for his or her bachelor's degree: *Carlos is an undergraduate at the University of Texas. He's in his second year there.*

**un·der·ground** /**uhnd**-ur-grownd/ *adjective*, *adverb* below the ground: *Moles live underground.* | *an underground river*

underground

Moles live underground.

**Un·der·ground Rail·road** /uhnd-ur-grownd **rayl**-rohd/ *noun* a secret system that helped slaves in the southern U.S. escape to a safe place in the north

**un·der·hand** /**uhnd**-ur-hand/ *adjective*, *adverb* if you throw a ball underhand, you keep your arm below your shoulder when you throw: *In softball, you throw the ball underhand to the batter.* ( ANTONYM: **overhand** )

**un·der·line**
/**uhnd**-ur-līn/ *verb* to draw a line under a word: *Underline any words you do not know.*

underline

# underlined

**un·der·mine**
/**uhnd**-ur-mīn/ *verb* to say or do something that makes someone or something less strong or effective over a period of time: *If you criticize him, you will undermine his confidence.*

**un·der·neath** /uhnd-ur-**neeth**/ *preposition*, *adverb* directly below or under something: *I found the book underneath your bed.* |

*We turned some rocks over to see what was underneath.*

**un·der·nour·ished** /uhnd-ur-**nur**-isht/ *adjective*
not healthy because you do not eat enough food or enough of the right type of food: *Many people in poor countries are undernourished because they cannot afford to buy food.*

**un·der·pants** /**uhnd**-ur-pantss/ *plural noun* a short piece of clothing that covers your body from your waist to the top of your legs and is worn under your clothes: *He put on his underpants and then his jeans.*

**un·der·pass** /**uhnd**-ur-pass/ *noun* a road or path that goes under another road or under a railroad: *The underpass is a safe way to get across the busy street.*

**un·der·priv·i·leged** /uhnd-ur-**priv**-uhl-ijd/ *adjective* very poor and not having the same advantages or chances that other people in society have: *The program helps underprivileged children do well in school, for example by helping with homework.* ( ANTONYM: **privileged** )

**un·der·shirt** /**uhnd**-ur-shurt/ *noun* a soft piece of clothing that you wear under a shirt: *He always wears an undershirt in the winter.*

**un·der·stand** /uhnd-ur-**stand**/ *verb*
(**understood** /uhnd-ur-**stud**/)
**1** to know the meaning of what someone is saying: *I don't understand the instructions.* | *She spoke clearly so that everyone could understand.*
▶ see **Thesaurus**
**2** to know how something works or why something happens: *Scientists are studying the brain to try to understand how it works.*
**3** to know how someone feels and why he or she behaves in a particular way: *I understand how you feel – the same thing happened to me before and I was pretty angry too.*

**Word Family:** understand

understand *verb* | misunderstand *verb* | understanding *noun*

**un·der·stand·a·ble** /uhnd-ur-**stand**-uhb-uhl/ *adjective* easy to understand: *Her anger is understandable. The people in the store were so rude to her.*

**un·der·stand·ing** /uhnd-ur-**stand**-ing/ *adjective*
● *adjective* someone who is understanding is kind and knows how you feel when you have problems: *Sam explained why his homework was late, and the teacher was really understanding.*
● *noun* an ability to understand something: *Most of the students seemed to have a good understanding of the story.*

**un·der·stood** /uhnd-ur-**stud**/ *verb* the past tense and past participle of **understand**

**un·der·tak·er** /**uhnd**-ur-tayk-ur/ *noun* someone whose job is to arrange funerals and get dead bodies ready to be buried

**un·der·wa·ter** /uhnd-ur-**wot**-ur/ *adjective*, *adverb* below the surface of the water: *You can use this camera underwater.*

**underwater**

You can use the camera underwater.

**un·der·wear** /**uhnd**-ur-wair/ *noun* clothes that you wear next to your body, under your other clothes: *The store sells panties, bras, and other underwear.*

**un·der·went** /uhnd-ur-**went**/ *verb* the past tense of **undergo**

**un·do** /uhn-**doo**/ *verb* (**undoes** /uhn-**duhz**/, **undid** /uhn-**did**/, **undone** /uhn-**duhn**/)
**1** to open something that is tied, fastened, or wrapped: *Isabel felt warm, so she undid the buttons on her coat.*
**2** to change something back to the way it was before: *I think I hurt Cindy's feelings. I wish I could undo what I said.*

**un·done** /uhn-**duhn**/ *adjective*
**1** not fastened or tied: *Your zipper's undone – pull it up.*
**2** not finished: *He went out to play with his friends and his homework was left undone.*
( ANTONYM: **done** )

**un·doubt·ed·ly** /uhn-**dowt**-id-lee/ *adverb*
definitely: *The school is undoubtedly one of the best in the city.*

**un·dress** /uhn-**dress**/ *verb* to take your clothes off: *We undressed and put on our pajamas.*
( ANTONYM: **dress** )

**un·eas·y** /uhn-**eez**-ee/ *adjective* worried or afraid about something: *I thought that I was lost, and I began to feel uneasy.*

**un·em·ployed** /uhn-im-**ployd**/ *adjective*
without a job: *My dad has been unemployed since the factory closed last year.*

**un·em·ploy·ment** /uhn-im-**ploy**-muhnt/ *noun*
**1** the condition of not having a job: *The factories in the city closed, and now there is a lot of unemployment there.* ( ANTONYM: **employment** )
**2** money that the government gives people who do not have jobs, so that they can buy food and pay for a place to live: *Adam lost his job, and now he is living on unemployment.*

**un·e·qual** /uhn-**eek**-wuhl/ *adjective* not the same or not equal: *The two bedrooms are of unequal size – mine is bigger.* ( ANTONYM: **equal** )

**un·e·ven** /uhn-**eev**-uhn/ *adjective*
**1** not flat or smooth: *She walked carefully over the uneven ground so that she wouldn't trip.*
( ANTONYM: **even** )
**2** good in some parts, and bad in others: *The quality of the songs is uneven; some of them are good, but some of them are awful.*

**un·ex·pect·ed** /uhn-ik-**spekt**-id/ *adjective*
surprising because of not being expected: *Our team had an unexpected win against the top team in the league.* ( ANTONYM: **expected** )
—**unexpectedly** /uhn-ik-**spekt**-id-lee/ *adverb* in an unexpected way: *My aunt arrived unexpectedly just as we sat down for dinner.*

**un·fair** /uhn-**fair**/ *adjective* not right or fair: *It's unfair that he got dessert, and I didn't.*
( ANTONYM: **fair** )
—**unfairly** /uhn-**fair**-lee/ *adverb* in an unfair way: *They unfairly blamed me for stealing the money when I hadn't touched it.*
—**unfairness** /uhn-**fair**-niss/ *noun* unfair treatment

**un·faith·ful** /uhn-**fayth**-fuhl/ *adjective* not loyal or faithful to a husband or wife: *David is an honest family man. He would never be unfaithful to his wife.* ( ANTONYM: **faithful** )

**un·fa·mil·iar** /uhn-fuh-**mil**-yur/ *adjective* if someone or something is unfamiliar, you do not recognize him, her, or it: *I wonder who this letter is from – the handwriting on the envelope is unfamiliar to me.* ( ANTONYM: **familiar** )

**un·fash·ion·a·ble** /uhn-**fash**-uhn-uhb-uhl/ *adjective* not popular now: *Her clothes were old and unfashionable, and looked like the dresses your grandmother wore when she was little.*
( ANTONYM: **fashionable** )

**un·fas·ten** /uhn-**fass**-uhn/ *verb* to open something that is fastened or tied: *Do not unfasten your seat belt until the plane has stopped moving.* ( SYNONYM: **undo** )
( ANTONYM: **fasten** )

**un·fa·vor·a·ble** /uhn-**fayv**-uhr-uhb-uhl/ *adjective* showing that people think someone or something is not good: *The movie got a lot of unfavorable reviews, so we decided not to go.*
( ANTONYM: **favorable** )

**un·fit** /uhn-**fit**/ *adjective* not good enough to do something or be used for something: *The food was unfit to eat.*

**un·fold** /uhn-**fohld**/ *verb* to open something that was folded: *I unfolded the letter and read it.*
( ANTONYM: **fold** )

**un·for·tu·nate** /uhn-**forch**-uhn-it/ *adjective*
happening because of bad luck: *The car accident was no one's fault – it was an unfortunate accident.* ( SYNONYM: **unlucky** ) ( ANTONYM: **fortunate** )

**un·for·tu·nate·ly** /uhn-**forch**-uhn-it-lee/ *adverb*
used to say that you feel sad or disappointed about something: *Unfortunately, I won't be able to come to your birthday party.*
( ANTONYM: **fortunately** )

**un·friend·ly** /uhn-**frend**-lee/ *adjective* not willing to be nice to and talk to people you do not know: *The people at the party were so unfriendly. No one smiled or talked to us.*
( ANTONYM: **friendly** )

**un·grate·ful** /uhn-**grayt**-fuhl/ *adjective* not wanting to thank someone who has helped you or been kind to you: *He's so ungrateful – he didn't even thank us for our help.*
( ANTONYM: **grateful** )

**un·hap·py** /uhn-**hap**-ee/ *adjective* (**unhappier, unhappiest**)
**1** not happy: *She was very unhappy when her dog died.* ( SYNONYM: **sad** ) ( ANTONYM: **happy** )
**2** thinking that something is not good or right: *Some members of the team are unhappy with the coach's decision and think he was wrong.*
( ANTONYMS: **pleased, satisfied** )
—**unhappiness** /uhn-**hap**-ee-niss/ *noun* an unhappy feeling
—**unhappily** /uhn-**hap**-uhl-ee/ *adverb* in an unhappy way

unhappy
happy | unhappy

**un·health·y** /uhn-**helth**-ee/ *adjective*
**1** likely to make you sick: *Eating a lot of junk food is very unhealthy.*
( ANTONYM: **healthy** )
**2** not physically healthy, and often sick: *She is very pale and looks unhealthy.*
( ANTONYM: **healthy** )

**un·help·ful** /uhn-**help**-fuhl/ *adjective* not helping you, or not useful: *The book is unhelpful and doesn't tell you anything new.*

**u·ni·corn**
/**yoon**-uh-korn/ *noun* a white horse with one horn on its head. A unicorn is not a real animal. It is only in stories.

unicorn

**u·ni·cy·cle**
/**yoon**-i-sīk-uhl/ *noun* a vehicle that is similar to a bicycle, but that has only one wheel: *The clowns were riding unicycles.*

**u·ni·form**
/**yoon**-uh-form/
● *noun* special clothes that people wear for some jobs, schools, or sports. For example, police officers and nurses wear uniforms: *Do you have to wear a school uniform?*
● *adjective* exactly the same in size, shape, or color: *Make sure all the pieces are a uniform length with no one piece longer than the other.*
—**uniformity** /yoon-uh-**form**-uht-ee/ *noun* the state of being the same: *He had dental work to improve the whiteness and uniformity of his teeth.*

uniform

uniform

**u·ni·fy** /**yoon**-uh-fī/ *verb* (**unifies, unified**) to join the different parts of a country or organization together to make a single country or organization: *After the Civil War, the U.S. needed to become unified again.*
—**unification** /yoon-uhf-uh-**kaysh**-uhn/ *noun* the act of unifying something: *The unification of East and West Germany began in 1989.*

**un·i·mag·in·a·ble** /uhn-i-**maj**-uhn-uhb-uhl/ *adjective* impossible to imagine: *Our modern world would be unimaginable to people who lived 500 years ago.* ( SYNONYM: **unthinkable** )

**un·im·por·tant** /uhn-im-**portn**'t/ *adjective* not important: *Most of what he said was unimportant, but he did tell us the date of the wedding.* ( ANTONYM: **important** )

**un·in·hab·it·ed** /uhn-in-**hab**-it-id/ *adjective* an uninhabited place has no one living there: *The house had been uninhabited for years and was starting to fall apart.* ( ANTONYM: **inhabited** )

**un·in·ten·tion·al** /uhn-in-**tensh**-uhn-uhl/ *adjective* not done deliberately: *I'm sure it was unintentional and she didn't want to upset you.*

**un·in·terest·ed** /uhn-**in**-trist-id/ *adjective* not interested: *He seemed uninterested in the movie and he kept looking at his watch.*
( ANTONYM: **interested** )

**u**

a b c d e f g h i j k l m n o p q r s t u v w x y z

**un·ion** /**yoon**-yuhn/ *noun*
**1** (also **labor union**) an organization that employees form to protect their rights: *The union has asked for better health benefits for all the workers.*
**2** a group of countries or states that have joined together: *France and Germany are both members of the European Union.*
**3** the act of joining things or people together to form a larger group: *Marriage is the union of two people who love each other.*
**4 Union** the states that stayed loyal to the United States government during the Civil War
( ANTONYM: **Confederacy** )

**u·nique** /yoo-**neek**/ *adjective* special and different from every other person or thing: *The teacher understands that every child is unique.*
—**uniquely** /yoo-**neek**-lee/ *adverb* in a unique way: *She is a uniquely talented singer.*

**u·ni·sex** /**yoon**-uh-sekss/ *adjective* suitable for men and women: *Both men and women can get their hair cut at the unisex hair salon.*

**u·ni·son** /**yoon**-uhss-uhn/ *noun* if a group of people does something in unison, they all do it at the same time: *The children stood up and sang the song in unison.*

**u·nit** /**yoon**-it/ *noun*
**1** one part in something larger: *The math textbook is divided into 12 units.* | *There are ten units in the apartment building.*
**2** a standard that people use to measure length, weight, etc.: *A "quart" is a unit of measurement for liquids.*

**u·nit cost** /**yoon**-it kost/ *noun* in math, the cost of each item when you have several of the same thing: *If you pay $2 for four pencils and each pencil is the same price, what is the unit cost of a pencil? (Answer: the unit cost is 50¢.)*

**u·nite** /yoo-**nīt**/ *verb*
**1** to join something together: *The atoms unite to form a molecule of water.*
**2** to make people have the same aims: *The country should try to unite and support the new president.*
—**unity** /**yoon**-uht-ee/ *noun* the situation when people all have the same aims: *There is a sense of unity in class – we all want to work together to learn.*

**u·nit·ed** /yoo-**nīt**-id/ *adjective*
**1** a united country is formed by two or more countries or states joining together: *There are 50 states in the United States of America.*
**2** if people are united, they have the same aims: *We are united in wanting our children to have a good education.*

**U·nit·ed Na·tions** /yoo-**nīt**-id **naysh**-uhnz/ *noun*
( ABBREVIATION: **U.N.** ) an organization that most of the countries in the world belong to. The United Nations tries to solve world problems in a peaceful way.

**u·nit frac·tion** /**yoon**-it frak-shuhn/ *noun* in math, a fraction that has the numerator 1: *1/2, 1/35,* and *1/100* are all unit fractions.

**u·nit square** /**yoon**-it skwair/ *noun* in math, a square whose sides all have the length 1. On a grid, the square would have the coordinates (0,0), (0,1), (1,1) and (1,0).

**u·ni·ver·sal** /yoon-uh-**vurss**-uhl/ *adjective* relating to everyone in a group or in the world: *The environment is a universal issue. It is important to everyone that we protect it.*
—**universally** /yoon-uh-**vurss**-uhl-ee/ *adverb* for or by everyone in a group or in the world: *He was a kind man who was universally liked.*

**u·ni·verse** /**yoon**-uh-vurss/ *noun* all of space, including all the stars and planets: *There are billions of stars in the universe.*

**u·ni·ver·si·ty** /yoon-uh-**vurss**-uht-ee/ *noun* (plural **universities**) a school where you study at a high level to get a degree: *Jennifer is studying Education at New York University.*

**un·kind** /uhn-**kīnd**/ *adjective* unfriendly or cruel: *Some of the children were very unkind and teased her a lot.* ( SYNONYM: **mean** )
( ANTONYM: **kind** )
—**unkindly** /uhn-**kīnd**-lee/ *adverb* in an unkind way: *They laughed unkindly at my mistake.*
—**unkindness** /uhn-**kīnd**-niss/ *noun* the quality of being unkind

**un·known** /uhn-**nohn**/ *adjective* not known: *For some unknown reason, William stopped coming to school.*

**un·law·ful** /uhn-**lo**-fuhl/ *adjective* against the law: *It is unlawful to drive without a license.*
( SYNONYM: **illegal** )

—**unlawfully** /uhn-**lo**-fuhl-ee/ *adverb* in a way that is unlawful: *He was arrested for unlawfully carrying a weapon.*

**un·lead·ed** /uhn-**led**-id/ *adjective* unleaded gas does not contain any lead

**un·less** /uhn-**less**/ *conjunction* used for saying that something must happen so that another thing can happen: *He won't go to sleep unless you tell him a story.*

**un·like** /uhn-**līk**/ *preposition*
**1** different from another person or thing: *Unlike most of the children, Margo walks to school.* ( ANTONYM: **like** )
**2** not typical of someone: *It's unlike Judy to leave without telling us.* ( ANTONYM: **like** )

**un·like·ly** /uhn-**līk**-lee/ *adjective* not likely to happen: *It's very unlikely that they'll win because they haven't been playing well.*

**un·load** /uhn-**lohd**/ *verb*
**1** to take things out of a vehicle: *The men were unloading a truck.* ( ANTONYM: **load** )
**2** to take something out of a machine, gun, or camera: *Will you unload the dishwasher?* ( ANTONYM: **load** )

**un·lock** /uhn-**lahk**/ *verb* to open the lock on something with a key: *He unlocked the door and went in.* ( ANTONYM: **lock** )

**un·luck·y** /uhn-**luhk**-ee/ *adjective* not lucky: *Some people think it's unlucky to walk under a ladder.* ( ANTONYM: **lucky** )

**un·mar·ried** /uhn-**marr**-eed/ *adjective* not married: *Ben is 40 and still unmarried.* ( SYNONYM: **single** )

**un·nat·u·ral** /uhn-**nach**-uhr-uhl/ *adjective* different from what is normal or natural: *Her hair was an unnatural color; she dyed it pink.* ( ANTONYM: **natural** )

**un·nec·es·sar·y** /uhn-**ness**-uh-sair-ee/ *adjective* not needed: *Paper and pencils will be unnecessary because we are taking the test on computers.* ( ANTONYM: **necessary** )
—**unnecessarily** /uhn-ness-uh-**sair**-uhl-ee/ *adverb* in a way that is not needed: *I try not to spend money unnecessarily on things I want but don't need.*

**un·of·fi·cial** /uhn-uh-**fish**-uhl/ *adjective* not

accepted or approved by anyone who is in charge: *We think the children did well on the tests, but that is unofficial because we have not received their scores yet.* ( ANTONYM: **official** )
—**unofficially** /uhn-uh-**fish**-uhl-ee/ *adverb* in an unofficial way: *Over 500 people were unofficially reported to have died in the earthquake.*

**un·pack** /uhn-**pak**/ *verb* to take everything out of a suitcase or box: *When we arrived at our hotel, we unpacked our bags.* ( ANTONYM: **pack** )

**unpack**

*She is unpacking her suitcase.*

**un·pleas·ant** /uhn-**plez**-uhnt/ *adjective* not nice or enjoyable: *The dog has an unpleasant smell. I think he needs a bath.* ( ANTONYM: **pleasant** )
—**unpleasantly** /uhn-**plez**-uhnt-lee/ *adverb* in an unpleasant way: *The water was unpleasantly cold.*

**un·plug** /uhn-**pluhg**/ *verb* (**unplugging, unplugged**) to take a plug out of a wall, and stop something electrical from working: *My computer wasn't working because someone had unplugged it.* ( ANTONYM: **plug in** )

**un·pop·u·lar** /uhn-**pahp**-yuhl-ur/ *adjective* not liked by many people: *The rules are very unpopular and most people want them to be changed.* ( ANTONYM: **popular** )
—**unpopularity** /uhn-pahp-yuh-**larr**-uht-ee/ *noun* the quality of being unpopular: *His unpopularity with voters makes him unlikely to win the election.*

**un·pre·dict·a·ble** /uhn-pri-**dikt**-uhb-uhl/ *adjective* changing a lot so you do not know what to expect: *The weather here can be very unpredictable – it can go from rain to sun within an hour.*

**un·pre·pared** /uhn-pri-**paird**/ *adjective* not ready to deal with something: *I was totally unprepared for the question and didn't know what to say.* ( ANTONYMS: **prepared, ready** )

a b c d e f g h i j k l m n o p q r s t **u** v w x y z

**un·pro·fes·sion·al** /uhn-pruh-**fesh**-uhn-uhl/ *adjective* not behaving in the way that people doing a particular job should behave: *It's very unprofessional to make a lot of personal phone calls at work.*

**un·rav·el** /uhn-**rav**-uhl/ *verb*
**1** if threads or a sweater unravel, the threads or yarn stop being twisted together: *The sleeves of my sweater are starting to unravel.*
**2** to find out the truth about something very complicated: *Detectives are still trying to unravel the mystery surrounding her death.*

**un·real** /uhn-**reel**/ *adjective* not really happening or existing: *I couldn't believe I'd won the prize. It all seemed so unreal!* ( ANTONYM: **real** )

**un·re·al·is·tic** /uhn-**ree**-uh-list-ik/ *adjective* unlikely to happen, even though you want it to: *It's unrealistic to expect every child to be good at sports.*

**un·rea·son·a·ble** /uhn-**reez**-uhn-uhb-uhl/ *adjective* not fair or sensible: *I think Mom's being unreasonable for not letting me go to Julio's birthday party.* ( ANTONYM: **reasonable** )
—**unreasonably** /uhn-**reez**-uhn-uhb-lee/ *adverb* in a way that is unreasonable

**un·rec·og·niz·a·ble** /uhn-rek-uhg-**nīz**-uhb-uhl/ *adjective* changed or damaged so much that you cannot recognize someone or something: *My dad now has a beard and a mustache and his face is almost unrecognizable.*

**un·re·lat·ed** /uhn-ri-**layt**-id/ *adjective* not connected: *Danny asked about the field trip during math – the question was totally unrelated to the lesson.* ( ANTONYM: **related** )

**un·re·li·a·ble** /uhn-ri-**lī**-uhb-uhl/ *adjective* not possible for you to believe or trust: *The buses here are very unreliable – they are never on time.* ( ANTONYM: **reliable** )

**un·rest** /uhn-**rest**/ *noun* a situation in which people protest or behave violently: *There is a lot of unrest in that part of the world because many people are very poor and they are not treated fairly.*

**un·roll** /uhn-**rohl**/ *verb* to open something that has been wrapped around itself, and make it flat: *The kids all unrolled their sleeping bags and got into them.* ( ANTONYM: **roll up** )

**un·ru·ly** /uhn-**rool**-ee/ *adjective* behaving badly or violently, and difficult to control: *Some of the kids were unruly, and they made a lot of noise and ran around in class.*

**un·safe** /uhn-**sayf**/ *adjective* dangerous: *It's unsafe to swim in the river because the water is very dirty.* ( ANTONYM: **safe** )

**un·sat·is·fac·to·ry** /uhn-sat-iss-**fakt**-uhr-ee/ *adjective* not good enough: *The food at the restaurant was unsatisfactory. We won't eat there again.* ( ANTONYM: **satisfactory** )

**un·screw** /uhn-**skroo**/ *verb* to open something by twisting it: *I can't unscrew the lid of this jar.*

**un·scru·pu·lous** /uhn-**skroop**-yuhl-uhss/ *adjective* behaving in an unfair or dishonest way and not caring about other people: *Some unscrupulous stores are charging a lot of money for the new toys because they are so popular.*

**un·self·ish** /uhn-**self**-ish/ *adjective* doing things for other people, rather than only doing things for yourself: *It was very unselfish of him to give us his candy.* ( ANTONYM: **selfish** )

**un·skilled** /uhn-**skild**/ *adjective* without any special training for a job: *Unskilled workers can only get jobs that do not pay much, such as at a car wash or burger restaurant.* ( ANTONYM: **skilled** )

**un·sta·ble** /uhn-**stayb**-uhl/ *adjective*
**1** not able to stay in the same position: *Be careful – the ladder's a little unstable.*
( ANTONYM: **stable** )
**2** not staying the same, and often changing suddenly or having problems: *The leaders of the country have changed again, and it is becoming more politically unstable.* ( ANTONYM: **stable** )

**un·stead·y** /uhn-**sted**-ee/ *adjective* shaking or moving in a way that is not controlled: *As the old man wrote the note, his hand was unsteady.*
( ANTONYM: **steady** )
—**unsteadily** /uhn-**sted**-uhl-ee/ *adverb* in an unsteady way: *After a month in bed he was walking very unsteadily.*

**un·suc·cess·ful** /uhn-suhk-**sess**-fuhl/ *adjective* not succeeding in doing something: *Jimmy tried to climb the tree, but he was unsuccessful.*
( ANTONYM: **successful** )
—**unsuccessfully** /uhn-suhk-**sess**-fuhl-ee/ *adverb* in

a way that is not successful: *She tried unsuccessfully to get out of her chair.*

**un·suit·a·ble** /uhn-**soot**-uhb-uhl/ *adjective* not good for a particular person or purpose: *Her high-heeled shoes were unsuitable for a long walk.* ( SYNONYM: **inappropriate** )
( ANTONYM: **suitable** )

**un·sure** /uhn-**shoor**/ *adjective* not sure about something: *If you're unsure about how to do the math problem, ask the teacher.*

**un·think·a·ble** /uhn-**thingk**-uhb-uhl/ *adjective* impossible to imagine: *It was unthinkable that our team could lose the game*
( SYNONYM: **unimaginable** )

**un·tie** /uhn-**tī**/ *verb* (**unties**, **untying**, **untied**) to undo string or rope that someone has tied in a knot: *Don't just pull your shoes off – untie them.*
( ANTONYM: **tie** )

untie

He untied his shoe.

**un·til** /uhn-**til**/ *preposition*, *conjunction*
**1** lasting up to a time or event and then stopping: *We worked until the house was clean.*
**2** before: *Dave won't be home until 10:00 tonight.*

**un·to** /**uhn**-too/ *preposition* an old word that means "to"

**un·true** /uhn-**troo**/ *adjective* not true: *He said that I cheated, but that is completely untrue.*
( SYNONYM: **false** ) ( ANTONYM: **true** )

**un·used** *adjective*
**1** /uhn-**yoozd**/ not used: *The room was empty and unused.*
**2** /uhn-**yoost**/ not having experience with something: *Felipe is from Mexico, and he's unused to our cold winters in Michigan.*

**un·u·su·al** /uhn-**yoozh**-oo-uhl/ *adjective* different from what is usual or normal: *It's unusual for Mrs. Norris to get so angry. Most of the time she's pretty calm.* ▶ see Thesaurus
—**unusually** /uhn-**yoozh**-oo-uhl-ee/ *adverb* differently than usual or normal: *Is something wrong with Joey? He seems unusually quiet.*

**un·want·ed** /uhn-**wahnt**-id/ *adjective* if something is unwanted, you do not want or need it: *She gave me a lot of unwanted advice. I'd already decided what to do.*

**un·wel·come** /uhn-**welk**-uhm/ *adjective* not wanted: *All the other people ignored me, and I felt unwelcome.* ( ANTONYM: **welcome** )

**un·well** /uhn-**wel**/ *adjective* sick: *She can't come to school today – she's feeling unwell.*

**un·will·ing** /uhn-**wil**-ing/ *adjective* not wanting to do something: *We weren't likely to win, but we were unwilling to give up.* ( ANTONYM: **willing** )
—**unwillingly** /uhn-**wil**-ing-lee/ *adverb* in an unwilling way: *He ate his meal unwillingly because he did not like eating vegetables.*

**un·wind** /uhn-**wīnd**/ *verb* (**unwound** /uhn-**wownd**/)
**1** to relax, especially after working hard: *My dad exercises after work to unwind.*
**2** to undo something that is wrapped around something else: *I unwound the bandage around my ankle.* ( ANTONYM: **wind** )

**un·wise** /unhn-**wīz**/ *adjective* not sensible: *It's unwise to keep a lot of money in your room – someone might steal it.*

**un·wound** /uhn-**wownd**/ *verb* the past tense and past participle of **unwind**

**un·wrap** /uhn-**rap**/ *verb* (**unwrapping**, **unwrapped**) to take off the paper or plastic that is around something: *Beth was unwrapping her birthday presents.* ( ANTONYM: **wrap** )

**un·zip** /uhn-**zip**/ *verb* (**unzipping**, **unzipped**) to pull down the zipper on a piece of clothing or a bag, so that it is open: *Lucy unzipped her jacket to show us her T-shirt.*
( ANTONYM: **zip up** )

unzip

He unzipped his jacket.

**up** /uhp/ *adverb, preposition, adjective*
**1** toward or in a higher place: *The paper is up on the top shelf.* | *The cat ran up the tree.*
( ANTONYM: **down** )
**2** to a higher level, amount, or number than before: *Can you turn up the TV? I can barely hear it.* | *The price of a candy bar has gone up from 50 cents to a dollar.* ( ANTONYM: **down** )
**3** until something is completely gone: *Eat your dinner up.* | *We used up all the glue.*
**4** to the place close to where someone or something is: *Dad drove up in the car.*
**5** used when a period of time is finished: *Time's up! Put down your pencils.*
**6** into a more upright position: *Sit up straight!*
**7** happening or doing something: *What's up? Why is everybody standing outside?* | *What are the kids up to in their room?*
**8** to a place that is further along the road: *We walked up the street together.*

> IDIOMS with **up**
> **it's up to you/him, etc.** used for saying who has to decide something: *It's up to you. If you want to go to the party, you can.*
> **up to 15/20, etc.** as many as 15 or 20, etc.: *We can take up to six people in our car.*
> **what's up?** used to say hello to someone, and ask what is happening: *Hi Mike! What's up?*

**up**

go up the stairs          go down the stairs

**up-** /uhp/

### Word Building

**up-** is a prefix.
**up**hill | **up**load | **up**stairs
**up-** means "toward a higher place or level." If you walk *uphill*, you walk toward the top of a hill. If you *upload* something, you move it from an individual computer to a computer network.

**up·beat** /uhp-beet/ *adjective* cheerful and confident that good things will happen: *The coach sounded upbeat about the team's chances of winning the game.*

**up·bring·ing** /uhp-bring-ing/ *noun* the way that your parents care for you and teach you to behave: *Mandy had loving parents and a very good upbringing.*

**up·com·ing** /uhp-kuhm-ing/ *adjective* happening soon: *The baseball team is getting ready for an upcoming game. They will play the Wildcats on Friday.*

**up·date** /uhp-dayt/
● *verb* to add the most recent information to something: *The school needs to update its records with parents' cell phone numbers.*
● *noun* the most recent information about something: *We have to give the teacher an update on how our science project is going.*

**up·front** /uhp-**fruhnt**/ *adjective* speaking in an honest way and not trying to hide anything: *The teacher was upfront about my chances of passing the test and said that I needed to work harder.*

**up·grade** /uhp-grayd/ *verb* to improve something, or to get something better instead: *The school is planning to upgrade its computer system and there will be a lot of new computers.*

**up·heav·al** /uhp-**heev**-uhl/ *noun* a very big change that often causes problems: *Going to live in a new place can be a big upheaval, especially if you have to change schools too.*

**up·hill** /uhp-**hil**/ *adjective, adverb* toward the top of a hill: *The road began to go uphill.* | *an uphill climb* ( ANTONYM: **downhill** )

**uphill**

uphill

downhill

**up·hold** /uhp-**hohld**/ *verb* (**upheld** /uhp-**held**/) to support a law or decision: *The job of the police is to uphold the law.*

**up·hol·ster·y** /uh-**pohlst**-uhr-ee/ *noun* material that people use for covering chairs: *The car seats have leather upholstery.*

**up·lands** /**uhp**-luhndz/ *noun* the parts of a country that are away from the ocean and are higher than the other areas: *Los Alamos is in the desert uplands in New Mexico.*

**up·load** /**uhp**-lohd/ *verb* to move information from your computer to the Internet or another computer: *Everyone can see my video now. I just uploaded it.* ( SYNONYM: **download** )

**up·on** /uh-**pahn**/ *preposition* on: *The ship sailed upon the sea. | The movie is based upon a true story.*

**up·per** /**uhp**-ur/ *adjective* in a higher position than another part of something: *His upper lip was bleeding.* ( ANTONYM: **lower** )

**up·per·case** /**uhp**-ur-**kayss**/
● *noun* letters written in their large form, such as "A," "D," and "G": *The first letter of a sentence is always in uppercase.*
( SYNONYM: **capital** ) ( ANTONYM: **lowercase** )
● *adjective* uppercase letters are written in their large form: *The first letter of your name is always an uppercase letter, for example Juan or Madison.*

**up·per class** /**uhp**-ur **klass**/ *noun* the group of people in a country who are very rich or who have a lot of power: *They were a wealthy family who had all the advantages of the upper class.*

**up·right** /**uhp**-rīt/ *adjective* straight up, not lying down or leaning: *She sat in an upright position, with her back flat against the back of the chair.*

**up·ris·ing** /**uhp**-rīz-ing/ *noun* a situation in which people in a country fight against their government because they disagree with it: *When there was not enough food to eat, the people began an uprising against the king.*
( SYNONYM: **rebellion** )

**up·roar** /**uhp**-ror/ *noun* a lot of noise, shouting, or angry protest about something: *When the band left the stage after playing only three songs, it caused an uproar.*

**ups and downs** /uhpss uhn **downz**/ *plural noun* good things and bad things that happen: *Every team has its ups and downs. Sometimes the team plays well, and sometimes people make mistakes.*

**up·set** /uhp-**set**/
● *adjective* sad, worried, or angry about something: *What's wrong? You look upset. | Julie was very upset about losing her purse.*
● *verb* (**upsetting**, **upset**)
**1** to make someone feel sad, worried, or angry: *Please stop upsetting your sister. Don't take her toys.*
**2** if something upsets a plan, it changes it and causes problems: *The rain upset our plans, and we had to cancel the picnic.* ( SYNONYM: **spoil** )

**up·side down**
/uhp-sīd **down**/ *adverb* with the top at the bottom, and the bottom at the top: *She was hanging upside down from the monkey bars.*
—**upside-down** /**uhp**-sīd down / *adjective* having the top at the bottom and the bottom at the top: *An "M" is like an upside-down "W."*

**upside down**

The picture is hanging upside down.

**up·stairs** /uhp-**stairz**/ *adjective, adverb* on or going toward a higher floor of a building: *Sally is upstairs in her room.* ( ANTONYM: **downstairs** )

**up·tight** /uhp-**tīt**/ *adjective* nervous and angry: *Dad gets so uptight when I'm late.*

**up to date**, **up-to-date** /uhp tuh **dayt**/ *adjective* most recent or modern: *We looked at a website for up-to-date information about the weather.*

**up·town** /uhp-**town**/ *adverb, adjective* in or to the northern part of a city center: *Miguel drove uptown to see his mother. | an uptown bus*

**up·ward** /**uhp**-wurd/ *adjective, adverb* toward a higher place or position: *The balloon moved upward into the sky.* ( ANTONYM: **downward** )

a
b
c
d
e
f
g
h
i
j
k
l
m
n
o
p
q
r
s
t
**u**
v
w
x
y
z

**u·ra·ni·um** /yu-**rayn**-ee-uhm/ *noun* a silver-white metal used for producing nuclear energy and weapons: *The atomic bomb was made out of uranium.*

**U·ra·nus** /yu-**rayn**-uhss/ *noun* the seventh planet from the Sun. Uranus is the third biggest planet in our solar system.

**Uranus**

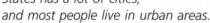

**ur·ban** /**urb**-uhn/ *adjective* relating to a town or city: *The United States has a lot of cities, and most people live in urban areas.*

ANTONYM: **rural**

—**urbanization** /urb-uhn-uh-**zaysh**-uhn/ *noun* a process in which urban areas get bigger: *Because of urbanization, houses and stores are being built on land that used to be farms, and more people move from the country to live in the cities.*

**urge** /urj/
● *verb* to advise someone very strongly to do something: *The piano teacher urged Nicholas to practice more.*
● *noun* a strong feeling that you want to do something very much: *She was so angry that she felt the urge to scream.*

**ur·gent** /**urj**-uhnt/ *adjective* if something is urgent, it is very important and someone needs to deal with it immediately: *He's hurt! Call an ambulance. It's urgent.*
—**urgently** /**urj**-uhnt-lee/ *adverb* in an urgent way: *"Come quickly, I need help!" she said urgently.*
—**urgency** /**urj**-uhnss-ee/ *noun* the need to do something as soon as possible: *He heard the urgency in her voice when she called for help.*

**u·rine** /**yoor**-in/ *noun* the liquid waste that comes out of your body when you go to the toilet
—**urinate** /**yoor**-uh-nayt/ *verb* to let urine come out of your body

**urn** /urn/ *noun*
**1** a container used for the ashes of a dead body
**2** a large metal container for hot coffee or tea

**us** /uhss/ *pronoun* yourself and another person. You use "us" after a verb or a preposition: *We went to the movies and Jack came with us.*

**U.S.** /yoo **ess**/ *noun* **the U.S.** the United States of America: *She lives in the U.S.*

**us·a·ble** /**yooz**-uhb-uhl/ *adjective* if something is usable, you can use it: *The computer is old, but it is still usable.*

**us·age** /**yooss**-ij/ *noun*
**1** the way that people use words in a language: *Sometimes words from other languages come into English usage. For example, "ketchup" comes from Malay.*
**2** the amount of something that is used: *Internet usage has increased in schools.*

**use**
● *verb* /yooz/
**1** if you use something, you do something with it: *Can I use your pen?* | *They used candles to light the room.* ▶ see **Thesaurus**
**2** to take something so that some or all of it is gone: *Big cars use a lot of gas.* | *I used up the shampoo when I washed my hair.*
● *noun* /yooss/
**1** the act of using something: *The use of sunblock helps prevent skin cancer.*
**2** a way of using something: *The tool has several uses. It works as a screwdriver and a drill.*
**3** if you have the use of something, you can use it: *Students have the use of computers after school to do their homework.*

IDIOMS with **use**
**it's no use** used when doing something will not have any effect: *It's no use. The door won't open however hard you push.*
**in use** if something is in use, someone is using it: *The library is in use all morning.*

**used** *adjective*
**1** /yoozd/ owned by someone else before you: *We bought a used car because we couldn't afford a new one.* SYNONYM: **second-hand**
**2** /yoost/ if you are used to something, you have done it or experienced it before, so it is not strange or surprising: *Jane is from Arizona, so she's used to hot weather.*

**used to** /**yoost**-uh, **yoost**-oo/ *verb* if something used to happen, it happened in the past but it does not happen now: *We used to live in California, but we moved last year.*

**use·ful** /**yooss**-fuhl/ *adjective* helping you to do or to get what you want: *That basket would be useful for picnics.* ( ANTONYM: **useless** )
▶ see Thesaurus
—**usefulness** /**yooss**-fuhl-niss/ *noun* how useful something is: *Some people question the usefulness of the tests.*

**use·less** /**yooss**-liss/ *adjective* not helpful or useful: *There's no ink in this pen – it's useless.*
( ANTONYM: **useful** )

**us·er** /**yooz**-ur/ *noun* someone who uses something such as a product or service: *A lot of computer users play games.*

**us·er-friend·ly** /**yooz**-ur **frend**-lee/ *adjective* easy to use: *The computer game teaches math in a user-friendly way.*

**ush·er** /**uhsh**-ur/ *noun* someone who shows people to their seats in a place such as a theater or church: *The usher showed us to our seats at the ballet.*

**u·su·al** /**yoozh**-oo-uhl/ *adjective* the same as what happens most of the time: *I sat in my usual seat in the front row.* | *Dad came home later than usual, at 8:00 instead of 6:00.*

**u·su·al·ly** /**yoozh**-oo-uhl-ee/ *adverb* if something usually happens, it almost always happens: *We usually have pizza and watch a movie on Friday.*
( SYNONYM: **normally** )

**u·ten·sil** /yoo-**tenss**-uhl/ *noun* a tool or object that you use for preparing or eating food: *Wash all the kitchen utensils carefully.*

utensil

kitchen utensils

**u·ter·us** /**yoot**-uhr-uhss/ *noun* the part inside a woman or female animal where a baby develops before it is born

**u·til·i·ty** /yoo-**til**-uht-ee/ *noun* (plural **utilities**) a service such as gas or electricity: *Is the cost of utilities included in the rent?*

**u·til·ize** /**yoot**'l-īz/ *verb* to use something: *Native American tribes utilized many plants as food.*

**ut·ter** /**uht**-ur/
● *verb* to say something: *No one uttered a word.*
● *adjective* complete or extreme: *We watched with utter amazement, as the magician made the coin disappear.*
—**utterly** /**uht**-ur-lee/ *adverb* completely or extremely: *He felt utterly exhausted.*

**U-turn** /**yoo** turn/ *noun* if you make a U-turn in a vehicle, you turn around and drive in the direction you came from: *She was going the wrong way, so she had to make a U-turn.*

a
b
c
d
e
f
g
h
i
j
k
l
m
n
o
p
q
r
s
t
u
**v**
w
x
y
z

# Vv

**vac-** /vac/

## Word Building

evacuate | **vac**ant | **vac**ation | **vac**uole | **vac**uum

These words all have the Latin word root **vac-** in them. **Vac-** means "empty." If the police *evacuate* a place, they tell everyone to leave that place, so that it is empty. A *vacant* apartment has no one living in it. A *vacuole* in a cell is a space in which the cell can keep water, nutrients, or waste material.

**va·can·cy** /**vayk**-uhnss-ee/ *noun* (plural **vacancies**)
**1** a room or apartment that is available for someone to stay in: *The motel has a "No Vacancy" sign, so we can't stay there tonight.*
**2** a job that is available for someone to start doing: *There weren't any vacancies at the factory.*

**va·cant** /**vayk**-uhnt/ *adjective* empty and available for someone to use: *The house has been vacant since the family moved away.*

**va·ca·tion** /vay-**kaysh**-uhn/ *noun* a time away from work or school when you can relax: *Where are you going on your summer vacation? | We've been working hard and really need to take a vacation.* ▶ see **Thesaurus**

**vac·cine** /vak-**seen**/ *noun* a substance that stops you from getting a disease. You swallow it or a doctor uses a needle to put it into your body: *She gets a flu vaccine each year.*
—**vaccinate** /**vakss**-uh-nayt/ *verb* to put a vaccine into someone's body: *Most children in this country are vaccinated against measles.*
—**vaccination** /vakss-uh-**naysh**-uhn/ *noun* the act of putting a vaccine into someone's body: *The doctor writes down the date of each vaccination.*

**vac·u·ole** /**vak**-yoo-ohl/ *noun* a space inside a cell that is full of liquid and that keeps nutrients or water for the plant or animal to use. Vacuoles can also hold waste products.

**vac·uum** /**vak**-yoom/
● *noun*
**1** (also **vacuum cleaner**) a machine that sucks up dirt and is used for cleaning floors with carpets on them: *If you get crumbs on the rug get the vacuum and clean them up.*
**2** a space that has no air or gas in it: *Outer space, away from the planets and stars, is a vacuum.*
● *verb*
to clean a carpet with a machine that sucks up dirt: *One of my jobs is to vacuum the floors.*

**vague** /vayg/ *adjective* not clear or certain: *Thomas said he had a good day at school, but he was vague about what he actually did.*
—**vaguely** /**vayg**-lee/ *adverb* in a vague way: *He looked vaguely familiar, but I couldn't remember his name.* ( SYNONYM: **unclear** )

**vain** /vayn/ *adjective*
**1** too proud of the way you look or what you can do: *She was very vain and always looking at herself in the mirror.*
**2** without success: *I tried in vain to convince Paul to come.*
—**vainly** /**vayn**-lee/ *adverb* without success: *He struggled vainly to escape.*

**val·en·tine** /**val**-uhn-tīn/ *noun*
**1** a card given on Valentine's Day: *Lucy made valentines for her friends.*
**2** someone you give a card or gift to on Valentine's Day: *Will you be my valentine?*

**Val·en·tine's Day** /**val**-uhn-tīnz day/ *noun* February 14, a day when people give cards, candy, or flowers to people they love: *My parents are going out to dinner for Valentine's Day.*

**val·id** /**val**-id/ *adjective*
**1** able to be used and legally accepted: *A U.S. passport is valid for ten years.* ( ANTONYM: **invalid** )
**2** reasonable and likely to be accepted: *You must have a valid reason for missing the test – for example because you are sick.* ( SYNONYM: **good** )

**val·ley** /**val**-ee/ *noun* a low area of land between hills or mountains: *The town is in a valley.*

valley

**val·ua·ble** /**val**-yuhb-uhl/ *adjective*
**1** worth a lot of money: *My mother's gold necklace is very valuable.* ( ANTONYM: **worthless** )
▶ see **Thesaurus**
**2** very useful: *Jess is the team's most valuable player. She always plays well.*
—**valuables** /**val**-yuhb-uhlz/ *plural noun* things that are valuable: *We put our valuables in a locker at the gym.*

**val·ue** /**val**-yoo/
● *noun*
**1** the amount of money that something is worth: *The value of the car is $5,000.*
**2** the importance or usefulness of something: *The trip to the farm was of great value – we learned so much about how food is produced.*
**3** a belief about what is right and wrong, or about what is important in life: *On our team, we work hard and try our best. These are our values.*
**4** in math, an amount: *If x + 5 = 7, then what is the value of x? (The value of x is 2.)* | *We learned about place value. In the number 30, the 3 represents three tens.*
● *verb*
**1** to think that something is important: *Maria's family really values education.*
**2** to say how much something is worth: *They valued the painting at $5 million.*

> **Word Family:** value
>
> **value** *noun* | **value** *verb* | **valuable** *adjective* | **invaluable** *adjective* | **valuables** *plural noun*

**valve** /valv/ *noun* a part of a pipe or tube that opens and closes to control the flow of liquid or gas passing through it: *The valve on the bike's tire opens when you pump air into the tire, and closes when you take the pump off.*
▶ see picture at **bicycle**

**vam·pire** /**vamp**-ī-ur/ *noun* an imaginary person who bites people's necks and sucks their blood: *"Dracula" is a famous vampire story.*

**van** /van/ *noun* a vehicle that is longer than a car, and is used to carry things or people. Some vans do not have windows in the back: *A van took us from the hotel to the airport.*

van

**van·dal** /**vand**'l/ *noun* someone who damages other people's property on purpose: *Vandals had broken the store's windows.*
—**vandalize** /**vand**'l-īz/ *verb* to damage other people's property on purpose: *Someone vandalized the school last night. The walls are covered with spray paint.*
—**vandalism** /**vand**'l-iz-uhm/ *noun* the crime of vandalizing property

> **Word Origin:** vandal
>
> **Vandal** comes from the name of a group of people called the Vandals. In the year 455 A.D., the Vandals attacked Rome and damaged the city very badly. In the 1600s, vandal started being used in English to mean people who damage things on purpose.

**va·nil·la** /vuh-**nil**-uh/ *noun* a substance used in sweet foods such as ice cream and cakes, that gives them a particular taste. Vanilla comes from the bean of a tropical plant: *For dessert, we had vanilla ice cream.*

**van·ish** /**van**-ish/ *verb* to disappear suddenly: *The clouds vanished and the sun came out.*

**van·i·ty** /**van**-uht-ee/ *noun* the quality of being too proud of your appearance or abilities: *The queen's vanity made her want to be the most beautiful woman of all.*

a b c d e f g h i j k l m n o p q r s t u **v** w x y z

**va·por** /**vayp**-ur/ *noun* a gas form of something that is liquid or solid at normal temperatures. Vapor is produced when the liquid or solid is heated. Vapor is often made of many very small drops of liquid that float in the air: *Steam is water vapor that is produced when water is boiled.*

**var·i·a·ble** /**vair**-ee-uhb-uhl/
● *adjective*
likely to change often or be different: *The weather is variable: one day it's raining and the next it's bright sunshine.* ( ANTONYM: **constant** )
● *noun*
**1** something that may be different in different situations: *In our science experiment, we measured how much plants grew. The variables were how much light the plant got, how much water we gave it, and how long we allowed it to grow for.*
**2** in math, a variable is a symbol that can stand for different amounts. A variable is usually written as a letter such as x or y: *In the problem "x + 2 = 10," x is a variable that equals 8.*

**var·i·a·tion** /vair-ee-**aysh**-uhn/ *noun* a difference between similar things: *There was a lot of variation in the test results. Some children did very well while other children did not.*

**var·ied** /**vair**-eed/ *adjective* including many different types of things or people: *The children have varied interests, including sports, music, and art.*

**va·ri·e·ty** /vuh-**rī**-uht-ee/ *noun* (plural **varieties**)
**1** a type of something that is different from other similar things: *There are many different varieties of apples, some with red and some with green skin.*
**2** a lot of different kinds of things: *We read a variety of books, such as fairy tales, biographies, and science books.*
**3** the differences within something that make it interesting: *Park rangers have a lot of variety in their work. They give talks, lead hikes, and even do scientific research.*

**var·i·ous** /**vair**-ee-uhss/ *adjective* several different: *We planted various kinds of flowers, including roses and daisies.*

**var·nish** /**varn**-ish/
● *noun* a clear liquid that you paint onto wood

to give it a shiny surface: *After Peter sands the wooden floor, he will apply varnish.*
● *verb* to put varnish on something

**var·si·ty** /**varss**-uht-ee/ *noun* (plural **varsities**) the varsity team at a school or college is the main team: *Mike plays on the varsity football team.*

**var·y** /**vair**-ee/ *verb* (**varies**, **varying**, **varied**)
**1** to be different from other things of the same type: *The rooms in the hotel vary in size, from small to very large.*
**2** to change often: *His mood varied: sometimes he was happy, sometimes he was sad.*
—**varying** /**vair**-ee-ing/ *adjective* different: *The arts camp is for children of varying ages, from kindergarten to fifth grade.*

**Word Family:** vary

**vary** *verb* | **variety** *noun* | **varied** *adjective* | **various** *adjective* | **variable** *adjective* | **variation** *noun*

**vase** /vayss/ *noun* a container for putting cut flowers in water: *She put the roses in a pretty vase.*

vase

vase

**vast** /vast/ *adjective* extremely large: *The Sahara is a vast desert that covers one quarter of all the land in Africa.*
( SYNONYMS: **enormous, huge** ) ( ANTONYM: **tiny** )
—**vastly** /**vast**-lee/ *adverb* very much: *Her reading has improved vastly this year.*

**vault** /volt/ *noun* a room with thick walls and a strong door. Money and jewels are kept in a vault so no one can steal them: *The gold is stored in a vault under the bank.*

**V-chip** /**vee**-chip/ *noun* a device in a television that blocks programs that parents do not want their children to see

**VCR** /vee see **ar**/ *noun* a machine used for recording television shows or watching videotapes

**veal** /veel/ *noun* meat from a young cow: *The sausage has pork and veal in it.*

**vege·ta·ble** /**vej**-tuhb-uhl/ *noun* a plant you can eat, such as a carrot or a cabbage: *My favorite vegetables are peas and carrots.* ▶ see picture on page **A7**

**veg·e·tar·i·an** /vej-uh-**tair**-ee-uhn/ *noun* someone who does not eat meat: *This dish is suitable for vegetarians because it contains no meat.*

**veg·e·ta·tion** /vej-uh-**taysh**-uhn/ *noun* the plants growing somewhere: *They pushed their way through the jungle vegetation.*

**ve·hi·cle** /**vee**-ik-uhl/ (also **motor vehicle** /moht-ur **vee**-ik-uhl/) *noun* something such as a car or bus that carries people or things: *A tractor is a type of vehicle that is used by farmers.*

**veil** /vayl/ *noun* a thin piece of material that women wear to cover their faces: *The bride wore a veil.*

**veil**

veil

**vein** /vayn/ *noun* one of the tubes in your body that carry blood to your heart: *Your veins look blue under your skin.* ▶ see picture at **heart**

**Vel·cro** /**vel**-kroh/ *noun trademark* pieces of special material that are used to fasten things. The small hooks on one piece stick to the other piece: *The sneakers fasten with Velcro, not with laces.*

**ve·loc·i·ty** /vuh-**lahss**-uht-ee/ *noun* (plural **velocities**) the speed at which something moves in a particular direction: *The rocket reached a velocity of 18,000 miles per hour.*

**vel·vet** /**velv**-it/ *noun* thick cloth with a soft surface on one side: *The king's chair was covered with red velvet.*

**vend·ing ma·chine** /**vend**-ing muh-sheen/ *noun* a machine that you can buy candy, drinks, and other things from: *I put my money in the vending machine and a candy bar dropped out.*

**ve·ne·tian blind** /vuh-neesh-uhn **blīnd**/ *noun* something that you let down to cover a window. A venetian blind is made from long horizontal pieces of plastic or wood.

**venge·ance** /**venj**-uhnss/ *noun* if you want vengeance, you want to do something bad to someone because he or she did something bad to you: *He wanted vengeance on the kids who bullied him, so he got them in trouble with the teacher.* ( SYNONYM: **revenge** )

**ven·i·son** /**ven**-uhss-uhn/ *noun* meat from a deer

**ven·om** /**ven**-uhm/ *noun* the poison of an animal such as a snake or spider. The animal puts the poison into other animals by biting or stinging them.

**vent** /vent/ *noun* a hole through which gas, smoke, or steam can go out, or fresh air can come in: *There's an air vent in the roof of the tent.*

**ven·ue** /**ven**-yoo/ *noun* a place where an organized event such as a concert takes place: *The hall would be a good venue for our concert.*

**Ve·nus** /**veen**-uhss/ *noun* the second planet from the Sun. It is between Mercury and the Earth.

**verb** /vurb/ *noun* a word that is used to say what someone or something does. "Write," "see," and "believe" are verbs: *In the sentence, "She plays the piano," "plays" is a verb.*

**ver·bal** /**vurb**-uhl/ *adjective*
**1** relating to words or using words: *She has good verbal skills and likes talking and writing.*
**2** spoken, not written: *Your parents must write a note saying you can go on the trip – their verbal permission is not enough.*
—**verbally** /**vurb**-uhl-ee/ *adverb* using words, especially by speaking to someone: *He passed on the message verbally rather than by writing an email.*

**ver·dict** /**vurd**-ikt/ *noun* the decision of a jury about whether someone is guilty of a crime: *We all waited for the jury to reach a verdict.*

**verge** /vurj/ *noun* **be on the verge of** to be going to do something very soon: *She was very upset and on the verge of tears.*

**ver·i·fy** /**verr**-uh-fī/ *verb* (**verifies**, **verified**) to check or prove that something is correct or true: *After they had verified the man's identity, they let him into the building.*
—**verification** /verr-uh-fuh-**kaysh**-uhn/ *noun* the act of verifying something: *I had to give the officer my ID card for verification.*

**ver·sa·tile** /**vurss**-uht'l/ *adjective* able to do a lot of different things or to be used in a lot of different ways: *He's a versatile actor who has done both serious movies and comedies.*
—**versatility** /vurss-uh-**til**-uht-ee/ *noun* the ability to be versatile: *The player has shown his versatility and can play center or guard.*

**verse** /vurss/ *noun*
**1** a set of lines that is one part of a poem or song: *We sang the first two verses of the song.*
**2** poetry: *The book of verse contained poems by many different people.*

**ver·sion** /**vurzh**-uhn/ *noun*
**1** one person's description of something that happened: *Kevin gave the teacher his version of what happened.*
**2** a form of something that is slightly different from other forms: *I prefer the original version of the song.*

**ver·sus** /**vurss**-uhss/ *preposition*
(ABBREVIATION: **vs.** or **v.**) against. This word is used when saying who is taking part in a game or a court case: *Tonight's game is the Knicks versus the Lakers.*

**ver·te·bra** /**vurt**-uhb-ruh/ *noun* (plural **vertebrae** /vertebrae/) one of the small bones down the center of your back: *You have 33 vertebrae in your spine.*

**ver·te·brate** /**vurt**-uh-brayt/ *noun* an animal that has a backbone: *Birds, fish, and mammals are all vertebrates.*

**ver·tex** /**vurt**-ekss/ *noun* (plural **vertices** /**vurt**-uh-seez/) a point where two straight lines meet, or where the sides of a shape meet: *A hexagon has six sides and six vertices.*

**ver·ti·cal** /**vurt**-ik-uhl/ *adjective* pointing straight upward: *Draw a vertical line from the top to the bottom of the paper.* (ANTONYM: **horizontal**)
—**vertically** /**vurt**-ik-lee/ *adverb* in a vertical way: *She was hanging vertically from the bars.*

**ver·ti·ces** /**vurt**-uh-seez/ *noun* the plural of **vertex**

**ver·ti·go** /**vur**-ti-go/ *noun* a feeling of fear and dizziness because you are looking down from a high place

**ve·ry** /**verr**-ee/
● *adverb*
**1** used for emphasizing another word: *It's a very good book.* | *I hope to see you again very soon.*
**2 not very** not at all: *I'm not very good at math. I can't even do simple addition.*
● *adjective*
**1 the very top/bottom/end/beginning** the farthest point: *There was a bird sitting at the very top of the tree.*
**2** exact: *I found the watch here, on this very spot.*

**Word Choice: very, too**

You use **very** to emphasize something that can be either good or bad: *It's very hot today.* | *I was going very fast on my skateboard.*

You usually use **too** to show that you do not like or approve of something: *I started going too fast on my skateboard.* | *My shoes are too small.* | *We were too late and missed the bus.*

**ves·sel** /**vess**-uhl/ *noun*
**1** a tube in your body that blood flows through: *A heart attack may be caused by a blocked blood vessel.*
**2** a ship: *He is now a sailor on a U.S. naval vessel.*

**vest** /vest/ *noun* a piece of clothing with no sleeves that you wear over a shirt: *He was wearing a dark suit with a matching vest.*

**vet** /vet/ *noun*
**1** a veterinarian: *Our cat is sick and he needs to go to the vet.*
**2** a veteran: *My grandfather was a Vietnam vet – he was a helicopter pilot.*

**vet·er·an** /**vet**-uhr-uhn/ *noun* someone who has been a soldier or sailor in a war: *Many war veterans marched in the parade.*

**Vet·er·ans Day** /**vet**-uhr-uhnz day/ *noun* a holiday in honor of people who were soldiers or sailors in wars. Veterans Day is November 11.

**vet·er·i·nar·i·an** /vet-uhr-uh-**nair**-ee-uhn/ *noun* a doctor for animals: *When our dog got sick we took him to the veterinarian.* (SYNONYM: **vet**)
—**veterinary** /**vet**-uhr-uh-nair-ee/ *adjective* relating

to the work of a veterinarian: *The veterinary clinic treats all kinds of animals.*

**veterinarian**

## ve·to /**veet**-oh/

- *verb* if someone with power vetoes something, he or she does not allow it: *I wanted to go to Hawaii, but my parents vetoed the idea because it was too expensive.*
- *noun* (plural **vetoes**) the action of vetoing something

## vi·a /**vī**-uh/ *preposition*

**1** if you go via a place, you travel through it or visit it on the way to another place: *We're going to Vermont via New York*
**2** using a particular method or person to pass something on: *The concert was broadcast around the world via satellite.*

## vi·a·duct /**vī**-uh-duhkt/ *noun* a long high bridge across a valley

## vi·brate /**vī**-brayt/ *verb* to move up and down or from side to side for a long time: *The top of the drum vibrates after you hit it.*
—**vibration** /vī-**braysh**-uhn/ *noun* the act of vibrating: *You can feel the vibrations from the engine.*

## vice /vīss/ *noun* a bad habit: *Her only vice was eating too much candy.*

## vice pres·i·dent /vīss **prez**-uhd-uhnt/ *noun*
**1** the person who is next in rank to the president of a country: *If the president dies, the vice president becomes president.*
**2** someone who is responsible for one part of a company: *He is vice president of sales at the company.*

## vi·ce ver·sa /vīss **vurss**-uh/ *adverb* used to

mean the opposite of the situation you have just described: *The girls may refuse to play with the boys, and vice versa, the boys may refuse to play with the girls.*

## vi·cin·i·ty /vuh-**sin**-uht-ee/ *noun* in the vicinity near a place: *People were scared because a wolf had been seen in the vicinity of the town.*

## vi·cious /**vish**-uhss/ *adjective*
**1** violent and likely to hurt someone: *She was bitten by her neighbor's vicious dog.*
**2** cruel and nasty: *He spread vicious lies about me.*
—**viciously** /**vish**-uhss-lee/ *adverb* in a vicious way: *She was viciously attacked.*

## vic·tim /**vikt**-im/ *noun* someone who has been hurt or harmed by something or someone: *Some flood victims were given shelter at a local school.* | *If you are a victim of bullying, get help from someone.*

## vic·to·ry /**vikt**-uhr-ee/ *noun* (plural **victories**) the act of winning a battle, game, or competition: *The team are celebrating their victory.* | *We'll keep fighting until we achieve victory.*
( SYNONYM: **win** ) ( ANTONYM: **defeat** )

## vid·e·o /**vid**-ee-oh/
*noun* a short recording of moving pictures: *You can see videos of people doing crazy things on the Internet.*

**video camera**

video camera

## vid·e·o cam·er·a
/**vid**-ee-oh kam-ruh/
*noun* a camera that you use to record moving images

## vid·e·o game /**vid**-ee-oh gaym/ *noun* a game in which you move controls and make pictures move on a screen: *He's playing a video game on the computer.*

## vid·e·o·tape /**vid**-ee-oh-tayp/
- *noun* a long band in a plastic case that you record moving pictures onto: *They showed us a videotape of their wedding.* ( SYNONYM: **tape** )
- *verb* to record something onto videotape: *Dad videotaped the school concert and I watched it again and again.*

**view** /vyoo/

● *noun*

**1** the things that you can see from a place: *The view from the top of the mountain was beautiful.*

**2** the ability to see something from a particular place: *I had a good view of the stage from my seat, so I could see all the actors clearly.*

**3** an opinion: *The magazine asked people about their views on marriage.*

● *verb*

**1** to have a particular opinion about something: *Some people view shyness as a problem, but shy people can be happy too.* ( SYNONYM: **regard** )

**2** to look at or watch something: *On the trip, you will be able to view bears and other animals.*

**view·er** /**vyoo**-ur/ *noun* someone who watches a television program: *The TV show has more than five million viewers.*

**view·point** /**vyoo**-poynt/ *noun* a particular way of thinking about something: *Parents should try to see things from their child's viewpoint.*
( SYNONYM: **point of view** )

**vig·i·lant** /**vij**-uhl-uhnt/ *adjective* watching carefully, so that you will notice if something bad happens: *You have to be vigilant so that you notice if any of your fish are getting sick.*
—**vigilance** /**vij**-uhl-uhnss/ *noun* vigilant behavior: *Vigilance from members of the public is very important in preventing crime.*

**vig·i·lan·te** /vij-uh-**lant**-ee/ *noun* an ordinary person, not a police officer, who tries to stop, catch, or punish criminals: *They formed a vigilante group to fight crime on the subway.*

**vig·or** /**vig**-uhr/ *noun* energy and determination

**vig·or·ous** /**vig**-uhr-uhss/ *adjective* using a lot of energy or effort: *Give the bottle a vigorous shake to mix the medicine thoroughly.*
—**vigorously** /**vig**-uhr-uhss-lee/ *adverb* in a vigorous way: *She nodded vigorously in agreement.*

**vil·la** /**vil**-uh/ *noun* a big country house

**vil·lage** /**vil**-ij/ *noun* a very small town: *My grandparents live in a small village in Mexico.*
—**villager** /**vil**-ij-ur/ *noun* someone who lives in a village

**vil·lain** /**vil**-uhn/ *noun* the bad character in a movie, play, or story: *The evil queen is the villain of the story.* ( ANTONYM: **hero** )

**vin·di·cate** /**vind**-i-kayt/ *verb* to show that someone was right, or did not do anything wrong: *After the game the coach said that his confidence in the team had been vindicated.*

**vin·dic·tive** /vin-**dikt**-iv/ *adjective* very mean to someone because you think he or she harmed you: *I think it's better to forgive people than to be vindictive.*

**vine** /vīn/ *noun* a plant with long stems that grow along the ground or climb up other plants, walls, or fences: *The house was covered in vines.*

vine

**vin·e·gar** /**vin**-ig-ur/ *noun* a sour liquid that is used in cooking: *You can make a salad dressing from olive oil and vinegar.*

**vine·yard** /**vin**-yurd/ *noun* a piece of land where someone grows grapes for making wine

vineyard

**vin·tage** /**vint**-ij/ *adjective* old and valuable or interesting: *He drives a vintage car from the 1940s.*

**vi·nyl** /**vīn**'l/ *noun* a strong plastic: *The seats in the diner were covered with vinyl, so they could be cleaned easily.*

**vi·o·la** /vee-**ohl**-uh/ *noun* a wooden musical instrument with strings that looks like a big violin. A viola has a lower sound than a violin.
▶ see picture at **violin**

**vi·o·late** /**vī**-uh-layt/ *verb* to break a law or rule: *He was punished for violating a team rule.*
—**violation** /vī-uh-**laysh**-uhn/ *noun* the act of breaking a law or rule: *The police arrested him for a traffic violation.*

**vi·o·lence** /**vī**-uhl-uhnss/ *noun*
**1** actions that hurt someone physically: *There was no excuse for violence – you shouldn't have hit him.*
**2** great force: *The violence of the storm increased and trees were blown down.*

**vi·o·lent** /**vī**-uhl-uhnt/ *adjective*
**1** involving actions that hurt someone physically: *I don't like violent movies that show a lot of people getting shot.*
**2** someone who is violent attacks and hurts other people: *He sometimes gets violent, and starts hitting people.* ▶ see **Thesaurus**
**3** happening with a lot of force: *The house was shaken by a violent earthquake.*
—**violently** /**vī**-uhl-uhnt-lee/ *adverb* in a violent way

> ### Word Family: violent
> **violent** *adjective* | **violently** *adverb* | **violence** *noun*

**vi·o·let** /**vī**-uhl-it/ *noun*
**1** a small purple flower with a sweet smell
**2** a purple color

violet

**vi·o·lin** /vī-uh-**lin**/ *noun*
a wooden musical instrument with four strings. You hold a violin under your chin and play it by pulling a bow across the strings: *Sarah is learning to play the violin.*
—**violinist** /vī-uh-**lin**-ist/ *noun* someone who plays a violin

viola
violin
violin

> ### Word Origin: violin
> **Violin** comes from an Italian word that means "little viola." **Viola** comes from a Latin word for a musical instrument with strings. This instrument may have been named after Vitula, who was the Roman goddess of joy.

**VIP** /vee ī **pee**/ *noun* someone who is famous or important, and is treated in a special way. VIP is short for "Very Important Person": *The red carpet is used when VIPs visit the theater.*

**vir·tu·al** /**vurch**-oo-uhl/ *adjective*
**1** on a computer, rather than in the real world: *The website allows you to take a virtual tour of the art gallery.*
**2** almost something: *My cousin's a virtual stranger – I've only met him once.*

**vir·tu·al·ly** /**vurch**-oo-uhl-ee/ *adverb* almost: *Samantha's dress is virtually the same as mine – its sleeves are slightly different.*

**vir·tu·al re·al·i·ty** /vurch-oo-uhl ree-**al**-uht-ee/ *noun* pictures and sounds on a computer that almost make you feel as if you are in a particular place: *Video games can give you exciting experiences in virtual reality, such as driving fast cars.*

**vir·tue** /**vurch**-oo/ *noun* a good quality that someone has: *Honesty is one of his virtues.*

**vir·tu·ous** /**vurch**-oo-uhss/ *adjective* behaving in a way that is usually good and right

**vi·rus** /**vīr**-uhss/ *noun*
**1** a living thing, too small to see, that causes an illness. Viruses can be spread from one person to another: *Colds are caused by a virus.*
**2** a program that gets onto your computer and stops it from working properly. Viruses are spread from one computer to another on the Internet: *It's important to protect your computer against viruses because you could lose all the information on your hard disk.*

715

a b c d e f g h i j k l m n o p q r s t u **v** w x y z

a
b
c
d
e
f
g
h
i
j
k
l
m
n
o
p
q
r
s
t
u
**v**
w
x
y
z

**vis-** /viz/, **vid-** /vid/

## Word Building

invisible | revise | vision | evidence | video

These words all have the Latin word root **vis-** or **vid-** in them. **Vis-** or **vid-** means "see." If something is *invisible*, you cannot see it. If you *revise* something you have written, you look at it again and change it to make it better. Your *vision* is your ability to see. The *evidence* in a court case is all the things a lawyer shows the court to try to prove that something is true.

**vi·sa** /**veez**-uh/ *noun* an official document or mark in your passport that allows you to enter or leave a country: *He came to the U.S. on a student visa.*

**vis·i·ble** /**viz**-uhb-uhl/ *adjective* able to be seen: *The house is visible from the road.*
(ANTONYM: **invisible**)
—**visibly** /**viz**-uhb-lee/ *adverb* in a way that you can see: *She seemed visibly upset by the news and she was crying.*
—**visibility** /viz-uh-**bil**-uht-ee/ *noun* the distance that you can see because of the weather: *It was very foggy, and the visibility was terrible.*

## Word Family: visible

**visible** adjective | **invisible** adjective | **visibly** adverb | **visibility** noun

**vi·sion** /**vizh**-uhn/ *noun*
**1** your ability to see: *I had my vision tested to find out if I needed glasses.* (SYNONYM: **sight**)
**2** an idea of what something should be like: *He has a clear vision of what he wants to do in the future.*

**vis·it** /**viz**-it/
● *verb*
**1** to go and see a person or a place: *We went to visit my aunt in Texas last year.*
**2** to talk to someone in a friendly way: *We watched TV while Mom visited with Mrs. Levinson.*
● *noun*
if you make a visit to a place or a person, you go

and see that place or person: *Did you enjoy your visit to Florida?*

**vis·i·tor** /**viz**-uht-ur/ *noun* someone who comes to visit a place or a person: *The Grand Canyon gets millions of visitors.*

**vi·sor** /**vīz**-ur/ *noun*
**1** the part of a hat that sticks out over your eyes: *He turned his cap around so the visor was at the back.*
**2** a part above a car's windshield that you pull down to keep the sun out of your eyes
**3** the part of a helmet that you pull down over your face ▶ see picture at **armor**

**vis·u·al** /**vizh**-oo-uhl/ *adjective* relating to seeing: *An alarm bell rings, and at the same time a red light gives you a visual warning.*
—**visually** /**vizh**-yoo-uhl-ee/ *adverb* in a way that relates to what you see: *The movie is visually spectacular.*

**vis·u·al·ize** /**vizh**-oo-uh-līz/ *verb* to form a picture of something in your mind: *I tried to visualize myself winning the race.*
(SYNONYM: **imagine**)

**vi·tal** /**vīt**'l/ *adjective* very important or necessary: *It's vital that you remember to water the plants every day.*
—**vitally** /**vīt**'l-ee/ *adverb* in a very important or necessary way: *It is vitally important that you follow the instructions exactly.*

**vi·ta·min** /**vīt**-uhm-in/ *noun* a natural chemical in food that keeps you healthy. Different types of food contain different vitamins: *Oranges contain vitamin C.*

**viv·id** /**viv**-id/ *adjective*
**1** giving you a very clear picture in your mind: *It was such a vivid dream that I thought it was real.* | *He wrote a vivid description of the things he had seen in Africa.*
**2** **a vivid imagination** the ability to imagine unlikely situations very clearly: *She has a vivid imagination and makes up very exciting stories.*
**3** vivid colors are very bright: *The parrot had vivid red and blue feathers.*
—**vividly** /**viv**-id-lee/ *adverb* in a vivid way: *I can vividly remember my first day at school.*

**vo·cab·u·lar·y** /voh-**kab**-yuh-lair-ee/ *noun* (plural **vocabularies**) all the words you know: *She* *wants to increase her vocabulary by learning new words.*

**vo·cal** /**vohk**-uhl/ *adjective* relating to the voice: *He had vocal training before becoming a professional singer.*

**vo·cal cords** /**vohk**-uhl kordz/ *plural noun* the parts in your throat that produce sound when you speak or sing. Air from your lungs makes your vocal cords move quickly.

**vo·cals** /**vohk**-uhlz/ *plural noun* the part of a pop song that is sung: *On this record, he does the vocals as well as playing the guitar.*

**vo·ca·tion** /voh-**kaysh**-uhn/ *noun* a job, especially one that you think is good and right for you: *For him, making music is a vocation, not just a way of earning money.*

**vogue** /vohg/ *noun* **be in vogue** to be fashionable: *Everyone is wearing canvas shoes because they are in vogue.*

**voice** /voyss/ *noun* the sound you make when you speak or sing: *"Hello," she said in a loud voice.*

> **IDIOMS with voice**
> **lose your voice** to become unable to speak: *He had a cold and had lost his voice.*
> **raise your voice** to speak loudly because you are angry or want someone to hear you: *My parents never argue or raise their voices to each other.*

**voice mail** /**voyss** mayl/ *noun* a system that records telephone messages so that you can listen to them later: *He wasn't there when I called, so I left a message on his voice mail.*

**void** /voyd/ *noun*
**1** if there is a void in your life or in a situation, someone or something important is missing: *When his best friend moved away, he tried to find a new friend to fill the void.*
**2** a large empty space: *We went up to the entrance of the cave and looked down into the void.*

**vol·a·tile** /**vahl**-uht'l/ *adjective*
**1** a volatile liquid or substance changes easily into gas: *Mercury is volatile at room temperature.*
**2** a volatile situation is likely to change suddenly and without warning

**3** a volatile person can suddenly become very angry

**vol·ca·no** /vahl-**kayn**-oh/ *noun* (plural **volcanoes** or **volcanos**) a mountain with a large hole at the top. Sometimes volcanoes send smoke or melted rock called lava out of the hole: *The volcano erupted and covered the town in ash.*
—**volcanic** /vahl-**kan**-ik/ *adjective* relating to volcanoes: *volcanic rocks*

> ## Word Origin: volcano
>
> **Volcano** comes from an Italian word that means "burning mountain." The Italians got this name from the Roman god Vulcan, who was the god of fire. The Romans believed that Mount Etna, which is a famous volcano in Italy, was where the god Vulcan worked.

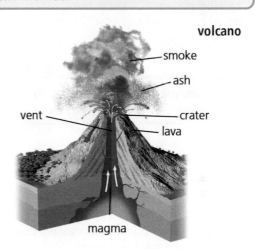

volcano
— smoke
— ash
vent —
— crater
— lava
magma

**vol·ley** /**vahl**-ee/ *noun* a large number of bullets, arrows, etc. that are fired at the same time: *The soldier fired a volley of shots into the air as a warning.*

**vol·ley·ball** /**vahl**-ee-bol/ *noun*
**1** a game played by two teams. The players hit a ball across a net with their hands, and try not to let it touch the ground: *They were playing volleyball on the beach.* ▶ see picture on page **A10**
**2** the ball used in this game

**volt** /vohlt/ *noun* a unit for measuring the force of an electric current: *The radio is powered by a 12-volt battery.*
—**voltage** /**vohlt**-ij/ *noun* the force of an electric current: *The lions are kept in an area surrounded by a high voltage electric fence.*

a b c d e f g h i j k l m n o p q r s t u **v** w x y z

**vol·ume** /**vahl**-yuhm/ *noun*
**1** the amount of sound that comes from a television, radio, etc.: *I can't hear the TV. Can you turn the volume up, please?*
**2** the amount of space that something fills or contains: *You find the volume of a box by multiplying the length by the width by the height.*
**3** the total amount of something: *We can't cope with such a large volume of work.*
**4** a book, especially one that is part of a set of books: *The encyclopedia was published in ten volumes.*

**vol·un·tar·y** /**vahl**-uhn-tair-ee/ *adjective* done because you want to and not because you must: *The test is completely voluntary – you don't have to take it.* ( ANTONYM: **compulsory** )
—**voluntarily** /vahl-uhn-**tair**-uhl-ee/ *adverb* because you want to and not because you must: *He quit the team voluntarily – no one made him leave.*

**Word Family:** voluntary
**voluntary** *adjective* | **voluntarily** *adverb* | **volunteer** *verb* | **volunteer** *noun*

**vol·un·teer** /vahl-uhn-**teer**/
● *noun*
**1** someone who willingly does something without being paid: *They don't have to pay wages because all the staff are volunteers.*
**2** someone who offers to do something: *The teacher asked for a volunteer to hand out the books.*
● *verb*
to offer to do something: *Ryan volunteered to help clean up after the party.*
● *adjective*
volunteer work is work that you do for no money: *She doesn't have a job but she does volunteer work in a hospital.*

**vom·it** /**vahm**-it/
● *verb* if you vomit, food comes up from your stomach and out through your mouth: *The food*
was so horrible it made me vomit.
( SYNONYMS: **throw up, be sick** )
● *noun* food that someone has vomited: *My sister threw up and there was vomit everywhere.*

**vote** /voht/
● *verb*
to show which person or plan you choose, for example by marking a piece of paper or raising your hand: *Who did you vote for in the election?* | *The class voted to spend the money on a new computer.*
—**voter** /**voht**-ur/ *noun* someone who votes: *The voters will decide who becomes president.*
● *noun*
**1** the choice of a voter: *The person who gets the most votes wins the election.*
**2** if there is a vote, people vote on something: *There's a choice of things to do, so let's take a vote on it.*

**vouch·er** /**vowch**-ur/ *noun* a piece of paper that you can use instead of money: *They gave me a $100 voucher to use at the department store.*

**vow** /vow/
● *noun* a serious promise: *When they got married, they wrote their own marriage vows.*
● *verb* to make a serious promise: *He vowed to make his parents proud of him.*

**vow·el** /**vow**-uhl/ *noun* one of the letters a, e, i, o, or u, and sometimes y, or the sounds that these letters represent: *You use "an," not "a," before words that begin with a vowel sound.*
( ANTONYM: **consonant** )

**voy·age** /**voy**-ij/ *noun* a long trip in a ship or a spacecraft: *The voyage from England to America took several weeks.*

**vs.** /**vurss**-uhss/ an abbreviation of **versus**

**vul·ner·a·ble** /**vuhl**-nuhr-uhb-uhl/ *adjective* easy to hurt or harm: *A snail is vulnerable when it comes out of its shell because there is nothing to protect it.*

**vul·ture** /**vuhlch**-ur/ *noun* a large wild bird that eats dead animals

a b c d e f g h i j k l m n o p q r s t u **v** w x y z

# Ww

**wack·y** /**wak**-ee/ *adjective* (**wackier**, **wackiest**)
unusual and funny or silly: *She's very wacky –
one time she dyed her hair pink.*

### Word Origin: wacky

**Wacky** is an American word that started
being used in the 1930s. Wacky came from
a British slang word that meant "fool." It
may have come from the idea that
someone who has been whacked (=hit) on
the head many times becomes silly or
foolish.

**wad** /wahd/ *noun* a
thick pile of paper or a
small soft ball of
something that has
been pressed together
tightly: *He had a wad of
dollar bills in his
pocket.* | *a wad of
chewing gum*

**wad**

a wad of bills

**wad·dle** /**wahd**'l/ *verb* to walk with short steps,
swinging from side to side: *The duck waddled
toward the pond.*

**wade** /wayd/ *verb* to walk through water: *He
waded across the river and the water came up to
his waist.*

**waf·fle** /**wahf**-uhl/
*noun* a type of thick
flat bread with a
pattern of deep squares
in it. People usually eat
waffles for breakfast.

**waffle**

**wag** /wag/ *verb*
(**wagging**, **wagged**) if
a dog wags its tail, it
moves it from side to side: *The dog was pleased
to see us and was wagging his tail.*

**wage** /wayj/
- *noun* the money that someone gets for doing
his or her job: *The workers at the factory wanted
higher wages.*
- *verb* to take part in a war or campaign: *Local
people waged a campaign to stop the factory
from being built.*

**wag·on** /**wag**-uhn/ *noun*
**1** a vehicle pulled by horses. Wagons were used
for carrying heavy things: *The pioneers traveled
in covered wagons.*
**2** a small low vehicle that children ride in or pull
along. A wagon has four wheels, and a long
handle at the front.

**wag·on train** /**wag**-uhn trayn/ *noun* a long line
of wagons. People traveled in wagon trains to
start living in the west of America in the 1800s.

**waist** /wayst/ *noun* the middle of your body,
below your ribs: *She fastened the belt around
her waist.*

**wait** /wayt/
- *verb*
**1** to stay somewhere or not do something until
something happens or comes: *We had to wait
20 minutes for the bus.* | *Wait here until I come
back.*
**2** **wait on** to serve food to someone in a
restaurant: *The waitress was busy waiting on
customers at another table.*

> **IDIOM with wait**
> **can't wait** used to say that someone is very
> eager to do something: *I can't wait to see
> what they bought me for my birthday!*

- *noun*
a time when you wait for something to happen
or come: *After a long wait at the hospital, I
finally had my hand bandaged.*

**wait·er** /**wayt**-ur/ *noun* a man who brings food
to the tables in a restaurant: *The waiter took our
order and went back to the kitchen.*

**wait·ing room** /**wayt**-ing room/ *noun* a room
for people to wait in, for example to see a
doctor

**wait·ress** /**waytr**-iss/ *noun* a woman who brings
food to the tables in a restaurant: *The waitress
brought our food very quickly.*

a
b
c
d
e
f
g
h
i
j
k
l
m
n
o
p
q
r
s
t
u
v
**w**
x
y
z

**wake** /wayk/ *verb* (**woke** /wohk/, **woken** /**wohk**-uhn/)
**1** to make someone stop sleeping: *Try not to wake the baby.*
**2 wake up** to stop sleeping: *What time did you wake up?*

**walk** /wok/
● *verb*
**1** to move forward by putting one foot in front of the other: *Do you walk to school or go by bus?* ▶ see **Thesaurus**
▶ see picture on page **A15**
**2 walk the dog** to take your dog for a walk, so that it has exercise: *People were walking their dogs in the park.*
● *noun*
a trip that you make by walking: *We went for a walk by the river.*

**walk·ie·talk·ie** /wok-ee **tok**-ee/ *noun* a small radio that you carry with you, and use to speak to someone who has the same type of radio

**wall** /wol/ *noun*
**1** one of the sides of a room or building: *There were lots of pictures on the walls.*
**2** something made of bricks or pieces of stone that separates one area from another: *He is building a wall around his yard.*

**wal·la·by** /**wahl**-uhb-ee/ *noun* an Australian animal that looks like a small kangaroo

**wal·let** /**wahl**-it/ *noun* a small flat case that you use for carrying paper money and cards: *He took a $100 bill out of his wallet.*

**wall·pa·per** /**wol**-payp-ur/ *noun* paper that you stick onto the walls of a room in order to decorate them: *The room has blue-and-white wallpaper and blue curtains.*

**wal·nut** /**wol**-nuht/ *noun* a nut with a large round shell. The part inside has a very uneven shape: *Decorate the top of the cake with walnut halves.* ▶ see picture at **nut**

**wal·rus** /**wol**-ruhss/ *noun* a large sea animal. Walruses have two long teeth called tusks coming down from the sides of their mouth. Walruses live in the Arctic.

walrus

**waltz** /woltss/ *noun* a formal dance done by two people together. Music for this type of dance has a pattern of three beats: *The bride and groom danced a waltz at their wedding reception.*

**wand** /wahnd/ *noun* a thin stick you hold in your hand when doing magic tricks: *The magician waved his wand, and the rabbit disappeared.*

**wan·der** /**wahnd**-ur/ *verb*
**1** to walk slowly, without any particular purpose: *We spent the whole day wandering around the city.* | *One kid wandered off and got lost.*
**2** if your mind or attention wanders, you stop paying attention to something and start thinking about other things: *The movie was boring and his mind started to wander.*

**wane** /wayn/ *verb*
**1** to become less: *He was getting tired, and his strength was waning.*
**2** when the Moon wanes, it seems to get thinner every night ( **ANTONYM: wax** )

**want** /wahnt/
● *verb* to feel that you will be happy if you have or do something: *Do you want some more soup?* | *I don't like it here – I want to go home.*
▶ see **Thesaurus**
● *noun* something that you want: *She understands her baby's needs and wants.*

**war** /wor/ *noun*
**1** a time when countries fight each other: *The soldiers are fighting in a war.* ( **ANTONYM: peace** )
**2** an attempt to stop something bad: *The police are fighting a war on crime.*

**Word Family:** war
**war** *noun* | **warfare** *noun* | **warrior** *noun*

**ward** /word/
- *noun* a room in a hospital with beds for sick people: *There are ten patients on the children's ward.*
- *verb* **ward off** to stop something bad from affecting you: *The smell of this plant wards off insects.*

**-ward** /wurd/

## Word Building

**-ward** is a suffix.

back**ward** | down**ward** | east**ward** | for**ward** | out**ward** | to**ward**

**-ward** means "in a direction." If you take a step *backward*, you move to the area behind you. If you drive *eastward*, you move to the east. If you take a step *toward* something, you move to the area in front of you.

**war·drobe** /**word**-rohb/ *noun*
**1** the clothes that someone has: *Her wardrobe consists of jeans and T-shirts.*
**2** a large piece of furniture where you hang clothes: *He took his suit out of the wardrobe.*

**ware·house** /**wair**-howss/ *noun* a large building where a company keeps things before selling them: *The toys are taken from the company's warehouse to stores around the state.*

**war·fare** /**wor**-fair/ *noun* a type of fighting in a war: *The soldiers were specially trained for jungle warfare.*

**warm** /worm/
- *adjective*
**1** slightly hot: *The water should be warm, but not hot.* | *I'm warm enough – I don't need another blanket.* ( **ANTONYM: cool** )
**2** warm clothes stop you from feeling cold: *Put a warm sweater on – there's a cold wind.*
**3** friendly: *"Welcome to Boston," he said with a warm smile.*
- *verb*
**1** to make someone or something warmer: *She warmed her cold hands by the fire.*
**2 warm up** to do gentle exercises just before playing sports, running, or dancing: *The athletes were warming up by doing some gentle stretching exercises.*

**warm-blood·ed** /worm **bluhd**-id/ *adjective* warm-blooded animals have a body temperature that does not change much. They stay warm whether the temperature around them is hot or cold: *Mammals are warm-blooded, so they keep the same body temperature all day.*
( **ANTONYM: cold-blooded** )

**warm·ly** /**worm**-lee/ *adverb*
**1** in a friendly way: *She greeted us warmly with a friendly smile.*
**2** in clothes that keep you warm: *He was warmly dressed in a thick sweater and coat.*

**warmth** /wormth/ *noun*
**1** a medium amount of heat: *He felt the warmth of the sun on his face.*
**2** friendliness: *The owner of the hotel welcomed us with great warmth.*

**warm-up** /worm uhp/ *noun* a set of gentle exercises that you do just before playing sports, running, or dancing: *We start each dance class with a warm-up.*

**warn** /worn/ *verb* to tell someone that something bad might happen, so that he or she can avoid it: *I warned him not to go too close to the edge of the mountain because he might fall off.*

**warn·ing** /**worn**-ing/ *noun* something that tells you that something bad might happen, so that you can avoid it: *There are warnings about the dangers of smoking on every pack of cigarettes.*

**war·rant** /**wor**-uhnt/ *noun* an official piece of paper that allows the police to do something: *The police have a warrant for his arrest.*

**war·ran·ty** /**wor**-uhnt-ee/ *noun* (plural **warranties**) a promise by a company to fix or replace something if it breaks: *Our new computer has a three-year warranty, so the company fixed the problem for free.*
( **SYNONYM: guarantee** )

**war·ri·or** /**wor**-ee-ur/ *noun* a soldier who is very brave. People use "warrior" about soldiers in past times: *The story is about an Indian warrior who tried to protect his people.*

**wart** /wort/ *noun* a small hard lump on your skin. Warts are caused by a virus: *He had a wart on the bottom of his foot.*

a b c d e f g h i j k l m n o p q r s t u v **w** x y z

**was** /wuhz, wahz/ *verb* the past tense of **be** that is used after "I," "he," "she," and "it": *She was hungry.*

**wash** /wahsh/
● *verb*
**1** to clean your body or an object using water and soap: *Whose turn is it to wash the dishes?* | *I took a bath and washed my hair.* | *Go wash up for dinner.* | *Don't worry – mud washes out.*
**2** if a river or the ocean washes something somewhere, it pushes that thing there: *Strong waves washed the boat onto the shore.*
● *noun*
clothes and sheets that you have washed or that you need to wash: *I did the wash yesterday, so you should have plenty of clean shirts.*
SYNONYM: **laundry**

wash
He is washing a plate.

**wash·able** /**wahsh**-uhb-uhl/ *adjective* able to be washed without being damaged: *The sweater is machine washable and you can wash it with your other clothes in the washing machine.*

**wash·board** /**wahsh**-bord/ *noun* an uneven metal board for rubbing clothes on when washing them. People used washboards in the past.

**wash·cloth** /**wahsh**-kloth/ *noun* a small square piece of cloth that you use for washing yourself

**wash·er** /**wahsh**-ur/ *noun* a washing machine

**wash·ing ma·chine** /**wahsh**-ing muh-sheen/ *noun* a machine that washes clothes: *She put the dirty clothes in the washing machine.*
SYNONYM: **washer**

**was·n't** /**wahz**-uhnt/ *contraction* short for "was not": *He wasn't there.*

**wasp** /wahsp/ *noun* a black and yellow flying insect that can sting you

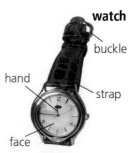
wasp

**waste** /wayst/
● *verb*
to use an amount of something in a silly or useless way, or to use too much: *Don't waste your money on clothes you won't wear.*
● *noun*
**1** the use of an amount of something in a silly or useless way: *Arguing with him is a waste of time – he won't change his mind.*
**2** things that are left after you have used something: *We should recycle more household waste such as empty bottles and cans.*

**waste·bas·ket** /**wayst**-bask-it/ *noun* a container for things that you want to get rid of, such as paper: *Put the candy wrapper in the wastebasket.*

**wast·ed** /**wayst**-id/ *adjective* not having a useful result: *It was a wasted trip because the store was closed.*

**waste dis·po·sal** /**wayst** di-spohz-uhl/ *noun* the activity of getting rid of unwanted things from houses, factories, etc.: *Rivers should not be used for waste disposal, because this causes pollution.*

**waste·ful** /**wayst**-fuhl/ *adjective* wasting something: *It's wasteful to throw away food that is good to eat.*
—**wastefulness** /**wayst**-fuhl-niss/ *noun* the quality of being wasteful: *People should be aware of the wastefulness of leaving the faucet running.*

**watch** /wahch/
● *verb*
**1** to look at someone or something: *Dad was watching his favorite TV show.* | *Watch me jump off this wall!*
▶ see **Thesaurus**
**2** to be careful when you are doing something, so that you do not hurt yourself or someone else: *Watch your head – the doorway's very low.* | *Watch out – don't trip over that rock!*
**3** to make sure that someone or something is not

watch
buckle
hand
strap
face

harmed: *Our neighbors watched the house for us while we were away.* | *It was amazing that we weren't hurt – I think God was watching over us.*
**4 watch for/watch out for** to be ready to notice something: *Watch for tracks left by wild animals.*

● *noun*
a small clock that you wear on your wrist: *When I looked at my watch, it was almost 12:30.*

> **IDIOM with watch**
> **keep watch** to look around so that you will see if someone is coming and can tell other people: *I kept watch to make sure no one saw us.*

## Word Choice: watch, look, see

You **watch** TV, a movie, or something that happens. You usually **watch** people or things that are moving: *They are watching TV.* | *Mom and Dad always watch me play basketball.*

You **look** at a picture, person, or thing because you want to. You usually **look** at people or things that are not moving: *Look at that car – it's pink!* | *Maria was looking at a picture book.* | *I looked out of the window.*

You **see** someone or something accidentally, or because you are trying to find a person or thing: *Josh saw a fire engine go by.* | *I can see three people by the tree.*

You can also say that you **saw** a movie, TV show, or game, or that you are going to **see** it in the future: *I saw the baseball game on TV last night.* | *Do you want to see a movie on Saturday?*

**watch·dog** /**wahch**-dog/ *noun*
**1** a dog that protects someone's home or property: *The watchdog barked when we went near the gate.* ( SYNONYM: **guard dog** )
**2** a person or group that makes sure that other people do not break rules: *The environmental watchdog group tries to stop companies from polluting land and water.*

**wa·ter** /**wot**-ur/
● *noun*
the clear liquid that you drink and use for washing: *He ran water into the bathtub.* | *The water in the ocean is salty.*

● *verb*
**1** to pour water on a plant that you are growing: *The plant died because I never watered it.*
**2** if your eyes water, they fill with tears because something is hurting them: *The smoke made my eyes water.*
**3** if your mouth waters, it fills with a liquid called saliva. It does this because you see or smell nice food: *The smell of the sausages made our mouths water.*

**wa·ter·col·or** /**wot**-ur-kuhl-ur/ *noun*
**1** a type of paint that is mixed with water: *He paints using watercolors.*
**2** a painting done using paint mixed with water: *She's doing a watercolor of a vase of flowers.*

**wa·ter cool·er** /**wot**-ur kool-ur/ *noun* a large container in an office where you can fill a cup with drinking water

**wa·ter cy·cle** /**wot**-ur sīk-uhl/ *noun* the way that water in the environment moves into the air and back again. Water in oceans, rivers, and lakes evaporates and becomes clouds. Then it falls as rain or snow.

**wa·ter·fall** /**wot**-ur-fol/ *noun* water from a river or stream that falls from a high place down to the ground: *The waterfall falls 300 feet into the valley.*

**waterfall**

**wa·ter foun·tain** /**wot**-ur fownt-uhn/ *noun* a piece of equipment in a public place that gives you water to drink: *I pushed the button on the water fountain and took a long drink.*
( SYNONYM: **drinking fountain** )

**wa·ter·front** /**wot**-ur-fruhnt/ *noun* land next to a lake, river, or ocean: *Her apartment is on the waterfront, so she has a view of the lake.*

**wa·ter·ing can** /**wot**-uhr-ing kan/ *noun* a container that you use for pouring water on plants. A watering can has a handle and a long spout.

a b c d e f g h i j k l m n o p q r s t u v **w** x y z

**wa·ter·logged** /**wot**-ur-lahgd/ *adjective* if something is waterlogged, it is so wet that you cannot walk on it or use it: *The children's play area is waterlogged after the rain.*

**wa·ter·mel·on** /**wot**-ur-mel-uhn/ *noun* a large round fruit with thick green skin. Inside, watermelons have sweet red flesh and a lot of black seeds: *Would you like a slice of watermelon?*

watermelon

**wa·ter polo** /**wot**-ur poh-loh/ *noun* a game played in a swimming pool. Two teams of players try to throw a ball into their opponent's goal.

**wa·ter·proof** /**wot**-ur-proof/ *adjective* waterproof clothing keeps you dry because water cannot pass through it: *It's raining hard. Do you have a waterproof jacket?*

waterproof

a waterproof jacket

**wa·ter qual·i·ty** /**wot**-ur kwal-uht-ee/ *noun* how clean the water in a river, lake, or ocean is: *The water quality of the lake is very good and there is no pollution.*

**wa·ter rights** /**wot**-uh rītss/ *plural noun* the right to use water from a river or lake: *Farmers would pay a lot for land with good water rights.*

**wa·ter·shed** /**wot**-ur-shed/ *noun*
**1** the area from which water goes into a river or a lake: *The watershed received so much rain that the river flooded.*
**2** high land between two river systems

**wa·ter ski·ing** /**wot**-ur skee-ing/ *noun* a sport in which you wear two long narrow pieces of plastic on your feet, as a boat pulls you along the water: *We went water skiing on the lake.*
—**water ski** /**wot**-ur skee/ *verb* to do water skiing
—**water skier** /**wot**-ur skee-ur/ *noun* someone who does water skiing

water skiing

**wa·ter table** /**wot**-uhr tayb-uhl/ *noun* the level below the surface of the ground, where there is water

**wa·ter·tight** /**wot**-ur-tīt/ *adjective* something that is watertight does not allow water to pass through it: *The roof must be watertight or it will leak.*

**wa·ter va·por** /**wot**-ur vayp-ur/ *noun* water in the form of very small drops in the air: *The air felt damp because of the water vapor in it.*

**wa·ter·way** /**wot**-ur-way/ *noun* a river or canal that boats can travel on: *A canal is a man-made waterway.*

**wa·ter·y** /**wot**-uhr-ee/ *adjective*
**1** containing too much water: *The soup tastes watery.*
**2** full of tears: *Her eyes were all watery and I know she had been crying.*

**watt** /waht/ *noun* a unit for measuring electrical power: *a 60-watt light bulb*

**wave** /wayv/
● *noun*
**1** a long high amount of water on the ocean: *We watched the waves crash on the beach.*
**2** a movement of your hand from side to side: *She gave us a wave as she drove away.*
**3** the form that energy, such as light or sound, travels in: *Sound waves travel faster through water than through air.*
**4** a sudden large amount of a feeling or activity: *A wave of unhappiness came over her.* | *During the crime wave, many cars were stolen.*
● *verb*
**1** to raise your arm and move your hand from side to side. You do this to say goodbye or hello to someone. You also wave to get someone to see you: *We waved goodbye to Andrea and she*

waved back. | Juan waved at us from across the gym.

**2** to move something you are holding from side to side: *The crowd cheered and waved American flags.*

**3** to move from side to side: *The branches were waving in the wind.*

**wave**

**wave·length** /**wayv**-lengkth/ *noun* the distance between matching points on one wave of light or sound and the next: *Red light has a longer wavelength than green light.*

**wav·y** /**wayv**-ee/ *adjective* wavy hair has curves

( ANTONYM: **straight** )

**wax** /wakss/

● *noun*

**1** a substance used for making candles and crayons. Wax is solid when it is cold, and soft or liquid when it is heated.

**2** a natural substance in your ears

● *verb*

when the moon waxes, it seems to get bigger every night ( ANTONYM: **wane** )

**way** /way/

● *noun*

**1** how you do something: *One way to keep food fresh is to freeze it.* | *She smiled at me in a friendly way.* ▶ see **Thesaurus**

**2** a road or path that you follow to get somewhere: *I'll show you the way to the library.*

**3** a particular direction: *Look both ways before you cross the street.*

**4** the distance between two places: *Houston is a long way from New York.*

**IDIOMS with way**

**by the way** used when you want to talk about a new subject: *Oh, by the way, did you finish that book I lent you?*

**in a way** used when something is partly true: *I enjoyed being sick in a way because I got to watch a lot of TV.*

**in the way** if something is in the way, it is in front of you and you cannot get past: *I couldn't put my bicycle in the garage because the car was in the way.*

**make your way** to go somewhere slowly or with difficulty: *He made his way to the front of the crowd.*

**on the way** while going somewhere: *We were talking about you on the way here.*

**out of the way** if something is out of the way, it is in a place where it is not stopping you moving or doing something: *I'll move this stuff out of the way, so that people can get past.*

**way of life** how someone or a group of people live, for example the things they normally do or the values they normally have: *The Native Americans had a very different way of life than the Pilgrims from England.*

● *adverb*

much: *These jeans are way too small for me – I can't get into them!*

**we** /wee/ *pronoun* the person who is speaking and one or more other people: *My sister and I are going to the park. We want to play on the swings.*

**weak** /week/ *adjective*

**1** not having much strength or energy: *Kate had the flu last week, and she still feels weak.* | *The batteries must be weak; the flashlight isn't very bright.* ( ANTONYM: **strong** ) ▶ see **Thesaurus**

**2** not having all the qualities something should have: *My orange juice tastes weak. Did you put water in it?* | *The dollar is weak right now. It is not worth as much as it used to be.*

( ANTONYM: **strong** )

**3** if someone is weak, he or she cannot make good decisions easily and other people can persuade him or her to do things that should not be done: *He was too weak to say no when the other boys wanted him to throw rocks at the window.* ( ANTONYM: **strong** )

a b c d e f g h i j k l m n o p q r s t u v **w** x y z

**weak·en** /**week**-uhn/ *verb* to make someone or something less strong: *The old buildings were weakened by the storms.* (ANTONYM: **strengthen**)

**weak·ness** /**week**-niss/ *noun*
**1** the state of being weak: *The illness causes weakness and tiredness.* (ANTONYM: **strength**)
**2** a bad quality or a problem in someone or something: *No one is good at everything – we all have weaknesses.* (ANTONYM: **strength**)

**wealth** /welth/ *noun*
**1** a large amount of money that someone has: *The family's great wealth came from finding oil on their land.*
**2** a large amount of something: *There is a wealth of information on the Internet.*

**wealth·y** /**welth**-ee/ *adjective* (**wealthier**, **wealthiest**) having a lot of money: *Wealthy people can buy things like expensive cars.*
(SYNONYM: **rich**) (ANTONYM: **poor**)

**weap·on** /**wep**-uhn/ *noun* something that people fight with, for example a knife or a gun: *A gun is a dangerous weapon.*
—**weaponry** /**wep**-uhn-ree/ *noun* weapons: *The army has modern weaponry, like machine guns and fighter jets.*

**wear** /wair/
● *verb* (**wore** /wor/, **worn** /worn/)
**1** to have clothes or jewelry on your body: *She's wearing a long black dress.*
**2** to have your hair in a particular style: *She usually wears her hair in a ponytail.*
**3 wear off** to become less strong or useful: *The effect of the drug is wearing off and the pain is starting to come back.*
**4 wear out** to use something so much that it becomes too damaged or weak to use: *Don't leave the flashlight on – you'll wear out the batteries.*
**5 wear out** to make someone feel very tired: *His mom has to take care of five kids and it's wearing her out.*
● *noun*
**1** a particular kind of clothes, or clothes for a particular activity: *The store sells casual wear such as jeans and T-shirts.*
**2** normal damage that something has because it has been used a lot: *The tire was showing signs of wear, so we got a new one.*

**wea·ry** /**weer**-ee/ *adjective* tired: *His eyes became weary and started to close.*

**wea·sel** /**weez**-uhl/ *noun* a small animal with a long body and short red-brown fur. Weasels eat small animals such as mice.

**weath·er** /**weth**-ur/
● *noun* the weather in a place is how warm or cold it is and whether it is raining, sunny, windy, etc.: *"What's the weather like today?" "It's snowing!"* | *When the weather is good, the children play outside.*
● *verb* if wood, stone, etc. weathers, its appearance changes because it has been outside in the wind, rain, and sun: *As the wood fence weathered, it changed from dark brown to a gray color.*

**weath·er fore·cast** /**weth**-ur for-kast/ *noun* a report on the television or radio that says what the weather will be like

**weath·er·ing** /**weth**-ur-ing/ *noun* the way that the surface of something changes, because of the effect of the rain, wind, or sun: *A common type of weathering is when water freezes in a crack in a rock. The frozen water pushes outward on the rock, making the crack bigger.*

**weath·er vane** /**weth**-ur vayn/ *noun* a metal object on the top of a building that moves to show the direction of the wind: *The weather vane on top of the barn shows there is a north wind.*

**weave** /weev/ *verb*
**1** (**wove** /wohv/, **woven** /wohv-uhn/) to make things such as rugs, cloth, or baskets. When you weave, you put threads or long strips of material under and over other threads or material: *The Navajo Indians still weave rugs with traditional patterns on them.*

**weave**

**2** to move somewhere by turning and changing direction a lot: *The motorcycle was weaving in and out of traffic.*
—**weaving** /**weev**-ing/ *noun* the activity of weaving

**web** /web/ *noun*

**web**

**1** a net of thin threads made by a spider to catch insects: *I watched the spider making its web.*
**2 the Web** the system that makes it possible for you to see and use information on the Internet: *I looked on the Web for information about penguins.*

web

SYNONYM: **Internet**

**web·cam** /web-kam/ *noun* a video camera on a computer that you can use to put pictures on the Internet

**web·site** /web-sīt/ *noun* a set of pages on the Internet that give you information about something: *The website had a lot of good math games.*

**we'd** /weed/ *contraction*

**1** short for "we had": *We'd forgotten our map.*
**2** short for "we would": *We'd like to see a movie tonight.*

**wed·ding** /wed-ing/ *noun* a ceremony in which two people get married: *The bride looked beautiful on her wedding day.*

**wedge** /wej/ *noun* a piece of something that is thick at one end and pointed at the other end: *Mrs. Lowe put a wedge of chocolate cake on my plate.*

**Wednes·day** /wenzd-ee/ *noun*

ABBREVIATION: **Wed.** the fourth day of the week. Wednesday is between Tuesday and Thursday: *Your piano lessons start Wednesday afternoon. | What time are you planning to come over on Wednesday?*

**Word Origin:** Wednesday

**Wednesday** is named for the god Wodan or Odin in an old religion. Many people in northern Europe believed in this religion before Christianity. Wodan was the most important god, and he was god of the sky and of war. Wednesday was Wodan's day. Wodan was married to the goddess Frige. Friday is named after Frige.

**weed** /weed/

● *noun* a wild plant that grows where you do not want it to grow: *The garden was full of weeds and looked very messy.*
● *verb* to pull weeds from the ground: *Dad was weeding the vegetable garden.*

**week** /week/ *noun*

**1** a period of seven days, usually from Sunday to Saturday: *We went on vacation for two weeks.*
**2** the part of a week when you go to work or school, usually from Monday to Friday: *I don't have much free time during the week.*

**week·day** /week-day/ *noun* any day of the week except Saturday and Sunday: *We go to school on weekdays.*

**week·end** /week-end/ *noun* Saturday and Sunday: *We're going to my aunt's house for the weekend. | I usually play soccer on weekends.*

**week·ly** /week-lee/ *adverb, adjective* once a week, or every week: *The teachers have weekly meetings.*

**week·night** /week-nīt/ *noun* any night except Saturday or Sunday: *Go to sleep now – it's a weeknight and you have school tomorrow.*

**weep** /weep/ *verb* (**wept** /wept/) to cry: *The family wept during the funeral.*

**weigh** /way/ *verb*

**weigh**

**1** to have a particular weight: *The baby weighed five pounds when he was born. | "How much do you weigh?" "I'm 120 pounds."*
**2** to measure how heavy someone or something is by using a scale: *The class weighed the apples and figured out how much they would cost.*

scale

The scale is used for weighing things.

**3** to think about something carefully before you decide what to do: *After weighing up all the alternatives, I decided that this one was the best computer for me.*

**weight** /wayt/ *noun*
**1** how heavy something or someone is: *The baby's weight was nine pounds.*
**2** if you lose weight, you become thinner. If you gain weight, you become fatter: *The doctor told John that he needs to lose weight.* | *When Mom stopped running every day, she gained weight.*
**3** a heavy piece of metal that people lift to make their muscles bigger: *Lifting weights makes your body stronger.*

**weight·lift·ing** /**wayt**-lift-ing/ *noun* the sport of lifting a bar with heavy metal objects on each end

**weird** /weerd/ *adjective* unusual and strange: *You look a little weird in that hat.* | *I had a weird dream that my dog was able to talk to me.*
( SYNONYM: **strange** )

**Word Origin:** weird

**Weird** comes from an Old English word, *wyrd*. In Old English, wyrd meant "fate" or "destiny" (="what is going to happen to you in your life.") Wyrd was also used as a name for the goddesses that people believed control your fate. By the 1400s, Scottish people used the word "weird" to mean a witch. Because people believed that witches look and act strangely, weird slowly started to mean "strange." By the 1800s, people had stopped using it about witches, and only used it about strange things or people.

**weird·o** /**weerd**-oh/ *noun* (plural **weirdos**) someone who behaves in a way that seems strange to other people: *He is such a weirdo – he's always talking to himself.*

**wel·come** /**welk**-uhm/
● *adjective*
**1** if you are welcome in a place, the people there are happy that you have come: *Anna smiled and made us feel welcome in her home.*
**2** if someone tells you that you are welcome to do something, he or she is telling you politely that you can do it: *You're welcome to stay for lunch – there's plenty of food.*

IDIOM with **welcome**
**you're welcome** used when replying politely to someone who has just thanked you: *"Thank you for your help." "You're welcome."*
● *verb*
**1** to say hello in a friendly way to someone who has just arrived: *He welcomed his guests at the door.*
**2** if you welcome something, you are happy if it happens because you think it is good: *The school always welcomes suggestions from parents.*
● *noun*
the way someone greets you when you arrive somewhere: *My aunt gave us a warm welcome when we arrived at her house.*

**weld** /weld/ *verb* to join metal objects to each other by heating them and pressing them together when they are hot: *The parts of the ship are welded together.*
—**welder** /**weld**-ur/ *noun* someone whose job is welding things

**wel·fare** /**wel**-fair/ *noun*
**1** money that the government gives to people who need it: *He lost his job at the factory and is now on welfare.*
**2** someone's health or happiness: *The most important thing is the children's welfare. They must be safe and have enough to eat.*

**well** /wel/
● *adverb* (**better**, **best**)
**1** in a good or satisfactory way: *Antonio speaks English very well. I didn't realize he is from Spain.* | *Did you sleep well?*
( ANTONYM: **badly** )
**2** in a thorough way: *Wash your hands well to get all the dirt off.*
( SYNONYM: **thoroughly** )

well

IDIOM with **well**
**as well** also: *I'd like a glass of milk and some cake as well.* ( SYNONYM: **too** )
● *adjective* (**better**)
healthy and not sick: *Steve went home early because he wasn't feeling very well.*
● *interjection*
**1** used before you say something, for example

because you are not sure what to say, you are surprised, or because you want to change what you are talking about: *Well, I guess I have to go now.*
**2** used to say that you accept a situation, even though it is not a good one: *I didn't hit the ball once. Oh well, I'll do better next time.*
● *noun*
a deep hole that people get water or oil out of. People dig wells deep into the ground: *She lowered the bucket into the well and drew out some water.*

## Word Choice: well, good

You use **well** when someone does something in a good way: *He plays basketball really well. | She did well on the test.*

You use **good** to talk about the quality of something or someone: *He's a good basketball player. | Her books are really good.*

**we'll** /weel/ *contraction* short for "we will": *We'll have to leave soon.*

**well-be·haved** /wel bi-**hayvd**/ *adjective* behaving in a good or polite way: *The children are well-behaved and always remember to say "please" and "thank you."* ( SYNONYM: **good** )

**well-be·ing** /wel bee-ing/ *noun* a feeling of being healthy and happy: *Exercise gives me a sense of well-being.*

**well-dressed** /wel **drest**/ *adjective* wearing clothes that look good and are fashionable: *A well-dressed man wearing a suit and tie came into the room.*

**well-known** /wel **nohn**/ *adjective* known about by many people: *Grandma is well-known for her excellent cooking.* ( SYNONYM: **famous** )
( ANTONYM: **unknown** )

**well-off** /wel **of**/ *adjective* having enough money to have a good life: *His parents are well-off and can afford to pay for his college.*
( SYNONYM: **rich** ) ( ANTONYM: **poor** )

**Welsh** /welsh/
● *adjective* relating to or coming from Wales: *Tom is Welsh – he was born in Wales.*
● *noun* the language spoken in Wales

**went** /went/ *verb* the past tense of **go**: *Tracy went to a different school last year.*

**wept** /wept/ *verb* the past tense and past participle of **weep**

**were** /wur/ *verb* the past tense of **be** that we use after "you," "we," and "they": *We were happy to be back home.*

**we're** /weer/ *contraction* short for "we are": *We're almost finished.*

**weren't** /wurnt/ *contraction* short for "were not": *I tried to call you, but you weren't home.*

**were·wolf** /**wair**-wulf/ *noun* a person in stories who changes into a wolf

## Word Origin: werewolf

**Werewolf** comes from two Old English words that mean "man" and "wolf." So, a werewolf was a man that could change into a wolf.

**west** /west/
● *noun*
**1** the direction in which the Sun goes down in the evening: *The sun sets in the west.*
**2** the western part of a country or area: *Pittsburgh is a city in the west of Pennsylvania.*
**3** the West the part of the U.S. that is west of the Mississippi River: *There are a lot of cattle ranches in the West, especially in Colorado and Wyoming.* ( ANTONYM: **eastern** )
**4** the West the countries in North America and the western part of Europe: *Our family is from India, but most of us live in the West now.*
● *adjective*
**1** in or to the west: *California is on the west coast of the United States.*
**2** a west wind comes from the west
● *adverb*
toward the west: *We left New York and drove west to Illinois.*

## Word Origin: west

**West** comes from an ancient word that probably meant "to go downward." The ancient word passed into Old English, which used west to mean the direction where the sun goes down.

a b c d e f g h i j k l m n o p q r s t u v **w** x y z

a b c d e f g h i j k l m n o p q r s t u v **w** x y z

**West Coast** /west **kohst**/ *noun* the part of the U.S. that is next to the Pacific Ocean

**west·ern** /**west**-urn/
● *adjective*
**1** in or from the west: *Buffalo is a city in western New York.*
**2** in or from the countries in North America and the western part of Europe: *The museum has many great works of Western art.*
**3** in or from the part of the U.S. that is west of the Mississippi: *The store sells western wear like cowboy hats, boots, and jeans.*
—**westerner** /**west**-urn-ur/ *noun* someone from the west of a country or from the countries in North America and the western part of Europe: *Many Westerners travel to Asia.*
● *noun*
a movie about cowboys in the western part of the U.S.A. in the 19th century: *We watched an old western on TV.*

**west·ward** /**west**-wurd/ *adverb, adjective* toward the west: *The train left New York and traveled westward toward California.*

**west·ward ex·pan·sion** /**west**-wurd ik-**spansh**-uhn/ *noun* in the United States, the movement of settlers into land in western North America in the 1800s. Settlers went to places such as Nebraska, Oregon, and Texas to have more land.

**west·ward move·ment** /**west**-wurd **moov**-muhnt/ *noun* another word for western expansion

**wet** /wet/
● *adjective* (**wetter**, **wettest**)
**1** covered in or full of water or another liquid: *They came in from the rain in wet clothes.* | *I washed my hair and it is still wet.*
( ANTONYM: **dry** ) ▶ see **Thesaurus**
**2** not yet dry: *The sign on the bench says "Wet Paint."* ( ANTONYM: **dry** )
**3** if the weather is wet, it is raining or it has been raining: *It's wet outside – wear your raincoat and boots.* ( SYNONYM: **rainy** )
( ANTONYM: **dry** )
● *verb* (**wetting**, **wet** or **wetted**)
to make something wet: *Wet the brush before you put it in the paint.* ( ANTONYM: **dry** )

**wet·land** /**wet**-luhnd/ *noun* an area of land that has a lot of water in it: *Marshes and bogs are both types of wetlands.*

**wet·suit** /**wet**-soot/
*noun* a piece of rubber clothing that keeps you warm when you go swimming or diving

**we've** /weev/
*contraction* short for "we have": *We've been friends for five years.*

**whack** /wak/
● *verb* to hit someone or something hard: *I swung the bat and whacked the ball over the fence.*
● *noun* a hard hit: *She gave him a whack on the head with the book.*

**wetsuit**

wetsuit

**whale** /wayl/ *noun* a very large animal that lives in the ocean. Whales look like fish, but they are mammals. Whales breathe air through a hole in the top of their head, and they can stay underwater for a long time

**whale**

**wharf** /worf/ *noun* (plural **wharves** /worvz/) a long flat structure that sticks out from the shore into water, so that boats can stop next to it: *His boat was tied up at the wharf.* ( SYNONYM: **pier** )

**what** /wuht, waht/ *pronoun, adjective*
**1** used in questions to ask for information about something: *What is your name?* | *What did Ellen say?* | *What color are her eyes?*
**2** used when you did not hear what someone said: *"The game starts at 3:00." "What?" "I said, the game starts at 3:00."*
( SYNONYMS: **excuse me, pardon** )

**3** the thing or things that have been said or described: *I didn't agree with what he said.* | *He told me what to do.*

**4** used to say strongly what you think: *"Would you like to have a picnic?" "Yes, what a great idea!"*

> IDIOMS with **what**
> **what about?** used to suggest or mention something: *What about your bike? Aren't you going to lock it up?*
> **what for?** used when asking for a reason for something or the purpose of something: *What's the red button on the camera for?*
> **what if?** used when asking about something that might happen: *What if he's not home when we get there?*

**what·ev·er** /wuht-**ev**-ur/ *pronoun, adjective* anything, or any kind of thing: *At a buffet meal, you can help yourself to whatever food you want.*

**what's** /wuhtss/ *contraction* short for "what is": *What's your name?*

**wheat** /weet/ *noun* a plant that farmers grow. The grain of the plant is used for making flour: *Bread is made from wheat flour.*

**wheel** /weel/ *noun*
**1** one of the round things under a car or bicycle that turns and makes it move: *A bicycle has two wheels.* ▶ see picture at **bicycle**
**2** a round object that you hold and turn to make a car move to the left or right: *He turned the wheel of his truck.* ( SYNONYM: **steering wheel** )

**wheel·bar·row** /**weel**-barr-oh/ *noun* a container with one wheel in the front and two long handles for pushing it. You use a wheelbarrow outdoors to move heavy things: *He took the dirt away in a wheelbarrow.*

**wheel·chair** /**weel**-chair/ *noun* a chair with wheels for people who cannot walk: *After he broke his back, he had to use a wheelchair.*

**wheel·ie** /**weel**-ee/ *noun* if you do a wheelie on a bicycle or motorcycle, you lift the front wheel in the air while you are riding, so that only the back wheel is on the ground: *Kurt knows how to do a wheelie on his bike.*

**wheeze** /weez/ *verb* to breathe with difficulty, making a sound in your chest: *He was wheezing after he climbed the stairs.*

**when** /wen/ *adverb*
**1** at what time: *When is your birthday?* | *I'll tell you when to stop.*
**2** at the time that something happens: *I was very tired when I got home.* | *He lived in Oregon when he was little.*

**when·ev·er** /we-**nev**-ur/ *adverb*
**1** at any time: *We can go whenever you are ready.*
**2** every time: *He felt pain in his leg whenever he kicked the ball.*

**where** /wair/ *adverb*
**1** used to ask or talk about a place: *"Where is Rachel?" "Upstairs, I think."* | *This is the house where my grandmother lives.*
**2** used when talking about one part of a story or movie: *I liked the part where the dog rescued the boy from the water.*

**where·as** /wair-**az**, wair-uhz/ *conjunction* used when saying that two situations are very different: *Jim was on time for the meeting, whereas all of the others were late.*

**wher·ev·er** /wair-**ev**-ur/ *adverb*
**1** in any place: *Sit wherever you want.*
**2** in every place: *They followed us wherever we went.*

**wheth·er** /**weth**-ur/ *conjunction*
**1** used when talking about a choice between different things: *I couldn't decide whether or not I wanted to go.* ( SYNONYM: **if** )
**2** used when saying that it is not important what someone wants or decides because something will happen anyway: *Whether you like it or not, you're going to have to take that test.*

**which** /wich/ *pronoun, adjective*
**1** used in order to say what things you mean out of a group: *There are three cups – which is yours?* | *I'm not sure which class she's in.*
**2** used when giving more information about something: *This is a new car which uses electricity, not gas.* | *We're going on vacation for two whole weeks, which will be really good.*

**which·ev·er** /wi-**chev**-ur/ *pronoun, adjective* any of a group of things or people: *For free reading, we can choose whichever books we want to read.*

a b c d e f g h i j k l m n o p q r s t u v **w** x y z

**while** /wīl/

- *conjunction*

**1** during the time that something is happening: *Someone called while you were out.* | *While she cooked dinner, we set the table.*
**2** although: *While it was a good school, I was not happy there.*

- *noun*

**a while** a period of time: *We waited a while, but Olivia never came.*

**whim·per** /**wimp**-ur/ *verb* to make low crying sounds: *The dog was whimpering because it had hurt its paw.*

**whine** /wīn/ *verb*

**1** to complain about something in a sad annoying voice: *"Stop whining and do your homework," the mother said to her child.*
**2** to make a long high sound because you feel pain or are unhappy: *The dog was whining outside, so I opened the door to let him in.*

**whip** /wip/

- *noun*

a long thin piece of leather or rope with a handle. A whip is used for making animals move faster.

- *verb* (**whipping**, **whipped**)

**1** to hit a person or animal with a whip: *He whipped the horse to make it run faster.*
**2** to quickly mix cream or the clear part of an egg until it is light and thick: *We had strawberries and whipped cream.* ( SYNONYM: **beat** )
**3** to move something fast and suddenly: *The wind whipped the paper out of his hand.*

**whirl** /wurl/ *verb* to make someone or something turn around quickly: *He whirled her around the dance floor.* ( SYNONYM: **spin** )

**whisk** /wisk/

- *verb*

**1** to stir liquids or soft foods together very quickly: *Whisk the eggs and sugar in a bowl.*
( SYNONYM: **beat** )
**2** to move or take someone somewhere very quickly: *He was whisked to the hospital.*

- *noun*

a small kitchen tool used for stirring liquids or soft foods. A whisk is made of curved pieces of wire: *I mixed the eggs and milk together with a whisk.*

**whisk·ers** /**wisk**-urz/ *plural noun*

**1** long hairs that grow near the mouth of some animals, such as cats: *Cats use their whiskers to feel their way around in the dark.*
**2** the hair that grows on a man's face: *Dad's rough whiskers rubbed against my face as he kissed me good night.*

**whis·per** /**wisp**-ur/

- *verb* to talk very quietly: *The girls were whispering to each other and giggling.* | *I saw him whisper something in her ear.*
- *noun* a very quiet voice: *"What's the answer?" she asked in a whisper.*

whisper

She is whispering in his ear.

**whistle** /**wiss**-uhl/

whistle

- *noun*

**1** an object that produces a high sound when you blow through it: *The teacher blew the whistle to start the race.*
**2** a high sound made by blowing air out through your lips, or by blowing  through a whistle: *Dan gave a whistle, and his dog came running back to him.*

- *verb*

to make a high sound by blowing air out through your lips, or by blowing through a whistle: *Dad was whistling a happy tune.* | *The referee whistled for the game to begin.*

**white** /wīt/

- *adjective*

**1** having the color of milk or snow: *Monica was wearing a white shirt.*
**2** belonging to the race of people who have pale skin: *The class has black, white, Hispanic, and Asian students.*

● *noun*

**1** the color of milk or snow: *The girls were dressed in white.*

**2** someone who belongs to the race of people who have pale skin: *Whites came to America from Europe.*

**3** the clear part of an egg that turns white when you cook it. The white is around the yellow yolk: *Beat together the egg whites and sugar.*
▶ see picture at **yolk**

**white·board** /**wīt**-bord/ *noun* a large board with a white smooth surface that teachers write on: *The teacher wrote the questions on the whiteboard.* ▶ see picture on page **A9**

**White House** /**wīt** howss/ *noun*

**1** the official home of the president of the United States. The White House is in Washington, D.C.: *We are going to take a tour of the White House.*

**2** the president of the U.S. and the people who work with the president: *The White House supports the new law.*

**whiz** /wiz/

● *verb* (**whizzing**, **whizzed**) to move very quickly: *Cars were whizzing past us.*

● *noun* someone who is very good at something: *My brother's a math whiz – he can solve any math problem.*

**who** /hoo/ *pronoun*

**1** used to ask or say which person is involved: *Who is that lady in the red dress?* | *I want to know who ate all the ice cream.*

**2** used for giving more information about someone you have mentioned: *Mark is visiting his cousins, who live in Chicago.*

**who'd** /hood/ *contraction*

**1** short for "who had": *There was a crowd of people who'd come to watch the game.*

**2** short for "who would": *Who'd like to go to the store with me?*

**who·ev·er** /hoo-**ev**-ur/ *pronoun*

**1** the person who: *Whoever broke this plate is going to be in trouble.*

**2** any person: *My parents said I could invite whoever I wanted to the party.*

**whole** /hohl/

● *adjective* all of something: *We spent the whole day at the beach.* | *Patty read her poem to the whole class.* ( SYNONYM: **entire** )

—**wholly** /**hohl**-ee/ *adverb* completely: *The writing is wholly her own. No one helped her.*

● *noun* a complete thing made of several parts: *Two halves make a whole.* | *The whole of my body hurt the next day, after all that exercise.*
▶ see picture at **quarter**

IDIOM with **whole**
**on the whole** generally or usually: *On the whole, children who read a lot are good at spelling.*

**whole num·ber** /hohl **nuhm**-bur/ *noun* in math, a number that does not contain fractions or decimals: *4 is a whole number, but 4.5 is not a whole number.*

**whole·sale** /**hohl**-sayl/ *adjective, adverb* if you buy something wholesale, you buy it in large quantities, so that you can sell it to people in a store: *The store buys clothes wholesale, then sells them in the store for a little bit more than it paid for them.*

**whole·some** /**hohl**-suhm/ *adjective*

**1** good for your health: *Cereal and fruit make a good wholesome breakfast before school.*

**2** having or showing behavior that is right and acceptable: *It's a wholesome family show about a family and their pets.*

**whole wheat** /hohl weet/ *adjective* whole wheat flour or bread is made using every part of the grain: *I had a turkey sandwich on whole wheat bread.*

**who'll** /hool/ *contraction* short for "who will": *Who'll take out the garbage?*

**whom** /hoom/ *pronoun* who – used as the object of a verb or preposition: *To whom am I speaking?*

**whoop·ing cough** /**hoop**-ing kof/ *noun* a serious disease that mainly affects children. It makes children cough and have difficulty breathing: *My mother had the measles and whooping cough when she was a child.*

**who's** /hooz/ *contraction*

**1** short for "who is": *Who's going to win the game?*

**2** short for "who has": *Mrs. Hicks is a teacher who's been at our school for many years.*

**whose** /hooz/ *adjective, pronoun*
**1** used in order to ask whom something belongs to: *Whose jacket is this?*
**2** used in order to say which person or thing you mean: *That's the girl whose mother teaches at our school.*

**who've** /hoov/ *contraction* short for "who have": *Sandra and Laurie are friends who've known each other for many years.*

**why** /wī/ *adverb* for what reason: *Why are you late?* | *Tell me why you are so upset.*

**wick·ed** /**wik**-id/ *adjective* bad or evil: *The wicked witch turned the boy into a frog.*

**wick·er** /**wik**-ur/ *adjective* made from thin branches woven together: *We sat in wicker chairs on the porch.*

**wide** /wīd/
● *adjective*
**1** measuring a large distance from one side to the other: *The river is too wide to swim across.*
( ANTONYM: **narrow** ) ▶ see picture at **narrow**
**2** measuring a particular distance from one side to the other: *The doorway is three feet wide.*
**3** including a lot of different things or people: *The camp has a wide variety of activities, such as art, games, and sports.*
● *adverb*
completely, or as much as possible: *The door was wide open.* | *It was midnight, but I was wide awake.*

**wide·ly** /**wīd**-lee/ *adverb* in a lot of places or by a lot of people: *The book is widely used in schools around the country.*

**wid·en** /**wīd**'n/ *verb* to make something wider: *They are going to widen the road by adding another lane.*

**wide·spread** /wīd-**spred**/ *adjective* happening in a lot of places: *The storm caused widespread damage in several states.*

**wid·ow** /**wid**-oh/ *noun* a woman whose husband has died

**wid·ow·er** /**wid**-oh-ur/ *noun* a man whose wife has died

**width** /width/ *noun* the distance from one side of something to the other: *They measured the width of the window.*

**wife** /wīf/ *noun* (plural **wives** /wīvz/) the woman that a man is married to: *Mr. Connors and his wife live in that big house.*

**Word Origin: wife**

When the word **wife** was used in Old English, it meant both the woman a man was married to, and just "a woman." The meaning "a woman" is still found in some words such as "housewife," but now we can't just use wife to mean woman.

**wig** /wig/ *noun* an object with hair on it that someone wears on their head. A wig can cover your own hair or be used when you have no hair: *She wore a clown wig at Halloween.*

wig
wig

**wig·gle** /**wig**-uhl/ *verb* to move something a little up and down or from side to side: *She wiggled her toes in the sand.*

**wig·wam** /**wig**-wahm/ *noun* a type of small house used in the past by some Native American tribes. Wigwams are made of wooden frames that are covered with bark and sometimes animal skins: *The tops of the wigwams come off – this was to let smoke out when people had fires.*

**Word Origin: wigwam**

**Wigwam** comes from a Native American language. It means "their house."

**wild** /wīld/
● *adjective*
**1** wild animals or plants are found in natural places and are not being taken care of by people: *Bears, wolves, and other wild animals live in this forest.* | *Wild strawberries grow by the side of the road.*
**2** not controlling your behavior or your strong feelings: *It was the last day of school, and the kids were a little wild.*
**3** a wild guess is one that you make without knowing any facts: *I made a wild guess at how many candies were in the jar.*

● *noun*
**the wild** natural conditions, where animals and plants are not taken care of by people: *In the wild, lions hunt in groups.*

**wild·cat** /**wīld**-kat/ *noun* an animal that is similar to a pet cat, but lives in forests, mountains, and other wild areas.

**wil·der·ness** /**wild**-ur-niss/ *noun* a large area of land that is natural, and where people do not live and there are no buildings: *Camping in the wilderness is a great way to see nature.*

**wild·flow·er** /**wīld**-flow-ur/ *noun* a flower that has not been grown by people: *In the spring, this field is full of wildflowers.*

**wild·life** /**wīld**-līf/ *noun* animals that are wild and are not taken care of by people: *The pictures were of Alaskan wildlife, such as bears and moose.*

**will** /wil/ (the short form of "will not" is **won't**) (the short form of "I will," "he will," "they will," etc. is **I'll, he'll, they'll, etc.**)
● *verb*
**1** used for talking about the future: *It will probably rain tomorrow.* | *Do you think the Lakers will win?*
**2** used to say what someone plans or agrees to do: *Cody won't clean his room.* | *I will help you.*
**3** used to tell or ask someone to do something: *Will you be quiet, please?*
**4** used for saying what is possible or what something can do: *The new plane will carry 550 people.*
● *noun*
**1** a strong wish to do something that you have decided to do: *She's very sick, but she hasn't lost the will to live.*
**2** a legal document in which you say who will have your money and property after you die: *My grandma left me $7,000 in her will.*

**will·ing** /**wil**-ing/ *adjective* if you are willing to do something, you will do it if someone wants you to do it: *I am willing to help in any way that I can.* ( ANTONYM: **unwilling** )
—**willingly** /**wil**-ing-lee/ *adverb* in a willing way: *The boys willingly help with the chores.*

**wil·low** /**wil**-oh/ *noun*
a tree with thin branches that bend easily. Willows have long narrow green leaves. Willows grow near lakes, ponds, or rivers.

willow

**will·pow·er**
/**wil**-pow-ur/ *noun* the ability to make yourself do something that is difficult or unpleasant: *Do you have the willpower to eat only one cookie?*

**wimp** /wimp/ *noun* someone who is afraid to do things: *Don't be such a wimp! You might like swimming if you try it.*

**win** /win/
● *verb* (**winning, won** /wuhn/)
**1** to be the best in a competition or game: *The Yankees won the game by one run.* | *Obama won the presidential election.* ( ANTONYM: **lose** )
**2** to get something as a prize for winning in a competition or game: *She won a gold medal in swimming at the Olympics.*
● *noun*
an occasion when you win a competition or game: *The team had its first win of the season. They beat the Wildcats 52 to 46.*
( SYNONYM: **victory** ) ( ANTONYM: **loss** )

**wind**
● *noun* /wind/
air outside that moves quickly: *A flag was waving in the wind.* | *A cold wind was blowing.*
▶ see **Thesaurus**
● *verb* /wīnd/ (**wound** /wownd/)
**1** to put something long around something else several times: *Wind the bandage around your arm.*
**2** to turn a handle around and around in order to make a clock or machine work: *Turn the key to wind up the toy car, then let the car go.*
**3** if a road or river winds, it curves many times: *The path winds up the mountain.*

**wind·chill fac·tor** /**wind**-chil fakt-ur/ *noun* the effect that the wind has on how cold a temperature feels when the wind is blowing: *It is 30 degrees today, but it feels much colder because of the windchill factor.*

a
b
c
d
e
f
g
h
i
j
k
l
m
n
o
p
q
r
s
t
u
v
**w**
x
y
z

**wind·ed** /**wind**-id/ *adjective* if you are winded, you are out of breath, usually because you have been running: *I was winded after running to school.*

**wind farm** /**wind** farm/ *noun* a place where wind is used to produce electricity: *The wind farm has a lot of wind turbines, which are turned by the wind.*

**wind·ing** /**wīnd**-ing/ *adjective* a winding road, path, or river has a lot of curves: *We drove along a winding road into the mountains.*

winding

a winding road

**wind in·stru·ment** /**wind** inss-truh-muhnt/ *noun* a musical instrument that you play by blowing through it. Flutes and clarinets are wind instruments.

**wind·mill** /**wind**-mil/ *noun* a tall structure with parts at the top called sails. The wind turns the sails around to produce power. A windmill is used to crush grain into flour or to produce electricity.

windmill

**win·dow** /**wind**-oh/ *noun*
**1** an opening with glass across it in a building or vehicle. A window is used for letting in air and light: *It was hot so I opened the window.* | *Abby looked out the window to see if it was still raining.*
**2** an area on a computer screen where you can use a particular program: *You can close the window by clicking on the X in the top right-hand corner.*

**Word Origin:** window

**Window** comes from two Old Norse words that meant "wind eye." Old Norse was spoken in Sweden and Denmark. The first windows were just holes in a roof or wall that you could look out of and that let the wind through.

**win·dow shop·ping** /**wind**-oh shap-ing/ *noun* the activity of looking at things in store windows without planning to buy them: *My friends and I went window shopping at the mall.*

**win·dow·sill** /**wind**-oh-sil/ *noun* a shelf at the bottom of a window: *The cat jumped up on the windowsill and looked out the window.*

**wind·pipe** /**wind**-pīp/ *noun* the tube through which air passes from your throat to your lungs

**wind·shield** /**wind**-sheeld/ *noun* the large window at the front of a car or other vehicle: *The windshield was dirty so you could hardly see through it.*

**wind·shield wip·er** /**wind**-sheeld wīp-ur/ *noun* a long thin object that moves across a windshield to push the rain off: *It started raining, and he turned on the windshield wipers.*

**wind·surf·ing** /**wind**-surf-ing/ *noun* the sport of moving across water by standing on a board and holding onto a sail
—**windsurf** /**wind**-surf/ *verb* to do windsurfing: *People windsurf on the lake.*
—**windsurfer** /**wind**-surf-ur/ *noun* someone who windsurfs

windsurfing

**wind tur·bine** /**wind** tur-bīn/ *noun* a large machine like a windmill, used for producing electricity from the wind: *Wind turbines only produce electricity when the wind is blowing.*

**wind·y** /**wind**-ee/ *adjective* if it is windy, there is a lot of wind: *It was a windy fall day, and the wind was blowing the leaves off the trees.*

**wine** /wīn/ *noun* an alcoholic drink made from grapes: *They had a glass of wine with dinner.*

**wing** /wing/ *noun*
**1** one of the parts of a bird's or insect's body that it uses to fly: *The eagle opened its wings and flew away.* ▶ see picture at **hornet**
**2** one of the two flat parts that stick out of the sides of an airplane: *The engines are attached to the airplane's wings.* ▶ see picture at **airplane**

**wink** /wingk/
● *verb* to close and open one eye quickly. You wink to show that you are joking or being friendly: *She smiled at me and winked.*
● *noun* the movement you make with your eye when you wink: *"Hi there, Suzy," he said, giving her a wink.*

**win·ner** /win-ur/ *noun*
**1** someone who wins a competition, race, or game: *The winner of the game is the person who gets the most points.*
**2** something or someone that is likely to be successful: *Her new book looks like another winner – everyone wants to read it.*

**win·ning** /win-ing/
● *adjective*
**1** the winning person or thing is the one that wins a competition, race, or game: *Everyone cheered when Sandy scored the winning goal.*
**2** a winning smile is attractive and makes people like you: *Rosy was a friendly girl with a winning smile.*
● *plural noun*
**winnings** money that you win in a game or competition: *Dad won first prize in the competition and he bought a new computer with his winnings.*

**win·ter** /wint-ur/ *noun* the season between fall and spring. The weather is coldest in winter: *In winter it snows and there is ice on the lake.*
▶ see picture at **season**
—**wintry** /win-tree/ *adjective* very cold, like the weather in winter: *It was a wintry day, so we put on warm jackets, hats, and gloves.*

**wipe** /wīp/ *verb*
**1** to clean something by moving a cloth, sponge, or your hand over it: *I wiped the dishes and put them away in the cupboard.* | *Could you wipe off the table? It's dirty.*

**2** to dry or clean something by rubbing it on something soft: *She wiped her hands on her apron and picked up the phone.*
**3 wipe out** to destroy something completely: *The dinosaurs were wiped out millions of years ago and they all disappeared. No one knows why this happened.*

**wip·er** /wīp-ur/ *noun* a long thin object that moves across a windshield to push the rain off
SYNONYM: **windshield wiper**

**wire** /wī-ur/ *noun*
**1** a long thin piece of metal that looks like string: *The fence was made of wire between wooden posts.*
**2** a long thin piece of metal that carries electricity or a telephone signal: *a telephone wire*
—**wiring** /wī-uhr-ing/ *noun* all the electrical wires in a building or machine: *The wiring in the house is very old and needs to be replaced.*

**wire**

wire

The fence is made of wire.

**wis·dom** /wiz-duhm/ *noun* good judgment and sensible ideas: *My grandfather is full of wisdom, so we often ask for his advice.*

**wis·dom tooth** /wiz-duhm tooth/ *noun* one of the four large teeth at the back of an adult's mouth

**wise** /wīz/ *adjective*
**1** sensible: *If you have a fever, it is wise to stay in bed.* ( ANTONYM: **unwise** )
**2** able to make good decisions and give good advice: *He was a wise leader who always made the right decisions.*
—**wisely** /wīz-lee/ *adverb* in a wise way: *Try to use your money wisely and don't spend it all at once.*

a b c d e f g h i j k l m n o p q r s t u v w x y z

## -wise /wīz/

### Word Building

-wise is a suffix. It is used in adjectives and adverbs.

**1** clock**wise** | length**wise** | like**wise** | other**wise**

-wise means "in the same way or direction as." If something moves *clockwise*, it goes around in a circle in the same direction as the hands of a clock move. If you fold a piece of paper *lengthwise*, you fold it along its length. If someone stands up, and other people do *likewise*, they stand up in the same way as the first person.

**2** time-**wise** | money-**wise** | health-**wise**

-wise means "concerning" or "relating to." If you ask how you are doing *time-wise*, you want to know if you have enough time to finish something. If it is better *health-wise* to drink less soda, it is better for your health to drink less soda.

## wish /wish/

● *verb*

**1** to want something to happen. You often wish for something that you think is unlikely: *I wish Grandma and Grandpa were here.*

**2** to say that you hope someone will be happy or lucky: *Mom said goodbye and wished me good luck on the test.*

**3** if you wish to do something, you want to do it: *Call this number if you wish to reserve a ticket.*

● *noun*

**1** something that you want to have or to happen: *On her birthday she got her wish and her parents gave her a cute little dog.*

**2** if you make a wish, you ask for something to happen and you believe that magic or luck will make it happen: *This is a magic stone. When you touch it you can make a wish.*

IDIOM with **wish**

**best wishes** a phrase that you write before your name at the end of cards and letters: *Best wishes, Angela*

## wit /wit/ *noun*

**1** the ability to say things that are funny and smart: *Dave has a quick wit and can always think*

of something funny to say.

**2 wits** your ability to think quickly and make the right decision: *In team sports you have to use your wits so you are ready for whatever happens next.*

IDIOM with **wit**

**scare you out of your wits** to frighten you very much: *I heard a loud crash which scared me out of my wits.*

## witch /wich/ *noun* a woman who has magic powers, especially in stories. Witches usually use magic to do bad things: *The witch said some strange words and changed the prince into a frog.*

—**witchcraft** /**wich**-kraft/ *noun* the use of magic to do bad things: *People accused her of witchcraft but she was not a witch.*

## with /with/ *preposition*

**1** used when saying that people or things are together: *He lives with his parents.* | *We are having pizza with mushrooms.*

**2** doing something together: *If you have a problem, talk with your teacher.*

**3** using something: *Dry your hands with a towel.*

**4** having something: *She's tall with dark brown hair.*

**5** in a way that shows a feeling or attitude: *You should always treat animals with kindness.*

**6** relating to someone or something: *Mom was angry with me.* | *I'm pleased with the result of my test.*

**7** supporting someone in a decision or argument: *I'm with you on this – I agree that we should go camping.*

## with·draw /with-**dro**/ *verb* (**withdrew** /with-**droo**/, **withdrawn** /with-**dron**/)

**1** to take money out of a bank account: *Mom withdrew $1,000 from the bank to pay the builder.* (ANTONYM: **deposit**)

**2** if soldiers withdraw from an area, they leave it: *At the end of the war, U.S. troops withdrew from the the country and came home.*

**3** to stop taking part in a competition or race: *She decided to withdraw from the race because of a leg injury.*

## with·draw·al /with-**dro**-uhl/ *noun*

**1** if you make a withdrawal. you take money out of your bank account: *Frank made a withdrawal of $100 from the machine outside the bank.*

**2** a situation in which soldiers are removed from an area: *U.S. forces will start their withdrawal from the country in January.*

**with·er** /**with**-ur/ *verb* if a plant withers, it becomes dry and it starts to die: *I forgot to water the plant and it withered and died.*

**with·hold** /with-**hohld**/ *verb* (**withheld** /with-**held**/) to refuse to give something to someone: *He knows who stole the car but is withholding the information.*

**with·in** /with-**in**/ *adverb, preposition*
**1** before a time ends: *You can go to the park, but come back within an hour.*
**2** less than a specific distance from a place: *Our house is within a mile of the school.*

**with·out** /with-**owt**/ *preposition*
**1** not having something or someone with you: *I went to the pool without my swimming things so I couldn't swim today.*
**2** not doing something: *We left the store without buying anything because they didn't have shoes in my size.*

**with·stand** /with-**stand**/ *verb* (**withstood** /with-**stud**/) to not be harmed or affected by something: *The tent is designed to withstand strong winds so it did not blow down in the storm.*

**wit·ness** /**wit**-niss/
● *noun*
**1** someone who saw an accident or a crime happen: *There were two witnesses and they both said that the accident was not his fault.*
**2** someone who gives evidence in a court of law: *Witnesses must swear to tell the truth to the court.*
● *verb*
to see an accident or a crime happen: *The robbery was witnessed by five people who were in the bank.*

**wit·ty** /**wit**-ee/ *adjective* good at talking in a funny or interesting way: *He's very witty and is always saying funny things.*

**wives** /wīvz/ *noun* the plural of **wife**

**wiz·ard** /**wiz**-urd/ *noun*
**1** a man in a story who has magic powers: *The wizard said some magic words, and then he suddenly disappeared in a cloud of smoke.*

**2** someone who is very good at doing something: *Dad's a computer wizard and I'm sure he can fix the problem.*

> **Word Origin:** **wizard**
>
> **Wizard** comes from a Middle English word that meant "wise." In the 1400s, a wizard was a wise man who knew a lot about plants and animals, and who did scientific experiments. In the Middle Ages, people thought science was a little like magic. By the 1500s, "wizard" meant a man with magic powers.

**wob·ble** /**wahb**-uhl/ *verb* to move from side to side so that something might fall: *The tower of blocks wobbled and then fell.*
—**wobbly** /**wahb**-lee/ *adjective* moving from side to side and likely to fall: *The ladder was wobbly and I was worried that it would fall over.*

**wok** /wahk/ *noun* a large frying pan that is shaped like a bowl. You use a wok in Chinese cooking to cook small pieces of meat or vegetables quickly.

wok

**woke** /wohk/ *verb* the past tense of **wake**

**wo·ken** /**wohk**-uhn/ *verb* the past participle of wake

**wolf** /wulf/ *noun* (plural **wolves** /wulvz/) a wild animal that looks like a large dog and hunts in groups

wolf

**wom·an** /**wum**-uhn/ *noun* (plural **women** /**wim**-in/) an adult female person: *Mrs. Stokes is a very nice woman.*

a b c d e f g h i j k l m n o p q r s t u v **w** x y z

**wom·en** /**wim**-in/ *noun* the plural of **woman**

**won** /wuhn/ *verb* the past tense and past participle of **win**

**won·der** /**wuhnd**-ur/
● *verb*
to want to know something that you are not sure about: *I wonder why he's late – he promised to be here half an hour ago.*
● *noun*
**1** a feeling of admiration and surprise: *The kids stared at the animal in wonder – it was amazing.*
**2** something that people admire a lot: *The way birds fly together in a group is one of the wonders of nature.*

IDIOM with **wonder**
**no wonder** used for saying that something does not surprise you: *No wonder you are tired if you stayed awake until after midnight.*

**won·der·ful** /**wuhnd**-ur-fuhl/ *adjective* very good or enjoyable: *I hope you have a wonderful vacation!* ( SYNONYM: **great** )

**won't** /wohnt/ *contraction* short for "will not": *The test tomorrow won't be difficult.*

**wood** /wud/ *noun*
**1** the hard material that trees are made of. Wood is used for making furniture or burning on fires: *The doors are made of wood.*
**2 woods** a small forest: *A lot of wild animals live in the woods.*

**wood**

the woods

**wood·chuck** /**wud**-chuhk/ *noun* a small animal with thick brown fur and big front teeth: *Woodchucks live in holes in the ground.*
( SYNONYM: **groundhog** )

**wood·en** /**wud**'n/ *adjective* made from wood: *In the kitchen there was a wooden table.*

**wood·land** /**wud**-luhnd/ *noun* land with a lot of trees growing on it: *In the south, there is a lot of woodland, with pine and maple trees.*

**wood·peck·er**
/**wud**-pek-ur/ *noun* a bird with a long pointed beak. A woodpecker uses its beak to make holes in trees to get insects.

**woodpecker**

**wood·winds**
/**wud**-windz/ (also **the wood·wind sec·tion** /**wud**-wind sek-shuhn/) *plural noun* the group of musical instruments in an orchestra that are played by blowing and pressing on keys to cover holes. These instruments include the flute, the clarinet, the oboe, and the bassoon.

**woodwinds**

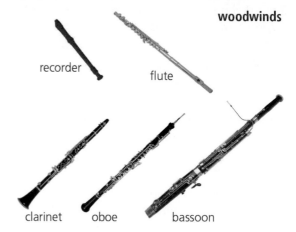
recorder
flute
clarinet
oboe
bassoon

**wool** /wul/ *noun* the hair on a sheep. People use wool for making clothes and fabrics: *This sweater's made of wool so it is very warm.*
—**woolen** /**wul**-uhn/ *adjective* made of wool: *Grandma has promised to knit me a new woolen scarf.*

**word** /wurd/ *noun*
**1** a group of sounds or letters that have a meaning: *"Oui" is a French word that means "yes."* | *For homework, we had to learn all the words of the poem.* ▶ see **Thesaurus**
**2** a short talk with someone: *The principal wants to have a word with your parents.*
**3** news or a message: *Is there any word about Grandma? I hope she's feeling better.*

**give your word** to promise someone something: *I won't tell anyone else what happened – I give you my word.*

**in your own words** describing something in your own way, and not repeating what you have read or heard: *Read the story and then write it again in your own words.*

**keep your word** to do what you have promised: *I trust him completely – he always keeps his word.*

**word pro·ces·sor** /**wurd** prahss-ess-ur/ *noun* a computer program that you use for writing —**word processing** /**wurd** prahss-ess-ing/ *noun* the activity of writing using a word processor

**word·search** /**wurd**-surch/ *noun* a game in which you look for words that are hidden among other letters

**wore** /wor/ *verb* the past tense of **wear**

**work** /wurk/

● *verb*

**1** to do a job to earn money: *Mom works as a nurse at the hospital.*

**2** to spend time and effort trying to do something: *My sister's working hard to get into college.*

**3** to have the effect that you want: *The medicine didn't work. I still have a bad cough.*

**4** if a machine works, it operates correctly: *The elevator wasn't working so we had to use the stairs.*

**5 work out** to find the answer to a question or problem: *Can you work out what 30 x 15 is?*

**6 work out** to do exercises for your body: *A lot of people go to the gym to work out.*

**7 get worked up** to become upset: *She got very worked up when she lost her key, and started crying.*

● *noun*

**1** a job that you do to earn money: *When he first started work, he earned $150 a week.*

▶ see **Thesaurus**

**2** something that needs a lot of time and effort: *We had to dig a hole and it was hard work.*

**3** something you produce when you are working or studying: *My teacher says that she is pleased with my work.*

**4** something that an artist produces that is very good or beautiful: *Many of her paintings are great works of art and are very valuable.*

**at work** doing your job, or in the place where you do your job: *He gets up early and he's at work in his office by eight o'clock.*

**out of work** if you are out of work, you do not have a job: *The factory shut down and a lot of people were out of work.*

**work·book** /**wurk**-buk/ *noun* a school book with questions and exercises in it: *For your homework, please do exercise five in your workbooks.*

**work·er** /**wurk**-ur/ *noun*

**1** someone who does a job, but who is not a manager: *He got a job as a farm worker, picking fruit.*

**2** a female bee, ant, or other insect that does all the work but does not lay eggs

**work eth·ic** /**wurk** eth-ik/ *noun* a belief in the importance of hard work: *My parents work hard because they have a strong work ethic.*

**work·ing** /**wurk**-ing/ *adjective*

**1** having a job: *Working parents often have to pay someone to take care of their kids.*

**2** relating to work: *His working hours are from 9:00 to 5:00 each day.*

**work·ing class** /**wurk**-ing **klass**/

● *noun* all the people who usually work with their hands, and who do not have much money or power: *He is from the working class – his father is a truck driver.*

● *adjective* relating to the working class: *He was a working class kid, but he became a famous singer.*

**work·load** /**wurk**-lohd/ *noun* the amount of work that you must do: *Teachers have a heavy workload and they often have to grade students' homework in the evenings.*

**work·man** /**wurk**-muhn/ *noun* (plural **workmen** /**wurk**-muhn/) a man who works with his hands building or repairing things: *The workmen are building a new apartment block.*

**work·out** /**wurk**-owt/ *noun* a series of exercises you do to keep your body fit: *My brother goes to the gym to do a workout every day.*

**work·sheet** /**wurk**-sheet/ *noun* a piece of paper with questions and exercises on it for students: *I finished three worksheets in math today.*

a b c d e f g h i j k l m n o p q r s t u v **w** x y z

**work·shop** /**wurk**-shahp/ *noun*
**1** a meeting where people learn how to do something, by talking about it and practicing it: *On Saturday, Mom and I went to a photography workshop.*
**2** a room or building where people make or repair things: *Dad has a workshop in our yard where he makes things out of wood.*

**world** /wurld/ *noun*
**1** the Earth that we live on: *The Nile is the longest river in the world.* ( SYNONYM: **Earth** )
► see **Thesaurus**
**2** all the people or countries on Earth: *News of the disaster shocked the whole world.*
**3** a particular part of the Earth, which includes several countries: *He is very interested in the Arab World and he has always wanted to visit Egypt.*
**4** the animal/plant/insect world all animals, plants, or insects as a group: *I like watching programs about the animal world, especially about lions and tigers.*
**5** an area of activity: *My sister says she would like a job in the world of fashion.*

**world rec·ord** /wurld **rek**-urd/ *noun* a score or time that is better than anyone else has ever achieved: *His time for running the 100 meters is a new world record – no one has ever run faster than him.*

**world·wide** /wurld-**wīd**/ *adjective*, *adverb* everywhere in the world: *The band became famous worldwide and they sold millions of records.*

**World Wide Web** /wurld wīd **web**/ *noun* the system that connects computers around the world together so people can find information on the Internet ( SYNONYM: **Web** )

**worm** /wurm/ *noun* a long thin creature that lives in the soil. Worms have a soft body and no legs. ( SYNONYM: **earthworm** )

**Word Origin:** **worm**

In Old English, **worm** was used as a name for many different types of animals. A worm could be the soft thin creature that lives in the soil, like we say today. Or a worm could be a snake, a scorpion, or even a dragon!

**worn** /worn/
● *verb* the past participle of wear
● *adjective* something that is worn has been used a lot and looks old or damaged: *Nick was wearing an old worn sweater with a hole in it.*

**worn out** /worn **owt**/ *adjective*
**1** very tired: *We walked all day and we were worn out when we got home.*
( SYNONYM: **exhausted** )
**2** something that is worn out is old and does not look good anymore: *You can't wear that old jacket – it's worn out.*

**wor·ried** /**wur**-eed/ *adjective* unhappy or anxious because you think something bad might happen: *When he didn't return home from school, his parents were very worried.*
► see **Thesaurus**

**wor·ry** /**wur**-ee/
● *verb* (**worries**, **worrying**, **worried**) to feel unhappy or anxious because you think something bad might happen: *I'm sure you'll pass the test so you don't need to worry.*
—**worrier** /**wur**-ee-ur/ *noun* someone who worries a lot: *Angela's a worrier – even little things make her anxious.*
—**worrying** /**wur**-ee-ing/ *adjective* making you worry: *It's worrying if people are late and you don't know why.*
● *noun* (plural **worries**) a problem that makes you feel unhappy or anxious: *If you have any worries, come and talk to me about them.*

**worse** /wurss/
● *adjective*
**1** not as good as something else: *My brother's spelling is worse than mine.* ( ANTONYM: **better** )
**2** more unpleasant or severe: *The rain got worse so we had to go indoors.* ( ANTONYM: **better** )
**3** more sick than you were before: *I feel much worse today than I did yesterday.* ( ANTONYM: **better** )
● *adverb*
more badly: *Our team didn't play well but the other team played even worse.* ( ANTONYM: **better** )
● *noun*
something that is worse: *We were already very upset by what had happened, but worse was to come.*

**wors·en** /**wurss**-uhn/ *verb* to become worse: *The weather worsened and it started to rain very heavily.*

**wor·ship** /**wursh**-ip/
● *verb* (**worshiping** or **worshipping**, **worshiped** or **worshipped**) to show great respect for God or a god by praying or singing: *People come to church to worship God.*
● *noun* the act of worshiping God or a god: *The chapel is used for worship.*
—**worshiper**, **worshipper** /**wursh**-ip-ur/ *noun* someone who worships God or a god: *The church was full of worshipers.*

**worst** /wurst/
● *adjective* worse than all the others, or worse than at any other time: *Zero is the worst score you can get.* | *The traffic is worst in the morning because everyone is going to work.*
( ANTONYM: **best** )
● *adverb* worse than anyone or anything else: *Our town was worst affected by the storms and many houses were badly damaged.*
● *noun* the one that is worse than all the others: *I don't like green vegetables but spinach is the worst.*

**worth** /wurth/
● *preposition*
**1** having a specific value: *The painting is worth a lot of money – maybe over $100,000.* | *Each question is worth four points.*
**2** if something is worth doing, it is interesting or good to do: *This book's really worth reading – it's great.*
● *noun*
**1** an amount of something that has a particular value: *I bought $6 worth of bananas.*
**2** how useful someone or something is: *He has already shown his worth to the team.*

**worth·less** /**wurth**-liss/ *adjective* having no value: *These coins are worthless because they are not used anymore.*

**worth·while** /wurth-**wil**/ *adjective* if something is worthwhile, it is useful or enjoyable: *The trip to the museum was a worthwhile experience and the children learned a lot.*

**wor·thy** /**wurth**-ee/ *adjective*
**1** good enough to deserve something: *It is a very useful book and it is certainly worthy of your attention.*
**2** deserving respect or support from people: *The money is for a worthy cause – it's to help poor children.*

**would** /wuhd, wud/ *verb*
**1** the past tense of **will**, used for describing what someone said or thought in the past: *I knew I would pass the test!*
**2** used in sentences with "if," when talking about something that could happen but is unlikely: *If I were rich, I would buy a house with a swimming pool.*
**3** used when politely offering someone something: *Would you like a cookie?*
**4** used when politely asking someone to do something: *Would you open the door, please?*
**5** used when saying that something happened regularly in the past: *When we lived in California, we would go to the beach every weekend.*
( SYNONYM: **used to** )
**6** used when saying that someone refused to do something: *I told him to stay at home but he would not listen and he went out anyway.*

**would·n't** /**wud**'nt/ *contraction* short for "would not": *She said she wouldn't be able to come to my party.*

**would've** /**wud**-uhv/ *contraction* short for "would have": *I would've sent her a card if I had known it was her birthday.*

**wound**
● *noun* /woond/
a deep cut in your skin. A wound is often made by a knife or bullet: *The bullet hit him in the shoulder and caused a serious wound.*
● *verb*
**1** to injure someone, especially with a knife or gun: *Several people were wounded in the bomb attack.*
**2** to upset someone: *His cruel remarks wounded her.*
**3** /wownd/ the past tense and past participle of **wind**
—**wounded** /**woond**-id/ *adjective* injured by a weapon: *There were hundreds of wounded soldiers in the hospital.*

**wove** /wohv/ *verb* the past tense of **weave**

**wo·ven** /**wohv**-uhn/ *verb* the past participle of weave

**wow** /wow/ *interjection* you say "wow" when you think something is impressive or surprising: *Wow! Look at that huge truck!*

**wrap** /rap/
- *verb* (**wrapping**, **wrapped**)

**1** to put paper or material around something to cover it: *I wrapped the birthday present in red paper. | She wrapped her baby in a blanket.*
**2** to hold someone by putting your arms around him or her: *She wrapped her arms around me and hugged me tightly.*

- *noun*

**1** thin clear plastic that you put around something to keep it clean: *Mom covered the food with a plastic wrap and put it in the fridge.*
**2** a type of sandwich that consists of a tortilla folded around meat or cheese or other food: *For lunch I had a cheese wrap.*

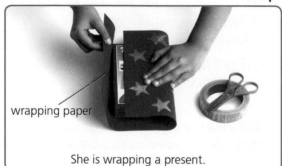
**wrap**

wrapping paper

She is wrapping a present.

**wrap·per** /**rap**-ur/ *noun* the paper or plastic that covers something you buy: *Andrew took the chocolate out of its wrapper and ate it.*

**wrap·ping pa·per** /**rap**-ing payp-ur/ *noun* colored paper that you use to wrap presents: *The gift was covered in silver wrapping paper.*

**wreath** /reeth/ *noun* a circle of leaves or flowers that are wound together: *They had a Christmas wreath on their door.*

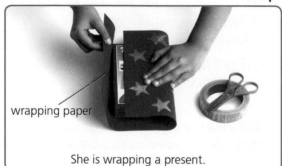
**wreath**

wreath

**wreck** /rek/
- *verb*

to destroy something completely: *A truck was wrecked in an accident on the highway.*

- *noun*

**1** a bad accident with cars or airplanes: *Two guys were killed in a car wreck.* ( SYNONYM: **crash** )
**2** a car, airplane, or ship that is very badly

damaged in an accident: *The wreck lay at the bottom of the ocean for hundreds of years.*

**wreck·age** /**rek**-ij/ *noun* the broken parts of a vehicle or building after a crash or explosion: *The wreckage of the plane was spread over a wide area.*

**wren** /ren/ *noun* a small brown bird with a loud song. Wrens have a short tail that points up in the air.

**wren**

**wrench** /rench/
- *verb*

**1** to pull something suddenly and with force: *The drawer was locked but I managed to wrench it open.*
**2** to injure a part of your body by twisting it suddenly: *I looked over my shoulder too quickly and wrenched my neck.*

- *noun*

a metal tool that you use to make metal nuts tighter. A wrench has a curved open part at the end that fits around the nut.

**wrench**

**wres·tle** /**ress**-uhl/ *verb*

**1** to fight by holding someone and trying to push him or her to the ground: *My brother and I were wrestling with each other but he was stronger so he won.*
**2** to try to solve a problem by thinking very hard about it: *Laura has been wrestling with the problem of which college she wants to go to.*
—**wrestler** /**ress**-lur/ *noun* someone who wrestles as a sport
—**wrestling** /**ress**-ling/ *noun* the sport in which two people wrestle

**wretch** /rech/ *noun* someone you feel pity for who is in a very bad situation

**wretch·ed** /**rech**-id/ *adjective* very unhappy because you are poor, lonely, sick, etc.: *The slaves had wretched lives and many of them were treated very badly.*

**wring** /ring/ *verb*
(**wrung** /ruhng/) to twist a wet cloth so that water comes out of it: *Wring out your swimsuit before you put it in your swimming bag.*

wring

She is wringing the cloth.

**wrin·kle** /**ringk**-uhl/ *noun*
**1** a line on your face that you get when you are old: *Mom puts this cream on her face to stop her from getting wrinkles.*
**2** a fold in a piece of clothing that you do not want: *She stood up and smoothed the wrinkles in her dress.*
—**wrinkled** /**ringk**-uhld/ *adjective* covered with wrinkles: *His skin is old and wrinkled.*

**wrist** /rist/ *noun* the joint between your hand and your arm: *He wears his watch on his left wrist.* ▶ see picture on page **A13**

**wrist·watch** /**rist**-wahch/ *noun* a watch that you wear on your wrist: *Alan looked down at his wristwatch. It was twenty after two.*

**write** /rīt/ *verb* (**wrote** /roht/, **written** /rit'n/)
**1** to make letters or words on paper, using a pen or pencil: *Don't forget to write your name at the top of the page.* ▶ see **Thesaurus**
**2** to produce a letter to send to someone: *I'm writing to Grandma to thank her for my birthday present.*
**3** to produce a story, book, or song: *He's written a lot of good children's books.*

**Word Origin: write**

The Old English word that **write** comes from meant "to scratch" words or pictures into something hard. People in those times did not have paper and pencils. If they wanted to write something, they had to cut the letters into a piece of stone or wood.

**writ·er** /**rīt**-ur/ *noun* someone who writes books: *That writer is famous for his books about animals.* ▶ see **Thesaurus**

**writ·ing** /**rīt**-ing/ *noun*
**1** words that are written or printed: *This writing is in Spanish so I can't understand it.*
**2** the way someone writes with a pen or pencil: *My teacher says I need to make my writing smaller and neater.*
( SYNONYM: **handwriting** )
**3** the activity of writing stories and books: *David has a very good imagination and he loves writing.*

**writ·ten** /**rit**'n/ *verb* the past participle of **write**

**wrong** /rong/ *adjective*
**1** not correct: *28 is the wrong answer. The right answer is 27.* ( ANTONYM: **right** )
▶ see **Thesaurus**
**2** not morally right: *It's wrong to tell lies. You should always tell the truth.* ( ANTONYM: **right** )
**3** not appropriate: *A lot of people think pink is the wrong color for boys.* ( ANTONYM: **right** )
**4** if there is something wrong with a machine, it is not working properly: *There's something wrong with this computer – it won't start.*
**5** making you feel pain or unhappiness: *You look sad. Is there something wrong?*

**wrong·ly** /**rong**-lee/ *adverb* in a way that is not correct or not fair: *I guessed wrongly. I thought Jane was the older sister but she's the younger one.*

**wrote** /roht/ *verb* the past tense of **write**

**wrung** /ruhng/ *verb* the past tense and past participle of **wring**

**WWW** /duhb-uhl-yoo duhb-uhl-yoo **duhb**-uhl-yoo/ *noun* the abbreviation for **World Wide Web**

a b c d e f g h i j k l m n o p q r s t u v **w** x y z

a b c d e f g h i j k l m n o p q r s t u v w **x** y z

# Xx

**x·ax·is** /**ekss** akss-iss/ *noun* the line that goes from left to right on a graph: *Draw a graph and mark the x-axis with the numbers one to ten.*

**x·co·or·di·nate** /**ekss** koh-ord'n-it/ *noun* the position of a point in relation to the x-axis on a graph: *In the pair (2,4) the x-coordinate is 2.*

**X·mas** /**kriss**-muhss/ *noun* an informal way of writing "Christmas": *Merry Xmas!*

**X-ray** /**ekss** ray/ *noun*
**1** a special beam of light that can pass through solid objects. X-rays are used for photographing the inside of the body, especially bones.
**2** a photograph of the inside of someone's body, taken with an X-ray: *The X-ray showed that the bone was broken.*

X-ray

**xy·lem** /**xīl**-uhm/ *noun* the part of a plant stem that carries water from the roots to the rest of the plant

**xy·lo·phone** /**zīl**-uh-fohn/ *noun* a musical instrument with a set of metal or wooden bars that you hit with a stick. Each bar is a different length and produces a different note.

xylophone

# Yy

**-y** /ee/

**yacht** /yaht/ *noun* a boat used for sailing or racing: *It was a sunny day and there were a lot of yachts on the bay.*

yacht

**yam** /yam/ *noun* another word for a sweet potato

**yank** /yangk/ *verb* to pull something quickly and with force: *Mom yanked me back and the car just missed me.*

**Yan·kee** /**yangk**-ee/ *noun*
**1** a name for someone from the U.S.
**2** a name for someone from the northern states of the U.S., used by people from the southern states
**3** a soldier who fought for the Union during the American Civil War. The Union was the northern states of America.

**Word Origin:** Yankee

No one is sure where the word **Yankee** comes from. It could come from Dutch or from Native American languages. When British people first started using the word Yankee about Americans, they thought it was a mean insulting name. Americans took the name for themselves to show that they did not care what the British thought.

**yard** /yard/ *noun*
**1** the land around a house, usually covered with grass: *The kids were playing in the back yard.*
**2** a unit for measuring length. A yard is 3 feet or 0.9144 meters: *We measured our classroom and it is ten yards long.*

**yard·stick** /**yard**-stik/ *noun*
**1** a special stick that is one yard long. You use a yardstick for measuring things.
**2** something you use as a standard for judging or comparing things: *The test results are a yardstick for measuring the children's progress.*

**yar·mul·ke** /**yahm**-uhlk-uh/ *noun* a small round cap that some Jewish men and boys wear on their heads

**yarn** /yarn/ *noun* thick thread that you use for knitting: *Grandma bought some red yarn to make a sweater.*

yarn

**yawn** /yon/ *verb*
● *verb* to open your mouth wide and breathe in deeply because you are tired or bored: *I was so tired I couldn't stop yawning.*
● *noun* an act of yawning: *"Goodnight," Mom said with a yawn.*

yawn

**y-ax·is** /**wī** akss-iss/ *noun* the line that goes from top to bottom on a graph: *Mark the y-axis with the months of the year.*

**y-co·or·di·nate** /**wī** koh-ord'n-it/ *noun* the position of a point in relation to the y-axis on a graph: *In the pair (2,4) the y-coordinate is 4.*

**yd.** the written abbreviation of **yard**

**yeah** /**ye**-uh/ *adverb* yes: *"Do you like Bobby?" "Yeah, he's great."*

**year** /yeer/ *noun*
**1** a period of 12 months or 365 days: *We moved to this house last July and we've been living here for one year.*
**2** the period from January 1 to December 31: *"Which year were you born?" "In 2001."*
**3** used for talking about someone's age: *My sister is 12 years old.*
**4** **years** a very long time: *I haven't seen my cousins for years because they live in Australia.*

**year·book** /**yeer**-buk/ *noun* a book that a school produces every year. A yearbook contains information about the students and their activities: *There's a picture of my brother playing baseball in his high school yearbook.*

**year·ly** /**yeer**-lee/ *adjective*, *adverb* every year: *The fourth of July parade is a yearly event.*

**yeast** /yeest/ *noun* a substance you use when you make bread, to make the dough rise

**yell** /yel/
● *verb* to shout something very loudly: *I yelled at Sam to wait, but he kept on running.*
● *noun* a loud shout: *Dad gave a yell from the kitchen window to say that supper was ready.*

a b c d e f g h i j k l m n o p q r s t u v w x **y** z

**yel·low** /yel-oh/ *noun, adjective* the color of a lemon or a banana: *In spring, the plant has yellow flowers.*

**yel·low jack·et** /yel-oh jak-it/ *noun* a type of wasp with yellow and black stripes on its body, that can sting you

**yes** /yess/ *adverb*
**1** said to show that something is true: *"Are you feeling better?" "Yes, thanks."* ( ANTONYM: **no** )
**2** said to agree with something: *"I like the red T-shirt best." "Yes, I do too."* ( ANTONYM: **no** )
**3** said to accept an invitation or offer: *I asked Greg to my party and he said yes.* ( ANTONYM: **no** )
**4** said to show that you are excited about something: *Yes! I scored a goal!*

**Word Origin:** yes

**Yes** comes from Old English. When yes was first used, it was a really strong way of saying yes. The normal way of saying yes was "yea." Now, we normally use yes, and yea is only used in some formal situations, such as voting in Congress.

**yes·ter·day** /yest-urd-ee/ *adverb, noun* the day before today: *Yesterday was March 31, so it's April 1 today.*

**yet** /yet/
● *adverb*
**1** until now or before now: *I haven't finished my homework yet.*
**2** used for saying that something could still happen: *The game's not over so we may yet win.*
**3** in addition to what has already happened: *He was late for class yet again so his teacher got angry.*
● *conjunction*
but – used when what you say next is surprising: *It was very late at night yet none of the kids were tired.*

**yield** /yeeld/
● *verb*
**1** to produce something: *In science, the class did an experiment that yielded an interesting result.*
**2** to do what someone wants, although you do not want to: *The king finally yielded to their demands and allowed the prisoners to be released.*

● *noun*
the amount that something produces: *Farmers want high yields of crops from their land.*

**yo·ga** /yohg-uh/ *noun* a set of exercises that relax your mind and keep your muscles strong. Yoga helps you to bend and move your body easily. Yoga comes from the Hindu religion: *She does yoga every morning because it helps to keep her body in good condition.*

yoga

**yo·gurt** /yohg-urt/ *noun* a thick liquid food that is made from milk. Yogurt has a slightly sour taste: *Fruit with yogurt is very good for you.*

**yoke** /yohk/
● *noun* a wooden bar that keeps two animals together when they are working and pulling heavy loads: *Farmers used to put a yoke on oxen when they were plowing the fields.*
● *verb* to put a yoke on two animals

**yolk** /yohk/ *noun* the yellow part of an egg: *I dipped my toast in the egg yolk.*

yolk

yolk

white

**Word Origin:** yolk

In Old English, **yolk** means "the yellow part." It comes from the Old English word for yellow.

**Yom Kip·pur** /yahm kip-ur/ *noun* a day that is an important Jewish holiday. On Yom Kippur Jewish people do not eat. They pray to God to forgive them for the things they have done wrong.

**you** /yuh, yoo/ *pronoun*
**1** the person or people someone is talking to: *Hi Jason, how are you?*
**2** people in general: *Exercise is good for you.*

**you'd** /yuhd, yood/ *contraction*
**1** short for "you would": *You'd like Thomas if you met him. He's great.*
**2** short for "you had": *I wish you'd told me you weren't coming.*

**you'll** /yuhl, yool/ *contraction* short for "you will": *If you keep trying, you'll get it right soon.*

**young** /yuhng/
● *adjective*
**1** having lived or existed for only a short time: *She's only five so she's still very young.* | *All these trees are still very young.* ( ANTONYM: **old** )
► see **Thesaurus**
**2** seeming or looking like a young person: *If people get plenty of exercise, it helps them stay young.*
● *plural noun*
an animal's young are its babies: *A mother tiger feeds her young for about three to six months.*

**young**

old

young

**young·ster** /**yuhng**-stur/ *noun* a child or a young person: *Youngsters have a lot more energy than adults.*

**your** /yur, yoor, yor/ *adjective* belonging to the person or people you are speaking to: *I like your new sneakers.*

**you're** /yur, yoor, yor/ *contraction* short for "you are": *If you're hungry, have an apple.*

**yours** /yoorz/ *pronoun* something belonging or relating to you: *Is this bag yours, Naomi?*

**your·self** /yur-**self**/ *pronoun* (plural **yourselves** /yur-**selvz**/)
**1** used to show that the person you are talking to is affected by his or her own action: *Be careful with that knife or you will cut yourself.*
**2** if you do something by yourself, you do it alone or without help: *This drawing is very good. Did you do it by yourself?*

**youth** /yooth/ *noun* (plural **youths** /yoothz/)
**1** the time when you are young: *My dad lived in Mexico in his youth, but he moved here when he was 25.*
**2** a boy or young man: *A gang of youths tried to steal her purse.*
**3** young people: *The youth of today are very concerned about protecting the environment.*

**youth·ful** /**yooth**-fuhl/ *adjective* typical of young people: *The students were full of youthful energy.*

**you've** /yuhv, yoov/ *contraction* short for "you have": *You've got mud on your pants.*

**yo-yo** /**yoh**-yoh/ *noun* a toy made of two circular parts that go up and down a length of string. You hold and move the string to make the yo-yo move.

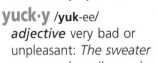

**yo-yo**

**yuck·y** /**yuk**-ee/ *adjective* very bad or unpleasant: *The sweater was a yucky yellow color and I didn't like it at all.*

**yum·my** /**yuhm**-ee/ *adjective* tasting very good: *This chocolate cake is yummy.*

a b c d e f g h i j k l m n o p q r s t u v w x **y** z

**a b c d e f g h i j k l m n o p q r s t u v w x y z**

# Zz

**zeal** /zeel/ *noun* a strong feeling of interest in something and a strong effort to do it: *He has a real zeal for learning and he has worked hard to improve his grades this year.*

**zeal·ous** /zel-uhss/ *adjective* very interested in something, or doing something with a lot of energy: *a zealous fan*

**ze·bra** /zee-bruh/ *noun* an African animal that looks like a horse with black and white stripes

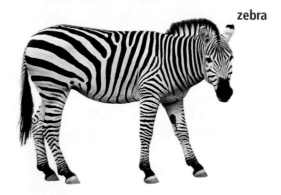
zebra

**ze·ro** /zeer-oh/ *number*
**1** the number 0: *My phone number ends with a zero.*
**2** 0 degrees in the Fahrenheit or Celsius systems of measuring temperature. In the Celsius system, water freezes at 0 degrees: *The temperature was 5° below zero last night.*
**3** the lowest possible amount or level of something: *The chance of winning the lottery is almost zero.*

**ze·ro prop·er·ty** /zeer-oh prahp-urt-ee/ *noun* in math, the rule that says if you add a number to zero, the answer is that number. Also, the rule says that if you multiply a number by zero, the answer is zero: *The zero property of addition means that 4 + 0 = 4. The zero property of multiplication means that 4 x 0 = 0.*

**zig·zag** /zig-zag/ *noun* a line that turns sharply from one side to the other several times, like a Z: *The trail goes in a zigzag up the side of the canyon. | a zigzag pattern*

zigzag

**zinc** /zingk/ *noun* a white metal that is a chemical element

**zip** /zip/ *verb* (**zipping, zipped**)
**1** to close or fasten something with a zipper: *Zip up your coat; it's cold outside.*
ANTONYM: **unzip**
**2** to go somewhere very quickly: *Two boys zipped past me on their bikes.*

zip

He is zipping his jacket.

**zip code** /zip kohd/ *noun* a number that you put at the end of an address on an envelope. The zip code shows the exact area to deliver the envelope to.

**zip·per** /zip-ur/ *noun* something you use for fastening clothes and bags. A zipper has two lines of metal or plastic that fit together: *Pull up the zipper on your coat.*

**zit** /zit/ *noun* a small raised spot on your skin: *Many teenagers get zits on their faces.*
SYNONYM: **pimple**

**zo·di·ac** /zohd-ee-ak/ *noun* **the zodiac** a circle made of 12 areas of the sky, through which the planets, the Moon, and the stars seem to travel. Each area has a special sign. Some people believe that the sign you were born under affects your personality: *Virgo is the sixth sign of the zodiac.*

**zom·bie** /zahm-bee/ *noun* in stories and movies, a dead body that moves by magic: *In the movie, the zombies attack people and turn them into zombies too.*

**zone** /zohn/ *noun* an area where a particular thing happens or where there are special rules: *Los Angeles is in an earthquake zone. | The red lines show that this is a no-parking zone.*

**zoo** /zoo/ *noun* a place where many different animals are kept, so people can go and see them: *We saw elephants and monkeys at the zoo.*

---

**Word Origin:** zoo

The idea of a **zoo** is a very old one, but it was mostly rich people such as kings who could collect animals. In the 1800s, cities started building places where ordinary people could see animals. They called these places zoological parks. Zoological comes from the Greek words for "animals" and "the study of a subject." People soon shortened the word to "zoo."

---

**zo·ol·o·gy** /zoh-**ahl**-uhj-ee/ *noun* the study of animals and their behavior: *Anne wants to be a veterinarian so she's studying zoology at college.*

**zoom** /zoom/
- *verb*
**1** to go somewhere very quickly: *The rocket zoomed into the sky.*
**2** if a camera zooms in or out, it makes the thing you are taking a picture of seem larger or smaller: *I zoomed in on a bird I could see high up in a tree.*
- *noun* (also **zoom lens** /**zoom** lenz/)
a part on some cameras that makes things that are far away look like they are closer: *The zoom makes things look five times bigger than they really are.*

**zuc·chi·ni** /zoo-**keen**-ee/ *noun* a long smooth green vegetable ▶ see picture on page **A7**

# Writer's Thesaurus

# Aa

## admire *verb*

to like and respect someone because you think that person is very good or good at doing something: *I admire my mother because she works so hard for our family.*

▶ **idolize** to admire someone very much and think that he or she is perfect: *She is a famous singer and she is idolized by millions of fans.*

▶ **look up to** to like and respect someone who is older than you, or who has authority over you: *When Jesse was a little boy, he looked up to his older brother and copied everything he did.*

▶ **revere** to have great respect for a leader, writer, or artist, especially one who has died: *Martin Luther King was revered for his role in the Civil Rights Movement.*

## advantage *noun*

something that is good or useful about something: *One of the advantages of living in a big city is that there are lots of exciting things to do. | He is tall and that is an advantage in basketball.*

( ANTONYM: **disadvantage** )

▶ **benefit** a good effect that something has: *Regular exercise has many benefits and is good for your health.*

▶ **good point** something that is good about something: *My phone has some good points: it is cheap and easy to use. The main bad point is that it doesn't look very nice.*

▶ **merit** a good feature that something has, which you think about when you are comparing it with other things: *We talked about the merits of the two schools. My school has the best playground, but the other school has big classrooms.*

## advice *noun*

an opinion that you give someone about what he or she should do: *I didn't know what to do, so I asked my father for his advice.*

▶ **tip** a useful piece of advice, especially about how to do something better: *The coach can give you some tips on how to improve your tennis.*

▶ **suggestion** an idea that someone suggests: *Does anyone have a suggestion for a good place to eat?*

## allow *verb*

to say that someone can do or have something: *Sandra's parents do not allow her to watch TV after eight o'clock. | Bikes are allowed in the park.*

▶ **let** to allow someone to do something: *Thanks for letting me borrow your pen. | Our teacher lets us choose the books we are going to read.*

▶ **permit** to allow someone to do something. **Permit** is often used on official signs about rules: *Students are not permitted to eat or drink in the classroom.*

▶ **give permission** to allow someone to do something. Usually a teacher, parent, or manager does this: *My teacher will give me permission to leave school early.*

## alone *adjective, adverb*

without any other people: *Katie ran up to her bedroom because she wanted to be alone. | Can I talk to you alone for a minute?*

▶ **lonely** unhappy because you are alone: *I feel so lonely without my best friend.*

▶ **solitary** a solitary person or thing is the only one you can see in a place: *A solitary tree is standing on top of the hill.*

▶ **by yourself/by myself/by himself etc.** alone, or without other people helping you: *I tied my shoelaces by myself! | The children are all by themselves in the big house.*

a
b
c
d
e
f
g
h
i
j
k
l
m
n
o
p
q
r
s
t
u
v
w
x
y
z

**a**

b
c
d
e
f
g
h
i
j
k
l
m
n
o
p
q
r
s
t
u
v
w
x
y
z

## anger *noun*

angry feelings: *His voice was full of anger because he felt that he had been treated unfairly.*

▶ **rage** very strong anger: *I was filled with rage when I found out they had lied to me.*

▶ **fury** very strong anger: *"How dare you?" she yelled, shaking with fury.*

▶ **frustration** a feeling of being a little angry because you cannot do what you want: *When the little boy could not have his toy, he kicked the table in frustration.*

## angry *adjective*

feeling like you want to shout or hurt someone: *Mom was angry at me for making such a big mess.*

▶ **mad** angry: *Michael got mad at them because no one was listening to him.*

▶ **upset** angry and worried or sad about something: *Mom was upset when I went to the park without telling her.*

▶ **annoyed** a little angry about something that is not very serious: *I think he was annoyed with me because I asked too many questions.*

▶ **irritated** a little angry about something that is not very serious, especially something that keeps happening: *The teacher gets irritated when students are late.*

▶ **furious** very angry: *Dad will be furious when he finds out that you lost his new camera.*

▶ **in a bad mood** behaving in an unfriendly way and becoming angry easily, often for no reason: *Ellen keeps criticizing me all the time – is she in a bad mood today?*

## animal *noun*

a creature that breathes and moves: *My favorite animal is a horse.*

▶ **mammal** an animal that drinks its mother's milk when it is young: *Cats, dogs, cows, and horses are all mammals.*

▶ **invertebrate** a creature that does not have a backbone: *Worms are invertebrates.*

▶ **vertebrate** a creature that has a backbone: *Mammals are vertebrates, and so are fish and birds.*

▶ **arthropod** a type of invertebrate such as a spider or beetle that has a hard skeleton on the outside of its body, and pairs of legs: *Some arthropods such as crabs and lobsters live in the water.*

▶ **reptile** an animal such as a snake or lizard whose body is covered in scales. Reptiles are cold-blooded and most reptiles lay eggs containing their babies: *Snakes and other reptiles lie in the sun to warm up their bodies.*

▶ **amphibian** an animal, such as a frog, that starts its life living in water. When it is young, an amphibian breathes through gills like fish do. Amphibians later grow legs, breathe air, and live on land: *The smallest amphibian in the world is a tiny frog that lives in Cuba.*

▶ **marsupial** a type of animal that carries its babies in a pocket on the front of its body: *Kangaroos and other marsupials live in Australia.*

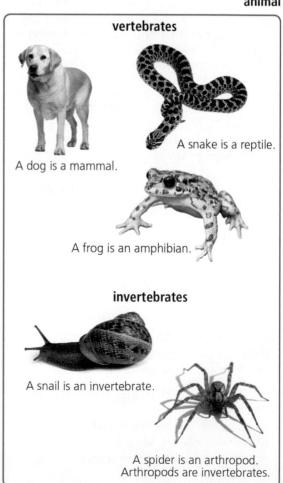

**animal**

**vertebrates**

A dog is a mammal.

A snake is a reptile.

A frog is an amphibian.

**invertebrates**

A snail is an invertebrate.

A spider is an arthropod.
Arthropods are invertebrates.

## answer *verb*

to say something after someone asks you a question or speaks to you: *The teacher answered my question and now I understand.* | *I said "hello" to her, but she didn't answer.*

▶ **reply** to answer. You often use **reply** when telling what someone said: *"Can I come too?" I asked. "Yes," she replied.* | *He didn't reply to my email.*

▶ **respond** to answer someone by saying or doing something: *When I asked him what time it was, he responded by pointing at the clock on the wall.*

▶ **write back** to write a letter or email to someone who has written to you: *When I send my friend an email, she always writes back.*

## area *noun*

a part of a town, country, or place: *The schools in our area are very good.* | *There is a play area for children, with swings and a sandbox.*

▶ **region** a large area that is part of a country or of the world: *The southeastern region of the United States includes Tennessee, Georgia, Alabama, and Mississippi.*

▶ **zone** a type of area where something happens, or where there are special rules: *Much of California is in an earthquake zone.* | *This is a no-parking zone. Drivers are not allowed to park their cars here.*

▶ **district** an area of a city or town: *My dad works in the city's business district.* | *There are a lot of old buildings in Boston's historic district.*

▶ **neighborhood** a small area of a city or town, where people live: *I like my neighborhood because the people are very friendly.*

## argue *verb*

if people argue, they shout or say angry things because they do not agree with each other: *My parents always argue with each other about money.*

▶ **fight** to argue, often in a very angry or excited way sometimes also hitting or kicking: *The kids started fighting in the back of the car and Dad told them to be quiet.*

▶ **disagree** to have a different opinion from someone about something, and sometimes to argue about it: *We disagreed about what movie we wanted to see.*

## argument *noun*

if people have an argument, they shout or say angry things because they do not agree with each other: *Mom and Dad had a big argument about money.*

▶ **fight** a situation in which people argue with each other in a very angry way, sometimes also hitting or kicking: *The two girls had a fight and now they are not talking to each other.*

▶ **disagreement** a situation in which people disagree or argue: *I had a disagreement with my mother about whether I could stay up late to watch a TV show.*

▶ **controversy** a lot of disagreement among people about something important: *The plan to build a new airport has caused controversy. Some people like the idea, but others are worried about airplane noise.*

## arrive *verb*

to get to a place: *James arrives at school at 8:30 a.m. every day.* | *What time does the bus arrive in Chicago?* (**ANTONYM: leave**)

▶ **get** to arrive somewhere: *What time did you get home?* | *By the time I got to the store it was closed.*

▶ **reach** to arrive somewhere, especially after a long or difficult trip: *It took them three days to reach the top of the mountain.*

▶ **land** if an airplane lands, it arrives on the ground at an airport: *The plane landed at 11:00 in the morning.*

a
b
c
d
e
f
g
h
i
j
k
l
m
n
o
p
q
r
s
t
u
v
w
x
y
z

a
b
c
d
e
f
g
h
i
j
k
l
m
n
o
p
q
r
s
t
u
v
w
x
y
z

### art *noun*

things such as paintings, drawings, and sculptures: *The museum has a big collection of modern art.*

▶ **painting** a picture that someone paints: *The children's paintings were drying on a rack.*

▶ **drawing** a picture you make with a pen or pencil: *He used colored pencils for his drawing of a boat.*

▶ **sculpture** a work of art that someone shapes from materials such as stone, metal, or wood: *There is a sculpture of a lion in front of the library.*

▶ **ceramics** pots, bowls, and other things that are made from clay: *In art we looked at ceramics and then made some beautiful pots.*

art

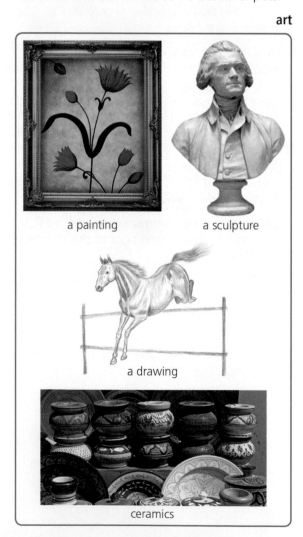

a painting       a sculpture

a drawing

ceramics

### artificial *adjective*

artificial things or flavors are not real or natural, but made by people: *Real flowers are nicer than artificial ones.* | *There are no artificial flavors in the juice.* ( **ANTONYM: natural** )

▶ **man-made** man-made materials or lakes are made by people and are not made naturally: *The new campsite has a man-made lake.* | *Man-made fibers like nylon are easy to wash.*

▶ **synthetic** a synthetic material is not natural and is made by people in a factory: *The shoes were made from some kind of synthetic material, not leather.*

▶ **false** false teeth or nails are made to look like real ones: *The old man has false teeth.*

▶ **imitation** imitation leather, jewelry, or guns are made to look like real ones: *My jacket is made of imitation leather, not real leather.*

▶ **virtual** made or done on a computer rather than in the real world: *We took a virtual tour of the Statue of Liberty.*

### ask *verb*

to say something that is a question: *I will ask her if she wants to go to the party.* | *You can ask your teacher to help you.*

▶ **question** to ask someone a lot of questions, in order to find out what this person knows about something: *Police are questioning a man about the robbery.*

▶ **consult** to ask someone for advice: *You should consult your doctor before you start a diet.*

▶ **inquire** to ask for information: *He inquired about the time of the next plane to Boston.*

▶ **beg** to ask for something that you want or need very much: *She begged me to help her.* | *People are begging for money in the street.*

▶ **demand** to ask for something in a very firm or angry way: *Angry parents will demand an explanation for closing the school.*

▶ **request** to ask for something, especially permission to do something: *Visitors must request permission if they want to take any photographs.*

# Bb

**baby** *noun*

**baby person**:

▶ **baby** a very young child, usually between the ages of zero and 12 months: *Babies cry when they are hungry.*

▶ **toddler** a baby who has learned to walk, usually between the ages of 12 months and two years: *The toddler walked toward me and then fell down.*

▶ **infant** a baby. **Infant** is a formal word: *Lay the infant on its back to sleep.*

**baby person**

a baby             a toddler

**baby animal**:

▶ **young** the babies of an animal or bird: *The young stay in the nest for six or seven weeks.*

▶ **kitten** a young cat

▶ **puppy** a young dog

▶ **lamb** a young sheep

▶ **piglet** a young pig

▶ **calf** a young cow

▶ **foal** a young horse

▶ **chick** a young bird

▶ **duckling** a young duck

▶ **colt** a young male horse

▶ **kid** a young goat

▶ **cub** a young lion, tiger, or bear

**baby animal**

a kitten       a puppy

a lamb       a piglet

a chick

a foal       a calf

**bad** *adjective*

not good: *I got a bad grade on my test. I got a D. | It's bad to lie to people. You should always tell the truth.* (ANTONYM: **good**)

▶ **awful** very bad: *The movie was awful. It was so boring. | What is that awful smell?*

▶ **terrible** very bad: *It was a terrible day. Everything went wrong.*

▶ **horrible** very bad in a way that shocks or upsets someone: *The weather has been horrible. It has rained all week.*

▶ **disgusting** smelling or tasting very bad: *The fish was disgusting and I couldn't eat it.*

a
**b**
c
d
e
f
g
h
i
j
k
l
m
n
o
p
q
r
s
t
u
v
w
x
y
z

## bag *noun*

a container used for carrying things: *He opened the bag of jelly beans and gave me one.* | *I carried some shopping bags for Mom.*

▶ **purse** a bag that women use to carry money and other things: *She always keeps a comb and a mirror in her purse.*

▶ **wallet** a small flat container where you keep money and plastic cards: *Do you have a $10 bill in your wallet?*

▶ **sack** a strong bag for storing or carrying food: *We bought a sack of potatoes.*

▶ **backpack** a bag that you carry on your back: *I carry my school books in my backpack.*

▶ **suitcase** a large bag with a handle. You carry clothes in a suitcase when you travel: *Don't forget to pack your suitcase – we're going on vacation tomorrow!*

▶ **luggage** the bags that you take with you when you are traveling: *We put our luggage in the back of the car.*

## beautiful *adjective*

very nice to look at. You use **beautiful** to describe a woman, girl, place, or thing: *She is very beautiful and has long dark hair and brown eyes.* | *You can see a beautiful view of the Grand Canyon.* | *They live in a beautiful old house.*

( ANTONYM: **ugly** )

▶ **handsome** nice to look at. You usually use **handsome** to describe a man: *Your dad looks very handsome in his army uniform.*

▶ **pretty** nice to look at. You use **pretty** to describe a woman, girl, or thing: *She has a pretty face.* | *The pink and blue curtains are very pretty.*

▶ **good-looking** nice to look at. You use **good-looking** about men or women: *John is tall and good-looking.*

▶ **cute** nice to look at. You use **cute** to describe a baby or animal that you want to cuddle. You also use **cute** about a person that you like: *What a cute little kitten!* | *My sister thinks you're cute!*

▶ **gorgeous** nice to look at, used to describe people or things: *I think Leonardo DiCaprio is gorgeous!* | *She was wearing a gorgeous blue dress.*

## become *verb*

to start to be: *The man became angry and started shouting at me.* | *She wants to become a doctor.* | *The stream became a river.*

▶ **get** to become: *I always get nervous before tests.*
You only use **get** before an adjective. You can use **become** before an adjective or a noun.

▶ **grow** to gradually change and become different: *In October, the weather starts to grow colder.* | *As you grow older, you start to forget things.*

▶ **go** to become a different color, or to become blind, deaf, or crazy: *The sun disappeared and the sky went gray.* | *Grandpa is going deaf, so he doesn't always hear things.*

▶ **turn** to change and become different: *In the fall, the leaves turn red and gold.* | *The weather turned colder.*

▶ **change into** to become something completely different: *The prince changed into a frog.* | *This sofa changes into a bed.*

## beginning *noun*

the first part of something: *We moved to San Diego at the beginning of the year.* | *I arrived late and I missed the beginning of the movie.*

( ANTONYM: **end** )

▶ **start** the beginning, especially the time or the way something begins: *The start of the show is at two o'clock.* | *It was a bad start when I was late on my first day of school.*

▶ **origin** where something came from or began: *The origin of the word Sierra is Spanish.*

▶ **starting point** the event or situation from which something starts happening: *The unfair taxes were the starting point for the American Revolution.*

## big *adjective*

if something is big, it has a large size: *Their house is very big – it has eight bedrooms.* | *Houston is a big city and over two million people live there.*

( ANTONYM: **small** )

▶ **large** **large** means the same as **big**. You can say *a big house* or *a large house*.
In some sentences, it is better to use **large**, not **big**.
You say *a large number*: *There are a large number of girls in the class.* You do not say "a big number of girls."
You say *a large amount*: *He eats a large amount of food.* You do not say "a big amount of food."

▶ **huge** very big: *Elephants are huge animals.* | *The palace is huge. It has over 100 rooms.*

▶ **enormous** very big. **Enormous** means the same as **huge**: *The tree was more than 300 feet tall.* | *The store has an enormous variety of toys.*

▶ **gigantic** very very big. **Gigantic** is even bigger than **huge** or **enormous**: *A gigantic storm blew down all the houses.*

▶ **vast** a vast area of land is very big: *The forest is vast and continues for hundreds of miles.*

## boat *noun*

a thing that you use to travel over water: *We went up the river by boat.* | *a fishing boat*

▶ **ship** a large boat that carries people and things on the ocean: *The ship is crossing the Atlantic.*

▶ **yacht** a boat used for sailing or racing: *He is sailing around the world in a yacht.*

▶ **sailboat** a small boat with one or more sails. When the wind pushes against the sails, the sailboat moves across the water: *The wind filled the sails and the sailboat began to move across the lake.*

▶ **canoe** a light narrow boat that you move through the water using a paddle: *They paddled up the river in their canoe.*

▶ **rowboat** a small boat for one or two people that you move through the water using oars: *We went out in the rowboat to fish.*

▶ **ferry** a boat that regularly takes people across an area of water and back again: *There's a ferry to the island that leaves once an hour.*

**boat**

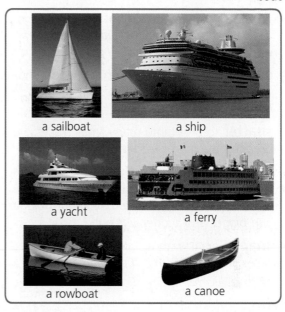

a sailboat

a ship

a yacht

a ferry

a rowboat

a canoe

## boring *adjective*

not interesting: *I didn't like the show. It was for grown-ups and was really boring.*

( ANTONYM: **interesting** )

▶ **dull** boring because nothing exciting happens: *It was a dull game because no one scored any goals.*

▶ **tedious** boring, and continuing for a long time: *The car trip was long and tedious.*

▶ **monotonous** boring because the same thing keeps happening, and nothing changes: *Factory work is very monotonous and you have to do the same thing again and again.*

## brave *adjective*

not afraid to do something difficult or dangerous: *You have to be brave to be a soldier.*

▶ **courageous** very brave: *The firefighters received medals for their courageous actions.*

▶ **daring** if you are daring, you try to do something, even though you know it is risky and things could go wrong: *One of the boys did a daring jump from high in the tree and we were worried that he had hurt his leg.*

▶ **bold** brave and confident: *I wasn't bold enough to tell her what I really thought.*

a b c d e f g h i j k l m n o p q r s t u v w x y z

a
**b**
c
d
e
f
g
h
i
j
k
l
m
n
o
p
q
r
s
t
u
v
w
x
y
z

## break *verb*

to separate into pieces: *If the cup falls on the floor, it will break. | I broke my arm when I was skateboarding.*

▶ **crack** to break in a way that makes a line on the surface: *The ice on the lake cracked when I walked on it.*

▶ **smash** to break violently, or with a loud noise: *The police smashed the door down with a hammer.*

▶ **shatter** to break into many small pieces: *He dropped the mirror, and it shattered into a thousand pieces.*

▶ **burst** if a balloon, bag, or pipe bursts, it breaks open suddenly: *The balloon got bigger and bigger and suddenly it burst.*

▶ **snap** to break with a short loud noise: *The sticks were so dry that they snapped in half easily.*

## bright *adjective*

shining with a lot of light: *I can see the bright lights of the city.*

▶ **sunny** if the weather is sunny, there is a lot of sunshine: *The sky is very blue and I think it will be sunny and warm today.*

▶ **strong** strong sun or sunshine is very bright and hot: *In the middle of the day, the sun is very strong.*

▶ **brilliant** very bright in a way that is beautiful: *The moon is shining and there are thousands of brilliant stars in the sky.*

▶ **dazzling** very bright, so that you cannot see clearly for a short time: *The headlights of the car were dazzling and I couldn't see the driver.*

▶ **shiny** having a smooth surface that reflects the light: *My new bicycle is red and shiny.*

## build *verb*

to make a building, bridge, or other structure: *They are going to build a new house next to our house. | The girl built a tower out of blocks.*

▶ **construct** to build something big or complicated: *The tunnel through the mountain took years to construct.*

▶ **assemble** to put the different parts of something together: *It's easy to assemble the shelves with a few simple tools.*

▶ **put up** to build a wall, fence, small building, or statue: *Dad put up a fence in our backyard. | A statue was put up in his honor.*

## burn *verb*

to destroy or damage something with fire or heat: *She put the letters on the fire and burned them. | Try not to burn the toast.*

▶ **scorch** to burn the surface of something and make it change color: *Mom scorched my shirt when she was ironing it so there is a brown mark on it now.*

▶ **scald** to burn yourself with hot liquid or steam: *I scalded my hand with some boiling water from the pan.*

▶ **singe** to burn something slightly by touching something hot: *I singed my hair when I stood too close to the candle flame.*

▶ **be on fire** if something is on fire, flames are burning and destroying it: *The house is on fire! There is smoke coming from the window!*

## butterfly *noun*

an insect with large and usually colored wings

▶ **caterpillar** the young form of a butterfly: *Caterpillars eat the leaves of plants and sometimes damage crops.*

▶ **chrysalis** a butterfly at the time when it has a hard covering and is changing from a caterpillar into an adult

**butterfly**

a caterpillar

a chrysalis

a butterfly

## buy *verb*

to get something by paying money for it: *My parents will buy me a new bike!* (ANTONYM: **sell**)

▶ **get** to buy something, especially something ordinary that you use every day: *Can you go to the store and get some milk? | I need to get some new clothes.*

▶ **purchase** to buy something. **Purchase** is a very formal word: *They purchased the house last year.*

▶ **stock up** to buy a lot of something, so that you can use it later: *In the fall we stock up on firewood for the winter.*

▶ **import** to buy a lot of goods from another country: *The U.S. imports seven billion barrels of oil a year, mostly from the Middle East.*

# Cc

## cake *noun*

a sweet food made by baking a mixture of flour, butter, sugar, and eggs: *There are ten candles on his birthday cake. | Would you like a piece of cake?*

▶ **pie** a dessert that consists of pastry that has fruit or a custard filling inside it. You bake the pie in a round dish in the oven: *Can I have another slice of apple pie? | We had pumpkin pie at Thanksgiving.*

▶ **cookie** a small flat cake that is baked until it is hard: *Mom's making chocolate chip cookies.*

▶ **cupcake** a small round sweet cake that usually has frosting on the top. Frosting is a thick sweet substance made from sugar: *I like cupcakes with a lot of frosting on them.*

▶ **muffin** a small round cake. Muffins often have fruit such as blueberries in them: *The blueberry muffins are nice and moist.*

▶ **doughnut** a small round cake that usually has a hole in the middle and that is cooked in hot oil: *I have a bag of doughnuts for us to share.*

**cake**

a cake  
a pie  
cookies  
a cupcake  
a muffin  
a doughnut

## calculate *verb*

to find out a number or amount using mathematics: *Calculate how many apples you can buy with $4, if they cost 50 cents each.*

▶ **estimate** to guess at a number or amount, using the information you have: *The teacher asked us to estimate how many jelly beans were in the jar.*

▶ **add** to put numbers together to get the total. The symbol that tells you to add numbers is +: *If you add 5 and 3, the sum is 8. (5 + 3 = 8)*

▶ **subtract** to take one number away from another number. The symbol that tells you to subtract numbers is −: *If you subtract 2 from 7, the difference is 5. (7 − 2 = 5)*

▶ **multiply** to add a number to itself a particular number of times. The symbol that tells you to multiply numbers is ×: *3 multiplied by 4 is 12.*

▶ **divide** to find how many times a bigger number contains a smaller number. The symbol for divide is ÷: *18 divided by 6 is 3.*

a b **c** d e f g h i j k l m n o p q r s t u v w x y z

**a b c d e f g h i j k l m n o p q r s t u v w x y z**

## calm *adjective*

not angry or upset: *Mom is calm and she never gets angry with anyone.*

▶ **relaxed** feeling comfortable because you are not worried about anything: *We all felt relaxed on vacation.*

▶ **laid-back** always relaxed and not worried about things: *Joe's parents are laid-back and don't mind if he watches a lot of TV.*

▶ **peaceful** if a place is peaceful, it is quiet and it makes you feel calm: *On weekends the town is peaceful because there isn't much traffic.*

## careful *adjective*

thinking about what you are doing, so you do not make mistakes or damage things: *Be careful not to get any dirt on your clothes.* | *The vase was very fragile and I was careful not to drop it.*
( **ANTONYM: careless** )

▶ **cautious** careful because you want to avoid danger or problems: *My aunt is a cautious driver so she drives very slowly.*

▶ **conscientious** careful to do everything that you have been asked to do in the correct way: *Michael is a conscientious student who does all of his homework.*

▶ **meticulous** very careful to make sure that every small detail is right: *Her meticulous drawings show every part of the plants clearly.*

## careless *adjective*

not thinking about what you are doing, so that you make mistakes or damage things: *She is careless about spelling so there are lots of mistakes in her essay.* ( **ANTONYM: careful** )

▶ **clumsy** moving in a careless way so that you often drop, hit, or break something: *He is clumsy and often knocks things over.*

▶ **reckless** careless and dangerous: *Reckless driving causes a lot of accidents.*

▶ **thoughtless** not caring about the effect of your actions on other people's feelings: *It was thoughtless of you not to call us, because we were very worried.*

▶ **irresponsible** behaving in a bad and careless way that could cause something bad to happen: *It's irresponsible to get a dog if you don't have time to take care of it.*

## castle *noun*

a large stone building with high walls or water around it. Castles were built in the Middle Ages to protect the people inside during wars: *The castle had a tall round tower at each corner.*

▶ **fort** a strong building used by soldiers to defend a place in past times: *The soldiers built a fort to protect the settlers.*

▶ **palace** a large house for a king, queen, or other ruler: *The princess lived in a beautiful palace with 50 rooms.*

**castle**

a palace          a castle

a fort

## catch *verb*

to stop or get a person or animal that wants to escape from you: *It was hard to catch him because he ran so fast.* | *Our cat is always catching mice.*

▶ **arrest** if the police arrest someone, they take that person to the police station because they believe he or she has done something illegal: *He was arrested for stealing a car.*

▶ **capture** to catch a person or animal in order to keep him, her, or it somewhere: *He was captured by enemy soldiers and kept as a prisoner for three years.*

▶ **trap** to catch an animal in a trap: *The hunters used to trap animals to get their skins.*

## cave *noun*

a big hole in the side of a cliff or under the ground: *We explored the cave using flashlights.*

▶ **cavern** a big cave: *They discovered an enormous cavern, deep under the ground.*

▶ **tunnel** a long hole through a mountain or under the ground: *The subway tunnel goes under the street.*

▶ **burrow** a hole in the ground that a rabbit or other small animal lives in: *The rabbit went down into its burrow.*

cave

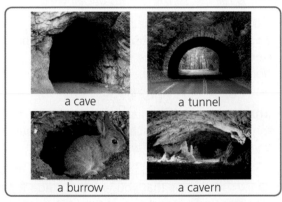

a cave     a tunnel
a burrow     a cavern

## change *verb*

to become different, or to make something different: *The school has changed a lot and there are many more students. | I want to change my hairstyle to have short hair.*

▶ **alter** **alter** means the same as **change**. You often use **alter** about small changes: *It started raining, so we altered our plans and had the party inside the house.*

▶ **adjust** to change something a little, to make it better: *You can adjust the height of the chair so that you are comfortable.*

▶ **convert** to change something so that you can use it for something else: *They converted the old factory buildings into apartments. | Your body converts sugar into energy.*

▶ **transform** to change someone or something completely: *In the chrysalis, the caterpillar transforms into a beautiful butterfly.*

## cheap *adjective*

costing very little money: *The dress was cheap – it only cost me $5.* ( ANTONYM: **expensive** )

▶ **inexpensive** not costing a lot of money: *The jewelry is inexpensive but it still good quality.*

▶ **low** low prices, rents, and costs are cheap: *The restaurant's prices are low and you can get a burger for under $3. | The rent on our apartment is very low.*

▶ **reasonable** a reasonable price seems fair and not too high: *A hundred dollars is a reasonable price for a new bicycle.*

▶ **economical** an economical car uses less fuel. An economical way of doing something saves you money: *Our car has a small engine and is more economical than other cars because it doesn't use as much gas. | It's more economical to buy a big bottle of shampoo because it lasts a long time.*

▶ **affordable** if something is affordable, most people have enough money to pay for it: *The store sells designer clothes at affordable prices.*

## choose *verb*

to decide to have something or do something: *A lot of students choose to study Spanish. | I chose a book on dinosaurs.*

▶ **pick** to choose a person or thing from a group: *The magician asked him to pick a card from the deck. | I hope the coach picks me for the basketball team.*

▶ **select** to choose a person or thing, especially in a careful way: *Look at the pictures, and then select the one that you want to talk about.*

▶ **elect** to choose a leader or a representative by voting: *We elected a new president in 2008.*

▶ **appoint** to choose someone to do an important job: *The president appointed a new Supreme Court judge.*

a
b
c
d
e
f
g
h
i
j
k
l
m
n
o
p
q
r
s
t
u
v
w
x
y
z

a
b
c
d
e
f
g
h
i
j
k
l
m
n
o
p
q
r
s
t
u
v
w
x
y
z

## clean *verb*

to remove the dirt from something: *Dad will pay me $5 to clean his car.* | *Bobby never cleans his room so it's really dirty.*

▶ **wash** to clean something using water and soap: *I always wash my hands before I eat.* | *Can you wash the dishes?*

▶ **wipe** to clean something by moving a cloth across it: *The waitress wiped the table with a cloth.*

▶ **brush** to clean something using a brush: *You need to brush your teeth every day to keep them healthy.*

▶ **scrub** to wash something by rubbing it hard with a brush or cloth: *I scrubbed the bathtub until it shined.*

▶ **polish** to rub something to make it shiny: *He polished his shoes until they were shiny.*

clean

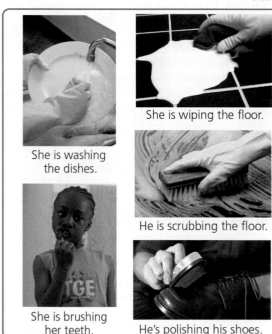

She is washing the dishes.

She is wiping the floor.

He is scrubbing the floor.

She is brushing her teeth.

He's polishing his shoes.

## close *verb*

to make a door, window, or your eyes stop being open: *I closed the window to keep out the noise of the traffic.* | *The baby slowly closed his eyes and started to sleep.* (**ANTONYM: open**)

▶ **shut** **shut** means the same as **close**. You often use **shut** when you close something quickly and firmly: *Shut the door and lock it.*

▶ **slam** to shut something with a loud noise, usually because you are angry: *He walked angrily out of the room and slammed the door.*

▶ **draw** to close curtains by pulling them across a window: *Draw the curtains before you go to bed.*

▶ **fasten** to join together the two sides of a belt or a piece of clothing: *Fasten your seatbelt before we start driving.*

## clothes *plural noun*

things that you wear, for example a sweater or a skirt: *It is raining so my clothes are all wet.*

▶ **clothing** **clothing** means the same as **clothes**. You use **clothing** when talking about **clothes** in general: *The store sells men's clothing.* | *It's important to take plenty of warm clothing when you go skiing.*

▶ **uniform** special clothes that people wear for some jobs, sports, or schools: *The Cub Scout uniform is a blue shirt and blue pants or shorts.* | *Police officers usually wear uniforms.*

▶ **costume** clothes that you wear on stage for a play or a performance: *The actors are wearing beautiful costumes.*

## cold *adjective*

having a low temperature: *It's cold in the mountains in winter.* | *Drink your hot chocolate before it gets cold.* (**ANTONYM: hot**)

▶ **cool** a little cold, in a way that seems nice: *There is a nice cool breeze.* | *I want a cool drink.*

▶ **chilly** chilly weather feels a little cold: *It was chilly outside in the evening, so I had to wear a sweater.*

▶ **freezing** very cold: *There was no heat so the room was freezing.*

▶ **icy** icy wind or water is very cold: *He put his hand into the icy water of the lake.*

▶ **frosty** if the weather is frosty, it is cold and things are covered in a thin powder of white ice: *It was a frosty morning in January.*

## comfortable *adjective*

comfortable clothes, furniture, or rooms make you feel relaxed: *The chair is really soft and comfortable.* | *I want some comfortable shoes that won't hurt my feet.*

▶ **cozy** warm and comfortable: *It is very cozy in front of the fire.* | *My bed is nice and cozy.*

▶ **snug** small and comfortable: *The cabin only has one bedroom but it's very snug in winter.*

▶ **luxurious** very expensive and comfortable: *The movie star lives in a luxurious apartment in Manhattan.*

## competition *noun*

an event in which people or teams try to be the best at doing something: *She came second in a gymnastics competition.* | *I got first prize in the competition.*

▶ **contest** a competition in which a group of judges decide the winner: *I decided to enter the school poetry contest.*

▶ **race** a competition in which people try to run, drive, swim, or ride faster than each other: *He won the race with a time of 9.69 seconds.*

▶ **championship** a competition to find the best player or team in a sport: *Nadal is expected to win the tennis championship this year.*

▶ **tournament** a competition in which many players or teams compete against each other until there is one winner: *They are playing the final game of the chess tournament.*

▶ **league** a group of sports teams that play against each other: *Our high school baseball team finished second in the league.*

## complain *verb*

to say that you are annoyed or not satisfied with something: *One of the neighbors complained about the noise from our party.* | *She complained to the waiter about the soup because it was cold.*

▶ **grumble** to keep complaining about something in a bad-tempered way: *He grumbles about having to get up in the morning.*

▶ **whine** to complain about something in an annoying way: *Stop whining about how hungry you are!*

▶ **object** to say that you do not agree with a plan: *When I suggested calling our basketball team the Tigers, no one objected.*

▶ **protest** if people protest, they show in public that they do not agree with something: *People stood outside the store to protest against the sale of fur coats.*

## confused *adjective*

if you are confused, you do not know what to do, or do not understand something: *She got confused and went to the wrong house.*

▶ **puzzled** confused because you cannot understand why something has happened: *I was puzzled when she said she didn't want to be my friend anymore.*

▶ **bewildered** very confused: *He was bewildered by all the questions they were asking him.*

## continue *verb*

to not stop: *The rain will continue all morning.* | *He continued talking for another few minutes.*

▶ **go on** **go on** means the same as **continue**: *We went on playing our game.* | *The party will go on until midnight.*

▶ **carry on** **carry on** means the same as **continue**: *We carried on driving for another ten miles.*

▶ **keep** to continue to do something for a long time, or to do something many times: *Keep driving till you come to the next traffic lights.* | *He kept saying he was sorry.*

▶ **last** to continue for a period of time: *The game lasted three hours.*

**cook** *verb*
to make food ready to eat by heating it: *She cooked us a great meal.* | *I cook the mushrooms in a frying pan.*

► **bake** to cook something such as bread or a cake in an oven: *Let's bake a cake for Sam's birthday.*

► **roast** to cook meat or vegetables in an oven: *We always roast a turkey for Thanksgiving.*

► **fry** to cook something in hot oil or butter: *I fried some bacon for breakfast.*

► **boil** to cook food in boiling water: *Boil the spaghetti for eight minutes.*

► **broil** to cook food directly over or under flames or heat: *She broiled the chicken until the skin was crisp.*

► **poach** to cook eggs or fish in a little water or liquid: *I poached the eggs in some water.*

**copy** *noun*
something that is made to look exactly the same as something else: *The picture is a copy of a painting by Picasso. The original painting is in the Museum of Modern Art.*

► **photocopy** a copy of a piece of writing or a picture that you make using a machine called a photocopier: *I made a photocopy of the letter.*

► **duplicate** an exact copy of something: *He gave me a duplicate of his front door key.*

► **fake** a copy of an object that is intended to deceive people: *The $50 billl was a fake!*

► **forgery** a copy of a document, painting, or piece of paper money that is intended to deceive people: *The signature on the check wasn't hers. It was a forgery!*

**cost** *noun*
the amount of money you must pay for something: *My dad says he will pay for the cost of fixing my bicycle.*

► **price** the amount of money you must pay to buy something, especially in a store: *This store's prices are much lower than other stores' prices.*

► **charge** the amount of money you must pay to use or do something: *There is a charge for entry to the museum.*

► **fee** the amount of money you must pay to join a club, go to some schools, have medical treatment, or visit a lawyer: *The membership fee for the club is $25 a year.* | *The insurance company paid all her medical fees when she was in the hospital.*

► **rent** the amount of money you must pay each month to live in a place: *The rent on our apartment is $800 a month.*

► **fare** the amount of money you must pay to travel by bus, train, or airplane: *Mom gave me money for the bus fare.*

**country** *noun*
a large area of land with its own government: *Canada is a very big country.*

► **nation** a country, and the people in it: *We learned about the history of our nation.*

► **state** a country, or part of a country that has its own government. You use **state** to mean a country when you are talking about politics that involves other countries: *The president had meetings with the leaders of other states.* You use **state** about a part of a country especially when you are talking about America: *Chicago is in the state of Illinois.*

► **colony** a country that is controlled by a more powerful country: *The United States used to be a colony of Great Britain.*

► **land** a country. **Land** is used especially in stories: *He told them of his adventures in foreign lands.*

**crime** *noun*
an action that the law does not allow, for example stealing something or attacking someone: *He was sent to prison as a punishment for his crime.* | *The police's job is to fight crime.*

► **offense** a crime. You often use **offense** when talking about less serious actions, for example driving too fast, or parking illegally: *It is an offense to park here without a permit.*

► **robbery** a crime in which someone steals something, usually in a violent way: *There was a robbery at the bank and the robbers took over $1 million.*

▶ **burglary** a crime in which someone steals things from a house or office when no one else is there: *The best way to prevent a burglary is to get a good alarm system for your house.*

▶ **murder** the crime of deliberately killing someone: *He went to trial for the murder of a young woman.*

▶ **mugging** the crime of attacking and robbing someone in the street: *This is a dangerous area of the city, because there are a lot of muggings here.*

## criminal *noun*

someone who breaks the law: *Criminals should be punished and put in jail.*

▶ **thief** someone who steals things: *A thief stole her handbag.*

▶ **robber** someone who steals something, usually in a violent way: *The robber threatened the store manager with a gun.*

▶ **burglar** someone who goes into a building to steal things when no one else is there: *The burglars got into the house through a window and took the computer.*

▶ **mugger** someone who attacks and robs people: *The mugger hit him and stole his phone.*

▶ **murderer** someone who kills someone else on purpose: *The murderer will stay in prison for the rest of his life.*

## cry *verb*

to produce tears from your eyes, especially because you are unhappy or in pain: *The little boy was crying because he was lost.*

▶ **weep** to cry a lot, especially because you are very unhappy: *Everyone at the funeral was weeping.*

▶ **sob** to cry in a noisy way: *Sarah was sobbing noisily on the phone, and it was difficult to understand what she was saying.*

▶ **bawl** to cry very loudly: *She fell and hurt her knee and started to bawl.*

▶ **burst into tears** to suddenly start crying: *When I asked my sister why she was unhappy, she burst into tears.*

## cut *verb*

to remove or divide something using a knife or scissors: *She cut the cake in two. | They are cutting down all the trees. | Can you cut another slice of pizza for me?*

▶ **slice** to cut something into thin flat pieces: *I sliced the cheese and put it in my sandwich.*

▶ **chop** to cut something into pieces using an ax or a knife: *Joe is outside chopping wood. | Chop the onions up into small pieces.*

▶ **saw** to cut wood using a tool that you push forward and backward: *My dad sawed the wood in half.*

▶ **carve** to cut wood or stone into a shape, or to cut slices from a large piece of cooked meat: *He was carving a piece of wood into the figure of a deer. | Shall I carve the turkey now?*

**cut**

She is slicing bread.

He is chopping wood.

He is sawing wood.

He is carving wood.

a b **c** d e f g h i j k l m n o p q r s t u v w x y z

a
b
c
**d**
e
f
g
h
i
j
k
l
m
n
o
p
q
r
s
t
u
v
w
x
y
z

# Dd

## damage *verb*

to cause harm to something: *The storm damaged the roof of the school.* | *Our car was damaged in the accident.*

▶ **break** to damage something so that it does not work or it cannot be used: *I dropped my camera on the floor and I broke it.* | *Don't bend the ruler, or it will break!*

▶ **scratch** to damage a painted or polished surface by making long thin marks on it with something sharp or rough: *Be careful not to scratch the table with those scissors.*

▶ **crack** to break something and make it have a line on its surface: *He fell against the mirror and cracked the glass.*

▶ **smash** to deliberately break something using a lot of force: *The burglars smashed a window to get inside the house.*

▶ **vandalize** to deliberately damage buildings or vehicles in a public place: *Someone vandalized the school last night. The walls are covered with spray paint.*

## damp *adjective*

slightly wet: *Mom washed my clothes this morning, and they are still damp.* | *The grass was damp so I didn't want to sit on it.* ( ANTONYM: **dry** )

▶ **moist** slightly wet, especially in a nice way. You use **moist** when talking about food: *The cake was nice and moist.*

▶ **clammy** **clammy** skin feels cold and wet because you are sweating: *I was nervous and my hands were clammy.*

▶ **humid** if the weather is humid, the air feels hot and full of moisture: *It gets very hot and humid in New Orleans in July, so it can be uncomfortable.*

## dance *noun*

an event or party where people move their bodies in time to music: *The dance will take place in the school gymnasium.*

▶ **ball** a large formal event, where people dance and wear formal clothes: *The princess wore a beautiful silver gown to the ball.*

▶ **prom** a formal dance party for students in high school: *She went to the prom with her boyfriend.*

▶ **ballet** a type of artistic performance in which movement and dancing are used to tell a story: *My sister wants to become a ballet dancer.*

## dangerous *adjective*

likely to cause death or serious injury: *The river is a dangerous place for swimming because it is very deep.* ( ANTONYM: **safe** )

▶ **risky** if something is risky, there is a chance that something bad will happen if you do it: *It was too risky to leave the money in my room, so my mom put it in the bank.*

▶ **poisonous** containing something that will make you very sick or kill you: *The berries are poisonous so you must not eat them.* | *Some snakes are poisonous.*

▶ **toxic** toxic chemicals are very poisonous: *The factory dumped toxic chemicals in the river and killed all the fish.*

## dark *adjective*

if a place is dark, there is little or no light: *The sun has gone down and the sky is dark.*
( ANTONYM: **light** )

▶ **gloomy** not bright or cheerful: *The doctor's office was a gloomy room with gray walls.*

▶ **shady** a **shady** place is protected from the light of the sun: *There is a shady spot under the trees.*

▶ **dim** **dim** light is not bright, and you cannot see clearly: *The light was dim so I couldn't read my book.*

## dead *adjective*

no longer alive: *His grandmother has been dead for five years.* (ANTONYM: **alive**)

▶ **deceased** dead. **Deceased** is a very formal word: *The house belonged to her deceased grandparents.*

▶ **extinct** if a type of animal is extinct, it no longer exists: *The dinosaurs became extinct millions of years ago.*

## decide *verb*

to choose what you are going to do: *I decided to take the bus to school.*

▶ **make up your mind** to decide what to do, especially after thinking about it for a long time: *I can't make up my mind about what I want for my birthday.*

▶ **resolve** to decide that you will definitely do something in the future: *He resolved to go on a diet when he put on weight.*

▶ **conclude** to decide that something is true, based on the facts that you know: *All the lights in the house were off, so I concluded that she wasn't home.*

▶ **rule** to make an official decision about something, especially in a court of law: *The judge ruled that the thieves should go to prison.*

## defeat *verb*

to win against someone in a game, war, or election: *The Dolphins defeated the Jets 24–17.*

▶ **beat** to defeat someone: *I always beat my brother at chess.*
**Beat** means the same as **defeat**. When you are talking about wars and battles, you normally use **defeat**, not **beat**: *George Washington defeated the British at the battle of Princeton in 1778.*

▶ **conquer** to defeat a group of people in a war and take their land: *The Spanish conquered large parts of South America.*

▶ **overcome** to fight and win against someone, especially after using a lot of effort: *The soldiers overcame the enemy after a fierce battle.*

## delicious *adjective*

delicious food tastes very good: *This chocolate ice cream is delicious. Can I have some more?*

▶ **tasty** **tasty** food has a nice strong taste: *My aunt cooked us a tasty bean stew.*

▶ **mouth-watering** **mouth-watering** food looks or smells very good and makes you want to eat it: *The cakes looked mouth-watering and I wanted to try them all.*

## description *noun*

a statement that tells you about someone or something: *The teacher asked us to write a description of what was happening in the picture.*

▶ **report** a description that gives facts and information about someone or something: *His school report says that he is a very good student and he tries very hard in class. | There was a report about the school project in the local newspaper.*

▶ **commentary** a spoken description of what is happening during a race or sports event: *I listened to the commentary on the baseball game on my dad's car radio.*

## destroy *verb*

to damage something so badly that it no longer exists or cannot be repaired: *The fire destroyed most of the house. | The bridge was destroyed in the earthquake.*

▶ **wreck** to damage something badly so that it is in pieces: *His car was wrecked in a crash. | The storm wrecked hundreds of homes.*

▶ **demolish** to knock down a building or wall. People often demolish old buildings to build new ones: *The old houses were demolished so a new apartment building could be built.*

▶ **devastate** to destroy everything in a large area: *The earthquake devastated large areas of the city and many people were left without homes.*

▶ **ruin** to damage something so that it looks very bad: *During the flood, water came into the house and the carpet was ruined.*

a
b
c
**d**
e
f
g
h
i
j
k
l
m
n
o
p
q
r
s
t
u
v
w
x
y
z

a
b
c

**d**

e
f
g
h
i
j
k
l
m
n
o
p
q
r
s
t
u
v
w
x
y
z

**die** *verb*

to stop living: *My grandmother died last year.* | *People are dying because they do not have enough food.* ( ANTONYM: **live** )

▶ **be killed** to die in an accident or an attack: *The car hit a tree and three people were killed.* | *Eight soldiers were killed when the bomb exploded.*

▶ **pass away** to die. You use **pass away** when you want to be polite: *The doctor told us that Aunt Louise had passed away in the night.*

**different** *adjective*

not the same: *The two girls look very different from each other. One is tall, and the other is short.* ( ANTONYM: **same** )

▶ **distinctive** different and easy to recognize: *Pineapple has a distinctive taste which makes it different from other fruits.*

▶ **alternative** an **alternative** way of doing something is a different one that you can use: *The road was blocked, so we had to find an alternative route to school.* | *Oil and coal cause a lot of pollution, so scientists are trying to find alternative sources of energy.*

▶ **various** of several different kinds: *There are various ways to cook eggs. You can boil them, fry them, or you can use them to make an omelet.*

▶ **unique** very special and different from every other person or thing: *He has his own unique way of playing the guitar. No one else plays like him.*

**difficult** *adjective*

not easy to do or understand: *The questions on the test were difficult and I couldn't answer them all.* ( ANTONYM: **easy** )

▶ **hard** difficult or tiring: *It's hard to understand people if they talk fast.* | *I had a hard day at school today and I need to rest.*

▶ **tough** very difficult because you have to use a lot of effort: *My dad has a tough job. He works as a doctor in a busy hospital.*

▶ **tricky** difficult because you could easily make a mistake: *Finding your way out of the forest can be tricky, especially at night. It's easy to get lost.*

▶ **complicated** difficult to understand because it has many parts: *Chess is a complicated game because there are a lot of rules.*

**dirty** *adjective*

not clean: *My jeans are dirty because I played baseball in them.* ( ANTONYM: **clean** )

▶ **filthy** very dirty: *John never cleans his room and it looks filthy.*

▶ **muddy** covered with mud: *Take your muddy shoes off before you come into the house!*

▶ **dusty** covered with dust: *I found some dusty old books that nobody had touched for years.*

▶ **greasy** covered with oil or grease: *His hair is greasy because he hasn't washed it for a long time.*

▶ **polluted** polluted air or water has a lot of harmful chemicals in it: *The river is polluted and a lot of the fish have died.*

**disadvantage** *noun*

a bad feature of something, which makes it seem less good: *The disadvantage of the car is that it uses a lot of fuel.* | *In class, we discussed the advantages and disadvantages of nuclear energy.* ( ANTONYM: **advantage** )

▶ **drawback** a disadvantage. You use **drawback** when something is good in other ways: *The only drawback of the best camera is the price.*

▶ **catch** a problem that you do not realize at first: *Three dollars for a T-shirt sounds cheap, but there is a catch. The material tears easily.*

**disappear** *verb*

if something disappears, you can no longer see it, or it stops existing: *The cat disappeared over the wall.* | *Much of the forest has disappeared because the trees have been cut down.*

▶ **vanish** to disappear suddenly or mysteriously: *I left the money on my desk and now it has vanished.* | *The clouds vanished and the sun came out.*

▶ **fade** to slowly disappear. You use **fade** about light, colors, or feelings: *It was getting late, and the light was beginning to fade from the sky.* | *My hopes of passing the test are fading.*

▶ **become extinct** if a type of animal **becomes extinct**, it disappears because they have all died: *If the ice in the Arctic melts, polar bears will become extinct.*

## discover *verb*

to find something for the first time, especially new information or a new place: *Scientists have discovered a new star.* | *We discovered that we went to kindergarten together.*

▶ **invent** to think of something completely new, especially a product or machine: *Alexander Graham Bell invented the telephone in 1876.*

▶ **find out** to get new information about something: *Your homework is to find out three facts about lions.*

▶ **detect** to find something that is not easy to notice: *Dogs can detect the smell of food from far away.*

## discussion *noun*

a meeting at which people talk about their ideas or opinions about something: *We had a discussion about the best place to have the party.*

▶ **debate** a discussion in which a group of people talk about their opinions about a subject and say why they agree or disagree: *In class, we had a debate on whether TV is good for us or not.*

▶ **talks** discussions between representatives of governments, companies, or groups, so that they can reach an agreement about something: *The company is having talks with the union about pay.*

▶ **negotiations** **negotiations** means the same as **talks**: *The United States and Russia are having negotiations about reducing the number of nuclear weapons.*

## disease *noun*

a type of illness, especially one that spreads from one person to another, or that affects a part of your body: *Chickenpox is a disease that is common among young children.* | *Michael suffers from a rare skin disease.*

▶ **illness** a problem with your health that makes you feel sick, especially one that makes it difficult for you to work or have a normal life: *She has missed a lot of school because of illness.* | *My grandpa died after a long illness.*

▶ **bug** a disease that is not serious. It spreads from one person to another, often in the air or in food: *There is a bug going around the school, and a lot of students have been sick.*

▶ **virus** a very small living thing that causes a disease and spreads from one person to another. A virus is too small to see: *The virus that causes the flu started in pigs and it now affects humans.*

## dishonest *adjective*

someone who is dishonest deceives people, for example by lying, stealing, or cheating: *He is dishonest. He steals things from other students in his class.* ( ANTONYM: **honest** )

▶ **devious** good at secretly thinking of ways of tricking people: *Paula is very devious. She sometimes pretends to be sick, so that she can avoid going to school.*

▶ **untruthful** not telling the truth: *She found out that her son had been untruthful. He had lied about the money.*

▶ **corrupt** using your power dishonestly, especially in order to get money: *A corrupt police officer took money to help the prisoners escape from the jail.*

▶ **suspicious** behaving in a way that looks dishonest: *The two boys were standing next to my bike in a very suspicious way. I thought they were going to steal it.*

a
b
c
d
e
f
g
h
i
j
k
l
m
n
o
p
q
r
s
t
u
v
w
x
y
z

**do** *verb*

you **do** an activity or a type of work: *I'm helping Mom do the cooking.* | *Have you done your homework yet?*

► **take** you **take** a test, bath, shower, or walk: *I have to take a math test tomorrow.* | *She takes a shower every morning before breakfast.*

► **give** you **give** a talk, speech, or performance: *The principal always gives a speech at the beginning of the school year.* | *The band gave an amazing performance.*

► **perform** you **perform** a task, duty, or operation: *A team of surgeons performed the operation on the patient.* | *The machine can perform several tasks at once.*

► **carry out** you **carry out** an experiment or research: *In science, we carried out experiments with the magnets.*

► **commit** a criminal **commits** a crime, robbery, or murder: *The police do not know who committed the crime.*

**doctor** *noun*

someone whose job is treating people who are sick: *I had a fever, so my mom took me to the doctor.*

► **physician** **physician** means the same as **doctor**: *Dr. Meadows is our family physician and we always go to see her when we are sick.*

► **surgeon** a doctor who cuts into someone's body in the hospital, in order to fix or remove something: *The surgeon performed an operation to remove a bullet from the soldier's chest.*

► **specialist** a doctor who knows a lot about a type of illness or injury: *After Grandpa's heart attack, he saw a heart specialist.*

► **dentist** a doctor who takes care of people's teeth: *The dentist took out one of my teeth.*

► **veterinarian** a doctor who treats animals: *Veterinarians say that you must not give your pet too much food.*

► **psychiatrist** a doctor who treats people who have a mental illness: *He was very depressed, so his parents took him to see a psychiatrist.*

**dog** *noun*

an animal that people keep as a pet or to guard a building: *I'm taking the dog for a walk in the park.*

► **puppy** a very young dog: *Their dog gave birth to six little puppies.*

► **hound** a dog used for hunting: *The hounds can easily smell a rabbit or a fox.*

► **Seeing Eye dog** *trademark* a dog that is trained to walk with a blind person and guide him or her: *She takes her Seeing Eye dog with her and he helps her to cross the street.*

► **guard dog** a dog that is trained to guard a place: *There was a fierce-looking guard dog behind the gate.*

**dog**

a puppy    a hound

a Seeing Eye dog    a guard dog

**dream** *noun*

something that you imagine when you are sleeping: *I had a strange dream last night.*

► **nightmare** a very bad and very frightening dream: *I had a nightmare about getting lost in a forest.*

► **daydream** thoughts about nice things that you imagine happening, which make you forget what is happening around you: *Neil was in a daydream, so he didn't hear the teacher call his name.*

## drink verb

to take liquid into your mouth and swallow it: *I drink orange juice at breakfast time.*

▶ **sip** to drink small amounts of something: *She sipped her hot chocolate because it was very hot.*

▶ **swig** to drink large amounts of liquid from a bottle: *The boy was swigging lemonade from a big bottle.*

▶ **gulp down** to drink all of something very quickly: *Dad gulped down his coffee and rushed out of the house.*

▶ **lap** if an animal laps water or milk, it drinks the water or milk using its tongue: *The cat laps milk from its bowl.*

# Ee

## early adverb

before the usual or right time, or near the beginning of the day: *I arrived at school a few minutes early.* | *My dad gets up early and leaves the house at six o'clock.* ( ANTONYM: **late** )

▶ **ahead of schedule** before the time when something was planned to happen: *The builders finished the work ahead of schedule.*

▶ **on time** at the right time, and not early or late: *He's a good student, and he turns in his assignments on time.* | *The plane was on time.*

▶ **first thing** immediately after you get up, or as soon as you start work or school: *I'll call you first thing in the morning.*

## easy adjective

not difficult: *It was an easy question, and everyone knew the answer.* | *My phone number is easy to remember: it's 234-1234.*
( ANTONYMS: **difficult, hard** )

▶ **simple** not complicated and not having a lot of parts: *The simple jigsaw puzzle had only eight pieces.*

▶ **straightforward** easy to do or understand: *The test is straightforward, You should be able to answer the questions easily.*

▶ **user-friendly** easy to use: *This camera is user-friendly. You just have to press one button to take a picture.*

## eat verb

to put food in your mouth and swallow it: *You need to eat your vegetables.*

▶ **have** to eat a meal or a kind of food: *I usually have dinner at seven o'clock.* | *We have pizza for lunch.*

▶ **feed on** if animals feed on something, they eat it: *Birds feed on insects and worms.*

▶ **munch** to eat something noisily, in a way that shows you are enjoying your food: *They munch potato chips while watching TV.*

▶ **nibble** to eat something by taking small bites: *The squirrel is nibbling on a nut.*

▶ **devour** to eat all of something very quickly: *The kids devoured the cookies in a few minutes.*

## edge noun

the part of something that is farthest from the center: *He sat on the edge of the bed.*

▶ **margin** the empty space at the side of a page of writing: *My teacher wrote "Good Work" in the margin.*

▶ **rim** the top edge of something round, for example a cup: *Her lipstick left a mark on the rim of the cup.*

▶ **border** an area around the edge, which has a different color or pattern from the rest of something. A **border** is also the line that separates two countries or states: *The blanket is yellow with a white border.* | *There is a long border between the U.S. and Canada.*

▶ **boundary** the line that separates two areas of land: *That hedge marks the boundary of our yard.*

▶ **curb** the part of a sidewalk that is next to the street: *It's dangerous to step off the curb without looking.*

a
b
c
d
e
f
g
h
i
j
k
l
m
n
o
p
q
r
s
t
u
v
w
x
y
z

a
b
c
d
e
f
g
h
i
j
k
l
m
n
o
p
q
r
s
t
u
v
w
x
y
z

**effect** *noun*
a change caused by something: *Sunlight can have harmful effects on your skin.*

▶ **impact** a big and important effect: *Moving to a new city had a big impact on my life.*

▶ **influence** an effect on what someone does or thinks: *Teachers can have a big influence on their students, and make them want to work hard.*

▶ **result** something that happens because of something else: *She has started exercising more, with good results. She is already healthier.*

▶ **side effect** an unwanted effect that medicine has on your body: *This medicine has some side effects, such as headaches.*

**embarrassed** *adjective*
feeling unhappy or nervous because you are worried about other people's opinion of you: *She was embarrassed when she forgot the words of the song.*

▶ **ashamed** feeling guilty and embarrassed because you have done something you know is bad or wrong: *He was ashamed of himself for lying to his mother.*

▶ **uncomfortable** feeling a little embarrassed or worried, and not relaxed: *I feel uncomfortable when everyone's looking at me.*

**empty** *adjective*
having nothing or no one inside: *The bottle is empty. Did you drink all the apple juice? | The classroom is empty and all the students have gone home.*

▶ **bare** a bare room or cupboard has very little in it. Bare walls have no pictures on them: *The cupboard was bare and there was no food to eat. | The walls looked bare, so we put up some of the students' paintings.*

▶ **blank** a blank screen or piece of paper has no writing or pictures on it. A blank disk or tape has nothing recorded on it: *She was staring at a blank sheet of paper because she did not know what to write.*

▶ **hollow** a hollow tree or wall is empty inside: *The insect lives in hollow trees.*

▶ **vacant** a vacant seat, room, or building is available for people to use: *The hotel doesn't have any vacant rooms.*

▶ **deserted** a deserted place is quiet because all the people have gone away: *The streets are deserted at four o'clock in the morning.*

**empty**

an empty wastebasket     a blank sheet of paper

a hollow tree     a bare room

lots of vacant seats     a deserted lounge at the airport

**end** *verb*
to stop happening: *The party ended at 6 o'clock. | The movie was great – I didn't want it to end!*

( **ANTONYMS: begin, start** )

▶ **come to an end** to end after a long time: *I was sad when the vacation came to an end.*

▶ **be over** if something is over, it has ended: *When the game was over, everyone congratulated the winner.*

## enemy *noun*

someone who wants to harm you: *The governor has many enemies who do not want him to be elected again.*

You also use **enemy** about the country or army that you are fighting against in a war: *U.S. soldiers defeated the enemy in battle.*

▶ **opponent** the person or group that someone is competing against in a game, competition, or election: *She is playing much better than her opponent, and she should win the game easily.*

▶ **rival** a person or group that tries to be more successful than another one: *The two schools are big rivals and they always want to do better than each other.*

## enough *adjective, pronoun*

as much or as many as you need: *Make sure that you take enough water with you.*

▶ **sufficient** **sufficient** means the same as **enough**: *Eight hours of sleep is sufficient for most adults.*

▶ **plenty** more than enough: *We have plenty of time to get to the airport before the flight.*

## enter *verb*

to walk, drive, or fly into a place: *Two men entered the room.* | *The sign by the road said "You are now entering California."*

( ANTONYM: **leave** )

▶ **go in/go into** to enter a place: *I went into the kitchen to get some juice.*

▶ **come in/come into** to enter the place where you are: *As soon as the teacher came into our classroom, everyone stopped talking.*

▶ **get in/get into** to enter a car, or to succeed in entering a place: *Mom told us to get in the car.* | *We couldn't get into our house because the door was locked.*

## escape *verb*

to leave a place where you do not want to be, or leave someone who is trying to catch you: *The mouse has escaped from its cage.* | *The robbers tried to escape, but the police caught them.*

▶ **get away** to escape from someone who is trying to catch you: *In the game, I tried to catch Sam, but he got away.*

▶ **flee** to leave a place very quickly to escape from danger: *People were told to flee the city before the hurricane hit.*

▶ **break out** to escape from a prison: *The prisoner planned to break out of the jail.*

## exciting *adjective*

making you feel excited: *Ice hockey is an exciting game to watch because it is very fast.*

▶ **thrilling** very exciting and enjoyable, often in a way that makes you feel a little nervous: *The rollercoaster ride was thrilling – we went so fast!*

▶ **dramatic** very exciting because things happen suddenly, and you do not know what will happen next: *In the movie, there was a dramatic car chase through the city.*

▶ **gripping** so exciting that you cannot stop watching or reading: *The story was very gripping and I wanted to know what happened at the end.*

## expensive *adjective*

if something is expensive, it costs a lot of money: *These basketball shoes are too expensive. I can't buy them.* ( ANTONYM: **cheap** )

▶ **high** high prices, costs, or taxes cost a lot of money: *The store's prices are very high compared to other stores.*

▶ **valuable** worth a lot of money: *My computer is the most valuable thing I own.*

▶ **fancy** fancy clothes, cars, or places look expensive: *She spends all her money on fancy clothes.* | *We dressed in our best clothes and went to a fancy restaurant to celebrate my dad's birthday.*

▶ **cost a fortune** if something costs a fortune, it is very expensive: *The house has eight bedrooms and a swimming pool – it must have cost a fortune.*

a b c d e f g h i j k l m n o p q r s t u v w x y z

a
b
c
d
e
**f**
g
h
i
j
k
l
m
n
o
p
q
r
s
t
u
v
w
x
y
z

## experience *noun*

something that happens to you, especially something unusual or important: *Meeting the president was a wonderful experience.*

▶ **adventure** an experience in which a lot of exciting and often dangerous things happen to you: *We had lots of adventures when we went camping in the mountains.*

▶ **ordeal** a very bad experience: *He is recovering after the ordeal of being trapped in an elevator.*

## explain *verb*

to give someone information so that he or she can understand something: *The teacher explained how to do the experiment. | Lisa explained why she was late and said that she had missed her bus.*

▶ **show** to explain how to do something, by doing it while someone watches: *Mom is going to show us how to make the cookies.*

▶ **demonstrate** **demonstrate** means the same as **show**: *The coach demonstrated the right way to hit the ball.*

# Ff

## fair *adjective*

treating everyone in the same way, or in a way that is right: *Why do I have to go to bed before Dan? It's not fair! | The election was fair – every vote was counted.*

▶ **equal** if people have equal rights or opportunities, they all have the same rights or opportunities: *The coach made sure that everyone had an equal opportunity to play in the game. | The Constitution guarantees equal rights for all U.S. citizens.*

▶ **reasonable** not too much or too little: *Fifty dollars seems like a reasonable price for a good coat.*

▶ **just** morally right and fair: *Many people are protesting because they do not believe it is a just war. | He was sick at the time of the test, so it was a just decision to let him take it again.*

▶ **impartial** not supporting any person or group: *The referee is supposed to be impartial and should not try to help one team win.*

## fall *verb*

to accidentally go down onto the ground: *I fell off my bike and hurt my knee.*

▶ **trip** to start to fall because you accidentally hit something with your foot: *She tripped over a tree root.*

▶ **slip** to start to fall because the ground is so smooth you accidentally slide on it: *Be careful you don't slip on the ice!*

▶ **collapse** to suddenly fall down onto the ground, especially because you are very weak or sick: *The old man collapsed and had to be taken to the hospital.*

▶ **lose your balance** to start to fall because you are standing on something high or narrow: *I was standing on top of a ladder when I lost my balance.*

fall

fall

trip

slip

## false *adjective*

not real. You use **false** about teeth or fingernails, or about a name or address: *My grandfather has false teeth.* | *The thief used a false name and said that he was called Brad Pitt.* ( **ANTONYM: real** )

▶ **fake** not real. Fake things are used especially to trick people: *We used fake blood to scare people at Halloween.*

▶ **imitation** imitation leather or jewelry is made to look like real leather or jewelry: *The diamonds are not real. They are only imitation and they were very cheap.*

▶ **counterfeit** counterfeit money is made to look exactly like real money in order to trick people: *Someone at the bank discovered that the $100 bill was counterfeit.*

## family *noun*

your family is your parents, brothers, sisters, etc.: *My little brother Julio is the youngest member of the family.*

▶ **relative** a member of your family, such as an aunt, uncle, or cousin: *Many friends and relatives came to the wedding.* | *I don't live in Mexico anymore, but I still have a lot of relatives there.*

▶ **ancestor** a member of your family who lived a long time before you were born: *His ancestors came to the U.S. from Germany over 100 years ago.*

▶ **descendant** someone who is related to a person who lived a long time ago: *My friend Megan is a descendant of one of the Pilgrims from the Mayflower.*

## famous *adjective*

if someone is famous, many people in a country or in the world know about him or her: *Johnny Depp is a famous actor who has appeared in many movies.* | *New York is famous for its tall buildings.*

▶ **well-known** if someone is well-known, many people know about him or her: *Grandma is well-known for her excellent cooking.* | *He was singing a well-known song.*

▶ **legendary** a legendary sportsperson or musician is very famous. You often use legendary about a person who lived in the past: *Michael Jordan is a legendary basketball player.*

▶ **eminent** an eminent scientist, politician, or writer is famous and respected for his or her knowledge: *The professor is an eminent scientist who has studied earthquakes for many years.*

▶ **notorious** someone notorious is famous for doing something bad: *On the Simpsons TV show, Homer Simpson is notorious for doing stupid things.*

## far *adverb*

a long distance away. You often use **far** in negative sentences and questions: *The school is not far from my house.* | *Is it far to the bank?* You also use **far** with "too": *It's too far to walk to the beach – let's take the bus.* ( **ANTONYM: near** )

▶ **a long way** a long distance: *It's a long way to the center of town.*

▶ **distant** a very long distance away: *I could see the light from a distant star in the night sky.*

▶ **remote** far away from other places and people, and difficult to get to: *The writer lives on a remote island off the coast of Maine.*

a b c d e f g h i j k l m n o p q r s t u v w x y z

a
b
c
d
e
**f**
g
h
i
j
k
l
m
n
o
p
q
r
s
t
u
v
w
x
y
z

**farm** *noun*
an area of land and buildings, where people grow crops or raise animals: *They grow wheat and corn on their farm.* | *He has a chicken farm.*

▶ **ranch** a large farm with cows, horses, or sheep: *There are hundreds of cows on their ranch in Texas.*

▶ **homestead** a farm and the area of land around it, where a family lives: *My grandmother still lives on the old family homestead in Nebraska.*

▶ **orchard** a place where people grow fruit trees: *You can pick apples at the orchard in the fall.*

▶ **vineyard** a place where people grow grapes to make wine: *There are vineyards in the Napa Valley, and the area is famous for its wine.*

**fast** *adverb, adjective*
moving or doing something quickly: *Don't drive so fast.* | *My brother is a fast runner.* ( ANTONYM: **slow** )

▶ **quickly** taking a short time to do something: *I quickly took a shower before school.* | *If you eat your food quickly you will feel sick.*

▶ **rapidly** quickly. You use **rapidly** especially about changes and increases: *The population of the world is increasing rapidly and there will soon be over seven billion people.* | *Babies grow rapidly in the first year.*

▶ **high-speed** a **high-speed** train or computer system is very fast: *The high-speed train can travel at over 300 miles an hour.* | *The computers have high-speed Internet access.*

**fasten** *verb*
to join together the two sides of a belt or a piece of clothing, so that you can use it: *Fasten your seat belts.* | *The skirt fastens in the back.*
( ANTONYM: **unfasten** )

▶ **tie** to fasten something by making a knot: *Can you tie your shoelaces?* | *She tied a scarf around her neck.*

▶ **zip** to fasten something with a zipper: *Zip up your jacket. It's cold outside.* | *We put our clothes in the suitcase and zipped it shut.*

▶ **button** to fasten something with buttons: *Mom helped my little sister button her coat.*

fasten

Fasten your seat belt. | She is tying her shoelaces. | He is zipping his jacket.

**fat** *adjective*
weighing too much for the size of your body: *I'm getting fat. I need to go on a diet.* ( ANTONYM: **thin** )

▶ **big** having a big body. **Big** sounds more polite than **fat**: *Everyone in my family is big. My dad weighs over 250 pounds.*

▶ **chubby** a little fat in a way that looks cute. You use **chubby** about a baby or child: *The baby has chubby cheeks.*

▶ **plump** a little fat, and having a nice round shape. You use plump especially about a woman: *My aunt is short and plump.*

▶ **heavy** someone who is **heavy** is fat. **Heavy** sounds more polite than **fat**: *Andy is heavy and he's trying to lose weight.*

▶ **overweight** weighing more than you should: *I'm about ten pounds overweight.*

▶ **obese** very fat, in a way that is dangerous to your health: *She was obese, so her doctor said that she had to stop eating too much.*

**fear** *noun*
the feeling you have when you are frightened of something: *The movie was scary and she covered her eyes in fear.* | *Fear of the dark is very common in children.*

▶ **fright** a sudden feeling of fear because you think something bad is going to happen: *She screamed with fright when the lights went out.*

▶ **terror** great fear: *The building was on fire and people screamed in terror. The firefighters came and everyone was safe.*

▶ **panic** a sudden feeling of fear and worry that makes you stop thinking clearly and sensibly: *When the fire bell rang, people ran in panic, not knowing what to do.*

▶ **horror** a feeling of great fear and shock, when something terrible happens: *I watched in horror as the car crashed into a tree.*

## feeling *noun*

something that you feel, for example sadness, happiness, or worry: *It was a great feeling to be back home.*

▶ **emotion** a strong feeling, for example love, hatred, or anger, that often has an effect on how you behave: *He could not control his emotions and started crying.*

▶ **sensation** the way your body feels when you experience or touch something: *The roller coaster ride gave me a strange sensation in my stomach.*

## find *verb*

to see someone or something that you were looking for, or to see something by chance: *We found him sitting under a tree. | I can't find my other shoe.*

▶ **locate** to find the exact place where someone or something is: *Rescue teams are trying to locate the missing plane.*

▶ **come across** to find someone or something, when you are not looking for them: *She came across the letters when she was cleaning the cupboard.*

▶ **spot** to see someone or something: *Can you spot the mistake in the first sentence? | Someone spotted him in the crowd and called the police.*

▶ **discover** to find something, especially a new place or a new way of doing something: *Who discovered America? | Scientists have discovered a new treatment for the disease.*

## finish *verb*

to stop doing or making something: *You have to finish your homework before you can go out and play. | When you finish reading the story, answer the questions.* (ANTONYMS: start, begin)

▶ **complete** to finish doing something, especially something that takes a long time: *It will take two years to complete the building.*

▶ **conclude** to finish something, especially something that you are writing or talking about: *He concluded his letter by saying that he hoped to be back in California very soon.*

▶ **terminate** to end an agreement: *If we are late paying the rent, the landlord will terminate our agreement to rent the house.*

## fire *noun*

flames that destroy things, or flames that you use for heating: *The house was destroyed by fire. | We lit a fire in the fireplace.*

▶ **flame** the bright part of a fire that you see burning in the air: *We saw flames coming from the roof of the burning building.*

▶ **blaze** a large and dangerous fire: *The firefighters are trying to control the blaze in the old factory.*

▶ **campfire** a fire that people make outside when they are camping: *At night, we sat around a campfire and sang songs.*

▶ **forest fire** a fire that causes a lot of damage to trees and forests: *A forest fire may start if the weather is hot and dry for a long time.*

## flat *adjective*

not sloping, or without any hills or raised parts: *The school has a flat roof. | In Ohio the land is very flat and good for farming.*

▶ **level** flat, with no part higher than the rest: *We put the tent up on level ground.*

▶ **horizontal** a horizontal line or position goes straight across, and is not sloping: *Draw a horizontal line across the paper. | His shirt had horizontal blue stripes across the chest.*

## flower *noun*

a pretty colored part on a plant. Flowers are made up of petals, and they produce the plant's seeds or fruit: *She picked a flower from the garden.* | *We gave my teacher a bouquet of flowers on her birthday.*

▶ **bud** a young flower or leaf that has just started growing and has a small round shape: *In spring, the buds on the trees start to open.*

▶ **blossom** a flower on a tree or bush: *In April, the cherry trees are covered with blossoms.*

▶ **bloom** if plants or trees are in bloom, they are producing flowers: *The orange trees are in bloom, so the air is filled with a wonderful smell.*

**flower**

buds

blossoms

The flowers are in bloom.

## fly *verb*

to travel through the air: *The plane is flying to Mexico City.* | *A bee flew into the classroom.*

▶ **float** to move slowly through the air: *The balloon floated up into the sky.*

▶ **soar** to fly high up in the air: *Eagles soar high in the sky.*

▶ **glide** to move slowly through the air without using an engine or without moving wings: *A swan glided down onto the lake.* | *The paper airplane glided through the open window.*

▶ **take off** if an airplane takes off, it leaves the ground and starts flying: *The plane took off from Los Angeles International Airport.*

## fog *noun*

a thick cloud near the ground which is difficult to see through: *The fog made driving very dangerous.*

▶ **mist** a cloud of tiny drops of water near the ground, which is not as thick as a fog. You often get mist near mountains, lakes, or the ocean: *The mountains are surrounded by mist.*

▶ **smog** a mixture of clouds and smoke in the air over cities, which is caused by cars and factories: *Los Angeles has a lot of smog because of all the traffic.*

▶ **haze** smoke, dust, or mist in the air, which is difficult to see through: *We could hardly see the horses through the haze of dust.*

## follow *verb*

to walk, drive, or run behind someone: *The little dog followed him everywhere.* ( ANTONYM: **lead** )

▶ **chase** to run after a person or animal that is trying to escape from you: *The fox chased the rabbit.* | *The police officer chased after the robbers.*

▶ **pursue** to follow someone in a determined way in order to catch him or her: *The Native American hunters pursued the buffalo.*

▶ **tail** to secretly follow someone in order to find out where he or she is going: *The robbers didn't realize that they were being tailed by a police car.*

## forbid *verb*

to order someone not to do something: *My mom forbid us to play in the street because she is worried about the traffic.* (**ANTONYM: allow**)

▶ **prohibit** if something is prohibited, it is not allowed because of a law or rule: *Smoking is prohibited in public places in New York City.*

▶ **ban** to say officially that people must not do, sell, or use something: *The book was banned in some countries.*

## foreigner *noun*

someone who comes from another country: *Foreigners from Europe and Asia come to visit New York City, and see the Statue of Liberty.*

▶ **immigrant** someone who comes to live in a country: *Maria is a Mexican immigrant who moved to California five years ago.*

▶ **refugee** someone who leaves his or her country because of danger or war: *The refugees had to leave their country during the war because their homes were destroyed.*

## forest *noun*

a large area of land covered with trees: *At one time forests covered most of the country. | When we were walking in the forest, we saw a deer.*

▶ **woods** a small forest: *We went to play in the woods near our house.*

▶ **jungle** a forest in a hot wet area, that has a lot of trees and plants growing close together: *Monkeys live in the jungle in Africa.*

▶ **rainforest** a forest in a part of the world where it is hot and rains a lot: *The rainforest in Brazil is very important for the environment because so many birds and animals live there.*

## forgive *verb*

to stop being angry with someone who has done something wrong: *Please forgive me for losing your ring.*

▶ **excuse** to forgive someone for something that is not very serious: *Please excuse me for being late. | Please excuse my handwriting. It is a little messy.*

▶ **pardon** to allow someone who is guilty of a crime to be free and not have to stay in prison: *After three years in jail, he was pardoned by the governor.*

## free *verb*

to let someone leave a place where he or she has been forced to stay: *The judge freed the prisoners and allowed them to leave the jail. | I freed the mouse from the trap.*

▶ **release** release means the same as **free**: *He will be released from prison in June.*

▶ **liberate** to free prisoners, or to free a country or city from the control of another group of people: *The prisoners of war were liberated when the war ended. | The Americans wanted to liberate their country from the British, and to have their own government.*

▶ **emancipate** to allow a group of people to be free and have the same rights as other people: *American slaves were emancipated after the Civil War, so they were not slaves anymore.*

## freedom *noun*

the right to do what you want, without other people stopping you: *His mother gives him a lot of freedom, so he can stay up as late as he wants. | People here have the freedom to follow the religion they choose.*

▶ **liberty** freedom for people in a country to do what they want, without the government telling them what to do: *We must not allow the government to take away our liberties. | In America, we have the liberty to choose where we want to live and work.*

▶ **independence** freedom from control by another country: *The United States declared its independence from Britain on July 4, 1776 and that is why we celebrate that day every year.*

a
b
c
d
e
f
g
h
i
j
k
l
m
n
o
p
q
r
s
t
u
v
w
x
y
z

## friend *noun*

someone you like and know well: *She invited all her friends to her birthday party.*

▶ **best friend** the friend who is most important to you: *Wendi is my best friend and we have known each other since we were in kindergarten.*

▶ **buddy** a friend who you know very well and who you like spending time with: *Joe is my buddy from the army.*

▶ **girlfriend** a girl or woman that someone has a romantic relationship with, or a girl or woman's female friend: *He went to see a movie with his girlfriend.* | *She is going to the mall with her girlfriends.*

▶ **boyfriend** a boy or man that someone has a romantic relationship with: *My sister's boyfriend is a senior in high school.*

▶ **acquaintance** a person you have only met a few times, but who is not really a friend: *He is just an acquaintance whom I have talked to on the bus.*

▶ **ally** a person or country that always helps and supports another person or country: *The United States and Great Britain are close allies, and they have fought together in many wars.*

## friendly *adjective*

behaving in a way that shows you like someone and want to talk to him or her: *The other students seem very friendly so I think I'm going to enjoy the class.* (ANTONYM: **unfriendly**)

▶ **nice** friendly and kind: *It was nice of you to invite me to your house to play.* | *Matthew is a really nice guy. He will do anything to help people.*

▶ **sociable** liking to spend time with other people and talk to them: *She's very sociable and plays with everyone.*

▶ **neighborly** friendly and helpful toward the people who live near you: *It was very neighborly of you to take care of our pets while we were on vacation.*

▶ **welcoming** friendly to people who have just arrived somewhere: *The teacher greeted the new students with a welcoming smile.*

## frightened *adjective*

feeling very nervous and worried because something bad might happen: *I am frightened of big dogs.* | *She had a frightened look on her face.*

▶ **scared** **scared** means the same as **frightened**: *Don't be scared. It's just a movie.* | *He looked very angry and I was scared of him.*

▶ **afraid** **afraid** means the same as **frightened**: *Children are often afraid of the dark.* | *I was afraid that I was going to fall off the ladder.*

▶ **terrified** very frightened: *We were terrified because we thought the boat was going to sink.*

## frightening *adjective*

making you feel afraid: *I got lost at the park and it was very frightening.*

▶ **scary** **scary** means the same as **frightening**: *The movie is really scary and you never know what is going to happen next.*

▶ **spooky** strange and frightening, especially because you think there is a ghost: *The old house was dark and spooky and no one ever went near it.*

▶ **terrifying** very frightening: *It was a terrifying experience because I thought the dog was going to bite me.*

## frog *noun*

a small green or brown animal that has long legs it uses for jumping. **Frogs** live on land and in water: *The frog jumped into the pond.*

▶ **toad** an animal that looks like a large frog with bumpy skin. **Toads** live mainly on land: *I found a big toad under a rock in our yard.*

▶ **tadpole** a small animal that grows to become a frog or a toad. A **tadpole** lives in water and has a large head and a long tail. As it grows, it stops having a tail and starts to grow legs: *It takes 12 weeks for a tadpole to become a frog.*

**frog**

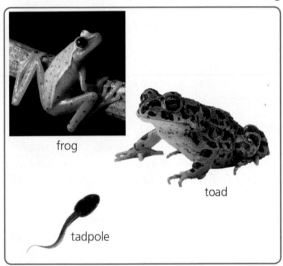

frog

toad

tadpole

## full *adjective*

containing as many things or people inside as possible: *The refrigerator is full of food.* | *The bus was full and I had to stand all the way home.*

**ANTONYM: empty**

▶ **packed** so full that no more people can get in: *The stadium is packed with baseball fans, and all the tickets for the game are sold out.*

▶ **overflowing** so full that liquid or other things come out over the top: *The bathtub was overflowing because someone forgot to turn the water off.*

▶ **bulging** if something is bulging, it is so full that the things inside change its shape: *His mouth was bulging with candy.*

▶ **stuffed** full of a lot of things: *The drawers were so stuffed with clothes that they would not shut.*

**full**

The glass is overflowing.

The escalator is packed.

## funny *adjective*

making you laugh: *My dad told us a funny joke and we all laughed.* | *I thought the show was really funny.*

▶ **amusing** making you smile: *Grandpa told us an amusing story about the time he fell into the lake.*

▶ **humorous** **humorous** means the same as **amusing**: *He gave a humorous speech about his days as a college student.*

▶ **witty** saying things that are amusing, intelligent, and interesting: *Martin is very witty and charming and I like being with him.* | *She made a witty remark.*

▶ **hilarious** very funny in a way that makes you laugh a lot: *The movie was hilarious! I couldn't stop laughing.*

a
b
c
d
e
f
**g**
h
i
j
k
l
m
n
o
p
q
r
s
t
u
v
w
x
y
z

# Gg

**game** *noun*

an enjoyable activity, in which you try to win or score points: *We played lots of games at Jacob's party.* | *My brother loves to play computer games.*

► **puzzle** a game in which you have to think hard to find the correct answer: *In the puzzle you have to find the difference between the two pictures.*

► **jigsaw puzzle** a picture that has been cut into pieces. You have to put the pieces together again: *This jigsaw puzzle has 1,000 pieces.*

► **crossword puzzle** a game in which you write the correct words into a pattern of squares: *The first word in the crossword puzzle has four letters, and the clue is "place to swim." The answer is "pool."*

► **wordsearch** a game in which you look for words that are hidden among other letters: *Can you find the five animal names that are hidden in the wordsearch?*

► **chess** a game for two people, played on a board that has a pattern of different colored squares. The goal of the game is to capture the other player's king: *Daniel is very intelligent and he always beats me at chess.*

► **checkers** a game for two people, played on a board that has a pattern of different colored squares. Each player has 12 round pieces. The aim of the game is to take all the other person's pieces: *Do you want to play another game of checkers?*

► **board game** a game that has a board that you move pieces around to try to win: *We played Monopoly and other board games.*

**get** *verb*

to be given something, or to buy something: *I got lots of presents for my birthday.* | *Let's go and get some food.*

► **receive** to be given something, or be sent something: *She received first prize in the competition.* | *I received a letter from the school the next day.*

► **obtain** to get something, especially by officially asking for it: *You can obtain a map from the tourist information center.*

► **earn** to get money for the work you do, or to get something good because of something you have done: *My sister earns $10 an hour for babysitting.* | *He studied hard and earned good grades.*

► **inherit** to get money or property after someone dies: *Jo inherited a lot of money from her mother.*

**ghost** *noun*

the spirit of a dead person, which some people believe exists and lives in a place: *In the old house, I thought I saw the ghost of a woman in a long white dress.*

► **phantom** a ghost, especially a frightening ghost that you cannot see clearly: *The phantom walked through the wall and disappeared.*

► **spirit** the part of a person that some people believe still exists after a person dies: *I think my grandmother's spirit is watching over me.* A **spirit** is also a creature without a physical body, which is believed to have special powers: *Some Native Americans believed that spirits controlled the weather.*

## gift *noun*

something that you give someone: *I have to buy a gift for my aunt for her birthday.*

▶ **present** **present** means the same as **gift**: *The watch was a present from my parents. | I get lots of Christmas presents.*

▶ **donation** money, things, or time that someone gives to an organization, in order to help people: *We gave donations of food to the food bank.*

▶ **reward** something that is given to someone for doing something good: *When your dog behaves well, give it a reward.*

## give *verb*

to let someone have something: *My parents gave me a bicycle for my birthday. | Can you give me his email address?* ( **ANTONYM: take** )

▶ **present** to give something to someone at a formal ceremony, in front of a lot of people: *The principal will present a certificate to the students who worked hardest this year.*

▶ **award** to give someone a prize: *Tyler was awarded a prize for his essay.*

▶ **hand out** to give something to every person in a group: *The teacher handed out the tests to the class.*

▶ **donate** to give money or other things, in order to help people: *A local company donated money to buy new sports equipment for the school.*

▶ **leave** if someone leaves you something, that person says that you should have it after he or she dies: *My grandma left me her pearl necklace.*

## glasses *plural noun*

something that you wear in front of your eyes to help you see better. Glasses consist of two thin pieces of glass or plastic, and a frame: *Grandpa's eyes aren't very good so he has to wear glasses to read.*

▶ **sunglasses** dark glasses that you wear to protect your eyes when the sun is bright: *The sunlight was very bright, so I put my sunglasses on.*

▶ **contact lenses** thin round pieces of plastic that you put onto your eyes to help you see clearly: *He wears contact lenses when he plays sports, so he won't break his glasses.*

▶ **goggles** special glasses that you wear to protect your eyes: *I wear goggles when I'm swimming, so the water doesn't get in my eyes.*

**glasses**

a contact lens

glasses

swimming goggles

sunglasses

## go *verb*

to move to another place: *I usually go to school in my mom's car. | It is late and I have to go home.*

▶ **travel** to make a trip somewhere: *My uncle has traveled all around the world.*

▶ **head** to go in a particular direction: *The settlers headed west to California.*

▶ **proceed** to go to a place. **Proceed** is often used when telling someone where to go: *Passengers for Miami should proceed to Gate 15.*

▶ **cross** to go across something: *You should always be careful when you cross the road. | George Washington crossed the Delaware River on December 25, 1776.*

▶ **return** to go back somewhere: *Britney returned to her home town of Kentwood, Louisiana.*

▶ **whiz** to go very quickly: *A police car whizzed past us with its lights flashing.*

▶ **crawl** to go very slowly: *The cars crawled along the freeway at five miles an hour.*

a b c d e f **g** h i j k l m n o p q r s t u v w x y z

a b c d e f **g** h i j k l m n o p q r s t u v w x y z

## good adjective

you use **good** when you like something, or you think that it is of a high standard: *The movie was really good and I enjoyed it a lot. | Did you have a good vacation? | The teacher said my essay was good and I got an A.* ( ANTONYM: **bad** )

▶ **nice** good. You use **nice** when you like or enjoy something: *It's nice to see you again. | Have a nice vacation!*

▶ **neat** good. You use **neat** when you are talking to your friends, when you like something a lot: *My brother showed me a neat computer game.*

▶ **fine** fine things are of good quality. Fine weather is sunny: *The museum has some fine paintings. | The weather was fine and the sun was shining all day.*

▶ **great** very good or enjoyable: *We had a great time at the beach.*

▶ **excellent** very good and of a high standard: *The food was excellent. It tasted really good.*

▶ **wonderful** very very good: *There is a wonderful view of the mountains from the hotel.*

## government noun

the people who are in charge of a country or state: *In Mexico, the government gives money to help poor farmers.*

▶ **administration** the U.S. president and the people who work for him or her: *Most Americans think that the administration is doing a good job.*

▶ **democracy** the system in which people choose their government by voting: *In a democracy, people can vote to change the government if they do not like it.*

▶ **monarchy** the system in which a country is ruled by a king or queen: *England has had a monarchy for over 1,000 years.*

▶ **dictatorship** the system in which a country is ruled by a leader with complete power, who has not been elected by the people: *The country is ruled by a military dictatorship and people who don't like the government are put in prison.*

## great adjective

very good: *I really like her songs. They're great! | We had a great vacation in Florida.*
( ANTONYM: **horrible** )

▶ **excellent** very good and of a high standard: *The food is excellent. It tastes really good. | He is an excellent guitar player.*

▶ **wonderful** very good: *San Francisco is a wonderful place to live. There are a lot of things you can do there.*

▶ **terrific** very good. **Terrific** means the same as **wonderful**: *She looks terrific in her new dress.*

▶ **fantastic** very good. You use **fantastic** especially when you are excited about something: *The team did a fantastic job so the coach is really pleased with them.*

▶ **fabulous** very good. **Fabulous** means the same as **fantastic**: *There is a fabulous view of the Grand Canyon.*

## ground noun

the surface of the Earth: *When we woke up, there was snow on the ground.*

▶ **floor** the surface that you stand on inside a building: *The children left all their toys on the floor.*

▶ **land** an area of ground that belongs to someone, or the part of the Earth that is not covered by water: *The land belongs to the school. | Turtles lay their eggs on land, not in the ocean.*

▶ **soil** the substance on the ground in which plants grow: *Cover the seeds with soil.*

▶ **dirt** dirt means the same as **soil**: *He had dirt on his pants from sitting on the ground.*

▶ **earth** earth means the same as **soil**. You use **earth** to talk about growing plants: *The earth here is very good for growing corn.*

## group *noun*

**a group of people**:

▶ **crowd** a large group of people: *A crowd has gathered to watch the parade.*

▶ **audience** the group of people who are watching a movie, concert, or play: *The audience cheered when the band started to play.*

▶ **team** a group of people who play a sport or game, or work together: *I hope our team wins the game.*

▶ **crew** the people who work on a ship or airplane: *The cook is an important member of the ship's crew.*

▶ **gang** a group of people who do things together, especially criminals: *A gang of robbers stole over $1 million from the bank.*

▶ **band** a group of musicians who play popular music together: *My brother plays the guitar in a band.*

**a group of animals**:

▶ **herd** a group of cows, deer, elephants, or other big animals: *A herd of cows is eating grass in the field.*

▶ **flock** a group of sheep, goats, or birds: *A flock of birds flew over our house.*

▶ **pack** a group of wild animals that hunt together: *The wolves hunt together in packs.*

▶ **school** a group of fish: *A school of fish is swimming in the water next to our boat.*

▶ **swarm** a group of bees or other insects: *A swarm of bees was buzzing around the tree.*

**a group of things**:

▶ **bunch** a group of fruit or flowers: *I always give my mother a bunch of flowers on Mother's Day.*

▶ **set** a group of things of the same type, which you use together: *Dad has a set of tools in the garage.* | *I got a chess set for my birthday.*

▶ **collection** a group of similar things that you collect because you like them: *He has a large collection of comic books.*

▶ **bundle** a group of things that are tied together: *I tied the newspapers together in a bundle.*

▶ **pile** a group of things that are placed one on top of the other: *He always leaves his clothes in a pile on the floor.*

▶ **stack** a pile of flat things that are placed on top of each other: *There was a stack of books on the desk.*

## grow *verb*

to get bigger: *The tree grew from 5 feet to 20 feet tall.* | *Children grow quickly and they always need new clothes.*

▶ **expand** if a substance expands, it gets bigger: *Metal expands when it gets hot.*

▶ **develop** to gradually change into something bigger, better, or more serious: *He is developing into an excellent basketball player.* | *The argument developed into a fight.*

▶ **mature** if something matures, it reaches its full size or its final form: *Cheese takes several months to mature before you can eat it.*

## guess *verb*

to say that you think something is true, when you cannot be sure you are right: *I guess he is about 20 years old.*

▶ **estimate** to guess the amount, cost, or size of something: *I estimate that the tree is 100 feet tall.* | *They estimated the cost of the repairs to be $6,000.*

▶ **speculate** to talk about what you think might happen or has happened: *People will speculate about the cause of the fire.*

▶ **suppose** to think that something is probably true: *There's no more pizza left. I suppose Lisa has eaten the last piece.*

▶ **assume** to think that something is probably true, especially when you are deciding what to say or do: *I assumed that the woman next to him was his wife. I called her "Mrs. Johnson."*

▶ **conclude** to decide that something must be true, after thinking about it or discussing it: *He couldn't find his coat anywhere, so he concluded that someone must have stolen it.*

a
b
c
d
e
f
**g**
h
i
j
k
l
m
n
o
p
q
r
s
t
u
v
w
x
y
z

a
b
c
d
e
f
g

**h**

i
j
k
l
m
n
o
p
q
r
s
t
u
v
w
x
y
z

# Hh

### hair *noun*

the mass of things like thin threads that grow on your head or your body: *My brother has short dark hair.* | *She brushed her hair in front of the mirror.*

▶ **fur** hair that covers an animal's body: *Our cat's fur is nice and soft.*

▶ **beard** hair that grows on a man's chin: *The old man had a long white beard.*

▶ **mustache** hair that grows above a man's mouth: *He has a thin mustache.*

▶ **sideburns** hair that grows on the sides of a man's face: *Elvis Presley had long black sideburns.*

▶ **eyebrow** a line of hair that grows above your eye: *He raised his eyebrows because he was surprised.*

▶ **eyelashes** the hair around the edges of your eyes: *She is very pretty and has long dark eyelashes.*

### happen *verb*

you use **happen** about an event that was not planned or expected: *The accident happened on my way home from school.* | *There's white paint in your hair. How did that happen?*

▶ **occur** **occur** means the same as **happen**. It is more formal: *Earthquakes sometimes occur in this area.*

▶ **take place** you use **take place** about an event or ceremony that is planned: *The parade takes place every year in July.* | *The wedding will take place in our church.*

▶ **come about** to happen. You use **come about** when explaining why something happened: *The discovery of gold came about when the men were building a mill.*

▶ **come true** if your wish or dream comes true, it happens: *My wish came true and I got a new computer for my birthday.*

### happy *adjective*

feeling good, for example because something good has happened to you, or because you are satisfied with your life: *She is happy at her new school.* | *We're a very happy family and we enjoy spending time together.* | *The movie has a happy ending.* ( ANTONYM: **sad** )

▶ **cheerful** looking happy or sounding happy: *Mom always looks cheerful and she never seems to worry about anything.* | *She is a cheerful girl who smiles a lot.*

**hair**

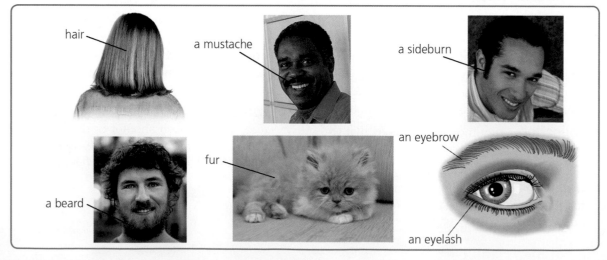

hair
a mustache
a sideburn
an eyebrow
fur
a beard
an eyelash

▶ **pleased** happy because something good has happened, or because you like something: *I'm pleased that my friends are here for my birthday.* | *We're very pleased with our new home. It has everything we want.*

▶ **glad** happy because something good has happened: *I'm glad that you passed the test.* | *She was glad when the rain stopped.*

▶ **content** feeling happy with your life and not wanting anything to change: *He was content with life on the farm, and he didn't want to live anywhere else.*

▶ **joyful** making you feel very happy: *The wedding was a joyful occasion for all the family.*

## hard *adjective*

not easy to do or understand: *It's hard to understand people if they talk fast.* | *The test was hard.* ( ANTONYM: **easy** )

▶ **difficult** **difficult** means the same as **hard**: *The questions on the test were difficult and I couldn't answer them.*

▶ **tough** very difficult because you have to use a lot of effort: *My dad has a tough job. He works as a doctor at a busy hospital.*

▶ **tricky** difficult because you could easily make a mistake: *Finding your way out of the forest can be tricky, especially at night. It's easy to get lost.*

▶ **complicated** difficult to understand because it has many parts: *Chess is a complicated game and there are a lot of rules.*

## hat *noun*

a piece of clothing that you wear on your head: *I put on my hat because it was very cold outside.*

▶ **cap** a cloth hat with a curved part that sticks out at the front: *Andy wears a Yankees baseball cap.*

▶ **helmet** a hard hat that protects your head when you are doing an activity such as bicycling or climbing: *You should wear a helmet when you ride your bicycle.*

▶ **cowboy hat** a wide round hat with a tall stiff top, which cowboys wear: *Jake came to the party in a cowboy hat.*

▶ **beret** a round soft hat that fits tightly on your head: *The army officer was wearing a green beret.*

▶ **top hat** a tall hat that men used to wear in the past: *Abraham Lincoln often wore a top hat.*

▶ **hard hat** a hat made of hard plastic, which protects your head from falling objects: *Building workers wear hard hats.*

**hat**

a cap    a cowboy hat

a helmet    a beret

a hard hat    a top hat

## hate *verb*

to dislike someone or something very much: *I hate spinach. It tastes horrible.* | *"Go away!" she screamed. "I hate you!"* ( ANTONYM: **love** )

▶ **can't stand** to dislike someone or something very much: *Katie is nice, but I can't stand her brother.*

▶ **detest** to hate someone or something very much: *I detest the mean way he talks to my mother.*

▶ **loathe** to hate someone or something very much: *My sister loathes housework so she refuses to do it.*

▶ **despise** to hate and have no respect for someone or something: *I despise people who are unkind to animals.*

a b c d e f g **h** i j k l m n o p q r s t u v w x y z

**healthy** *adjective*
physically well and strong: *Eating fruit and vegetables helps you stay healthy.* (ANTONYM: **sick**)

▶ **well** healthy. You use **well** when saying that someone looks or feels healthy: *Laura didn't go to school because she wasn't feeling well.*

▶ **fine** healthy and happy. You use **fine** when someone asks "How are you?": *"How are you?" "Fine, thanks."* | *My family is doing fine.*

▶ **better** less sick than before: *I had to stay in bed for two days, but I'm better now.*

▶ **physically fit** having a strong healthy body because you exercise regularly: *My brother's physically fit because he goes to the gym every day.*

**hear** *verb*
to notice a sound with your ears: *I can hear a strange noise in the kitchen.*

▶ **listen** to pay attention to something, using your ears: *I listen to music on the radio.*

▶ **catch** to hear what someone says: *Can you say that again? I didn't catch what you said.*

▶ **overhear** to accidentally hear what other people are saying to each other: *I know Maria is having a party because I overheard her telling Katie about it.*

**help** *verb*
to do something that makes it easier for another person to do something: *I help my mom with the housework.*

▶ **give someone a hand** to help someone carry something or do physical work: *Can I give you a hand with your suitcase? It looks heavy.*

▶ **do someone a favor** to do something to help someone you know well because he or she asks you: *Would you do me a favor and open the door for me?*

▶ **support** to help someone during a difficult time in his or her life: *If I have any problems, I know my family will always support me.*

▶ **assist** to help someone, especially by doing part of his or her work: *Her job is to assist the teacher during the class.*

▶ **aid** to help something to happen, or to help someone to do something: *This computer game will aid children with their learning.* | *If you breathe deeply, it can aid relaxation.*

**hide** *verb*
to put something where people cannot see it or find it: *I hide my candy in the closet, so that my sister cannot find it.*

▶ **conceal** to hide something carefully: *She concealed the money in a secret drawer.*

▶ **disguise** to make yourself look different because you want to hide who you are: *He put on a wig and disguised himself as a woman.*

▶ **camouflage** to make someone or something difficult to see, by using colors or patterns that are similar to the things around them: *Soldiers camouflage themselves by wearing brown and green clothes, so that the enemy will not see them.*

▶ **cover up** to hide the truth, by preventing someone from finding out what really happened: *The company tried to cover up the bad safety report, but the newspapers found out about it.*

**high** *adjective*
measuring a long way from the bottom to the top. You use **high** about mountains, walls, or fences: *Mount Everest is the highest mountain in the world.* | *The prison is surrounded by high walls.* (ANTONYM: **low**)

▶ **tall** measuring a long way from the bottom to the top. You use **tall** about people, plants, or narrow buildings and objects: *My dad is very tall. He is six feet five inches tall.* | *Sequoia trees are the tallest trees in the world.*

▶ **high-rise** a **high-rise** building is tall and modern and has a lot of floors: *There are many high-rise office buildings in New York City.*

▶ **majestic** big, tall, and impressive: *The mountains in Yosemite are very majestic.*

## hit *verb*

to quickly move your hand or an object against someone or something, with a lot of force: *I hit the ball over the fence.* | *Don't hit the dog, Becky; you might hurt him.*

▶ **punch** to hit someone or something with your fist: *The boys had a fight, and Alex punched David in the face.*

▶ **slap** to hit someone with the flat part of your hand: *He pushed her, and she slapped his face.*

▶ **beat** to hit someone or something many times: *The man was beating the horse with a stick so I told him to stop.*

▶ **bang** to hit something in a way that makes a loud noise: *He was shouting and banging his fist on the table.*

▶ **knock** to hit a door with your hand so that the people inside can hear you: *I knocked on the door, but no one answered.*

▶ **tap** to hit someone or something gently, especially to get someone's attention: *She tapped me on the shoulder and said "hi!"*

## hold *verb*

to have something in your hands or arms: *I want to hold the baby.* | *The teacher was holding a pile of books.*

▶ **grip** to hold something very firmly: *Sophie gripped her camera tightly so that no one could take it.*

▶ **grab** to quickly take something in your hand: *"I'm late," Rod said, grabbing his bag and running out the door.*

▶ **seize** to take something in your hand quickly and with a lot of force: *Mom seized Bobby's arm to stop him from running into the street.*

▶ **hug** to put your arms around someone to show that you like him or her very much: *We hugged each other and then said goodbye.*

## hole *noun*

an empty space in the ground, or in something that is torn or broken: *Our dog likes digging holes and burying old bones in them.* | *My T-shirt has a hole in it where it tore.*

▶ **gap** a space between two things or two parts of something: *Suzy has a gap between her two front teeth.* | *The cat gets into our yard through a gap in the fence.*

▶ **cavity** a hole in a tooth: *The dentist says I have a cavity in one of my teeth.*

▶ **leak** a small hole that lets liquid or gas flow out of something: *There's a leak in the pipe so there's water all over the floor.*

▶ **slot** a narrow hole in a machine where you put money: *I put the coins in the slot in the vending machine and got a candy bar.*

▶ **crater** a round hole in the ground, made by something falling, or by an explosion: *The surface of the Moon is covered in craters.*

## honest *adjective*

someone who is honest does not lie, cheat, or steal: *Ricky is completely honest. I'm sure he didn't take the money.* ( **ANTONYM: dishonest** )

▶ **truthful** saying what is true and not trying to hide the facts: *Be truthful. Did you throw the rock at the window?*

▶ **sincere** someone who is sincere really feels or believes something, and does not just pretend to feel or believe it: *She sounded sincere when she thanked us for our help.*

▶ **frank** speaking in an honest and direct way about something that is difficult to talk about: *The teacher was frank with him when she told him that his work needed to improve.*

▶ **trustworthy** able to be trusted: *They need someone who is trustworthy to take care of the kids.*

a b c d e f g h i j k l m n o p q r s t u v w x y z

**a b c d e f g h i j k l m n o p q r s t u v w x y z**

## horrible *adjective*

very bad: *The weather is horrible. It's raining all the time.* ( ANTONYM: **great** )

▶ **terrible** very bad: *The movie was terrible. The story didn't make any sense.*

▶ **awful** very bad: *I woke up with an awful headache.*

▶ **disgusting** smelling or tasting very bad: *The fish tastes disgusting. I can't eat it.*

▶ **revolting** smelling, tasting, or looking very bad: *The walls were painted a revolting brown color.*

## horse *noun*

a large animal that people ride or use for pulling carriages: *In the old days, people used horses instead of cars.*

▶ **pony** a type of small horse: *Sophia loves riding and she wants to have her own pony.*

▶ **racehorse** a horse that runs in races: *The racehorses are getting ready for the start of the race.*

▶ **foal** a very young horse: *The foal stayed close to its mother.*

▶ **colt** a young male horse

▶ **stallion** an adult male horse

▶ **mare** a female horse or donkey

▶ **donkey** an animal like a small horse with long ears. **Donkeys** are sometimes used for carrying things.

▶ **mule** an animal that has a horse and a donkey as its parents. **Mules** are sometimes used for carrying things.

## hot *adjective*

having a high temperature: *It's really hot today. It's over 80°. | I'm hot. Can I take my sweater off? | Would you like a hot drink to warm you up?* ( ANTONYM: **cold** )

▶ **warm** slightly hot, especially in a pleasant way: *It's nice and warm in the house. | We made a fire to keep ourselves warm.*

▶ **lukewarm** lukewarm liquid is only slightly warm, and is not as hot as it should be: *The soup was only lukewarm.*

▶ **scalding** scalding liquid is so hot that it burns your skin: *I spilled scalding coffee all over my knee and it was very painful.*

▶ **humid** if the weather is humid, the air feels warm and wet: *In the rainforests of South America, the weather is very humid.*

▶ **feverish** if you are feverish, your skin feels hot because you are sick: *He feels feverish and he has a temperature of 102°.*

**horse**

a horse
a racehorse
a pony
a donkey
a foal

## house *noun*

a building that you live in, especially with your family: *We live in a house on Pine Street. | Do you want to come to my house after school?*

▶ **home** the place where you live: *They have a nice home | Welcome to our home!*

▶ **apartment** a set of rooms in a large building, where someone lives: *Our apartment is on the fifth floor of the building.*

▶ **condominium/condo** an apartment in a building with several other apartments. Condominiums are sometimes on two levels: *I live in a condo with a pool that we share.*

▶ **townhouse** a house in a group of houses that share one or more walls: *They live in a three-bedroom townhouse.*

▶ **row house** one house in a row of houses that are joined together: *We live in a row house and we have neighbors on either side of our house.*

▶ **ranch house** a long house that is all on one level: *They live in a three-bedroom ranch house.*

▶ **cabin** a small house made of wood in a forest or the mountains: *We stayed in a log cabin in the mountains.*

▶ **mansion** a very big expensive house: *The movie star lives in a mansion in Beverly Hills.*

▶ **residence** a big house where someone lives, especially someone important: *The party took place at the mayor's residence.*

▶ **mobile home** a small metal house that can be moved on a truck: *A mobile home is cheaper to buy than a house.*

▶ **shack** a small building that has been badly built: *The people live in shacks with no electricity or running water.*

▶ **hut** a very simple building made from wood, mud, or straw: *In Africa, some people live in mud huts far away from cities.*

## hurt *verb*

to make someone feel pain, or damage part of someone's body: *Don't hold my arm so tightly. You're hurting me! | I fell off my bicycle and hurt my leg.*

▶ **injure** to hurt someone badly, especially in an accident: *He was playing football when he injured his leg.*

▶ **wound** to hurt someone with a weapon: *The soldier was wounded by a bullet in the war.*

▶ **break** to hurt a part of your body by breaking a bone in it: *Nicky broke her leg when she was skiing.*

▶ **sprain** to hurt part of your body by suddenly twisting it: *Tom sprained his wrist when he was playing tennis.*

▶ **bruise** to hurt part of your body when you hit something, so that a dark mark appears on your skin: *I walked into a branch and bruised my forehead.*

**house**

a house     a cabin     an apartment     a hut

a row house     a shack     a mobile home

# Ii

## ice *noun*

frozen water: *In winter, the lake is covered in ice.* | *Do you want ice in your water?*

▶ **icicle** a long pointed piece of ice that hangs down from something: *It was a cold winter's day and icicles were hanging from the roof of the house.*

▶ **frost** ice that looks like white powder and covers things outside when it is very cold: *The next morning was very cold so the grass was covered in frost.*

▶ **hailstone** a small drop of hard frozen rain: *There was a storm outside and I could hear hailstones hitting the windows.*

ice

icicles                    ice

## idea *noun*

something that you think of, especially a plan or suggestion that you tell someone about: *"I think we should have pizza!" "That's a good idea!"* | *I like the idea of going to the beach.*

▶ **thought** something that comes into your mind when you think about something: *Her mind was filled with thoughts about the dance.*

▶ **theory** a set of ideas that is used to explain why something happens: *There are many theories about how the universe began.*

▶ **concept** a general idea about what something is like: *The concept of freedom is very important to Americans and they always want to defend it.*

▶ **impression** your opinion or feeling about someone or something: *I had the impression she was very intelligent, because she got all the answers right on the test.*

## immediately *adverb*

very quickly and with no delay: *If you get ketchup on your clothes, you should clean it off immediately.*

▶ **instantly** almost as soon as something else happens: *As soon as I saw the worried look on Mom's face, I instantly knew that something was wrong.*

▶ **at once** immediately, because something is very urgent: *The doctor came at once and gave him medicine to stop the pain.*

## increase *verb*

to get bigger, or to make something bigger: *When we measured the bean plants, they had increased in size.* | *My parents increased my allowance from $3 to $4.* ( **ANTONYM: decrease** )

▶ **rise** to increase. You use **rise** about the temperature, level, or standard of something: *The weather report says that the temperature will rise to 90° today.* | *The level of the ocean is rising because of climate change.*

▶ **grow** to increase, especially gradually over a period of time: *The number of students has grown from 1,000 to 3,000 in the last 10 years.*

▶ **double** to become twice as big: *The price of this ice cream has doubled. It used to be $2 and now it is $4.*

▶ **shoot up** to increase suddenly by a large amount: *The cost of a chocolate bar has shot up from 50c to 95c.*

▶ **raise** to make prices, taxes, or standards increase: *Some people want the government to raise taxes.*

## information *noun*

details about someone or something: *You can find lots of useful information on the Internet.* | *Where can I get some information about Ben Franklin?*

▶ **fact** a piece of information that is true about someone or something: *One fact about China is that more people live there than in any other country.*

▶ **data** facts, numbers, and other information that have been collected and stored, especially on a computer: *Scientists are collecting data about pollution levels in the city.*

▶ **evidence** things that show that something is true, or that someone did something: *They found evidence that people lived there thousands of years ago.* | *There is no evidence that he committed the robbery.*

## injury noun

damage to part of your body because of an accident or an attack: *The injury to her leg happened in the car accident.*

▶ **wound** an injury, especially a deep cut in your skin made by a knife or a bullet: *The soldier had a bullet wound in his chest.*

▶ **cut** a long thin hole in your skin caused by a sharp object, from which blood comes out: *Mom put a bandage over the cut on my arm.*

▶ **bruise** a dark mark on your skin that you get when you fall or get hit: *I have a bruise on my knee from when I fell down.*

▶ **bump** a raised area on your skin that you get when you fall or get hit: *I had a big bump on my forehead after I hit my head on the cupboard door.*

## intelligent adjective

able to learn and understand things quickly: *You have to be intelligent to be a doctor.* | *Some birds are very intelligent and they can copy the sound of human voices.* ( ANTONYM: **stupid** )

▶ **smart** able to think and learn quickly and find ways to solve problems: *My brother is smart, so he do can his math homework quickly.*

▶ **clever** intelligent and good at thinking of ways of doing things. You often use **clever** about people tricking other people: *He's clever! Somehow he gets his sister to do his chores for him.*

▶ **bright** intelligent. You use **bright** about children and young people: *She's a bright kid and is doing very well at school.*

▶ **brilliant** very intelligent and good at your work: *Marie Curie was a brilliant scientist who made important discoveries.*

▶ **wise** able to make good decisions and give sensible advice because you have a lot of experience of life: *My grandfather is a wise old man who has taught me many things.*

## interested adjective

if you are interested in something, you want to know more about it: *I'm interested in football and often go to watch games.* ( ANTONYM: **uninterested** )

▶ **fascinated** very interested: *Many children are fascinated by dinosaurs.*

▶ **absorbed** very interested in something you are doing, especially so that you do not notice anything else: *I was so absorbed in watching a television show that I didn't hear the doorbell ring.*

▶ **be obsessed with** to be too interested in something, so that you cannot stop thinking about it, often in an unhealthy way: *He's obsessed with computer games and never plays outside.*

▶ **curious** if you are curious about something, you want to find out more about it, especially because it seems strange or unusual: *I'm curious to find out what happens at the end of the movie.*

## interesting adjective

if something is interesting, it keeps your attention because it seems exciting, or it tells you things you did not know about: *I'm reading an interesting book about space.* ( ANTONYM: **boring** )

▶ **fascinating** very interesting: *He has had a fascinating life and met lots of famous people.*

▶ **absorbing** interesting in a way that keeps your attention completely: *The book was so absorbing that I didn't want to stop reading it!*

▶ **intriguing** interesting because you want to find out more: *The story is intriguing because you try to solve the mystery along with the characters in the book.*

a
b
c
d
e
f
g
h
i
j
k
l
m
n
o
p
q
r
s
t
u
v
w
x
y
z

a
b
c
d
e
f
g
h
i

**j**

k
l
m
n
o
p
q
r
s
t
u
v
w
x
y
z

**invent** *verb*
to think of or make something completely new, for example a new machine or game: *Alexander Graham Bell invented the telephone in 1876. | Basketball was invented by a Canadian called James Naismith.*

▶ **discover** to find a new substance, fact, or method that no one has found before: *Sir William Herschel discovered the planet Uranus in 1781. | Scientists have discovered a cure for the disease.*

▶ **create** to make or design something new, especially in art or literature: *The students created their own costumes for the school play. | The writer Mark Twain created the character Huckleberry Finn.*

▶ **devise** to invent a way of doing something: *The teacher devised a math game to help us learn the times tables.*

▶ **make up** to invent a story, song, or excuse: *Mom makes up stories for us at bedtime. | He was late for school so he made up an excuse about his alarm clock not working.*

# Jj

**jewelry** *noun*
things such as rings and necklaces that you wear for decoration: *My aunt wears a lot of gold jewelry. She has a gold ring and four gold bracelets.*

▶ **ring** a piece of jewelry that you wear on your finger: *He has a wedding ring on his finger.*

▶ **bracelet** a piece of jewelry that you wear around your wrist: *Dad gave Joanne a silver bracelet for her birthday.*

▶ **earring** a piece of jewelry that you fasten to your ear: *Sally was wearing a pair of gold earrings.*

▶ **necklace** a piece of jewelry that you wear around your neck: *Mom is wearing a diamond necklace.*

▶ **pendant** a jewel or small decoration that hangs from a chain around your neck: *Maria was wearing a pendant around her neck.*

▶ **brooch** a piece of jewelry with a pin on the back, that women fasten to their clothes: *She pinned a brooch shaped like a flower to her jacket.*

**jewelry**

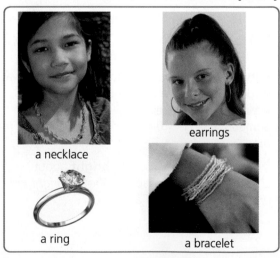

a necklace

earrings

a ring

a bracelet

## job *noun*

the work that you do regularly to earn money, especially when you work for a company or organization: *Mom has a full-time job in a supermarket.* | *He had several jobs after he left high school.*

▶ **work** activities that you do to earn money: *My father started work when he was 15.*

▶ **profession** a job that needs special education and training, for example being a teacher, doctor, or lawyer: *She wants to work in the legal profession, so she is going to law school.*

▶ **occupation** someone's job. You use **occupation** on official documents: *Write your name, address, and occupation at the top of the form.*

▶ **career** a type of work that you do for a long time, often for most of your life: *I'm interested in a career as a teacher.*

## join *verb*

to make two things become connected together, so that they form a single thing: *I used a nail to join the two pieces of wood together.* | *The gym is joined onto the school.*

▶ **connect** to join two parts of something together, often with a wire or pipe: *You can connect a speaker to your MP3 player.* | *The pipe connects the gas tank to the engine.*

▶ **attach** to join one thing to another, so that it stays in position. You often use **attach** when you can separate the two things later: *She attached the photo to the letter with a paper clip.*

▶ **link** to connect machines, systems, or computers, so that electronic signals can pass from one to another: *All the computers in the library are linked to the Internet.*

▶ **fasten** to join together the two sides of something such as a belt or a knot: *Fasten your seat belts, because the plane is ready to take off.*

## joke *noun*

something funny that you say or do to make people laugh: *Dad tells silly jokes to make us laugh.*

▶ **gag** a short joke, especially one told by a professional entertainer: *The comedian told a funny gag and everyone laughed.*

▶ **pun** a joke made by mixing up two different meanings of the same word, or two words with the same sound: *"Ice cream or I scream" is a good pun.*

▶ **practical joke** a trick that you do to surprise someone and make other people laugh: *He put a plastic spider on her desk as a practical joke.*

▶ **prank** a trick, especially one that makes someone look silly: *As a prank, he phoned one of his friends and pretended to be a radio show host.*

## judge *noun*

one of the people who decide who is the winner of a game or competition: *The judges decided that her essay was the best.*

▶ **umpire** the person who makes sure that a sport such as tennis or baseball is played correctly: *The umpire at first base said the runner was out.*

▶ **referee** someone who makes sure that players obey the rules in sports such as football, basketball, and boxing: *The referee stopped the game because one of the players was injured.*

a
b
c
d
e
f
g
h
i
**j**
k
l
m
n
o
p
q
r
s
t
u
v
w
x
y
z

a
b
c
d
e
f
g
h
i
j
k
l
m
n
o
p
q
r
s
t
u
v
w
x
y
z

**jump** *verb*

to push yourself up into the air or over something using your legs: *How high can you jump?* | *Jumping on a trampoline is a lot of fun.*

► **leap** to jump up high or a long way: *The horse leaped over the fence.* | *The monkeys were leaping from tree to tree.*

► **spring** to jump or move somewhere suddenly: *I watch the cat spring up onto the sofa.*

► **hop** if a person hops, he or she jumps on one leg. If a frog, insect, or rabbit hops, it suddenly jumps somewhere: *He was hopping around because he had hurt his foot.* | *The frog hopped into the pond.*

► **skip** to move forward with quick jumps from one foot to the other: *The girls were skipping down the street.*

► **dive** to jump into water with your arms and head first, not your feet: *I like diving into the pool.*

jump

The boy is jumping.

The girls are skipping.

He is diving.

The boy is leaping.

# Kk

## keep *verb*
to put something in a place, so that you can find it there later when you need it: *I keep the scissors in the desk drawer.*

▶ **save** to keep something, so that you can use or enjoy it later: *I save some money every week, because I want to buy a new bike later.*

▶ **store** to keep something somewhere, especially for a long time: *My old books are stored in a box in the garage.*

▶ **file** to keep documents in a place, often using an organized system: *I file all my essays in a special folder on my computer.* | *The students' reports are filed alphabetically.*

▶ **collect** to keep a particular type of thing because you are interested in it: *One of my hobbies is collecting stamps.*

▶ **hoard** to keep a lot of something and hide it somewhere: *Some animals hoard food so that they can eat it during the winter.*

## kind *adjective*
showing that you care about other people and want to help them: *A kind boy helped the old lady to cross the street.* | *It's kind of you to help.*

( ANTONYMS: **unkind, mean** )

▶ **nice** friendly and kind: *The teachers at my school are nice. They always answer questions.*

▶ **generous** kind because you give people money or presents: *My grandpa is very generous and he often buys us presents.*

▶ **thoughtful** thinking of things you can do to make other people happy or feel good: *It was thoughtful of you to send David a card when he was sick.*

▶ **considerate** thinking about other people's feelings and careful not to do anything that will upset them: *Our neighbors are considerate and keep their TV turned down.*

## king *noun*
a man who is in charge of a country because he is from a royal family: *King George III was king of England during the American Revolution.*

▶ **monarch** a king or queen: *Queen Elizabeth II is the British monarch.*

▶ **ruler** someone such as a king, president, or general who has official power over a country and its people: *The king was a good ruler who was kind to his people.*

▶ **emperor** the ruler of an empire: *Julius Caesar was a Roman emperor.*

▶ **prince** the son of a king or queen: *In the story, the prince falls in love with Cinderella.*

## know *verb*
to have knowledge or information about something: *My brother knows a lot about baseball and he can tell you all the best players.* | *Do you know what the capital city of France is?*

▶ **realize** to know that something is true: *I didn't realize that it was so late.* | *Do you realize how much this will cost?*

▶ **be aware** to know that a situation or a problem exists: *You need to be aware that cars don't always stop, so you must look both ways before you cross the street.*

▶ **can tell** to know that something is true because you can see signs that show this: *His eyes are red so you can tell that he has been crying.*

▶ **be familiar with** to know something well because you have seen it or used it before: *I am familiar with horses because I grew up on a farm.*

a
b
c
d
e
f
g
h
i
j
k
**l**
m
n
o
p
q
r
s
t
u
v
w
x
y
z

### knowledge *noun*

the things that you know about something: *I have a basic knowledge of Spanish and I can say "buenos días" and "muchas gracias." | The teacher was impressed by Tina's knowledge of art.*

▶ **wisdom** the ability to make good decisions, based on your knowledge and experience of life: *My grandfather is full of wisdom, so I often ask him for his advice.*

▶ **expertise** special skills or knowledge that you learn from experience or training: *I need someone with technical expertise to fix my computer.*

**Ll**

### land *noun*

an area of ground: *They want to use the land for a new swimming pool.*

▶ **territory** land that a country controls: *Alaska became U.S. territory in 1867.*

▶ **the grounds** the land around a big building: *The photograph shows the president and his family in the grounds of the White House.*

▶ **farmland** land that is used for farming: *This area is farmland and people grow wheat and corn.*

### language *noun*

the system of words, phrases, and grammar that the people who live in a country use to speak and write to each other: *She can speak three languages: English, Spanish, and Japanese.*

▶ **dialect** a form of a language that is spoken by the people who live in one area of a country. The dialect uses some different words and a different pronunciation: *The people speak a dialect of English which includes some French words.*

▶ **slang** very informal spoken language used by a group of people, for example young people: *You shouldn't use slang when you are writing essays. | "Awesome" is a slang word which means "very good."*

▶ **mother tongue** the first language that someone learns as a child: *I was born in Mexico, so my mother tongue is Spanish.*

### laugh *verb*

to make a sound with your voice because you think something is funny: *His jokes always make me laugh.*

▶ **giggle** to laugh quickly in a high voice because something is funny, or because you are nervous or embarrassed: *A group of girls giggled when he spilled the milk on his pants.*

▶ **chuckle** to laugh quietly because you are reading or thinking about something funny: *She chuckled to herself while she was reading the cartoon.*

▶ **snicker** to laugh quietly in an unkind way, for example when someone is hurt or embarrassed: *He snickered when his sister fell over and got mud on her new dress.*

▶ **roar with laughter** to laugh very loudly: *His pants fell down and the audience roared with laughter.*

### learn *verb*

to get knowledge about a subject or about how to do something: *She has been learning English for six years. | I'm learning how to play the guitar.*

▶ **study** to spend time learning about a subject, by reading books, or going to classes at school or college: *I need to study for my English test. | My brother is studying math in college.*

▶ **master** to learn to do something very well, for example playing a musical instrument, or speaking a language: *It can take years to master the violin.*

▶ **train** to learn the skills that you need in order to do a job: *Katie is training to be a nurse.*

## leave *verb*

to go away from a place or person: *Before you leave the house, make sure all the windows are shut. | I have to leave soon or I'll be late for school.* (ANTONYM: **stay**)

▶ **emigrate** to leave your own country, in order to live permanently in another country: *In 2005, his family emigrated to the U.S. from Colombia.*

▶ **go away** to leave your home and go to another place for a few days or weeks: *We're going away for the weekend to visit some friends in Chicago.*

▶ **depart** to leave a place. You use **depart** especially about trains, airplanes, and buses: *The train for Denver will depart from track 9.*

▶ **take off** if an airplane takes off, it leaves the ground: *Our plane took off late because of bad weather.*

▶ **set sail** to leave a place in a boat: *Columbus set sail from Spain in 1492.*

## lie *noun*

something that you say, which you know is not true: *She's always telling lies. I don't believe a word she says.* (ANTONYM: **the truth**)

▶ **fib** a small lie, especially one that a child tells someone: *He didn't want to go to the movies with Joe, so he told a fib and said he had to visit his aunt.*

▶ **white lie** a lie that does not harm anyone, especially one that you tell to avoid hurting someone's feelings: *I told a white lie and said her new dress looked nice, because I didn't want to upset her.*

▶ **tall tale** something that someone tells you, which is difficult to believe: *My dad is always telling tall tales about his school days, like the time when he scored six home runs.*

## lift *verb*

to move something to a higher position: *Can you help me lift this box onto the table?*

▶ **raise** to move something to a higher position for a short time, before lowering it again: *Raise your hand if you know the answer. | The batter raised his bat, ready to hit the ball.*

▶ **pick up** to lift something up from the ground or a table, especially something small or light: *He picked up the letter and put it in his pocket.*

▶ **hoist** to lift up something heavy, or pull something up with ropes or special equipment: *He hoisted the sack over his shoulder. | They hoisted the flag up the flagpole. | The crane began hoisting the containers onto the ship.*

**lift**

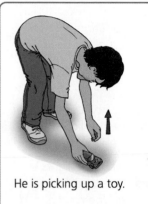

He is picking up a toy.

He is lifting a box.

The crane is hoisting the bricks.

She raised her bat ready to hit the ball.

a b c d e f g h i j k **l** m n o p q r s t u v w x y z

### light *noun*

something that produces light for you to see, especially from electricity: *Please turn off the lights when you leave the classroom.*

▶ **lamp** a type of light that you can put on a table or stand on the floor: *I have a lamp next to my bed, which I use for reading.*

▶ **flashlight** a small electric light that you carry in your hand: *I used my flashlight to see into the cave.*

▶ **candle** a thing that you burn to produce light. A candle consists of a stick of wax with string through the middle: *There are nine candles on my birthday cake.*

▶ **lantern** a lamp you can carry, consisting of a glass or metal container with a light inside: *The miners used lanterns which were lit by candles.*

▶ **headlight** one of the two large lights at the front of a vehicle: *Cars have their headlights on at night, so drivers can see the road ahead.*

▶ **streetlight** a light at the top of a tall post in a street: *There are two men standing under the streetlight next to our house.*

**light**

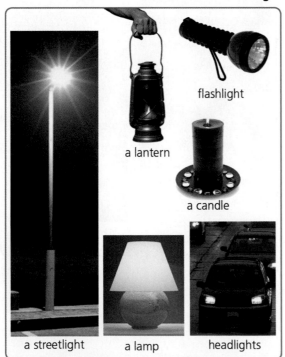

flashlight

a lantern

a candle

a streetlight     a lamp     headlights

### like *verb*

to think that someone or something is good or nice: *I like Mexican food. | She likes all the other students in her class.* (ANTONYM: **dislike**)

▶ **prefer** to like someone or something more than another person or thing: *I prefer the blue dress. It's prettier than the other one. | Do you prefer milk or apple juice?*

▶ **enjoy** to like doing something or watching something: *I enjoyed the game. It was really exciting.*

▶ **love** to like someone or something very much: *I love chocolate chip cookies.*

▶ **adore** to like someone or something very much: *I adore my grandma. She is really nice.*

▶ **be fond of** to like someone or something, especially someone you have known for a long time, or something you have had for a long time: *I'm very fond of my dad and I don't like it when he goes away.*

▶ **be addicted to** to like doing something so much that you spend all your free time doing it: *My brother's addicted to computer games. He sits in his room for hours playing them.*

### line *noun*

a long thin mark on a surface: *The teacher asked us to draw a straight line. | There is a yellow line down the middle of the road.*

▶ **stripe** a straight line of color, usually part of a pattern where the line is repeated many times: *The American flag has red and white stripes on it.*

▶ **streak** a line of a different color from the rest of something: *Mrs. Brooks has brown hair with gray streaks in it.*

▶ **crease** a line on clothes or paper, where it has been folded: *He folded the paper and made a crease in it.*

▶ **wrinkle** a line on your face, which you get when you are old, or a line on a piece of clothing where it has been crushed: *You'll have to iron the skirt to get the wrinkles out.*

## liquid *noun*

a substance such as water, that is not a solid or a gas: *Milk is a white liquid.*

▶ **fluid** **fluid** means the same as **liquid**. You use **fluid** when you are talking about liquids in machines or people's bodies: *You need to drink plenty of fluids when you're exercising. | Brake fluid was leaking out from under our car.*

▶ **solution** a liquid that has another substance dissolved into it. This word is used especially in chemistry: *We made a solution of salt and water.*

▶ **juice** the liquid from fruit and vegetables: *Mom, can I have a glass of apple juice, please?*

▶ **sap** a sticky liquid in plants. The sap carries food up through the plant: *The syrup is made of sap from maple trees.*

## list *noun*

a set of things that you write down, one below the other: *I'm making a list of the people I want to invite to my party.*

▶ **checklist** a list that helps to remind you of all the things you need to do: *The checklist is of all the things you need to take on vacation.*

▶ **index** an alphabetical list of names and subjects at the back of a book. The index shows the page on which they are mentioned: *I looked for his name in the index.*

▶ **catalog** a list of all the things that a store sells, or all the books in a library: *Mom and Dad ordered a new sofa from the catalog.*

▶ **roll** a list of the names of everyone in a class: *When the teacher calls the roll, you say "here" when she says your name.*

▶ **roster** a list of the names of the people in a class, team, or organization: *Make sure that your name is on the team roster.*

▶ **schedule** a list of the times of trains, buses, or airplanes, or a list of the times when something will happen: *The schedule says that the next train is at 8:30. | The schedule says that the beginners swimming class starts at 4:30.*

▶ **menu** a list of the food that you can eat in a restaurant: *I looked at the menu and ordered ice cream.*

## listen *verb*

to use your ears so that you hear what someone is saying, or a sound: *Listen carefully to what the teacher says. | I like listening to music.*

▶ **pay attention** to listen carefully to what someone is saying: *I have some important information to give you, so please pay attention.*

▶ **eavesdrop** to secretly listen to other people talking: *She was hiding behind a door and eavesdropping on Sue and Tim's conversation.*

## live *verb*

to have your home somewhere: *I live in Los Angeles.*

▶ **stay** to live in a place for a short time, especially as a visitor or guest: *We stayed in a hotel near the beach.*

▶ **inhabit** if a group of people or animals inhabit a place, they live there: *The island is inhabited by sheep. | The first people to inhabit North America probably came from Siberia.*

▶ **settle** to start to live permanently in a country or city after you have lived in other places: *After living in New York and Chicago, we finally settled in San Francisco.*

▶ **grow up** to live somewhere when you are a child: *She grew up in Canada.*

## lonely *adjective*

unhappy because you are alone or do not have any friends: *There was nobody else in the house, and Ben felt lonely.*

▶ **lonesome** **lonesome** means the same as **lonely**: *Karen was lonesome when her sister went away to college.*

▶ **homesick** unhappy because you are away from your home, your family, and your friends: *After a few days at camp, he started to feel homesick for his family.*

▶ **isolated** lonely because your situation makes it difficult for you to meet people: *Some people feel isolated because their families live far away.*

a
b
c
d
e
f
g
h
i
j
k
**l**
m
n
o
p
q
r
s
t
u
v
w
x
y
z

a
b
c
d
e
f
g
h
i
j
k
l
m
n
o
p
q
r
s
t
u
v
w
x
y
z

**long** *adjective*
continuing for many minutes, hours, days, or years: *The movie is very long. It lasts over two hours.* (ANTONYM: **short**)

▶ **lengthy** a **lengthy** discussion or delay continues for longer than you expect: *The teachers had a lengthy meeting with the boy's parents.* | *The accident is causing lengthy delays on the freeway.*

▶ **long-running** a **long-running** show or argument continues for a long time: *The program is one of the longest-running shows on TV.*

▶ **long-winded** a long-winded speech, answer, or explanation is too long and boring: *He gave a long-winded speech that seemed to go on for hours.*

▶ **interminable** very long and boring, so that you think that something will never end: *The trip seemed interminable, so I was glad when we finally got off the plane.*

**look** *verb*
to use your eyes so that you can see someone or something: *She looked at me and smiled.*

▶ **watch** to look at something that is moving, or to look at a game, television show, or movie: *I watched the baseball game on TV.* | *I watched him drive away in his car.*
You say *I watched TV.* You do not say "I looked at the TV."

▶ **glance** to look at someone or something for a short time: *Kevin glanced at the clock as he walked past it.*

▶ **peek** to quickly look at something that you should not look at: *When his mother was out of the room, he opened her bag and peeked inside.*

▶ **peer** to look very carefully because you cannot see something clearly: *We peered through a hole in the fence to see what was on the other side.*

▶ **stare** to look at someone or something for a long time without moving your eyes, often because you are surprised or angry: *Don't stare at people. It's rude.*

▶ **gaze** to look at someone or something for a long time, with feelings of love, or when you are thinking about something else: *She was gazing into the baby's beautiful brown eyes.*

**loud** *adjective*
making a lot of noise: *The TV's too loud. Turn it down.* | *There was a loud cheer from the fans when their team scored.* (ANTONYM: **quiet**)

▶ **noisy** making a lot of noise. You use **noisy** about people, machines, and places that are too loud: *Our neighbors are very noisy so it is hard for me to sleep sometimes.* | *The old car had a noisy engine.*

▶ **deafening** very loud, especially so that you cannot hear anything else: *The noise of the planes was deafening.*

▶ **piercing** a **piercing** sound is very high and loud: *I suddenly heard a piercing scream.*

**love** *verb*
to like someone very much and care a lot about that person: *She kissed him and said "I love you!"* | *I love my dad. He's a really nice guy.*
(ANTONYM: **hate**)

▶ **adore** to love someone very much: *She adores her grandchildren so she often buys presents for them.*

▶ **be in love** to love someone in a romantic way: *Stephen is in love with Suzy and he wants to marry her.* | *They are very much in love, and they are always holding hands.*

**lucky** *adjective*
if you are lucky, good things happen to you by chance: *I was lucky and guessed the right answer to the question.* | *It was lucky that you remembered to bring the map. Otherwise, we would be lost.* (ANTONYM: **unlucky**)

▶ **fortunate** **fortunate** means the same as **lucky**: *I was fortunate to get a ticket to the concert because there weren't many tickets left.*

▶ **miraculous** if something is miraculous, it is very lucky because you avoid something very bad in a way that is almost unbelievable: *The car crash was bad, but we had a miraculous escape and no one was hurt.*

# Mm

**make** *verb*

to produce something, especially by putting different parts together: *My mom makes all her own clothes.* | *The company makes computers.*

▶ **build** to make a house, road, bridge, or tunnel: *Our house was built five years ago.*

▶ **construct** to build something especially something big: *Two new schools will be constructed.*

▶ **manufacture** to make things in factories in large amounts: *The toys are manufactured in China.*

▶ **create** to make something new and original: *He created a new computer game.* | *L. Frank Baum created the "The Wizard of Oz" books.*

▶ **form** to make something as the result of a chemical reaction or natural process: *Ice forms on the lake during the winter.*

▶ **generate** to make electricity, power, or heat: *People can use wind power to generate electricity.*

**many** *adjective, pronoun*

a large number of people or things. **Many** is usually used in questions and negative sentences: *Did you get many presents for your birthday?* | *There aren't many cars on the road today.* | *We have lived here for many years.* ( ANTONYM: **few** )

▶ **a lot** a large number of people or things: *She has a lot of friends at school because she's very popular.*

▶ **several** more than a few, but not a very large number: *I have visited Chicago several times and I know the city well.*

▶ **plenty** a large number, which is as much as you need: *She has plenty of books to read at home. She doesn't need any more.*

▶ **countless** a very large number, which is more than you can easily count: *I have already told him countless times to stop talking.*

**mark** *noun*

a small area where the surface of something is dirty or damaged: *There are marks on the door where the cat has been scratching it.* | *How did you get that dirty mark on your T-shirt?*

▶ **stain** a mark that is difficult to remove: *He had grass stains on the knees of his pants.*

▶ **spot** a small mark in the shape of a circle: *The dog is white with black spots.*

▶ **blemish** a mark on something, which spoils the way it looks: *The pears have blemishes on them, but they taste good.*

▶ **bruise** a purple or red mark that you get on your skin, when you fall or hit something: *After I fell off my bike, my arms were covered in bruises.*

▶ **scar** a permanent mark on your skin, after a cut or wound has healed: *She still has a scar from the operation on her stomach.*

▶ **freckles** small brown spots on your face or your arms: *People with red hair often have freckles.*

**mark**

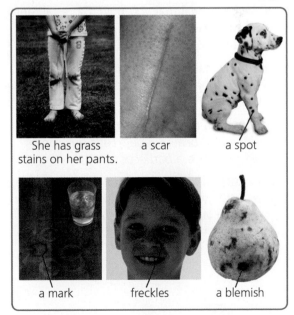

She has grass stains on her pants.    a scar    a spot

a mark    freckles    a blemish

a b c d e f g h i j k l **m** n o p q r s t u v w x y z

a
b
c
d
e
f
g
h
i
j
k
l

**m**

n
o
p
q
r
s
t
u
v
w
x
y
z

## mathematics *noun*

the study of numbers and shapes: *My brother is good at mathematics and he likes solving problems.*

▶ **math** math is short for **mathematics**: *Gina's favorite subject is math because she likes working with numbers.*

▶ **arithmetic** the activity of adding, subtracting, multiplying, or dividing numbers: *Let's do some arithmetic. What is 27 plus 13?*

▶ **algebra** a type of mathematics that uses letters and symbols to represent numbers, for example 2x + 5 = 11: *You use algebra to figure out how far a car will travel in 30 minutes at 10 miles an hour.*

▶ **geometry** the study of shapes, lines, and angles: *In geometry we learned how to calculate the area of a triangle.*

## meal *noun*

the food that you eat at regular times each day: *The whole family has a meal together in the evenings.*

▶ **snack** something small, for example cookies or chocolate, that you eat between meals: *We have a snack in the morning. Maybe a banana or some potato chips.*

▶ **takeout** a meal that you buy at a restaurant to eat at home: *I don't feel like cooking. Let's get a takeout.*

▶ **picnic** a meal that you prepare at home and take somewhere to eat outdoors: *We can make sandwiches and have a picnic on the beach.*

▶ **barbecue** a meal that you cook and eat outside: *It's a beautiful day. Let's buy some steaks and have a barbecue.*

▶ **banquet** a large formal meal for many people, often with important people there: *There was a banquet in Washington in honor of the new president.*

meal

She is having a snack.

The family is having a picnic.

They are having a barbecue.

## mean *adjective*

behaving in a way that is not kind or nice to someone: *The other kids were mean to her and called her names.* (ANTONYMS: nice, kind)

▶ **unkind** unkind means the same as **mean**: *Amy wanted to play with you and you said no. That was unkind.*

▶ **nasty** deliberately mean, in a way that seems shocking: *She keeps saying nasty things to me like, "you're too fat!"*

▶ **cruel** very mean, and deliberately trying to hurt or upset someone: *He was a cruel man who did not give his dogs enough to eat.*

▶ **thoughtless** not thinking about other people's feelings: *It was thoughtless of me not to thank Grandma for the birthday present.*

## medicine *noun*

something that you take when you are sick, to help you get better: *The doctor gave me some medicine to make the pain go away.*

▶ **drug** a medicine, or a substance used for making medicines: *Scientists have found a new drug that can be used to treat cancer.*

▶ **medication** medicine that you take regularly for a health problem: *My grandpa is on medication for his heart.*

## meeting *noun*

an occasion when people meet in order to discuss something: *The teachers had a meeting to talk about the new tests.*

▶ **appointment** an arrangement to meet someone at a particular time: *I have a doctor's appointment at 5:00.*

▶ **date** an arrangement to go somewhere with someone whom you like in a romantic way, for example to see a movie or eat a meal: *Steve asked Suzie if she wanted to go on a date with him.*

▶ **play date** an arrangement to play with a friend at a particular time: *My mom made a play date for me with Sofia.*

▶ **interview** a meeting at which someone is asked a lot of questions: *In the interview, the actor talked about his new movie.* | *My mom has a job interview tomorrow.*

▶ **conference** a large meeting that lasts several days. People listen to talks and discuss ideas: *Scientists are holding a conference about the environment.*

## middle *noun*

the part that is closest to the center of something: *David was standing in the middle of the room.*

▶ **center** **center** means the same as **middle**. You often use **center** about the middle of a town or city, or a point that is exactly in the middle: *There's a park in the center of town.* | *Draw a line through the center of the circle.*

▶ **heart** the middle of a place. You use **heart** when saying that a place is good or interesting because it is in the middle: *The town is in the heart of Texas.*

▶ **core** the middle part of an apple or pear, or of the Earth: *He threw the apple core in the wastebasket.*

## mind *noun*

the part of you that you use for thinking and imagining things: *Her mind was filled with thoughts about the party, so couldn't sleep.*

▶ **brain** the organ in your head that controls how you think, feel, and move: *His brain was damaged when he was a baby, so he has difficulty walking.*

▶ **memory** the part of you that you use for remembering things: *Grandpa has a terrible memory. He forgets people's names.*

## mistake *noun*

something that is not correct: *His homework was full of spelling mistakes.*

▶ **error** **error** means the same as **mistake**: *Writing "there" when you mean "their" is a common error.* | *The accident was caused by human error.*

▶ **misprint** a mistake in the way a word has been printed: *There was a misprint on the menu, and instead of "fries" it said "flies."*

▶ **typo** a mistake in the way something has been typed: *His report was full of typos, like "hse" instead of "she."*

## modern *adjective*

using the most recent designs, methods, or ideas: *Modern planes can fly very fast.* | *Modern technology has made many household jobs much easier.* ( ANTONYM: **old-fashioned** )

▶ **contemporary** contemporary art, music, or literature was produced and written recently: *The museum has a show of contemporary art.*

▶ **up-to-date** if something is up-to-date, it includes the the most recent information, or it is in the latest style: *You need to check that your software is up-to-date.*

▶ **advanced** using very modern technology: *The car has an advanced safety system. It brakes automatically if it gets too close to the car in front.* | *The U.S. has some of the most advanced hospitals in the world.*

▶ **high-tech** using very modern electronic equipment: *The kitchen is very high-tech. The fridge will order your food for you!*

a b c d e f g h i j k l **m** n o p q r s t u v w x y z

a
b
c
d
e
f
g
h
i
j
k
l

**m**

n
o
p
q
r
s
t
u
v
w
x
y
z

**money** *noun*

coins and pieces of paper that you use to buy things: *I don't have enough money to buy a new computer.*

▶ **cash** coins and paper money that you use for buying things: *Mom pays for things using a credit card rather than cash.*

▶ **currency** the type of money that a country uses: *The U.S. currency is the dollar.*

▶ **change** coins, or the money that you get back when you pay more than something costs: *He emptied all the change out of his pockets.* | *The sales clerk handed me my change.*

▶ **coin** a piece of money made of metal: *Suzie put some coins in the soda machine.*

▶ **bill** a piece of paper money: *I paid for the meal with a ten-dollar bill.*

▶ **penny** a coin worth one cent: *I save all my pennies in a jar.*

▶ **nickel** a coin that is worth five cents: *Two nickels make ten cents.*

▶ **dime** a coin that is worth ten cents: *Dad put a dime in the parking meter.*

▶ **quarter** a coin that is worth 25 cents: *I had a couple of quarters in change.*

**mountain** *noun*

a very high hill: *Denali is the highest mountain in North America.* | *We are going camping in the mountains.*

▶ **hill** an area of high land. A **hill** is smaller than a **mountain**: *From the top of the hill you can see the ocean.*

▶ **volcano** a mountain that has a hole at the top, through which smoke and hot liquid rock come out: *The volcano erupted and destroyed the forest below.*

▶ **summit** the top of a mountain: *After a long climb, he reached the summit of the mountain.*

**mountain**

lava

a volcano

the summit

hills

a mountain

**move** *verb*

to change from one place or position to another: *Every time I move, my arm hurts.* | *The cars are moving very slowly.*

▶ **sway** to move slowly from one side to the other: *The palm trees sway in the wind.*

▶ **rock** to move repeatedly from one side to another, with small gentle movements: *Grandma was rocking in her chair on the porch.*

▶ **wobble** to move unsteadily from side to side: *The ladder began to wobble and then it fell over.*

▶ **fidget** to keep moving your fingers, hands, or feet because you are bored or nervous: *The children were bored with the movie, so they began to fidget in their seats.*

▶ **budge** if something will not budge, it will not move: *The table is very heavy and I can't make it budge.*

**movie** *noun*

moving pictures that tell a story: *My favorite movie is "Pirates of the Caribbean."*

▶ **film** **film** means the same as **movie**: *The film won the "Best Picture" award.*

▶ **comedy** a funny movie that makes people laugh: *We watched a comedy about a dog that can talk to people.*

▶ **thriller** a movie that has an exciting story, in which you do not know what will happen next. A thriller is often about a crime: *The movie is a thriller about a man whose wife disappeared.*

▶ **western** a movie about cowboys: *The cowboys take cattle from Texas to Montana in this western.*

▶ **cartoon** a movie with characters that are drawings and are not real: *The kids are watching a Walt Disney cartoon.*

▶ **romance** a movie about the love between two people: *In this romance, she falls in love with a man she meets at work.*

▶ **horror movie** a movie that makes you feel frightened because dangerous and frightening things happen to the characters: *I don't like horror movies because they give me bad dreams.*

▶ **action movie** a movie that has a lot of exciting scenes in it, for example people fighting and chasing each other in cars: *My brother likes action movies with lots of car chases.*

▶ **science fiction movie** a movie about life in the future, often with people or creatures who live in other parts of the universe: *We saw a science fiction movie about monsters from outer space.*

## music *noun*

the sounds that people make when they play instruments or sing: *I like listening to pop music.*

▶ **tune** a series of musical notes that are nice to listen to: *Can you play this tune on the piano?*

▶ **melody** the main notes in a song or piece of music: *The song has a nice melody.*

▶ **song** a short piece of music with words: *I sang the song and my sister played the guitar.*

## musician *noun*

someone who plays a musical instrument, especially as a job: *She wants to be a musician and play in an orchestra.*

▶ **player** someone who plays a musical instrument: *He is a great guitar player.* | *The piano player played my favorite song.*

▶ **band** a group of musicians who play rock, jazz, or folk music together: *My brother plays the drums in a band.*

▶ **orchestra** a large group of musicians who play classical music together: *I play the violin in the school orchestra.*

▶ **composer** someone who writes music: *Mozart is a famous composer who began writing music as a child.*

**musician**

an orchestra

a band    a trombone player

# Nn

## name *noun*

what someone or something is called: *"What's your name?" "Joshua."* | *Do you know the name of this flower?* | *My name is Maddy.*

▶ **family name/last name/surname** the name that you share with other people in your family: *My family name is Palmer.*

▶ **first name/given name** the name that your parents choose for you. In English, your first name comes before your family name: *His first name is Paul.*

▶ **middle name** the name between your first name and your family name, which many people do not use: *The baby's middle name is Rosa, like my mother's first name.*

▶ **nickname** a name that your friends or family use instead of your real name: *Teddy is his nickname. His real name is Edward.*

▶ **maiden name** a woman's family name before she marries and chooses to use her husband's name: *Mom is Mrs. Parker, but her maiden name was Johnson before she married Dad.*

a b c d e f g h i j k l m **n** o p q r s t u v w x y z

a
b
c
d
e
f
g
h
i
j
k
l
m

**n**

o
p
q
r
s
t
u
v
w
x
y
z

## natural *adjective*

existing in nature, and not made by people: *Wool is a natural material because it comes from sheep.* | *The Grand Canyon is one of the wonders of the natural world.* ( ANTONYM: **artificial** )

▶ **wild** wild plants and animals are not grown or taken care of by people: *In spring, the mountainside is covered with wild flowers.* | *The forest is full of wild animals such as deer and bears.*

▶ **pure** not mixed with anything else: *I drink pure orange juice with no added sugar.* | *The air in the mountains is pure because there is no pollution.*

▶ **organic** grown or produced without using chemicals: *Some people prefer organic vegetables because they think chemicals are harmful to the environment.*

## near *adverb, preposition, adjective*

only a short distance from someone or something: *The park is near my house so I often go there after school.* | *Is there a library near here?*
( ANTONYM: **far** )

▶ **close** very near someone or something: *I stayed close to Dad, because I didn't want to get lost.* | *We can all fit in the back of the car if we sit close together.*

▶ **nearby** near where you are, or near your home: *Is there a grocery store nearby?* | *My friend Daniel lives in a nearby town.*

▶ **not far** not a long distance away, and easy to get to: *Let's go to my house, because it's not far from here.*

▶ **local** local stores, schools, and other things are in the area where you live: *On Sundays, we go to a local church.*

▶ **neighboring** a neighboring country, state, or town is next to another country, state, or town: *We went to Indiana and the neighboring states of Ohio and Illinois.*

## necessary *adjective*

if something is necessary, you need to do it or have it: *If necessary, I can ask my mom to lend me the money.* | *You can find the necessary information on the Internet.*
( ANTONYM: **unnecessary** )

▶ **essential** very necessary because you cannot do something without it: *Yeast is essential for making bread, because the bread will not rise without it.*

▶ **vital** very necessary and important because there will be serious problems if you do not do it or have it: *It is vital that he takes his medicine every day.* | *The police found a vital piece of evidence which helped them to solve the case.*

▶ **compulsory** if something is compulsory, you must do it or have it because of a rule or law: *School is compulsory until you are 16.*

## need *verb*

if you need something, you must have it: *I need a new pen because this one is broken.* | *You need three eggs to make this cake.*

▶ **require** to need something. **Require** is a formal word: *If you have a dog, it requires food, clean water, and exercise every day.*

▶ **be desperate for** to need or want something very much: *It was very hot and we were desperate for something to drink.*

▶ **can't do without** to need something very much because it is very useful to have: *My sister can't do without her cell phone because she uses it a lot.*

▶ **lack** to not have something that you need: *Tom lacks confidence, so he finds it difficult to talk to people.*

## nervous *adjective*

worried or frightened: *I always feel nervous before I go to the dentist.* ( ANTONYM: **calm** )

▶ **anxious** very worried about something: *I was anxious about being late for school.*

▶ **tense** worried and unable to relax, so that you become angry or upset easily: *We were waiting for news from the hospital, and everyone was tense.*

▶ **jumpy** nervous and easily surprised by sudden sounds or movements: *It was dark in the forest and I felt jumpy.*

**new** *adjective*
recently made, produced, or bought: *I like your new shirt.* | *The band has a new song.*
( ANTONYM: **old** )

▶ **brand-new** new and never used before: *The apartment is brand-new, so we are the first people to live there.* | *My shoes are shiny and brand-new.*

▶ **original** new and different from what other people do: *His style is original. No one else plays the guitar like he does.*

▶ **fresh** fresh food is good because it has been picked or made recently. Fresh ideas or ways of doing something are new and different: *I picked these strawberries this morning, so they are fresh.* | *When we moved to Utah, it was a fresh start for all of us.*

▶ **recent** made or done a short time ago: *This is a recent photograph of our house. Mom took it last week.*

▶ **latest** most recent: *Her latest movie is better than her other ones.* | *Have you heard the latest news? There's going to be a big storm this weekend.*

**nice** *adjective*
**person**:
▶ **nice** friendly and kind: *Our new teacher seems nice.* | *He's a nice guy. He helps other people.*

▶ **friendly** nice and wanting to talk to people you do not know well: *Our new neighbors are friendly.*

▶ **charming** polite and friendly, in a way that makes people like you: *She is very charming so it's easy for her to persuade other people to do things for her.*

▶ **likable** nice and easy to like: *Cinderella is the only likable character in the story.*

▶ **sweet** very kind and gentle: *My grandma is a sweet lady.* | *Did you buy these flowers for me? You are sweet!*

▶ **great** very nice. You use **great** when you like or admire someone very much: *I really like Raoul. He's a great guy.*

**something you like or enjoy**:
▶ **nice** good or enjoyable: *There's a nice breeze, so it doesn't feel too hot.* | *We had a nice time at the beach.*

▶ **enjoyable** making you have fun and be happy: *The school trip was enjoyable so everyone had a good time.*

▶ **good** having a pleasant flavor: *The cookies are really good.*

▶ **great** very good or enjoyable. You use **great** when you like something a lot: *It's a great movie. You have to see it!* | *Have a great vacation.*

**noise** *noun*
a sound, especially one that is loud, annoying, or strange: *I can't sleep because of the noise of the traffic outside my window.* | *What's that strange noise? It sounds like a cat.*

▶ **sound** something that you hear: *I can hear the sound of the wind in the trees.*

▶ **racket** a very loud and annoying noise: *The kids are making a racket upstairs.*

▶ **roar** a loud continuous noise, for example from an engine, waves, or a crowd: *You can hear the roar of the plane's engines when it takes off.*

▶ **commotion** if there is a commotion, some people suddenly start moving around and shouting or arguing: *We heard a crash and a sudden commotion in the street outside.*

**normal** *adjective*
usual or expected: *It isn't normal to have snow in July.* ( ANTONYM: **unusual** )

▶ **ordinary** not special or different from usual: *We live in an ordinary house on an ordinary street.*

▶ **regular** not special or different from usual. **Regular** means the same as **ordinary**: *He became a millionaire, but he is just a regular guy.*

▶ **average** typical and around the usual level or amount: *She is five feet tall, which is the average height for her age.*

▶ **standard** usual. You use **standard** about the size, shape, or price of something, or a way of doing something: *The standard width for a door is 30 inches.* | *These are the standard tests that all the kids take.*

▶ **routine** normal and not happening for any special reason or problem: *I went to the dentist for a routine check.*

a b c d e f g h i j k l m **n** o p q r s t u v w x y z

a
b
c
d
e
f
g
h
i
j
k
l
m
n
o
p
q
r
s
t
u
v
w
x
y
z

**notice** *verb*

to see, feel, or hear something: *I noticed that she looked sad.*

▶ **spot** to notice or recognize someone or something, especially when you only see them for a short time: *He spotted one of his friends in the crowd. | I spotted a spelling mistake in the newspaper.*

▶ **detect** to notice something, especially something that is difficult to notice: *The equipment can detect small changes in temperature.*

▶ **observe** to notice something by carefully watching or studying what is happening: *Did you observe anything strange about the man's behavior?*

▶ **become aware** to gradually begin to notice something: *I became aware that there was another person in the room.*

**number** *noun*

a word or symbol that shows a quantity: *Choose a number between one and ten. | We live in apartment number eight.*

▶ **odd number** a number that cannot be divided by two, such as 1, 3, 5, 7, 9, etc.: *There are 25 children, which is an odd number.*

▶ **even number** a number that can be divided by two, such as 2, 4, 6, 8, etc.: *There are an even number of children, so they can work in pairs*

▶ **fraction** a part of a whole number, for example 3/4 or 1/2. The fraction 2/3 means that you have 2 of the 3 parts of something.

▶ **decimal** a number such as 0.8 or 2.63. You write money in decimal numbers, for example $1.25.

▶ **prime number** a number that can only be divided by itself and the number one: *Eleven is a prime number.*

▶ **figure** a number written as a sign, not a word: *Add together all the figures in the right-hand column. | Sixty is written 60 in figures.*

▶ **digit** a number between 0 and 9: *I can't remember the last digit of his telephone number.*

**often** *adverb*

many times: *I often go swimming after school.*

▶ **frequently** **frequently** means the same as **often**: *The buses are frequently late.*

▶ **regularly** often and at regular times: *Buses go downtown regularly, every ten minutes.*

▶ **constantly** very often, especially when this is annoying or causes problems: *My brothers are constantly fighting with each other.*

▶ **again and again** used when you do something many times, or something annoying happens many times: *I tried calling Mom again and again but she didn't answer her phone. | Joey asked the same question again and again.*

**old** *adjective*

an old person or thing has lived or existed for a long time: *My grandmother is old. She's is almost 98. | The old shed is falling down.*

( ANTONYMS: **young, new** )

▶ **elderly** old. You use **elderly** when talking politely about an old person: *An elderly man with gray hair was sitting on the bench.*

▶ **elder** your elder sister or brother is older than you: *I'm nine years old and my elder sister is eleven.*

▶ **ancient** thousands of years old: *The explorers found an ancient temple that was built over 2,000 years ago.*

▶ **antique** antique furniture or jewelry is old and often valuable: *I have an antique gold ring that belonged to my great-grandmother.*

**old**

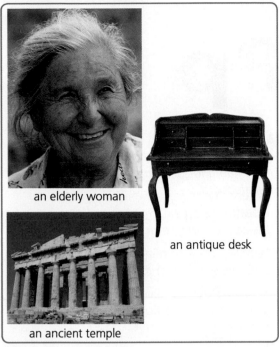

an elderly woman

an antique desk

an ancient temple

## open *verb*

to move something so that it is not closed:
*I opened the door and went in. | Open your eyes!*

**ANTONYM: close**

▶ **unlock** to turn the lock on something with a key, so that you can open it: *Dad turned the key to unlock the garage door.*

▶ **unwrap** to take off the paper or plastic that covers a package: *I wanted to unwrap my birthday presents.*

▶ **undo** to open something that is fastened or tied: *I can't undo the knot in this rope. | Jason undid the buttons on his shirt and took it off.*

▶ **unfasten** to open something that is fastened or tied: *The car is stopped, so you can unfasten your seatbelts.*

▶ **unzip/unbutton/untie/unbuckle** to open something, especially clothing: *Unzip your jacket now. | Can you unbutton your shirt? | Your shoelace is untied.*

▶ **unscrew** to open a lid on a bottle or container by twisting it: *Can you unscrew the lid on this jar for me?*

## open *adjective*

not closed: *I leave the window open at night when it's hot. | She stared at me with her mouth open.*

▶ **unlocked** not locked with a key: *Don't leave the door unlocked when you go out.*

▶ **unfastened** not fastened or tied: *His belt was tight, so he left it unfastened.*

▶ **undone** not fastened or tied: *Your zipper is undone.*

▶ **ajar** a door that is ajar is open a little bit: *I'll leave the door ajar so the cat can come in.*

**open**

The door is open.

The door is ajar.

## opinion *noun*

what you think about someone or something: *My brother and I have different opinions about almost everything. | In my opinion, she's right.*

▶ **view** your opinion about an important subject: *My view is that all children have the right to a good education.*

▶ **belief** a strong feeling that something is true or right: *People have different religious beliefs and we should respect that.*

▶ **attitude** the way you think or feel about something, and how this affects your behavior: *Ben has a good attitude toward school so he gets good grades.*

▶ **point of view** an opinion, that is based on your own situation: *From my point of view, I think it's a good idea to start school at nine o'clock instead of eight.*

a b c d e f g h i j k l m n o p q r s t u v w x y z

a
b
c
d
e
f
g
h
i
j
k
l
m
n
o
**p**
q
r
s
t
u
v
w
x
y
z

**organization** *noun*
a group of people, companies, or countries that has formed for a particular purpose: *The organization helps children improve their math and reading skills.* | *The United Nations is an international organization.*

▶ **club** a group of people who meet to do an activity or sport: *I am a member of the tennis club.*

▶ **society** an organization of people who have the same interest or purpose: *The Wildlife Society aims to protect animals, birds, and plants in this area.*

▶ **institution** a big organization such as a college, hospital, or bank: *Schools, colleges, and universities are all educational institutions.*

▶ **association** a big organization of people who do the same type of work or activity: *The American Medical Association says that washing hands helps prevent colds and flu.* | *The National Basketball Association runs professional basketball.*

▶ **charity** an organization that collects money to help people: *The charity helps children who come from poor families.*

▶ **party** an organization of people with the same political ideas: *Most congressmen and congresswomen are from the Democratic Party or the Republican Party.*

# Pp

**pain** *noun*
the feeling you have when part of your body hurts: *I had a lot of pain in my arm after I fell off my skateboard.*

▶ **headache** a pain in your head: *She has a bad headache and a fever.*

▶ **toothache** a pain in your tooth: *I had a toothache, so Mom took me to the dentist.*

▶ **stomachache** a pain in your stomach: *He has a stomachache because he ate too many cookies.*

▶ **backache** a pain in your back: *You can get a backache if you sit at your computer for a long time.*

▶ **earache** a pain in your ear: *Sometimes when I get a cold I get an earache too.*

▶ **twinge** a sudden slight pain that disappears quickly: *I get a twinge in my knee when I am walking downstairs.*

▶ **cramp** a bad pain that you get in a muscle: *If you sit too long in one position, you can get a cramp in your leg.*

**painful** *adjective*
making you feel pain in part of your body: *I twisted my foot and it was very painful.*

▶ **sore** painful, especially because of an infection: *She has a sore throat and can't eat anything.*

▶ **stiff** if part of your body is stiff, it is difficult to move and feels slightly painful: *We walked for eight hours and the next day our legs felt stiff.*

▶ **tender** if part of your body is tender, it is painful when you touch it: *The cut on my finger is red and tender.*

▶ **itchy** if your skin feels itchy, it feels uncomfortable and you want to scratch it: *A mosquito bit my leg and now it is itchy.*

## part *noun*

one of the pieces or areas that form the whole of something: *You put all the parts of the puzzle together to make a picture.* | *She lives in a different part of town from me.*

▶ **piece** a part of something that is cut or broken from the rest: *Do you want another piece of pizza?* | *There were pieces of broken glass on the floor.*

▶ **section** one of the parts that something is divided into: *The book is in the children's section of the library.* | *The test has two sections: reading and writing.*

▶ **department** a part of an organization: *He teaches in the science department at the high school.*

▶ **chapter** one of the parts of a book: *I'm reading the last chapter of the book.*

▶ **scene** a part of a play or movie, which happens in one place: *I liked the battle in the final scene of the movie.*

▶ **episode** a part of a story on the television or radio, which you can see or hear on different days, or every week: *The next episode of the show is on Saturday.*

## party *noun*

a social event where people talk, drink, eat, and dance, often at someone's house: *Can you come to my birthday party?*

▶ **celebration** a party or other special event to celebrate something: *When his brother came home, they had a big celebration.* | *Thanksgiving is a special celebration in America.*

▶ **shower** a party for a woman who is going to get married or have a baby: *She got clothes for the baby from friends who came to her baby shower.*

▶ **costume party** a party where people dress like a famous person or a character in a story: *I went to the costume party dressed as a fairy.*

▶ **house-warming** a party that you have when you move into a new house: *We're having a house-warming next week, in our new home.*

## people *plural noun*

men, women, and children in general: *All the people we met in Mexico were really nice.* | *A lot of people are frightened of snakes.*

▶ **population** the number of people who live in an area or country: *The population of Texas is around 25 million.*

▶ **the public** the ordinary people of a country, rather than the government or other important people: *The Library of Congress is open to the public.*

▶ **the human race** all the people in the world, considered as a group: *Most of the human race now lives in cities.*

▶ **man/mankind** all the people in the world, considered as a group. You use **man** or **mankind** especially when talking about their development: *Man has lived here for thousands of years.*

▶ **humankind** all the people in the world, considered as a group. Many people prefer to use **humankind** instead of **man** or **mankind** because it sounds like it includes women as well as men: *Humankind must work together to protect the Earth.*

## perfect *adjective*

something that is perfect is extremely good and could not be better: *He speaks perfect Spanish.* | *Thanks for the birthday present. It's perfect!*

ANTONYMS: **imperfect, flawed**

▶ **just right** very suitable for something: *Your blue dress would be just right for the party.*

▶ **ideal** very suitable in every way. You often use **ideal** about someone or something you imagine: *My ideal home would have a swimming pool and a movie theater.* | *The hotel is ideal for families with young children.*

▶ **flawless** perfect, with no marks or small mistakes: *He gave a flawless performance on the piano.*

a b c d e f g h i j k l m n o **p** q r s t u v w x y z

a
b
c
d
e
f
g
h
i
j
k
l
m
n
o
**p**
q
r
s
t
u
v
w
x
y
z

## persuade *verb*

to make someone decide to do something or make someone change his or her mind, by saying that it is a good idea or asking many times: *I tried to persuade Dad to come and play baseball with us.*

▶ **encourage** to try to persuade someone to do something: *My mom always encourages me to eat healthy foods.*

▶ **convince** to make someone feel sure that something is true or the right thing to do: *He convinced the jury that he was innocent.*

▶ **coax** to try to make someone do something by talking gently and kindly: *We tried to coax her to eat a little, but she was too upset.*

▶ **talk someone into** to persuade someone to do something that he or she does not want to do: *I didn't want to go to the movie, but my friends talked me into it.*

## phrase *noun*

a group of words that are used together, but are not a full sentence: *In the sentence "I saw Andy on the way home," "on the way home" is a phrase.*

▶ **expression** a group of words that has a special meaning: *The expression "all by myself" means "completely alone."*

▶ **idiom** a group of words with a meaning that is different from the usual meaning of the words: *"On top of the world" is an idiom that means "very happy."*

▶ **cliché** something people say that is boring because it has been said or used so many times before: *"Boys are better than girls at math" is a cliché and it isn't true.*

▶ **saying** a well-known phrase that gives advice or information about life: *I'm glad you came. You know the old saying – "better late than never."*

▶ **proverb** a well-known phrase that gives advice or information about life. **Proverb** means the same as **saying**: It often has a rhyme in it: *"An apple a day keeps the doctor away" is a proverb which means that eating apples is good for your health.*

▶ **slogan** a short statement that is easy to remember, used in advertisements and politics: *The slogan for this new fruit snack is "Healthy snacks for healthy kids."*

## picture *noun*

a drawing, painting, or photograph: *Do you like my picture of Dad? | I took a lot of pictures with my new camera.*

▶ **painting** a picture that someone has painted: *He does paintings of ships using oil paints.*

▶ **drawing** a picture that someone has drawn with a pencil or pen: *In class we had to make a drawing of a flower.*

▶ **sketch** a quick drawing that does not have a lot of details: *She did a sketch of the cat before it ran away.*

▶ **portrait** a painting, drawing, or photograph of a person: *On the wall, there is a portrait of Abraham Lincoln.*

▶ **illustration** a picture in a book: *My sister likes picture books with colorful illustrations.*

▶ **cartoon** a funny drawing in a newspaper: *Have you seen this funny cartoon of the president?*

▶ **photograph/photo** a picture you take using a camera: *This is a photograph of my family.*

picture

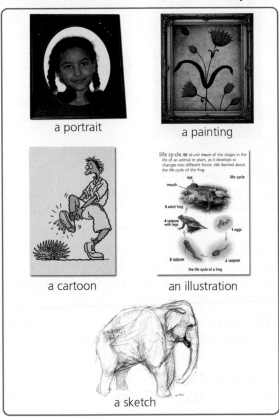

a portrait

a painting

a cartoon

an illustration

a sketch

▶ **chunk** a thick piece that does not have an even shape: *Cut the pineapple into chunks.* | *There's a big chunk of rock in the middle of the road.*

▶ **scrap** a small piece of paper, cloth, or food: *She tore off a scrap of paper and wrote her address on it.* | *I gave the dog a few scraps of meat.*

▶ **fragment** a very small piece that has broken off something: *The astronauts came back from the moon with fragments of moon rock.*

▶ **speck** a very small piece of dirt or dust: *Sarah brushed a speck of dirt off her skirt.*

piece

a slice of pizza

fragments of a vase

a chunk of bread

a scrap of paper

a lump of coal

## piece *noun*

a part of something that has been cut or broken from the rest: *Do you want a piece of cake?* | *Be careful! There are pieces of broken glass on the floor.*

▶ **slice** a flat piece of food that you cut from a bigger piece: *She put a slice of bread in the toaster.*

▶ **crumb** a very small piece of bread or cake that has fallen off a bigger piece: *I dropped crumbs all over the floor when I was eating my toast.*

▶ **lump** a small piece of something solid: *Each child had a lump of clay to play with.*

a
b
c
d
e
f
g
h
i
j
k
l
m
n
o
**p**
q
r
s
t
u
v
w
x
y
z

**place** *noun*
an area, building, city, or country: *They live in a place called Duluth. | I keep my journal in a secret place.*

▶ **position** the place where someone or something is, in relation to other things: *From my position behind the sofa, I could hear everything they said. | Put the plant in a position where it will get plenty of light.*

▶ **location** the exact place where someone or something is: *Dad found the exact location of the hotel on a map.*

▶ **point** an exact place on a line, road, river, or path: *At this point, the river divides in two.*

▶ **spot** a place where you can do something or where something happened: *It's a great spot for a picnic. | It was at this spot that the Pilgrims landed.*

▶ **site** an area of ground where something important happened, or where something is built: *The field is the site of a famous battle. | This area will be the site of the new school.*

**plant** *noun*
a living thing that has leaves and roots: *Plants need water and light to grow.*

▶ **weed** a wild plant that grows where you do not want it: *If you don't take care of the garden, it soon gets covered in weeds.*

▶ **herb** a plant that you use for giving more taste to food, or for making some medicines: *The spaghetti has the herbs basil and oregano in it.*

▶ **bush** a large plant with a lot of branches: *I didn't want Rachel to see me, so I hid behind a bush.*

▶ **crop** a plant such as corn or wheat, which farmers grow: *The land around here is good for growing crops.*

plant

a bush

herbs

**polite** *adjective*
behaving well, in a way that shows you respect other people: *Remember to be polite and to say please and thank you.* (ANTONYM: **rude**)

▶ **well-behaved** a well-behaved child is polite and does not cause trouble or make a lot of noise: *It's a good school and the students are well-behaved.*

▶ **tactful** careful not to say or do something that will upset someone: *I was tactful and I didn't say anything about her weight.*

▶ **courteous** polite in a formal way, when you are with someone you do not know: *The man was courteous and he opened the door for me.*

**politician** *noun*
someone who works in politics, especially someone who is elected: *He became a politician because he wanted to help society.*

▶ **statesman** a political leader that people admire: *Senator Kennedy was a great statesman.*

▶ **governor** the person who is in charge of a state in the U.S.: *McDonnell was elected governor of Virginia.*

▶ **mayor** the person who is in charge of the government of a town or city: *The mayor of Chicago plans to spend $1 billion on new schools.*

▶ **senator** a member of the Senate. Each state has two senators: *Obama was a senator from Illinois before he became president.*

▶ **congressman** a man who is a member of the House of Representatives: *The Republican congressman voted against the bill.*

▶ **congresswoman** a woman who is a member of the House of Representatives: *Mrs. McKinney was the state's first black congresswoman.*

## practice *verb*

to do something regularly in order to improve your skill at it: *I practice the piano every day because I want to play in the concert.*

▶ **train** to prepare for a sports competition by exercising and practicing: *Terry is training for the race, so he runs every day.*

▶ **rehearse** to practice for a play or concert, before people come to see it: *We're rehearsing the school play, which the parents will come to see.*

## praise *verb*

to say that someone has done something well, or that something is good: *Dad is a really good cook, so I praise his cooking.*

▶ **congratulate** to tell someone that you think it is good that he or she has achieved something: *My teacher congratulated me for passing the test.*

▶ **compliment** to say that you think someone looks nice or is good at doing something: *Everyone complimented her on her new dress because she looked good in it. | I want to compliment you on your excellent English.*

▶ **flatter** to say nice things to someone, especially when you do not really mean what you are saying: *You look pretty. I'm not trying to flatter you; you really do look good.*

## prejudice *noun*

an unfair attitude to one group of people in society, which is not based on facts or reason: *There is still prejudice against disabled people, so it can be difficult for them to find jobs.*

▶ **discrimination** unfair treatment of one group of people in society: *Women suffered from discrimination and they were paid less than men.*

▶ **bias** an unfair opinion about someone that makes you treat that person differently: *The newspaper seemed to have a bias toward Republicans, so they reported more good stories about Republicans than Democrats.*

▶ **racism** an unfair attitude to a group of people because they belong to a different race from you: *Because of racism, black people didn't have the same rights as white people.*

▶ **sexism** an unfair attitude to people because they are women, or because they are men: *She accused him of sexism when he said that men were better drivers than women.*

▶ **bigotry** a strong and unfair dislike of people from other races, religions, or countries, and often angry behavior toward them: *His speeches are full of bigotry and religious hatred.*

## press *verb*

to push something with your finger, or to push something against something else: *You press this switch to make the lights come on. | I pressed my ear to the door and listened to what they were saying.*

▶ **push** to move something down or away from you using your hand or finger: *Push the red button to start the DVD player.*

▶ **squash** to make something become flat by pressing it against something else: *He sat on her hat and squashed it.*

▶ **crush** to press very hard on something and break or damage it: *The tree fell down and crushed the car.*

▶ **squeeze** to press something on both sides with your fingers or hands: *If you squeeze the toy, it makes a funny noise. | Squeeze a lemon and add the juice to the cake mixture.*

▶ **pinch** to press someone's skin between your finger and thumb: *Ouch! Eric pinched me!*

## prize *noun*

something that you win in a game, competition, or race: *Jason won first prize in an art competition.*

▶ **award** a prize for doing something well: *The show won an award for the best television drama. | She received the best player award.*

▶ **medal** a flat piece of metal that you get as a prize, or for doing something brave: *Lewis won the gold medal in the long jump. | Her dad got a medal for bravery in the war.*

▶ **reward** money or a present that you are given for doing something good: *Our neighbors are offering a reward to anyone who finds their lost cat.*

▶ **honor** something that is given to you to show that a lot of people admire what you have done: *He was awarded the Purple Heart, which is a top military honor.*

a b c d e f g h i j k l m n o **p** q r s t u v w x y z

**a b c d e f g h i j k l m n o p q r s t u v w x y z**

## problem *noun*

something that causes trouble, or makes it difficult for you to do something: *We had problems with our car, and we asked a mechanic to look at it.* | *Crime is a serious problem in this part of the city.*

▶ **difficulty** a problem that makes it difficult for you to do something: *Suzy has difficulty with spelling, so the teacher is giving her extra help.*

▶ **issue** a subject or problem that people need to discuss and deal with: *Global warming is an important issue that affects our world today.*

▶ **bug** a small problem in a computer program that stops it from working well: *My computer isn't working right and I think it has a bug.*

▶ **drawback** a disadvantage that something has, which makes it seem less good: *The main drawback of this television is that the screen is too small.*

## program *noun*

a show on television or the radio: *The program is about a girl who is an ordinary teenager in the daytime and a famous singer at night.*

▶ **show** a play or performance on television or the radio. **Show** means the same as **program**: *The show is about three brothers who play in a band together.*

▶ **drama** a program in which actors perform a story: *My favorite show is a TV drama that takes place in a hospital.*

▶ **documentary** a program that gives information about a subject or situation: *I watched a documentary about China.*

▶ **cartoon** a program with characters that are pictures and not real: *The cartoon is about a cat and a mouse, in which the mouse always tricks the cat.*

▶ **series** a set of TV programs with the same characters or the same subject. The series is usually on the television at the same time every week or every day: *There are two TV series I watch every Thursday night.*

▶ **the news** a television or radio program that tells you what is happening in the world or in your area: *The plane crash was on the news.*

▶ **soap opera** a story about the lives of a group of people, which is shown for many years: *The show is a soap opera about a family of doctors who live in a town called Salem.*

▶ **game show** a program in which people take part in games in order to win prizes: *If you answer all the questions on the game show correctly, you can win a million dollars.*

▶ **talk show** a program in which famous people answer questions about themselves: *The actor will be on the talk show to talk about his new movie.*

## promise *verb*

to say that you will definitely do something: *Dad promised he would take me to watch the baseball game on Saturday.*

▶ **swear** to make a very serious promise, especially publicly or in a law court: *In court, you have to swear that you will tell the truth.*

▶ **take an oath** to make a very serious promise publicly: *Each new president has to take an oath to serve the United States faithfully.*

▶ **vow** to promise to do something, in a very definite way: *I hated the place so much that I vowed that I would never go back there again.*

▶ **pledge** to promise publicly to do something, especially to help someone: *The president pledged to end the war.*

▶ **guarantee** to say that something will definitely happen, especially when you feel very certain of this: *I guarantee that you will enjoy the movie.*

▶ **give someone your word** to promise something in a very sincere way: *I give you my word that I won't tell anyone about your secret.*

## protect *verb*

to stop someone or something from being harmed or damaged: *A cat will fight to protect her kittens.* | *The young plants need to be protected from the wind.*

▶ **shield** to protect something by putting another thing in front of it: *I raised my hand to shield my eyes from the sun.*

▶ **defend** to protect someone or something from attack: *They built the fort to defend the city.*

▶ **guard** to protect a place or person by staying nearby and watching carefully for danger: *Soldiers guard the building day and night to stop people from getting in.* | *The president is carefully guarded wherever he goes.*

▶ **preserve** to protect something from being harmed or changed too much, for example to protect an area of land or people's traditional culture: *They want to preserve the forest and stop people from cutting down all the trees.* | *The Native Americans want to preserve their culture.*

## proud *adjective*

pleased because you, someone in your family, or your country has achieved something good: *Mom and Dad were very proud of me when I won the race.* | *I'm proud to be an American and I think this is a great country.*

▶ **pleased** happy that you or someone you know has achieved something good: *My parents were pleased that I had worked so hard.*

▶ **vain** very pleased with yourself and the way you look, in a way that annoys people: *Sarah is vain. She's always looking in the mirror.*

▶ **arrogant** rude and unfriendly because you think you are more important or know more than other people: *I don't like him because he's arrogant and he always thinks he's right.*

▶ **conceited** too proud of what you can do or how you look, so you think that you are better than other people: *He's very conceited. He thinks he's the best player on the team.*

## pull *verb*

to move something toward you or down, using your hands: *You pull the rope to make the bell ring.* | *He pulled the blanket off the bed.*

▶ **drag** to pull something heavy along the ground: *We tried to drag the table across the room.*

▶ **tug** to pull something suddenly and hard: *Don't tug on my hair! It hurts!*

▶ **heave** to pull or lift something heavy with a lot of effort: *I heaved the suitcase up the stairs.*

▶ **haul** to pull or carry something heavy, often using a rope: *Dad and I pulled on the rope and hauled the boat up the beach.*

▶ **tow** to pull a vehicle along using a rope or chain: *The truck towed our car to the next town, after the engine stopped working.*

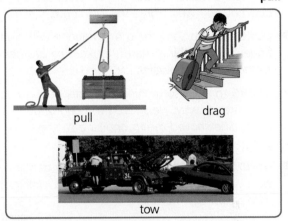

pull

pull

drag

tow

## punishment *noun*

something that is done to punish someone: *The teacher made Joey stay after school as a punishment for being rude.*

▶ **penalty** a punishment for not obeying a law or rule: *The maximum penalty is 12 years in jail.*

▶ **fine** money that you pay as a punishment for breaking a law or rule: *Dad had to pay a fine because he was driving too fast.*

▶ **sentence** a punishment that a judge gives to someone who is guilty of a crime: *The judge gave the thief a three-year prison sentence.*

## purpose *noun*

the reason for doing something: *The purpose of going to school is to get a good education.*

▶ **aim** something that you are trying to achieve: *His aim is to become a doctor, so he's studying hard.*

▶ **goal** something important that you hope to achieve in the future, even though it may take a long time: *Their goal is to set up a base on the Moon.*

▶ **objective** something that you are trying to achieve in your work: *The main objective of the fair is to raise money for the school.*

a b c d e f g h i j k l m n o **p** q r s t u v w x y z

**push** *verb*
to move something or someone away from you using your hands or arms: *Push the door to open it.* | *He pushed me and I fell down onto the ground.*

▶ **press** to push something with your finger, for example a button or bell: *If you press the doorbell and wait, someone will come.*

▶ **poke** to push something or someone with your finger or something sharp: *I poked my brother to see if he was awake.*

▶ **shove** to push something or someone hard or in a careless way: *He shoved the bag under his bed.* | *She shoved me to one side so she could get to the front of the line.*

▶ **nudge** to push someone next to you gently with your elbow: *Andrew nudged me. "Look who's coming," he said.*

push

press

push

nudge

poke

**put** *verb*
to move something to a place or position: *Can you put your homework on my desk, please?*

▶ **place** to put something carefully in a particular position: *She placed the flowers in the center of the table.*

▶ **lay** to put something or someone carefully on a flat surface: *She laid the baby on the bed.* | *Open the map and lay it on the table.*

▶ **stick** to put something somewhere quickly or carelessly: *Just stick the bags in the corner.*

▶ **dip** to put something in a liquid for a very short time and take it out again: *I like to dip my cookies in my milk.* | *I dipped my feet in the ocean.*

▶ **hang** to attach something to a hook or line: *We hang our coats on the hooks on the wall.* | *Can you hang the wet clothes on the line?*

▶ **lean** to put something in a sloping position against a wall or other surface: *Dad leaned the ladder against the wall and climbed up it.*

# Qq

**question** *noun*
something that you ask someone, when you are either speaking or writing: *Do you have a question about the homework?* ( ANTONYM: **answer** )

▶ **query** a question in which you ask for more information about something: *If you have a query, please ask me at the end.*

▶ **request** a question in which you ask for something officially: *Raoul was having problems at school, so his parents made a request for a meeting with the teacher.*

▶ **demand** if you make a demand for something, you ask for it in a very firm way: *His mother's demand was that he do his homework before dinner.*

**quick** *adjective*
taking only a short time: *What's the quickest way to your house?* | *We did a quick review of the vocabulary we had learned.*

▶ **short** lasting only a short time: *There will be a short break of 15 minutes for lunch.* | *We watched a short program about China.*

▶ **brief** brief means the same as **short**: *There was a brief silence and then the music began.* | *We made a brief visit to Mexico for only two days.*

▶ **rapid** very quick. You use **rapid** especially about changes and increases: *There has been a rapid increase in the number of students.* | *She made a rapid recovery from her illness.*

▶ **hasty** doing something too quickly, without thinking carefully enough: *I made a hasty decision, and now I wish I could change it.*

## quiet *adjective*

making or having very little noise: *We have to be quiet because the baby is sleeping.* | *Their house is on a quiet street outside of town.*

▶ **silent** making or having no noise at all: *Eric was silent for a long time, and then he asked me a question.* | *The house was silent because everyone had gone out.*

▶ **low** a low voice or sound is quiet and deep: *They were talking in low voices, so it was difficult to hear what they were saying.* | *The volume is too low. Can you turn up the radio?*

▶ **soft** quiet and pleasant to listen to: *The child listened to his mother's soft voice as she read him a story.* | *Soft music came from the CD player.*

▶ **faint** quiet and difficult to hear, especially because the sound comes from a long way away: *I can hear the faint sound of traffic, even though the freeway is over a mile away.*

▶ **peaceful** a **peaceful** place is quiet and calm in a pleasant and relaxing way: *It was peaceful under the trees in the park.*

▶ **still** completely quiet and with no activity: *In the early morning, the town was still.*

## quit *verb*

to stop doing something, or to leave your job: *My mom quit smoking last year.* | *He quit his job and went back to college.*

▶ **resign** to say officially that you are going to leave your job: *She resigned from her job because she didn't like her boss.*

▶ **retire** to stop working, usually because of old age: *My grandfather will retire at the age of 65.*

▶ **give up** to stop doing something, or stop trying to do something: *Mom gave up her job when I was a baby, but now she is back at work.* | *Don't give up! It takes practice to learn how to ride a bike.*

▶ **drop out** to stop going to school or doing an activity, before you have finished it: *Jerry dropped out of high school when he was 16, and now he regrets it.* | *The runner had to drop out of the race because of an injury.*

# Rr

## rain *noun*

water that falls from clouds in the sky: *If the rain stops, we can go out.* | *People were waiting for the bus outside in the rain.*

▶ **drizzle** light rain with very small drops: *It's not raining hard. It's only a light drizzle.*

▶ **sleet** a mixture of snow and rain: *The weather became colder and the rain turned to sleet.*

▶ **hail** small hard balls of frozen rain that fall from the sky: *The hail was the size of peas.*

▶ **shower** a short period of rain: *Tomorrow there will be heavy showers followed by sunny periods.*

▶ **downpour** a lot of rain that falls in a short time: *Kerrie got wet because she was caught in a downpour on the way home.*

a b c d e f g h i j k l m n o p q **r** s t u v w x y z

a
b
c
d
e
f
g
h
i
j
k
l
m
n
o
p
q
**r**
s
t
u
v
w
x
y
z

**read** *verb*
to look at and understand the words in a book, magazine, etc.: *I want to read a book about George Washington.*

▶ **flip through** to turn the pages of a book or magazine quickly, looking for things that might interest you: *She flipped through a magazine as she waited.*

▶ **skim** to read something quickly in order to find something: *I skimmed through the list, but my name wasn't there.* | *Skim the paragraph to get a general idea of the meaning.*

▶ **pore over** to read something very carefully for a long time: *My dad pored over the instructions to find out how to put the table together.*

**ready** *adjective*
if you are ready, you have done everything you need to prepare for something: *It takes her a long time to get ready for school in the morning.*
(**ANTONYMS: unready, unprepared**)

▶ **prepared** ready to deal with something because you are expecting it or have made careful preparations: *I had an umbrella so I was prepared for the rain.*

▶ **all set** completely ready for something that is just about to happen: *The team is all set for tonight's game and I'm sure they can win.*

▶ **ripe** ripe fruit is ready to eat: *The apples will be ripe in about a month.*

**real** *adjective*
not false or artificial: *Are those flowers real or artificial?* | *People call her J.Lo, but her real name is Jennifer Lopez.* (**ANTONYMS: false, fake**)

▶ **genuine** real. You use **genuine** especially about valuable things, or about feelings: *If the painting is genuine, it is worth a lot of money.* | *Her surprise was genuine. She wasn't expecting me to be there.*

▶ **authentic** real. You use **authentic** especially when something is typical of a place or a period in history: *The restaurant serves authentic Mexican food.* | *The actors in the play were wearing authentic 19th century costumes.*

▶ **actual** real. You use **actual** when something is different from what people say or imagine: *The actual cost of the computer is higher than the price in the advertisement.*

▶ **sincere** behaving in a way that shows your real feelings, and not pretending: *She is a sincere and loyal person.* | *Brian was sincere when he apologized.*

▶ **true** having the good qualities that a particular type of person or thing should have: *Maggie is a true friend. She helps me when I need her.* | *He's a true Red Sox fan who never misses a game.*

**reason** *noun*
a fact that explains why something happens, or why you do something: *The reason she is upset is because she can't find her cat.* | *There are lots of good reasons for studying Chinese.*

▶ **explanation** something that helps you understand why something has happened: *The teacher gave an explanation of the math problem.*

▶ **excuse** the reason you use to explain why you did not do something. An **excuse** is often a reason that is not completely true: *When he's late, he makes up an excuse about problems with his dad's car.*

▶ **motive** the reason why someone does something, especially something bad or dishonest: *The motive for the crime was money.*

▶ **justification** a reason for doing something that seems wrong: *His justification for eating the cake was that he didn't know it was for the party.*

▶ **grounds** a reason that makes it right or fair to do something: *If you cheat on a test, the principal has grounds to punish you.*

## recently *adverb*

a short time before now, especially a few days, weeks, or months ago: *The Smiths recently returned from a vacation in Hawaii.* | *There has been bad weather recently.*

▶ **lately** **lately** means the same as **recently**: *Have you seen Matthew lately?* | *I haven't seen any good movies lately.*

▶ **just** very recently, for example only a few minutes, hours, or days ago: *I'm not hungry. I just had a snack.* | *I just heard Kelly is moving soon.*

▶ **freshly** cooked, painted, or picked very recently: *I love the smell of freshly baked bread.* | *The house was freshly painted.*

▶ **the other day** used when telling someone about something that happened a few days ago: *I saw Monica the other day at church.*

## reduce *verb*

to make something less or smaller: *The school plans to reduce the number of children in the class from 25 to 20.* | *More police officers on the streets might help reduce crime.*

( ANTONYMS: **increase, raise** )

▶ **lower** to reduce the level, amount, or price of something: *Bake the pie for ten minutes at 425° and then lower the heat to 350°.* | *They should lower the price because $100 is too much for a doll.* ( ANTONYM: **raise** )

▶ **cut** to reduce something, especially by a large amount: *The store has cut prices by 50%.* | *The company cut hundreds of jobs to save money.*

▶ **relieve** to make pain or an unpleasant feeling less strong: *The doctor will give you medicine to relieve the pain.* | *We played games to relieve the boredom.*

## remember *verb*

if you remember something, it is in your mind or comes into your mind: *I remember my first day at school very well.* | *Do you remember Andrew? He was in your class a few years ago.*

( ANTONYM: **forget** )

▶ **recall** **recall** means the same as **remember**. You use **recall** especially about facts, information, or names: *Do you recall the name of that boy we played with on vacation?*

▶ **reminisce** to talk or think about nice things that happened in the past: *My mom and her sisters reminisced about their childhood.*

▶ **memorize** to learn words, music, or facts so that you can remember them later: *The teacher asked us to memorize the poem and say it in front of the class.*

▶ **remind** to make someone remember to do something: *Remind me to clean the fish tank tomorrow.*

## remove *verb*

to take something away, either to another place, or so that it no longer exists: *She removed the pie from the oven and put it on the table to cool.* | *It is difficult to remove stains from the carpet.*

▶ **take off** to remove clothes, or to remove things from a surface: *I took off my clothes and got into the shower.* | *Take the sheets off the bed and I'll wash them.*

▶ **get rid of** to throw away or take away something you do not want: *I cleaned my room and got rid of old toys.*

▶ **delete** to remove words from a piece of writing, or remove files from a computer: *I deleted one paragraph from the essay.* | *Don't delete the file, because you might need it later.*

▶ **erase** to remove pencil marks by rubbing them with an eraser, or to remove information recorded on a computer or disk: *If you write in pencil, it's easy to erase mistakes.* | *You can erase what you have recorded by pressing this button.*

▶ **cut** to remove a part from a movie, book, or speech: *I cut the last part of my speech because I thought it was too long.*

a
b
c
d
e
f
g
h
i
j
k
l
m
n
o
p
q
**r**
s
t
u
v
w
x
y
z

a
b
c
d
e
f
g
h
i
j
k
l
m
n
o
p
q

**r**

s
t
u
v
w
x
y
z

## repair *verb*

to make something be in good condition again after it was broken or damaged: *Jimmy knows how to repair cars.* | *We need to get the computer repaired because it isn't working.*

▶ **fix** **fix** means the same as **repair**: *Dad, can you fix the camera? Something is wrong with it.* | *We have to get the bike fixed before you can ride it.*

▶ **patch** to put a small piece of material over a hole to cover it: *Mom patched my pants because there were holes in the knees.*

▶ **renovate** to repair an old building and put it back into good condition: *They renovated the old house before they moved in.*

▶ **restore** to repair something old so that it looks the same as it did originally: *The theater was built in 1920, and it has been restored to its original beauty.* | *She restores old paintings.*

## result *noun*

something that happens because of something else: *His success is the result of many years of hard work.*

▶ **consequence** something that happens later because of someone's actions, especially something bad: *One consequence of misbehaving in class is that the teacher will phone your parents.*

▶ **outcome** the final result after other things have happened: *You can never be sure of the outcome of a game until it is finished.*

## rich *adjective*

having a lot of money: *He's rich so he doesn't have to work anymore.* | *The United States is one of the richest nations in the world.*

( ANTONYM: **poor** )

▶ **wealthy** rich. You use **wealthy** especially about a person, family, or place that has been rich for a long time: *She comes from a wealthy family who own a big oil company.* | *Monica lives in a wealthy part of the city.*

▶ **well-off** having enough money to have a good life, with all the things you want: *He is a lawyer, so he is well-off.*

▶ **prosperous** a **prosperous** person or place is rich and successful: *My grandfather is a prosperous farmer who owns a lot of land.* | *The city is becoming prosperous because of all the computer companies in the area.*

## right *adjective*

not wrong: *"He is six years old, isn't he?" "That's right."* | *I hope I made the right decision.* | *I agree with her, because she is right.* ( ANTONYM: **wrong** )

▶ **correct** **correct** means the same as **right.** It sounds more formal: *The correct answer is 27.* | *The coach showed me the correct way to hold the tennis racket.*

▶ **accurate** exactly correct. You use **accurate** especially about measurements: *Use a ruler to make sure that your measurements are accurate.*

## river *noun*

a long wide area of water that flows into a lake or an ocean: *The Mississippi River flows along the borders of ten states.*

▶ **stream** a very small narrow river: *I jumped over the stream.* | *They drank water from mountain streams.*

▶ **creek** a stream or narrow river: *You can step on these rocks to get across the creek.*

▶ **tributary** a river that flows into a larger river: *The Jari River is a tributary of the Amazon.*

▶ **estuary** the wide part of a river where it goes into the ocean: *The estuary has a mixture of fresh and salt water.*

▶ **delta** an area of low watery land where a big river spreads out into smaller rivers that flow into the ocean: *The Mississippi River delta is in Louisiana.*

**river**

a delta

a river        a stream

## road *noun*

a surface that cars and trucks drive on, which goes from one place to another: *My dad drives slowly when there is ice on the road.* | *The park is down a gravel road.*

▶ **street** a road in a town or city with houses or stores on each side: *We both live on the same street.*

▶ **avenue** a street. **Avenue** is used in the names of streets in a town or city: *We went for a walk along Fifth Avenue in New York City.*

▶ **boulevard** a wide road in a city: *There were trees on both sides of the boulevard.*

▶ **highway** a wide fast road that connects cities or towns: *The speed limit on most highways is 65 miles per hour.*

▶ **freeway** a wide fast road between or through cities or towns that takes traffic into and out of a big city: *We took the freeway to downtown Los Angeles.*

▶ **turnpike** a highway that drivers have to pay to use: *How much does it cost to drive along the New Jersey Turnpike?*

## rough *adjective*

not flat or smooth. You use **rough** especially about the ground or a road, or about someone's skin: *A rough dirt road leads to the farm.* | *Her hands are rough because she does a lot of hard work.* (ANTONYM: **smooth**)

▶ **uneven** an **uneven** surface has parts that are not all the same level. You use **uneven** especially about the ground: *Be careful here, because the sidewalk is very uneven and you might fall over.*

▶ **bumpy** a **bumpy** road or path is very rough, and makes you go up and down when you travel on it: *The road was bumpy, so I was starting to feel sick.*

▶ **coarse** **coarse** cloth has a rough surface that feels slightly hard: *The sacks are made of coarse brown cloth.*

## round *adjective*

shaped like a circle or ball: *They are sitting at a round table.* | *The moon looks perfectly round tonight.*

▶ **circular** shaped like a circle: *The dancer moved her arms in a circular motion.*

▶ **curved** shaped like part of a circle, and not straight: *The wild sheep has curved horns.*

▶ **spherical** shaped like a ball: *The Earth is spherical.*

▶ **oval** shaped like a long narrow circle: *She has an oval face.*

## rude *adjective*

not polite: *It's rude to stare at people.* | *He was rude to his mother when he said that she was stupid.* (ANTONYM: **polite**)

▶ **impolite** **impolite** means the same as **rude**. It sounds more formal: *It's impolite to interrupt people when they are speaking.*

▶ **insulting** very rude and not showing respect: *I think his jokes are insulting to women.*

▶ **offensive** making people feel upset or angry, especially because you use rude words or do not show respect for other people: *People can't use swear words on TV because it is offensive.*

a
b
c
d
e
f
g
h
i
j
k
l
m
n
o
p
q
r
s
t
u
v
w
x
y
z

a
b
c
d
e
f
g
h
i
j
k
l
m
n
o
p
q
r
**s**
t
u
v
w
x
y
z

**rule** *noun*

a statement that says what you are allowed to do: *Do you want me to explain the rules of the game? | It's against the rules to run inside the school buildings.*

▶ **law** a rule that everyone in a country must obey: *It is against the law to steal money from people.*

▶ **regulation** an official rule, which is part of a set of rules made by a government or organization: *Pets are not allowed in the restaurant because of health and safety regulations.*

▶ **restriction** an official rule that limits what people can do: *Because of restrictions on what you can take onto the plane, you can only take one small bag.*

**run** *verb*

to move very quickly using your legs: *I ran to school because I was late.*

▶ **jog** to run at a slow steady speed for exercise: *Julie jogs in the park every morning.*

▶ **sprint** to run as fast as you can for a short distance: *Jeff caught the ball and sprinted down the football field.*

▶ **race** to run somewhere as quickly as you can, especially because you have to do something urgently: *We had to race to the bus stop to catch the bus.*

▶ **charge** to run quickly and with a lot of energy, with the result that you might knock someone over: *The bulls charged toward me and I had to jump over the fence.*

▶ **bolt** to suddenly run somewhere very quickly, especially to escape: *The dog bolted out of the house and across the street.*

▶ **gallop** if a horse gallops, it runs very quickly: *The horses gallop toward the finish line.*

run

He is running.     He is jogging.

The horse is galloping.

# Ss

**sad** *adjective*

not happy: *She felt sad as she waved goodbye to her grandparents.* (**ANTONYM: happy**)

▶ **unhappy** **unhappy** means the same as **sad**: *She's unhappy because her dog is sick.* In some sentences, it is better to use **sad**, not **unhappy**. You say *a sad song, a sad story, a sad movie.*

▶ **miserable** very sad: *He's miserable because his dog ran away and is lost.*

▶ **disappointed** sad because something you wanted did not happen: *Katie was disappointed when she did not pass the test.*

▶ **depressed** very unhappy for a long time: *She started to feel depressed when some of the children would not stop being mean and calling her names.*

## salary *noun*

the money that people get each year for doing their job, especially people who work in offices. People usually get paid part of their salary each month: *Some lawyers earn a big salary.*

▶ **wages** the money that people earn each hour for doing their job, especially people who work in factories or stores. People usually get paid their wages each week: *The workers at the factory want higher wages.*

▶ **pay** the money that is paid for a job: *The pay is $18 an hour.*

▶ **income** the money that you get regularly, from your job and from other things: *They spend most of their income on food and rent.*

## same *adjective*

not different: *We were both wearing the same shoes.* ( **ANTONYM: different** )

▶ **similar** almost the same as someone or something else: *Their dog is similar to ours, but ours is a darker color.*

▶ **alike** similar to each other: *Steve and his brother look alike.*

▶ **identical** exactly the same in every way: *The girls are twins and look identical, so it is difficult to know which one is which.*

▶ **matching** having the same color, style, or pattern as something else: *She was wearing a diamond necklace with matching earrings.*

## say *verb*

to tell someone something, using words: *She says she feels sick. | Did he say anything about me?*

▶ **shout** to say something very loudly: *"I'm home," Dana shouted.*

▶ **cry** to say something loudly, especially when you are excited or upset: *"Stop!" she cried.*

▶ **comment** to say something about something: *"It's very big," he commented | They commented on how much I had grown.*

▶ **remark** to say something about a person or thing: *Mom remarked that I look tired. | "It was fun," the girl remarked.*

▶ **demand** to ask for something in a firm way: *"I want you to clean your room," demanded Mom.*

▶ **mention** to talk about someone or something, without giving a lot of information: *He mentioned that his sister was in college.*

▶ **quote** to say or write exactly what someone else has written: *She quoted some words from the Bible in her speech.*

▶ **announce** to tell people about something publicly or officially: *They announced that the plane was three hours late.*

▶ **predict** to say that something is going to happen in the future: *I predict that our team will win the competition.*

## secret *adjective*

if something is secret, only you or only a few people know about it: *I will hide the money in a secret place so that no one can find it.*

▶ **private** secret and not for other people to know about: *Go away! We're having a private conversation!*

▶ **confidential** if information is confidential, you must not show it or talk about it to other people: *A doctor should not tell people confidential information about patients.*

▶ **classified** if information is classified, the government wants it to be kept secret: *He was accused of giving classified information to a foreign government.*

▶ **clandestine** a clandestine organization or meeting is one that is secret: *The two spies had a clandestine meeting.*

## see *verb*

to use your eyes to look at and notice people or things: *I can see a bird in the tree. | She can't see very well, so she has to wear glasses.*

▶ **watch** to look at something that is moving, or to look at a game, television show, or movie: *I watched the dog chase the cat across the yard. | My dad likes to watch basketball.*

▶ **spot** to suddenly see someone or something, especially someone or something you are looking for: *I spotted a spelling mistake in my essay.*

▶ **notice** to see something and realize that it is there: *I noticed a blue mark on my shirt.*

▶ **witness** to see an accident or a crime happen: *The police talked to everyone who witnessed the accident.*

a b c d e f g h i j k l m n o p q r **s** t u v w x y z

## sharp *adjective*
having a thin edge or point that can cut things easily: *She cut the tomatoes into slices using a sharp knife.* ( **ANTONYM: blunt** )

▶ **pointed** having a point at the end: *Sharks have pointed teeth.*

▶ **prickly** having a lot of sharp points: *The plants have prickly leaves, to prevent animals from eating them.*

▶ **spiky** having long points that stick out: *A porcupine has a spiky coat, so don't touch it.*

▶ **jagged** having a sharp uneven edge: *The jagged rocks made a hole in the boat.*

**sharp**

a sharp pencil          The dog has pointed ears.

prickly leaves          Porcupines are spiky.

jagged mountains

## shine *verb*
to produce bright light, or to reflect a lot of light: *It is warm when the sun shines.* | *She polished the table until it shone.*

▶ **flash** to shine brightly for a short time or several times: *Lightning flashed in the sky.* | *The red light on the machine was flashing.*

▶ **twinkle** to shine with a light that keeps changing from bright to less bright: *The stars twinkle in the night sky.*

▶ **flicker** to burn or shine with a light that is not steady: *The wind made the candle flame flicker.*

▶ **sparkle** to reflect a lot of small flashes of light: *The lake sparkled in the sunshine.*

▶ **glitter** **glitter** means the same as **sparkle**: *Her diamond jewelry glittered under the lights.*

## shout *verb*
to say something very loudly: *There is no need to shout.* | *"Wait for me!" she shouted.*

▶ **yell** to shout very loudly, especially when you are angry or excited: *Dad got mad and started to yell at us.*

▶ **call** to shout something in order to get someone's attention: *I heard someone call my name.*

▶ **scream** to shout in a loud high voice because you are afraid, hurt, or excited: *When the boy fell in the lake, his sister screamed for help.*

▶ **cheer** to shout to show that you like something: *Everyone cheered when the band came on stage.*

▶ **cry** to say something loudly: *"This is awful!" she cried.*

## sick *adjective*
having a disease or illness: *Ethan wasn't in school today because he's sick.* ( **ANTONYMS: well, healthy** )

▶ **ill** **ill** means the same as **sick**: *She went to the doctor because she was ill.*

▶ **not very well** a little sick: *I'm not feeling very well. I think I'll go back to bed.*

▶ **weak** not having much strength: *She was so weak she couldn't walk.*

▶ **feverish** having a higher temperature than normal: *He was feverish and his forehead felt hot.*

▶ **sickly** a sickly child is often sick: *He is a sickly boy who is often absent from school.*

## sleep *verb*

to lie down with your eyes closed and your mind and body not active: *I didn't sleep well last night. The noise kept me awake.*

▶ **be asleep** to be sleeping: *The baby is asleep so be quiet.*

▶ **doze** to sleep lightly for a short time, especially when you are sitting in a chair: *After lunch, Grandpa dozes on the couch.*

▶ **take a nap** to sleep for a short time during the day: *She was tired when she got home, so she took a nap.*

▶ **oversleep** to sleep for longer than you intended, especially when this makes you late: *If I oversleep I will be late for school.*

## slowly *adverb*

at a slow speed: *A snail moves slowly.* | *The teacher speaks slowly so that all the students can understand her.* ( ANTONYM: **fast** )

▶ **gradually** happening slowly, over a long period of time: *His health gradually improved over the next few weeks.*

▶ **little by little** slowly, in a series of small amounts or stages: *Little by little, she learned more about him.*

## small *adjective*

not large: *I only want a small piece of cake.* | *These shoes are too small for me.*
( ANTONYMS: **big, large** )

▶ **little** **little** means the same as **small**. You often use **little** after another adjective, when saying how you feel about something: *What a cute little dog!* | *The little boy began to cry.* In some sentences, it is better to use **small**, not **little**.
You say *a small amount.* You do not say "a little amount."
You say *a small number.* You do not say "a little number."

▶ **tiny** very small: *Babies have tiny fingers.*

▶ **microscopic** so small that you cannot see it without a microscope: *There are microscopic creatures living in the pond water.*

▶ **miniature** made much smaller than the usual size: *She puts miniature furniture in her dollhouse.*

▶ **minor** small and not serious or important: *Luckily, his injuries are minor.* | *We had a few minor problems, but nothing serious.*

▶ **slight** very small and not serious or important: *There will be a slight delay before the show starts.*

## smell *noun*

something that you notice by using your nose: *I noticed a strong smell of paint in the room.*

▶ **scent** a nice smell from flowers and plants, or the smell left by an animal: *The scent of the pine trees reminded him of home.* | *Cats use scent to mark where they live.*

▶ **fragrance** a nice smell: *The roses have a lovely fragrance.*

▶ **perfume** a nice smell: *The air was full of the perfume of flowers.*
You also use **perfume** to mean a liquid with a nice smell that women put on their skin: *The woman was wearing perfume.*

▶ **aroma** a nice smell from food or coffee that is being made: *I love the aroma of freshly baked cookies.*

▶ **odor** a bad smell: *The odor of the garbage made him feel sick.*

## smile *verb*

if you smile, you have a happy expression on your face and your mouth curves up: *I want you all to smile for the camera.*

▶ **grin** to give a big happy smile: *He grinned when he found out that he passed the test.*

▶ **beam** to smile in a very happy way because you feel pleased or proud: *Her parents beamed with pride when she went up to get her award.*

▶ **smirk** to smile in an unpleasant way, especially because you are pleased that something bad has happened to someone: *William smirked because I was in trouble but he wasn't.*

a b c d e f g h i j k l m n o p q r **s** t u v w x y z

**a b c d e f g h i j k l m n o p q r s t u v w x y z**

**snow** *noun*

soft white pieces of frozen water that fall from the sky when it is very cold: *There is snow in winter so many people go skiing there.*

▶ **sleet** a mixture of snow and rain: *The weather got colder and the rain changed to sleet.*

▶ **frost** a white powder of ice that covers things when it is very cold: *The trees look beautiful when they are covered with frost.*

▶ **hail** small hard balls of frozen rain that fall from the sky: *The hail was the size of peas.*

▶ **snowflake** a small piece of snow that falls from the sky: *I tried to catch a snowflake, but it melted in my hand.*

▶ **blizzard** a very bad storm with a lot of snow and wind: *A blizzard makes driving dangerous, because people can't see where they are going.*

snow

snow

a snowflake

a blizzard

**soft** *adjective*

not hard or firm, but easy to press: *Peaches should be soft and juicy when you eat them.* | *My cat has soft white fur.* ( ANTONYM: **hard** )

▶ **tender** tender meat and vegetables are easy to cut and nice to eat: *The steak was tender and delicious.* | *Cook the carrots until they are tender.*

▶ **soggy** soft and wet in an unpleasant way: *The French fries are cold and soggy and I don't want to eat them.* | *The ground is too soggy to play football.*

**sound** *noun*

something that you hear: *A strange sound woke me up in the night.* | *I like the sound of the saxophone.*

▶ **bang** a sudden loud noise: *The balloon burst with a bang.*

▶ **crash** a sudden loud noise when something falls or breaks: *There was a loud crash when the plates hit the floor.*

▶ **roar** a loud continuous noise: *I can hear the roar of the traffic outside.* | *There was a flash of light and then the roar of thunder overhead.*

▶ **squeak** a short high sound: *My new sneakers make a funny squeak when I walk.*

▶ **creak** a long high sound, for example when an old door opens: *The door opened with a creak.* | *She heard a creak on the stairs, so she knew that her parents were going to bed.*

▶ **beep** a high electronic sound that a machine makes: *I heard a beep coming from your cell phone.*

▶ **splash** the sound that water makes when something hits it: *I jumped into the pool with a splash.*

▶ **thud** a low sound that something heavy makes when it falls onto a surface: *The box fell off the shelf and landed with a thud.*

▶ **echo** a sound that you hear again, especially after it comes back off a wall or a mountain: *If you shout in a tunnel, you will hear the echo of your voice.*

**speak** *verb*

to produce words with your voice, or to talk to someone: *She has a sore throat and it is hard for her to speak.* | *He can speak Spanish very well.* | *I spoke to Ava to arrange a time to meet.*

▶ **talk** to say things to someone, especially when you are having a conversation: *We talked about Ellen's party.* | *I need to talk to you about something.*

▶ **whisper** to speak very quietly, so that other people cannot hear you: *Suzie whispered something in her friend's ear, but I couldn't hear what it was.*

▶ **mumble** to speak quietly and not clearly, in a way that is difficult to understand: *Don't mumble, Matthew! No one can hear what you are saying.*

▶ **mutter** to say something quietly and in a way that is difficult to hear clearly, especially because you are angry: *"I won't do it," she muttered as she went out of the door.*

▶ **stammer** to speak with a lot of pauses and repeated sounds: *"I'm s-s-s sorry," he stammered nervously.*

## star *noun*

a point of light in the sky at night. Stars are made of burning gases: *We looked up at the stars in the night sky.*

▶ **sun** the yellow ball of light in the sky during the day. It is made of fire and gives out light and heat. Our planet, the Earth, moves around the sun: *The sun rises in the east and sets in the west.*

▶ **planet** a large round object in space that moves around the Sun, for example the Earth, Mars, or Saturn: *Do you think there is life on other planets?*

▶ **asteroid** a mass of rock that moves around the sun: *Most asteroids are found between Mars and Jupiter.*

▶ **constellation** a group of stars that form a pattern and that have a name: *This map of the sky shows the constellations.*

▶ **galaxy** a very large group of stars: *Our Sun is in a galaxy that is called the Milky Way.*

## start *verb*

to begin happening, or to begin doing something: *The movie starts at three o'clock. | I started writing a story. | Let's start the game.*

ANTONYMS: **end, stop, finish**

▶ **begin** begin means the same as **start**: *School begins in September. | It is beginning to rain.*

▶ **set off** to start a trip somewhere: *We packed our suitcases in the trunk of the car and set off.*

▶ **break out** if a fire, fight, or disease breaks out, it starts: *No one knows how the fire broke out. | There was an argument and a fight broke out.*

▶ **open** to start to be available for people to use, or to make something start: *The new swimming pool will open next month. | My dad opened a pizza restaurant.*

## steal *verb*

to take something that belongs to someone else: *The thieves tried to steal the car by breaking one of the windows.*

▶ **take** to steal or borrow something without asking someone's permission: *Someone has taken my lunch box! I left it on this table and now it's gone.*

▶ **rob** to steal money or other things from a person, bank, or store: *The men robbed a bank and escaped with over $1 million.*

▶ **mug** to attack someone in the street in order to steal something: *Someone tried to mug her and steal her purse.*

▶ **burglarize** to enter a house or other building to steal things: *A thief burglarized the house and stole all her jewelry.*

## stop *verb*

to not continue happening or doing something: *I wish the rain would stop. | The teacher came in, so we all stopped talking.* ANTONYMS: **start, begin**

▶ **quit** to stop doing something, especially because you do not want to do it anymore, or because it is annoying: *He decided to quit his job and go back to college. | Quit making that terrible noise!*

▶ **give up** to stop doing something that is too hard or that you do a lot: *Dad gave up smoking last year. | I didn't want to give up, but the puzzle was too hard.*

▶ **take a break** to stop doing something for a short time, in order to rest: *We will finish exercise 3 and then we can take a break.*

▶ **pause** to stop talking or doing something for a short time, in order to do something else: *They paused to watch a bird fly overhead.*

▶ **cease** to stop happening. **Cease** is a formal word: *Suddenly the rain ceased and the sun came out.*

a
b
c
d
e
f
g
h
i
j
k
l
m
n
o
p
q
r
**s**
t
u
v
w
x
y
z

**storm** *noun*

if there is a storm, there is a lot of wind and rain or snow: *The storm blew down a tree outside our house.*

▶ **thunderstorm** a storm with thunder and lightning: *I'm scared of thunderstorms because they are so loud.*

▶ **blizzard** a very bad storm with a lot of snow and wind: *A blizzard makes driving difficult because you cannot see where you are going.*

▶ **hurricane** a storm with very strong fast winds. **Hurricanes** start in the Atlantic Ocean or in the Caribbean Sea: *The hurricane destroyed thousands of homes in Florida.*

▶ **typhoon** a storm with very strong fast winds. **Typhoons** start in the Pacific Ocean: *In Asia, there are dangerous typhoons between May and November.*

▶ **tornado** a very violent storm that sucks things up from the ground. The air spins and moves very quickly: *Some tornadoes reach speeds of 300 miles per hour.*

**story** *noun*

a description of events which is told to entertain people: *I'm reading a story about a girl who wants to be a dancer.*

▶ **tale** a story, especially about exciting imaginary events: *The book is a tale of pirates and adventure. | In the fairy tale, Jack climbs to the top of a giant beanstalk. | In American folk tales, Paul Bunyan is a giant who combs his beard with a pine tree.*

▶ **myth** an old story about gods, magical creatures, or the beginning of the world: *In the ancient Greek myth, Hercules is a great hero and he is the son of the god Zeus.*

▶ **legend** an old story about a person or place, in which strange things happen, or people have magical powers: *According to the legend, the boy was raised by a family of wolves.*

▶ **fable** a story that teaches us something about life. A **fable** often has animals in it: *In the fable of the ant and the grasshopper, the ant is successful because he works hard.*

▶ **fiction** books and stories about people or things who are not real: *I like to read fiction, especially stories about children who have adventures.*

▶ **anecdote** a short story about something that happened, which you tell to amuse people: *He told an anecdote about the time he got stuck in the mud.*

**strange** *adjective*

different from usual, in a way that makes you a little frightened or surprised: *There's a strange insect in the bathroom. | It's strange that she didn't call to say that she was late.*

ANTONYMS: **normal, usual**

▶ **unusual** different from what is usual or normal: *Bright pink is an unusual color.*

▶ **weird** very strange: *I had a weird dream last night. I dreamed that I was talking to a bear.*

▶ **peculiar** strange, especially in a way that makes you feel uncomfortable: *This meat tastes peculiar. Do you think it is OK to eat?*

▶ **mysterious** very difficult to understand or explain because you know very little about it: *It is mysterious that no one ever came back to live in that house.*

▶ **eccentric** behaving in a way that seems strange and a little bit crazy: *Jake is a little eccentric, because he always wears different colored socks.*

**strong** *adjective*

**strong person**:

▶ **strong** having good muscles, especially so that you can lift heavy things: *My dad is very strong, so he can lift me up on his shoulders.*

ANTONYM: **weak**

▶ **powerful** very strong. You use **powerful** about someone's body, arms, muscles, etc.: *He has a big powerful body, and he looks like a football player.*

▶ **muscular** having big muscles that look strong: *Joe is muscular because he goes to the gym three times a week.*

a b c d e f g h i j k l m n o p q r **s** t u v w x y z

## strong thing:

▶ **strong** not easy to break or damage: *The rope is strong enough to hold your weight.*

> ( ANTONYM: **weak** )

▶ **tough** **tough** material is difficult to damage or tear: *Jeans are made from denim, which is very tough.*

▶ **heavy-duty** strong enough to use a lot, or for very hard work: *My dad wears heavy-duty boots when he is working in the factory.*

▶ **indestructible** impossible to break or destroy: *Wooden toys are almost indestructible.*

## stupid *adjective*

not intelligent or not sensible: *My younger sister is always doing stupid things, like pouring water into her shoes.*

▶ **dumb** **dumb** means the same as **stupid**: *Everyone laughed at me and I felt dumb.*

▶ **silly** a little stupid. **Silly** sounds much gentler than **stupid**: *That was a silly mistake.* | *Don't be silly. It's only a spider and it won't hurt you.*

▶ **foolish** behaving in a way that is not sensible, or is dangerous: *It was foolish to run across the street.*

▶ **crazy** not sensible at all. You use **crazy** when you are surprised by someone's behavior, or by what someone has said: *You're crazy if you go out in this bad weather.* | *It sounds like a crazy idea to me.*

## successful *adjective*

if you are successful, you achieve what you want to do: *His second attempt to reach the top of the mountain was successful.* | *She is a successful singer who has sold two million records.*

▶ **effective** producing the result that you want: *The medicine was effective and she got better quickly.*

▶ **promising** good and likely to be successful: *Lucy is a promising piano player who may become a concert pianist.*

▶ **victorious** if you are **victorious**, you win a game, war, battle, or election: *Washington's army was victorious and they defeated the British.* | *The victorious team receives a silver cup.*

## suggest *verb*

to tell someone your ideas about what he or she should do: *If the movie starts at 7 o'clock, I suggest that we meet at 6:30.*

▶ **recommend** to advise someone to do something because you know it is good: *I recommend that you read this book because it's really good!* | *A friend recommended the game to me.*

▶ **nominate** to say that someone or something should get an important job or prize: *The other players nominated him for team captain.* | *The movie has been nominated for an award.*

## sure *adjective*

knowing or believing that something is true: *I'm sure that you'll pass the test.*

▶ **certain** completely sure: *Don't go on the trip unless you are certain that you want to.*

▶ **positive** completely sure that something is true, especially when other people are doubtful: *"Are you sure that you mailed the letter?" "I'm positive."*

▶ **convinced** believing firmly that something is true, even if you do not have any proof: *His family is convinced that he is innocent.*

## surprised *adjective*

having the feeling that people have when something unusual happens: *I'm not good at football, so I was surprised when they picked me for the team.*

▶ **shocked** surprised and upset by something bad that happens: *Everyone was shocked when they heard he was hurt.*

▶ **astonished** very surprised: *I was astonished when I saw how big the fish was.*

▶ **amazed** very surprised. **Amazed** means the same as **astonished**: *I was amazed by how much the meal cost, because it was over $100.*

▶ **startled** surprised and a little frightened because something suddenly happens: *Tom was startled by the sound of someone knocking on the window.*

a b c d e f g h i j k l m n o p q r s **t** u v w x y z

**surprising** *adjective*
if something is surprising, you do not expect it: *It is surprising that many children don't know that milk comes from cows.*

▶ **shocking** surprising and upsetting: *There were some shocking pictures of the city after the earthquake.*

▶ **amazing** very good, especially in a surprising way: *This cake tastes amazing!*

▶ **extraordinary** very unusual and surprising: *The girl has an extraordinary talent for math.*

▶ **astonishing** very surprising and hard to believe: *The car was moving at the astonishing speed of 200 miles per hour.*

# Tt

**take** *verb*
to move someone or something from one place to another: *I will take my umbrella with me in case it rains. | Dad took me home in his car.*

▶ **bring** to take something to the place where you are now, or to the place where you are going to with someone: *Bring me your homework, please. | You can bring your friends to the party.*

▶ **accompany** to go somewhere with someone: *The blind man has a dog that accompanies him wherever he goes.*

▶ **drive** to take someone somewhere in a car or truck: *Sometimes Mom drives me to school.*

▶ **deliver** to take a letter or package somewhere: *The mailman delivered the letter to the wrong address.*

▶ **transport** to take a lot of things somewhere in a truck, train, ship, or airplane: *The toys are transported by ship to the U.S. from China.*

**talk** *verb*
to say things to someone: *The boys talked about last night's football game. | I need to talk to you about your schoolwork.*

▶ **speak** to produce words with your voice, or talk to someone: *She has a sore throat and can't speak. | He can speak Spanish very well. | I spoke to Ava and arranged a time to meet.*

▶ **chat** to talk in a friendly way to someone you know well: *Mom and her friends meet to chat and drink coffee.*

▶ **discuss** to talk about something, especially in order to make a decision or make plans: *We discuss where we want to go on vacation.*

▶ **communicate** if people communicate, they say or write things to each other: *We communicate by phone or by email.*

▶ **gossip** to talk about other people's private lives when they are not there. When people **gossip**, they sometimes say things that are not true: *People gossip about Mrs. Stern because she has 12 children.*

▶ **whisper** to talk very quietly, so that other people cannot hear you: *You have to whisper when the baby is asleep.*

**taste** *noun*
the feeling that you get when your tongue touches food or drink: *Most people like the taste of chocolate.*

**different types of taste**:

▶ **sweet** containing a lot of sugar: *He likes chocolate and other sweet foods.*

▶ **salty** containing a lot of salt: *The chips are salty, and they are making me thirsty.*

▶ **spicy** containing a lot of spice, especially when this makes your mouth feel hot: *The enchiladas were nice and spicy.*

▶ **hot** hot means the same as **spicy**: *If you eat a hot chili pepper, it will make your mouth burn.*

▶ **bitter** bitter coffee or chocolate has a strong taste that is not sweet and is not very pleasant: *Some types of coffee have a bitter taste.*

▶ **sour** having a strong sharp taste like a lemon, which is usually not very nice: *The apple sauce is sour, so you will want to add sugar to it.*

▶ **bland** having very little taste: *Pasta is bland, so you need cheese or tomato sauce with it.*

## teacher *noun*

someone who teaches people as a job, especially in classes in a school: *Our teacher gives us a lot of homework.*

▶ **instructor** someone who teaches a practical skill or a sport: *The driving instructor is teaching him how to park the car.* | *The swimming instructor will show us how to do the crawl.*

▶ **coach** someone who trains a sports team or a sports player: *The coach makes us practice hitting baseballs.*

▶ **tutor** someone who teaches a subject to one student or only a few students: *My brother has extra math classes from a tutor at home.*

▶ **professor** a teacher at a university: *Professor Alvarez teaches Spanish at the University of Chicago.*

▶ **lecturer** a teacher at a university who gives talks to big groups of students: *She's a lecturer in economics at Stanford University.*

## tell *verb*

to give someone information by talking or writing to them: *Can you tell me how much the tickets cost?* | *One of my friends told me about the movie.*

▶ **warn** to tell someone that something bad or dangerous may happen, so that he or she can avoid it: *She warned me not to go swimming in the lake because it is very deep.*

▶ **reveal** to tell people about something that was a secret: *Everyone was surprised when he revealed that he is a millionaire.*

▶ **announce** to tell a lot of people about something publicly or officially: *They announced that the plane was going to be late.* | *Katie and Joe announced that they are getting married.*

▶ **inform** to tell someone officially about something, for example by writing a letter to them or by telephoning them: *Please inform the office if you are going to be late for school.*

▶ **break the news** to tell someone some news, especially bad news: *I lost Dad's camera, but I didn't want to break to the news to him!*

## test *noun*

a set of questions or activities to measure your knowledge or skill: *I got a good score on my math test.* | *She passed her driving test on the first try.*

▶ **exam** an important test in high school or college: *High school students take exams at the end of each semester.*

▶ **quiz** a short test that a teacher gives to a class: *Every week, the teacher gives us a spelling quiz.*

## thin *adjective*

not having much fat on your body: *She is tall and thin.* | *My grandpa has a very thin face.*

( ANTONYM: **fat** )

▶ **slim** thin in a way that looks good: *Exercise is a good way to stay slim.*

▶ **skinny** very thin, especially in a way that looks unhealthy: *Young boys are often skinny, but they put on weight as they get older.*

▶ **slender** thin in a way that looks good. You use **slender** especially when someone is tall and thin, or when someone has long thin arms or legs: *Her arms are long and slender.*

## think *verb*

to use your mind to have ideas, remember things, or solve problems: *I want you to think about what I said.* | *Have you thought about going to college when you're older?*

▶ **consider** to think about something carefully before deciding what to do: *She considered the idea of moving to New York.*

▶ **concentrate** to think very carefully about what you are doing: *I can't concentrate on my work because there is too much noise.*

▶ **have something on your mind** to be thinking about something, so that you feel worried about it: *Her dad has just lost his job, so she has a lot on her mind.*

a
b
c
d
e
f
g
h
i
j
k
l
m
n
o
p
q
r
s
**t**
u
v
w
x
y
z

a
b
c
d
e
f
g
h
i
j
k
l
m
n
o
p
q
r
s

**t**

u
v
w
x
y
z

**throw** *verb*

to make something go through the air, by moving your arm and letting it go out of your hand: *Throw the ball to me, and I will catch it.*

▶ **toss** to throw something in a careless way: *Tammy tossed her coat on the bed.*

▶ **fling** to throw something quickly with a lot of force: *The boy was flinging a tennis ball into the air and then catching it.*

▶ **pitch** in baseball, to throw the ball for a player to hit: *Scott pitches for his baseball team.*

▶ **pass** to throw the ball to another member of your team in a game, for example in basketball: *Kate passed the ball to me, and I scored.*

**tired** *adjective*

feeling that you want to sleep or rest: *I was tired so I got ready for bed.*

▶ **sleepy** feeling that you want to sleep very soon, so that your eyes start to close: *It was eight o'clock and she felt sleepy.*

▶ **drowsy** starting to sleep, especially because you are in a warm place, or because you have eaten or drunk something: *The car was nice and warm, and I felt drowsy.*

▶ **exhausted** very tired, so that you cannot do any more: *By the end of the game, I was exhausted and I wanted to sit down.*

▶ **worn out** **worn out** means the same as **exhausted**: *When the children came home from camp, they were worn out.*

▶ **weary** very tired because you have been traveling a long way, worrying a lot, or doing something for a long time: *They were weary after the long trip from New York. | Grandfather worked hard all his life, and now he is old and weary.*

**touch** *verb*

to put your fingers or hand onto something or someone for a short time: *Don't touch the paint, because it's still wet! | She touched his arm to get his attention.*

▶ **stroke** to move your hand gently over someone's hair or body in a loving way: *Mother sat with me when I was sick and stroked my hair.*

▶ **pet** to move your hand over an animal's fur to show that you like it: *I like to pet the cat because her fur is so soft.*

▶ **scratch** to rub your skin with your fingernails because it feels uncomfortable: *Try not to scratch those bug bites on your arm.*

▶ **pat** to touch someone lightly with your hand flat, in a friendly way: *I pat the dog on the head. | The coach patted me on the back when I came off the field.*

▶ **tickle** to move your fingers lightly on parts of someone's body to try to make him or her laugh: *Dad tickled us under our arms.*

**town** *noun*

a place with many buildings and streets where people live and work. A **town** is smaller than a **city**: *They live in a small town in Oregon. | We spent our vacation in a town on the coast of Maine.*

▶ **city** a very large town: *New York is the biggest city in the United States. | There are a lot of apartment buildings in the city.*

▶ **village** a very small town: *My grandparents live in a village in Mexico.*

▶ **capital** the city where a country's or state's main government is: *Tokyo is the capital of Japan. | At school we learned all of the state capitals.*

**travel** *verb*

to go from one place to another: *I like to travel by train.*

▶ **take** if you take the bus, airplane, or train, you go somewhere by bus, airplane, or train: *It's quicker if you take the bus.*

▶ **drive** to travel in a car: *We're going to drive to the beach and have a picnic.*

▶ **fly** to travel in an airplane: *Antonio will fly to Mexico City to see his family.*

▶ **sail** to travel by boat or ship: *He got in the boat and sailed across the lake.*

▶ **bike** to travel by bicycle: *I bike to school with my friends.*

▶ **commute** to go in a car, bus, or train every day to get to work: *My dad commutes to work by car.*

## trip *noun*

a visit to a place that you travel to: *We are going to the museum on a school trip. | I had a great trip to Florida and I want to go back again.*

▶ **journey** a long trip from one place to another: *The book is about the men's journey across North America.*

▶ **voyage** a long trip in a ship or a space vehicle: *Christopher Columbus made his first voyage to the New World in 1492. | The voyage to Mars takes about nine months.*

▶ **tour** a trip to several different places in a country or area: *We went on a tour of Washington, and visited the White House, and the Capitol Building.*

▶ **cruise** a vacation on a large boat: *My family is going on a cruise around the Caribbean islands.*

▶ **expedition** a long and carefully planned trip, often to a dangerous or unknown place: *Lewis and Clark led the expedition across North America to the Pacific Ocean.*

## try *verb*

to make an effort to do something: *Try to do the math homework, and I'll help you.*

▶ **attempt** to try to do something, especially something difficult or dangerous: *She will attempt to climb Mount Everest. | The skater is going to attempt a new kind of jump.*

▶ **do your best** to try as hard as you can to do something: *I'll do my best to finish the essay by tomorrow morning.*

▶ **make an effort** to try hard to do something, especially something that you do not want to do: *You should make an effort to be nicer to your sister.*

## turn *verb*

to move around in a circle: *The wheels of the train started to turn. | She turned the key and opened the door.*

▶ **go around** **go around** means the same as **turn**: *I watched the hands on the clock go around until it was ten o'clock.*

▶ **spin** to turn around many times very quickly: *The skaters spin around on the ice.*

▶ **rotate** to move in a circle around a fixed central point: *The tires rotate around the axle.*

▶ **twist** to turn something firmly, so that it moves around: *To open the bottle, you have to twist the cap off.*

▶ **whirl** to make someone or something move around quickly: *He whirled her around the dance floor.*

## type *noun*

a group of people or things that are similar to each other in some way: *At the aquarium you can see many different types of fish.*

▶ **kind** **kind** means the same as **type**: *"What kind of food do you like?" "I like pizza."*

▶ **sort** **sort** means the same as **type**: *"What sort of tree is this?" "I think it's a maple tree."*

▶ **category** one of the groups that something is divided into: *The teacher asked us to read books from each category: fiction, science, and history.*

▶ **species** a group of plants or animals that are all similar and can produce young animals or plants of the same type: *Dogs and wolves belong to the same species.*

▶ **brand** a type of product made by a company, especially one that you use every day such as clothes or food: *This brand of toothpaste is cheaper than the others.*

▶ **make** a type of product made by a company, especially a machine or a car: *"What make is your dad's car?" "It's a Ford."*

a
b
c
d
e
f
g
h
i
j
k
l
m
n
o
p
q
r
s
t
**u**
v
w
x
y
z

# Uu

## understand *verb*
to know the meaning of what someone is saying: *The teacher spoke clearly so that everyone could understand.*

▶ **comprehend** to understand something . You use **comprehend** especially when something is difficult to understand: *I can't comprehend why he spent so much money on a new cell phone.*

▶ **follow** to understand instructions, a story, or what someone is saying: *The instructions for the game are easy to follow. | I'm sorry, I didn't follow you. Can you say that again?*

▶ **see** to understand what someone means, or the reasons for something: *Do you see what I mean? | I can see why she doesn't like him, because he is really annoying.*

▶ **figure out** to think about something complicated until you understand it: *I can't figure out how to solve this math problem.*

## unusual *adjective*
different from what is usual or normal: *It's unusual for Mrs. Norris to get so angry. | She has an unusual name. It's Hepzibah.*

( ANTONYMS: **usual, normal** )

▶ **rare** if something is rare, it does not happen often, or there are only a few: *The disease is rare and only a few people get it. | Tigers are becoming rare and they need to be protected from hunters.*

▶ **special** different from usual, and better or more important: *We wanted to do something special for mom's birthday, so we had a surprise party.*

▶ **extraordinary** very unusual or surprising: *The firefighter showed extraordinary bravery in rescuing the child from a burning house.*

▶ **exceptional** very good in a way that is unusual: *The coach says that Dan is an exceptional player, one of the best he has ever seen.*

## use *verb*
if you use something, you do something with it: *Many people use bicycles to get to school. | We use candles to light the room.*

▶ **consume** to use an amount of something, especially fuel, energy, or resources: *The U.S. consumes more energy than any other country in the world.*

▶ **utilize** to use something that is available to you. **Utilize** is a formal word: *Native Americans utilized every part of the buffalo, for food, clothing, and other things.*

▶ **exhaust** to use all of something: *They exhausted their supply of food so there was none left.*

## useful *adjective*
helping you to do or to get what you want: *The book is full of useful ideas for teachers. | This bag is useful for carrying school books.*

( ANTONYM: **useless** )

▶ **handy** useful and easy to use: *We got Mom a handy gadget for peeling vegetables. | The magazine has handy hints for making cookies.*

▶ **invaluable** very useful: *The Internet is an invaluable tool to find information.*

▶ **versatile** able to be used in a lot of different ways: *She is a versatile player who can play well in different positions.*

# Vv

## vacation *noun*

a period of time when you do not have to work or go to school: *During summer vacation, I went to stay with my aunt.*

You also use **vacation** about a period of time when you go to a different place for enjoyment: *We are going on a two-week vacation to Mexico.*

▶ **break** a short vacation from work or school: *We spent spring break in Florida.*

▶ **leave** a period of time when someone does not have to work, especially someone in the army or the navy: *His dad is home on leave from the army.*

▶ **honeymoon** a vacation that people take after they get married: *My parents went to Italy on their honeymoon.*

▶ **holiday** one of the days when no one has to go to work or school: *Thanksgiving is a holiday when families and friends get together for a big meal. | May 5 is a national holiday in Mexico.*

## valuable *adjective*

worth a lot of money: *The ring is made of gold so it's very valuable.*

▶ **precious** a precious metal or stone is very rare and expensive: *The bracelet has diamonds and other precious stones in it.*
A precious person or thing is very special and important to you: *The doll is precious to me because it belonged to my grandmother.*

▶ **priceless** very valuable. You use **priceless** about something that is so valuable that you cannot say how much it is worth: *The museum has many priceless works of art.*

## violent *adjective*

using force to hurt or kill people: *People who commit violent crimes go to prison.*

▶ **aggressive** behaving in an angry way, and wanting to argue or fight with people: *The truck driver suddenly became aggressive and shouted at us.*

▶ **fierce** a fierce animal looks frightening and likely to attack people: *The house is guarded by a fierce dog.*

▶ **brutal** very violent and cruel: *The war was long and brutal.*

▶ **gory** a gory movie or picture has a lot of violence and blood in it: *I don't like horror movies because they are too gory.*

a
b
c
d
e
f
g
h
i
j
k
l
m
n
o
p
q
r
s
t
u
**v**
w
x
y
z

a
b
c
d
e
f
g
h
i
j
k
l
m
n
o
p
q
r
s
t
u
v
**w**
x
y
z

# Ww

## walk *verb*
to move forward by putting one foot in front of the other: *Be careful when you walk across the street.*

▶ **tiptoe** to walk very quietly on your toes, so that you do not disturb someone: *We tiptoed out of the room because we didn't want to wake the baby.*

▶ **creep** to walk slowly and quietly, so that someone does not notice you: *It is funny to creep up behind someone and say "boo!"*

▶ **limp** to walk with difficulty because you have hurt your leg or foot: *The cat is limping because he has a cut on his paw.*

▶ **stroll** to walk in a slow relaxed way: *They strolled through the park in the sunshine.*

▶ **wander** to walk slowly around a place, without having a clear idea of where you want to go: *We like to wander around the mall, looking in the store windows.*

▶ **march** to walk with regular steps. You use **march** especially about a group of soldiers or a band: *The high school band will march in the parade.*
**March** also means to walk in a determined or angry way: *She marched into the office and demanded to see the principal.*

▶ **go hiking** to go for a long walk in the country or the mountains: *On weekends, we go hiking in the mountains.*

## want *verb*
to feel that you will be happy if you have or do something: *I want a new bike. | The little boy wants his mother. | We want to go to the beach.*

▶ **would like** a polite way of saying that you want something: *I would like some chocolate ice cream, please. | Would you like to come to the park with us?*

▶ **wish** to feel that you want something to happen, especially when you know that it is not possible: *I wish I was taller. | I wish it was Saturday tomorrow.*

▶ **be dying for** to want something very much: *It is very hot and I am dying for a drink of water.*

## watch *verb*
to look at something that is moving, or to look at a game, television program, or movie: *I watched the dog chase the cat across the yard. | I watch television when I get home from school.*

▶ **see** to watch something. You use **see** when talking about something you watched in the past, or something you are planning to watch in the future: *I saw a good movie last night. | Do you want to see the game tomorrow?*

▶ **keep an eye on** to watch someone or something and make sure that he, she, or it is safe: *Mom asks me to keep an eye on the baby when she's in the next room.*

▶ **observe** to watch someone or something carefully over a period of time: *We will plant seeds and observe them to see which ones grow best.*

▶ **spy on** to watch someone secretly to find out what he or she is doing: *Someone was spying on us from an upstairs window.*

## way *noun*
how to do something: *What's the best way to tie your shoes? | There are lots of ways to learn a language.*

▶ **method** a way of doing something, especially one that is well known and often used: *Some farming methods are bad for the environment.*

▶ **means** a method or system that you use to do or get something: *Email is an important means of communication.* | *In those days, the horse was the only means of transportation.* | *He will use any means to get what he wants.*

▶ **technique** a special way of doing something, which uses a special skill: *Doctors are using a new technique for treating heart problems.*

## weak *adjective*

**person**:

▶ **weak** not having much strength or energy: *I feel weak because I haven't eaten all day.*
(ANTONYM: **strong**)

▶ **feeble** very weak: *She was sick and too feeble to raise her arm.*

▶ **frail** thin and weak, especially because you are old: *My grandmother is a frail lady so she can't walk far.*

▶ **delicate** weak and becoming sick easily and often: *He was a delicate child and he often had colds.*

**thing**:

▶ **weak** not strong: *The branch was too weak to support his weight.* | *He has a weak heart.*
(ANTONYM: **strong**)

▶ **fragile** easy to break. You use **fragile** when you must handle something carefully: *Be careful, the glass is fragile.*

▶ **flimsy** very thin and badly made, and easy to break: *The chair is flimsy, so don't stand on it.*

▶ **delicate** delicate things are made of very thin material. They look nice, but they are not strong: *She had a delicate silver necklace around her neck.*
Delicate skin is easily damaged: *This soap is good for delicate skin.*

## wet *adjective*

covered in water or another liquid: *Don't sit on the grass, because it's wet.* (ANTONYM: **dry**)

▶ **damp** a little wet: *Wipe the counter with a damp cloth.*

▶ **moist** a little wet. You use **moist** especially when this is what you want: *Make sure that the soil is moist before you plant the seeds.*

▶ **soggy** wet and soft. You use **soggy** especially when this is not what you want: *The ground is still soggy after the rain, so we can't play baseball.* | *The cereal is soggy because it has been in the milk too long.*

▶ **soaked** completely wet: *It started to rain and everyone got soaked.*

▶ **drenched** completely wet. **Drenched** means the same as **soaked**: *The car splashed water all over me and I was drenched.*

## wind *noun*

air outside that moves and blows things around: *The wind blew the leaves off the trees.*

▶ **breeze** a gentle wind: *The cool breeze keeps us from getting too hot.*

▶ **gust** a sudden strong wind: *A gust of wind made the door bang shut.*

▶ **gale** a very strong wind: *The fence was blown down in a gale.*

▶ **hurricane** a storm with very strong fast winds. **Hurricanes** start in the Atlantic Ocean or in the Caribbean Sea: *Hurricane Katrina caused a lot of damage to the city of New Orleans.*

▶ **tornado** a violent storm that sucks things up from the ground. The wind spins around and moves very quickly: *A tornado sucked part of the roof into the air.*

## word *noun*

a group of sounds or letters that have a meaning: *"Bonjour" is a French word that means "hello."*

▶ **term** a word or phrase used in a technical or scientific subject: *"Hypertension" is the medical term for high blood pressure.*

▶ **jargon** technical words used by people who do a particular job, or are interested in a particular subject. **Jargon** is difficult for ordinary people to understand: *The instructions were written in technical jargon, so I couldn't understand them.*

▶ **slang** very informal words used by a group of people, for example young people: *You shouldn't use slang words like "awesome" in your essays.*

a b c d e f g h i j k l m n o p q r s t u v **w** x y z

a
b
c
d
e
f
g
h
i
j
k
l
m
n
o
p
q
r
s
t
u
v
w
x
y
z

**work** *noun*
an activity that you do to earn money: *Dad wears a suit for work.*

▶ **schoolwork** work that students do for school: *Staying up late affected her schoolwork, because she kept falling asleep in class.*

▶ **homework** work for school that students do at home: *The teacher gave us math problems for homework.*

▶ **housework** work that needs to be done in your home, for example washing and cleaning: *Mom asked me to help with the housework, so I cleaned the bathroom.*

▶ **chores** jobs that you have to do regularly, especially jobs in the home such as cleaning: *On Saturday mornings we do our chores. My chore is to clean the car.*

▶ **assignment** a piece of work that you have to do for school: *Your homework assignment is to write an essay about the American Revolution.*

**world** *noun*
the planet we live on: *Mount Everest is the highest mountain in the world.*

▶ **planet** a large round object in space that moves around a sun: *Mars is the fourth planet from the Sun.*

▶ **Earth** the planet we live on. You use **Earth** especially when talking about space and the other planets: *The rocket has now returned to Earth.* | *The Earth goes around the Sun.*

▶ **globe** the world. You use **the globe** when talking about all of the surface of the world: *Using the Internet, we can communicate with people all over the globe.* | *She lives in Australia, which is on the other side of the globe from us.*

**worried** *adjective*
not happy or relaxed because you think something bad has happened or might happen: *I'm worried that I will make a mistake on the test.*

▶ **anxious** **anxious** is very similar to **worried**. **Anxious** sounds stronger than **worried**, and you are often **anxious** for a longer time: *His parents are anxious because his Mom has lost her job.*

▶ **concerned** worried about a problem: *People are becoming more concerned about the environment.*

▶ **nervous** worried about something you have to do: *I am always nervous when I go on stage.*

▶ **uneasy** a little worried because you feel that something is not right: *I felt uneasy when she didn't answer her phone, when I knew she was home.*

▶ **stressed** worried because you have too much work, or a problem is difficult to deal with: *My dad is feeling stressed about his work and he needs a vacation.*

**write** *verb*
to put letters or words on paper, using a pen or pencil: *Write your name at the top of the page.* | *The children are learning to read and write.*

▶ **sign** to write your name on something: *Your parents have to sign a permission slip to say you can go on the field trip.*

▶ **type in** to write something on a computer: *Type in your password.*

▶ **fill out** to write information on a form or other official document: *I had to fill out an application form for swimming lessons.*

▶ **make a note of** to write information that you will need later: *Make a note of the math problems that you need to do for homework.*

▶ **scribble** to write something quickly in a messy way: *I scribbled my email address on a piece of paper.*

▶ **jot down** to write something quickly: *Let's jot down a few ideas for our writing assignment.*

## writer *noun*

someone who writes books, plays, poems, or newspaper articles: *J.K. Rowling is my favorite writer, and I have read all of the Harry Potter books.*

▶ **author** someone who writes books, or a particular book: *Jeff Kinney is the author of the "Diary of a Wimpy Kid."*

▶ **novelist** someone who writes novels: *Mark Twain is a famous novelist, who wrote "The Adventures of Tom Sawyer."*

▶ **playwright** someone who writes plays: *"Romeo and Juliet" was written by the English playwright William Shakespeare.*

▶ **scriptwriter/screenwriter** someone who writes the words for a movie or television show: *The scriptwriter decided to give the movie a happy ending.*

▶ **poet** someone who writes poems: *Robert Frost was an American poet who often wrote about nature.*

▶ **reporter** someone who writes reports for newspapers, magazines, television, or radio: *The reporter asked the president for his opinion about the situation.*

## wrong *adjective*

not correct: *You're wrong! I'm not nine, I'm eight. | You lose a point for every wrong answer.*

ANTONYMS: **right, correct**

▶ **incorrect** incorrect means the same as **wrong**. You usually use **incorrect** about answers and information: *The phone number she gave me was incorrect, so I couldn't call her.*

▶ **false** not based on true facts: *On the test, you have to say whether the statement is true or false.*

▶ **inaccurate** inaccurate information is not exactly right: *It's an old book so some of the information is inaccurate.*

▶ **misleading** likely to make someone believe something that is not true: *The title of the book is misleading, because it makes you think the book is about birds when it is about football.*

# Yy

## young *adjective*

someone who is young has only lived for a short time: *Young babies sleep most of the time. | I was the youngest student in the class.* ( ANTONYM: **old** )

▶ **little** very young: *When I was little, I used to sleep in my parents' room. | Who's the little girl in the red shirt?*

▶ **teenage** between 13 and 19 years old: *Some teenagers from the high school come to our school to help us with our reading.*

▶ **immature** behaving in a way that is not sensible and is typical of someone who is much younger: *He is so immature! He is twelve, but he still has temper tantrums.*

▶ **childish** childish means the same as **immature**: *Katie is childish because she still plays with dolls at age 15.*

a b c d e f g h i j k l m n o p q r s t u v w x **y** z

# Picture Dictionary

frog

newt

salamander

toad

lizard

alligator

turtle

snake

crocodile

rabbit

bison

cow

bat

beaver

bear

sheep

wolf

fox

raccoon

anteater

cougar

elephant

zebra

giraffe

dolphin

whale

bass

salmon

flounder

goldfish

trout

tuna

shark

catfish

shrimp

manatee

crab

mussel

lobster

starfish

eel

sea urchin

bald eagle

bluejay

cardinal

hummingbird

crow

duck

flamingo

crane

magpie

mockingbird

ostrich

owl

parakeet

parrot

peacock

woodpecker

penguin

pigeon

raven

sparrow

swallow

swan

pelican

bee

wasp

butterfly

moth

hornet

caterpillar

fly

mosquito

grasshopper

cricket

cockroach

beetle

ant

praying mantis

ladybug

firefly

dragonfly

snail

centipede

earthworm

## Flowers

daisy

crocus

azalea

lily

tulip

orchid

rose

carnation

daffodil

foxglove

sunflower

chrysanthemum

violet

iris

water lily

dandelion

## Trees and Plants

cactus

willow

pine

holly

fir

maple

palm tree

sequoia

chestnut

oak tree

# Fruit and Vegetables

## Fruit

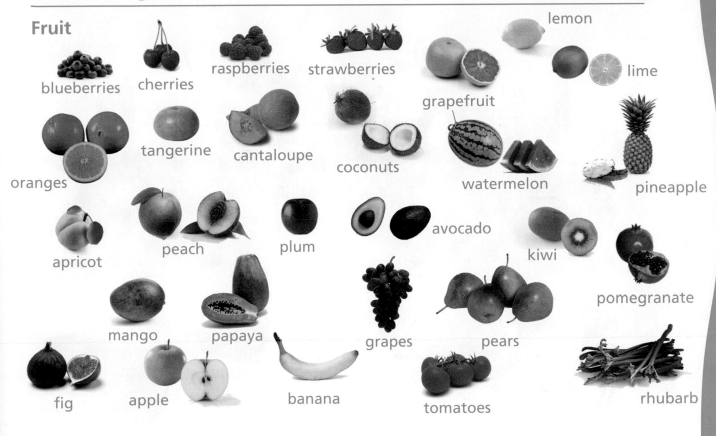

blueberries

cherries

raspberries

strawberries

lemon

lime

grapefruit

oranges

tangerine

cantaloupe

coconuts

watermelon

pineapple

apricot

peach

plum

avocado

kiwi

pomegranate

mango

papaya

grapes

pears

fig

apple

banana

tomatoes

rhubarb

## Vegetables

asparagus

eggplant

beet

corn

zucchini

garlic

onions

carrots

green onions

broccoli

cauliflower

lettuce

spinach

potatoes

pumpkin

green beans

mushrooms

peas

cucumber

squash

sweet potato

turnips

celery

peppers

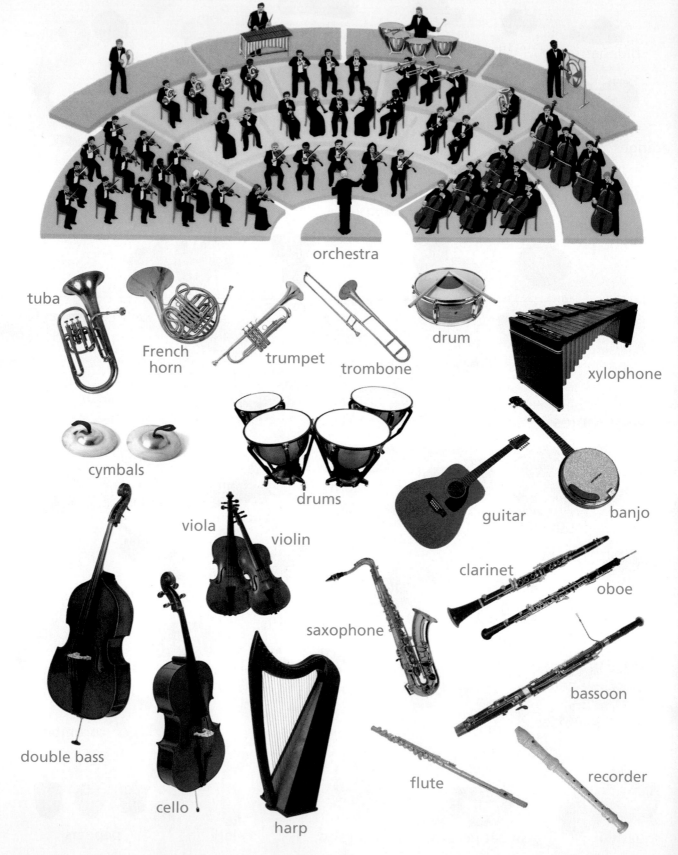

orchestra

tuba

French horn

trumpet

trombone

drum

xylophone

cymbals

drums

guitar

banjo

viola

violin

clarinet

oboe

saxophone

bassoon

double bass

cello

harp

flute

recorder

calculator

colored pencils

compass

globe

crayons

eraser

felt tip pens

glue

notebook

paintbrushes

paints

paper clips

pen

pencil

pencil case

pencil sharpener

ruler

scissors

tape

stapler

computer

whiteboard

football

baseball

basketball

hockey

softball

volleyball

soccer

running

skiing

tennis

golf

sailing

rowing

surfing

swimming

coast

desert

forest

lake

mountains

swamp

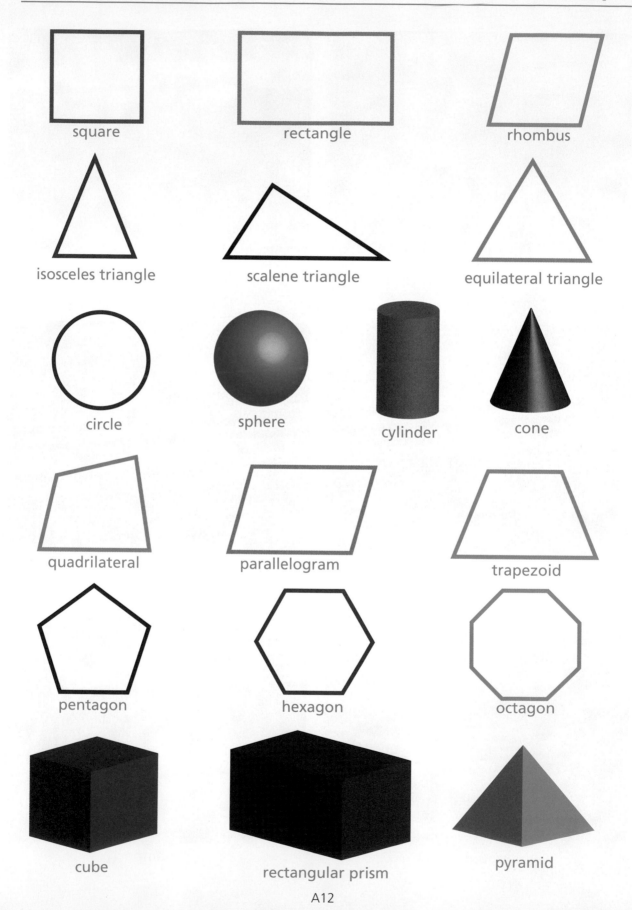

square

rectangle

rhombus

isosceles triangle

scalene triangle

equilateral triangle

circle

sphere

cylinder

cone

quadrilateral

parallelogram

trapezoid

pentagon

hexagon

octagon

cube

rectangular prism

pyramid

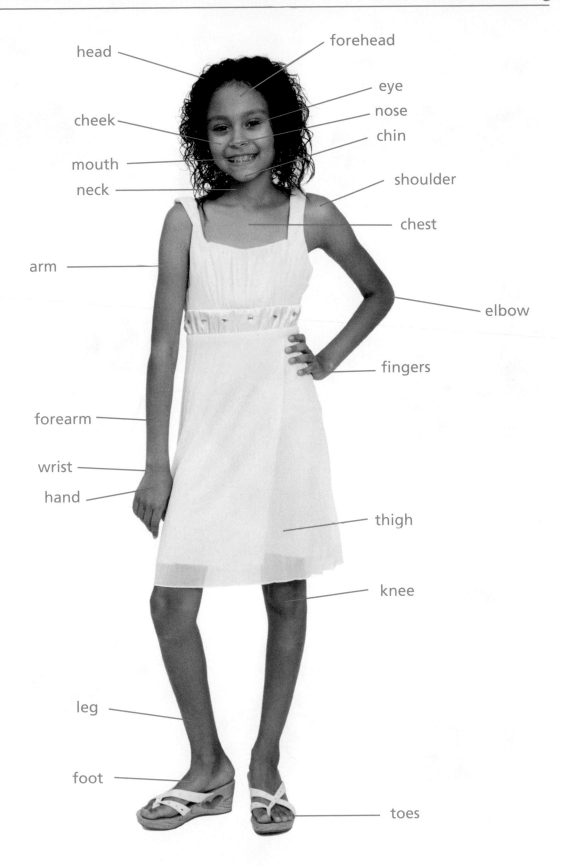

head

forehead

cheek

eye

nose

mouth

chin

neck

shoulder

chest

arm

elbow

fingers

forearm

wrist

hand

thigh

knee

leg

foot

toes

clap

tap

pinch

hold hands

scratch

point

pet

tickle

wave

pick up

lift

carry

hold

tiptoe

walk

march

jog

run

throw

catch

fall

drop

hop

trip

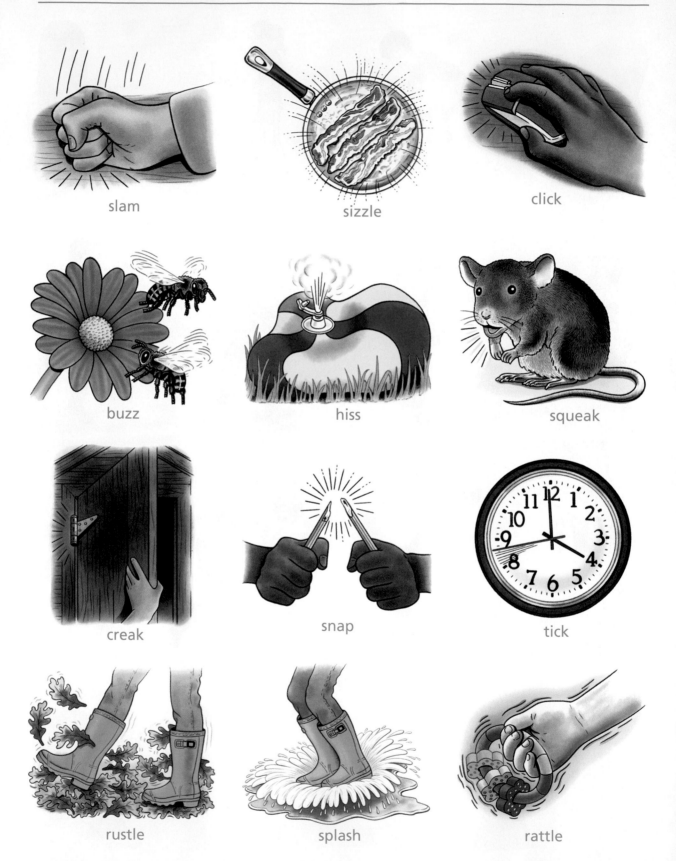

slam

sizzle

click

buzz

hiss

squeak

creak

snap

tick

rustle

splash

rattle

# Reference Section

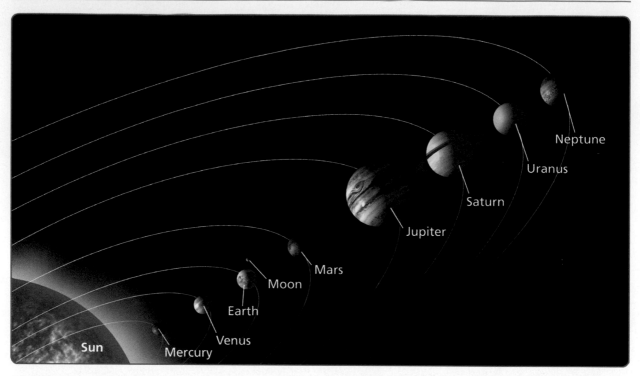

Our solar system is the Sun and all the objects that **revolve** around or **orbit** (= move around) it. The Sun is a star. It is made up of very hot gases. It is much bigger than any of the planets, but it is very far away so it looks small. Plants and animals need energy from the Sun to live and stay warm.

There are eight planets in our solar system. They move around the Sun in paths called "orbits." They look like stars in the night sky. The planets and the Moon do not produce their own light. They reflect light from the Sun.

**Mercury** is the nearest planet to the Sun. It is much smaller than Earth. It orbits the Sun once every 88 days.

**Venus** is the second planet from the Sun. It is the brightest object in the night sky besides the Moon. It is slightly smaller than Earth. It orbits the Sun once every 225 days.

**Earth** is the third planet from the Sun. It takes one year for Earth to revolve around the Sun. While Earth revolves, the seasons change. Earth and the other planets also rotate (= spin on an imaginary line) as they revolve. It takes 24 hours for Earth to rotate once. This rotation causes day (= when that part of Earth is facing

the Sun) and night (= when that part of Earth is facing away from the Sun).

**The Moon** is not a planet. It revolves around Earth, not the Sun. It revolves around Earth once every 28 days, about one month. It is made of rock.

**Mars** is the fourth planet from the Sun. It has a reddish color. It is much smaller than Earth. It takes nearly two years to orbit the Sun. It has two moons of its own.

**Jupiter** is the fifth planet from the Sun. It is the largest planet in the solar system. It is made of gas instead of rock or solid material. It orbits the Sun once every 12 years. Jupiter has at least 63 moons.

**Saturn** is the sixth planet from the Sun. It is the biggest planet after Jupiter, and it is also made of gas. It orbits the Sun once every 30 years. It has large rings of ice, rock, and dust around it and at least 61 moons.

**Uranus** is the seventh planet from the Sun. It is made of gas. It has at least 27 moons. It takes 84 years to orbit the Sun.

**Neptune** is the eighth planet from the Sun. It is made of gas. It has at least 13 moons. It takes nearly 165 years to orbit the Sun.

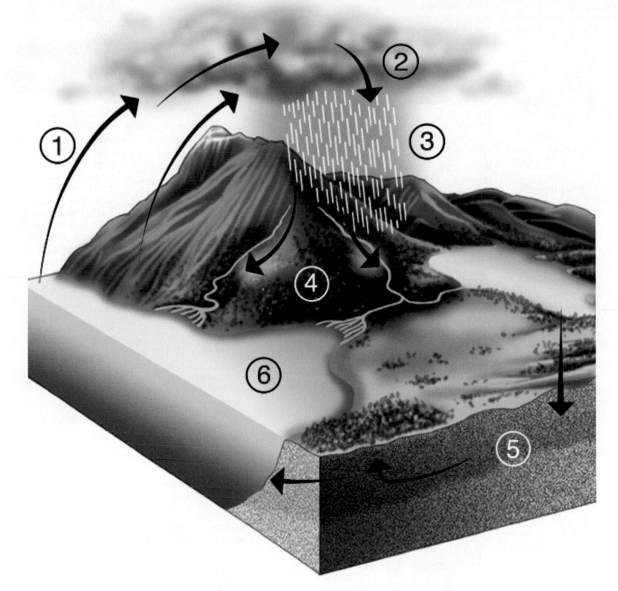

**1. Evaporation**
Heat from the Sun changes water in lakes and oceans into a gas. This gas is called "water vapor." Water vapor mixes with the air through the process of evaporation.

**2. Condensation**
Water vapor rises into the air and becomes cooler. The cool vapor condenses and becomes liquid again. Drops of water come together and form clouds.

**3. Rain**
The drops of water join together and get bigger and heavier. Finally they fall to the Earth as rain. Rain in low temperatures becomes snow, sleet, or hail.

**4. Run-off**
Some of the water from rain and melted snow, sleet, and hail runs off the land into streams, rivers, lakes, and oceans.

**5. Groundwater**
Some of the water on the land soaks into the ground. Plants, animals, and people use this groundwater to live and grow. Some of the groundwater also flows into streams, rivers, lakes, and oceans.

**6. Ocean**
Some of the water from the sky falls directly into streams, rivers, lakes, and oceans and collects there. The Sun heats water in the lakes and oceans and the water cycle begins again.

# The 50 States of the U.S.

## Alabama
(traditional abbreviation: Ala. | postal abbreviation: AL)

**Capital:** Montgomery
**Largest city:** Birmingham
**Another important city:** Mobile

Alabama was the 22nd state to join the United States, in 1819.
The name "Alabama" comes from the name of the Alabama Indian tribe that lived in the area.
Huntsville, Alabama, is called the "Rocket City" because of its work for the U.S. space program.
Someone from Alabama is called an "Alabamian" or "Alabaman."

## Alaska
(postal abbreviation: AK)

**Capital:** Juneau
**Largest city:** Anchorage

Alaska was the 49th state to join the United States, in 1959.
The name "Alaska" comes from an Aleut word that means "great land" or "mainland."
Alaska has the largest area of any state.
Someone from Alaska is called an "Alaskan."

## Arizona
(traditional abbreviation: Ariz. | postal abbreviation: AZ)

**Capital:** Phoenix
**Largest city:** Phoenix
**Another important city:** Tucson

Arizona was the 48th state to join the United States, in 1912.
We do not know exactly where the name "Arizona" comes from. It may come from an Aztec Indian word meaning "where silver comes from" or from a Pima or Tohono O'odham Indian word meaning "small spring."
The Grand Canyon is in Arizona.
Someone from Arizona is called an "Arizonan."

## Arkansas
(traditional abbreviation: Ark. | postal abbreviation: AR)

**Capital:** Little Rock
**Largest city:** Little Rock

Arkansas was the 25th state to join the United States, in 1836.
The name "Arkansas" comes from a Sioux Indian word that means "downstream place" or "south wind."
Arkansas contains the only active diamond mine in North America.
Someone from Arkansas is called an "Arkansan."

## California
(traditional abbreviation: Calif. | postal abbreviation: CA)

**Capital:** Sacramento
**Largest city:** Los Angeles
**Other important cities:** San Diego, San Jose, San Francisco, Fresno

California was the 31st state to join the United States, in 1850.
The name "California" comes from the name of an island in an old Spanish story. At first, explorers thought that California was an island.
California has the largest population of any state.
Los Angeles, California, is the second largest U.S. city.

Someone from California is called a "Californian."

## Colorado
(traditional abbreviation: Colo. | postal abbreviation: CO)

**Capital:** Denver
**Largest city:** Denver

Colorado was the 38th state to join the United States, in 1876.
The name "Colorado" comes from a Spanish word that means "red."
Colorado is the highest of all the states.
Someone from Colorado is called a "Coloradan."

## Connecticut
(traditional abbreviation: Conn. | postal abbreviation: CT)

**Capital:** Hartford
**Largest city:** Bridgeport

Connecticut was the fifth state to join the United States, in 1788.
The name "Connecticut" comes from an Indian word that means "beside the long tidal river."
The first telephone network was installed in New Haven, Connecticut, in 1878.
Someone from Connecticut is called a "Connecticuter" or "Nutmegger."

## Delaware
(traditional abbreviation: Del. | postal abbreviation: DE)

**Capital:** Dover
**Largest city:** Wilmington

Delaware was the first state to join the United States, in 1787.
Delaware was named for the Delaware River and Bay. These places were named after Lord de la Warr, the governor of Jamestown, Virginia, in 1610.
Nylon was produced for the first time in Delaware.
Someone from Delaware is called a "Delawarean."

## Florida
(traditional abbreviation: Fla. | postal abbreviation: FL)

**Capital:** Tallahassee
**Largest city:** Jacksonville
**Other important cities:** Miami, Tampa

Florida was the 27th state to join the United States, in 1845.
The name "Florida" comes from part of a Spanish phrase that means "flowery Easter."
United States space flights leave from the NASA Kennedy Space Center near Cape Canaveral, Florida.
Someone from Florida is called a "Floridian."

## Georgia
(traditional abbreviation: Ga. | postal abbreviation: GA)

**Capital:** Atlanta
**Largest city:** Atlanta

Georgia was the fourth state to join the United States, in 1788.
Georgia was named for King George II of England.
Georgia is the country's largest producer of peanuts, pecans, and peaches.
Someone from Georgia is called a "Georgian."

## Hawaii
(postal abbreviation: HI)

**Capital:** Honolulu
**Largest city:** Honolulu

Hawaii was the 50th state to join the United States, in 1959.
We do not know exactly where the name "Hawaii" comes from. It may come from a Hawaiian word that means "homeland."
Underwater volcanoes formed the islands of Hawaii. The state produces more than a third of the world's pineapples.
Someone from Hawaii is called a "Hawaiian."

## Idaho
(postal abbreviation: ID)

**Capital:** Boise
**Largest city:** Boise

Idaho was the 43rd state to join the United States, in 1890.
The name "Idaho" was made up. The man who made it up said it was a Shoshone Indian word that meant "gem of the mountains," but this was not true.
Idaho is the country's largest producer of potatoes.
Someone from Idaho is called an "Idahoan."

## Illinois
(traditional abbreviation: Ill. | postal abbreviation: IL)

**Capital:** Springfield
**Largest city:** Chicago

Illinois was the 21st state to join the United States, in 1818.
The name "Illinois"

comes from an Algonquin Indian word that means "warriors."

Illinois was the home of President Lincoln. Chicago, Illinois, is the third largest U.S. city.

Someone from Illinois is called an "Illinoisan."

## Indiana
**(traditional abbreviation: Ind. | postal abbreviation: IN)**

**Capital:** Indianapolis
**Largest city:** Indianapolis

Indiana was the 19th state to join the United States, in 1816.

The name "Indiana" means "land of Indians." The Indianapolis 500 sports car race happens here every year.

Someone from Indiana is called an "Indianan," an "Indianian," or a "Hoosier."

## Iowa
**(postal abbreviation: IA)**

**Capital:** Des Moines
**Largest city:** Des Moines

Iowa was the 29th state to join the United States, in 1846.

The name "Iowa" comes from the name of the Ioway Indian tribe that lived in the area. Iowa is the country's largest producer of corn and soybeans.

Someone from Iowa is called an "Iowan."

## Kansas
**(traditional abbreviation: Kans. | postal abbreviation: KS)**

**Capital:** Topeka
**Largest city:** Wichita

Kansas was the 34th state to join the United States, in 1861.

The name "Kansas" comes from the name of the Kaw or Kanza Indian tribe that lived in the area. Kansas is the country's largest producer of wheat. Smith Center, Kansas, is the geographical center of the United States (not including Alaska and Hawaii).

Someone from Kansas is called a "Kansan."

## Kentucky
**(traditional abbreviation: Ky. | postal abbreviation: KY)**

**Capital:** Frankfort
**Largest city:** Louisville

Kentucky was the 15th state to join the United States, in 1792.

The name "Kentucky" may come from an Iroquoian Indian word that means "land of tomorrow."

The Kentucky Derby is the oldest horse race in the U.S.

Someone from Kentucky is called a "Kentuckian."

## Louisiana
**(traditional abbreviation: La. | postal abbreviation: LA)**

**Capital:** Baton Rouge
**Largest city:** New Orleans

Louisiana was the 18th state to join the United States, in 1812. Louisiana was named for King Louis XIV of France. Louisiana is the only state that is divided into parishes instead of counties. The world-famous festival of Mardi Gras is celebrated in New Orleans every year.

Someone from Louisiana is called a "Louisianan."

## Maine
**(postal abbreviation: ME)**

**Capital:** Augusta
**Largest city:** Portland

Maine was the 23rd state to join the United States, in 1820.

Sailors first used the name "Maine" to refer to the "mainland" and not nearby islands. Maine is farther east than any other state. It belonged to Massachusetts before it became a state.

Someone from Maine is called a "Mainer."

## Maryland
**(traditional abbreviation: Md. | postal abbreviation: MD)**

**Capital:** Annapolis
**Largest city:** Baltimore

Maryland was the seventh state to join the United States, in 1788. Maryland was named for Queen Henrietta Maria, the wife of King Charles I of England.

The U.S. Naval Academy is at Annapolis, Maryland. Maryland gave some of its land to form Washington, D.C.

Someone from Maryland is called a "Marylander."

## Massachusetts
**(traditional abbreviation: Mass. | postal abbreviation: MA)**

**Capital:** Boston
**Largest city:** Boston

Massachusetts was the sixth state to join the United States, in 1788.

The name "Massachusetts" comes from the name of the Massachusetts Indian tribe that lived in the area. The name means "at the big hill."

The Pilgrims had the first Thanksgiving in Plymouth, Massachusetts, in 1621.

Someone from Massachusetts is called a "Massachusettsan" or a "Bay Stater."

## Michigan
**(traditional abbreviation: Mich. | postal abbreviation: MI)**

**Capital:** Lansing
**Largest city:** Detroit

Michigan was the 26th state to join the United States, in 1837.

The name "Michigan" comes from an Ojibwe Indian word that means "big lake."

Michigan is the country's largest producer of cars.

Someone from Michigan is called a "Michigander" or "Michiganian."

## Minnesota
**(traditional abbreviation: Minn. | postal abbreviation: MN)**

**Capital:** St. Paul
**Largest city:** Minneapolis

Minnesota was the 32nd state to join the United States, in 1858.

The name "Minnesota" comes from a Dakota Sioux word that means "sky-tinted water." Minnesota is called the "Land of 10,000 Lakes" because of the many lakes there.

Someone from Minnesota is called a "Minnesotan."

## Mississippi
**(traditional abbreviation: Miss. | postal abbreviation: MS)**

**Capital:** Jackson
**Largest city:** Jackson

Mississippi was the 20th state to join the United States, in 1817.

The name "Mississippi" comes from an Ojibwe Indian word that means "big river."

Root beer was invented in Biloxi, Mississippi, in 1898.

Someone from Mississippi is called a "Mississippian."

## Missouri
**(traditional abbreviation: Mo. | postal abbreviation: MO)**

**Capital:** Jefferson City
**Largest city:** Kansas City
**Another important city:** St. Louis

Missouri was the 24th state to join the United States, in 1821. Missouri was named for the Missouri Indian tribe. The name means "town of the large canoes." Missouri shares its borders with eight other states. The most powerful earthquake in the U.S. happened in New Madrid, Missouri, in 1811.

Someone from Missouri is called a "Missourian."

## Montana
**(traditional abbreviation: Mont. | postal abbreviation: MT)**

**Capital:** Helena
**Largest city:** Billings
The name "Montana" comes from the Spanish for "mountain."
Glacier National Park is in Montana.
Someone from Montana is called a "Montanan."

## Nebraska
**(traditional abbreviation: Nebr. | postal abbreviation: NE)**

**Capital:** Lincoln
**Largest city:** Omaha
Nebraska was the 37th state to join the United States, in 1867.
The name "Nebraska" comes from an Otos Indian word that means "flat water."
Nebraska is the only state with a one-house legislature (= institution for making laws), instead of both a house and a senate.
Someone from Nebraska is called a "Nebraskan."

## Nevada
**(traditional abbreviation: Nev. | postal abbreviation: NV)**

**Capital:** Carson City
**Largest city:** Las Vegas
**Another important city:** Reno
Nevada was the 36th state to join the United States, in 1864.
The name "Nevada" comes from the name of the Sierra Nevada mountain range. "Nevada" is a Spanish word that means "covered in snow." The Mojave Desert and Hoover Dam are in Nevada.
Someone from Nevada is called a "Nevadan."

## New Hampshire
**(traditional abbreviation | postal abbreviation: NH)**

**Capital:** Concord
**Largest city:** Manchester
New Hampshire was the ninth state to join the United States, in 1788.
New Hampshire was named for Hampshire in England.
New Hampshire's state motto is "Live Free or Die." The first free public library in the U.S. started here in 1833.
Someone from New Hampshire is called a "New Hampshirite."

## New Jersey
**(traditional abbreviation: N.J. | postal abbreviation: NJ)**

**Capital:** Trenton
**Largest city:** Newark
New Jersey was the third state to join the United States, in 1787.
New Jersey was named for the Island of Jersey between England and France.
A higher percentage of people in New Jersey live in cities than in any other state.
Someone from New Jersey is called a "New Jerseyan" or "New Jerseyite."

## New Mexico
**(traditional abbreviation: N. Mex. | postal abbreviation: NM)**

**Capital:** Santa Fe
**Largest city:** Albuquerque
New Mexico was the 47th state to join the United States, in 1912.
New Mexico is named for Mexico. The name "Mexico" comes from an Aztec Indian word that means "place of Mexitli" (an Aztec god).
The Rio Grande (river) forms the southern border of New Mexico.
New Mexico has a higher percentage of Hispanic residents than any other state.
Someone from New Mexico is called a "New Mexican."

## New York
**(traditional abbreviation: N.Y. | postal abbreviation: NY)**

**Capital:** Albany
**Largest city:** New York City
New York was the 11th state to join the United States, in 1788.
New York was named for the Duke of York (brother of King Charles II of England).
New York City is the largest city in the U.S. Niagara Falls is between New York state and Ontario, Canada.
Someone from New York is called a "New Yorker."

## North Carolina
**(traditional abbreviation: N.C. | postal abbreviation: NC)**

**Capital:** Raleigh
**Largest city:** Charlotte
**Another important city:** Winston-Salem
North Carolina was the 12th state to join the United States, in 1789.
North and South Carolina were named for King Charles I of England. The name "Carolina" comes from the Latin word for "Charles."
The Wright brothers flew the first airplane at Kitty Hawk, North Carolina, in 1903. North Carolina is the country's largest producer of tobacco.
Someone from North Carolina is called a "North Carolinian."

## North Dakota
**(traditional abbreviation: N. Dak. | postal abbreviation: ND)**

**Capital:** Bismarck
**Largest city:** Fargo
North Dakota and South Dakota were the 39th and 40th states to join the United States in 1889.
The name "Dakota" comes from a Sioux Indian word that means "friend."
North Dakota grows more sunflowers than any other state.
Someone from North Dakota is called a "North Dakotan."

## Ohio
**(postal abbreviation: OH)**

**Capital:** Columbus
**Largest city:** Columbus
**Other important cities:** Cleveland, Cincinnati, Toledo
Ohio was the 17th state to join the United States, in 1803.
The name "Ohio" comes from an Iroquoian Indian word that may mean "big river."
Ohio is called the "Buckeye State" because of the many Ohio buckeye trees there.
Someone from Ohio is called an "Ohioan."

## Oklahoma
**(traditional abbreviation: Okla. | postal abbreviation: OK)**

**Capital:** Oklahoma City
**Largest city:** Oklahoma City
**Another important city:** Tulsa
Oklahoma was the 46th state to join the United States, in 1907.
The name "Oklahoma" comes from two Choctaw Indian words that mean "red people."
Oklahoma has a larger Native American population than any other state.
Someone from Oklahoma is called an "Oklahoman."

## Oregon
**(traditional abbreviation: Oreg. | postal abbreviation: OR)**

**Capital:** Salem
**Largest city:** Portland
Oregon was the 33rd state to join the United States, in 1859.
We do not know exactly where the name "Oregon" comes from. It may come from a French word that means "hurricane," or it may be the result of mistake on a map in the early 1700s. Crater Lake, the deepest lake in the U.S., is in Oregon.
Someone from Oregon is called an "Oregonian."

## Pennsylvania
**(traditional abbreviation: Pa. | postal abbreviation: PA)**

**Capital:** Harrisburg
**Largest city:** Philadelphia
**Another important city:** Pittsburgh

Pennsylvania was the second state to join the United States, in 1787. Pennsylvania was named for William Penn. The name "Pennsylvania" comes from a Latin word that means "Penn's woodland."
The Declaration of Independence was signed in Philadelphia in 1776.
Someone from Pennsylvania is called a "Pennsylvanian."

## Rhode Island
**(traditional abbreviation: R.I. | postal abbreviation: RI)**

**Capital:** Providence
**Largest city:** Providence

Rhode Island was the 13th state to join the United States, in 1790.
Rhode Island was named for the Greek island of Rhodes.
Rhode Island is the smallest state in the U.S.
Someone from Rhode Island is called a "Rhode Islander."

## South Carolina
**(traditional abbreviation: S.C. | postal abbreviation: SC)**

**Capital:** Columbia
**Largest city:** Columbia
**Another important city:** Charleston

South Carolina was the eighth state to join the United States, in 1788.
North and South Carolina were named for King Charles I of England. The name "Carolina" comes from the Latin word for "Charles."
The first battle of the Civil War happened at Fort Sumter in South Carolina.
Someone from South Carolina is called a "South Carolinian."

## South Dakota
**(traditional abbreviation: S. Dak. | postal abbreviation: SD)**

**Capital:** Pierre
**Largest city:** Sioux Falls

North Dakota and South Dakota were the 39th and 40th states to join the United States in 1889.
The name "Dakota" comes from a Sioux Indian word that means "friend."
Mount Rushmore (a mountain with four presidents' faces carved on it) is in South Dakota.
Someone from South Dakota is called a "South Dakotan."

## Tennessee
**(traditional abbreviation: Tenn. | postal abbreviation: TN)**

**Capital:** Nashville
**Largest city:** Memphis

Tennessee was the 16th state to join the United States, in 1796.
Tennessee was named for the Cherokee Indian village Tanasqui. We do not know what the name means.
Nashville, Tennessee, is an important center for the country music industry.
Someone from Tennessee is called a "Tennessean."

## Texas
**(traditional abbreviation: Tex. | postal abbreviation: TX)**

**Capital:** Austin
**Largest city:** Houston

**Other important cities:** San Antonio, Dallas, Fort Worth, El Paso

Texas was the 28th state to join the United States, in 1845.
The name "Texas" comes from a Caddo Indian word that means "friends."
Texas was an independent country from 1836 to 1845, when it became a state. It is the second largest U.S. state in size after Alaska. Texas is the country's largest producer of cattle.
Someone from Texas is called a "Texan."

## Utah
**(postal abbreviation: UT)**

**Capital:** Salt Lake City
**Largest city:** Salt Lake City

Utah was the 45th state to join the United States, in 1896.
The name "Utah" comes from an Apache Indian word that means "people of the mountains."
The first settlers of Utah were members of the Mormon Church.
Someone from Utah is called a "Utahan."

## Vermont
**(traditional abbreviation: Vt. | postal abbreviation: VT)**

**Capital:** Montpelier
**Largest city:** Burlington

Vermont was the 14th state to join the United States, in 1791.
The name "Vermont" comes from a French phrase that means "green mountain."
Vermont is the country's largest producer of maple syrup.
Someone from Vermont is called a "Vermonter."

## Virginia
**(traditional abbreviation: Va. | postal abbreviation: VA)**

**Capital:** Richmond
**Largest city:** Virginia Beach
**Another important city:** Norfolk

Virginia was the tenth state to join the United States, in 1788.
Virginia was named for Queen Elizabeth I of England. She never married and was called the "Virgin Queen."
Eight U.S. presidents were from Virginia. The Pentagon in Arlington, Virginia, is the largest office building in the world.
Someone from Virginia is called a "Virginian."

## Washington
**(traditional abbreviation: Wash. | postal abbreviation: WA)**

**Capital:** Olympia
**Largest city:** Seattle

Washington was the 42nd state to join the United States, in 1889.
Washington was named for the first U.S. president, George Washington.
Washington is the country's largest producer of apples.
Someone from Washington is called a "Washingtonian."

## West Virginia
**(traditional abbreviation: W. Va. | postal abbreviation: WV)**

**Capital:** Charleston
**Largest city:** Charleston

West Virginia was the 35th state to join the United States, in 1863.
Virginia was named for Queen Elizabeth I of England. She never married and was called "The Virgin Queen."
West Virginia was formed from the western part of Virginia that did not want to leave the Union during the Civil War.
Someone from West Virginia is called a "West Virginian."

## Wisconsin
**(traditional abbreviation: Wis. | postal abbreviation: WI)**

**Capital:** Madison

**Largest city:** Milwaukee

Wisconsin was the 30th state to join the United States, in 1848.
The name "Wisconsin" comes from an Algonquian Indian word. We do not know exactly what it means.
Wisconsin is the country's largest producer of cheese.
Someone from Wisconsin is called a "Wisconsinite."

## Wyoming
**(traditional abbreviation: Wyo. | postal abbreviation: WY)**

**Capital:** Cheyenne

**Largest city:** Cheyenne

Wyoming was the 44th state to join the United States, in 1890.
The name "Wyoming" comes from a Delaware Indian word that means "on the big plains." The name was first used for the Wyoming Valley in Pennsylvania.
Wyoming has the smallest population of any state.
Someone from Wyoming is called a "Wyomingite."

# Key Events in American History

**from prehistoric times** – **Native Americans** settle the Americas.

**around 1000 A.D.** – **Leif Ericsson**, a Norseman, lands in Newfoundland, now part of Canada.

**1492** – **Christopher Columbus** sails from Spain to the New World. He tells other Europeans about it.

**1513** – **Juan Ponce de León** lands in Florida.

**1565** – **Saint Augustine, Florida**, becomes the first permanent settlement in North America. It belongs to Spain.

**1607** – **Jamestown**, in **Virginia**, becomes the first permanent English settlement in North America.

**1619** – The first **African slaves** are traded in Virginia. Slavery spreads to all the colonies. Africans are brought to America against their will and sold as slaves.

**1620** – **The Pilgrims** land in **Plymouth, Massachusetts**, and begin a settlement. The Pilgrims celebrate the first Thanksgiving with local Native Americans in 1621.

**1775–1783** – **The 13 American colonies** fight the **American Revolution** to become independent from Great Britain.

**1776** – Members of the Continental Congress sign the **Declaration of Independence on July 4th**. This action is remembered every year on the Fourth of July (= Independence Day).

**1787** – Representatives of the colonies write the **U.S. Constitution**.

**1793** – The states approve the **Bill of Rights** (= the first ten amendments to the Constitution).

**1800** – The **U.S. capital** moves from Philadelphia, Pennsylvania, to Washington, D.C.

**1803** – The United States buys the **Louisiana Territory** from France. The area extends from the Mississippi River to the Rocky Mountains.

**1804** – **Meriwether Lewis** and **William Clark** leave St. Louis, Missouri, to find **a land route to the Pacific Ocean**.

**1808** – A U.S. law makes slave trade illegal. Slavery continues, especially in the Southern states, until 1865.

**1812–1815** – The United States fights against Great Britain in the War of 1812. The war is about shipping rights and control of western land. Francis Scott Key writes "The Star-Spangled Banner," the country's national anthem (= song), in 1814 during one of the battles.

**1819** – Spain gives Florida to the United States in a treaty.

**1830** – **President Andrew Jackson** signs a law that forces many **Native Americans** in the eastern part of the United States to move west of the Mississippi River.

**1845** – The United States makes **Texas** part of the country.

**1846** – The United States adds the **Oregon** Territory to the country. This area includes today's states of Idaho, Washington, and Oregon and parts of Montana and Wyoming.

**1846–1848** – The United States fights the **Mexican War**. At the end of the war, the United States pays Mexico $15 million and takes land that includes today's California, Nevada, Utah, most of New Mexico and Arizona, and parts of Colorado and Wyoming.

**1848** – **Gold is discovered in California**. Soon many people go to California to look for gold in the California Gold Rush.

**1861–1865** – **The Union** (= northern states) **fights the Confederacy** (= the southern states) in the American Civil War to prevent them from leaving the country and to end slavery. The 11 southern states that try to leave the country are South Carolina, Mississippi, Florida, Alabama, Georgia, Louisiana, Texas, Virginia, Arkansas, North Carolina, and Tennessee. **In 1863**, **President Abraham Lincoln** signs an order **to free the slaves** in the Confederate states. **In 1865**, Confederate General Robert E. Lee surrenders to Union General Ulysses S. Grant at Appomattox, Virginia. **In 1865**, the 13th Amendment to the Constitution makes **slavery illegal** in all states.

**1867** – The United States buys **Alaska** from Russia.

**1869** – The **railroad** across the country is completed at Promontory Summit, Utah.

**1870** – The **15th Amendment** to the Constitution gives men of all races (not just whites) the **right to vote**.

**1896** – The **U.S. Supreme Court** decides that keeping people of different races separate is constitutional. This leads to many racist laws.

**1898** – The United States fights Spain in the **Spanish–American War**. After the War, the United States takes control of Cuba, the Philippines, Puerto Rico, and Guam.

**1898** – The United States takes over **Hawaii**.

**1917–1918** – The United States fights in **World War I** against Germany and Austria–Hungary.

**1919** – The **19th Amendment** to the Constitution gives **women the right to vote**.

**1929** – The **U.S. stock market crashes**. This leads to the **Great Depression**, a period of very bad economic times that lasts until World War II.

**1941–1945** – The United States fights in **World War II** with Great Britain, France, and the Soviet Union against Germany, Japan, and Italy. In 1945, the United States drops two atomic bombs on the cities of Hiroshima and Nagasaki in Japan. This ends the war.

**1945–1991** – Tensions between the United States and the Soviet Union near the end of World War II lead to the **Cold War**. During this period, the two countries do not fight each other directly. Instead, they each try to limit the influence of the other by developing strong relationships with other countries. The Cold War ends when the Soviet Union stops existing.

**1950–1953** – The United States fights in the **Korean War** against North Korea.

**1954** – The U.S. Supreme Court decides that **separate schools for children of different races are unconstitutional**.

**1961–1973** – The United States military fights against North Vietnam in the **Vietnam War**.

**1968** – **Martin Luther King, Jr.**, is shot and killed. King was an African–American leader in the fight for civil rights for people of all races.

**1969** – **U.S. astronaut Neil Armstrong** walks on the moon.

**1989** – The **Berlin Wall** that divides the city of Berlin, Germany, comes down. This is an important event in the ending of the Cold War between the United States and the Soviet Union.

**1991** – The United States leads the fight against Iraq in the **Gulf War** after Iraq invades Kuwait.

**2001** – **Terrorists** fly airplanes into the **World Trade Center in New York City** and the **Pentagon in Washington, D.C.** Another plane crashes in Pennsylvania. The World Trade Center towers are destroyed and many people are killed. In response, the United States and other countries begin military attacks on Afghanistan.

**2003** – The United States leads an invasion of Iraq. Fighting continues for many years.

**2008** – Barack Obama is elected the first African–American president of the United States.

# U.S. Presidents

## 1. George Washington
**President from 1789 to 1797**

**born:** February 22, 1732
**died:** December 14, 1799
**Party:** None
**Important Facts:** Before becoming president, Washington was the leader of the Continental Army (= the name of the American army) during the Revolutionary War and defeated the British army. He was in charge of the group that wrote the U.S. Constitution in 1787. Because he was the first president, he helped decide what a president does.

## 2. John Adams
**President from 1797 to 1801**

**born:** October 30, 1735
**died:** July 4, 1826
**Party:** Federalist
**Important Facts:** Adams was a member of the first and second Continental Congresses. He helped write the Declaration of Independence. He was vice president while George Washington was president.

## 3. Thomas Jefferson
**President from 1801 to 1809**

**born:** April 13, 1743
**died:** July 4, 1826
**Party:** Democratic–Republican
**Important Facts:** Jefferson was the main author of the Declaration of Independence. While he was president, the U.S. made the Louisiana Purchase. This included a lot of land west of the Mississippi River. He also sent Lewis and Clark to find a way across this land to the Pacific Ocean. After being president, he started the University of Virginia.

## 4. James Madison
**President from 1809 to 1817**

**born:** March 16, 1751
**died:** June 28, 1836
**Party:** Democratic–Republican
**Important Facts:** Madison was the main author of the U.S. Constitution. He wrote the first ten amendments to the Constitution. These amendments are called the Bill of Rights. He was president during the War of 1812 against Great Britain.

## 5. James Monroe
**President from 1817 to 1825**

**born:** April 28, 1758
**died:** July 4, 1831
**Party:** Democratic–Republican
**Important Facts:** While Monroe was president, the U.S. gained control of Florida. He is most famous for the Monroe Doctrine. This plan says that the U.S. did not want European countries to be involved in any countries in North or South America.

## 6. John Quincy Adams
**President from 1825 to 1829**

**born:** July 11, 1767
**died:** February 23, 1848
**Party:** Democratic–Republican
**Important Facts:** Adams was the son of the second president, John Adams. He did many different jobs in government before becoming president.

## 7. Andrew Jackson
**President from 1829 to 1837**

**born:** March 15, 1767
**died:** June 8, 1845
**Party:** Democrat
**Important Facts:** When Jackson was younger, he was a successful general in the War of 1812 against Great Britain. He was a tough but popular leader and had the nickname "Old Hickory." His face is on the twenty-dollar bill.

## 8. Martin van Buren
**President from 1837 to 1841**

**born:** December 5, 1782
**died:** July 24, 1862
**Party:** Democrat
**Important Facts:** Van Buren helped organize the modern Democratic Party from the old Democratic–Republican Party. A major economic depression after the Panic of 1837 happened while he was president.

## 9. William Henry Harrison
**President in 1841**

**born:** February 9, 1773
**died:** April 4, 1841
**Party:** Whig
**Important Facts:** Harrison became president at age 68. Soon after, he caught a cold, developed pneumonia, and died after only 32 days in office.

## 10. John Tyler
**President from 1841 to 1845**

**born:** March 29, 1790
**died:** January 18, 1862
**Party:** Whig

**Important Facts:** Tyler was the first vice president to become president because the previous president died in office. While he was president, the U.S. government claimed Texas as part of the United States.

## 11. James K. Polk
**President from 1845 to 1849**

**born:** November 2, 1795
**died:** June 15, 1849
**Party:** Democrat
**Important Facts:** Polk increased the size of the U.S. by making an agreement with Great Britain for the Oregon Territory in the Northwest. He also bought land in the Southwest from Mexico to end the Mexican–American War.

## 12. Zachary Taylor
**President from 1849 to 1850**

**born:** November 24, 1784
**died:** July 9, 1850
**Party:** Whig
**Important Facts:** Taylor was in the military for 40 years before he was president. He became sick and died after being president for only 16 months.

## 13. Millard Fillmore
**President from 1850 to 1853**

**born:** January 7, 1800
**died:** March 8, 1874
**Party:** Whig
**Important Facts:** Fillmore became president when Taylor died and was never elected president. He was the last president from the Whig party. Many historians think he was one of the worst U.S. presidents.

## 14. Franklin Pierce
**President from 1853 to 1857**

**born:** November 23, 1804
**died:** October 8, 1869
**Party:** Democrat
**Important Facts:** Pierce's support for slavery in the West made him unpopular in the North. He was from the North, but later he supported the South during the Civil War. Many historians think he was one of the worst U.S. presidents.

## 15. James Buchanan
**President from 1857 to 1861**

**born:** April 23, 1791
**died:** June 1, 1868
**Party:** Democrat
**Important Facts:** Buchanan tried to keep peace between Northern and Southern states before the Civil War, but his decisions made both sides angry. Many historians think he was one of the worst U.S. presidents.

### 16. Abraham Lincoln
**President from 1861 to 1865**

**born:** February 12, 1809
**died:** April 15, 1865
**Party:** Republican
**Important Facts:** As president during the Civil War, Lincoln led the Northern states against the Southern states. He did not want the South to form a separate country. He also ended slavery in the United States. A man shot and killed Lincoln because he was angry about the North winning the war.

### 17. Andrew Johnson
**President from 1865 to 1869**

**born:** December 29, 1808
**died:** July 31, 1875
**Party:** Union
**Important Facts:** Johnson became president after Lincoln was killed. He worked to bring the Southern states quickly back into the nation after the Civil War. Many historians think he was one of the worst U.S. presidents.

### 18. Ulysses S. Grant
**President from 1869 to 1877**

**born:** April 27, 1822
**died:** July 23, 1885
**Party:** Republican
**Important Facts:** During the Civil War, Grant was the top general of the Union Army. He helped the Northern army win, and he became very popular. While he was president, he allowed dishonest and illegal behavior in the government.

### 19. Rutherford B. Hayes
**President from 1877 to 1881**

**born:** October 4, 1822
**died:** January 17, 1893
**Party:** Republican
**Important Facts:** The election for president in 1876 was very close. In the end, members of Congress decided to make Hayes president. He ended Reconstruction (= the period of national control of the South after the Civil War).

### 20. James A. Garfield
**President in 1881**

**born:** November 19, 1831
**died:** September 19, 1881
**Party:** Republican
**Important Facts:** Four months after Garfield became president, he was shot. He died two months later.

### 21. Chester A. Arthur
**President from 1881 to 1885**

**born:** October 5, 1829

**died:** November 18, 1886
**Party:** Republican
**Important Facts:** As president, Arthur worked well with Congress. He improved the system for giving government jobs.

### 22. Grover Cleveland
**President from 1885 to 1889**

**born:** March 18, 1837
**died:** June 24, 1908
**Party:** Democrat
**Important Facts:** People considered Cleveland very honest. He supported the use of gold instead of silver to measure the value of the U.S. dollar.

### 23. Benjamin Harrison
**President from 1889 to 1893**

**born:** August 20, 1833
**died:** March 13, 1901
**Party:** Republican
**Important Facts:** Harrison signed an important law to prevent businesses from becoming too powerful. He also signed a law to raise taxes on imports.

### 24. Grover Cleveland
**President from 1893 to 1897**

**born:** March 18, 1837
**died:** June 24, 1908
**Party:** Democrat
**Important Facts:** Cleveland was the 22nd and 24th president. He is the only president to be elected two times, not one after the other. During his second term, the country had very bad economic problems.

### 25. William McKinley
**President from 1897 to 1901**

**born:** January 29, 1843
**died:** September 14, 1901
**Party:** Republican
**Important Facts:** The economy improved while McKinley was president. He led the country in the Spanish–American War. Later he made the Philippines, Puerto Rico, Guam, and Hawaii part of the United States. He was shot and killed while he was president.

### 26. Theodore Roosevelt
**President from 1901 to 1909**

**born:** October 27, 1858
**died:** January 6, 1919
**Party:** Republican
**Important Facts:** Roosevelt was the youngest president in U.S. history. He took control of the Panama Canal Zone and started building the canal (= artificial river). He started the

National Forest service and made many areas national parks. He also helped end a war between Russia and Japan.

### 27. William Howard Taft
**President from 1909 to 1913**

**born:** September 15, 1857
**died:** March 8, 1930
**Party:** Republican
**Important Facts:** Taft worked to prevent companies from becoming too big and powerful. He encouraged U.S. businesses to invest in foreign countries. He later became chief justice of the U.S. Supreme Court.

### 28. Woodrow Wilson
**President from 1913 to 1921**

**born:** December 28, 1856
**died:** February 3, 1924
**Party:** Democrat
**Important Facts:** Wilson led the country in World War I against Germany. He later worked to start the League of Nations, an organization of many different countries dedicated to a more peaceful world.

### 29. Warren G. Harding
**President from 1921 to 1923**

**born:** November 2, 1865
**died:** August 2, 1923
**Party:** Republican
**Important Facts:** Harding's government is remembered for the dishonest and illegal activities of one of its members in the Teapot Dome Scandal. Harding died of a heart attack after serving two years as president.

### 30. Calvin Coolidge
**President from 1923 to 1929**

**born:** July 4, 1872
**died:** January 5, 1933
**Party:** Republican
**Important Facts:** Coolidge opposed government involvement in business. He tried to limit the size and control of government.

### 31. Herbert Hoover
**President from 1929 to 1933**

**born:** August 10, 1874
**died:** October 20, 1964
**Party:** Republican
**Important Facts:** Hoover became president soon after the stock market crash of 1929. He could not prevent the Great Depression (= very bad economic time) from becoming worse.

# U.S. Presidents

### 32. Franklin D. Roosevelt
**President from 1933 to 1945**

**born:** January 30, 1882
**died:** April 12, 1945
**Party:** Democrat
**Important Facts:** Roosevelt was elected president four times (no other president was elected more than twice). He was president during the Great Depression (= very bad economic time) and started many programs to control the banks and give people jobs. He led the U.S. during World War II, but he died before it ended.

### 33. Harry S. Truman
**President from 1945 to 1953**

**born:** May 8, 1884
**died:** December 26, 1972
**Party:** Democrat
**Important Facts:** Truman was president when World War II ended. He worked to rebuild Europe after the war. He supported the creation of the United Nations. He was very opposed to communism. Because of this, he supported the creation of the North Atlantic Treaty Organization (= organization of democracies against the Soviet Union). He also entered the U.S. in the Korean War. In the U.S., he supported the rights of people of all races and allowed them all to serve together in the military.

### 34. Dwight D. Eisenhower
**President from 1953 to 1961**

**born:** October 14, 1890
**died:** March 28, 1969
**Party:** Republican
**Important Facts:** During World War II, Eisenhower was a general and the leader of all the Allies' military forces in Europe. As president, he continued opposition to the Soviet Union. He also started the Interstate Highway System (= system of large roads across the country).

### 35. John F. Kennedy
**President from 1961 to 1963**

**born:** May 29, 1917

**died:** November 22, 1963
**Party:** Democrat
**Important Facts:** Kennedy supported an unsuccessful invasion of Cuba (= attempt to take control of it by military force). The next year, he avoided a nuclear war with the Soviet Union over missiles (= military weapons) in Cuba. He supported protecting the rights of African Americans. He was shot and killed while he was president.

### 36. Lyndon B. Johnson
**President from 1963 to 1969**

**born:** August 27, 1908
**died:** January 22, 1973
**Party:** Democrat
**Important Facts:** Johnson supported programs to improve education, help poor and old people, and protect the rights of people of all races, especially African Americans. He also increased the U.S. involvement in the Vietnam War.

### 37. Richard M. Nixon
**President from 1969 to 1974**

**born:** January 9, 1913
**died:** April 22, 1994
**Party:** Republican
**Important Facts:** Nixon first increased U.S. involvement in the Vietnam War, but later ended U.S. involvement. He started a relationship with China and improved the U.S. relationship with the Soviet Union. Nixon was involved in dishonest and illegal activity in the Watergate scandal. Because of this, he resigned (= quit).

### 38. Gerald R. Ford
**President from 1974 to 1977**

**born:** July 14, 1913
**died:** December 26, 2006
**Party:** Republican
**Important Facts:** Ford pardoned Nixon (= allowed him not to be punished) for his illegal activity. Ford worked to continue improving the U.S. relationship with the Soviet Union. While he was president, the U.S. economy got very bad.

### 39. Jimmy Carter
**President from 1977 to 1981**

**born:** October 1, 1924
**Party:** Democrat
**Important Facts:** As president, Carter returned the Panama Canal Zone to Panama. He also helped bring peace between Egypt and Israel. He failed to save U.S. hostages (= prisoners) in Iran. In the U.S., he was not able to solve many economic problems.

### 40. Ronald Reagan
**President from 1981 to 1989**

**born:** February 6, 1911
**died:** June 5, 2004
**Party:** Republican
**Important Facts:** Reagan was a movie actor before he was a politician. As president, he lowered taxes and limited the government's control of the economy. The economy improved. He increased spending on military weapons to use against the Soviet Union. His actions helped end the Cold War with the Soviet Union.

### 41. George H. W. Bush
**President from 1989 to 1993**

**born:** June 12, 1924
**Party:** Republican
**Important Facts:** Bush was Ronald Reagan's vice president. He ordered military action in Kuwait and Iraq. The economy got worse and Bush approved an increase in taxes.
As president, he ordered military action in Kuwait and Iraq. Before his election, Bush promised not to raise taxes. But the economy got worse and Bush approved an increase in taxes. This is one of the reasons he was not elected a second time.

### 42. William J. ("Bill") Clinton
**President from 1993 to 2001**

**born:** August 19, 1946
**Party:** Democrat
**Important Facts:** The economy improved and was very strong while Clinton was president. He supported changes in the health care and welfare (= money for poor people) systems. He was put on trial in the Senate for dishonest actions, but the Senate decided that he was not guilty.

### 43. George W. Bush
**President from 2001 to 2009**

**born:** July 6, 1946
**Party:** Republican
**Important Facts:** Bush is the son of the 41st president, George H. W. Bush. He was president when terrorists attacked the U.S. on September 11, 2001. Bush ordered attacks on Afghanistan and Iraq. While he was president the nation's debt got much bigger. The economic situation in the U.S. became its worst since the Great Depression.

### 44. Barack H. Obama
**President since 2009**

**born:** August 4, 1961
**Party:** Democrat
**Important Facts:** Obama is the first African–American president. His father was from Kenya, his mother was from Kansas, and he was born in Hawaii. After becoming president, he put a lot of effort into trying to improve the economy.

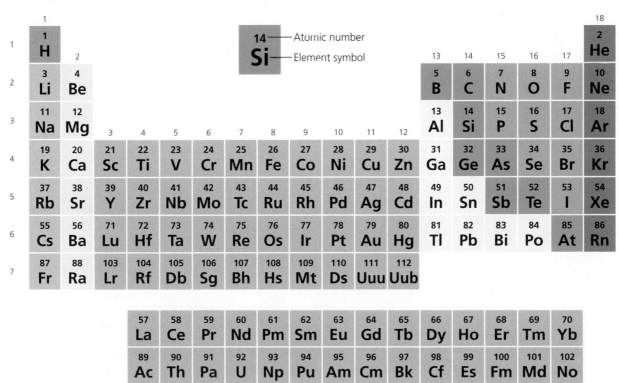

## Weights and Measures

**U.S. Customary System**

**Units of length**

| | | |
|---|---|---|
| 1 inch | = 2.54 cm | |
| 12 inches | = 1 foot | = 0.3048 m |
| 3 feet | = 1 yard | = 0.9144 m |
| 1,760 yards (5,280 feet) | = 1 mile | = 1.609 km |
| 2,025 yards (6,076 feet) | = 1 nautical mile | = 1,852 m |

**Units of weight**

| | | |
|---|---|---|
| 1 ounce | = 28.35 g | |
| 16 ounces | = 1 pound | = 0.4536 kg |
| 2,000 pounds | = 1 ton | = 907.18 kg |
| 2,240 pounds | = 1 long ton | = 1,016.0 kg |

**Units of volume (Liquid)**

| | | |
|---|---|---|
| 1 fluid ounce | = 29.574 ml | |
| 8 fluid ounces | = 1 cup | = 0.2366 l |
| 16 fluid ounces | = 1 pint | = 0.4732 l |
| 2 pints | = 1 quart | = 0.9463 l |
| 4 quarts | = 1 gallon | = 3.7853 l |

**Units of volume (Dry measure)**

| | | |
|---|---|---|
| 1 peck | = 8,809.5 cm³ | |
| 4 pecks | = 1 bushel | = 35,239 cm³ |

**Units of area**

| | | |
|---|---|---|
| 1 square inch | = 645.16 mm² | |
| 144 square inches | = 1 square foot | = 0.0929 m² |
| 9 square feet | = 1 square yard | = 0.8361 m² |
| 4,840 square yards | = 1 acre | = 4,047 m² |
| 640 acres | = 1 square mile | = 259 ha |

**Temperature**

| | |
|---|---|
| degrees Fahrenheit | $= (°C \times 9/5) + 32$ |
| degrees Celsius | $= (°F - 32) \times 5/9$ |

**Metric System**

**Units of length**

| | | |
|---|---|---|
| 1 millimeter | = 0.03937 inch | |
| 10 mm | = 1 centimeter | = 0.3937 inch |
| 100 cm | = 1 meter | = 39.37 inches |
| 1,000 m | = 1 kilometer | = 0.6214 mile |

**Units of weight**

| | | |
|---|---|---|
| 1 milligram | = 0.000035 ounce | |
| 1,000 mg | = 1 gram | = 0.035 ounce |
| 1,000 g | = 1 kilogram | = 2.205 pounds |
| 1,000 kg | = 1 metric ton | = 2,205 pounds |

**Units of volume**

| | | |
|---|---|---|
| 1 milliliter | = 0.03 fluid ounce | |
| 1,000 ml | = 1 liter | = 1.06 quarts |

**Units of area**

| | | |
|---|---|---|
| 1 square centimeter | = 0.1550 square inch | |
| 10,000 cm² | = 1 square metre | = 1.196 square yards |
| 10,000 m² | = 1 hectare | = 2.471 acres |

## Periodic Table of the Elements

# Affixes and Word Roots

## Prefixes

| Prefix | Examples |
|---|---|
| anti- | antidote, antibody, anti-war |
| bi- | bicycle, binoculars, biweekly |
| co- | cooperate, co-star, correspond |
| counter- | counterattack, counterterrorism |
| e- | email, e-commerce, e-learning |
| ex- | ex-wife, ex-boyfriend, ex-president, exhale, exclude, explode |
| fore- | forecast, forehead, foresee |
| il-, im-, in-, ir- | illegal, immature, immigrant, impolite, import, incorrect, invisible, irregular, irresponsible, include, inhale |
| mal- | malnutrition, malpractice |
| mega- | megabyte |
| mid- | middle, midnight, midway, Midwest |
| min-, mini- | miniature, minimum, miniskirt, minority, minus |
| mis- | misbehave, mislead, misspell, mistake, misunderstand |
| multi- | multicultural, multimedia, multiple, multiracial |
| non- | nonfiction, non-living, nonsense, nonstick, nonstop |
| out- | outdated, outdoors, outfield, outgoing, outstanding |
| over- | overcrowded, overdo, overeat, overpopulation, overtime, overalls, overcase, overcoat, overlap, overboard, overflow, overhand, overhead |
| post- | postpone, post-World War II, post-1990 |
| pre- | predict, prefix, prepare, preschool, prevent, pre-1990 |
| pro- | projector, promote, proceed, progress, pro-democracy, pro-family, pro-war |
| re- | recycle, reelect, reflect, remember, repeat, retreat |
| tri- | triangle, triathlon, triceratops, tricycle, trio, triple |
| un- | unclear, unhealthy, unable, undress, uncover, unfasten |
| under- | underarm, underline, underneath, underwear, underwater, underestimate, undernourished, underprivileged |
| up- | upcoming, uphill, upload, upstairs |

## Suffixes

| Suffix | Examples |
|---|---|
| -able | washable, portable, valuable, adorable, comfortable |
| -al | logical, magical, structural |
| -an/ian | American, San Franciscan, vegetarian, electrician, Victorian, Christian |
| -ed | chased, started, walked, finished, bored, excited |
| -ee | employee, nominee, refugee |
| -ence | difference, intelligence, patience, conference, experience, reference |
| -er | baker, member, player, reporter, teacher, bigger, higher, quieter, stronger, wider |
| -ess | actress, waitress, stewardess, goddess |
| -est | biggest, highest, quietest, strongest, widest |
| -ful | awful, beautiful, helpful, joyful, wonderful |
| -hood | childhood, likelihood, livelihood, parenthood, neighborhood, statehood |
| -ible | audible, convertible, divisible, edible, invisible, possible |
| -ic | allergic, athletic, historic, scientific |
| -ify | simplify, clarify, horrify, magnify |
| -ing | helping, throwing, walking, taking, clapping, sitting, winning |
| -ish | Jewish, Scottish, Polish, yellowish, fortyish, tallish |
| -ism | communism, feminism, Buddhism, optimism, heroism, patriotism |
| -ist | artist, Buddhist, dentist, guitarist, novelist, scientist |
| -ity | simplicity, activity, creativity, impossibility |
| -ive | active, creative, expensive, imaginative, sensitive, talkative |
| -less | breathless, careless, motionless, painless, spotless |
| -ly | carefully, correctly, quickly, slowly, strongly |
| -ment | agreement, disappointment, government, movement, payment |
| -ness | awareness, blindness, carelessness, fairness, friendliness, rudeness, sickness |
| -or | actor, doctor, professor, sailor, sculptor |
| -ous | adventurous, anxious, courteous, dangerous, marvelous, religious |
| -proof | fireproof, foolproof, waterproof |
| -s, -es, -ies | pens, planets, times, glasses, boxes, heroes, days, ladies, puppies, hits, catches, flies |
| -ship | championship, citizenship, friendship, membership, sportsmanship |
| -sion | admission, confusion, decision, permission, supervision, discussion |
| -tion | abolition, admiration, celebration, motion, perfection, separation |
| -ward | backward, downward, eastward, forward, outward, toward |
| -wise | clockwise, lengthwise, likewise, otherwise, time-wise, money-wise, health-wise |
| -y | angry, curly, hairy, hungry, sleepy |

# Word Roots

| Root | Examples |
|---|---|
| audi- | audience, auditorium, audiovisual, audible, audition |
| auto- | automobile, autobiography, autograph, automatic |
| bio- | biology, biography, biome |
| cent- | cent, century, centimeter, centipede |
| circ-/circum- | circuit, circulate, circumference |
| commun- | communicate, community, communism |
| contra-/contro- | contradict, controversy, contrary |
| -cycl/cycl- | bicycle, cyclone, recycle |
| dec- | decade, decagon, decibel, decimal |
| -dict/dict- | contradict, dictate, dictionary, predict, verdict |
| eco- | ecology, ecosystem, economy |
| exter-/extr- | exterior, extract, extraordinary, extraterrestrial, extreme |
| geo- | geology, geometry, geography |
| -graph | autograph, biography, geography, graph, paragraph, telegraph |
| homo- | homograph, homophone, homonym |
| inter-/intr- | intermission, interrupt, international, introduce, intrude |
| -ject | inject, projector, reject |
| kilo- | kilobyte, kilogram, kilometer, kilowatt |
| log-/-log | dialogue, logic, logo, monologue |
| -logy/-ology | biology, etymology, geology, mythology, paleontology |
| -meter/-metr- | barometer, metric, diameter, geometry, perimeter, thermometer |
| micro- | microbe, microchip, microphone, microscope, microwave |
| mono- | carbon monoxide, monologue, monopoly, monotonous |
| -nym | acronym, antonym, homonym, pseudonym, synonym |
| oct- | octagon, October, octopus |
| para- | paragraph, parallel, paramedic, paraphrase, parasite |
| -phone | earphones, homophone, microphone, phonics, saxophone, telephone |
| photo- | photocopier, photograph, photosynthesis |
| poly- | polyester, polygon |
| -port/port- | export, import, passport, portable, support, transport |
| quart-/quad- | quart, quarter, quarterback, quadrant, quadrilateral |
| -scope | horoscope, kaleidoscope, microscope, periscope, stethoscope, telescope |
| scrib-/scrip- | describe, manuscript, prescription, script, scribble, scripture |
| semi- | semicircle, semicolon, semifinal, semi-metal |
| sub- | subdued, submarine, submerge, subscribe, subtitles, subway |
| super- | superb, superficial, superhero, superior, supermarket, supervisor |
| tele- | telegraph, telephone, telescope, television |
| terr- | extraterrestrial, terrain, territory |
| therm- | thermal, thermometer, thermostat |
| trans- | transcontinental, transfer, translate, transmit, transparent, transportation |
| vac- | evacuate, vacancy, vacant, vacation, vacuole, vacuum |
| vis-/vid- | invisible, revise, television, vision, visit, evidence, video |

# Academic Words

## The Academic Word List

**Averil Coxhead**, Massey University, New Zealand

Averil Coxhead is a lecturer in English for Academic Purposes at Massey University, New Zealand. She compiled the AWL in 2000. For further information on the AWL, go to Averil's website at http://language.massey.ac.nz/staff/awl.

The Academic Word List (AWL) is a list of 570 word families that are commonly found in academic texts. This list was selected by examining a large corpus (or collection) of written academic texts and selecting the words that occurred:

1 in texts from all four academic faculty sections: Arts, Commerce, Law, and Science

2 over 100 times in the corpus overall

3 at least ten times in each academic faculty section

4 outside the 2,000 most frequent words on Michael West's "General Service List" (GSL). The GSL includes everyday words such as **I**, **house**, and **do**.

These principles ensured that only words that occurred reasonably frequently in a variety of study areas were selected.

The AWL targets vocabulary that occurs most often in written academic texts. These words also occur in newspapers but not as often as they do in textbooks. The AWL words appear even less in fiction. If your focus is learning academic vocabulary, you need to make sure you read academic textbooks so that you encounter these words in context.

The AWL is organized into word families. Word families are made up of the "parent word" and "family members." Take, for example, the word **dominate**. Its family members include *dominance*, *domination* and the adjective *dominant*.

If you learn the verb **dominate**, you will be able to recognize other family members such as *domination* when you encounter them in your reading. These words are closely related and the meaning is likely to be the same or similar. When you are looking for words in this dictionary, think about other word family members too.

In order to read and write successfully you need to be able to recognize as many words as possible in your textbooks and use as many as possible in your writing. The bigger your vocabulary, the more you will be able to cope with the high reading and writing demands of your studies.

The *Longman Elementary Dictionary and Thesaurus* is specifically for Elementary level students, and we have omitted some words from the full Academic Word List, because they are not very common and they are very high level. For example, we have included **coincidence** and **coincide**, but not **coincident**. We have included **structure**, but not **unstructured**. Both **coincident** and **unstructured** are very specialized words that students at this level are unlikely to need to know.

---

abandon, *verb*
abnormal, *adjective*
abnormally, *adverb*
abstract, *adjective*
academic, *adjective*
academy, *noun*
access, *noun, verb*
accessible, *adjective*
accommodate, *verb*
accompany, *verb*
accumulate, *verb*
accumulation, *noun*
accuracy, *noun*
accurate, *adjective*
accurately, *adverb*
achieve, *verb*
achievement, *noun*
acknowledge, *verb*
acknowledgement, *noun*
acquire, *verb*
acquisition, *noun*
adapt, *verb*

adaptable, *adjective*
adaptation, *noun*
adequate, *adjective*
adequately, *adverb*
adjacent, *adjective*
adjust, *verb*
adjustment, *noun*
administration, *noun*
administrator, *noun*
adult, *noun*
affect, *verb*
aid, *noun, verb*
alter, *verb*
alteration, *noun*
alternate, *verb, adjective*
alternative, *noun, adjective*
alternatively, *adverb*
ambiguous, *adjective*
amend, *verb*
amendment, *noun*
analysis, *noun*
analyst, *noun*

analyze, *verb*
annual, *adjective*
annually, *adverb*
anticipate, *verb*
anticipation, *noun*
apparent, *adjective*
apparently, *adverb*
appendix, *noun*
appreciate, *verb*
appreciation, *noun*
approach, *verb, noun*
appropriate, *adjective*
appropriately, *adverb*
approximate, *adjective*
approximately, *adverb*
arbitrary, *adjective*
area, *noun*
aspect, *noun*
assemble, *verb*
assembly, *noun*
assess, *verb*
assessment, *noun*
assign, *verb*

assignment, *noun*
assist, *verb*
assistance, *noun*
assistant, *noun*
assume, *verb*
assumption, *noun*
assurance, *noun*
assure, *verb*
attach, *verb*
attachment, *noun*
attain, *verb*
attainment, *noun*
attitude, *noun*
author, *noun*
authority, *noun*
automatic, *adjective*
automatically, *adverb*
automation, *noun*
availability, *noun*
available, *adjective*
aware, *adjective*
awareness, *noun*
beneficial, *adjective*

benefit, *noun, verb*
bias, *noun*
biased, *adjective*
bond, *noun*
brief, *adjective*
briefly, *adverb*
bulk, *noun*
bulky, *adjective*
capability, *noun*
capable, *adjective*
capacity, *noun*
categorize, *verb*
category, *noun*
cease, *verb*
challenge, *noun, verb*
challenger, *noun*
challenging, *adjective*
channel, *noun*
chapter, *noun*
chart, *noun*
chemical, *noun, adjective*
circumstances, *plural
    noun*
cite, *verb*
civil, *adjective*
clarification, *noun*
clarify, *verb*
clarity, *noun*
classic, *adjective, noun*
classical, *adjective*
clause, *noun*
code, *noun*
coherent, *adjective*
coherently, *adverb*
coincide, *verb*
coincidence, *noun*
collapse, *verb*
colleague, *noun*
commence, *verb*
commencement, *noun*
comment, *noun, verb*
commentary, *noun*
commentator, *noun*
commit, *verb*
commitment, *noun*
communicate, *verb*
communication, *noun*
community, *noun*
compensate, *verb*
compensation, *noun*
complex, *adjective, noun*
complexity, *noun*
compound, *noun*
comprehensive,
    *adjective*
comprise, *verb*
computer, *noun*
conceive, *verb*

concentrate, *verb*
concentration, *noun*
concept, *noun*
conclude, *verb*
conclusion, *noun*
conduct, *verb, noun*
conference, *noun*
confirm, *verb*
confirmation, *noun*
conflict, *noun, verb*
conform, *verb*
consent, *noun, verb*
consequence, *noun*
consequently, *adverb*
considerable, *adjective*
considerably, *adverb*
consist, *verb*
consistency, *noun*
consistent, *adjective*
constant, *adjective*
constantly, *adverb*
constitute, *verb*
constitution, *noun*
constitutional, *adjective*
construct, *verb*
construction, *noun*
consult, *verb*
consultant, *noun*
consultation, *noun*
consume, *verb*
consumer, *noun*
consumption, *noun*
contact, *verb, noun*
contemporary, *adjective,
    noun*
context, *noun*
contract, *noun, verb*
contradict, *verb*
contradiction, *noun*
contradictory, *adjective*
contrary, *noun, adjective*
contrast, *noun, verb*
contribute, *verb*
contribution, *noun*
contributor, *noun*
controversial, *adjective*
controversy, *noun*
convention, *noun*
converse, *verb*
conversely, *adverb*
conversion, *noun*
convert, *verb*
convince, *verb*
convinced, *adjective*
convincing, *adjective*
cooperate, *verb*
cooperation, *noun*
cooperative, *adjective*

coordinate, *verb, noun*
coordinated, *adjective*
coordination, *noun*
core, *noun, adjective*
corporation, *noun*
correspond, *verb*
correspondence, *noun*
couple, *noun*
create, *verb*
creation, *noun*
creative, *adjective*
creatively, *adverb*
creativity, *noun*
creator, *noun*
credit, *noun, verb*
criteria, *plural noun*
crucial, *adjective*
cultural, *adjective*
culture, *noun*
currency, *noun*
cycle, *noun*
cyclic, *adjective*
cyclical, *adjective*
data, *noun*
debate, *noun, verb*
decade, *noun*
decline, *verb, noun*
deduce, *verb*
deduction, *noun*
define, *verb*
definite, *adjective*
definitely, *adverb*
definition, *noun*
demonstrate, *verb*
demonstration, *noun*
demonstrator, *noun*
denial, *noun*
deny, *verb*
depress, *verb*
depressed, *adjective*
depressing, *adjective*
depression, *noun*
derive, *verb*
design, *noun, verb*
designer, *noun*
despite, *preposition*
detect, *verb*
detection, *noun*
detective, *noun*
detector, *noun*
device, *noun*
devote, *verb*
devoted, *adjective*
devotion, *noun*
dimensions, *noun*
diminish, *verb*
discriminate, *verb*
discrimination, *noun*

display, *noun, verb*
disposable, *adjective*
disposal, *noun*
dispose, *verb*
dissimilar, *adjective*
distinct, *adjective*
distinction, *noun*
distinctive, *adjective*
distinctly, *adverb*
distort, *verb*
distortion, *noun*
distribute, *verb*
distribution, *noun*
diverse, *adjective*
diversity, *noun*
document, *noun*
domain, *noun*
domestic, *adjective*
dominance, *noun*
dominant, *adjective*
dominate, *verb*
domination, *noun*
draft, *noun, verb,
    adjective*
drama, *noun*
dramatic, *adjective*
dramatically, *adverb*
dramatist, *noun*
dramatization, *noun*
dramatize, *verb*
dynamic, *adjective*
economic, *adjective*
economical, *adjective*
economically, *adverb*
economics, *noun*
economist, *noun*
economy, *noun*
edit, *verb*
edition, *noun*
editor, *noun*
editorial, *noun, adjective*
element, *noun*
eliminate, *verb*
emerge, *verb*
emphasis, *noun*
emphasize, *verb*
enable, *verb*
encounter, *noun, verb*
energetic, *adjective*
energetically, *adverb*
energy, *noun*
enforce, *verb*
enforcement, *noun*
enormous, *adjective*
enormously, *adverb*
ensure, *verb*
environment, *noun*
environmental, *adjective*

# Academic Words

environmentally, *adverb*
equation, *noun*
equip, *verb*
equipment, *noun*
equivalent, *adjective, noun*
erode, *verb*
erosion, *noun*
error, *noun*
establish, *verb*
establishment, *noun*
estimate, *verb, noun*
ethic, *noun*
ethical, *adjective*
ethically, *adverb*
ethnic, *adjective*
ethnicity, *noun*
evaluate, *verb*
evaluation, *noun*
eventual, *adjective*
eventually, *adverb*
evidence, *noun*
evident, *adjective*
evidently, *adverb*
evolution, *noun*
evolutionary, *adjective*
evolve, *verb*
exceed, *verb*
exclude, *verb*
excluding, *preposition*
exclusion, *noun*
exclusive, *adjective*
exclusively, *adverb*
exhibit, *verb, noun*
expand, *verb*
expansion, *noun*
expert, *noun, adjective*
expertise, *noun*
exploit, *verb*
exploitation, *noun*
export, *verb, noun*
exporter, *noun*
expose, *verb*
exposure, *noun*
external, *adjective*
extract, *verb*
facilitate, *verb*
facility, *noun*
factor, *noun*
feature, *noun, verb*
federal, *adjective*
fee, *noun*
file, *noun, verb*
final, *adjective, noun*
finally, *adverb*
finance, *noun, verb*
financial, *adjective*
financially, *adverb*

flexibility, *noun*
flexible, *adjective*
focus, *verb, noun*
focused, *adjective*
format, *noun*
formula, *noun*
found, *verb*
foundation, *noun*
founder, *noun*
framework, *noun*
function, *noun, verb*
functional, *adjective*
fund, *noun, verb*
fundamental, *adjective*
fundamentally, *adverb*
furthermore, *adverb*
gender, *noun*
generate, *verb*
generation, *noun*
global, *adjective*
globally, *adverb*
globe, *noun*
goal, *noun*
grade, *noun, verb*
grant, *verb, noun*
guarantee, *noun, verb*
guidelines, *plural noun*
highlight, *noun, verb*
hypothesis, *noun*
identical, *adjective*
identification, *noun*
identify, *verb*
identity, *noun*
ignorance, *noun*
ignorant, *adjective*
ignore, *verb*
illegal, *adjective*
illegally, *adverb*
illogical, *adjective*
illustrate, *verb*
illustration, *noun*
image, *noun*
imagery, *noun*
immature, *adjective*
immigrant, *noun*
immigrate, *verb*
immigration, *noun*
impact, *noun, verb*
implement, *verb, noun*
implication, *noun*
imply, *verb*
impose, *verb*
imprecise, *adjective*
inaccuracy, *noun*
inaccurate, *adjective*
inadequate, *adjective*
inadequately, *adverb*
inappropriate, *adjective*

inappropriately, *adverb*
incapable, *adjective*
incentive, *noun*
incident, *noun*
incidentally, *adverb*
inclination, *noun*
inclined, *adjective*
incoherent, *adjective*
incoherently, *adverb*
income, *noun*
incompatible, *adjective*
inconsistent, *adjective*
incorporate, *verb*
indefinite, *adjective*
indefinitely, *adverb*
index, *noun*
indicate, *verb*
indication, *noun*
indicative, *adjective*
indicator, *noun*
individual, *adjective, noun*
individuality, *noun*
individually, *adverb*
inevitable, *adjective*
inevitably, *adverb*
infer, *verb*
infinite, *adjective*
infinitely, *adverb*
initial, *noun, adjective*
initially, *adverb*
initiate, *verb*
initiation, *noun*
initiative, *noun*
injure, *verb*
injured, *adjective*
injury, *noun*
innovate, *verb*
innovation, *noun*
input, *noun*
insecure, *adjective*
insecurity, *noun*
insert, *verb*
insertion, *noun*
insight, *noun*
insignificant, *adjective*
inspect, *verb*
inspection, *noun*
inspector, *noun*
instance, *noun*
institute, *noun*
institution, *noun*
instruct, *verb*
instruction, *noun*
instructor, *noun*
insufficient, *adjective*
insufficiently, *adverb*
integrate, *verb*

integrated, *adjective*
integration, *noun*
integrity, *noun*
intelligence, *noun*
intelligent, *adjective*
intelligently, *adverb*
intense, *adjective*
intensely, *adverb*
intensify, *verb*
intensity, *noun*
interact, *verb*
interaction, *noun*
interactive, *adjective*
intermediate, *adjective*
internal, *adjective*
internally, *adverb*
interpret, *verb*
interpretation, *noun*
interval, *noun*
intervene, *verb*
intervention, *noun*
invest, *verb*
investigate, *verb*
investigation, *noun*
investigator, *noun*
investment, *noun*
investor, *noun*
invisibility, *noun*
invisible, *adjective*
involve, *verb*
involved, *adjective*
involvement, *noun*
irrational, *adjective*
irrelevant, *adjective*
isolate, *verb*
isolated, *adjective*
isolation, *noun*
issue, *noun, verb*
item, *noun*
job, *noun*
journal, *noun*
justifiable, *adjective*
justification, *noun*
justify, *verb*
label, *noun, verb*
labor, *noun, verb*
layer, *noun*
lecture, *noun, verb*
lecturer, *noun*
legal, *adjective*
legally, *adverb*
legislate, *verb*
legislation, *noun*
legislator, *noun*
legislature, *noun*
liberal, *adjective, noun*
liberalism, *noun*
liberate, *verb*

license, *noun, verb*
likewise, *adverb*
link, *verb, noun*
locate, *verb*
location, *noun*
logic, *noun*
logical, *adjective*
logically, *adverb*
maintain, *verb*
maintenance, *noun*
major, *adjective*
majority, *noun*
manipulate, *verb*
manipulation, *noun*
manual, *adjective, noun*
manually, *adverb*
margin, *noun*
mature, *adjective, verb*
maturity, *noun*
maximum, *adjective,
    noun*
mechanism, *noun*
media, *plural noun*
medical, *adjective*
medium, *adjective*
mental, *adjective*
method, *noun*
methodical, *adjective*
migrant, *noun*
migrate, *verb*
migration, *noun*
military, *adjective, noun*
minimal, *adjective*
minimize, *verb*
minimum, *adjective,
    noun*
ministry, *noun*
minor, *adjective, noun,
    verb*
minority, *noun*
misinterpret, *verb*
misinterpretation, *noun*
mode, *noun*
modification, *noun*
modify, *verb*
monitor, *verb*
motivate, *verb*
motivation, *noun*
motive, *noun*
mutual, *adjective*
negative, *adjective*
negatively, *adverb*
network, *noun*
neutral, *adjective*
neutralize, *verb*
nevertheless, *adverb*
nonetheless, *adverb*
normal, *adjective*

normality, *noun*
normally, *adverb*
notion, *noun*
nuclear, *adjective*
objective, *noun*
obtain, *verb*
obvious, *adjective*
obviously, *adverb*
occupant, *noun*
occupation, *noun*
occupy, *verb*
occur, *verb*
odd, *adjective*
odds, *plural noun*
ongoing, *adjective*
option, *noun*
optional, *adjective*
outcome, *noun*
output, *noun*
overall, *adjective*
overlap, *verb*
overseas, *adjective,
    adverb*
panel, *noun*
paragraph, *noun*
parallel, *adjective, noun*
participant, *noun*
participate, *verb*
partner, *noun*
partnership, *noun*
passive, *adjective, noun*
passively, *adverb*
perceive, *verb*
percent, *noun*
percentage, *noun*
perception, *noun*
period, *noun*
periodic, *adjective*
periodical, *noun*
persist, *verb*
persistence, *noun*
persistent, *adjective*
perspective, *noun*
phase, *noun, verb*
phenomenal, *adjective*
phenomenon, *noun*
philosopher, *noun*
philosophical, *adjective*
philosophy, *noun*
physical, *adjective, noun*
physically, *adverb*
plus, *preposition, noun,
    adjective*
policy, *noun*
portion, *noun*
pose, *verb, noun*
positive, *adjective*
positively, *adverb*

potential, *noun,
    adjective*
potentially, *adverb*
precede, *verb*
precise, *adjective*
precisely, *adverb*
precision, *noun*
predict, *verb*
predictable, *adjective*
prediction, *noun*
presumably, *adverb*
presume, *verb*
presumption, *noun*
previous, *adjective*
previously, *adverb*
primarily, *adverb*
primary, *adjective*
prime, *adjective, noun*
principal, *noun, adjective*
principle, *noun*
prior, *adjective*
prioritize, *verb*
priority, *noun*
procedure, *noun*
proceed, *verb*
process, *noun, verb*
professional, *adjective,
    noun*
prohibit, *verb*
prohibition, *noun*
project, *noun, verb*
projection, *noun*
promote, *verb*
promotion, *noun*
proportion, *noun*
prospect, *noun*
psychological, *adjective*
psychologist, *noun*
psychology, *noun*
publication, *noun*
publish, *verb*
publisher, *noun*
purchase, *verb, noun*
pursue, *verb*
pursuit, *noun*
quotation, *noun*
quote, *verb, noun*
radical, *adjective*
radically, *adverb*
random, *adjective*
randomly, *adverb*
range, *noun, verb*
ratio, *noun*
rational, *adjective*
rationally, *adverb*
react, *verb*
reaction, *noun*
recover, *verb*

recovery, *noun*
refine, *verb*
refined, *adjective*
regime, *noun*
region, *noun*
regional, *adjective*
register, *noun, verb*
registration, *noun*
regulate, *verb*
regulation, *noun*
reinforce, *verb*
reject, *verb*
rejection, *noun*
relax, *verb*
relaxation, *noun*
relaxed, *adjective*
relaxing, *adjective*
release, *verb, noun*
relevant, *adjective*
reliable, *adjective*
reliably, *adverb*
reluctance, *noun*
reluctant, *adjective*
reluctantly, *adverb*
rely, *verb*
removable, *adjective*
removal, *noun*
remove, *verb*
require, *verb*
requirement, *noun*
research, *noun, verb*
researcher, *noun*
residence, *noun*
resident, *noun*
residential, *adjective*
resolution, *noun*
resolve, *verb*
resource, *noun*
respond, *verb*
response, *noun*
restore, *verb*
restrain, *verb*
restrained, *adjective*
restraint, *noun*
restrict, *verb*
restricted, *adjective*
restriction, *noun*
retain, *verb*
reveal, *verb*
revealing, *adjective*
revenue, *noun*
reversal, *noun*
reverse, *verb, noun,
    adjective*
reversible, *adjective*
revise, *verb*
revision, *noun*
revolution, *noun*

# Academic Words

revolutionary, *adjective*
rigid, *adjective*
role, *noun*
route, *noun*
schedule, *noun*
scheme, *noun*
section, *noun*
secure, *adjective*
securely, *adverb*
security, *noun*
seek, *verb*
select, *verb*
selection, *noun*
sequence, *noun*
series, *noun*
sex, *noun*
sexism, *noun*
shift, *verb, noun*
significance, *noun*
significant, *adjective*
similar, *adjective*
similarity, *noun*
similarly, *adverb*
simulate, *verb*
simulation, *noun*
site, *noun*
sole, *adjective*
solely, *adverb*
somewhat, *adverb*
source, *noun*
specific, *adjective*
specifically, *adverb*
specify, *verb*
sphere, *noun*
spherical, *adjective*
stability, *noun*
stabilize, *verb*
stable, *adjective*
statistic, *noun*
straightforward,
    *adjective*
strategic, *adjective*
strategy, *noun*
stress, *noun, verb*
stressful, *adjective*
structural, *adjective*
structure, *noun, verb*
style, *noun*
stylish, *adjective*
submit, *verb*
subsequent, *adjective*
subsequently, *adverb*
substitute, *noun, verb*
substitution, *noun*
sufficient, *adjective*
sufficiently, *adverb*
sum, *noun, verb*
summarize, *verb*

summary, *noun*
survey, *noun, verb*
survival, *noun*
survive, *verb*
survivor, *noun*
suspend, *verb*
suspension, *noun*
sustain, *verb*
sustainable, *adjective*
symbol, *noun*
symbolism, *noun*
symbolize, *verb*
tape, *noun, verb*
target, *noun*
task, *noun*
team, *noun*
technical, *adjective*
technique, *noun*
technological, *adjective*
technology, *noun*
temporarily, *adverb*
temporary, *adjective*
tense, *adjective*
tension, *noun*
terminal, *noun, adjective*
text, *noun, verb*
theme, *noun*
theory, *noun*
thereby, *adverb*
thesis, *noun*
topic, *noun*
trace, *verb, noun*
tradition, *noun*
traditional, *adjective*
traditionally, *adverb*
transfer, *verb, noun*
transform, *verb*
transformation, *noun*
transit, *noun*
transition, *noun*
transmission, *noun*
transmit, *verb*
transport, *verb*
transportation, *noun*
trend, *noun*
trigger, *noun, verb*
ultimate, *adjective*
ultimately, *adverb*
unaware, *adjective*
unbiased, *adjective*
unconstitutional,
    *adjective*
underestimate, *verb*
undergo, *verb*
unification, *noun*
uniform, *adjective, noun*
uniformity, *noun*
unify, *verb*

unique, *adjective*
uniquely, *adverb*
unpredictable, *adjective*
unreliable, *adjective*
unstable, *adjective*
utility, *noun*
utilize, *verb*
valid, *adjective*
variable, *adjective, noun*
variation, *noun*
varied, *adjective*
vary, *verb*
varying, *adjective*
vehicle, *noun*
version, *noun*
via, *preposition*
violate, *verb*
violation, *noun*
virtual, *adjective*
virtually, *adverb*
visibility, *noun*
visible, *adjective*
visibly, *adverb*
vision, *noun*
visual, *adjective*
visualize, *verb*
visually, *adverb*
volume, *noun*
voluntarily, *adverb*
voluntary, *adjective*
volunteer, *noun, verb*
welfare, *noun*
whereas, *conjunction*
widespread, *adjective*

| Verb | Past Tense | Past Participle | Present Participle |
|------|-----------|-----------------|--------------------|
| arise | arose | arisen | arising |
| awake | awoke | awoken | awaking |
| be | was *or* were | been | being |
| bear | bore | borne | bearing |
| beat | beat | beaten | beating |
| become | became | become | becoming |
| begin | began | begun | beginning |
| bend | bent | bent | bending |
| bet | bet | bet | betting |
| bid | bid | bid | bidding |
| bind | bound | bound | binding |
| bite | bit | bitten | biting |
| bleed | bled | bled | bleeding |
| blow | blew | blown | blowing |
| break | broke | broken | breaking |
| breed | bred | bred | breeding |
| bring | brought | brought | bringing |
| broadcast | broadcast *or* broadcasted | broadcast *or* broadcasted | broadcasting |
| build | built | built | building |
| burn | burned *or* burnt | burned *or* burnt | burning |
| burst | burst | burst | bursting |
| buy | bought | bought | buying |
| cast | cast | cast | casting |
| catch | caught | caught | catching |
| choose | chose | chosen | choosing |
| cling | clung | clung | clinging |
| come | came | come | coming |
| cost | cost | cost | costing |
| creep | crept | crept | creeping |
| cut | cut | cut | cutting |
| deal | dealt | dealt | dealing |
| dig | dug | dug | digging |
| dive | dived *or* dove | dived | diving |
| do | did | done | doing |
| draw | drew | drawn | drawing |
| dream | dreamed *or* dreamt | dreamed *or* dreamt | dreaming |
| drink | drank | drunk | drinking |
| drive | drove | driven | driving |
| eat | ate | eaten | eating |
| fall | fell | fallen | falling |
| feed | fed | fed | feeding |
| feel | felt | felt | feeling |
| fight | fought | fought | fighting |
| find | found | found | finding |
| fit | fit *or* fitted | fit *or* fitted | fitting |
| flee | fled | fled | fleeing |
| fling | flung | flung | flinging |
| fly | flew | flown | flying |
| forbid | forbid *or* forbade | forbidden | forbidding |

# Irregular Verbs

| Verb | Past Tense | Past Participle | Present Participle |
|---|---|---|---|
| forecast | forecast | forecast | forecasting |
| foresee | foresaw | foreseen | foreseeing |
| forget | forgot | forgotten | forgetting |
| forgive | forgave | forgiven | forgiving |
| freeze | froze | frozen | freezing |
| get | got | gotten | getting |
| give | gave | given | giving |
| go | went | gone | going |
| grind | ground | ground | grinding |
| grow | grew | grown | growing |
| hang (= clothes/pictures) | hung | hung | hanging |
| hang (= kill someone) | hanged | hanged | hanging |
| have | had | had | having |
| hear | heard | heard | hearing |
| heave | heaved *or* hove | heaved *or* hove | heaving |
| hide | hid | hidden | hiding |
| hit | hit | hit | hitting |
| hold | held | held | holding |
| hurt | hurt | hurt | hurting |
| keep | kept | kept | keeping |
| kneel | knelt *or* kneeled | knelt *or* kneeled | kneeling |
| knit | knit *or* knitted | knit *or* knitted | knitting |
| know | knew | known | knowing |
| lay | laid | laid | laying |
| lead | led | led | leading |
| leap | leaped *or* leapt | leaped *or* leapt | leaping |
| leave | left | left | leaving |
| lend | lent | lent | lending |
| let | let | let | letting |
| lie (= say something untrue) | lied | lied | lying |
| lie (= be on your bed/the floor) | lay | lain | lying |
| light | lit *or* lighted | lit *or* lighted | lighting |
| lose | lost | lost | losing |
| make | made | made | making |
| mean | meant | meant | meaning |
| meet | met | met | meeting |
| mislead | misled | misled | misleading |
| mistake | mistook | mistaken | mistaking |
| misunderstand | misunderstood | misunderstood | misunderstanding |
| mow | mowed | mown *or* mowed | mowing |
| outgrow | outgrew | outgrown | outgrowing |
| overcome | overcame | overcome | overcoming |
| overdo | overdid | overdone | overdoing |
| overeat | overate | overeaten | overeating |
| overhear | overheard | overheard | overhearing |
| oversleep | overslept | overslept | oversleeping |
| overthrow | overthrew | overthrown | overthrowing |
| pay | paid | paid | paying |
| plead | pleaded *or* pled | pleaded *or* pled | pleading |

| Verb | Past Tense | Past Participle | Present Participle |
|---|---|---|---|
| prove | proved | proved *or* proven | proving |
| put | put | put | putting |
| quit | quit | quit | quitting |
| read | read | read | reading |
| redo | redid | redone | redoing |
| relay | relaid | relaid | relaying |
| repay | repaid | repaid | repaying |
| rewind | rewound | rewound | rewinding |
| rewrite | rewrote | rewritten | rewriting |
| ride | rode | ridden | riding |
| ring | rang | rung | ringing |
| rise | rose | risen | rising |
| run | ran | run | running |
| saw | sawed | sawed *or* sawn | sawing |
| say | said | said | saying |
| see | saw | seen | seeing |
| seek | sought | sought | seeking |
| sell | sold | sold | selling |
| send | sent | sent | sending |
| set | set | set | setting |
| sew | sewed | sewn *or* sewed | sewing |
| shake | shook | shaken | shaking |
| shed | shed | shed | shedding |
| shine | shone | shone | shining |
| shoot | shot | shot | shooting |
| show | showed | shown | showing |
| shrink | shrank *or* shrunk | shrunk | shrinking |
| shut | shut | shut | shutting |
| sing | sang | sung | singing |
| sink | sank | sunk | sinking |
| sit | sat | sat | sitting |
| sleep | slept | slept | sleeping |
| slide | slid | slid | sliding |
| slit | slit | slit | slitting |
| sneak | sneaked *or* snuck | sneaked *or* snuck | sneaking |
| sow | sowed | sown *or* sowed | sowing |
| speak | spoke | spoken | speaking |
| speed | sped *or* speeded | sped *or* speeded | speeding |
| spend | spent | spent | spending |
| spill | spilled *or* spilt | spilled *or* spilt | spilling |
| spin | spun | spun | spinning |
| spit | spit *or* spat | spit *or* spat | spitting |
| split | split | split | splitting |
| spread | spread | spread | spreading |
| spring | sprang | sprung | springing |
| stand | stood | stood | standing |
| steal | stole | stolen | stealing |
| stick | stuck | stuck | sticking |
| sting | stung | stung | stinging |

# Irregular Verbs

| Verb | Past Tense | Past Participle | Present Participle |
|---|---|---|---|
| stink | stank or stunk | stunk | stinking |
| stride | strode | stridden | striding |
| strike | struck | struck or stricken | striking |
| string | strung | strung | stringing |
| swear | swore | sworn | swearing |
| sweep | swept | swept | sweeping |
| swell | swelled | swollen | swelling |
| swim | swam | swum | swimming |
| swing | swung | swung | swinging |
| take | took | taken | taking |
| teach | taught | taught | teaching |
| tear | tore | torn | tearing |
| tell | told | told | telling |
| think | thought | thought | thinking |
| thrive | thrived or throve | thrived | thriving |
| throw | threw | thrown | throwing |
| thrust | thrust | thrust | thrusting |
| undergo | underwent | undergone | undergoing |
| understand | understood | understood | understanding |
| undo | undid | undone | undoing |
| unwind | unwound | unwound | unwinding |
| uphold | upheld | upheld | upholding |
| upset | upset | upset | upsetting |
| wake | woke | woken | waking |
| wear | wore | worn | wearing |
| weave | wove | woven | weaving |
| weep | wept | wept | weeping |
| wet | wet or wetted | wet or wetted | wetting |
| win | won | won | winning |
| wind | wound | wound | winding |
| withdraw | withdrew | withdrawn | withdrawing |
| withhold | withheld | withheld | withholding |
| withstand | withstood | withstood | withstanding |
| wring | wrung | wrung | wringing |
| write | wrote | written | writing |

# Longman Elementary Dictionary and Thesaurus
## Picture Credits

The publisher would like to thank the following for their kind permission to reproduce their photographs:
(Key: b-bottom; c-centre; l-left; r-right; t-top)

**Action Plus Sports Images:** Neil TIngle 305, A10 (hockey); **Alamy Images:** Aerial Archives 339, Aflo Foto Agency A10 (skiing), Arco Images GmbH 346c (above), Peter Arnold, Inc A3 (manatee), 341r, ArteSub 15b, Big Cheese Photo LLC 217l, Steve Bly 300, bobo 628bl, ClassicStock 659t, Judith Collins 83c, CountryStock 480, David R. Frazier Photolibrary, Inc. A9 (whiteboard), James Davis Photography 317c, 796l, E.R. Degginger 295t, Dex Image 453b, Ian Evans 423, Matt Fowler Photography 327t, Sean Gladwell 138, Glow Images 482, 808bl, Golden Pixels LLC 791 (top hat), H Lansdown 661t, Bill Heinsohn 141tl, David Hosking 93t, Ilene MacDonald 677b, 823, Image Source Pink 227, 528b, 780 (fasten), 780tl, Chloe Johnson 448c, Jupiterimages / Pixland 433b, Kim Karpeles A10 (running), Scott Kemper 49, Kevin Foy 640, Eileen Langsley / Figure Skating 234l, Craig Lovell / Eagle Visions Photography 303l, 810 (hills), David Lyons 292r, Michael Matthews 16t, Nature Picture Library 304, Werner Otto 327b, PetStockBoys 306cr, 765 (burrow), Photofrenetic 75tr, 782 (buds), Picture Partners 358b, Radius Images 488c, RTimages 270b, RubberBall 160b, The Print Collector 3, Anthony Thorogood 86tr, Top-Pet-Pics 294b, Greg Vaughn 395t, David Wall 86tl, Westend61 GmbH 320b, WILDLIFE GmbH A3 (eel), 198, Worldspec / NASA 285b;
**Arcticphoto: Bryan & Cherry Alexander** 340b; **Ardea:** John Daniels 55, Karl Terblanche 23t, M. Watson A2 (anteater); **Art Directors and TRIP photo Library:** Ark Religion / Dinodia Picture Library 659b; **Corbis:** 219, 245r, A27 (31), A28 (42), Birgid Allig / zefa 178, 800b, Scott Andrews / Science Faction 612t, Apis / Sygma A28 (34), Heide Benser 143t, Hal Beral / zefa 445, Bettmann A26 (2), A26 (3), A26 (5), A26 (7), A27 (18), A27 (26), A27 (28), Christophe Boisvieux 38b, Brooklyn Museum 487r, Brooks Kraft A28 (44), Car Culture 223, Chris Carroll 351br, 800tl, Caterina Bernardi 695, Michele Constantini / PhotoAlto 311, Daniel J. Cox 160t, Jim Craigmyle 374, cultura 672, David Puu 677t, Dennis Van Tine / Retna Ltd A28 (43), Odilon Dimier / PhotoAlto 306cl, Edward Bock 725r, Eric Audras / PhotoAlto 150, Macduff Everton 250, 764 (fort), Randy Faris 581t, John-Francis Bourke / zefa 89cl, Todd Gipstein 293b, A. Green 109tl, David Gubernick / AgStock Images 12, Charles Gullung / zefa 399l, Image Source 654r, 675b, JLP / Jose L. Pelaez 405t, John Henley 685b, 811br, Joseph Sohm / Visions of America 699t, Joson / zefa 586r, Kulka / zefa 487l, Lester Lefkowitz 148hr, Charles & Josette Lenars 139tr, Look Photography / Beateworks 631, John Lund 6, Massimo Listri 668l, Michele Westmorland 678t, Moodboard 108, 234r, Larry Mulvehill 84t, Oscar White A27 (23), Philip Kaake 685t, Carl & Ann Purcell 332b, Rainer Elstermann 679b, Rick Gomez / Comet 195t, Robert Harding World Imagery 679t, Ron Chapple 634, 828 (stream), Paul Souders 269, Keren Su 418t, Vince Streano 242tl, 726, Bob Winsett 317t, Jim Wright / Star Ledger 143c; **DK Images:** 10, 89t, A3 (flounder), A3 (salmon), A8 (orchestra), 187l, 242br, 345t, 453t, 458, 473tl, 473c, 514t, 516b, 551, 562t, 747t, 811t, 824 (pushing), Peter Anderson 58bl, A2 (bison), Andy Crawford and Tim Ridley 727b, Tai Blanche 195c, 798 (earrings), Paul Bricknell 186b, Geoff Brightling 20 (newt), A1 (newt), Demetrio Carrasco. Courtesy of Boston EMS Ambulances 18, Peter Chadwick 517l, Andy Crawford 106b, 359b, 461l, 534, 580, 660b, 688tr, 724b, 746bl, 749r, Dave King A2 (bear), A3 (shark), 164b, 180b, 241l, 256, 272, 281tr, 366, 368b, 618b, 629, 670, 744cl, 763 (pie), Philip Dowell 346c, Mike Dunning 295, Ellis Nadler 819 (cartoon), Neil Fletcher 414b, Trish Gant 141b, Geoff Brightling 20 (newt), A1 (newt), Steve Gorton and Karl Shone 494r, Frank Greenaway 112, David Johnson 331, Colin Keates / Dorling Kindersley, Courtesy of the Natural History Museum, London 251, Dave King A2 (bear), A3 (shark), 164b, 180b, 241l, 256, 272, 281tr, 366, 368b, 618b, 629, 670, 744cl, 763 (pie), Dave King / Jeremy Hunt - modelmaker 582, Cyril Laubscher A4 (duck), A4 (parakeet), A4 (parrot), 191l, 465r, 467, David Murray and Jules Selmes 186t, 278b, 474t, Nelson Hancock / Rough Guides 651, Gary Ombler 57, 388bl, Susanna Price A8 (cymbals), 253b, 287, 807 (freckles), Tim Ridley 14t, Dave Rudkin 540, Kim Sayer 79, 758 (sculpture), Steve Gorton 618t, 701, Harry Taylor 394l, Jerry Young 20 (toad), A1 (toad), 370, 493, 673, 785 (toad); **FLPA Images of Nature:** Mike Parry / Minden Pictures A2 (whale); **Getty Images:** Allsport Concepts A10 (soccer), Asia Images / Yukmin 800tr, Alistair Berg / Photonica 558b, Greg Ceo / Taxi 294tl (harp), Colin Anderson 807 (stain), Jim Cummins / Taxi 533t, Hulton Archive A26 (1), A27 (16), A28 (32), A28 (40), Hulton Archive / Library of Congress A28 (35), Dave & Les Jacobs / Blend Images 170, Jeffrey Coolidge 766 (wiping), Joos Mind / Riser 168, Christina Kennedy / DK Stock 405b, Andy Crawford / Dorling Kindersley 192t, Dave King / Dorling Kindersley RF 414tl, Flynn Larsen / UpperCut Images 516t, Mark Lund 807 (mark), Tara Moore / Taxi 410, 766 (brushing), Piotr Powietrzynski 732t, Lars Klove Photo Service / Riser 368t, Steve Shott / Dorling Kindersley 524br, 693, Hugh Sitton / Stone 433tr, Sports Illustrated A10 (volleyball), Tom Bean / Stone 159, 828tr, Brian Summers / First Light 549tr, Brad Wilson / Taxi 333r; **Hemera Photo Objects:** 4, 72r, 75, 75 (hairbrush), 75 (paintbrushes), 75 (toothbrush), 95 (chair), 95 (folding chair), 95 (rocking chair), 95 (wheelchair), A3 (lobster), A3 (mussel), A4 (ostrich), A6 (rose), A7 (oranges), A9 (calculator), A9 (compass), 100tl, 111, 184t, 270cr, 290, 291br, 310cl, 310cr, 346t, 355t, 355c, 360b, 373cl, 380b, 388 (magnify), 406, 422t, 422b, 424, 449, 454b, 479, 491, 542 (alligator), 542 (crocodile), 542 (lizard), 542 (snake), 549bl, 555b, 569, 584b (shellfish), 603t, 613, 622, 630, 662, 690, 719b, 722b, 747b, 748b, 763 (doughnut), 763 (muffin), 794 (horse), 815 (desk ), 819 (pizza); **iStockphoto:** 9, 15t, 40, 43tr, 51t, 65, 87tr, 87b, 89cr (pencil case), 93b, 99t, A2 (cow), A2 (elephant), A3 (starfish), A4 (cardinal), A4 (crane), A5 (bee), A5 (cricket), A5 (dragonfly), A5 (hornet), A6 (carnation), A6 (crocus), A6 (daffodil), A6 (foxglove), A6 (oak tree), A6 (orchid), A6 (sunflower), A6 (swquoia), A6 (waterlily), A7 (apricot), A7 (banana), A7 (beetroot), A7 (cantaloupe), A7 (coconut), A7 (cucumbers), A7 (fig), A7 (Green onions), A7 (peach), A7 (pineapple), A7 (sweet potato), A8 (cello), A8 (drum), A9 (colored pencils), A9 (felt tip pens), A9 (glue), A9 (paperclips), A9 (pencil ), A9 (pencil case), A9 (scissors), A9 (stapler), 113t, 121, 141tr, 146l, 148bl, 155, 185, 190t, 192b, 196, 199t (fried), 201, 202, 210tl, 210tr, 228, 229l, 231t, 237, 238, 240, 241br, 243, 252l, 253cl, 253cr, 257, 268tr, 268bl, 271, 282, 289t, 291bl, 295b, 296, 298tr, 299b, 308b, 310bl, 317br, 332t, 354b, 373cr, 373bl, 388tl, 389, 399r, 403l, 412, 433tc, 442 (cashew), 442 (hazelnuts), 443tl, 448b, 461c, 463t (jeans), 498t, 515 (puppet), 527c (below), 532b, 533b, 548b (ribbon), 548b (rosette), 549tl, 568b, 572t, 589b, 591b, 606, 624, 642, 643b, 660t, 661b, 686bl (fire truck), 686bl (fork-lift truck), 686bl (towtruck), 759 (chick), 761 (ferry), 761 (yacht), 780tc, 790 (sideburn ), 791 (fur), 834t, A10 (golf), A10 (sailing), A10 (swimming), Ana Abejon 367, Monika Adamczyk A7 (blueberries), adrian beesley 795 (mobile home), Roberto Adrian 433tl, Elena Aliaga 68t, Brandon Alms A5 (firefly), Andyd 490c, andydidyk 795 (hut), Angel_a 791 (beret), Antagain A5 (wasp), 722t, Mark Aplet 145 (paper cup), AVAVA 713t, bacalao64 645, Ron Bailey 394r, Frédéric De Bailliencourt 317bl, Roumen Baitchev 43b, Don Bayley 44b, 342, Beata Becla 137, Rob Belknap A10 (basketball), John Bell 527t, Frank van den Bergh 208, 231b, Bernhard Richter 759 (lamb), Robert Blanchard A2 (raccoon), 522bl, Rodrigo Blanco 48t, blaneyphoto 635r, 748t, Blaz Kure 815 (temple), Olivier Blondeau 87r (below centre), Ronald Bloom 17, Michael Bodmann 33b, Franck Boston 686bl (truck), James Boulette 525b, Cheryl Bowman 357t (gauze), Brandon Laufenberg 804 (headlights), Andrew Brown 236c, Karel Broz A4 (swallow), Jani Bryson 357br, 495t, Wiktor Bubniak 67t, Andrzej Burak 550, Sascha Burkard 490b, Dmitriy Buyanskiy 375t, Steve Byland 58t, Ilker Canikligil 145 (cup & saucer), Ken Canning 420t, Nancy Catherine 86b, Lya Cattel 432t, cbabbitt 725l, Daniel Chadwick A7 (raspberries), Sam Chadwick 563, Norman Chan 106t, Yungshu Chao 360t, Libby Chapman 623t, Chepko 689b, Chris Hepburn 766 (washing), Gene Chutka 76b, Marcus Clackson A6 (holly), 306t, 832 (prickly), Cathleen Clapper 559, Claudia Dewald 787br, Clint Scholz 759 (piglet), Colleen Butler 803br, Chris Crafter 101, Heather Craig 293c, creativebloke A4 (swan), 648, Les Cunliffe 82t, 623b, Rhienna Cutler 44t, 74, 591l, Antonio D'Albore 414tr, dageldog 628br, Dainis Derics 782 (blossoms), Jennifer Daley 574t, Daniel Loiselle 766 (scrubbing), Chepko Danil 574b, Liza David 303r, Beverly Guhl Davis 494l, Catherine dee Auvil A6 (violet), 715t, Openko Dmytro 462t, DNY59 A9 (ruler), 558tl, dolah A3 (tuna), 689t, dr. Le Thanh Hung 285cl, 488r, Alexandra Draghici 154, Olena Druzhynina 249l, Godfried Edelman 448tr, EEI_Tony 689c, 765 (tunnel), Mike Eikenberry 598, Laura Eisenberg 54, ejs9 723, Elena Elisseeva 442 (walnuts), elrphoto 759 (foal), 794 (foal), emyerson 684, Eric Isselee 43tl, 99b, A2 (cougar), A4 (Owl), A4 (raven), 100br, 135, 194, 274c, 313, 460l, 495r, 527c (above), 597bl, 832 (spiky), ericfoltz 636c, Donald Erickson 442 (peanuts), 485b (sink pipe), Roberto Anguita Escribano 139b, Tiago Estima 463t (scissors), 568t, Justin Eubank A1 (turtle), Mark Evans 167t, 798 (ring), Stanislav Fadyukhin 308t, Mehdi Farahmandfar 340t, filo 655b, Trevor Fisher A6 (tulip), 688b, Susan Flashman 25 (orangutan), Steffen Foerster 440, Steven Foley 92b, 765 (cave), forgiss 736br, foto IE 776 (deserted), Stanislav Fridkin A7 (pumpkin), 514b, Jill Fromer 498l (coffee pot), Caroline Garcia 68 (jewelry box), Andy Graff A2 (fox), 252t, 455, Pascal Genest A10 (football), Andrea Gingerich 276, Li Kim Goh A10 (tennis), Krzysztof Gorski 442 (chestnuts), Joe Gough 199t (poached), Ken Graff 432bl, Bill Grove A7 (melon), 724tl (slices), Mehmet Salih Guler 666, Richard Gunion 345b, Simon Gurney 571bl, Izabela Habur 244r, Thomas Harris A3 (bass), Heiko Bennewitz 749l, 759 (baby ), Johann Helgason A11 (swamp), Jon Helgason 596l (roller skates), Darren Hendley 420b, Henk Badenhorst 804 (streetlight), John Hess A8 (drums), Kris Hollingsworth 398, Thomas Hottner 20 (amusement park), Andrew Howe A4 (magpie), 388br, Juha Huiskonen 548t, Charles Humphries 581bl, Innershadows 627, Ivan Ivanov 473tr, jackhollingsworth. com, LLC A13 (girl), Jorgen Jacobsen 381, Jacom Stephens 798br (bracelet), James McQuillan 804 (candle), Jerry Callaghan 744b, Erick Jones 164t, jpbcpa 724tr, Juanmorino 804 (flashlight), Leanne Kanowski 615t, Torsten Karock A2 (wolf), Britta Kasholm-Tengve 443b, Kate Leigh 633tr, Murat Giray Kaya 23c, 529t, Robert Kelsey A10 (softball), Patrik Kiefer 24t, 417t, KingWu 727t, Sven Klaschik 81t, A6 (cactus), Koksharov dmitry 804 (lamp), Elena Korenbaum 200, 815tl, Radoslaw Kostka 286, Sergey Kulikov 68 (tool box), John Kuo 91b, Dmitry Kutlayev 570, Rebekah Lane 20 (frog), 341l, Adam Larsen 451, laughingmango 746br, Sergey Lavrentev 373t, Lawrence Freytag 828 (river), Lawrence Sawyer 67br, 746t, Scott Leigh 377, Monika Lewandowska 396r, Tom Lichtman 602t, Liliboas 650b, lise gagne 626l, Guillermo Lobo 31, Sean Locke 45t, 808r, Uwe lol 156, LPETTET 653, 784 (tadpole), Kyle Maass A11 (mountains), Mona Makela 422c, manley620 707, Mark Wragg 763 (cupcake), Georgy Markov